AUSTRALIAN
CRICKET
THE GAME AND THE PLAYERS

AUSTRALIAN
CRICKET
THE GAME AND THE PLAYERS

JACK POLLARD

FOREWORD BY
SIR DONALD BRADMAN
EDITED BY
IAN MOIR

HODDER AND STOUGHTON
SYDNEY AUCKLAND LONDON TORONTO

For Barbara

First published in 1982 by
Hodder and Stoughton (Australia) Pty Limited,
2 Apollo Place, Lane Cove, NSW 2066
in association with the
Australian Broadcasting Commission
145–153 Elizabeth Street, Sydney, NSW 2000

©text, Jack Pollard, 1982

Editor: Ian Moir
Designer and Production Manager: Linda Williams

Typeset in 10/11pt Dominante Light at
Griffin Press Limited, Netley, South Australia 5037

Printed and bound at Griffin Press Limited, Netley,
South Australia 5037

National Library of Australia Cataloguing-in-Publication entry

Pollard, Jack, 1926– .
    Australian cricket.

    Limited ed. consists of 452 signed copies.
    Bibliography.
    ISBN 0 340 28796 9.
    ISBN 0 340 33067 8 (limited ed.).

    1. Cricket—Australia—History.
    I. Australian Broadcasting Commission.
    II. Title.

796.35'8'0994

Reprinted 1982

FOREWORD

by Sir Donald Bradman

Among Australian sportswriters the name of Jack Pollard stands high. After the production of this book I hope and believe his reputation will stand even higher, for here is a comprehensive and detailed review of Australian cricket that should be on the shelves of all cricket devotees.

Jack Pollard has already produced countless numbers of books, the sales of which exceed one million copies. They range from cricket to football, tennis, swimming, bowls, horse racing, golf—you name it—but strangely enough his biggest sellers have been on fishing, a pastime which, as a small boy, I loved, but regrettably have been unable to pursue. Having read several of Jack's books I know they are always interesting and I confess to having read his book *Six and Out* several times. Despite his obvious versatility, Jack's perennial love is cricket and he really puts his heart into works on this subject.

As England was the cradle of cricket one can well understand that country spawning the majority of great reference works. One of these was *A History of Cricket*, first published in 1926 by the late H. S. Altham, a man of immense knowledge, charm and wisdom. Years later it reappeared in two volumes which were divided

(i) up to World War I by H. S. Altham and

(ii) from then up to roughly the date of publication by the renowned writer and broadcaster, E. W. Swanton, who styled himself the "junior author". I had the great honour and privilege of writing a Foreword for each volume.

Of more recent origin is a magnificent production called *Barclay's World of Cricket* with the same E. W. Swanton as general editor and John Woodcock, The London Times cricket correspondent, now Editor of *Wisden*, as associate editor.

There have been many attempts at an Australian cricket history of which the best in my possession, produced in 1959, was by my late friend and mentor A. G. ("Johnnie") Moyes. One of the tragedies of every cricket history is that it so quickly becomes out of date. Harry Altham for instance had no opportunity to concern himself with any reference to Kerry Packer or World Series Cricket. And though his literary skill paid tribute to the life of Victor Trumper, sadly Altham died before Ian Botham began his first class career.

Jack Pollard has attempted a different style or concept of a history from Moyes by embracing details of individual careers—rather like a "Who's Who"—together with the broadest canvas of information concerning the game itself and many of the historic organisations and clubs associated with it. It was my privilege to read proofs of a large percentage of these entries. If any inaccuracies are located (and it would be miraculous if there weren't any) they will not have occurred because of any lack of research and diligence on the part of the author. Every Australian Test player is covered, as is every first-class cricketer of note.

An example of this may be told concerning the late Archie Johnson. In *Wisden*'s Births & Deaths, he is referred to as A. A. I was intimately associated with Archie until his sad and unfortunate death, was one of the pall bearers at his funeral, and always believed he was Archibald Alexander. But for the sake of authenticity Jack Pollard went to the extent of locating Archie's birth certificate which lists but the one name, Archibald. Archie's surviving sister said, "Archie felt out of place in a team with so many second initials and adopted our father's name 'Alexander'" in what she delightfully called a 'teenage whim'.

Cricket is a remarkable game. No sport can rival it as a topic of conversation and it remains supreme as a vehicle for literature. The works of the late Sir Neville Cardus are renowned for their mastery of the English language as much as for their revelations about cricket. Challenges to the very existence of the game may be found right from its inception. The first and perhaps most serious was in the early days when cricket was declared an illegal pastime. That hurdle surmounted, its survival has been subsequently questioned on several occasions. As long ago as 1822, one John Willes was "no balled" for throwing, i.e. in those days, round-arm bowling. Up to that stage bowling had always been under-arm. Writers of the day condemned the new style, one claiming "the new style is fatal to all scientific play, putting a premium on chance hits, and placing scientific defence at a discount". But the reformers were not dismayed. They persisted.

In 1864, over-arm bowling was allowed for the first time. Some detractors immediately forecast doom because, so they said, the pace which the bowlers could generate from this new method of delivery would ruin batsmanship. The most effective answer to such a prophesy came from the bat of England's great champion, Dr W. G. Grace. In consecutive innings for the Gentlemen against the Players in 1871, 1872 and 1873, he scored 217, 77, 112, 117, 163, 158, and 70. One old player of the period immediately went to the other extreme by saying Grace "killed professional fast bowling; for years they were almost afraid to bowl within his reach". In the world of 1982 some people are decrying the predominance of the speed merchants. But that is another story. There are many examples of writers foreshadowing the demise of cricket because, so they said, it "lacked public appeal", "the standard of play has declined", and so on. But the game is still very much alive, coping with changes in the rules, limited over matches, coloured clothing and other trends. Not only does cricket attract large audiences to major games, it has developed a television audience of vast proportions.

One of the greatest regrets of my life is that I did not read enough about cricket and the wonderful characters who trod the turf at Lords, Adelaide and other places long before I did. It would have so enriched my life when I played against Wilfred Rhodes had I known as much about him as I now do. And this remorse extends to those who so uplifted and graced the cricket world by their portrayal of its virtues, their written and spoken words, men like the great Lord Birkett whose speeches at cricket functions were a joy and a revelation. I cannot too strongly urge the youth of today to read and digest all they possibly can about cricket, and this volume by Jack Pollard is an invaluable contribution to that vast field of literature which awaits the enthusiast.

Nobody but a dedicated cricket lover could possibly have spent the time required to produce this mine of information. I congratulate Jack and thank him for producing a reference work of great interest and incalculable value.

CONTENTS

Foreword by Sir Donald Bradman   v

List of Colour Illustrations   x

Preface   xii

Acknowledgements   xiv

The players, administrators, historic
matches and tours, development
of the states, and important records   17

Addendum   1157

Bibliography   1159

LIST OF COLOUR ILLUSTRATIONS

Between pages 64 and 65

Terry Alderman in action against England during the Fourth Test at Edgbaston in 1981.

Russell Drysdale's famous painting, *The Cricketers*.

Rodney Marsh making one of his rare Test match stumpings. Marsh diving full length to catch Alan Knott off Jeff Thomson.

Between pages 256 and 257

Greg Chappell plays a carefully controlled back foot defensive shot.
Ian Chappell plays his famous sweep shot.

The 1878 Australian Team playing a match against Wilsher's Gentlemen at Chilham Castle, Kent.

Left-arm spinner Ray Bright at the point of delivery.
Ian Davis in a Sydney night match.

Opposite page 336

Alan Border clips a ball away to square leg.

Opposite page 337

Mick Malone shows his copybook style.
Garry Gilmour follows through after the delivery of one of his left-arm medium pacers.

Opposite Page 368

Australian slips fieldsmen Ian Redpath, Doug Walters, Greg and Ian Chappell.
Terry Alderman clean bowls English opener Graham Gooch.

Opposite page 369

Rick Darling goes down after being hit by England's fast bowler Bob Willis.

Opposite page 496

David Hookes hammers a ball past point.
Bruce Laird driving through mid-off.
Rick Darling moves off as he turns a ball to leg.

Opposite page 497

Alan Border dives wide to reach a slips catch off Thomson.
A jubilant moment for the Australian fieldsmen as Ashley Mallet claims a victim.

Leg Spinner Jim Higgs in action.
Tony Greig under fire from Jeff Thomson.
Opposite page 528

Martin Kent glides a ball down to deep fine leg.
The only Australian 'keeper to score a test century, Rodney Marsh, clubbing a ball to leg boundary.
Opposite page 529

David Ogilvie shows the agression that brought him six first class centuries.
Ian Redpath drives through the covers.
Opposite page 624

Dennis Lillee in action against England.
The well known Lillee appeal.
Opposite page 625

Rod Marsh taking a catch to dismiss Gooch off Jeff Thomson.
Opposite page 656

Jeff Thomson's famous delivery stride with the front-arm well up.
Len Pascoe's powerful arm action in closeup.
Opposite page 657

Kim Hughes drives a ball for four at Birmingham.
The 1979 World Cup finalists at Lord's.
Bob Simpson seen square cutting in Sydney. Max Walker delivers a ball in his unique style.
Between pages 800 and 801

John Snow clashes with a spectator during the Sydney Test in 1970–71.
The Hill at Sydney during the Seventh Australia-England Test in 1970–71.
Opposite page 976

Terry Alderman makes England 'keeper Paul Downton one of his nine victims in the first Test at Nottingham in 1981.
Geoff Lawson throws his front arm and leg high in an action shot.
Opposite page 977

Bruce Laird pulls a ball to the leg boundary.
Rick McCosker cuts a ball down to the third man fence.
Opposite page 1008

Rodney Hogg, one of Australia's fastest bowlers in recent years.
Opposite page 1009

Doug Walters driving during a one day game in Sydney.
Graeme Wood, talented left-handed opener, turns a ball to leg.
Between pages 1056 and 1057

A lithograph by Charles Troedel of the Melbourne Cricket Ground, 1864.

Steve Rixon and slips fieldsman Bob Simpson alert for the next ball during a match in Sydney.

xi

PREFACE

The records and players' averages in this book have all been calculated up to the end of the 1981–82 Australian cricket season, and include the 11-match tour of New Zealand by the Australian team that immediately followed.

I have adhered to the traditional definition of a first-class match as one played over a minimum of three days by teams of 11 players. Apart from occasional references to players' clubs and limited over performances, the text concerns first-class games. WSC three-day matches are not regarded as first-class and have not been included in the players' records.

Every cricketer who has played in a Test for Australia is included in the book, together with his complete statistics, dates of birth and death, and his most notable performances. Many others who have been influential in the development of Australian cricket by giving outstanding service to State teams or in committee rooms are also included. Sometimes it has been very difficult to decide whether a cricketer should be included.

There are some marked differences in this book compared with previously published works containing cricket records. We have found notable differences in the ages some cricketers gave and their birth certificates. Changes in ages and averages are so numerous I believe the book offers a new perspective for cricket's statisticians. We have confirmed, for example, that Hanson Carter, Archie Jackson and Charles Kelleway did not have second christian names, although most books have suggested them. "Alick" Bannerman is five years older in our book than in others, Bert Ironmonger four years older, B. J. Kortlang turned out to be Henry Frederick Lorenz Kortlang. Our composition of some early Australian teams that toured England also differs from those shown in some State Association yearbooks.

Some of the entries in this book also differ from those in *Wisden* and other English books of statistics because of the match that was or was not started at Melbourne on the scheduled dates, December 31, 1970, to January 5, 1971. The toss was made, the teams announced, but as the players took the field the rain came down and no play was possible. The match was abandoned on the third day. The Australian Cricket Board ruled that as the toss had been made the match should be credited to all the selected Australians as a Test appearance. None of the English authorities agree with the ACB ruling because not a ball was bowled.

The ACB ruling is important to the players. John Gleeson, one of the Australians involved, qualified for the ACB Provident Fund because this match gave him 30 Tests. Umpire Tom Brooks in Australian records is credited with 24 Tests because of his brief appearance in this match. Rodney Marsh broke the Australian Test appearance record by playing in his 80th Test in Sydney in 1981–82 if the ACB ruling is accepted, but in Adelaide in the next Test that season if the English view is applied. I have gone along with the ACB ruling, so all our records differ from those accepted in England by one Test for the 11 players and two umpires concerned, but we have pointed this out in their career records.

All the Australian State Associations now have statisticians whose role it is to keep the record straight. Some of them have a difficult job because they have inherited inaccurate records, but I have found them all co-operative and express my thanks for their assistance. It was pleasing to learn that Mr Alan Barnes, a former secretary, is working on a history of the Australian Cricket Board, a difficult but essential job if the history of Australian cricket is to be told accurately for future generations.

Jack Pollard

ACKNOWLEDGEMENTS

The author and publisher would like to sincerely thank the following for their assistance in the long task of compiling the text, photographs and statistics in this book:

STATISTICIANS All the members of the Association of Cricket Statisticians who have answered persistent queries, but especially Roger Page, the Australian co-ordinator of the Association's work, Ernie Cosgrove, the New South Wales Cricket Association scorer, Alf Sherwood, the official Australian team scorer, Robert Spence for his researches into Queensland players' performances, Cliff Winning, for his tireless work on New South Wales cricket, Ian McLeod at the Victorian Cricket Association's office, Harold Merritt, South Australia, and the indefatigable Western Australian Cricket Association statistician, Bill Reynolds. In addition, we have received help from Mervyn Shaw and Richard Finlay on Tasmanian cricketers and from Greg McKie and his wife Ann with their assistance on various problems. Throughout the preparation of the text, the author was assisted by the work of David Roylance, who has deservedly built a wide reputation for his expert knowledge of cricket history.

PHOTOGRAPHS All the families of famous cricketers who donated photographs: Lady Drysdale for permission to use one of the paintings by her late husband, Sir Russell Drysdale, for the cover and inside; Patrick Eagar, the noted English cricket photographer whose work has helped revolutionise cricket coverage; Ken Piesse, for permission to use many pictures from the Australian *Cricketer*; Martin King, for his outstanding original work in colour; the photographic section of the Australian National Library; Frank Bohlsen, for his shots of Australian players and matches; Ken Kelly for his photographs of Australians in England—Harrow Mechanics Institute; and the libraries of the Brisbane *Courier-Mail*, the Sydney *Daily Mirror*, the Sydney *Morning Herald*, the Melbourne *Age*, the *Herald & Weekly Times* group, the Adelaide *News*, the

Adelaide *Advertiser*, the *West Australian*, *Canberra Times*,
the *Examiner* Launceston and the *Mercury*, Hobart.

CRICKET WRITERS

The late Ray Robinson read much of the manuscript and offered invaluable advice, as well as opening his own library of
cricket books and papers for our inspection; Phil Wilkins, of
The Australian also provided advice freely; Tom Goodman
made several important suggestions; David Frith in London
helped solve some problems.

CRICKET ORGANISATIONS

The secretaries of all the English County cricket clubs who
have so willingly responded to our enquiries; the staff at
Lord's for their unfailing co-operation; the secretaries and
staff of the Australian Cricket Board, the Queensland Cricket
Association, the New South Wales Cricket Association, the
Victorian Cricket Association, the South Australian Cricket
Association, the Western Australian Cricket Association, and
the Tasmanian Cricket Council; the Australian Women's
Cricket Council.

CRICKETERS

Many of the cricketers in the book have seen the text describing their careers and we thank them for their helpful
comments; Alan McGilvray, Keith Miller and Bill O'Reilly
have been full of encouragement and advice, Miller in particular a great source of material on wartime events affecting
cricketers; Ian Johnson at the Melbourne Cricket Ground, Gil
Langley from Adelaide, Johnny Gleeson, David de Cavalho,
John Eldershaw, of I Zingari; Ronald Cardwell, of the Australian Cricket Society; and before they died, Halford Hooker,
Jack Fingleton, Ken Mackay, Bruce Dooland and Clarrie
Grimmett.

SPECIAL THANKS

Sir Donald Bradman, A.C. for his generous Foreword and
for much helpful advice; Patrick Mullins, for access to his
cricket library in Brisbane; Roger Page, for assistance freely
given from vast collection of cricket books and papers and
through his contacts among cricket statisticians; Bill Hunt,
Curator of the Sydney Cricket Ground Museum, for so many
kind acts. Barbara Pollard for typing, proof-reading and many
years of encouragement and support. Mr Phil Hitchins, a
former South Australian cricket administrator for his invaluable reminiscences of South Australia's noted players; Jim
Pollard, for his expert researches.

XV

Australian cricket has had very few first-class matches that have been abandoned. The most recent examples were the Third Test against England in 1975 when vandals dug up the Leeds pitch and smeared oil on it, and the 1979 WSC match at Georgetown, Guyana, when Ian Chappell's rebels were unable to complete their match against the West Indies.

When vandals stopped play at Leeds, Australia needed 225 to win on the final day with seven wickets in hand. The vandals badly damaged the pitch during darkness to draw attention to the alleged wrongful imprisonment of George Davis. The match was abandoned as a draw but heavy rain fell from noon and would have prevented either team winning.

Rioting interrupted play several times on the WSC West Indies tour, and at Georgetown spectators, angered by the lack of information about a resumption of play after rain, hurled seats and bricks on to the field, destroyed records of the host club, ransacked the pavilion, and kept players virtual prisoners in the dressing-rooms. The umpires refused to extend the hours of play to make a result possible. The previous season (1978) one umpire refused to "make up" time lost during rioting so the Fifth Test between Bob Simpson's Australians and the West Indies was left as a draw.

The first major match involving Australians to be abandoned was the Test at Old Trafford, Manchester in 1890, when rain prevented play. This occurred again at Old Trafford, Manchester in July 1938, and at Melbourne in December, 1970, when the toss was made and teams nominated, but rain prevented play and the match was declared off on the third day of continual rain. A limited over match was played on what would have been the fifth day.

In the Sheffield Shield competition, the last match of the 1901–02 season between Victoria and South Australia was abandoned. The Shield had already been decided in New South Wales' favour and it was decided that following the tour by England both players and spectators would be exhausted. The same thing happened at the end of the 1903–04 summer when the match between Victoria and South Australia was not played after a tour by England, with New South Wales certain Shield winners.

In a match that finished on December 1, 1920, Victoria (310 and 724) beat South Australia by 385 runs. South Australia then went by train to Sydney for a match against New South Wales that was due to start on December 3. The SACA asked for a postponement until December 4 to allow their players to recover from their long stint in the field at Melbourne. The NSWCA refused. New South Wales then scored 802 (Bardsley 235) and dismissed South Australia for 191 (Mailey 8 for 81). South Australia followed on but at none for 6 heavy rain set in. The South Australians had had enough. At the request of the SACA the match was abandoned but New South Wales was credited with a win.

Apart from these abandoned matches, MCC and Victoria "mini tours" of Tasmania around 1920–22 were abandoned due to shipping strikes and an influenza epidemic. This meant that Tasmania was isolated from first-class cricket from 1914–15 to 1921–22.

Only three Sheffield Shield matches have been abandoned without a ball being bowled—all involving Victoria and Queensland.

Chairs and broken benches litter the Bourda ground in Guyana, where vandals ransacked the pavilion

Formed in 1857 by Scotch College students, this club played an important role in pioneering cricket in Melbourne. Members met originally in Dight's Paddock, Abbotsford, and practised for some time on ground at the south-east corner of Albert and Clarendon Streets, East Melbourne. As membership increased they used a pitch on what was called Richmond Paddock, near the entrance to Melbourne Cricket Ground. In 1860, the club changed its name to East Melbourne and played on ground set aside for its use on Capt. Lonsdale's cow paddock. The area was a bog in winter and trees, heavy blue-stone boulders and fences, had to be removed to get the ground into shape. In 1865, the club built a pavilion and the ground became the scene of many historic matches including those between Smokers and Non-Smokers in 1886–87. Famous early players were in the club's teams, including Horan, Boyle, Laver, McAlister and Arnold Seitz. Between 1860–61 and 1905–06, East Melbourne won the premiership outright 18 times.

ABBOTSFORD CRICKET CLUB

A Victorian fast-medium pace bowler and right-handed batsman who began in first-class cricket at the age of 20 and retired four years later at the peak of his career. Between 1928 and 1932 he played four Tests for Australia, two in Australia against MCC, one in England in 1930, and one against South Africa. He came into Test cricket after only six first-class matches, replacing Jack Gregory, who had broken down in the First Test against Percy Chapman's 1928–29 touring team.

The 6 ft, 13 stone a'Beckett, born at East St Kilda, had won his colours at cricket, athletics and Australian Rules football at Melbourne Grammar School. He played cricket while he studied law at Melbourne University and retired when he was admitted to the bar. He was a blonde-headed fast-medium swing bowler with whip off the pitch. Those who watched him in his two Tests against Chapman's team predicted he would do well in England in 1930, when he was one of Woodfull's young hopefuls but he played in only one Test, finishing the tour with 19 wickets at 33.10, scoring 397 runs at 24.81 in first-class matches.

When a'Beckett returned home the Victorian Amateur Football Association withheld for a time his permit to play football, claiming he had violated his amateur status by accepting expenses on cricket tours. They were over-ruled and a'Beckett played football that season, but a broken bone in the head influenced his decision to retire—another such injury could have permanently disabled him—and concentrate on law. He was the sixth generation of a'Becketts in the legal profession—two great-uncles had been Supreme Court judges.

a'BECKETT, Edward Lambert ("Ted") 1907–

First-class Averages: Batting, 1,636 runs at 29.21; Bowling, 105 wickets at 29.16.

Tests (4): 143 runs at 20.42; 3 for 317 at 105.66.

Four a'Becketts have played for Victoria, but E. L. (Ted) was the only Test player. The family record for the State goes back to 1851 when **Edward Fitzhaley a'Beckett** (1836–1922) and his brother **Malwyn** (1834–1906) played for Victoria. E. F. a'Beckett was only 15 years and 349 days when he made his debut for the State. He made five runs at 1.25 in four innings, and took two wickets at a cost of 21 runs, Malwyn a'Beckett's figures were two wickets for 10. Ted a'Beckett's son, **Edward Clive** (1940—) was a prominent St Kilda cricketer in the 1960's, but was disappointing in two matches for the State, scoring only three runs at 1.50, and failing to take a wicket in conceding 39 runs. All the a'Becketts were right-handers.

ABORIGINALS IN AUSTRALIAN CRICKET

Aboriginals took so readily to cricket in the early years of white settlement it is disappointing that they do not figure more prominently in the records of first-class matches and hardly at all in international games. The first settlers who taught the Aboriginals cricket often included them in teams that established the game's popularity in Australia. Sometimes they were included by the owners of large holdings simply to make up the numbers, fielding in the deep, going in last, and not being offered a bowl, but many of them showed a marked aptitude for all aspects of the sport. They appeared to enjoy it and their whippy arms enabled them to quickly master basic skills.

In 1835, when the Hobart club met the Carlton club in two matches an Aboriginal named "Shiney" went down in the records as one of the Carlton side—and made three consecutive ducks. When pastoral land in the Edenhope and Harrow regions of Victoria was taken up around 1844–46, the Aboriginals Peter and Bullocky played regularly in teams raised on the properties. By 1865 there were records of Aboriginal teams defeating whites in the Edenhope area. Johnny Taylor, an Aboriginal cricketer in the New South Wales country near where Canberra is now, made history in 1869 when he scored 35 runs in a four-ball over when there were no boundaries and all hits had to be run out. An Aboriginal team from New Norcia to the north of Perth toured the colony extensively in the late 1880s. Similar tours by Aboriginal sides occurred in South Australia. Only in Tasmania, where the Aboriginal population was systematically wiped out in the 1830s and 1840s, did the cricket prowess of Aboriginals fail to win admiration.

William Hayman was so impressed by their skills in the Edenhope district of Victoria where he had a holding that he sent photographs of them to a man called Rowley, proprietor of a refreshment pavilion at Melbourne Cricket Ground, offering to sponsor a match in Melbourne. Tom Wills, of Australian Rules fame who had played first-class cricket in England,

Johnny Mullagh, star Aboriginal cricketer
Photo Harrow Mechanics Institute

20

was appointed to coach the Aboriginals after they had played together for three years. The Melbourne match was conceived more as a contribution to Aboriginal welfare than as a financial venture.

The Aboriginals played preliminary matches in Edenhope, where Tom Wills gave them expert coaching, and then left for Melbourne to play a Melbourne Cricket Club team at the MCG on Boxing Day, 1866. Several of Melbourne's best players were away in Sydney representing Victoria against NSW and *The Argus* was critical of the club for electing the noted bowler James a playing member two days before the match solely to strengthen the MCC side.

The match attracted 10,000 spectators to the ground with other people stealing a free look from trees outside the ground. The crowd completely over-awed the Aboriginals who batted first and were all out for 39. Bullocky and Mullagh reached double figures after Cuzens, one of the big hopes of the Aboriginal players, was out without scoring when he opened the innings. It was the first time the Aboriginals had had an audience of any size and although the big crowd cheered everything they did, the Aboriginals could not settle down. Mullagh got the MCC openers cheaply but Dick Wardill made 45 before the club were all out for 100. Cuzens took 6 for 24. Mullagh made 33 in the second innings and Wills helped with 25 not out but Melbourne CC won the match by nine wickets early on the second day.

The Melbourne *Herald* said: "That they have been thoroughly acquainted with various points of the game was manifestly evident by the manner in which they conducted themselves in the field. Mullagh and Bullocky showed themselves to be no mean batsmen. They not only stopped balls but hit them, showing good direction and strong defence. The fielding was very fair." After the match there was a sports meeting at which Mullagh threw a cricket ball 110 yards. Tarpot gave an exhibition of running backwards at speed, and Mullagh cleared 5ft. 3in. in the high jump.

The fame of the Aboriginal players spread quickly and when the Victorian team played Sixteen of Tasmania on January 17, 1867, Mullagh and Cuzens were picked in the Victorian team. On the day of the match Mullagh was ill and Bullocky took his place. Tasmania won by five wickets and *The Age* blamed the absence of Mullagh as one of the chief causes of Victoria's defeat.

At this point a "Captain" W. Edward Brougham Gurnett appeared in Melbourne and persuaded Hayman and Wills to sign a contract for a year long tour by the Aboriginal team through the colonies and to England. Hayman returned to Edenhope to recruit more players and the Aboriginal team went to Geelong, Bendigo and Ballarat for matches, returning to Melbourne to win a game against a County of Bourke XI.

The public were not enthusiastic about the trip to England, fearing that the Aboriginals were being exploited. Their suspicions deepened when some of Gurnett's cheques were dishonoured and he had to make special arrangements with his creditors before he could leave Victoria.

The Aboriginal players moved on to Sydney where they were beaten by 132 runs by the Albert Club, Redfern, in a match that proved a financial disaster. Plans for a Brisbane match fell through because of exorbitant demands for financial guarantees from "Captain" Gurnett and the team returned to Melbourne destitute. The Hamilton *Spectator* commented: "It is evident that Hayman and his blacks entrusted themselves to hands which were not quite trustworthy". The players were not paid, some became ill, and four of the original team members, Paddy, Jellico, Sugar and Watty, died.

Despite these enormous setbacks, Charles Lawrence, the former all-England player, persisted with his view that the Aboriginal team would prove a worthy investment if taken to England. Alderman George Smith, a former Mayor of Sydney, and G. W. Graham assisted with finance, and good crowds watched matches in Victoria aimed at raising funds for the trip to England. But the Aboriginal Protection Board opposed further tours, fearing another debacle comparable with the earlier trip to Sydney. A Dr Molloy, from the Sydney suburb of Balmoral, wrote to the Board claiming that the change of climate on a trip to England would prove fatal to the players, but all objections were ignored and the team slipped out of Melbourne for matches in Sydney before boarding the Parramatta on February 8, 1868, for the long voyage to England. They were ten years ahead of the first white Australian team to tour England.

In England the team set a remarkable record for stamina, playing 47 matches between May and October, winning 14, losing 14, with 19 drawn. They were on the field 99 days out of a possible 126 and played in 15 different counties. They played 11 matches in September and six in October in cold conditions far more difficult than those encountered by any white Australian side. There were no tea breaks and lunch was taken some time between 2 and 3 p.m. for 35 minutes. They were not provided with lunch and had to take their chances with spectators who crowded the refreshment tents.

One of the players, King Cole, died of tuberculosis in London in June and two others, Sundown and Jim Crow, were sent home sick in August. Of the remaining 11 Aborigines, Red Cap and Tiger played in all 47 matches, Twopenny in 46, Cuzens in 46, Dick-a-Dick and Johnny Mullagh in 45. Three others and Charles Lawrence, the white man, played in 40 matches or more. The white umpire, William Shepherd, an old Surrey professional who travelled with the side, had to play in seven matches and captained the team when Lawrence was rested.

English newspapers largely ignored them after showing some interest in the early matches, but English spectators gave them an enthusiastic welcome. They drew crowds of more than 5,000 several times although a summer of extremes deterred would-be spectators. Those journalists who did report on their matches praised their "gentle and by no means unintellectual appearance," and their "long, wiry beards". The *Rochdale Observer* called them "stalwart men" of "manly, dignified and pleasantly confident gait and bearing". At York the Aboriginals were barred from the luncheon tent, but most centres looked after them well. The Surrey club entertained the whole side to dinner.

Originally the Aboriginals' tour was to involve only 10 matches but the popularity of the team kept attracting additional fixtures. Even the MCC committee, which had voted against a match at Lord's, reversed their decision. D. J. Mulvaney, who produced a delightful book on the Aboriginals' tour, noted that at Lord's their opposition included an earl, a viscount, a lieutenant-colonel and a captain.

MCC scored 164 and 120, with Cuzens taking 10 wickets for 117 runs in the match. The Aboriginals made 185 in their first innings, Mullagh top-scoring with 75, but they collapsed for 45 in their second knock. Mullagh, star of the entire tour, made 21 of these, Cuzens 12. Despite criticism of the crudity of their play the Australian Aboriginals were seldom overwhelmed and, as Mulvaney has stressed, at Reading it was the home side which sent down 20 wides, and lost by an innings and 218.

FIGURES FOR ALL MATCHES

Name	I.	NO	HS	Runs	Ave.	W.	Runs	Ave.
Bullocky	64	4	64*	576	9.66 :	4	46	11.50
J. Cuzens	80	6	87	1367	18.48 :	114	1296	11.37
Dick-a-Dick	71	2	27	309	4.59 :	5	96	19.20
Charley Dumas	64	12	17*	212	4.07 :	—	—	—
Jim Crow	20	5	14	49	3.26 :	—	—	—
King Cole	12	2	18	75	7.50 :	1	34	34.00
C. Lawrence	69	14	63	1192	21.67 :	250	3022	12.09
Mosquito	49	25	8*	89	3.70 :	—	—	—
J. Mullagh	74	4	94	1670	23.85 :	245	2489	10.16
Peter	64	7	30	279	4.86 :	—	—	—
Red Cap	80	6	56	654	8.83 :	54	576	10.66
Tiger	76	4	32	444	6.16 :	—	—	—
Twopenny	76	7	35*	578	8.37 :	35	242	6.91

Also batted: W. S. Norton, 2 innings for 11 runs; W. Shepherd, 11 innings for 64 runs; G. H. Shum-Storey, one inning for 16 at 16.00; Sundown, three innings for one run.

Also bowled: W. Shepherd, six wickets for 124.

Note: The analysis is incomplete for two innings in which Lawrence took seven wickets and Mullagh 12, to give each bowler 257 wickets. The above averages are from C. H. G. Pridham and vary from those in **Sporting Life**, October 28, 1868, as used by D. J. Mulvaney.

According to cricket historian Arthur Haygarth, the Aboriginals played their matches for £200 down or, alternatively, for all the match proceeds out of which they donated £20 to the host club. Haygarth described the tour as "very lucrative". Other contemporary writers said that although the tour was a financial success expenses were so high there was little profit. The tour statistics show that the side included several players who completely failed to match the performances of Cuzens, Mullagh and Lawrence, and to a lesser extent, those of Bullocky, Red Cap and Twopenny.

Apart from the Aboriginals' cricketing skills, their display of Aboriginal sports after every match was a big attraction for the English public. Dick-a-Dick endeared himself to the crowds with his speed in running backwards. Another of Dick-a-Dick's feats was to fend off cricket balls thrown at him from about 20 yards away, defending himself with a parrying shield. Boomerang and spear throwing continually delighted spectators, but at Bootle there was a minor disaster when one of Mullagh's boomerangs veered off-course, struck a man on the head, cutting through his hat and inflicting a severe wound across his brow. The Marylebone club did not want the usual "sports" to be held at Lord's but, to please the crowd they went ahead anyway, and so infectious was the mood they created that at one of their meetings W. G. Grace, then a youth of twenty, joined in with a display of his own. He threw a cricket ball 116, 117 and 118 yards with successive attempts and he also threw the ball 109 yards one way and 105 yards back.

In late October, 1868, the team left England on board the *Dunbar Castle* for the long trip home. When they arrived in February, 1869, they were required to play almost immediately, but a match in Sydney was washed out. A three-day match with Victoria was drawn and the tour finished with another drawn match against a team selected from members of the Duke of Edinburgh's ship, *H.M.S. Galatea's* crew, and members of the garrison regiment. The Duke of Edinburgh watched the match in which the Aborigines scored 331 for the loss of nine wickets. Lawrence and Cuzens each made more than fifty, but the military team replied by making five for 293.

The side then dispersed, the *Hamilton Spectator* praising Hayman, Lawrence and Smith on the team's record and on the way in which the team had been looked after. Unfortunately, the team members did not maintain their cricketing interest and some died within a few years.

Cuzens played in the trial match in 1869–70 between the Victorian Eleven and the "Next Sixteen". Wills dismissed him for a single, and it came as no surprise to find Cuzens omitted from the Victorian side chosen to meet New South Wales in February, 1870. Lawrence made his last appearance for NSW in that match, two months after his forty-second birthday. Twopenny also played for NSW, his only game for the colony,

Above: *Aboriginals playing cricket at Point Macleay, South Australia, probably in the 1870s.* Below: *The Aboriginal team that played at Melbourne Cricket Ground on Boxing Day 1866.* (L to R) *Captain, Officer, Sugar, Jellico, Cuzens, Neddy, Mullagh, Bullocky, Tarpot, Sundown, Peter, umpire.*

but he had a rough time. Charles Gordon made 121 for Victoria, and Twopenny had 56 runs hit off him without taking a wicket. He scored eight in the first innings, but in the second knock Wills clean-bowled him for a duck. Some critics claimed Twopenny threw the ball.

Nearly a decade later Johnny Mullagh played his only match for Victoria, against the 1879 English team led by Lord Harris. The Englishmen scored 248, of which his lordship's share was 67. Mullagh held a catch, but only bowled three overs, and finished with 0 for 8. The Victorians then collapsed, to be out for 146. Tom Emmett took 6 for 41 for Lord Harris' side, while Tom Horan topscored for Victoria with 46. Mullagh went in ninth, scoring four and the Victorians followed-on. Emmett, bowling well, took another five wickets. Mullagh held the innings together with an elegantly played hand of 36, and a collection of £50 was made for him. Lord Harris' team won by six wickets.

Cuzens died from dysentery in March, 1871. For a period after the tour he had been a ground bowler for the Melbourne Club. Twopenny ended his days working as a station hand in the Molonglo area, near Canberra, and died in 1883, another victim of the white man's curse, alcohol. The captain, Lawrence, ran hotels in Sydney before settling in Melbourne. He died in 1916.

Mullagh, the team's hero, died in 1891 at the age of fifty. He was highly respected in the Edenhope area, where he lived alone on Edgar's Pine Hills property. Sensitive about racial discrimination, which had been rare on the English tour, Mullagh once threw his wicket away in a match in Victoria after the opposing captain had called him a "nigger". The Edenhope sports ground was named after Mullagh and a memorial was also erected. "Long after all memory of his team-mates has faded," wrote D. J. Mulvaney, "Mullagh remains the dominant force in the folklore of this pastoral region".

Despite the promising showing by the Aboriginal team of 1868, few Aboriginals since then have figured in Australian first-class cricket. Those that have usually have been the centre of controversy, pace bowlers who operated from short runs. **Jack Marsh** played six matches for NSW, scoring 40 runs at an average of 5.00, and taking 34 wickets at 21.47; **Alex Henry**, who bowled barefoot in club matches, played for Queensland in seven matches between 1901–02 and 1904–05, including a match against NSW when Jack Marsh also played, the only time Aboriginals have opposed each other in Australian first-class cricket; **Eddie Gilbert**, one of the few bowlers to dismiss Bradman for a duck, took 87 wickets for Queensland at 28.97; and **Ian King** who took 30 wickets for Queensland at 28.36 and scored 65 runs at 8.12. And last but by no means least, **Faith Thomas**, an Aboriginal fast bowler from Adelaide who played for the Australian women's cricket team.

The most attractive of all Australia's first-class cricket grounds, and one of the most appealing in the world. It is the only major cricket ground in Australia called "The Oval", a legacy of the influence a Surrey migrant had on the South Australian Cricket Association when The Oval was opened in 1873. The bill to grant the Association a lease of the twelve acres on which Adelaide Oval began was introduced into the State Parliament by John Darling, whose son Joe later captained both the State and Australia. The Oval was established largely through the efforts of H. Yorke Sparks, who became secretary of the Association (the second) soon after The Oval was opened. Much of the advice on pitches and soil came from Englishman James Lillywhite.

Adelaide Oval, fittingly, has an English charm, with the spire of St Peter's Cathedral rising above the scoreboard and the Lofty Mountains stretching away to the north. In the 109 years since it opened, most of the great players of Australian cricket have performed at Adelaide Oval. The first Test on the ground was played in 1884 and the first Sheffield Shield match in the 1890s, with local players Giffen, Lyons, Jarvis, Darling and Hill doing so well they became heroes of the State. Dr W. G. Grace protested loudly when he was given out

ADELAIDE OVAL

Adelaide Oval, with St Peters in the background.

caught for six runs on the ground. Clem Hill made 365 not out there v. NSW in 1900–01 which in 1981 was still the highest score made on the ground by a South Australian. Don Bradman made 369 for South Australia against Tasmania in 1935–36 but he was born in New South Wales.

When the first secretary of the SACA, J. Pickering, inspected the ground that became Adelaide Oval with surveyor H. M. Addison they marked out the boundaries that were later officially adopted. Apparently neither could cut or hook for the boundaries are uncommonly short square of the wicket. When H. Yorke Sparks succeeded Pickering as SACA secretary, he bought 150 old iron posts which he had screwed into the ground. He then bought some chain for £17 which he donated to the association, which could not afford to pay for it. Sparks and his brother then threaded the chains through the posts, thus originating the term "a hit to the chains".

Expert opinion on what was the best grass to plant differed. The local botanist, Dr Schomburgk, favoured planting couch because English clover and rye grasses would not withstand mid-summer heat. On advice from Melbourne that English grasses did well if properly watered, couch was planted. A long argument over the rental the SACA should pay was resolved when the Lord Mayor of Adelaide ruled that the association should pay seven pounds a year for the first seven years and fourteen pounds a year for the seven years after that. A cheap price for a ground which cricketers consider is rivalled for splendour only by the Newlands ground at Cape Town, South Africa, among the world's major Test arenas. The SACA negotiated a fresh 25-year lease with the Adelaide City Council in 1980 requiring annual payments "far in excess of a peppercorn rental".

AGES OF AUSTRALIAN CRICKETERS

Don Blackie was the oldest and Ian Craig the youngest Australian to play in a Test. Blackie played his first Test at 46 years 253 days in 1928 v. England, Craig his first at 17 years 239 days in 1953 v. South Africa. Bert Ironmonger made his Test debut at 46 years 237 days and continued until he was 50 years and 327 days. This compares with W. G. Grace who was 50 years and 320 days in his final England v. Australia Test in 1899. Oldest player to make his debut in Test cricket was James Southerton, who was 49 years and 119 days when he played for England in the first of all Tests at Melbourne in 1877.

The youngest player to appear in a first-class match in Australia was L. J. Junor, who played for Victoria in 1929–30 v. Western Australia at 15 years 265 days. Clayvell Lindsay ("Cyril") Badcock was only 50 days older when he played for Tasmania against Victoria in 1929. Craig was 16 years 249

Left: *Ian Craig, Australia's youngest Test cricketer and youngest Test captain.* Below: *John Marshall, at 58 the oldest player to appear in first-class cricket in Australia.*

days when he scored 91 on his first appearance for NSW at Sydney in 1952 against South Australia. Craig remains Australia's youngest captain—22 years 188 days—a record he earned playing against South Africa at Johannesburg in 1957, and he was the youngest player from any country to make a double century in first-class cricket—17 years 239 days—when he scored 213 not out for NSW v. South Africa in 1953.

Oldest Australian first-class cricketer was wicketkeeper-batsman John Marshall, who played for Tasmania in 1853–54 at 58. Another who appeared in first-class matches when past 50 was G. Moore, of NSW.

YOUNGEST AUSTRALIAN FIRST-CLASS CRICKETERS

L. J. Junor	Victoria v. West Australia, 1929–30	15 years 265 days
C. L. Badcock	Tasmania v. Victoria, 1929–30	15 years 315 days
E. F. a'Beckett	Victoria v. Tasmania, 1851–52	15 years 349 days
C. Hill	South Australia v. West. Australia 1892–93	16 years 9 days
I. D. Craig	NSW v. South Australia, 1951–52	16 years 249 days

OLDEST AUSTRALIAN FIRST-CLASS CRICKETERS

J. Marshall	Tasmania v. Victoria, 1853–54	58 years
G. Moore	NSW v. Victoria, 1872–73	52 years 325 days
H. Ironmonger	Victoria v. NSW, 1933–34	51 years 298 days
D. D. Blackie	Woodfull's XI v. Richardson's XI, 1933–34	51 years 231 days
C. V. Grimmett	South Australia v. NSW, 1940–41	49 years 62 days

YOUNGEST AUSTRALIAN TEST CRICKETER ON DEBUT

I. D. Craig	v. South Africa, 1953	17 years 329 days

OLDEST AUSTRALIAN TEST CRICKETER ON DEBUT

D. D. Blackie	v. England, 1928	46 years 253 days

YOUNGEST AUSTRALIAN TEST CAPTAIN

I. D. Craig	v. South Africa, 1957	22 years 188 days

OLDEST AUSTRALIAN TEST CAPTAINS

S. E. Gregory	v. England, 1912	42 years 130 days
R. B. Simpson	v. West Indies, 1978	42 years 91 days

YOUNGEST AUSTRALIAN TO SCORE A MAIDEN TEST CENTURY

R. N. Harvey	v. India, 1947–48 (153)	19 years 121 days

OLDEST AUSTRALIAN TO SCORE A MAIDEN TEST CENTURY

A. J. Richardson	v. England, 1926 (100)	37 years 351 days

Note: The 1935–36 Australian team in India (semi-official, with no Tests) included a number of veterans, including the manager, F. A. Tarrant, who played in the first-class fixture against the Maharajah of Pataila's XI, aged 55 years 37 days. Tarrant first played for Victoria in 1898. Also on this tour:

*C. G. Macartney made his last first-class appearance against All India at the age of 49 years 226 days;

* H. Ironmonger made his last first-class appearance against All India aged 53 years 305 days.

ALBERT CLUB, THE
One of the most famous Australian clubs in the early days of cricket, the Albert Club was founded in 1852, and helped foster interest in cricket before inter-Colonial matches began. Many of the finest players in Sydney appeared for the Alberts, including Dave Gregory, Fred Spofforth, Billy Murdoch, H. Massie, Harry Moses, Nat Thompson and the Bannermans. The Alberts published a strict set of rules for members in which it was stressed that white hats, white trousers and blue shirts had to be worn, the captain having the right to a distinguishing colour of his own.

The Albert Club played matches against clubs such as the Warwick, Belvidere, of Carlton and National or against Sydney University, and even sent a team to Tasmania. The match against the National Club in 1862 finished in uproar when the Nationals refused to continue because 12 men were on the field when their batsman Newcombe was caught. The Alberts offered to let Newcombe return when the umpires ruled that the catch had been fairly taken, but Newcombe refused. The umpires then ruled that the Nationals had lost the match, by failing to continue.

30

The Alberts played a draw with Northern Tasmania on their Tasmanian trip in 1875 and defeated Southern Tasmania by eight wickets. The club then won a match against the full Tasmanian side by 126 runs, Spofforth taking 8 for 48 and 6 for 3. Dave Gregory and Murdoch were in the Albert team.

The Albert Club's habit of charging 20 per cent of the gate takings for the use of their playing field at Redfern—the club had leased the land for 21 years early in the 1860s at £100 a year—indirectly led to the establishment of the Sydney Cricket Ground. Clubs that could not play on The Domain—it could not be fenced—were disgruntled by the Albert club's charges and approached the Minister for Lands, Thomas Garrett. He granted a lease of the ground known as the Civil and Military Ground, where services teams played cricket and the Alberts sometimes appeared. In 1875 three trustees were appointed to what by then was known as the Association Ground, Richard Driver, president of the NSWCA, Phil Sheridan of the NSWCA, and W. W. Stephens, who represented the minister.

The first game on the Association Ground was played in 1877 and the following year the first intercolonial match to be played at this new ground took place. By then the Albert Club's lease on its ground had lapsed and the site of the Albert's playing field later was sold off for building blocks.

A skilful, persistent Western Australian right-arm fast-medium bowler who in 1981 took 42 wickets in six Tests against England, a record for an Australian bowler in England. He had served a seven-year apprenticeship in first-class cricket before he achieved this feat, improving his skills and adding an inswinger and a leg-cutter to the outswinger he had had since he was a dramatic success in schoolboy cricket.

Tall, fair-skinned, with a healthy mop of brown hair, Alderman is one of a cricket-mad family from the Perth suburb of Subiaco. His father Bill played for the State Colts in 1946–47, his brother John plays first grade with him in the Subiaco-Floreat side, and his sister Denise is a high-scoring batswoman for Australia's World Cup squad. The Alderman children spent their summers playing cricket in their backyard, with cousins and friends making up the numbers. Later Terry was a star bowler for Aquinas College.

Terry made his debut for Western Australia a few months after his 18th birthday, taking 5 for 65 in New South Wales' first innings at Sydney early in the 1974–75 season. He broke down with a hamstring injury in the second innings and before he had had time to be hailed as a "find" was on the plane back to Perth. Similar injuries hampered him for years. Understandably, he sometimes held back and did not bowl at

**ALDERMAN,
Terence Michael,
1956–**

First-Class Averages
Batting, 236 runs at 6.38;
Bowling, 271 wickets at
23.08.

Tests (14): 44 runs at 5.5;
63 wickets at 26.22.

31

full pace. He also showed a lack of enthusiasm for hard work both in matches and at the practice nets.

His strike rate was impressive, however, and Western Australians pressed for his inclusion in the Australian team. Only the presence of splendid bowlers like Lillee, Thomson, Pascoe, Hurst, Hogg and Lawson kept him out. After his debut match coup of 5 for 65, his best performances included another 5 for 65 against New South Wales at Perth in 1976–77, 6 for 63 against South Australia at Perth in 1978–79, 5 for 47 against the West Indies at Perth in 1979–80, 6 for 80 against Queensland at Perth in 1979–80. He has never been a batsman of account but is a safe field and a sure catch.

In the Australian winter of 1980, Alderman went to Scotland to play league cricket as a professional. He returned a different bowler, tougher in mental outlook, eager for work, and with a variety of additional deliveries, which he had worked hard to perfect during his sojourn in Scotland. Ian Brayshaw, a close observer of Western Australian cricket, noted that Alderman had slightly more pace and his gasps at the delivery stride were clearly heard in broadcasts as he bent to his work on the WACA ground.

Just before the Australian team to tour England in 1981 was chosen, Western Australia played vital matches against New South Wales and Queensland in Perth in which they clinched the 1980–81 Sheffield Shield. Alderman took 12 wickets in those two games to make certain of his place in the side for England. Behind him was a record of 171 wickets for his State. The English tour proved a turning point in his career thanks to the realisation that he could do more off the seam than by swinging the ball. He took 51 wickets on the tour at 20.86, finishing ahead of the great Dennis Lillee on the tour averages. His 10 innings with the bat yielded only 34 runs at 6.80 but he proved a reliable slips and gully fieldsman, taking 13 catches. His 42 Test wickets broke the record of 41 Rodney Hogg had set in the 1978–79 series against England and was six ahead of Arthur Mailey's 36 in 1920–21 in five Tests, the long-time record for a series against England.

Alderman attributed his success to sharing the new ball with Lillee and to Lillee's advice that he should bowl off a longer run and try to hit the seam. He was rewarded by being named one of the five Cricketers-of-the-Year in the 1982 *Wisden*, which said no blame could be laid on Alderman for Australia's failure to regain The Ashes. "He stamped himself as a seam bowler of the highest quality," *Wisden* said. Alderman was nowhere near as penetrative at home against Pakistan and the West Indies in 1981–82 when injuries hampered him, but he did take 14 for 87 for WA against NSW at Perth. His form improved, however, when he got on to the softer pitches in New Zealand in 1982 and he again moved the ball sharply from the seam, taking eight further Test wickets.

A hard-hitting Victorian right-hand batsman, handy change round-arm bowler, smart field and sure catch between 1875 and 1884 who is best remembered as the manager of three important touring teams. He managed the Australian teams which toured England in 1880 and 1884 under W. L. Murdoch and in 1882–83 managed the Hon. Ivo Bligh's English team in Australia. Alexander played in two Tests, one at The Oval in 1880, the first ever test played in England, and the other at Adelaide in 1884.

In the great match at The Oval, he joined Murdoch on the third day when Australia, with eight out, still needed 84 to avoid an innings defeat. He had scored only 10 runs in his previous four knocks in England, but he contributed 33 in a stand of 52. W. H. Moule then helped Murdoch to add 88, leaving England with 57 to get. England lost five wickets getting them. Alexander, who played for the Melbourne Club, took six wickets on that tour at 33.83 runs.

ALEXANDER, George
1851–1930

First-Class Averages:
Batting, 466 runs at 15.53;
Bowling, 33 wickets at 18.39.

Tests (2): 52 runs at 13.00; 2 wickets at 46.50.

A strongly-built Victorian fast bowler who figured in widely discussed incidents during the controversial Bodyline tour by Jardine's England team in 1932–33. He was not a tall man but he had a wide chest and powerful arms and could intimidate the best of batsmen through sheer pace. And he could go on bowling lively deliveries just short of express pace for long periods.

Alexander, born at Ascot Vale, Victoria, started to play cricket at 16 when he joined Essendon's third grade side in Melbourne. He played for Essendon firsts for 16 years and was Victoria's opening bowler for seven Shield seasons. He made his debut for the State in 1929 and was fast enough by 1932 to take 7 for 95 against New South Wales and keep Ernie McCormick out of the Victorian team.

His performance against New South Wales won him a place in the Fifth Test at Sydney. He hit England's captain Jardine three times in one over and also broke Wyatt's bat, but the English batsmen mastered him and that was his only Test. Jardine brought guffaws from spectators by walking down the pitch to pat down a spot where he indicated Alexander had pitched the ball—at a place closer to Alexander than to Jardine's stumps.

Alexander's selection to provide pace to match Larwood's proved a brave failure in his only Test, with his bowling figures 1 for 154 and his batting 17 not out and 0.

Alexander toured India in 1935–36 in the team captained by Frank Tarrant, and served with the AIF in Crete, the Middle East and the Pacific Islands during World War II. He settled in Euroa after the war and served as a councillor there for more than 30 years. He was responsible for three England teams

ALEXANDER, Harry
Houston ("Bull")
1905–

First-Class Averages:
Batting, 228 runs at 6.16;
Bowling, 95 wickets at 33.91

Tests (1): 17 runs at 17.00; 1 wicket at 154.00

playing in Euroa where the ground sports one of the best turf wickets in Australia and a stand named "The H. H. Alexander Pavilion".

ALLAN, Francis Erskine, 1849–1917

First-Class Averages: Batting, 371 runs at 10.91; Bowling, 123 wickets at 13.31.

Tests (1): 5 runs at 5.00; 4 wickets at 20.00.

One of the first internationally praised Australian bowlers, a fast-medium left-hander who imparted disconcerting swing to the ball. He was the mainstay of the Victorian attack for years after his debut but he made the mistake of withdrawing from the first of all Tests, declaring that he could not spare the time. He said he had to go to an agricultural show that was on at the time and could not miss the chance of mixing with old friends, which must rank as one of cricket's great misjudgments. One writer labelled him the "bowler of the century". When Allan played his one Test against England at Melbourne in 1879 he scored five runs in his only innings, and took 4 for 80.

Allan, born at Allansford, Victoria, was at his best before Tests and international tours began. He was a natural bowler who could spin the ball at speed as well as bend it, a first-rate rifle shot and angler, and a right-handed batsman with a style peculiarly his own whom team-mates called "the crouching panther" because of his odd stance.

Allan was one of the major hopes of the first Australian team to visit England in 1878 under Dave Gregory, but he detested the bleak English weather and failed to do himself justice. Harry Boyle took over as partner to Spofforth, though Boyle had been inferior to Allan back in Australia. But on one gloriously hot day at Lord's Allan unveiled his full powers, taking 3 for 27 and 7 for 76, Australia winning by 98 runs.

Englishmen who saw him that day were unanimous that they had never seen a bowler of such pace get so much work on the ball. Although form like this largely eluded him in England, he finished with 26 wickets at 23.28 in all matches.

Allan was responsible for many fine bowling displays including 8 for 35 and 5 for 25 in the Melbourne match in 1871–72, and 8 for 20 at Sydney in 1868–69. Other fine efforts included 9 for 46 and 5 for 24 for Victoria v. 16 of Tasmania in 1867–68 and all 10 wickets for his hometown of Warrnambool against a strong Coranderrk (Victorian country) aboriginal team in 1884.

Many oldtime Australian cricket writers gave Allan, 6 ft 1 ins, the credit—not Spofforth—for pioneering fast swing bowling.

ALLAN, Peter John 1935–

A right-handed Queensland fast-medium bowler who took more wickets for the State than any bowler except Ron Oxen-

34

ham and Geoff Dymock, but is remembered most for one memorable season when he really got his act together. In 1965–66, Allan, a big, strong seam bowler of rare stamina, became one of only three bowlers who have taken all ten wickets in a Sheffield Shield innings.

Allan took 10 for 61 off 126 balls against Victoria at Melbourne, figures that had a special sweetness as he had been unable to get past the Victorian State practise squad in three seasons in Melbourne. Only Tim Wall, with 10 for 36 for South Australia against New South Wales at Sydney in 1932–33, and Ian Brayshaw, with 10 for 44 for Western Australia v. Victoria at Perth in 1967–68, have taken all 10 wickets in a Shield innings. Only Allan has performed the feat at the MCG.

Allan made his debut for Queensland in 1959–60 and played in three Shield matches. He was transferred in his job to Melbourne for the next three years but could not get a turn in representative matches. He returned to Queensland in 1963–64 and was a regular member of the State team until his retirement after the 1968–69 season. The year of his ten-wicket haul, he was chosen for his sole Test against Mike Smith's English team at Brisbane, taking 2 for 83. He didn't bat. He was 12th man for the Second Test, and was chosen for the fourth Test but had to withdraw through injury.

He toured the West Indies with Australia in 1965 but did not play in a Test. He played in only four matches and bowled only 65 overs on the entire tour, taking five wickets for 209 runs at 41.80.

First-Class Averages: Batting, 689 runs at 10.60; Bowling, 206 wickets at 26.10.

Tests (1): Did not bat, 2 wickets at 41.50.

A Sydney-born fast bowler who played in 25 Tests for England. Allen captained England against the land of his birth five times. Popular with team-mates and opponents alike, he gained added respect from Australians by refusing to bowl at the body during the Bodyline series. In 1936 he brought the MCC team to Australia, losing a marvellous rubber 3–2 after winning the first two Tests, every match providing a result.

He was an enormously exciting fast bowler, running full tilt at the stumps and turning side-on in the classical delivery stride, coiled like a spring as he let the ball go. His Bodyline tour bag of 21 Test wickets was richly deserved and often forgotten, but he did far more for cricket when he returned to Australia in 1936 as England's captain. His warmth and enthusiasm for the re-establishment of cricket's virtues, helped stabilise international cricket when further arguments would have been disastrous.

Allen played for Eton, Cambridge University and Middlesex, and became president of the MCC during 1963–64. Over the years he has done many favours for Australian cricket, particularly in helping to put Australia's case at Lord's on con-

ALLEN, George Oswald Browning ("Gubby"), 1902–

A fine action study of "Gubby" Allen, a fast bowler with a splendidly smooth action. Note how the umpire is watching the back crease not the front for a no-ball.

troversial issues. In all first-class matches, he scored 11 centuries. In 25 Tests he made one century. He held 131 catches in first-class games. Allen scored 9,232 runs in his first-class career and took 778 wickets. Of these he scored 750 runs and took 81 wickets in Test matches. He is a nephew of Reginald Charles Allen.

ALLEN, Reginald Charles, 1858–1952

First Class Averages: Batting, 382 runs at 12.32.

Tests (1): 44 runs at 22.00.

A resolute right-hand batsman for New South Wales before the Sheffield Shield competition began who played in the final Test against Shrewsbury's touring English side in 1886–87. Allen, born in Sydney, scored 14 in the first innings and a brave 30 in the second innings being finally caught by team-mate C. T. B. Turner fielding as a substitute as Australia failed by 71 runs to score the 221 needed for victory. Allen's sole Test was notable for the absence from the Australian side of Spofforth, who had played his last Test, and of the Notts all-rounder Barnes from the English team—Barnes had injured his hand throwing a punch at Australia's McDonnell, hitting a wall instead of McDonnell. Allen played in only 17 first-class matches.

36

A right-hand batsman and leg-break bowler who, with his son Ross, boosted the reputation of Toowoomba cricket by turning in some outstanding performances for Queensland. Tom played 43 matches for Queensland between 1933–34 and 1939–40, scoring 1,869 runs at 24.27. His four centuries did a lot to lift Queensland batsmanship in the State's early years in the Shield competition.

Tom Allen's highest score was 146 in a Queensland total of 528 at Brisbane in 1935–36 which caused the shock defeat of New South Wales. He followed it with an innings of 100 against Victoria at Melbourne and 54 against South Australia at Adelaide. In 1936–37, he made 101 against Victoria at Melbourne and in 1938–39 put on 165 for the second wicket with Bill Brown against Victoria in Melbourne in scoring 136. In the return match against Victoria that summer he made 79 in Brisbane.

The Allens played most of their cricket in Toowoomba on matting but when Tom went to Brisbane in 1936–37 for a season in club cricket he scored 419 runs at 83.80, highest score 155 not out, in seven innings for South Brisbane. Tom and a host of Allens were stalwarts of Queensland country carnivals for many years, and the family did a lot for cricket in outlying areas. **Ross Allen** (1939), a right-hand fast medium bowler and right-hand batsman, played one Shield match for Queensland in 1962–63, taking 2 for 62 and scoring 18 runs for once out. The Toowoomba Allens are not related to Test fast bowler Peter Allen.

ALLEN, Thomas 1912–1954

First-Class Averages:
Batting, 1,869 runs at 24.27;
Bowling, 20 wickets at 48.10.

A combative, talkative left-hander who, in between working as a blacksmith's striker, boilermaker's assistant, car greaser, professional boxer, dancehall bouncer, chicken farmer, deep-sea fisherman and cider-brewer, found time to give some of the most notable performances in the history of English county cricket. He never played for Australia but he was superior to many who did. He played for New South Wales 12 times, scoring three centuries in wartime matches, but moved to England when he missed selection in Bradman's 1948 side. There he became a legend, both for his repartee and prolific run-scoring when he was a batsman of some antiquity.

Alley as a batsman was busy, brimful of strokes from the first ball he faced, seldom seeking time to play himself in. He could play the left-hander's cuts without hint of edging them, drove forcefully in front of the stumps and pulled and hooked with unerring precision. At full flight, he rarely swung at a ball and missed, and bad balls invariably went for four. He bowled accurate left-arm swingers and cutters and mixed them up cleverly. In 1960 he bowled 14 consecutive maiden

ALLEY, William Edward, 1919–

First-Class Averages:
Batting, 19,612 runs at
31.88;
Bowling, 768 wickets at
22.68.

overs for Somerset. He was an outstanding gully fieldsman. As befitted a player with his background he had wrists of steel.

Alley, later a Test umpire, always played cricket aggressively. "Never bowl your granny a full toss even on her birthday," was the way he expressed his approach. In his prime only Fred Trueman matched him as a talker. Trueman once bowled a bouncer that whistled over the aged Alley's head. Alley advanced down the pitch and threatened to wrap the bat round Trueman's head if he did it again. At the end of the over, Trueman confided in his team-mates, "Yon Aussie seems a—good bloke, but he don't 'arf—swear". It was Alley who, when he had an lbw appeal turned down bowling for Somerset, called "Are you blind?" to the umpire. The umpire said, "What did you say?" and Alley replied: "Oh, don't tell me you are deaf, too".

Alley was born on the Hawkesbury River north of Sydney and went to school at Brooklyn, where one of his class-mates was the famous Australian boxer, Vic Patrick. His first job was on a Hawkesbury oyster farm. When he began playing grade cricket for Sydney's Petersham club, he left home before seven each Saturday morning and returned on the paper train early Sunday morning. He went to live in Sydney when he became a professional boxer. He had won all 28 of his pro. fights and was hailed as a potential champion when he bent down to pick up a ball at cricket practise and was hit a shocking blow by a wild shot from an adjoining net. His jaw was so badly broken he could not fight again and doctors needed 20 stitches to repair his mouth.

He was an exciting figure in Sydney grade cricket, scoring heavily week after week. He played on 12 occasions for New South Wales, usually as an opener, but when Arthur Morris returned from the war the State selectors dropped him down the list, a move that cost him all chance of Test selection. When his first wife died tragically, he went off to play in the Lancashire League. He played successfully for Colne for five seasons from 1948 and then with Blackpool for four. He married a Lancashire girl and fathered three sons.

Alley wanted to play county cricket for Lancashire with Ken Grieves but Lancashire rejected him because he was too old so he went to Somerset where another Sydney grade mate, Colin McCool, had done so well. Alley, at an alleged 38, was a spectacular success from his first match with Somerset and he spent the next few years travelling happily around England in a red van that carried a mattress in the back, for use after the pubs shut.

The runs kept flowing and wickets tumbling, and he bought a small holding near Taunton, where he had an orchard, raised sheep and poultry and made good use of his press for producing "scrumpy", or cider. Once a week he had a "parish pump" meeting with the local farmers in the village pub. He even learned to outplay the locals in their ancient game of nine-pin skittles. Somerset had not known a character like him since "Sammy" Woods, the legendary Australian.

With McCool and Alley firing, Somerset moved off the bottom of the County table. They were fifth in 1962, third in 1963. In 1961, after McCool returned to Australia, the Somerset committee awarded Alley a benefit year after only four years service. He returned the compliment by scoring 3,019 runs in all games during the season, including a record 2,761 in County games and a record 11 centuries. That was the year he scored 134 and 95 against Richie Benaud's Australians playing for Somerset and a further century against the Australians playing for Gilligan's XI.

In 1962 he narrowly missed the double of 2,000 runs and 100 wickets in an English season, scoring 1,915 runs and taking 112 wickets. He backed himself for $1,000 with a book-making firm to complete the double of 1,000 runs and 100 wickets in 1962 and as he expressed it, "I walked it in".

By now doubts were frequently raised in newspapers about

A typically pugnacious shot of Bill Alley turning a ball to leg. He was a batsman who kept the score moving.

Alley's age. Colin McCool said, "If Bill was born in 1919 like he says, he must have been in first year at school when he came into grade cricket". Asked about his age, Alley said, "I still haven't found my birth certificate".

Somerset's committee inadvisedly read the newspaper reports about "Grandpa Bill" and notwithstanding a magnificent 110 in partnership with young Greg Chappell against Kent they let him go at the end of the 1968 season, offering him a contract merely for one-day matches. "They know what they can do with their offer," said Alley. "It is either a deal to play a full season's County cricket or nothing." He had made a mammoth 19,612 runs in first-class cricket at an average of 31.88, and taken 768 wickets at 22.68. For New South Wales he made 597 of those runs at 42.64.

In 1969, he turned to umpiring and by 1974 he was given a Test. He umpired the First Test between England and Australia at Nottingham in 1981. He is ranked as a completely impartial umpire even when he umpires Australian team fixtures, but he may have let his gift for repartee compromise him when he umpired one or two big matches with his countryman and old Lancashire league rival, Cec Pepper.

ALL-ROUNDERS

George Giffen, who gave some of the finest allround performances in the history of Australian cricket.

Australia has never been short of players who could bat, bowl and field with almost equal proficiency. Over the years the contribution of high class all-rounders has been one of Australian cricket's strengths, a tradition that probably began with George Giffen, a dominant figure on the last four of his five tours of England whether batting or bowling. The famous English cricket authority H. S. Altham considered that Giffen's performance in scoring 271 runs and then taking 16 wickets for 166 runs for South Australia against Victoria in 1891–92 at Adelaide the greatest all-round performance in recorded cricket at any level. Giffen topped both batting and bowling averages for the 1886 Australian team in England with outstanding figures. He scored 1,454 runs and took 162 wickets. Here are some of the most memorable achievements by Australian all-rounders:

1,000 Runs and 100 Wickets In Tests: Seven Australians have achieved this distinction. Their figures are:

	M	Runs	HS	Ave.	100	Wkts.	Ave.	No. of Tests to Double
R. Benaud	63	2201	122	24.45	3	248	27.03	32
A. K. Davidson	44	1328	80	24.59	—	186	20.53	34
G. Giffen	31	1238	161	23.35	1	103	27.09	30
I. W. Johnson	45	1000	77	18.51	—	109	29.19	45
R. R. Lindwall	61	1502	118	21.15	2	228	23.03	38
K. R. Miller	55	2958	147	36.97	7	170	22.97	33
M. A. Noble	42	1997	133	30.25	1	121	25.00	27

Benaud, who heads this table, further enhanced his value by taking 65 Test catches.

40

Superb all-rounder Richie Benaud padding up before going in to bat at the SCG nets.

Best All-Round Performances In A Test Series: By Giffen and Benaud. In the 1894–95 series against England, Giffen scored 475 runs at 52.77 in five Tests and took 34 wickets at 24.11. In the five Test 1957–58 series against South Africa, Benaud scored 329 runs at 54.83 and took 30 wickets at 21.93. Giffen made a topscore of 161, Benaud 122. Giffen took five wickets in an innings three times, Benaud five wickets in an innings four times.

A Century And Five Wickets In A Test: Charlie Kelleway was the first Australian to perform this feat when he scored 114 and took 5 for 33 against South Africa in the Triangular series at Old Trafford. Jack Gregory scored 100 and took 7 for 69 against England at Melbourne in 1920–21. Keith Miller scored 109 and took 6 for 107 against the West Indies at Kingston in 1954–55. Richie Benaud made 100 and took 5 for 84 against South Africa at Johannesburg in 1957–58.

Warwick Armstrong demonstrates his versatility. Left he drives a ball powerfully to the fence during the final Test in 1921; Right he delivers a right-arm legspinner, lumbering to the stumps but sustaining a good length, all 22 stone of him.

100 Runs And 10 Wickets In The Same Match: Alan Davidson scored 44 and 80 and took 5 for 135 and 6 for 87 against the West Indies in the tied Test at Brisbane in 1960–61.

Best All-Round Performances By Wicket-Keepers: Rod Marsh heads the list, with more than 300 dismissals and more than 3,000 runs in Test cricket, followed by Bert Oldfield, with 1,427 runs and 130 Test dismissals. Marsh took 25 Tests to reach the 100 dismissals and 1,000 runs double, Oldfield 41.

Most Under-Rated Australian All-Rounder: Most cricket historians disregard the all-round skills of Ken "Slasher" Mackay in assessing this unique cricketer. Admittedly, he developed late as a fast-medium bowler but he should never be considered solely as a batsman with a lot of weird habits. He scored 10,823 runs and took 251 wickets in first-class cricket, and in Test matches he scored 1,507 runs and took 50 wickets with a best performance of 6 for 42. Mackay never made a Test century although he made 13 Test scores of 50.

Best All-Round Performance On An English Tour: By Warwick Armstrong, who, in 1905 on his second tour of England, scored 2,002 runs and took 130 wickets in all matches. His 303 not out against Somerset was the highest score until then by an Australian on tour in England. His bowling figures include 7 for 16 v. Gloucestershire, 5 for 29 v. Derbyshire, 6 for 25 v. Surrey, 8 for 50 against Middlesex, and 6 for 32 followed by 6 for 60 against Lancashire.

Best Debut By An All-Rounder: Probably the most impressive was by Keith Miller who scored 79 and took 7 for 60 in his first Test in 1946–47 against England. He finished second in the batting averages to Bradman in that series with 384 runs at 76.80 and second in the bowling averages to Lindwall with 16 wickets at 20.87. Miller's injured back often prevented him finishing with the figures he deserved but he still had a decisive influence on many big matches. In the Third Test at Sydney in 1950–51 for instance, he took 4 for 37 and made 145 not out. In all first-class matches Miller scored 14,183 runs, took 497 wickets, and held 136 catches.

Best "Double" By An Australian: In 1950 at Masterton, New Zealand, Alan Davidson took 10 for 29 off 81 balls against Wairarapa, with the last batsman smashing down all three stumps as he tried to dodge a Davidson bouncer. Davidson followed with an innings of 157 not out in only 109 minutes. But unfortunately this was not a first-class match. According to *Wisden*, the only comparable feat was by E. M. Grace who in 1862 scored 192 not out and then took 10 wickets in the second innings of a 15–a-side match.

ALLSOPP, Arthur Henry, 1908–

First-Class Averages: Batting, 1,469 runs at 45.90.

A classy country-bred right-hand batsman who had trouble overcoming his Boys' Home background but played some sparkling innings in the 1930s for New South Wales and Victoria. He was born in the NSW mining town of Lithgow and went to Dr Parsonage's home for delinquent boys at an early age. He went into the NSW side from country cricket in 1929–30 but found it more convenient to travel from the home at Leeton to play for Victoria from the 1933–34 season.

"Boy could he bat," said former team-mate Bill Hunt. "He was right up there in the class of Archie Jackson and Bradman and McCabe, but unfortunately a few bad reports went in about him and the people who ran Australian cricket were not prepared to be sympathetic to a bloke who had really tough beginnings. He was a great guy and the authorities made a big mistake in the way they treated him."

Allsopp was a particularly powerful hitter of the ball who excelled on the drive. He kept wicket for Leeton, but fielded on the off for NSW and Victoria. He played no club cricket in NSW but appeared for Richmond in Melbourne district matches. His innings of 146 in 180 minutes in 1934–35 was regarded as the innings of the season. In 1935–36, Frank Tarrant included him in his side on the tour of India. He played for NSW from 1929 to 1930–31 and for Victoria in 1933–35.

43

**ANDREWS, Charles William ("Cassie")
1901–1962**

First-Class Averages:
Batting, 2,246 runs at
31.65;
Bowling, 6 wickets at
31.83.

A right-hand opening batsman and right-arm medium-pace bowler for New South Wales and Queensland through the 1930s, who learnt cricket in the Maitland district. His place in Australia's cricket history rests on his seventh wicket partnership with E. C. Bensted in 1934–35, only nine runs short of the then world record* for that wicket, and in 1981 still the highest seventh wicket stand in Australian first-class matches.

In an earlier match, in 1930, he opened for New South Wales with Bradman against Queensland and scored 56. Bradman was out for three in the first innings and made 452 not out in the second innings, for a long time the world's highest first-class score. Andrews played cricket for New South Wales from 1928 to 1931 and for Queensland from 1931 to 1937.

After his move to Queensland in 1931 Andrews made his debut for the State at the age of 30, hitting 110 against Victoria at Brisbane. He continued to play for Queensland until 1936–37, scoring 1,826 for the State in 30 Shield matches, top-score 253 (average 33.81), and made 116 runs in matches against visiting MCC teams. He seldom bowled but took six wickets for Queensland at 30.33 apiece and 0 for 10 for New South Wales.

**ANDREWS, Thomas James Edwin
1890–1970**

A dashing right-handed batsman of crowd pleasing style with splendidly free strokes, and a nimble close to the wicket fieldsman who played 16 Tests for Australia and 74 first-class matches for NSW. He was a busy batsman, adept at stealing singles, and could subdue the best attacks with an easy confidence that was a trademark of his cricket. But he did not score a Test century. He was regarded as an unlucky batsman often being dismissed within sight of a century. In England in 1921 he was out for 92 and 94 against England.

He was one of those batsmen who seem destined to lose their wickets to remarkable catches. Several of his nine dismissals while in the nineties came from spectacular catches. In all first-class matches he scored 12 centuries and two double centuries, and over 8,000 stylish runs. His genius in the field lifted the performance of every side in which he played, for he had a famous throwing arm that forced even the most fleet-footed batsmen to remain at the crease, afraid of the wicked returns he rifled in only millimetres over the stumps. He not only saved numberless runs, but had the gift of arousing spectators to a pitch of joyous enthusiasm that only superlative fielding can inspire.

* The world record seventh wicket partnership, set in 1902, was 344 by K. S. Ranjitsinhji and W. Newham, for Sussex against Essex. This was broken in 1954–55 by D. St E. Atkinson and C. C. Depeiza who made 347 for the West Indies v. Australia, at Bridgetown, Barbados.

Andrews' first-class career lasted from 1913 to 1931. He went from the Petersham first grade side to the NSW team in 1913, toured England twice (in 1921 and 1926), New Zealand once (1924), South Africa once (1921), and Malaya with Oldfield's team in 1927. He was chosen for the Australian tour of South Africa in 1914 that had to be abandoned because of the war. In 1919–20, he began with a century against South Australia at Sydney and followed with 247 not out v. Victoria, highest score of his career. In all of those years and on so many contrasting cricket fields, his cavalier approach set Australian cricket in a special place for those who watched.

The 1928–29 season was his last in first-class cricket, but he was still good enough in 1929–30 at the age of 40 to score 1,150 runs for Petersham at an average of 88.46—the highest summer aggregate to that time in Sydney grade cricket. In his 13 Tests against England and three against South Africa, he scored 592 runs at an average of 26.90. His one Test wicket for 116 runs did not show his value as a leg-break bowler. For

First-Class Averages:
Batting, 8,095 runs at 39.48;
Bowling, 95 wickets at 32.10.

Tests (16): 592 runs at 26.90; 1 wicket for 116 runs.

Tommy Andrews moves out to drive, swinging the bat freely. He was a lovely stroke player, unlucky to miss a Test century.

NSW, he had 115 innings, scored 4,869 runs, average 44.66, and took 82 wickets at 29.42.

None of these figures convey the style and easy confidence of the man, nor do they show his immense value to teams such as Armstrong's memorable 1921 side. Andrews lacked the desire to show the endurance of a Ponsford, Bradman or Woodfull, but he relished opportunities for shot-making. Arthur Mailey rated him an invaluable team player because of his lively personality and competitive nature. He was capable of a spate of joyous strokes or of producing superb catches or run outs when his team faced a crisis. Andrews always chuckled over the fact that when he made 164 for Australia against Middlesex in 1926 he was caught three times off no balls. That day at least cricket's gods were kind to him. Tommy Andrews was a stonemason by trade who made the headstones for Archie Jackson and Victor Trumper when their graves were moved to Waverley cemetery in Sydney. His family owned a number of funeral parlours.

APPEARANCE RECORDS, BY AUSTRALIAN CRICKETERS

Rodney Marsh in 1981–82 became Australia's longest-serving international cricketer when he appeared in his 80th Test match, but there is doubt about where he achieved the record. Australian statisticians, adhering to a ruling by the Australian Cricket Board, have Marsh achieving the record in Sydney when he played in the Second Test against the West Indies, but English authorities consider Marsh set the record one Test later in Adelaide against the West Indies. There is no argument about Marsh holding the record as he played a further three Tests soon afterwards in New Zealand, reaching a total of 83 or 84, depending on which side of the dispute you consider valid.

The disagreement stems from the abandoned Third Test between England and Australia at Melbourne, when the scheduled dates were December 31, 1970, to January 5, 1971. Both teams and the 12th-men were announced, and the toss was made, but as the players took the field—Ray Illingworth sent Australia in after winning the toss from Bill Lawry—with the umpires Tom Brooks and Lou Rowan, heavy rain began. The rain continued until the third day. Sir Donald Bradman, then chairman of the ACB, called a special meeting at the ground which was attended by Sir Cyril Hawker, president of the MCC, the MCC team manager, D. G. Clark, and G. O. Allen, treasurer of the MCC. This meeting agreed that the Test be abandoned and the result be declared a draw.

The ACB has confirmed the decision in various ways many times since. Tom Brooks has been officially given 24 Tests, which enables him to share the Test appearance record for umpires with the late George Borwick. Johnny Gleeson was

46

paid his entitlement from the ACB Players' Provident Fund because he had reached the statutory 30-Test mark, which included the washed out Melbourne Test. An extra Test was added to the MCC schedule and designated the Seventh Test. And the ACB credited all 12 players named in the Australian team with a Test appearance although they did not take the field.

Marsh was one of the 12 Australians awarded a Test, although some of them did not even change into their cricket clothes. Hence ACB records show him having played his 80th Test at Sydney, while English authorities who have never accepted the Melbourne washout as a Test consider Marsh played his 80th Test one match later in Adelaide. *Wisden's Cricket Almanack*, noted historians Bill Frindall, Irving Rosenwater, and other renowned English statistical authorities, show that six Tests were played in 1970–71, whereas the ACB has ruled that seven Tests took place that summer.

Whatever side you take, Marsh definitely owns the Australian Test appearance record, which he achieved in his 11th season of first-class cricket in a career that began in 1970–71. Neil Harvey took from 1948 to 1963 to establish the previous appearance record of 79 Tests for Australia. Apart from Harvey and Marsh, the Australians who have played in most Tests are:

G. S. Chappell 76; I. M. Chappell 75; K. D. Walters 74; W. M. Lawry 67; I. R. Redpath 66; D. K. Lillee 63; R. Benaud 63; R. B. Simpson 62; R. R. Lindwall 61; G. D. McKenzie 60; S. E. Gregory 58; K. R. Miller 55; W. A. S. Oldfield 54; D. G. Bradman 52; A. T. W. Grout 51; W. W. Armstrong 50.

Most Consecutive Test Appearances: 71 by Ian Chappell between 1965–66 at Adelaide and the Melbourne Test in 1975–76.

Most Test Appearances As Captain: 42, by Greg Chappell between 1975 and 1982, followed by 38 by Bob Simpson, who captained Australia 28 times before his first retirement in 1967–68 and his remarkable comeback a decade later to captain Australia 10 more times in 1977–78. Ian Chappell captained Australia in 30 Tests and Bill Woodfull was captain in 25 consecutive Tests. None of these figures include limited over matches in which captains are under continual pressure.

APPEARANCE RECORDS—FOR THE STATES

Les Favell played 143 matches for South Australia. At the end of the 1981–82 Australian season this was more than any other cricketer has played for any State. John Inverarity had played in 142 State matches up to that time, but this was split up between appearances for Western Australia and South Australia. Indeed Sam Trimble made more appearances for Queensland than Inverarity did for WA. The record:

Queensland: 133 first-class appearances by Sam Trimble, comprising 123 Sheffield Shield games and 10 other first-class matches for Queensland. Trimble also played 11 times for Australian elevens to give him 144 appearances in all first-class games. Ken Mackay made 109 appearances for Queensland and 201 in all first-class matches.

New South Wales: 103 appearances by K. D. Walters in all matches for the State. Brian Booth came next with 93 appearances for NSW.

Victoria: Bill Lawry made a record 99 appearances for Victoria in a career that comprised 249 first-class matches in all.

South Australia: Les Favell played 143 times for SA, 121 times in Shield games and 22 others. He was closely followed by Neil Dansie with 124 State appearances, 107 of them in the Shield.

Western Australia: R. J. ("John") Inverarity played in 119 matches for WA, 109 of them in the Shield. Since he joined South Australia he has played 23 times for his new State. Taking into account matches for Australia and representative games, he has played 193 first-class matches.

Tasmania: G. T. James and R. O. G. Morrisby both played 35 first-class matches for Tasmania, but this record should soon be broken now that Tasmania has won full Shield status.

John Inverarity, long-serving first-class cricketer, gets a ball away for Australia against Hampshire in 1972.

Several Australian-born cricketers have played for another country apart from their own. J. J. Ferris played for Australia in 1886–90 and for England in 1891–92; W. E. Midwinter, Australia 1876–86 and England 1881–82; W. L. Murdoch, Australia 1876–90, England 1891–92; A. E. Trott, Australia 1894–95, England 1898–99; S. M. J. Woods, Australia 1888, England 1895–96. Victorian-born Murdoch lived and worked in NSW and captained Australia in 16 Tests against England between 1880 and 1885 and again in 1890. He played for NSW, Sussex, London County, the Gentlemen and for England in a Test against South Africa, but never appeared for his home State, Victoria. Midwinter remains the only player to play both for and against Australia.

Left: *Billy Murdoch, Australian captain.*
Far left: *Powerful allrounder Albert Trott.*

ARCHDALE, Helen Elizabeth ("Betty"), 1907–

The captain of the first English women's cricket team to tour Australia, who later became a wellknown headmistress, television and radio commentator, and author. She has repeatedly been asked to adjudicate on questions of morality, but seldom on cricket. Shining through this varied career is a well honed commonsense.

As a cricketer, she was sound, unspectacular and mindful of the overall tactics of each match. Women's cricket was fortunate to have her at the centre of events in 1934–35 when international women's cricket began. Her English team were unbeaten in 21 matches, winning 15 and leaving six unfinished. England won the first two Tests and drew the third. Each member of the 1934–35 team paid £80 for her fare to Australia and the Australian Women's Cricket Association went ahead with the tour although it had only £1 in the bank. The tour's success was due to Archdale's captaincy and the brilliance of some of her players such as Betty Snowball, Molly Hide and

49

Myrtle Maclagan, who achieved a tour average of 63.25, and at Sydney scored the first Test century—119—in women's cricket.

Betty Archdale, who played for Kent, returned to England with her team and in 1937 was called to the bar in London. She came to Australia in 1946 as principal of the Women's College within the University of Sydney, and in 1958 became headmistress of the exclusive Abbotsleigh girls' school in the Sydney suburb of Wahroonga. Her place in cricket history is secure as the first woman to score a century in first-class cricket and the first to captain an international team on tour.

ARCHER, Kenneth Alan, 1928–

First-Class Averages: Batting, 3,774 runs at 29.95; Bowling, 13 wickets at 53.69.

Tests (5): 234 runs at 26.00.

A forceful right-hand opening batsman and sometimes off-spin bowler who played five Tests for Australia between 1950 and 1952. He was a superb fieldsman who was once offered a contract to play baseball in America. His cricket career would have been more successful had he been able to carry on after scoring an attractive 30 or 40. In an era of top-class Australian talent his value as a team player became expendable and selectors turned to other players like his younger brother Ron.

Ken, born at Yeerongpilly, played for Colts, University and South Brisbane clubs, a radio executive who made 58 appearances for Queensland after his debut at 18 in 1946–47. He toured South Africa in the 1949 Australian team and was twelfth man in all five Tests. He finally won a Test place against England in the Second Test in 1950, scoring 26 and 46.

Ken Archer was recalled for two Tests in 1951 against the West Indies but again failed to get the big scores needed to hold his place. Strangely, for such a brilliant fieldsman, he did not take a Test catch. He kept playing for Queensland until 1956 captaining his State 20 times, opening the batting for 11 years.

ARCHER, Ronald Graham, 1933–

First-Class Averages: Batting, 3,768 runs at 31.93; Bowling, 255 wickets at 23.36.

Tests (19): 713 runs at 24.58; 48 wickets at 27.45;

A right-arm fast medium bowler of quality and a hard-hitting middle-order right-hand batsman who played 19 Tests for Australia in the 1950's. Injuries to his spine and knee cartilages forced him to retire prematurely at 25 when his best cricket appeared just ahead of him. He was an outstanding all-round sportsman who excelled at Australian rules football, rugby and baseball and was hailed early in his career as a budding Keith Miller. His injuries and weight problems prevented him reaching that high pinnacle.

Archer and his brother Ken learned the fundamentals of cricket from their father, a Brisbane furniture factory manager and first grade cricketer. Ron represented Queensland three times in schools' carnivals while still in primary school, in 1945, 1947 and 1948. He was the first player after the second

50

war to win a place in the Queensland Shield team while still at school. In his State debut in 1952, he took 5 for 45 and 3 for 87. He played for Queensland in schools' rugby as a centre-threequarter.

Archer, a bulky figure even in his early matches in big cricket, was 6 ft 1 in. tall, with an ability to move the ball sharply either way. He was at his best with the new ball but with Lindwall, Miller and Davidson in the Australian team he did not often get it. As a batsman, he made a habit of never reading the scoreboard while he was batting. "I'm not game to look," he said. "It brings bad luck. I was skittled three times in a row after looking at the board, so I don't do it anymore."

Archer went to England twice, in 1953 under Lindsay Hassett and in 1956 under Ian Johnson. On his first trip he scored 627 runs at 36.88, topscore 108 against Worcestershire and took 57 wickets at 16.87. He went back to England in 1956 a regular Test player and in the Test at The Oval took 5 for 53, his career best figures, finishing the tour with 649 runs at 30.90, best score 148 against Glamorgan, and with 61 wickets at 22.23. Only Miller (21) took more than his 18 wickets in the Tests.

Archer also toured the West Indies with the Australian side in 1954–55 where he made the highest score of his Test career, 128 in an Australian total of 758 that included five centuries in the Test at Kingston. His hard-hitting brought him 364 runs at 60.66 in the five Tests of that series. In all first-class matches between 1951 and 1958, he made four centuries. He scored 1,675 runs at 32.84 and took 91 wickets at 24.63 in 35 matches for Queensland. He made one Test century and took 20 Test catches. He has worked in radio and television since his retirement and is now head of a Brisbane TV station.

ARMSTRONG, THE FAMILY

Three brothers from the Toowong club in Brisbane, all of whom played for Queensland as right-hand batsmen in the first decade of this century, before the State joined the Sheffield Shield competition.

Edward Killeen Armstrong (1881–1963) played three matches for Queensland in the 1905–06 season. **William Anthony Armstrong** (1886–1955) made his debut for the State in 1907–08 and appeared in five matches. **George Gort Armstrong** (1884–1956) played two matches for the State in 1909–10.

Despite their outstanding family record all the Armstrongs found their opponents from southern States too experienced, and could not reproduce their high scores of club games, though they did contribute a sprinkling of useful scores. They were not related to T. G. Armstrong and W. W. Armstrong who played for Victoria.

**ARMSTRONG,
Warwick Windridge,
1879–1947**

First-Class Averages:
Batting, 16,158 runs at
46.83;
Bowling, 832 wickets at
19.71.

Tests (50): 2,863 runs at
38.68; 87 wickets at
33.59.

A perverse, irascible Victorian allrounder who played for Australia in 50 Tests, ten of them as undefeated captain, winning eight and drawing two of these matches. He had some monumental clashes with officials, but was widely admired by fellow cricketers and by cricket fans. He stood 6 ft 2 ins and when he was picked from the Victorian XI to make his debut for Australia in 1902 against England, aged 23, he weighed 10 stone. When he retired from first-class cricket at 42, he was 22 stone and was known as "The Big Ship", a weight increase due largely to his fondness for whisky. He was notorious for his forthright opinions.

Armstrong toured England with four Australian teams, 1902, 1905, 1909 and 1921, three of them winning sides. He was one of the rebels who refused to go in 1912 under the Board of Control's terms. His greatest personal success was in 1905 when he scored 2,002 runs and took 130 wickets in an English season, a show of allround strength nobody has equalled. On the 1921 tour he led Australia with great common sense but the side was so strong it settled the Ashes in three straight Tests, all before the end of the third day. There is no evidence to support the view that he was an inspired captain, however, or that he is entitled to rank with Bradman, Benaud, or Ian Chappell as one of the great Australian captains. But he was unrivalled among cricketers who could buck officialdom and win the argument.

He was born at Kyneton, north-west of Melbourne, and learned to play cricket as he was educated at Cumloden School, Alma Road, and at University College, Armadale, on the southern side of the Yarra. He became a powerful hitter, especially on the drives, using his long reach shrewdly, but he also could cut with a daintiness surprising in such a vast man. From an uncommonly long approach, he bowled leg-breaks out of the back and top-spinners over the top of his big right fist. Despite his bulk, his action was neat and fluent and he could sustain a tight length for hours. He took more than 100 wickets three times on English tours, in 1905, 1909 and 1921, and critics said he would have taken even more had he not resorted to negative leg theory. In 1905, for instance, when England won the Trent Bridge Test by 213 runs, Armstrong held them up by bowling wide of the leg stump for 52 overs that included 24 maidens and produced 1 for 67.

Armstrong, a kind-hearted man despite his bossiness, worked at the Melbourne ground as pavilion clerk early in his career. He was never forgiven by the influential Victorian Cricket Association secretary Ernie Bean for joining the players who dropped out of the 1912 Australian trip to England, but in guerilla war with Bean that lasted for almost a decade invariably bested his man. The crucial years of his career were 1920 and 1921 when Bean tried to prevent him going to England as captain.

Armstrong started the 1920 Australian summer with innings of 157 and 245 not out for Victoria against South Australia, and he followed up with a marvellous knock of 158, top-score in the match, in the First Test against England at Sydney. His driving in this match was spectacular and with England's fieldsmen right out on the boundary he still struck 17 fours. He took six wickets in the Second Test and made 121 in the Third, Australia winning The Ashes in three Tests. The captaincy for the tour of England appeared his, but Bean was not finished.

On the day before the Victoria-New South Wales match at Sydney Armstrong did not practise and was seen at Randwick races. Just before the match began Armstrong withdrew. The Victorian selectors responded by dropping him from the side to play an England XI the next week in Melbourne, and refused to give a reason for his omission. Irate Armstrong supporters immediately organised a protest meeting and set the time for the meeting as 3 p.m. on the Saturday of the match against England outside the MCG. Bean responded by refusing to allow the protesters the customary pass-out tickets, which meant they had to pay to return to the ground after the protest.

"Patsy" Hendren was in dashing form as time for the protest meeting arrived but 8,000 spectators still left the ground to hear the protest convenor, H. D. Westley. Inside the ground as Hendren passed 200, there were cries of "Give Ernie Bean a bowl". England made 445 for five wickets that day, which in effect only emphasised the folly of omitting Armstrong. This was compounded when the next meeting of the VCA was told by the State side doctor, Roy Park, and by the vice-captain Edgar Mayne that heavy bruising to Armstrong's leg caused his late withdrawal in Sydney, with their concurrence.

Armstrong's appearance in the fourth Test set off another demonstration by his supporters as he went in to bat, fortified by stiff whiskies, Australia 5 for 153. The legend is that Bean stood gloating at the gate as Armstrong went in, a sight that sobered the big man, who went out and made 123 not out, returning to find Bean the teetotaller drunk in the pavilion.

Despite this marvellous display when the chips were down, the late Johnny Moyes wrote that Armstrong only received the captaincy for England by "the narrowest possible margin". In England Armstrong was quickly into stride, demanding that drinks be served for his players in the Lord's dressingroom. The MCC secretary, F. E. Lacey, said the bar was the proper place for serving drinks, but Armstrong won the point. Then he challenged the fixture list that denied the Australians a rest day before the Tests. Again he won the argument and most of the counties Australia played before the Tests agreed to curtail play or drop a day's play. By the time Gregory and McDonald started dusting the aged English batting lineup and Mailey hoodwinked what was left, Armstrong became a special kind of demon to some Englishmen.

Armstrong's second last Test in 1921 was one of his most memorable, for it was in this match that he informed England's captain Lionel Tennyson that Tennyson could not declare at 5.50 p.m. on the second day after there had been no play on the first day. The rule book was consulted with both teams off the field and Armstrong, who had relied on the advice of Hanson Carter, was found to be correct. Armstrong, who had bowled the last over before the break, bowled the first when play resumed—the only known instance of a bowler sending down successive overs in a Test. Armstrong's last Test at The Oval in 1921 was also badly affected by rain on the first day. With England concentrating on a draw, he showed his disapproval by resting his regular bowlers and retiring to the outfield where he startled both players and spectators by reading a newspaper. When Mailey asked him why he read the paper, the big man said: "To see who we were playing".

Armstrong's 1921 team lost only two of 39 matches, matching the 1902 Australian side's record. The defeats came right at the end of the tour at Eastbourne and Scarborough. On that final trip to England, Armstrong established links with the Glasgow whisky industry which, when he returned to Australia, helped make him rich. He was the ideal man to sell the product. Once when the VCA executive queried the cost of a bottle of whisky he kept to entertain visitors to the dressing-room, Victorian 'keeper Jack Ellis said: "Why get his back up for the sake of a few lousy bob. Give him two bottles". Armstrong gave up his job as pavilion clerk to become the Victorian agent of Peter Dawson distillery. "Stork" Hendry moved from Sydney to take over as pavilion clerk in 1922 and Warwick commenced a fruitful business career.

For Victoria, between 1898 and 1921, Armstrong scored 6,732 runs at an average of 52.18, with a highest score of 250. For Australia, from 1901–1921, he scored six 100s.

As a captain, Armstrong had a few inspired moments, such as the day he began with Mailey's spin when England expected pace and Mailey obliged with an invaluable wicket, but in the main he was content to lead a team of talented cricketers by arguing for more privileges for them, which automatically won him support. He only got to England as captain on the casting vote of the Tasmanian delegate to the Australian Board but there was little doubt that he was the man for the job. He took his team on a lengthy tour, which involved matches in Kalgoorlie and Perth, 38 in England, and six in South Africa on the way home. His photographs show a man of dramatic bulk but in fact he moved with surprising light-footedness although English historians cannot be blamed for calling him a monolithic obelisk. Probably the best thing he

54

did for his 1921 team was to persuade Ted McDonald on the voyage to England to get into superb physical condition. Every day Armstrong joined McDonald for two hours in the stokehold of the ship. Armstrong's weight remained unaltered, but McDonald was raring to go when the Australians arrived.

He married Aileen O'Donnell, tiny daughter of a Gundagai grazier, and settled in the Sydney suburb of Darling Point. They had a son who was a good swimmer. Warwick wrote some stinging commentaries on Tests for big fees. When he died at 68, he left £90,000 in his will. The respect he commanded from his players because of his long service, the manner in which he fought to improve his players' conditions, and his success over humdrum administrators have combined to make Armstrong a brilliant captain. There is great doubt about his standing as a captain, however, because he only had to lead brilliant cricketers and never had to mould beaten and demoralised sides back to the top as did Benaud and Ian Chappell.

ASHES, THE Symbol of supremacy between England and Australia cricket teams. The Ashes originated at The Oval when Australia defeated a full strength England team on August 29, 1882, the first time this had been achieved in England. Australia won by seven runs and next day the *Sporting Times* printed a mock obituary by Shirley Brooks, son of an editor of *Punch*, which read:

IN AFFECTIONATE REMEMBRANCE
OF
ENGLISH CRICKET
WHICH DIED AT THE OVAL
ON
29*th August* 1882,
Deeply lamented by a large circle of sorrowing friends and acquaintances.
R. I. P.

N.B.—The body will be cremated, and the ashes taken to Australia.

The following Australian summer, the Hon. Ivo Bligh, later Lord Darnley, took a team to Australia. Australia won the first Test but after England won the final two Tests. Mrs Annie Fletcher, wife of J. W. Fletcher, secretary of the Paddington

*The original Ashes urn.
Replicas have been made but
the original never moves from
The Cricket Museum at
Lord's.*

Cricket Club, suggested to Bligh when he visited the Fletcher's Woollahra house in Sydney that they should burn a pair of bails for him to take home as a momento of the tour. Bligh liked the idea so Mrs Fletcher had the well known artist Blamire Young sketch a design for a bag in which to keep the ashes. Mrs Fletcher worked the design herself in velvet. But when Bligh showed the bag to some ladies in Melbourne they did not like it, and they bought him an urn for the ashes.

When Bligh died in 1927, the ashes, by a bequest in his will, were given to the MCC who have retained them in the original urn in a place of honour at Lord's. Many replicas have been made but the MCC have always retained the original. In 1953, The Ashes urn was moved from the Long Room at Lord's to the Imperial Cricket Museum nearby, along with Mrs Fletcher's velvet bag, together with the scorecard of Australia's win in the 1882 match.

The original Ashes were a joke that was forgotten until 1894 when Clarence P. Moody published his book *Australian Cricket and Cricketers* which set out to establish which matches were and which were not Test matches between England and Australia. Moody revived the Ashes story, which in origin was not more than a long-winded Victorian jest. Ten years after Moody's book appeared English captain "Plum" Warner was searching round for a title for his book on his team's tour of Australia in 1903–04 when he settled on *How We Recovered The Ashes* and gave the term "Ashes" the status of a spiritual trophy that was never intended by the women who burnt the bails. Indeed newspaper accounts of matches between Australia and England between 1882 and 1894 make no mention of the term "Ashes", though they unanimously accepted the term "Test matches".

In 1970, Rowland Bowen, editor of the English magazine "Cricket Quarterly", urged that The Ashes be abolished. "Some think it would be a pity to abolish what has become so traditional", wrote Bowen, a noted individualist. "But when traditions have such phoney origins, there can be no objections to getting rid of them. It all began as a joke, and then because of an historical mistake it became a fetish, and it is time it was abolished."

In 1979–80 English officials disappointed Australian cricket fans by refusing to put The Ashes at stake following the peace settlement between official cricket and Packer, claiming the Australian visit by the England team was an experimental one which had not been officially scheduled. The results of the 1979–80 Tests were officially recognised, however, and the Australian public remained indifferent to the fact that The Ashes were not at stake. A precedent had been set in 1975, when, after the inaugural World Cup, Australia agreed to stay in England and play a series of four Tests—without any suggestion that The Ashes would not be at stake.

ATKINSON, James Archibald ("Snowy") 1896–1956

First-Class Averages: Batting, 1,408 runs at 32.74; Bowling, 4 wickets at 74.0.

Arguably Tasmania's finest cricket captain, and the first batsman in that State to score 1,000 runs in club cricket in three successive seasons—1927–28 to 1930–31. He was born at Beaconsfield in Victoria, where he played four first-class matches, scoring 135 runs in six innings. "Snowy" Atkinson was 6 ft tall, an orthodox right-hand batsman who excelled on wet or turning pitches, a useful change bowler, and an agile close to the wicket fieldsman who took 33 catches. As a wicket-keeper he made two stumpings. He was an outstanding Australian Rules footballer. His major contribution was in helping to develop young cricketers. Two of his proteges, Cyril Badcock and Laurie Nash, became Test players.

ATTENBOROUGH, Geoffrey Robert, 1951–

First-Class Averages: Batting, 738 runs at 10.39; Bowling, 193 wickets at 31.96.

A willowy South Australian left-arm fast-medium swing bowler who, in nine years of first-class cricket, took a commendable number of wickets. He was a critic of the lack of support for South Australia's aspiring youngsters. He made his debut for South Australia in 1972–73 after a sequence of impressive performances for the Sturt club. In 57 matches for his State, his best analysis was 7 for 90 against Victoria in 1977–78. He batted right-handed and had a topscore of 54 against Victoria in 1978–79.

ATTENDANCES

Australian teams and Australian grounds hold most of the records for Test cricket attendances and gate takings. This is largely because one arena, the Melbourne Cricket Ground, dwarfs most of the traditional Test venues around the world. The MCG has held 121,696 spectators for an Australian Rules match whereas Lord's seldom fits that many in for an entire five-day match. The MCG, close to the centre of the city and well served by all forms of transport, can be highly depressing for players, however, with only a few thousand spectators present and vast areas of its grandstands untenanted. It lacks charm and its main atmosphere comes when a well-primed crowd starts to chant in support of bowlers like Lillee.

First Crowd Count: Admission charges were introduced in Australia for the first Victoria versus New South Wales match at Melbourne in 1855–56, 111 years after spectators were first charged admission in England.

Highest Single Day Test Crowd: 90,800 for the second day of the West Indies versus Australia Fifth Test at Melbourne in 1961. This remains a world record for any cricket match.

Highest Test Series Audience in Australia: 943,513 for the five Tests of the England-Australia series in Australia in 1936–37. Two of the five Tests were played in Melbourne.

Highest Test Aggregate in Australia: 350,534 spectators who saw the Third Test between England and Australia in 1936–37. On the third day a then record of 87,798 people attended. The previous record had been 68,238 for the Third England–Australia Test of the Bodyline series.

World Record One Day Crowd: 78,142 people set a world record for one-day limited match on January 11, 1982 at Melbourne Cricket Ground between Australia and West Indies.

Biggest Crowds For A Night Match: 52,053 for the West Indies v. Australia match at Sydney Cricket Ground on January 19, 1982. This was only a little better than the crowd for the first ever floodlit match at the SCG on November 28, 1978, when the gates were opened to admit people still trying to get in after 44,374 had paid.

Centenary Test Attendance: Officials predicted more than 100,000 people would attend on one day of a cricket match for the first time during this lavishly promoted match at MCG but they were disappointed. Crowds did average almost 50,000 daily, however, with 247,873 attending the five-day match.

ATTENDANCE RECORDS CAPITAL CITIES

Apart from the Melbourne Cricket Ground and its unique array of concrete stands, the 1982 trend at Australia's major cricket arenas was to provide more comfort and a wider range of facilities. Crowd capacity at the 'Gabba has been reduced by providing splendid club and stand facilities offering barbecues and excellent menus. The Brewongle Stand at Sydney—a big success in providing fine views of play from good seats with refreshments close at hand, and architecturally pleasing—has cut the capacity of the SCG. This trend towards modernised facilities has increased revenue and made grounds more viable—but will make many of the old crowd records unapproachable.

Brisbane: 23,647 for the Australia v. West Indies World Series Cup match on January 17, 1982. People were told the day before the game not to go to the ground without tickets as every space had been sold. Before the new stands were built, a crowd of 47,000 crammed into the 'Gabba for an England-Australia Rugby League Test.

Sydney: 58,446 at the SCG for the second day of England v. Australia in 1928. Altogether 169,537 attended the match. It is doubtful if the SCG would hold that many now the Brewongle stand and tougher police safety standards operate.

Melbourne: 90,800 for the deciding Fifth Test between Australia and West Indies in 1961.

Adelaide: 50,962 for the Saturday of the Bodyline Test played between January 13 and 19, 1933, when 172,926 attended the entire match. A photograph of this crowd hangs in the SACA office at the ground to convince those who claim it was impossible. Even in the stands people stood up for the entire day. Biggest crowd for a one day match at Adelaide was

24,606 for the England v. West Indies match on January 16, 1980, the sole crowd record not involving an Australian team.

Perth: 24,151 is the biggest single day crowd for a Test—on December 15, 1974, England v. Australia. Biggest one day crowd in Perth exceeded this: 26,446 for Australia v. West Indies in a WSC match on December 20, 1981, when many spectators who broke down fences were not counted as they did not pay.

Hobart: 11,001, for the Saturday of a match between John Goddard's West Indians team and Tasmania in 1951–52. The Gillette Cup final in 1978–79 drew just a few short of this record, 10,800.

AUSTRALASIAN CRICKET COUNCIL

Forerunner to the Australian Board of Control and the present Australian Cricket Board, but an organisation that carried little authority, was not recognised at Lord's by the MCC, and was unpopular with the players. The Council organised the 1893 Australian tour of England, and according to George Giffen upset leading players by instructing the selectors—Giffen, Blackham, Turner, Harry Trott, Alick Bannerman and Lyons—that it should include Arthur Coningham, the former Queensland player then appearing for NSW.

South Australian members of the 1893 Australian team to England, G Giffen, A H Jarvis, J Lyons and W Giffen, who strongly opposed the Australasian Cricket Council's attempt to appoint the team captain.

60

The Council, formed in 1892, comprised four representatives from the New South Wales, Victorian and South Australian cricket associations. Its aims were to regulate and control international tours, to arrange inter-Colonial matches, to amend and interpret the Laws of Cricket, and to settle disputes between associations represented on the Council. New Zealand was not represented on the Council, but it was clearly hoped that she would join when the Council's name was decided. The Council had only a few meetings and was disbanded in 1898, when W. O. Whitridge, of South Australia, was chairman, and John Creswell, of Adelaide, secretary. Its main progress to that point had been to list the 22 umpires from the member States who were acceptable for representative matches.

George Giffen wrote in his book *With Bat And Ball* that the captains of seven of the first eight Australian teams to tour England were chosen by the players. The exception was in 1886 when the Melbourne Cricket Club made the appointment of H. J. H. Scott as captain and Ben Wardill as manager, appointments with which the players agreed. "The Cricket Council resolved in 1896 (ninth team) to take the reins into its hands," wrote Giffen. "In common with many other cricketers I cannot see what the council has to do with the matter. If it financed the tours, the position would be entirely different, but it did not take on its shoulders one iota of financial responsibility, and as in former years the players had to bear the whole responsibility."

The Council lacked funds to finance tours but hoped to get some from the first tours it organised. The players made it clear to their State associations that a Council that was unable to finance tours could not control them and the Council was disbanded. By the time the tenth and eleventh Australian teams went to England in 1899 and 1902 B. J. Wardill was again manager and the Melbourne Cricket Club again held power. The major lasting contribution of the Council was the instigation of the Sheffield Shield for competition between States. This followed the gift in 1892 of £150 by Lord Sheffield.

Cricket has been played in the ACT since the Ginninderra Club began at Ginninderra Station near the village of Hall on the highway between Canberra and Yass in 1854. The Ginninderra team comprised: W. Davis, W. Campbell, W. Bowyer, J. Shumack, R. Shumack, M. Southwell, D. Cameron, W. Creswell, Mason and Bobby and Jimmy Taylor. Bobby (wicket-keeper) and Jimmy Taylor (batsman) were aboriginals. Soon after the foundation of the Ginninderra club, clubs were organised at Queanbeyan, and then at Cooma, Braidwood, Bungendore, Gundaroo and Tuggeranong. Later clubs appeared at

AUSTRALIAN CAPITAL TERRITORY, CRICKET IN

Woden, Yarralumla, Bredbo, Michelago and at Duntroon. The Ginninderra club changed its name to the One Tree Hill CC in 1877, and from this club the Hall CC had its origin some years later. The One Tree Hill club, continued to exist, however, until the early 1930s.

The Australian Capital Territory Cricket Association was formed in 1921 as the Federal Territory Cricket Association. The foundation clubs were Ainslie, Westridge, Canberra, Duntroon Cadets, Queanbeyan, Hall and Eastlake. By the start of the 1927–28 season 16 affiliated clubs fielded teams. The ACT competition was open to all teams within a 15-mile radius of Canberra Post Office. Matches were played on one afternoon between October and April. Premierships were decided initially on a simple points system but later semi-finals and finals were introduced. Many new fields appeared while the city was being built, usually close to the camps of construction workers. Matches were played mainly on concrete, which the clubs laid themselves, or on antbed (clay) strips covered with coir or Kippax matting. The Ainslie club's antbed pitch at its home ground on the Yass road was renowned as a batsman's paradise. A good turf wicket became available at Duntroon Military College and was used by the ACT association for matches against visiting teams.

The development of cricket in the ACT depended heavily on visiting teams until the population built up and could support its own competition. Regular matches were played against teams from the Stragglers' club in Sydney, managed by Neil Blue, a vice-president of the NSWCA, and against sides led by Arthur Mailey, Alan Kippax and later, by Jack Chegwyn. Mailey's side for a match against an ACT team in April, 1928, included Tommy Andrews, Don Bradman and Jack Ellis. Teams from Yass, Goulburn, Cooma, Tumut, Young and other country centres also sent teams to Canberra. In 1927 the Federal Parliament transferred to Canberra and brought with it a permanent population that transformed cricket in the ACT. District cricket was introduced in two grades, but with the rapid expansion of population and new suburbs ACT cricket officials had plenty of problems fashioning a competition suitable to the ACT's needs.

The ACT competition was completely recast after the 1968–69 season, old clubs were dissolved and new ones formed, and new district boundaries established. From the start the need for all the best clubs to play on turf was fostered. Manuka Oval was returfed and remodelled in 1929–30 when practice wickets were laid down and the ground was fenced. The ACT association celebrated by staging a carnival over the 1930 Easter weekend during which Neil Blue from the Stragglers club in Sydney performed the first hat-trick on Manuka Oval. Turf wickets were also reconditioned at Northbourne Oval, Queanbeyan Park and Kingston Oval and with the return of Duntroon Military Academy to Canberra in 1937–38, the Duntroon turf wickets became available. After World War II, concrete pitches were replaced by turf at Ainslie and Reid Park ovals.

The ACT association pressed for many years for recognition of the nation's capital as a venue for international cricket. Attempts to get the MCC in 1928–29, West Indies in 1930–31, South Africa in 1931–32 and MCC in 1932–33 to include a Canberra match in their itineraries all failed. Then in 1932–33 after Prime Minister Joe Lyons had approached Lords, the manager of the MCC team "Plum" Warner, D. R. Jardine, G. O. Allen, and the Nawab of Pataudi motored to Canberra to inspect facilities. But the ACT association had withdrawn its affiliation to the NSWCA in 1931 and although it rejoined in 1934, this probably delayed a visit by a tourist side. Finally the MCC team captained by "Gubby" Allen played a two-day match against a NSW Country team on Manuka Oval in February, 1937. The Country XI was captained by C. J. ("Clem") Hill, who had played for NSW before moving to Canberra. Since then MCC, India, West Indies, Pakistan, and New Zealand teams have played periodically in Canberra, and while Sir Robert Menzies was Prime Minister seven matches between overseas sides and the Prime Minister's XI were staged. The practice was discontinued when Menzies retired and the

Manuka Oval, Canberra, scene of many highly enjoyable matches between overseas touring teams and the Prime Minister's XI.

ACT association again had to fight for inclusion in touring team's schedules.

The ACT association in 1981–82 had a turnover in excess of $100,000-a-year, conducted a strong junior competition in seven age groups starting from under 10s, ran a twilight competition, and a district competition in five grades. An intensive coaching scheme saw former State player Ray Flockton appointed Director of Coaching in June, 1980, but despite his success his appointment ended with a government fiscal cut. The ACT association has among its members a strong women's association and a well organised umpire's association. Canberra remains one of the most pleasant cities in Australia for watching and playing cricket, as the dozens of country teams and State players who go there each year will confirm—and Manuka Oval one of Australia's most attractive cricket fields.

AUSTRALIAN CLUB, THE One of the first clubs in the colony of New South Wales, founded in 1826, 23 years after the first recorded match in the colony in 1803. The Australian Club, formed the same year as the Military club, consisted of native-born youths. The club did invaluable pioneering work, taking teams into outlying areas and playing matches against teams from Maitland and other centres.

AUSTRALIAN CRICKET BOARD The controlling body for Australian cricket since 1905, comprising delegates from six States whose decisions are administered by a management staff in Melbourne after 75 years of being run by secretaries, many of them honorary. Representatives of the Board's member associations are a hard-working lot, usually former district cricketers of moderate skill. It is rare to find outstanding players such as Sir Donald Bradman and Phil Ridings ready to give the immense amount of time involved in Board membership, though Test players are often the most vocal critics of the Board. Originally formed simply to control overseas tours by Australian teams and hand the profits back to State associations and their clubs, the Board also organises Australian tours by two or three international teams a year, a National Youth Cricket Council, under-19 and under-21 competitions and tours, and a national coaching programme. Delegates receive their expenses and good seats at big matches but are unpaid for countless hours of committee work. They usually have served lengthy apprenticeships in administrative work with their home clubs and State associations.

The Board's executive committee of one delegate from each

Terry Alderman, the record-breaking fast-medium bowler in action against England during the Fourth Test at Edgbaston in 1981.

*Russell Drysdale's famous
painting, The Cricketers.*

Above: Rodney Marsh making one of his rare Test match stumpings to dismiss Tony Greig off Ashley Mallett's bowling. Below: A superb action shot of Marsh diving full-length to catch Alan Knott off Jeff Thomson at Melbourne in 1974.

State meets regularly in capital cities—in 1980 it met for the first time outside Australia, in London—programming tours up to ten years in advance and trying, with the players' help, to regulate behaviour. Full Board meetings are held at least twice a year. The discussions around the conference table are earnest and dedicated, repeatedly underlining a wisdom that stems from delegates' business experience, and over the years some colourful personalities have reigned. The historical irony is that despite the Board's best endeavours the ACB does not share the universal respect of cricketers enjoyed by the Marylebone Cricket Club at Lord's. A major reason for this is that most of the Board's discussions are closed and cricket followers are rarely told how the Board reaches its decisions, a procedure that survives because of the Board's past distaste for the small but persistent sensationalist Australian press. Another reason is that the ACB has a stormy past.

The Board had a turbulent foundation after 74 Test matches had been played, 16 English teams had toured Australia, and 11 Australian teams had visited England. But having survived and won acceptance as the fully representative administrative authority for Australian cricket, the Board has retained complete control over the State associations and their member clubs.

Despite 77 years of scrupulously honest management, direct contributions to clubs that supported the Board's formation have been meagre and irregular. The money always seems to be spent before it finds its way to the district clubs. In NSW funds were used to buy Cricket House (rentals from which carried the NSWCA through many hard years), to set up country cricket programmes, to pay umpires' fees, and the costs of running grade competitions. Australian clubs receive no income at all from a successful overseas tour by an Australian team—but a poor "drawing" series in Australia can mean the associations have to meet substantial losses. The Sheffield Shield, vital producer of Test players, runs at a substantial loss partly due to competition from international tours. Sponsorships from corporate advertisers have helped reduce this loss, but the theory district clubs had that they would benefit financially from the Board's existence has never worked out.

In 1982, the ACB handled several million dollars a year, and fed back its net profits to the State associations after paying for ground rentals, team travel and accommodation, and big payments to players. The States' share of these profits broadly reflect their importance in first-class cricket, but the bigger their share of profits the more they have to find when a call is made to the States to finance an Australian team abroad. The manner in which the States spend their share of Board profits is left to them. Despite misgivings about the involvement of cigarette companies, cricket in Australia was booming at the

65

end of 1981–82 season. Record numbers were playing the game, crowd records were regularly broken, particularly at one-day games, the Board's revenue from colour TV rights was at a record level, and in at least two big cities plans were going ahead for new stands at major venues. The WSC protest against the Board's authority was over, and judging from the cash flow the States were enjoying, the Board's handling of this, its biggest crisis, could not have been as ill-judged as some commentators suggested.

WSC's aim always was to secure immediate exclusive TV rights. They fought very hard in the two years duration of World Series cricket and won. In those two years Australian cricket lost an estimated one million dollars, WSC four million dollars. With the money essential for cricket's administration ebbing away, the Board came under intense pressure from all the nations who play the game to compromise. The Board, bound by a contract with the Australian Broadcasting Commission, said it had no mandate to give the television rights away to an entrepreneur. Finally the International Cricket Conference chairman Charles Palmer gave the ACB permission to independently negotiate a settlement. For some State associations, deeply worried about future funding, the settlement came just in time.

The amount WSC pays to exclusively market colour TV of the Board's major matches—they collect all revenue from TV advertising—is far in excess of the $80,000 yearly paid by the ABC for black and white rights before WSC began. Apart from paying heavily for commercial rights, WSC is contracted to help promote the game. It certainly has been less than active in promoting Sheffield Shield matches. The Board is free to arrange team and competition sponsorships independently of WSC's PBL Marketing organisation, but the bulk of this sponsorship money goes to the players, not the Board, as prize-money.

International cricket began for Australians when some of the best players gambled their own money to make overseas tours. When the players' investment paid off with regular shares of tour profits, moves began among destitute clubs for a national control body that could hand profits back through State associations to the clubs. An Australasian Cricket Council functioned between 1892 and 1898, when tour financing and arrangements reverted to the players. Rumours spread about how well some players did financially from tours to England. Finally discussions began in Sydney in January, 1905, for the formation of a body that would take control from the players, and a draft constitution was discussed by representatives of the NSW, Queensland, Victorian and South Australian associations. South Australia's delegates to that meeting strongly urged some form of player representation on the new Board.

At about this time Australia's best players became concerned that the proposed visit to Australia by an England side in 1906–07 might be in jeopardy. Joe Darling, the reigning Australian captain, held a meeting in Adelaide at which well known players agreed to send a letter to the Melbourne Cricket Club agreeing to play against England if a team toured. The Melbourne club had organised some earlier English visits and had helped sponsor Australian tours of England.

When the NSW association learned that M. A. Noble, R. A. Duff, V. T. Trumper, J. R. Mackay, G. L. Garnsey, J. A. O'Connor, A. Diamond, A. Cotter, A. J. Hopkins and the Rev. E. F. Waddy had signed what amounted to an agreement with the Melbourne club, they immediately called on the players to withdraw their promise. Only the Rev. E. F. Waddy retracted, and at a lively NSWCA meeting the others were disqualified at the NSWCA's pleasure. District clubs held emergency meetings and all except Paddington supported the NSWCA action. Paddington at first refused to suspend Noble and Trumper, but under pressure from the association passed a motion suspending them at a later meeting. In Adelaide Joe Darling and Clem Hill responded by announcing they would not play in NSW until the suspensions were lifted and in the face of this the NSWCA backed down.

The first meeting of the Australian Board of Control for International Cricket was held at Wesley College, Melbourne, on May 6, 1905. Representatives from the NSW and Victorian associations were the foundation members and included two who were to play a major role in shaping what the Board became—Ernest Edward Bean, then honorary secretary of the VCA who worked for the government printing works, and William Percy McElhone, a Sydney solicitor and master of controlling debates. Others included A. W. Green (NSWCA), L. A. Adamson (VCA), the first Board president, H. R. Rush (VCA), F. A. Iredale (NSWCA), G. P. Barbour (NSWCA), E. F. Mitchell (Melbourne Cricket Club) with G. M. College and J. Allen acting as observers for Queensland. South Australia's representatives, J. Darling, H. Blinman, and G. M. Evans refused to join the Board because it denied players any representation. South Australia also objected to any interference with the financial arrangements for Australian tours of England and said it would not join until the Board defined what it meant by "financial control".

Queensland joined the Board on September 22, 1905, and went along with the Board's decision in return for a promise that Brisbane would get a Test when English teams visited Australia. It was a promise that took until 1928–29 for the Board to honour. The QCA also professed that its players would get more chance of touring with teams announced shortly before departure instead of six months beforehand as had been the case when the players ran their own tours.

Tim Caldwell, former ACB chairman, and one of those who has helped restructure the administration of Australian cricket.

An invitation to send a team to Australia in 1906–07 was declined by the MCC at Lord's on the grounds that the new Board was not fully representative of Australian cricket. The MCC was clearly aware that Joe Darling and Clem Hill in Adelaide were urging the SACA not to have anything to do with the new Board until it allowed players financial control of overseas tours and gave the players a voice on the Board. The proposed tour by England in 1906–07 was postponed while both sides discussed their problems.

Darling was obviously not a committee type. In the reminiscences published by his son, he said: "I will never forget the last inter-State match I played in Sydney against NSW. South Australia were fielding and getting some leather hunting. The weather was extremely hot and when we adjourned for tea we found McElhone and some leading notoriety seekers present with some dead head friends who had rushed the afternoon tea provided for the players. The waiters were very busy and with this crowd we could not get a look in sideways. I got up and walked over to the large tea urn, called two mates I could rely on at a pinch, and we took possession of the tea urn, and served the players and kept the dead heads waiting."

Darling said he was disgusted by the way in which the Board conducted its affairs when he attended as a South Australian observer, and claimed the minutes of the meetings were false. "Everything on the agenda was discussed privately at a prior meeting of the delegates from Victoria, NSW and Queensland," Darling said of one meeting. "Some delegates, particularly Bean and McElhone, boasted that they would drive out of the game all the players who signed themselves as ready to play against an MCC side organised by the Melbourne Cricket Club."

To stave off the threat of the Melbourne CC organising another English tour, the Board widened its membership by inserting a clause in its constitution which said profits from tours would be divided equally by players in the team. South Australia accepted this and joined the Board on April 20, 1907. Tasmania joined on August 9, 1907, and Western Australia on October 15, 1914, with WA's entry delayed, according to Darling, by the fear that WA might vote against the NSW-Victoria bloc.

England's 1907–08 tour of Australia proceeded but the star players' resentment over their lack of a real voice on the Board remained. This friction increased when the Board handled a tour of England for the first time in 1909. The Board refused to make the customary cash advances to selected players to cover pre-tour expenses, and appointed their own man, Peter McAlister, as tour treasurer. The players elected Frank Laver as manager. When tour arrangements were well advanced the Board welshed on its promise not to interfere

with players' tour terms by demanding five per cent of the first £6,000 earned by the team and 12.5 per cent of all profits over that amount. Instead of a share of profits, the Board offered all players the option of accepting a lump sum of £400, plus all expenses.

In between his managerial duties, Laver managed to head the tour bowling averages by taking 70 wickets. He played in four Tests and took 8 for 31 in England's first innings in the Manchester Test. McAlister, who had been appointed vice-captain of the team ahead of more experienced and popular players like Victor Trumper and Warwick Armstrong, proved a batsman below international class. He failed to reach 50 in any of his eight Tests. Although he was the team's designated treasurer, he disclosed when the side arrived home that he had kept no financial records. The Board then asked Laver for his books on the tour but Laver refused to hand them over as they contained private entries and comments reserved for team members. Laver offered to attend a Board meeting and answer all questions on costs but the Board rejected this offer.

When the time came to prepare Australia's team for England in 1912, a South Australian delegate, G. Mostyn Evans, proposed that the selected players appoint their own manager on the same financial terms as themselves. The Board's Victorian treasurer, Harry Rush, then announced that the regulation giving the players the right to appoint a manager had "been swept away". When the Board voted for its own manager, the Victorians, Bean and Rush, wanted Peter McAlister, but the NSW delegates pushed for chairman McElhone's nomin-

69

ee, Ernest Hume, of Sydney. Piqued that McElhone would not back McAlister, the Victorians refused to vote for Hume and the upshot was that a completely unexpected candidate, Queenslander G. S. Crouch, who had played a few games for his State but had no English experience, was given the job.

Realising they had been double-crossed and that all the assurances they had received when the Board was formed had proved worthless, six famous players wrote to the Board saying the appointment of Crouch was illegal. They said that if the players were not allowed to appoint their own manager, a breach of faith with them would have occurred and none of them would be available to tour England if selected. The letter was signed by Victor Trumper, Warwick Armstrong, Vernon Ransford, Albert Cotter, Clem Hill and Hanson Carter. The Board stood firm and the team went to England without Australia's six finest players. It is generally regarded as the worst side Australia ever sent away. The team's tour lost £1,286. The Board won the challenge to its authority.

A sensational climax to the power struggles of 1912 occurred on February 3 that year when two Australian selectors fought in the NSWCA's offices. The combatants, Peter McAlister and Clem Hill, met with Frank Iredale to pick the team to play England in the Fourth Test at Melbourne. McAlister was immediately critical of Hill's captaincy.

Hill: "The Australians wouldn't have gone to England under you."

McAlister: "I'm a better captain than you and Trumper put together. You're the worst captain I've ever seen."

Hill: "If you keep on insulting me I'll pull your nose."

McAlister: "You are the worst captain I've ever seen."

Angrily Hill reached across the table and slapped McAlister's face. McAlister claimed he had been hit while his hands were down. Hill lowered his arms and said, "My hands are down now". McAlister rushed around the table and grappled with Hill. Locked together they swayed around the room, fighting and wrestling, spattering the room with blood, which stained the clothing of witnesses Iredale and Board secretary Sydney Smith. After 15 minutes McAlister was on his back with Hill standing over him. Iredale and Smith moved in and separated them and Hill left the room, with McAlister calling "coward" as Iredale and Smith slammed the door. McAlister's nose and face were cut but Hill bore no marks. Later *The Australasian* printed a blow-by-blow account of the scrap in which Iredale was asked how long it lasted. "About 20 minutes, I should think," said Iredale. "It all occurred as quick as lightning. They were both game and determined. We are all very sorry about the whole affair, and I don't think anyone regrets it more than the participants."

The wounds created by the 1912 row have been a long time healing despite the Board's efforts to improve its standing.

The Board's name was changed from the Australian Board of Control for International Cricket to the Australian Cricket Board in 1973, when an updated constitution was adopted. Over the years the McElhones, Beans and Rushes have been replaced but conciliation and forebearance have never been the Board's strong points.

Crouch in his report to the Board on the 1912 tour of England—his team won only nine matches, lost eight, and left 20 unfinished—made scathing comments about the behaviour of certain players. The Board appointed a committee in December, 1912, to investigate the conduct of players and two months later team captain Syd. Gregory, "Barlow" Carkeek, T. J. Matthews and David Smith were summoned to explain incidents on the tour. All bar Smith attended. The committee issued a statement saying many of the stories being circulated about the players were grossly exaggerated and unfair, but their report to the Board was never made public.

Sydney Smith, doyen of Board Officials

The Board's thoughtless handling of players continued in 1928–29 when Arthur Mailey was suspended for writing an article about a match in which he played for NSW at Brisbane. Mailey depended for his livelihood on journalism and cartooning, and he retired immediately, leaving the clear impression that he had been driven out of cricket. The Board denied Mailey a testimonial match until long after players like Tommy Andrews, Vic Richardson, Alan Kippax and others over whom he had priority were awarded them.

The player-writer problem remained a headache for the Board when it withheld £50 of Don Bradman's allowance for the 1930 tour of England, ruling that he had broken his tour agreement by writing about the tour before the team arrived home. Bradman disagreed because serialisation of a book he had written on his life had nothing to do with the tour. Cricket was fortunate Bradman was only fined and not banished like Mailey.

The Board's London representative Dr Robert McDonald reported before the 1934 tour that an MCC sub-committee agreed that a direct assault on a batsman by a bowler was against the best interests of the game—but declined to give any promises that bowling of the type Australian batsmen had endured in 1932–33 would not be repeated. Although a majority of members wanted to hold out for a guarantee of some kind, the Board meekly sent a cable accepting the MCC's invitation to tour. Later it was disclosed that several members of the Board had not agreed to the cable before it was sent and the fiery Queenslander E. E. Hutcheon told Board chairman Aubrey Oxlade: "The responsibility of letting Australian players down is on your shoulders".

After Australia lost the first two Tests of the 1936 series against England Bill O'Reilly, Stan McCabe, Fleetwood-Smith and Leo O'Brien were summoned to a meeting with Board

71

chairman Dr Robertson. At the meeting Dr Robertson read an essay about players who did not give full support to their captain, drank too much liquor, or were not in the best condition. One of the players asked Dr Robertson if any of them were being accused of these things. "I can assure you there are no accusations whatsoever," said Dr Robertson.

A player: "In that case, sir, this is just tiggy-touchwood, and we might as well go."

The meeting broke up but as they reached the door the players were advised not to say anything about the meeting. Out in the streets they saw newspaper posters that read "Board Carpets Four Test Men". Dr Robertson was the Board chairman whose comments on the Australian team resounded around the world in September, 1937. "I doubt if England will ever produce a team to make an even go with Australian cricketers," he said. "In my lifetime, they are not going to produce a team equal to ours." Before another September was out England gave the 1938 Australian team the worst trouncing in Test history at The Oval, scoring 7 for 903 to win by an innings and 579 runs.

The Board has taken a long time to improve its own publicity. There has been a sharp improvement recently, but newspapers criticising the Board are a regular part of the Australian season. Long time Board member J. S. Hutcheon, a Brisbane lawyer known as "Czar-Czar", refused the distinguished MCC member Charles Fry entry to the Brisbane members' reserve on the ground that he was a journalist. When fast bowler Harold Larwood arrived at the Brisbane ground to comment on Tests against India in 1947–48, an attendant barred his way. "Twenty years too late," commented Neville Cardus. Nobody did more than Hutcheon to win the Board a poor press.

At the end of the 1956 Australian tour of England the Board fined Keith Miller £100 because a book he had written was serialised before the tour ended. Ray Lindwall was fined £50 for the same offence, but there was no explanation for the discrepancy in the fines. Just as misguided was the Board's decision in gagging Richie Benaud, the team captain, during the 1961 English tour when he was receiving a highly favourable press. The Board instructed him that henceforth all statements had to come from team manager Syd Webb, who was unaware of journalists' needs.

Sid Barnes went to court when a Sydney club official announced that Barnes had been omitted from the Australian team's South African tour in 1949 "for reasons other than cricket." The court found in Barnes' favour and agreed that the comment was an unjustified slur on his reputation as a cricketer and on his standing in the community. Several Board members had the unhappy experience of being cross-examined about Barnes' behaviour. Barnes has gone but other players have appeared to harass the Board, including Ian Chappell, Dennis Lillee and his fancy footwork with Miandad and the use of his aluminium bat. These were minor irritations, however, compared with the WSC breakaway.

Restructuring of the Board began before WSC appeared, but its arrival accelerated the changes aimed at streamlining management and helped modernise the Board. Meetings with players have become more frequent, and the recommendations of the Australian captain are now given careful consideration. The Board has had to come to grips with a big cash flow, constantly escalating costs and modern sports promotion techniques that demand instant decision-making. Under chairman Phil Ridings, it now has a management setup that cannot be compared with the old honorary secretary control system. And the players have the voice in Board decision-making they have always sought.

The Australian Cricket Board today is more than a body that controls overseas tours—the original reason for its formation. It now looks after all aspects of Australian cricket from junior development all the way through a cricketers' career until he receives his retirement pay. The criticisms of the Joe Darlings, Sid Barnes's and Ian Chappells probably have helped reshape the Board into an organisation that can genuinely help every Australian who plays the game.

The first cricket matches in Australia are believed to have been played in 1803 when the Sydney settlement was only fifteen years old. Cricket could have been played in Sydney before then but if so it was not recorded. The first players are believed to have been officers of the ship *Calcutta*, which reached Sydney in December 1803, and civilians who found time for recreation. *Sydney Gazette*, January 8, 1804, reported:

> "The late intense weather has been very favourable to the amateurs of cricket who have scarce lost a day for the last month. The frequent immoderate heat might have been considered inimical to the amusement, but was productive of very opposite consequences, as the state of the atmosphere might always regulate the portions of exercise necessary to the ends of this laborious diversion was originally intended to answer."

A government order of October 6, 1810, by which Governor Macquarie named Hyde Park, referred to that area as having previously been known by the common names of "The Exercising Ground," "The Cricket Ground," and "The Race Course," so cricket seems to have been generally played by 1810. In 1821, Macquarie ordered 12 cricket bats and six balls for the Reverend Thomas Reddall's school at Macquarie Fields, near what is now Ingleburn Army Camp.

AUSTRALIAN CRICKET—ITS ORIGINS AND EVOLUTION

Tasmania, then Van Diemen's Land, had an important pioneering role and cricket was played in Hobart in the 1820s. Hobart Town CC was formed in 1832 and the Launceston CC, founded in 1843, still exists. In January 1935, officers of HMS *Hyacinth* combined with the 21st Regiment to form the United Services XI to play Hobart Town CC. Newspaper scores of the game were studded with errors, but the *Hyacinth*'s team was clearly overwhelmed. Hobart Town CC made 83 and 84, the *Hyacinth*'s team 39 and 21. The following month the Hobart Town CC changed its name to the Derwent CC.

On the mainland the first clubs in Sydney included the Military CC, the Currency CC and the Australian CC, for Australian-born players only, which began in 1826, the same year organised cricket began in Hyde Park. After a match among members of the Australian Club on New Year's Day, 1827, it was stated that the Windsor CC had declined to play against their brother amateurs in Sydney. Thus it appears that the Windsor CC must have been formed around the same time as the Australian CC. The Sydney CC was founded in 1829 but did not last long after its players were ejected from "a government paddock on the other side of the turnpike," apparently an area near the present Central railway station.

Recorded references to cricket in Sydney increased after 1830 when, on February 27, the *Sydney Gazette* carried this report: "The cricket match on the Race Course yesterday, eleven aside, the competitors being equal numbers of military experts at the game and of native-born youths, lasted from 11 o'clock in the forenoon till 5 o'clock in the evening. At 2 o'clock it was thought the natives had no chance, and that they must be beat. However, as the day's play advanced the Australians recovered all they had lost in the morning and at length won the game. A prettier day's play than this was certainly never witnessed in this colony. At 4 o'clock it was estimated that there were upwards of 100 spectators on the ground." Stakes for this match were said to have been £20 a side. The final scores were: Civilians 76 and 136, the 57th Regiment 101 and 87, with the Civilians winning by 24 runs. The *Sydney Monitor* recorded another tense match for ten guineas (£10.10.0) a side on March 3, 1830, when "the Natives" (95 and 75) defeated "the Soldiers" (82 and 52) by 36 runs. The *Monitor* said there was heavy betting on this match, not only in money, but also in property such as pigs, sawn timber, dripstones, boots, maize, snakeskin shoes, butter and fish.

Participants in these matches did not wear gloves or pads. The civilians went on to the field bareheaded or wore cabbage-tree hats trimmed with ribbons and with streamers behind. Players in the military teams wore tall black hats. As the colony's population grew, there were some interesting arrivals. Edward Gregory, who was to have seven sons, five of

74

whom played representative cricket, arrived around 1813, and played cricket in Sydney in the 1820's. When a club was formed at Liverpool one of its leading players was Australian-born Robert Still, one of the first exponents of round-arm bowling, a skill he had been taught by the brothers John and William Hardy, who were generally said to have introduced this style to Australia. John Hardy played for Cambridge against Oxford in 1829 and arrived in Australia with his brother soon afterwards.

The Australian Club, whose members met at Flood's Inn in George Street, Sydney, beat the Military on December 9, 1833, by eight wickets, with a brand of fielding described as "the best ever seen to that time". For the return match in February, 1834, the Military practised hard, whereas the club's players "indulged in a great deal of laziness". It was a tense affair because "when the Military went in against 14 notches, no less than six wickets were defunct with only 10 runs". The Military hung on to win by four wickets and later won a third match by 18 runs. By then decorations had sprung up in Sydney public houses illustrating scenes from Hyde Park cricket matches and panoramic views of Lord's.

Before one match at Sydney in 1834 the Supreme Court had to be adjourned to allow lawyers in a suit to take their place on the cricket field. Judge Dowling agreed to the adjournment despite the objection of Dr Wardell, a leading barrister of the time, who interjected with: "To play cricket, no doubt," when told that professional men retained in the case were otherwise required. From Hyde Park the important Sydney matches moved to the Domain and later to the Albert Club's ground at Redfern. Matches between Marrieds and Singles and Smokers versus Non-Smokers were common.

The game was just as popular in other parts of the colony. Soon after John Batman stepped on to "the site for a village", wickets were laid on Batman's Hill where Spencer Street station now stands. Cn November 15, 1838, Australia's most distinguished cricket club, the Melbourne CC, was formed, with A. M. Mundy, C. F. Mundy, F. A. Powlett, Robert Russell and G. B. Smyth its first members. Powlett was a relative of the Rev. Charles Powlett, one of the leading members of England's Hambledon Club. The *South Australian Gazette* and *Colonial Register* on October 19, 1839, advertised for players ready to join the London Tavern CC. In Perth, cricket began with a match between mechanics and master builders working on the new Government House in April, 1835. In Queensland cricket thrived long before the district of Moreton Bay became Queensland in 1859.

As the settlements in Sydney, Port Phillip, Moreton Bay, Van Diemen's Land, South and West Australia grew, cricket in England made striking advances. The round-arm style of bowling was officially accepted in 1835 and six years later the

Duke of Wellington ordered that cricket pitches were to be an adjunct to every military barracks. In Sydney the transportation of convicts stopped in 1840. In Nottingham in 1846 William Clarke founded the "All-England XI", which did invaluable work in popularising cricket. When Clarke died, George Parr took over much of the management of the team, and from its members came most of the players who comprised Parr's team that toured Australia in 1863–64.

One of the most stirring early matches in Sydney was played in May, 1834, between "eleven officers and migrants and eleven natives". In hoisting their flag above their tent before play began the natives accidentally reversed the cornstalk emblem. One of the best known native players, Harry Hilliard, wrote in a publication called *Old Times* how the native-born players practised in an old graveyard near where St Andrew's Cathedral now stands in George Street, Sydney. To make more space they moved tombstones aside and they were often chased by police. The cricketers were too nimble for the police and escaped behind the Baptist Church, but they sometimes left their bats behind and had to go to the police to claim them.

Publicans quickly recognised the opportunities cricket offered them to promote business. The Currency Club was promoted by William Tunks, whose hotel in Castlereagh Street, Sydney, was the regular meeting place of members. Tunks was later Mayor of St Leonard's, on the northern side of Sydney Harbour and had a park named after him in that district which today attracts hundreds of cricketers. Richard Tress, publican at the Cricketers' Arms, Sydney, sponsored an open challenge for a single wicket match for any sum, against any man in the colony.

One of the first country towns in Australia to organise a cricket club was Maitland, where on February 5, 1845, the *Maitland Mercury* reported that Holdstock's team defeated Honeysett's by 10 runs. The *Mercury* said the difference between the teams lay in the skill of the winning side's long stop, Crumpton, who conceded only seven byes, whereas the opposition conceded 21 byes. The Maitland club had 44 active members at the time.

From the matches between soldiers attached to barracks and those between a variety of clubs, inter-colonial matches developed between Victoria and New South Wales. The advent of these matches in 1855–56 gave Australian cricket first-class status for the first time. Six years later, however, when H. H. Stephenson brought the first English team to Australia the standard had not improved at all. Indeed it was not until 1873–74 when the third English team, led by Dr W. G. Grace, arrived, that any marked advance became apparent. Grace was such a tough exponent of all the finer points the locals had to improve or be completely overwhelmed. The first

English team (Stephenson's) lost only two matches, the second under Parr was unbeaten, but from the time Grace's side arrived the Australians started to look more capable of winning, largely because of the coaching from Caffyn and Lawrence, members of Stephenson's side nine years earlier, who had stayed in Australia to give cricket tuition.

The improvement enabled the Australians to graduate from matches in which they fielded 16 or more players against 11 in the touring sides to mostly eleven-a-side games. By the time James Lillywhite's all-professional team toured in 1876–77 the Australians were considered good enough to play a full strength English XI on equal terms. The match was variously advertised as "All England versus All Australia" and "United England versus United Australia," and later became known as the first of all Test matches.

This match, the first of all the contests between England and Australia, was won by Australia by 45 runs, but it was not until a South Australian, Clarence P. Moody, published the first of his four books that the term Test match was recognised and the Melbourne match universally accepted as the first Test.

"Most interesting and important of the hundreds of matches played in England and Australia by visiting elevens to one country or the other, were those which by common consent were aptly styled Test matches," Moody wrote in *Australian Cricket and Cricketers*, published in 1894. "Many of these matches excited transcendent interest. It is difficult to draw an arbitrary line between Test matches in the fullest sense of the word and those in which so-called weak Austra-

The first international cricket match in Australia, showing the match at Melbourne Cricket Ground between H. H. Stephenson's All-England team and 18 of Victoria, with the new stand in the background. England made 305, Victoria 118 and 98. Photo Public Library of Victoria.

77

lian teams took part, but the delicate task must be undertaken."

Moody accepted all the matches played in England by sides representing England and Australia, but disregarded the matches played in Australia in 1887–88 when two English teams visited Australia because "no particular pains were taken to secure the best eleven of Australia against them separately." The match between Australia and a combination of the two English teams was recognised. He also discounted the three matches played by the 1886 Australian team against the English team after their return from England because Giffen was unfit, and Scott, the captain, and Bonnor had been left in England, so that the Australian eleven that took the field did not represent the full strength of the original 1886 Australian team.

He went through all the so-called international matches Australia had played to that point, judging each with great commonsense, until he ended with a list of 38 that could properly be called Tests. England had won 20; Australia 12, with six drawn. Moody's assessment of which matches should be accepted as Tests was universally agreed on from the time his book appeared, but it took a little longer before his use of the term "Ashes" was accepted as the symbol of Australian or English supremacy.

Indeed the Ashes originally referred to England's defeat at The Oval in 1882 and to the one series in Australia involving Ivo Bligh's victories in two Tests in 1882–83 and were forgotten for twenty-one years. Then Sir Pelham Warner, searching for a title to his book on how England won three of the five Tests in 1903–04, settled on *How We Won the Ashes*. This revived the term and the "Ashes" became the trophy for which the two countries play (at least in theory—the original trophy containing the Ashes never leaves London).

In the evolution of Australian cricket, however, one victory stands out as more important than any Test. By defeating an MCC team made up of the finest players in England on May 27, 1878, the first Australian team to tour England established the reputation of Australian cricket at a single stroke. Denied a Test match in a long, 37-match programme, the Australians under Dave Gregory made the most of their first appearance at Lord's by defeating MCC in a single afternoon. "The Australians drove in their brake on to Lord's ground, practically unrecognised by the 500 or so spectators that had by then mustered," wrote Harry Altham. "Twelve hours later England was ringing with the news that the flower of English cricket had been beaten in a single day, and the crowds came flocking to the Tavistock Hotel in Covent Garden to look at the men who had thus flung open a new era in the history of the game."

The match began just after noon and in 10 overs the Australians dismissed MCC for 33. Australia then scored 41 for a first innings lead of eight runs. News of the sensational cricket had spread around London and when the second MCC innings began 5,000 spectators watched. Spofforth, who had taken 6 for 4 in the first innings, had W. G. Grace missed off his first ball and bowled him with his second. This time Boyle took the bowling honours with 6 for 3 and MCC were all out

Played at Lord's on May 27, 1878.
W. G. Grace won the toss from Dave Gregory and batted.

MARYLEBONE CLUB AND GROUND

W. G. Grace	c Midwinter, b Allan	4	b Spofforth		0
A. N. Hornby	b Spofforth	19	b Boyle		1
C. Booth	b Boyle	0	b Boyle		0
A. Ridley	c A. Bannerman, b Boyle	7	b Boyle		0
A. J. Webbe	b Spofforth	1	b Spofforth		0
F. Wild	b Boyle	0	b Boyle		5
W. Flowers	c & b Spofforth	0	b Boyle		11
G. G. Hearne	b Spofforth	0	b Spofforth		0
A. Shaw	st Murdoch, b Spofforth	0	not out		2
G. F. Vernon	st Murdoch, b Spofforth	0	b Spofforth		0
F. Morley	not out	1	c Horan, b Boyle		0
	Extras	1	Extras		0
		33			**19**

	O	M	R	W	O	M	R	W
Allan	9	4	14	1	—			
Boyle	14	7	14	3	8.1	6	3	6
Spofforth	5.3	3	4	6	9	2	16	4

AUSTRALIANS

C. Bannerman	c Hearne, b Morley	0	b Shaw	1
W. E. Midwinter	c Wild, b Shaw	10	not out	4
T. P. Horan	c Grace, b Morley	4	not out	7
A. Bannerman	c Booth, b Morley	0		
T. W. Garrett	c Ridley, b Morley	6		
F. R. Spofforth	b Shaw	1		
D. W. Gregory	b Shaw	0		
H. F. Boyle	c Wild, b Morley	2		
W. L. Murdoch	b Shaw	9		
F. E. Allan	c & b Shaw	6		
G. H. Bailey	not out	3		
	Extras	0	Extras	0
		41	One wicket for	**12**

	O	M	R	W	O	M	R	W
A. Shaw	33.2	25	10	5	8	6	4	1
F. Morley	33	19	31	5	8	4	8	0

Australia won by nine wickets in 3 hours 40 minutes.

for 19 shortly after five o'clock. Wanting 12 to win, the Australians lost Bannerman for one but at twenty minutes to six Horan made the winning hit.

Punch magazine greeted this historic win with these lines:

The Australians came down like a wolf on the fold,
The Marylebone cracks for a trifle were bowled;
Our Grace before dinner was very soon done,
And Grace after dinner did not get a run.

To the end of the 1981–82 Australian cricket season Australians have played 426 Test matches against all the nations that play international cricket. Australia was ahead against all countries, having beaten England, South Africa, the West Indies, New Zealand, India and Pakistan more frequently than Australia has lost to any of them. It was a significant contribution to a wonderful game but any jubilation at this achievement should be tempered by the fact that the first English team was brought to Australia (for the start of big cricket) by Spiers and Pond, who did so hoping to promote their Melbourne restaurant business. The English cricket team was only the second choice after author Charles Dickens had declined to come. Melbournians could easily have watched Dickens recite instead of English cricketers batting.

Here is Australia's record of the now universally accepted 'Test' matches:

	Tests Played	Won	Lost	Drawn	Tied
v. England	247*	93	82	72	—
v. South Africa	53	29	11	13	—
v. West Indies	52	26	13	12	1
v. New Zealand	15	8	2	5	—
v. India	39	20	8	11	—
v. Pakistan	20	9	5	6	—
TOTALS	426	185	121	119	1

For more complete details on Australia's performances in international cricket, see the entries under the various cricket nations, England, India, Pakistan, New Zealand, South Africa, West Indies, plus those on the Netherlands, Fiji, Sri Lanka, and the United States.

* This includes the 1970–71 match at Melbourne abandoned before a ball was bowled, but after the toss was made.

The first match played on level terms under first-class conditions by teams representing Australia and England was not recognised as the first of all Tests until some years later. Three of Australia's best bowlers at the time, Allan, Spofforth and Evans, and one of her finest batsmen, Billy Murdoch, did not play. England was without her best amateurs in an all-professional team, and the teams only wicket-keeper, Pooley, had been detained by police in New Zealand. Jupp kept wicket for England in his place. Five of the Australian team, Bannerman, Horan, Kendall, Midwinter and Thompson, were born in Britain.

Played at Melbourne Cricket Ground on March 15, 16, 17, 19.

AUSTRALIA

C. Bannerman	retired hurt	165	b Ulyett		4
N. Thompson	b Hill	1	c Emmett, b Shaw		7
T. P. Horan	c Hill, b Shaw	12	c Selby, b Hill		20
D. W. Gregory*	run out	1	(9) b Shaw		3
B. B. Cooper	b Southerton	15	b Shaw		3
W. E. Midwinter	c Ulyett, b Southerton	5	c Southerton, b Ulyett		17
E. J. Gregory	c Greenwood, b Lillywhite	0	c Emmett, b Ulyett		11
J. M. Blackham†	b Southerton	17	lbw, b Shaw		6
T. W. Garrett	not out	18	(4) c Emmett, b Shaw		0
T. Kendall	c Southerton, b Shaw	3	not out		17
J. H. Hodges	b Shaw	0	b Lillywhite		8
Extras	(B 4, LB 2, W 2)	8	(B 5, LB 3)		8
		245			104

	O	M	R	W	O	M	R	W
Shaw	55.3	34	51	3	34	16	38	5
Hill	23	10	42	1	14	6	18	1
Ulyett	25	12	36	0	19	7	39	3
Southerton	37	17	61	3				
Armitage	3	0	15	0				
Lillywhite	14	5	19	1	1	0	1	1
Emmett	12	7	13	0				

ENGLAND

H. Jupp†	lbw, b Garrett	63	(3) lbw, b Midwinter		4
J. Selby	c Cooper, b Hodges	7	(5) c Horan, b Hodges		38
H. R. J. Charlwood	c Blackham, b Midwinter	36	(4) b Kendall		13
G. Ulyett	lbw, b Thompson	10	(6) b Kendall		24
A. Greenwood	c E. J. Gregory, b Midwinter	1	(2) c Midwinter, b Kendall		5
T. Armitage	c Blackham, b Midwinter	9	(8) c Blackham, b Kendall		3
A. Shaw	b Midwinter	10	st Blackham, b Kendall		2
T. Emmett	b Midwinter	8	(9) b Kendall		9
A. Hill	not out	35	(1) c Thompson, b Kendall		0
James Lillywhite*	c and b Kendall	10	b Hodges		4
J. Southerton	c Cooper, b Garrett	6	not out		1
Extras	(LB 1)	1	(B 4, LB 1)		5
		196			108

	O	M	R	W	O	M	R	W
Hodges	9	0	27	1	7	5	7	2
Garrett	18.1	10	22	2	2	0	9	0
Kendall	38	16	54	1	33.1	12	55	7
Midwinter	54	23	78	5	19	7	23	1
Thompson	17	10	14	1				
D. W. Gregory					5	1	9	0

FALL OF WICKETS

	A	E	A	E
Wkt	1st	1st	2nd	2nd
1st	2	23	7	0
2nd	40	79	27	7
3rd	41	98	31	20
4th	118	109	31	22
5th	142	121	35	62
6th	143	135	58	68
7th	197	145	71	92
8th	243	145	75	93
9th	245	168	75	100
10th	—	196	104	108

Umpires: C. A. Reid and R. B. Terry.

Australia won by 45 runs.

81

AUSTRALIAN CRICKET SOCIETY

An Australian offshoot of a group founded in England in 1945 to provide contact between cricket lovers of all ages, regardless of their sex or cricket ability, and to contribute some form of repayment for the pleasure they have had from the game. In 1982, there were branches of the Society in every Australian State except Tasmania. Each branch holds quarterly meetings for members which are addressed by cricket celebrities, holds an annual dinner, sponsors awards for young cricketers, plays social matches throughout the year, and stages inter-State trips for their teams.

The English branch of the Cricket Society grew out of the Society of Cricket Statisticians, formed in November, 1945. It became clear that many cricket fans were not as interested in statistics as in watching the game and enjoying its literature. In October, 1948, the Cricket Statisticians voted to become the Cricket Society. The Society survived various troubles including a court case and a vote of no confidence in the committee, and in 1970 celebrated its silver jubilee. There are now four branches in England, with membership of each increasing each year.

From the English Society, branches sprang up in Rhodesia and Australia. The Australian Cricket Society was formed in November, 1967, by Andrews Joseph, of Victoria, who became this body's first secretary. Since then membership has steadily increased, with membership in Victoria now close to 500. The second branch was formed at Newcastle, NSW, in May, 1972, and subsequently branches were set up in the ACT (1973), Sydney (1973), Brisbane (1975), Perth (1976) and Adelaide (1977).

Members received regular issues of the Branch journal *Hill Chatter*, and in Melbourne *Pavilion* and *Extra Cover*, which regularly include articles by Ray Robinson, Frank Tyson and the noted statistician, David Roylance. The Cricket Society Library has more than 800 cricket books, which members are able to borrow without charge. In 1974, the Australian Cricket Society took a team made up of its members around the world, in 1978 to New Zealand, and in 1981 an ACS team toured USA and the Caribbean. The Society also runs cut-price trips to England in the years of Australian tours. In 1982, membership of any of the ACS's branches cost $3.50 joining fee, with an annual fee of $5.50. A practical contribution by the Society has been their restoration of graves of prominent cricketers, including that of W. E. Midwinter in the Melbourne General Cemetery, which was derelict and difficult to find before the Society moved in to arrange for it to be properly kept and sign-posted. In Sydney the Society proposes to erect plaques in Hyde Park, the Domain, Centennial Park and other places where cricket was pioneered. Plaques may also be put up at the former homes of famous early players.

B

A record-breaking Tasmanian-born right-handed batsman hailed as a potential champion as a teenager, whose seven Tests proved a poor record of his obvious talents. He made some of the highest scores in the history of Australian first-class cricket, mostly for his adopted South Australia, but could not do it in international matches.

There was an air of dominance about Badcock as he strode to the crease, less than medium height, wide-shouldered and sturdy, that excited spectators from the time he first appeared for the northern Tasmanian club, Esk. He made more than 1,000 runs in each of his first three seasons with the club, and gave impressive displays for Tasmania, for whom he first played at 15. (See Ages, of Cricketers.) In the 1932–33 season he made 57 in the first innings against Jardine's MCC side, and batted throughout Tasmania's second innings for 43 not out. In 1934 at 20, he made 25, 107, 274 and 71 not out against a strong Victorian Colts team, average 159, scoring more than half Tasmania's runs in the two games.

Badcock's scoring had mainland States chasing him, and he moved to South Australia after the 1933–34 season. He made his Test debut for Australia in 1936, the year in which he scored 325 for South Australia at Adelaide against Victoria. Although he had to work hard to overcome a weakness against spin, he looked as impregnable as Woodfull and as full of runs as Bradman. Even his gait was impressive as he moved confidently about the ground. Oldtimers said they had seen nothing like the Badcock presence on Australian fields since W. G. Grace.

His footwork was quick, classical, and he turned balls off his body with Kippax-like ease. He was more correct and less impish than Bradman, driving superbly, cutting so hard fieldsmen could not get a hand to the ball. He exuded class and personality all his own but apart from 118 against England at Melbourne in 1937 when he put on 161 with Ross Gregory, his Test efforts were disappointing. Selectors moved

BADCOCK, Clayvell Lindsay ("Jack") 1914–

First-Class Averages: Batting, 7,571 runs at 51.54.

Tests (7): 160 runs at 14.54.

him around in the order trying to help him, but he could not get a start. On tour in England in 1938, he scored freely against the counties, scoring 1,659 runs at 43.65, topscore 198, but scored 9, 5, 0, 0, 4, 5 not out, 0 and 9 in Tests.

And yet at home in 1938–39 he was able to score 271 not out against New South Wales at Adelaide and 236 against Queensland at Adelaide. In 1940 he hit three centuries in a month against Victoria, two in the same match at Melbourne (120 and 102) and one in Adelaide (172). He retired at 27 because of persistent lumbago after heading the South Australian batting averages in 1940–41, with 554 runs at 69.25 for the season.

BAILEY, George Herbert, 1853–1926

First-Class Averages: Batting, 367 runs at 16.68; Bowling, 4 wickets at 25.50.

A member of the first Australian team to visit England in 1878, who played an important role in lifting Tasmanian cricket standards. He was a free, wristy batsman of style, an excellent field, and a useful slow bowler.

Bailey was born in Colombo, educated in England, where he had his cricket grounding, and came to Australia when he took an appointment with a bank. He lived for 12 years in Launceston, before settling in Hobart. He made 281 runs for the pioneer Australian team in England at 14.78 in all matches, with 106 against XVIII of Hastings his best score. He was invited to go to England again in 1880, but withdrew for business reasons.

He played in many matches between North and South Tasmania, distinguishing himself in the game at Hobart in 1892–93. The North, left with 307 to make to win, won by eight wickets, Bailey (139) and C. Rock (113) adding 226 for the first wicket. In 1880–81, he had played an innings of 227 n.o. for Derwent v. Break-o'-Day at Hobart, and in 1907 he made 156 n.o. for Newtown at the age of 54.

BAKER, Glen George, 1915–1943

First-Class Averages: Batting, 1,531 runs at 31.24; Bowling, 13 wickets at 42.92.

A splendid allrounder from Townsville who gave Queensland valuable service in the 1930's. As a teenager he was so keen to improve he practised with all six Townsville clubs. He died of malaria on active service at Buna, New Guinea, aged 28. He was a right-handed batsman who hit the ball hard and with style. His highest score was 157 in first-class cricket. He bowled a brisk medium pace and had a good leg-break. He played for Townsville and Easts in Brisbane.

BALDRY, Robert John, 1950–

A right-hand batsman who scored more than 1,000 runs for Victoria in the early 1970's, contributing some useful innings without scoring a century. Baldry, born in the country town of Warragul, won State selection with consistent batting for Collingwood, for whom he played for 14 seasons. His highest score was 90 in a four-year first-class career. He did not bowl.

First-Class Averages: Batting, 1,220 runs at 27.72.

BANNERMAN, Alexander Chalmers, ("Alick") 1854–1924

First-Class Averages: Batting, 7,816 runs at 22.14; Bowling, 22 wickets at 29.81.

Tests (28): 1,108 runs at 23.08; 4 wickets at 40.75.

One of the great stonewallers of Australian cricket. Unlike his brother Charles, he never made a Test century, but he won many matches for Australia and New South Wales with his unique brand of stubborn defence. In the early days of Australian cricket, the shotmakers in our teams received all the praise when Australia won, but more often than not it was "Alick" Bannerman plodding away at the other end who had worn out opposing bowlers and fieldsmen.

Giffen described Bannerman's habit of watching carefully for loose balls on the legside at the start of an innings or when a bowler first came on. "I have seen him score three fours in an over with leg hits and then, when the bowlers found their lengths, and with their direction improved, bat half an hour without making a solitary notch," said Giffen. "Unquestionably, he was the best batsman of the barndoor class against whom I bowled, but he was more than a stonewaller, for when opportunities occurred he could hit very hard." He was a brilliant field and an intense student of cricket. When he was chosen in the first official Australian team to tour England in 1878* he had not at that time played inter-colonial cricket, the equivalent of State cricket.

He made six trips to England, also touring with Australian teams in 1880, 1882, 1884, 1888 and 1893. He was in the side that beat England at Lord's in 1878 in an afternoon, played in the first ever Test in England at The Oval in 1880, and was in the 1882 team that beat England at The Oval by seven runs. Bannerman's catch to dismiss W. G. Grace proved the turning point of that epic struggle. In 1891–92 at Sydney, Bannerman batted seven and a half hours for 91 against Lord Sheffield's side, clinching the series for Australia, scoring only five from 204 balls bowled at him by Attewell.

Bannerman had very strong forearms and a powerful back. Everything about him was disciplined except his droopy moustache. There was a time when he played in an Australian team with a player who relieved the tedium between overs or waiting for incoming batsmen by singing music hall ditties. Bannerman stood it for a few overs but finally went to the singer and said, "If you want to play cricket, play it; and if

* For reasons best known to himself, A. C. Bannerman gave a number of different years for his date of birth, including 1854, 1856 and 1859. The Association of Cricket Statisticians believes the most likely date was 1854, which would have made him 23 when he first toured England.

you want to sing, go and sing, but for Heaven sake don't sing comic songs in the slips!"

Between 1879 and 1893 Bannerman played 50 innings in 28 Tests. In all first-class matches between 1877 and 1894 he made five centuries. He was coach to the New South Wales Cricket Association on retirement.

Sydney Pardon in his *Wisden* obituary of "Alick" Bannerman recorded how seriously Bannerman took his cricket. "It was said of him, not ill-naturedly, that when in the match with England at The Oval in 1888 he was out to the finest of catches at cover slip ever brought off by George Lohmann, he talked about his bad luck, and of nothing else, for the rest of the afternoon." Pardon gave this list of Bannerman's centuries:

134 Australia XI v. Rest of Australia, Sydney, 1888–89.

133 Australia v. Oxford & Cambridge Past And Present, Portsmouth, 1893.

117 New South Wales v. Victoria, Melbourne, 1889–90.

105 Australia v. Derbyshire, Derby, 1893.

101 Not out New South Wales v. Victoria, Melbourne, 1882–83.

BANNERMAN, Charles, 1851–1930

First-Class Averages: Batting, 1,687 runs at 21.62.

Tests (3): 239 at 59.75.

A celebrated Australian cricketer who in 1877 plundered distinguished English bowlers Shaw, Southerton and Lillywhite to score 165 not out in the first ever Test, the match that started international cricket. Nobody else in the Australian team scored more than 20 runs, but Bannerman's knock caused England's defeat by 45 runs. Bannerman retired with a split finger after opening Australia's innings. He made 126 of his runs on the first day. He had received the first ever ball in Test cricket from England's Alfred Shaw. He was dropped by Armitage off Shaw before he reached double figures. The ball lobbed up from the bat but the simple catch struck Armitage in the stomach. He was particularly severe on Armitage's lobs, and Armitage became so frustrated he tried to lob the ball over Bannerman's head, before finally resorting to grubbers. On the second day Yorkshireman Ulyett broke open Bannerman's finger and he left the field, his place in cricket history secure. The next best Australian score in the innings was 18 not out from Garrett.

Bannerman played in two further Tests against England. Ill-health caused his early retirement. For years it was socially important to reveal at Australian parties that you had seen Charles Bannerman make the first Test 100. Unlike his brother "Alick", who was born in Sydney, Bannerman was born in England—at Woolwich in Kent. Bannerman was also the first Australian player to score a century in Canada (125 at Montreal in 1878), and the first Australian to score a century in New Zealand (125 at Invercargill in 1878). He received

86

£83/7/6 for his 165 at Melbourne, subscribed by spectators.

Charles Bannerman, who was coached by Englishman William Caffyn, headed the Australian batting averages and aggregates in all matches on the first official tour of England in 1878 with his century against Leicestershire the first three figure score by an Australian. He scored 723 runs at 24.10, almost twice as many as the next highest scorer on the tour, T. P. Horan, who had a total of 377. His brother "Alick" was also in that first Australian team, which made the Bannerman's the first of a long list of brothers who have won fame at cricket for Australia. Charles Bannerman received £490 when the NSW trial match in November, 1922, between teams captained by Herbie Collins and Charlie Macartney was made his benefit match. This was the first cricket match in the world that was given a radio commentary.

Charles Bannerman, who hit the first Test century, talking to a youthful Don Bradman in 1929–30. Bannerman died soon afterwards, Bradman went on to unprecedented success.

**BARBOUR,
THE FAMILY**

E. P. Barbour

An outstanding professional family who in the days when serious cricket could be pursued as a hobby, built a big reputation through their playing skills and intimate knowledge of the game. They had the happy knack of mixing academic attainment with their cricket field pleasures.

George Pitty Barbour (1867–1951), known as "Boss", was born at Williamstown, Victoria and educated at Sydney Grammar School and in classics at Sydney University. He was in the 1883 cricket team at Grammar, said to be the school's best-ever. He played club cricket with Burwood and was in the first grade side in 1903–04 and 1905–06 when it won the premiership. His eldest son, **Eric Pitty Barbour** (1891–1934) was the first grade team's scorer, his father the shrewd and far-sighted captain. "Boss" Barbour represented Burwood on the NSWCA from 1902. He was a member of the Australian Board of Control and chairman in 1908–09. He also represented NSW at Rugby Union in 1888 and tennis in 1891.

G. P. Barbour became headmaster of Toowoomba Grammar School in 1910 and over 25 years built it into one of the finest public schools in Queensland, emphasising hard work and disciplined study. He had five daughters and three sons and he taught the boys the fundamentals of cricket, continuing to play himself in Toowoomba. In 1911 and 1924 he captained Toowoomba teams against touring English sides. In the annual match between Toowoomba and South Brisbane, played on Christmas Day and Boxing Day, 1925, G. P. Barbour and E. W. ("Eddie") Kann, later a prominent sportswriter, put on 244 for the first wicket in 124 minutes. G. P. was only a month off his 59th birthday and made 60. Kann then put on a further 202 in 60 minutes with Frank Drews before Barbour retired him at 250 (41 fours).

Eric Barbour was Dux of Sydney Grammar School, where his aggregate of 2,146 runs in the 1908–09 season was a school record. He played for NSW while studying medicine at Sydney University between 1908 and 1914, and was chosen for the Australian tour of South Africa in 1914 that had to be cancelled because of World War I. He graduated in 1915. He played only 23 first-class matches but in that time made five centuries and 1,577 runs at 46.38, topscore 160. He was a medical officer in France and played for the AIF against England. He and Dr Roy Park were members of the AIF Sports Control Board in England, which in 1919 selected and organised the notable First AIF team. Doctors Barbour and Park both declined to join the team as they had to return home to re-establish their medical practices.

E. P. Barbour wrote on cricket for the *Sunday Mail* and *Sydney Morning Herald* and published two books on the game, *The Making Of A Cricketer*, which remains a fine coaching manual, and *Anti-Bodyline*, in association with Alan Kippax. In the 1920's he warned of the dangers to cricket's good fellowship of the continual use of the bouncer. "The deliberate banging down of the ball less then halfway up the pitch is not cricket," he wrote. "If continued and if allowed to extend to all grades of cricket, the end result of such tactics will be the disappearance of every champion after he has put up with two or three years of assault and battery. A more serious aspect still is the imminent danger to the good fellowship and friendly rivalry that has always been associated with cricket." Prophetic words, written before the Bodyline tour and before batsmen resorted to wearing helmets. E. P. Barbour captained Randwick to the Sydney first grade premiership in 1931–32.

Another son, **Robert Roy Pitty Barbour** (1899–   ) was a consistent wicket-taker for the old Burwood club before it became Western Suburbs, taking 100 wickets at 21.02, and twice heading the club's bowling averages. R. R. P. Barbour played six first-class matches between 1919 and 1923 and scored 172 runs at 15.63, topscore 41. He usually batted at No. 4 and was a relief medium-pacer. He attended Queensland University, where he won a Rhodes scholarship, and went to Balliol College, Oxford. On his return from Oxford he was a master at Geelong Grammar, where he coached the First XI from 1924 to 1928. He then transferred to Adelaide University and while he was there played grade cricket for Sturt. His son Peter was director-general of the Australian Security Intelligence Organisation in 1970–75. The eldest of G. P. Barbour's three sons, Frederick Pitty Barbour, was killed in World War I.

BARDSLEY, Warren
1882–1954

A distinguished Australian left-handed batsman, and probably the best of our left-handers on turning pitches. He usually went in first. He was the first batsman to make a century in each innings of a Test, and one of the few to bat right through a Test innings. He scored more than 2,000 runs on tour in England three times and made 53 first-class centuries, six of them in Tests.

Bardsley was born in New South Wales, the son of William Bardsley, teacher, and his wife Rachael, and grew up in the Sydney suburb of Forest Lodge, where his father was school principal and taught for 40 years. "Tibby" Cotter, Charles Kelleway, and Bert Oldfield went to the same school. Bardsley recalled pupils at his father's school using six longstops to Cotter's playground bowling. Warren, oval-faced, solemn, a non smoker, teetotaller and vegetarian, with heavy, arched eyebrows, came into big cricket from the Glebe club in 1903–04 when he first played for New South Wales. He built his scores calmly, thoughtfully, with an air of having plenty in reserve. He seldom took opposing attacks apart. His footwork was quick and tidy, especially on spinning pitches, and his bat was perfectly straight in defence and attack. He drove

First-Class Averages: Batting, 17,025 runs at 49.92.

Tests (41): 2,469 runs at 40.47.

superbly off the front foot and could play back to force the
ball off his pads with wrists that had developed power at ju-
jitsu. He held the bat high on the handle, foregoing a right-
hand batting glove. He was taught to write with the right-
hand at school, but threw with his left hand from the outfield,
where he was efficient and safe. His career was characterised
by a fierce dedication to practise.

He wore a bulky Australian cap pulled well down on his forehead and when bowlers gave him a bouncer he had a way of tossing his head contemptuously as he let the ball pass a metre or so from his cap. His Test career lasted 17 years and it was a splendid testimony to his tradesmanlike technique that at the age of 43 he could score 193 not out in an innings of 6 hours 30 minutes at Lord's in 1926, subduing an England attack of Tate, Root, Larwood, Kilner and Woolley.

Bardsley's Test career began in 1909 with the Thirteenth Australian team to tour England. He topped the Australian batting averages on the tour with 2,180 runs at 46.38 in all matches, topscore 219. Against Essex, with Australia 2 for 8, Bardsley and Ransford put on 355 runs in 200 minutes. For the rest of their careers, their methods as high-scoring left-handers were repeatedly compared. Bardsley's 46 in the Second Test at Lord's helped give Australia a first innings lead of 89 and set up a win, with Ransford scoring 143 not out. In the Fifth Test at The Oval, Bardsley followed a first innings of 136 with 130 in the second, adding 180 for the first wicket with Syd Gregory. He batted for 3 hours 45 minutes in each innings and became the first player to score a century in each innings of a Test.

He returned home a celebrity and in 1910–11 Australian season continued his heavy scoring by making 573 runs at 63.66 in the series against South Africa, who were visiting Australia for the first time. At Sydney in the First Test he made 132, featuring with some devastating on-side hitting in a partnership of 224 with Clem Hill.

This outstanding start to his international career was followed by the only series in Bardsley's career in which he failed. He was one of an array of outstanding Australian batsmen who could not cope with the bowling of S. F. Barnes and Frank Foster in the 1911–12 series in Australia against England. Barnes and Foster, at a time when one new ball was used for each innings, proved one of England's greatest bowling combinations, England winning four Tests in a row after "Ranji" Hordern mastered them in the First Test. Four times in the first four Tests Bardsley was out to balls that swung in from his leg stump and hit the off stump. After eight innings that included two ducks and only one score over 30, he was dropped for the Fifth Test. He spent countless hours for the rest of that summer in the nets with fast left-hander Bill Whitty firing the ball across his body as he worked to eliminate his weakness.

He went back to England with the 1912 Australian team that had to be reconstructed following defections by six star players, topping the batting averages again, this time with 2,441 runs at 51.93 in all matches, highest score 184 not out. He was the most prolific batsman in all three sides during the Triangular tournament played that year in England, scoring

392 runs at 65.33, including 164 against South Africa at Lord's where he put on 242 with Kelleway.

By now he was rated a better batsman in England than he was at home and this certainly seemed valid on his last two trips to England. In 1921, he made 2,218 runs at 55.45 in all matches, topscore 209, and in 1926 he scored 1,558 runs at 50.25 in all matches, best score 193 not out. His footwork and sound technique enabled him to score comfortably as team-mates struggled against the turning ball or those that moved off the seam. The ease with which he handled damp pitches was attributed to a childhood habit of early morning practice on dewy strips.

He toured South Africa in 1921–22 under Herbie Collins but was not among our Test century-makers. In all he scored three Test hundreds against South Africa, 132 in 1910–11 at Sydney, 121 in 1912 in the Triangular series at Manchester and 164 in the same series at Lord's. In just 17 innings against South Africa he made 982 runs at 61.37.

In a first-class career that lasted 24 years (1903–1927), Bardsley scored 53 centuries. In between this marvellously sustained scoring, he gave outstanding service as a player and a selector to New South Wales and to the Glebe and Western Suburbs clubs in Sydney. From 1898 to 1932–33, he made 12,110 runs for both clubs at an average of 50.45. For New South Wales, he scored 6,419 runs at 53.04 in 83 matches, best score 235. In one of the longest careers among all our first-class cricketers, he did not bowl a single over. He worked originally as a clerk in government departments and later as an agent for English firms. He married Gertrude Cope at 62 and she survived him on his death nine years later.

BARING, Frank Albert, 1890–1961

First-Class Averages:
Batting, 1,846 runs at 32.96;
Bowling, 5 wickets at 57.00.

A tall, powerful right-hand batsman and occasional off-break bowler for East Melbourne and Victoria. *Wisden* called him the best Australian batsman on bad pitches after the death of Victor Trumper. His batting was notable for the manner in which he used his long reach to pull and drive and smother dangerous deliveries. He was a splendid field.

Baring, who played for East Melbourne, was born at Hotham East. He appeared for Victoria between 1911 and 1928, and in 1914 made 122 against New South Wales at Melbourne. He was chosen in the Australian team whose proposed tour of South Africa in 1914–15 was cancelled because of the war. In 1918, he made 131 against New South Wales at Melbourne.

F. A. Baring played Australian Rules for Victoria and district baseball for East Melbourne. His brother, **Hugh Thomas Baring** (1907–1968), was a right-hand batsman from the North Melbourne club, who played three innings for Victoria in the 1929–30 season, scoring 33 runs at 11.00.

A hard-working former first-grader from the Mosman club in Sydney, who was secretary of the Australian Cricket Board in some of the most turbulent years of its history. Barnes, who had been secretary of the New South Wales Cricket Association since 1949, took over as secretary of the ACB in 1960 on the day the Australia-West Indies match at Brisbane ended in cricket's first tie, and held the job for 21 years, retiring a few months earlier than planned because of a stroke. He is regarded as one of the most industrious and conscientious officials the game has ever had in Australia, genial but cautious in his dealings with the world's cricket writers and completely trustworthy.

BARNES, Alan Roberts ("Justa"), 1916–

Barnes played in the Mosman team captained by Stan McCabe that won the 1938–39 Sydney premiership. He put on 222 in 106 minutes with "Ginty" Lush for the eighth wicket in 1939–40 and 99 runs in 78 minutes with pace bowler George Bennett for the tenth wicket against Marrickville. He was appointed assistant secretary of the NSWCA in 1946 under the gruff, remote Harold ("The Fuhrer") Heydon, after wartime service with the RAAF in Malaya. He took over as NSWCA secretary three years later when Heydon retired and then succeeded Jack Ledward as ACB secretary. NSW won nine successive Sheffield Shield competitions when he was NSWCA secretary, one fewer than Surrey's record of 10 successive English county championships. As ACB secretary, Barnes had to deal with the cancellation of South Africa's planned tour of Australia in 1971–72 and with the WSC rebellion against the Board's authority. Although he was appointed to carry out the Board's policy, there were countless occasions when he had to make on the spot decisions for Australian cricket. He was made a Life Member of the Marylebone Cricket Club for his services to the game.

Barnes was the NSW team manager in Brisbane in 1963–64 when Queenslander Peter Burge came in for the tea adjournment on the second day with his score 180 not out. Burge had just shared a huge opening stand with opener Ray Reynolds, who made 121. Burge collapsed into a chair and Barnes asked if he was going to join the other players in a cup of tea. "No, I'm stuffed," said Burge. "I feel more like a double rum." Barnes had no rum but he did have a bottle of Scotch, so he gave Burge a healthy slosh of it. Revitalised, Burge went on to make 283 run out, the highest score by a Queenslander in first-class cricket. Burge batted seven and a half hours and hit 42 fours. But Barnes' men were not done. Bob Simpson scored 359 and NSW reached 661, returning as first innings winners.

A colourful, over-confident right-hand opening batsman whose brilliance as a strokemaker, short leg fieldsman, and

BARNES, Sidney George, 1916–1973

First-Class Averages:
Batting, 8,333 runs at
54.11;
Bowling, 57 wickets at
32.21.

Tests (13): 1,072 runs at
63.05; 4 wickets at 54.50.

proficiency as a leg-spinner and wicket-keeper were forgotten amid his brash newspaper comments on the game. He was bombastic and he was tough, and nobody ever quite knew how to react to him.

Barnes was born in humble circumstances into a sheep farming family in a remote country district of Queensland. His father died before he was born, and the family moved to Sydney. Barnes was a back streets urchin from the Sydney suburb of Stanmore who was transformed by his first trip to England into the team's most fashionable dresser, right down to his diamond-patterned socks. He was chosen for the 1938 Australian tour of England, aged 21, after only eight first-class matches but broke his wrist on the voyage to England. Yet in the brief period before the second world war he proved himself one of the most gifted natural cricketers Australia has known, a magnificent off-side player who could hook and pull with fearsome power, drive with devastating effect, cut, glance and sweep brilliantly. He did not make a century on that first trip to England, largely because of his injury, but he knew he was among the world's best players.

Grieving over his lost opportunities in the long break war forced on big cricket, he worked out a run-getting style he believed was foolproof. He gave up hooking and cutting behind point and did not square cut until he scored 40, and seldom ventured down the track as he had in his youth. He taught himself to watch the ball more closely than any other batsman of his time, picking up late swing and turn with consummate ease.

Came the peace and he was ready to make his bid for the fame and the fortune he was sure his talents deserved. No more were the casual clothes of his youth seen as he entered our cricket grounds to polish his skills, usually with a retinue of hand-picked bowlers. Now he was in Savile Row suits and beautifully tailored flannels. Few more exciting cricketers have ever performed in our practice nets. When grade players were limited to a 10 minute net, Barnes would bat for an hour and a half but such was the brilliance of his stroke play those whose own practise was cut short by his lack of consideration forgave him. Then he had to spoil it by placing silver coins on his stumps and challenging bowlers to earn the coins by bowling him.

Barnes had no feeling for mateship or protocol among club cricketers and whichever the club for whom he played he left a multitude of tales about his misdeeds. He was always determined he would get to the top and club cricket was to him simply a step towards the inevitable. He seldom stayed to do his share of practise bowling, preferring to rush off to some business deal rather than to send down a few overs of the leg-breaks that did not turn but fizzed off the pitch fast enough to take Test wickets.

Manchester policemen carry Sid Barnes from the field in the 1948 Test at Old Trafford after Barnes had been hit fielding at silly short-leg to Ian Johnson's bowling.

He was an incorrigible stealer of the strike when batting, turning his back or adjusting his gloves rather than run when his partner called. Even in the Test arena he stole the strike from players like Bradman and Morris. This was the man who in 1947 hit 40 off an over from State fast bowler "Ginty" Lush, with four sixes and four fours, the man known to have opened several first grade innings by pulling the first ball for six.

Barnes, black-haired, bushy-browed, was not a tall man at 5 ft 8 in, but he was wide-shouldered and stocky at 12 st 7 lb. He was always in peak physical shape and could bat for hours without stress. When Australia's Test batting lineup had to be reshuffled after the war, he made the switch from first wicket down to opener at the age of 30 without problems, getting his head down closer to the ball, shortening his backswing but not his ambition.

He was exempt from the services as he and golfer Norman von Nida produced supplies vital to our war effort. He made several centuries in the war years in well under even time but when the serious business of international cricket began again he was all dour defence and the hardest batsman in Australia to get out. "At times he walls himself up inside his own fun factory so that he cannot get out to deliver the goods," said Ray Robinson. "One of his specialties has been to get the ball round the corner just as it was about to hit him below the belt—when all the other runs dried up he always had one on the hip."

Barnes' highest score against England in 1946–47 was one of the most controversial Test innings of all time. He opened the innings with Morris, upset the crowd by appealing continuously against the light, and stayed until Australia's score

Barnes swings a ball to fine leg for NSW against Queensland. Don Tallon is the 'Keeper, McCool the slip.

96

had reached 564, playing through eight interruptions—through lunch and tea breaks, overnight stops and light appeals. He batted for 10 hours 42 minutes for 234, the same score as Bradman, with whom he shared the world record fifth wicket partnership of 405. Only two batsmen in history had ever batted longer, Merchant of India, for 359 not out in 10 hours 45 minutes in 1943, and Len Hutton for 364 in 13 hours 17 minutes against Australia in 1938. Barnes' 200 took 9 hours 30 minutes, the then slowest double century in Anglo-Australian Tests.*

Barnes, who had married a Scots theological professor's daughter, promised his wife he would score a century in the Lord's Test in 1948. He was out in the first innings for a duck. Once back in the pavilion he asked team-mates who had bet against him scoring 100 if they wanted to double their bets. He took 4 hours 15 minutes to get the century in the second innings before he started to loft his drives and play the pull shot. Englishmen were surprised that he had developed from the predominantly off-side player they had seen in 1938 into a batsman who could stroke the ball all round the wicket.

Another shock on the 1948 tour was Barnes' fielding at short leg. He stood about a metre from the edge of the pitch in a position that forced batsmen to worry about him as Miller, Lindwall and Johnston moved in to unleash their thunderbolts. His reflexes were lightning-fast. He was less than five metres from the bat and he undoubtedly added menace to the Australian attack. Finally in the Manchester Test he overdid it by standing in close for Ian Johnson's loopy off-breaks and Dick Pollard buried a hefty swipe into his ribs. Barnes was carried off by four policemen. He tried to bat next day but collapsed again. He was still unfit for the Leeds Test a fortnight later and this undoubtedly spoilt his tour figures. He finished with 1,354 first-class runs at 56.41.

Amid all his expertise, Barnes couldn't resist clowning. He batted with a toy bat at Bradman's Melbourne Testimonial, insisting it was legal, signed his autograph with a rubber stamp, jumped the turnstiles when attendants demanded his ticket at the MCG, and once went on as twelfth man bearing brushes, combs, perfume sprays, and clothes brushes for his team-mates. He would start to walk towards the pavilion when he hit a bump ball and would give his cap to umpires pretending he was coming on to bowl. He made good money showing his movies of the 1948 tour, with spectators content that they had as much value for their admission price from Barnes' wisecracks as from the film.

Barnes started the practice of Australians going to the Lancashire League in between Australian seasons when he

---

* Since then Hanif Mohammad, Pakistan v. West Indies in 1957–58, batted 16 hours 10 minutes for 337.

signed for Burnley. In 1949–50 he declared himself unavailable for Australia's South African tour, saying he could not afford to go for the £450 out-of-pocket allowance. That was virtually the end of his first-class career, but by then he had been publicised so much for his pranks and his clashes with officialdom that he was able to return to England in 1953 as a commentator. He rubbished all his old mates and claimed they boozed away a Test win by nightclubbing until the small hours when they had the Lord's match won.

His book *Eyes On The Ashes* on the tour aroused so much controversy a Sydney paper signed him up as a columnist and there he sniped away at all and sundry almost until his death, from an overdose of sleeping pills. Barnes' 13 Tests produced three centuries and five scores over 50, and he made 14 catches. In all first-class matches between 1936 and 1953 he scored 26 centuries. Nobody who saw him at his amazing prime doubts that those figures would have been a whole lot better had he attacked more often.

BARNETT, Benjamin Arthur, 1908–1979

First-Class Averages: Batting, 5,531 runs at 27.51; Dismissals, 358 (216 caught, 142 stumped).

Tests (4): 195 runs at 27.85; Dismissals, 5 (3 caught, 2 stumped).

A wicket-keeper who batted effectively left-handed. He was a shock selection for the 1934 Australian team to England. The first telegram of congratulations he received was from Charlie Walker, the South Australian 'keeper he had beaten for the job as Oldfield's deputy. Barnett was young and cheerful, curly-haired, bright in conversation, with a flair for amateur acting and conjuring that enlivened the long voyage to England. He learned a lot of lessons in England, not the least of them in diplomacy, and became a keen student of good form on and off the field.

Barnett was only a moderately performed cricketer when he was picked for England in 1934 but he had established a reputation for his skill in 'keeping to spinners, a big advantage with Grimmett in the touring team. He also took the unpredictable Fleetwood-Smith tidily, which no doubt influenced the selectors when they had to decide between Barnett and Walker. Barnett had begun at school as a slow bowler and knew the breed well.

Barnett's 1934 English tour was seldom impressive and his selection ahead of Don Tallon in 1938 also created much controversy, particularly in Queensland where some newspapers were quite irate. Apart from his two trips to England, Barnett visited South Africa in 1935–36 with Richardson's Australian side, and in 1953–54, when he was in his forties went to India with a Commonwealth team.

Barnett, Hawthorn-East Melbourne's first Test player, made 131 against Tasmania at Hobart in his debut for Victoria in 1929–30 and in 73 games for Victoria scored 2,773 runs at an

98

average of 28.88, with two centuries. He settled in England after World War II and captained Buckinghamshire.

Ben Barnett's major contribution to Australian cricket was his off the field charm, for he represented Australia at many important international cricket conferences for almost half a century, and handled this difficult job with tact and skill. He was also an able representative of Australian tennis at European conference tables. He returned to Australia not long before his death.

BARRETT, Dr John Edward, 1866–1916

First-Class Averages:
Batting, 2,039 runs at 25.81;
Bowling, 21 wickets at 16.00.

Tests (2): 80 runs at 26.66.

A 6 ft 1 in left-handed batsman with a strong defence and unfailing patience, who bowled medium pace from a high action, could hit when required, but was a duffer in the field. He started with South Melbourne CC, and played in turn for Melbourne University, Sydney University, Victoria and Australia's 1890 touring side in England.

At 17, he played for Fifteen of Victoria v. The Fourth Australian touring team, and in his first match for Victoria the following season he took 5 for 31 and 6 for 49 against South Australia. Medical studies kept him out of big matches until he went to England with the 1890 side and finished second to Murdoch in the batting averages with 1,305 runs at 22.89, compared with Murdoch's 1,459 at 23.53, which topped the Australian averages.

His highest scores were 97 and 73 not out v. an England XI at Manchester, and 96 v. Oxford and Cambridge. In the Test at Lord's he was 67 not out, the first Australian to carry his bat through a Test innings. His work as a doctor shortened his cricket career.

Right, Dr John Barrett, the first Australian to carry his bat through a Test innings. Far Right, C. Barstow, a devastating bowler in Brisbane club cricket.

BARSTOW, Charles Banks, 1883–1935

First-Class Averages:
Batting, 187 runs at 6.44;
Bowling, 78 wickets at 28.12.

One of the best bowlers Queensland has produced. Brisbane-born Barstow played 22 matches for Queensland. He bowled right-arm medium leg-breaks. Fingerspin and flick were his assets, and on badly-prepared pitches that gave him assistance he could be irresistible. On hard, unresponsive pitches he sometimes introduced what critics called "a dropping ball" that was really a fast-actioned wrong'un. His first-class appearances were limited in the years before Queensland was admitted to the Sheffield Shield, but in Brisbane club cricket he was devastating. Between the summers of 1901–02 and 1929–30, he took 1,073 club wickets.

Barstow's best season was 1913–14 when he took 101 wickets for Toombul at 8.80 each. In 1909–10, Barstow took all 10 wickets for South Brisbane against Oxley for only 34 runs. He repeated the feat in 1921, playing for Toombul against University, the ten wickets costing only 16 runs this time. In 1908–09, also for South Brisbane, he had 8 for 1 against Toombul, clean bowling six batsmen. No other Queenslander approaches Barstow's record of having played in 16 first grade premiership teams in 25 seasons in Brisbane first grade, divided between the Woolloongabba, South Brisbane, North Brisbane and Toombul clubs. He was the supreme grade cricketer.

BARTON, the Rt. Hon. Sir Edmund, PC, GCMG, 1849–1920

First Prime Minister of Australia and the only Prime Minister to have umpired in first-class cricket. Barton played for Sydney University against Melbourne University and periodically umpired inter-State matches. Barton was the umpire at the other end at Sydney in 1879 when the crowd rioted after umpire George Coulthard gave local idol Murdoch run out. Barton steadfastly defended Coulthard's decision and the behaviour of the English players in the nasty recriminations that followed. When the English captain Lord Harris protested to Barton that the Australian players had forfeited the match by leaving the field, Barton said, "I'll give it to you if they don't come back in two minutes." But before the Australians could return a further invasion of the field occurred and finally play had to be called off for the day, with spectators refusing to vacate the playing area.

BATTING

Since Charles Bannerman faced the first ball bowled in the first of all Tests at Melbourne at 1 p.m. on Thursday March 15, 1877, Australians have brought a distinctive approach to batsmanship and cricket is the richer for it. Australian batsmen have brought character, flair, some style, and a lot of ingenuity to the task of batting in international matches before large crowds against skilful bowlers, the disasters of 1981 in England notwithstanding.

Among many superb innings since Bannerman started it all, several stand out as classics. Stan McCabe's 187 not out against England's Bodyline attack at Sydney in 1932, his 189 not out at Johannesburg against South Africa in 1935 and his 232 against England at Nottingham in 1938 will always be remembered. All who saw Victor Trumper score 185 not out against England at Sydney in 1903 thought it was the best of Trumper's many great knocks, but he followed it with a superlative innings of 74 out of a total of 125 on a vile sticky

101

wicket at Melbourne, enhancing his reputation as the best bad pitch batsman ever in Australia.

Bradman surpassed McCabe and Trumper in consistency and high scoring, if not in style, but he also played a string of classic innings. His 334 against England at Leeds, followed by 254 at Lord's and 232 at The Oval in his triumphant 1930 tour were each masterpieces of stroke-making without mistakes. But I fancy that Bradman's 173 not out on the last day at Leeds in 1948 gave him greater pleasure.

Australia's left-handers have done us proud, with Joe Darling, Clem Hill, Vernon Ransford and Warren Bardsley playing many knocks brimful of character and exciting strokes. Arthur Morris carried on this tradition and in 1948 at Leeds made 182 at Headingley in a show of consummate batsmanship. Neil Harvey, a marvel of timing and placement of shots, underlined the value of left-handers, as did Bill Lawry in his famous innings at Lord's in 1961 when he scored 130 on the ridge in a total of 238, batting for six hours and ten minutes.

For the right-handers, Hassett's magical footwork, Miller's blazing shotmaking, took over from Ponsford and Woodfull's

Below: One of Australia's greatest opening pairs, Bill Woodfull and Bill Ponsford, going out to bat against Worcestershire at the start of the 1934 Australian tour of England.

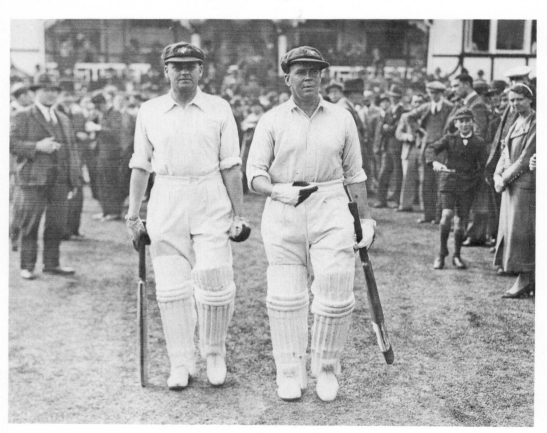

Bob Simpson and Bill Lawry going to the wicket at Old Trafford in 1964 when they had a record opening stand of 201. Simpson made 311, a score only Bradman has surpassed in Tests, Lawry 106.

amazing efficiency. Bob Simpson's great powers of concentration were followed by Doug Walters' flashing bat. Walters had willing disciples in Ian and Greg Chappell, who have both played a string of classic innings, give or take a hook caught on the boundary. Kim Hughes and Alan Border have begun their bid to be included among our great batsmen.

From Archie Jackson's brilliant driving and cutting to Kippax's sophisticated hooking and late cutting, all of them different in style, all of them contributing to the tradition Bannerman started. Detailed below are some of the highlights.

NOTABLE BATTING ACHIEVEMENTS

First Century in First-Class Cricket: 110 by R. W. Wardill, for Victoria against NSW in 1867. Wardill committed suicide by throwing himself in the Yarra River in 1873.

First Test Century: 165 retired hurt, by Charles Bannerman, for Australia against England, First Test at Melbourne, 1877.

First Australian To Bat Through An Innings: Billy Midwinter, who was born in England, scored 16 not out in batting through an innings of 76 as a member of the 1878 Australian team against Nottinghamshire.

First Australian To Bat Through An Innings In A Test: Dr J. E. Barrett, 67 not out in an Australian total of 176 against England in 1890 at Lord's.

First Century Partnership For Australia: By Tom Horan and George Giffen, who scored 107 for the fifth wicket against England in 1881–82 at the MCG. Horan made 124, Giffen 30.

Lowest Innings Total By An Australian Team: 18 against MCC at Lord's in 1896 (J. T. Hearne 4 for 4, A. Pougher 5 for 0) in Australia's first innings. G. Giffen was absent.

Lowest Innings Total Against An Australian Team: 17 by Gloucestershire at Cheltenham, 1896 (H. Trumble 6 for 8, T. McKibbin 4 for 7).

Lowest Total By An Australian Test Team: 36 against England at Birmingham in 1902 (Rhodes 7 for 17, Hirst 3 for 15).

Lowest Total Against An Australian Test Team: 36 by South Africa at Melbourne, 1932 (Ironmonger 5 for 6, Nash 4 for 18, McCabe 1 for 4).

Fewest Runs In A Day By An Australian Test Team: 80 by

Below, Alan Kippax walking out to bat in England in 1934; Right, Bradman pulling a ball to leg on his last English tour in 1948.

Australia against Pakistan at Karachi, 1956–57. Pakistan made 2 for 15 for stumps, providing a day's total of 95 runs.

Lowest Total In An Australian First-Class Game: 15 by Victoria against MCC in 1903–04. Victoria batted one short.

Lowest Match Aggregate Involving Australians: 105 runs on a day in which 31 wickets fell, Australia v. MCC at Lord's in 1878. MCC made 33 and 19. Australia scored 41 and took 20 minutes to score the 12 runs required to win.

Lowest Match Aggregate In A Test: No Test match has produced as few runs as the match at Melbourne in 1931–32 in which Australia scored 153, South Africa 36 and 45, the 29 wickets were lost yielding 234 runs. Australia batted one short.

Highest First-Class Score By An Australian: 452 not out by D. G. Bradman, for New South Wales v. Queensland, Sydney, 1929–30, in 6 hours 55 minutes, with 49 fours. This is 47 short of Hanif Mohammed's world record.

Highest Score By An Australian In Tests: 334 by D. G. Bradman against England at Leeds, 1930. Bradman was 309 not out at the end of the first day's play after scoring a century before lunch. He added 25 before he was out on the second day.

Only Australian To Pass 400 Twice: Bill Ponsford, who made 437 for Victoria against Queensland in 1927–28 at Melbourne, in 10 hours 20 minutes, with 42 fours, and 429 for Victoria against Tasmania, 1922–23, in 8 hours, with 42 fours.

Highest Score By An Australian In England: 345 by Charles Macartney against Nottinghamshire at Nottingham in 1921. This is also the highest score ever made in one day in a first-class match. Macartney reached 345 in just under four hours, with 4 sixes and 47 fours.

First Australian To Score 300: William Lloyd Murdoch, with 321 for New South Wales v. Victoria in 1881–82 at The Sydney Cricket Ground.

FULL LIST OF AUSTRALIANS WHO HAVE BATTED THROUGH A TEST INNINGS

Dr. J. E. Barrett	67* in 176 v. England	Lord's, 1890
W. W. Armstrong	159* in 309 v. Sth Africa	Johannesburg, 1902
W. Bardsley	193* in 383 v. England	Lord's 1926
W. W. Woodfull	30* in 66 v. England	Brisbane, 1928–9
W. M. Woodfull	73* in 193 v. England	Adelaide, 1932–3
W. A. Brown	206* in 422 v. England	Lord's, 1938
W. M. Lawry	49* in 107 v. India	Delhi, 1969
W. M. Lawry	60* in 116 v. England	Sydney, 1970–1
I. R. Redpath	159* in 346 v. New Zealand	Auckland, 1974

Centuries By Australians In Test Debut: C. Bannerman, J. Burke, G. S. Chappell, H. Collins, G. Cosier, R. Duff, H. Graham, R. Hartigan, A. Jackson, W. Ponsford, K. D. Walters and Dirk Wellham. Duff and Ponsford also scored centuries in their last Tests. Neil Harvey scored 100 in his first Test against England, his third Test altogether.

105

Most Centuries In Succession By An Australian: Six by D. G. Bradman in 1938–39, the first for Bradman's XI against Keith Rigg's XI at Melbourne, followed by five for South Australia.

Australians Who Have Scored 300 In A Test: D. G. Bradman at Leeds in 1930 and 1934. R. B. Simpson at Manchester in 1964 and R. M. Cowper at Melbourne in 1965–66.

Most Runs In A Day By An Australian Side: Australia scored 721 in a day's play against Essex at Southend in 1948, reaching this score in 348 minutes. This total has not been exceeded by the aggregate of two sides batting in a single day. It is note-worthy that K. R. Miller made a duck in a scorecard that read:

S. G. Barnes, hit wkt. b R. Smith	79
W. A. Brown, c Horsfall b Bailey	153
D. G. Bradman, b P. Smith	187
K. R. Miller, b Bailey	0
R. A. Hamence, c P. Smith b R. Smith	46
S. J. E. Loxton, c Rist b Vigar	120
R. A. Saggers, not out	104
I. W. Johnson, st Rist b P. Smith	9
D. T. Ring, c Vigar b P. Smith	1
W. A. Johnston, b Vigar	9
E. R. H. Toshack c Vigar b P. Smith	4
Extras (b 7, n-b 2)	9
Total	**721**

Highest Innings Total By Australia In A Test: The first Australian team to tour West Indies in 1955 under Ian Johnson scored an Australian Test record 8 for 758 declared at Kingston, Jamaica in June that year. Scorecard:

C. C. McDonald, b Worrell	127
L. Favell, c Weekes b King	0
A. R. Morris, lbw b Dewdney	7
R. N. Harvey, c Atkinson b Smith	204
K. R. Miller, c Worrell b Atkinson	109
R. G. Archer, c Depeiza b Sobers	128
R. R. Lindwall, c Depeiza b King	10
R. Benaud, c Worrell b Smith	121
I. W. Johnson, not out	27
Extras	25
Total (for 8 wkts dec.)	**758**

Highest Innings Total Against Australia: 7 for 903 declared by England at The Oval in August, 1938.

Highest Individual Test Score Against Australia: 364 by Len Hutton out of England's 7 for 903 declared at The Oval in August, 1938.

Highest First-Class Score By Australia: In matches other than Tests, Australia's best innings total was 843 v. Oxford and Cambridge Universities Past and Present at Portsmouth in 1893.

Highest Australian Totals Without a Century: 476 against England at Adelaide in 1911–12 when Clem Hill's 98 was top-score, and 9 for 450 against South Africa at Sydney, 1963–64, when Richie Benaud's 90 was the topscore.

RECORD TEST PARTNERSHIPS BY AUSTRALIANS

Wkt.

1st	382	W. M. Lawry and R. B. Simpson, v. WI (Bridgetown), 1964–65
2nd	451	W. H. Ponsford and D. G. Bradman, v. Eng. (Oval), 1934
3rd	295	C. C. McDonald and R. N. Harvey, v. WI (Kingston), 1954–55
4th	388	W. H. Ponsford and D. G. Bradman, v. Eng. (Leeds), 1934
5th	405	S. G. Barnes and D. G. Bradman, v. Eng. (Syd.), 1946–47
6th	346	J. H. W. Fingleton and D. G. Bradman, v. Eng. (Melb.), 1936–37
7th	217	K. D. Walters and G. J. Gilmour, v. NZ (Christch.), 1976–77
8th	243	C. Hill and R. J. Hartigan, Eng. (Adel.), 1907–8
9th	154	S. E. Gregory and M. McC. Blackham, v. Eng. (Syd.), 1894–95
10th	127	J. M. Taylor and A. A. Mailey, v. Eng. (Syd.), 1924–25

HIGHEST TOTALS FOR AUSTRALIA

758 for 8	v W. Indies	Kingston	1954–55
729 for 6 dec.	v England	Lord's	1930
701	v England	Oval	1934
695	v England	Oval	1930
674	v India	Adelaide	1947–48
668	v W. Indies	Bridgetown	1954–55
659 for 8 dec.	v England	Sydney	1946–47
656 for 8 dec.	v England	Old Trafford	1964
650 for 6	v W. Indies	Bridgetown	1964–65
645	v England	Brisbane	1946–47

The longest innings for Australia is 12 hours 58 minutes when they made 656 for 8 dec. at Old Trafford in 1964.

Youngest Australian To Score A Double-Century: D. G. Bradman who was 21 years 307 days in his 254 at Lord's in 1930.

Youngest Australian To Score A Triple-Century: D. G. Bradman who was 21 years 318 days in his 334 at Headingley in 1930.

Photographer George Beldam's famous shots of Victor Trumper's classical straight drive. Absence of fieldsmen suggest that the photographs were specially posed.

YOUNGEST AUSTRALIAN TEST CENTURY SCORERS

The following centuries were scored by batsmen under the age of 21.

Year	Name	Age	Score	Against	Venue
1947–48	R. N. Harvey	19 years 121 days	153	India	Melbourne
1928–29	A. Jackson	19 years 152 days	164	England	Adelaide
1948	R. N. Harvey	19 years 290 days	112	England	Headingley
1965–66	K. D. Walters	19 years 357 days	155	England	Brisbane
1928–29	D. G. Bradman	20 years 129 years	112	England	Melbourne
1950–51	J. W. Burke	20 years 240 days	101*	England	Adelaide
1897–98	C. Hill	20 years 317 days	188	England	Melbourne

Oldest Australian To Score A Century: W. Bardsley, who was 43 years 201 days when he reached his century in his 193 at Lord's in 1926.

SCORES OF 300 OR MORE BY AUSTRALIANS

452*	D. G. Bradman	NSW v. Qld	Sydney	1929–30
437	W. H. Ponsford	Vic v. Qld	Melbourne	1927–28
429	W. H. Ponsford	Vic v. Tas	Melbourne	1922–23
383	C. W. Gregory	NSW v. Qld.	Brisbane	1906–07
369	D. G. Bradman	SA v. Tas.	Adelaide	1935–36
365*	C. Hill	SA v. NSW	Adelaide	1900–01
359	R. B. Simpson	NSW v. Qld.	Brisbane	1963–64
357	D G. Bradman	SA v. Vic.	Melbourne	1935–36
352	W. H. Ponsford	Vic. v. NSW	Melbourne	1926–27
345	C. G. Macartney	Aust. v. Notts.	Nottingham	1921
340*	D. G. Bradman	NSW v. Vic.	Sydney	1928–29
336	W. H. Ponsford	Vic. v. SA	Melbourne	1927–28
334	D. G. Bradman	Aust. v. England	Leeds	1930
325*	H. S. T. Hendry	Vic. v. NZ	Melbourne	1925–26
325	C. L. Badcock	SA v. Vic.	Adelaide	1935–36
321	W. L. Murdoch	NSW v. Vic.	Sydney	1881–82
315	A. F. Kippax	NSW v. Qld.	Sydney	1927–28
311	R. B. Simpson	Aust. v. England	Manchester	1964
307	R. M. Cowper	Aust. v. England	Melbourne	1965–66
304	D. G. Bradman	Aust. v. England	Leeds	1934
303*	W. W. Armstrong	Aust. v. Somerset	Bath	1905
300*	V. T. Trumper	Aust. v. Sussex	Hove	1899

Note: South African Barry Richards scored 356 while playing for South Australia against Western Australia at Perth in 1970–71.

LOWEST TOTALS FOR AUSTRALIA

36	Edgbaston	1902
42	Sydney	1887–88
44	Oval	1896
53	Lord's	1896
58	Brisbane	1936–37
60	Lord's	1888

All these scores were recorded against England.
The shortest innings for Australia is 71 minutes, when they made 58 at Brisbane in 1936–37.

108

Fewest Runs In A Day By An Australian First-Class Side: 105 by Queensland in 1958–59 against MCC.

Highest Total In A Single Innings In Australian Cricket: Victoria scored 1,107 against New South Wales at Melbourne in 1926–27. When the teams met four weeks later at Sydney, Victoria were out for 35. Victoria scored 1,059 against Tasmania in 1922–23, at Melbourne.

Monopolised The Scoring: P. S. McDonnell made 82 out of 86 for Australia v. North of England in 1888. W. Howell made 95 out of 109 for New South Wales v. England, 1897–98, R. Benaud made 97 out of 117 for Australia v. England, 1956. J. Lyons made 149 out of 181 for Australia v. MCC, 1893. These are the best examples of batsmen monopolising the scoring, but a feat that also rates high was A. Kippax's 238 out of 307 runs for the last wicket for New South Wales against Victoria, 1928–29.

Slowest Scoring By An Australian In First-Class Cricket: Paul Nicholls batted 114 minutes for four runs for Western Australia against South Australia in 1971–72, the slowest innings in Shield matches.

LONGEST INNINGS FOR AUSTRALIA IN TESTS

Year	Name	Time Taken	Score	Against	Venue
1964	R. B. Simpson	12 hours 42 minutes	311	England	Old Trafford
1965–66	R. M. Cowper	12 hours 07 minutes	307	England	Melbourne
1946–47	S. G. Barnes	10 hours 42 minutes	234	England	Sydney
1965–66	R. B. Simpson	9 hours 07 minutes	225	England	Adelaide
1958–59	C. C. McDonald	8 hours 07 minutes	170	England	Adelaide
1884	W. L. Murdoch	8 hours 05 minutes	211	England	Oval

LONGEST PERIODS TAKEN ON FIELD OF PLAY

Year	Name	Time Taken	Against	Venue
1964	R. B. Simpson	27 hours 59 minutes (Whole match except for 16 mins.)	England	Old Trafford

SLOWEST CENTURIES

Year	Name	Time Taken	Score	Against	Venue
1968	W. M. Lawry	350 minutes	135	England	Oval
1953	A. L. Hassett	346 minutes	115	England	Trent Bridge
1946–47	A. L. Hassett	344 minutes	128	England	Brisbane
1964	R. B. Simpson	330 minutes	311	England	Old Trafford

SLOWEST DOUBLE CENTURIES

Year	Name	Time Taken	Score	Against	Venue
1964	R. B. Simpson	608 minutes	311	England	Old Trafford
1946–47	S. G. Barnes	570 minutes	234	England	Sydney
1965–66	R. M. Cowper	535 minutes	307	England	Melbourne
1965–66	R. B. Simpson	483 minutes	225	England	Adelaide

Richie Benaud lofts a ball into the outfield. He made 121 when Australia scored her highest Test total, 8 for 758, at Kingston.

BEAMES, Percival James, 1911–

First-Class Averages: Batting, 1,186 runs at 51.56; Bowling, 7 wickets at 22.42.

A fast-scoring right-hand batsman and right-arm medium pace bowler for Victoria between 1933–34 and 1945–46, when he captained the State team. He was cricket writer for the Melbourne *Age* for 30 years, and scoped the world during the England-Australia Test at Melbourne in 1954 when he broke the story about illegal watering of the pitch. Beames was the only writer who learned that curator Jack House, a crony from his football years, hosed the wicket on the rest day, Sunday, after big cracks appeared on it late on Saturday afternoon.

Beames scored three centuries for Victoria, two of them among the fastest on record in inter-State matches. He went in to bat 13 minutes before lunch at Launceston against Tasmania on Boxing Day, 1938, and by tea had scored 122. He added 104 more by stumps to finish the day on 226 not out. He was a fine exponent of late cuts and square cuts, and fast footwork enabled him to get into position early for powerful hooks. He was given out lbw at 93 but the Tasmanian captain Ron Morrisby refused to let him depart and told the umpire Beames had hit the ball. Barry Scott, the last man in, made four while Beames went from 169 to 200 in 28 minutes. Beames followed this with 169 not out in his next innings against Tasmania at Hobart, during which he put on 100 in 34 minutes with Ian Johnson.

Beames, born in Ballarat and educated at Ballarat College, had one season with South Melbourne in 1929, but when he settled in Melbourne played all his football and cricket for the Melbourne club. He was a tough, fast rover whose football depended on quick wits and speedy feet. He made his sole Shield century, 104 against South Australia at Melbourne, in the same match in which Keith Miller made his maiden first-class century. In his best years, competition for State team spots was fierce. He had a period in 1938 when he was not dismissed in scoring 400 runs for Victoria, but when the team to travel to Sydney was selected he missed out.

BEARD, Graeme Robert ("Agatha") 1950–

A tall, sunny-natured all-rounder with an ability to adapt and experiment when he was bowling and a flair for scoring valuable middle order runs with the bat. At 30, he toured England with the 1981 Australian team with three Tests behind him and a better record in one day matches than the first-class variety which go three days or more. This was not a criticism of his stamina but more a compliment to his consistency in bowling a good line and length.

Beard, a teacher at Avalon Primary School in Sydney, won selection in Manly first grade at 19 as a leg-spinner. But Manly already had successful spinners in Peter Philpott, Terry Lee, Tom Spencer and Mick Pawley, so Beard concentrated on his batting and did well enough to win selection for New South Wales against West Indies in 1975 in place of an injured Doug Walters. He made a "pair," but recovered from the shock of it to score 75 and 16 against Victoria.

Frustrated by Manly's surplus of spinners, he started bowling off-cutters and inswingers. Continually experimenting, he added an outswinger and a leg-cutter to his armory, but his batting fell away and the New South Wales selectors overlooked him in 1976–77 and for most of the following summer. He kept plugging away at the nets, trying different grips and by the start of the 1978–79 season, the wickets started to come. He bowled splendidly for 31 overs against Western

First-Class Averages:
Batting, 1,441 runs at 23.62;
Bowling, 125 wickets at 28.19.

Tests (3): 114 runs at 22.80; 1 for 110.

111

Australia in Perth to take 4 for 78. Against Tasmania at Sydney he took eight wickets and finished the season with 26 wickets.

When the WSC players returned for the 1979–80 season, he was dropped to the State Seconds but before the season was out he had advanced from this obscurity to Test status. First he was reinstated to the State side, balancing an attack that included pace men Pascoe and Lawson and spinners Hourn and Holland. He even introduced a delivery called the "Cho" ball, tucking a finger under the ball in the style of "Cho" Gleeson and spinning it in from the leg. New South Wales players called him "Agatha" after the mystery writer Agatha Christie.

When Ashley Mallett and Jim Higgs dropped out of the tour of Pakistan, he went as a replacement, partnering Ray Bright in all three Tests and scoring handy runs. Back in Australia, he bowled splendidly in one day matches but found Australian hard pitches unresponsive to his bag of tricks. Selectors probably had to decide between him and Yardley for the 1981 team to England, and plumped for Beard and his flair for experimentation.

Beard did not play in a Test on the tour of Sri Lanka and England and in 10 matches scored 144 runs at 16.00 and took 21 wickets at 29.90, best figures 5 for 69 against Sri Lanka. His results were equally modest in Australia in 1981–82 when he made 378 runs at 34.36 and took 22 wickets at 33.95. Only once in the season did he take five wickets in an innings—5 for 67 against Queensland in Brisbane. Beard announced his retirement from first-class cricket in 1982.

BECKER, Gordon Charles, 1936–

First-Class Averages: Batting, 2,227 runs at 27.49; Dismissals: 138 (116 catches, 22 stumpings).

An outstanding wicket-keeper-batsman for Western Australia who toured South Africa with the Australian team in 1966–67. Becker, who began with West Perth before transferring to the Perth club, made three centuries and 13 scores over 50 in 52 first-class matches. He scored 130 against NSW at Perth in 1964–65, his career highest of 195 against India at Perth in 1967–68, and 112 against Queensland at Brisbane in 1968–69. He was a member of the WA team that won the Sheffield Shield in 1967–68. In South Africa in 1966–67, he had a big chance to press his Test claims following the retirement of Wally Grout but Brian Taber was preferred for the Tests. He never got another chance, though he continued to take magnificent catches and score centuries for the Perth club in grade cricket. Becker played in only five of the 17 first-class games on his South African tour, but took 10 catches and made four stumpings. He scored 68 runs at 11.33 in seven innings, topscore 16. He became a State selector after he retired.

Gordon Becker

A broad-shouldered Victorian allrounder whose career typified that of thousands of Australians who have to decide between cricket and football. Bedford, an outstanding centreman and rover for South Melbourne Australian Rules club, looked probable Test cricket material when he first played for Victoria in 1966, but despite an innings of 134 not out in 1969 at Melbourne against Western Australia and some handy bowling analyses never fulfilled his cricket potential. In football, however, he won the highest honour—the 1970 Brownlow medal for the best and fairest player in the Victorian Football League.

BEDFORD, Peter Lawrence Anthony, 1947–

First-Class Averages: Batting, 1,602 runs at 28.10; Bowling, 45 wickets at 33.40.

BELVIDERE CUP The symbol of Sydney grade cricket supremacy, presented each year to the first grade premiers. From the start of grade competition in 1893–94 until the 1902–03 season, winners of Sydney's first grade premiership received the H. V. Hordern Shield. It was then discovered that under Dr Hordern's "deed of gift" a team that won the Shield three times kept it. Paddington had achieved this by winning the 1900–01 premiership so the Shield was belatedly handed over to the club. The Rawson Cup then became the prize for first grade supremacy until North Sydney won it outright in 1912–13. Then in 1919 the Percy Arnott Cup was presented until Waverley won it outright in 1922. From then until 1931 there was no first grade trophy.

At this stage Dr Percy Charlton, an original member of the Belvidere CC, donated a trophy won by his club back in 1882. Dr Charlton said that it was the wish of the surviving members of the Belvidere CC that the trophy be henceforth known as the Belvidere Cup and that it should be presented to the Sydney premiers each year. The Cup has remained the trophy for which grade clubs compete each summer. In the 1950s members of the Paddington Cricket Club, celebrating at Paddington Town Hall, found the Hordern Shield in the bowels of the Town Hall when they went looking for a punch bowl. They had the Hordern Shield restored, and handed it to the New South Wales Cricket Association, in whose rooms it now stands.

BENAUD, John
1944–

First-Class Averages: Batting, 2,888 runs at 36.55; Bowling, 5 wickets at 35.20.

Tests (3): 223 runs at 44.60; 2 wickets at 6.00.

Younger brother of Richie whose preference for his career as a journalist cut short a first-class cricket career that was sprinkled with big hitting and took him to the captaincy of New South Wales and into three Tests for Australia. John, who learned the game as Richie had done from father Lou, was a spectacular grade cricketer first for Cumberland, then on his return from England with Randwick, Penrith and finally with Cumberland.

John Benaud, a free-thinker like his brother, made headlines in 1969–70 when he was suspended by the New South Wales Cricket Association from all grade and association matches because he and members of the New South Wales team he captained disobeyed an instruction from the association's executive not to wear ripple-soled boots. Eight members of the New South Wales team wore the shoes that were really a slipper. When John Benaud requested an interview to explain the players' preference for the smaller shoe, Sid Webb, a member of the NSWCA executive, kept referring to him as "Richie."

John Benaud, tall, pugnacious, determined to play attractive cricket, appeared in 34 matches for New South Wales, and made 2,042 runs at 36.46, best score for the State, 134 against Victoria at Melbourne in 1969–70. He made one overseas tour with an Australian team—with the side that went to the West Indies in 1972–73, when Australia won the only Test to provide a result. His best effort in Tests was 142 in Melbourne against Pakistan including 93 before lunch after just being told he had been dropped for the next Test. He is currently Executive Editor of the tabloid Sydney Sun.

John Benaud, hooks a ball to the fence for NSW against Queensland.

After the NSWCA banned cut-down ripple soled shoes in 1969–70, the NSW team responded by offering their footware for sale outside the dressing-room door at the SCG.

BENAUD, Richard ("Richie"), 1930–

First-Class Averages:
Batting, 11,719 runs at 36.50;
Bowling, 945 wickets at 24.73.

Tests (63): 2,201 runs at 24.45; 248 wickets at 27.03.

A first-class allrounder, dynamic as a gully fieldsman, and among the best-ever in that position, a punishing batsman who hit some stirring sixes, severe on the drive and pull, a very shrewd leg-spinner, and a great captain. He was only a moderate performer when he began in first-class cricket, but he played 63 Tests for Australia and for most of his 12-year span was the hardest worker in big cricket at the practise nets. From a high, fluent action he made the ball bounce high, even if it did not turn far, and teased with flight and pace variations. Late in his career Bruce Dooland taught him the "flipper," a wrong-un with topspin. His involvement with Packer's breakaway World Series Cricket has, for some cricket devotees, tarnished his high reputation.

Benaud was a lucky cricketer, but cricket was luckier that in 1958 when international matches were in the doldrums he became Australia's captain. For his instinctively aggressive approach to cricket and his skill in the neglected chores of public relations revitalised Test cricket wherever his team played. He lost only four of his 27 Tests as Australia's captain, two to England, and one each to West Indies and India, a marvellous record for any captain. Probably only Ian Chappell matched Benaud among Australia's recent captains.

Richie Benaud leaps high to his left to bring in a brilliant one-hand catch off his own bowling to dismiss England opener Peter Richardson.

Typical of the Benaud approach was Australia's win at Manchester in 1961 against England. Midway through the last afternoon, he decided that England had to be bowled out, for if they continued at a normal rate they would win with time to spare. Instead of playing safe, he attacked and his fieldsmen responded with some spectacular catching. Shrewdly pitching his leg breaks into patches roughened by the boots of Trueman and other English pace bowlers, he got one to spin round Peter May's legs and bowl May for a duck. Australia won by 51 runs to clinch The Ashes. His crucial decision was to bowl around the wicket. This helped give him the angle which, exaggerated by spin out of the rough, finished off May.

Benaud was a skilled hand at persuading his players to play as a team rather than concentrate on individual deeds, and he could extract every bit of ability and stamina from them. Many times he got Davidson to keep going for an extra 40 minutes with pleas of "Just one more over, Al, pal." Ken Mackay transformed himself into a very useful medium pace bowler for Benaud's Test side and never quibbled about batting at No. 8 although he had scored more than 6,000 runs going in earlier in the order for Queensland. Tactically, it could be argued that Benaud was never bested, though he did disappoint right at the end of his career when he submitted to a tame draw in Sydney against Dexter's MCC team. The only criticism of his captaincy that persisted was that he was far too demonstrative in hugging bowlers and fieldsmen who had just dismissed a batsman. Many oldtimers claim he started the modern habit of bowlers rushing to embrace catchers.

Richie Benaud went to Parramatta High School and learned the game from his school-teacher father Louis, a descendant of a family that migrated to Australia in a sailing ship from La Rochelle. Lou, a slow leg-break bowler, is one of the few to take all 20 wickets in a match, and a veteran first-grader.* Richie worked at first in the business department of the old *Sydney Sun*, handling reporters' expense accounts and later was put under the guidance of some tough old police rounds writers. He made his debut for New South Wales in 1948–49, and played his first Test for Australia against West Indies in 1951–52 at the age of 21. He made three tours of England, in 1953, 1956 and in 1961 as captain.

Selectors persevered with him despite early failures but it was not until 1957–58 in South Africa that they were rewarded. From then to the end of his Test career in 1963–64 he gave a succession of outstanding performances. In his 63 Tests he became the only player to take more than 200 wickets and score more than 2,000 runs. His record of 248 Test wickets was not beaten until Dennis Lillee moved ahead of him in 1980–81.

* Lou Benaud took 20 wickets for 65 runs with his leg-breaks playing for Penrith Waratahs against St Marys in the 1922–23 season.

A superb shot of Richie Benaud going out to bat at the Sydney Cricket Ground.

He took 10 wickets in a Test once and 16 times took five wickets or more, best effort 7 for 72, each wicket costing 27.03 runs. He also held 65 Test catches, many of them spectacular efforts, and almost all of them in the gully position. The left-handed catch with which he dismissed Cowdrey from a full-blooded drive at Lord's in 1956 ranks among the finest in modern times.

Benaud (pronounced Benno) became Australian captain in curious circumstances when Ian Craig, who had taken the Australians to New Zealand and South Africa in 1957, contracted hepatitis in 1958. Most critics considered Neil Harvey was certain to get the job, but under Benaud Australia did not

Benaud bowling his spinners for Australia against Sussex at Hove in 1961 following a series of shoulder troubles.

119

lose a Test series and won many exciting victories. In 1960–61 Benaud's team played the most entertaining series in modern times against West Indies, captained by Frank Worrell. The series started with Test cricket's first tie and ended with a world crowd of 90,800 packing into Melbourne Cricket Ground for the second day of the Fifth Test.

Benaud was always one of the boys, but sufficiently apart from the team to maintain discipline without embarrassment. When he gave his players instructions, it was short, staccato stuff life: "I want runs, but don't get out!" or "I want wickets, and no runs." At Dacca in Pakistan he told "Slasher" Mackay to bowl at the stumps and on no account bowl outside the off-stump. One ball in Mackay's next 45 overs in stifling heat drifted outside the off-stump and Saeed clipped it for four. Richie walked over to "Slasher" and said, "What's the matter, getting tired?" When Mackay bowled Saeed soon after, Richie pumped him on the back. "That's where I wanted it," he said.

For New South Wales in 86 matches, Benaud scored 9 centuries. For thrills, however, nothing quite matched his batting in the final match of the 1953 Australian tour of Scarborough when he hit a then world record of 11 sixes in an innings which also yielded nine fours, making 102 in boundaries in an innings of 135. This innings began slowly until Len Hutton baited Benaud with a jibe about playing for a good average. Stung by Hutton's words Benaud gave spinners Roy Tattersall and John Wardle a fearful hiding with his lofted driving, and even hooked Alec Bedser for six. In all first-class matches he scored 23 centuries. Shoulder trouble hastened his retirement.

Richie was never as penetrative a bowler as Grimmett but he was just as cunning. He lived for cricket and his long absences on tours helped destroy his first marriage to a very attractive blonde, Marcia Lavender. They had two boys, Gregory and Jeffrey, and Richie took them around England before his divorce on the grounds of desertion. At 36, he married Daphne Surfleet, a former secretary to the doyen of English cricket writers, E. W. Swanton, and probably the world's most knowledgeable cricket lady. Their public relations company, apart from its WSC contracts, is an outstanding success.

Richie's involvement with World Series Cricket as a public relations consultant cost him many friends. He was, however, a free agent who accepted a challenge for a new employer and made a success of the job. His success in public relations, as a columnist and TV commentator has been a memorable feat by a resourceful man. He took on a demoralised lot of cricketers as Australia's captain and transformed them into winners. His struggle with cricket's establishment over his role in the WSC affair is still going on, but one can be sure he will be just as resolute in the fight for common sense.

Until the introduction by State associations and the Australian Cricket Board of Players' Provident Funds, it was the custom to reward prominent players for long service by granting them testimonial matches. Stan McCabe and Bill O'Reilly in 1956–57 were the last to be given an official benefit match. All around Australia outstanding players have frequently had matches to boost unofficial benefit funds since then—but the

BENEFIT MATCHES FOR AUSTRALIAN CRICKETERS

The 1946–47 Australian team on the steps of a Sydney clothing factory after receiving one of the benefits of Test selection, a sports coat and pair of slacks.

matches have been staged without the official sanction of the ACB and the State associations. The Provident Funds, prize-money, and match fees are generous, and as they operate for both State and Test players, officials believe that involvement in benefit matches would needlessly complicate arrangements for TV and advertising fees.

Benefit matches have produced some strange incidents, such as Sid Barnes batting in the Bradman benefit with a mini bat only a few inches long. Often the organisers have stage-managed what was shown to spectators by taking off a hostile bowler who may have dismissed a drawcard and replacing him with a bowler the drawcard could punish. Bill O'Reilly got rid of Badcock, Robinson and Morrisby for seven runs during the Bardsley-Gregory benefit at Sydney in 1936. Vic Richardson apologised for taking him off when Bradman came in. "I didn't get a go at Bradman until he was 70 or 80 and he made 212," says O'Reilly.

Australian cricket's most successful benefit match was held in Melbourne after the return of the 1948 team from England. The team's captain, Don Bradman, had just retired and even in America the newspapers were full of his amazing achievements. The match attracted a gate of £5,185 and Bradman received £9,342 after donations were added. Nobody present objected when Col McCool's normally brilliant hands failed to catch Bradman in the outfield when Bradman was on 97.

The first recorded benefit match for an Australian cricketer was for Richard Coulstock at Melbourne in the 1857–58 season, but the amount he received is unrecorded. Other cricketers to have benefits in the 19th century included T. F. Wray (Victoria), G. H. S. Trott (Victoria), E. J. Gregory (NSW), H. F. Boyle (Victoria), S. Cosstick (Vic. and NSW), W. Swain (Qld), C. Bannerman (NSW) and J. P. Carew (Qld). Wicket-keeper J. J. Kelly (NSW) was the first Australian to be given a first-class match at his benefit, in 1905–06, when the proceeds reached £1,400.

Australians have figured in many lucrative testimonial matches overseas, going back as far as 1893 when the match between England and Australia at The Oval was played for the benefit of J. M. Read, a famous Surrey player and raised £1,200. The Surrey club was extremely grateful for this gesture and has remained a staunch supporter of Australian cricket ever since. In 1948, the match between Australia and Lancashire formed part of Cyril Washbrook's benefit year and helped boost his receipts to £14,000 sterling. The Australians were glad to play in these matches but they envied the English players' right to take their benefits tax-free. Not the least attraction for Australians who have played league cricket in England are the collections taken on the ground for players who hit 50s and 100s or take more than five wickets.

Apart from benefit matches, some Australian players have received handsome gifts for feats that thrilled spectators. Don Bradman collected £1,000 for his Test record 334 in 1930 at Leeds. Others have received watches, tiepins, clocks, tankards, cars, suits and cases of wines. Sid Barnes was a master at converting autographed bats into rolls of valuable cloth when good cloth was scarce in Australia. Bradman recalls in his autobiography an advertisement that appeared in a Gloucestershire paper during his 1934 tour of England which read: "If Don Bradman comes to Jones' Garage he can have a second-hand Austin 7 for a present (1 dozen still in stock)." He didn't collect it.

BENEFIT MATCHES FOR FIRST-CLASS PLAYERS

Season	Player	Match, Venue	Amount Raised
1905–06	J. J. Kelly	NSW v. Australia, Sydney	£1400
1906–07	S. E. Gregory	NSW v. Rest, Sydney	£630
1907–08	J. McBlackham	Victoria v. MCG, Melbourne	£1359
1907–08	M. A. Noble	Australia v. Rest, Sydney	£2000
1909–10	C. T. B. Turner	NSW v. Rest, Sydney	£331
1910–11	T. S. Warne	Australia v. Rest, Melbourne	£234
1912–13	V. T. Trumper	NSW v. Rest, Sydney	£2950
1921–22	W. W. Armstrong	Public Subscription	£2500
1921–22	F. Iredale	Australia v. Rest, Sydney	£1741
1922–23	C. Bannerman	Collins XI v. Macartney's XI, Sydney	£490
1922–23	G. Giffen	South Australia v. Victoria, Adelaide	£2020
1924–25	W. P. Howell	NSW v. Australian XI, Sydney	£950
1926–27	C. G. Macartney	Rest v. Australians	£2598
1930–31	J. S. Ryder	Woodfull's XI v. Ryders XI, Melbourne	£2463
1933–34	D. D. J. Blackie, H. Ironmonger	Woodfull's XI v. V. Y. Richardson's XI, Melbourne	£908 each
1933–34	E. Jones	South Australia v. NSW, Adelaide	£1000
1933–34	H. J. Collins, C. Kelleway, T.J., E. Anders	NSW v. Rest, Sydney	£500 each
1934–35	W. M. Woodfull, W. H. Ponsford	Woodfull's XI v. V. Y. Richardson's XI, Melbourne	£1042 each
1936–37	W. Bardsley, J. M. Gregory	Bradman's XI v. V. Y. Richardson's XI, Sydney	£762 each
1937–38	V. Y. Richardson, C. V. Grimmett	Bradman's XI v. V. Y. Richardson's XI, Adelaide	£1028 each
1948–49	A. J. Richardson	South Australia v. Victoria, Adelaide	£2130
1948–49	D. G. Bradman	Bradman's XI v. Hassett's XI, Melbourne	£9432*
1948–49	A. F. Kippax, W. A. Oldfield	Hassett's XI v. Morris's XI Sydney	£3015 each**
1953–54	A. L. Hassett	Hassett's XI v. Morris's XI, Melbourne	£3503***
1955–56	A. A. Mailey, J. M. Taylor	Johnson's XI v. Lindwall's XI, Sydney	£3591 each****
1956–57	S. J. McCabe, W. J. O'Reilly	Harvey's XI v. Lindwall's XI, Sydney	£3570 each*****

*Gate receipts for this match were £5185
**After deducting expenses of £900
***Donations took Hassett's benefit up to £5000
****After deducting expenses of £1900
*****After deducting expenses of £2300
Note: Not all these matches were first-class.

When the Victor Trumper testimonial was launched in 1912–13, the public contributed handsomely, subscriptions including cheques from the Rugby League star Dally Messenger, "Plum" Warner in England and Mr Justice Street, later Chief Justice of NSW. To this was added the receipts from the match, cheques from State associations, and receipts from the sale of photographs of Trumper which were sold on The Hill by players who appeared in the testimonial match. One of the entries in the book listing donations to the Trumper Testimonial Fund read: "One of Trumper's pupils, one shilling;" another simply: "A Newcastle schoolboy." Trumper's testimonial raised £2,950/13/3.

Trustees were appointed by the NSW Cricket Association in 1913 to hold and invest the money raised for Trumper. Income from the trust fund was paid to Trumper until he died in 1915, and after his death, his wife, Sarah Ann Trumper, received 12 guineas a month until her death in 1966. Children of the marriage then were paid monthly sums from the fund until Victor Trumper, jnr was paid $2537.93 and the fund wound up.

One of the intriguing sequels to the Trumper testimonial was a court case in which Thomas John Houghton claimed £111/7/– commission from the sum collected in public subscriptions. Houghton alleged that he lived from working as an organiser and had been approached to help with the Trumper fund by Hanson Carter who said the fund would be a flop if left to the NSWCA. He claimed he had worked for five months raising money. The court agreed with Trumper that he was in no way indebted to Houghton and threw the action out. Trumper himself later sent an old mate to the trustees of his fund saying the man had fallen on hard times, but the trustees declined to help.

BENSTED, Eric Charles, 1901–1980

First-Class Averages: Batting, 2,700 runs at 26.73; Bowling, 76 wickets at 43.34.

A useful right-handed allrounder for Queensland from 1923 to 1936, a tall, handsome figure who took 38 catches and had best bowling figures of 4 for 28 in 58 first-class matches for his State. He was born at Killarney. He scored three centuries for his State, 145 against South Australia in 1931–32, 155 against New South Wales in 1934–35, and 102 against New South Wales in 1935–36. He took 76 wickets for Queensland at a time when southern States boasted some of the most prolific batsmen (Bradman, Ponsford, McCabe, Brown, Kippax) of all time. He is best remembered for a stand of 335 for the seventh wicket with C. W. Andrews out of a Queensland total of 495 against New South Wales in 1934–35. Andrews, an ex-Sydney player, made 253, Bensted 155, and their partnership was only nine short of the then world record for the seventh wicket by Ranjitsinhji and Newnham for Sussex in 1902. Bensted played

124

for Toombul and Northern Suburbs clubs, Brisbane and was discovered playing in Warwick by one of Roger Hartigan's touring teams.

BETTING, ON AUSTRALIAN CRICKET

Spectators gambled on the outcome of matches and on the performances of players from the start of inter-Colonial cricket in Australia. The first Australian cricket annual, *Australian Cricketer's Guide*, published in Melbourne in 1856–57, included rules for cricket betting modelled on those that applied in England. Fortunately, the English scandals over matches being rigged by titled gamblers were not repeated in Australia. Bookmakers were present at the first inter-Colonial match between New South Wales and Victoria in Melbourne at the Richmond Paddock, but have long since been outlawed from our cricket grounds by the gaming laws of the individual States.

The Victorians encouraged gambling on the result when they placed an advertisement in the Melbourne *Argus* in 1856 challenging neighbouring colonies to play them for £500. In Sydney an enthusiastic group of cricketers gathered by William Tunks voted to accept the challenge but declined to play the Victorians for money. They were not overawed by the tal-

Dennis Lillee bowling against England at Trent Bridge, showing the betting tent in the background.

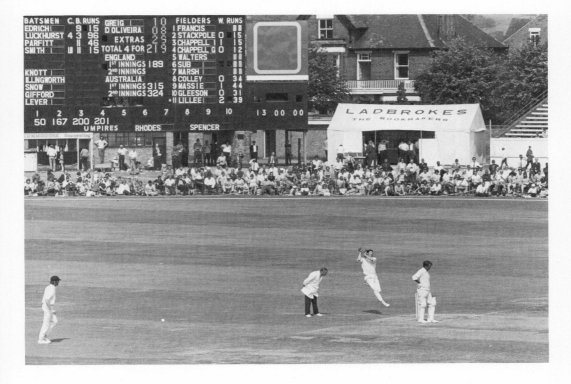

ents of the Victorians, merely convinced that playing for money was not for gentlemen. Tunks took the hat round to raise the money for the trip to Melbourne and added a substantial donation of his own.

The Argus said, "In the pluckiest manner, and at every disadvantage, an XI of New South Wales, was found to take up the 'Berlin' and waiving pecuniary considerations, the members of the Sydney Club have come to Melbourne determined to win. Of late years cricket, like chess, has invariably been a game of love, money a thing unmentionable. The stake is now for the supremacy of local play, and the broader grounds upon which the contest is placed are decidedly more calculated to produce better sport."

Before play began bets of 2 to 1 against the NSW team were freely taken. An argument over who had the right to bat first stimulated betting even further. The Victorian team argued that as they won the toss they should decide who batted first. The NSW players claimed the visiting team always had the choice of batting first or sending in their opponents, and asked Victoria to bat, a step which shortened the odds wagered about Victoria to 3 to 1 on. Victoria were out for 63 and 28. NSW scored 76 and 7 for 16 to win the match and their supporters' bets.

The *Australian Cricketer's Guide* for 1859, published a list of rules for cricket betting which began:

1. No bet on any match is payable unless it is played out or given up.

2. If the runs of one player are betted against those of another, the bet depends on the first innings unless otherwise specified.

3. If a bet be made on both innings, and one party beat the other in one innings, the runs of the first innings shall determine it.

Rule 42 in this list stipulated that umpires were not allowed to bet, and added that this rule was explicit as the natural consequence of allowing betting would be "the probable leaning to self-interest and a possible injustice." The Guide recommended the immediate sacking of any umpire who gambled on match results.

The riot at Sydney in 1878–79 during the match between Lord Harris' England XI and NSW was largely attributable to incitement by bookmakers in the Sydney pavilion. Angry mobs of members as well as outer ground spectators invaded the pitch and threatened the players after the England side's umpire gave Billy Murdoch run out. Mounted police had to restore order and no further play was possible that day after Lord Harris was struck by a spectator.

At the Imperial Cricket Conference in 1921, Australian captain Warwick Armstrong advocated that umpires should not be appointed until the day of a match. "The umpires are paid so little for their services and, as there is a lot betting on Tests, it would be wise to remove them from temptation," Armstrong said. Lord Harris said that the issue was so serious that he would like it to be held over until the next day while inquiries were made. Next day he told the conference he had been unable to find any evidence of betting on big cricket. To which Armstrong replied, "Well if you'd like £500 on the next Test I can get it on for you."

Betting on cricket was confined to bookmakers' offices until the revision of the English gaming laws in the 1970s. These days bookmakers' tents are erected at the grounds to take bets on the play, with popular ex-players like Godfrey Evans present to encourage bettors. Not all English counties allow betting tents on their grounds, for some are unhappy about simply receiving a fee from bookmakers without a percentage of the tents' turnover. Among Test match grounds, Old Trafford is the only one that does not permit betting tents. On the 1981 Australian tour of England one English paper claimed Australian players had won big money by backing England at long odds just before a dramatic Australian slump. The Australian players indignantly denied this. So far there has been no move to follow England by providing cricket fans with betting facilities at the grounds, but bets are still laid with bookmakers at their sporting clubs.

BETTINGTON, Dr Reginald Henshall Brindley, 1900–1969

First-Class Averages:
Batting, 3,314 runs at 27.38;
Bowling, 357 wickets at 23.79.

The first Australian to captain Oxford University at cricket, a captivating all-round sportsman richly enjoyed by spectators for the loudness and piercing clarity of his appeals when bowling. Bettington went straight to Oxford from the King's School, Parramatta, and won colours in his first year, 1920, in cricket and Rugby and golf. He played in the forwards at Rugby against Cambridge, kicking goals left foot.

On wickets that gave the slightest assistance he could turn his leg-breaks and googlies sharply. In his first year in first-class cricket, he took 7 for 47 and 5 for 42 against Somerset, 5 for 48 against Essex, and 5 for 48 against Warwickshire. Reg Bettington made the ball buzz like a top, wrote noted English critic R. C. Robertson-Glasgow. "At the moment of delivery there was a sharp snapping sound. There was another even sharper snapping sound when he asked for lbw or a catch at the wicket. A Bettington appeal brought all Sydney to the Oxford parks."

Bettington, who was accompanied to Oxford by his brother B. J., was dark-complexioned, immensely strong, 6 ft 3 ins tall and bowled at a normal leg-breaker's pace off a longish run. Jack bowled spinners at a brisk medium pace. At Eastbourne in 1920 Reg was the centre of a controversial incident when Oxford were set to get 179 to defeat H. D. Leveson-Gower's XI,

and reached the target with Reg on 99. E. Smith bowled another ball which Bettington hit for two runs to reach what was called "a totally illegitimate century."

In 1923, when Reg took over the Oxford cricket captaincy, he took 3 for 19 and 8 for 66 against Cambridge, playing the leading role in Oxford's win by an innings and 227 runs—the largest margin in the history of the match. He also took 6 for 71 v. Hampshire, 5 for 22 and 4 for 91 v. Surrey, and a total of 61 wickets that summer at 16.55. From the University he went to London's St Bartholomew's Hospital, where he qualified as a doctor, and assisted Middlesex and played for The Gentlemen v. The Players. In 15 County championship matches, he took 54 wickets at 29.44 each and made 605 runs at 30.25.

His best figures were at Lord's when he followed an innings of 95 against Sussex by taking 6 for 78. He also took 6 for 76 v. Somerset on the same ground. In all first-class cricket, Bettington, who once hammered a six into the press box at The

128

Oval, scored four centuries, and took five wickets in an innings 21 times. Later Bettington played five matches for NSW, scoring 152 runs at 19.00, and taking 10 wickets at 50.60 each. His duties as an ear, nose and throat specialist restricted his cricket, but he excelled as a golfer, winning NSW and Australian titles.

In the 1932 Australian amateur championship final at Adelaide, noted left-hander Harry William was four up on Bettington with seven holes to play. Bettington reeled off five successive birdies and set a stymie to win six holes in a row and the title 2 and 1. Bettington died tragically when his car plunged 100 feet on to a railway line at Gisborne, New Zealand, where he had been a specialist for many years. A street leading to his beloved Oatlands golf course in Sydney was named after him.

BEVAN, Hubert George ("Hugh"), 1932–

First-Class Averages: Batting, 331 runs at 8.27; Bowling, 121 wickets at 34.99.

A lively fast-medium left-arm bowler for Western Australia when that State was building its strength in the 1950s and 1960s. He took five wickets or more in an innings seven times, and did it against every State, before Tasmania joined in regular first-class cricket. He was given a Test "trial" at Melbourne in 1963–64 against South Africa but failed to take a wicket. Bevan's best figures were 6 for 22 against Queensland at Perth in 1963–63. He also took 5 for 55 against New Zealand at Perth in 1961–62, and 6 for 93 against South Africa at Perth in 1963–64. He was unimpressive with the bat, seldom reaching double figures, best score 26. He gave North Perth enthusiastic service in club cricket, heading the Perth first grade bowling averages in 1957–58 with 45 wickets at 12.13. He became a State selector on retirement.

BIG HITTING AND FAST SCORING

Nothing in cricket delights spectators more than big-hitting, and most of the great Australian sides have included at least one batsman who could lift the ball into the crowd, however big the ground. Big hitters have a key role in the game and have had a significant tactical part in Australia's international successes.

Australian captain Joe Darling played an important part in helping big hitters. He had the Laws of Cricket altered to give batsmen six for hits over the fence. When Darling first went to England with the 1896 Australian team, batsmen scored only four for hits over the fence, the same as for hits along the turf to the boundary. In Australia, batsmen got five for hits over the fence. To score six, both in England and Australia, batsmen had to hit the ball right out of the ground. In one match at Crystal Palace Darling was given four for a hit over the fence. "I asked Dr Grace how much further I had to hit it to get six and he replied, 'About another 100 yards,'" wrote Darling in his *Test Struggles, On and Off the Field*. Had that happened the hit would have gone right out of the Melbourne Cricket Ground, Darling said. At a dinner given by the Surrey club for the Australians in 1899, the Surrey president deplored slow, tedious play by batsmen. Responding on behalf of the Australians, Darling urged English authorities to alter the Laws to give six for every hit over the boundary.

"My suggestion led to a lot of discussion, with the result that I was asked to write to the MCC to seek agreement on the suggestion in Tests," said Darling. On his return to Australia, he got the South Australian Cricket Association to alter the laws of cricket to award batsmen six for hits over the fence. In moving the motion, he pointed out that by only awarding five for hits over the fence, the batsman was penalised by losing the strike. The SACA was the first cricket association to allow six for hits over the fence, and the other Australian States and England followed later.

Longest Hit in Australian Cricket: J. E. C. Moore hit a ball a measured 170 yards 1 ft 5 ins in a minor cricket match at Griffith, NSW, in 1930. This remains the longest authenticated hit in any level of Australian cricket. For many years Moore's blow was considered to rate second only to a hit of 175 yards by the Rev. W. Fellowes on the Christchurch ground at Oxford in 1856, but doubts have recently been raised about the authenticity of Fellowes' hit, and a blow of 168 yards 2 ft by C. I. Thornton in 1871, on the Hove ground, is now generally accepted as the longest hit in English cricket.

Early Australian Big Hitters: George Bonnor, John James Lyons, Albert Trott, Sammy Woods, Alan Marshal, Victor Trumper and Bill Howell were all mighty hitters in the first fifty years of first-class cricket in Australia. Most of them were physical giants who excelled at big hits straight down the ground rather than long pulls or hooks square of the wicket.

Bonnor's Legacy: For consistency in big hitting most oldtimers gave preference to Bonnor because his hitting was repeated all over the world. He hit a ball that travelled 147 yards before it bounced, at Mitcham Green, near London, in 1880, which was measured by fellow cricketer James Southerton. At Melbourne during practise he was credited with hits of 160 yards and 150 yards.

Albert Trott at Lord's: Lillywhite's *Scores and Biographies* records that in scoring 164 for Middlesex against Yorkshire at Lord's in 1899, Trott scored 26 runs in four minutes. One drive off Wainright hit the pavilion seats with such force it rebounded almost to the stumps. Playing for MCC v. Australia at Lord's in 1899, Trott drove a ball from Monty Noble over the pavilion. The ball struck the pot of one of the chimneys and disappeared behind.

130

Albert Trott at Taunton: In a partnership of 96 in 35 minutes with C. M. Wells, Trott hit successive balls out of the ground into the river for six each. The following year (1900) against Yorkshire at Leeds, Trott made 50 in 22 minutes for Middlesex while G. MacGregor made two.

Albert Trott in his early days. He was then a batsman who planned his innings and took his time. Later, as he put on weight, he became an unashamed big hitter, recording some enormous blows on English grounds.

South Australia's Jack Lyons: W. J. Ford, the great English hitter who played first-class cricket from 1873 to 1899, rated the South Australian J. J. Lyons one of the three best hitters of that period. Ford, in *Giants of the Game*, written in 1899, said: "The pace at which Lyons scored was remarkable, as few balls, whatever their length, escaped punishment, and no ring, whatever its size, seemed too big for him." At Sydney, in 1891–2, Lyons drove a ball with such power that it broke an iron fence post in front of the pavilion. In an innings of 149 at Lord's in 1893, during which he added 181 for the first wicket with A. C. Bannerman, Lyons hit balls on to the roof of a temporary stand, over the awning in front of the grandstand, over spectators by the old tennis court, and into the enclosure in front of the Players' room.

Trumper at Redfern Oval: Playing against Redfern on Redfern Oval in 1902, Victor Trumper put on 517 with Dan Gee, scoring 22 fives and 39 fours in an innings of 335. For much of the innings the only fieldsmen close to the wicket were the bowler and wicket-keeper. Even the slips were out on the fence. Australian captain Herbie Collins, who watched that display, said so many of Trumper's hits landed on the bowling green adjacent to Redfern Oval, the lawn bowlers gave up trying to continue their game and watched Trumper instead. One of Trumper's fives, a drive over mid-on, went out of the ground, across the road and broke a window on the second floor of a shoe factory facing the ground. This hit was estimated to have travelled 150 yards and would have gone further if it had not struck the building. When the South Sydney Leagues' Club bought the factory site in 1963 the window was preserved by the club as a memorial to Trumper's hitting.

"Sunny Jim" Mackay at Manly: J. R. M. Mackay, from Sydney's Burwood (later Western Suburbs) club, became a renowned big-hitter from the time he joined the side in 1902–3, from the country town of Uralla. At Manly in 1905–6, in an innings of 156 not out, he hit eight balls out of the ground for five each from Middle Harbour bowler J. Randall. One of these landed on the balcony of a house 60 yards outside the ground. G. P. Barbour, a respected critic, wrote that another blow, which struck the Presbyterian manse 50 yards from the ground in that knock against Middle Harbour was the biggest hit he ever saw.

Here are some of the biggest recorded hits at Australia's major centres:

Brisbane: Victor Trumper hit four sixes and 25 fours in an innings of 207 not out in Brisbane in May, 1906. One of his hits went well over the fence at the 'Gabba into Stanley Street, the first time such a blow had been recorded. J. N. Crawford, playing for an Australian XI against England in December 1911, hit a ball into the Alliance Hall in Stanley Street. Cec Pepper hit seven sixes, six off spinner Bill Tallon and one off left-

An artist's impression of Victor Trumper's mighty blow at Redfern Oval.

hander Charles Christ, in an innings of 81 for NSW against Queensland in November, 1939. Some of the sixes cleared the wooden structure since replaced by the Clem Jones stand, one landed in Vulture Street, two in Stanley Street. Victoria's Barry Scott hit a ball out of the 'Gabba into Vulture Street playing against Queensland in January, 1940.

Since World War II the mayhem has continued at the 'Gabba. In the 1946–47 series against England, Keith Miller hit a no-ball from leg-spinner Doug. Wright on to the top of the old 'Gabba Members' Stand. South Australian John Lill hit Queensland spinner John Freeman on to the top of the Leslie Wilson stand in January, 1962. Gary Sobers, during an innings of 196, hit John Mackay over the roof of the same stand, out across Vulture Street into the service station in January, 1963. Vivian Richards hit a ball on to the roof of the new Clem Jones stand on the Stanley Street side of the 'Gabba during the QCA Centenary match in October 1976, a blow that would have carried into the street before the stand was built. In the same innings Richards hit a ball into the car park behind square leg at the Vulture Street end.

Sydney: Victor Trumper, who made many of his longest hits on sticky wickets, faced the Victorian bowlers Jack Saunders and Frank Laver on an SCG "sticky" in 1905–06, hitting one ball from Saunders into the Showground before Saunders bowled him for 101. "Farmer Bill" Howell hit a ball high into the back of the Sheridan stand in a Shield game in 1901–2. Then in December, 1946, there was Keith Miller's superb blow off Ernie Toshack which hit seats in the M. A. Noble stand about five rows from the back. The ball was still rising when it struck the seats and ricocheted around them. Miller also hit a ball on to the Hill, a feat later emulated by Johnny Martin. Gary Sobers, playing for the West Indies against Australia in 1960–61, shaped to pull a ball to the square leg boundary, but the ball's flight deceived him and turned out to be of fuller length that he expected. Sobers changed to a full-blooded drive virtually in mid-stroke and hit the ball high into the Sheridan stand. Alan Davidson in 1954–55 hit a full toss from Colin Cowdrey on to the roof of the old Brewongle stand and straight drove the next ball on to the wall at the back of the Hill, with the ball still rising on impact. The first blow hit a ridge a yard from the top of the Brewongle stand, which stopped it from landing in the street.

Keith Miller batting for the Dominions against England at Lord's in 1945 when he gave the grandstands a dusting in an innings of 185.

There has often been talk about players who hit the Sydney Cricket Ground clock, but the truth is that this has never been done. Don Bradman and Walter Hammond both landed sixes on the roof of the Members' stand on which the clock stands, and the Pakistani fast bowler Farooq hit a ball from Johnny Martin on to the roof of the Ladies' stand, but the clock has always remained intact. The famous West Indian hitter Learie Constantine tried hard to hit the clock in 1930–31 but he failed. Constantine, like Martin and Brian Booth later on, did land a ball on to the roof of the Hill (the old Bob Stand) stand which just failed to clear the roof and fall in the Showground. The nearest any batsman has come to the "clock stroke" was during the 1914–1918 War when E. T. Hall, batting for the Burwood club, hit the rim of the clock face, and when champion Rugby League footballer Dally Messenger hit the clock tower in a World War I social cricket match.

Melbourne: The most sustained exhibition of big-hitting on the Melbourne Cricket Ground occurred in 1926–27 when Jack Ryder hit six sixes, all driven, in an innings of 295. One blow struck a verandah rail of the Smokers' pavilion (since replaced) but the four shots that most delighted spectators landed in the outer ground near where Bay 11 patrons sit today. Nothing as dramatic as Ryder's hitting was seen at the MCG until David Hookes hit Tony Greig for five successive fours in the Centenary Test in 1976–77, but all of Hookes' strokes sped along the turf to the fence.

The MCG is one of the world's sternest tests for big-hitters. Shots that would be worth six on other grounds are caught there in the outfield. Nothing in the history of the MCG matches the blow by George Bonnor in 1881 when he struck a ball from the English bowler Bates out of the ground over the skittle alley and 20 yards beyond into Richmond Paddock—a shot of approximately 150 yards.

Ken Barrington, an English batsman who took his time, hit a most uncharacteristic six off spinner Tom Vievers into the MCG members' stand to reach his century in 1965–66 in the Fifth Test against Australia; surprisingly the second time he had reached a Test century in this fashion. In a limited over match against England in 1978–79, Victorian strongman Trevor Laughlin and big Gary Cosier hit enormous sixes into the members' stand—but just to clear the fence at the MCG is an exceptional feat.

Adelaide: The boundaries are so short square of the wicket at the Adelaide Oval that blows into the stands or into the area around the Victor Richardson gates on the opposite side of the ground are fairly common. The old-time batsman Jimmy Reedman was notorious for striking the ball into the stands and that great exponent of the left-hander's pull shot, Clem Hill, was credited with several blows into the street behind where the Richardson gates now stand. One of the most im-

Doug Walters lifts a ball from Peter Sleep high out to the boundary for NSW against SA in Sydney. He once hit a ball right out of the SCG No. 2 into Kippax Lake.

pressive onslaughts at Adelaide Oval came from New Zealander Dick Motz, who in 1967–68 hit six sixes, five off Ian Chappell and one off Ashley Mallett, in an innings of 94. But veteran cricket fans at the ground consider big Joel Garner's straight hit for six off Bruce Yardley in the Australia v. West Indies Third Test in 1981–82 one of the longest hits seen in Adelaide. Garner's blow travelled an estimated 140 yards before it bounced, landing in the crowd at deep long-on.

Perth: The WACA ground is almost as difficult as the MCG for batsmen keen to land the ball in the crowd. Western Australian captain Barry Shepherd thumped six sixes over the fence on his way to 207 in a day against Queensland in 1961–62. Tom Vievers was the unfortunate bowler. Jeff Thomson made one of the biggest ever hits at the WACA in 1979–80 when he landed a ball on the aluminium window base of the members' bar, momentarily scaring drinkers who watched the ball zooming towards them. The most frequently discussed big hit at the WACA, however, was Doug Walters' last ball of the day six off Bob Willis in the Second Test at Perth in 1974–75. This blow disappeared into a horde of spectators who invaded the pitch as Walters reached his century in the tea to stumps session.

136

Australians have had a flair for scoring quickly since the early days of the game. In big cricket George Bonnor, Victor Trumper, D. R. A. Gehrs, Charlie Macartney and Don Bradman have the best records for consistently fast scoring. In district and country cricket matches all over Australia, there have been countless instances of every ball in an over being hit for six. Gehrs scored the fastest first-class century in Australia, 119 in 50 minutes for South Australia v. Western Australia in 1912–13.

At all levels of Australian cricket our research has shown that the fastest century officially recorded was at Cairns on February 18, 1910, by Laurence Campbell ("Laurie") Quinlan, who reached 100 in 18 minutes off six ball overs. Quinlan was playing for Trinity CC, who were out for 71 in the first innings of the match. Their opponents, Mercantile CC, responded with 222, Trinity went in to bat the second time with time running out.

Quinlan, a renowned hitter who played most of his cricket in Townsville and Cairns, went in to bat at 4.41 p.m. and was not out on 100 when Trinity's second innings was closed at 4.59 p.m. Left to score 123 in 65 minutes to win outright, Mercantile scored 5 for 127, so Quinlan was on the losing side. Scores in the match were:

Mercantile 222 and 5 for 127	
Trinity 1st Innings	71
Trinity Second Innings	
Burke b. Archibald	101
Hill b. Archibald	1
Rodgers c. sub. b. Archibald	39
Quinlan not out	100
Creagh c. sub b. Archibald	0
Brennan not out	10
Sundries	22
Innings Declared Closed	4 for 273

Quinlan's hits were 2, 6, 2, 4, 1, 1, 6, 2, 3, 6, 4, 4, 3, 6, 2, 6, 6, 4, 1, 4, 4, 2, 4, 6, 4, 6, 1.

Don Bradman in his book *Farewell to Cricket* records that in an innings for New South Wales at Blackheath he scored 102 in three overs during an innings of 256, which included 14 sixes and 29 fours. With Wendell Bill as Bradman's partner, this was the scoring sequence:

First Over	6,6,4,2,4,4,6,1
Second Over	6,4,4,6,6,4,6,4
Third Over	1,6,6,1,1,4,4,6

"The scoring shots made by Wendell Bill in those three overs were the first and fifth singles in the third over", Bradman wrote. "Residents of Cairns, north Queensland, claim that the fastest 100 ever made was scored there by Laurie Quinlan in 18 minutes. No time was recorded at Blackheath, though I think it must have been less than 18 minutes."

In Sydney first grade cricket the fastest recorded century was by Jim Minter, who in the 1937–38 season made 100 in 34

Laurie Quinlan

minutes, with 14 fours, a five and one six. Minter batted for 12 minutes for 23 not out on the first day. On the second day three wickets fell quickly and Minter was held up waiting for incoming batsmen, one of whom, Dick Nutt, batted two minutes for a duck—but that two minutes counted on Minter's time. He moved to his century in 22 minutes, however, adding 78 runs to the 23 he had made the previous week. Minter was finally out for 141, having put on 109 in 40 minutes with Bill Hunt. In 1981 Northern Districts batsman Peter Taylor hit 101 in 38 minutes, with 16 fours, fastest Sydney first grade century since Minter's.

There is no record of other fast scorers surpassing Minter's effort but Victor Trumper had passages of play on his way to huge grade scores that must have matched it. When Trumper scored 189 not out for Paddington against Waverley on 1 October 1904, for example, he hit 15 fives and 22 fours. In successive scoring shots, Trumper scored 5,4,4,4,4,4,1,4,5,4,5,5,5,5,5 and later hit 4,4,5,4,5,5,5,5,4,5.

Another innings that compares with Minter's effort, though not a century, was Laurie Hawkins' 92 not out for Millfield in a Maitland district match against Aberdare in 1910. Hawkins hit 10 sixes, four fours, three twos, with the rest singles, and scored 36 in one over of six balls, all sixes. Stumps were drawn at 6 p.m., Hawkins having batted since 5.35, so his knock took 25 minutes.

Here are some of the outstanding fast scoring performances:

Fast Scoring By An Australian Team: An Australian representative team on tour in New Zealand in the summer of 1913–14 scored 9 for 922 in a mere 5 hours 30 minutes. During this innings Victor Trumper and the Englishman J. N. Crawford added 298 runs in 69 minutes against Canterbury. They put on 50 runs twice in periods of only 10 minutes. This scoring spree exceeded that at Southend in 1948 when Australia scored 721 in a day against Essex.

Fast Scoring By Australia In Tests: At Sydney in 1910–11, Australia made 6 for 494 on the first day against South Africa. In 1934 in The Oval Test against England, Australia scored 2 for 475 on the first day. At Headingley in 1930, Australia reached 3 for 458 in a day against England. At Headingley against England in 1934, Australia advanced from 3 for 39 to 4 for 494 on the second day, scoring 455 for the loss of one wicket.

Most Runs In A Day By An Australian Test Batsman: 309 by Bradman (334) out of a total of 456 against England at Leeds in 1930. Bradman also made 271 out of 455 for Australia against England at Leeds in 1934.

Fast Fifties By Australians In Tests: Charlie Macartney made 56 in 35 minutes against South Africa at Sydney in 1910–11; Jack Gregory scored 50 in 35 minutes on his way to 119 against

South Africa at Johannesburg in 1921–22; J. J. Lyons made 50 in 36 minutes on his way to 55 against England at Lord's in 1890; Jack Ryder made 50 in 36 minutes on his way to 79 against England at Sydney in 1928–29.

Fastest Fifty Against Australia: J. T. Brown made 50 in 28 minutes for England against Australia at Melbourne in 1894–95.

Fast Test Centuries By Australians: Jack Gregory scored 100 of his 119 against South Africa at Johannesburg in 1921–22 in 70 minutes. Richie Benaud scored 100 in 78 minutes in 1954–55 on his way to 121 against the West Indies at Kingston. Joe Darling took 91 minutes to make 100 of his 160 against England at Sydney in 1897–98.

Fast Double Centuries By Australians: 131 minutes by V. T. Trumper (293) for an Australian XI v. Canterbury at Christchurch, 1913–14; 214 minutes by Bradman (334) against England at Leeds, 1930; 223 minutes by McCabe (232) against England at Nottingham, 1938; 226 minutes by Trumper (214 not out) against South Africa at Adelaide, 1910–11.

Fast Triple Centuries By Australians: 205 minutes by C. G. Macartney (345) for Australia v. Notts, 1921; 336 minutes by Bradman (334) against England at Leeds, 1930. Bradman's first 100 took 99 minutes, his second 115 minutes, his third 122 minutes.

The longest hits at the Sydney Cricket Ground.

Right, Ian Redpath, who hit 32 off an over for Australia against Orange Free State in 1969–70; Above, Stan McCabe, who figured in many fast scoring partnerships for NSW and Australia.

Other Fast Innings: 35 in 14 minutes by Bill Howell against England at Sydney, 1901–02.

Fast Partnerships: 42 in 16 minutes for the 9th wicket by Fred Freer and George Tribe against England at Sydney, 1946–47; 77 in 28 minutes for the 10th wicket by Stan McCabe and Fleetwood-Smith against England at Nottingham, 1938; 86 in 44 minutes for the third wicket by Greg and Ian Chappell against New Zealand at Wellington, 1973–74.

Other fast partnerships include 169 in 53 minutes by H. L. Collins and V. T. Trumper, for NSW v. Tasmania at Hobart in 1912–13; 336 in 145 minutes by W. H. Ponsford and H. S. B. Love, for Victoria versus Tasmania at Melbourne in 1922–23; and 433 in 180 minutes by V. T. Trumper and A. Sims for Australians v. Canterbury at Christchurch, New Zealand in 1913–14.

Most Runs In An Over: Technically, there is no limit to the runs that can be scored from an over if the bowler keeps bowling no-balls. The highest score our researchers have been able to find from an eight ball over at any level of Australian cricket was 62 by H. Morley in a Queensland country match in 1968–69. The bowler, R. Grubb, sent down four no-balls. Morley struck nine sixes and two fours and missed the other ball altogether.

Most Runs From An Eight Ball Over For Australia: 32 by Ian Redpath who hit four sixes and two fours off N. Rosendorff in a most uncharacteristic innings for Australia against Orange Free State at Bloemfontein in 1969–70. Redpath advanced his score by 51 runs in 12 minutes after reaching his century.

Most Runs From A Six Ball Over: Don Bradman scored 30 (4,6,6,4,6,4) from an over by leg-spinner A. P. ("Tich") Freeman playing for Australia v. an England XI at Folkestone in 1934. Gary Sobers hit the maximum with 36 for a six ball over for Nottinghamshire against Glamorgan in 1968 at Swansea. The bowler was M. A. Nash.

Most Runs From A Four Ball Over: Australian George Bonnor took 20 (6,4,4,6) from a four ball over by A. P. Lucas for an Australian XI v. I Zingari at Scarborough in 1888.

Most Runs From An Over In Australian Grade Cricket: Since district cricket began, Sid Barnes' 40 off an eight-ball over from "Ginty" Lush (four sixes, four fours) in Sydney in 1937–38 is the highest.

Most Personal Boundaries In An Innings: 55 by C. W. Gregory in a knock of 383 for NSW v. Queensland at Brisbane in 1906–07, followed by C. G. Macartney with 51 in an innings of 345 for Australia v. Nottinghamshire in 1921, and 50 by Bradman in his innings of 369 for South Australia v. Tasmania in 1935–36.

BILL, Oscar Wendell, 1910–

A right-handed opening batsman who figured in several absorbing events in Australian cricket, the best performed of a fascinating family of cricket lovers. Wendell was the son of a University lecturer, born in Birmingham, England, who had taken degrees in Arts, Economics and Philosophy at Glasgow University. The Bill boys played grade cricket for Waverley for many years.

Wendell gave his devotion to cricket, Waldo to his career in shipping. Wendell played 23 matches for New South Wales, scoring two centuries, 153 in 1930–31 against Queensland at Brisbane and 100 in the same summer against Victoria at Sydney. He was Bradman's partner at Blackheath when Bradman made a century in three overs. Bill scored singles off the first and fifth balls of the third over, while Bradman made 102 off the rest.

Wendell Bill was also involved in the curious affair at Sydney in 1929 when he fielded for almost four days without getting a bat. When the MCC v. New South Wales match began, the MCC had only 11 fit players and when one was injured soon after the start, Wendell, who was New South Wales' 12th man, took the field in his place. New South Wales batted for two days. When MCC batted, Oldfield was soon hurt, Allsop went behind the stumps, and Wendell went on as Oldfield's

First-Class Averages: Batting, 1,931 runs at 37.86.

141

replacement. MCC batted for two days, with Wendell still on the field.

Many accounts of his matches give the impression that Wendell is part of Bill's surname. In fact, he only added his christian name in the scorebooks to distinguish between himself and his brother, Waldo. Otherwise the Waverley score sheets would have had two "W. Bills." Both were outstanding baseballers. Wendell pitched for NSW, Mosman and Waverley, and Waldo was a stalwart of the Waverley baseball club. Wendell Bill toured India in 1935–36 in the Australian team captained by Jack Ryder, scoring 740 runs and finishing second to Ryder in the averages.

BIZZELL, Graham Maurice, 1941–

First-Class Averages: Batting, 1,182 runs at 27.48; Bowling, 1 for 68.

An unlucky wicket-keeper and right-handed batsman who had 30 matches for Queensland in the seasons between 1961–62 and 1965–66, topscore 101 not out. He was born in Beenleigh but was not considered a bowler, and took 20 catches. He gave some dazzling displays for University behind the stumps, but there was no way selectors would drop Wally Grout, then the world's No. 1 'keeper, to play him, though one critic suggested they should. He married a sister of Test spinner Tom Vievers.

BLACKHAM, John McCarthy, 1854–1932

First-Class Averages: Batting, 6,395 runs at 16.78; Bowling, 2 wickets at 69.00; Dismissals: 451 (272 caught, 179 stumped).

Tests (35): 800 runs at 15.68; Dismissals: 60 (36 caught, 24 stumped).

An original Australian hero comparable with Phar Lap, Les Darcy and Boy Charlton. The great South Australian allrounder, George Giffen, described Blackham as the prince of wicket-keepers. Blackham kept wicket for Australia for twenty years and in that time revolutionised the job. He stood up on the stumps and eliminated the need for a longstop with his safe hands, sustaining a reputation for alert stumpings, catching and pressuring batsmen through 35 Tests. In England on one of his trips there a group of clergymen complained that he was a danger to the wellbeing of cricket, encouraging as he did the abolition of long-stop, the clergy's traditional fielding spot in village teams.

Blackham, born in the Melbourne suburb of Fitzroy, worked in Melbourne as a bank clerk, a black-bearded figure who looked the essence of reliability as he pushed sovereigns across the counter. He grew a beard at the age of 23 and wore it all his life, a swarthy figure with tiny cap, feet splayed far wider than modern 'keepers advocate, and when he caught the ball and whipped off the bails in one motion he thrilled spectators who had never seen this before. He made his debut for Victoria in 1874–75 and played in all the important early Tests that shaped the whole future of international cricket.

He was Australia's 'keeper in the very first Test match in

1876–77 despite objections from demon bowler Fred
Spofforth, who refused to play when Billy Murdoch was not
appointed 'keeper. He played in all of the first eight teams
Australia sent to England and was a dramatic success in the
very first Test in England when he and his English counterpart, Lyttleton, both gave memorable displays. Sometimes on
these tours he would field while Murdoch kept wicket.

Blackham's eagerness to stand right up on the stumps
wearing little more than gardening gloves to take Spofforth,

*Jack Blackham, first
wicket-keeper to stand up to
the stumps.*

Boyle and the other early Australian pace bowlers added menace to their bowling and played a major part in many important Australian victories. He appeared in more Tests than any Australian of his period and was affectionately known to spectators near the end of his long career as "Old Jack," the same sobriquet bestowed on the great racehorse, Carbine. He was a very handy left-hand batsman, with no pretentions to style, whose plucky slogging often saved Australia. He asked one of his captains why a man had been placed behind him. "Put him out where he can do some good," he said.

"One could not help admiring him as he stood behind the stumps at critical periods of a game," wrote Giffen. "With dark eyes as keen as a hawk, and regardless of knocks, he would take the fastest bowling with marvellous dexterity, and woe betide the batsman who even so much as lifted the heel of his back foot as he played forward and missed the ball."

Blackham, who had been discovered by Conway, manager of the first Australian XI, was a man of highly strung temperament, who could not bear to watch a close finish. Instead he would with clenched hands and chin on his chest pace up and down the dressing-room in a way that had newspapers talking of him as a "caged lion." He was a first-class judge of the opposition and few players could more quickly detect a weakness in a batsman.

On his first trip to England in 1878 Blackham stumped six and caught four in a match against 18 of Stockport. In 1884, when Australia defeated the Gentlemen at Lord's by 46 runs, Blackham stumped the last three batsmen. In 1883, when Ivo Bligh's English team played a fine match against Australia, Blackham scored 57 and 58 not out, Australia winning by four wickets. In the First Test at Sydney against Stoddardt's team in 1894, Blackham added 154 for the ninth wicket with Syd Gregory, for Australia to reach a total of 586 after being 3 for 21. This was Blackham's last Test and his 74, his highest Test score. He suffered a severe knock in this match which prevented him wicket-keeping again.

Blackham, who had taken over as Victoria captain in 1882–83 and held the job for five summers, was Australia's captain on his last tour of England in 1893. He had a disastrous time because of his tendency to mourn over temporary setbacks, and in two months lost a stone in weight. In all, he captained Australia eight times for three wins, three losses and two draws.

Blackham's 20 years of first-class cricket produced one century—109 for Victoria against New South Wales in 1884—and saw him dismiss 451 batsmen. In 45 matches for Victoria, he made 1,600 runs at 22.85. His strike rate was not high by comparison with modern 'keepers at less than two victims per Test, but he set the standard for wicket-keeping proficiency that many Australian 'keepers have followed.

A bow-legged, engaging Victorian right-arm off-break bowler notorious for his impassioned appeals and for his debut in Test cricket at 46 years and 253 days. Nobody has ever offered a satisfactory explanation of why selectors of Australia's teams rejected Blackie in his younger days. He had retired from cricket and was spending his Saturday afternoons gardening when he was enticed to make a comeback by playing grade cricket for St Kilda. There he joined "Dainty" Ironmonger in one of cricket's most incongruous partnerships but a joyful one for devotees. They had such a merry time the Victorian selectors picked Bendigo-born Blackie for the State team. Then he was chosen for Australia. It was too late. After three Tests against Percy Chapman's tourists, Blackie departed the Test cricket scene, an enigma.

Blackie's supporters claim he was treated shabbily in his youth by selectors who considered his type of bowling old fashioned. Blackie started his run near mid-off, which in the 1920's was considered a joke but was emulated by many

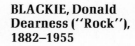

BLACKIE, Donald Dearness ("Rock"), 1882–1955

First-Class Averages: Batting, 548 runs at 12.17; Bowling, 211 wickets at 24.10.

Tests (3): 24 runs at 8.00; 14 wickets at 31.71.

bowlers in the 1960's and 1970's. He invariably shared a joke with the mid-off fieldsmen. He curved the ball in to the wicket and was full of subtlety, both in his variations of spin and in length. He was a keen exponent of flight.

Blackie's long career in cricket began when he won the batting and bowling trophy at the Punt Road State school, South Yarra, at the age of 12. He became an apprentice with the Electric Light Co. when he left school but was put on the night shift and could not play cricket. When he got on to the day shift at the age of 17, he joined South Yarra club and played in a matting wicket competition. He won a gold medal for the best all-rounder in his first season, and in 1904-05 joined the Hawksburn club as an all-rounder. Hawksburn won the Melbourne first grade premiership in his first year with them. Blackie had been with the club four seasons when it changed its name to Prahran Cricket Club.

He was fortunate to have the assistance of "Barlow" Carkeek, the wicket-keeper, and the Rush brothers, who coached him on finer points. He could turn the ball both ways, with the off-break his stock delivery and four times before World War I he won the Prahran averages. After the war he worked in the country and did not return to Melbourne until 1922, when he was persuaded to join the St Kilda club. His partnership with Ironmonger became a grade cricket legend, for even on shirtfront wickets they turned the ball sharply, tall, lean men with strong fingers who mixed clever flight with nip off the pitch, and could bowl all day. The *Australian Cricketer* magazine in 1933 calculated that he had bowled 40,521 balls in all cricket over his career.

Johnnie Moyes' explanation of how Blackie got his nickname was that Blackie had a habit of calling people "Rock," particularly when he could not remember a man's name. The "Rock" stuck and was taken up by Blackie's fellow cricketers. In 33 matches for Victoria he took 158 wickets. When he smiled it was impossible to worry about such things as the validity of his birth certificate.

BODYLINE The word used to describe the most controversial type of bowling in cricket history. Many English cricket enthusiasts still do not understand its true meaning, though to Australians who saw Bodyline used by the 1932–33 MCC team captained by the haughty, scholarly lawyer Douglas Jardine it remains the most dangerous and unsportsmanlike form of attack known to cricket. Origin of the word is debatable but the history of this form of attack went back to the 1911–12 summer in Australia when the English team captained by Pelham Warner had to curb Victor Trumper and other splendid Australian stroke players. They did it mainly by bowling

146

deliveries on the leg stump that moved into the batsmen and sometimes kicked up at the torso. Left-handed F. R. Foster (32 wickets) and right-handed S. F. Barnes (34 wickets) took 66 wickets in the series, Foster usually taking his wickets bowling to a packed legside field. Foster battered Trumper's ribs, skilfully lifting the ball of a good length—but his attack with Barnes was not a physical threat to batsmen.

The 1932–33 English team faced a similar problem in restricting Bradman. Jardine did it by intensifying Foster's field placings and adding a threat of injury to batsmen. Between them Harold Larwood and Bill Voce clinched the Test series just as Foster and Barnes had done. Larwood took 33 wickets in the Bodyline series, but Voce, the ideal foil to Larwood, managed only 15 in four Tests. Many shrewd judges considered Voce's role in aiming at the batsmen in the Bodyline series prevented him reaching his full potential, and this was borne out four years later in Australia when he took more wickets (26 at 21.53) than anyone on either side. In the Second Test in 1936–37 he dismissed O'Brien, Bradman and McCabe in four balls.

Just as the legside field placings for Foster and Barnes had been contrived to prevent Trumper scoring heavily, so Bodyline was invented solely for Bradman's benefit. And not without cause, for he had gone through the 1930 tour in England with a string of unforgettable scores: 334 at Leeds, 254 at Lord's, 232 at The Oval, 131 at Trent Bridge (all Tests), 236 at Worcester, 205 at Canterbury, 191 at Southampton, 185 at

Bill Woodfull ducks under a Larwood bouncer during the Bodyline series. Note the six fieldsmen close in on the legside, with only one fieldsman in front of the wicket on the offside.

Leicester, and 117 at Taunton. Only once in that memorable 1930 tour had Bradman appeared uneasy against English bowling, it was this brief period of concern amid all his incredible feats of machine-like scoring that produced Bodyline bowling and threatened the long history of matches between England and Australia.

The over that started it all was nearly not bowled at all. Rain fell at The Oval when Bradman and Archie Jackson were in command. They left the field and further play that day appeared unlikely until the umpires surprisingly decided to go back only five minutes from stumps. The Australians were disgruntled at the decision, and Bradman and Jackson went very slowly out to the wicket so that only one over would be possible. Larwood bounced the ball into the batsman's body and as it lifted nastily from the damp pitch Bradman, for the first time Englishmen could recall, clearly flinched.

Not long after that the dour, introverted Douglas Jardine, captain of the MCC team to tour Australia in the summer of 1932–33, invited Larwood, his Nottinghamshire pace bowling partner Voce, and their county captain, Arthur Carr, to dine with him at the Piccadilly Hotel, London. They discussed ways of ending Bradman's dominance and those few minutes at The Oval when Bradman had drawn away from Larwood's good length bouncers.

"I told Jardine that I thought Bradman had flinched, and he said he was aware of that," said Larwood in his book *The Larwood Story*. "There had been a lot of talk among cricketers about this match and I had heard it said that Bradman could well have a weakness against fast rising deliveries on the leg stump."

Jardine had not played in the match at The Oval but he had a very reliable grapevine. One theory is that the idea was suggested to Jardine by George Duckworth, who had kept wicket for England at The Oval and had seen Bradman recoil. Before he died Archie Jackson said that Duckworth had been the first to notice Bradman's reaction.

When Jardine asked if Larwood thought he could bounce the ball up into the body on the leg stump so that Bradman had to play his shots to leg, Larwood said he believed it could be done. Larwood was a professional, trained to do his job in a tradesmanlike manner, and he did not consider there was anything new in what he had been asked to do. Foster had done it in Australia in 1911–12, Fred Root had confined Bardsley, Macartney and other Australians with it in 1926 in England. Larwood, in fact, thought Voce would be more successful with leg theory than himself, because Voce, a burly 6 ft 3 in with unlimited stamina, had had far more practise with this form of attack.

"For all I knew Bradman might hit me all over the leg side," wrote Larwood. "But it was worth the effort."

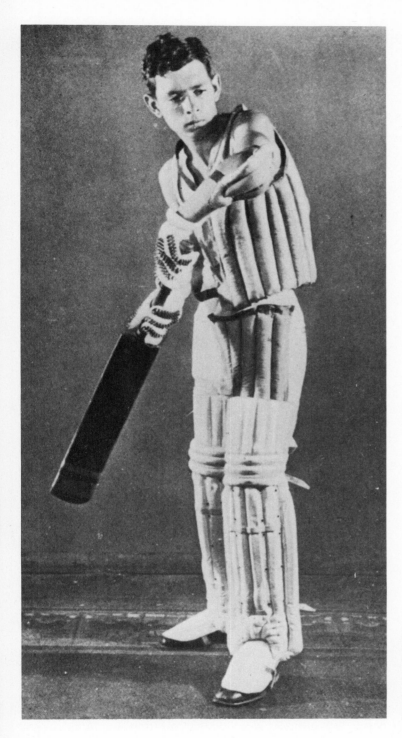

Some of the padding designed to combat bowlers who attacked the batsman's body, including instep pads which would be handy against the modern "sandshoe ball." Curiously, the model has no helmet.

After that dinner Jardine began to call in to F. R. Foster's flat in St. James to discuss leg theory field placings with him. Foster wrote about these meetings in an Australia paper after the Bodyline furore flared. "If I had known for what purpose Jardine wanted my leg-side placings, I would never have given them to him," said Foster. Jardine also got from Bill Ferguson, the famous scorer, diagrams of the Australian batting stars' Test innings which showed their most productive strokes.

Jardine's temperament contributed to the Bodyline furore. From the time the English team left for Australia he ruled it with an iron will. He declined a gift of a bottle of Scotch for every man in his side (to safeguard their fitness), confiscated Freddie Brown's golf clubs (encourages cross-bat shots), clashed with Pressmen at the first stop in Perth (MCC were not in Australia to provide stories), and took his side on the field there 20 minutes late (no explanation given). To Australians who imagined themselves to be friendly, open people, the stuffy, pretentious Jardine was the type of Englishman they delighted in spoofing. Jardine read Chaucer in spare moments, wore a Harlequin cap, often ignored hands offered for a handshake, and openly resented Australian barrackers.

The English team kept their plan in wraps until the fifth match of the tour, the match against an Australian XI at Melbourne. Here they unleashed Bowes, Larwood, Voce and Allen, in all-out bid to break Bradman's confidence. Lisle Nagel made a match of it by taking 8 for 32 in the MCC's second innings and the Englishmen were all out for 60. Set to get 125 the Australian XI lost Bradman and Woodfull for 19 when rain washed out play. Jardine rested while this match was played, leaving Bob Wyatt to put his plan into effect. But even after this one showing, it was obvious that this was not the customary form of leg theory, for now batsmen could only protect themselves at the risk of offering a catch to one of the seven men on the legside.

Bodyline depended entirely on the field placings. If the batsman swung or hooked at the fast rising deliveries, he had to elude the fieldsmen on the leg boundary. If he defended against the kicking ball, it was only a question of time before one flew from the edge of the bat to one of the fieldsmen close in on the legside. The only other way to play it was to duck when you could and let the deliveries which couldn't be avoided smack against the chest or ribs. The trap could only be set while the Englishmen continued with only two fieldsmen on the offside. And it only worked with a bowler of exceptional pace like Larwood, who had the marvellous control that enabled him to keep the ball on the leg stump and to make it rear from a good length.

Bradman offered to play in the First Test at Sydney but the Board of Control's doctors Aspinal and Holmes a'Court declared him unfit. He watched the Test from the stand, visiting a radio station to broadcast his impressions of play, and then had a fortnight recuperating for the Second Test. Larwood at Sydney had his most successful Test against Australia, with 5 for 96 and 5 for 28, and, despite McCabe's legendary 187 not out in the first innings, Australia lost by 10 wickets. McCabe gambled by hooking and swinging from under the kicking ball and he got away with it, bouncing his hooks short of leg boundary fieldsmen or over their heads.

Reporters tried hard to find a word which would neatly describe Larwood's bowling and the field placings. They tried "shock attack," "human skittles," "fast leg theory," and others, but they seemed inappropriate. The former Australian captain Joe Darling called it "Bradman Theory." There are many versions of who first thought of the word "Bodyline." Larwood thought it was the Sydney *Sun's* Claude Corbett, but Jardine probably was more accurate in thinking it was Hugh Buggy, then the Melbourne *Herald* cricket writer. Former Test cricketer Jack Worrall after the Australian XI-England match spoke of "half-pitched slingers on the body line." Buggy had read an article by R. E. W. Wilmont, in the opposition Melbourne *Argus* that said England's attack was "on the line of the body." To save money in those days of high telegram costs Buggy condensed Worrall's words to "Bodyline," and overnight the word became infamous.

When Bradman rejoined the Australian team for the Second Test at Melbourne his fellow players were simmering with anger over what they regarded as the unsportmanlike English attack. Their bitterness found sympathetic outlet among Australians still suffering the frustrations of the Depression—dole queues, relief work, evictions, semi-starvation. Gusts of applause greeted Bradman all round the MCG as he strode to the wicket with his own reputation and Australia's Ashes hopes on the line.

Bowes bounced the first ball down the legside at his left hip. Bradman danced to the off to hook. But the ball came off the pitch far slower than Bradman expected and he was almost through his shot when he touched it on to his stumps. Only then did experts realise how unusually slow the wicket was. Indeed the English players considered it had been deliberately drugged to extract pace from their four fast bowlers.

Queues almost a mile long waited for the ground to open, and during the night after the second day's play the night-watchman at the MCG spotted two men scaling the wall. He drew his revolver and fired in the air and they dropped down inside the ground right into his arms, looking down the barrel of his revolver. They explained they had only wanted to see Bradman bat in Australia's second innings. The groundsman marched them straight out of the ground.

One of the most curious aspects of the Bodyline tour was that it occurred when radio description of play was first introduced. There were no Board of Control restrictions on players commenting on play and at the end of each day the players who had enjoyed some success went on the air to discuss their success.

Bradman's second innings rates among his best, for it was played amid unprecedented tension before 68,000 spectators, with most of Australia's population following every ball. For the first time he exploited a field set without a single player on the off-side in front of point, even if he slashed the ball into the open spaces from outside leg stump. His 103 not out in an innings in which seven of his team-mates made only ten runs between them, coupled by O'Reilly's 10 wickets, and courageous knocks from Fingleton and McCabe, clinched victory for Australia and set the stage for the climatic fireworks of the Bodyline series in Adelaide.

By now all Australia's batting stars had been hit hard and often and it was clear the bowling was deliberately aimed at their bodies. Vic Richardson, a powerful hooker, told newspapers he took guard a foot outside the leg stump and Larwood's deliveries still came straight at him. Woodfull, cricket's quiet man, took some stunning blows that had him clutching his chest in pain. But it was the eagerness with which the bowlers tried to hit Bradman as he ducked and weaved and tried to make himself a moving target that convinced fans England's bowlers were deliberately trying to strike the batsmen.

In the Second Test McCabe and Richardson had come very close to forcing Jardine to forsake Bodyline when they hooked so strongly the inner ring of on-side fieldsmen were forced to retreat for their own safety. They had Bodyline beaten, it seemed, when Jardine took a marvellous catch off Voce to dismiss McCabe. Larwood believes Bodyline would have been discarded altogether had McCabe and Richardson had another hour together.

Before the Adelaide Test began newspapers reported a clash between Gubby Allen, who had been born in Australia, and Jardine, over Allen's refusal to bowl Bodyline. Allen allegedly said he would prefer to be sent back to England on the next boat rather than bowl it. Australia's batsmen now were wearing pads to cover the ribs and heart, a pad over the elbow, and reinforced thigh guards as well as the customary groin guard.

For this Test 400 mounted police were marshalled at the No. 2 ground ready for trouble and 400 more foot police formed the Oval pickets. England batted first and scored 341 and midway though the second day Woodfull and Fingleton opened the most controversial of all Test innings. Fingleton was out to Allen with only one run scored. Larwood bowling with four slips, then hit Woodfull a tremendous blow over the heart with the last ball of his second over. Spectators booed

152

and catcalled all round the ground as the Englishmen moved in to sympathise with Woodfull. Accounts of the incident said Woodfull was ashen and groggy.

Larwood had started his approach run for the first ball of his next over when Jardine clapped his hands and stopped him. Jardine signalled the off-side fieldsmen over to the leg-side into the Bodyline positions. The unhappy timing of this switch in view of Woodfull's distress sent the crowd wild. Even in the Members' enclosure quietly-spoken, retiring characters were transformed into hooting figures as they counted the Englishmen out. As Larwood ran in to bowl the howling mob counted to ten in a screaming crescendo as he let go. He now had six short legs, two men deeper at square leg and a mid-wicket for the top edge or half hook. For a time it seemed certain many of the crowd would jump the fence.

Woodfull continued to be hit by deliveries just short of a length as he struggled gamely to 22. Ponsford took a beating, offering his ample backside to bumpers, sustaining bruises all over his body as he battled to 85. Disdainful of the uproar which broke loose each time a player was hit Jardine persisted with his leg-side attack, phlegmatic, absolutely dedicated to winning. When Woodfull was out to Allen, the English managers Pelham Warner and R. C. N. Palairet went to the Australian dressingroom to sympathise with him over the blows he had taken. Woodfull had just showered and was receiving treatment for his bruises, one a very livid mark under the heart.

Bill Woodfull grimaces with pain immediately after being hit over the heart batting against Larwood at Adelaide.

"We have come to say how sorry we are and to offer our sympathy," said Warner.

"I don't want to see you, Mr. Warner," said Woodfull. "There are two teams out there. One is trying to play cricket and the other is not. The game is too good to be spoilt. It is time some people got out of it."

This encounter and the clear implication of Woodfull's words were later dispatched around the world. Woodfull was very upset that it leaked out but he publicly denied that he apologised to Warner for what had been said.

Bodyline, contrary to the general belief, was not used continuously, but in spells that enabled Jardine to rest Larwood and Voce. Oldfield was hit a sickening blow on the skull when Larwood was bowling to an orthodox off-side field. Oldfield admitted it was his own fault. He tried to hook a straight ball, misplaced his feet, and the ball hit him as he spun round at the completion of the stroke. Although his cap peak took some of the force from the blow, Oldfield's right frontal bone sustained a linear fracture. A doctor who examined Oldfield said that if the blow had been an inch lower, it might have been critical.

On the third day of the match the Board of Control met at the Adelaide ground. Warner and Palairet were told the Board proposed to send a cable to the MCC protesting about

Right, Pelham Warner, manager of the English "Bodyline" tourists. Far Right, Don Bradman playing the type of shot he used to counter Bodyline, body well away from the ball.

the type of attack England was using. Warner asked if they might have the chance to see the cable as they might be able to suggest a useful phrase or word. Reporters covering the series—English newspapers were poorly represented at this, the biggest of all cricket stories, a mistake they have not repeated since—were summoned to the conference room and given the text of the cable. It read:

"Bodyline bowling has assumed such proportions as to menace the best interests of the game, making protection of the body by the batsman the main consideration. This is causing intensely bitter feeling between the players, as well as injury. In our opinion it is unsportsmanlike. Unless stopped at once it is likely to upset the friendly relations existing between Australia and England."

Pressmen were flabbergasted that such a cable should already have been sent, but no more so than Warner and Palairet who had not had the chance to offer an opinion on it before it was sent. Newspapers condemned the tactless wording of the cable. In one paper a judge was quoted as saying Bodyline was covered by criminal law. Five days after the Board of Control cable was sent, after England had won by 338 runs, the MCC sent this reply:

"We, Marylebone Cricket Club, deplore your cable. We deprecate your opinion that there has been unsportsmanlike play. We have fullest confidence in captain, team and managers, and are convinced they would do nothing to infringe either the Laws of Cricket, or the spirit of the game. We have no evidence that our confidence has been misplaced. Much as we regret accidents to Woodfull and Oldfield, we understand that in neither case was the bowler to blame.

"If the Australian Board of Control wishes to propose a new law or rule it shall receive our careful consideration in due course. We hope the situation is not now as serious as your cable would seem to indicate, but if it is such to jeopardise the good relations between English and Australian cricketers, and you consider it desirable to cancel remainder of programme, we would consent but with great reluctance."

By now arguments engendered by Bodyline caused fights in pubs. Cries that the Australians were squealers echoed back and forth in cables from England. Amid stories that there was dissension in the English team over the legality of Bodyline the managers issued a statement saying the side was in harmony and behind Jardine to a man.

The exchange of cables between the Board of Control and the MCC overshadowed a fascinating duel between Bradman and Larwood. Bradman had returned from his seaside holiday between the First and Second Tests determined that whatever else he did he must not allow himself to be hit because

155

of the possibility of injury. He felt Australia's hopes of winning The Ashes were best served if he made himself a moving target, and he did bring off some spectacular tennis shots only a man with his amazing co-ordination could have played.

"When he began moving to the leg to hit me to the off, I couldn't let him get away with it," Larwood said in *The Larwood Story*. "The captain had set my field and I had to bowl to it. When Don tried to counter me in this way it became a matter of him or me. I used to try to sense what Don was going to do. If I saw him trying to move back to the leg in that split second before delivery I used to follow him a little bit. I suppose it amounted to bowling at the man. But he made it that way."

Jardine and his players were so annoyed over the Board of Control's first cable claiming their bowling had been unsportsmanlike they agreed not to take the field for the Fourth Test at Brisbane unless it was withdrawn. The Board did this in the last of its series of cables to the MCC and the Brisbane match went on. The Board was taking too much money from the series to abandon the Tests as the first MCC cable had offered.

The Test was incredibly grim. Paynter was in hospital with a fever when he heard that the MCC had lost 6 for 216 chasing Australia's first innings 340. He got out of bed and went out to the match to score an invaluable 83, a sick, ghost-like figure to whom Woodfull showed moving consideration. Jardine was so determined not to get out he faced 82 balls without scoring and didn't make a run for 82 minutes. Apparently spurning the gamble of hooking, McCabe in Australia's second innings ducked six deliveries in succession without offering a stroke.

Australia after seeming to have made the match safe when it reached 3 for 251 in the first innings, collapsed then and again in the second innings when it scored 175. England won by six wickets and with this win took home The Ashes. But that did not spoil the crowd for the Fifth Test in Sydney, where every available space was crammed with spectators arguing about Bodyline. Every ball Larwood pitched short drew a tremendous roar. Yabba was there but nobody could hear him in the din.

Larwood did not want to play in the Fifth Test because he was bone-weary from long spells on the hard grounds, but Jardine insisted, using Bodyline whenever the chance offered although The Ashes had been won. Larwood's admirable 98 shocked Australians when England were struggling in the chase for Australia's first innings total of 435. Larwood was cheered round all the ground for his aggressive batting when Ironmonger caught him—a reception that delighted him.

In Australia's second innings, Larwood was in full flight, after dismissing Richardson for his second duck of the match, when he broke down. His left foot was so painful because of the fracture of two small bones beneath the toes he could barely walk. Jardine insisted that he finish the over. Larwood said he couldn't last the five balls left. Jardine told him he *had* to bowl them. So Larwood stood at the crease and swung his arm and Woodfull politely patted the five balls straight back to him. Even then Jardine would not let Larwood leave the field. Jardine wanted to retain the psychological advantage of having Larwood on the field while Bradman was batting. For two overs Bradman attacked, relieved to have Larwood out of action. When Verity bowled Bradman for 71, Jardine clapped his hands. "Righto, Harold, you can go now," he said. Bradman and the half-walking, half-limping Larwood went off together without speaking a word, Bradman partly tamed by Bodyline, Larwood never again to enter a Test arena.

The dismissal of Larwood for 98 in the Fifth Test of the Bodyline series to one of the few catches "Dainty" Ironmonger held in important matches. Larwood had gone in as a nightwatchman.

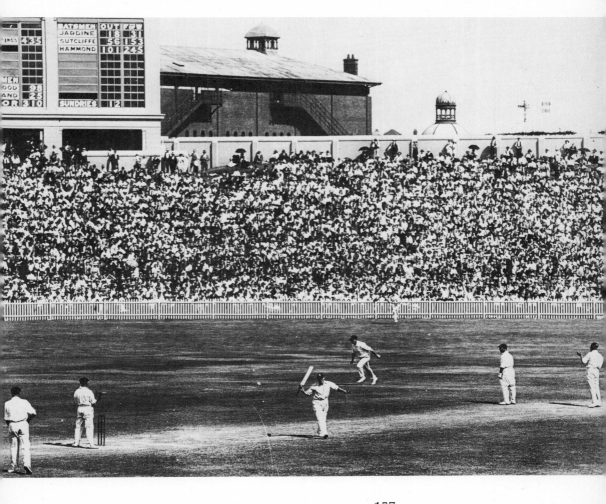

**BOGLE, James,
1890–1963**

First-Class Averages:
Batting, 911 runs at
45.55; Bowling 3 wickets
at 32.00.

A steady, high-scoring left-handed batsman who did not often try fancy shots and had a brief but impressive career with New South Wales just after World War I. He played only three seasons of first-class cricket before he left to set up a medical practice at Port Douglas in far north Queensland, but he left memories of big scoring that oldtimers discussed 60 years later. Although naturally left-handed, he threw a cricket ball and played all other sports right-handed.

Bogle was born at Mossgiel, a small town near Hay in western NSW, where his father owned the main store. He taught at Sydney Church of England Grammar School while he studied Arts and Medicine at Sydney University. He won Blues in five sports, cricket, baseball, swimming, rugby and tennis. After scoring 1,000 runs in a first grade season for University, he made his first appearance for NSW in 1918–19 before the Sheffield Shield competition resumed after the war, scoring 145 in NSW's second innings and adding 157 for the fourth wicket with Tommy Andrews against a Victorian attack that included Ted McDonald. Andrews saved him from destroying himself when he saw Bogle feeling for balls outside the off-stump. This outstanding debut earned Bogle 6 lb of tobacco from a Sydney tobacco firm.

In Bogle's second season for NSW in 1919–20, he scored 200 against South Australia at Adelaide, batting strongly in stands of 203 for the second wicket with Bardsley and 166 for the fourth wicket with Andrews. He made 103 in 1920–21 at Sydney against South Australia, starting a run feast that took NSW's total to 802. Despite this string of big scores he was not among 24 players named for a Test trial. The Sydney newspapers were outraged and called for the sacking of NSW selector Herbie Collins. Bogle toured New Zealand in an Australian side in 1921 and was in the Australian XI that defeated New Zealand in an unofficial Test by an innings and 227 runs.

After he graduated Bogle spent two years as Resident Medical Officer at Royal Prince Alfred Hospital in Sydney before moving to the far north and disappearing from big cricket. He is remembered in the north for devastating hitting in social matches and for his valuable coaching. Frank Sides, later a prominent batsman for Queensland and Victoria, was one of Bogle's patients as a boy and the doctor taught him the rudiments of batting. Bogle was Medical Superintendent at Brisbane General Hospital for two years, but went north again to Babinda, near Cairns. Then he moved to Beaudesert, south of Brisbane, where he figured in important lawn bowls events and yarned incessantly with his patients about cricket. Bogle scored three centuries in first-class cricket, all for NSW.

One of the heaviest hitters of all time, a right-hander in whose hands the bat looked like a child's toy, a heavily-bearded giant of 6 ft 6 in and 16 stone, variously labelled as the "Colonial Hercules," "The Australian Giant" and "Bonnor The Basher." Australian bush cricket has never known anything like him.

His batting style was neither elegant nor scientific, but he was unexcelled as a hitter. At Mitcham Green, near London, in 1880, he hit a ball 147 yards on the full—fellow cricketer James Southerton measured the distance. At Melbourne he was credited with hits of 150 and 160 yards, during practise. He could also throw the ball enormous distances and had throws of 120 and 131 yards. On the voyage to England in 1882 he bet £5 he could throw a ball 100 yards on the day of the Australian team's arrival. The bet was decided at Raglan Barracks, Devonport, where Bonnor threw a ball 104 yards before it bounced.

Around the world Bonnor set the standard for big-hitting which others tried to match. English batsman A. C. MacLaren, on a visit to a ground in Philadelphia, USA, was told that Bonnor had landed a ball on a faraway roof marked by a blue tile. "I'll break the next one to it," joked MacLaren and he very nearly did, too. "My eye was out," said MacLaren. "I missed by several tiles."

Twice in Tests Bonnor was out to sensational catches after quite remarkable blows. At The Oval in 1880, he skied a ball so high the batsmen had turned for their third run when W. G.'s brother, G. F. Grace, caught it, a wonderful piece of judgment by a fieldsman who made a duck in both innings. A Mr. Frederick Gale chained the distance of the hit with two of The Oval ground staff and measured it at 115 yards. When team-mates sympathised with Bonnor in the dressing-room, he said: "Hard luck, nothing. I should have hit the perisher."

At Lord's in 1884 George Ulyett caught and bowled Bonnor off a half-volley that Bonnor cracked so hard spectators behind the bowler parted to avoid being hit by a stroke they believed would clear the fence. At The Oval, Bonnor hit a ball over the pavilion and right through the secretary's window. At Melbourne in 1881, he hit a ball from the English bowler Bates over the skittle alley and beyond into Richmond Paddock.

Bonnor, born at Bathurst in the New South Wales mid-west, was the innocent country boy drawn to the big city limelight because of his tremendous hitting powers. His weakness was his yearning to be regarded as an elegant, stylish batsman. Often he went to the wicket determined to prove he was not just a big hitter, but these quests for orthodoxy were invariably frustrated. "Bonnor was a born hitter," wrote George Giffen. "He had a distinct mission as a demoraliser of bowlers and fieldsmen and if he had always adhered to the strict

BONNOR, George John, 1855–1912

First-Class Averages: Batting, 4,820 runs at 21.23; Bowling, 12 wickets at 39.16.

Tests (17): 512 runs at 17.06; 2 wickets at 42.00.

159

160

terms of his commission he would have made a great many more runs. Nevertheless he often pulled Australia out of a tight spot. He was one of the finest specimens of manhood. When, exerting all the strength in that Herculean frame, he smote the bowling, it was a sight for the gods."

Bonnor, whose father came from Herefordshire and mother from Lancashire, toured England in five Australian teams. His highest scores were 122 not out for Australia against I Zingari in 1882, 124 for Non-Smokers against Smokers in 1884, 119 for Australia v. The Gentlemen at Lord's in 1888, and 115 for Australia v. Yorkshire in the same year. In 1882, he made 66 out of 79 runs added in 30 minutes for Australia against Cambridge Past And Present at Portsmouth. He made 782 runs in all matches at 16.63 in 1880, 815 runs at 20.37 in 1882, 937 runs at 19.12 in 1884, 581 runs at 18.76 in 1886 and 1,204 runs at 19.73 in 1888. Figures for his last four tours are for first-class matches.

At home his scoring was equally dramatic. He made 267 not out in a couple of hours for Bathurst against Oriental CC. At Melbourne in 1882–83 when Australia beat England by nine wickets in the First Test, Bonnor made 85, lofting a number of balls over the boundary. Playing for Australia at Melbourne in the Second Test in 1882–83, Bonnor went in to bat after England's Billy Bates had dismissed McDonnell and Giffen with successive balls. England's captain Walter Read moved in to very short mid-on for the hat-trick ball. Bonnor lunged forward with that great stride of his and popped up an easy chance to give Read a catch and Bates the first hat trick in Tests by an English player.

Bonnor made only one century in Tests, a magnificent 128 out of 169 at Sydney in 1884–85. He was dropped at slip on 99. Australia won the match by eight wickets, thanks entirely to his remarkable knock, which began when Australia were 6 for 119 and 150 behind. In all first-class matches between 1880 and 1890 Bonnor made five centuries. He made a remarkable 127 catches in first-class cricket and one stumping. He died at Orange, New South Wales, the achievements in country cricket thick upon him.

BOON, David Clarence, 1960–

A right-handed Tasmanian batsman whose hard-hitting stroke play and sound temperament have impressed mainland critics since he won selection in the Australian Under-19 representative team. He has a wide range of powerful strokes to the legside and can now cut and drive efficiently. He is a useful fieldsman in any position.

Boon made his debut for Tasmania in 1978–79, and passed

First-Class Averages: Batting, 1,429 runs at 36.64; Bowling, 1 wicket for 55.

Left: George Bonnor, the 16 stone giant from Bathurst in whose hands critics said the bat looked like a matchstick.

Dave Boon goes down on knee to sweep.

1,000 runs in first-class cricket during the 1981–82 season. He has proved particularly useful to Tasmania in one-day matches or in situations where runs are required quickly. In the 1980–81 season he took part in two partnerships that established Tasmanian records, putting on 174 for the fourth wicket with Brian Davison against Victoria at Hobart, and 158 with David Smith against South Australia at Devonport.

Boon's prospects of winning selection in Tests were restricted to Tasmania's five first-class matches until the State was granted full Sheffield Shield status from 1982–83. Many observers believe that he tried to rush things when his chances were limited to five matches a summer and he said that if Tasmania had not won full Shield status he would have tried to move to a mainland State where he would have had more opportunities to prove himself.

Boon, who comes from Launceston, has some brilliant club knocks to his credit. He played in England in 1981 on a Tasmanian government cricket scholarship and believes that playing a season with the northern League club Netherfield and in the Lancashire Second XI helped tighten his technique. "I was very much an on-side player, but now I am playing shots all round the wicket," said Boon, who has had offers from NSW, Victoria and WA. All Tasmanian cricket fans are hopeful that he will stay now that he can match his skills against mainland Australian team candidates on level terms.

BOOTH, Brian Charles, ("Sam") 1933–

One of a long list of players who have graduated to the Australian team from beginnings in country cricket. He was a graceful right-handed batsman, born in the New South Wales country town of Bathurst, who represented Bathurst High School and played first grade hockey and cricket in Bathurst. In 1947, he was included in a country squad that went to Sydney Cricket Ground for special coaching. He played for Combined New South Wales Country against Combined Sydney in 1950 and in 1952 joined the St George club in Sydney. He made his debut for New South Wales in 1954–55 but missed the following season because of his selection as an inside left for the Australian Olympic Hockey team which competed at the 1956 Melbourne Games.

Booth was for a time the most successful batsman in Australia, a tall, upright player whose strokes flowed fluently from a fairly rigid stance. Among the batsmen of his time only Harvey and O'Neill gave as much pleasure to spectators, for he was noted for his rescue efforts, batting at No. 4 or No. 5. He drove and cut with style, fielded skilfully and mixed freely with opponents and team-mates.

He toured New Zealand in 1960 with an Australian team and did well enough to win selection in the 1961 Australian

First-Class Averages: Batting, 11,265 runs at 45.42, Bowling, 16 wickets at 59.75.

Tests (29): 1,773 runs at 42.21; 3 wickets at 48.66.

163

team in England, where he played in two Tests. In 1964 he was vice-captain of the Australian team in England, India and Pakistan. He was also vice-captain to Bob Simpson in the West Indies in 1964–65, where he played one of his finest innings, partnering Bob Cowper to resist a fierce onslaught by Hall and Griffith in a stand of 228. In 1965–66, he took over the Australian captaincy when Simpson dropped out firstly with a broken wrist, in the first Test and then in the third with chicken pox. Booth made a lasting impression for his sportsmanship by standing at the England dressing-room door and shaking hands with the England players one by one as they came off the field.

From captain Booth was dropped when the Australian side was re-shaped as a result of that England victory. He was 32 and still full of splendid strokes as he showed by continuing in first-class cricket for a further three years. He was a much respected cricketer whose gestures of fair play perhaps gave selectors the impression he was not tough enough for Tests, an Anglican parish councillor who amid dressing-room ribaldry and blue language always conducted himself quietly. Cricketers everywhere knew him as "Sam," a nickname his father had given him as a child. After he saved Australia in one Test with a typical gutsy century sportswriter Robert Gray called him "Sam Booth, Australia's one-man Salvation Army."

Booth played for New South Wales 93 times, more often than any player of his era after making his debut when summoned to the SCG from a school playground where he was duty master. He made frequent appearances at church and youth rallies, appearing with the Reverend David Sheppard at Sydney Town Hall, and at a Methodist Church in Port of Spain when Conrad Hunte preached the sermon. He was first chairman of the Youth Advisory Committee which sought to tackle teenaged unemployment and vandalism. He was also an unfortunate victim of the arbitary rules for the Test players' provident fund. He was one Test short of qualifying for a payment of $50 a Test or $1,500. After his last Test, he made his highest score in first-class cricket, 214 not out against Central Districts at Palmerston North, when he toured with an Australian Second team in 1967.

Booth made 25 first class centuries, five of them in Tests, with 112 at Brisbane and 103 at Melbourne in successive Tests in the 1962–63 series against England his most notable efforts. He had a highest Test score of 169, with 10 scores over 50. He took 17 Test catches. For New South Wales, he appeared in 93 matches, scoring 5,577 runs at 43.57, best score 177. He was a noted outfielder, once running out Sobers and Butcher in a day's play of a Test at Queen's Park, Jamaica, with returns that thudded into Wally Grout's gloves right over the bails.

Brian Booth, a delightfully fluent strokemaker, plays an off-drive on his way to 112 against England at Brisbane in 1962–63.

A versatile, gutsy, hard-hitting left-hand batsman, brilliant fieldsman with a whiplash throw, and a useful left-arm finger spinner. He has opened the batting and gone in at No. 3 and No. 6 for Australia but did not confirm his place in the Australian team until the trip to India and Pakistan in 1980 when he was the success of the tour and jumped to a top spot among the world's left-handed batsmen.

Border, the second of four boys whose father is a wool trader, grew up in a house opposite Mosman Oval in Sydney and spent most of his childhood leisure hours on the ground. Allan played first grade baseball for Mosman from the age of 15 until he moved to Queensland at the start of the 1980–81 cricket season. He played cricket for the Mosman club from the age of eight, graduating to the lower grades at 13, and making his debut in first-grade at 16 while he was still at school.

BORDER, Allan Robert, 1955–

First-Class Averages: Batting, 6,680 runs at 46.71; Bowling, 42 wickets at 35.29.

Tests (42): 3,048 runs at 48.38; 12 wickets at 30.67.

Border went to North Sydney Boys High School and played cricket for Combined High Schools in the inter-State carnival in 1972–73. His brother John pitches for Mosman firsts baseball team, and his brother Brett plays lower grade cricket for Mosman. Allan played for Gloucestershire Second XI in 1977 and Lancashire League cricket for East Lancashire in 1978.

He is a compact moustachioed figure eager to pull, drive and cut, who has a constant struggle to avoid nicking high rising deliveries outside his off-stump. He is not the first left-hander to have this problem, but a remarkably high percentage of the pitches on which he has played his big cricket have helped pace bowlers achieve lift and bounce. In matches

Alan Border looks anxiously towards Mike Brearley in the slips after edging a ball from Mike Hendricks. Border appears to have since overcome an early problem outside the off-stump.

against England when he first came into Test cricket in 1978–79, he frequently succumbed to balls on or outside the off stump, but he got a splendid 115 at Perth the same season against England when he was badly cut near the eye when past his century, trying to hook a bouncer. It turned out a match-winning hand, Australia winning by 138 runs. He also contributed 63 at Melbourne in the Third Test in 1979–80 in the match Australia won by eight wickets.

Border did reasonably well on tour in India in 1979 under Kim Hughes' captaincy, scoring 749 runs in 10 matches at 39.42 with two centuries, but he really starred on tour in Pakistan in 1980 under Greg Chappell, heading the averages with 674 runs at 112.33. Most of the Australians considered this tour a farce, with the wickets the worst they had ever played on and Border, like Greg Chappell, said he had no wish to return to Pakistan. Border was named man-of-the-match in the Third Test at Lahore, where he scored 150 not out in the first innings and 153 in the second innings. He averaged 131.66 in the three Tests, scoring 395 runs.

He returned home an established Test star and did not let his fans down despite the difficulties involved in switching States. He gave Queensland their money's worth and in a summer of good scoring produced a gem of an innings for 124 against India in the third Test at Melbourne. Whenever Greg Chappell was dismissed cheaply, Australia's hopes in the big matches swung to Border.

In England in 1981 under Hughes, Border alone of the established batsmen, came through with his reputation enhanced. He had a marvellous Test series. His 63 in the first innings of the First Test at Nottingham when Australia were 4 for 23 took Australia to within six runs of England's total, an insignificant deficit from which Australia went on to win. He followed with 64 in the Second Test at Lord's, 40 in the Fourth Test at Birmingham, 123 not out in the Fifth Test at Old Trafford, and 106 not out and 84 in the Sixth Test at The Oval. From the start of his knock in the second innings of the Fifth Test until he was finally out in the second innings of the Sixth Test he defied the English attack for 15 hours while scoring 313 runs, batting with a broken bone on his lefthand and a big chip in his favourite bat. On the entire tour of Sri Lanka and England he made 826 runs at 45.88, with three centuries, an effort for which Wisden made him one of the five Cricketers-of-The-Year for 1982.

At home in 1981–82 when Greg Chappell had his remarkable series of ducks and Kim Hughes showed his customary inconsistency, Australian hopes against Pakistan and the West Indies invariably rested with Border. He did not disappoint, and in between the Tests gave some fine exhibitions for Queensland. After the 1982 tour of New Zealand he was appointed Australia's vice-captain for the tour of Pakistan.

BOWLING   After the first of all Tests at Melbourne in March, 1877, public subscriptions were opened to reward three players who had played the most significant roles in Australia's surprise win over England by 45 runs. Charles Bannerman received £83.7.6 for scoring 165 in Australia's first innings, Blackham for his brilliant wicket-keeping, and Tom Kendall for taking 7 for 55 off 33.1 overs shared £23.5.0 when England faced the comparatively easy task of scoring 154 in the final innings. Kendall's bowling enabled Australia to win by 45 runs and came at a more tension-packed time of the match than when Bannerman made his century, but he got less than a sixth of Bannerman's reward.

Australian cricket fans' appreciation of our batsmen and bowlers has continued in about the same ratio ever since. Batsmen get all the glamorous lead roles, bowlers the bit parts, and our best bowlers have all had a laconic fortitude in their makeup that allowed them to accept this unfair secondary place in the public's esteem. Television has helped correct this with its dramatic closeups of bowlers' sweating to bring batsmen undone, but I fancy most fans would rather see a Greg Chappell cover drive hit the fence than a Lillee outswinger force a slips catch.

Australian bowlers have sweated under conditions favouring batsmen for 130 years, largely because of a climate that virtually guarantees hot weather and grasses and soils that produce hard, billiard table surfaces on which deviation is difficult to obtain. The size of the stumps has been increased, various leg-before-wicket laws have been tried and pitches for big cricket alternately covered and uncovered. In the early days a new pitch was cut for each innings, but the batting strips lasted so well this was soon dispensed with. Some remarkable collapses were seen on uncovered pitches when hot sun shone on rain-soaked surfaces, and Australian "sticky" wickets became notorious thoughout the cricket world. Unfortunately, the necessity for ensuring as much play as possible to keep gatemoney rolling in forced pitches to be covered. We no longer have spectacles like that at Melbourne in 1903–04 when Victoria were all out on a "sticky" against England for 15, with one batsman contributing nine of them.

When the first inter-Colonial matches were played all bowling was underarm, but round-arm bowling with the arm above the elbow was legalised in England and we followed. On the goldfields of Victoria there were a high number of skilful round-arm bowlers among the diggers. Even then there were outraged claims that bowlers who lifted their arms up around the shoulder instead of letting them go in true round-arm style were "throwing". Australia's first bowling hero, Gideon Elliott, was a round-armer whose action would amaze today's spectators. With Elliott, Tom Wills, who learned to bowl in England, and Sam Cosstick, hurling down

168

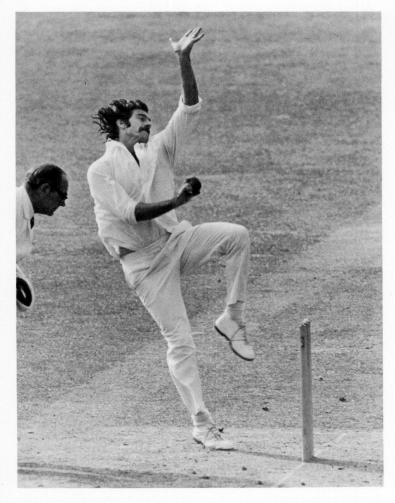

their round-armers with deadly effect, young Australians had fine examples to follow and they learnt a lot, too, from the bowlers in the visiting English teams of 1862, 1864 and 1873.

Australia's cricket history since then has underlined more than batting, bowling is an individual art. There has never been a convincing duplicate of an Australian Test bowler. All our great bowlers had an instinctive approach to bowling and stuck to it. Some of the failures included bowlers who tried to alter their action to conform to text book notions about bowling. But the best bowling style has always been the one that surprises the batsman, the one that conceals the bowler's intentions until the ball is on its way.

Spofforth did it with a big leap that made it hard to judge the pace at which he was about to bowl. C. T. B. Turner let the ball go with his body almost front-on to the batsman. Mailey lulled victims with deliberate long-hops and full tosses, joining the applause when he was hit for four. "Ranji" Hordern and Arthur Mailey perfected the right-armers' googly. "Chuck" Fleetwood-Smith tried unorthodox left arm spin. Bill O'Reilly came off a gallumping approach run and his finger work was such even great players could not pick if he was going to bowl an off-break, leg-break or wrong-un. Monty Noble used a strange baseballer's grip to make his inswingers dip in late. Grimmett and McCool were virtual roundarmers. Iverson and Gleeson tried something different. Victorian "Froggie" Thomson's approach bamboozled many batsmen; they could never tell which stride or whirl would produce a delivery!

When you examine Australia's bowling coups in big cricket, it is significant how often they were achieved by partnerships. From our baptism in big cricket Spofforth depended on Harry Boyle or Frank Allan sustaining pressure at the other end, Turner needed Ferris, Gregory frightened batsmen out while McDonald bowled them, Grimmett and O'Reilly formed a superb liaison with spin, Lindwall and Miller did it with pace, and later Lillee and Thomson gave batsmen some of the same. Success came largely because batsmen had no respite from our attack.

Here are the achievements that stand out in more than 100 years of scheming by our bowlers to hoodwink their more glamorous opponents:

MOST WICKETS IN A TEST

16–137	R. A. Massie	v. Eng.	(Lord's)	1972*
14–90	F. R. Spofforth	v. Eng.	(The Oval)	1882
14–199	C. V. Grimmett	v. SA	(Adel.)	1931–32

*On Test debut.

AUSTRALIANS WHO HAVE BOWLED UNCHANGED THROUGH A TEST

This has been done seven times by Australian Bowlers, the last time in 1901–02. The full list is:

		Total		
G. E. Palmer (7–68) & E. Evans (3–64)	v. Eng.	133	Sydney	1881–82
F. R. Spofforth (5–30) & G. E. Palmer (4–32)	v. Eng.	77	Sydney	1884–85
C. T. B. Turner (6–15) & J. J. Ferris (4–27)	v. Eng.	45	Sydney	1886–87
C. T. B. Turner (5–36) & J. J. Ferris (5–26)	v. Eng.	62	Lord's	1888
G. Giffen (5–26) & C. T. B. Turner (4–33)	v. Eng.	72	Sydney	1894–95
H. Trumble (3–38) & M. A. Noble (7–17)	v. Eng.	61	Melbourne	1901–02
M. A. Noble (5–54) & J. V. Saunders (5–43)	v. Eng.	99	Sydney	1901–02

Note: Australian J. J. Ferris did it with F. Martin while playing for England against South Africa in 1891–92. A. R. Trott did it with S. Haigh for England v. South Africa, 1898–99.

Clarrie Grimmett, born at Caversham, near Dunedin, bowling for Australia against England on the 1934 tour. He was a virtual round-armer who varied his flight by raising or lowering his arm.

Richie Benaud, who was Australia's highest Test Wicket-taker until Dennis Lillee took the record.

THREE WICKETS IN FOUR BALLS

The eight Australians who have taken three wickets in four consecutive balls are:

F. R. Spofforth	(7–44)	Aust. v. England	The Oval	1882
F. R. Spofforth	(4–54)	Aust. v. England	Sydney	1884–85
W. P. Howell	(4–18)	Aust. v. Sth Africa	Cape Town	1902–03
W. J. O'Reilly	(7–189)	Aust. v. England	Old Trafford	1934
R. R. Lindwall	(4–52)	Aust. v. England	Adelaide	1946–47
R. Benaud	(4–15)	Aust. v. West Indies	Georgetown	1954–55
J. W. Martin	(3–56)	Aust. v. West Indies	Melbourne	1960–61
K. D. Mackay	(4–57)	Aust. v. England	Edgbaston	1961
G. D. McKenzie	(5–33)	Aust. v. West Indies	Port of Spain	1964–65
D. K. Lillee	(6–66)	Aust. v. England	Manchester	1972
D. K. Lillee	(5–58)	Aust. v. England	The Oval	1972

AUSTRALIAN TEST BOWLING

	Balls	Runs	Wkts	Ave.
D. K. Lillee	16532	7568	328	23.07
R. Benaud	19093	6704	248	27.03
G. D. McKenzie	17681	7328	246	29.78
R. R. Lindwall	13666	5257	228	23.05
C. V. Grimmett	14573	5231	216	24.21
A. K. Davidson	11665	3828	186	20.58
J. R. Thomson	8959	4620	172	26.86
K. R. Miller	10474	3905	170	22.97
W. A. Johnston	11048	3825	160	23.90
W. J. O'Reilly	10024	3254	144	22.59
H. Trumble	8099	3072	141	21.78
M. H. N. Walker	10094	3792	138	27.47
A. A. Mallett	9990	3940	132	29.84
M. A. Noble	7109	3027	121	25.01
I. W. Johnson	8773	3182	109	29.19
G. Giffen	6325	2791	103	27.09
A. N. Connolly	7818	2981	102	29.22
C. T. B. Turner	5195	1670	101	16.53

Qualification 100 wickets.

OUTSTANDING TEST BOWLING ANALYSES

O	M	R	W				
7.4	2	17	7	M. A. Noble	v. Eng.	(Melb.)	1901–02
18	11	15	6	C. T. B. Turner	v. Eng.	(Syd.)	1886–87
16	8	15	6	M. H. N. Walker	v. Pak.	(Syd.)	1972–73
16	7	17	6	W. J. Whitty	v. SA	(Melb.)	1910–11
2.3	1	2	5	E. R. H. Toshack	v. Ind.	(Bris.)	1947–48
7.2	5	6	5	H. Ironmonger	v. SA	(Melb.)	1931–32
15.1	7	14	5	T. W. Wall	v. SA	(Bris.)	1931–32
12	5	14	5	W. J. O'Reilly	v. NZ	(Well.)	1945–46
15	8	15	5	D. K. Lillee	v. Eng.	(Edg.)	1975

MOST WICKETS FOR EACH STATE IN FIRST-CLASS CRICKET

New South Wales	A. Mailey	334
Victoria	A. N. Connolly	330
South Australia	C. V. Grimmett	668
Queensland	G. Dymock	309
Western Australia	G. A. R. Lock	316
Tasmania	E. A. C. Windsor	126

173

Most Wickets For Fewest Runs In A Test: Ernie Toshack took 5 for 2 for Australia v. India at Brisbane in 1947–48.

Most Wickets In A Test Innings: 9 for 121, by Arthur Mailey v. England at Melbourne, 1920–21.

Most No Balls In A Match By An Australian: 35 from 20 overs by Ernie McCormick in 1938 in the opening match of the Australian tour against Worcestershire.

Best Test Bowling Average By An Australian: By J. J. Ferris, whose 61 wickets for Australia and England cost 12.70 runs each, followed by A. E. Trott, whose 26 wickets for Australia and England cost 15.00 apiece.

Best Test Bowling Average Solely for Australia: By C. T. B. Turner, whose 101 Test wickets cost 16.53 each. Next best was Bert Ironmonger with 74 Test wickets at 17.97.

Best Test Striking Rate: Of the Australians who have taken 25 wickets or more in Tests, A. E. Trott had the best striking rate, with a wicket every 36.46 balls, followed by J. J. Ferris with a wicket every 37.73 balls.

Most Wickets Per Test: J. J. Ferris took an average of 6.77 wickets in every Test in which he played, C. T. B. Turner 5.94 wickets in each of his Tests, J. V. Saunders 5.64, D. K. Lillee 5.21, W. J. O'Reilly 5.33, H. Ironmonger 5.28, F. R. Spofforth 5.22 and C. V. Grimmett 5.84.

Most Economical Australian Bowlers: Of the Australians who have bowled more than 2,000 balls in Tests, H. Ironmonger was the most economical, conceding 28.32 runs every 100 balls in taking 74 wickets at 17.97. K. D. Mackay conceded 29.71 runs per 100 balls in taking 50 wickets at 34.42 and E. R. Toshack conceded 31.49 runs per 100 balls in taking 47 wickets at 21.04.

Highest Australian Test Wicket-Takers: D. K. Lillee, with 328 wickets in 63 Tests followed by Richie Benaud with 248 wickets in 63 Tests, Graham McKenzie with 246 in 60 Tests, Ray Lindwall with 228 in 61 Tests and C. V. Grimmett 216 in 37 Tests.

Highest Australian Wicket-Taker In All First-Class Matches: Clarrie Grimmett, with a total of 1424 in his first-class career.

Most Overs Bowled In A Test Match: Tom Veivers in the Fourth Test at Manchester in 1964 bowled 95.1 overs or 571 balls, only 17 balls short of Sonny Ramadhin's all-time Test record. L. O'B. Fleetwood-Smith bowled 87 six-ball overs, 522 balls, v. England in the England first innings at The Oval in 1938; W. J. O'Reilly bowled 85 six-ball overs, 510 balls, in the same innings. In 1886, T. W. Garrett bowled 99 four-ball overs, 396 balls, v. England at The Oval.

Most Overs In An Australian First-Class Match: Clarrie Grimmett bowled 106 overs or 848 balls for South Australia v. New South Wales in 1925–26.

Bowled Successive Overs: When England's captain Lionel

An intriguing shot of Ray Lindwall in action in England in 1948. The ball is still in his hand, with the front foot well over the batting crease, a delivery that would now be no-balled.

Tennyson wrongly declared England's first innings closed at Manchester in 1921, wicket-keeper Hanson Carter drew attention to the fact that it was against the agreed tour regulations. Australian captain Armstrong, who had bowled the last over before the England players went off, had such faith in Carter's knowledge of the rulebook he went and explained to Tennyson that his closure was out of order. England resumed batting and Armstrong inadvertently bowled the first over. This is the only recorded instance of a bowler sending down successive overs in Tests.

Fastest Australian Bowler: Unproved because so many of the past speedsters could not be properly timed. But it is interesting that Jeff Thomson was timed at 147 kilometres per hour or 91 miles per hour at Perth in 1978 in a contest with WSC pace bowlers.

Best Bowling By An Australian On Test Debut: 16 wickets for 137 runs by R. A. L. Massie against England in 1972 at Lord's. Massie took 8 for 84 and 8 for 53, swinging the ball about so much England players kept inspecting the ball in disbelief.

175

He could never do it again and the apparent reason is that humid conditions at Lord's for that match were perfect for swing bowling.

Wicket With First Ball In Tests: An Australian, left-arm fast bowler Arthur Coningham, was the first player to take a wicket with his first ball in Test cricket. He did it at Melbourne in 1894–95 against England. Since then nine bowlers from other countries have achieved the feat—but no other Australians.

Most Test Wickets In A Day: In the 1901–02 season 25 wickets fell for 221 runs on the first day of the Second Test between England and Australia. Australia were all out for 112, with S. F. Barnes taking 6 for 42, C. Blythe 4–64. Monty Noble, 7–17, and Hugh Trumble, 3–38, then routed England for 61. Australia sent in nightwatchmen but at stumps were 5 for 48 in the second innings. Australia finally won the match by 229 runs, with Noble taking 13 for 77. Only Australian Test to compare with this for dismissals was the Third between Australia and the West Indies at Adelaide in 1951–52 when 22 wickets fell in a day for 207 runs.

Eleven Bowlers In A Test Innings: The only occasion this has

Rodney Hogg's all-out aggression is dramatically shown in his great summer in 1978–79 when he took 41 wickets in six Tests against England.

happened was in the third Test at The Oval in 1884 when Australia scored 551 runs, and all the English team bowled and in the second Test at Faisalabad in 1980 when only one Australian bowler, Geoff Dymock, took a wicket as Pakistan scored 2–382.

Most Wickets By An Australian In A Test Series v. England: 42 in six Tests in 1981 by Terry Alderman, one more than Rodney Hogg's 41 in six Tests against England in 1978–79. Arthur Mailey bowled in only four Tests of the 1920–21 series against England when he set the previous series record of 36 wickets. In 1894–95, George Giffen took 34 wickets in a five Test series v. England. Dennis Lillee took 39 wickets in six Tests in 1981, and Jeff Thomson took 33 wickets in five Tests against England in 1974–75.

Most Wickets In A Series v. West Indies: 33 by Clarrie Grimmett in 1930–31 and by Alan Davidson in 1960–61.

Most Wickets In A Series v. South Africa: 44 by Clarrie Grimmett in five Tests, 1935–36, followed by 37 by Bill Whitty in five Tests, 1910–11. Grimmett's bag was two ahead of Alderman's 42 v. England in 1981, and remains the highest aggregate in a Test series by an Australian.

Most Wickets In A Series v. India: 29 by Alan Davidson and Richie Benaud, 1959–60.

Ten Wickets In An Innings By Australians: 10 for 66 by G. Giffen for Australia v. The Rest, 1883–84; 10 for 28 by W. Howell for Australia v. Surrey, 1899; A. Trott 10 for 52 Middlesex v. Somerset 1900; F. A. Tarrant took 10–90 Maharajah of Cooch Behar's XI v. Lord Willingdon's XI at Poona, 1918–19; 10 for 66 by A. Mailey for Australia v. Gloucestershire, 1921; 10 for 37 by C. Grimmett for Australia v. Yorkshire, 1930; 10 for 36 by T. Wall for South Australia v. New South Wales, 1932–33; 10 for 61 by P. Allen for Queensland v. Victoria, 1965–66; 10 for 44 by I. Brayshaw, for Queensland v. Victoria, 1967–68.

The Over: The over consisted of four balls in England from 1744. In May, 1889, this was increased to five balls, and in May, 1900, to six balls. In Australia, six-ball overs began in December, 1884, and were increased to eight balls in December, 1918, when the Laws of Cricket were altered at the Imperial Cricket Conference to provide for eight-ball overs for all matches played in Australia. The Australian Board of Control reverted to six-ball overs for certain matches between 1920 and 1933, but the eight-ball over lasted until 1979–80 when Australia reverted to the more widely used six-ball over.

Best Bowling In First-Class Debut: By Harry Hay, who in his first match for South Australia took 9 for 67 in an innings, including a hat-trick, against England in 1902–03.

Most Bowlers In A First-Class Match: The Australian Record is 17, which has happened five times, but not since an Australian XI match against New Zealand in 1921.

First Hat-Trick In Australian First-Class Cricket: By G. H. B.

Gilbert for NSW against Victoria at Melbourne in 1857–58. Gilbert was a cousin of W. G. Grace.

Most Expensive Bowling: Arthur Mailey's 4 for 362 off 64 overs, no maidens, for New South Wales v. Victoria in 1926–27 is the most runs conceded by one bowler in a first-class match. L. O'B. Fleetwood-Smith had a poorer average when he took 1 for 298 against England at The Oval in 1938.

Four Wickets In Four Balls: This feat has been accomplished only once by an Australian in Australia—by J. E. H. Hooker, for New South Wales v. Victoria, 1928–29. Australians A. E. Trott (1907), F. A. Tarrant (1907) and A. K. Walker (1956) all performed the feat in England.

Most Wickets For Fewest Runs: S. Cosstick bowled 21 overs for Victoria v. Tasmania at Melbourne, 1868–69, finishing with 6 for 1. Gideon Elliott took 9 for 2 off 19 overs for Victoria v. Tasmania at Launceston in 1857–58.

BOYLE, Henry Frederick, 1847–1907

First-Class Averages: Batting, 1,711 runs at 10.24; Bowling, 370 wickets at 15.38.

Tests (12): 153 runs at 12.75; 32 wickets at 20.03.

A heavily bearded right-arm roundarm medium pace bowler who played in many of the vital early first-class matches that shaped cricket's future. With Fred Spofforth, he formed Australia's first exciting bowling combination. Between them they gave performances that stirred public imagination and helped build the initial interest in international cricket. One of Harry Boyle's most enduring contributions to big cricket was that he virtually invented the silly mid-on position. Although he took many severe blows, he was absolutely fearless positioned two or three metres from the bat. He took so many catches in that position in the early days of England-Australia cricket, the spot became known as "Boyley's mid-on." Some English batsmen lost their nerve because of his presence so close to them.

Boyle was born in Sydney but lived all his life in Victoria. In 1873 he played for the Eighteen of Victoria that beat Dr. Grace's England team with an innings to spare, Boyle bowling down the great doctor's stumps. A story had been spread that Grace had backed himself for £50 to £500 that he would not be bowled on the Australian tour, so that when Boyle hit Grace's leg stump in this very first match, the crowd were overjoyed. Grace, who was on his honeymoon, told Boyle at a farewell dinner for the Englishman: "If you Australians ever come to England, and your bowlers are as good there as they have been here, you will make a name for yourself." Prophetic words!

Tall for a round-armer, with high bounce off the pitch, Boyle first became associated with Spofforth in the great adventure that was the first Australian tour of England in 1878. Heading off from Australia after a heavy programme of home matches, including a trip to New Zealand, they journeyed to

178

England through the United States. James Lillywhite, manufacturers of sporting goods, sponsored the team to England, and arranged the programme. Boyle and Spofforth quickly became the foundations of the Australian attack. Boyle took 64 wickets in 11-a-side matches on the tour, and 197 wickets at 7.43 in all matches.

Boyle and Spofforth shook English cricket to its foundations when on May 27, 1878, they humbled the best team England could muster in a single day. England batted first and were dismissed for 33, Spofforth taking 6 wickets for four runs off 5.3 overs, Boyle, 3 for 14 off 14 overs. Australia responded with 41, Alfred Shaw at one time bowling 13 overs for one run. Shaw finished with 5 for 10 off 33 overs. Spectators who had

Harry Boyle is the heavily-bearded figure at the rear with Fred Spofforth. Billy Murdoch and Alick Bannerman are in front.

heard news of these sensational events hurried to the ground from all over London.

Before 5,000 spectators Spofforth began against W. G. Grace, who was missed off his first ball and bowled by his second. His third ball bowled A. J. Webbe. At the other end Boyle bowled Booth and Ridley in his first over. By five o'clock they had England out for a total of 19, with Boyle's figures reading: 8.1 overs, 3 runs, 6 wickets. Spofforth took 4 for 16. Australia scored the 12 runs needed to win for the loss of Bannerman by 5.40 p.m.

The Australians lost only four of their 19 11-a-side matches on the tour but Boyle and Spofforth by their performances in that remarkable day at Lord's had shocked insular English fans and had a dramatic effect on the evolution of the game. On the whole trip Boyle's 64 victims in 11-a-side matches cost him only 9.68 runs apiece. His length was immaculate, his flight and leg-spin subtle, and he was always at the stumps, bowling for hours on a steady line and length.

Much has been written about the Boyle-Spofforth partnership, but if one studies that tour closely, it becomes apparent that Australia in fact had a great quartet of bowlers to make an international impact for the first time, with Allan and Garrett itching for the ball and able to perform almost as well with it when Boyle and Spofforth were spelled. And they were blessed with an understanding captain in Dave Gregory, who always had his fieldsmen keenly supporting this superb quartet.

Boyle's second trip to England in 1880 was marred by the Australians' late arrival. Most English counties had completed their programmes not knowing if the Australians would arrive, and as a result the Australians had difficulty securing matches. They played mostly against club teams in London and the midlands and went until August that year without really being tested. They even advertised for opponents in the English newspapers. Finally, Lord Harris was persuaded to captain an England side comprising the best available amateurs and professionals in the first of all Tests on English soil against the Australians.

Spofforth could not play through injury and England scored 420 in the first innings. Australia replied with 271 and had reached 6 for 170 by the end of the second day. Here Murdoch gave a marvellous display in adding 140 runs with the support only of tailenders. England had only 57 to get but Boyle produced an inspired effort with Palmer to dismiss the first five Englishmen for 20 runs. Every ball was packed with tension and Boyle produced a spell of sustained accuracy that had the big crowd agog with admiration. England got home but the great rivalry between the two countries that had begun in Melbourne had been rekindled.

The climax of Boyle's career came in The Ashes match at

The Oval on Boyle's third tour of England in 1882, a trip on which Boyle again did remarkable work, bowling 1,208 overs, and taking 144 wickets at 11.68. Massie and Bannerman opened the historic match at The Oval to the bowling of Peate and Ulyett but by lunch Australia was 6 for 48. The innings ended at 63, England responding with 101, a lead of 38. Rain delayed play the next day and here Australia had a great chance to score, with the ball like soap in the bowler's hands but the pitch still firm. Massie made 55, chancing his arm to put Australia ahead, but the innings finished with our lead a mere 84 runs.

In the ten minute break in the dressing-room Spofforth called to his team-mates that "this thing can be done", and they went down the steps on to the field determined to do so. Boyle bowled then as he never had before, with maiden following maiden. But Grace and Ulyett added 36 runs and with 34 needed England had eight wickets in hand. Boyle then had Grace caught and Spofforth dismissed Ulyett. With the score at 60 Boyle and Spofforth bowled 12 successive maiden overs.

This was the desperate half hour in which a spectator dropped dead and another gnawed the top off his umbrella handle. Spofforth ended up the hero with 14 wickets in an almost unbelievable Australian victory by 7 runs, England scoring 77 in the final innings. But it was Boyle, steady as a rock at the other end who helped Spofforth do it, and Boyle who took the final wicket.

Boyle, who always stood up very straight in team pictures, made two further tours of England after that dramatic trip but he was never quite the same bowler. In 1884 he took 67 wickets but in 1888, when he was player-manager, aged 41, only 11. Few cricketers have seen more eventful matches, fewer still have had such an influence on the creation of international cricket as we know it.

On all his trips to England, he took 669 wickets in all matches at 9.55 each. The record of his first-class catches shows that he held 125, most of them at what is known now as silly mid-on.

BRADMAN, Sir Donald George, A.C. Kt, 1908–

First-Class Averages: Batting, 28,067 runs at 95.14; Bowling, 36 wickets at 37.97.

Tests (52): 6,996 runs at 99.94; 2 wickets at 36.00.

Cricket's most successful batsman, and with Dr W. G. Grace the most influential figure the game has known. Others have scored more runs and more centuries by playing more matches, but nobody has matched his feat of scoring a century at an average of better than every third time he batted. He made 117 first-class centuries, including one innings of 452 not out (still the highest first-class score on turf), six innings over 300 and 37 over 200. Fielding in the outfield or covers he scurried brilliantly, gathering and throwing with applause-winning dexterity, but he dropped a few catches—attributed to his unusually small hands. He was occasionally used as a bowler and his right-arm leg-spinners yielded 36 first-class wickets, two in Tests. His batting was so proficient many of his 16 first-class ducks received more publicity than his centuries.

Bradman's batting skill should not be allowed to overshadow his success as a captain, selector, administrator, commentator, speechmaker and businessman. From humble beginnings in a small country public school, he achieved distinction in all of these fields that fully honour his position as the only Australian knighted for his services to cricket (in 1949). He was made a Companion of the Order of Australia in 1981, the second highest award that can be granted in the Australian honours list and one which ranks six places higher in the Australian Order of Precedence than a knight bachelor.

Bradman's right-hand batting was criticised for its lack of style but it had a character all its own, sparked by a gamin-like compulsion to express his authority from the time he

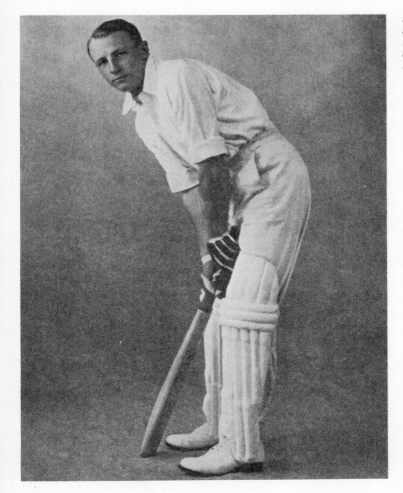

Don Bradman in 1930, showing the beautifully relaxed stance and alertness that became the scourge of English bowlers.

took guard. No other batsman scored so often from the first ball received, no other found gaps in the field as regularly as he did, and no one punished tired bowlers at the end of a day as he did. No other batsman hit the ball along the ground as consistently as Bradman, who only lifted his shots when his side was dominating a match. He was run out only once in Tests and only four times in 338 first-class innings. Two-thirds of his first-class centuries were chanceless. He top-scored in 24 of his 52 Tests. A non-smoker who enjoyed a pot of tea more than a few beers, he remains cricket's supreme disciplinarian. In 1982, at the age of 73, his handwriting remained as clear and defined as when he first handed Australia's batting order to scorers.

He was a cricket phenomenon, an innocent country boy eager to attack the world's finest bowlers with astonishing confidence, whose enjoyment in run-getting crowds shared.

He smiled a lot as a boy to whom a long train trip was an adventure, but much of the laughter faded as he was harried by
officials and team-mates and misquoted by newspapers. Nobody ever suffered more from the Australian habit of mali-
ciously gossiping about national heroes. Very little of it was
justified, but it turned him into a man who kept his secrets,
an iron-willed figure in public who treasured his home life.
But no Australian hero has put back into his field of endeavour as much as Bradman has done. He deserves his privacy,
for this is a man who had to get team-mates to unstrap his
pads when he batted himself into exhaustion in Australia's
cause.

Bradman was born on August 27, 1908, at 89 Adam Street,
Cootamundra, in the house of the local midwife, Mrs Eliza
Ellen Scholtz, but neither he nor his parents ever lived in Cootamundra. His father, George Bradman, was the son of a English migrant from an area on the borders of Cambridgeshire
and Suffolk formed by the villages of Horseneath and Haver-
hill. Don's grandfather, Charles, was a farm labourer who was
attracted to New South Wales by gold strikes near Bathurst.
Don's mother was a Whatman, a family with a long history in
the Bowral-Mittagong district.

After his birth at "Granny" Scholtz's house in Cootamundra,
Bradman went home to the family cottage at Yeo Yeo, be-

Bradman playing an off-drive gives the stroke a full swing of the bat, body balanced well up on the toes.

tween Wallendbean and Stockinbingal, where Don's father was a successful wheat and sheep farmer. Don's brother Victor was just over six feet tall like their father, and Don's three sisters, Islet, Lillian and May, were all above average height. Don was the smallest in the family, the same height (5 ft, 6¾ in) as his mother. When he was two, the seven Bradmans moved to Bowral from Yeo Yeo because it was felt the climate in the southern highlands would improve his mother's uncertain health. Married in 1893 at 17, Don's mother enjoyed a happy marriage until her death a few days before Christmas, 1944. His father died in 1961 at 85.

Don's father turned to carpentry in Bowral and did a lot of work for Alf Stephens, one of the town's leading builders and the president and captain of the Bowral Cricket Club. Don described in his book *Farewell To Cricket* how he attended Bowral Intermediate High School, where there was no sports coach, though the headmaster sometimes played football or cricket with the boys. After school Don amused himself by hitting a golf ball against the brick base of an 800–gallon water tank with a small stump. There were no neighbourhood boys of similar enthusiasm close enough to join him in play and he formed himself into Test teams, batting in turn for Jack Gregory, Herbie Collins and the rest of Australia's current Test heroes.

At the family house in Shepherd Street (and later when they moved to Glebe Street which runs alongside the cricket ground now known as Bradman Oval), the Bradmans held regular musical evenings, and Don's sister Lillian taught him the piano. In the backyard Don's mother bowled left-armers to him each afternoon after school. Don was a choirboy at St Jude's Church, Bowral, where he went to Sunday school. He was a champion runner at school never beaten by a boy his own age, played for the school Rugby League side, and was as good a tennis player as a cricketer. On leaving school he played tennis for two years before returning to cricket. He thought he might become a house decorator.

Victor Bradman, Don's brother, was an average cricketer, and his father George never made a century in his life. The cricket talent in the family came from his mother's relatives, the Whatmans. His uncles George and Richard Whatman were intensely keen. George, an opening batsman and splendid wicket-keeper, was the power behind Bowral cricket for some years and, with Alf Stephens who let Don practise on his backyard pitch, helped enormously in Don's development. Don revelled in all sport and became the scorer for Bowral teams, travelling to matches sitting on a wooden box in a lorry that ran on solid rubber tyres. He played when the team was short but he was so small one of the players took pity on him and cut a piece off an old bat and presented it to Don. In 1921, Don's father took him to Sydney to watch two days of the England-Australia Test during which he watched every ball as Macartney scored a glorious 170.

Playing for Bowral against a Wingello side that had beaten Moss Vale in the final the previous year, Bradman first met Test bowler Bill O'Reilly at the end of the 1925–26 summer. Bradman was 17 and some of his teammates were in their forties. On the first Saturday, batting on the Bowral ground, Bradman was twice dropped in slips off O'Reilly but reached 234 not out, hitting four sixes and six fours in his last 50. Although he was bowled around his legs by O'Reilly's first ball the following week on the Wingello ground, his score received wide publicity. He followed it with an innings of 300 against Moss Vale in that year's final. Under the rules the match continued on succeeding Saturdays.

Opening the batting, Don made 80 not out on the first Saturday, went on to 279 not out the next week when he added 323 with George Whatman (277), and was finally out for 300 on the third Saturday, when Bowral's score reached 9 for 672. Dick Whatman could not bat because he broke a toe after play began. Don's brother Vic was clean bowled for one run. Moss Vale were dismissed for 134 in the first innings and 200 in the second, giving Bowral a win by an innings and 338 runs. The match lasted for five Saturday afternoons and was the easiest win in the history of the Berrima District Cricket Association. The "Boy from Bowral" legend had begun.

Bradman's prolific scoring in bush cricket earned him an invitation to attend the Sydney Cricket Ground nets in October, 1926. He went in the train with his father not knowing that the State selectors had called this special series of practices mainly because they were alarmed at the lack of bowling talent. In his first appearance on a turf wicket, he made a big impression, and this in turn won him an invitation to play in a Possibles v. Probables match designed to give aspiring youngsters a chance of selection in the State side. He made 37 not out in that match, his first on turf. Behind the scenes one of the three State selectors, "Mudgee" Cranney tried to persuade the committee of his Sydney club, Cumberland, to pay Bradman's expenses to Sydney by train from Bowral to play for the club in each round of grade matches. The club decided it did not have the money. On learning of this, another State selector, Dick Jones, went to the committee of the St George Club and urged them to select Bradman.

St George accepted Jones' advice and Bradman made his first grade debut at the age of 18 on November 27, 1926, at Petersham Oval against Petersham. Batting at No. 5, he scored 110 in even time, his first century on a turf pitch. He followed two days later with an innings of 98 for Country against City and this won him selection for NSW Seconds against Victoria Seconds on New Year's Day, 1927. He made 43 before accidentally treading on his wicket making a pull shot to the boundary. At the end of the season, he returned to Bowral to break his own district record with a score of 320 not out against Moss Vale in the final of the district competition. He kept travelling to Sydney at the start of the 1927–28 season to play each Saturday for St George, but when the NSW practice squad was announced, he was not among the 29 names.

But before the season was very far advanced Jack Gregory and "Hammy" Love, dropped out of the NSW team for the southern tour and Bradman, who had missed selection for the northern trip to Queensland, were chosen with St George clubmate Albert Scanes to fill in. The team went to Adelaide via Broken Hill and on to Melbourne, quite a trip for a lad who had never ventured outside his State. The NSW side included a champion leg-puller in Halford Hooker, who kidded Bradman that piano playing built up his back muscles. He had no sooner got Bradman to the piano in the team's hotel than he coaxed young spinner Hughie Chilvers out on to the floor to tap dance, baited by the challenge that he could not

Bradman leaves the field with Sid Barnes in 1946–47 at Sydney. Both scored 234 in an Australian total of 659.

187

dance as fast as Bradman could play. In view of the tough negotiator and boardroom debater Bradman later became, it is enchanting to recall him hammering away at the piano keys while Chilvers danced furiously.

Bradman made his first-class debut in Adelaide against South Australia on a wicket as hard as the concrete on which he had played in Bowral. He went in at No. 7, after his captain Alan Kippax had retired with sunstroke, and was 65 not out at stumps on the first day. He went on next day to 118, a chanceless knock of 188 minutes. To veteran spectators his confidence in his own ability was remarkable, as was his throwing from the boundary. His enthusiasm for the game, his bright, happy demeanour were quite infectious and made an immediate impact on spectators. People who saw him and Archie Jackson chasing the ball at practice said they were like a couple of playful puppies. He made 33 in the NSW second innings and 31 and 5 in Melbourne against Victoria, and returned to Sydney with his place in the NSW side confirmed. He was bowled for a duck from the first ball he received in a first-class match on Sydney Cricket Ground by Queensland's Frank Gough. But in the last match of the summer he scored 134 not out against Victoria, the first of many centuries on the SCG.

Bradman's biographer, Irving Rosenwater, believes that the jokes teammates played on Bradman in his first season of first-class cricket intensified his fierce desire to do well. "He did not forget these incidents at his expense as he looked back on his first season, and determined to answer them the way he knew best—with the bat," Rosenwater wrote, adding that in Bradman's first big season the NSW Cricket Association paid State team players £1 a day expenses in Sydney and £1/5/– when they were away.

A few days after his 20th Birthday Bradman left Bowral to live in Sydney, taking a job as secretary to the newly opened Sydney office of his Bowral employer, real estate agent Percy Westbrook. At the kind invitation of Mr and Mrs Frank Cush, he moved into their home at Frederick Street, Rockdale, ending all doubts about his eligibility to play for St George under the residential rule that applied for Sydney grade cricketers. In his first grade match of the 1928 season, Bradman made 106 not out against Gordon at Chatswood, but he failed (14 and 5) in a trial to guide selectors in picking a side to play Chapman's MCC side. Bradman made his bid for Test selection with innings of 131 and 133 not out for NSW against Queensland, a performance that secured his place in the NSW team to play the MCC in Sydney. MCC scored 7 for 734. Bradman made 87 in the first innings and when NSW followed on saved the match with an unbroken stand of 249 for the fourth wicket with Kippax, Bradman finishing with 132 not out, a fine feat for a boy of 20.

Bradman lifts his bat to acknowledge the crowd's applause after reaching 300 at Leeds in 1930.

In his Test debut he was out for 18 and 1. England batted on despite a lead of 399 on the first innings and set Australia 742 runs to win in the final innings. Australia were caught on a sticky wicket—which Bradman had never seen before—and lost by 675 runs. When "Farmer" White had Bradman caught in the second innings, Maurice Tate called: "What do you mean by stealing my rabbit?" It was a tough entry to Tests, but from that day onward the "rabbit" was no laughing matter for English bowlers. He was 12th man for the second Test at Sydney but fielded for 11 hours because of an injury to Ponsford. Australia were heavily defeated again, this time by eight wickets. Recalled for the third Test at Melbourne

Bradman made 79 and 112 and was never again excluded from an Australian team, except through illness.

When Bradman scored his maiden Test century with a drive past mid-on for an all-run four, he was cleverly farming the strike to prevent the English bowlers attacking Ron Oxenham at the other end. Bradman was then 20 years, 129 days, the youngest player ever to score a century in Tests (to that time). Oxenham's age was 37. The crowd cheered Bradman's century for so long the English players sat down. In Sydney when his century came up on the scoreboard outside the Sydney *Sun* office, men and women danced in the streets, cars honked their horns and tram drivers clanged their bells. For all who watched, the surety of Bradman's stroke play and the confidence with which he attacked the bowling when moving down the pitch were astounding in one so young.

Bradman's international baptism had seen him field while Hammond played innings of 225, 251, and 200 and he now set about emulating this high scoring. At Sydney early in 1929 he made 340 not out for NSW against Victoria, the highest score to that time at the SCG, surpassing Billy Murdoch's 321 of 1882. In the fourth Test at Adelaide he made 40 and 58, batting with Archie Jackson in the first innings as Jackson reached his superb century, and being run out by an injudicious call from Oldfield in the second. This knock gave Jackson, 19, the record for the youngest-ever Test century-maker, an honour which Bradman had taken a month earlier. Australia lost again, but returned to the winning list when Bradman scored 123 in the fifth Test at Melbourne, passing the record for most runs in an Australian season by taking his total to 1,690, average 93.88. From his debut in November, 1928, until his retirement in August, 1948, Bradman scored a century in 13 of the 17 Tests Australia won against England. In all he made 19 centuries against England, eight of them extending beyond 200, and two past 300.

Strangely enough, doubts were expressed about his prospects of success in England when he set off for his first tour in 1930. The Surrey captain Percy Fender claimed Bradman hit across the ball too much to sustain his prolific Australian run-getting in England. Only one day's play was possible in the match between Australia and Surrey but Bradman made 252 not out, the second 100 in 80 minutes, with Fender powerless to halt the slaughter.

The previous summer in Sydney Bradman had made the world record score of 452 not out in 415 minutes. He was 205 not out on Saturday night, rested all day Sunday at the Cushs', and went on to the fastest quadruple century (377 minutes) ever made by any batsman, before tea on Monday. He hit 49 fours in his 452, scoring at 65.34 runs an hour, without a single wild stroke.

"Mr and Mrs Cush offered me the peace and comfort of their
own home in order that I might pursue my normal occupation and at the same time not lose opportunities in cricket,"
Bradman wrote in *Farewell To Cricket*. "Their help and guidance was of enormous value to me." When he set off for his
first trip to England Bradman had left real estate for a job
with Mick Simmons sports store, the shop in which he had
chosen his first cricket bat, his mother's reward for the 300 he
made for Bowral against Moss Vale.

Only four of the 1930 Australian side had been to England
before and the team were given little chance of success. But
such was the brilliance of Bradman's batting and the skill of
Woodfull's captaincy the tour was a great triumph for Australian cricket. Bradman began with 236 in the first game against
Worcestershire and followed with 185 not out against Leicestershire. At Nottingham in the first Test he had appeared
likely to win the match for Australia when Walter Robins deceived him with a googly when he was 131. At Lord's in the
second Test he made 254, victim of a magnificent Percy
Chapman catch. At Leeds in the third Test he scored 334, then
the highest score in Tests. Many English experts rated this 334
as the finest innings ever played in England.

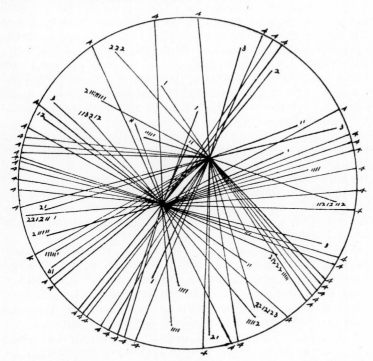

*Scorer W. H. Ferguson's diagram showing how Bradman scored his 334 runs
against England at Leeds in 1930. He hit 46 fours, six threes, 26 twos and 80
singles, seldom lifting the ball.*

Bradman went to the wicket after Archie Jackson was out in the second over. He moved to 50 in 49 minutes and his century in 99 minutes (out of 127 scored). He was 105 at lunch, 220 at tea, and 309 by the end of the day. He was out after adding 25 the next morning, having hit 46 fours and figured in stands of 192 with Woodfull and 229 with Kippax. He was still several weeks away from his 22nd birthday, but in this, only his seventh Test, he passed 1,000 Test runs. In the drawn fourth Test Peebles fooled him with a googly as Robins had done, but in the fifth Test at The Oval, Don did it again, scoring 232 as he turned the match Australia's way, Australia winning the series 2–1. Bradman had scored 974 runs in the Tests at an average of 139.14. In first-class matches on the tour he made 2,960 runs at 98.66, with ten centuries. In addition he had established himself as a great fieldsman, whether gathering, throwing or catching. At Manchester his catch at long leg to dismiss Sutcliffe was a superlative effort.

There followed a series at home against the West Indies in which he made 223 in the third Test and 152 in the fourth Test, and his first duck in Tests when he was yorked in the fifth Test by a slower ball from pace bowler Griffith. The West Indies star Learie Constantine reported ecstatically on Bradman's ability to contacts in the Lancashire League and, before the 1931–32 season began, rumours that Bradman would switch to the League studded the sports pages. In the end, Associated Newspapers, Radio 2UE, and the department store chain, F. J. Palmer, combined to make an offer that kept him in Australia. On the field Bradman began with his famous duck against Eddie Gilbert at Brisbane but quickly made amends with scores of 226, 112, 2, 167 and 299 not out against the touring South Africans.

In April, 1932, Bradman married Jessie Menzies, daughter of a Mittagong farmer, whom he had known at school in Bowral. Don was 10 months older than Jessie, who as a child had stayed with the Bradmans in Bowral. They were married at St Paul's Church, Burwood, in Sydney, by the Rev. Canon Ernest Selwyn Hughes, vice-president of the Victorian Cricket Association. After a whirlwind trip to America he returned to the biggest test of his career—Bodyline.

The Bodyline method of attack was invented to curb Bradman's consistent high-scoring. It had its birth in a few short-pitched deliveries sent down to him at The Oval in 1930. The Bodyline series, which England won 4–1 and is dealt with elsewhere, proved Bradman mortal, for he averaged only 56.57, thanks to a score of 103 not out. A disgrace to the people who conceived it, Bodyline created bitterness between the game's two leading countries previously unknown in international cricket. Bradman played in the last four Tests in the Bodyline series after missing the first through illness and scored over 50 four times, mainly using a method whereby he

192

stepped away towards square leg and cut—the technique now frequently used by players in one day games to try and thwart legside bowling.

Thirty years later in his book *The Larwood Story* written in association with Kevin Perkins, Larwood said, "Let me confirm what so many people have always believed—Bodyline was devised to stifle Bradman's genius." Outside of the Tests Bradman's prolific scoring continued unabated in the Bodyline summer. He scored runs galore for NSW and in other first-class fixtures.

Bradman moved out of the St George district when he married and this caused him to switch to the North Sydney club at the start of the 1933–34 season. In his second innings for his new club he made 127 in 90 minutes against Western Suburbs. In Shield cricket he began with 200 against Queensland at Brisbane, scoring 294 for the second wicket with Billy Brown, the last 94 in 41 minutes. He followed with 76 against South Australia, 187 and 77, both not out, against Victoria, and 253 in the return match against Queensland in Sydney, where he added 363 for the third wicket with Kippax. A back injury then prevented him appearing in any further grade cricket for North Sydney, and restricted him to only one more appearance for NSW in which he made 128 against Victoria at Sydney.

Don Bradman and his wife Jessie returning to Australia after their honeymoon trip to America in 1932 just before the Bodyline series against England.

Bradman's contract with Associated Newspapers, Radio 2UE and F. J. Palmer ended on February 1, 1934. A few days later it was announced that he would join the Adelaide stock-broking firm of H. W. Hodgetts & Co. on his return from the 1934 tour of England and that he would play for South Australia from the start of the 1934–35 season. Harry Hodgetts was one of SA's delegates to the Board of Control. When the Board announced the team for England, Bradman was vice-captain, a clear indication that he was being groomed for the Australian captaincy. Bradman had furthered his cricket education

Bradman's dramatic dismissal in the first innings of the second Bodyline Test in 1932–33 when he nicked a ball from Bill Bowes and was out first ball for a duck. He made 103 out of 191 in the second innings.

194

in August, 1933, by passing "with credit" the examination of the NSW Umpires' Association.

Woodfull persuaded him to play in the opening match of the 1934 English tour at Worcester to end reports that he was unfit. Bradman made 206 at around a run a minute. He had his first match as captain of a first-class side in the drawn match at Leicester. In the Leeds Test, Bradman made 304, and in the Oval Test 244, but for the first time he showed some uncertainty, particularly against Verity, Yorkshire's left-arm spinner, and the word spread that Bradman disliked a sticky wicket. Another reason why Bradman did not excite people in 1934 as he had done in England in 1930 was that Ponsford scored almost as heavily and Bradman's achievements no longer appeared unique. But Bradman's aggregate of runs for the 1934 Tests, 758, was far ahead of any teammate. He hit the ball in the air far more than four years earlier and in the match at Folkestone against an England XI hit "Tich" Freeman for 30 runs off a six-ball over, on his way to 149 not out, which included four sixes. There was no longer any need for him to confirm his place in teams and this freedom revealed one of the fastest scorers Australian cricket had known. The speed of his scoring won as many matches as his huge scores.

A jubilant Bill O'Reilly has an lbw appeal against Bradman upheld. Bradman has always rated O'Reilly the best bowler he faced.

195

Throughout the 1934 tour of England he was in poor health and at the end of it he collapsed and almost died. Doctors diagnosed acute appendicitis, and on the operating table it was found to be almost gangrenous. The emergency operation, performed within an hour of Bradman's entry into a London nursing home, prevented peritonitis. All visitors were forbidden except the Australian manager, Harold Bushby, who was allowed to see him for just a few moments. Blood transfusions were necessary and as Bradman weakened official bulletins had to be issued to reduce the phone calls that jammed the switchboard. In Australia, rumours spread that Bradman had died. In Fleet Street cricket writers went to their typewriters to write his obituary. Jessie Bradman, who had been aware of his indifferent health, rushed to London to be with him.

Sir Douglas Shields, a distinguished Melbourne-born surgeon, performed the operation on Bradman and protected him from all visitors except Bushby in the critical days just afterwards. Slowly, Bradman recovered and after a holiday in Switzerland and on the Riviera went to his father-in-law's farm at Mittagong for three months to recuperate. He played no Shield cricket at all in the 1934–35 season on medical advice, and he was unable to accept his nomination as an Australian selector because of his inability to watch players in contention for Australia's 1935–36 tour of South Africa. Vic Richardson, who replaced Bradman as a national selector, took the team to South Africa without Bradman.

Bradman, who was taught the piano by his sister, playing for Arthur Chipperfield and "Chuck" Fleetwood-Smith in 1934 at their London hotel. A few days later he was rushed to hospital.

After seven months' rest Bradman began his new job in H. W. Hodgett's stockbroking office in Adelaide in 1935. This was what he had been looking for when he left Sydney— work that secured his future without any cricket in his daily routine. To regain fitness he took up squash and at his first attempt won the South Australian amateur championship, beating Davis Cup tennis player Don Turnbull in the final. In Sydney after he left, the NSWCA had its worst season financially for many years, with gate takings in sharp decline. In Adelaide officials looked to a boost in the State's cricket finances when Bradman made his debut for SA in November, 1935. In his first three innings for SA, Bradman made 117, 233 and 357, when he added 109 before lunch on the second day. In March, 1936, he scored 369 for SA against Tasmania at Adelaide, putting on 356 with Hamence for the third wicket in 181 minutes. He hit 46 fours and four sixes in this knock, which remains the highest score for SA.

Bradman began his career as Australian captain with losses in the first two Tests against "Gubby" Allen's 1936–37 English team when Australia were caught on sticky wickets in both matches, but led his team to an exciting series win. All attendance records were broken as Australia struggled to win the last three Tests. More importantly, Bradman and Allen restored the friendly atmosphere—missing from the Bodyline series—in which hard-fought, tense Tests should be played. They have remained close friends amid all the problems that have arisen over chucking, dragging, covering pitches, time wasting, the WSC signings etc., and this has been highly beneficial to the game. The enthralling 1936–37 series produced the only instance in international cricket in which a team has recovered to win after losing the first two Tests. To help achieve it, Bradman played innings of 270, 212 and 169 in the last three Tests, and in none of these innings did he give a chance.

By now Bradman's influence on gate takings was enormous, with people who normally did not watch cricket flocking to the grounds to see him, particularly women. Even in Adelaide club matches for Kensington his failures were rare as he clobbered bowlers of all types for an apparently endless stream of fours and sixes. In 1938, he made his third trip to England, his first as captain, leading a side he had helped select. He had matured markedly as a strategist and was to win 21 of his last 22 Tests as Australian captain.

For the third successive trip he began with a double century against Worcestershire, scoring 258 at just over 50 an hour without a chance.

During the tour he averaged 115.66, which remains the best-ever average for a season in England, scoring 2,429 runs and 13 centuries in the summer. He scored 1,000 runs before the end of May in just seven innings. It was the second time he had made 1,000 in May. No other cricketer has done it twice although batsmen such as Hobbs, Grace, and Woolley had 20 or more chances compared with Bradman's four chances.

The first two Tests were drawn, the Test at Manchester abandoned through rain without the toss being made, and Australia retained the Ashes at Leeds in one of the best Tests ever played. Set to score 105 for victory in the final innings, Australia lost five wickets in reaching 107, Hassett batting gamely for 33 as rain clouds threatened. With the Ashes secure Australia made the mistake of going into the final Test at The Oval with only three regular bowlers and England declared at 7 for 903. In this match Hutton surpassed Bradman's Test record of 334 by scoring 364 in 796 minutes. Bradman fractured his ankle while bowling and Fingleton was unable to bat through injury, England winning by a mammoth margin of an innings and 579 runs. It was Australia's heaviest defeat ever by England.

In his first six innings of the 1938–39 season in Australia, Bradman scored 118, 143, 225, 107, 186, and 135 not out to equal C. B. Fry's record for the most centuries in succession in first-class matches. The feat was matched in the 1970–71 English season by South African Mike Proctor. Bradman's five centuries in a row for South Australia that season enabled South Australia to win the Shield for the second time in four years. Strangely, he was beaten that year on the casting vote of the

Bradman bowled by left-arm spinner Hedley Verity at Lord's in 1938 for 18. He made 102 not out in the second innings.

The end of Bradman's Test career. Needing four runs to average 100 in Tests, he was bowled second ball for a duck.

chairman when he applied for the job as secretary at the Melbourne Cricket Club, the job going to Vernon Ransford.

War began on September 3, 1939, but the government asked for the 1939–40 Shield competition to continue. Bradman, whose son John had been born in July, 1939, celebrated with an astounding innings of 188 for the Kensington club, scoring the last 52 in two overs. It was the prelude to a brilliant season in which he made 1,475 runs at 122.91, highest score 267. Sir Donald rates his two innings in that marvellous season against NSW at Adelaide as his best in Shield matches. He made 251 not out and 90 not out against O'Reilly at his peak.

Bradman enlisted in the RAAF but after a delay in his formal enlistment switched to the Army as a physical training instructor with the rank of lieutenant. He played only one first-class match during World War II—for his own XI against a Stan McCabe XI for charity. In a regulation Army test at Frankston, Victoria, his eyesight was found to be below average, a result that was no surprise to Bradman though it amazed sports fans. His new work produced a succession of muscle problems diagnosed as fibrositis. He had three spells in hospital before he was invalided out of the Army in June, 1941. Yet again he went back to Bowral to recuperate, unable to lift his arm to comb his hair, and forced to get his wife to shave him. After the birth of his daughter Shirley in 1941, he returned to work in stockbroking and in 1943 was elected a member of the Adelaide Stock Exchange. In July, 1945, the stockbroking firm of H. W. Hodgetts, his employer, collapsed, and Bradman went into business on his own. When the South

199

Australian Cricket Association voted on a successor to Hodgetts as the State's representative on the Board of Control, they chose Bradman.

Despite misgivings about his health, Bradman decided to give himself a fair trial in the nets before formally retiring. He agreed to play for South Australia against the Services XI because it was for charity. His 112 in that match was just what Bradman needed to regain his old spark at the age of 37 and six years after his last first-class century. He felt bone weary and had torn a muscle but a century on Adelaide Oval was better than all the treatments he had had for fibrositis in the war years. He groped his way through a century against England at Brisbane in the 1946–47 season Test that restored big cricket to the front pages.

He captained Australia throughout the series against Hammond's side, in the series against India in 1947–48, wherein he scored his 100th first-class century at Sydney, and led the superb 1948 Australian team on an unbeaten tour of England during which he scored 11 more centuries, including 138 in the Nottingham Test and 173 not out in the enthralling Leeds Test. His Test career ended when he was bowled by Hollies for a duck at The Oval, needing just four runs to average exactly 100 in his Test career. His first-class career ended at Adelaide in March, 1949, when he played for South Australia v. Victoria for A. J. Richardson's testimonial.

After his cricket career ended Bradman concentrated on his business and family life. He gave up stock and share broking in 1954 to devote adequate time to the many company directorships which he was offered. But he still found time to give magnificent service as a selector. He served two three-year terms as chairman of the Australian Cricket Board, wrote two superb commentaries on Tests between England and Australia (1953 and 1956), made a 100 break at billiards, and at an age when most players are past their peak reduced his golf handicap to scratch.

BRATCHFORD, James David, 1929–

First-Class Averages: Batting, 1,628 runs at 22.92; Bowling, 123 wickets at 30.37.

A right-handed all-rounder from Brisbane's Toombul club who achieved the double of 1,000 runs and 100 wickets for Queensland in the 1950's. He came into the State side at the same time as Peter Burge. Between 1952 and 1960 he scored two centuries, topscore 143 and three times took five wickets or more in an innings, best return 6 for 57. He took 30 catches. In 1959–60 Bratchford shared a record sixth wicket stand of 211 with Tom Vievers against South Australia at Brisbane.* In this his final season, he captained his State.

*This is the highest sixth wicket partnership for Queensland in Australia, but R. McDonald and O. Cowley made 238 for the sixth wicket for Queensland against Hawke's Bay on tour in New Zealand in 1896–97.

Probably the best all-rounder to play for Western Australia, who since his retirement has become a leading commentator. He was one of three bowlers to take all 10 wickets in a Sheffield Shield innings, a right-arm medium pace bowler with fine control of swing and cut whose accuracy worried the best batsmen in Australia. His batting in the middle of the order improved enormously over his long period in first-class cricket. Brayshaw's all-round ability was a big factor in Western Australia's splendid Sheffield Shield performances over the past decade.

Brayshaw did not play in a Test. His close friend John Inverarity rates him a far better player than many who have represented Australia. "He was certainly a most valuable member of the West Australian side," said Inverarity. "There were times in his last season in 1977–78, when Western Australia won the Shield, when his knee injury really played up, and I couldn't bowl him as much as I wanted to. But he would

BRAYSHAW, Ian James, 1942–

First-Class Averages: Batting, 4,325 runs at 31.80; Bowling, 178 wickets at 25.08.

never complain. If it was bothering him before he went in to bat, he would take a couple of pain-killing tablets. He would never talk about it. Just go out there and do his best."

Brayshaw and Inverarity first became associated in the First XI at Perth's Scotch College, where they played together for three seasons, starting in 1957–58. They played together for most of 21 seasons, starting with the Claremont Cottesloe first-grade side and later in the State side. Brayshaw made his debut for Western Australia in 1960–61. He joined Tim Wall and Peter Allan as taker of all ten wickets in an innings in Western Australia's opening match of the 1967–68 season at Perth against Victoria. Helped by some brilliant fielding (Inverarity at slip and Becker the wicket-keeper both held two spectacular catches), he finished with this analysis:

17.6 overs 4 maidens 44 runs 10 wickets.

This effort enabled Western Australia to win the match after they had been dismissed in their first innings for only 161.

Brayshaw went to England in 1968 and 69 to play in the Lancashire League and gain experience in his career as a journalist and this has undoubtedly paid off in his rising reputation as a cricket commentator. He is fair and constructive in his criticisms. He has set himself high standards and never wavers from them. On the field he was always at his best when Western Australia needed him most and he sacrificed many big scores because Western Australia needed runs fast before a declaration. He made three first-class centuries.

Brayshaw's figures show that he gave unrivalled service to Western Australia for almost 17 seasons. He made 108 catches, the majority of these in the slips, though he was a fine fieldsman at mid-off. Brayshaw tells how he dropped the great South African Barry Richards when Richards had made 160 in a Western Australia v. South Australian Shield game at Perth. "Oh well, he can't make many more," Brayshaw told himself. Richards was out next day for 356. At the instigation of his fellow players, the WACA granted him unofficial approval for a testimonial fund in 1980–81 which raised $15,000.

BRIGGS, Ronald Edward ("Biggles"), 1929–

First-Class Averages: Batting, 1,089 runs at 47.34.

A stocky, right-hand opening batsman who scored three centuries for New South Wales in 1950 but could not overcome tough opposition to win Test selection. His career was a tribute to the comprehensive organisation of Australian cricket. From school matches in the Bankstown district he played junior cricket, then in the A. W. Green Shield (under 18) and on up through third grade, second grade to Marrickville firsts and, in 1948, to the NSW Colts XI. His teammates in that side included Richie Benaud, Jim Burke and Graeme Hole. In his first Colts match, Briggs made 155 at The 'Gabba. Next he played in Sydney sides against Country and finally the NSW team.

Briggs, a school teacher, made 121 in his first first-class match, aged 22, at Perth against WA, but with Barnes and Morris available again he found himself 12th man for the following match against South Africa at Sydney. Whenever Barnes decided he would not play, Briggs got a berth. He made his career highest score of 136 against SA at Sydney in 1953–54 and made 100 against Queensland at Brisbane in 1954–55, the season he played for an Australia XI against Hutton's MCC side. He even gave up table tennis after winning a NSW title to concentrate on cricket, but he could not make the final jump to Tests. He played for the Bankstown club—he captained them to a premiership in 1958—for the first 14 years of its existence, retiring in 1963. His son, Gregory, went to Pakistan with the Australian Under-19 team, combining left-arm spinners with his right-hand batting (topscore so far 180).

BRIGHT, Raymond James ("Candles"), 1954–

An orthodox left-arm finger spinner who by sheer determination has put together an impressive record in big cricket. Many bowlers of greater hostility have not played for Australia. In 1981 he was picked to tour England with the Australian side without having played in a single Test the previous summer in Australia, a surprise selection but one that had some excellent results.

Bright's selection for the English tour was all the more fortunate when one studied his action. He had completely lost the curve and dip of his earlier days, probably because of too many appearances in one day matches, with skilful flight and drift gone from his bowling mixture. In England, however, he drifted the ball in, and kept on the stumps, giving batsmen very little outside the off-stump and restricting possible shots to leg-side sweeps or edges. It was shrewd, tight bowling without hostility. Bright is an efficient right-hand batsman with a record of gritty innings when his side badly needed runs and a spendid gully fieldsman.

Bright, born in the Melbourne suburb of Footscray, first played for Victoria in 1972–73 when he was 18. He virtually forced his way into the State squad by taking 46 wickets at 17.00 in his first 20 matches in district cricket. He went to Sri Lanka with the Australian schoolboys team in 1972. In the winter he played Australian Rules for South Melbourne. He toured New Zealand in 1974 with Ian Chappell's Australian side, winning preference at 19 over established spinners like

First-Class Averages: Batting, 2,445 runs at 20.38; Bowling, 288 wickets at 28.82.

Tests (14): 269 runs at 14.15; 34 wickets at 33.12.

Terry Jenner and Malcolm Francke, but he did not play in a Test. Later in 1974 he quit his job as a teacher in Melbourne to gain experience playing for Ramsbottom in the Lancashire League.

He is a consistent wicket-taker for Victoria in first-class matches. He returned to New Zealand in 1976–77 for a short tour, finishing with 25 wickets at 14.64 to top the bowling averages. He made his Test debut in 1977 against England when he toured with Greg Chappell's side, taking 39 wickets at 20.61 to lead the bowling averages. He also had a useful batting average on that tour, 26.09, with a top score of 53 not out.

The following summer in Australia he joined World Series Cricket, for whom he was one of the most dedicated players,

204

training far harder than previously. In two seasons with WSC, he took 43 wickets at 29.23—second only to Lillee among Australia's wicket-takers—and scored 541 runs at 23.52. When "peace" was declared he went to Pakistan with the official Australian team in 1980 and in three Tests took 15 wickets. His career best figures are 7 for 87 in the First Test of 1980 against Pakistan at Karachi.

Despite modest returns with bat and ball during the 1981–82 Australian summer he was chosen to tour New Zealand with Greg Chappell's Australian team at the season's end. He took two wickets at 78.00 on the tour and scored 27 runs at 27.00, and did not play in a Test. At the end of the tour former Test captain Bill Lawry commented: "Bright may not be remembered for his bowling, but he may create a record or two . . . say . . . play more Tests than he will take wickets."

BRISBANE CRICKET GROUND ("The 'Gabba")

Australia's most major improved cricket venue, in the Brisbane suburb of Woolloongabba, and the scene of some of the most dramatic events in our cricket history. The 'Gabba, first dedicated as a cricket ground in 1895, was not given a Test until November-December 1931, when South Africa played Australia. It remained a stark, unattractive venue for big cricket until 1975 when a new grandstand complex was completed. The Queensland Cricketers' Club, which has rooms at the ground, and the 'Gabba Greyhound Racing Club, which conducts meetings on a grass track circling the ground, made important financial contributions to the improvements.

The 'Gabba has a deserved reputation for providing shocks, dating back to the years when uncovered pitches were exposed to tropical thunderstorms. No cricketer's education was complete without a match on a 'Gabba "sticky". When rain fell there for the 1946–47 series Test against England, and the ground was buffeted by 80 mph winds, hail and almost three inches of rain that dried out under a fierce sun in time for play on the fifth morning.

For many years the Queensland Cricket Association preferred to use the palm-fringed Exhibition Ground, a splendid arena with superior facilities to the 'Gabba, for important matches. The first inter-Colonial matches at Brisbane were at the Exhibition Ground and Brisbane's first two Test matches—Australia v. England in 1928, and Australia v. West Indies in 1930–31—were at the Exhibition Ground. But patrons of agricultural shows used their membership of the Exhibition Ground to secure free admission to the cricket, and this loss of revenue finally caused the QCA to concentrate on development of the 'Gabba.

First Big Game at The 'Gabba: In 1897 between a combined

205

team of NSW and Queensland players and A. E. Stoddart's visiting English team.

Bodyline Test at The 'Gabba: The Fourth Test of the Bodyline series was conducted in heat that had most players wearing wide-brimmed sunhats and sweat chokers around the neck. The Lancashire lefthander Eddie Paynter, confined to hospital with tonsillitis, left his bed to put on a crucial 92 for the ninth wicket with Hedley Verity, England winning the match by six wickets. A remarkable total of 93,143 spectators attended the match.

Cricket's First Tied Test: The West Indies Test at the 'Gabba in 1961 ended in a tie when the last four Australian wickets fell for seven runs. The groundsman failed to carry out Australian captain Richie Benaud's request to cut the clover grass in the outfield and apparent boundaries were saved.

Meckiff's Dismissal From Tests: Umpire Col Egar called Ian Meckiff for throwing four times in the 1963 Australia v. South Africa Test at the 'Gabba, ending Meckiff's Test career.

Ground Development: Since 1971 more than $3.5 million has been spent on developing the 'Gabba, which is controlled by a government appointed trust. The Clem Jones Stand and the Sir Gordon Chalk Building were opened in 1975, the Sir Leslie Wilson Stand and the Arthur Dibdin complex a year earlier.

Brisbane Cricket Ground, better known as "The Gabba" during an Australian v. West Indies Test.

An aerial view of The Gabba before some of the present stands were built. It is much harder now to hit the ball into adjacent streets.

A tall, willowy all-rounder who batted left-handed and had a prodigious throwing arm that made him one of Australia's notable outfieldsmen. In a throwing contest at the Melbourne Cricket Ground in 1933, Bromley moved up to the starting line and let go a throw that hit a safety barrier erected to protect spectators 130 yards away, a feat that left organisers disorganised. He had enormous palms and when he took a catch, the ball disappeared but it was his low trajectory throws that bulleted in just over the stumps that excited crowds.

Bromley, born at Fremantle, Western Australia, playing for Fremantle club in Perth, made his first-class debut for Western Australia in 1929–30. He scored a promising 78 for Western Australia against South Africa in 1931–32, and after 12 first-class innings for the State transferred to Victoria in 1932 to get more opportunities. With a big reputation, he found it easy to get lots of runs for St Kilda in Melbourne grade matches and forced his way into the State side, immediately impressing with an innings of 84 against New South Wales after Bill O'Reilly had dropped him at one at second slip. That

BROMLEY, Ernest Harvey ("Slogger"), 1912–1967

First-Class Averages: Batting, 2,055 runs at 28.54; Bowling, 39 wickets at 42.33.

Tests (2): 38 runs at 9.50.

207

knock won him a Test place in the Fourth Test against Jardine's side but shrewd bowlers quickly revealed his weakness in swishing at balls outside his off-stump.

Bromley clinched his selection in the 1934 Australian team to England with a magnificent innings of 161 against South Australia at Melbourne in 1933 and he also had an outstanding 102 v. New South Wales at Melbourne in 1934. He had a barndoor defence early in his innings and later drove and pulled with power. But he scored only 312 runs in 20 innings on the 1934 tour of England, average 16.42, with bowlers and wicket-keepers finishing ahead of him. Shield cricket turned out to be the limit of his powers, with the innings of 161 that earned him his trip to England his career highlight. His two Test appearances brought a topscore of 26. For St Kilda he scored 2,949 runs between 1932–33 and 1948–49 at around 35. He was generally considered to lack a "killer instinct" but could really cut loose when he was in the mood. His best scores for St Kilda included 168 in 1932–33, 156 n.o. in 1933–34, 184 in 1938–39. His bowling in district cricket brought 98 wickets.

BROOKS, Thomas Francis 1919–

First-Class Averages: Batting, 192 runs at 16.00; Bowling, 65 wickets at 22.50

A spirited right-arm fast bowler for New South Wales who later became a first-class umpire and was involved in many controversial incidents. He was a splendid bowler who moved the ball appreciably in the air and played in the Manly first grade side with Keith Miller, Peter Philpott, and Jimmy Burke. He made his debut for New South Wales in 1946–47 and appeared in 16 first-class matches, with 6 for 54 against South Australia in 1949–50 his best figures. He started his club career in 1939 with Waverley but switched to Manly after World War II.

Brooks, a tall, reserved man, made his debut as a first-class umpire in 1967–68 and umpired three international matches between Australia and a World XI in 1971-72. He was one of the umpires when Ray Illingworth took the England team from the field in the Test at Sydney in 1970–71 and was strongly criticised for not taking any action against John Snow in that match because of Snow's alleged intimidatory bowling. Snow was called for his offence during the tour by Lou Rowan and Max O'Connell, but Brooks let him bowl persistent bouncers in Sydney and eventually tail-ender Terry Jenner received a nasty blow on the head and was taken from the field. Rowan, the umpire at the other end, clashed with Snow and Illingworth, and after an altercation between Snow and a spectator, the Englishmen finally walked off the field.

At that point, England clearly forfeited the match, for the walk-off was a clear breach of the laws, but Rowan did the sensible thing by informing the English players they had to return or forfeit the game. Brooks went on to umpire 23 Tests. He was also due to have officiated in the abandoned Test at Melbourne in 1970–71. In 1977 he umpired in England under an exchange agreement. He retired from umpiring after the Second Test between Australia and England in 1978, admitting that his nerve had cracked in that game ("I could feel myself going"), a sad end to his Test umpiring. He quit umpiring in all first-class matches after the New South Wales v. Queensland match in January 1979, but still umpires grade matches in Sydney.

BROWN, William Alfred, 1912–

A classy right-hand opening batsman who played for Australia between 1934 and 1948 and scored more than 1,000 runs on each of his three tours of England. He was a superb player of swing bowling, watching the ball right on to the bat, body well behind it, but his batting success sprung from his great strength on the on-side. From the glance to fine leg round to the straight drive past the bowler he played all the onside strokes perfectly. Further, he had a rare skill in getting the bumped ball quickly to the ground, especially when it was directed at his body. Many thought he would have handled Bodyline better than the Australian openers in that series.

Brown, born at Toowoomba, Queensland, played for Marrickville district club in Sydney and did so well at a young age he was the baby of every team he played in. He was tall, lean, with fair curly hair and won admirers in both sexes. He made his debut for New South Wales in 1932 and by the time he was selected at the age of 21 for his first trip to England in 1934 in preference to Jack Fingleton, he had scores of 205 against Victoria and 154 v. Queensland against his name. In the field he resembled Fingleton and had the same skill in picking up and returning with fluent grace.

In 1934 in his Test debut at Trent Bridge at 21, he made 73, figuring in a partnership of 112 with McCabe, Australia winning by 238 runs. In the Third Test at Old Trafford he made 72, finishing the tour with 1,308 runs, highest score 119, average 38.47. On the 1938 tour he showed the benefit of that experience by finishing second to Bradman on the tour averages, with 1,887 runs at 57.18, highest score 265 not out. After the war he did almost as well, averaging 57.92 on the 1948 tour, top score 200, aggregate 1,448, opportunities strictly limited.

Brown achieved a special kind of notoriety when he scored a century on his first appearance at Lord's in 1934, the only batsman in the Australian team who could handle the great English left-arm bowler Hedley Verity on a rain-affected wicket tailor-made for Verity's skills. The second time Brown appeared at Lord's, in 1938, he made a double century, emulating Bardsley and Woodfull by carrying his bat through the

First-Class Averages: Batting, 13,838 runs at 51.44; Bowling 6 wickets at 18.33.

Tests (22): 1,592 runs at 46.82.

Australian innings. He saved Australia in the 1938 Test from following-on and in doing so probably saved the rubber, too. Before that memorable 206 not out at Lord's, Brown made 133 at Nottingham, and immediately after his Lord's innings he made 265 not out against Derbyshire.

Just before the war Brown, a sports store proprietor, moved from Sydney to Queensland where he played a major role in building up the cricket strength of that State. He was immediately successful, partnering G. Cook in a first wicket stand of 265 against New South Wales at Sydney in 1938–39. His captaincy of the Queensland side was like the man himself, sound, considered and lacking in flamboyance and with the talent at his disposal, highly effective. But his departure to the northern State gave him limited chances to play in front of Australian selectors and Morris and Barnes quickly moved ahead of him for the Australian openers jobs when the war ended. Barnes and Morris, it was claimed, had a faster scoring rate.

At 35, he made his third tour of England in 1948 and made eight centuries at the rate of one every third match. He was one of the finest fieldsmen in a highly talented side. He subdued the bowling almost every time he opened for Australia but only played two Tests on the 1948 tour, an indication perhaps of the difference in strength between Australia's 1938 and 1948 teams.

In his 22 Tests between 1934 and 1938, Brown, a copybook stroke player all the way, had nine scores over 50 and four centuries. He made 14 Test catches but did not bowl. His best score for New South Wales was 205 v. Victoria in 1933–34, and his best for Queensland was 215 v. Victoria at Brisbane in 1938–39. He played 189 first-class matches between 1932 and 1950 with 39 centuries.

BRUCE, William
1864–1925

First-Class Averages:
Batting, 5,731 runs at
23.97; Bowling, 143
wickets at 29.67.

Tests (14): 702 runs at
29.25, 12 wickets at
36.66.

A graceful left-handed batsman who visited England with the Australian teams of 1886 and 1893 and could score quickly when set. He was the first in a long line of magnificent left-handers to be sent to England. He also bowled left-arm slows, and was an efficient, energetic fieldsman, with reliable catching hands and surprisingly strong ambidextrous throws. He played 250 innings in all first-class matches and to all of these he brought dedication and style in years when pitches were far from well prepared.

Bruce, born at South Yarra, began his cricket with Scotch College, Melbourne, and in 1881 was granted an honorary membership of Melbourne CC as the outstanding cricketer of the year at the school. He first played for Victoria the following year. In 1884, he scored 328 not out for Melbourne against Hotham. In 1892, he made 260 for Melbourne vs St Kilda.

On the Australian team's 1886 visit to England he scored 106 against C. I. Thornton's XI at Chiswick on a tour which saw him compile 706 runs at 15.68. In 1886–87 at East Melbourne, he made 131 in a first wicket partnership of 196 with Shrewsbury for Non-smokers against Smokers. On Australia's 1893 tour of England he made 1,311 runs at 24.27, with a top score of 191 v. Oxford and Cambridge Universities' Past and Present at Portsmouth. He took 13 wickets on his first trip to England, 34 on the second.

William Bruce, the first in a long line of outstanding Australian left-handed batsmen.

In his long career for Victoria, Bruce, a wellknown solicitor, made just one century and four in all first-class games. He did quite a lot of bowling for his State. He took a keen interest in coaching other left-handers and helped Vernon Ransford a lot as a junior. He was found drowned at Melbourne, aged 61.

BRYANT, THE FAMILY   The three sons of a Western Australian timber merchant and tug–o'–war champion who made a major contribution to cricket in the west as players and administrators. Their father was a 6 ft 2 ins powerhouse of a man whose tug-o'-war team was unbeaten for 25 years. The family lived in the centre of Perth and the boys were educated at Catholic schools by brothers who encouraged their cricket development.

Richard John Bryant, born in 1904, was the eldest, and the only bowler in the family. He once clean bowled Walter Hammond with a right-arm legbreak. Dick, a solicitor, was a famous cover point, rated the best in Australia by touring English players. He scored 950 runs for WA at 20.65, topscore 103 against Victoria at Melbourne in 1933–34. He took 19 wickets for the State at 35.68.

William James Bryant, a chemist, was born in 1906, had only two innings for WA, scoring six runs at 6.00, and did not bowl. He headed the Perth first grade batting averages and aggregates in 1926–27 with an impressive 761 runs in 17 innings at 47.5, topscore 151.

Frank Joseph Bryant, born in 1909, was a publican and the most successful cricketer in the family. In the years before WA entered the Shield competition, he played 58 innings in 32 first-class matches, scoring 1,495 runs at 26.69, with three centuries. His best score was 155 for an Australia XI against Bombay in 1935–36 when he toured India in Jack Ryder's unofficial side. He made 113 not out against Victoria at Perth in 1927–28 and 115 against Victoria at Melbourne in 1933-34. In compiling his 1927–28 century, he put on 238 with W. McRae and this is still the WA record for the second wicket. After his retirement Frank Bryant became a prominent administrator. He is a Western Australian delegate to the Australian Cricket Board, and managed Australian teams to New Zealand in 1966–67, 1969–70 and 1974.

The Bryant brothers had three sisters, all still alive in their eighties in 1982. The Bryant brothers were all right-handed batsmen. They played originally for East Perth but joined Mount Lawley when that club was formed in 1924–25. All three played in the club's premiership side in 1927–28. Both Dick and Frank were State selectors and managed WA sides on tours of eastern States.

A big, happy-go-lucky Queensland left-hand batsman who occasionally bowled right-arm medium-pacers. Between 1963 and 1971 Buckle, who came from the University club of Brisbane, played 23 first-class matches for Queensland. He made two centuries, the best a hard-hitting effort for 207 against Western Australia in 1964–65 on the first Sunday cricket was permitted in Queensland. A bout of glandular fever upset his career and his batting lacked the same sparkle after he recovered. Buckle, a commerce graduate, later became a State selector, and is involved in the administration of the Greg Chappell cricket school in Brisbane.

BUCKLE, William Harvey, 1943–

First-Class Averages: Batting, 1,114 runs at 28.56.

A wicket-keeper batsman from the South Perth club who played 63 first-class matches in the 1950s. Only Rodney Marsh has improved on his performance behind the stumps for WA. Buggins, a right-hand batsman, had a topscore 60 not out. He bowled three balls for WA and holds the record for the State's best bowling average in first-class cricket, 1 for 1, figures quiz masters sometimes recall.

BUGGINS, Bruce Leonard, 1929–

First-Class Averages: Batting, 1,192 runs at 14.36. Dismissals 164 (144 catches, 20 stumpings).

A stocky left-hand batsman who scored five first-class centuries for Queensland. He bowled left-arm medium pacers but was not required at the first-class level. Bull, who in 68 first-class matches between 1956 and 1967 often opened with Sam Trimble, produced the outstanding performance of his career in 1965–66 against Victoria at Melbourne when he batted through the Queensland innings for 167 not out, his highest score. This was the match in which Peter Allen took 10 for 61—two excellent performances.

BULL, Desmond Frederick Earl, 1935–

First-Class Averages: Batting, 3,292 runs at 29.92.

Among the highest scoring of all Queensland batsmen, as befitted a player with brilliant driving power plus an ability to pull and hook strongly and glance delicately against the highest quality of bowling. Few Australians have hit the ball harder, and none has dominated proceedings as Burge did in Sheffield Shield matches in the last seasons of his career. Initially, he had a lot of prejudice to overcome because his father was a leading administrator, but as soon as you saw him drive straight back past the bowler, you realised he had won his place in Australian sides on merit.

He was born at Buranda, Queensland, and educated at Queensland Church of England Grammar School, Brisbane. He made his debut for Queensland at 20 in 1952–53 and, after a shaky debut for Australia against England in 1954–55, many

BURGE, Peter John Parnell, 1932–

First-Class Averages: Batting, 14,640 runs at 47.53; Bowling, 1 wicket at 129.

Tests (42): 2,290 runs at 38.16.

thought him fortunate to be chosen in the 1955 team to tour the West Indies, which his father managed. But he gave good value all the way scoring 177 against British Guiana. He toured England in 1956 and scored 780 runs on the tour at 35.45, with a topscore of 131 against Nottinghamshire. In 1956–57 he scored 210 for Queensland against Victoria after being dropped first ball.

By the time he went back to England in 1961 for his second tour he had become one of the most dangerous batsmen in the world, and he scored 1,376 runs at 55.04. His 181 in the Fifth Test at The Oval was the highest score of the tour and included a brilliant stand of 123 with Norman O'Neill, who made 117. But even more important an innings for Australia was his batting at Lord's in the Second test. He strode to the wicket with Australia at 4 for 19, requiring a further 52 to win, with Statham and Trueman at their best. In a gem of an innings he drove and hooked Australia to victory by five wickets.

In the summer of 1963–64 Burge made his highest first-class score, 283 against New South Wales, a superb display of ferocious driving on either side of the stumps, muscular hooks and pulls. He went back to England for his third visit in 1964, scoring 1,114 runs at 37.13, this time swinging the Headingley Test Australia's way with a magnificent 160, one of the classical centuries which included 24 fours. His daring assault on the second new ball saw him add 105 with Neil Hawke and 89 with Wally Grout. He batted for 5 hours 15 minutes.

Burge's last Test century came in 1965–66 at Melbourne

where he turned in another match-saving knock against England, adding 198 with Doug Walters on his way to 120 after Australia followed-on. This was his fourth century in 42 Tests. All his centuries were against England. For Queensland his 24 centuries remain a record for the State as does his highest score of 283. In all first-class matches Burge made 38 centuries.

Burge, an accountant in Brisbane, failed to match his skills with the bat as a cricket commentator, though he probably was paid more. In recent years he has devoted himself to his interests in trotting.

BURKE, James Wallace, 1930–1979

A stubborn, determined opening batsman in 19 successive Tests for Australia who showed such courage on the field that it was a shock to all cricket addicts when he shot himself. Jimmy was a great lover of cricket, but a perverse batsman when you bowled to him and a highly suspect bowler of off-breaks. After he batted for two days at Sydney Cricket Ground for just over 100, a spectator called, "I wish you were a statue and I was a pigeon, Burke." Jimmy enjoyed the joke with the crowd, put his head down, tugged on his bulky cap, and called for a new block from the umpire.

Burke, black-haired, lantern-jawed, bowled his decidely jerky breaks right through the midst of cricket's biggest chucking controversy without being called, picking up 53 Shield wickets and virtually destroying some Sydney first-grade sides when many experts believed he should not have been allowed to bowl at all. His bowling action was described by English critic Ian Peebles as looking like a policeman applying his truncheon to a particularly short offender's head. In the 1950s when NSW had a fine pace attack that included Tom Brooks, Alan Davidson, Pat Crawford and Alan Walker, Western Australia's openers got through a fiery opening session and Burke was given the ball. After one over the batsmen conferred. "Burkey's chucking them for sure," said one. "Shut up, for goodness sake or they'll take him off," said the other.

Jimmy Burke was born at Mosman and learned to play cricket in the Manly area and at Sydney Grammar School. He made his debut for NSW at 18, and first played for Australia a year later in 1950–51, joining an exclusive list of batsmen who have made a century in their first Test by scoring 101 not out. His most fruitful season was in 1956 in England when he headed the Australian Test and tour averages and aggregates. He made 1,339 runs on the trip, best score 194, average 47.82. For a number of years he formed a very successful opening pair with Colin McDonald.

First-Class Averages: Batting, 7,563 runs at 45.01; Bowling, 101 wickets at 29.12.

Tests (24): 1,280 runs at 34.59; 8 wickets at 28.75.

215

In a career that stretched from 1950 to 1959 Burke added two further Test centuries to that in his first Test, 161 against India at Bombay in 1956, and 189 against South Africa at Cape Town in 1957. His best Test bowling figures were 4 for 37. He made eight centuries for NSW, with a topscore of 220 in 1956–57. In 1958–59, he won a special place in the record books by taking 250 minutes to score 28 not out against the MCC, following a deathly slow Trevor Bailey knock. This was an even slower effort than "Slasher" Mackay's 31 in 264 minutes at Lord's two years earlier.

Jimmy Burke, left, going out to bat with Colin MacDonald. They formed one of Australia's most successful opening partnerships.

After he retired Burke became an ABC commentator. It saddened all followers of cricket when, because of financial pressures, he bought a rifle in a Sydney gunshop, took it home to Manly in the ferry and suicided. He was facing a major hip operation that meant the end of his beloved golf, but had this genial man hung on for just a few more months his investments in gold futures could have made him a rich man.

BURN, Edwin James Kenneth, 1862–1956

A vigorous, self-coached right-hand batsman who scored 42 centuries at various levels of cricket, two of them exceeding 350. He topped the Tasmanian Cricket Association's batting averages 11 times, but will be remembered more as the player at the centre of the worst selection blunder in Australian cricket history.

Burn, born at Richmond about 15 miles from Hobart, started playing senior cricket at 15 and scored his first century at 17, a raw, unpolished hitter. After a tour of New Zealand in 1883-84 under J. G. Davies, he loomed as a Test prospect. He made 100 against Vernon's touring English side, but disappointed in a trial in Sydney for selectors to pick the 1888 side for England.

The 1890 Australian team for England was chosen by a group of leading players from Victoria and New South Wales, who disagreed over who should be Blackham's deputy wicket-keeper. The Victorians wanted John Harry and the New South Welshmen S. Deane and the team left Sydney on the long voyage to England with the issue unresolved. When the team reached Melbourne Blackham, Australia's senior cricketer, plumped for Burn and a message was sent to Hobart inviting him to join the side. At two days notice Burn decided to accept and went to Adelaide on a ship which crossed the path of that carrying the Australian side, presenting himself on the wharf with the words, "Here I am—but I have never kept wicket in my life."

The Australians tried several team members as a substitute for Blackham but even in light-hearted shipboard games, Burn refused to put on the gloves. He had a miserable tour, playing in only six of the first 21 first-class matches, as Roger Page has recorded, and invariably being sent in late during one of the wettest English seasons.

Burn played in two Tests, scoring 41 runs in four innings, and 355 runs at 10.14 on the entire tour. He was very useful at the end of the trip, according to Page, when the hard-worked main players tired. At Lord's he snapped the bat handle while taking block. Given a new bat he was bowled first ball, final score: two bats, no runs, no contact.

On his return home at the end of that tour Burn rejected an offer from East Melbourne, preferring to remain in Tasmania

First-Class Averages: Batting, 1,750 runs at 21.34.

Tests (2): 41 runs at 10.25.

where he proceeded to build a remarkable club record. He scored seven centuries in 1895–96, and in 1899–1900 he made 1,200 runs at an average of 133. In 1896, he made 87 against the Australian team, who said the innings was second only on their entire tour to Ranjitsinhji's. In 1907–08, he made 112 against the touring MCC. He was an astute captain of Tasmania for 20 years, giving nothing away. Roger Page in his *History of Tasmanian Cricket* calculated that Burn played 365 innings over 26 years in all cricket scoring 16,142 runs at 51.20 retiring in 1909. His highest scores were 365 and 351 but in first-class cricket he was restricted to two centuries, top-score 119. He made 873 runs at 32.30 against Victoria and failed to reach double figures only four times.

The Tasmanian team that Ken Burn led against the MCC at Hobart in 1904: Standing (L to R) Umpire C. McAlley, N. Dodds, Scorer W. Eltham, D. R. Smith, P. Facy (STCA Secretary), D. G. Paton, Umpire Watt; Sitting, H. Hale, L. A. Cuff, E. A. Windsor, K. E. Burn, C. J. Eady, G. K. D. Bailey; Front, O. H. Douglas, R. J. Hawson.

A wicket-keeper for New South Wales, Victoria and in two Tests for Australia. He kept wicket in his first Test in 1886–87 but fielded while Jack Blackham kept in his second Test in 1887–88, finding a place in the Australian team because of his sound batting. He failed to deliver and scored only four runs in his two Tests.

Burton appeared for Victoria in two matches in 1888–89 and scored 26 runs at 13.00. In 1895, he toured New Zealand with a NSW team and eventually settled there. In a first-class career that lasted from 1885 until 1896, Burton often looked a potential star but he made only 300-odd runs with a best score of 38. He played for Carlton and East Sydney clubs in Sydney and for Melbourne when he went south. He died at Wanganui in New Zealand in 1929, leaving doubts about his age. Most statisticians opt for 1866 as his birth date.

BURTON, Frederick James, 1866–1929

First-Class Averages: Batting, 376 runs at 13.42; Dismissals, 29 (23 catches, 6 stumpings).

Tests (2): 4 runs at 2.00; Dismissals, 2 (1 catch, 1 stumping).

A forcing right-hand batsman, top-class slips field and lively pace bowler who played regularly for Tasmania against Victoria, visiting English teams, and New Zealand and in one match for Victoria in 1872. He was one of a notable Tasmanian cricket family, son of Charles Butler, father of the Tasmanian Bar, and brother of C. W. Butler, for a time the best batsman in Southern Tasmania. He was president of the Tasmanian Cricket Association, of which his father was vice-president, for many years. His best performances were 5 for 7 in 1879–80 for Southern Tasmania v. Northern Tasmania at Hobart, and 6 for 0 off 19 balls in the same match in 1881–82. His father Charles, a founder of the Break-o'-Day club, was a trustee of the Tasmanian Cricket Association for 38 years. E. H. Butler had several near misses when Australian teams where chosen and in 1877 visited England, playing for the Gentlemen v. Players at the Old Princes ground in London, and in a number of other matches. In a career from 1872 to 1883, Butler played eight first-class matches.

BUTLER, Edward Henry, 1851–1928

First-Class Averages: Batting, 98 runs at 7.00; Bowling, 7 wickets at 19.42.

C

**CAFFYN, William
("The Surrey Pet"),
("Terrible Billy"),
1828–1919**

First-Class Averages:
Batting, 5,885 runs at
17.99; Bowling, 577
wickets at 13.46.

A legendary English cricketer who made a major contribution to Australian cricket in our crucial early years. When he decided to stay in Australia, he was acknowledged as one of the masters of cricket. On his return to England he could not recapture his place in the Surrey XI, for his best years had been spent in Australia. Caffyn was probably the best all-rounder in the Surrey team that twice beat a full strength England side. Yet many Englishmen gloated when he could not win back his County place, such was the opposition to those who played cricket for money.

Caffyn was not highly paid in Australia. The Melbourne Cricket Club persuaded him to remain in Australia for £300-a-year at the end of his second tour of Australia with George Parr's team in 1863–64. He had toured two years previously with H. H. Stephenson's side that was sponsored by the Melbourne restaurateurs, Spiers & Pond. Later he had signed with the Warwick Club in Sydney at a yearly salary of £300. Then he went to the Albert Club, which played for a time on the Civil and Military ground that is now Sydney Cricket Ground. Caffyn, whose wife opened a hair-dressing shop in Sydney, made his debut for New South Wales in 1865. He coached Australia's first great batsman, Charles Bannerman.

Caffyn had first played for Surrey in 1849. The next year he topped the County's batting averages. He was the leading bowler in the team and, until he left for Australia, the finest batsman. He was an attractive batsman, free-scoring, impish, and a superb exponent of the cut on firm pitches. On rough pitches he was judged inferior to George Parr, Richard Daft, and the first Tom Hayward, but to no others. After he agreed to play in Australia, English writers cast doubts about his ability on rough pitches and on his roundarm bowling style. But even his critics never doubted his fielding skills, for in his period he was the outstanding exponent of catching, throwing, and reading a batsman's intentions.

Caffyn, a small, compact, active man did not coach with

long periods of oral instruction but preferred to take a session bowling or batting in the nets where his pupils could learn from his example. He was proud of the role the Surrey CC played in developing Australian cricket and that it had fallen to two Surrey players, himself and Charles Lawrence, to be the first instructors of the game in the colony. Four of Caffyn's children, three boys and a girl, were born in Australia but two of the boys died here.

Caffyn returned to England in 1872 and played several times for Surrey that year and in 1873, but it was too late for him to make a fresh start. His day was done. He had made three overseas trips with English teams, to America in 1859, and Australia in 1861–62 and 1863–64. All his best performances were before he settled to coaching in Australia. For New South Wales, he had only nine innings, all against Victoria, scoring 114 runs at 12.66, best score 38, and took 2 wickets at 38.50.

The team organised by eccentric Nottinghamshire furniture millionaire Sir Julien Cahn in the decade before World War II which included four leading Australian players. The team had its headquarters at Sir Julien's private grounds in Nottingham, where it staged midweek and weekend matches throughout the English summer, and it made frequent overseas tours. The players were drawn from all the cricket nations and had all their expenses, plus an annual retainer, paid by Sir Julien, who occasionally captained the side, batting in pneumatic pads pumped up by his chauffeur just before he went to the crease.

The Australians who played in Sir Julien's team were Vic Jackson, "Ginty" Lush, Harold Mudge and Jack Walsh, all of them outstanding in NSW teams and not far from Test selection. They were all approached and signed as amateurs for Sir

CAHN, Sir Julien's Eleven

Sir Julien Cahn's cricket team in 1938 (L to R): Back row, G. Woolf (manager), E. Watts (Surrey), B. Oldfield (Lancs), J. Hardstaff (Notts), E. Phillipson (Lancs), A. Dyson (Glamorgan), J. G. Lush (NSW), J. Walsh (NSW), E. Astill (Assist. manager); Front row, S. Dempster (NZ), H. Mudge (NSW), C. Maxwell (Notts), C. Goodway (Warwick.), Sir Julien Cahn, G. Heane (Notts, capt.), V. Jackson (NSW), P. Smith (Essex).

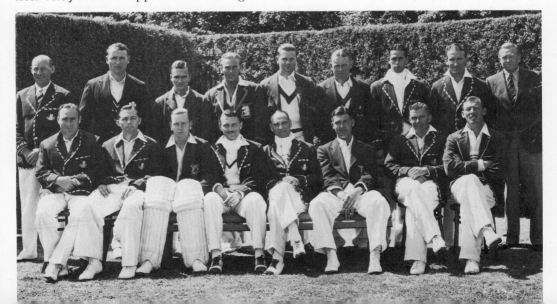

Julien's team by the former Test player Alan Fairfax, who lived in England and acted as Sir Julien's Australian agent. They joined an outstanding cricket team which between 1923 and 1941 played 565 matches and lost only 16. Their teammates included South Africans Dennis Morkel and Bob Crisp, New Zealanders Stuart Dempster, Roger Blunt and Giff Vivian and Englishmen Walter Robins, Ian Peebles and Paul Gibb, all of them Test players.

They played their home games at West Bridgford, just down the road from Trent Bridge, and on the pitch in the grounds of Sir Julien's stately home, Stanford Hall, where Sir Julien, a member of the Magic Circle, entertained them with card tricks and a trick using his magic phonograph. Stanford Hall had its own seal pond where two seals, Aqua and Ivy, went through their tricks for the cricketers.

Sir Julien Cahn's eleven toured Jamaica in 1929, Argentina in 1930, North America and Bermuda in 1933, Ceylon, Malaya and New Zealand in 1939, usually reinforced by top-class English players such as Joe Hardstaff, Buddy Oldfield and Peter Smith. Mudge and Walsh joined the team in 1937, Lush and Jackson the following year. They played in perfect conditions on wickets superior to most County grounds and wore Sir Julien's colours of black, pink and pale blue, with a pink fox's head on their breast pockets. Sir Julien's flag in the same colours fluttered from the masthead wherever they appeared, and Sir Julien always had his mascot, a wooden fox with a movable tail, speared into the ground close to the pavilion. When things went poorly, which was not very often, he would lower the tail.

In these surroundings Walsh blossomed to one of the best spin bowlers in the world, spinning his leg break more than anyone in England and bowling two varieties of wrong-uns, one he did not attempt to disguise and another that he slid from the tops of his fingers. In 1938, he took 218 wickets for Sir Julien's side, and did so well that Harold Mudge, a fine spinner who had routed the MCC side at Sydney, bowled only 50 overs in the season. Lush bloomed as a pace bowler who could take early wickets and score centuries in better than even time with the bat. Jackson and Mudge became splendid all-rounders. All four were superb in the field.

The team broke up when World War II began, Sir Julien terminating all contracts, and the players returning to their native countries. Sir Julien died in 1944, a month short of his 62nd birthday, and with his death one of the romances of cricket ended. None of the Australian members of his team became Test players, although Walsh and Jackson later had splendid careers with Leicestershire. None of them regretted not staying at home to push their Australian team claims, for they considered they had played cricket in greater luxury and better conditions than any Test team enjoys.

An all-rounder who was a first-rate right handed batsman and right-arm fast medium bowler. He played in 33 matches for New South Wales between 1888 and 1896 and in three Tests for Australia. His Australian Test career was short but included a memorable performance in the Third Test against England at Adelaide in 1894–95 when he made his highest Test score of 41 in last wicket stands of 81 in the first innings and 64 in the second innings, both with A. E. Trott. He topped it off by taking 5 for 37 in England's first innings, his best Test bowling figures. Australia won by 382 runs.

Callaway, born in the Sydney suburb of Redfern, twice toured New Zealand with New South Wales teams and eventually settled there, playing for Canterbury and New Zealand between 1900 and 1907 against English and Australian teams. He was not related to Norman Frank Callaway, born at Hay, New South Wales, in 1895, who scored 207 for New South Wales against Queensland in 1914–15, and was killed in action in France in 1917.

CALLAWAY, Sydney Thomas, 1868–1923

First-Class Averages: Batting, 1,747 runs at 16.79; Bowling, 320 wickets at 17.06.

Tests (3): 87 runs at 17.40; 6 wickets at 23.66.

A tall, powerful fast-medium right-arm bowler with a copybook action and an ability to swing the ball away from batsmen. He has never quite been able to recapture the magic of his initial first-class season in 1976–77 when he took 31 wickets in six Shield matches for Victoria. His figures that season included 8 for 42 against Queensland, 4 for 55 and 5 for 15 against South Australia, and 5 for 73 against New South Wales. He has been something of a court jester in Victorian cricket because of his pranks.

Callen, born at Yarck, a tiny hamlet 20 kilometres from Alexandra, Victoria, moved to Melbourne at the age of four. He learned to play cricket from his father whom he followed into Carlton district teams. He made his Test debut at Adelaide in 1977–78 where he bowled pluckily for 55 overs, taking over as our spearhead when Thomson could not bowl, finishing with six wickets at 31.83.

He went to the West Indies with the Australian team in 1978 but fell out of a tree while trying to get some coconuts, sustaining small fractures of the spine. "I didn't tell Bob Simpson because he's a bit serious and I don't think he would have fallen over laughing," said Callen, whose back problems caused him to give up a contract to play County cricket for Somerset. He took only 11 wickets at 50.18 runs each on the West Indies tour. But this moustachioed sometime male model has recovered enough to take his first-class total of wickets to 155. He played for Ramsbottom in the Lancashire League in 1981. He was selected for the Australian tour of Pakistan in 1982 after bowling with his old hostility in Australia in 1981–82.

CALLEN, Ian Wayne 1955–

First-Class Averages: Batting, 464 runs at 12.89; Bowling, 155 wickets at 27.42.

Tests (1) 26 runs, N.A.; 6 wickets at 31.83.

CAPTAINS, OF AUSTRALIA

Captaincy of the Australian Test cricket team remains the most prestigious job in Australian sport. British Open golf champions, Wimbledon title winners, and riders of the Melbourne Cup winners are temporarily hero-worshipped, but none of them enjoy the status of a successful Australian cricket captain. The job enjoys this special place in Australian society for good reasons—the men who have held it have had a unique blend of toughness and skill, and in building up Australia's exceptional record they helped give a young country an identity all could appreciate.

From the time Dave Gregory took over in the first of all Test matches at Melbourne and then took the first Australian touring team to England, all of the 37 men who have held the job have had a special aura. They were elected in the early days by their fellow players and in the main the administrators of Australian cricket have respected the tradition of giving the job to the cricketer most respected by his teammates. Unlike the English habit of appointing a captain—often not among the best players in England—who then helps select the English team, the Australian captains have all had to win their place in the team before they were appointed. There are no passengers among Australia's captains but England has had quite a few so-called "non-playing" captains. Nobody could imagine an English team setting off for overseas without a nominated captain but that happened several times with early Australian teams, the players preferring to elect a skipper once they were at sea.

The rugged individualism Australia's cricket captains have moulded into the team effort has made them better known than many Prime Ministers. Sir Donald Bradman is certainly more frequently discussed in Australian dining-rooms than any politician, even including Sir Robert Menzies. Probably only Billy Hughes in his heyday started the arguments sparked by the Chappells. Bradman got 17 lines more than Stalin in the last edition of Australia's *Who's Who* before World War II.

Neville Cardus wrote in the 1964 edition of *Wisden* that both England and Australia, cricket's longest-standing rivals, had produced tough men and men who were not so tough. "On the whole I fancy the Australians have put forward the tougher," Cardus wrote. "Even Richie Benaud, friendly, smiling, has proved himself fairly uncompromising and tactically ungenerous. He is, however, a shining light of magnanimity amongst the dark lanterns of Collins, Armstrong, Bardsley and Co." Australians would be historically correct in arguing that they were taught that the tough way was how to approach captaincy by W. G. Grace. If there had been any relaxation since Grace then Douglas Jardine certainly reminded Australians of the Grace philosophy.

Beneath their tough exteriors, however, there have been

many warm, generous men among Australian cricket captains. In the main they have been successful but most of them knew how slim was the margin between success and failure. Sir Donald Bradman gave a classic example in his book *Farewell to Cricket* when he recalled the Leeds Test in which Warren Bardsley was dismissed first ball, and Macartney was dropped off the fifth ball of the match. Macartney went on to score a century before lunch. "The English skipper was in trouble," wrote Sir Donald, "but had that slips catch from Macartney been held he might have been a hero."

Greg Chappell has captained Australia more often than any other player. In New Zealand in 1982 he led Australia for the 42nd time, three times more than Bob Simpson and 12 times more than his brother Ian—but who could argue that he has been a superior captain to Bradman who led Australia in 24 Tests, or Richie Benaud who did the job so well for 28 Tests? Certainly Greg Chappell occasionally shows more strain from captaincy than any of his predecessors, which probably is due to the greater number of international matches these days and the additional tension of so many one-day matches.

Neil Harvey, who won his only Test as Captain.

225

AUSTRALIA'S CAPTAINS

Season	Where played	Australian Captain	Opposing Captain	Total	W	L	D
1876–77	Australia	D. Gregory	J. Lillywhite	2	1	1	–
1878–79	Australia	D. Gregory	Lord Harris	1	1	–	–
1880	England	W. Murdoch	Lord Harris	1	–	1	–
1881–82	Australia	W. Murdoch	A. Shaw	4	2	–	2
1882	England	W. Murdoch	A. N. Hornby	1	1	–	–
1882–83	Australia	W. Murdoch	Hon. Ivo Bligh	4	2	2	–
1884	England	W. Murdoch	A. Hornby (1) / Lord Harris (2)	3	–	1	2
1884–85	Australia	W. Murdoch (1) / T. Horan (2) / H. Massie (1) / J. Blackham (1)	A. Shrewsbury	5	2	3	–
1886	England	H. Scott	A. G. Steel	3	–	3	–
1886–87	Australia	P. McDonnell	A. Shrewsbury	2	–	2	–
1887–88	Australia	P. McDonnell	W. W. Read	1	–	1	–
1888	England	P. McDonnell	W. G. Grace (2) / A. G. Steel (1)	3	1	2	–
1890	England	W. Murdoch	W. G. Grace	2	–	2	–
1891–92	Australia	J. Blackham	W. G. Grace	3	2	1	–
1893	England	J. Blackham	A. E. Stoddard (1) / W. G. Grace (2)	3	–	1	2
1894–95	Australia	J. Blackham (1) / G. Giffen (4)	A. E. Stoddart	5	2	3	–
1896	England	H. Trott	W. G. Grace	3	1	2	–
1897–98	Australia	H. Trott	A. C. MacLaren (3) / A. E. Stoddart (2)	5	4	1	–
1899	England	J. Darling	W. G. Grace (1) / A. C. MacLaren (4)	5	1	–	4
1901–02	Australia	J. Darling (3) / H. Trumble (2)	A. C. MacLaren	5	4	1	–
1902	England	J. Darling	A. C. MacLaren	5	2		1
1902–03	S. Africa	J. Darling	H. M. Taberer (1) / J. H. Anderson (1) / A. E. Halliwell (1)	3	2	–	1
1903–04	Australia	M. A. Noble	P. F. Warner	5	2	3	–
1905	England	J. Darling	Hon. F. S. Jackson	5	–	2	3
1907–08	Australia	M. A. Noble	A. O. Jones (2) / F. L. Fane (3)	5	4	1	–
1909	England	M. A. Noble	A. C. MacLaren	5	2	1	2
1910–11	Australia	C. Hill	P. W. Sherwell (S.A.)	5	4	1	–
1911–12	Australia	C. Hill	J. W. H. T. Douglas	5	1	4	–
1912	England	S. Gregory	C. B. Fry	3	–	1	2
		S. Gregory	F. Mitchell (2)* (SA) / L. J. Tancred (1)*	3	2	–	1

*South Africans in triangular tournament in England.

Season	Where played	Australian Captain	Opposing Captain	Total	W	L	D
1920–21	Australia	W. Armstrong	J. Douglas	5	5	–	–
1921	England	W. Armstrong	J. Douglas (2) / Hon. L. Tennyson (3)	5	3	–	2
1921–22	S. Africa	H. Collins	H. W. Taylor	3	1	–	2
1924–25	Australia	H. Collins	A. E. R. Gilligan	5	4	1	–
1926	England	H. Collins (3) / W. Bardsley (2)	A. W. Carr (4) / A. P. F. Chapman (1)	5	–	1	4
1928–29	Australia	J. Ryder	A. P. F. Chapman (4) / J. C. White (1)	5	1	4	–
1930	England	W. Woodfull	A. P. F. Chapman (4) / R. E. S. Wyatt (1)	5	2	1	2
1930–31	Australia	W. Woodfull	G. C. Grant (W.I.)	5	4	1	–

Year		Australian Captain	Opposing Captain				
1931–32	Australia	W. Woodfull	H. B. Cameron (S.A.)	5	5	–	–
1932–33	Australia	W. Woodfull	D. R. Jardine	5	1	4	–
1934	England	W. Woodfull	{ C. F. Walters (1) R. E. S. Wyatt (4)	5	2	1	2
1935–36	S. Africa	V. Richardson	H. F. Wade	5	4	–	1
1936–37	Australia	D. Bradman	G. O. Allen	5	3	2	–
1938	England	D. Bradman	W. R. Hammond	4	1	1	2
1946	N. Zealand	W. Brown	W. A. Hadlee	1	1	–	–
1946–47	Australia	D. Bradman	{ W. R. Hammond (4) N. W. D. Yardley (1)	5	3	–	2
1947–48	Australia	D. Bradman	L. Amarnath (India)	5	4	–	1
1948	England	D. Bradman	N. W. D. Yardley	5	4	–	1
1949–50	S. Africa	L. Hassett	A. D. Nourse	5	4	–	1
1950–51	Australia	L. Hassett	F. R. Brown	5	4	1	–
1951–52	Australia	{ L. Hassett (4) A. Morris (1)	{ J. Goddard (W.I.) (4) J. Stollmeyer (1)	5	4	1	–
1952–53	Australia	L. Hassett	J. Cheetham (S.A.)	5	2	2	1
1953	England	L. Hassett	L. Hutton	5	–	1	4
1954–55	Australia	{ I. Johnson (4) A. Morris (1)	L. Hutton	5	1	3	1
1954–55	W. Indies	I. Johnson	{ D. Atkinson (3) J. Stollmeyer (2)	5	3	–	2
1956	England	I. Johnson	P. B. H. May	5	1	2	2
1956–57	Pakistan	I. Johnson	A. H. Kardar	1	–	1	–
1956–57	India	{ I. Johnson (2) R. Lindwall (1)	P. Umrigar	3	2	–	1
1957–58	S. Africa	I. Craig	{ J. McGlew (1) C. van Ryneveld (4)	5	3	–	2
1958–59	Australia	R. Benaud	P. B. H. May	5	4	–	1
1959–60	Pakistan	R. Benaud	{ Fazal Mahmood (2) Imtiaz Ahmed (1)	3	2	–	1
1959–60	India	R. Benaud	G. S. Ramchand	5	2	1	2
1960–61	Australia	R. Benaud	F. M. Worrell	5	2	1	1*

*Australia tied with West Indies at Brisbane.

Year		Australian Captain	Opposing Captain				
1961	England	{ R. Benaud (4) N. Harvey (1)	{ M. C. Cowdrey (2) P. B. H. May (3)	5	2	1	2
1962–63	Australia	R. Benaud	E. R. Dexter	5	1	1	3
1963–64	Australia	{ R. Benaud (1) R. Simpson (4)	T. L. Goddard (S.A.)	5	1	1	3
1964	England	R. Simpson	E. R. Dexter	5	1	–	4
1964–65	India	R. Simpson	Nawab of Pataudi	3	1	1	1
1964–65	Pakistan	R. Simpson	Hanif Mohammad	1	–	–	1
1964–65	Australia	R. Simpson	Hanif Mohammad	1	–	–	1
1964–65	W. Indies	R. Simpson	G. S. Sobers	5	1	2	2
1965–66	Australia	{ B. Booth (2) R. Simpson (3)	M. J. K. Smith	5	1	1	3
1966–67	S. Africa	R. Simpson	P. van der Merwe	5	1	3	1
1967–68	Australia	{ R. Simpson (2) W. Lawry (2)	{ C. Borde (India) (1) N. of Pataudi (3)	4	4	–	–
1968	England	{ W. Lawry (4) B. Jarman (1)	{ M. C. Cowdrey (4) T. W. Graveney (1)	5	1	1	3
1968–69	Australia	W. Lawry	G. S. Sobers	5	3	1	1
1969–70	India	W. Lawry	N. of Pataudi	5	3	1	1
1969–70	S. Africa	W. Lawry	A. Bacher	4	–	4	–
1970–71	Australia	{ W. Lawry (5) I. Chappell (1)	R. Illingworth	6	–	2	4
1972	England	I Chappell	R. Illingworth	5	2	2	1
1972–73	Australia	I. Chappell	Intikhab Alam	3	3	–	–
1972–73	W. Indies	I. Chappell	Rohan Kanhai	5	2	–	3
1973–74	Australia	I. Chappell	B. E. Congdon (NZ)	3	2	–	1

Lindsay Hassett, Captain on 24 occasions.

1974	N. Zealand	I. Chappell	B. E. Congdon	3	1	1	1
1974–75	Australia	I. Chappell	J. H. Edrich (1) M. H. Denness (5)	6	4	1	1
1975	England	I. Chappell	M. H. Denness (1) A. W. Greig (3)	4	1	–	3
1975–76	Australia	G. Chappell	C. H. Lloyd	6	5	1	–
1976–77	Australia	G. Chappell	Mustaq Mohammad	3	1	1	1
1976–77	N. Zealand	G. Chappell	G. Turner	2	1	–	1
1976–77	Australia	G. Chappell	A. W. Greig	1	1	–	–
1977	England	G. Chappell	J. M. Brearley	5	–	3	2
1977–78	Australia	R. Simpson	B. S. Bedi (India)	5	3	2	–
1978	W. Indies	R. Simpson	C. H. Lloyd (2) A. Kallicharran (3)	5	1	3	1
1978–79	Australia	G. N. Yallop	J. M. Brearley	6	1	5	–
1978–79	Australia	G. N. Yallop (1) K. J. Hughes (1)	Mushtaq Mahammad	2	1	1	–
1979–80	India	K. J. Hughes	S. Gavaskar	6	–	2	4
1979–80	Australia	G. Chappell	C. H. Lloyd	3	–	2	1
1979–80	Australia	G. Chappell	J. M. Brearley	3	3	–	–
1979–80	Pakistan	G. Chappell	Javed Miandad	3	–	1	2
1980	England	G. Chappell	I. Botham	1	–	–	1
1980–81	New Zealand	G. Chappell	G. Howarth	3	2	–	1
1980–81	India	G. Chappell	S. Gavaskar	3	1	1	1
1981	England	K. J. Hughes	I. Botham (2) J. M. Brearley (4)	6	1	3	2
1981–82	Pakistan	G. Chappell	Javed Miandad	3	2	1	–
1981–82	West Indies	G. Chappell	C. H. Lloyd	3	1	1	1
1982	New Zealand	G. Chappell	G. Howarth	3	1	1	1

AUSTRALIAN CAPTAINS REVIEWED

Dave Gregory

From their debut in international cricket at Melbourne in 1877, Australia's cricket captains have all been men of widely-admired integrity whose presence commanded respect. **Dave Gregory** began the tradition of calm judgement and firm but considerate handling of a first-ever Test team whose ages were mostly under 25. He may have been a father figure as the only man in the team over 30 but he joined in the fun after the match. When the team for the Second Test was chosen, he dropped his brother Ned and brought in Murdoch and Spofforth, but insisted that Blackham continue to keep wicket.

At a time when captains wearied spectators by persevering with bowlers who delivered a series of maiden overs, big Dave changed the bowling promptly in his quest for wickets. He varied his field to cope with the peculiarities of batsmen, kept his players alert and disciplined, setting an example with some marvellous slips catching. Only once on Australia's first tour of England did he err in his appraisal of a batsman's strengths—on the day Edward Lyttelton showed why he was regarded as one of the best cutters in cricket by scoring 72, without a third man to cut off his fours. It was a fine achievement for him to take a team of 11 men, all of them unaccustomed to English conditions, through 41 matches, winning 19 of the 26 that were finished. The players deserved every penny of the £750 each they collected when they got home for they had completely shaken England's insular attitude and established the appeal of big cricket that still exists.

Billy Murdoch, who succeeded Dave Gregory, had the same commanding presence. He brought a lawyer's perspicacity to his captaincy and the experience gained in leading teams in Cootamundra, Grenfell, Yass, Temora and Junee. He had the mental agility expected of a man who had to match tactical know-how with W. G. Grace, a pleasant disposition and the essential coolness in a crisis. His high scoring despite the burdens of captaincy started a preference for batsmen as Australia's captain that only a few bowlers have been able to change.

Murdoch retired to his legal practice at Cootamundra after playing in 16 successive Tests, 14 as captain, dropping out after the first Test of the 1884–85 series after a dispute between players and officials over terms. Murdoch missed the next 13 Tests and two tours of England. He was coaxed into reappearing at 36 and such was his popularity he was given a standing ovation as he led Australia on to the field for the First Test at Lord's in 1890. He led Australia in 16 Tests altogether, winning five, losing seven and drawing four. George Giffen wrote that Murdoch's loss to Sussex's county team after the 1890 series was calamitous.

Dr Henry Scott, whose side was crippled by injuries in 1886.

When Murdoch first gave up the Australian captaincy after the Victorian Cricket Association refused a players' demand for half the gate takings from the Second Test in 1884–85, **Tom Horan**, a highly respected Irishman from County Cork was given the Australian captaincy. He was given a team that included nine new Test players and five who never played for Australia again. When England won by 10 wickets, the captaincy passed to **Hugh Hamon Massie** for one match, Massie's last Test. **Jack Blackham** led Australia in the Fourth Test in which he squared the series at two–all, but the selectors reverted to Horan for the deciding Fifth Test. England won again to clinch a series in which Australia's captain was changed for every Test.

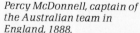

Percy McDonnell, captain of the Australian team in England, 1888.

To take the fifth Australian team overseas in 1886, the organisers, the Melbourne Cricket Club, picked **Henry James Herbert Scott**, then completing a degree in medicine. He led the side with great purpose and sportsmanship but he lacked experience and when injuries crippled his team Scott had to recruit players. Team manager Ben Wardill had to play in one match at 44 and team doctor Roly Pope played in four. Without Spofforth as his spearhead because of a dislocated finger and Bonnor as his big hitter after July, Scott was further undermined by quarrels among players and England won all three Tests.

Greek scholar **Percy Stanislaus McDonnell** took over for the next six Tests between 1886–87 in Australia and the 1888 tour of England, but could only win one of them. He was prob-

Hugh Trumble, who won both his Tests as captain.

ably too young for the job at 26 and was asked to lead a team in which there were several players with more Test experience than himself. McDonnell was the second and last Australian captain born overseas. He was born in Kensington in London. He was a strong hitter of the ball but even his superior intellect could not break Australia's losing sequence in seven successive Tests.

After Murdoch had returned in 1890 for two Tests as captain, Blackham regained the captaincy he had held for one Test seven summers earlier. Between 1891–92, when he broke Australia's losing run by winning two Tests to one against Grace's side, Blackham captained Australia for eight Tests, but he was never an ideal captain despite his vast knowledge of the game because of his nervous, excitable temperament. Injury finally forced him out of Test cricket and **George Giffen**, a letter sorter at the Adelaide GPO, took over for the last four Tests of 1894–95, after an election among the players. He managed to peg England back from two-nil up to a 3–2 Tests loss, but his leadership was not a good reference for skipper-bowlers as he bowled himself far too much. Giffen's idea of giving himself a break was to go on at the other end. Giffen's side lost the series when Yorkshireman J. T. Brown hit 50 in 30 minutes and a century in 95 minutes in the final Test in a last-day stand of 210.

Harry Trott made four visits to England with Australian teams and captained the side on the last trip in 1896, when he took over from Giffen. He made his Test century in England and was ranked one of the best leg-spinners in the world but he had to be persuaded to accept his election by the players as captain. "Blessed with a humour that nothing could ruffle," said *Wisden*, "Harry Trott was always master both of himself and his team, whatever the position of the game." England won the 1896 series 2–1, but Trott's side put the steel—and the humour—back into Tests. Back in Australia Trott's team won the 1897–98 series against England 4–1, to give him a record of 5 wins to 3 in the eight Tests in which he was captain.

Joe Darling, elected by team-mates to succeed Trott on the tour to England in 1899, held the job for 21 Tests. His teams won seven Tests, drew nine and lost five. He was revered by his players and won two successive series in England, but he could be a tough disciplinarian, especially with players who had too much to drink. In return for his players' devotion, Darling worked tirelessly for improved conditions and terms. Darling had 15 children, but finished second in the virility stakes to Dave Gregory, who had 16. Amiable **Hugh Trumble** substituted for Darling as captain in 1901–02 and won both his Tests. Darling returned to the job for the next two series and Trumble never got another chance.

Monty Noble had played in 22 Tests when he took over as captain from Joe Darling in 1903–04. Noble was something of

George Giffen, a captain who kept himself bowling too long.

Darling led 4 teams to England.

a martinet who stopped play to rebuke his players for talking to spectators and asked them to stop drinking and smoking on the night before a Test and right through it. He won the toss in 11 of his 15 Tests as captain and had a record of eight wins, five losses and two draws. **Clem Hill**, who succeeded Noble for two series, had a wife who was so keen on cricket she kept the score and at the end of the day badgered Clem about so-called scoring mistakes. Clem's teams won the 1910–11 series against South Africa 4–1 but lost the 1911–12 series against England by the same margin.

When Hill and five other outstanding players declined to tour in the famous 1912 feud with the Australian Board of Control, **Syd Gregory** became Australia's 14th captain. He had the sad task of leading an ill-disciplined scratch side that won only nine of its 37 matches on tour in England in 1912. The team's eight losses included two to counties, Surrey and Hampshire. They won two Tests against South Africa and drew one in the triangular tournament but went without a win against England, who won one and drew two.

After World War II, Australian cricket enjoyed a succession of outstanding captains. **Herbie Collins** did a fine job with the first AIF team, then played under **Warwick Armstrong**'s no nonsense brand of captaincy in 1920–21 in Australia, and on the triumphant tour of England in 1921. Armstrong was unbeaten in Tests as the leader of a brilliant array of players. The 1921 side lost only two matches, the first to McLaren's all-amateur side at Eastbourne. They had a run of 34 matches without defeat. In 10 Tests as captain, Armstrong won eight and drew two.

Syd Gregory, captain of perhaps the worst team Australia has ever sent overseas.

Collins took over as captain on the way home from England when Armstrong was unfit for the matches in South Africa. He was in charge for 11 Tests, losing only the Fourth Test at Melbourne to Arthur Gilligan's England side and the Fifth Test at The Oval in 1926, and winning five Tests and drawing four. Collins' luck in winning the toss was legendary. His place as captain was taken for two Tests while he was injured in 1926 by **Warren Bardsley**, whose two matches as captain produced draws. Bardsley was then 43.

Australia at this stage had built up an ascendancy in international cricket, stretching back to the triangular series in 1912, but that all stopped when **Jack Ryder** became captain in 1928–29. He was the victim of some strange selections and of an outstanding English team led by Percy Chapman and lost the first four Tests, England winning the series 4–1.

Bill Woodfull, one of the great captains, took over in England in 1930 when Australia was given little chance. Thanks

Jack Ryder, who captained Australia in 1928–29 against Percy Chapman's English team.

233

Arthur Morris, Australian captain in two Tests.

largely to Woodfull's captaincy and Bradman's prolific run-getting, Australia caused an upset by winning the rubber 2–1, with two Tests drawn. Woodfull's side followed with a 4–1 win over West Indies, 5–0 over South Africa, lost the Bodyline series to Jardine's team, and went to England again in 1934 to win the series 2–1, when few expected them to recover quickly from the Bodyline defeats. Woodfull won 14 of his 25 Tests as captain, lost seven and drew four. When he retired, **Vic Richardson** took Australia to South Africa, winning four Tests, with one drawn.

Don Bradman followed Richardson and in 24 Tests as captain between 1936–37 in Australia and the end of the 1948 tour of England led Australia in 24 Tests (one was washed out in 1938 at Manchester), for 15 wins, three losses and six draws. Sandwiched in between Bradman's superb displays of captaincy was **Bill Brown**'s sole Test as leader in 1946 in New Zealand, when Australia won the only Test.

Lindsay Hassett, who had received only one vote when Brown was appointed to take the side to New Zealand, succeeded Bradman as captain. Several of the great players Bradman had led in 1948 were declining when Hassett took charge but he still managed to win 14 of his 24 Tests as captain, losing only four, with six draws. Hassett had a real flair for captaincy and on several occasions made brilliant tactical moves and it was unjust that he should retire as the captain of the side that lost The Ashes in 1953 after Australia had held them for 20 years.

Ian Johnson's appointment ahead of Morris and Miller was controversial as many argued Johnson could not be certain of his place in the Australian team. In 17 Tests as captain, Johnson had a record of seven wins, five losses and five draws. His 1956 team had the worst record in England for 30 years, winning only nine of its 31 games, largely because of a policy of playing key batsmen and bowlers into form and not trying for wins in the early matches. **Arthur Morris** (two matches for two losses) and **Ray Lindwall** (one match for a draw) took over the captaincy when Johnson or Hassett were unfit for Test duty.

When Johnson and the other stars of the immediate post-war period retired, **Ian Craig** led a reconstructed team to South Africa in 1957–58. He was the youngest-ever Australian captain and had only six Tests behind him. Team-mates still called him "The Colt," but they knew he had not sought the position and Craig's tact enabled him to get through the series with three wins and two draws, content that Australia was well on the way back to former glory. But hepatitis prevented Craig continuing in the job, and the Board surprised by appointing **Richie Benaud** to succeed him when Neil Harvey was the senior player. It turned out an inspired choice and Harvey is to be admired for the wholehearted support he

234

gave Benaud in putting Australia back on top in world cricket.

Benaud's captaincy in 28 Tests saw Australia win 12, tie one, and lose only four, with 11 unfinished. Tactically, he compared with Darling, Armstrong, Collins, and Bradman among the great Australian captains, but more importantly his teams never lost a series and brought big crowds back to Tests at a time when cricket's popularity was waning. The only criticism of his captaincy was his encouragement of hugging and embracing bowlers or fieldsmen who dismissed rival batsmen.

Dour, stoical **Bob Simpson** took over from Benaud without a Test hundred to his name but he embellished his maiden Test century at Old Trafford in 1964 by carrying on to 311. Simpson's reign as captain fell into two parts. In the first between 1963–64 and 1967–68, he led Australia 29 times, and in the second when he came back from retirement in 1977 to 1978 he did the job 10 times. In 1965–66 against England, Simpson missed the first Test through a broken wrist and the third through chickenpox. **Brian Booth** replaced him for one draw and one loss.

After Simpson retired for the first time **Bill Lawry**, Melbourne pigeon fancier, captained Australia for 25 Tests with modest results: nine wins, eight losses, eight draws. Lawry was sacked part the way through a Test series, the only Test captain to suffer this ignominy. His replacement, **Ian Chappell**, had an unenviable job, for he took over an untried lot, demoralised by the thrashing 4–0 Australia had received in South Africa. He proved a superb leader and in the opinion of experts such as Alan McGilvray rates slightly ahead of Benaud and Bradman because of the record he built from nothing. Chappell was captain 30 times for 15 wins, five losses and 10 draws.

Ian Chappell lessened the strain of captaincy by handing over to his vice-captain, his brother Greg, in lesser games, although Ian played in some for match practice. This groomed **Greg Chappell** for the big job. Formal approval came from the ACB when Greg had played in 34 Tests. He was 27.

Greg Chappell had already built an impressive record as Australia's captain when he joined WSC. This gave **Graham Neil Yallop** an unexpected opportunity to take over after only nine matches' experience as captain of Victoria. England won 5–1 against Yallop's team of inexperienced cricketers. Yallop had had trouble throughout controlling Rodney Hogg, his main spearhead and had little or no idea of when to bowl legspinner Jim Higgs. Yallop's reign as captain ended in the same season it began with his record as a captain: six losses and one win from seven matches. In 1980 he asked to be relieved as captain of Victoria.

Graham Yallop, who captained Australia in 1978–79.

Yallop's deputy in those seven disastrous Tests was
Kimberley John Hughes, who took over as Australia's captain when Yallop was forced out of the last Test in 1978–79
against Pakistan because of a leg injury. Hughes had never
captained a first-class team in his career and no Western
Australian had ever before been Australian captain. Ray
Robinson called Hughes the least experienced captain in 102
years of Test cricket, but despite this he did a sound job reviving the players' enthusiasm enough for Australia to square
the two Test series against Pakistan in Australia.

236

Sportswriters appreciated Hughes' frankness; he made no excuses when Australia were outplayed in the 1979 Prudential Cup matches in England. He then took an Australian team to India on an 11-match tour that included six Tests. India won two and the rest were drawn but it was not Hughes' fault for he made 594 runs in the Tests, a record for an Australian in India.

Hughes led the 1981 Australian team to England when Greg Chappell declined to tour. Australia could easily have won the series 3–0 but England staged a remarkable recovery to save the series after sacking their star player Ian Botham as captain. Many considered Hughes, who had been loyal to establishment cricket throughout the WSC affair and endured tough tours of India and England, deserved to retain the job, but when Greg Chappell was available again he regained the captaincy in Australia in 1981–82. Despite a harrowing sequence of ducks, Chappell won the series against Pakistan and held the world's No. 1 team, the West Indies to one-all. He then took Australia to New Zealand, where Australia recovered to draw the series.

ACB had a golden chance to reward Rodney Marsh's long service by awarding him the captaincy for the 1982 tour of Pakistan when Greg Chappell again declined to tour. Marsh wrote a splendid letter to the ACB suggesting that if they did not make him captain it would be best for the future of Australian cricket to disregard him for the vice-captaincy and groom a younger player. A single vote is believed to have given the captaincy once again to Hughes, with Alan Border vice-captain. Most fans wondered how often a player like Chappell could give up the coveted Australian captaincy and get it back when he was ready to play.

MOST APPEARANCES AS TEST CAPTAINS

Player	Eng	WI	SA	NZ	IND	PAK	Total
				Opponents			
G. Chappell	10	12	—	8	3	9	42
R. Simpson	8	10	9	—	10	2	39
I. Chappell	16	5	—	6	—	3	30
R. Benaud	14	5	1	—	5	3	28
W. Woodfull	15	5	5	—	—	—	25
W. Lawry	9	5	4	—	7	—	25*
D. G. Bradman	19	—	—	—	5	—	24
L. Hassett	10	4	10	—	—	—	24
J. Darling	18	—	3	—	—	—	21
I. Johnson	9	5	—	—	2	1	17
W. Murdoch	16	—	—	—	—	—	16
M. A. Noble	15	—	—	—	—	—	15
K. J. Hughes	6	—	—	—	6	1	13
H. Collins	8	—	3	—	—	—	11
W. Armstrong	10	—	—	—	—	—	10
C. Hill	5	—	5	—	—	—	10

* Lawry was also captain in the abandoned Test at Melbourne in 1970–71.

**CARKEEK, William
("Barlow"), 1878–1937**

First-Class Averages:
Batting, 1,388 runs at
12.17; Dismissals 159
(114 caught, 45
stumped).

Tests (6): 16 runs at 5.33,
6 catches.

A blacksmith turned wicket-keeper who toured England with two Australian teams, a short, big-shouldered man with vast hands who was neat but uninspired behind the stumps as he manfully struggled to uphold the high standards of his predecessors, Blackham, Jarvis, Kelly and Carter. He was a left-handed batsman of modest ability.

Carkeek, born at Walhalla, Victoria, played for Hawksburn and Prahran, and came into the Victorian side in 1903–04 when both New South Wales and Victoria were pushing their players for national selection. He went to England as Carter's deputy on the 1909 English tour and got his big chance when Carter dropped out of the 1912 team along with Trumper, Hill, Armstrong, Ransford and Cotter in a disagreement with the

238

Board of Control. In 1911–12, he put on 141 with Armstrong for the ninth wicket against South Australia, a big improvement on his first match in 1903–04, when he was one of six batsmen dismissed for a duck in a Victorian total of only 15.

He was unlucky to encounter miserable weather on his second tour of England for the triangular series, which turned out a dismal flop. Australia won two Tests and drew one against a poor South African side, and lost one and drew two of the three Tests against England. Carkeek went with the Australian team to North America during the 1912 tour.

Carkeek was chosen in the Australian team whose tour of South Africa in 1914–15 was abandoned because of World War I.

One of the most successful all-rounders to play for Queensland, a free scoring right-hand batsman with an outstanding cover drive, severe on slow bowling but a little suspect against pace bowling of the highest class. He was a brilliant fieldsman who took a memorable slips catch in his first Test. His medium pace bowling demanded careful watching as he moved the ball in the air and off the seam with shrewd variation.

Carlson, born at Kedron, Queensland, was unfortunate that 11 distinguished seasons with Queensland led into his worst form slump in his benefit season, 1980–81. What should have been a summer of tribute to his undoubted skills turned sour when he was dropped for three home matches and announced his retirement from first-class cricket. He had sadly failed to live up to his Test potential.

Only a few weeks before the chairman of Carlson's benefit committee, Allan Pettigrew, had acclaimed Carlson's performances for his State as among the most imposing on record. "He ranks among the top three all-rounders to play for Queensland," said Pettigrew, comparing Carlson with Ken Mackay and Ron Oxenham.

Carlson had carried the "golden boy" tag in Queensland cricket from the time he played for Queensland schoolboys as a 58 inch high wicket-keeper at the age of 12. He became captain of the Australian schoolboys team and by the age of 16 was in first grade. He was chosen for the Colts, a side which plays in the Brisbane first grade competition to give promising youngsters nominated by their home clubs the chance to play regularly together. He hit his first century for Queensland against NSW at 20 in 1971–72. By then he had grown to 6 ft 1 in, a robust freckle-faced figure who seemed assured of a long career in Tests.

But he had to play through almost ten seasons of first-class

CARLSON, Philip Henry, 1951–

First-Class Averages: Batting, 4,167 runs at 28.34; Bowling, 124 wickets at 24.96.

Tests (2): 23 runs at 5.75; 2 wickets at 49.50.

Phil Carson bowling for Queensland at the MCG against Victoria.

cricket before he got his Test chance against the 1978–79 England team. He proved to be uncertain against an England attack that carried an excellent array of pace bowlers.

In January, 1979, Carlson became only the second Australian to score a century and take 10 wickets in the same match when he took 5–46 and 5–27 and scored 102 not out against New South Wales. Only other Australian to perform the feat was George Giffin in 1891–92. He must have been close to selection for at least two Australian tours of England but was overlooked. Certainly less talented players made trips overseas in our national teams during his years in first-class cricket.

240

An outstanding family of Victorian-born cricketers from Bacchus Marsh.

John Carlton (1865 or 1866–1945) began the family's impressive record when he appeared for Victoria in the 1890–91 season. He took 5 for 26 and 7 for 53 that season against Tasmania with his right-arm fast-medium deliveries. From the North Melbourne club, he took a total of 48 wickets, in 17 first-class matches at 27.58 and scored 172 runs at 7.47 between 1890 and 1896. He played one match for Queensland in 1894.

Alfred Robert Carlton (1868–1941) first played for Victoria in 1892–93. He took 16 wickets for Victoria at 22.43 with right-arm off-breaks, and scored eight runs at 4.00. He played for the Carlton club.

William Carlton (1876–1959), younger brother of J., and A. R. Carlton, played for North Melbourne and made his debut for Victoria in 1888–89 as a specialist right-hand batsman scoring 727 runs at 23.45, topscore 88 not out, and took 27 wickets at 19.7 in 19 matches between 1898 and 1913.

Thomas Andrew Carlton (1890–1973), nephew of J., and A. R., and W. Carlton, played for North Melbourne and made his debut for Victoria in 1919–20, scoring 110 runs at 18.33 and taking 15 wickets at 32.53. He played for the New Zealand team that toured Australia in the 1913–14 season, and between 1909–10 and 1921–22 appeared for Canterbury, Otago and South Island representative teams. Between 1928–29 and 1931–32, Thomas, the only left-hander in the family, played for South Australia scoring 384 runs at 12.38 and taking 77 wickets at 28.40. In 1928–29, he took 5 for 64 for South Australia against England at Adelaide. In all first-class matches he scored 1,153 runs at 15.37 and took 186 wickets at 24.48, in a career that stretched from 1909 to 1932.

A remarkable student of cricket, an exceptional coach with a flair for innovation, as well as an enterprising right-hand opening batsman. He left a lasting influence on field placements for fast bowlers, now universally known as the "Carmody field" when up to eight fieldsmen cluster in catching positions behind the stumps. His career in big cricket was severely restricted by World War II in which he rose to be a Flight-Lieutenant, and he never played in a Test.

Carmody was developed by the Mosman club in Sydney, a brilliant shotmaker not afraid to loft the ball over fieldsmen. He joined Mosman in 1930 and scored 5,724 runs for the club. He topped the first grade aggregate in 1937–38 and 1940–41, and still holds the record of 1,606 for most runs scored in the Poidevin-Gray competition. He played first grade at 16 and was never dropped from the side, playing in two premiership

CARMODY, Douglas Keith, 1919–1977

First-Class Averages: Batting, 3,496 runs at 28.89; Bowling, 3 wickets at 62.33.

Keith Carmody, Western Australia's first Sheffield Shield captain, plays the sweep shot.

teams, the first in 1935–36 under Ben Salmon, and the second in 1938–39 under Stan McCabe.

He was shot down and taken prisoner during a daylight low level raid on German E-Boats over the North Sea in 1944. His health was badly affected by his time in a prison camp, but he resumed playing after his release, first for the RAAF, then for the Australian Services team captained by Lindsay Hassett. Carmody was vice-captain. He made his debut for NSW in 1939–40, and played for his home State 13 times. He played in 65 first-class matches for NSW, Western Australia and Australian Services and captained Western Australia to their first Shield win in 1947–48. As the Western Australian State coach he initiated coaching programmes that laid the foundation for Western Australia's impressive strength in Shield cricket.

He was New South Wales coach for a time after his return from Western Australia, and until his death from cancer at 58 retained a unique ability to disturb prominent students of the game with his flair for innovation, proposals for dismissing top run-scorers, methods of countering the bouncer, and the weaknesses in some cricket coaching. He could suggest a fault in the techniques of batsmen who appeared apparently impregnable to the average grade player. Right or wrong he always advocated trying something unusual, something even great players would not expect.

CARRIGAN, Aubrey Herbert, 1917–

First-Class Averages: Batting, 2,883 runs at 35.59; Bowling, 31 wickets at 47.06.

A hard-hitting right-hand batsman who made four centuries for Queensland in compiling almost 3,000 runs in the six seasons immediately after World War II. His cut past point was hit with memorable power and he pulled and drove with force that warmed fieldsmen's hands. He was a personality cricketer with a fondness for mocking slang and he was the man who christened Ken Mackay "Slasher" after Mackay made 30 not out and 63 not out in two laborious knocks in his first Shield game. To see Carrigan and Queensland teammate Rex Rogers together chasing runs was a sight for the gods of cricket, for they were both fearsome hitters.

Carrigan, who played for Northern Suburbs and Toombul clubs in Brisbane, was one of the few men to outsmart the late Sid Barnes. When Carrigan was Queensland's captain, Barnes went to him in the 'Gabba dressing-room as NSW skipper and suggested they toss without going on to the field. Carrigan, who knew the pitch was sodden, agreed. Barnes won the toss and decided to bat and couldn't believe it when he saw the water on the pitch. "That's not wet for Brisbane," said Carrigan. Barnes had the last laugh. The pitch played placidly and Barnes made a century.

Carrigan always performed well against touring teams. He

made a century in 1945–46 against Hammond's England team after Queensland had lost 2 for 23, and in 1951–52 he flogged the renowned West Indian spin attack of Ramadhin and Valentine for 169 in a Queensland score of 455. This was the highest of his four first-class centuries. He was such a crowd-pleaser he should be considered unlucky not to have appeared in Tests, playing as he did for a losing team when his best years had been ruined by World War II. He bowled right-arm medium pacers, best result 4 for 95, and he took 21 catches.

CARROLL, Eugene Vincent ("Hughie") 1885–1965

A Victorian right-hand batsman who played 37 matches for the State in the first decade of this century and made a big reputation after he retired as a coach at the South Melbourne club. Lindsay Hassett, Ian Johnson and Keith Miller were among his proteges. He first played for Victoria in 1905–06. The following season he scored a match-winning 112 for Victoria in the Christmas match against New South Wales in Melbourne. When Victoria defeated NSW for the first time in 16 years in 1908–09, he made a bright 60. "Hughie" Carroll's brother, **Edmund Louis ("Eddie") Carroll** (1886–1959), played four matches for Victoria in 1912, scoring 135 runs at 19.28, topscore 43.

First-Class Averages: Batting, 1,706 runs at 26.24; Bowling, 5 wickets at 38.20.

CARROLL, Sydney Joseph, 1922–

A lovely stroke player who captained New South Wales to six successive Sheffield Shield competition wins and might easily have been chosen for Australia at any time in the 1950s when he scored six first-class centuries. He was one of the most appealing right-hand batsmen in Australian cricket and only the presence in the national team of some brilliant players kept him out of Tests.

Carroll, who was developed by the Gordon club in Sydney, played in the Gordon teams that won the grade premiership in 1945–46 and 1947–48. He was a consistently high scorer in district cricket and forced his way into the NSW side in 1945–46. He formed a successful opening partnership with Jimmy Burke from their first match together when they put on 149 against South Australia at Adelaide. Carroll made 92.

He was a strong driver who despatched half-volleys with immaculate timing, and could cut and pull freely. He made his initial first-class century (102) against Queensland at Sydney in 1951–52, and his highest score in first-class matches (126) at Sydney against Queensland in 1952–53. He took over as NSW captain when Keith Miller and Ronnie James retired in 1952–53 and triumphed as a skipper until he retired in 1958–59. His most impressive season was 1957–58 when he

First-Class Averages: Batting, 2,811 runs at 39.59.

scored 700 runs in 14 innings, with centuries against Western Australia and South Australia. In 25 seasons for Gordon—retiring at the end of the 1965–66 season—he scored more runs for the club than any other player, surpassing Charlie Macartney's record club aggregate, with 11,314 runs at 35.36. He scored more than 500 runs in a first grade season nine times.

CARTER, Hanson ("Sammy"), 1878–1948

First-Class Averages: Batting, 2,897 runs at 20.11; Dismissals, 271 (182 catches, 89 stumpings).

Tests (28): 873 runs at 22.97; Dismissals 65 (44 catches, 21 stumpings).

One of New South Wales and Australia's most successful wicket-keepers, the last to wear open-slatted pads in Tests, and the first to squat on his haunches as the bowler turned to run in. Carter was an undertaker, a vocation that prevented him practising regularly, and he sometimes went straight

Hanson Carter and the characteristic squat that he introduced to wicket-keeping.

from the cemetery to the cricket in a hearse. He had only one christian name but was so widely known as "Sammy" or "Sep" his name was often printed as H. S. Carter. He was a widely accepted authority on the Laws of Cricket (See Armstrong, W. W.)

Carter was born in Halifax, Yorkshire, and settled in the Sydney suburb of Waverley. He had the distinction in the 1921 Test at Headingley of being the only Yorkshireman in a Test, though he was on the Australian side. He toured England three times with Australian teams, in 1902, 1909 and 1921, and probably would have gone in 1912 had he not joined the rebels Ransford, Hill, Trumper, Armstrong and Cotter in their stand against the Australian Board of Control.

He was a useful batsman, who once took 21 off an over from Wilfred Rhodes. He could clump the ball hard over his front shoulder to the fine leg fence—his famous "shovel shot." In 1908 in the Sydney Test, he made 61 for Australia to win by two wickets after appearing beaten. Carter made two first-class centuries, both for NSW. He played first-class cricket for 27 years, retiring at 47, making a comeback at 54 to join Arthur Mailey's team in America and Canada in 1932.

Carter was a lean, short (5 ft 5 in) figure, who moved with dramatic little steps between overs as he changed ends. He refused to stand back to all but the fastest bowling, but his usual stance was taken about a metre behind the stumps. This gave him a fraction longer to sight snicked balls and provided him with some remarkable catches, but it meant that he had to "stalk" the batsmen, moving forward quickly for stumpings.

CAUSBYS, THE

Two South Australian right-hand batsmen, who made a big impact in inter-State matches in the 1960s and 1970s without winning national team selection. They were cousins.

John Phillip Causby (1942–) was a stocky (5 ft 10 in, 13 stone) opening batsman, born at Woodville, who went straight into Adelaide A Grade cricket with Woodville from Prince Alfred College. He first played for SA in 1960–61 and made 3,067 runs for the State in 63 matches at 28.98. His best innings were 137 against NSW in 1967–68 when he put on 281 with Les Favell for the first wicket and 115 against WA at Adelaide in 1968–69 when he batted down the list.

Barry Leon Causby (1948–) started his career at Gawler but spent his teenage years in Western Australia. He played for WA Colts in 1972–73, scoring 66 and 99. He made his debut for SA in 1973–74 and in 32 first-class matches has made 1,722 runs at 30.22, topscore 174 against Victoria at Adelaide in 1977–78. His best season was 1977–78, when he made 642 runs for the State at 45.85.

CENTENARY, TEST THE (1977) The most spectacular cricket match ever staged in Australia and with the tied Test in Brisbane the most famous of all Australian matches. The match was held on the Melbourne Cricket Ground, scene of the first of all Tests 100 years earlier, the brainchild of a president of the Melbourne Cricket Club, Hans Ebeling. The organisers assembled a great array of famous players in Melbourne to celebrate 100 years of Test cricket between England and Australia. By an astonishing coincidence Australia won the match played from March 12 to 17, 1977, by the same 45–run margin they had won by in 1877.

The organisation Ebeling's idea aroused was virtually flawless. Invitations went out to 244 surviving participants in the 100 years of Anglo-Australian Tests, and all except 26 who were too old or infirm to travel gathered for a reunion unsurpassed in cricket history. Australian Jack Ryder, 87, was the oldest former Test player present, and he died a month later. Percy Fender, at 84, was the oldest of the English contingent, all of whom travelled together to Melbourne in a special Qantas flight. Fender was almost blind and brought his grandson to lead him about and describe events to him. The old players, many of them grey-haired and frail and completely unrecognisable from their playing days, attended, but none enjoyed it more than Eddie Paynter, the Lancashireman who in 1932–33 left his hospital bed in Brisbane to make what turned out to be a match-winning 83. He, too, died soon afterwards.

"The cumulative effect of all these men under the same roof, lunching, dining, watching the play, reminiscing, recalling old triumphs—and failures—across 40 or 50 years produced an atmosphere of almost unbelievable nostalgia," wrote the famous English critic John Arlott. "It was an historic triumph and, on a human level, unforgettably reassuring and stimulating for some fine cricketers who had thought themselves forgotten."

The game itself matched the occasion, although after two days, with Australia batting for the second time on 3 for 104, there was doubt that it would last beyond three days. There was talk of playing an exhibition match to fill in the time before the Queen's scheduled arrival on the fifth day. But the tension that had ebbed and flowed around the ground subsided enough for the players to settle and produce a string of heroic performances that took the match into the fifth day. The final day was tense, memorable, with both sides capable of winning.

Play began with Tony Greig winning the toss and sending Australia in to bat. Australia contributed to their own down-

Above: Rodney Marsh and Rick McCosker going out to bat in the Centenary Test. Despite a broken jaw McCosker helped Marsh become the first Australian wicket-keeper to score a century in a Test against England. Bottom: Cosier ends Randall's brilliant innings of 174 with a smart catch.

THE CENTENARY TEST Played at Melbourne Cricket Ground on March 12, 13, 14, 16, 17, 1977.

AUSTRALIA

I. C. Davis	lbw b Lever	5		c Knott, b Greig	68
R. B. McCosker	b Willis	4	(10)	c Greig, b Old	25
G. J. Cosier	c Fletcher, b Lever	10	(4)	c Knott, b Lever	4
G. S. Chappell(C)	b Underwood	40	(3)	b Old	2
D. W. Hookes	c Greig, b Old	17	(6)	c Fletcher, b Underwood	56
K. D. Walters	c Greig, b Willis	4	(5)	c Knott, b Greig	66
R. W. Marsh†	c Knott, b Old	28		not out	110
G. J. Gilmour	c Greig, b Old	4		b Lever	16
K. J. O'Keeffe	c Brearley, b Underwood	0	(2)	c Willis, b Old	14
D. K. Lillee	not out	10	(9)	c Amiss, b Old	25
M. H. N. Walker	b Underwood	2		not out	8
Extras	(B 4, LB 2, NB 8)	14		(LB 10, NB 15)	25
		138		(9 wickets declared)	**419**

	O	M	R	W	O	M	R	W
Lever	12	1	36	2	21	1	95	2
Willis	8	0	33	2	22	0	91	0
Old	12	4	39	3	27.6	2	104	4
Underwood	11.6	2	16	3	12	2	38	1
Greig					14	3	66	2

ENGLAND

R. A. Woolmer	c Chappell, b Lillee	9		lbw b Walker	12
J. M. Brearley	c Hookes, b Lillee	12		lbw b Lillee	43
D. L. Underwood	c Chappell, b Walker	7	(10)	b Lillee	7
D. W. Randall	c Marsh, b Lillee	4	(3)	c Cosier, b O'Keeffe	174
D. L. Amiss	c O'Keeffe, b Walker	4	(4)	b Chappell	64
K. W. R. Fletcher	c Marsh, b Walker	4	(5)	c Marsh, b Lillee	1
A. W. Greig(C)	b Walker	18	(6)	c Cosier, b O'Keeffe	41
A. P. E. Knott†	lbw b Lillee	15	(7)	lbw b Lillee	42
C. M. Old	c Marsh, b Lillee	3	(8)	c Chappell, b Lillee	2
J. K. Lever	c Marsh, b Lillee	11	(9)	lbw b O'Keeffe	4
R. G. D. Willis	not out	1		not out	5
Extras	(B 2, LB 2, W 1, NB 2)	7		(B 8, LB 4, W 3, NB 7)	22
		95			**417**

	O	M	R	W	O	M	R	W
Lillee	13.3	2	26	6	34.4	7	139	5
Walker	15	3	54	4	22	4	83	1
O'Keeffe	1	0	4	0	33	6	108	3
Gilmour	5	3	4	0	4	0	29	0
Chappell					16	7	29	1
Walters					3	2	7	0

FALL OF WICKETS

	A	E	A	E
Wkt	1st	1st	2nd	2nd
1st	11	19	33	28
2nd	13	30	40	113
3rd	23	34	53	279
4th	45	40	132	290
5th	51	40	187	346
6th	102	61	244	369
7th	114	65	277	380
8th	117	78	353	385
9th	136	86	407	410
10th	138	95	—	417

Umpires: T. F. Brooks and M. G. O'Connell.

Australia won by 45 runs.

248

fall with some undisciplined strokes but England fielded and bowled splendidly to have Australia out for 138. Greg Chappell batted valiantly to save his side before he became Underwood's 250th Test victim, and McCosker had his jaw smashed by a ball that deflected on to his stumps. With the crowd roaring at every delivery, Lillee and Walker blitzed England for 95 on the second day, with Marsh passing Wally Grout's record of 187 Test dismissals.

The third day produced some fine batting, with Marsh only five runs away from the first century by an Australian 'keeper at stumps. Hookes, playing in his initial Test, hit Greig for five successive fours in a blazing 56, and Davis (68) and Walters (66) chimed in with splendid strokes. After Marsh had reached his century, McCosker came in to join him with his jaw bandaged for all to see, batting at No. 10. Cheered every time he made contact, McCosker made a valuable 25 in a thrilling ninth wicket stand of 54 with Marsh that enabled Greg Chappell to declare at 9 for 419, leaving England to get 463 in around 11 hours. Marsh remained unbeaten on 110. By stumps on the fourth day England had climbed to 2 for 191, thanks to Randall's 87 not out.

The fifth day brought a gradual increase in excitement. Amiss and Randall added 166 before Amiss was out, Randall having reached his maiden Test century through a mixture of audacious hooks and flowing drives. Lillee knocked Randall down with a vicious bouncer but he bounced up grinning and rubbing his head. Lillee's stamina was stretched to the limit as he bowled on. Randall was given out caught behind on 161 but sportingly Marsh recalled him. He added only 13 more. England batted defiantly on, with Knott (42) and Greig (41) pushing the score along but at 5.12 p.m. Lillee trapped Knott lbw and Australia had won by the same 45 run margin of 100 years (less two days) earlier. England's 417 was the highest fourth innings total since Tests began.

Within weeks the euphoria of Melbourne was transformed to dismay as it was realised that many of the players in that historic match had had WSC contracts in their bags when they played at Melbourne. But the Centenary Test should always remain a tribute to Hans Ebeling and the imaginative and efficient manner in which he made his concept a reality.

Three years later England staged a Centenary Test to commemorate the first Test in England against Australia. Once again surviving players were flown in from around the world, but the venue was switched to Lord's instead of The Oval, where Australia's first ever Test in England was played, simply because Lord's had bigger stands for spectators and was better equipped to handle the vast crowds expected. Nostalgia reigned again and spectators saw some spectacular hitting from Kim Hughes and Graeme Wood, but heavy rain curtailed play on the second and third days and the match fizzled out in a draw. For Australian fans at least, it always lacked the tension of Melbourne's Centenary match.

Scores: Australia 5–385 dec. (Wood 112, Laird, 24, G. Chappell 47, Hughes 117, Border 56 not out, Old 3–91) and 4–189 dec. (G. Chappell 59, Hughes 84, Old 3–47) drew with England 205 (Boycott 62, Gower 45, Pascoe 5–59, Lillee 4–43) and 3–244 (Boycott 128 not out, Gatting 51 not out, Lillee 1–53, Pascoe 1–73, Mallett 1–61.

Umpires: Bird, Constant.

CENTURIES BEFORE LUNCH

Hugh Hamon Massie was the first Australian to perform this feat. In his first innings in England against Oxford University at Christ Church Ground, Oxford in 1882, he reached 100 by lunchtime out of a total of 0–145. Massie went on to 206, making his second hundred while his team-mates added only 12 runs. The feat has been achieved an additional 31 times in first-class matches by Australians since then. Victor Trumper did it twice, Charlie Macartney three times, Arthur Morris twice, Neil Harvey twice, but Bradman tops the list with four performances of the feat. Australians are extremely proud that Trumper, Macartney and Bradman were the first to achieve the feat in Tests. In 1938 when Charlie Barnett scored 98 before lunch for England in the First Test at Nottingham the Australians fielded brilliantly to stop him stealing singles and retain Australia's record. "We were jealous of Australia's record," said Bradman. Majid Khan broke Australia's Test monopoly by scoring 108 not out for Pakistan v New Zealand at Karachi in 1976–77.

AUSTRALIANS TO SCORE A CENTURY BEFORE LUNCH
(i) ON THE FIRST DAY

H. H. Massie	Australians v. Oxford	206	Oxford	1882	
V. T. Trumper	Australia v. England	104	Manchester	1902	
V. T. Trumper	Australians v. Gloucestershire	108	Bristol	1905	
A. J. Richardson	South Australia v. MCC	280	Adelaide	1922–23	
C. G. Macartney	Australia v. England	151	Leeds	1926	
J. M. Gregory	NSW v. New Zealanders	152	Sydney	1927–28	
D. G. Bradman	Australia v. England	334	Leeds	1930	
D. G. Bradman	Australians v. Leveson-Gowers XI	132	Scarborough	1934	
A. R. Morris	Australians v. Gloucestershire	290	Bristol	1948	
C. C. McDonald	Australians v. Cambridge University	100	Fenners	1961	
R. M. Cowper	Australians v. Pearce's XI	110	Scarborough	1964	

(ii) ON OTHER DAYS

C. Hill	Australia v. South Africa	142	Johannesburg	1902–03	3rd
W. Bardsley	Australia v. South Africa	164	Lord's	1912	2nd
C. G. Macartney	NSW v. Wellington	120	Wellington	1923–24	3rd
C. G. Macartney	NSW v. Otago	120	Dunedin	1923–24	2nd
A. Punch	NSW v. Otago—same innings	176	Dunedin	1923–24	2nd
D. G. Bradman	NSW v. Queensland	452*	Sydney	1929–30	3rd
S. J. McCabe	Australia v. South Africa	189*	Johannesburg	1935–36	4th
D. Tallon	Combined XI v. NSW	152	Brisbane	1940–41	3rd

250

K. R. Miller	Dominions v. England	185	Lord's	1945	3rd
D. G. Bradman	Australians v. Lancashire	133*	Manchester	1948	2nd
A. R. Morris	NSW v. Queensland	108*	Sydney	1948–49	3rd
R. N. Harvey	Australians v. Glamorgan	180	Swansea	1953	2nd
J. W. Burke	Australians v. Somerset	125*	Taunton	1956	3rd
L. E. Favell	Australians v. Griqualand West	190	Kimberley	1957–58	3rd
R. N. Harvey	Australians v. Nottinghamshire	140	Trent Bridge	1961	2nd
R. B. Simpson	Australians v. Somerset	125	Taunton	1964	3rd
K. D. Walters	Australia v. Rest of the World XI	137	Melbourne	1971–72	5th
K. R. Stackpole	Australians v. Sussex	154*	Hove	1972	3rd
I. M. Chappell	SA v. Victoria	141*	Adelaide	1973–74	3rd
M. K. Kent	Queensland v. Pakistan	122*	Brisbane	1976–77	3rd
D. W. Hookes	SA v. Queensland	105	Adelaide	1976–77	4th
G. S. Chappell	Australia v. New Zealand	176	Christchurch	1981–82	2nd

* Not out.

Notes:
1 In many cases the exact score in the morning session cannot be ascertained, so the final score has been listed.
2 C. G. Macartney's scores against Wellington and Otago were made in consecutive innings on the tour.
3 On the second day of NSW's match against Otago in 1923–24, 649 runs were made in a day. Punch reached his century before lunch in 120 minutes, with 116, while Macartney started the day 19 not out, and 91 minutes later was out for 120. Punch and Macartney added 230 for the 2nd wicket.
4 The most runs before lunch in a Test in Australia is 98 by C. H. Lloyd, West Indies v. Australia (Perth), 1975–76. The most runs by an Australian at home is 93 by John Benaud, against Pakistan at Melbourne in 1972–73.
5 A. J. Richardson's 280 against MCC in 1922–23 included the first ever century before lunch in Australian first-class matches.

Charlie Macartney, who scored 100 before lunch three times once for Australia and twice for New South Wales.

CHADWICK, Derek, 1941–

First-Class Averages: Batting, 4,080 runs at 34.28.

A right-hand batsman who joined a select group of Australian cricketers when he scored 129 on his debut for Western Australia against Queensland at Brisbane in 1963–64. Batting in the middle of the order, he followed this with innings of 58 and 114 against Victoria. At that stage he appeared a future Test player but his batting fell away and he was dropped from the WA side midway through the 1966–67 season. Brought back in 1968–69 as an opener he proved a solid partner for big-hitting Englishman Colin Milburn. At Brisbane that season Chadwick and Milburn scored 328 for the first wicket against Queensland at Brisbane. Milburn scored 243, Chadwick 91, and their partnership remains the highest for any wicket for Western Australia.

Chadwick went to New Zealand with an Australian team in 1970, but failed to press claims for a Test place. He had scored exactly 1,000 runs in 1969–70—755 for the State at 58.1, and 245 for Scarborough in grade cricket at 34.50. He went back to Brisbane in 1970–71 to make his highest first-class score, 137. He played 69 first-class matches and took 45 catches for the State. He was a heavy scorer in club cricket and in 1973–74 headed the Perth first grade batting aggregates with 678 runs at 42.37 for Scarborough. He made nine first-class centuries and scored 50 or more 15 times.

Derek Chadwick lifts a ball high over the bowler's head to the mid-off boundary.

A left-handed batsman who scored heavily for Hawthorn and East Melbourne clubs in the decade after World War II and despite limited opportunities made valuable runs for Victoria. He scored three first-class centuries, 122 against Tasmania in 1950–51, 114 against South Australia in 1951–52 and 102 against South Australia in 1953–54. He was involved in two century partnerships with Neil Harvey, 114 against Tasmania in 1953–54 and 110 against England in 1953–54, both for the fourth wicket. In 1950–51 he put on 108 for the fourth wicket with Sam Loxton against South Australia.

CHAMBERS, John Leslie, 1930–

First-Class Averages: Batting, 1,457 runs at 33.11.

One of three brothers who have dominated Australian cricket headlines for 15 years. Technically, Greg is one of the most proficient right-handed Australian batsmen of all time, immensely strong in a wide variety of on-side shots and powerful on all the drives in front of the stumps on the off-side. Only an occasional tendency to edge deliveries just outside the off stump robs him of copybook perfection. An ex-spinner, he is also a subtle bowler of medium pace cut and swing and an outstanding fieldsman, particularly at close-in positions.

Tall, lean, bearded, he is the second son of Martin and Jeanne Chappell, born at Unley, South Australia, and educated at St Leonards Primary School, followed by secondary schooling at Prince Alfred College in Adelaide. He played for the Glenelg Club while he was still at school in 1960 and made his first-class debut for South Australia in 1966–67 against Victoria, aged 18, while his elder brother Ian was in South Africa with the Australian side. Greg made 53 and 62 not out. All the Chappell boys were coached by their family friend Lynn Fuller, and by the coach at Prince Alfred College, Chester Bennett. Their grandfather, Vic Richardson, seldom said much but undoubtedly helped by inspiration.

Greg Chappell went to England to play for Somerset in 1968 and 1969, which resulted in an overall tightening of his technique, especially against medium-pacers who cut the ball off damp pitches. He was playing for Somerset while brother Ian was scoring centuries for the 1968 Australian team in England. He went to England as a leg-spinner and returned as a medium pace swing bowler. His strokeplay blossomed and at 22 he was chosen for his initial Test for Australia in 1970, the first Test staged at Perth. It was a brave selection as Chappell had scored 6, 25 not out, 25, 5 and 11 for South Australia in the matches before that Test. He went to the crease with Australia 5 for 107 and England on top. He was out for 108 with the score at 326. He has gone on like that in Tests, repeatedly rescuing Australia with impeccable batsmanship.

On his first tour of England in 1972 Greg showed remarkable maturity for a 22-year-old, heading the Australian aver-

CHAPPELL, Gregory Stephen, 1948–

First-Class Averages: Batting, 22,786 runs at 52.75; Bowling, 282 wickets at 28.06.

Tests (76, plus 1 abandoned): 6,293 runs at 53.33; 46 wickets at 37.22.

ages with 1,260 runs in 18 innings, seven of them over 50. Of his four centuries on the tour, two were superb performances, studded with classical strokes that helped a much maligned Australian side draw the series, although England retained The Ashes. His 131 in the Second Test at Lord's was a masterly knock, with Australia 2 for 7 chasing 272 when he went to the crease. But that innings was only slightly superior to his century in the Fifth Test at The Oval when he joined brother Ian at the wicket with Australia 2 for 34. They added 201 runs in a partnership as impressive for the Chappell brothers' defiant spirit as it was for their strokeplay. The win their batting brought started a revival in Australia's big cricket fortunes that lasted for several years.

Greg returned to Australia a much improved player, bat and pad far closer together in his defensive shots, confidence high as he unwound his attacking strokes. In the first match of the 1972–73 season he hit a glorious 129 against New South Wales for South Australia. For the next match against Queensland he and Ian were joined in the South Australian team by younger brother Trevor. Greg made 77 in that match, Trevor 67. No wonder English cricket writers call them Australia's counterpart of the Grace family.

In 1972–73 Greg went to the West Indies in the side captained by his brother, an arduous, difficult tour which saw the breakdown of the two bowling heroes of Australia's previous English tour, Bob Massie and Dennis Lillee. In the face of these setbacks Greg revelled in the need for total dedication and became the first Australian to score 1,000 runs in first-class matches on a Caribbean tour. He made 1,110 at 69.37, with Ian our second best run-scorer with 862 runs at 61.57. Against all the odds, with a make-shift attack comprising Max Walker, Jeff Hammond, Terry Jenner and Kerry O'Keeffe, Australia won the series 2–0.

At Wellington in 1973–74 Greg scored 247 not out and 133 in the same Test against New Zealand in which Ian made 145 and 121, with Greg elegant and stylish, Ian rugged and ebullient, their understanding between wickets flawless. This was the tour in which streakers started to upset Greg. He has since applied the bat to the backside of several other streakers, the exhibitionists who run naked on to the field. They were initially a novelty because of their shamelessness but most cricket fans now support Greg Chappell's impatience when they interrupt the game.

The 1974–75 season in Australia saw the continuation of Greg's stylish batting and the defeat of Mike Denness' England team by Australia. With the Chappells leading the run-scoring and Lillee and Thomson taking the wickets and handing out the knocks, Australia won 4–1 before vast crowds.

On the Australian tour of England, which followed immediately afterwards, Ian Chappell's individual approach to the

The Chappell family.

game reached a climax in the match at Swansea. After the toss had been made he told the team: "Greg will be captain to-day. I want to relax and give myself a chance to go into the First Test mentally fresh." Ian then went out on to the boundary to field. Australia won a poor series 1–0 and on his return home Ian resigned the captaincy, having given his brother a golden run for the job.

As Australian captain Greg was less flamboyant than his brother, but just as subject to strain. He often looked pale and wan after he moved to Queensland, where he was made State captain, but from the start he gave Queensland great value for the big money that lured him from Adelaide. In his first match as Australian captain, he made 123 and 109 not out at Brisbane against Clive Lloyd's West Indies side, establishing a supremacy that carried Australia to a 5–1 win over what had been rated a great team, helped by the bowling of Lillee, Thomson, Walker and Gilmour.

In 1977 when news of World Series Cricket broke, Greg was ·captaining Australia in England in a series eventually won by a moderate English team led by Mike Brearley. Greg made 1,182 runs at 59.10, with five centuries, on the tour, but with 13 of the 17 players having signed contracts with Packer before the side reached England, it proved hard for them to keep their minds on their performances and they performed accordingly. For the first time since 1886 England won three Tests in England, taking back The Ashes for only the third time in England this century. Even Greg Chappell's old County, Somerset, beat the Australians—for the first time ever.

Ray Robinson disclosed in a revised edition of his book on Australian captains that Greg Chappell was the last player to join Packer's WSC. The offer came at a time when Greg was having difficulty justifying playing cricket without helping his family's security and when he found communication with Board chairman Bob Parish almost impossible. Greg was dismayed when news of the Packer signings broke in May instead of after the English tour. Greg told Robinson: "WSC was foreign to all I had known about cricket. I understand how people were shocked because that's how I felt at first. For people to whom cricket was almost a religion, we were heretics."

In the split between traditional cricket and WSC, Ian and Greg Chappell were in the forefront of all the rebels' planning. Without them, the breakaway would never have worked. Significantly, Ian resumed the Australian team captaincy, and Trevor Chappell, who earlier had moved to Western Australia, joined WSC. There followed a two year kaleidoscope of one night stands under lights, exhilarating batting and bowling and spectacular catching, as a whole new television approach to cricket emerged. Before unruly and noisy crowds, Greg and Ian Chappell and Dennis Lillee matched the charisma of Vivian Richards, Clive Lloyd and the towering West Indian pace bowlers.

Greg went to the West Indies with the Australian side his elder brother captained in 1979, when riots disrupted two of the five WSC Tests. When peace was declared Ian immediately returned the Australian captaincy to Greg after clashing with an umpire at Hobart. Greg captained Australia in 1979–80, losing 2–0 to West Indies and winning 3–0 over England, Ian playing under him in Ian's final Test. Then early in 1979 Greg took Australia to Pakistan, where he passed 5,000 runs in his Test career. Pakistan won a lifeless series on deadpan wickets 1–0. Greg made 381 runs at 76.20 in the three Tests.

Greg refused to admit his health was troubling him but often in the middle he appeared close to exhaustion. He took a spell at the end of 1979 to allow Kim Hughes to take an Australian side to India but returned for the 1980–81 season for the matches against New Zealand and India. Traditional cricket appeared to have settled down again, with praiseworthy friendliness between rebels and administrators when, in February, 1981, Greg Chappell was at the centre of an incident that caused the entire game to erupt once again. After a marvellous day's play in a one-day match at Mel-

Left: Greg Chappell plays a
carefully controlled
backfoot defensive shot to
a high rising ball.

Below: Ian Chappell plays
his famous sweep shot.

This painting from the Kim Nankivell collection in the Australian National Library, Canberra, shows the 1878 Australian team playing a match against Willsher's Gentlemen at Chilham Castle, Kent. The artist has been identified only by the initials, W. A. N.

bourne, with New Zealand needing six runs for a tie, Greg ordered his brother Trevor to bowl the last ball underarm and along the ground. A stunned New Zealand batsman blocked it.

Uproar followed. On television, Richie Benaud called the underarm delivery "the most gutless thing I have ever seen on a cricket field." In New Zealand Prime Minister Muldoon called it an act of cowardice and said it was no wonder the Australians played in yellow togs. The Australian Board of Control considered sacking Greg Chappell but finally reprimanded him and advised him of the Board's strong feelings that Australian captains should uphold the spirit of the game at all times. Greg admitted he had erred and said, "It is something I would not do again."

One State wanted the victory to Australia in the match annulled and the match replayed but as underarm bowling was still within the laws under which the match had been played the Australians retained their $35,000 first prize. Newspapers were innundated with protests over Greg's action. The *Sydney Morning Herald* suggested that instead of mullygrubbers such deliveries should be called money-grubbers. The Board of Control promptly took the right to bowl underarm out of the laws for one-day matches. Nothing like the Chappells' underhand delivery had mixed politics and sport since the Bodyline crisis.

Most Australians were so embroiled in the controversy they hardly noticed that Australia beat New Zealand in the next two games and then polished off a disappointing India, who capped an easily forgotten season when their captain Sunny Gavaskar initially ordered his batting partner to walk off the field in protest after Gavaskar had been given out lbw.

At the end of the 1980–81 Australian season Greg Chappell declared himself unavailable for the 1981 tour of England and Kim Hughes took over as Australian captain. There was keen debate over whether Hughes should continue in the job but the selectors gave Chappell back the captaincy for the 1981–82 season. Greg opened with a marvellous double century in Brisbane, but then had one of the most astounding sequences of ducks ever suffered by a first-class batsman. In Tests and one-day matches he was out for a duck seven times in the season. He led Australia against Pakistan, the West Indies and in New Zealand, where his sportsmanship overcame heckling by crowds keen to remind him of the underarm incident. At the end of the New Zealand tour only Bradman was ahead of him in runs scored for Australia. At that point Greg Chappell had scored 68 first-class centuries, 20 of them in Tests. He was also within striking distance of Bob Simpson's Test catching record (110), with 106 Test catches to his credit. He prefers to captain the Australian team from the slips but is also a brilliant outfielder.

CHAPPELL, Ian Michael ("Chappelli") 1943–

First-Class Averages: Batting, 19,680 at 48.35; Bowling, 176 wickets at 37.57.

Tests (75 plus 1 abandoned): 5,345 runs at 42.42; 20 wickets at 65.80.

A gritty right-hand batsman, outstanding slips fieldsman, occasional leg-spinner, and a great captain. No player has had more influence on Australian cricket over the past 20 years but it is doubtful if he has used his unique position in the best interests of himself or of the game. He has been an exciting player to watch in all he did but one cannot discard his long, consistent history of unfortunate behaviour which suggests that his judgement often was astray.

One of Chappell's greatest admirers, Alan McGilvray, who rates Chappell's captaincy ahead of that of Bradman or Benaud, strongly regrets much of Chappell's behaviour. "Many of the things Ian has done were completely unnecessary," McGilvray said.

Chappell was the figurehead in the top Australian players' bid to get more money from the receipts of major matches that led to the WSC breakaway. It also led to English critics like Robin Marlar labelling Ian Chappell "a barbarian." Indeed it is amusing to read the attempts of English writers such as Marlar, Swanton and Woodcock to assess Chappell's makeup. They had never encountered anybody like him; he was outside their terms of reference.

Ian is the tough, chunky, heavily moustached, eldest son of a remarkable cricket family. His father, Martin, was a seasoned grade cricketer in Adelaide who married Vic Richardson's daughter, Jeanne, and brought up his family in north Glenelg. The three Chappell boys learned their cricket on a backyard pitch laid down by their dad, who often pelted the ball hard at them as they batted. This helped improve their approach to pace bowling as they had to either play shots or be hit.

"To me a fast bowler is like an animal," Chappell said in an interview. "If he smells fear he will be after you twice as hard. People make a fuss about batsmen being intimidated by fast bowlers. It's a load of rubbish. That's been going on since the game was first played."

Ian went to the Prince Alfred College, Adelaide, like his brothers, but received very little coaching from his famous grandfather. Martin Chappell introduced his sons to cricket and baseball and then left them to it. A friend, Lynn Fuller, took over Ian's coaching when Ian was five. Every Sunday for 11 years Ian went to Fuller's backyard pitch for three hours' coaching, with the emphasis on defensive strokes.

At Prince Alfred College, the headmaster was former New Zealand Test cricketer John Dunning. The sportsmaster was ex-South Australian captain Chester Bennett. Between them they kept the Chappell boys busy on the cricket and baseball field. Years later Ian escorted Bennett around Lord's and introduced him to the Australian players as the master who had taught him English. "So you're the bloke that taught him those terrible words," said Dennis Lillee.

Ian left school at 17 to work as a share clerk with a stock-broker and at 19 played in the Lancashire League. He was a sales representative for a chocolate firm in Adelaide and then a tobacco company. At 18, he made his debut for South Australia in 1961–62, replacing Garfield Sobers who had to fly home to the West Indies to play in a Test series. His skills as a leg-spinner helped win him his place in the side. He was always a brilliant slips field. He scored his maiden first-class century, 149, against New South Wales at Adelaide in 1962.

From the start of his career, Ian was a compulsive hooker, a shot that brought him a lot of runs but also frequently caused his dismissal. When he broke into the Australian team in 1964–65, Bob Simpson suggested he drop the shot and he did for a time until Bradman recommended that he play it, reasoning that it was not the shot that was at fault but the placement and execution of it. Chappell became known for his pugnacious driving on both sides of the wicket, for his precise cutting and glancing and for powerful pull shots, but the hook was always his most characteristic stroke for it stressed that he was a fighter, a bonny man for a crisis.

After one Test against Hanif Mohammad's Pakistani side in

Ian Chappell goes down on one knee to sweep a ball past England wicket-keeper David Bairstow.

*Ian Chappell removed a
stump and placed it wide on
the offside where he alleged
New South Wales bowlers
were pitching most deliveries.
The umpire ordered him to
restore it to its original place.*

1964–65, he seemed a strong chance for selection in the Australian team to tour the West Indies at the end of the season, but he missed selection. Noted critic Phil Wilkins believes that was a blessing in disguise, for the Australians took a fearful hammering from the pace barrage of Wes Hall and Charlie Griffiths, losing a rugged series 2–1.

Bil Lawry took over the Australian captaincy from Simpson in 1967–68, and Chappell became the heir apparent. On his first tour of England in 1968 Ian topped the Australian averages with 1,261 runs at 48.50, topscore 202 not out against Warwickshire at Edgbaston. He was the success of the tour, Australia retaining The Ashes by drawing the series 1–1, with three Tests drawn. When Brian Taber replaced Jarman behind

260

the stumps in the following series at home against the West Indies, Chappell replaced Jarman as vice-captain.

He made five centuries that summer against the West Indies, including 117 in the First Test and 165 in the Second Test in a brilliant display of consistent, attractive batsmanship, and followed with 138 and 99 in successive Tests for Australia in India. Lawry was unwise enough to call Chappell the best batsman in the world on all types of pitches when the Australians reached South Africa. For the only time in his career, Ian faltered, but throughout a poor tour was never allowed to forget Lawry's words, with Australia taking her worst thrashing in postwar cricket.

Despite his personal disappointments in South Africa and the collapse of the Australian side's morale under Lawry, Chappell has remained loyal to Lawry. Even when he replaced Lawry as Australian captain after four Tests against Illingsworth's England side, he called the manner of Lawry's dismissal shameful. Chappell lost a dramatic match at Sydney and with it The Ashes in his first Test as captain, a result that may have been reversed had he had Lawry's skill with the bat to counter the pace of John Snow. But with his appointment a new spirit and dedication began to transform the Australian team.

Starting from defeat, he built an Australian side over the next few years that bordered on greatness and gave spectators tremendous pleasure wherever they played. Unfortunately, the revival was accompanied by a loss of decorum on and off the field by cheroot-smoking Chappell and many of his players. Sloppy dressing at social functions became customary, "sledging" reappeared, and there was frequent public use of the colourful Chappell vocabulary.

Ian Chappell was a problem for the Board of Control from the time he took over the Australian captaincy. He refused to conform, ran the team his own way, but he inspired devotion from his players no other cricketer has received. After he pleaded guilty and was fined for an "unlawful assault" on an official on the riot-disrupted tour of West Indies in 1979 the WSC team united behind him and played very well to level the series in the last Test. Ian played 75 Tests for Australia, 72 before he defected to WSC and three under his brother Greg's captaincy after peace was declared in 1979–80. All the honours open to Australian cricketers have gone to him except the respect of those who revere the game for the standards it sets in good behaviour.

In his last first-class season in 1979–80 he was unable to curb his misbehaviour. He was suspended after abusing an umpire in Hobart and again for the same offence in Adelaide. In Sydney in the South Australia-New South Wales match, friends like Lennie Pascoe objected to the rudeness of his "sledging," which included references to Pascoe's ancestry.

Many old internationals were relieved when he retired finally in 1980, a sad end to a brilliant career. In 1980–81, he formed part of Kerry Packer's TV commentary team, and in 1981 he was given his own sports show. To his credit he offers balanced, objective commentaries on TV and in his newspaper articles. Indeed some of his newspaper work rates as the best by a former player since Bradman produced his famous Test commentaries for the London *Daily Mail*, well-considered, thought-provoking pieces that are good for cricket.

His suspension from his job as a Channel 9 television commentator in 1981 disappointed all who thought he had reached maturity following the collapse of his marriage. For a man who takes infinite pains with his hairdo, he can be extremely careless with his tongue. He may not have known he was on air but it will be intriguing to see if he can fulfil his promise not to swear at all inside the studio doors.

Between 1961 and 1980 he scored 59 first-class centuries, 14 of them in Tests. He captained Australia 30 times for 15 wins, 10 draws and five losses. He captained SA from 1970–71 to 1975–76 and again in 1979–80 winning the Shield in 1970–71 and in 1975–76.

CHAPPELL, Trevor Martin, 1952–

First-Class Averages: Batting, 3,201 runs at 31.38; Bowling, 25 wickets at 24.00.

Tests (3): 79 runs at 15.80.

Youngest of the three brothers who created an Australian record by all playing for Australia, a right-handed batsman, medium-pace bowler and superb cover fieldsman who has appeared for three Australian States. He is quieter of manner and better behaved than his brothers but in an extended trial has not shown their rich flair for the game—he is a very useful player in any team and deserved Test selection on the 1981 Australian team of England which gave the three Chappells a record that may never be broken.

Trevor was brought up with his brothers in North Glenelg, Adelaide, and went to the same school, Prince Alfred College, where cricket coach Chester Bennett rated him superior to his brothers at the same age. Like his brothers he owes a lot to his father Martin's instincts for cricket. Martin played district cricket for Sturt and married the captain of the first grade side's daughter, Jeanne Richardson. Martin was a leading catcher in South Australian baseball and second baseman in the State's Claxton Shield team. Trevor and his brothers all have the same reliable baseballer's throwing arms and fielding skill. Martin scored more runs than any player in the Adelaide district competition in 1950–51 with 513 runs at 42.75, but failed to win State selection as a cricketer.

After a brilliant start in schoolboy cricket Trevor has had a long struggle to emerge from his brothers' shadows. He failed by only 25 runs to score 1,000 runs for Prince Alfred College in the 1969–70 season when he made 227 in the annual match against St Peter's College. At 18, he toured the West Indies with the Australian schoolboys' team. When he first played for South Australia in 1972–73 against Queensland, Ian and Greg were already famous. Trevor made a praiseworthy 67 but the going was tough. Between 1972–73 and 1975–76, Trevor played in 17 first-class matches for South Australia, scoring 603 runs at 20.10, highest score 70 against Western Australia. He played for Walsden in the Central Lancashire League in 1975 and for East Lancashire in the Lancashire League in 1976 and 1977. He also appeared for Lancashire County Second XI in 1975. Overseas experience developed his bowling and improved his defence as a batsman.

He switched to Western Australia and made his debut for that State against his old team, South Australia, in 1976–77 at Perth. In four innings for Western Australia he made 160 runs at 40.00, highest score 57. He was one of the 28 Australian players who joined World Series Cricket and in four appearances in WSC internationals made 127 runs at 15.87.

Trevor Chappell hooks Hohns to the boundary for New South Wales against Queensland at the Gabba.

On the instructions of his brother Greg, Trevor Chappell bowls the last ball of the one-day match against New Zealand.

In 1979–80 he made his debut for New South Wales against Western Australia and in that match played the finest innings of his career, scoring 150 in the second innings as NSW brought off a thrilling win by scoring in better than even time for much of the last day. Since then he has confirmed his value in the NSW side, contributing useful runs and wickets and saving countless runs with his brilliant fielding. He is a particularly valuable one-day player, pressuring batsmen with his superb gathering and throwing and making scoring difficult with a good length mixture of medium pace swingers.

His inclusion in the 1981 Australian team for England was criticised as it was thought he had been included mainly for limited over matches but by the time the First Test was played at Nottingham he forced his way into the side with his all-round skills. He capped a strong debut by hitting the winning runs in a well disciplined knock of 20 that guided Australia to a four-wicket win. A lift in the batting order to No. 3 for NSW has undoubtedly improved his batting. Trevor was 28 when he made his Test debut, Ian 21, and Greg 22. Martin and Jeanne Chappell were in the crowd at Nottingham to watch Trevor's debut. Technically, the Chappell brothers had already beaten the record when Trevor was chosen as Australia's 12th-man at Christmas, 1980, but they are not the kind of family to count a record like that until all three actually played in a Test. Before Trevor became the third Chappell to play Test cricket ten sets of brothers had played for Australia.

In the period of insecurity that preceded his Test selection

264

Trevor clearly felt the strain of being the last of a famous family. "I'd rather be Bill Smith, or just an ordinary bloke," he said once when he was making his way up. Nothing he has done in big cricket has quite matched that superb century for NSW on his debut when he did not play a false stroke until he was out, but he can be proud of his first-class centuries, a sprinkling of wickets and some splendidly executed run-outs.

CHARLESWORTH, Richard Ian ("Ric"), 1952–

A pugnacious left-handed batsman whose versatility has prevented him concentrating fully on his cricket. He is also Australia's hockey captain, and his commitments to the build-up towards an Olympic hockey gold medal has been total. He is an outstanding fieldsman with 35 first-class catches to his name as well as an impressive record of consistency with the bat which has brought 16 scores over 50 with the bat and one century in ten years of first-class cricket.

Charlesworth, son of **Lester Charlesworth**, a Western Australian representative (494 runs at 32.53 from 1949 to 1951), plays for West Perth. He went from club cricket into the WA Colts side in 1972–73 and captained the Colts in 1974–75 when he made 106 against Victorian Colts. He made his debut for the WA senior team in 1972–73, but scored ducks in his first three first-class matches and did not play in 1974–75. Since then he has been used both as an opener and in the middle order. His best season was 1977–78 when he scored 702 runs at 41.29.

He was absent throughout the 1981–82 first-class cricket season on hockey tours, but right at the end of the season played some impressive innings in district cricket, and moves began to get him to return to State cricket in 1982–83. Ric headed the Perth first grade averages two seasons in a row for West Perth, in 1975–76 (59.50) and 1976–77 (78.85), emulating a feat his father had performed for that club in 1952–53 when Lester averaged 56.20.

First-Class Averages: Batting, 2,327 runs at 30.22.

CHARLTON, Dr Percy Chater, 1867–1954

First-Class Averages: Batting, 648 runs at 12.46; Bowling, 97 wickets at 19.96.

Tests (2): 29 runs at 7.25, 3 wickets at 8.00.

A fine all-rounder for New South Wales and Australia who gave outstanding service to club administration in Sydney. He was a useful medium-pace bowler, smart fieldsman and splendid right-hand batsman. He was a member of the 1890 Australian team in England and played two Tests on the trip. Frank Iredale rated him with Trumble and Jack Gregory as a slips field. He took 38 catches in 40 first-class matches.

He played his early cricket for Ivanhoe and Belvidere clubs in Sydney and at 21 he distinguished himself by taking 7 for 61 for Eighteen Sydney Juniors against the visiting England team. He played for New South Wales in inter-colonial matches for a few years and then in one Shield match when the competition began in 1892–93. In England, under Murdoch's captaincy, he scored 534 runs at an average of 14.83, topscore 75 not out against Leicestershire, and took 42 wickets at 19.04 apiece.

Ill-health and his work as a doctor interferred with his appearances in big matches but he played regularly for I Zingari until he left for England in 1903–04 and when he returned in 1909–10. He was a delegate to the NSWCA from 1892 to 1904, representing the Belvidere club, I Zingari and North Sydney. He was made a Life Member of the NSWCA in 1927. He remained vice-president of I Zingari for 23 years until his election as president in 1928, and continued as president until elected Patron in 1947. On his death I Zingari elected him Patron in Perpetuity so that his 57 year association with I Zingari could continue. The club said of him, "He touched nothing he did not adorn."

Albert Cheetham an outstanding allrounder who opened the batting for NSW just before World War II.

266

An outstanding all-rounder for the Balmain club in Sydney, in 24 matches for New South Wales and in the Services XI matches that helped revive big cricket after World War II. He was a tall, punishing right-hand opening batsman who dropped down the order for the Services and a fast-medium bowler of fine control and nip from the pitch.

Cheetham, born in the Sydney suburb of Ryde, came to notice in 1931–32 with an innings of 105, brimful of brilliant strokes for Balmain's Poidevin-Gray side against Northern Districts when he was 16. Two years later he scored 139 for Balmain first grade against Manly. He was in the NSW Second XI in 1935–36 and made his debut for the State in 1936–37. In 1937–38 he opened for NSW in three Shield games and against the visiting New Zealand side. In 1938–39, he scored three centuries and took a hat-trick for Balmain. He appeared to be progressing towards Test status in the 1939–40 season when he scored 332 runs for NSW and took 13 wickets but World War II upset his career.

After service in the AIF, he played in three of the Victory Tests for the Australian Services side captained by Lindsay Hassett. He finally settled in Melbourne, leaving those who saw his thrilling stroke play as a teenager to sigh over what might have been. His highest first-class cricket score was 85.

CHEETHAM, Albert George, 1915–

First-Class Averages: Batting, 899 runs at 20.90; Bowling, 42 wickets at 36.11.

One of the outstanding frontiersmen of Australian cricket who for 40 years took star-studded teams into the bush and helped develop country cricket to a stage where it supplies a surprising number of international players. Chegwyn was robbed of regular Shield selection by World War II. After playing for New South Wales Seconds in 1939–40 he played five matches for NSW in the next two years. In 1941–42 he set records for the highest first grade aggregate (939 runs), and the highest individual score (201 not out) for the Randwick club. In all, he made 11,943 runs in his career with Randwick, including 11 centuries.

But it was his work in organising teams of outstanding players, sprinkled with promising youngsters, on country trips that was so valuable to Australian cricket.

Such was his love of the game that in the years before television, he presented our heroes to people who otherwise would never have seen them in dozens of country centres. He started with a visit to Canberra in 1939, with a team that included McCabe and O'Reilly and kept going bush until he was 78. He has a long list of Test players whom he first spotted and recommended to his fellow State selectors, Doug Walters and Steve Rixon among them. As a talent spotter, he had few peers. In his 24 years as a New South Wales selector, New South Wales won the Shield nine times.

CHEGWYN, John William ("Cheggy") 1909–

First-Class Averages: Batting, 375 runs at 46.87.

CHILVERS, Hugh Cecil, 1902–

First-Class Averages: Batting, 548 runs at 16.11; Bowling, 151 wickets at 26.39.

An outstanding slow leg-break bowler for New South Wales whose skills were cruelly overlooked by Australian team selectors. Between 1929 and 1937 he played 34 first-class matches, 32 for New South Wales and in a decade of brilliant Australian batsmanship he repeatedly fooled the best in the land. Bill O'Reilly rated him the best spin bowler never to play for Australia.

Chilvers, born at Sawbridgeworth, England, came to Australia at an early age. He graduated from Pennant Hills club near Sydney to Northern Districts firsts and won State selection in 1929–30. He had a curious bouncing gait that never failed to amuse spectators but such was the whip from the pitch of his leg-breaks and his sustained accuracy he was no joke for batsmen. He took a long time to become a regular member of the New South Wales team despite many fine performances on unresponsive pitches.

In 1929–30 he had a fine double against South Australia with 4 for 57 and 4 for 38. The next season he took 5 for 68 and 2 for 81 against South Australia and in two matches against West Indies for New South Wales took 15 wickets, 4 for 84, 5 for 73, 3 for 56 and 3 for 53. In 1932–33 against England at Sydney he took 5 for 73 and 3 for 29. He was an excellent fieldsman of happy disposition and a useful batsman. He strongly challenged for a position in the 1934 and 1938 Australian teams that visited England. In 1935, when the Australian Board found itself unable to accept India's request to send a team, Frank Tarrant organised an unofficial team to play in India while Australia's Test side toured South Africa. Chilvers was among the players Tarrant invited, but the Board refused to allow Chilvers to tour India on the grounds that he might be wanted by his State. Famous cricket writer Ray Robinson commented, "The sight of Chilvers continuing to play for the Northern Districts club until he was 56 should have been an annual reproach to officials who denied this honest toiler his only chance for a trip abroad. In my opinion officialdom has shown no poorer spirit in the past 20 years." After World War II Chilvers remained a formidable proposition for rising young batsmen in Sydney grade cricket. He reverted to the Pennant Hills team in the Shire's competition in his veteran years, by which time he was said to have two types of wrong-un mixed with his leg-breaks.

CHIPPERFIELD, Arthur Gordon ("Chipper"), 1905–

A dashing but inconsistent right-hand batsman chosen for an Australian tour of England after only three first-class innings, partly because he was regarded as without peer as a slips fieldsman. He bowled useful right-arm slows, and took valuable wickets on the few occasions O'Reilly or Grimmett were rested in big matches.

268

Chipperfield was born in the Sydney suburb of Ashfield but was mistakenly hailed as a country player because he played and coached a lot in Newcastle in his early years. When he joined Sydney's Western Suburbs club in 1926–27, the club captain, Warren Bardsley, described him as superior to Jack Gregory in the slips. He batted with sporadic brilliance, hitting the ball powerfully in front of the wicket, using his feet admirably.

In 1932, when England played Newcastle in the midst of the Bodyline tour, Chipperfield made 152 against an attack of the highest quality. But he did not make the New South Wales team until the 1933–34 season. His three innings for New South Wales had produced 105 runs when he was chosen for the 1934 tour of England. He only made nine in the key match against Victoria but bowled smartly against Woodfull for several overs and also took three superb slips catches, his all-round ability apparently earning him the tour spot.

In his first Test in England, he frequently lofted the ball at Trent Bridge, and reached 99 at lunch on the second day. He was out to Farnes' third ball after the interval, caught behind, and he remains the only Australian to score 99 in his Test debut. He followed with 37 not out on a turning wicket at Lord's in the Second Test, in which he had a spell of 34 overs for 3 for 91, and justified his tour selection by scoring 899 runs on the trip at 40.86, top score 175 v. Essex.

In his first Test against South Africa at Durban in 1936, he scored 109, his highest Test score and lone century, earning the right to plant a tree at the ground. The following season in Sydney he had 8 for 66 for an Australian XI against England. He went to England a second time in 1938, but was hampered by appendicitis, scoring 424 runs at 28.26, topscore 104 not out. One of his best efforts was at Brisbane in 1936–37 when Australia were caught on a "sticky" and were all out for 58. "Chipper" made 26 of them unconquered.

Between 1933 and 1940 he scored nine first-class centuries top score 175. After his retirement he became an ardent amateur fisherman. For connoisseurs, Chipperfield moving to a slips catch was one of the wonders of cricket—and he took them without falling down, somersaulting or even hugging a team-mate.

First-Class Averages: Batting, 4,295 runs at 38.34; Bowling, 65 wickets at 39.72.

Tests (14): 552 runs at 32.47; 5 wickets at 87.40.

CHRISTIAN, Arthur Hugh, 1877–1950

A successful left-hand all-rounder for Victoria and Western Australia in the early years of this century. He was a prolific performer in club cricket, batting in the middle of the order and bowling slow-medium spinners. He graduated from the strong East Melbourne XI to the Victoria team in 1903–04 and had proved his value when he went to live in WA. He took 5 for 24 for Victoria against Queensland in Melbourne, forming

First-Class Averages: Batting, 960 runs at 22.85; 102 wickets at 24.43.

269

a hostile all left-handed attack with Saunders. He made his debut for WA in 1906–07 and in the 1908–09 season figured in a sensational incident when he withdrew as WA captain after the first of three scheduled matches against SA.

Christian complained over what he considered was unfair criticism and declined to lead the WA side after the first match was drawn. He took 25 of the 46 wickets that fell to WA in the three matches, including 11 for 200 at Fremantle and 11 for 123 at Perth. In all he took five wickets or more six times in an innings in first-class matches. With the bat his highest score was 98. He was good enough to take 6 for 40 for WA against NSW at Sydney in 1912 when NSW was out for 95, of which Trumper made 51. Christian then scored 30 out of WA's first innings score of 102 and 55 out of 83 in the second innings of the drawn match.

CHRISTY, James Alexander Joseph, 1904–1971

A right-handed South African Test batsman who, after an impressive tour of Australia in 1931–32, played the 1934–35 season with Queensland. He made three centuries for South Africa in Australia, including a thriller in the tour match against Western Australia, at Perth, but in 25 innings for Queensland failed to reach three figures. He played with the Colts club in Brisbane and did valuable coaching. His 13 matches for Queensland yielded 596 runs at 29.80, topscore 80 and five wickets at 44.60. In a first-class career that produced 11 centuries and covered 10 Tests he scored a total of 3,670 runs at 37.07, topscore 175. One of his best innings was his 119, when he added 181 for the first wicket for South Africa against Victoria at Melbourne in 1931–32.

CLARK, Wayne Maxwell, 1953–

First-Class Averages: Batting, 530 runs at 12.33; Bowling, 158 wickets at 29.06.

Tests (10): 98 runs at 5.76; 44 wickets at 28.75.

A big-framed right-arm fast-medium bowler of swing and cut from Western Australia, who, with an action similar to that of Graham McKenzie, handled long spells for Australia with admirable stamina. He was introduced into the Australian side in 1977–78 following the creation of the WSC sides.

Clark, born in Perth, first played for Bassendean-Bayswater and then for West Perth. He had his first match for Western Australia in 1974–75 and made his debut in Tests three years later. A feature of his bowling was a vicious bouncer. When doubts arose about the legality of this delivery he lost his Test place to Rodney Hogg, whose remarkable success restricted Clark to State matches.

Clark made his first overseas tour with Bob Simpson's side to the West Indies in 1978, taking 31 wickets at 23.32 on the trip. His action came under close scrutiny in the West Indies, where umpires watched films of his delivery stride but

270

finally cleared him because of a back injury which may have caused him to jerk. He took 15 wickets in four Tests on the tour, a fairly good result. Since then further back problems have restricted his prospects of test appearances but he has performed manfully for Western Australia in first-class matches.

CLAXTON, Norman ("Norrie"), 1877–1951

First-Class Averages: Batting, 2,090 runs at 29.43; Bowling, 66 wickets at 35.56.

A dapper Adelaide stockbroker who gave valuable service to South Australian cricket as a player and administrator. He is regarded as one of Australia's most versatile exponents of sport, a man comparable with Reg ("Snowy") Baker, Fitz Lough, Sir Henry Braddon, Wal Mackney and Vic Richardson, who all excelled in several sports. Claxton, a bachelor, was a fine Australian Rules footballer with North Adelaide, an A-grade hockey player, winner of major bike riding events, a splendid athlete, and an outstanding baseballer who donated the Claxton Shield, Australia's premier baseball trophy, in 1934. As a cricketer he batted right-handed with surprising elegance and bowled useful fast-medium pacers.

Claxton, son of an auctioneer, first showed promise in Adelaide district cricket in the late 1890's. He scored more than 500 runs for North Adelaide at an average of 48.00 in 1900 and made his debut in the South Australian team in 1903. Newspapers described him as a popular cricketer "of sanguine temperament," who batted and bowled optimistically. His batting yielded 2,090 runs over seven first-class seasons and in three of them he averaged better than 40. His bowling was steady but lacked penetration against class batsmen who abounded in State teams at that time, but in 1903–04 at Adelaide he took 5 for 129 against New South Wales, and 5 for 56 against England. In 1904–05 he took 5 for 130 against Victoria. His fielding saved countless runs and batsmen feared his throwing arm.

The highlight of his cricket career came at Melbourne in December 1905, when he swung the match against Victoria in South Australia's favour by batting six hours for 199 not out, a stubborn knock brimful of character, in which he hit 22 boundaries, scoring most of his runs on the offside. He managed the 1913 SA team on its eastern tour, and was a selector with Joe Darling, Clem Hill and George Giffen in 1902–05 and 1907–09. He was a committee-man of the SACA for 20 years and did much to foster cricket among high school pupils. He topped the Adelaide first grade batting averages in 1908–09, with 68.14 and the bowling averages in 1903–04 (11.72) and 1904–05 (11.92).

Claxton joined the Adelaide Stock Exchange in 1910 and in a varied business life developed properties in Alice Springs and northern SA, and was a partner in a firm that dredged

Darwin Harbour. He was the winner of the Bay Sheffield sprint cycle race in 1900 using the name "F. Pierce," and the Bendigo cycling championship in 1901 and captained the North Adelaide Cycling Club from 1917 until his death. He was always immaculately tailored, with a flower in his buttonhole, and left an estate of £27,118.

COACHING IN AUSTRALIA

Organised instruction of aspiring cricketers in Australia began at the end of the first English tour in 1862 by H. H. Stephenson's team, when the Surrey allrounder **Charles Lawrence** agreed to remain in Australia. Lawrence, shrewd and knowledgable, accepted an offer from the Albert club in Sydney to become Australia's first professional coach. His appointment had an influence on all the leading players in the colony, not just on those he tutored at the Albert club, for he improved field placings, running between wickets, and kept fieldsmen alert for their captain's signals, all points that could be copied by observant opponents.

In 1863–64, the second English team under George Parr toured Australia, and this time another Surrey stalwart, **William Caffyn**, was persuaded to remain in Australia and become coach to the Melbourne Cricket Club at a fee of £300-a-year. Between them Lawrence and Caffyn, helped by the Australian-born **Tom Wills**, when he returned home from schooling in England, laid the foundation for a dramatic improvement in Australian standards. Even on the simplest points such as arranging practice sessions so that each man had a bat and a bowl, they were enormously helpful and soon clubs all through the colonies followed the procedures they laid down.

Caffyn took a personal interest in coaching Charles Bannerman, the first Australian batting hero. He was quick to spot a talented batsman or bowler to whom he could give special instruction and although his wife disliked the warm Australian climate and had the misfortune to have two of her sons die in Australia, Billy thoroughly enjoyed his years in Australia. In 1899 he wrote of his coaching days in Australia in his book *71 Not Out*.

"They were delightful pupils, always willing to be shown a new stroke, quick to do their best to retrieve an error, never taking an offence at having a fault pointed out, never jealous of one another. When I remember all this, it is not so much a surprise to me to see what Australian cricket has become."

Lawrence and Caffyn were professionals and their instinct for cashing in on their skills undoubtedly rubbed off on their pupils. Wills had absorbed the true spirit of amateurism at Rugby School and in his brief stay at Cambridge but following the massacre of his relatives in Queensland he, too, was

272

quick to cash-in on his ability as a cricket coach. Both Lawrence and Wills gave a lot of time to coaching the Aboriginal cricketers who toured England. Wills often played as a guest in country teams outclassed by visiting English sides, instructing the locals as well as reinforcing their batting and bowling strength.

The improvement these three were able to achieve with players who came under their influence made all cricket clubs aware that the appointment of a good coach assisted success. In 1877, when the newly-formed South Australian Cricket Association asked James Lillywhite and James Southerton to choose a competent coach for them in England, they selected **Jesse Hide**, of Sussex. He arrived in Adelaide in 1878, stayed for three years at a salary of £200 a year, and laid the foundation for future successes by that State. Hide's job included acting as curator and adviser on turf pitches. He did a good job helping South Australians catch up on cricketers in eastern Australia. In Queensland the QCA set out to attract good coaches from the south almost from its inception. **Ned Sheridan** was among the first to go north from Sydney to coach in Brisbane. Among other early migrants to Queensland from the south were **James Moore**, an ancestor of Charlie Macartney from Maitland, who remained in Brisbane after the first inter-Colonial match and assisted in coaching, and **N. E. Tooth**, a former captain of Glebe Cricket Club in Sydney, who coached young players in the Maryborough district for years. **Sydney Donahoo**, a skilful left-hand batsman from Victoria, was another whose instruction vastly improved Queensland cricket. In 1907 the QCA engaged **Syd Redgrave**, who had played for three seasons in the NSW team, as coach and he did invaluable work for years.

In NSW, the work begun by Caffyn and Lawrence was carried on by the **Gregorys** and the **Bannermans**, who at various times were official coaches to the NSWCA. Another outstanding Sydney coach was **Jimmy Searle**, who had toured New Zealand with the NSW team in 1893–94. Searle was forced to give up playing and concentrate on coaching when he severely injured a leg in a collision with the boundary fence in a trial match for English tour aspirants. Searle concentrated his coaching on public schools. But the man who really established the job as NSWCA coach as a role of great prestige was **George Garnsey**, former NSW right-hand batsman and leg-spin bowler. Garnsey had rare patience and a gift for communication and developed ambitious coaching programmes and edited the NSWCA's coaching magazine. The popularity of Garnsey's coaching classes was matched, however, by those conducted by another former State player **Les Gwynne**. Schoolboys travelled from all over Sydney to attend the classes Gwynne and **George Lowe** ran on Saturday mornings at Manly Oval.

In Western Australia, the first professional coach was **W. V. Duffy**, who took up his appointment to the Metropolitan club in Perth in 1887. The club had asked Harry Boyle and "Tup" Scott, the Australian Test players, to advise them on the choice of a coach and they reported that Duffy, "a highly efficient allround man" living at East Melbourne, was ready to take the job for £100 for the season. Duffy did valuable work in the clearing and preparation of pitches as well as coaching and playing in the first inter-Colonial match between WA and SA, when he led the WA attack and topscored with 44 in the WA second innings, SA winning by an innings. **Arthur Richardson**, Test allrounder, strongly influenced a whole generation of WA cricketers in his job as WACA coach between 1927 and 1929. **Trevor Rowlands**, a teacher at Haile, WA's oldest public school, also built a reputation for his coaching acumen in the 1930s, coaching some outstanding boys, captaining and State team, and also guiding senior West Perth club players. This work was carried on after World War II by **Keith Carmody**, **Peter Loader** and **Tony Lock**.

Arthur Richardson also coached in his home State of South Australia for a spell, and was followed by **"Nip" Pellew** and **Clarrie Grimmett**. Since 1970, the former Middlesex player **Ernest Clifton** has been the SACA coach and he has become heavily involved in schemes to coach the coaches aimed at ensuring that schoolmasters and others who take a team have whatever help they need.

In Tasmania early cricket instruction was limited to the study of coaching manuals sent from England, and when copies of John Nyren's *The Young Cricketer's Tutor* containing the laws of cricket and directions on how the game should be played went on sale in Hobart in 1835 they were soon sold out. But the first man to inspire the youth of the colony to emulate his words and deeds with the bat was **William Holden Walker**, who did more than anybody to establish cricket in Tasmania at a time when north and south were bitterly quarreling. Walker, who had played for the Islington Albert Club in London before migrating to Tasmania in 1859, had what Roger Page described in his history of Tasmanian cricket as a "great gift of inspiring youth with a feeling of admiration for his powers as a batsman, bowler and wicket-keeper". Walker's good-humoured tuition as captain of the State team markedly improved techniques in Tasmania.

Tasmania's first professional coach was **Tom Kendall**, who had taken 7 for 55 with his left-arm bowling in the first Test at Melbourne in 1877. Kendall was chosen in the first Australian team for England but when the team reached Perth was sent back to Melbourne for reasons other than cricket. At that stage the TCA signed him up to coach in

Hobart. To get full benefit from Kendall's appointment as coach a five-day bazaar was held in Hobart during which £1,300 was raised to pay for practice pitches, drainage and fencing of Hobart Oval, terraced walks and a ladies' stand. Kendall's coaching inspired a whole generation of Tasmanian cricketers, one of whom, **John Henry Savigny** became an outstanding coach himself. Savigny was considered a splendid batsman by all the leading English and Australian cricketers who saw him, but he was content not to seek international honours and devoted himself to coaching the young.

Tasmania has sustained a policy of appointing leading international players to coaching jobs ever since Kendall's time. **Alan Knott**, England and Kent, was the Northern Tasmanian Cricket Association's coach in 1969–70; **Richard Hadlee**, New Zealand and Nottinghamshire, was NTCA coach in 1979–80; **John Hampshire**, England, Yorkshire and Derbyshire, had three seasons as the TCA coach from 1966–67; **Rohan Kanhai**, West Indies and Warwickshire, was coach to the Devonport club in 1969–70; **Peter Lever**, England and Lancashire, was coach to the NTCA in 1971–72; **Khalid** ("Billy") **Ibadulla**, Pakistan and Warwickshire, was coach at Devonport in 1969–70; **Sadiq Mohammad**, Pakistan and Gloucestershire, was coach to the Latrobe club for three seasons from 1973–74; **Parves Jamil Mir**, Pakistan and Glamorgan, was Wynyard club's special schoolboy coach in 1979–80; **Paul Allott**, England and Lancashire, was coach to the TCA in 1980–81. This concentrated coaching paid off when Tasmania was granted full Sheffield Shield status from 1982–83 and should pay big dividends in the future.

On the mainland the most successful of recent coaches have been **Peter Philpott**, who played eight Tests for Australia as a leg-spinner, **Frank Tyson**, former England and Northants fast bowler, and **Brian Taber**, former Australian Test 'keeper and organiser of the National Coaching Plan. Philpott has had great success in coaching schoolboys and young grade players and although his appointment as the first coach to the Australian team in 1981 in England was not a raging success, the team captain, Kim Hughes, strongly urged continuation of this appointment. Tyson coached at Carey, a leading Melbourne grammar school, before taking the job as the Victorian Cricket Association's official coach. Taber, with the assistance of the NSWCA coach **Peter Spence**, has the backing of a wealthy tobacco firm in arranging courses for coaches at Schools, Clubs, Districts, State, and National levels. The courses are free and mean that nobody given a team to coach in any part of Australia, regardless of the level, need do so without proper qualifications. There has always been a great natural character among Australia's best players, many of whom reached Test status without any

275

coaching whatever. Some oldtimers are sceptical about how much can be achieved by intensified coaching and fear the spirit and flair of Australian cricket may disappear. The important aspect of the scheme, however, is that it is entirely voluntary, with expert coaching now available to any boy who feels he needs it.

COHEN, Morton Barnett ("Mort"), 1913–1968

First-Class Averages: Batting, 574 runs at 31.88; Bowling, 5 wickets at 23.80.

One of the most colourful personalities of NSW cricket for many years, a wily, resourceful cricketer, notorious for his scheming and for his knowledge of the game's finer points. He played the game with great verve and gamesmanship. He opened for NSW with Harold Mudge and Arthur Morris, and in 1940–41 made a century for the State in a big opening stand with Morris.

Cohen was educated at Sydney Boys' High and Sydney University, where he graduated as Bachelor of Economics. He played with Paddington when Monty Noble was captain and learned a lot of tricks from State selector Billy Wells. When he became captain of Paddington in the war years, he won a reputation among all clubs for the distance he bowled wide of the stumps. Few could bowl an outswinger so consistently close to a wide without being called as Cohen. "Bowling for a rupture," one critic labelled it. His defensive field placings were equally frustrating.

In one grade final against Cohen's Paddington side, North Sydney needed only 14 runs from three eight ball overs to win, but with Cohen bowling a width and his fieldsmen cleverly blocking every shot were never in the hunt. For NSW, he is remembered for purposeful stands in which he used the sweep shot to great effect, although an opening bat. He became a Life Member of the NSWCA, a member of the SCG Trust and was MP for Bligh in the State's Legislative Assembly on his death. Arthur Morris was one of his scrutineers at election booths.

Cohen was always mindful of cricketers' off the field problems and tried to assist them in their employment or studies. When Ray Flockton won a lucrative prize in the New South Wales State Lottery, Cohen helped him invest it wisely. In these affairs he worked closely with Paddington's keeper Geoff See, an astute accountant.

When the NSWCA merged his beloved Paddington with Glebe and called the amalgamation "Sydney," Cohen failed in the courts in a move to block the merger. Cohen, an accountant who made a lot of money in minerals, directed that $500 of the $105,743 he left in his will be invested on a trophy for the best all-rounder each season in the Paddington first grade side—but that team no longer existed, and the money was returned to his wife and children.

276

An organisation which aims to give the average club cricketer a chance to tour overseas. Their teams play in the far
flung corners of the cricket world in places like Bahrein, Hollywood, Berlin, Calgary, Paris, Jakarta, Dusseldorf and The
Hague as well as in the lovely villages of England, and the
traditional big match venues in Britain, Pakistan and India.
The players pay all their own expenses and the ability to do
this and show that they have played to a reasonable standard
at school or in a district club is now the only yardstick in arranging touring sides.

The idea and the name came from Graeme Wallace-Smith,
a Geelong College old boy who went farming in South Australia and made a tour of Britain in 1956 with a South Australian
Country XI. He enjoyed it so much he thought it would be a
fine idea to go again with a group of players like himself who
could handle themselves in a cricket match but did not aspire
to State or Test team trips. Graeme believed that factions
might develop if the tours were open to everybody and to
avoid the in-fighting he thought would occur limited selection for the first tour to old private school boys. His fears
proved groundless, on the first trip in 1959, but it gave the
group its name with more than 3,500 letters going out to old
boys of private schools around Australia. These days touring
players ready to pay for their trip who can play to an acceptable standard are included, regardless of where they went to
school.

Some very good players have gone on Old Collegian tours,
including Test batsman Leo O'Brien. They are not an organisation that brandishes names about but you can bet that either
"Sonny" or David de Carvalho are not far away when tours are
planned. It is an admirable organisation but I believe a
change of name should be one of the priorities once they get
through whatever tour or reunion they are planning now.

The AOC, now well known among Australia's club cricketers, has made four tours of India, one to New Zealand in
1969, one exclusively to the UK in 1977, and world tours in
1959, 1960, 1964, 1968, 1976 and 1980.

**COLLEGIANS, THE
AUSTRALIAN OLD**

A handsome, dark-haired all-rounder for Mosman, New
South Wales and Australia, a powerful hitter and a fast-
medium bowler of surprising nip who could move the ball
around in helpful conditions. He captained New South Wales
with great flair in four matches in 1976–77.

Colley, born at Mosman, was an outstanding pitcher for the
district's baseball club, which showed in his powerhouse
throwing at cricket. He was selected in Mosman's first grade
side at 15 and showed his potential by taking a hat-trick in
his first match against Balmain. But he was casual in an out-

**COLLEY, David John,
1947–**

First-Class Averages:
Batting, 2,374 runs at
23.74; Bowling, 236
wickets at 31.60.

Tests (3): 84 runs at 21.00;
6 wickets at 52.00.

277

David Colley bowling his right-arm medium-pacers.

look without ambition for higher honours, and it was not until former English Test player Barry Knight became captain that he started to settle to his responsibilities.

He was close to State selection for three seasons before he finally made it at 22 after seven summers in first grade. He had played for New South Wales Colts in 1965, 1967, 1968 and in 1970 when he was captain. In his Shield debut he did not take a wicket as Dave Renneberg's opening partner against Western Australia, but he made 46 runs with aggressive batting. Knight moved him up the batting order at Mosman and this helped Colley's concentration.

He made his debut in Tests while he was with the 1972 Australian team in England. He was a shock selection for this tour but quickly showed that he was a far more hostile bowler under English conditions than in Australia. Against Gloucestershire at Bristol, he took 5 for 27, and he finished the tour with 32 wickets and 266 runs at 22.16. His three Test appearances were highlighted more by his dashing hitting than by his bowling. At Trent Bridge he made a valuable 54 in what turned out to be his highest Test score. At home after that trip he never again showed the same zeal and was often critical of payments to players, at a time when the New South Wales and Australian treasurers were struggling to meet costs. A nagging back injury further restricted his chance of getting back into Tests.

Colley scored one century for New South Wales—101 against South Australia at Adelaide in 1970–71. His first-class results were disappointing for such an obviously gifted player.

278

A right-arm fast-medium bowler who turned in impressive performances for East Melbourne and Victoria at the turn of the century. He took five wickets in an innings 11 times for his State after making his debut in 1899–1900 at the age of 19. He troubled all the finest batsmen of his period, bowling at a lively pace and moved the ball appreciably. At Melbourne in 1902–03 he took 6 for 54 against a New South Wales line-up that included Trumper, Duff and Noble.

Collins had some enthralling duels with Duff and Trumper and did well enough to be talked of as a Test prospect. In 1901–02 when Maclaren's English team toured Australia he took 5 for 58 against them at Melbourne, and in 1902–03 when Lord Hawke's side played three matches in Australia on the way home from New Zealand, he took 7 for 61 as Victoria won by seven wickets. But Fred Collins never got a Test chance and during World War II was killed in Belgium, aged 36.

COLLINS, Frederick Bisset, 1881–1917

First-Class Averages: Batting, 390 runs at 7.95; Bowling, 146 wickets at 26.10.

One of Australia's most successful cricket captains, some say the wisest, an introverted enigma of a man whose spiritual homes were the gaming tables of Monte Carlo, the dog and racing tracks where he fielded as a bookmaker, the sleazy gambling joints of Sydney's King's Cross and London's Soho, a two-up school in Flanders trenches, and anywhere a game of poker was on. He gambled with his own fortunes but protected Australia's cricket prestige with a Scrooge-like intensity. As a cricketer he considered all the factors carefully before he moved. As a gambler, he bet impulsively.

He batted right-handed and opened with unlimited patience, imperturbable in a crisis, at first inspection apparently strokeless, but somehow able to score 32 first-class centuries. He owed everything to steadfastness of character. He was lucky to get the Australian captaincy, but he exploited his good fortune and set standards probably only Noble, Bradman, Benaud and Ian Chappell have matched among Australian captains. Win or lose a fortune at the gaming tables or in a big match, his face remained impassive.

He was born in the Sydney suburb of Darlinghurst, not far from where his father conducted an accountancy business. He bowled left-arm spinners for the Paddington club (and later for Waverley) and batted with little backswing, realising quite early that deflections were safe, brave swings for boundaries risky. He prodded and nudged his way to so many good scores he was chosen at 19 for the New South Wales' southern tour. In his initial first-class match at Adelaide, he was clean-bowled by J. N. Crawford for three. His four innings on that trip brought only 32 runs. He continued to score well in Sydney grade matches, however, and at 20 was picked for four matches for NSW, including the Sydney game against

COLLINS, Herbert Leslie ("Horseshoe" "Squirrel"), 1889–1959

First-Class Averages: Batting, 9,924 runs at 40.01; Bowling, 181 wickets at 21.38.

Tests (19): 1,352 runs at 45.06; 4 wickets at 63.00.

South Africa. He opened the batting with Bardsley with whom he played many long innings.

Australia's batsmen were destroyed in 1911–12 by the English bowlers Barnes and Foster. Collins appeared in only one match that season and failed but he later confessed he made a careful study of the England side's field placements. He played his first complete season of top-class cricket in 1912–13, finishing with a flourish at Hobart against Tasmania by scoring 282, highest score of his career, and his initial first-class century. He kept that form in 1913–14 when he went to New Zealand with an Australian team that included Trumper, Armstrong, Noble, Mailey, Ransford and J. N. Crawford. That same year he toured Canada and the US with Edgar Mayne's side.

Collins was a Lance Corporal in the Australian Lighthorse, having served in France, when World War I ended. Charles Kelleway, a captain, and the only player in the side with extensive Test experience (15 Tests), led the original AIF side for six matches before the commander of Australia's forces in Europe, Field-Marshall Birdwood, called Collins in and asked him to take over. Birdwood knew Collins was the captain the players wanted. The first AIF team lost only four of 28 first-class matches and defeated the MCC at Lord's. Collins bowled more than 700 overs of left-arm spinners in taking 106 wickets for the AIF team, including 8 for 31 against Somerset, although he sometimes looked pasty and drawn at the start of the day's play after overnight sessions at the gaming tables.

Herbie Collins at Leicester in 1921.

Australian cricket had been dealt a savage blow by the bad behaviour of the 1912 team, whose poor playing record was compounded by the easy-going nature of their captain Syd Gregory. Collins played a major role in restoring our lost prestige with his unselfish leadership of the first AIF side, and another strong personality, Warwick Armstrong, carried on the good work. Collins played in his first Test at 31 in the 1920–21 series against England, beginning with innings of 70 and 104 and finished the series with 557 runs. In the Third Test he batted 258 minutes for 162, helping to boost Australia's score to 354.

He broke his thumb in the First Test of the 1921 tour of England and missed the next two Tests. Returning in the Fourth Test after Australia had beaten England in eight successive postwar matches, he ensured that Australia, outplayed at last, was not beaten. His 40 runs took 289 minutes and he was at the crease for all bar 29 minutes of the 318 minutes it took Australia to reach 175 and make certain of a draw. He scored 1,222 runs in all matches on the 1921 tour at 33.94.

When Armstrong retired Collins took over the Australian captaincy. He celebrated with an innings of 203 against South Africa at Johannesburg and then made 114 and 60 against

280

Gilligan's English side in the First Test at Sydney in 1924, cleverly shielding new player Ponsford from the threat of Maurice Tate as they put on 190 for the second wicket and Ponsford reached 110. Collins' undemonstrative nature and innate fairness endeared him to his players. He never moaned and he had the good fortune to have the players who could deliver on the odd occasions that he gambled. When Gilligan's men need only 27 runs to win the Adelaide Test with two wickets, Collins surprised by throwing the ball to Mailey, whose facility to bowl full tosses was well known. Oldfield caught Freeman off Mailey to give Australia victory and The Ashes by 11 runs. At the other end Jack Gregory had had Gilligan caught off what he admitted was an accidental slower ball. Australia won the series 4–1.

Collins' team knew him as a man who would bet on anything, but who refused to play poker with them in the dressing-room. He saw no fun in an expert taking money from novices. When he was appointed a selector by the NSWCA he looked for combinations rather than stars and once dropped a player who had made 200 because his presence upset the balance of the team. He made a painstaking study of all the dangerous players opposed to Australia, always trying to find a weakness in their stroke play or temperament that could be exploited. After a day's play he would sit quietly by himself going through the lessons of the day, the last man to shower.

Collins working as a bookmaker at a Sydney pony race meeting.

Arthur Mailey always said Collins could see better at night than by day and said Collins' eyes glowed at night. Collins was a chain-smoker but had little use for alcohol except for a celebration glass of champagne. He had a period as a steward at Sydney's pony races and later took out a bookmaker's licence but neither role appealed to him as much as punting. He worked for a long time as a commission agent laying-off for bookmakers that were over-committed on certain horses, placing huge sums of money with ice-cold precision. His appetite was sparse and never likely to add to his frail but wiry frame.

By the time the Australian team reached England in 1926, Collins was suffering frequent pain from neuritis and arthritis. Gregory, his key bowler, was suffering from a leg injury, and the general strike made travelling from match to match arduous. Collins never complained, though he missed two Tests while he was in hospital. Bardsley led the team in his absence. Here Collins' luck finally ran out and England won a thrilling match by 289 runs to clinch its first series win against Australia since 1912. It was his final Test. Of the 11 Tests in which he had captained Australia only two were lost, while five were won and four drawn. Despite his illness Collins made 875 runs at 31.25 on the 1926 English tour and topped the bowling averages with 14 wickets at 14.92 in all matches.

Collins married the daughter of a race club steward when he was 51, his bride 24. The marriage lasted just over 11 years and produced a son. Through World War II Collins was an Army sergeant stationed at Sydney's Victoria Barracks and able to work as a commission agent each Saturday at the races. Divorced at 64, he frequented the gambling clubs around Kings Cross, playing poker through the nights. He gave up smoking but his lungs finally gave out and he died at the age of 70.

In a first-class career that stretched from 1909 to 1926, Collins seldom bowled long spells after his marathon effort for the first AIF team. No innings in his career was as valuable as that 40 runs in almost five hours that saved the Manchester Test in 1921.

CONINGHAM, Arthur, 1863–1939

First-Class Averages: Batting, 896 runs at 15.71; Bowling, 112 wickets at 23.24.

Tests (1): 13 runs at 6.50; 2 wickets at 38.00.

A colourful, left-handed, all-round sportsman, whose skill as a cricketer was not fulfilled because of his headlined activities in other fields. He was a solid, free hitting batsman, the first to score a century for Queensland, and he took a wicket with his first ball in Test cricket with one of his fast medium-pacers. His fielding in the slips was often brilliant. He was also a prominent runner who set records for several distances and over hurdles, a winning clay target and live-bird shooter, outstanding billiards player, oarsman and Rugby player of high repute.

Coningham was born at Emerald Hill, Melbourne, son of a brass-finisher and his wife Jane, both English. He played for the Melbourne Cricket Club and then went to Queensland. In 1891 he gave a unique performance for Stanley in the Aitchison Ale Trophy competition against Albert, scoring 26, which was the entire innings total. Nobody else scored and there were no extras. His scoring shots were 6, 4, 5, 5, 3, 2, 1.

Perhaps his best performance with the ball after moving to New South Wales was when he took 4 for 90 and 5 for 79 against Victoria at Sydney in 1892–93. He was chosen in the 1893 Australian team that toured England and on the day the team left he married English girl Alice Stamford. He impressed English critics who were puzzled why he was not used more. Part of the answer was that Coningham was a firebrand. Tall, dark haired and blue eyed, and immensely attractive to women, he absented himself from the team without notice and in a match at Lord's conducted in very cold weather gathered some twigs and fallen branches and lit a fire at one end of the ground to warm himself. He was also a brave man, diving into the Thames on one occasion to rescue a boy in difficulties in conditions only a strong swimmer could have mastered. He scored only 249 runs at 13.10 on the tour in all matches, but finished ahead of G. Trott and Giffen in the bowling averages with 31 wickets at 18.09. In the match against Liverpool and District, Coningham bowled through the innings with R. W. McLeod.

He made his debut for Queensland in 1893–94 on his return from England and played in three matches over the next four seasons, scoring the first ever first-class century for Queensland against NSW at Sydney, when he made 151 in the first innings and followed with 51 in the second. He appeared in his sole Test in 1894–95 at Melbourne, opening dramatically by having the legendary Archie Maclaren caught by G. H. S. Trott from the first ball of the match. He returned to play in NSW and in 1899 he set up as a bookmaker on the flat at Randwick with his bag inscribed in big white letters CONINGHAM THE CRICKETER. He ran a tobacconist business that failed and made money gambling on his ability at billiards and at shooting birds.

In 1899 he sued his wife for divorce on the ground of adultery, naming Father D. F. O'Haran, administrator of St Mary's Cathedral in Sydney and private secretary to Cardinal Moran, as his wife's lover. Coningham said O'Haran was the father of the youngest Coningham child and claimed £5,000 damages from Father O'Haran. Coningham's barrister, Hyman ("Smudgy") Moss, bowed out of the case when Coningham admitted sharing his bedroom with his wife after divorce proceedings had begun. Coningham then conducted his own case. Cyril Pearl, in his book *Wild Men of Sydney*, wrote: "Coningham, who had faced Dr Grace's umbrageous beard calmly, now showed no awe of the horsehair wig and fierce mustachios of Mr Jack Want, K.C., Father O'Haran's advocate."

The first hearing of the case learned from a doctor that Coningham was the improbable father of the child he alleged O'Haran sired "because of an injury from a cricket ball he had received in 1899." The court conflict between cricketer and priest—Cardinal Moran himself was cross-examined at length—almost overshadowed the federation of Australia ceremonies.

The jury could not agree at the first trial and the judge discharged them and ordered a retrial. At the even more spectacular second trial three months later Coningham, now supported by the Presbyterian Church, had to be relieved of a loaded revolver in court as he conducted his case. Again he was extremely eloquent and prone to quote great poets, but this time the jury dismissed the case against Father O'Haran. At this point Coningham threw himself at the priest, breaking court furniture as he resisted attempts to stop him. Later conspiracy on both sides was established.

Coningham then took his family to New Zealand where he worked as a book salesman and went to gaol for six months for fraudulent conversion of £6/3/–. His wife divorced him in 1912 on the ground of his adultery in a beach hut, with

Coningham admitting having pointed a revolver at her and Mrs Coningham denying she had broken a water bottle over his head. "In Sydney, my wife said she did and the jury said she didn't," he said. "In Wellington, I said I didn't and a jury said I did." He was admitted to Ryde mental home in Sydney in 1937 and died there two years later. Air Marshal Sir Arthur Coningham, RAF, born in Brisbane in 1895 and killed in an air crash near the Azores in 1948, was his son.

CONNOLLY, Alan Norman, 1939–

First-Class Averages: Batting, 1,073 runs at 8.79; Bowling, 676 wickets at 26.58.

Tests (29): 260 runs at 10.40; 102 wickets at 29.22.

A large, amiable, well-built right-arm fast medium bowler who mixed cut and swing with clever changes of pace and set batsmen of all cricket nations plenty of problems. He was a key figure in many of his 29 Tests and in most of the matches he played for Victoria over an impressive 12-year period. Few bowlers of his type have matched his subtlety. He was not a batsman who scored runs regularly but he had enough character to bat out the last 25 minutes of a Test match in 1969 at Adelaide against the West Indies and save Australia from defeat. No bowler had taken more wickets for Victoria.

Connolly, born at Skipton, Victoria, played his way through the ranks of the South Melbourne club to the Victorian team in 1959. He gave the State tremendous service in between Test and tour commitments, and taking 330 wickets for the State at 27.04, 12 times taking five wickets or more in an innings, and playing important roles in three teams that won the Sheffield Shield. Among his best efforts were 6 for 55 and 4 for 40 against Western Australia in 1963–64, 9 for 67 against Queensland in 1964–65, 4 for 83 and 5 for 100 against South Australia in 1966–67, 6 for 104 and 7 for 61 against South Australia in 1967–68, 7 for 101 against Western Australia in 1967–68.

Connolly made his Test debut in 1963–64 against South Africa, starting with the Brisbane Test in which Ian Meckiff played his last Test. His 88 Test overs that summer produced only six wickets, best effort 2 for 49. He went to England in the 1964 Australian team but his chances were restricted by the success of McKenzie (29 Test wickets), Hawke (18) and Corling (12). Connolly took 28 wickets at 30.53, playing in only 15 of the 30 first-class matches because of a back injury. He recovered enough to play two Tests in India as McKenzie's opening partner, taking 3 for 66 and 3 for 24 at Bombay.

He missed the 1965 tour of the West Indies but was recalled for one Test against England in 1965–66, taking 1 for 128. In 1966–67 he was overlooked for the tour of South Africa but was brought back into the side for the Indian tour of Australia in 1967–68, taking eight wickets in three Tests at 31.25. But by now he had developed into a bowler of extreme accuracy and cunning and in England in 1968 he played in all five Tests, heading the averages by taking 23 wickets at 21.69, including 5 for 72 in the Fourth Test. His success continued in Australia in 1968–69 against the West Indies, with a further 20 wickets at 31.40 in Tests.

Connolly's last tour, to South Africa in 1969–70, again saw him head the averages. He took 20 Test wickets at 26.10, with 6 for 47 in the Fourth Test at Port Elizabeth his finest Test performance, although Australia lost by 323 runs. Connolly signed for Middlesex in 1969 but because of persistent back trouble retired after two of his three contracted seasons. Bill Lawry sometimes recalls in his commentaries that Connolly once bowled until there was blood inside his boots.

Alan Connolly at the point of delivery.

A well performed Melbourne cricketer who conceived the idea of sending the first Australian team to England. He was promoter and manager of that first team in 1878, and later wrote expertly on the game for Melbourne newspapers.

Conway, born at Fyansford, learned cricket at Melbourne Church of England Grammar School, and at 19 played for Eighteen of Victoria against H. H. Stephenson's English tourists in Melbourne, taking 4 for 60 with his pace bowling and scoring only one run. He developed into a sound batsman, outstanding slips field, and an able captain, and in a career that took in a lot of club cricket was captain of South Melbourne for many years.

He played nine matches in first-class cricket after making his debut in 1861. His best performances for Victoria were in 1865, when he took 5 for 39 against New South Wales in Melbourne and followed with eight wickets and an innings of 33

CONWAY, John
1842–1909

First-Class Averages:
Batting, 156 runs at 11.14;
Bowling, 32 wickets at 13.25.

in Sydney between the same sides. He was an outstanding judge of young cricketers and was the first to recognise the promise of Horan and Blackham. His place in cricket stems from his bright idea of sending a side to England. He wrote for many years on cricket for Sydney and Melbourne newspapers and edited Conway's Australian Cricket Annual.

COOK, Geoffrey Glover, 1910–

First-Class Averages: Batting, 3,453 runs at 29.76; Bowling, 125 wickets at 35.50.

One of the most consistent Queensland cricketers before World War II, a busy, pugnacious right-hand batsman and right-arm medium pace bowler who, when he did not make runs, usually took wickets. He scored three centuries for Queensland between 1931–32 and 1946–47, and his best bowling figures were 6 for 94. In 1938–39 he put on 265 for the first wicket with Bill Brown against New South Wales at Sydney, and this remains the highest opening stand for Queensland. At the age of 36 he batted for seven and quarter hours against Hammond's English team at Brisbane in 1946 for 169 not out in a total of 400. He bowled in an era of brilliant Australian batsmanship on unresponsive pitches.

Geoff Cook's father, **Bernard William** ("Barney") **Cook** (1879–1944), played seven matches for Queensland between 1909 and 1912, scoring 61 runs at 6.10 and taking 20 wickets at 18.00, best figures 5 for 34. "Barney" Cook was a pirate broadcaster who gave descriptions of Brisbane cricket matches to commercial radio listeners at a time when the Australian Broadcasting Commission had exclusive rights to big games. He operated from precarious positions outside the 'Gabba, often harrassed by police, and amused listeners when his son erred by muttering "Oh no, not like that, Geoff!" into the microphone.

COOPER, Bransby Beauchamp, 1844–1914

First-Class Averages: Batting, 1,610 runs at 20.64; Dismissals, 61 (41 catches, 20 stumpings).

Tests (1): 18 runs at 9.

An attractive, hard-hitting, right-hand batsman who, after a successful career on the playing fields of Rugby, for Middlesex and Kent and in representative matches with W. G. Grace, played a leading role in early big cricket in Australia. He played eleven times for Victoria in Inter-Colonial matches against New South Wales. In 1873, he scored 84 in a total of 266 for Eighteen of Victoria against W. G. Grace's English team, the Eighteen winning by an innings and 21 runs. He was a handy wicket-keeper, if below top-class.

In March, 1877, Cooper played for Australia in the first ever Test against England, scoring 15 and 3. Australia won by 45 runs thanks to Charles Bannerman's 165 and Tom Kendall's outstanding bowling. Cooper was a true blue English amateur, never afraid to attack, though he could defend patiently when required. He had a stabilising influence on aspiring Victorian players.

He was born in India, educated at Rugby, for whom he played at Lord's in 1860 against MCC. In 1864 he played in the first match for the newly formed Middlesex County Club. In 1865 he made 70 for the Gentlemen v. Players at Lord's, making his first appearance with W. G. Grace, then 17. In 1869 he partnered Grace in a stand of 105 for the first wicket for Gentleman v. Players, scoring 40 while Grace hit 83. Three weeks later Cooper and Grace added 283 for Gentlemen of the South v. Players of the South in 220 minutes, Cooper scoring 101, Grace 180. In July, 1869, Grace made 122 in a total of 173 for South v. North, Cooper's 23 being the only other score of double figures.

Cooper settled in Australia in 1869 and died at Geelong without ever returning to England.

A slow bowler with a huge leg break who took up cricket at the age of 27 when his doctor advised him to get more exercise. Within three years of joining South Melbourne club as a rank beginner he was chosen for Victoria against Lord Harris' team in 1878–79. He played in two Tests after this late start, became Victoria's captain, a State selector and a vice-president of the VCA, but he was not a native Australian. He was born at Maidstone, Kent, and his parents settled in Australia when he was eight years old.

Cooper let the ball go from a full extension of his 5 ft 9½ ins and took many wickets through sheer surprise at the width of his breaks. He was often expensive and wicket-keepers had trouble adjusting to his turn, conceding many byes. But he took many prize wickets.

In the Test against Ivo Bligh's team at Melbourne in 1881–82, he took 3 for 80 and 6 for 120, and for Australia against Fifteen of South Australia two seasons later he took 15 wickets for 194 runs, including 8 for 128 in an innings. He was chosen for the 1884 Australian team to England when several stars dropped out and there was much speculation about how English batsmen would handle his vast breaks, but he badly injured his bowling hand on the voyage to England and was a tour failure. He bowled only 136 overs on the whole tour, taking seven wickets at 46.42 apiece, and he only batted nine times.

At his best Cooper was a remarkable bowler, capable of subduing first-class batsmen with only two fieldsmen on the offside as he concentrated on leg theory. He was a poor batsman but brilliant point fieldsman. When he returned from England after the 1884 trip he retired to get his exercise in games that accommodated his injured hand.

COOPER, William Henry, 1849–1939

First-Class Averages: Batting, 247 runs at 10.29; Bowling, 71 wickets at 24.49.

Tests (2): 13 runs at 6.50; 9 wickets at 25.11.

In one match against New South Wales in his third season in cricket he took 7 for 37 in an innings, taking a prize for the best bowling performance in the game in the face of competition from Australia's best bowlers.

CORLING, Grahame Edward, 1941–

First-Class Averages: Batting, 484 runs at 10.52; Bowling, 173 wickets at 32.05.

Tests (5): 5 runs at 1.66; 12 wickets at 37.25.

One of the least exploited talents in Australian cricket since World War II, a right-arm opening bowler with a copybook action that was all style, but was seen in only five Tests. Corling had stamina, and an astute mentor in Bobby Simpson, but after touring England as the youngest member of the 1964 side dropped out of Test cricket, content to play Shield and grade cricket, which he did with great cheerfulness and spirit.

Corling had the ideal action to produce inswing and outswing, releasing the ball high up, arm extended, always in control, accurate in line and length. In heavier, darker atmospheres than Australia's blue skies provide, he should have been sensational, for on the occasional day when our clouds helped him he beat the bat with consummate ease.

COSIER, Gary John, 1953–

First-Class Averages: Batting, 5,005 runs at 32.92; Bowling, 75 wickets at 30.68.

Tests (18): 897 runs at 28.93; 5 wickets at 68.20.

A burly, red-haired right-hand batsman and slow-medium pace bowler who played some swashbuckling innings for three Australian States and for Australia. He could hit the ball vast distances and had the bulk and physical power that needed no backswing as he swatted the ball over the fence. He was the 11th Australian to score a century on his Test debut. He bowled from a short, jerky approach as if his boots were full of nails and in humid conditions could swing the ball sharply. He has surprising talent as a singer and was an unashamed wisecracker. In the field he was quite sharp in the close-in positions despite his bulk. Selectors gave him numerous chances to develop his big-hitting but he failed too often to retain a permanent place in the Test team.

From his early days with the Northcote club in Melbourne, Cosier's strength made him a potential match-winner in the George Bonner mould. In his short but merry career in big cricket, he played some memorable blows. He was an immense hitter in the practice nets but messed things up when he was most needed in important matches, though he did get to be Australia's vice captain when the WSC players were unavailable.

Cosier, born in the Melbourne suburb of Richmond, toured the West Indies in the Australian Schoolboys' side in 1969–70 and at 17 was twelfth-man for Victoria. He played for Victorian Colts in 1971–72 and made his debut that year in the Victorian senior team. He scored 93 runs in two State matches, including 34 v. South Australia at Adelaide. He missed the next two seasons and when he returned it was with South Australia. He scored 1,504 runs for SA in 23 matches at 35.81, topscore 130 against the West Indies in 1975–76. In his first Test at Melbourne that season against the West Indies he made 109. A succession of failures followed and in eight Shield innings at the start of the 1976–77 season he made only 80 runs. The selectors persevered with him, however, and in January, 1977, he made 168 against Pakistan at Melbourne, his highest Test score, taking the Pakistani attack apart after spectators had booed him at the start of his innings.

At the start of the 1977–78 Australian season he signed a 10-year contract with a Queensland firm, reported by newspapers to be worth half a million dollars. He made his debut for Queensland against Victoria at Brisbane becoming the sixth player to appear for three States (P. S. McDonnell, K. H. Quist, W. H. McDonald, N. J. Hawke and G. D. Watson were the others). He was considered lucky to have played in the Centenary Test in March, 1977, and failed to distinguish himself in England that year or in the West Indies in 1978. But Kim Hughes rated him a potential matchwinner when Australia went to England for the 1979 World Cup matches. "I reckon Coze will eat bowlers like Geoff Miller for breakfast," said Hughes. Cosier flopped again.

He returned to Melbourne at the start of the 1980–81 season and was made captain of his old club, Northcote, winning the Jack Ryder medal with 467 runs and 20 wickets after his six seasons away. But by the end of the season he had lost his place in the Victorian side. He has played 91 first-class matches, with seven first-class centuries. Sadly he appeared finished as a representative cricketer before he was 30.

COSSTICK, Samuel, 1836–1896

First-Class Averages: Batting, 315 runs at 9.84; Bowling, 106 wickets at 9.41.

An important figure in building the strength of cricket in Victoria in its formative years. He was a professional on the staff of the Melbourne Cricket Club for many years and first played for Victoria in 1861, appearing against English teams in 1862, 1863 and 1873. For Victoria against Tasmania in 1869, Cosstick took 6 for 1, one of the most sensational bowling performances for the State.

Cosstick, born at Croydon, Surrey, was a fine round-arm bowler whose job was to keep the Melbourne CC's ground in order, to play in all the club's matches, and to bowl to members every afternoon from 2.30 p.m. until 7 p.m. His salary was £3/10/– a week. On Boxing Day, 1873, he combined with Harry Boyle and Frank Allan to dismiss Dr Grace's visiting English XI for 110 and 132, giving Eighteen Of Victoria victory by an innings and 24 runs. Dr Grace's team played 22-man sides at Ballarat, Stawell and Warrnambool and Allan and Cosstick kept appearing for every match. At Ballarat, where W. G. Grace made 126 and G. F. Grace 112 in an England total of 470, the local cricket reporter said: "The sun shone infernally, the eleven scored tremendously, we fielded abominably, and all drank excessively." After the Stawell match Dr Grace had to give his players a warning about drinking while matches were in progress.

Cosstick, who gave the Melbourne club's first curator Rowland Newbury great assistance at the MCG, was involved in two nasty incidents with Dr Grace. Playing for a Combined XV against England in Sydney, Cosstick claimed the wrong umpire gave him out and refused to budge. Dr Grace simply led his side from the field. In Melbourne, apparently annoyed about being heavily punished, he shied three balls directly at Grace. Sam was taken off and refreshments called for and during the interval Sam was placated enough not to try to maim Dr Grace again. Cosstick was one of the umpires in the second of all Tests in 1877. He died at West Maitland, NSW.

COTTAM, John Thomas, 1867–1897

A right-hand batsman who represented Australia in one Test against England at Sydney in 1886–87. He was then 19. Cottam, born in the inner Sydney suburb of Strawberry Hill, played for the Warwick and Sydney clubs, and showed immense promise from an early age. He had a polished style and a powerful physique, and was extremely popular with all cricketers. He went to New Zealand with the New South Wales team in 1889–90 and was the outstanding batsman on the tour. His figures—286 runs in all matches at an average of 26.00—were far better than they looked, as most matches were played on very rough pitches. He drifted out of cricket after the New Zealand tour and died of typhoid fever at Coolgardie in 1897, aged 29.

First-Class Averages: Batting, 273 runs at 22.75; 3 wickets at 32.66.

Tests (1): 4 runs at 2.00.

COTTER, Albert (''Tibby''), 1883–1917

A Sydney-born fast bowling idol before World War I, doted on by spectators because of his habit of breaking batsmen's stumps. At 5 ft 8 ins, he was no giant, but he was enormously strong around the chest and shoulders, rather like Larwood, and at his peak he bowled at a furious pace, giving such energy to the task that he was as dangerous at the end of a hard day as at the start.

Cotter, son of affluent parents like most of Australia's first-class players in his period, went to Forest Lodge Primary School and Sydney Grammar School, and played district cricket for Glebe. He was a really menacing batsman if he got a start and hit 152 runs one afternoon against Waverley which included 16 sixes and six fours and took only 70 minutes. There are also more than 20 recorded instances of his snapping a stump or shattering a bail when one of his fireballs struck them.

He toured England with the 1905 team after making his debut for New South Wales four years earlier, taking 121 wickets in all matches at 20.19, a tour bag that was only exceeded by Armstrong with 130 wickets. He was a great favourite with crowds and one of the main reasons for the 1905 side's wide popularity. He went back to England for a second tour in 1909 when he took 64 wickets at 29.09 in all matches.

Cotter was the Jeff Thomson of his day, spraying the ball a

First-Class Averages: Batting, 2,484 runs at 16.89; Bowling, 442 wickets at 24.37.

Tests (21): 457 runs at 13.05; 89 wickets at 28.64.

lot, but bowling with extreme pace, and he opened the bowling for Australia for eight years between 1904 and 1912 with great zest and enthusiasm. In the fifth Test at Melbourne in 1903–04 Australia regained The Ashes thanks to his 8 for 65 in the match. At Worcester in 1905, he took a total of 12 for 34, and in 1909 he was largely responsible for winning the Headingley Test in taking 5 for 38 in England's second innings.

Cotter was one of the six famous players who in 1912 rebelled over the Board of Control's conditions for the tour of England and withdrew from the side. In 1917, as a Trooper in the Australian Light Horse, he raised his head over the rim of a trench at Beersheba to verify what his periscope had told him and was shot dead by a sniper. He was 34.

"Tibby" Cotter took 295 wickets at 20.20 for the Glebe club between 1900–01 and 1914–15. His best season was 1906–07 when he took 37 wickets and scored 731 runs. In a Test career that lasted from 1904–12 he took five wickets or more in an innings seven times, with 7 for 148 his best figures. On April 29, 1911, he took four in four balls for Glebe versus Sydney at Wentworth Park.

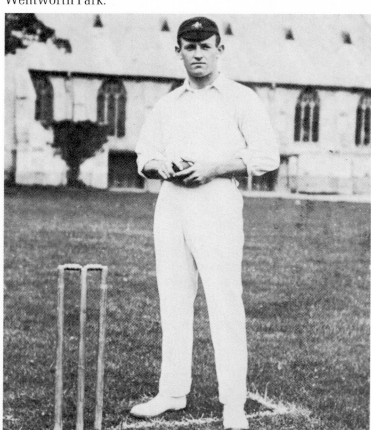

A splendid study of 'Tibby' Cotter, the Sydney fast bowler.

A fiery, controversial South Australian fast bowler in the years leading up to World War II. He was a lift driver with the Shell oil company in Adelaide. The fairness of his bowling action caused widespread discussion but he was only no-balled for throwing once in a first-class career. His pace invariably unsettled opening batsmen. His best figures were 5 for 49 against Queensland in 1938–39. In 1940–41, he headed the South Australian bowling averages with 11 wickets at 24.90.

Cotton was a legendary cricketer in the Prospect club in Adelaide. Ray Sutton, in his book *Great Prospects*, covering a half-century of The Prospect club's endeavours (1928–29 to 1978–79) said: "Harold Cotton possessed true pace by any fast bowling standards, and earned the respect of district and inter-State players alike for his ability as a front-line attack bowler. Old club players tell many stories of their aversion to facing him in the practice nets and the testing of their courage when he was in full flight." Cotton took 115 wickets for Prospect at 15.90 apiece.

COTTON, Harold Norman Jack, 1914–1968

First-Class Averages: Batting, 147 runs at 10.50; Bowling, 76 wickets at 27.81.

A controversial but much admired figure in the early days of international cricket. He was a sound batsman, handy medium-pace bowler and superb field, who played for Victoria in 1880 and 1881 and once for Australia against England in 1882 at Melbourne. He reversed the customary sequence by playing in a Test after umpiring in one. It was an umpiring decision, however, that brought Coulthard his notoriety for he was the man who gave Billy Murdoch run out against England at Sydney in 1879, and touched off the worst riot Australian cricket has known, almost snuffing out big cricket before it had had a chance to flourish. He died of tuberculosis, aged 27.

COULTHARD, George, 1856–1883

First-Class Averages: Batting, 92 runs at 11.50; Bowling, 5 wickets at 25.00.

Tests (1): 6 runs, N.A.

An excellent all-rounder of the early 1960's from a family devoted to the ideals of amateur sport, who, in the weeks leading up to the WSC breakaway, worked for the dissenting cricketers. For some Cowper's involvement demonstrated more forcibly than any other factor how completely the Australian Board of Control had misjudged the top players' desire to win fairer rewards for their play. For he was the son of a pillar of amateurism, from a family steeped in the lore of playing sport for fun without financial reward.

In 1965–66, Cowper made 307 against England at Melbourne, the highest Test score in Australia. He was a splendid slips fieldsman and took many valuable wickets with drifting slows. He bowled, wrote, played squash and golf right-

COWPER, Robert Maskew ("Wallaby") 1940–

First-Class Averages: Batting, 10,595 runs at 53.78; Bowling, 183 wickets at 31.19.

Tests (27): 2,061 runs at 46.84; 36 wickets at 31.63.

Cowper driving a ball through mid-off.

handed, but batted left-handed. His batting technique was helped, he believed, by his strong right-arm.

Bob's father, Dave, was a pre-war Rugby international who took over as Australia's captain in South Africa in 1933 when the skipper Alec Ross was injured. Cowper was largely responsible for Australia winning two of the five Tests convincingly, by 21 to 6 and 15 to 4. Dave Cowper, a successful district cricketer with Hawthorn, also managed an Australian Rugby team to England, and Bob took his nickname "Wallaby" from his family's association with the amateur code. Bob also played rugby for Victoria and Australian Universities. His brother David kept wicket for Victoria against MCC in 1966. His brother Trevor played Rugby for Victoria.

Bob attributed much of his success in cricket to the coaching he received from John Miles at Melbourne's Scotch College, and from former inter-State pace bowler Barry Scott at Melbourne University, where Bob took a degree in commerce. Bob made his debut for Victoria in 1959–60 and was chosen in the 1964 Australian team for England, with five first-class centuries in his credentials—114 not out v. Western Australia at Perth in 1960–61, 132 not out v. South Australia at Melbourne in 1962–63, 195 not out v. Western Australia in 1962–63 at Melbourne, 141 not out v. Queensland in 1962–63 at Melbourne, and 167 in 1963–64 v. Western Australia at Melbourne. He made his Test debut at Leeds on that tour, which helped develop his talents and make him Australia's leading run-scorer the following year in the West Indies, where he scored 854 runs at 61, 417 of them with two centuries in the Tests. That performance and the two centuries he scored in 1964–65 for Victoria—104 not out v. Queensland at Brisbane and 192 against New South Wales at Melbourne—caused forecasts that he would captain Australia.

However, his form slumped and he began to fiddle at the crease, taking 200 minutes to make 99 in the Second Test

294

against England in 1965–66 at Melbourne. He made 60, top-score for Australia in the Third Test at Sydney but it took over four hours and he was made the scapegoat for Australia's defeat by an innings when he was dropped for the Fourth Test. Reinstated for the Fifth Test at Melbourne, he took 310 minutes to reach 100, a further 225 minutes to get to 200, passed Bradman's record score for a Test in Australia, and when Knight bowled him for 307, he had batted 12 hours 7 minutes, hitting 20 fours.

In 1966–67, he branched out as a bowler, subduing stroke-makers of class such as Graeme Pollock and Colin Bland, drifting the ball across the batsman with deliveries he had learnt in a season in the Lancashire League. He also bowled useful spells for Victoria in Shield cricket. He played the last of his 27 Tests in 1968, finishing with five centuries and 10 scores of more than 50. Ten of his total of 26 first-class 100s were in Shield matches for Victoria, best score 195 not out. Right at the end of his career he played three matches for Western Australia.

He became an investment counsellor and a tough negotiator after his retirement. He worked for the WSC cricketers and represented them at Australian Cricket Board meetings in an unpaid capacity.

CRAIG, Ian David, 1935–

The youngest Australian to play in a cricket Test and the youngest Australian Test captain. He was an attractive, compact right-hand batsman of slight, almost frail build, whose career unhappily did not fulfil the rich promise of his early days, partly because of a severe bout of hepatitis when he should have been at the peak of his powers. He represented Australia and New South Wales in schoolboy baseball and despite his size was a dashing schoolboy rugby player. He had a charm remindful of Lindsay Hassett's and the same unspoken cunning.

Craig, born at Yass, New South Wales, first won selection for New South Wales at 16 years 249 days after a remarkable career at North Sydney Boys' High under great headmaster Arthur Henry, and in his initial grade matches with the Mosman district club. At Sydney in 1952–53 against South Africa he scored a thrilling 213 not out in a New South Wales total of 7 for 416 declared, scoring 63 of the runs added in an 81-run stand with Jim Burke and 98 of the runs made in a 159-run partnership with Keith Miller. "For a boy of his age, it was unbelievable," said Miller. "He hit almost every shot in the meat of the bat, very little that was streaky or off the edge, and had composure through it all that many veterans could not have matched." This innings won Craig a place in the Australian team at the age of 17 years 239 days.

First-Class Averages: Batting, 7,328 runs at 37.96; Bowling, 1 wicket at 127.00.

Tests (11): 358 runs at 19.88.

The celebrity status a double century brought Craig added to the pressure he faced in every first-class innings. He scored 53 and 47 in his Test debut, a total that has continued to reappear in a trick question on quiz shows—Did Ian Craig score a century in his first Test?—but found the going very hard after that. In England in 1953, Lindsay Hassett did his best to protect him from the vast army of sportswriters who covered every move Craig made, but the pressure told. Craig made only 429 runs at 16.50 and 14 of his 16 teammates finished above him on the tour averages.

After Craig had nicked a catch into the gully in yet another failure, Hassett found him in the dressing-room mourning over it all. "No point in sitting here, feeling sorry for yourself," said Lindsay. "Come and watch how Miller plays the shot by getting right over the top of the ball." They went up into the stands and sat and watched Miller nick the ball as Craig had done straight into gully's hands.

Craig launched himself into his studies as a chemist at the end of that tour and did not play cricket seriously again until 1955–56, when he emerged as a model cover-driver, with crisp on-side shots and footwork that got him quickly to any likely half-volleys. In Lindsay Hassett's benefit match he hit Ian Johnson for four sixes in five balls, looking to have plenty of time to play his shots and placing bat on to ball with timing that made these hits look easy.

Struggling for form in England, Craig often fell to glorious catches like this one by Surrey's silly-mid-on.

On his second tour of England in 1956 shrewd bowlers again showed up his weakness against the ball pitched outside the off stump that cut a bit. The poor fellow was expected to behave like Bradman every time he batted. He made 872 runs on the tour at 36.33, topscore 100 not out, and only three players finished above him on the Australian batting averages. He appeared to be fighting his way out of trouble, though he clearly lacked ruthlessness, and he did well on the way home against India and Pakistan and impressed with his team spirit.

In 1957–58, when all the immediate postwar heroes departed, Craig was sent to South Africa as captain of an untried side. He helped build a team spirit on that tour that overcame the absence of Miller, Johnson, Hassett, Morris, Johnston and other great players, although he was then only 22. He was undefeated in five Tests as Australia's captain. The following season in Australia when Craig was struck by a severe bout of hepatitis, his successor, Richie Benaud, was one of the first to pay tribute to Craig's work. There was an air of authority about this Congregational lay preacher, a trait all the great captains have had, that selectors could not be blamed for following.

After his recovery from illness he opened with success for New South Wales but the responsibilities of his job in marketing pharmaceutical goods and his marriage prevented him applying himself to a comeback to Test cricket. Despite his bad luck, he continued to enjoy weekly grade matches with Mosman and captained New South Wales until 1961–62. In one of the highlights of his career he put on 323 with Neil Harvey for the second wicket against Queensland in 1960–61. He scored 15 centuries between 1951 and 1962 in all first-class matches.

CRANNEY, Harold ("Mudgee"), 1886–1971

First-Class Averages: Batting, 856 runs at 31.70; Bowling, 2 wickets at 59.00.

One of a well-known family of cricketers, a hardhitting batsman and handy slow bowler from Sydney's Central Cumberland club who opened the batting for New South Wales. He was among the first to spot the tremendous potential of Don Bradman.

Cranney played with Cumberland for many years and did a lot to foster cricket in the district. He first came to notice in first-class cricket in 1913–14 with an innings of 67 against Tasmania at Sydney. He scored 70 and 144 in a fine double against South Australia at Adelaide in 1921–22. He had a great love for the bush and bush cricketers were his special concern. He was one of three State selectors who watched Bradman's first appearance at the Sydney nets (Johnnie Moyes and R. L. Jones were the others) and resigned at the end of that season to settle in Tamworth.

CRAWFORD, John Neville, 1886–1963

First-Class Averages:
Batting, 9,470 runs at
32.76; Bowling, 815
wickets at 20.06.

An English schoolboy prodigy who had a row with his county and spent 10 years playing in South Australia. He was an all-rounder, a scholarly figure who wore glasses, batted right-handed and bowled medium pace. In England he is regarded as one of the finest schoolboy cricketers of all time. He went straight from school at Repton into a Test series against South Africa and played 12 Tests. He first played for his county at 17 and at 19 he achieved the double of 1,000 runs and 100 wickets in the season. He toured South Africa in 1905–06 with the MCC before he was 20, and in 1907–08 headed the English team's bowling averages in Australia with 30 wickets at 24.79.

In 1909, he incurred the displeasure of the Surrey committee by refusing to captain the county against the touring Australians because several of Surrey's best professionals were omitted. Surrey barred him from their side, which interrupted his English career, and Crawford accepted a place on the teaching staff of St Peter's College, Adelaide, and during the next few years often played dominating roles in matches for South Australia.

Batting from an extremely upright stance, with lovely footwork, he scored two centuries for South Australia and 11 times took five wickets or more in an innings. In 1911–12 for an Australian XI against the visiting English side, he made 110 in even time against an attack comprising S. F. Barnes, Frank Foster, Wilfred Rhodes, J. W. Hearne and Frank Woolley. In 1911–12 he made 126 for South Australia v. Victoria in Adelaide, and in 1912–13 he made 163 v. Victoria at Adelaide. In 1914, on tour in New Zealand with an Australian team, Crawford and Victor Trumper put on 298 for the eighth wicket in 69 minutes against a South Canterbury XV at Temuka, adding 50 in nine minutes with M. A. Noble. Crawford made 354.

After war service, Crawford healed his breach with Surrey and in 1919 made a brilliant 144 for the county against the First AIF team, scoring 73 out of 80 runs added in 35 minutes for the last wicket, driving Jack Gregory back over his head for six. His best bowling efforts in Australia included:

8 for 66 v. Victoria at Adelaide in 1912–13.
6 for 97 v. Victoria at Adelaide in 1913–14.
7 for 78 v. New South Wales at Adelaide in 1913–14.
7 for 92 v. New South Wales at Sydney in 1909–10.
6 for 59 v. New South Wales at Adelaide in 1909–10.
6 for 141 v. New South Wales at Adelaide in 1911–12.

Crawford's father, a parson, and two brothers, R. T. and V. F. Crawford, were outstanding cricketers, noted for big hitting, all appearing in County cricket. Between 1904 and 1921 he scored 15 centuries, and while he was in Australia made 1,642 at 41.05 and took 122 wickets at 25.13 in first-class matches. He toured America in 1914 with the Australian team, scoring prodigiously. In his 12 Tests he made 469 runs at 22.33 and took 39 wickets at 29.48.

A tall, powerful right-arm fast bowler who toured England, India and Pakistan with the 1956 Australian team. He forced his way into the Australian team with some impressive bowling for New South Wales and appeared the logical successor to Ray Lindwall in the Test team but a series of muscular problems frustrated his efforts.

Crawford made his debut for NSW in 1954–55 and took 34 wickets for the State in a highly promising start including 6 for 59 and 6 for 55 against Queensland. The next season he took 33 wickets, including 5 for 75 against South Australia. On hard, fast pitches he generated true pace. He toured England through the wettest summer on record, however, and seldom achieved the same hostility. He took 31 wickets on the English part of the tour at 27.45 and scored 101 runs at 12.62. Only in the match against Surrey when Australia lost to a County side for the first time in 44 years did he bowl as fast as he had done at home. When Surrey required only 20 runs to win in the last innings, Crawford and Lindwall bowled with tremendous pace and it took Surrey 55 minutes to get them. His best figures on the tour were 4 for 31 against Lancashire and 4 for 28 against Oxford University.

He made his Test debut at Lord's but after only 29 balls pulled a muscle and did not bowl again in the match. On the way home he played in the three Tests against India but found the matting pitches just as unresponsive as the damp strips in England. He took 3 for 32 in the First Test and 3 for 28 in the Second Test, finishing with a modest three-Test bag of seven wickets. Probably the highlight of his whole tour was a breezy partnership of 87 runs with Ian Johnson for the ninth wicket in the Madras Test, a stand which helped Australia to win by an innings and five runs.

Crawford was the bowler in the first match of the 1955–56 season at Brisbane when "Slasher" Mackay walked in to bat about three minutes before the Melbourne Cup was due to be run. The NSW captain Keith Miller and the Queensland captain Don Tallon took the players from the field to listen to the race. The start was delayed several minutes but it was almost ten minutes before the players got back in to their positions, with Mackay, who had got a duck in the first innings and dropped two outfield catches (off Crawford shots), fuming about the delay. Crawford bowled a superb inswinger first ball that moved in from 18 inches outside the off-stump to scatter Mackay's stumps and give him a pair for the match. The air at the 'Gabba turned a shade of blue as Mackay went off voicing his opinion of Crawford.

CRAWFORD, William Patrick Anthony, 1933–

First-Class Averages: Batting, 424 runs at 19.27; Bowling, 110 wickets at 21.02.

Tests (4): 53 runs at 17.66; 7 wickets at 15.28.

CRESWELL, John
1859–1909

A pioneer merchant and shipping agent who became a household word in South Australia as secretary of the South Australian Cricket Association between 1883–1909. He worked tirelessly for the improvement of Adelaide Oval and during his time new stands and gardens were built. He was responsible for England playing their first match at Adelaide Oval against Australia in 1884–85, when the Adelaide *Advertiser* praised the improvements he had made at the ground, reported that the wicket was ideal for batting, and that Creswell's marquees for smokers were "popular with those addicted to the weed." Creswell was a fine shot, a bowls player with his own private green, and an authority on greyhounds. He managed the company that built Plympton greyhound track, was secretary of the Chamber of Commerce, secretary of the Vinegrowers Association, and South Australia's representative on the English Board of Trade. He was also secretary of the Australasian Cricket Council during its short life. The John Creswell Stand at Adelaide Oval honours his contribution to cricket.

CRIPPIN, Ronald James
1947–

First-Class Averages:
Batting, 899 runs at
25.68.

A highly talented right-hand opening batsman who retired from the New South Wales team just when it seemed his batting was nearing the maturity that would carry him into the Test team. He tried a comeback after a period out of big cricket but his change of heart came too late at 31 and a career of rich potential was left unfulfilled. Few players with as much talent have appeared in Australian cricket since World War II but throughout his sporting career Crippin just could not seem to get a lucky break.

Crippin's unlucky story bore a remarkable similarity to that of his father Archie, an outstanding Rugby Union winger for St Joseph's College in Sydney, who turned to Rugby League and played three Tests against England in 1936, aged 19. Archie had a dramatic fend and one day a rival grabbed his arm and slammed him into the turf. A recurring shoulder injury finished his career at 20. Ron inherited his father's football skill and played for the Randwick club briefly before South Sydney League officials signed him up. He broke his left shoulder twice, dislocated it, and found it was calcified. He cracked his ribs, broke his nose twice and gave up his football boots in a hospital ward to concentrate on cricket. In 1969–70, he made 712 runs for Randwick and in 1970–71 he made his debut for NSW.

From the start of his first-class career Crippin's flair was unmistakable. He was one of those rare players who always appeared to have a lot of time in which to play his strokes and he timed the ball so well that it really flew to the boundary. He was a fearless hooker and his name was frequently mentioned as one who might be included in the 1973 Australian team for the West Indies. He probably listened to too many people who told him to restrict his hooking, advice that created indecision in a natural hitter.

He missed selection for the West Indies, which in retrospect was a tour that could have made him into a star performer, and in the following season was flattened by a ball from Alan Hurst playing against Victoria at the SCG. Halfway through a hook shot to a Hurst bumper, he remembered the so-called experts' advice on restraining his shotmaking, tried to check the shot, and collected the ball just over the right eye. The wound required 21 stitches. A fortnight later he walked out on to the SCG and hit a dynamic 112 for NSW in a Gillette Cup semi-final against Western Australia, a knock that confirmed his place as one of the most exciting stroke players in Australia.

At the end of the 1973–74 season he retired for the first time, but in October, 1978, he was back. He started by being run out in a one day match when Andrew Hilditch admired his shot and didn't move for an easy single. Then Crippin was floored in a Shield game by a Wayne Clark bouncer, attempting to hook, and went to hospital for 10 more stitches. He batted on in the same innings and, still groggy, was run out again. His vision remained blurred for some days and John Dyson took his place. Crippin then retired for the last time.

"I have had trouble with torn ligaments in my right shoulder from a fall while skiing; I was hit in the mouth by a ball from a kid whose name I didn't even know and then thought every toe on my foot had been broken when I was hit by a ball from Steve Bernard. It was the last straw when I didn't even see the ball from Wayne Clark. I can't understand why I was hit, but I decided it was for the last time," he said.

CROCKETT, Robert, 1863–1935

A softly-spoken imperturbable character who was inspired to take up umpiring cricket matches by the brave example of "Dimboola Jim" Phillips, the South Australian who declared war on 19th century throwers. Crockett, known as "Chief Justice," umpired Australian first-class cricket matches for 38 years, a tribute to his resilience. In 1926, admirers gave him a cheque for £1,043 in appreciation of his services to cricket, during the tea interval of a Melbourne match. Crockett pocketed the cheque, thanked all present, looked at his watch, and announced that it was time for play to resume. He was that sort of chap, precise, unemotional, lacking in sentiment.

The most intense of all the controversies Crockett endured came in 1903–04 when Australia raised their best team in years to play "Plum" Warner's Englishmen. Australia included Trumper, Duff and Noble and their following was such that

10,000 people gathered outside the office of a Sydney newspaper where scores of the SCG matches were posted. Warner's side led by almost 300 runs on the first innings, Foster 287, but on the fourth day Trumper and Hill staged a thrilling revival for Australia. Trumper took 16 off the first five balls of an over from Braund. They ran four off the next ball and tried for a fifth run but Hill was ruled run out by Crockett. As Hill walked off, the crowd on The Hill started to chant, "Crock, Crock, Crock." Noble, the next Australian batsman in, apologised to the opposing captain Warner, but the uproar continued with people in the Members' stand joining in. Crockett, disdainful of it all, walked calmly to his position as rowdies in the crowd called that they would see him outside after play.

The demonstration did not ruffle Crockett but it started a move for tighter control of cricket crowds in Australia. The London *Times* suggested Test matches in Australia should be suspended until players could be certain the Sydney larrikinism would not be repeated. In 1907–08, Crockett was involved in another memorable incident when he refused to signal a boundary after a fieldsman kicked the ball into the fence to prevent the striker taking a single and retaining the strike at the end of the over. Crockett said the kick was contrary to the spirit of the game. He was applauded for his courage. He was a stickler for decorum. Between 1901–02 and 1924–25, Crockett umpired 32 Tests. He was highly regarded by all players for his accuracy and impartiality. He retired through failing sight and started making his own cricket bats from Tasmanian willow. They were still in demand after his death.

There were no colourful mannerisms in Crockett's umpiring, no playing to the crowd with exaggerated hand signals. After each day's play he retired to a small room, just behind the Australian dressing-room at the MCG to talk over the match. To be invited to the "Chief Justice's" room was a special privilege.

CROMPTON, Colin Neil, 1937–

First-Class Averages: Batting, 2,162 runs at 31.79; Bowling, 8 wickets at 48.37.

A determined left-handed batsman who played some valuable innings for Melbourne and Victoria. He was a fine team batsman who figured in many useful partnerships, but scored only three centuries. He made 529 runs at 40.69 in his initial season in first-class cricket, 1957–58, and looked a player of rich promise. He was involved in three century stands that season, 211 with John Shaw against NSW, 133 with Ian Huntington against Western Australia, and 125 with John Shaw against Queensland, all of them for the second wicket, and made 124 against NSW and 101 against WA. He hit the ball harder than most openers, pushed the score along briskly, and was quite a smart fieldsman with 47 first-class catches to his name.

CUFFE, John Alexander, 1880–1931

First-Class Averages: Batting, 7,476 runs at 22.25; Bowling, 738 wickets at 25.47.

A right-hand batsman and slow or medium pace left-arm bowler, born in Toowoomba, where he did well enough on matting wickets against visiting English teams to win selection for Queensland in 1901–02. He later played in Sydney but after one game for New South Wales went to England, where he had an outstanding career with Worcestershire.

Jack Cuffe played for Worcestershire from 1903 to 1914 and in 215 matches for the County scored 7,404 runs at 22.78, with four centuries, best score 145. He also took 716 wickets at 25.36, taking five wickets or more in an innings 31 times, best analysis 9 for 38. He held 123 catches for the County, and in 1911 achieved the double of 1,000 runs and 100 wickets. His partnership of 181 with R. D. Burrows against Gloucestershire in 1907 remains the Worcestershire record for the ninth wicket. He subsequently played Lancashire League cricket and in the 1920s stood as a first-class umpire.

CUNNINGHAM, Kenneth George, 1943–

First-Class Averages: Batting, 5,144 runs at 37.00; Bowling, 45 wickets at 33.40.

A pugnacious left-hand batsman and right-arm change bowler who made up in application what he lacked in style. He cut and hooked his way to more than 5,000 runs for South Australia in a career that stretched to 89 matches, topscore 203. He learned cricket at Ascot Park Primary School and played his way through grade matches with the Adelaide district club to the South Australian captaincy. In lean years his spirit helped the South Australian team compete keenly against States with far more talent. Highspot of his career came in 1966–67 when he became one of the select few to score a century in each innings of a Shield match, scoring 107 and 101 not out against Western Australia in Adelaide.

CURRENCY CLUB

The Currency Cricket Club was one of the most important of the clubs that sprang up in Sydney before inter-Colonial cricket began. Promoted by onetime publican William Tunks, it had a strong influence in popularising inter-club matches. It played its first match in January, 1844, when it lost to Cumberland by 80 runs, but by 1845 it was able to defeat Victoria Club, the City club and the Union club in successive matches. The club mainly recruited its players from Australian-born youths, and often followed a policy of dropping from its team players who spilt a catch. The alternative to being dropped was to receive a punching, a disciplinary approach that would be difficult to follow today. One of the best players for the Currency club was Henry Hilliard, who made his highest score of 94 for the club. Hilliard's ability was well known to the Currency players as he had taken 13 wickets against them for the City club before switching clubs.

D

DANSIE, Hampton Neil ("Nodder"), 1928–

First-Class Averages:
Batting, 7,543 runs at
34.40; Bowling, 88
wickets at 33.20.

A right-hand batsman who clubbed, pulled and cut his way through 107 matches for South Australia without getting a chance to play for Australia. His 124 appearances in all matches for South Australia is surpassed only by Les Favell's 143 appearances.

Dansie's devotion to South Australian cricket was matched by his bewildering list of sporting roles. Over 30 years he was involved in a variety of sports as a first grade Australian Rules footballer for Norwood (1946–49), first grade baseballer for Kensington and Norwood (1950–54), coach of Norwood seconds to a League football premiership (1957–60), coach of the South Australian State amateur football team (1963–68), coach of the Australian amateur football side (1969 and 1972), treasurer to the South Australian Sportsman's Association, secretary of the Australian Sportsman's Association, and as a player for Todmorden in the Lancashire League (1955–56–57). He also coached the South Australian State women's cricket team (1958–72), played first grade cricket for 30 years with Kensington and East Torrens (1943–1973), was secretary of the East Torrens CC, and a South Australian cricket selector.

Dansie, born at Nuriootpa in the far north of South Australia, learned to play cricket on a concrete pitch at Stone Hut. His grandfather Sam, who played for a Broken Hill side against the MCC at the turn of the century, laid down the pitch near the general store which he ran, so that a team of Dansie's could take on other local family teams. Neil's development was rapid after the family moved to Adelaide in the early war years and he played his first grade match for Kensington against Prospect in 1943, aged 15, scoring the first two of the 5,895 runs he made in district cricket at an average of 29.7, with seven centuries.

Dansie, 5 ft 8 ins tall, 12 stone, played his first match for South Australia at Perth in 1949–50. He made 18 centuries in all for South Australia during his first-class career (1949–1967). He topped the State's batting aggregate in

304

1950–51 and twice headed the bowling averages (1960–61, 1962–63).

Former Australian wicket-keeper Barry Jarman christened him "Nodder" because of his habit of giving a reflex nod of agreement when deep in conversation. Johnny Moyes found that he had an inclination to worry too much. He retired in 1973 from district cricket and football but returned in 1976 as a State selector, replacing longtime team-mate Les Favell. Dansie, a qualified accountant, non-drinker and non-smoker, spent most of his working life with government departments, and then took the appointment as bursar to Norwood High School. There he coaches under-age cricket and football sides.

DARLING, Joseph ("Paddy"), 1870–1946

A teak-tough South Australian-born pastoralist, sports store proprietor, and politician, who ranks with Clem Hill, Vernon Ransford, Warren Bardsley, Arthur Morris, Neil Harvey, Bill Lawry and Alan Border among Australia's finest left-handed batsmen and among Australia's greatest captains. He was the sixth son of the Honourable John Darling, merchant-farmer and member of the South Australian Legislative Council. Joe was only ten months old when his father introduced a Bill into the house of Assembly granting a lease on parklands that became known as Adelaide Oval. He followed his father's interest in politics, became an independent member of the Tasmanian Legislative Assembly in 1920, and one of the instigators of the 1922 movement to form the Country Party.

Joe Darling was born at Glen Osmond, SA, and educated at Prince Alfred College, Adelaide, where he became devoted to cricket. On the day before his 15th birthday he went on to Adelaide Oval and scored 252 for his school against the Collegiate School of St Peter, batting for six hours and offering only two chances in surpassing the record of 209 not out set by George Giffen. This innings won him a place in the Fifteen of South Australia and Victoria that played the Australian team on Adelaide Oval in March, 1886. Joe scored only 16 but he did it in such a style he was hailed by the senior players as a budding champion.

John Darling strongly objected to his son's fondness for sport, however, and took him out of cricket and Australian Rules football teams when he finished school to spend 12 months at Roseworthy Agricultural School. Joe worked in a bank and then was appointed manager of one of the family's wheat farms. He was out of cricket for two years but returned in the summer of 1893–94 to open a sports store in Rundle Street, Adelaide. He immediately proved his merit as a batsman and was chosen for inter-Colonial cricket, an event he celebrated by marrying Alice Minna Blanche Francis; they

First-Class Averages: Batting, 10,637 runs at 34.42.

Tests (34): 1,657 runs at 28.56.

305

had 10 sons and five daughters. After distinguishing himself against A. E. Stoddart's English team in 1894–95 he was chosen for the first of his four English tours in 1896. He went as captain in 1899, 1902, and 1905.

On those four visits to England, Darling won a universal reputation for his stoutness of character and became known as a man who scorned any underhand act. He was so tough that even Ernie ("Jonah") Jones, famous for his physical powers, succumbed to him in a dressing-room wrestle. Against Leicestershire in 1896 he took part in three stands of over 100 in making 194, his highest score in England. When Australia were set 123 to win against Cambridge University in 1899, Joe scored 60 not out and Jack Worrall 53 not out to give Australia a 10 wickets win. In 1905, against the Gentlemen at Lord's, Darling (117 not out) put on 273 unbeaten with Warwick Armstrong (248 not out), and the same season he and Monty Noble added 275 for the fifth wicket against Sussex at Hove. Darling made 21 first-class centuries in all with a mixture of courage, patient defence and fierce hitting.

His best year was at home in 1897–98, when his Test scores were 7 and 101 at Sydney, 36 at Melbourne, 178 at Adelaide, 12 and 29 at Melbourne, and 14 and 160 at Sydney. He made his 160 out of 253 in 165 minutes when Australia needed 275 to win, hitting 30 fours, Australia winning a thriller by six wickets. His highest score in first-class matches was his 210 for South Australia against Queensland in 1898–99. Between 1893 and 1908 while he ran his Adelaide sports store, Joe made merry against all types of bowling in club cricket. He averaged 144 for East Torrens in 1899–1900, 96.66 for Adelaide in 1896–97, and 86.20 for Sturt in 1904–05. He scored 235 not out for Adelaide v. Port Austral in 1897, when he had to stop batting because of the illness of one of his children, and 259 not out for East Torrens v. Port Adelaide in 1899. On Hindmarsh Oval in 1908, he contributed 77 not out in a total of 2 for 93 which included two sundries.

In September, 1908, Darling sold up his Adelaide shop and left to settle in Tasmania, where he pioneered the eradication of the rabbits that over-ran his own and other properties, worked for over 25 years on the committee that ran the Royal Hobart Show, and was a pillar of the Tasmanian Stockowners' and Orchardists' Association. He built up one of the best flocks in the State with South Australian merino rams and his wool topped the Hobart sales several times. In 1920, he introduced subterranean clover to Tasmania.

He held his seat in the Tasmanian parliament from 1921 until his death in 1946, a forceful no-nonsense speaker who spared neither friend nor foe. In the 1930s he won small farmers an exemption from land tax and in 1945 his charges of maladministration led to the appointment of a Royal Commission whose findings, after his death, proved a minister and

A youthful Joe Darling faces the bowling in England where his feats won him a place among Australia's great left-handers.

two others guilty of accepting bribes. One of his closest friends in parliament was C. J. Eady, the high-scoring batsman who had toured England with Joe in 1896. Originally, Joe lived in the Tasmanian midlands on a property called "Stonehenge" bought for him by his father, but in 1919 he moved to Claremont House at Claremont. When he heard a radio description of Jardine's field placings in 1932–33, he is said to have leapt from his chair and before a ball was bowled say, "My God, they're going to bowl at our batsman's body."

On his three tours of England as Australia's captain Darling helped bring changes in the conduct of matches that later were written into the laws. He persuaded the MCC to award six for hits over the fence or over the ropes whereas the ball had previously to be hit right out of the ground to earn six. He helped make it mandatory for captains to exchange the names of their twelve players before matches began to prevent the use of a brilliant fieldsman as twelfth man for a player who left the field, but who took no other part in the match. And he had the law on declarations altered after an incident in the First Test at Nottingham in 1899.

Darling declared Australia's innings closed at lunch but W. G. Grace, realising England's only chance was a draw, demanded an extra ten minutes for rolling the pitch. Darling had the law changed so that no additional time could be taken for rolling if the declaration was made within 15 minutes of the start of the luncheon interval. Noticing that English bowlers stayed on the field to fill their tracks with sawdust when rain drove players from the field, Darling had the instructions to umpires amended to read: "In order to facilitate play at the earliest moment in wet weather, the umpires shall see that foot marks made by bowlers and batsmen are cleaned out, dried, and filled with sawdust at any time in the match, although the game is not actually in progress."

One of Joe's great coups was in overcoming his father's objections to cricket. When the old wheat-buyer finally relented and went to watch his son, Joe made a century against Stoddart's team on Adelaide Oval. Thrilled by his son's display, the Hon John Darling went into the dressing-room and gave Joe a gold watch and a cheque representing a pound for every run Joe had scored. The elder Darling became so keen on cricket he followed his son to the major grounds in Melbourne and Sydney. But when Joe made 178 against England at Adelaide in 1897–98 he reduced his cheque to £78 or £1 for every run over 100. "One has to be canny with Joe. He bats better when the silver is up," he said.

Joe Darling, nicknamed "Paddy" because of his resemblance to the great boxer Paddy Slavin, continued scoring heavily in Tasmanian club cricket right through middle age. For Claremont in 1921, he made 100 in an hour, including 29 runs off an eight-ball over. At 52, he made 133 not out, with seven sixes and 12 fours, for Break-o'-Day, who made 6 for 219 after being set to make 203 to win in 90 minutes. He was always a batsman of resource, a great driver on the offside who could cut harder behind point than any of his contemporaries, and he was one of the finest of all Australian fieldsmen at mid-on or in the deep. He was the great-uncle of W. M. ("Ric") Darling, who has played 14 Tests for Australia and fields in such commanding style.

Joe Darling captained Australia 21 times between 1899 and

308

1905 when he quit because he said it was not fair to his wife to continue. On his four tours of England he made 109 catches, and countless friends. It was Joe Darling who, after losing every toss in the Tests against England in 1905, appeared at the door of the English dressing-room for the Festival match at Scarborough wrapped only in a towel. "I can't beat 'Jacker' (F. S. Jackson) at tossing, so I thought I'd wrestle him for first innings," he said.

An attractive batsman for Australia in 12 Tests between 1932 and 1937, one of an array of Victorian left-handers that included Leo O'Brien, Ernie Bromley, Ian Lee, George Newstead and Frank Sides. He was regarded as the most promising left-handed colt produced in Australia after the first war but developed slowly. When he first came into big cricket he had the reputation of a dasher prone to flick at balls outside the off-stump or to try leg-glancing good length balls on the middle stump.

The 1931–32 season was the turning point in his career as he scored 473 runs in first-class matches at an average of 47.30. Darling and McCabe were considered the only Australian batsmen who did not become "bumper happy" in the Bodyline series. This boosted his confidence and poise, and he was chosen in the 1934 Australian team to tour England, scoring 1,022 runs at an average of 34.06, topscore 117.

Darling was often described as an all-rounder but there was little merit in his bowling. His action was crude and he let go fast medium deliveries right-handed without any guile or deliberation, with surprise his main weapon. In his early days he was a very fast outfielder but he slowed down through increasing weight and later fielded best close in where his agility and anticipation paid off. He took two remarkable legside catches in the 1936–37 Test at Melbourne to dismiss Hammond and Leyland on a "sticky" wicket.

Darling began his grade career with South Melbourne, but later played with the Melbourne club, who made him a clerk at the MCC office. At South Melbourne, he played with Dr Roy Park, "Snowy" Davidson and Frank Morton, three highly colourful characters. For South Melbourne, he scored 1,632 runs between 1926–27 and 1930–31 at 34.74, with 117 in 1930–31 his best score. For Melbourne between 1931–32 and 1936–37 he scored 1,193 runs at 51.87, topscore 127, missing the 1936–37 season when he was touring South Africa with Vic Richardson's team. Darling, who played in all five Tests in South Africa, was batting with Stan McCabe at Johannesburg in 1935 when the famous appeal against the light by the fielding side was made, the South African captain, H. F. Wade, alleging that his fieldsmen were in danger from McCabe's fero-

DARLING, Leonard Stuart, 1909–

First-Class Averages: Batting, 5,780 runs at 42.50; Bowling, 32 wickets at 47.00.

Tests (12): 474 runs at 27.88.

cious hitting. The appeal was upheld, with McCabe on 189, Darling 37.

At the end of the 1936–37 season Darling went to Adelaide, where he married and dropped right out of first-class cricket.

For Victoria, Darling's highest score was 185 against Queensland in Brisbane in 1932–33, but probably his most meritorious innings was his 103 for Victoria against England at Melbourne the same year. He had three Tests scores over 50 in 18 innings, topscore 85. In all first-class matches he made 16 centuries.

DARLING, Warwick Maxwell ("Rick") 1957–

First-Class Averages: Batting, 4,730 runs at 37.54.

Tests (14): 697 runs at 26.80.

A right-hand opening batsman of obvious quality even at the highest levels of cricket, whose talents have been wasted by his failure to find a regular place in the batting order and his compulsive hooking. Darling has been flattened many times in first-class matches trying to hook bouncers but he keeps getting up to play the shot again. The introduction of the batting helmet has improved his confidence and possibly has kept him alive. At the end of the 1981–82 season he had had seven summers of first-class cricket, but with the return of WSC players it had been three summers since he appeared in the last of his 14 Tests. He is among the most nervous of the world's first-class cricketers, as highly-strung as a concert violin, given to biting his nails before he bats, though he no longer has dizzy spells.

Darling, born in Waikerie, South Australia, is a great-nephew of Joe Darling. At his best he is all flair and excitement, as the *Adelaide News'* Mike Coward described it. "For those who have seen this young man during a command performance, it is difficult to accept that he is not regularly required in the Test arena," said Coward. "He strongly denies he is emotionally ill-equipped to play Test cricket, yet he is still shackled with an identity crisis as a cricketer."

Darling learned to play cricket at his family's home at Ramco on the Murray River and played for the Salisbury district club in 1970–71. He still loves the river, the water-skiing, trail-bike riding, and fishing but he has learned to adjust to life in Adelaide where he works as a public relations officer for a Building Society, the official sponsors of South Australian cricket. He is desperately keen to get back into the Australian Test side.

Darling won his place in the Australian team as an opener. He says he has no objection to facing fast bowling, but he loathes opening. His dislike of opening flared on the Indian tour in 1979. Darling said he could not cope with spending hours in the fierce sun and then immediately opening the Australian innings. Captain Kim Hughes agreed to drop him down the order. He was notably unproductive as a middle

Rick Darling goes down after a ball from Bob Willis hit him on the helmet.

order batsman, and has since returned to opening for South Australia, with some dramatic results in 1981–82. His omission from the Australian team to tour Pakistan in 1982 dismayed many followers of the game. Darling has played in two Test series against India (1977–78, 1979), one against West Indies (1978) one against England (1978–79), and one against Pakistan (1978–79).

English fast bowler Bob Willis hit him just above the heart early at Adelaide in the Fifth Test in 1979, a blow described as "near fatal." Gum he was chewing lodged in the back of his throat but John Emburey cleared the obstruction and got him breathing again. Darling is probably the best and most exciting cover fieldsman in Australia today.

311

**DAVIDSON, Alan Keith
("Davo"), 1929–**

First-Class Averages:
Batting, 6,804 runs at
32.86; Bowling, 672
wickets at 20.90.

Tests (44): 1,328 runs at
24.59; 186 wickets at
20.58.

A match-winning all-rounder of enormous strength, the delight of small boys across Australia in a first-class career that extended from 1949 until 1963. From a 15 pace run, he bowled fast-medium left-arm with a wheeling action, moving the new ball late in the air and either way off the pitch. With the bat, co-ordination of wrists, hands and arms enabled him to play a wide range of attacking strokes with exceptional power, and it was unjust that he did not make a Test century. In the field he took some of the finest catches the game has seen, moving with uncanny anticipation.

Davidson came from Lisarow, a small country town five miles from Gosford, New South Wales, and learned the game on a pitch he dug himself out of the side of a hill. "I burrowed out the pitch on a hillside and although it was a good flat strip, when I missed the stumps I had to chase the ball down the hill," he said. He bowled left-arm leg-breaks, but when his uncle needed a pace bowler for a Gosford team "Davo" volunteered for the job and seldom bowled spinners after that.

He was a splendid Rugby League player and went through Gosford High School teams in cricket and football to the New South Wales Combined High Schools team in which he met Richie Benaud and Graeme Hole for the first time. In the summer of 1948–49 he went to Sydney to further his career and quickly won a place in the New South Wales side. He was dropped from the State team in 1951–52 but returned the following season after a spectacular New Zealand tour to win back his State berth and to play his first Test against England. In New Zealand with the Australian Second XI he took 10 for 29 off 81 deliveries against Wairarapa at Masterton and scored 157 not out, a memorable double in representative cricket.

Initially, Davidson had a supporting role to that great pace trio, Lindwall, Miller and Johnston but as they declined he took over as the spearhead of the Australian attack and for a time ruled as the best new ball bowler in cricket. He had discarded football to concentrate on cricket but he still trained with the Western Suburbs Rugby League club in Sydney. Against England in Australia in 1958–59, he took 24 wickets, against England in England in 1961, he took 23 wickets and against England in Australia in 1962–63 he took a further 24 wickets, all the time catching magnificently, throwing superbly and scoring useful runs with the bat.

His best effort with the bat was in 1961 at Manchester when he and McKenzie added 98 for the last wicket, Davidson scoring 77 not out. In that innings as in many others he made some amazing hits right out of the ground. At Sydney against Cowdrey he pulled one ball high on to the roof of the stand and straight drove the next on to the wall at the back of the hill, with the ball still rising on impact.

Towards the end of his career Davidson used to hobble a lot

312

in the midst of long bowling spells. His captain, Richie Benaud, would put his arm around Davo's large girth and say, "Just one more over, Al, pal," and keep him going for another hour or so that way. Benaud knew Davidson was a match-winner and a great team man and that every over he could extract from Davidson improved Australia's chances. "Davidson may have limped more than most of his contemporaries when bowling but he had a heart bigger than most of them," said Benaud. On the Australian tour of South Africa in 1957–58, the Australian team all chipped in to buy Alan Davidson a massage table. They figured that he spent so much time on the table he deserved one of his own.

In the tied Test at Brisbane in 1960–61 against the West Indies, Davidson became the first player to score 100 runs and take 10 wickets in a Test match. He played 193 first-class matches between 1949 and 1963, scoring nine centuries and taking 168 catches, best bowling 7 for 31, for New South Wales. After his retirement he left a job in a bank to become director of Rothman's National Sports Foundation. He has been president of the NSWCA for some years and a national selector.

DAVIES, Sir John George, 1846–1913

First-Class Averages: Batting, 149 runs at 14.90; Bowling, 6 wickets at 6.33.

A former Speaker of the Tasmanian Parliament and Mayor of Hobart who represented Tasmania 15 times and captained the State team that visited New Zealand in 1884. He was always closely identified with southern Tasmanian cricket and played a big part in persuading the government to clear and fence the area that became Hobart Oval, on a spot overlooking the city with views of the River Derwent and Mount Wellington. On the day Davies said the ground was ready for play the top-dressing cut up badly and E. H. Butler bowled 19 balls without conceding a run and took six wickets.

Davies played for Tasmania against four English touring teams between 1873–74 and 1887–88. He set something of an endurance record by playing for South versus North 24 times between 1865 and 1889. He failed to score 10 times and averaged 12.05 for 37 completed innings. In the 1863 match he scored eight runs in two hours. He had more influence in cricket committee rooms than on the results of matches. He was a wellknown cricket writer in Tasmania and managed an Australian rifle shooting team at Bisley.

DAVIES, Geoffrey Robert, 1946–

A valuable allrounder who was on the fringe of Test selection several times in the 1960s after outstanding performances for New South Wales. Many less talented players have appeared for Australia. He was an attractive right-hand shotmaker

First-Class Averages:
Batting, 3,903 runs at
36.13; Bowling, 107
wickets at 32.18.

who timed the ball splendidly, a right-arm leg-spinner, and a slips fieldsman of high standard. There was an unmistakable quality about his cricket but he never wore the bulky green Test cap of Australia.

Davies was born in the Sydney suburb of Randwick and went to the Coogee Primary School, where he bowled medium-pace. At Randwick High School he switched to leg-spinners and won a place in the NSW Under 14 side with promising batting and bowling. At 12, he played in the Randwick club's fourth grade and at 16 he played in his initial first grade match. By the time he was 20 he was a first-class cricketer and experts praised his allround skills.

Former Test star Bill O'Reilly was the most vociferous of the critics who stressed that Davies' cricket had the stamp of genuine class and deserved more opportunities. Davies, 6 ft tall, but a rather lean 11 stone, was twice chosen for NSW in 1964–65 but both times was twelfth man. In 1965–66, he played three Shield games and took 3 for 30 in the match against the MCC. In 1966–67 he made 557 runs, including two centuries in first-class matches, 123 v. Queensland and 101 v. South Australia, and took 17 wickets. This won him a place in the Australian team that visited New Zealand in 1967, where he had knocks of 91 and 89 and took 20 wickets.

At the end of the New Zealand trip he went to England to further his experience in League cricket with East Lancashire, scoring 695 runs and taking 40 wickets in the season. He continued to take wickets and make runs for NSW but not enough to force his way into the Australian side. He made 112 against Queensland in 1967–68 and his career highest score, 127, against Victoria at Melbourne in 1968–69, finishing with six first-class centuries in all. He twice took five wickets in an innings for NSW and held 70 catches, drifting out of big cricket when he settled in the Blue Mountains west of Sydney.

DAVIS, Ian Charles
1953–

A slightly-built, fair-haired, trimly-moustached right-hand opening batsman who played for Australia at the age of 20 and has led an erratic career ever since. At his best, he times his drives, glances and cuts impressively and with the unhurried grace of a class batsman, but he has been unable to string good scores together, and this inconsistency has given him problems with selectors. He is an outstanding fieldsman in any position.

Davis, born at North Sydney, made his debut for New South Wales in 1973–74 against Western Australia at Perth, and played for Australia the same season against New Zealand at Melbourne. He looked a hot property, and played the 1975–76 season in Queensland. Despite an innings of 91 for NSW against England in 1974–75 he lost his Test place, but returned to score 105 against Pakistan at Adelaide in 1976–77. In the Centenary Test at Melbourne he made a valuable 68 in Australia's second innings.

He went to England with the Australian team in 1977, but disappointed, scoring 608 runs at 30.40, with a topscore of 83. He played in three Tests on the tour but scored only 107 runs at 17.83, apparently unable to handle the ball cutting off the pitch. Following the tour he joined WSC, and since the settlement he has been unable to win back his place in the Australian team. He has tended in recent years to be critical of selection policies and this may not have helped him.

First-Class Averages: Batting, 4,508 runs at 33.89.

Tests (15): 692 runs at 26.61.

DAVISON, Brian Fettes, 1946–

An aggressive right-hand batsman who has led Tasmania with great flair for two seasons. He bowls lively right-arm medium pacers, fields energetically and ensures that his team-mates do the same. He is one of the most craftsmanlike cricketers to play in Australia, a no-nonsense professional who has scored more than 21,000 runs in all first-class matches and relishes a tough, hard-fought match.

Davison was born in what was then called Rhodesia but is now Zimbabwe. He has applied for permanent residency in Australia and after interviews with officials from the Department of Immigration believes his wife and two children will be allowed to emigrate to Australia. He plays for Leicestershire in northern summers and made his highest first-class score, 189, for Leicestershire against Australia in 1975. He made his first-class debut for Rhodesia in 1967–68 and first played for Tasmania in 1979–80, taking over from Jack Simmons as captain the following season. He made his highest score for Tasmania, 173, against Victoria in 1980–81. In more than 360 first-class matches, his best bowling figures were 5 for 52 for Rhodesia against Griqualand West in 1967–68. In 1980–81 he made four centuries in successive matches in scoring 700 runs for Tasmania in 10 innings.

DE COURCY, James Henry, 1927–

A classy right-hand batsman, one of many Australian team players produced in the Hunter Valley of New South Wales, whose brief Test career failed to convey his ability to charm spectators with strokes all around the ground. He played all his club cricket in Newcastle and held his place in the New South Wales side for 10 seasons despite the lack of regular encounters with top-class bowling. This probably accounted for his habit of getting away to promising starts without reaching big scores. He made six centuries in first-class cricket, an inadequate return for a batsman of such obvious talents.

First-Class Averages: Batting, 3,778 runs at 37.04.

Tests (3): 81 runs at 16.20.

De Courcy first appeared for NSW in 1947–48, aged 20. In 1950–51 he made a stylish 72 not out for NSW against the MCC. He went to England with Hassett's Australian team in 1953, scoring 1,214 runs at 41.86, scoring well enough in the County matches to play in the last three Tests. He began with a bright innings of 41 at Old Trafford but failed in the other five innings. He made 204 against Combined Services and three other tour centuries. In 1953–54 he made 405 runs in State games for NSW. He played a delightful innings of 95 against Victoria in 1954–55 when NSW were set 400 to win and reached 363.

DELL, Anthony Ross
1947–

First-Class Averages:
Batting, 169 runs at 5.63;
Bowling, 137 wickets at
26.70.

Tests (2): 6 runs, NA; 6
wickets at 26.66.

A heavyweight Queensland fast left-arm bowler who pussy-footed up to the bowling crease with a strange, staccato approach in which he never seemed to get his paces right. He had the physique to do great things but could never get his run and his arm action co-ordinated often enough to justify Test permanency despite considerable coaching by people like Ray Lindwall. He moved the ball disconcertingly off the pitch and in the air on the few occasions the components of his delivery came together. Dell, born in England at Lymington, Hampshire, played for Queensland over five summers and six times took five wickets in an innings. He was a genuine tailender with the bat. In his first Test appearance he opened the Australian attack with Dennis Lillee in the final Test against England in 1970–71. He later played a Test against New Zealand in 1973–74. He was a fine stamp of a man, well-liked but with troublesome feet that clearly stemmed from his enormous bulk. Not a man to run a quick three with, but a delightful companion in after match gatherings.

DIAMOND, Austin,
1874–1966

First-Class Averages:
Batting, 1,681 runs at
32.96.

A resourceful, Yorkshire-born right-hand batsman who was one of the personalities of New South Wales cricket for more than 30 years, widely known for his vast cricket knowledge as well as for his batting and agile fielding. He made four splendid centuries for NSW, including a double century, and countless runs in club cricket for Leichhardt—Balmain, Burwood—Western Suburbs and Gordon. His heavy black moustache and dour demeanour were familiar to hundreds of district players and his name is perpetuated in the diamond monogram for cap and blazer of the Western Suburbs club.

Diamond, born in Huddersfield, played for Leichhardt from 1896 to 1903, in which year he joined Burwood where he played a valuable role in the side captained by G. P. Barbour. He first played for NSW in 1899–1900. He batted with a mixture of strong defence and powerful aggression, holding the bat on the bottom of the handle. In 1905–06 he had to retire after scoring 164 against South Australia at Adelaide and rush back to Sydney following the death of his brother. In 1906–07 he made 138 in a second wicket stand of 193 with Hopkins against SA, and 210 not out, his career best, against Victoria, both at Sydney. In 1911–12, he made 105 not out against Queensland in Sydney.

Diamond was a member of E. R. Mayne's team that toured America between May and September, 1913. The team won 49 of its 53 matches and Diamond contributed 803 runs in fine style. He was in the Western Suburbs premiership sides of 1903 and 1906, taking over the captaincy from G. P. Barbour in 1906–07 and retaining the job until 1916 when he joined the AIF. He returned to the West captaincy in 1919, but the following season transferred to Gordon. In 13 seasons with Wests he scored 4,694 runs at 31.71, all in first grade. The club adopted his name as its emblem in a special motion at the annual meeting in 1918. He twice played for NSW against his native England, scoring 41 in four innings. He held 35 catches in first-class matches.

An inspiring personality who chose banking instead of cricket after showing great promise before and after World War I. He was a fast bowler whose opportunities in big cricket were limited first by "Tibby" Cotter and later by Jack Gregory.

Docker began with the Burwood club—later renamed Western Suburbs—in the Sydney grade competition in 1906, and made his debut for New South Wales against Queensland in 1909–10, taking 9 for 132. He became a captain with the first AIF and after playing several services matches at Lord's was one of the instigators of the tour by the first AIF team. He opened the bowling in the first match played by the AIF team, with Kelleway bowling at the other end. Docker took 5 for 34 and Jack Gregory did not bowl. *Wisden* records that although Docker took 5 for 41 and made 52 not out a week later against Cambridge University, it had by then become apparent that Gregory was a far more formidable proposition for batsmen.

Docker had a further good performance when the AIF side reached South Africa, where he took 5 for 20 against Transvaal. He played in the AIF's Australian matches but injuries restricted his later appearances. In 1918 he played for the Dominions XI against England in three one day matches. The Docker family were involved in New South Wales cricket as far back as 1863. Cyril's younger brothers Keith and Phillip were prominent cricketers in the State, but none of the family achieved Test status. Cyril Docker played 23 first-class matches for the first AIF side and had 24 in all.

DOCKER, Cyril Talbot, 1884–1975

First-Class Averages: Batting, 371 runs at 16.86; Bowling, 58 wickets at 18.81.

DOLLERY, Keith Robert, 1924–

First-Class Averages: Batting, 958 runs at 11.97; Bowling, 227 wickets at 26.51.

The nomad son of a Queensland stationmaster who bowled right-arm fast-medium for Queensland, Auckland (NZ), Tasmania, Stockport in the Central Lancashire League, and for the Warwickshire County club. He moved the ball both ways when conditions suited him and took hat-tricks against Kent and Gloucestershire during his six seasons with Warwickshire, letting the ball go from a spendid high action, exploiting every inch of his 5 ft 10 in frame.

Dollery, born at Cooroy, Queensland, moved around the State to fit in with his father's transfers but spent most of his schooldays at Indooroopilly State School and Mackay High School. He made his debut for Queensland in 1947–48 but after two matches decided to use his cricketing skills—he was also a handy late order right-hand batsman—to see the world. In 1949–50 he played for Auckland in New Zealand and in 1950–51 bobbed up in the Tasmanian side. When Freddie Brown's MCC side visited Hobart that summer, Dollery at one stage had 3 for none against them.

Talking to spinner Eric Hollies after the match, Keith learned that his namesake Tom Dollery captained Hollies' County team, Warwickshire, back in England. This led to Warwickshire offering Keith a trial and he went to Stockport in the Central Lancashire League while he qualified for the County. He played friendly matches for Warwickshire from 1951 and became a full-time professional when he qualified in 1953. He began by taking 94 wickets in his first season despite frequent injuries. In all first-class matches for Warwickshire until his retirement in 1956 he took 215 wickets at 25.81, best figures 8 for 42 against Sussex. He also scored 927 runs at 12.70, highest score 41. He married a Stockport girl, fathered three daughters, and returned to live in Sydney, where he sells hearing aids.

DONNAN, Henry ("Harry"), 1864–1956

First-Class Averages: Batting, 4,262 runs at 29.19; Bowling, 29 wickets at 41.06.

Tests (5): 75 runs at 8.33.

A fascinating figure in Australian cricket, probably our last outstanding round-arm bowler. He was a right-hand batsman of extraordinary patience who for many years was regarded as the best defensive batsman in Australia. He made it his job to wear down the bowling for batsmen who followed and his scoring was agonisingly slow.

Donnan, born at Liverpool on the outskirts of Sydney, first came to notice at Sydney Grammar School with a series of striking performances bowling round-arm. Not long after leaving school he joined the Colonial Sugar Refinery's head office and worked for them for the next 42 years. He married Syd Gregory's sister, the daughter of Ned Gregory, herself an outstanding cricketer who once hit a ball over the fence at Sydney Cricket Ground in a ladies' match, the wicket having been prepared by her father, then the ground's curator.

318

Donnan, only 5 ft 6 ins tall, was slow to develop as a batsman and did not reach the front rank of Australian batsmen
until he was 32, when he played innings of 160 and 46 for New
South Wales against Victoria at Melbourne, 93 against South
Australia at Adelaide, and 48 and 67 not out against South
Australia at Sydney. This splendid sequence of scores won
him a place in the Australian team to tour England in 1896,
and he promptly justified his inclusion by scoring 88 for the
tourists against the Rest Of Australia in Sydney, just before
sailing. He showed plenty of courage on the tour and some
fine offside strokes but was sloppy in the field. He made 1,009
runs in all matches on the tour at 23.46, including 167 against
Derbyshire.

Back in Australia he continued to show good form for New
South Wales but was not chosen again to tour. At Adelaide in
1898–99, he opened for New South Wales and was 160 not out
when the innings ended at 374, but despite his efforts South
Australia won by 57 runs. He and his brother-in-law had
some big partnerships in Sydney grade cricket, and in 1894
put on 309 for Sydney against Combined Country, each retiring unbeaten on 201. In 1897, Donnan made 308 in a total of
613 for South Sydney against North Sydney. He also made 353
in a St George junior association match for Bexley Oriental in
1908 at the age of 44, adding 426 for the fourth wicket with
Alan Cooper (228).

Donnan did not take a wicket with his round-armers in his
five Tests. As his career progressed his early hostility with
the ball was overshadowed by the advent of the over the
shoulder bowlers. In all first-class matches between 1887 and
1901, he scored with six centuries. Undoubtedly, he would
have played many more matches for Australia but for his
poor fielding.

A great right-arm leg spinner who enjoyed more success in
England than any post-war bowler of his type but played
only three Tests for Australia. He was a dogged batsman,
strong in driving and cutting, and fielded splendidly close to
the stumps. He played for Australia at baseball, was a seven
handicap golfer, and as a keen cricket theorist had a big influence on the development of young Australian bowlers on
tour in England. Dooland is credited with teaching the "flipper," a wrong-un that gains topspin off the pitch, to Richie
Benaud.

Dooland, born in Adelaide, learned to bowl on a concrete
pitch laid down in the family backyard by his father, Walter
Dooland, who from the beginning encouraged Bruce to spin
the ball. He progressed from Thebarton Central School to
Adelaide High School and at 15 set a bowling record by

DOOLAND, Bruce
1923–1980

First-Class Averages:
Batting, 6,907 runs at
24.40; Bowling, 1,016
wickets at 21.98.

Tests (3): 76 runs at 19.00;
9 wickets at 46.55.

taking 72 wickets in eight matches. He joined West Torrens to play grade cricket and impressed selectors of the South Australian team who invited him to play against New South Wales at the age of 17, but Dooland's bank employers refused him leave.

His first–class debut was delayed by service in a commando unit in the Pacific until 1945–46, when he took the first hat-trick in postwar Shield matches for South Australia against Victoria. He went to New Zealand in 1946–47 with the Australian team and in 1947, played for Australia in the Third Test against Hammond's English team, taking 4 for 69, and staying at the crease while McCool reached his century. He had 3 for 133 in the Fourth Test but in the Fifth was replaced by Tribe who had been dropped for Dooland in the Third Test. His success in Shield matches continued but such was the spin bowling talent in Australia at the time he played in only one more Test, the Third against India in 1947–48 at Melbourne.

As the 1948 Australians moved triumphantly around England, with Bradman making very little use of leg-spinners McCool and Ring, Dooland played out the season with East Lancashire. He had four years with the club which twice won the Lancashire League Cup while he was with them. Nottinghamshire invited him to join them and he made his debut for the county in 1953 at Trent Bridge against Kent. In his first two seasons of county cricket Dooland took 172 wickets at 16.58 in 1953, and 196 wickets at 15.48 in 1954. His 368 wickets in two seasons was the best performance by a leg-spinner in England since "Tich" Freeman retired in 1936. In naming Dooland one of its five cricketers of the year 1954, *Wisden* said he "did much to restore right–arm leg-break and googly bowling to an important part of the strategy of the game."

Tall (6 ft), athletic, with long arms and powerful fingers, he varied his flight and pace cleverly, bouncing the ball awkwardly from a fluent, high action. The leg-break was his stock ball, with occasional top-spinners thrown in and, occasionally, the wrong-un. He had some amazing successes, including 16 for 83 against Essex in 1954, 22 for 97 in two matches against Somerset in 1953 and 13 wickets against both Leicester and Northants. In 1953 and 1954 he played for Players against Gentlemen at Lord's and in 1950–51 he toured India with the Commonwealth side, making two centuries in the unofficial Tests. Much to the disappointment of the Nottinghamshire committee, he returned to Australia after the 1957 season so that his children could be educated in Australia. He twice completed the double of 100 wickets and 1,000 runs in a season. He took five wickets or more in an innings 76 times during his career.

Bruce Dooland's finger-tip control is vividly shown in this shot as he released the ball.

Australians are not immune to the common cricket disease of failing to score. Statisticians have calculated that about 10 per cent of batsmen in all cricket countries head back to the pavilion without a run to their name, and even the greatest Australian has done so. Spectacles or the failure to score in both innings of a match have been registered regularly since P. S. McDonnell became the first Australian to do so in January, 1883, against England. Talk to the average youngster learning the game and the conversation quickly turns to golden (first ball), silver (second ball) and bronze (third ball) ducks.

South Australian bowler Alby Wright holds the world record for most ducks in succession in first-class cricket, with six in 1905–06. In Wright's defence it should be stressed that he had a highest score of 53, although batting was clearly not his specialty (average 7.58 in 52 innings). He made up for it by taking 106 wickets at 30.81 for SA. Another prominent bowler, Victorian Jim Higgs, made an entire tour of England without scoring a run in 1975, but he only had two innings, finishing with one duck and one nought not out.

The most sensational ducks are seldom those by tailenders, however, but those suffered by brilliant batsmen. Warren Bardsley, a great opener, recorded one of Test cricket's most dramatic ducks in 1926 when he was out to the first ball of the Test at Leeds, which led to Charlie Macartney at first drop scoring a famous century before lunch. Some notable ducks involving Australians:

• The first ever Test duck—by E. J. Gregory at Melbourne in 1878.

• First Spectacles—by P. S. McDonnell in 1883 at Sydney, followed by team-mate T. W. Garrett in the same match. Australian Edwin Evans had spectacles at Lord's in 1886 and by the turn of the century P. McShane, A. C. Bannerman, Jack Worrall, M. A. Noble and S. E. Gregory had all joined the Australian spectacles club.

• Eight Australians were out for a duck in 1896 when the MCC dismissed Australia for 18. The scorecard read: J. J. Kelly 8, H. Graham 4, G. H. S. Trott 6, S. E. Gregory 0, F. A. Iredale 0, C. Hill 0, H. Trumble 0, J. Darling 0, C. J. Eady 0, T. R. McKibbin 0, G. Giffen absent 0; Extras 0. Total 18. Australia had seven ducks in one innings in 1878 at The Oval against The Players, when E. Barrett took all 10 wickets for 43 runs.

• Australia dismissed seven batsmen for ducks on the same (1878) tour in an innings of 19 by MCC And Ground. Sixteen players made ducks in that match, Australia winning outright in 4 hours 30 minutes.

• In the three completed innings of the 1888 England v. Australia Test at Manchester, 13 players failed to score, two of them "not out."

• Father and son, E. J. and S. E. Gregory, were both out for a duck in their Test debuts for Australia. Another member of the family, J. M. Gregory, cousin of Syd, also got a duck in his Test debut in 1920–21.

• At Leeds in 1899, there were six Australian ducks in the Test against England.

• On an ill-prepared pitch at Brisbane in 1931–32, Bradman fell down twice avoiding Eddie Gilbert fliers, with slips and the wicket-keeper closer to the boundary than the stumps. Gilbert took 2 for 0, including Bradman, in his first over. "Luckiest duck I ever made," said Bradman.

• Master batsman Bill Lawry made his first duck in his 103rd Test innings. This was two innings better than Arthur Morris' record of going without a duck until his 101st Test knock.

• In the Second Test against England at Sydney in 1936–37, three Australians, Bradman, McCabe and Leo O'Brien were all out for ducks in the same over on a sticky wicket.

• Stan McCabe always tried to encourage young batsmen dismissed for a duck by explaining to them that he made a duck in his first match for St. Joseph's College in Sydney, a duck in his first game for the Mosman club and a duck in his first innings for NSW. In his first Test McCabe hit a four from the first ball he received and was out next ball.

• Prolific Melbourne batsman Bill Ponsford was out for a duck only eight times in 235 innings and like Bradman's ducks, these got bigger headlines than his high scores.

• Don Bradman went to the wicket at The Oval in 1948 for his last Test innings requiring only four runs to average 100 in Tests, but was clean bowled for a duck by Eric Hollies.

• Jack Moroney, a heavy scorer in grade and inter-State cricket just after World War II was out for a duck in each innings of his first Test against England at Brisbane in 1950–51.

• Victorian pace bowler Alan Hurst made six ducks and one nought not out in 12 innings in the 1978–79 series against England.

• Clem Hill, Billy Brown, Norm O'Neill and Brian Booth are among the noted Australian batsmen who made ducks in their first innings in first-class cricket.

• Australian captain Greg Chappell, who has averaged 52.75 runs for every innings in his first-class career, had an astonishing seven ducks in the 1981–82 Australian season. Experts could not recall a worse record of ducks by a first-class batsman in the whole history of the game in Australia. And Chappell had begun with a double century in his first knock of the season!

• First Australian captain to register spectacles was Joe Darling in the 1902 Test at Sheffield, the sole Test played in that city.

• Victor Trumper had spectacles at the MCG against England in 1907–08.

• First Australian to achieve spectacles against South Africa was Bert Oldfield at the MCG in 1931–32, while the late Wally Grout was the first Australian to suffer the fate against the West Indies—at the SCG in 1960–61. Ken Mackay was the first Australian exponent of spectacles against India, a disaster he suffered in the Test at Kanpur in 1959–60.

DUFF, Reginald Alexander, 1878–1911

First-Class Averages: Batting, 6,589 runs at 35.04; Bowling, 14 wickets at 34.14.

Tests (22): 1,317 runs at 35.59; 4 wickets at 21.25.

An attacking, stylish right-hand batsman with a wide array of strokes he was eager to play, who formed one of cricket's greatest opening pairs with Victor Trumper. Duff was adept at driving the rising ball and relished rushing the score along, a dapper little man with a defiant thick upper lip, a superlative outfielder of exceptional speed of foot with a splendid throwing arm.

Duff toured England twice in Australian teams, in 1902 and 1905, when he was the only player to score a century in the Tests and Australia's only player to average over 40. His 146 at The Oval enabled Australia to reach 363 in a drawn match. This is still regarded as one of the great Test innings. Duff was not as sound as Trumper on damp pitches but he still managed to score more than 1,000 runs on both his trips to England.

He was a realist about who was the dominant partner in this remarkable partnership. As he padded up before going out to bat in one Test, he said, "Victor is taking me for a run again." But he complimented Trumper with exceptional judgement of a run, and bowlers seldom had a break from the elegant stroke play by Trumper when they bowled Duff's end.

One of the innings that helped make Duff's name was his 104 in the second innings of his first Test in 1901–02 at Melbourne. He batted at No. 7 in the first innings and topscored with 32. He and Armstrong were held back in the second innings until a wet pitch dried and he batted at No. 10. Duff made 104, Armstrong 45 not out and Australia won the game by 229 runs. This knock made Duff one of the exclusive group who have scored a century in their first Test. In 1982 he remained the only Australian to score a Test century going in at No. 10.

Duff impressed the famous English critic and player C. B. Fry. "Reggie Duff had a face like a good-looking brown trout and was full of Australian sunshine," Fry wrote. Duff earned this accolade by scoring 1,507 runs at 28.43 compared with Trumper's 2,570 at 48.49 in 1902 in England, and 1,395 at 29.68 compared with Trumper's 1,754 at 36.54 in 1905.

Sydney, with its hard pitches, was his spiritual home, however. He scored 3,406 runs in all for North Sydney club in district games at 38.27, topping the first-grade averages in 1899–1900 when he scored 562 runs at 62.40. On the Sydney

Cricket Ground he showed all his assured footwork on the drive and was full of enterprise. When NSW made 918 against South Australia on the SCG in 1900–01, Duff started the run riot with a dazzling 119. He made 132 there against Victoria in 1902–03, 132 against South Australia the same season, and 271 against South Australia in 1903–04. At Sydney he had stands of 298 against South Australia and 267 against Victoria, with Trumper. The only century he scored outside of Sydney in Shield matches was his 102 against Victoria at Melbourne in 1902–03.

Duff played 121 first-class matches between 1898 and 1908 and made 10 first-class centuries in all. His brother **Walter Scott Duff** (1875–1921) was a capable batsman for North Sydney for several seasons and played three times for NSW.

324

An attractive right-hand batsman from South Australia who toured New Zealand in the team captained by Billy Brown in 1949–50. He was born at Eudunda at the lower end of the Barossa Valley and played originally with the Senior Colts side in the Adelaide district competition. He went into the State side in 1948–49. At Adelaide Oval in 1949–50 he made a match-saving 121 not out against Victoria, and his 458 runs that season in first-class cricket earned him a trip to New Zealand, but he appeared in only four first-class tour matches, scoring 80 runs at 20.00. He finished his career with Port Adelaide.

DULDIG, Lance, 1922–

First-Class Averages: Batting, 2,027 runs at 32.17.

A right-hand batsman and right-arm fast medium bowler for Queensland, Victoria and in one Test for Australia. He played in 71 first-class matches, turning in fine performances with the ball. His bowling dominated his efforts in first-class cricket.

Born in Brisbane, he began with the Eastern Suburbs club as a teenager and first played for Queensland in 1964–65, continuing with his home State until he moved to live in Melbourne. He played for Victoria in the 1971–72 and 1972–73 seasons. In 1970–71, he took 8 for 55 and 5 for 70 for Queensland against Victoria, a match coup that won him his sole Test cap but he bowled in only one innings. He had little chance despite other fine efforts such as 5 for 21 for Victoria against Queensland and 5 for 16 for Victoria against New South Wales.

DUNCAN, John Ross Frederick, 1944–

First-Class Averages: Batting, 649 runs at 8.42; Bowling, 218 wickets at 31.19.

Tests (1): 3 runs at 3.00; 0 wickets for 30.

The Sydney-born grandson of an Irish Chieftain exiled to Australia for his part in the Irish insurrection of 1798. His grandfather Michael Dwyer was one of the boldest Irish leaders and held out in the Wicklow mountains for five years before he was deported in 1804 to Australia, where he died in 1826. Known as "E.B." despite his seven Christian names, he learned to play cricket in Sydney and made a big impression on "Plum" Warner when England toured Australia in 1903–04. "E.B." Dwyer bowled right-arm at a brisk pace but lacked consistency. He played for Redfern Wednesday Cricket Club in Sydney and later with Redfern. Warner urged him to go to England and in the spring of 1904 he turned up on the Lord's groundstaff. C. B. Fry saw him bowl and persuaded him to join Sussex.

E. B. Dwyer played club cricket in Brighton while he qualified for county cricket. In his first season with Sussex in 1906, he took 96 wickets at 26.80 each, which included a memorable coup against Middlesex. He took 7 for 56 and 9 for 44 for 16 wickets in a match that saw the powerful Middlesex side out

DWYER, John Elicius Benedict Bernard Placid Quirk Carrington, 1876–1912

for less than 100 in both innings and defeated outright. In 1907, he took 58 wickets at 27.65, including 6 for 25 against South Africa, who were out for 49. But in 1908 and 1909 he played in only a few matches before he dropped out of the side. His career best figures were 9 for 35 against Derbyshire at Brighton. In all first-class matches he took 179 wickets at 27.93 and scored 986 runs at 11.87, topscore 63 not out. He died at 36 in Crewe, where he was engaged as a professional.

DYMOCK, Geoffrey 1945–

First-Class Averages: Batting, 1,518 runs at 14.45; Bowling 425 wickets at 27.78.

Tests (21): 236 runs at 9.44; 78 wickets at 27.11.

Queensland's greatest wicket-taker, a cheerful, even-tempered left-arm medium-pace bowler who improved with age. He was about to retire several times when a further big haul of wickets kept him playing. He bowled classical left-arm pace across the right-hand batsman's body from a 16-stride approach, varying his speed with a characteristic hip turn in an easy action devoid of frills. He was a tradesman who never showed petulance, and brought intense concentration to his work as a stock bowler admired for the economy of his bowling over 11 seasons for Queensland and in 21 Tests for Australia. He may have got his big chance to play in a lot of those Tests because of World Series Cricket but Australia lost nothing by playing him.

Dymock, a mathematics master born at Maryborough, Queensland, was the backbone of the Queensland attack for a long time and sometimes had contentious decisions given against him. But he never resorted to "sledging" or histrionics, and when he took an important Test wicket there was no hugging or back-slapping. And when a batsman was beaten but escaped through good fortune, there were no grimaces or rude gestures.

After appearing for Queensland Colts and Queensland Country in 1968–69, he played for Milnrow in the Lancashire League in 1970 and 1971, when he also played for Worcestershire Second XI. This prepared him for his debut for Queensland in 1971–72. He made his Test debut in 1973–74 against New Zealand at Adelaide, taking 2 for 44 and 5 for 58, but was not considered hostile enough for WSC to sign in 1977, and with Hughes, Cosier and Serjeant was one of the four among the Australian touring party's 17 players in England in 1977 who were not recruited. He had always taken second place to bowlers like Lillee and Thomson in big matches, but now he had his chance to bowl long spells. He bowled particularly well in Australia in 1978–79 against England, had a splendid tour of India in 1979, and sustained his outstanding form in 1979–80, when he virtually won the Perth Test with 3 for 52 and 6 for 34 against England. He finished that season with 28 wickets in five Tests against England and the West Indies at 19.60. His 6 for 34 at Perth remain the best figures in that city by a bowler from any country in a Test.

326

Part of Dymock's improvement at an age when most cricketers are ready to retire came from his development of an inswinger to go with the away swing he always had bowled. His
ability to bring the ball back surprised the top batsmen of his
era and helped Queensland to a top place among Sheffield
Shield contenders. He was one of the first players picked for
the Centenary Test trip to England in 1980. A lot of sound
judges were surprised at his omission from Australia's 1981
team to England, if only because his left-arm attack was likely to be more penetrative under English conditions and provide a more varied attack.

Dymock took 10 wickets in a Test once, with best Test figures of 7 for 67. In all first-class matches he took five wickets
in an innings 13 times. His only first-class century came in a
Shield match against South Australia at Brisbane a few
weeks before he finally retired, when, batting with characteristic determination and from a straight, upright stance, play-

Geoff Dymock bowled with this kind of determination throughout the hardest of days.

327

ing down the line, he reached 101 not out. The rejoicing over this feat by a cricketer who always gave his best had hardly subsided when he played for Queensland in the McDonald's Cup final shortly afterwards, Queensland winning the trophy for the second successive year. Dymock took 309 first-class wickets for Queensland at 27.53.

DYSON, John, 1954–

First-Class Averages: Batting, 4,976 runs at 38.28; Bowling, 1 wicket at 20.

Tests (19): 779 runs at 25.13.

A right-hand opening batsman who in six summers of first-class cricket has had to repeatedly overcome setbacks. At his best he is a splendid timer of the ball, particularly on the straight drive, and has an attractive array of strokes. But he has often looked stodgy and strokeless because of his dedication to the task of giving his team a good start. His attitude in curbing his shotmaking while he doggedly holds up an end has earned him comparisons with England's Geoff Boycott. Like Boycott he lifts the bat a lot in his stance, often leaving it six inches off the ground.

Dyson, a physical education teacher at Caringbah, NSW, was born in the Sydney suburb of Randwick and has played for Sutherland and Randwick clubs. He made a painstaking start to his Shield career with New South Wales in 1977–78. In the match against Western Australia at Perth he delayed NSW's defeat with a long, sometimes laborious innings of 102 that caused one Perth newspaper to label him a strokeless wonder. By the end of the season he had two first-class centuries, having made 103 not out against Victoria at Sydney.

In 1977–78, after the WSC breakaway, he was chosen for three Tests against India. He batted soundly against the Indian medium-pacers but was found wanting against the spin of Bedi and Venkataraghavan and Chandrasekhar. The following season his highest score was 197 against Tasmania. He confirmed his place in the side in 1979–80 as he settled down to top the NSW batting aggregate with 729 runs at 42.88 and a top score of 99. These figures won him a place in the Australian team for the Centenary Test tour of England in 1980.

His stance in England was more upright with not so much bend in the knees and he edged the ball far less than previously. English experts were impressed and he came home a far more assured cricketer. With Bruce Laird missing most of the 1980–81 Australian season through injury, Dyson became a regular Test opener, though his opening spot was taken by other batsmen in one-day matches. He went back to England in 1981 under Kim Hughes but had a disappointing tour, despite a hard-earned 102 in the Leeds Test. He took the catch of the 1981–82 season, leaping high off the ground while moving backwards to grasp an outfield skier off Yardley's bowling at the SCG.

328

Above: *John Dyson, a former soccer goalie, leaps high to take a brilliant outfield catch in the Sydney Test against the West Indies in 1981–82.*
Right: *John Dyson gets both feet off the ground to keep down a high rising ball from Wayne Prior at the SCG.*

E

EADY, Charles John, 1870–1945

First-Class Averages:
Batting, 1,490 runs at
22.92; Bowling, 135
wickets at 23.30.

Tests (2): 20 runs at 6.66;
7 wickets at 16.00.

A large, impressive man who performed efficiently for Tasmania as an all-rounder for two decades, but who will always be remembered for his innings of 566 in 473 minutes. He made it in a total of 911 at Hobart in March and April 1902, for Break-O'-Day against Wellington. Eady hit 13 fives and 68 fours, and added 429 for the seventh wicket with W. Abbott, who made 143. Play was spread over four afternoons while Eady achieved this, which remains the highest score in club cricket anywhere in the world.

Eady, the son of a butcher, left school at 13 and at 14 began playing cricket for Lefroy club's junior team. He switched to the Break-O'-Day club in 1890. By choosing to live in Tasmania, Eady enormously restricted his cricketing opportunities. When he did get a chance in big matches on the mainland, he was inclined to cramp his natural hitting style and defend, which he could do with skill. He was an outstanding fieldsman in any position, a solicitor who was as crafty in the courts as he was in handling Break-O'-Day sides, and later a prominent parliamentarian. He was a tremendous hitter of the ball, but this should not be allowed to overshadow his skill as a bowler. He headed the Southern Tasmanian averages four times as a batsman—but 12 times as a bowler.

Eady only toured England once—with the 1896 Australians—but ill health prevented him showing his best and he made only 290 runs at 13.18 and took 16 wickets at 25.50. Despite this disappointing tour, he received several offers from English counties, which he declined. His reputation was secure in his feats at home. He made 88 not out for Tasmania against Victoria in 1892–93, and 187 for Southern Tasmania against Northern Tasmania in 1892–93 but club cricket was his domain. Apart from his 566, he also scored 231 for Break-O'-Day against Derwent in 1898–99, 229 not out against Derwent and 218 not out against Wellington in successive knocks in 1898–99, 218 against Derwent in 1890–91, 205 and 120 not out v. Wellington in 1897–98. In 1905–06 he took all ten wickets for 42 runs for South Hobart against East Hobart.

330

For Tasmania against Victoria at Melbourne in 1894–95 he took 8 for 34, for Southern Tasmania against Queensland in 1896–97 he had 13 for 139, and for Tasmania against Victoria in 1906–07, he took 13 for 185. He bowled in matches between North and South Tasmania for 20 years. In 1908, he and Ken Burn put on 122 for the fourth wicket for Tasmania against England at Hobart.

Eady, who stood 6 ft 3 ins and weighed 15 stone, was the

first Australian to score a century in each innings of a first-class match, a feat he accomplished in 1894–95 when he made 116 and 112 not out against Victoria at Hobart. He also scored a century against Victoria in 1901. After his retirement in 1908 he continued to take a keen interest in cricket and was for a time chairman of the Australian Board of Control. He was president of the Amateur Sports Federation of Tasmania from 1910 till 1933 and for shorter periods of the Tasmanian Amateur Boxing Association, and the Tasmanian branch of the Royal Lifesaving Society. He was an active member of the Derwent Rowing Club and was secretary of the Tasmanian Amateur Jockey Club from 1917 to 1927, and a judge for various racing clubs. He was a first-class Australian Rules footballer, known for his high marking, captained the Holbrook club in 1890, and played for Southern Tasmanian teams several times against Victoria. He was also a member and then president (1944) of the Tasmanian Legislative Council, after serving as chairman of committees (1937–44).

In cricket, first-class and club, Eady scored 12,776 runs at 43.50 and 1,171 wickets at 14.20.

EASTWOOD, Kenneth Humphrey, 1935–

First-Class Averages: Batting, 2,722 runs at 41.87; Bowling, 6 wickets at 63.83.

Tests (1): 5 runs at 2.5; 1 wicket at 21.00.

One of the most curious selections of all time for an Australian Test team. He was a solid left-hand Victorian opening batsman who had shown he could take hard knocks without flinching when the national selectors preferred him to his State captain Bill Lawry for the Seventh Test against England at Sydney in 1970–71.

Eastwood, born at Chatswood, New South Wales, made his debut for Victoria in 1959–60 and in 42 first-class matches scored nine centuries. The best of his nine centuries for Victoria was 177 against New South Wales in 1970–71. He also made two double centuries, a factor which no doubt influenced the selectors who picked him for an Ashes deciding Test—201 not out against New South Wales in 1970–71 at Sydney, and 221 in 1970–71 against South Australia at Adelaide.

Although he appeared outclassed at the Test level, Eastwood left behind plenty of bowlers in State cricket who have cause to remember his powerful hitting when he was set. He was probably too old at 35 when given his Test chance. After his retirement from big cricket he became a respected official, and continued to make runs for Footscray, for whom he scored 7,000 runs, including a club record 153. He also took more than 100 wickets with his occasional slows. He played a major role in Footscray's first pennant win in 1979–80 when he was the club's senior coach. He ended his 26-year association with Footscray at the age of 46 when he joined Sunshine United in the Sunshine Cricket Association for the 1981–82 season.

An efficient fast-medium swing bowler who gave Australia and Victoria outstanding service, not the least of it off the field as the instigator of the 1977 Centenary Test in Melbourne. He was one of four famous Australian bowlers who toiled all Christmas Day 1928 bowling to Alan Kippax and Hal Hooker when they scored 307 runs for the New South Wales 10th wicket, a world record that still stands. The other bowlers were Bert Ironmonger, Ted a'Beckett and Hunter Hendry. Ebeling had a 57-year association with the Melbourne Cricket Club and helped give that club distinction unmatched by any other Australian cricket club. He was president when he died.

Ebeling, born at Avoca, Victoria, won the Melbourne Cricket Club's bowling averages the first summer he played for the club after leaving Caulfield Grammar School, 1922–23. He rolled up to the wicket to bowl, stiff-legged and wobbling, propping off one leg at a time, arms hanging down his sides, and let the ball go with a very quick action. His stock ball moved in from the off but he swung it either way and made the batsman play at almost every ball. His accuracy was sustained. He was a handy batsman, very strong on the legside and often contributed valuable runs near the end of his team's innings.

His business commitments prevented him devoting much time to cricket early in his career and after his debut in 1923–24 he did not play regularly for several seasons, though he did tour New Zealand with a Victorian team in 1924–25. But in 1933–34 he played in two Testimonials and five Shield games and impressed enough in these seven outings to win a place in the 1934 Australian team that toured England. He took 62 wickets at 20.83 and scored 265 runs at 14.72 on that trip and won praise from such great names as Jack Hobbs, who rated him one of the best medium pace swing bowlers he had faced.

Ebeling's skills as a diplomat and strategist were strongly tested in his years as Victoria's captain but he handled Fleetwood-Smith's spin bowling and his bird noises from the outfield better than anyone else. He had survived the 1934 tour of England as Bill O'Reilly's room-mate. In 1935–36 he turned down an invitation to tour South Africa with the Australians because of business pressures.

In 1936 Ebeling clashed with Bradman after Ernie McCormick bounced a couple at Bradman. Bradman claimed McCormick was bowling Bodyline, but Ebeling said it was for the umpires to decide and he could not agree that McCormick was bowling Bodyline as he had only two fieldsmen on the on side. Bradman was adamant, so Ebeling said, "You captain your side and I'll captain mine." The umpires made no move to warn McCormick.

After he retired from big cricket he devoted his time to the

EBELING, Hans Irvine, 1905–1980

First-Class Averages: Batting, 1,005 runs at 14.15; Bowling, 217 wickets at 26.58.

Tests (1): 43 runs at 21.50; 3 wickets at 29.66.

Melbourne Cricket Club committee and to developing the MCG as a cricket museum. He suggested playing the Centenary Test in 1977 and more than two years of planning paid off when the greatest-ever gathering of star players assembled in Melbourne for the match. Hans and his wife Myra were perfect hosts in what is regarded as cricket's entrepreneurial masterpiece.

For Victoria his best bowling figures were 7 for 33 against Queensland in 1928–29, which included a hat-trick. He led Victoria to win the Sheffield Shield in 1933–34 and 1934–35.

EDWARDS, Alan Robert, 1921–

First-Class Averages: Batting, 2,325 runs at 32.29; Bowling, 14 wickets at 24.00.

A left-handed batsman and left-arm slow bowler who was the first to score a century in each innings of a match for Western Australia. He was a schoolboy prodigy for Christian Brothers College in the Darlot Cup, a fine deflector of the ball who since his retirement has served for many years as a WA selector.

Edwards, who played for the North Perth and West Perth clubs, made his debut for WA in 1946–47. He made 104 against Victoria at Perth in 1947–48, but the highlight of his career came in the 1950–51 season when he scored 103 in the first innings against Queensland in Perth and followed with 105 in the second innings. He was a fine fieldsman and held 35 catches in his 44 matches for WA.

EDWARDS, John Dunlop, 1862–1911

First-Class Averages: Batting, 961 runs at 13.72; Bowling, 7 wickets at 27.71.

Tests (3): 48 runs at 9.60.

A member of the 1888 Australian team that toured England, a free-hitting right-hand batsman, with a solid defence, a useful leg-break bowler and an impressive fieldsman. He made a big reputation while at Wesley College, Melbourne, and was offered honorary membership of Melbourne CC, but he never quite fulfilled his early promise. For Sandhurst against North Bendigo in 1888, he scored 254 not out, and later that year went to England with Australia. He disappointed, scoring only 527 runs at 12.85, missing a number of matches through a hand injury. His highest score was 65 for Victoria against England in 1881–82.

EDWARDS, Ross, 1942–

A strongly-built, fair-headed Western Australian right-hand batsman who gave up wicket-keeping to become one of the most brilliant cover point fieldsmen Australia has produced. He scored two notable Test centuries when Australia badly needed runs, and save 30 or more runs an innings in the field. Often when the fast bowlers were on he was the only Australian fieldsman in front of the wicket patrolling the offside su-

334

perbly. His judgement, pick up and throw were so rapid batsmen refused runs they would have taken to lesser fieldsmen.

Edwards, born in the Perth suburb of Cottesloe, is the son of E. K. Edwards, who kept wicket for Western Australia in 1948–49. Ross, who learned much of his cricket with Fremantle club, made his debut for Western Australia in 1964-65, substituting as wicket-keeper for Gordon Becker and batting at No. 10. He lost his place when Becker returned and thereafter played as a batsman. He was a regular member of the 1967–68 side that won the Shield under Tony Lock, contributing 396 runs at 28.29. In 1968–69 he made 117 not out in a Western Australian score of 6 for 594 at Sydney and finished that season with 488 runs at 56.00.

After scoring four centuries for Western Australia in 1971–72, he toured England with the 1972 Australian side as a batsman, frequently proving himself a cricketer of character. When Bruce Francis fell ill before the Third Test at Trent Bridge he made 170 not out as a stop-gap opener, not giving a chance in 330 minutes. He scored 747 runs on the tour at 32.47 and on every ground on which he appeared was cheered for his spectacular patrolling of cover and mid-off.

He went to the West Indies in 1972–73, acting as reserve wicket-keeper, a self-effacing character who was never a great batsman but always rose to the big challenges when they came. He had become a qualified accountant and found it difficult to find time in his job for cricket but he went back into the Test team against England in 1974–75, scoring 115 in the Second Test at Perth, where he became the first West Australian to make a Test 100 in his home State.

In 1957 he returned to England for his second tour, at 32 the oldest member of the Australian side. He began with 56 in the First Test, and in the Second Test rescued Australia from 7 for 81 with an innings of 99 that lifted the score to 268. He hit 15 fours and was out lbw to part-time bowler Bob Woolmer. In Prudential Cup matches he made 80 not out against Pakistan and 58 against West Indies. When he returned home he had lost his job through going on tour and felt obliged to retire in the interests of his family. In 1977, he was able to recoup some of his financial losses by playing WSC cricket. He now lives in Sydney, where he turns out regularly for Northern Districts, enthusiasm and rosy cheeks undimmed.

Between 1964 and 1980 he made 14 centuries in first-class cricket, took 111 catches and made 11 stumpings.

First-Class Averages: Batting 7,345 runs at 38.29.

Tests (20): 1,171 runs at 40.37.

A left-hand opening batsman who repeatedly made an attractive start without going on to his century. He passed 50 eleven times for Western Australia but scored only two hundreds. In three Tests for Australia against England in

EDWARDS, Walter John, 1949–

First-Class Averages:
Batting, 1,371 runs at
30.46; Bowling, 2
wickets at 70.50.

Tests (3): 68 runs at
11.33.

1974–75, he twice helped Ian Redpath put on more than 60 but his best score in Tests was only 30.

Edwards, who began in grade cricket with Midland-Guildford, made his debut for WA in 1973–74 against New Zealand at Perth, scoring 32 and 67. He made 122 against South Australia at Perth that season, and 153 against NSW at Sydney in 1975–76, the innings that earned him Test selection. He was dropped after the third Test, Rick McCosker replacing him as Redpath's opening partner.

He continued to give WA good starts but dropped out of first-class cricket after the 1975–76 season through trouble with his eyes. He played for University for a time and now captains North Perth, wearing glasses.

ELLIOTT, Gideon
1828–1869

First-Class Averages:
Batting: 95 runs at 7.91;
Bowling, 48 wickets at
4.93.

An English-born right-hand batsman and right-arm fast round-arm bowler who set the record for a Victorian bowler in first-class cricket by taking 9 wickets for 2 runs against Tasmania in February, 1858. He also made the highest score, 28, in that game. It is not clear from reports of the match that he bowled 19 overs (76 balls) of which 18 overs were maidens, and apparently the two runs scored from his bowling came from one shot. Tasmania were dismissed for 33, of which 14 were extras.

Elliott, born in Surrey, died in the Melbourne suburb of Richmond. He played district cricket for Richmond and Melbourne. His first-class career spanned the years 1855 to 1861. Apart from his 9 for 2 against Tasmania, he took 7 for 27 and 3 for 7 against New South Wales in 1855–56, 5 for 17 against New South Wales in 1857–58, and 2 for 13 followed by 6 for 23 against New South Wales in 1859–60.

Elliott was Victoria's spearhead in the first intercolonial match against NSW on the Richmond Paddock, but his 10 wickets for 34 runs could not prevent a NSW win. He bowled fast and straight and the *Australian Cricketer* said "the batsmen require a sharp eye to dispose of his shooters." His brother was killed when aboriginals attacked a party led by Horatio Wills, Tom Wills' father, while on its way overland to Queensland.

ELLIS, John Leslie
("Nana") 1890–1974

A highly efficient wicket-keeper who made three overseas tours with Australian teams. He was Oldfield's deputy on the 1926 tour of England by Collins' team, toured New Zealand in 1924–25 with Victoria, and India in 1935–36 with Tarrant's team. He was good enough to send "Hammy" Love, who had gone to Victoria to get more opportunities because of Oldfield's masterly form in New South Wales, back to Sydney.

Outstanding Australian left-hander Alan Border clips a ball away to square leg in England in 1981.

Left: Economical medium-pace bowler Mick Malone shows his copybook style.

Right: Gary Gilmour follows through after the delivery of one of his left-arm medium-pacers.

Ellis made his debut for Victoria in 1918 and played until 1936. He scored two first-class centuries. When Victoria made the world record total of 1,107 in 1926–27, an Ellis pull shot off Tommy Andrews brought up the 1,000th run. "Come on, there's three in it," he cried. "Three to me and 1,000 up. Long live Victoria."

Ellis, who played for Prahran district club from 1917 to 1932, headed Prahran's batting averages in 1919–20 with 68.00, and played for three Prahran premiership sides. He made 80 stumpings and 71 catches for the club over 15 years, excelling in his 'keeping to spinners such as Grimmett. He had a reputation for ungentlemanly comments about batsmen from behind the stumps, but he was always a happy, jovial figure.

Ellis once kept wicket for Victoria at Melbourne wearing brown pads. He was a contractor and he had grabbed the pads belonging to one of his labourers who played park cricket. Sometimes when Bill Woodfull won the toss and batted, Ellis, realising he would not be required for a while, went off and inspected some of the jobs around Melbourne that his company were working on. Ellis was the player who jumped the fence in Adelaide to exchange blows with a spectator whose comments had been annoying him. Hal Hooker told how Ellis greeted him when he went in as last man for New South Wales: "Have a go, Hal, the bowling's rubbish." Hooker proceeded to stay put until he and Kippax had produced a world record tenth wicket stand of 307, a partnership that deprived Ellis and his team-mates of their Christmas Day celebration lunch.

First-Class Averages: Batting, 2,351 runs at 21.18; Dismissals 293 (186 catches; 107 stumpings).

An inconsistent right-arm spin bowler of lively pace who went to England for the 1912 Triangular series with Syd Gregory's Australian team. He took 67 wickets on the tour in all matches at 23.89, best effort 12 for 110 against Northants. He played in two Tests against England and two Tests against South Africa, but with little success. *Wisden* described him as a bowler "of uncertain length." But he did play in the match at Old Trafford in which T. J. Matthews got two hat-tricks in an afternoon for Australia.

"Sid Emery in his day was probably the most devastating bowler of the bosey ever seen," wrote "Johnnie" Moyes. "He bowled at medium pace rather than slow, spun the ball prodigiously, could make it fly back at unseemly angles and had life and fire that made him unplayable when he found his control. Unfortunately, these occasions were rare, but at Melbourne in the first innings against Victoria in 1909–10 he took 7 for 28 in the first innings of 93 and 5 for 85 in the second when Victoria made 185."

Arthur Mailey called Emery "Mad Mick" when they toured

EMERY, Sidney Hand 1886–1967

First-Class Averages: Batting, 1,197 runs at 18.41; Bowling 183 wickets at 23.93.

Tests (4): 6 runs at 3.00; 5 wickets at 49.80.

America together with an Australian team in 1913, and the name stuck. Monty Noble told Emery he would be a great bowler if he could learn to control his googly. "I'd be a great man if I could learn to control myself," said Emery. He was fined five dollars when he was five minutes late for one match in Canada. He grabbed his bat, sold it to a spectator, and paid the Australian manager, R. B. Benjamin, the five dollars.

Emery, a wild, relentless fellow with the strength of Tarzan, claimed that he once bowled "Plum" Warner with a full-pitcher after Warner made two strokes at the ball in 1912 at Lord's. In a Sydney club match when an umpire turned down his appeal against the light, Emery asked the umpire for a match, lit one, placed it gently on the bails, and resumed batting.

EMU CLUB, THE   An organisation aimed at providing opportunities for young bush cricketers in northern New South Wales, which, in a short period, has developed State and Australian team players. The Emu Club is a carefully planned body with strict conditions of membership which regularly conducts tours to Tasmania and New Zealand and undertakes a world tour every four or five years. All the club's activity is pitched at assisting players under 21, though senior members frequently join the tours. The Emus operate one of most novel fundraising schemes in Australian cricket by running its own herd of cattle and selling off the progeny of that herd.

The Emus were founded in 1950, the brainchild of J. S. White, a prominent NSW cattle-breeder and former outstanding GPS athlete. White took a team of young country lads each Christmas from around his property at Muswellbrook to play a team organised by Ike Rowland in Tamworth. Encouraged by the eagerness of the young players to improve their standards he founded the Emu Club.

The club divides NSW into areas, the Hunter Valley, the North Coast, Northern Tablelands and the North West. Each of these areas organises an Under 21 team and the four teams play a round robin over Christmas at Tamworth. From these matches North and North-West Colts teams are selected to tour either Tasmania or New Zealand. When they have completed these trips the players are then eligible to become members of the Emu Club and for overseas tours. The Emus went on their first overseas trip to Singapore and Malaya in 1959 in a goodwill venture supported by the Australian government and the then Minister for External Affairs, R. G. Casey. They made their first world tour in 1961.

Test players Johnny Gleeson, North Coast, Doug Walters, Upper Hunter, and Rick McCosker, Northern Tablelands, were all first spotted playing for the Emus, as was State player Tim Grosser. Gleeson was the first Emu to win Test selection. He toured New Zealand in 1951 as a wicket-keeper batsman and went to Malaya the same year as the second 'keeper and batsman. In 1961 he went on a world tour with the Emus and on that trip developed his famous unorthodox spinners. He became a prolific wicket-taker in the Tamworth area on his return and after Keith Stimson, captain of the Balmain club in Sydney, had reported favourably on his efforts for a Combined Country side in Sydney in 1965, he joined Balmain. Within two seasons he was in the Test side.

The Emus found that the staging of their annual carnival and entertaining visiting teams was costly and set themselves to raise $10,000 to invest, with the interest to be used to pay expenses. Members were invited to lend money to the club for the purchase of a herd of cows and calves, the money to be repaid when the calves were sold. In the first year, 1967, $1,200 was raised and 22 cows and calves bought. After that most of the cows calved regularly and the club owned outright the original cows and the calves at foot. Members of the Emu Club touring teams, always smartly turned out, with the Emu emblem on their blazers and caps, have their overheads paid for by that herd.

ENGLAND VERSUS AUSTRALIA

Since Test cricket began at Melbourne on March 15, 1877, Australia's matches against England have always aroused stronger emotions among Australian cricket followers than those against other countries. Most of Australia's players in the early Tests had strong family ties in England and the two countries played 30 Tests before another country, South Africa, began playing Test cricket. South Africa came into Tests in 1888–89 when they played England at Port Elizabeth, but England had played Australia regularly for 11 years before then. And Australia had been visited by 17 English teams before the first tour by another country—by South Africa in the 1910–11 Australian summer.

Australia got away to a good start in the matches against England, probably because the first English teams were organised by individuals who had a tour profit uppermost in their minds. "Plum" Warner's 16th English touring team was the first to visit Australia that was selected and organised by the Marylebone Cricket Club, which was more mindful of England's prestige and insisted more on sending the best possible teams than had the entrepreneurs.

Australia has retained the slight edge established by winning the first of all Tests, but has taken some fearful hidings from English teams. The record shows that 247 Tests have now been played against England, Australia winning 93,

England 82, with 72 drawn. The matches have seldom been one-sided, most have been closely-contested and the results seem to count more among the players than do the outcome of Tests against other countries.

The highest attendance for a cricket match anywhere in the world was for an England-Australia Test in 1936–37 at Melbourne, when 350,000 attended and close to one million people watched the rubber. Close scrutiny of cricket tactics show that most innovations came in England-Australia matches. The first time a side placed eight fieldsmen in the slips area was in a 1953 England-Australia clash. Silly mid-on was developed as a standard fielding position in England-Australia matches and was originally "Boyley's mid-on," because Australia's Harry Boyle was the first to venture in so close. When Ian Chappell's team defeated England in 1974–75 84 of the 110 English wickets that fell in the series fell to catches, most of them in the 'keeper-to-gully sector. Seven English batsmen were out lbw, 16 had their stumps removed and three were run out.

Greg Chappell took seven slips catches in the Perth Test of that series against England, a record for a single Test. Similarly, Jack Gregory's record of 15 catches in a Test series was set against England (in 1921), and many of Australian wicket-keepers' best performances were achieved against England. Indeed Australia's main phase of superiority over England has been in the field, where Australian throwing arms, developed on vast, spacious grounds, have achieved greater accuracy and speed. In batting, there has been very little in it. England had the first world famous batsman in Dr W. G. Grace, but Don Bradman later matched his stature in the game. Great bowlers have appeared in about equal numbers for both countries and there has been little to choose between the wicket-keepers.

The men who began the England-Australia tradition were far from representative of English and Australian cricket. All the best amateurs, including W. G. Grace, were absent from England's team in the first-ever Test and the Australian side was really only a combination of Sydney and Melbourne's best players, with the exception of Allan, Spofforth, Evans and Murdoch. Four of the Australian players in that first Test, Bannerman, Kendall, Midwinter and Thompson, were born in England, and a fifth, Horan, was born in Ireland. But they began a history of keen rivalry that is never quite reproduced when Australia plays another country. Here is a summary of 105 years of England versus Australia cricket:

ENGLISH TEAMS IN AUSTRALIA

Spiers & Pond, proprietors of the Cafe de Paris in Bourke Street, Melbourne, brought the first English team to Australia to promote their catering business. They sent a Mr W. B. Mallam to England to negotiate a team's visit when Charles

Dickens failed to answer their invitation for a speaking tour. Mallam went to Birmingham where the North were playing the South and all the best players in England were assembled. At dinner he invited the best of the two teams to tour Australia with first-class expenses plus £150-a-man. George Parr and his northern team-mates scoffed at the offer, so Mallam concentrated on William Burrup, the Surrey secretary, and H. H. Stephenson, the Surrey captain who was skippering the South.

Stephenson accepted Mallam's terms and assembled a team comprising William Caffyn, Charles Lawrence, W. Mortlock, T. Sewell, G. Griffith, W. Mudie, and H. H. Stephenson from Surrey, T. Hearne from Middlesex, E. Stephenson and R. Iddison from Yorkshire, G. Bennett from Kent and G. ("Tiny") Wells from Sussex. Mudie was so thin he was known as the "Surrey Shadow." They left England in the schooner *Great Britain* on October 18, 1861, and arrived in Melbourne on Christmas Eve to a tumultuous welcome. There were more than 10,000 people on the wharf to cheer

FIRST ENGLISH TEAM, 1862

H. H. Stephenson

The first England team to tour Australia, on board their ship in Melbourne. Standing (L to R): R. Iddison, G. Griffith, C. Mudie, H. H. Stephenson (centre), G. Wells (with ball), E. Stephenson (with bat), T. Hearne; Seated, W. Caffyn, G. Bennett, T. Sewell (with ball); Seated on the deck, C. Lawrence, W. Mortlock.

them ashore and they rode through Melbourne amid scenes of rejoicing to the Cafe de Paris, drawn by four magnificent greys. The Melbourne *Herald* said there had been no welcome like it since the Athenians arrived in Corinth.

The team's captain, Heathfield Harman Stephenson (1833–1896) was a popular figure and the English players were agreeably surprised to find that none of the social barriers encountered by professionals in England existed in Australia. "Scarcely a day passed without our being entertained to champagne dinners, luncheons or breakfasts," wrote Caffyn. But from the start the "needle" atmosphere that has characterised Australia-England cricket emerged as visitors and hosts jockeyed for an advantage. Stephenson said that although his team had agreed to play against Twenty Two Melbournians in the first match his players were weary after the long sea voyage and refused to have more than 18 in the Melbourne team. The Melbourne *Herald* attacked Stephenson's attitude but Spiers & Pond agreed to reduce the Melbourne side to 18.

The Englishmen were astonished at the style of that match against an Australian colony from January 1–4, 1862. Colourful marquees and awnings topped by flags circled the Melbourne Cricket Ground, where a new stand with accommodation for 6,000 had just been completed. The underneath of the new stand was reserved for publicans who advertised that they would have 500 cases of beer for the match. For hours before the match every road to the MCG was blocked with carriages, buggies and even bullock waggons. At the ground there were shooting galleries, hurdy-gurdies, fruit and sweet stalls, Aunt Sallies, and small boys selling cards carrying photographs of the players. A painter who brought his high ladder did a thriving business helping spectators climb to positions in the trees. The Melbourne *Herald* estimated the crowd at 15,000 but some said it was far higher.

The Melbourne and Districts captain George Marshall won the toss and gave this historic match a good start by scoring 27, but the locals were all out for 118, with six ducks. Griffith took 7 for 30, Bennett 7 for 53, with three run outs. The English team responded with 305, of which "Terrible Billy" Caffyn made 79 and Griffith "the Lion Hitter" 61. Melbourne were all out for 92 in the second innings, with 10 ducks, Sewell took 7 for 20, giving Stephenson's side victory by 95 runs. More than 45,000 people paid to see the match and takings paid all the expenses for the entire tour. When the match finished early, the enterprising Spiers & Pond organised the first balloon ascent ever seen in the colony. The balloon was called "All England" and had pictures of Queen Victoria and the English cricketers painted on the outside. The balloon was aloft for 35 minutes, drifting all over Melbourne before the balloonists, Mr and Mrs Brown, brought it down in Albert Street.

342

Stephenson's team played 13 matches as scheduled, plus two scratch games. The itinerary included a match labelled "Surrey versus The World," in which the six Surrey players, assisted by the best local players took on their team-mates, and five locals. Team captain Stephenson proved a fine speechmaker and a round-arm fast bowler with a pronounced break-back, who could bat, bowl or keep wicket. His star was William Caffyn, who headed the tour batting averages with 419 runs at 23.27. Caffyn and Iddison did the bulk of the bowling, delivering more than 400 overs each. Caffyn had 80 wickets at 6.18, Iddison 103 at 6.61.

Of the 13 matches England played, 11 were against 22, one against 18, and only the Surrey v. The World affair 11-a-side. England won five of the matches against 22, lost two and four were drawn. They won the match against 18 and Surrey v. The World was drawn. Spiers & Pond made £11,000 profit on the tour, and the Melbourne Cricket Club was so pleased by the matches on their ground they paid the English team a bonus of 100 sovereigns. The tour brought big improvements in local coaching methods and produced a bonus when Charles Lawrence remained in Australia to coach. When the team arrived home Roger Iddison was asked his opinion of Australian cricketers. "Well, oi doan't think mooch of their play, but they're a wonderful lot of drinking men," he said.

SECOND ENGLISH TEAM, 1864

G. Parr

George Parr, who had rejected Mallam's invitation to tour Australia with the first English team, captained the second touring team, which this time included all the best professional talent in England, plus the noted amateur E. M. Grace. Caffyn was the only member of the original English team to join Parr's side. Parr, a Nottinghamshire legend known as the "Lion Of The North," was one of the finest batsmen in cricket and the greatest legside hitter England had known. He invented the sweep shot. At Trent Bridge on the Bridgford Road side of the ground later Australian players were intrigued to find an old elm known as "Parr's Tree," where many of his shots landed. Parr's 1864 team was entirely sponsored by the Melbourne Cricket Club.

They began with a draw against Twenty Two of Victoria, needing nine runs to win with six wickets left when the umpires called time precisely at six o'clock. Then they played at Sandhurst, where they won easily and at Ballarat where one spectator walked much of the 300 miles he travelled to see them play. After beating Twenty Two of Ararat (Tinley the lob bowler got them out as fast as they came in), the Englishmen made a quick trip to New Zealand to play four matches, three of which they won, with one drawn. They returned for matches in Sydney and Melbourne, Geelong and Ballarat where Bob Carpenter made history by scoring 121, the first century by an English player in Australia. They played 12 matches in Australia altogether, all against teams of 22, winning seven and drawing five. Bob Carpenter topped the batting averages in all matches on the tour, compiling 399 runs at 22.11. An interesting performer was Tom Hayward, uncle of the famous Surrey batsman, who made 326 runs on the tour at 18.11, best score 61. Most of the bowling was done by Tinley with his lobs, and he took his 171 wickets at a cost of only 3.65 apiece. Each English player made £250 from the tour after expenses, with big crowds attending in a carnival atmosphere wherever they played. Caffyn stayed in Australia to coach when the team left.

THIRD ENGLISH TEAM, 1873–74

W. G. Grace

Ten years after Parr's team the third English team arrived under the captaincy of W. G. Grace to find that Caffyn and Lawrence had done a fine coaching job in improving standards, particularly in the main centres. Grace accepted the invitation to tour from a syndicate of Melbourne Cricket Club members. The voyage out lasted 52 days and Grace's players were taken straight from the boat to watch a match at South Melbourne Cricket Ground where their hosts bragged about their crowd control. Within a few minutes an umpire's decision was challenged, spectators broke on to the playing area, and the match had to be abandoned. "I am sorry to say that was a foretaste of some experiences which subsequently fell our lot," Grace wrote. In the same book he described how one of his players bluffed an umpire after being bowled in a country match, replacing the bails and explaining that he always had a trial ball. Grace's teams lost their first match to an Eighteen of Victoria by an innings and 24 runs, a result which hardly prepared the Englishmen for a wearisome coach ride through heat and dust over lumpy roads to Ballarat. In a temperature of 100 degrees Fahrenheit, W. G. Grace made 126, his brother G. F. Grace 112, and England 440. Ballarat scored 276 and the match was drawn.

A "wretched trip" took them to Sydney for a loss to 18 of NSW that included Spofforth. The next match against Maitland was washed out by floods but then they were dragged out to Bathurst by coach for an eight wickets' win. Back in Sydney they had a good win over a Combined NSW-Victoria XV. This was the match in which a NSW batsman was persuaded in the pavilion that he had been unfairly given out and returned to continue batting. With three batsmen at the crease, W. G. took his men from the field until sanity prevailed and the dismissed batsman departed.

The inexperience of the tour programmers showed as Grace and his men were taken back to Melbourne in choppy seas for a game against Victoria, shipped to Hobart to beat Tasmania and then submitted to a wild voyage to Adelaide, the first English team to visit South Australia. But the SACA had declined to pay the guarantee required by the Melbourne club

344

syndicate and the tourists had to go in a coach driven by Clem Hill's father to Kadina, 100 miles down Yorke Peninsula, whose cricket club had agreed to pay the guarantee. "When we reached Kadina, we went out to search for the cricket ground," Grace wrote. "And a search it really proved. We came to an open space and when we asked to be directed to the cricket ground were told this was it. There was scarcely a blade of grass to be seen, while the whole area was covered by small stones. On the morning of the match, a bushel of pebbles was swept up." The match was just as farcical. Twenty-two of Kadina were dismissed for 42 and 13, with 16 batsmen failing to score in the second innings. England won by an innings and nine runs.

By now the SACA had agreed to pay £110 and half the gate to Grace's team for a match with Twenty-two of Adelaide. The English players arrived at 3.30 pm on the day they were due to play, delayed by rough roads. In the first appearance by an English team on Adelaide Oval, the South Australians were dismissed for 63 and 82, England winning by seven wickets. The Adelaide match was a big financial success and the organisers paid £150 compensation to the Kadina club who had lost £700 on their pioneering venture. Grace's team played 15 matches, winning 10, losing three, with two draws. W. G. Grace led the batting averages with 711 runs, including an innings of 126, at 35.55. James Lillywhite topped the bowling averages in taking 172 wickets at 2.29 each.

Lillywhite's team comprised professionals from Sussex, Yorkshire, Surrey and Nottinghamshire, four of whom had visited Australia with the previous English side captained by W. G. Grace (Lillywhite, Greenwood, Jupp and Southerton). The tour was notable for the introduction of what became Test cricket. England were at a disadvantage as they had only arrived the day before the first Test after a rough voyage from New Zealand with most of the side badly seasick. England won the return Test at Melbourne a fortnight after the first by four wickets to finish one-all in the series.

The two Melbourne Tests ended Lillywhite's career in international cricket but he later helped foster Anglo-Australian tours by making advance arrangements for Australian teams in England. He accompanied four more teams to Australia, sometimes acting as umpire. His authority was widely respected and when he was asked to rule on the legitimacy of the young South Australian pace bowler Whitridge, he passed his delivery as fair. Whitridge was never again accused of an unfair action. Lillywhite's team in Australia had the services of some fine players, including George Ulyett, who topped the batting averages with 768 runs in all games at 22.58, and Alfred Shaw who took 231 wickets at 3.82. Lillywhite did well with his left-arm medium pacers, taking 138

FOURTH ENGLISH TEAM, 1876–77

J. Lillywhite

345

wickets at 4.57. The team played 23 matches, three against 11, and 20 against the odds, they won one of the 11–a-side matches, lost one and drew one. Of the matches against the odds they won 10, drew seven and lost three. C. Bannerman's 165 retired against them in the First Test was the first three figure score against an English touring team.

FIFTH ENGLISH TEAM, 1878–79

Lord Harris

The Melbourne Cricket Club's efforts to secure a tour by an all-amateur English team proved successful with the visit by Lord Harris' team. Isaac Walker was originally invited to bring out the team but had to decline. Lord Harris, in assembling his side, found it essential to include two professional bowlers, George Ulyett and Tom Emmett, in place of amateur bowlers of quality who could not spare the six months for the trip. Lord Harris' tourists arrived in Adelaide as the first Australian team to England arrived home in Sydney.

The tour began with an easy win over Eighteen of South Australia, with Emmett taking 9 for 45 and 5 for 58. In Melbourne a Victorian Fifteen held England to a creditable draw, Donald Campbell scoring a magnificent 128 in Victoria's second innings. The eagerly awaited Test match between the Australian side just back from England and Harris' tourists began dramatically when England collapsed at 4 for 26. Spofforth then performed the hat-trick to send England to 7 for 26 and the innings ended at 113 after some hurricane hitting by Absolom for 52. In the Australian innings "Monkey" Hornby bowled seven successive overs of grubbers, all maidens, and bowled Allan, but Australia reached 256, a lead of 143. Spofforth again bowled superbly in England's second innings to finish with 7 for 62 and match figures of 13 for 110. Australia won by 10 wickets. Among Spofforth's victims was F. A. Mackinnon, The Mackinnon of Mackinnon, 35th Chief of the Clan Mackinnon, whom Spofforth bowled in each innings.

Lord Harris had engaged a young Victorian, George Coulthard to accompany his side as umpire. A ground bowler with the Melbourne Cricket Club, Coulthard played a few times for Victoria and in 1881–82 appeared in one Test against England. He went with Lord Harris' team to matches against NSW in Sydney, which NSW won by five wickets, and then on to Bathurst for a game with a local Eighteen, back to Sydney, and a game against Twenty Two at Sydney's Victoria Barracks, before the return match with NSW.

Reporting the first day of the match which saw England dismissed for 267 the *Sydney Morning Herald* mentioned a blatant umpiring error by Coulthard and strongly objected to the "impunity with which open betting was carried out in the pavilion." The *Herald* said betting was carried on with a disdain for signs prohibiting it that was characteristic of the fraternity who make gambling a trade. Next day the gamblers prospered as NSW tumbled to be out for 177. NSW followed-on, but within a few minutes a riot began when Murdoch was given run out by Coulthard. The hooting began among gamblers in the pavilion, with a wellknown bookmaker urging on the hecklers. Spectators rushed on to the ground demanding that the decision be reversed. In defending Coulthard from attack, Lord Harris was struck by a larrikin with a stick. Hornby dragged Lord Harris' assailant from the ground and after half an hour the ground was cleared. The Englishmen decided there was no reason to replace Coulthard. Two attempts to resume play failed when the mob rushed the ground and play was abandoned for the day.

Next day's papers in reporting the riot said two Englishmen had insulted the crowd by calling them "nothing but sons of convicts." Dave Gregory had caused unpleasantness in England by complaining about umpiring decisions, and his insistence during the Sydney riot that Coulthard be replaced increased English bitterness. The match was finished with Coulthard umpiring, England winning easily.

Lord Harris' team went off to Melbourne while two offenders in the Sydney riot were convicted and fined. The Melbourne matches winding up the tour were affable and the Melbourne Cricket Club gave Lord Harris and his side a farewell dinner. The team won two 11-a-side matches and lost three, including the Test. The 13 matches against the odds resulted in five wins to England, five draws and three losses. Hornby and Emmett headed the averages for the tour—Hornby finishing on top in the batting with 574 runs at 33.76 and Emmett on top in bowling with 137 wickets at 8.49. Without the two professionals, it was a very weak team.

SIXTH ENGLISH TEAM, 1881–82

A. Shaw

This team was comprised entirely of professionals, with Lillywhite, Selby, Shaw, Emmett and Ulyett returning after earlier visits. The antagonism Murdoch's 1880 team had encountered in England following the Sydney riot had largely been forgotten, although Australians were puzzled to find the controversial Bill Midwinter a member of this English side. They played five matches in America on their way to Australia and began the Australian visit with a series of matches against local Twenty-Twos in Maitland, Newcastle, Orange and Bathurst, where a local lad named Charles Turner took 17 English wickets for 69 runs in the match.

In the first of the main matches, more than 30,000 people saw England beat NSW by 68 runs, 20,000 attending on the Saturday. England played Victoria in a thriller. Victoria led by 105 runs on the first innings and England followed-on. On a damp pitch Shrewsbury made a masterly 80 not out and Victoria were set 94 to win. Peate and Bates had the first six Victorians out for seven runs. Boyle then hit a lusty 42, but the innings ended at 75 to give England victory by 18 runs, Peate taking 6 for 30.

The First Test at Melbourne was drawn, with Australia 156 runs short of a win with seven wickets left. Shaw took his side to New Zealand for seven matches—five wins, two draws—and then returned to play Australia again in Sydney. Evans and Palmer bowled unchanged to dismiss England for 133 and despite a second innings opening stand of 122 by Ulyett and Barlow, Australia won by five wickets, Palmer taking 11 for 165 in the match.

The tourists played two Test matches against the Australian team that Murdoch was about to take to England. In Sydney, Murdoch's side were lucky to win by six wickets. McDonnell hit a brilliant 147 for Australia in the first innings in a 199 fourth wicket stand with Alick Bannerman that gave Australia a total of 260—no other batsman got to double figures. The second match at Melbourne was drawn. Ulyett's laborious 149 was the initial Test century for England in Australia. Shaw's team played 18 matches, winning eight minor matches, losing three, with seven drawn. They lost two and drew two of the four Tests. Ulyett was the leading batsman with 1,424 runs at 33.11 in all matches while Peate took 264 wickets in all matches at 5.84. Pilling kept brilliantly throughout the tour, which was a tremendous financial success.

SEVENTH ENGLISH TEAM, 1882–83

Hon. Ivo Bligh

Ivo Bligh's team had an eventful voyage to Australia in which their ship collided with a sailing vessel near Colombo. Fast bowler F. Morley was badly injured in the collision and could not bowl in more than half the team's matches in Australia. Bligh sustained a hand injury and could not play in the first five matches. Bligh, later the 8th Earl of Darnley, captain of Cambridge University and of Kent CC, had the job of recovering The Ashes. The notice that created The Ashes had appeared in the *Sporting Times* during the previous English summer. Australia won the First Test through a solid batting display that featured some enormous hitting by Bonnor. "Joey" Palmer took 10 for 126 in the match, for once outshining Spofforth.

In the Second Test the English bowler Billy Bates achieved the first hat-trick for England in Test cricket by dismissing McDonnell, Giffen and Bonnor. Bligh's clever captaincy gave Bates his third wicket, for when Bonnor walked in Bligh positioned Walter Read close in on the legside, knowing that Bonnor invariably played defensively forward to the first ball he received. Bates bowled slightly short of a length, Bonnor could not reach it on the half volley, and the ball popped into Read's hands. England won the match by an innings and 27 runs, Bates taking 14 for 102, and then went to a 2–1 lead by winning the Third Test by 69. This was the last scheduled Test and after the match some ladies burned a bail and presented Bligh with The Ashes urn.

348

Later Bligh agreed to play a further Test, which was won by Australia despite a fine 135 by A. G. Steel. The captains experimented by using a different pitch for each innings in this match. Some experts have argued that as the series against Bligh ended 2–2 The Ashes should have remained in Australia, but Bligh took them home in his luggage and presented them to the MCC at Lord's. Bligh's team played seven matches on level terms and 10 against the odds, winning four of the 11-a-side matches and losing three. Of the matches against the odds, five were drawn and five won. A. G. Steel topped the batting averages, scoring 551 runs in all matches at 30.61, and capped a fine tour by also heading the bowling averages with 152 wickets at 6.57.

The Seventh English team in Australia (L to R): Back row, W. Barnes, F. Morley, C. T. Studd, G. F. Vernon, W. W. Read (seated); Centre, C. B. Studd, E. F. S. Tylecote, Hon. Ivo Bligh, A. G. Steel, C. F. H. Leslie (standing); Front, R. G. Barlow, W. Bates.

EIGHTH ENGLISH TEAM, 1884–85

A. Shrewsbury

The all professional eighth English team to tour Australia was promoted by James Lillywhite, Alfred Shaw and Arthur Shrewsbury and included three other previous tourists, Billy Bates, George Ulyett and William Scotton. They began in Adelaide where Ulyett made 100 against Fifteen of South Australia. At Melbourne they ran into trouble with rain and by the refusal of members of Murdoch's team that had recently toured England to play. The Australians wanted a share of the match proceeds, a demand that got no public support, but most of the leading Australian players kept up the demand throughout a troublesome season.

Before the First Test at Adelaide—the first ever played on that ground—the Australians asked for half the proceeds. They were offered 30 percent and refused. Finally the South Australian Association took over financial arrangements for the match and paid each team £450, much to the disgust of the Englishmen. Murdoch further insisted that Lillywhite could not umpire in the match, although it was impossible in the time available to get experienced umpires from Melbourne or Sydney. England won by eight wickets despite McDonnell's brilliant 124. McDonnell was run out at 83 in the second innings through a blatant error by Giffen and deprived of the honour of being the first to score a century in each innings of a Test.

When the team for the Second Test was announced, Murdoch's men were all missing, for they still declined to appear without a share of the gate. The Victorian Cricket Association disqualified all the Victorians who refused to appear. Australia took the field with an entirely new side and lost by 10 wickets. England scored 401 in the first innings thanks to a knock of 121 by J. Briggs. By refusing to play Jack Blackham ended his run of having played in all the first 17 Tests.

Australia won the Third Test by only six runs, one of the smallest margins in history. England did well to get so close after losing the first three wickets of their first innings in four balls from Spofforth. Bannerman and Bonnor agreed to play in this game but Murdoch stayed in Cootamundra. Massie led Australia. Blackham took over the captaincy in the Fourth Test and levelled the series at two Tests apiece after Bonnor hit a 128, the first 100 in 100 minutes. A dispute-studded series ended when England won the Fifth Test by an innings and 98 runs, Shrewsbury becoming the first captain to make a Test century (105 not out). In the five Tests 28 players batted for Australia and 20 bowled. England fielded an unchanged team throughout the series. Right to the end there was trouble, with umpire J. Hodges refusing to take the field after the tea interval on the third day of the Fifth Test because of English complaints over his decisions.

Big crowds watched all England's 33 matches, which featured some amazing statistics in up-country matches. But nothing matched English bowler Robert Peel's feat at Moss Vale where his 18 wickets for seven runs against Twenty Two of Moss Vale gave him an average of 0.388 runs per batsman! England won six of the eight 11-a-side matches, lost two and won 10 of the 25 matches against the odds and drew 15. On the intervention of the Englishmen the VCA lifted the disqualifications on the players who demanded more pay.

There were 13 players in this side but Lillywhite and Shaw, who sponsored the trip with Shrewsbury, seldom played. When Barnes was injured in Melbourne, his place in the team was taken by R. Wood, a former Lancashire player living in Melbourne. This was Lillywhite's fifth visit to Australia, Bates and Shaw's fourth, and the third by Barnes, Barlow, Scotton and Shrewsbury. Only Gunn, Lohmann and Sherwin were new to Australia.

Shrewsbury struck form with a century in the first match at Adelaide and continued in that style to top the tour averages with 980 runs in all matches at 33.79, topscore 144. Johnny Briggs topped the bowling averages with 179 wickets in all matches at only 7.94, while four bowlers topped the 100 wickets, dismissing batsmen in matches against the odds in country centres with consumate ease. But the locals were starting to show occasional fight. At Parramatta Turner took 6 for 20 and 7 for 34 and Ferris 4 for 50 and 3 for 49 and England were beaten by the Eighteen by six wickets.

At Sydney in the First Test Turner and Ferris made exciting debuts, dismissing England for 45, which is still the lowest score by England in a Test in any country. Percy McDonnell was the first captain to invite the opposition to bat after winning the toss, but England won the match by 13 runs in a tense finish. England went on to win the two Test series by winning the Second Test in Sydney by 71 runs. The season ended happily with the Smokers v. Non-Smokers match comprising mixed sides of English and Australian stars. In the final innings, Scotton played a ball a foot or two in front of him, picked it up and put it in his pocket. Amid laughter he was given out for handling the ball. The Englishmen played 29 matches in all, winning six of the 10 rated first-class, with two draws and two losses. They played 19 matches against the odds, winning six, with 13 draws.

The 1887–88 Australian season saw tours by two English teams, one sponsored by the Melbourne Cricket Club and captained initially by M. B. Hawke, and then on the death of his father in England, by G. F. Vernon, the other sponsored by the old firm of Shaw, Shrewsbury and Lillywhite and captained by C. A. Smith, later Sir Aubrey Smith the film actor. Both teams comprised both amateurs and professionals. Towards the end of a season in which Turner established a record that has never been approached by taking 106 first-class wickets at 13.59, the two English touring teams combined to put their best eleven into a Test at Sydney. Australia's total of 42 in the first innings of that Test remains the lowest score in any Test in Australia and was Australia's lowest in all Tests until England dismissed Australia for 36 at Birmingham in 1902. Turner's 12 for 87 remains the best figures for a Test at Sydney but were not good enough to prevent England win-

NINTH ENGLISH TEAM, 1886–87

A. Shrewsbury

TENTH AND ELEVENTH ENGLISH TEAMS, 1887–88

G. F. Vernon (Lord Hawke)

C. A. Smith

ning by 126 runs. Shrewsbury topscored in the match with 44, with only 374 runs scored in four completed innings.

Vernon's team played 26 matches in all, winning six of the eight against 11-a-side, with one drawn and one lost. In 18 matches against the odds, they won five and 13 were drawn. A. E. Stoddart topped the batting averages with 1,188 runs in all matches at 38.32 and Bobby Peel topped the bowling averages with 213 wickets at 7.53. Smith's side played 22 matches, winning five of the seven against 11-a-side, losing two. They won seven and drew eight of the 15 matches against the odds. Shrewsbury topped the batting averages for Smith's team with 1,113 runs at 37.10, with Briggs (208 wickets at 6.50) and Lohmann (210 wickets at 8.12) doing most of the bowling.

C. Aubrey Smith, English Test cricketer and noted actor on the stage and in films.

This team was financed by Lord Sheffield, who accompanied the team and led by the legendary Dr W. G. Grace, who made a grand 159 not out early in the tour in the match against Victoria. The tourists began by beating South Australia, NSW and Victoria handsomely. In the First Test Bannerman batted for 435 minutes for 86 runs, scoring 45 and 41, and Grace in his first Test in Australia scored 50. Australia won by 54 runs thanks to Turner's 5 for 51 in England's second innings. Australia then made the rubber safe by winning the Second Test by 72 runs, Bobbie Abel becoming the first batsman to bat through a Test innings in scoring 132 not out. Bannerman batted all the third day for 67, and Johnny Briggs ended Australia's second innings with a hat-trick. Stoddart made a brilliant 134 in an England total of 499 in the Third Test, setting up an England win by an innings and 230 runs.

By now the good doctor had become accustomed to Australian roads and he entertained large crowds at Parramatta, Camden, Bowral, Goulburn and Ballarat. He was full of advice for young Australian cricketers and only occasionally challenged umpires or resorted to the gamesmanship for which he was famous. To commemorate a happy tour Lord Sheffield donated the £150 which was used to buy the Sheffield Shield. His team played 27 matches, winning six and losing two of the 11-a-side games, and remaining unbeaten in matches against the odds, with seven wins and 12 draws. W. G. Grace headed the batting averages with 921 runs at 32.89 in all games, and three bowlers, Briggs (140 at 7.66), Lohmann (155 at 8.50) and Attewell (100 at 9.33) shared the honours in all tour matches.

Stoddart's first touring side found a marked improvement in standards. South Australia beat them in the second match of the tour despite a century by J. T. Brown in an English total of 477. Joe Darling made his bid for stardom with 117. Giffen took 11 wickets and had innings of 64 and 58 not out. All the matches against NSW and Victoria were tough matches from here on, but Queensland was still building its strength.

The First Test at Sydney went to England when heavy rain fell during the night with Australia on 2 for 113 needing 177 to win. Warm sun on the soaked pitch produced an ideal surface for Briggs and Peel and they bowled England to a 10 run win. Australia wanted 428 to win the Second Test at Melbourne and at 1 for 190 had a chance, but they faltered, to lose by 94 runs. Australia won the Third Test by 382 runs in a triumphant debut for Albert Trott, who scored 38 not out and 72 not out and took 8 for 43 in England's second innings of 143. The Fourth Test saw Trott carry on with 85 not out and Harry Graham contribute a brilliant century. England were then bowled out twice in a day. In this Test Briggs became the first English bowler to take 100 Test wickets and Turner the first

353

Australian to do so. The Fifth Test produced one of the most brilliant innings in Test history by J. T. Brown, who made 140. His first 50 took only 28 minutes.

England won eight and lost four of the 12 matches on level terms and drew 10 and won one of the 11 matches against the odds. Stoddart topped the batting averages with 1,332 runs at 47.57 in all matches, W. Humphreys the bowling with 79 wickets at 11.78.

FOURTEENTH ENGLISH TEAM, 1897–98

A. E. Stoddart

Stoddart's second team were soon tested, for in the opening first-class match Clem Hill scored 200 in a South Australian score of 408 and Ernie Jones bowled really fast. But Ranjitsinhji played a charming innings of 189 not out to save the match. England then showed strength by beating Victoria and NSW, McLaren scoring 142 and 100 against NSW and Ranjitsinhji 112 not out.

The Sydney Cricket Ground Trust took the unprecedented step of postponing the start of the First Test without consulting the captains and play did not begin until Monday. By then Ranjitsinhji, who had been ill with no chance of playing on Friday, had recovered. He went in late on the Monday and took his score to 175 on the Tuesday. He had thus made a century in his first Tests in England and Australia. Joe Darling became the first left-hander to make a Test century but England won by nine wickets. Australia responded with an innings and 55 runs win in the Second Test, when Ernie Jones became the first bowler no-balled for throwing in a Test. With the series deadlocked at 1–1, Australia then won three Tests in a row, thanks largely to the batting of the left-handers Darling and Hill, Darling scoring three centuries in the series.

Stoddart's team won four, lost five and drew three of its 11-a-side matches and won eight of the 10 matches against the odds, with two unfinished. Ranjitsinhji topped the batting averages by a slim margin, finishing with 1,372 runs at 54.88 runs in all matches, compared with 1,413 runs at 54.34 by Archie MacLaren. Stoddart topped the bowling with 35 wickets at 8.80, but Tom Richardson took most wickets, 65 at 26.63.

FIFTEENTH ENGLISH TEAM, 1901–02

A. C. MacLaren

Australia beat MacLaren's team 4–1 in the Tests in perhaps its best display to that time. England lost Barnes through injury during the Third Test at Adelaide and he took no further part in the tour, but Australia consistently showed superior all-round strength, particularly in fighting a way out of difficulty. England won the first Test when Barnes in the first innings and Braund in the second bowled Australia out for small scores. After that it was all Australia. Duff made a century in his debut in the Second Test in which Trumble took a hat-trick. Hill got his third successive ninety in the Third Test, and in the Fourth Howell made 35 in 14 minutes being out off the 15th ball he received. The Fifth Test saw the start of the famous Trumper–Duff opening partnerships. Hill reached 500 runs in the series without a century. MacLaren topped the English batting averages with 929 at 58.06 and Barnes the bowling with 41 wickets at 16.48. England won five and lost six of the 11 matches played on level terms and won three and drew eight of the matches against the odds.

The Fifteenth English team in Australia (L to R): Back row, C. Blythe, S. F. Barnes, A. A. Lilley, T. Hayward; Centre, J. Gunn, H. G. Garrett, C. MacGahey, A. C. Maclaren, C. Robson, A. O. Jones, L. C. Braund; Front, W. G. Quaife, J. T. Tyldesley.

SIXTEENTH ENGLISH TEAM, 1903–04

P. F. Warner

This was one of the great English teams and, significantly, the first to be selected and organised by the Marylebone Cricket Club. Australia were fortunate to only go down 2–3 in the Tests for England had great batting strength and truly hostile attack in which Bosanquet, inventor of the googly, came on to mystify batsmen who survived the fine bowling of Hirst, Arnold, Braund and Rhodes.

At Sydney in the First Test Foster, in his Test debut, batted for seven hours for 287 in an England total of 577. Facing a first innings deficit of 292 after Australia had made 285, Trumper and Hill were scoring rapidly when umpire Crockett gave Hill run out. The crowd immediately demonstrated against the decision calling "Crock," "Crock," "Crock," and yelling for Crockett to be replaced. The other batsmen capitulated and Trumper was left on 185 not out, England winning by five wickets. In the Second Test, Rhodes set a record against Australia by taking 15 wickets in the match, England winning by 185 runs. Australia won the Third Test by 216 runs when both Trumper and Syd Gregory both made their fourth centuries in Tests. Bosanquet chimed in with 6 for 51 in the Fourth Test to seal the rubber for England. Australia regained some prestige by winning the Fifth Test by 218 runs when Trumble took his second Test hat-trick on a pitch that Cotter had cut up after rain. England played 20 matches, winning eight, losing two and drawing one of those played on level terms, and winning two of the matches against the odds, with seven unfinished. Rhodes took 76 wickets in all matches at 15.53, 31 of them in Tests. Tom Hayward make 1,181 runs at 49.20 in all matches.

SEVENTEENTH ENGLISH TEAM, 1907–08

A. O. Jones

Australia reversed the 4–1 defeat suffered against Warner's team with a splendid all-round display, winning all bar the Second Test when Hazlitt threw wildly from cover point with a run-out certain. The English batsmen, Barnes and Fielder, scampered through for the winning run and Test cricket's first tie was postponed. This was the first English touring team to play in Perth, the Western Australian side acquitting itself well in the opening match of the tour thanks to 5 for 132 by left-arm spinner Christian. George Gunn was not in the original English touring party but was in Australia for health reasons and was brought into the England side at the last minute for the First Test. He topscored in both innings but could not prevent an Australian win. The Second Test went to England by one wicket when Barnes and Fielder put on 39 for the last wicket.

Hill batted with extraordinary pluck to prevent England taking a winning position in the Third Test, leaving the field several times though illness and vomiting by the side of the pitch during a stand of 243 with Hartigan, who had a century on his debut. In the Fourth Test Saunders bowled Australia to victory after Crawford took 5 for 48 in Australia's first innings, Saunders finishing with match figures of 9 for 104. Saunders was again the match-winning bowler in the Fifth Test, although Crawford matched his eight wickets. Of the 19 matches England played, only one (a draw) was against the odds, England winning seven and losing four of the 11-a-side matches, with eight drawn. Gunn headed the batting averages with 831 runs in all matches at 51.93, and Blythe topped the bowling with 48 wickets at 20.12.

EIGHTEENTH ENGLISH TEAM, 1911–12

J. W. H. T. Douglas

Pelham Warner arrived in Australia as captain of the 18th English team but became ill after the first match and did not play again on the tour. J. W. H. T. Douglas took over the captaincy and this is always referred to as Douglas' team, for he led the team with skill and made a major contribution to its success with his own batting and bowling. It was a season of turmoil for Australia's leading players. The dispute with the

356

Board Of Control simmered throughout and undoubtedly affected the key players' form.

"Ranji" Hordern hoodwinked the England batsmen in the First Test, taking 5 for 85 and 7 for 90, but once Hobbs, Hearne, Rhodes and Foster had worked out Hordern's googly technique, England were overwhelmingly superior, winning the last four Tests convincingly. Barnes and Foster proved magnificent bowlers for England, moving the ball sharply either way off good pitches. In the Fourth Test Hobbs (178) and Rhodes (179) put on a record 323 for the first wicket. Foster bowled Bardsley around his legs twice in this match and Bardsley was dropped from the Fifth Test.

Hobbs made 662 runs in the Tests at 82.75 and scored 1,156 in all matches on the tour. Rhodes scored 463 runs at 57.87 in the Tests and made 1,164 runs on the tour. Barnes took 34 wickets in the Tests at 22.88 and Foster 32 at 21.62. Trumper made the only Test century for Australia but only scored 269 in nine innings. Hordern was the best Australian bowler with 32 wickets at 24.37. For Hill, Cotter, Trumper and Ransford the series was a disappointing end to outstanding Test careers. Douglas' side played 18 matches, 15 on level terms and only three against the odds, winning 12, losing one and drawing two of the 11-a-side matches and leaving all the matches against the odds drawn.

English cricket took a lot longer to recover from World War I than Australian cricket, which was helped tremendously by the success of the First AIF team. This team's tour around England and through South Africa and the Australian States not only revived interest in cricket, but it left Australia with a match-winner in Jack Gregory and several other fine players.

Douglas was a popular and shrewd captain and his side had no trouble defeating WA, SA and Victoria. The loss to NSW by six wickets clearly showed the problems that lay ahead in the Tests, however, for Macartney and Collins were in brilliant form as they added 244 of the 344 runs NSW needed to win for the first wicket. In the First Test Collins made a resolute century in his initial Test and Armstrong drove with tremendous power for 158 in around 200 minutes. The weakness in England's bowling exposed, Gregory and Pellew proceeded to centuries in the Second Test, Collins, Kelleway, Armstrong and Pellew centuries in the Third Test, Armstrong a century in the Fourth Test, and Macartney a brilliant 170 in the Fifth Test, Australia taking the rubber 5–0.

England played 22 matches, all on level terms for the first time, winning nine, losing six, with seven drawn. Only Hendren reached 1,000 runs in all matches, scoring 1,178 at 61.47, topscore 271. Rhodes topped the bowling averages with 18 wickets at 26.61 and all the other bowlers' wickets cost more than 30 runs apiece.

NINETEENTH ENGLISH TEAM, 1920–21

J. W. H. T. Douglas

**TWENTIETH
ENGLISH TEAM,
1924–25**

A. E. R. Gilligan

Gilligan's team began with four matches in WA, an indication of that State's growing strength. The MCC then beat SA, lost to Victoria, beat NSW, had the match with Queensland ruined by rain, and drew with an Australian XI. The First Test at Sydney went into the seventh day before Australia won by 193 runs, Collins and Ponsford contributing centuries, and Taylor and Mailey adding a record 127 for the last wicket. Taylor finished with 108, Mailey 46 not out. England made 411 in the final innings, with Sutcliffe 115 in his first Test against Australia and Woolley 123 in 150 minutes, a great losing effort.

Sutcliffe repeated the dose with 176 and 127 in the Second Test but Australia still won by 78 runs due to centuries by Ponsford and Victor Richardson and a fine 90 by Taylor. Ryder made 201 not out in the Third Test but England recovered gamely to go down by only 11 runs, this time scoring 363 in the final innings. England ended an Australian sequence of 16 Tests without defeat by winning the Fourth Test by an innings and 29 runs, Sutcliffe scoring his four century in the rubber. Grimmett took 11 wickets (5 for 45 and 6 for 37) in his debut in the Fifth Test, setting up an Australian win and a 4–1 result in the series.

Sutcliffe's batting and the start of his association with Hobbs were the feature of England's tour. Sutcliffe made 734 runs in the Tests and 1,626 at 73.90 in all games. Tate was the best of England's bowlers with 81 wickets in all at 17.66 and 38 wickets in the Tests. The team won 8 matches, lost 6, drew 9, all of them 11-a-side.

**TWENTY-FIRST
ENGLISH TEAM,
1928–29**

A. P. F. Chapman

Chapman's team began with an unhappy injury in the first match against WA in Perth, Geary sustaining a blow on the nose that kept him out for a month. When MCC compiled 734 against NSW at Sydney it was clear the team had exceptional batting strength. Hammond and Hendren put on 333 in 230 minutes, but NSW also scored heavily, Bradman (132 not out) and Kippax (136 not out) seeing out time with NSW three for 364 in the second innings.

England won the First Test at Brisbane by 675 runs when Australia were caught on a sticky wicket and had batsmen absent injured. The Second Test was almost as one-sided England winning by eight wickets after scoring 636 in the first innings, Hammond contributing 251. Kippax, Woodfull, Ryder and Bradman all scored centuries in the Third Test but England immense batting strength prevailed by three wickets, Hammond scoring his second successive double century (200). The Fourth Test was distinguished by one of the classic Test centuries, Archie Jackson's 164, but England still won by 12 runs thanks to scores of 119 and 177 by Hammond. The Fifth Test lasted eight days, with Hobbs scoring a century in his 47th year, Leyland 137. Centuries by Woodfull (102) and Bradman (123) helped Australia to win by five wickets. Chapman's team won 10 of its 24 matches, drew 13, and lost 1. Hammond made 1,553 in all matches at 91.35, J. C. White topped the bowling averages with 65 wickets at 22.63.

This was the most contentious cricket tour Australia has known and always will be recalled as "The Bodyline Tour." Firm friendships were broken, players bitterly accused each other of poor sportsmanship, and the administrators of cricket in England and Australia exchanged sharply-worded cables. More bruises were sustained in this season than in any season since, even including those when Lillee and Thomson were in their prime. Jardine's team played 22 matches, for 10 wins, 10 draws, one loss and one tie, the first by an English team in Australia. Victoria needed eight runs to win off the last over in the return match at Melbourne against England and made seven of them, Victoria finishing with eight wickets in hand. Only Sutcliffe, with 1,318 runs at 73.22, made 1,000 runs for England on the tour, though Hammond had the highest score of 203, and seven players made centuries. Verity and Larwood topped the bowling averages with 49 wickets at 16.93.

TWENTY-SECOND ENGLISH TEAM, 1932–33

D. R. Jardine

G. O. Allen's team performed the important task of restoring peaceful relations with Australia and they did this admirably. All the bitterness of the previous tour by Jardine's side was forgotten in a tense, exciting series that broke all attendance records to that time. Allen could count himself unlucky not to have won the series after leading 2–0 but Australia recovered to win 3–2 when Bradman found his form at the right time.

TWENTY-THIRD ENGLISH TEAM, 1936–37

G. O. Allen

After a spin around the States from Perth the MCC went into the First Test at Brisbane in indifferent form but they lifted their standard to give a spirited showing throughout the series. The First Test started with Worthington dismissed off the first ball from McCormick, but at 3 for 20, Leyland and Barnett added 99, Leyland going on to a fine 126. McCormick, after bowling at great pace, was attacked by lumbago and had to retire. Fingleton got his fourth successive Test century in Australia's first innings but was out first ball in the second when Australia was caught on a sticky wicket and were out for 58.

England pressed home their advantage in the second Test at Melbourne where Hammond made 231 not out and set up a win by an innings and 22 runs and a 2–0 lead in the series. In the Third Test England was caught on a damp pitch but Allen delayed his closure until 9 for 76 by which time the pitch had dried. Many thought he should have closed earlier and given excellent wet pitch bowlers like Verity and Voce a chance at the Australians. Bradman led the Australian win with 270 and followed with 212 in the Fourth Test, also won by Austra-

359

lia. The Fifth Test was no contest after Australia scored 604, Bradman making 169, McCabe 112, and Badcock 118. The five Tests attracted 943,513 spectators, the highest attendance for any Test rubber.

England won only six of its 24 matches, lost five and 13 were drawn. Seven of the 24 matches were not first-class. Barnett made most runs in all matches for England, 1,375 at 55.00, topscore 259, but Hammond had a better average with 1,205 at 66.94. Farnes headed the bowling averages with 41 wickets in all matches at 20.65.

TWENTY-FOURTH ENGLISH TEAM, 1946–47

W. R. Hammond

This team had the worst record of any English team to tour Australia, winning only two of its 23 matches, with three losses and 18 draws. The team included only four players, Hammond, Voce, Fishlock and Hardstaff, who had toured previously in Australia but had some interesting newcomers to Australia in Compton, Hutton, Edrich, Wright and Washbrook. Australia's Test team had only Bradman, Hassett and Barnes left from the 1938 side but once again a services team tour uncovered a match-winner in Keith Miller. Australia won the First Test by an innings and 332 runs, their first win over England at Brisbane. After Australia scored 645 the match was played between thunderstorms and England had to bat twice on a rain-damaged pitch. Miller and Toshack both took nine wickets in the match, England scoring 141 and 172. Barnes and Bradman both scored 234 in the Second Test at Sydney, where Evans conceded no byes in Australia's score of 659. England lost by an innings and 33 runs, with the spin of Johnson in the first innings and McCool in the second too much for them. The Third and Fourth Tests were drawn and England succumbed again to McCool's leg-spin in the final innings of the Fifth Test, to give Australia a 3–0 win in the series.

Hammond's team did a splendid job re-establishing international cricket in Australia, attracting big crowds and putting cricket back into the headlines. Hutton (1,267 at 70.38) and Compton (1,432 runs at 65.09) were the most successful English batsmen and Wright the most successful wicket-taker (51 wickets at 33.80). Bedser found Australia's hard pitches unresponsive but laboured manfully. The team's fielding was far below Australia's standard and did not match that of most of the States.

TWENTY-FIFTH ENGLISH TEAM, 1950–51

F. R. Brown

Freddie Brown's team had an array of outstanding batsmen, but lacked penetration in bowling and did not field as well as their opponents in Tests. But they had the satisfaction of ending Australia's run of 29 Tests without defeat (24 wins, 5 draws). The recall of Freddie Brown at the age of 40 to captain England to Australia produced a dynamic leader. He played some exciting innings and had some happy results with the

360

ball, playing every game belligerently as befitted a man who had been captured at Tobruk and returned to cricket almost five stone lighter. He was a real John Bull-type figure with his pipe and knotted kerchief and Australians loved him.

Led for the first time at home by Hassett, Australia won the first four Tests, Iverson enlivening proceedings in each of these matches with his unorthodox spinners. In the Fifth Test Brown inspired his team to victory by eight wickets, thanks to an innings of 156 not out by Simpson who scored all bar 10 of a last-wicket stand of 74 in 55 minutes with Tattersall. It was the first time England had beaten Australia since 1938. Brown's team played 25 matches, 14 of them first-class, won seven, lost four and drew 14. Hutton headed the batting averages with 1,199 runs at 70.52 in all matches. Simpson made the topscore of 259. Bedser was the highest wicket-taker with 51 wickets at 20.03.

The negative approach of Len Hutton's team did not prevent big crowds attending the matches, though it did irk the Australian batsmen trying to push the scoring rate along. Hutton was the first professional to captain a team sponsored by the MCC and he made sure he did not encourage those who claimed his appointment was a mistake. He approached every match grimly determined not to take a single risk. Hutton's trump was pace bowler Frank Tyson who, with the series evenly balanced at one Test all, produced a devastating spell to take 6 for 16 off 51 balls and finish with 7 for 27, winning the Third Test for England and virtually clinching the series. None of the oldtimers who watched could recall bowling as fast as Tyson's in that spell. Tyson had demonstrated his special brand of pluck in the Second Test when he was knocked unconscious by a Lindwall bouncer and returned to bowl with great speed and give England a thrilling victory. But it was at Melbourne that he delivered the decisive blow. Others have taken more than the 28 wickets Tyson took in that series but nobody has so thoroughly demoralised Australian batsmen. Compton led the batting averages with 799 runs in first-class matches at 57.07, and Tyson did all the damage with his 51 first-class wickets at 19.92. Hutton's team won 13 of its 23 matches, lost two and left eight unfinished.

The tour by Peter May's English team was marred by arguments about "chuckers." The Englishmen did not protest officially but were unhappy about the actions of Meckiff, Rorke, Slater and in a minor way by that of Burke. Australians in return were still not satisfied with Lock's action, although it was said to have been remodelled. England failed to get away to good starts throughout the tour and although their openers clearly were below international class one of the suspect bowlers usually secured the early wickets. The first Test was

TWENTY-SIXTH ENGLISH TEAM, 1954–55

L. Hutton

TWENTY-SEVENTH ENGLISH TEAM, 1958–59

P. B. H. May

cursed with the slowest half-century in all first-class cricket when Trevor Bailey batted for 357 minutes to reach 50 and 458 minutes to make 68 before Mackay bowled him. Bailey faced 425 balls and scored off 40 of them. Australia won that Test and the next when Davidson took three wickets in one over and had match figures of 9 for 105. The Third Test was drawn when Benaud declined the challenge of scoring 150 in 110 minutes. Australia regained The Ashes by winning the Fourth Test, with McDonald scoring 170 and Benaud taking 9 for 173 in the match. Australia made it 4–0 with a nine wickets' win in the Fifth Test, McDonald scoring 133. Bailey, in his final Test, achieved spectacles. The team played 23 matches, winning 10, losing four and leaving nine unfinished. Three of the wins were in matches that were not first-class. May was the only batsman to make 1,000 runs—1,197 at 57.00. Laker topped the bowling averages with 38 wickets at 17.23.

TWENTY-EIGHTH ENGLISH TEAM, 1962–63

E. R. Dexter

"Lord Ted" Dexter's bid to regain The Ashes failed after a disappointing rubber that produced three draws and a win to each side. Neither England nor Australia was able to dismiss the opposition batsmen cheaply enough to set up a win in the drawn matches. England, managed by the premier nobleman, the Duke of Norfolk, had five batsmen who scored more than 1,000 runs on the 27-match tour in which only three matches were lost, with 12 won and 12 unfinished. Ten of the 16 players in the England side made tour centuries, but only David Allen took more than 50 wickets (58 at 19.41). Fourteen 50s were scored in the First Test and that set the pattern of batting supremacy for the entire series. Trueman helped pave the way to England's sole Test win by taking 8 for 147 in the Second Test, just as Davidson set up Australia's Third Test win with match figures of 9 for 79. In the drawn Fourth Test Barrington became the second batsman in England-Australia matches (Joe Darling in 1897–98 was the first) to reach his century with a six. Dexter got 481 Test runs, a record for an English captain in Australia, without scoring a century, but Barrington headed the tour averages with 1,775 runs at 77.17.

TWENTY-NINTH ENGLISH TEAM, 1965–66

M. J. K. Smith

Another England team strong in batting but unable to get the opposition out cheaply often enough to win the rubber. Titmus was the most successful English bowler with 45 wickets at 27.82 but Barrington headed the English bowling averages with 18 wickets at 22.61. There were seven totals over 400 in five Tests. For Australia the series was enlivened by Walters, who scored 155 in his first Test, aged 19 years 357 days, and 115 in his second Test. Overall it was a dour series with batsmen taking a long time to get their runs. Lawry batted 419 minutes for 166 in the First Test, Bob Barber 291 minutes for 185 in the Third Test, Simpson 547 minutes for 225 in the Fourth Test, and Cowper 727 minutes for 307 in the Fifth

Test. One of the few innings for spectators to cheer about was Barrington's 115 in the Fifth Test. He reached his century again with a six off 122 balls. Ten of the 17 English players made centuries on the 23-match tour, the English winning 13 matches, losing two and leaving eight unfinished. John Edrich made most runs for England—1,274 at 50.96—but the bowlers always struggled for wickets.

Far Left: M. J. K. Smith, whose team failed to recover The Ashes; Left, R. Illingworth, whose team succeeded.

An incident-packed tour that produced the longest Test series on record. Six Tests were scheduled but when the third was washed out after the toss had been made the Australian Cricket Board organised a seventh. Throughout the series England's fast bowler John Snow aroused spectators, bowling with fire and a liberal sprinkling of bouncers. Few could recall a bowler with such a low arm action who could make the ball kick so viciously off a good length, and he gave Australian batsmen a thorough dusting. The first two Tests were drawn, Stackpole scoring 207 after a lucky run-out decision favoured him at 18, and Walters (112) in the first, Redpath (171) and Greg Chappell (108) scored centuries in the second. The third saw umpires on the field, but not a ball was bowled. England won the Fourth Test despite a dogged effort by Lawry who batted through the Australian second innings for 60. The Fifth and Sixth Tests produced 111 and 104 from Ian Chappell but were both drawn, leaving the Seventh Test to decide the rubber. There was a sensation before this match when the Australian Cricket Board sacked Bill Lawry as Australia's captain. In his first Test as captain Ian Chappell sent England to bat, a decision which seemed justified when England were bundled out for 184. On the second day Snow's bouncers were widely hooted and when he flattened Jenner with a short-pitched delivery that cannoned off Jenner's head a barrage of cans and fruit landed on the field. With further missiles ballooning on to the ground Illingworth led his team from the field. Snow, who had been grabbed by a spectator as the cans bounced on to the field, fractured his finger in Australia's se-

THIRTIETH ENGLISH TEAM, 1970–71

R. Illingworth

cond innings when he crashed into the boundary fence. In the end it was the spin of Illingworth and Underwood that brought Australia undone and gave England a memorable series in which they did not have a single lbw appeal upheld. England won 10 of the 25 tour matches, losing two, with 13 unfinished. Boycott headed the batting averages with 1,697 runs at 94.27, topscore 173, and Underwood was the most dangerous bowler with 44 wickets at 23.75.

THIRTY-FIRST ENGLISH TEAM, 1974–75

M. H. Denness

England had a major problem throughout this tour—a captain who could not make enough runs to justify his Test place and whose captaincy did not compensate for that as Brearley's did more recently. Australia produced one of its finest teams, with Thomson and Lillee a devastating opening pair whatever opening batsmen England used, and an array of strokemakers who could bat well in a crisis. Australia won the First Test when Lillee and Thomson took 13 wickets between them, the Second Test when Lillee and Thomson took 11 wickets, the Third was drawn with Lillee and Thomson taking 12 wickets, and Australia won the Fourth and Fifth with Lillee and Thomson taking 10 and then 11 wickets. With Australia in an unbeatable position Denness made 188 and Fletcher 146, Thomson having torn fibres in his shoulder playing tennis in Adelaide during the Fifth Test. Left to open without his usual partner, Lillee took only one wicket, England winning by an innings. None of the English batsmen made 1,000 runs in the 24-match tour. England won eight, lost six and drew nine matches, with one abandoned. Tony Greig topped the batting averages on his first trip to Australia with 836 runs at 46.44. Derek Underwood was the best bowler with 40 wickets at 26.98.

THIRTY-SECOND ENGLISH TEAM, 1977

A. W. Greig

This English team visited Australia after a tour of India and Sri Lanka mainly to play the Centenary Test at Melbourne. They were a splendid bunch of cricketers, pugnaciously led by Greig and brimful of crowd-pleasers like Randall, Knott, Willis and Old. They were not lacking in intestinal fortitude either and gave a great occasion the spirited cricket it deserved. They drew the warm-up match against Western Australia at Perth. Brearley headed the batting averages for the two-match trip with 174 runs at 58.00, but Randall made more runs with 225 at 56.25, with Old the leading wicket-taker (9 at 22.33).

THIRTY-THIRD ENGLISH TEAM, 1978–79

J. M. Brearley

Mike Brearley's team beat a half-strength Australia 5–1, but the Australian captain Graham Yallop said the result would have been reversed had Ian Botham been in the Australian team. He did not mention the absence from the Australian team of the WSC players whose loss hit Australia far harder than England. Both teams lacked high-scoring batsmen, although Randall made a gutsy 150 in the Fourth Test. Australia's sole success was Rodney Hogg, who grabbed a remarkable 41 wickets in his first full series. Jim Higgs took 19 Test wickets but England had five bowlers who took 16 wickets, including spinners John Emburey and Geoff Miller. Mike Brearley was one of the most unsuccessful of English captains with the bat but was far superior to Yallop as a tactician. Apart from Botham, David Gower was England's star with 420 Test runs at 42.00.

Australia, with the WSC players back, thoroughly outplayed Mike Brearley's team. None of the Englishmen scored 200 runs in the three Tests, all won comfortably by Australia. Botham and Underwood were the only English bowlers to take 10 Test wickets. Brearley found Greg Chappell a far tougher opposing captain than Yallop had been on his previous Australian trip. Ian Chappell returned to Tests after four years under his brother's captaincy. Lillee disappointed his admirers by trying to insist on using an aluminium bat in the Perth Test, where Dymock took the honors with nine wickets, including 6 for 34 in the second innings. Only eight of England's 21-matches were first-class, which was hardly an adequate preparation for the Tests. England refused to put The Ashes at stake as this series was not officially scheduled and was held to heal the wounds caused by the WSC.

THIRTY-FOURTH ENGLISH TEAM, 1979–80

J. M. Brearley

The first Australian tour of England went ahead barely 20 years after the first inter-Colonial matches despite the undisguised opposition of the colonial cricket associations, who declined to help in any way. The Australians were partly sponsored by James Lillywhite, who had captained England in the first two Tests against Australia in 1876–77, and booked matches in advance for the team. The team's manager, John Conway, of Melbourne, was the other major sponsor and he received some financial help from T. S. Wills, noted cricketer and originator of Australian Rules Football. Conway organised the tour finances on a joint stock basis, each member contributing pro rata towards expenses and sharing in any profits. The team played matches in Australia before leaving and after returning, went to New Zealand and back before going to England, and played six matches in America after leaving England. They left to a lukewarm send-off, but were warmly welcomed home.

Authorities disagree on the number of matches the team played but there is no reason to doubt Conway's figure of 41 matches as he was closest to arrangements. The discrepancy arose when four of the 37 matches in the schedule finished within two days. The team played 17 first-class matches, two others against 11-a-side, and 22 against the odds or exhibition games, winning 19, losing seven and leaving 15 drawn. They

AUSTRALIAN TEAMS IN ENGLAND

FIRST AUSTRALIAN TEAM, 1878

D. W. Gregory

lacked depth in batting, with seven of the top side worth "about 30 runs between them." They fielded splendidly throughout and Blackham was a fine 'keeper, but Dave Gregory's field placements showed inexperience when the best English batsmen appeared. The attack, based on four bowlers, Spofforth, Boyle, Garrett and Allan, was the team's strength and many sides could not cope with them at all.

The team was badly weakened by the loss of Midwinter after only nine matches (See, Midwinter, W. E.) and had to call on Victorian medical student H. W. Tennant, the first-ever Australian tour replacement. They lost the opening match of the tour in cruel conditions at Nottingham, but on May 27, 1878, at Lord's, established the reputation of Australian cricket by beating the finest players in England in a match against MCC And Ground in three hours 40 minutes. This win destroyed English complacency about their world leadership in cricket and helped attract big crowds for much of the tour. Next came easy victories over Yorkshire and Surrey. More than 30,000 people atttended the two days of the Surrey game at which crowds held up at turnstiles broke through fences. Spectators crowding on to the playing area reduced the field to half its normal size.

Against an Eighteen of Elland, Boyle achieved the astound-

The First Australian team to tour England (L to R): Back row, J. M. Blackham, T. Horan, G. H. Bailey, J. Conway (manager), A. C. Bannerman, C. Bannerman, W. L. Murdoch; Centre, D. W. Gregory (captain); Front, F. R. Spofforth, F. Allan, W. E. Midwinter, T. W. Garrett, H. F. Boyle.

ing feat of taking seven wickets with his last eight balls. At Longsight the locals included W. G. Grace in their Eighteen. The next match against Middlesex at Lord's produced the famous incident in which W. G. Grace "kidnapped" Midwinter and set up a grudge match against Gloucestershire before a huge crowd at Clifton, where the locals had never lost. Australia won by 10-wickets with hours to spare, Spofforth taking 12 wickets in the match. The 13-month tour ended with a few more matches in Australia. The entire venture was a big financial success, but the sportsmanship of the Australians left sour feelings in England and America. Only two weeks after the team dispersed Lord Harris arrived at the head of an English team for an Australian tour in which Australian behaviour was again condemned.

First-class match averages for the first Australian team:

FIRST AUSTRALIAN TEAM AVERAGES

Name	I.	NO	HS	Runs	Ave.	W.	Runs	Ave.
C. Bannerman	31	1	133	723	24.10	—	—	—
J. M. Blackham	22	9	53	256	19.60	1	4	4.00
W. Midwinter	10	2	32	124	15.50	8	58	7.25
G. H. Bailey	24	5	41	281	14.78	2	62	31.00
T. Horan	30	2	69	377	13.46	8	143	17.87
W. L. Murdoch	28	4	49	319	13.29	5	80	16.00
F. R. Spofforth	28	2	56	335	12.88	107	1254	11.71
A. C. Bannerman	26	3	71*	261	11.34	—	—	—
T. W. Garrett	27	1	43	282	10.84	38	396	10.42
F. E. Allan	26	6	78	212	10.60	26	605	23.26
D. W. Gregory	25	2	57	233	10.13	—	—	—
H. F. Boyle	23	6	18	119	7.00	64	620	9.68
J. Conway	2	–	46	58	29.00	—	—	—
H. W. Tennant	2	–	6	7	3.50	—	—	—

SECOND AUSTRALIAN TEAM, 1880

W. L. Murdoch

The second Australian tour of England was organised with the help of the colonial cricket associations, but arrived in England to find that most counties had omitted them from their schedule of matches because of the uncertainty over their arrival. Many enthusiasts argued that the tour was too soon after the riot at Sydney during the match with Lord Harris's team and that an Australian side would not be welcome in England. Murdoch was a surprise appointment as captain as most felt Harry Boyle would get the job. The team was managed by George Alexander, the Victorian allrounder, and Thomas Groube went as a last-minute replacement when illness prevented Charles Bannerman from touring. Arthur ("Affie") Jarvis, the replacement wicket-keeper for Blackham, became the first South Australian to tour. The most surprising selection, however, was George Bonnor, who had not played in a first-class match when the team left.

The Australians were confined initially to matches against clubs in northern England and the Midlands, and like Gregory's side two-years earlier, were forced to advertise for matches. The match against Yorkshire was classed "unoffi-

cial." When a Canadian team arrived the counties soon altered their fixture lists to give the Canadians matches. Murdoch offered to play an England XI with all proceeds going to a cricketers' benevolent fund but the idea met with little enthusiasm. W. G. Grace tried to arrange a match at Lord's but this fell through, largely because of the antipathy of the Marylebone Cricket Club committee. Finally Lord Harris, the man who was at the centre of the Sydney riot that caused all this hostility towards the Australians, intervened and organised a match at The Oval, after pressure from W. G. Grace and the Surrey secretary, C. W. Alcock.

This match became the first of all Tests in England. W. G. Grace made 152 and Billy Murdoch topped it with 153 not out, but Australia could not overcome the absence through injury of Spofforth. Three Graces were in the English team, the first time three brothers played together in a Test. England opened with a stand of 91 by W. G. and E. M. Grace before 20,814 spectators and then W. G. and Alfred Lucas added 120 for the second wicket. Lord Harris contributed 52 and the youngest Grace, G. F., a duck and England were finally out for 420.

Australia were all out on the second day for 149, with 19,863 in attendance, and had to follow on 271 runs behind. They began badly, losing 3 for 14, but Murdoch and McDonnell put on 83 for the fourth wicket. At 8 for 187, Alexander defended grimly while Murdoch attacked but when Alexander was out England were still 32 in front. Moule then stayed with Murdoch who passed his century in a gallant last-wicket stand of 88, which ended with Barnes bowled Moule for 34. Chasing 56, England lost 5 for 36, but Frank Penn and W. G. then hit England to victory. The Australians received £1,110 as their share

Above: A splendid shot of Australian slips fieldsmen Ian Redpath, Doug Walters, Greg and Ian Chappell alert for a catch from Lillee's bowling. Below: Terry Alderman clean bowls English opener Graham Gooch during the Fifth Test at Old Trafford in 1981.

Australian opening batsman Rick Darling goes down after being hit by England's fast bowler Bob Willis in the Third Test at Melbourne in 1978.

Played at The Oval, London, on September 6, 7, 8, 1880.

In this the fourth match between Australia and England on level terms under first-class conditions, W. G. Grace scored the first-ever Test century by an Englishman.

THE FIRST TEST IN ENGLAND

ENGLAND

E. M. Grace	c Alexander, b Bannerman	36	(6) b Boyle	0
W. G. Grace	b Palmer	152	(7) not out	9
A. P. Lucas	b Bannerman	55	c Bannerman, b Palmer	2
W. Barnes	b Alexander	28	(5) c Moule, b Boyle	5
Lord Harris (c)	c Bonnor, b Alexander	52		
F. Penn	b Bannerman	23	(4) not out	27
A. G. Steel	c Boyle, b Moule	42		
Hon. A. Lyttelton†	not out	11	(1) b Palmer	13
G. F. Grace	c Bannerman, b Moule	0	(2) b Palmer	0
A. Shaw	b Moule	0		
F. Morley	run out	2		
Extras	(B 8, LB 11)	19	(NB 1)	1
		420	(5 wickets)	**57**

	O	M	R	W	O	M	R	W
Boyle	44	17	71	0	17	7	21	2
Palmer	70	27	116	1	16.3	5	35	3
Alexander	32	10	69	2				
Bannerman	50	12	111	3				
McDonnell	2	0	11	0				
Moule	12.3	4	23	3				

AUSTRALIA

A. C. Bannerman	b Morley	32	c Lucas, b Shaw	8
W. L. Murdoch (c)	c Barnes, b Steel	0	(3) not out	153
T. U. Groube	b Steel	11	(4) c Shaw, b Morley	0
P. S. McDonnell	c Barnes, b Morley	27	(5) lbw, b W. G. Grace	43
J. Slight	c G. F. Grace, b Morley	11	(6) c Harris, b W. G. Grace	0
J. M. Blackham	c and b Morley	0	(7) c E. M. Grace, b Morley	19
G. J. Bonnor	c G. F. Grace, b Shaw	2	(8) b Steel	16
H. F. Boyle	not out	36	(2) run out	3
G. E. Palmer	b Morley	6	c and b Steel	4
G. Alexander	c W. G. Grace, b Steel	6	c Shaw, b Morley	33
W. H. Moule	c Morley, b W. G. Grace	6	b Barnes	34
Extras	(B 9, LB 3)	12	(B 7, LB 7)	14
		149		**327**

	O	M	R	W	O	M	R	W
Morley	32	9	56	5	61	30	90	3
Steel	29	9	58	3	31	6	73	2
Shaw	13	5	21	1	33	18	42	1
W. G. Grace	1.1	0	2	1	28	10	66	2
Barnes					8.3	3	17	1
Lucas					12	7	23	0
Penn					3	1	2	0

FALL OF WICKETS

	E	A	A	E
Wkt	1st	1st	2nd	2nd
1st	91	28	8	2
2nd	211	39	13	10
3rd	269	59	14	22
4th	281	84	97	31
5th	322	84	101	31
6th	404	89	143	—
7th	410	97	181	—
8th	410	113	187	—
9th	413	126	239	—
10th	420	149	327	—

Umpires: H. H. Stephenson and R. Thoms.

England won by five wickets.

of the Test receipts, but a more important outcome was that Australia's cricketers had re-established their popularity with their fighting recovery.

Murdoch's captaincy and good humour prevented any recurrence of the bitterness the earlier Australian team had aroused, and memories of the Sydney riot were forgotten. The team played 37 matches, won 21, lost 4, and had 12 draws. Eleven of these matches were first-class against 11-a-side, 26 against the odds. Of the matches against the odds, 16 were won, two lost, eight drawn. Once again Blackham's work as the No. 1 'keeper had all England's prominent 'keepers re-examining their technique. The team played 10 matches in New Zealand on the way home, winning six, with three drawn, losing only to a Twenty-Two of Wanganui. Once again the tour was a big financial success.

SECOND AUSTRALIAN TEAM AVERAGES

Name	I.	NO	HS	Runs	Ave.	W.	Runs	Ave.
W. L. Murdoch	19	1	153*	465	25.83	—	—	—
P. S. McDonnell	19	1	79	418	23.22	0	73	—
F. R. Spofforth	9	1	44	169	21.12	46	396	8.60
A. C. Bannerman	12	1	38	196	17.81	3	126	42.00
A. H. Jarvis	11	1	41	167	16.70	0	5	—
H. F. Boyle	17	4	69	195	15.00	39	616	15.79
G. Alexander	14	1	47	190	14.61	6	203	33.83
G. E. Palmer	13	6	23	101	14.42	80	890	11.12
J. M. Blackham	18	3	42*	205	13.66	—	—	—
T. U. Groube	19	3	61	210	13.12	—	—	—
W. H. Moule	9	3	34	75	12.50	4	69	17.25
G. Bonnor	17	1	35	145	9.06	—	—	—
J. Slight	6	–	21	41	6.83	—	—	—
W. A. Giles	1	–	3	3	3.00	—	—	—

THIRD AUSTRALIAN TEAM, 1882

W. L. Murdoch

One of the best teams Australia has ever sent to England. Batting techniques had vastly improved on those shown by earlier teams, with Murdoch outstanding. Field placements and team discipline were of a high order and in Blackham the team still had a superb 'keeper. The team impressed by the speed with which they got into position in the field, their throwing was splendid, but again they irritated English commentators with their "commercial spirit." They went ten weeks without defeat after beating Oxford University by nine wickets in the first match when Massie scored 206 out of 265 runs made in three hours. They thrashed Sussex by an innings and 355 runs, Palmer achieving a hat-trick and Murdoch scoring 286 not out in a total of 643.

The Australians lost to Cambridge University, for whom C. T. Studd made a century and the Queenslander R. C. Ramsay took 12 wickets. An admirable sequence of 14 wins in 19 matches against county teams followed. The Gentlemen were beaten by an innings, Giffen taking 8 for 49. Horan scored centuries against Gloucestershire and a United XI. In the

370

Middlesex match Blackham was injured, with byes reaching 29, top-score in a total of 104. In the match won by Cambridge University Past and Present, Bonnor played a remarkable innings of 66 runs out of 79 in scarcely half an hour.

The Test at The Oval was full of incident, with the English selectors careful to ensure they picked the strongest possible side. Murdoch won the toss and batted but Australia managed only 63, of which Blackham made a brave 17. Spofforth bowled unchanged in England's first innings to restrict England's lead to 38. On the second morning a wet, easy pitch helped the Australians, Massie scoring 55 out of 66 scored by the openers in less than an hour. Further rain fell with Australia 5 for 99. When play resumed after lunch Murdoch scored a single to the legside, and Jones grounded his bat inside the crease and then went back along the pitch to pat down a bump. W. G. Grace at once broke down the wicket and Jones was given out. Grace was within his rights, but his lack of sportsmanship annoyed the Australians, who were all out for 122.

Requiring 85 to win, England reached 4 for 65. "Suddenly a new phase came over the innings," wrote C. P. Moody. "The batsmen could not get the ball past fieldsmen. Spofforth was bowling the most remarkable break-backs at tremendous pace; Boyle, from the other end, maintained a perfect length; Blackham with matchless skill took every ball that passed the batsman . . . every fieldsman strained his nerves to the ut-

The Third Australian Team to visit England (L to R): Standing, T. W. Garrett, G. J. Bonnor, H. F. Boyle, H. H. Massie, G. E. Palmer, C. W. Beal (manager), J. M. Blackham; Seated, G. Giffen, F. R. Spofforth, T. Horan, P. S. McDonnell, W. L. Murdoch, A. C. Bannerman.

most. A dozen successive maidens were sent down. Something of the spirit of the struggle pervaded the thousands of spectators, and their oppressive silence was punctuated by a mighty shout when Lyttelton broke the spell with a single." The single had been pre-arranged because Spofforth wanted a bowl at Lyttelton. Four more maidens followed and then Spofforth bowled Lyttelton. It was 5 for 66, with 19 needed.

Lucas hit Boyle for four and immediately Spofforth struck back by dismissing Steel and Read in one over. Seven for 70, with 15 needed. Then came a two and three byes off Spofforth before Lucas played Spofforth into his stumps and was replaced by C. T. Studd, who had scored centuries against Australia in two earlier matches.

"Now Boyle's pertinacious accuracy was rewarded," Moody wrote in his *Australian Cricket And Cricketers*. "Off the first ball of his over Barnes was caught off the glove by Murdoch at point. Edmund Peate, last man in, swished the first ball to leg for two, flukily played the next one, tried to hit the last ball of the over, but missed, and it bowled him. The game was won by seven runs."

On the way to this historic win Spofforth bowled 10 maidens in his last 11 overs and took four wickets for two runs off his last seven balls. This gave him 7 for 44 for the innings and 14 for 90 for the match. When Peate was criticised for not giving his partner C. T. Studd a chance to score the runs, he said, "Mr Studd was so nervous I did not feel I could trust him to score the runs." One spectator died in the excitement, another is said to have gnawed the handle off his umbrella. "Men who were noted for their coolness at critical moments were trembling like a leaf, some were shivering as if with cold, some even fainted," said the Surrey secretary C. W. Alcock. The next day the mock obituary notice that started The Ashes legend appeared in the *Sporting Times* (See The Ashes).

After winning the sole Test the rest of the tour was an anticlimax for the Australians, who ended with wins in 18 of their 33 first-class matches, four losses and 11 draws. They played 38 matches in all, for 23 wins, four losses and 11 draws. The team was enormously strong in bowling but perhaps lacked the batting strength needed to justify inclusion in the great Australian teams. Nothing can detract from their win in the Test at The Oval, however, achieved in intensity "that converted the English batsmen as they went in to bat into ashen grey figures with throats too parched to speak." The scorer's hand trembled so that he wrote Peate's name as "Geese," and when Peate's wicket fell the crowd sat voiceless and stunned before they broke over the ground to cheer the men who had won and to carry Spofforth shoulder high from the field. The 1882 team's manager, Charles William Beal (1855–1921) also managed the 1888 team. He was 27 on the 1882 tour and remains the youngest-ever Australian team manager.

372

THIRD AUSTRALIAN TEAM AVERAGES

Name	I.	NO	HS	Runs	Ave.	W.	Runs	Ave.
W. L. Murdoch	61	5	286*	1711	30.55	1	47	47.00
T. Horan	52	5	141*	1175	25.00	—	—	—
H. H. Massie	61	4	206	1405	24.64	0	18	—
A. C. Bannerman	56	2	120*	1201	22.24	4	112	28.00
G. Bonnor	47	7	122*	815	20.37	—	—	—
G. Giffen	52	4	81	873	18.18	32	728	22.75
P. S. McDonnell	55	3	82	900	17.30	2	60	30.00
J. M. Blackham	43	7	62	612	17.00	—	—	—
S. P. Jones	32	1	59	370	11.93	1	85	85.00
T. W. Garrett	48	6	59	496	11.80	128	1759	13.74
G. E. Palmer	32	8	35	266	11.08	138	1731	12.54
H. F. Boyle	45	13	39*	300	9.37	144	1682	11.68
F. R. Spofforth	45	11	37	282	8.29	188	2282	12.13
C. W. Beal	2	0	5	5	2.50	—	—	—

This was another fine pioneering team, strong in batting and fielding, shrewdly led by Murdoch and manager George Alexander, but a little thin on bowling, with Garrett missing and Boyle past his prime. The side's strength was demonstrated when it assembled in Melbourne to play The Rest. Murdoch scored 279 not out, McDonnell 111 in Australia's total of 619. In the return match at Sydney, Giffen took all 10 wickets for 66 to dismiss The Rest for 113. All but four of the 1882 team returned to England, Henry Scott, William Cooper and George Alexander replaced Massie, Garrett and Horan. Midwinter, forgiven over the 1878 "kidnapping," replaced Jones. Cooper broke a finger on the voyage to England and was unfit for most of the tour.

With three Tests scheduled for the first time on an Australian tour, the tour started badly as the key players struggled to find form. They lost three of the first six matches, including the match against MCC in which W. G. Grace, A. G. Steel and William Barnes scored centuries. At Birmingham in a match against an England XI the pitch was so poor the match was finished in six hours, Australia winning by four wickets. Spofforth's match figures were 14 for 37, including a second innings effort in which he bowled 8.3 overs, six of them maidens, and took 7 for 3, and had the England XI out for 26. In the match against Lancashire Giffen took a hat-trick and scored 113 before play was washed out.

In a match against the Gentlemen, W. G. Grace and C. T. Studd started the chase for 188 to win in the final innings with an opening stand of 60. Spofforth then took seven wickets to restrict the Gentlemen to 141, Australia achieving a fine victory by 47 runs. In this match umpire Farrands disallowed a catch in the slips, a decision which caused Spofforth to bowl at his fastest with Blackham standing back and six men in the slips.

The First Test was notable because Lord Harris declined to captain England following the selection of Crossland, a notor-

FOURTH AUSTRALIAN TEAM, 1884

W. L. Murdoch

373

ious "chucker." A. N. Hornby took over the captaincy but Crossland was replaced by Barlow. The Test ended in a draw after Australia led by 87 on the first innings. England won the Second Test by an innings and five runs, when Australia, trailing by 150 runs, made only 145 in the second innings on a crumbling pitch. In the Third Test Australia were 2 for 363 at the end of the first day but had to bat out the innings under laws that then prevailed which prevented a declaration. Every player in the English team bowled as Australia reached 551, Murdoch scoring 211. England responded with 346 and were 2 for 85 when the match ended in a draw, England winning the series with one win and two draws.

The 1884 Australians played 32 matches in a tour that involved only 11-a-side matches for the first time, winning 18, losing seven and leaving seven unfinished. By now it was clear the two countries were evenly matched, for Australia had had by far the best of the two drawn Tests although they lost the series. The tour ended with a highly successful match between Smokers and Non-Smokers in which Bonnor made 124 out of 156 scored by the Non-Smokers while he was at the crease. He hit 16 boundaries and even walloped Spofforth for six.

FOURTH AUSTRALIAN TEAM AVERAGES

Name	I.	NO	HS	Runs	Ave.	W.	Runs	Ave.
W. L. Murdoch	50	5	211	1378	30.62	0	25	—
P. S. McDonell	54	2	103	1225	23.55	0	27	—
H. J. H. Scott	51	8	102	973	22.62	3	157	52.33
G. Giffen	51	1	113	1052	21.04	82	1623	19.78
A. C. Bannerman	52	2	94	961	19.22	2	32	16.00
G. C. Bonnor	52	3	95*	937	19.12	6	219	36.50
W. Midwinter	46	4	67	800	19.04	15	440	29.33
J. M. Blackham	44	3	69	690	16.82	1	8	8.00
G. E. Palmer	47	10	68*	493	13.32	132	2131	16.14
F. R. Spofforth	46	6	54	488	12.20	216	2642	12.23
W. H. Cooper	9	6	8*	33	11.00	7	325	46.42
H. F. Boyle	38	14	48	262	10.91	67	1143	17.05
G. Alexander	5	1	10*	20	5.00	2	24	12.00

FIFTH AUSTRALIAN TEAM, 1886

H. J. H. Scott

This was the first Australian team to go to England under the auspices of a cricket club, the Melbourne CC, which organised the tour to return the visit by Lord Harris's side to Australia in 1878–79. All the four Australian teams that preceded it to England were sponsored by private entrepreneurs. The Melbourne CC opted for an all amateur touring party, which meant that Alec Bannerman was unavailable. Boyle, McDonnell and Murdoch were also unavailable and the club appointed Henry Scott captain of a side that included eight players who had previously toured and four newcomers in William Bruce, Edwin Evans, John Trumble and John McIlwraith. The team was managed by Major Ben Wardill, a former Victorian player and secretary of the Melbourne CC.

374

Friction developed among the players before a match was played and Scott soon had his hands full adjudicating in disputes. "The cares of leadership affected his run-getting, for quarrels among the players were many, and he did not have sufficient strength of character to cope with the situation," wrote cricket historian Haygarth. The Australians played bravely in the first Test but were overwhelmed in the next two. Giffen was virtually the only success on the tour, heading both bowling and batting averages. At one stage he took 40 wickets in five successive innings against Derbyshire, Cambridge University and Lancashire. The loss of Spofforth with an injured hand for much of the tour badly weakened the Australians.

The tour was a remarkable success, however, in attracting crowds. More than 33,000 paid to see the three days of the Lord's Test. The team played 39 matches, 38 against 11-a-side and one against the odds, winning nine, losing seven, with 22 drawn, and the match against the odds lost. Generally, the Australian bowlers took a hammering in the important matches, with W. G. Grace's 170 in the Third Test typical of the high scores English batsmen enjoyed.

FIFTH AUSTRALIAN TEAM AVERAGES

Name	I.	NO	HS	Runs	Ave.	W.	Runs	Ave.
G. Giffen	63	9	119	1453	26.90	159	2711	17.05
S. P. Jones	64	2	151	1498	24.16	7	297	42.42
H. J. Scott	64	5	123	1289	21.84	1	12	12.00
G. E. Palmer	56	4	94	1028	19.76	106	2328	21.96
G. J. Bonnor	34	3	49	581	18.76	—	—	—
J. W. Trumble	52	8	56*	823	18.70	30	803	26.76
A. H. Jarvis	50	6	96*	780	17.72	1	24	24.00
J. McIlwraith	39	7	62*	532	16.62	—	—	—
J. M. Blackham	50	5	71	731	16.24	0	36	—
W. Bruce	48	3	106	706	15.68	13	620	47.69
T. W. Garrett	48	8	49*	561	14.02	123	2221	18.05
E. Evans	41	15	74*	347	13.34	28	588	21.00
F. R. Spofforth	28	7	37*	163	7.76	89	1528	17.16
R. J. Pope	8	4	12	31	7.75	—	—	—

Only Harry Boyle of the famous bowlers who had established Australia's international reputation survived in this side and he was a long past way his best. Apart from Bonnor, Bannerman, Jones and McDonnell, none of the batsmen had experience of English conditions. Giffen declined to tour, and Ferris and Turner had to get the opposition out because there was nobody else in the team who could bowl straight or to a length, although Harry Trott's wayward legbreaks occasionally dismissed good players. The work load undertaken by Turner and Ferris was astounding. Australia won the First Test at Lord's, but lost by more than an innings in the other two Tests. The side was promoted and managed by C. W. Beal, who carefully kept secret the nature of Jones' illness. Had it

SIXTH AUSTRALIAN TEAM, 1888

P. S. McDonnell

become known that Jones had smallpox the whole tour could have been ruined. The team played 40 matches against 11-a-side, won 19, lost 14 and drew 7.

SIXTH AUSTRALIAN TEAM AVERAGES

Name	I.	NO	HS	Runs	Ave.	W.	Runs	Ave.
P. S. McDonnell	62	1	105	1393	22.83	0	28	—
G. J. Bonnor	64	3	119	1204	19.73	2	66	33.00
G. H. S. Trott	65	2	83	1212	19.23	48	1145	23.85
A. C. Bannerman	63	7	93*	943	16.83	3	117	39.00
S. P. Jones	20	2	61	303	16.83	10	134	13.40
C. T. B. Turner	60	2	103	807	13.91	314	3492	11.12
J. J. Lyons	43	6	84	489	13.21	18	514	28.55
J. D. Edwards	53	12	50*	527	12.85	1	40	40.00
A. H. Jarvis	52	2	39	597	12.18	—		
J. J. Ferris	61	16	39	528	11.73	220	3103	14.10
J. Worrall	61	10	46	561	11.00	24	455	18.95
J. M. Blackham	58	1	96	548	9.61	1	26	26.00
H. F. Boyle	29	11	36	153	8.50	11	203	18.45
S. M. J. Woods	10	—	18	54	5.40	11	298	27.09

The Sixth Australian team to tour England, whose manager, C. W. Beal (in top hat), kept an important secret.

SEVENTH AUSTRALIAN TEAM, 1890

W. L. Murdoch

Murdoch had to be persuaded to tour, but Giffen refused once again, leaving Australia with a side largely inexperienced in English conditions. Walters, Burn and Gregory were failures. Ferris and Turner again saved Australia's prestige, sharing the 430 wickets they took together. The team fielded badly and lacked support bowlers. Murdoch and the left hander, Dr Barrett, showed character and Trott and Lyons batted well. For Australia the most encouraging aspect of a disappointing tour was the improved form of Harry Trott and newcomer Hugh Trumble. The team played 38 matches, all against 11-a-side, won 13, lost 16, and drew nine, under the managership of Harry Boyle.

376

SEVENTH AUSTRALIAN TEAM AVERAGES

Name	I.	NO	HS	Runs	Ave.	W.	Runs	Ave.
W. Murdoch	64	2	158*	1459	23.53	—	—	—
J. Barrett	64	7	97	1305	22.89	6	89	14.83
G. H. S. Trott	65	1	186	1273	19.89	23	610	26.52
J. Lyons	65	1	99	1142	17.84	43	989	23.00
J. M. Blackham	51	5	75	728	15.82	—	—	—
C. T. B. Turner	60	—	59	910	15.16	215	2725	12.67
J. J. Ferris	56	13	54*	647	15.04	215	2838	13.20
P. C. Charlton	47	11	75*	534	14.83	42	800	19.04
S. E. Gregory	60	15	59*	568	12.62	—	—	—
S. P. Jones	35	2	98	400	12.12	—	—	—
K. E. Burn	39	4	35*	355	10.14	—	—	—
F. H. Walters	43	3	53*	402	10.05	—	—	—
H. Trumble	50	12	34*	310	8.15	53	1138	21.47
R. J. Pope	4	—	6	6	1.50	—	—	—
H. F. Boyle	1	—	3	3	3.00	—	—	—

This side had a big weakness in the lack of a fast bowler to take advantage of hard, fast pitches. Turner was not the threat he had been on the two previous tours. Giffen could not really penetrate against the best batsmen, Harry Trott's leg-spinners were costly, and Hugh Trumble was only just emerging as a match-winning bowler. Most of the teams they faced had at least one quality pace bowler. The team played 36 matches on level terms, with 18 wins, 10 losses and eight draws. Of the three Tests, one was lost and two narrowly saved as draws. Blackham captained the side nervously. Graham, Lyons, Trott, Bannerman, Giffen, Bruce and Syd Gregory all made 1,000 runs and scored centuries. Australia's manager was V. Cohen. Australia made 843, then a record for a first-class innings, against Oxford and Cambridge Past And Present. The team visited America on the way home and was the first beaten in America—by the Gentlemen of Philadelphia.

EIGHTH AUSTRALIAN TEAM, 1893

J. M. Blackham

EIGHTH AUSTRALIAN TEAM AVERAGES

Name	I.	NO	HS	Runs	Ave.	W.	Runs	Ave.
H. Graham	53	3	219	1435	28.70	0	22	—
J. J. Lyons	56	2	149	1527	28.27	2	94	47.00
G. H. S. Trott	59	2	145	1437	25.21	60	1141	19.01
A. C. Bannerman	50	1	133	1229	25.08	—	—	—
W. Bruce	59	5	191	1311	24.27	34	770	22.64
S. E. Gregory	53	4	112	1162	23.71	1	54	54.00
G. Giffen	53	1	180	1220	23.46	142	2580	18.16
H. Trumble	50	12	105	874	23.00	120	2005	16.70
R. W. McLeod	46	11	47*	633	18.08	46	1132	24.60
W. Giffen	20	4	62	245	15.31	—	—	—
J. M. Blackham	33	12	42	288	13.71	—	—	—
C. T. B. Turner	43	4	66	521	13.35	149	2124	14.25
A. Coningham	22	3	46	249	13.10	31	561	18.09
A. H. Jarvis	19	4	10	61	4.06	—	—	—

Harry Trott proved an astute leader for a new generation of Australian batsmen, with Clem Hill, Joe Darling and Frank Iredale outstanding successes. Giffen continued his allround excellence, and Trumble and McKibbin troubled all batsmen.

NINTH AUSTRALIAN TEAM, 1896

G. H. S. Trott

377

But the big difference compared with previous Australian teams was the pace bowling of Ernie Jones. The Tests were tremendous tussles, England winning the first by dismissing Australia for 53 in the first innings, Australia the second after struggling to make the 125 needed for victory. England won the rubber by winning the third Test, Australia failing to score the 111 needed to win in the final innings, being all out for 44 on a difficult pitch. The team, managed by Harry Musgrove, played 34 matches, all on level terms, winning 19, losing six, with nine unfinished.

NINTH AUSTRALIAN TEAM AVERAGES

Name	I.	NO	HS	Runs	Ave.	W.	Runs	Ave.
S. E. Gregory	48	2	154	1464	31.82	—	—	—
J. Darling	53	1	194	1555	29.90	1	28	28.00
C. Hill	46	3	130	1196	27.81	0	4	—
F. A. Iredale	51	3	171	1328	27.66	—	—	—
G. H. S. Trott	54	5	143	1297	26.46	44	928	21.09
G. Giffen	49	1	130	1208	25.16	117	2257	19.29
H. Donnan	44	1	167	1009	23.46	5	231	46.20
H. Trumble	43	11	45*	628	19.62	148	2340	15.81
H. Graham	32	2	96	547	18.23	1	19	19.00
J. J. Kelly	38	8	45	490	16.33	—	—	—
A. E. Johns	12	6	31*	84	14.00	—	—	—
E. Jones	41	6	40	482	13.77	121	1940	16.03
C. J. Eady	24	2	42	290	13.18	16	408	25.50
T. R. McKibbin	34	11	28*	175	7.60	101	1441	14.26

TENTH AUSTRALIAN TEAM, 1899

J. Darling

One of the best of all Australian teams, strong in every department. They won the Test series against England, and lost only three of their 35 matches, winning 16 and playing 16 draws. For the first time in England five Tests were played, Australia winning one and having the better of most of the four draws. Victor Trumper, in only his third international

The Tenth Australian team to visit England (L to R): Standing, V. T. Trumper, H. Trumble, A. E. Johns, W. P. Howell, B. Wardill (manager), M. A. Noble, F. Laver, C. E. McLeod; Seated, J. J. Kelly, C. Hill, J. Worrall, J. J. Darling, F. A. Iredale, E. Jones; Front, S. E. Gregory.

match, scored 135 at Lord's, where Ernie Jones bowled breathtakingly fast and Australia won handsomely by 10 wickets. This win started a long history of Australian success at Lord's. Darling's captaincy was wise and efficient, his batting skilful and courageous. Trumper batted with an artistry nobody before or since has matched. Noble showed superb allround skill, as did Trumble. "Farmer Bill" Howell took 117 wickets, Jones 135, and the catching and throwing of the team were outstanding, with wicket-keeper J. J. Kelly matching the skill Blackham and Jarvis had shown on earlier tours. Ben Wardill managed the team skilfully.

TENTH AUSTRALIAN TEAM AVERAGES

Name	I.	NO	HS	Runs	Ave.	W.	Runs	Ave.
J. Darling	56	9	167	1941	41.29	0	10	—
C. Hill	23	1	160	879	39.95	1	16	16.00
M. A. Noble	50	7	156	1608	37.39	82	1878	22.90
J. Worrall	39	5	128	1202	35.35	1	104	104.00
V. Trumper	48	3	300*	1556	34.57	1	29	29.00
F. Laver	38	10	143	859	30.67	23	619	26.91
F. Iredale	38	3	115	1039	29.68	1	11	11.00
H. Trumble	51	8	100	1183	27.51	142	2618	18.43
S. E. Gregory	49	6	124	1181	27.46	0	73	—
J. J. Kelly	39	6	103	768	23.27	0	16	—
E. Jones	35	4	55	552	17.80	135	2849	21.10
C. E. McLeod	38	7	77	544	17.54	81	1860	22.96
W. P. Howell	40	11	49*	307	10.58	117	2381	20.35
A. E. Johns	8	3	27*	50	10.00	—	—	—

ELEVENTH AUSTRALIAN TEAM, 1902

J. Darling

Joe Darling was again captain and Ben Wardill a manager whose watchfulness and tact helped overcome earlier English misgivings about the commercial attitude of the Australians. At the start of the Great Age of Batsmanship, Trumper "entranced the eye, inspired his side, demoralised his enemies and made run-getting appear the easiest thing in the world." He scored 2,570 runs on the tour although he sometimes threw his hand away when he reached 100. Nobody else in the Australian side approached his average or his tally. Noble, by now a superb player, took the allround honours in a team of stars, but Armstrong, on his first English tour, was little behind him. The tour produced many memorable events, none greater than Clem Hill's catch to dismiss Lilley, running flat out around the square leg boundary at Old Trafford, with England eight runs from winning and two wickets in hand. On the strength of that great catch Australia won by three runs. Saunders, a left-arm bowler of the highest class throughout the tour, took the final wicket that gave Australia The Ashes. England won the final Test when Wilfred Rhodes and George Hirst, with 15 needed, nine wickets down, decided "to get them in singles." They made it only moments before torrential rain fell and rang down the curtain on a magnificent series. This Australian team played 39 matches, all eleven a side, won 23, drew 14 and lost only 2.

ELEVENTH AUSTRALIAN TEAM AVERAGES

Name	I.	NO	HS	Runs	Ave.	W.	Runs	Ave.
V. Trumper	53	0	128	2570	48.49	20	415	20.75
M. A. Noble	48	5	284	1416	32.93	98	1945	19.84
C. Hill	52	1	136	1614	31.64	4	59	14.75
R. A. Duff	58	5	183	1507	28.43	4	48	12.00
W. W. Armstrong	51	10	172*	1087	26.51	81	1410	17.40
A. J. Hopkins	54	8	105*	1192	25.91	38	669	17.60
J. Darling	51	5	128	1113	24.29	—	—	—
S. E. Gregory	52	6	86	999	21.71	0	21	—
H. Trumble	30	6	68	429	17.87	140	1998	14.27
J. J. Kelly	33	8	75	368	14.72	2	13	6.50
E. Jones	21	1	40	254	12.70	71	1456	20.50
H. Carter	20	5	31	121	8.06	0	7	—
W. P. Howell	24	6	16	95	5.27	68	1215	17.86
J. V. Saunders	34	9	9	84	3.36	127	2168	17.07

TWELFTH AUSTRALIAN TEAM, 1905

J. Darling

After Australia had beaten England in four Test series in six years, the MCC decided that England's cricket prestige had taken such a battering from Australia, honour could only be restored by taking the conduct of tours out of the hands of private entrepreneurs and ensuring that the best players appeared in every Test. Individuals haggling over tour terms ended; Tests became true contests of strength. The new English captain, F. S. Jackson, won seven tosses against our captain Joe Darling during this tour, five of them in Tests. Cotter bowled very fast throughout the tour—again emphasising the value to teams touring England of a front-rank pace bowler. The Australians scored wonderfully well against the counties, with nine batsmen hitting centuries. Armstrong made 303 not out against Somerset and a fine 248 against The Gentlemen. Noble made six centuries on the tour. But they could not do it in the Tests and England held The Ashes by winning the series 2–0, with three draws. Armstrong irked English critics by bowling leg theory to a packed on-side field for hours at a time, but headed both batting and bowling averages. The team won 16 of 38 matches, lost 3, drew 19.

TWELFTH AUSTRALIAN TEAM AVERAGES

Name	I.	NO	HS	Runs	Ave.	W.	Runs	Ave.
W. W. Armstrong	48	7	303*	2002	48.82	130	2288	17.60
M. A. Noble	49	2	267	2084	44.34	59	1558	26.40
J. Darling	51	7	117*	1696	38.54	0	10	—
C. Hill	49	3	181	1731	37.63	0	16	—
V. Trumper	49	1	110	1754	36.54	0	4	—
R. A. Duff	47	—	146	1395	29.68	12	326	27.16
A. J. Hopkins	42	5	154	1094	29.56	27	825	30.55
S. E. Gregory	31	3	134	717	25.60	0	47	—
D. R. A. Gehrs	33	4	83	612	21.10	1	33	33.00
G. E. McLeod	41	6	103*	700	20.00	80	1833	22.29
J. J. Kelly	33	11	74*	407	18.50	—	—	—
A. Cotter	43	3	48	737	18.42	121	2444	20.19
F. J. Laver	35	6	78	440	15.17	115	2092	18.19
P. M. Newland	16	7	25*	95	10.55	—	—	—
W. P. Howell	30	9	46	192	9.14	71	1377	19.39

Noble took over as captain, with Frank Laver making his second English tour as player-manager, and Peter McAlister
joining the team as player-treasurer. The side started disastrously, losing three matches, including the First Test by 10
wickets, inside the first month, but recovered to win the Second and Third Tests and draw the last two. They suffered
their fourth defeat only at the very end of the tour at Scarborough. The side fielded superbly and though the batting
lacked distinction it was sound enough to match an England
team that had declined since 1905. Ransford made a century
in his first Test at Lord's and he proved a worthy substitute for
Hill and Darling. Macartney was a surprise as a bowler, winning the Leeds Test with 11 for 85. Bardsley was full of strokes,
a tremendous success on his first tour and the only batsman
to score more than 2,000 runs. In the final Test at The Oval he
made a century in each innings. Noble was an admirable captain. The team won 13, lost 4 and drew 22 of its 39 matches.

THIRTEENTH AUSTRALIAN TEAM, 1909

M. A. Noble

THIRTEENTH AUSTRALIAN TEAM AVERAGES

Name	I.	NO	HS	Runs	Ave.	W.	Runs	Ave.
W. Bardsley	51	4	219	2180	46.38	0	7	—
W. W. Armstrong	43	9	110*	1480	43.52	126	2046	16.23
V. S. Ransford	45	4	190	1783	43.48	1	27	27.00
V. Trumper	45	2	150	1435	33.37	1	151	151.00
P. A. McAlister	33	5	85	816	29.14	1	0	—
M. A. Noble	48	5	131	1109	25.79	25	928	37.12
S. E. Gregory	42	7	74	684	19.54	1	84	84.00
C. G. Macartney	40	7	124	638	19.33	71	1240	17.46
R. J. Hartigan	33	1	115	603	18.84	0	4	—
H. Carter	33	7	61	408	15.69	—	—	—
A. J. Hopkins	31	3	56*	432	15.42	58	1191	20.53
J. A. O'Connor	29	7	39	295	13.40	85	1619	19.04
F. Laver	19	4	25	162	10.80	70	1048	14.97
A. Cotter	32	—	37	335	10.46	64	1862	29.09
W. Carkeek	17	4	37	107	8.23	—	—	—
W. J. Whitty	26	8	21	136	7.55	77	1573	20.42

One of the worst teams Australia ever sent overseas, largely
because of the withdrawal of Trumper, Hill, Cotter, Ransford,
Armstrong, and Carter. Their absence, following a dispute
with the Australian Board of Control, came at a time when
Australia needed all her best players to overcome the heavy
defeats handed out by Warner's England team in the Australian summer of 1911–12. Syd Gregory captained the side on
his eighth English tour during which the Australians played
six Tests in an experimental "triangular" tournament, three
each against England and South Africa. For the first time the
Australians were managed by a Board of Control appointee,
G. S. Crouch. Whitty bowled manfully and Hazlitt joined him
in taking more than 100 wickets on the trip, but against the
full strength of England's batting they could not overcome
the lack of a penetrative opening bowler like Cotter. Wet
weather ruined the series as much as the South Africans' lack

FOURTEENTH AUSTRALIAN TEAM, 1912

S. E. Gregory

Back Row:- R. B. M... ... ... J. Crouch (manager).
Second Row:- J. W. Mac... ... ... W. J. Whitty ... ... (captain), W. Bardsley, C. G. Macartney, G. R. Hazlitt.
Front Row:- H. Webster. C. B. Jennings (vice-captain). T. J. Matthews.

The Australian team that competed in the triangular tournament. Leg-spinner T. J. Matthews, who took two hat-tricks on the same day, is in front at right.

of form. After two rain-affected draws against England, Australia went down in the decisive final Test when they were dismissed for 65 chasing 310 to win in the last innings. Bardsley again topped 2,000 runs, and Macartney was an admirable allrounder. The side won only nine of its 37 matches, with 20 draws and eight losses. They beat South Africa twice in the Tests, lost one against England and played three drawn Tests.

FOURTEENTH AUSTRALIAN TEAM AVERAGES

Name	I.	NO	HS	Runs	Ave.	W.	Runs	Ave.
W. Bardsley	53	6	184*	2441	51.93	—	—	—
C. G. Macartney	50	1	208	2207	45.04	43	703	16.34
C. Kelleway	49	7	114	1300	30.95	47	1144	24.34
S. E. Gregory	47	2	150	1055	23.44	—	—	—
C. B. Jennings	51	4	82	1060	22.55	—	—	—
E. R. Mayne	44	3	111	877	21.39	0	35	—
R. B. Minnett	42	5	65*	734	19.83	41	970	23.65
T. J. Matthews	36	4	93	584	18.25	85	1647	19.37
H. Webster	14	5	26	139	15.44	—	—	—
S. H. Emery	29	9	37*	279	13.95	67	1601	23.89
D. Smith	25	2	100	316	13.73	1	22	22.00
W. J. Whitty	36	9	33	282	10.44	109	1971	18.08
W. Carkeek	29	12	27	156	9.17	—	—	—
J. W. McLaren	17	1	40	132	8.25	27	620	22.96
G. R. Hazlitt	38	8	35*	230	7.66	101	1915	18.96

FIFTEENTH AUSTRALIAN TEAM, 1921

Among the greatest Australian cricket teams, strong in every phase of the game, with the inimitable Syd Smith, secretary of the Board of Control from 1911 to 1926, as manager. In Gre-

382

gory and McDonald, Australia had a match-winning opening bowling pair. They humbled the best of England's batting, just as Barnes and Foster had destroyed Australia in 1911–12 in Australia. McDonald took more wickets (150) but Gregory with his high bounding approach was more frightening, and they bruised and battered England's batsmen to such an extent England used 30 players in the five Tests, Australia winning the rubber 3–0. Australia was so strong it omitted Arthur Mailey from the First Test but he still finished with 146 wickets on the tour.

Eleven Australians made centuries on the tour, with Macartney's 345 against Nottingham in a day a highlight. In the Fourth Test Armstrong bowled two successive overs, the first and only instance of this in international cricket, when England declared and left the field and then found the declaration was illegal. It was a magnificent fielding side, without a batting duffer, and had an outstanding captain in Armstrong and fine 'keepers in Carter and Oldfield. Of the 38 matches played, they won 22, drew 14 and lost two (only at the end of the tour), and until the 1948 side came along were regarded as the best team Australia ever sent to England. After the side returned home the Board of Control showed its appreciation of its performance by granting each of the 15 players a bonus of £300.

FIFTEENTH AUSTRALIAN TEAM AVERAGES

Name	I.	NO	HS	Runs	Ave.	W.	Runs	Ave.
C. G. Macartney	42	2	345	2335	58.37	8	264	33.00
W. Bardsley	44	4	209	2218	55.45	0	13	—
W. W. Armstrong	40	8	182*	1405	43.90	106	1554	14.66
J. Ryder	33	6	129	1032	38.22	24	586	24.41
E. R. Mayne	20	2	157*	654	36.33	0	45	—
J. M. Gregory	35	2	107	1171	35.48	120	1993	16.60
T. J. Andrews	44	4	132	1358	33.95	4	215	53.75
H. L. Collins	37	1	162	1222	33.94	2	272	136.00
J. M. Taylor	39	2	143	1116	30.16	4	79	19.75
H. L. Hendry	30	7	56*	634	27.56	42	1095	26.07
C. E. Pellew	39	3	146	924	25.66	2	127	63.50
W. A. Oldfield	23	6	123	419	24.64	—	—	—
H. Carter	19	1	57	378	21.00	—	—	—
A. A. Mailey	34	13	46	263	12.52	146	2889	19.78
E. A. McDonald	29	6	36	284	12.34	150	2467	16.44

Herbie Collins took over the captaincy from Armstrong and Oldfield the No. 1 'keeper's role from Carter. Lacking a hostile opening attack—McDonald had settled in Lancashire and Gregory had a bad knee—the team depended on the spin of Grimmett and Mailey. They bowled splendidly, Mailey taking 141 tour wickets, Grimmett 116, but all the guile of team captain Herbie Collins could not quite overcome the absence of a hostile partner for Gregory on pitches unresponsive to spin. After four drawn Tests England won back The Ashes by taking the Fifth Test. Woodfull, on his first English tour, topped the batting averages. Both Woodfull and Johnny Taylor had scores of 201 in a team which had ten century-makers. Macartney again proved his class as an allrounder and in the Fourth Test scored his third consecutive Test century. Chapman led a superb English side with rare skill. The Australians played 40 matches, won 12, drew 27 and lost only that final Test. Syd Smith was manager for the second time.

SIXTEENTH AUSTRALIAN TEAM AVERAGES

Name	I.	NO	HS	Runs	Ave.	W.	Runs	Ave.
W. M. Woodfull	36	5	201	1809	58.35	—	—	—
C. G. Macartney	35	4	160	1698	54.77	56	904	16.14
W. Bardsley	35	4	193	1558	50.25	—	—	—
W. H. Ponsford	30	5	144	1064	42.56	2	42	21.00
T. J. Andrews	41	5	164	1460	40.55	11	339	30.81
J. M. Gregory	31	6	130*	930	37.20	36	1173	32.58
J. Ryder	39	7	109	1145	35.78	27	907	33.59
H. L. Hendry	10	1	81	320	35.55	1	117	117.00
A. J. Richardson	33	9	100	766	31.91	63	1113	17.66
H. L. Collins	29	1	99	875	31.25	14	209	14.92
J. M. Taylor	41	3	201	1080	28.42	1	18	18.00
J. L. Ellis	17	5	43	338	28.16	—	—	—
W. A. Oldfield	24	6	62	442	24.55	—	—	—
S. C. Everett	12	2	100	219	21.90	27	705	26.11
C. V. Grimmett	23	3	41	303	14.42	116	1996	17.20
A. A. Mailey	24	6	21	121	6.72	141	2637	18.70

The 16th Australian team that toured England in 1926, with poker-faced captain Herbie Collins in the centre of the middle row.

SEVENTEENTH AUSTRALIAN TEAM, 1930

W. M. Woodfull

Bradman's amazing scoring won all the headlines on this tour, but Woodfull's captaincy won all the praise from the players. Taking a side of unseasoned players—only Oldfield, Grimmett, Ponsford and Woodfull himself had been to England before—into a series against an England side that had won the two previous rubbers, Woodfull recovered The Ashes

384

two Tests to one. Bradman scored 974 runs in the Tests at 139.14, including 232 in the crucial Fifth Test. Grimmett was again a match-winner, taking 142 wickets on the tour at an economical 16.79, and the Queenslander Percy Hornibrook did well with 93 wickets. The team included six century-makers but a youthful Stan McCabe failed to get one, best score 96. At Trent Bridge McCabe was brilliantly caught by S. H. Copley, a member of the Nottinghamshire ground staff, who was fielding as a substitute for the injured Sutcliffe. Copley made a lot of ground and caught the ball diving full-length, rolling over but retaining possession. McCabe was on 49 and Australia appeared likely to score the 428 required to win. The catch proved the turning point and Australia were dismissed for 335—93 short. Ponsford and Woodfull repeatedly gave the team valuable starts, Ponsford playing one innings of 220 not out. But it was Bradman's tour, with his 334 at Leeds the highest score inTest cricket to that time. The team was managed by W. L. Kelly and played 34 matches, winning 12, losing one, with one tie, one abandoned and 19 unfinished.

SEVENTEENTH AUSTRALIAN TEAM AVERAGES

Name	I.	NO	HS	Runs	Ave.	W.	Runs	Ave.
D. G. Bradman	36	6	334	2960	98.66	12	297	24.75
A. F. Kippax	32	7	158	1451	58.04	4	91	22.75
W. M. Woodfull	26	1	216	1434	57.36	—	—	—
W. H. Ponsford	33	4	220*	1425	49.13	0	6	—
A. Jackson	35	3	118	1097	34.28	0	8	—
S. J. McCabe	33	2	96	1012	32.64	29	723	24.93
V. Y. Richardson	32	1	116	832	26.83	0	8	—
A. Fairfax	27	6	63	536	25.52	41	1238	30.19
E. L. a'Beckett	21	5	67*	397	24.81	19	629	33.10
W. A. Oldfield	17	5	43*	225	18.75	—	—	—
P. M. Hornibrook	26	8	59*	232	12.88	93	1721	18.50
C. V. Grimmett	23	3	50	237	11.85	142	2385	16.79
A. Hurwood	19	1	61	188	10.44	28	736	26.28
T. W. Wall	19	6	40*	107	8.23	56	1664	27.71
C. W. Walker	14	5	10*	43	4.77	—	—	—

EIGHTEENTH AUSTRALIAN TEAM, 1934

W. M. Woodfull

An eventful tour saw Australia regain The Ashes—lost in 1932–33—under Woodfull's captaincy, thanks to the prolific scoring of Bradman, Ponsford and McCabe, backed by outstanding efforts from the spinners O'Reilly, Fleetwood-Smith and Grimmett. The Australian attack, in retrospect, appears badly unbalanced, with none of the medium-pacers or opening bowlers penetrating against top English batsmen, but after heavy scoring by a superb array of gifted batsmen the spinners had enough runs to do the job. The team was managed by Tasmanian Harold Bushby, who had done much to find employment for cricketers during the Depression years. He handled a delicate situation in England following the Bodyline friction with firmness and tact. Australia won the First Test, England the Second, and the next two were drawn. In the decisive Fifth Test, Ponsford and Bradman followed their partnership of 388 in the Fourth Test by putting on 451 for Australia's second wicket. Ponsford made 266, Bradman 244, Australia 701, and victory was ours by 562 runs. This was Ponsford's last Test and he made it count, leaving the field, out hit-wicket, having seen 472 runs scored while he was at the crease.

Against the cream of English batting, O'Reilly, Grimmett and Fleetwood-Smith each took 100 wickets at less than 20 runs each—a statistic to reflect on when discarding good spinners for English tours. Admittedly, spinners of the class of this team's threesome are rare, but it is nonsense to suggest good spinners are passengers on English tours. The team fielded brilliantly, was capably led, and had a superfine No. 1 'keeper in Oldfield. They played 34 matches, won 15, drew 18 and lost only one, the Second Test. It was a tremendous performance for a team that had been demoralised in the previous (Bodyline) series against England.

EIGHTEENTH AUSTRALIAN TEAM AVERAGES

Name	I.	NO	HS	Runs	Ave.	W.	Runs	Ave.
D. G. Bradman	27	3	304	2020	84.16	—	—	—
W. H. Ponsford	27	4	281*	1784	77.56	—	—	—
S. J. McCabe	37	7	240	2078	69.26	21	798	38.00
W. M. Woodfull	27	3	228*	1268	52.83	—	—	—
A. F. Kippax	23	4	250	961	50.57	0	13	—
A. G. Chipperfield	26	4	175	899	40.86	12	595	49.58
W. A. Brown	36	2	119	1308	38.47	—	—	—
L. S. Darling	31	1	117	1022	34.06	9	334	37.11
B. A. Barnett	20	6	92	470	33.57	1	3	3.00
W. J. O'Reilly	18	9	30*	237	26.33	109	1870	17.15
W. A. Oldfield	16	3	67	295	22.69	—	—	—
E. H. Bromley	20	1	56	312	16.42	5	245	49.00
C. V. Grimmett	20	3	39	255	15.00	109	2159	19.80
H. I. Ebeling	19	1	41	265	14.72	62	1292	20.83
T. W. Wall	12	3	24	84	9.33	42	1303	31.02
L. O'B. Fleet-wood-Smith	13	6	7*	24	3.42	106	2037	19.21

NINETEENTH AUSTRALIAN TEAM, 1938

D. G. Bradman

Bradman led Australia in England for the first time. The team's fast bowler, Ernie McCormick, encountered acute problems through dragging over the line and was no-balled so often he lost all confidence and hostility. The spinners had to again get the good batsmen out. O'Reilly probably never bowled better in his life than in the Leeds Test, when his 10 wickets helped Australia to a five wickets win—just before heavy rain came. This win enabled Australia to retain The Ashes. Six batsmen topped 1,000 runs on the tour, with Bradman again on top with 2,429 at 115.66, topscore 278.

McCabe played a legendary innings for 232 at Nottingham, slaughtering the bowling while protecting tailenders. England made 903 for 7 declared in the Fifth Test, Hutton reaching a world record 364. Fingleton, who had been left out of the 1934 tour, did well with 1,268 runs at 38.42. O'Reilly alone took more than 100 wickets. Barnett made useful runs but failed to match the standard of previous Australian 'keepers in England. Badcock hammered the County bowlers but flopped in the Tests. Overall a successful tour, with 20 wins in 36 matches and only two losses.

NINETEENTH AUSTRALIAN TEAM AVERAGES

Name	I.	NO	HS	Runs	Ave.	W.	Runs	Ave.
D. G. Bradman	28	7	278	2429	115.66	0	6	—
W. A. Brown	39	6	265*	1887	57.18	0	22	—
A. L. Hassett	33	3	220*	1595	53.16	1	78	78.00
C. L. Badcock	42	4	198	1659	43.65	0	56	—
S. G. Barnes	22	2	94	818	40.90	4	134	33.50
J. H. Fingleton	37	4	124	1268	38.42	2	17	8.50
S. J. McCabe	36	2	232	1239	36.44	14	524	37.42
B. A. Barnett	29	4	120*	737	29.48	—	—	—
A. G. Chipperfield	18	3	104*	424	28.26	6	155	25.83
M. G. Waite	33	3	77	760	25.33	57	1484	26.03
C. W. Walker	12	4	42	198	24.75	—	—	—
E. C. S. White	22	8	52	318	22.71	32	738	23.06
F. A. Ward	20	6	71	234	16.71	96	1823	18.98
W. J. O'Reilly	20	3	42	232	13.64	114	1818	15.94
L. O'B. Fleetwood-Smith	23	10	18	119	9.15	94	1785	18.98
E. L. McCormick	17	5	12	51	4.25	35	1210	34.57

Perhaps the greatest Australian cricket team. Eleven batsmen between them scored 50 centuries in the side's 34 matches. Seven players made 1,000 runs, with Sam Loxton just short when his nose was broken in the last match. The Australians scored 300 or more in 27 innings and, apart from Tests, no team reached 300 against them. They dismissed the opposition for under 200 no less than 34 times and for under 100 eight times. They scored 721 runs against Essex at Southend, a record for one day's first-class cricket.

The bowling was ideally balanced, with topclass new ball bowlers in Lindwall, Miller and Johnston, a left-armer of remarkable accuracy in Toshack, off spinner Johnson, leg-spinners McCool and Ring and medium-pacer Loxton. The batting was enormously strong from openers Morris and Barnes, down to tailenders with first-class centuries to their credit. Tallon was a brilliant wicketkeeper-batsman, Barnes the world's best short leg, Miller the world's most brilliant slip and the throwing of the whole side was spectacular and accurate. Of the 34 matches played, 25 were won, 17 by an innings, and nine were drawn.

The 1948 Australians were cleverly led throughout with most being ex-servicemen, clearly a big factor in uniting the side. The team scored 16,045 runs to their opponents 11,521 and averaged 48.77 per wicket against 19.42 by their opponents. In the Tests they scored 46.53 runs per 100 balls against England's 39.71. But the searing pace of Australia's opening attack was the key to the team's success. "Bombs against water

TWENTIETH AUSTRALIAN TEAM, 1948

D. G. Bradman

pistols," was how one English player described the opening attacks in the Tests. Australia was expertly managed by Keith Johnson, who had managed the Services XI with such skill and devotion.

TWENTIETH AUSTRALIAN TEAM AVERAGES

Name	I.	NO	HS	Runs	Ave.	W.	Runs	Ave.
D. G. Bradman	31	4	187	2428	89.92	0	2	—
A. L. Hassett	27	6	200*	1563	74.42	0	48	—
A. R. Morris	29	2	290	1922	71.18	2	91	45.50
W. A. Brown	27	2	200	1448	57.92	4	16	4.00
S. J. E. Loxton	23	6	159*	973	57.23	32	709	22.15
S. G. Barnes	27	3	176	1354	56.41	2	121	60.50
R. N. Harvey	27	6	126	1129	53.76	1	29	29.00
K. R. Miller	26	3	202*	1088	47.30	56	989	17.66
R. A. Hamence	22	4	99	582	32.33	7	151	21.57
I. W. Johnson	22	4	113*	543	30.16	85	1563	18.38
D. Tallon	13	2	53	283	25.72	—	—	—
R. R. Lindwall	20	3	77	411	24.17	86	1359	15.80
R. A. Saggers	12	3	104*	209	23.22	—	—	—
C. L. McCool	18	3	76	306	20.40	57	1018	17.85
W. A. Johnston	18	8	29	188	18.80	102	1699	16.65
D. T. Ring	14	5	53	150	16.66	60	1328	22.13
E. R. Toshack	12	3	20*	78	8.66	50	1069	21.38

The 1948 Australian team, the only side to tour England undefeated (L to R): Standing, R. N. Harvey, D. Tallon, D. Ring, I. W. Johnson, R. R. Lindwall, R. Saggers, W. A. Johnston, S. J. E. Loxton, K. R. Miller, E. R. Toshack; Seated, A. R. Morris, C. L. McCool, A. L. Hassett, D. G. Bradman, W. A. Brown, S. G. Barnes, R. A. Hamence.

TWENTY-FIRST AUSTRALIAN TEAM, 1953

A. L. Hassett

Hassett took over the captaincy from Bradman and Harvey assumed Bradman's role as main run-scorer. Six of the team made more than 1,000 runs but none of the bowlers reached 100 wickets. Lindwall was still a great bowler but Miller and Johnston were more injury-prone and not as penetrative as in 1948. Bill Johnston topped the batting averages going in last in all his 16 matches, thanks to a sole dismissal. England regained The Ashes by taking the Fifth Test after four draws.

388

Australia let England off the hook in the Second Test at Lord's. Chasing 343 for victory, England were 4 for 73 at the start of the final day and then, in one of the celebrated match-saving stands, Watson and Bailey batted most of the day to prevent Australia winning. Watson batted 5 hours 46 minutes, Bailey 4 hours 17 minutes.

England had in Trueman a bowler to match Australia's pace and in May and Graveney young strokemakers to support Hutton and Compton. Tallon was past his best, whereas Evans was at his peak for England. Of the 35 matches played, Australia won 16, drew 18 and lost one, but it was the one that counted in The Ashes battle.

TWENTY-FIRST AUSTRALIAN TEAM AVERAGES

Name	I.	NO	HS	Runs	Ave.	W.	Runs	Ave.
W. A. Johnston	17	16	28*	102	102.00	75	1580	21.06
R. N. Harvey	35	4	202*	2040	65.80	4	51	12.75
K. R. Miller	31	3	262*	1433	51.17	45	1015	22.55
A. L. Hassett	30	2	148	1236	44.14	3	76	25.33
J. H. De Courcy	31	2	204	1214	41.86	0	28	—
A. K. Davidson	30	7	104*	944	41.04	50	1050	21.00
A. R. Morris	37	3	126*	1302	38.29	1	30	30.00
R. G. Archer	25	8	108	627	36.88	57	962	16.87
G. B. Hole	33	—	112	1118	33.87	4	210	52.50
C. C. McDonald	24	1	125	717	31.17	—	—	—
R. Benaud	28	1	135	748	27.70	57	1270	22.28
J. C. Hill	19	8	51*	220	20.00	63	1328	21.07
G. R. Langley	19	3	46	273	17.06	—	—	—
R. R. Lindwall	25	1	62	400	16.66	85	1398	16.43
I. D. Craig	27	1	71*	429	16.50	0	23	—
D. T. Ring	20	4	88	252	15.75	68	1359	19.98
D. Tallon	16	2	83*	169	12.07	0	28	—

TWENTY-SECOND AUSTRALIAN TEAM, 1956

I. W. Johnson

Ian Johnson, fresh from triumphs as Australia's captain in the West Indies, encountered big problems as leader of this team, most of them handed out by English curators who insisted on preparing wickets that suited spinners Laker and Lock and did not help an Australian attack based on pace. But it was also evident to anybody who mixed with the team that the tremendous team spirit of the 1948 side was missing. Too many big names failed to support Johnson. Part of the problem was that several players in the team disagreed with Johnson's appointment and were not prepared to shrug it off and give their all. The team fielded well. Langley and Maddocks were efficient 'keepers but the young English batsmen May, Cowdrey and Sheppard outplayed Australia's newcomers. Ian Craig, after a disastrous first tour in 1953, had an improved record this time. Benaud gave an indication of what was to come by taking 60 wickets and scoring 871 runs. Overall the failure of Australia's spinners to match the hostility of Laker and Lock on turning pitches and supine batting by Australia enabled England to hold The Ashes. The batting at Manchester where Laker took 19 wickets for 90 runs in the

Fourth Test was a sad commentary on the Australians' inability to adjust to turning surfaces. Australian protests over the dust bowl pitch were skilfully handled by Johnson who managed to control the anger in his team. The team played 34 matches, won 11, drew 20 and lost 3.

TWENTY-SECOND AUSTRALIAN TEAM AVERAGES

Name	I.	NO	HS	Runs	Ave.	W.	Runs	Ave.
K. Mackay	28	7	163*	1103	52.52	8	269	33.62
J. W. Burke	35	7	194	1339	47.82	6	181	30.16
K. R. Miller	29	6	281*	843	36.65	50	984	19.68
I. D. Craig	29	5	100*	872	36.33	1	14	14.00
P. J. Burge	26	4	131	780	35.45	0	2	—
R. Benaud	29	4	160	871	34.84	60	1342	22.36
C. C. McDonald	35	—	195	1202	34.34	0	12	—
R. N. Harvey	32	1	225	976	31.48	1	24	24.00
R. G. Archer	25	4	148	649	30.90	61	1356	22.23
A. K. Davidson	13	3	75	270	27.00	26	586	22.54
J. Rutherford	33	5	98	640	22.86	3	152	50.66
G. R. Langley	13	8	41	112	22.40	0	2	—
R. R. Lindwall	18	6	116*	260	21.66	47	924	19.66
L. V. Maddocks	17	3	56	201	14.35	1	4	4.00
D. P. A. Crawford	15	7	19	101	12.62	31	851	27.45
I. W. Johnson	20	2	44	193	10.72	50	1352	27.04
J. Wilson	11	3	8*	23	2.88	43	993	23.09

TWENTY-THIRD AUSTRALIAN TEAM, 1961

R. Benaud

Success of this team's tour hung on a win at Lord's in the "Battle of the Ridge" and a magnificent victory by 54 runs in the Fourth Test at Old Trafford. In the Lord's Test Bill Lawry batted coolly under severe pressure for six hours, taking many bruising blows as Statham and Trueman made the ball fly. His 130 set up an Australian win that ended an English sequence of 18 Tests without defeat. At Old Trafford he again handled the English speedsters calmly, contributing 74 and 102. England had Australia apparently beaten in this match. Australia led by only 157 with one wicket left, and a full day to play. But Davidson (77 not out) and McKenzie added 98 for that wicket in a remarkable stand, Davidson hitting 20 off one over from David Allen. England required 256 to win in 230 minutes and when Dexter made a daring 76 in 84 minutes Benaud's famous luck seemed to have deserted him. But he got Dexter with a ball that popped and bowled May around his legs out of rough created by the fast bowlers off the second ball May faced. Close failed with a much criticised wild swing and, with Australia catching brilliantly, a match that had appeared within England's grasp, was won. It was a sensational victory and it won The Ashes for Australia. O'Neill and Lawry both made around 2,000 runs on their first tours of England in a side that had great batting depth. Lawry surprised critics in Australia as well as in England with his success at 24. Davidson was the best of a competent attack, Grout kept superbly. The ground fielding was outstanding but overall this has to go down as Benaud's tour. He took 61 wickets

390

and made 627 runs, not exceptional figures, but his captaincy ranks with the best by an Australian. The team lost only two of its 37 matches, won 14 and left 21 unfinished.

TWENTY-THIRD AUSTRALIAN TEAM AVERAGES

Name	I.	NO	HS	Runs	Ave.	W.	Runs	Ave.
W. M. Lawry	39	6	165	2019	61.18	1	33	33.00
N. C. O'Neill	37	4	162	1981	60.03	6	269	44.83
P. J. Burge	36	11	181	1376	55.04	0	13	—
R. B. Simpson	44	6	160	1947	51.23	51	1707	33.47
C. C. McDonald	26	7	140	913	48.05	0	14	—
B. C. Booth	32	3	127*	1279	44.10	0	37	—
R. N. Harvey	35	2	140	1452	44.00	4	93	23.25
B. N. Jarman	14	5	85	354	39.33	—	—	—
K. D. Mackay	25	3	168	683	31.04	52	1481	28.48
A. K. Davidson	25	5	90	607	30.35	68	1519	22.33
R. Benaud	32	7	80*	627	25.08	61	1443	23.65
A. T. W. Grout	21	3	49	299	16.61	—	—	—
F. M. Misson	15	3	33	194	16.16	51	1294	25.37
G. D. McKenzie	26	8	48	254	14.11	54	1561	28.90
R. A. Gaunt	12	6	30	77	12.83	40	875	21.87
I. W. Quick	18	9	18	108	12.00	50	1701	34.02
L. F. Kline	12	2	22*	68	6.80	54	1520	28.14

Bob Simpson took over from Benaud as Australia's captain and with agile fielding and accurate pace bowling swung the Test series Australia's way 1-nil, with four draws. Burge made a wonderful 160 in Australia's sole Test win. Simpson made 311 in an Australian score of 8 for 656 declared in the Fourth Test at Old Trafford, to which England replied with 611. Boycott, in his first series, made 113 batting in glasses in the drawn Fifth Test. Simpson's 311 was his maiden Test century in his 52 innings. It was the highest score in England by an Australian captain. His innings lasted 762 minutes—the long-

TWENTY-FOURTH AUSTRALIAN TEAM, 1964

R. B. Simpson

est ever against England. One of the successes of the tour was Bill Lawry, who showed outstanding pluck in many of his innings to finish with 1,601 runs at 42.13. The team lacked the opening bowling hostility it had when Davidson was in the side, but McKenzie, Hawke, Corling and Connolly bowled well enough to overcome the side's lack of a topclass spinner. Jarman and Grout were fine 'keepers, and of the 36 matches played the side won 14, lost 4 and drew 18.

TWENTY-FOURTH AUSTRALIAN TEAM AVERAGES

Name	I.	NO	HS	Runs	Ave.	W.	Runs	Ave.
R. B. Simpson	38	8	311	1714	57.13	32	1037	32.40
B. C. Booth	36	8	193*	1551	55.39	1	109	109.00
R. M. Cowper	29	4	113	1286	51.44	23	713	31.00
N. C. O'Neill	34	4	151	1369	45.63	6	356	59.33
W. M. Lawry	41	3	121	1601	42.13	0	32	—
P. J. Burge	34	4	160	1114	37.13	0	17	—
T. R. Veivers	28	7	79	725	34.52	52	1881	36.17
I. R. Redpath	37	4	162	1075	32.57	3	149	49.66
J. Potter	27	3	78	751	31.29	11	437	39.72
B. N. Jarman	17	2	105	417	27.80	0	7	—
R. D. H. Sellers	19	8	36	233	21.18	30	1130	37.66
J. W. Martin	23	4	70	362	19.05	35	1142	32.62
A. T. W. Grout	20	2	53	303	16.83	1	22	22.00
G. D. McKenzie	25	7	50	290	16.11	88	1996	22.68
N. J. Hawke	16	6	37	159	15.90	83	1649	19.86
A. N. Connolly	10	6	14	27	6.75	28	855	30.53
G. E. Corling	13	6	13	43	6.14	44	1403	31.88

TWENTY-FIFTH AUSTRALIAN TEAM, 1968

W. M. Lawry

On his third English tour, Lawry went as captain. He did not score as well as on his previous tours and he showed a lack of understanding on how to handle his spin bowlers, but he remained a cricketer of stature. His 1968 team was one of the most disappointing Australia has sent to England and few of the players showed their true potential. The weather caused the loss of many days' play and kept spectators away to an extent that the tour finances became a major worry to the team management. To correct this they asked all the counties they were to play from the beginning of June, to play on Sundays. Only Kent agreed, and on August 18, 1968, Australia played in England for the first time on a Sunday, at Canterbury. In the end big crowds at the Tests and the later matches gave the Australians a good tour profit.

Australia won only five of their matches against the 17 first-class county teams, and lost to Yorkshire and Glamorgan. But they retained The Ashes by drawing the Test series 1–1. Only Ian Chappell among the ten newcomers in the side made a favourable impression, though Walters and Sheahan had periods of brilliance. Injuries affected the performances of Cowper and Lawry. The attack, in damp conditions that should have assisted them, proved one of the weakest of all time. The side fielded well throughout, and in the 29 matches the team won 10, lost 3, drew 15, with 1 abandoned.

TWENTY-FIFTH AUSTRALIAN TEAM AVERAGES

Name	I.	NO	HS	Runs	Ave.	W.	Runs	Ave.
I. M. Chappell	30	4	202*	1261	48.50	18	529	29.38
W. M. Lawry	23	3	135	906	45.30	—	—	—
I. R. Redpath	37	3	135	1474	43.35	0	16	—
R. M. Cowper	24	4	148	744	37.20	32	771	24.09
K. D. Walters	32	2	95	933	31.10	5	353	70.60
A. P. Sheahan	32	3	137	817	28.17	—	—	—
H. B. Taber	16	2	81*	365	26.07	—	—	—
R. J. Inverarity	30	4	88	645	24.80	2	34	17.00
E. W. Freeman	14	—	116	326	23.28	31	873	28.16
L. R. Joslin	18	2	61	344	21.50	—	—	—
N. J. N. Hawke	18	5	47	267	20.53	35	749	21.40
A. A. Mallett	13	6	43*	106	15.14	44	1248	28.36
G. D. McKenzie	18	2	50	185	11.56	40	1250	31.25
B. N. Jarman	19	1	41	184	10.22	—	—	—
A. N. Connolly	18	8	22*	88	8.80	55	1157	21.03
J. W. Gleeson	18	3	19	122	8.13	58	1200	20.68
D. A. Renneberg	12	6	9*	27	4.50	41	1015	24.75

TWENTY-SIXTH AUSTRALIAN TEAM, 1972

I. M. Chappell

Ian Chappell's struggle to rebuild a national team that could win back lost prestige received a tremendous boost on this tour through the performance of Dennis Lillee, who took 31 wickets in the Tests and 53 on the tour. Bob Massie chimed in with a staggering bowling effort in his very first Test. Massie took 16 for 137, a useful contribution in any Test but absolutely incredible from a bowler who two years before had taken 3 for 166 in two matches for Northants Second XI and had not been offered a contract by the county. "Massie's match" plus Lillee's sustained excellence and a general improvement in the batting enabled Australia to square the rubber on the sixth afternoon of the final Test. The Fifth Test provided the first instance of brothers (Ian and Greg Chappell) scoring a century in the same Test innings, but it also proved to Ian Chappell that Australia was on the way back and that his team-building efforts were working.

Both Chappells scored more than 1,000 runs on the tour, as did Keith Stackpole, while Dougie Walters made more than 900 runs and nine of the batsmen in the team averaged over 30 runs an innings. The spinners Gleeson and Mallett gave the pace men strong support in a varied attack in which Inverarity proved a surprise with his drifting left-arm knuckle balls. Marsh set a record of 23 dismissals in the Tests and kept the side's ground fielding at a high level. Ross Edwards produced a once in a lifetime innings of 170 not out in the Trent Bridge Test, in which Stackpole underlined his consistency with a fine 114. Despite some difficulty against the nagging accuracy and subtle variation of Underwood and against the rising deliveries of Snow, Australia managed five Test centuries and for the first time in a five-Test rubber prevented England scoring any. The team played 26 matches, won 11, lost 5, and drew 10.

TWENTY-SIXTH AUSTRALIAN TEAM AVERAGES

Name	I.	NO	HS	Runs	Ave.	W.	Runs	Ave.
G. S. Chappell	28	10	181	1260	70.00	19	495	26.05
K. R. Stackpole	34	4	143*	1268	42.26	2	164	82.00
A. P. Sheahan	25	7	135*	721	40.05	1	20	20.00
K. D. Walters	29	5	154	935	38.95	2	117	58.50
R. W. Marsh	24	5	91	664	34.94	—	—	—
G. D. Watson	26	2	176	820	34.16	22	590	26.81
R. Edwards	18	3	170*	747	32.47	0	15	—
I. M. Chappell	34	1	118	1017	30.90	10	106	10.16
B. C. Francis	26	1	210	772	30.88	1	15	15.00
J. R. Hammond	6	3	36*	78	26.00	19	784	41.26
H. B. Taber	11	3	54	180	22.50	—	—	—
D. J. Colley	15	3	58*	266	22.16	32	979	30.59
R. J. Inverarity	29	8	54	453	21.57	35	954	27.25
A. A. Mallett	12	3	29	140	15.55	37	1161	31.37
J. W. Gleeson	12	4	30	88	11.00	41	955	23.29
R. A. L. Massie	10	1	18	45	5.00	50	896	17.92
D. K. Lillee	13	7	11*	30	5.00	53	1266	23.88

TWENTY-SEVENTH AUSTRALIAN TEAM, 1975

I. M. Chappell

The four Test series between two closely matched teams was played after the inaugural World Cup competition in which the West Indies defeated Australia in the final. (See World Cup.) The Test rubber was marred by the actions of vandals in the Third Test at Leeds when Australia led 1–nil and needed 225 to win with seven wickets in hand to go to a 2–0 lead. McCosker was on 95 not out and within sight of his first Test century when the match had to be abandoned. The vandals, who were campaigning for the release of a prisoner, badly damaged the pitch with knives and oil. Rain fell from 4 o'clock on the afternoon of the abandoned last day and a result may have been impossible—but players on both sides were deprived of what promised to be a thrilling struggle.

Back Row (L to R): D. McErlane (Physiotherapist), J. R. Thomson, D. K. Lillee, R. B. McCosker, A. G. Hurst, M. H. N. Walker, A. A. Mallett, R. D. Robinson, J. D. Higgs, D. K. Sherwood (Scorer). Front Row (L to R): G. J. Gilmour, K. D. Walters, R. Edwards, I. M. Chappell (Captain), F. W. Bennett (Manager), G. S. Chappell (Vice-Captain), R. W. Marsh, B. M. Laird, A. Turner.

There were two other draws apart from the Leeds Test, with McCosker scoring that elusive Test century in the fourth match with 127 of Australia's 532. He was involved in a second wicket stand of 277 with Ian Chappell after Australia's first wicket had fallen at seven.

The team played 15 first-class matches, winning eight, losing two and playing five draws. The losses to Kent and Leicestershire were particularly disappointing in view of the sides' fine efforts in beating the MCC, Glamorgan, Derbyshire, Northants, Somerset and Essex. The Australians scored 18 centuries in the 15 first-class games, Ian Chappell leading with four, and three batsmen averaged more than 50 an innings. Lillee and Thomson provided an outstanding opening attack that was seldom mastered, taking 37 Test wickets between them. Max Walker and Gary Gilmour gave excellent support. The fielding was of a very high standard, with the Chappells in the slips as good a twosome as Australia has ever had. McCosker was rewarded for his always sound technique by heading the Test batting averages and scoring more runs on the tour than any other Australian.

TWENTY-SEVENTH AUSTRALIAN TEAM AVERAGES

Name	I.	NO	HS	Runs	Ave.	W.	Runs	Ave.
K. D. Walters	18	5	103*	784	60.30	7	171	24.42
R. B. McCosker	20	2	127	1078	59.88	—	—	—
I. M. Chappell	19	—	192	1022	53.78	6	184	30.66
G. S. Chappell	20	3	144	762	44.82	5	152	30.40
G. J. Gilmour	14	5	102	389	43.22	28	855	30.53
R. Edwards	20	4	101*	675	42.18	0	27	—
R. D. Robinson	9	3	41	223	37.16	—	—	—
A. Turner	20	1	156	654	34.42	—	—	—
B. M. Laird	17	2	127	488	32.53	—	—	—
R. W. Marsh	17	2	65*	469	31.26	—	—	—
J. R. Thompson	10	4	49	186	31.00	34	1173	34.50
D. K. Lillee	9	4	73*	154	30.80	41	907	22.12
A. A. Mallett	12	8	25*	112	28.00	31	1239	39.96
M. H. N. Walker	12	3	25	134	14.88	36	1108	30.77
A. G. Hurst	4	1	10*	15	5.00	21	695	33.09
J. D. Higgs	2	1	—	—	—	27	890	32.96

TWENTY-EIGHTH AUSTRALIAN TEAM, 1977

G. S. Chappell

Greg Chappell on his first tour as Australia's captain led an uninspired side through 22 matches that mostly were as depressing as the weather. Australia won only five matches, lost to Somerset for the first time ever, and were even beaten by Minor Counties in a two-day game. Chappell, of course, had an impossible job once it became known early in May that 13 of his 17 players had signed to join WSC. Manager Len Maddocks went to great lengths to stress that the WSC contracts the side's best players had in their pockets had nothing to do with their poor form, and *Wisden* was right once again in suggesting there was a good deal of heresy in what the players did in England.

Once Lillee, Ian Chappell and Ross Edwards decided not to

tour the tour was in trouble. Thomson was never the same bowler with the pressure Lillee applied at the other end. Ian Chappell's positive captaincy was replaced by a brother then feeling his way as a skipper. Walters disappointed yet again in the matches that counted, and on his first Test appearance for Australia Richie Robinson had to be used as an opener. On the entire tour the Australians only once scored more than 400 in an innings—against the weak Nottinghamshire attack.

To cap all these woes, Australia dropped a lot of important catches, including one when Boycott was on 22 at Leeds. He went on to his 100th Test century. Only Greg Chappell scored more than 1,000 runs in first-class matches on the tour and only Max Walker took more than 50 first-class wickets, a sad contrast to the deeds of players in earlier Australian teams. Perhaps the one bright spot for Australia was the entry into Test cricket of Kim Hughes who made his debut in the final Test. The team won only five of 22 matches, lost four and drew 13.

TWENTY-EIGHTH AUSTRALIAN TEAM AVERAGES

Name	I.	NO	HS	Runs	Ave.	W.	Runs	Ave.
G. S. Chappell	25	5	161*	1182	59.10	6	305	50.83
K. J. O'Keeffe	19	12	48*	355	50.71	36	1054	29.27
R. D. Robinson	23	4	137*	715	37.63	—	—	—
C. S. Serjeant	22	2	159	663	33.15	—	—	—
D. W. Hookes	26	1	108	804	32.16	1	18	18.00
G. J. Cosier	20	1	100	587	30.89	0	37	—
I. C. Davis	20	—	83	608	30.40	—	—	—
K. J. Hughes	19	—	95	540	28.42	—	—	—
K. D. Walters	26	1	88	663	26.52	0	31	—
R. J. Bright	19	8	53*	287	26.09	39	804	20.61
R. B. McCosker	32	1	107	737	23.77	0	5	—
R. W. Marsh	24	2	124	477	21.68	0	6	—
M. H. N. Walker	17	2	78*	250	16.66	53	1231	23.22
G. Dymock	6	5	8*	16	16.00	15	498	33.20
M. F. Malone	10	3	46	95	13.57	32	847	26.46
J. R. Thomson	17	1	25	130	8.12	43	1296	30.13
L. S. Pascoe	9	3	20	44	7.33	41	941	22.95

TWENTY-NINTH AUSTRALIAN TEAM, 1981

K. J. Hughes

Australia could claim to have outplayed England for most of this astounding series, but in the end capitulated to Ian Botham's allround brilliance after he relinquished the England captaincy. Australia could have led 3–0, but collapsed under pressure in the second innings of the third and fourth Tests and in the first innings of the Fifth Test. England were in desperate trouble until Brearley, who on playing skills was not deserving of a Test berth, took over the captaincy and freed Botham to weave his magic. Kim Hughes, who failed badly with the bat, was a sensible, competent captain but in the end the series belonged to Botham.

England held vital catches under Brearley, who coaxed a big effort from pace bowler Willis in the final three matches. Alderman moved the ball appreciably throughout the series and finished ahead of Lillee, who bowled throughout in a yellow headband, among Australia's wicket-takers. Botham played a masterly innings of 118—off 102 balls, with 13 fours and six sixes—to clinch the Fifth Test and The Ashes for England, following his 149 not out in the Third Test when England recovered from 7 for 135 to score 356.

During the series Rodney Marsh became the best performed of all Test wicket-keepers when he took four catches in the first innings of the Third Test to pass Alan Knott's record 263 dismissals. England became only the second team in Test history to win after following-on as Botham hammered out 100 in the session between tea and stumps at Leeds. The first team to do it was A. E. Stoddart's team in 1894–95 at Sydney. John Dyson made a maiden century in his 12th Test, Dirk Wellham a century in his first Test, and Alan Border staked his claim to be ranked among the great left-handers. Michael Whitney, a left-arm pace bowler from Sydney who had played minor cricket with Fleetwood and a few games with Gloucestershire, was called into the team when Geoff Lawson and Rodney Hogg were injured and performed creditably in the last two Tests.

TWENTY-NINTH AUSTRALIAN TEAM AVERAGES

Name	I.	NO	HS	Runs	Ave.	W.	Runs	Ave.
D. Wellham	13	4	135*	497	55.22	1	11	5.50
A. Border	21	5	123*	807	50.44	2	65	32.50
G. Yallop	22	3	114	624	32.84	6	241	40.17
G. Wood	24	2	81	690	31.36	—	—	—
J. Dyson	20	1	102	575	30.26	0	2	—
K. Hughes	24	1	89	679	29.52	0	14	—
T. Chappell	18	2	91	409	25.56	0	18	—
R. Marsh	16	1	72*	368	24.53	1	0	—
G. Lawson	9	3	38*	140	23.33	25	652	26.08
M. Kent	15	—	92	347	23.13	—	—	—
D. Lillee	11	4	40*	158	22.57	47	1028	21.87
S. Rixon	9	2	40	146	20.86	0	19	—
G. Beard	9	2	36	131	18.71	16	559	34.93
R. Bright	16	1	42	280	18.66	40	1056	26.40
T. Alderman	10	5	12*	34	6.80	51	1064	20.86
R. Hogg	8	2	7	16	2.66	27	657	24.33
M. Whitney	5	—	4	5	1.00	11	327	29.73

A right-hand slow-medium bowler who at his prime varied his flight with great judgement and bowled to a consistent length. He was rated the best all-rounder in Australia in the 1870s, batting and bowling splendidly and fielding with great verve. Members of the first English teams to visit Australia said Evans could "pitch the ball on sixpence." He achieved some remarkable coups with Spofforth and did not suffer in comparison with the great man. He missed two tours of England while he was at his peak and by the time he made his first trip in 1886 he was 38 and his powers had waned.

EVANS, Edwin
1849–1921

First-Class Averages: Batting, 1,010 runs at 12.02; Bowling, 202 wickets at 16.58.

Tests (6): 82 runs at 10.25; 7 wickets at 47.42.

Evans, born at Emu Plains, New South Wales, first played for the State in 1874–75 against Victoria, helping to win the match by taking 6 for 25 in the second innings. He improved with every outing and in one match joined Spofforth in dismissing Victoria for 37. Against Lillywhite's team in 1876–77 and Lord Harris' side in 1878–79 he was as much feared as any Australian bowler. In 1884–85 at Sydney in the Third Test he took a brilliant catch off Spofforth at point to dismiss England's outstanding batsman Wilfred Flowers and win a thrilling victory for Australia by six runs.

When he went to England in 1886 he still bowled to a good length but he had lost the spin that had made him a terror for years in Australia. In a team disorganised by petty feuds, he took only 30 wickets on the tour at 20.50 and was given little work by a captain who had little faith in him (H. J. Scott). He made only 347 runs on the tour, in all matches, best score 74 not out, average 12.39. In eight matches in which he played on the trip, he did not get a bowl at all. He had left the trip too long.

Evans's fame as a cricketer won him a job as an inspector of selections settled on by early farmers. He spurned quiet mounts and took big, lively horses on which to ride round the selections. Banjo Paterson, famous poet, recalled trying to dissuade Evans from taking a gun with him on one snorting horse. "Evans said he could manage all right and turned out to be a first-class horseman," Paterson wrote. "Then he astounded us by taking his rifle and killing a kangaroo that was going past at full speed—a feat only attempted by very good professional kangaroo shooters. Evidently the keen eye that had made him a crack slips fieldsman was also useful looking along the sights of a gun."

EVERETT, Samuel Charles, 1901–1970

First-Class Averages: Batting, 617 runs at 14.69; Bowling, 134 wickets at 27.11.

A right-arm fast medium bowler and left-hand batsman for Petersham, New South Wales and the 1926 Australian team in England. He bowled at a speed comparable to that of Terry Alderman. He was never a hostile opening bowler but he had some big triumphs for New South Wales. His strong physique was ideally suited to his buccaneering batting style.

Everett first played for NSW in 1921–22 and soon showed that he was not easy to play if the pitch was a little worn or wet. In 1923–24 he took 6 for 54 against South Australia and on tour in New Zealand with the NSW side at the end of that summer he took 5 for 48 against New Zealand. In 1925–26 he took 5 for 84 against WA in Sydney and did well enough playing for The Rest against Australia to win selection in Collins' side for England. He was one of the tour failures, though illness upset his form. On a tour in which Mailey (141 wickets) and Grimmett (116) were desperate for support, he took only

398

27 wickets. His sole success on the trip came in the match at Hobart en route to England when he made a whirlwind 77, hitting 60 of them in boundaries with two sixes and 12 fours.

Everett took five wickets or more in an innings eight times in a first-class career that ended in 1929–30. His best figures, 6 for 23, came in 1929–30 against Queensland at Sydney but it was a match that saw all the headlines go to Bradman for his record 452.

EVERS, Harold Albert, 1876–1937

First-Class Averages: Batting, 624 runs at 22.28; Dismissals, 38 (22 catches, 16 stumpings).

A colourful personality who captained two Australian States and weighed as much as Warwick Armstrong (22 stone) although he jokingly insisted he was just over 18 stone. He kept wicket for New South Wales and Western Australia with an agility that belied his bulk. (When he went out to toss for WA in the match at Perth against Armstrong's 1921 team, the turf took a bad bruising, for their combined weight was around 45 stone.)

Evers was born at Newcastle, NSW, and played for the State at the age of 20, in 1896–97. He captained NSW in one match in 1901–02, but after only five first-class matches settled in WA, where his first-class opportunities were severely limited. He played 14 matches for WA, however, between 1905–06 and 1920–21, making his last appearance at 44. (He made almost as many stumpings as he took catches, none better than his stumping of Jack Ryder before 10,000 spectators at Perth when Ryder had made 102 for Armstrong's 1921 Australian team.)

F

FAIRFAX, Alan George, 1906–1955

First-Class Averages: Batting, 1,872 runs at 29.25; Bowling, 134 wickets at 27.11.

Tests (10): 410 runs at 51.25; 21 wickets at 30.71.

A valuable all-rounder for New South Wales and Australia. When Fairfax and Bradman were selected for Australia against England in the 1928–29 season, they were the first players from Sydney's famous St. George club to represent Australia. Fairfax did not match the run-getting prowess of his clubmate but he made four scores over 50 in 10 Tests, top-score 65. He was a useful medium-pacer and in his first-class career took 41 catches, some of them spectacular efforts.

Fairfax, a right-hander born in the Sydney suburb of Summer Hill, learned to play cricket with his brother Eric on a Bulli soil wicket their father laid down in the backyard of their Kogarah home. He was adept at all ball games, particularly snooker, billiards and baseball. He scored a century for New South Wales Colts against Queensland Colts in Brisbane at the start of the 1928–29 season, and on promotion to the Shield side batted and bowled consistently well. Against Victoria at Sydney he made 104 in a partnership of 161 for the second wicket with Bradman (340 not out).

He toured England with the 1930 Australian team, scoring 536 runs at 25.52 and taking 41 wickets at 30.19. His fielding at gully swung matches on that trip and many famous batsmen fell to his catches, including an amazed Wally Hammond. He was a room-mate of Archie Jackson and encouraged him through the tour. In the Fourth Test he made 49 and with Grimmett added 87 for the eighth wicket, lifting Australia to a respectable 345. In the Fifth Test, he made 53 not out. Having taken 4 for 101 in the Second Test, it fell to Fairfax to bowl Jack Hobbs for nine at The Oval in Hobb's last Test knock.

Fairfax returned to England early in 1932 and played for Accrington in the Lancashire League, and later set up an indoor cricket school in the basement of Thames House, London. He was badly knocked about during war service with the RAF and later spent seven years in hospital. When he recovered he became cricket writer for the big-circulation London Sunday paper, *The People*. He died of a heart attack soon after returning from covering an English tour of Australia.

A high-scoring right-hand batsman and right-arm medium-pace bowler who could not reproduce his district cricket form in State matches. In 1941–42 Fallowfield, a North Sydney-born allrounder who played for Northern Districts, scored five consecutive centuries in first grade and failed by only four runs to beat Victor Trumper's record of five centuries in a row when he was out for 96 in his sixth knock. He made his debut in 1934–35 for NSW, but in a career that covered 11 matches, scored only one first-class century, he could not overcome the array of talent challenging for State berths.

FALLOWFIELD, Leslie John, 1916–

First-Class Averages: Batting, 756 runs at 44.47.

Since first-class cricket began with the early inter-Colonial matches in the 1850s, Australian cricket has drawn a lot of its strength from a remarkable array of families. There are dozens of instances of fathers and sons representing their States and some of our finest players have been brothers. Uncles and cousins are liberally sprinkled through the scorecards of notable matches and there are even a few grandfathers and grandsons. The Davidson clan from the Gosford district of New South Wales have fielded an entire social team, with Test player Alan their most famous member. The Gregory family provided five brothers who played for NSW, and numerous cousins and uncles, but there is no record more imposing than South Australia's Hill family, who produced seven brothers that played first-class cricket.

The best family record in Tests was established in 1981 when Trevor Martin Chappell joined his brothers Ian Michael and Gregory Stephen Chappell by playing Test cricket for Australia. Ian and Greg Chappell also provide the only example of brothers captaining Australia, though brothers have captained some State teams. Trevor Chappell set the record for Australia's Test brotherhood when he appeared in three Tests against England, hitting the winning run in his Test debut at Nottingham. The Chappells' grandfather, Victor York Richardson, also captained Australia.

Since Dave and Edward Gregory began the tradition in 1877, a total of 10 sets of brothers have played for Australia. "Alick" Bannerman joined his brother Charles in 1879 and by the end of the 19th century six sets of brothers had played in Tests. The first to achieve it this century were the Harveys in 1948. The Chappells' record of supplying three brothers for Test duty is matched by only four families in the history of cricket—the Graces (E. M., G. F. and W. G.) and the Hearnes (A., F., and G. G.) in England, the Tancreds (A. B., L. J. and V. M.), of South Africa, and by the Mohammad family of Pakistan. Four Mohammads, Hanif, Mushtaq, Wazir and Sadiq, played in Tests, and a fifth brother, Raees, was 12th man for a Test and technically is credited with representing his country.

FAMILIES, IN AUSTRALIAN CRICKET

"Alick" Bannerman.

The three Chappell brothers appeared together in a match for South Australia, but this was far from unique as it had already been done by three Bryants for Western Australia, three Hills for South Australia, and three Harveys for Victoria.

AUSTRALIAN BROTHERS WHO HAVE WON TEST SELECTION

The Brothers	State		Span	Tests	Runs	Ave.	Wickets	Ave.
K. A. (Ken) Archer	(QLD)	18–1–1928	1950–51	5	234	26.00	did not bowl.	
R. G. (Ron) Archer	(QLD)	25–10–1933	1953–56	19	713	24.58	48	27.35
C. (Charles) Bannerman	(NSW)	23–7–1851	1877–79	3	239	59.75	did not bowl.	
A. C. (Alick) Bannerman	(NSW)	21–3–1854	1879–93	28	1108	23.08	4	40.75
R. (Richie) Benaud	(NSW)	6–10–1930	1952–64	63	2201	24.45	248	27.03
J. (John) Benaud	(NSW)	11–5–1944	1972–73	3	223	44.60	2	6.00
I. M. (Ian) Chappell	(SA)	26–9–1943	1964–80	75	5345	42.42	20	65.80
G. S. (Greg) Chappell	(SA, QLD)	7–8–1948	1970–82	76	6293	53.33	46	37.22
T. M. (Trevor) Chappell	(SA, WA, NSW)	21–10–1952	1981	3	79	15.80	did not bowl.	
G. (George) Giffen	(SA)	27–3–1859	1881–1896	31	1238	23.35	103	27.09
W. F. (Walter) Giffen	(SA)	10–9–1863	1887–1892	3	11	1.83	did not bowl.	
D. W. (Dave) Gregory	(NSW)	15–4–1845	1877–79	3	60	20.00	0-9	0-9
E. J. (Edward) Gregory	(NSW)	29–5–1839	1877	1	11	5.50	did not bowl.	
M. R. (Merv) Harvey	(V)	29–4–1918	1947	1	43	21.50	did not bowl.	
R. N. (Neil) Harvey	(V, NSW)	8–10–1928	1948–63	79	6149	48.41	3	40.00
R. W. (Robert) McLeod	(V)	19–1–1868	1892–93	6	146	13.27	12	32.00
C. E. (Charles) McLeod	(V)	24–10–1869	1894–1905	17	573	23.87	33	40.15
G. H. S. (Harry) Trott	(V)	5–8–1866	1888–98	24	921	21.92	29	35.13
A. E. (Albert) Trott	(V)	6–2–1873	1895	3	205	102.50	9	21.33
H. (Hugh) Trumble	(V)	12–5–1867	1890–1904	32	851	19.79	141	21.78
J. W. (John) Trumble	(V)	16–9–1863	1885–86	7	243	20.25	10	22.20

Notes: (1) I. M. Chappell and G. S. Chappell are the only Australian brothers to have captained their country. Other captains in the above list are R. Benaud, G. Giffen, D. W. Gregory, R. N. Harvey, G. H. S. Trott & H. Trumble. (2) A. E. Trott also played two Tests for England, against South Africa in 1898.

In inter-State cricket, the Hills and Gregorys set a high standard in family representation, but there are a lot of proud family achievements scattered round the States. For example, four Huttons, W. F. P. Hutton and his three sons, all played for South Australia. Test batsman Paul Sheahan followed his great-grandfather, W. H. Cooper, into Tests. Ian Johnson followed his father-in-law, Dr Roy Park, into Tests. The cousins Keith Rigg and Colin McDonald both played for Australia. Here is a selection of intriguing family representations around the States:

Queensland: Test players Ken and Ron Archer head the list of notable Queensland cricketing brothers. Other families included E. K., G. G. and W. A. Armstrong, who all played for the State; S. W. Ayres and his son R. W.; E. R. and G. S. Crouch; B. W. Cook and his son G. G.; the brothers E. H. and J. S. Hutcheon; L. P. D. O'Connor and his son B. R. D.; L. E. and R. K. Oxenham; N. T. and R. E. Rogers; the Tallon brothers Don and Bill; and the Toowoomba Allens, Tom and his son Ross.

New South Wales: The Gregorys have provided a bewildering array of State representatives, starting with A. H., C. S., D. W., and E. J., brothers who were followed by the brothers C. W. and S. E., both sons of E. J. Test fast bowler J. M. Gregory was the son of C. S. Other families represented in NSW include the brothers R. and W. Bardsley; J. and R. Benaud; B. C. J. and R. H. B. Bettington; A. R. and E. B. Docker, followed by E. B.'s nephews K. B., C. T. and P. T. Docker; the brothers R. A. and W. S. Duff; the brothers R. J. and T. J. Hartigan; the brothers H. V. and L. D. McGuirk; Alec Marks and his sons N. and L.; the three Minnett brothers, L. A., R. B. and R. V.; the brothers G. and J. Moore, followed by J. Moore's sons W. H. and L. Moore; E. G. and M. A. Noble; W. L. and E. Trenerry; E. L., E. F., and P. S. Waddy; Victor Trumper and his son Victor, jnr.

Victoria: The redoubtable Trott brothers, Harry and Albert, were the first brothers from Victoria to win international acclaim, while a third Trott brother, Fred, was on the ground staff at Lord's and later was a professional in Scotland. Other families prominent in Victoria were E. F. and M. a'Beckett, E. L. a'Beckett and his son E. C.; A. R., J. and W. Carlton; E. L. and E. V. Carroll who opened the batting for Victoria v. South Australia at Adelaide in 1912–13; D. R. and his son R. M. Cowper; the Harveys, C. E., M. R., R. and R. N.; the Hassett brothers R. J. and A. L.; J. J. Healy and his son G. E. J.; E. D. Heather and his son P. J.; the Horans T. P., and his sons J. F. and T. I. B.; the brothers J. D. and W. G. Kinnear; the brothers A. J. W. and H. C. Lansdown; C. C. McDonald and his brother I. H.; the three McLeod brothers, C. E., D. H. and R. W.; the brothers L. V. and R. I. Maddocks, and L. V.'s son I. L.; the twins L. E. and V. G. Nagel; the Raysons, W. J., his son M.W., and his grandson R. W.; the Rush brothers E. R. and T. R., and E. R.'s son J.; the Slight brothers J. and W.; K. W. Stackpole and his son K. R.; the brothers G. and J. H. Stuckey; G. E. Tamblyn and his son G. L.; W. A. Tarrant and his nephew F. A.; the Trumbles, H. and his brother J. W.; the brothers B. J. and R. W. Wardill; and T. S. Warne and his son F. B.

Tasmania: There are several remarkable cricket families scattered through Tasmania's cricket history, such as the Richardsons, who had seven family members play for the State; the Davises, four, and the Martin family, who had four who played for the State and one that played for Queensland. The other leading families were the brothers G. H. and J. L. A. Arthur, sons of C. Arthur; C. W. and E. H. Butler and his son E. L. A. Butler; the Thomases, M. R. and R. V.; C. E. and G. Vautin; D. D. and R. B. Wardlaw; K. R., N. R. and R. Westbrook; C. W. and N. V. Rock; and J. H. and W. H. Savigny.

South Australia: Seven Hill brothers played first-class cricket in a family of 16 that included eight girls. The SA representatives were Arthur, Clem, Henry, Leslie, Percival, Roland, and Stanley, who also played for NSW. Other outstanding SA families include L. W. and C. T. Chamberlain, the Giffen brothers G. and W. F., the Goodens, H. A., N. L., and J. E.; A., F. T. and R. Hack; the brothers B. W. and G. M. Hone; the Hutton family, W. F. P. and his sons, M. D., M. P., and N. H.; the Jarvis brothers A. H., F., and H. S. C.; the Leaks, B. H., E. H. and S.; the four Pellews, A. H., C. E., J. H. and L. V.; and the brothers Riding, K. and P. L.

Western Australia: The Bryant brothers, Frank, Dick and Bill were the first set of three together to play in a first-class match in Australia—in 1926–27 for WA v. SA—though this feat was later matched by the Harveys for Victoria and the Chappells for SA. Other outstanding family representation for WA include L. Charlesworth and his son R.; the brothers A. and I. Dick; E. K. Edwards and his son R.; M. Inverarity and his son J.; K. Meuleman and his son R.; C. MacGill and his son T.; E. McKenzie, his brother D., and his son G.; the Rigg brothers B. and H. W. H.; A. Robinson and his sons A. W. and G.; and the Prindiville brothers, K. and T.

This summary of family representation in Australian first-class cricket clearly demonstrates the influence cricket has had in an amazing number of families. It does not include families that have jumped about the States such as the Barbours (NSW and Qld), N. C. O'Neill and his son M. (NSW and WA), and the Loxtons (Vic and Qld). There certainly appears to be a strong desire among fathers who represented their States for their offspring to emulate them.

FAVELL, Leslie Ernest, 1929–

First-Class Averages: Batting, 12,379 runs at 36.63.

Tests (19): 757 runs at 27.03.

An instinctively aggressive, crowd-pleasing right-hand opening batsman whose technique sometimes strayed from the coaching manuals. He had a thrilling hook shot, an eagerness to cut hard, and was renowned for his sportsmanship and throwing skill. He toured all the cricket nations except England in Australian teams in a first-class career that brought 91 half centuries and 27 centuries, one of them in Tests.

Favell, born in the Sydney suburb of Arncliffe, was developed in the St George district. He won his promotion to St George first grade at 18 because the selectors wanted the best fieldsman. He moved to Adelaide at 22 to get more opportunities, leaving a State over-burdened with Test heroes, and made more runs for South Australia than any other batsman. He originally won selection in the South Australian team after selector Sir Donald Bradman saw him make 139 for East Torrens against Prospect. He made 86 and 164 in his first match for SA against his former mates from Sydney in 1951–52. He captained SA more often than anyone else—95 times, compared with 87 by Vic Richardson—and played 143 games in all for the State. He twice scored a century in each innings of a match for SA.

"Temperament dictated to technique in rewarding Favell with the highest aggregate by an Australian whom the selectors never gave an opportunity to tour England," wrote Ray Robinson. "Cricket-goers preferred him that way than if he had been a technocrat too canny to have taken risks." Favell's footwork was quick but his keenness to really hammer the ball frequently left a gap between bat and pad. When Barry Jarman, his Test and SA team-mate, hit a magnificent shot against NSW in Sydney in January, 1957, Favell, who had just made a century in each innings, commented: "I wish I could play a cover drive like that." Bradman, who was standing nearby, said, "If you got your feet closer to the ball you could."

Favell was an inter-State baseballer whom no batsman trusted for an extra run once the ball got near his hand. With the bat, he was eager to score while the ball was still red, and in 16 years of going in first he cut down many outstanding opening attacks. One of his favourite strokes was the drive straight down the pitch past the bowler, a renowned confidence-sapper for any bowler. "Keep 'em there," he would say as he came down to turn for two or three. Just before he went out to open an innings he would inform team-mates that all was well because "I have spoken to both edges of the bat."

In 1963–64 he captained South Australia with imaginative skill to win the Sheffield Shield for the first time in 11 seasons. Overseas he is remembered for innings such as his sparkling century against the President's XI at Ahmedabad, India, in 1959–60, and his 190 at better than a run a minute against Griqualand West, highest score on Australia's 1957–58 South Africa tour. He made 114 before lunch on his way to that score and put on 293 for the second wicket with Bob Simpson. He hit three sixes, one of them an extraordinary hook shot in response to a spectator's cry of "Give us a six." Another of his outstanding knocks was to hit 120 against the MCC at Adelaide in 1962–63.

When he first came into first-class cricket, Favell had a low, crouched stance and really choked down low on the bat handle with his grip. As he became more experienced, he taught himself to stand up straighter. After one innings against India at Madras, he moved slowly to 72 not out by the tea interval. "I don't think my upright stance was a factor in my slow scoring," he said, "but it does explain why I am still in."

He dropped himself as an opener for SA in 1967–68 after scoring 281 with John Causby. "When the medium-pacers all start looking like Tyson, it's time to drop down the order," he said. He kept going for a couple more seasons, retiring in his 41st year. He had scored a century against every Australian State, given endless pleasure to fans wherever he appeared, and set an example for sportsmanship which Bradman said

405

has never been bettered by anyone who has played the game. As a radio commentator he is honest, perceptive, and thousands of cricket lovers admire the sanity of his homespun summaries, even if his words lack the pyrotechnics he provided in his playing days.

FENNELLY, Sidney James, 1887–1964

First-Class Averages: Batting, 1,076 runs at 27.58; Bowling, 1 wicket at 114.

A former Sydney cricketer who settled in Brisbane and played 21 matches for Queensland before and after World War I. Fennelly, a right-hand batsman, is best remembered for a magnificent 131 in a Queensland total of 219 against a strong New South Wales side at Brisbane in 1912–13. "It was an innings Trumper himself would have been proud of," wrote Clem Hill. Fennelly so pleased the crowd a collection was taken up for him. He was a classy batsman from Valleys club who loved to use his feet and wrists, hit the ball very hard, and display his wide array of strokes. An injury to his skull deprived Queensland of his services after the 1920–21 season. Fennelly was also a brilliant fieldsman.

FERGUSON, William Henry ("Fergie"), 1880–1957

Australian cricket's great traveller. He spent 52 years as scorer and baggage master to touring teams in Australia, England, South Africa, West Indies and New Zealand, and claimed that on 43 tours he never lost a bag. He began as a clerk with a Sydney insurance office and persuaded his dentist, M. A. Noble, to recommend him to the authorities as scorer-baggage man for the 1905 Australian team. He was paid £2 a week for his first tour from which he had to cover his expenses and pay his boat fare. His skill with Australian teams led to other countries hiring him, and he was continually in demand.

He scored in 208 Tests and travelled more than 600,000 miles before air travel became routine. His scorebooks were immaculate and Test captains used his diagrams of batsmen's strokes to plan their field placings. He elevated the job of scoring to a comprehensive statistical exercise.

FERRIS, John James, 1867–1900

A one-time Sydney bank clerk who won undying fame as a left-arm opening bowler and formed with C. T. B. Turner one of cricket's greatest bowling partnerships. He bowled at a lively medium pace to an immaculate length, swung the new ball either way, and later spun it sharply, particularly if the pitch was damp. He varied his pace and flight cleverly. He was one of the few cricketers who have played Test cricket for two countries.

Ferris, born in Sydney, played for the Belvidere club, whose members nicknamed him "The Tricky." He first played for New South Wales in 1886 and in January, 1887, made a dramatic debut for Australia at Sydney in one of the most dramatic of all Tests. Australia won the toss and put the English batsmen in to face their new bowlers, Turner and Ferris. They bowled unchanged through the innings, often pitching into each other's footprints, and had England out for 45, still England's lowest Test total. Turner took 6 for 15, Ferris 4 for 27, and they were helped by some brilliant catches—two by Spofforth. Ferris followed with 5 for 76 in the second innings, but England won the match when Australia, set to get 111, were out for 97 in the final innings.

Ferris followed up his dream debut by taking 5 for 71 and 4 for 69 in his next Test at Sydney four weeks later but again his superb bowling with Turner (9 for 93) was wasted by our batsmen, England winning by 71 runs. In February, 1888, they teamed again, catching England on a rain-ruined pitch at Sydney, and this time had England out for 113, Turner 5 for 44, Ferris 4 for 60. But Australia made only 42 in the first innings and lost by 126 runs.

First-Class Averages: Batting, 4,264 runs at 15.67; Bowling, 813 wickets at 17.53.

Tests—Australia (8): 98 runs at 8.16; 48 wickets at 14.25. England (1): 16 runs at 16.00; 13 wickets at 7.00.

Critics reported that there was near panic among English batsmen facing Ferris and Turner on the 1888 tour by the Sixth Australian team. On this, the first of his two tours of England with Australia, Ferris bowled 2,222 four-ball overs, 998 maidens, and took 220 wickets at 14.10, at the age of 21. His accuracy was remarkable in one so young. He and Turner opened the bowling in almost every match knowing Australia had nobody else who could get good batsmen out. They had to do the job if Australia was to win.

In the opening match of the tour, Ferris and Turner took all 20 wickets for 161 and Australia won easily, although only two of her batsmen exceeded 20. Against Lancashire at Old Trafford, Ferris took 8 for 41. Finally the Test win Ferris and Turner deserved came in the Test at Lord's, with Turner taking 5 for 27 and 5 for 36, and Ferris 5 for 26 in the second innings, Australia winning by 61 runs.

On this 1888 trip it was generally agreed that Turner was the better of the pair but two years later, when both took 215 wickets, it was considered that Ferris, whose average was then 13.20, was the more to be feared. Between these tours Ferris had continued his fine form in 1890–91 by taking 15 for 54, including 8 for 12 in an innings, for New South Wales against Fifteen of Queensland in 1889–90 and 14 for 192, including 8 for 84, against South Australia in 1890–91.

Ferris agreed on his second English tour to return and qualify for Gloucestershire, after settling his affairs in Sydney. He played his last Test for Australia at The Oval in 1890, taking 9 for 74 in the match. There were numerous presentations for him in Sydney and he sailed back to England laden with gold watches and cigarette cases. While he was qualifying for

Gloucestershire, he went to South Africa with W. W. Read's English team, enhancing his reputation even further by taking 235 wickets on the trip, 13 of them in a Test for only 91 runs. There, unaccountably, his great skills deserted him, and he was never the same bowler again, though he improved markedly as a batsman.

In 1893 he made 1,056 runs in an English first-class season, including 106 for Gloucester at Hove against Sussex. He made several appearances for The Gentlemen against The Players and figured in a series of big partnerships with W. G. Grace. When he made 135 not out for Thornbury against Bath in 1893, he and Grace, 204 not out, scored 352 without being separated. Ferris returned to Australia late in 1895 still searching for his old magic, playing once for South Australia in 1895–96 and twice for New South Wales (1897–98). His old skill had gone. He went off to the Boer War and died at Durban in November, 1900, from enteric fever while serving with the Imperial Light Horse.

FIELDING RECORDS

Australia has produced many outstanding fieldsmen, players whose catches could swing a match or reduce the opposition's total by 20 or 30 runs by intercepting apparently certain boundaries, players of thrilling speed over the ground whose returns could cause vital run-outs. Some have excelled in the outfield with their gathering and throwing, others have excited crowds by picking up faint chances in the slips or at short leg. Think of a position on the cricket field and it is not difficult to name half a dozen Australians who have fielded there superbly. There have been Test series in which the important difference in well-matched sides has been that Australia fielded better than their opponents.

In the enthralling 1961 Australia-England Test at Manchester, when England needed 256 runs to win on the last day, Australia clinched The Ashes with a superlative display of fielding in support of some clever bowling. Simpson took two amazing catches in slips, Grout splendidly caught danger man Dexter, and O'Neill made a difficult catch from Close look easy at backward square-leg.

Australia's Influence On Fielding Strategy: Early Australian teams that toured England suffered from a lack of experience in field placements but they quickly learned the art of cutting off a batsman's best scoring shots. Australian Jack Blackham virtually eliminated the need for long stops in big matches. Harry Boyle influenced all captains in the positioning of fieldsmen at silly mid-on, which at one time was known as "Boyley's mid-on," a tradition carried on by Jack Fingleton and others who fielded close in on the legside to Bill O'Reilly. After World War II Australia influenced widespread use of the "Carmody field," in which up to six fieldsmen are placed in the slips area for pace bowlers.

Throwing Records: The longest throws attributed to Australian cricketers were those by George Bonnor and Ernie Bromley. Bonnor, 6 ft 6 ins, 16-stone, had measured throws of 131 and 120 yards before the ball bounced. In a throwing contest at Melbourne in 1933, Bromley threw a ball on to a barrier erected to protect spectators 130 yards from his starting point. For sustained accuracy from anywhere in the field even old-timers agree the most remarkable Australian throwing arm belonged to Neil Harvey. He threw with his right-arm, batted left-handed.

The "World Record" Throw: A newspaper called *The Peak Downs Telegram* published on February 16, 1872, reported that during a cricket match at Clermont, Qld, between sides called Town and Country, spectators were much impressed by the throwing skill of several players and particularly by that of Billy, an aboriginal who worked for Jack Thorn, owner

Australia's Jeff Thomson bowling to a "Carmody field," with six fieldsmen in catching positions from slips to point.

409

The anticipatory Australian slips in England in 1964, Bob Cowper, Brian Booth, Ian Redpath, Bill Lawry and Peter Burge.

of the Clermont Hotel. Between innings a contest was organised to assess how far the players could throw. Billy astonished everyone by throwing the ball 140 yards. Allegations were later made that the throw was not accurately measured because a tape was used, not as accurate a method as a chain. In March, 1873, the *Telegram* reacted to these charges of improper measurement by saying: "We have not the slightest doubt over the accuracy of the throw, which was witnessed by several gentlemen still in Clermont. Everyone who saw it said that it surpassed anything they deemed possible. The throw was actually measured at 142 yards 1 ft 6 in, but $2\frac{1}{2}$ yards were allowed for deviation in measurement using the tape." The newspaper said witnesses included C. J. Graham, MLA for Clermont, an old Cambridge cricketer and oarsman. A long correspondence on Billy's throw in Lillywhite's *Scores And Biographies* disclosed that several tapes, including a

410

brand new one, were used to measure the distance. All of the tapes confirmed the throw had gone at least 140 yards.

Ian Chappell gets both hands to his 100th Test catch, which dismissed West Indian Lawrence Rowe at Melbourne on Boxing Day, 1975.

Most Catches In a First-Class Career By An Australian: 610 by Ken Grieves between 1945–46, when he first played for New South Wales and 1964, when he completed 15 seasons with Lancashire.

Most Catches In An English First-Class Season: 63 by Australian Ken Grieves playing for Lancashire in 1963.

Most Catches In A Career In Australia: 383 catches by Bob Simpson, comprising 272 in all first-class matches in Australia and overseas while on tour with Australian teams, 110 official Test catches in all countries, plus one catch taken while acting as a substitute.

Most Catches By Australian On A Tour Of England: Hugh Trumble holds all the record for an Australian team tourist. He made 52 catches in 1893, 50 in 1890 and 48 in 1899. The next best were Jack Gregory with 45 in 1919 (AIF team), George Bonnor with 43 in 1884, Trumble with 39 in 1896, J. M. Gregory with 37 in 1921, and Bob Simpson (1964), Warwick Armstrong (1905), and Frank Iredale (1896) all with 36 catches on an English tour.

Most Catches In A Test Career By An Australian: 110 by Bob Simpson* in 62 Tests, followed by 106 by Greg Chappell in 76 Tests, and 105 by Ian Chappell in 75 Tests. They were all slips

*Simpson took another Test catch in 1958–59 against England at the SCG while fielding as a substitute.

411

fieldsmen. Simpson was first positioned in slips by Keith Miller when he went on as NSW's 12th man. He held 14 of the 15 chances that came his way in his initial first-class season for New South Wales in 1954–55.

Most Catches In An Innings: 5 by Victor Richardson against South Africa at Durban in 1935–36.

Most Catches In A Match: 7 by Greg Chappell against England at Perth in 1974–75. Jack Gregory, Ian Chappell, Vic Richardson, Neil Harvey and Davenel Whatmore all took six catches in a Test match.

Most Catches In A Test Series: 15, by Jack Gregory in 1920–21 against England in Australia (5 Tests). Greg Chappell held 14 catches in the six-Test series against England in 1974–75, while his brother Ian took 11 in the same series, giving the brothers 25 of the 110 wickets that fell in that series. Bob Simpson twice held 13 catches in a Test series—in 1957–58 against South Africa and in 1960–61 against West Indies, both five-Test series.

Most Catches In A Match By An Australian Team: In the Fifth Test between England and Australia at Melbourne in 1901–02, 16 English batsmen were out caught, which is still the Test record.

CAREER CATCHING PERFORMANCES—FIRST-CLASS

Fieldsman	Tests	Career Total (All Matches)	Fieldsman	Tests	Career Total (All Matches)
R. B. Simpson	110*	383	G. A. R. McKenzie	34	200
G. S. Chappell	106	336**	V. T. Trumper	31	171
I. M. Chappell	105	312	A. L. Hassett	30	170
I. R. Redpath	83	211	W. M. Lawry	30	123
R. Benaud	65	225	M. A. Noble	26	191
R. N. Harvey	64	228	R. R. Lindwall	26	123
K. R. Stackpole	47	166	S. C. Gregory	25	174
H. Trumble	45	329	V. Y. Richardson	24	211
W. W. Armstrong	44	274	P. J. P. Burge	23	166
A. K. Davidson	42	168	G. H. S. Trott	21	183
J. M. Gregory	37	195	A. C. Bannerman	21	154

* Simpson's total does not include one catch taken as a substitute fieldsman.
** Greg Chappell's career figures include catches taken during his two seasons with Somerset (1969 and 1970).

CATCHING PERFORMANCES BY AUSTRALIANS (MAINLY OVERSEAS)

Fieldsman	Career Total	Fieldsman	Career Total
K. J. Grieves	610	V. Jackson	250
A. E. Trott	449 (4)	G. Tribe	243
F. Tarrant	296	J. Walsh	209
W. E. Alley	293	B. Dooland	171 (3)
S. M. J. Woods	282 (5)	L. O. S. Poidevin	160
C. L. McCool	262 (14)	J. L. Livingston	149

The figures in brackets indicate Test catches.
Note: Wicket-keeping records are listed separately.

Australia and Fiji have not played an official Test but there have been several matches between Australian and Fijian players stretching back to 1905 when Joe Darling's team played a match in Fiji on the way to England. Fijian cricket administrators are hopeful that a good display by their team in the 1983 World Cup will encourage Australia to send official teams occasionally to Fiji.

A Fijian team visited Australia in March, 1908, and played matches against South Australia, Victoria, New South Wales and Queensland. The team comprised Ratu Kadavu Levu, Ratu Pope, Ratu Robonu, Toroca, Suma, Bainivanua, Liceni, Tara, Kikau, Manasa, Esala, Sokidi, Bulatoluu, Meleti Raimuria, Rev. Joni Rovai, Joni B. Sigila and Inoke. Ratu Kaduvu, a good batsman and an allrounder of merit, was the captain and Ratu Pope was the outstanding player.

In Adelaide the Fijians made 147, George Giffen, then 49, taking 6 for 58. South Australia replied with 198, Liceni taking 6 for 53. The Fijians then closed at 7 for 263, Sokodi scoring 86, Meleti 78. SA had scored 3 for 59 when the match ended. In Melbourne Victoria scored 367, Onyons 152, and 4 for 121, Fiji 262. At Sydney NSW made 440 and dismissed Fiji for 132, White taking 4 for 18. At Wollongong the Fijians scored 158 and the home side replied with 8 for 158, Ratu Pope taking 8 for 63. In Brisbane Queensland make 274, Ratu Pope taking 7 for 106 with his right-arm fast medium-pacers. Fiji scored 152 and Queensland declared their second innings closed at 7 for 165. Fiji narrowly escaped defeat and were 7 for 88 at stumps. Soon after this match, in the surf at Newcastle, NSW, Ratu Kadavu Levu saved the lives of two men carried out in heavy seas. The Fijians played a draw, scoring 159 against Northern Tasmania 155 and 4 for 79. The Fijians played in native costumes in all their matches, entering the field in single file wearing sulus or calf-length skirts, most of them sporting vast bushy hairdos and playing in bare feet.

The celebrated Australian cricketer Sammy Woods wrote of a visit to Fiji in 1910 in which he took 27 wickets in an innings before he was forced to leave with the score at 72 wickets for 175 runs, pursued out to sea to his cruise ship by Fijians with spears and arrows. Phillip Snow, an expert on Fijian cricket, discounted Woods' claims about the weapons because he said Fiji had forsaken cannibalism 35 years earlier, but Snow—in Barclay's *World of Cricket*—cited matches on Fijian village greens in which 90 fieldsmen, some lurking in trees or behind thatched houses, joined in. Syd. Gregory's Australian team played in Fiji on their way home from the triangular tournament in England in 1912 after matches in the US. Austin Diamond took a team of prominent Australian cricketers, including Mailey, Bardsley, Macartney and Armstrong, to play in Suva in 1913.

During World War II cricket matches between Australian

413

and New Zealand servicemen stationed in Fiji boosted local enthusiasm, and in 1946 a meeting in the bungalow of the Australian administrator, E. E. Turner, agreed to form a Fiji Cricket Association. The Australian Board of Control approved a 16-match tour of NSW by a Fiji Cricket Association team in 1959–60. The Fijian team won 10, lost five and drew one match, playing mainly in country centres. Highlight of the tour was a match against a NSW XI at the Sydney Cricket Ground when W. Apted top-scored with 67 in a Fijian first innings score of 163 against a side comprising J. Burke, R. Benaud, N. O'Neill, R. Gasnier, A. Davidson, K. Miller, N. Harvey, N. Marks, R. Madden, R. Flockton and E. Laidler. The NSW XI made 137 and lost on the first innings.

The Fijians brought kava out for their fieldsmen to drink at the breaks. One batsman was hit on his bare toes by a fiery Alan Davidson yorker, a blow that would have crippled a batsman wearing boots with a steel cap. He simply wriggled his toes and batted on immediately. Keith Miller scored 37 and hit a ball high in the air to a vacant space at deep mid-on. The Fijian fieldsman stationed at square leg ran almost 80 metres while the ball was in the air and caught Miller out on the mid-on fence. He later turned out to be an Olympic sprinter. Miller had ambled through for two when he was out.

FINGLETON, John Henry Webb ("Jack") 1908–1981

First-Class Averages: Batting, 6,816 runs at 44.54; 2 wickets at 27.00.

Tests (18): 1,189 runs at 42.46.

A forceful right-hand opening batsman who at his best was a fluent and polished performer, but had moods when he lapsed into stodgy, unattractive occupancy of the crease. Nobody doubted his pluck and he played some of the bravest innings in big cricket between the wars. He played for New South Wales for ten years and for Australia in five international series between 1931–32 and 1938, and in those matches was the centre of several famous incidents.

Fingleton, son of a member of State parliament, was educated at Waverley Christian Brothers College, and played grade cricket with the Waverley club. He was a superb fieldsman, fast to the ball, immaculate in gathering and throwing, and caused many run outs. On and off the field he was always splendidly tailored. He married well, taking as his wife Phillippa, daughter of Sir Kenneth Street, Chief Justice of New South Wales. He fathered three sons and two daughters.

He made his debut for New South Wales in 1930–31 and came into international cricket against South Africa in the Fifth Test in 1931–32. His first full Test series was against Jardine's team in 1932–33. He took a fearsome hiding from Voce in the match before the First Test, carrying his bat through the innings for 119 not out for New South Wales v. MCC. This began his reputation for courage and persuaded the top Australian batsmen to play in the Tests in an extraordinary array

414

of padding that included a pad that fitted round the neck and heart and protected the ribs on the side facing the bowler. In the Tests Fingleton won hordes of admirers for the manner in which he unflinchingly faced Larwood and Voce, who hit him repeatedly all round the body.

Sir Pelham Warner, the English manager, apparently mindful of Fingleton's training as a journalist, blamed Fingleton for publicising his clash with Australia's captain Bill Woodfull in the dressing-room at Adelaide. Fingleton had always spiritedly denied this charge. He said there were several players in the Australian team with close newspaper connections and believed the most likely source of the Warner-Woodfull quotes was Bradman.

In his book, *The Immortal Victor Trumper*, Fingleton wrote: "The story as told to me by Claude Corbett, then writing for the *Sydney Sun*, and a colleague of mine, was that Corbett got a ring that night at his hotel from Bradman who wanted to tell him something. Corbett arranged a rendezvous with Bradman on Adelaide's North Terrace, and while they sat there in a car Bradman told Corbett all about the Warner-Woodfull incident. Corbett said he thought the story was too hot to run on his own and gave it to all the press."

After missing the 1934 tour of England, Fingleton reached his peak as a batsman on the 1935–36 Australian tour of South Africa under the captaincy of Vic Richardson. He shrugged off the stubborn approach of the stonewaller for that of the punishing stroke-maker, and shared in a stand of 215 with Bill Brown, scoring 112, 108 and 118 in successive Test innings. He made it four Test centuries in a row by scoring 100 in Australia's first innings against "Gubby" Allen's MCC team in the First Test at Brisbane in 1936–37. This was the first instance on record of a batsman scoring four Test 100s in successive innings.

Jack Fingleton completes a hook shot against Surrey at The Oval in 1938.

In England on his sole tour there as a player in 1938, he sat down beside the pitch when spectators heckled him for slow scoring as he struggled to make Australia safe from defeat. He refused to resume until the crowd quietened. In between his cricket successes he worked as secretary to Billy Hughes, one-time Prime Minister of Australia, and became a highly respected writer on Australian politics.

Between 1928–29 and 1939–40, he made eight centuries for New South Wales, with a topscore of 160 and 22 centuries in all. During the early war years when he was playing with his brother Les for Waverley in Sydney grade cricket, the Paddington club captain, Mort Cohen, invited him to practise at Trumper Park when Fingleton said he could not get to Waverley Oval.

Bowlers like Jack Rayner, Jackie Clarke, Brian Flynn, Colin McCool, Ronnie James and Ray Flockton relished the chance of a crack at such a renowned Test player. Fingleton's stroke-

415

play in the half hour or so he batted to this mixture of representative bowlers was absolutely bewildering. He played every shot in the coaching manuals powerfully but with classical ease, graceful in his footwork, unerring in his timing. Seldom did a ball get past him.

I walked over to Billy Wells, Paddington club president and a State selector and told him I had never seen such brilliant shotmaking. Billy was unimpressed. "The greatest practice wicket batsman Australia has ever had—but watch how he goes tomorrow in his match when things really count," said Wells. Sure enough reports of next day's grade matches carried accounts of Fingleton's slow batting against bowlers who should not have got a ball past him. All of which has left me pondering for 40 years on what it is that converts practice net wizards into players who read all sorts of terrors into the bowling when formal play begins.

His lifelong friend Bill O'Reilly believed that Fingleton's approach to batting became more dour and cautious because of Fingleton's unjustified omission from Australia's 1934 tour of England. "That setback in his career left indelible scars on his cricket outlook," said O'Reilly. "The closing of official eyes to the amazing contributions he had made to Australia's 1932 efforts was not easily forgotten by Jack or his teammates." O'Reilly said Fingleton's fielding at short leg, almost within touching distance of the batsman, played an important part of his bowling success.

Jack Fingleton is one of the few Australians who have written well about cricket, though he has irked many of his readers with his jibes at Bradman. Lindsey Browne, cricket expert, music critic, and crossword puzzle wizard, called it "Bradmania." Fingleton said in *The Immortal Victor Trumper* that he and Bradman feuded for years because he believed Bradman should have cleared him of the suspicion of leaking the Warner-Woodfull quotes by telling the story of Bradman's meeting with Claude Corbett.

Fingleton, who made five Test centuries, shared in a record sixth wicket stand of 346 with Bradman in the 1936–37 Test series against England. Fingleton, who was trained on the old Sydney *Daily Guardian*, wrote some notable short profiles for the London *Sunday Times*, and had a deserved reputation for shrewd, penetrative radio commentaries despite an extremely coarse voice that was completely out of character in such a man. In between an arduous life as a political writer and cricket author, read by more Englishmen than Australians, he was responsible for his old Bodyline foe Harold Larwood migrating to Australia. He persuaded the then Prime Minister Ben Chifley to assist Larwood. Fingleton's brother Les, a former mayor of the Sydney suburb of Waverley, was a prominent executive of the NSW Cricket Association for many years. Jack Fingleton's best books, *Cricket Crisis*, *Brightly*

Fades The Don, The Ashes Crown The Year, Masters Of Cricket, The Greatest Test Of All, The Immortal Victor Trumper, and *Batting For Memory* will be read as long as cricket is played in Australia.

An all-rounder who did not win Test selection but went close. In 56 matches for Queensland from 1954 to 1967, his highest score was 103 and his best analysis 6 for 41. He batted in the middle order and bowled right-arm fast-medium. He toured New Zealand in 1959–60 with an Australian "B" team. Fisher, who played for Queensland at 19, swung the ball awkwardly when conditions favoured him and produced some remarkable figures for Western Suburbs, Brisbane, and Queensland Colts. He had eight wickets in his first-class debut in 1954–55 against New South Wales, 3 for 78 and 5 for 50. His father, **Alexander Fisher**, played three matches for Queensland in 1934–35.

FISHER, Barry
1934–1980

First-Class Averages:
Batting, 1,369 runs at 21.06; Bowling, 126 wickets at 32.15.

A right-hand batsman and right-arm fast-medium bowler who was one of nine Australians included in the Commonwealth team that toured India in 1949–50 when the Marylebone Cricket Club decided not to send a team. Fitzmaurice, born in Carlton, played for South Melbourne, appeared for Victoria in 1947–48 but left for the Lancashire League after only four matches. In India with Jock Livingston's Commonwealth team, he took 25 wickets in first-class matches at 24.56 and scored 176 runs at 13.53. Des Fitzmaurice made 1,196 runs for South Melbourne at 17.30 and took 179 wickets at 18.80. His brother, **Dudley James Anthony Fitzmaurice** (1913–) played four games for Victoria in the 1930s, and scored 230 runs at 57.50 in seven innings for the State.

FITZMAURICE,
Desmond Michael
John, 1917–1981

First-Class Averages:
Batting, 272 runs at 17.00;
Bowling, 28 wickets at 28.50.

Rated by some the most gifted, if not the most successful, spin bowler Australia has ever had, a complex figure who sang popular tunes and gave bird calls on the field and died a derelict after years on Melbourne's skid row. He was an expert on magpie calls, imitating the whipbird, and in producing unplayable deliveries when the mood struck him. Bill O'Reilly said that the ball with which Fleetwood-Smith bowled Wally Hammond, pitching outside the off stump and striking the middle and leg at Adelaide in 1937, was the finest ball he ever saw delivered in big cricket.

Fleetwood-Smith was born in the Wimmera town of Stawell, Victoria, where they run the professional footrace every

FLEETWOOD-SMITH,
Leslie O'Brien
("Chuck"), 1910–1971

First-Class Averages:
Batting, 617 runs at 7.34;
Bowling, 597 wickets at 22.64.

Tests (10): 54 runs at 9.00; 42 wickets at 37.38.

year and where his father owned the local newspaper. He wanted to concentrate on tennis and originally bowled right-arm for Xavier College, Melbourne. When he broke his right arm, he was compelled to switch to bowling left-arm and found unsuspected joy in fooling batsmen with what the kids called his "corkscrew" deliveries.

He first played for Victoria in 1931–32, taking 11 for 120 in his first match against South Australia. "He could spin the ball on a pitch of gramophone records," said former VCA secretary Jack Ledward. "It wasn't much use putting him on to bowl against tail-enders as he wasn't particularly interested in getting them out unless the match depended on it. But give him the ball when a top batsman looked likely to get a big score and he would spin the ball so much you could hear it humming in the air."

Fleetwood-Smith took 295 wickets for Victoria at 24.38. He took five wickets or more in an innings for the State a remarkable 31 times. He took some fearful hidings in among his great coups and became a nightmare for his captains, who never knew if he was in the mood for bowling or making bird calls. Cricket to him was a game of fun, not averages. He sometimes made cries of "Come on, Port Melbourne", at tense moments in the cricket. In between all this he had patches of sheer magic with the ball. In 1934–35, he took 26 wickets in seven days of Sheffield Shield cricket.

He went to England twice, in 1934 and 1938, and to South Africa in 1935–36. On his first English tour he finished second in the bowling averages with 106 wickets at 19.21, compared with O'Reilly's 109 wickets at 17.15. In 1938 he was third with 94 wickets at 18.98. His value cannot be expressed in these figures, however, as he could turn a match with one ball by bowling the opposition's star batsman.

In the Third Test at Melbourne in 1936–37, Fleetwood-Smith, a duffer with the bat, opened the batting on a wet pitch for Australia with O'Reilly, a lusty swiper. O'Reilly hit the first ball in the middle of the bat and was out caught and bowled to Voce. Fleetwood-Smith played and missed 26 balls before he snicked a catch off the 27th. At The Oval in 1938 Fleetwood-Smith and O'Reilly did the bulk of the bowling on an over-prepared pitch when England scored 7 for 903. Hutton's sole chance in his innings of 364 was a stumping at 40 off Fleetwood-Smith, who ended the innings with 1 for 298.

"I recall with glee the roar that my left-handed bowling partner let out late on the second day of England's innings, when he raucously informed me, fielding deep at the point, that he had managed to make his off-break turn," said O'Reilly. "He was the best left-handed spinner of his day, and if his temperament had allowed him to concentrate fully on developing his magnificent talents, he would have been rated the greatest spinner of all time."

418

Fleetwood-Smith's stock ball was an off-break that pitched just outside the right-hander's off stump and on pitches that gave any assistance whipped back quickly to test the skill of even great players of spin like Bradman, McCabe, Kippax and Fingleton, all of whom acknowledged his outstanding skill. His well disguised wrong-un went away quickly towards first slip, often bringing disaster to batsmen who failed to pick it and played for the off-break.

He had big, wide shoulders, powerful forearms and an exceptionally strong wrist. On turning pitches he spun the ball so much even top-class players had trouble getting the bat to him. He skipped a few steps, curled his arm spiderishly and flicked the ball up at the batsman with so much spin on it you could hear the ball buzzing. When he was in the mood, every ball whipped off the pitch. He was a handsome figure, with a trim black moustache, and very popular with the ladies, a man of presence with a wealthy background.

His biggest triumph came against England on a hard Adelaide pitch in the 1936–37 Test when he took 4 for 129 and 6 for 110, his 10 wickets winning the match for Australia by 148 runs. Stawell, Fleetwood-Smith's home town, staged a special welcome home for him as a result of that performance, presenting him with a wallet full of notes and an illuminated address. He was chaired through the town to a civic reception where the Mayor read a telegram from Don Bradman, which said: "Fleetwood-Smith's magnificent bowling in Adelaide thoroughly merits honour Stawell paying him."

Another highlight in Fleetwood-Smith's career was at the Scarborough Festival in 1938 when he made Maurice Leyland, who had scored seven centuries in Tests against Australia, look a novice as he repeatedly beat Leyland's bat. At the end of an over in which spectators laughed at Leyland's efforts to make contact with the ball, O'Reilly walked past Fleetwood-Smith and said, "Don't get him out yet, Chuck. He made us look fools often enough, so please let's keep him there for another half hour and make him look a complete idiot."

Keith Miller made his debut for Victoria just after that tour of England ended and he recalls a practice session in which "Chuck took me into a side net and said he'd bowl a few spinners at me." Miller could not detect which way the ball would spin but Fleetwood-Smith helped him by calling out which spinner he would bowl and then sending it down at a slower pace. "With O'Reilly, Grimmett and Frank Ward around these days, you won't survive unless you can handle spin," said Fleetwood-Smith. Miller listened to him whistling popular tunes as he ambled up to bowl in Shield matches but noticed that he never did it bowling to Bradman or batsmen with big reputations. Bowling to Bradman was very serious business and Fleetwood-Smith always enjoyed his duels with the great man.

Fleetwood-Smith married in 1935, and divorced in 1946 after service with the AIF. He had no children. When he first left school he had shown a distaste for work, and now that old urge to loaf returned. He drifted out of the sports pages into the wine bars and parks where "metho" drinkers gathered.

In April, 1969, he appeared in Melbourne City Court on a charge of vagrancy, and he was back in the headlines again. Old school mates and cricketers with whom he had played rallied to help, and the magistrate released him on a $20 good-behaviour bond. He told reporters after he left the court that all he wanted was a bed, a meal, and a few beers. He died two years later, having been spurred to make a fresh start by his court appearance, but failing to settle to regular work. "Too many friends, parties, and social drinks," he said.

FLOCKTON, Raymond George, 1930–

First-Class Averages: Batting, 1,695 runs at 41.34; Bowling, 27 wickets at 38.03.

A lean, sunny-natured allrounder who overcame, humble beginnings in his native Paddington to win recognition as an accomplished cricketer. His 264 not out for New South Wales against South Australia in 1959–60 is believed to be the highest score anywhere in the world by a player making his maiden first-class century. Flockton had begun as a barefoot kid in short pants who sneaked into Trumper Park on practice days and bowled leg-breaks for hours at the club's star batsmen. He was taken to grade games as a scorer and reserve player by club members who fed him up on the way home. He was a natural, stylish with the bat, fluent, high-actioned with the ball, and a fine field, but he lacked consistency in his early grade career.

He made his debut for NSW in 1951–52 but failed to deliver in occasional appearances over the next three seasons. In 1956 he spent a season with Colne in the Lancashire League and this seemed to give him the tough attitude his cricket had lacked. He returned to the NSW team in 1959–60 and remained a valued player until he retired in 1962–63. He had long since given up the leg-breaks that had branded him in the war years as a prodigy, preferring medium-paced swingers.

Working as a traffic cop outside the old Sydney Stadium on fight night, he went to the aid of a hawker whose barrow of peanuts was spread across the road by an impatient motorist. The grateful peanut vendor bought him a lottery ticket and with it Flockton won a share in £50,000. Later he worked in the bar at Sydney Cricket Ground, and in the 1970s went to Canberra as coach to the ACT Cricket Association, where he has done invaluable work. He had never got close to the Test career Paddington oldtimers like Billy Wells had tipped, but the hundreds of players like him who give everything, with an Australian blazer as their ambition, remain one of Australian cricket's great strengths.

420

A Newcastle-born wicket-keeper who gave New South Wales long service without winning Test selection or a place in a touring team. Between 1957–58 and 1963–64 Ford made 51 Sheffield Shield appearances, surpassing Bert Oldfield's NSW record by five matches, and played in 12 other representative games for the State. In those 63 matches he was a model of reliability and sportsmanship and periodically contributed useful runs batting at No 9 or No 10.

Ford moved from Newcastle to the Mosman club in Sydney to further his prospects of first-class selection and got his chance in the State team in unusual circumstances. The selectors first pick for the side was the Balmain 'keeper Keith Herron who had gone on holidays and neglected to leave a forwarding address. When Herron could not be found, Ford went into the NSW team and remained an automatic selection for seven years.

Thickset but agile, Ford was as athletic at the end of a hard day as at the beginning. Some of his 179 dismissals were the result of splendid anticipation and catching, and he was a swift, cool stumper. Test stars who played with him frequently argued that he was deserving of higher honours but the presence in the Australian team of players like Langley, Jarman and Grout kept him out. He had to be content with a tour of New Zealand with Ron Roberts' International team in 1961–62.

FORD, Douglas Allan, 1929–

First–Class Averages: Batting, 575 runs at 13.37; Dismissals, 179 (122 catches, 57 stumpings).

Doug Ford attempts a stumping for New South Wales.

FOTHERGILL, Desmond Hugh, 1920–

First-Class Averages: Batting, 1,404 runs at 39.00; Bowling, 6 wickets at 50.00.

A prominent Australian Rules footballer who scored runs consistently for Victoria in first-class cricket. Fothergill, who dead-heated for the Brownlow medal in 1939, forced his way into the State cricket team in 1938–39 with some strong performances for Northcote club as a right-hand batsman and leg-break bowler. He made 102 against South Australia at Adelaide in 1947–48 and in the match against India that season in Melbourne, scored a valuable 54 as Victoria recovered to save the game following a bad start in the chase for India's 403.

FOWLER, Edwin, 1841–1909

First-Class Averages: Batting, 478 runs at 18.38; Bowling, 22 wickets at 11.95.

A right-hand batsman with what *Wisden* described as a capital style who learned the game in England and distinguished himself in the first inter-Colonial matches. He played for Victoria against New South Wales at Melbourne in 1865 when William Caffyn appeared for NSW for the first time. Fowler contributed 37 to the Victorian total of 285 and Victoria won by an innings. In a single wicket match played immediately afterwards, Fowler scored 51 against Caffyn, Cosstick, Lawrence and Thompson. Many of Fowler's appearances were in matches against the odds, but he had 26 first-class innings for a topscore of 40. He kept wicket and bowled, taking 14 catches and four stumpings.

FRANCIS, Bruce Colin, 1948–

First-Class Averages: Batting, 6,183 runs at 33.97; 1 wicket at 15.

Tests (3): 52 runs at 10.40.

A pugnacious opening batsman who faced the furious pace of John Snow from a right-handed stance with admirable calm. He was tough and well coached, difficult to dislodge, but he lacked shots when he had subdued Test bowlers and they were gasping. Everybody who met him enjoyed the experience.

Francis, born in Sydney where he became a stalwart member of the Waverley club, signing up such notables as Tony Greig, graduated in economics from Sydney University. He was a powerful striker of the ball with a flair for the on-drive and lofted straight hits. He played the first of his 32 matches for New South Wales in 1968–69. In 1970 he played for Accrington in the Lancashire League, and in 1971 and 1973 had seasons with Essex, scoring 1,578 runs in 1971, with four centuries and 1,384 in 1973, with three centuries.

He first represented Australia in matches against the Rest Of The World in 1971–72, scoring 34 runs in three knocks before he broke a thumb. He was in the Australian team that toured England in 1972 under Ian Chappell, scoring well in matches against the counties, but never quite able to overcome class pace bowling from John Snow and others in important games, partly because of a tendency to walk across his stumps towards the off. He made his career best score of 210 not out against a Combined Oxford and Cambridge team in 1972.

Playing for Essex he confided in one of the umpires, fellow New South Welshman Cec Pepper, that he had been out 16 times that season leg before wicket. He immediately went in to bat, was hit on the pad and there was a noisy appeal. "That's 17 times, Bruce," said Pepper, giving Francis out. Apart from his broken thumb he seldom suffered physical injury but sometimes had to leave the field because of extreme migraines.

On his tour of England in 1972 Francis scored 772 runs at 30.88 and took one wicket for 15 runs. Among 13 first-class centuries, he made 126 and 105 against Queensland in the two games in 1969–70, and 132 against Victoria at Sydney in 1971–72.

FRANCKE, Frederick Malcolm, 1941–

An effervescent leg-spinner from Sri Lanka who gave Queensland invaluable service in the 1970s. He played all his cricket with great enthusiasm and gave the Queensland attack much-needed variety at a time when medium-pacers dominated. He was an efficient field who took some outstanding catches.

Francke made his debut for his native Sri Lanka, then called Ceylon, at the age of 15 years 6 months in a match against Madras for the Gopalan trophy. He played three first-class matches without success with the bat, but took 6 for 83 with his spinners against Mysore at Bangalore in 1957–58. He played in Cornish League cricket and for Cornwall in the minor counties' championship in the early 1960s.

He joined the Valley club in Brisbane and made his debut for Queensland in 1971–72 against the World XI at Brisbane, and was a regular in the Queensland side for the next six seasons. He toured South Africa in D. H. Robins' XI in 1974–75. Bowling turned out to be his strength, though he rarely had assistance from Australia's billiard-table pitches. He took five wickets or more in an innings eight times and held 31 catches. His best figures were 6 for 62 against South Australia at Adelaide in 1972–73 when he finished with 11 for 184 in the match.

First-Class Averages: Batting, 671 runs at 10.82; Bowling, 172 wickets at 30.45.

FREEMAN, Eric Walter, 1944–

A right-arm South Australian fast-medium bowler who played in contact lenses and was just as efficient at Australian Rules football as he was at cricket. He had a powerful physique, played every match enthusiastically, and had a big following among spectators, but in a period when Australia

First-Class Averages:
Batting, 2,244 runs at
19.17; Bowling, 241
wickets at 27.76.

Tests (11): 345 runs at
19.16; 34 wickets at
33.17.

was desperate for a hostile pace bowler, he was found wanting. He could bowl straight and steadily but he did not beat the bat often enough. He was an excellent field, and had a record of big hitting which produced two valuable Test fifties and a spate of sixes.

Freeman, born at Largs Bay, South Australia, was in and out of Test cricket within three years. He had a meteoric rise after taking 7 for 52 for South Australia against Queensland in 1966–67, and toured New Zealand with an Australian side that year. Between 1967 and 1970, he also toured England, India, and South Africa. In England in 1968, he took 31 wickets at 28.16, with 4 for 78 off 30.5 overs in the Third Test his best bowling effort. He hit a spectacular 116 against Northants in 90 minutes, with five sixes and 13 fours among his 326 runs at 23.28. It was the sole century of his career.

He took a pasting from the South Africans in 1969–70, when it became clear he lacked the penetration of a Test bowler, and he dropped out of international cricket on his return home. For South Australia, his best performance was against New Zealand in 1967–68 at Adelaide when he batted at No. 10 and made 50 and 39 and took 3 for 50 and 8 for 47, South Australia winning by 24 runs.

FREER, Frederick William, 1915–

First-Class Averages:
Batting, 1,284 runs at
32.10; Bowling, 104 runs
at 27.75.

Tests (1): 28 runs at n.a.;
3 wickets at 24.66.

A top quality right-arm medium to fast bowler of impressive stamina who had the misfortune to play when Miller, Lindwall and Bill Johnston were at their devastating peak. He replaced Lindwall, who was unfit, in the Second Test against England at Sydney in 1946–47, taking three good wickets and scoring handy runs without being dismissed. Freer, who had begun as a schoolboy with the Carlton club in Melbourne, went to play with Rishton in the Lancashire League in 1948. Rishton were last when he took over as professional and were first at the end of his initial season.

Freer toured India with the Commonwealth team in 1949–50 and made three centuries in the unofficial Tests, best score 132 against India at Bombay. He scored 769 runs and took 44 wickets on the tour and was rated the team's leading allrounder. He returned to play in Australia in the 1951–52 season but a leg injury began to worry him and he retired the following season.

Before he went to England Freer took 7 for 29 for Victoria against Queensland and 5 for 62 against New South Wales in 1945–46 and 6 for 63 against New South Wales in 1946–47. He was a fine field who scored eight centuries for Carlton. His 88 wickets at 12.50 in the 1943–44 season was a Melbourne pennant cricket record for many years. He was very well known in South Africa and India, where he coached during English winters.

A left-hand opening batsman from the Fitzroy club who figured in some valuable partnerships in 31 matches for Victoria between 1956–57 and 1962–63. He put on 167 against South Australia in 1959–60, 132 against South Australia in 1960–61 and 105 against New South Wales in 1960–61, all for the first wicket with Bill Lawry, and 169 for the second wicket with Lawry in 1961–62 against NSW. But he did not carry on to a century in any of those stands and his sole first-class hundred, 137, came against Tasmania at Launceston in 1959–60.

FURLONG, Ronald William, 1936–

First-Class Averages: Batting, 1,722 runs at 32.49.

Wicket-keeper "Jock" Livingston leads a Commonwealth team on to the field before the tour of India in 1949–50. Bruce Dooland is behind Livingston and Fred Freer is behind him on the right.

GAGGIN, William Wakeham, 1847–1925

First-Class Averages: Batting, 79 runs at 15.8.

A sound batsman and splendid fieldsman who represented Victoria several times. He was for many years the mainstay of the East Melbourne Cricket Club and between 1867 and 1881 made 3,978 runs for the club at an average of 23, and took 70 wickets at 10.42 each. Gaggin had 12 innings for Victoria in matches "With or Against the Odds" and scored 145 runs at an average of 12.08.

GANNON, John Brian ("Sam"), 1947–

First-Class Averages: Batting, 141 runs at 6.40; Bowling, 117 wickets at 30.47.

Tests (3): 3 runs at 3.0, 11 wickets at 32.82.

A tall, handsome, fast-medium left-arm bowler and nimble outfieldsman from the Perth suburb of Scarborough who was overshadowed early in his career by the presence of Lillee, Massie and Brayshaw in the West Australian team. He made his State debut in 1966–67 when his figures included 6 for 107 against South Australia but dropped out of big cricket after the 1972–73 season. He returned after an absence of four seasons and when Australia's leading pace bowlers switched to WSC won Test selection. He proved a lively, determined bowler of praiseworthy endurance and a rare crowd-pleaser whether bowling or fielding. He twice took five wickets in an innings in first-class matches, best figures 6 for 107 against South Australia in Adelaide in 1966–67. He played originally for the Subiaco-Floreat club but later changed to Scarborough.

GARRETT, Thomas William, 1858–1943

A Test all-rounder who improved with age, a highly successful captain of New South Wales teams, who batted right-handed and bowled right-arm medium fast. He was the most experienced player of his time apart from Blackham—in inter-colonial matches before the Sheffield Shield competition began. He repeatedly threatened to retire but was rated too shrewd a skipper by New South Wales selectors to be discarded. He was particularly wise in his handling of aspiring young bowlers.

George Giffen said of him: "Without being so deadly a bowler as Spofforth, Boyle or Palmer, he was often very successful and always very useful. Australia has not had many exponents of the off-theory principle of bowling, and Tom Garrett has been the wiliest of them. He would keep a fine length outside the off-stump and never minded being hit. Sometimes the ball would work a little from the pitch which victimised most of the batsmen."

As Garrett lost his expertise as a bowler, his skill as a batsman increased. He became quite a threatening batsman if he got a start, cutting firmly and hitting powerfully to leg. From a start in big cricket in which he was regarded as a "rabbit" with the bat, he progressed to make 131 against South Australia in 1896–97 at Sydney, the first century he had made since 1883, when he scored 163 against Victoria.

Tom Garrett, born at Wollongong, New South Wales, was a highly popular cricketer whose Test career began when he played against Lillywhite's England side in the first two Tests in 1876–77. He was only 18 years and 232 days old when he played in the first ever Test and in 1982 remained the youngest Australian to play in a Test v. England. (See Ages of Cricketers.) He toured England with the Australian team in 1878, again in 1882 when he played in the historic Ashes match, and for a third time in 1886. He was a skilful sprinter which helped his performance in the field.

In his prime as a bowler he used his 6 ft high frame well, releasing the ball from as high a point as he could reach, moving the ball quickly off the pitch, and swinging it either way in the right conditions. He took more than 100 wickets on the 1882 (128 at 13.74) and the 1886 (123 at 18.05) tours in all matches. In 1882, the four matches between Yorkshire and Australia brought him 27 wickets at around nine runs each.

Garrett played for Australia in seven Test series at home and finished with a career total of 19 Tests. His best series was in 1881–82 when he took 9 for 163 in the Third Test at Sydney and finished the series with 18 wickets at 20.38. In Tests, his best score was 51, he took seven catches, and 6 for 78 was his best analysis. Figures apart, he should be remembered for his clever captaincy.

First-Class Averages: Batting, 3,673 runs at 16.18; Bowling, 445 wickets at 18.77.

Tests (19): 339 runs at 12.55; 36 wickets at 26.94.

Clubs formed by the officers and soldiers stationed in Sydney and Hobart which played a big role in cricket in the colonies in the 1850s. Both were commanded by men who were very keen cricketers and the success of their teams brought rejoicing and liberal toasting in the barracks.

The formation of the Hobart Garrison Club in the 1840s by the commanding officer of the 96th Regiment, Col. Cumber-

GARRISON CLUBS

land, was an important early landmark in Tasmanian cricket as it increased interest in the game and led to the formation of clubs at Sorrell, New Norfolk, Green Ponds, Clarence Plains and Richmond. Officers such as Colonel Cumberland, Captains Denison, Miller and Eyton often played but the two sergeants, Miller and Windibank, carried the team. Occasionally Garrison and Derwent players combined to meet country teams.

The first match in Sydney at the back of the Victoria Barracks on what became the Sydney Cricket Ground was played in February, 1854, between soldiers from the Garrison Club and the Royal Victoria Club. The Garrison Club batted first and made 67 and 56. The Royal Victorians made 106 in their first knock and only had to score 18 runs in the second to win, but in a dramatic upset the Garrison Club got them out for 16. The last batsman was run out trying for a run that would have tied the scores. Privates Tester and Harefield were the Garrison Club heroes for taking all the Royal Victorian's wickets.

On December 6, 1856, the Garrison Club and the Royal Victorian Club played the first match ever on what became the Sydney Domain. This ground was set aside to give the cricketers of Sydney a field of their own away from the overcrowded Hyde Park. In the 1860s the Military and Civil Club took over from the Garrison Club and the Garrison Club's home ground just behind Victoria Barracks changed its name from the Garrison Ground to the Military and Civil Ground. The Garrison Races were held there and cricket matches continued there until they were moved to Moore Park and to the Cricket Ground.

GAUNT, Ronald Arthur, 1934–

First-Class Averages: Batting, 616 runs at 10.44; Bowling, 266 wickets at 26.85.

Tests (3): 6 runs at 3.00; 7 wickets at 44.28.

A strong, thickset right-arm fast medium bowler of determination and stamina whose career was dogged by problems with dragging. He frequently came under close inspection from umpires and bowled too high a percentage of no-balls. He batted left-handed with little success, but was an efficient field, holding 31 first-class catches. He took five wickets or more in an innings 10 times and made three overseas tours with Australian teams.

Gaunt, born at Yarlu, Western Australia, played for WA from 1955–56 to 1959–60. He toured New Zealand in 1956–57 and 1959–60 and South Africa in 1957–58, both teams captained by Ian Craig. He replaced Ian Meckiff in one of the South African Tests, taking 2 for 82. He moved to Victoria and first appeared for that state in 1960–61. He missed a place in the home series that year against the West Indies but a series of strong performances for Victoria earned him a place in the

1961 Australian team in England under Benaud. His best performance was 3 for 53 in the drawn Fifth Test, and he topped the tour bowling averages with 40 wickets at 21.87 in all matches. He took 2 for 137 in one Test against South Africa in 1963–64.

In 85 first-class matches red-haired Gaunt's best figures were 7 for 104 for WA against NSW at Sydney. He took five wickets or more five times for WA in taking 109 wickets at 26.55. For Victoria, he took five wickers or more three times and a total of 67 wickets at 26.35.

GEHRS, Donald Raeburn Algernon ("Algie"), 1880–1953

A dashing right-handed batsman for South Australia in the early years of this century, but a disappointment in matches for Australia. Gehrs blend of tight defence, clean, hard driving and strong pulls and hooks often proved match-winners for his State in a career that lasted from 1902 to 1921. He was taken to England in 1905, but could not produce the high scoring he unwound for his State.

His tour to England brought 612 runs, best score 83, average 21.10 in all matches. On the international level these were poor figures compared to his 3,387 runs for South Australia at 39.38, with a top score of 170 among his 13 centuries, many of them thrilling displays of stroke play. He was the first batsman to score centuries in each innings of a match for South Australia, 148 not out and 100 not out against Western Australia at Fremantle in 1906.

Gehrs was first tried in a Test against "Plum" Warner's 1903–04 MCC team. Australia won by 218 runs but Gehrs scored only eight runs in two innings. He played in a Test for Darling's touring Australians in England in 1905 but again flopped. At home he did better against South Africa in 1910–11 making four Test appearances, scoring 67 at Sydney and 58 at Melbourne.

For South Australia he was often the batsman on whom match-winning scores were built, three times heading the State's batting averages (1904–05, 1905–06 and 1908–09) despite the presence of high scoring batsmen like Clem Hill, Edgar Mayne and J. N. Crawford. In 1910–11, when South Australia made a great effort to retain the Shield they had won for the second time the previous season, Gehrs got to 94 with South Australia needing six runs to score 304 and win the match against Victoria at Adelaide. Amid wild cheering he lay back and hooked the ball high into the stand to finish on 100 not out in a style even Doug Walters could not have bettered. Gehrs topped the aggregate for Adelaide club cricket in 1912–13, scoring 763 runs in 11 innings for North Adelaide at an average of 69.36.

First-Class Averages: Batting, 4,377 runs at 33.67; Bowling, 7 wickets at 49.20. Tests (6): 221 runs at 20.09.

GIBBS, Lancelot Richard, 1934–

A right-arm off-spin bowler from Guyana who, in a first-class career that took him to every corner of the cricket world between 1953 and 1976, took 1,024 wickets and scored 1,729 runs. He averaged 27.22 runs per wicket and 8.55 runs an innings with the bat. He also took 309 wickets in 79 Tests and for a period was Test cricket's highest wicket-taker, Dennis Lillee passing his record in 1981–82. He played for Warwickshire for several seasons in the English County Championship.

In between Gibbs fitted in a season playing for South Australia in 1969–70, when he coached in Adelaide. He took 18 wickets at 33.27, but SA finished at the bottom of the Sheffield Shield competition. He was extremely popular among the schoolboys he coached and became widely respected by his fellow cricketers for his knowledge of racehorses.

GIBSON, George Watson Hogg, 1827–1910

First-Class Averages: Batting, 214 runs at 16.46.

A Jamaica-born right-handed batsman and wicket-keeper who played for Victoria between 1865 and 1872. In nine games, Gibson, who played for the Melbourne Club, had a topscore of 41, against New South Wales in 1872. For compiling this score, *Wisden* reported that he was presented with a bat made from a willow tree that grew in his Melbourne garden. He took four catches and made four stumpings.

GIFFEN, George 1859–1927

One of the finest all-rounders Australia has produced, a wide-shouldered, heavily-moustached 5 ft 10 in tall, 11 st 9 lb specimen with vast fists who performed with great spirit whether batting, bowling or fielding and behaved with dignity on and off the field. He was inclined to pick and choose which tours and big games suited him and sometimes refused to play unless his brother Walter, who was far below George's class, was also included in the Australian team.

He was called Australia's W. G. Grace and remains one of the few Australian players to have a grandstand named after him (at Adelaide Oval). He was the first of seven Australians to have scored 1,000 runs and taken 100 wickets in Tests. He broke new ground when in 1898 he published a book on cricket, still an invaluable work for historians, as fascinating as the man, warm-hearted, blunt and to the point, and respectful of cricket's enduring virtues. And what an industry that book started!

Giffen, born in Adelaide, started his career with the Norwood club but later played for West Adelaide. He headed the South Australian batting averages seven times between 1887–88 and 1902–03 and topped the bowling averages 11 times between 1880–81 and 1902–03. In 1890–91, he topped the Adelaide "A" grade batting averages with 195.66. In 1876–77, he headed the "A" grade bowling averages with an average cost per wicket of 3.88. For Norwood, he took all 10 wickets against Adelaide in 1893 and then scored 172 not out. In 1890 for the same club he made 296 against South Adelaide in adding 345 for the fourth wicket with J. E. Godden. For West Adelaide, he made 167 not out while he and E. Bailey put on 308 for the second wicket.

He made his debut for South Australia in 1880 and made the first of his five tours of England two years later, a right-arm slow-medium bowler of off-breaks and cutters who flighted the ball cleverly and varied his pace, and an accomplished right-hand batsman who defended stoutly and was alert for chances to produce flowing, heavily-struck drives. He was a fine field in any position.

For years at a spell he virtually *was* the South Australian team, with the outcome of that State's matches depending on his performance. On the international level he was sometimes overshadowed by Spofforth, Ferris, Turner, Trumble and Palmer but he had some great moments. He performed the hat-trick and scored 203 for South Australia against Vernon's English team in 1887–88 at Adelaide and twice took hat-tricks for Australian teams—against Lancashire at Manchester in 1884, and against an England XI at Wembley in 1896. At Sydney in 1895 he helped get England out for 65 and 72 by taking 3 for 14 and 5 for 26!

The finest performance of Giffen's career came in the 1891–92 Australian summer when he scored 271 for South Australia against Victoria and then took 16 wickets for 166 runs, a feat which noted English historian Harry Altham said was "surely the greatest all-round performance in recorded cricket history of any class". Altham, incidentally, was firmly of the opinion that Giffen was Australia's best-ever all-rounder, though many would prefer Monty Noble.

Giffen toured England in 1882, 1884, 1886, 1893 and 1896, and declined to tour twice, in 1888 and 1890. He also visited the US, Canada and New Zealand. Brother Walter went in 1893 with not much to recommend him but big scores in Adelaide club matches. George turned the ball far more in England, shrewdly giving it air, and developed a superb high slower ball that secured many caught-and-bowled dismissals. When he spread that vast hand around the ball it almost disappeared among fingers he had developed as a postal worker.

On his first tour of England in 1882, George said he learned how to groom himself well for all occasions and how to adhere to basic principles such as bowling to a line and length and playing straight with the bat. He made 873 runs on that tour at 18.18 and took 32 wickets at 22.75 in all matches, bowling a third the number of the overs bowled by Spofforth, Boyle, Palmer and Garrett. In low-scoring matches, it was hard to get the ball.

First-Class Averages: Batting, 11,757 runs at 29.61; Bowling, 1,022 wickets at 21.31.

Tests (31): 1,238 runs at 23.35; 103 wickets at 27.09.

He scored 180 against Gloucestershire at Bristol and 171 against Yorkshire at Bradford, both in 1893. On his last tour of England in 1896 he played a major role in Australia's thrilling three wicket win over England at Old Trafford, scoring 80 in a 131-run partnership with Frank Iredale which helped Australia to what turned out to be a match-winning total of 412, and then helping to tie the Englishman down with clever bowling.

At home he often was a match-winner. When Australia won the Second Test at Sydney in 1891–92, he followed his first innings 4 for 88 with 6 for 72, helping to bundle England out for 157 when they needed 230 to win. He made his sole Test century at Sydney in 1894–95 when he added 171 with Iredale and 139 with Syd Gregory to reach 161. Seven times in Tests he took five wickets or more in an innings, with 7 for 117 and 7 for 128 his best figures. In 53 Test innings he made more than 50 six times. He took 24 Test catches. He was still playing for South Australia in 1902–03 when almost 44, scoring 81 and 97 not out and taking 15 wickets for 185 against Victoria. He later became a respected coach.

Giffen captained Australia four times in 1894–95 for two wins and two losses. In one of the matches he lost as captain he scored 108 runs and took 5 for 236 but England won by six wickets. He was not a good captain because he never knew when to take himself off. To Giffen, a change of bowling simply meant changing ends.

For the Fourth Australian team against The Rest at Sydney in 1883–84, he took all ten second innings wickets for 66 runs off 26 overs, the first time a bowler had taken 10 wickets in an innings in a first-class match in Australia. He bowled throughout the innings and only two other bowlers, Palmer and Boyle, were used. But perhaps the best demonstration of Giffen's value was in England in 1886 when he in five successive innings took 40 wickets for 222 runs.

Giffen made 18 centuries, including four double centuries and seven centuries for South Australia, top score 271 against Victoria in 1891–92. He also took five wickets or more in an innings an astonishing 48 times.

GIFFEN, Walter Frank, 1863–1949

First-Class Averages: Batting, 1,178 runs at 15.92.

Tests (3): 11 runs at 1.83.

A right-handed batsman, brother of George, whose promising career was upset when he lost the tops of two fingers on his left hand in an accident at an Adelaide gasworks. Walter had shown that he was an above average batsman who could hit hard when required, but whose strength lay in his resolute defence. He was an exceptional outfielder, with a powerful throw.

Walter played 13 matches for South Australia, top score 89.

He was educated at Caler's College and played for Mitcham in Adelaide district cricket. On the strength of his heavy scoring in district cricket, he was chosen in 1893 to tour England with the Eighth Australian team under Blackham. His elder brother George was said to have insisted on Walter's inclusion in the team for England. Walter scored 245 runs, best score 62, average 15.31 in all matches.

GILBERT, Eddie, 1908–1978.

First-Class Averages: Batting, 224 runs at 7.22; Bowling, 87 wickets at 28.97.

A dynamic Aboriginal fast bowler who at his prime ranked second only to Bradman among Queensland fans. He bowled at sizzling pace after taking only four or five paces up to the stumps, but was moody and unpredictable and did not always let them fly. He was endowed with very long arms and wiry frame and achieved his pace with a right arm that swung in such a blur it was difficult to assess claims that he threw. He did not swing the ball, relying on pace. A shoulder injury restricted his first-class career to five years. He came from the Barambah Aboriginal settlement (later Cherbourg) and lived there for most of his life as a ward of the State.

Just before Christmas, 1931, Gilbert had Bradman out for a duck after five balls of what Bradman said was the fastest bowling he ever faced. Gilbert hit Bradman with the fourth delivery and had him caught by wicket-keeper L. W. Waterman off the next ball. A few minutes earlier Waterman had caught Wendell Bill off Gilbert. At the end of the match the New South Wales team manager, A. L. Rose accused Gilbert of throwing and claimed his bowling was a blot on the game. Rose said four of NSW's leading players were emphatic that Gilbert threw. Bradman wrote later that Gilbert's bowling looked fair from the pavilion but that "when batting against him if he did not actually throw then he certainly jerked it."

Gilbert was a quiet, unassuming figure, 5 ft 8 ins tall and weighing around 9 stone. He won his way into country representative teams with striking figures for Barambah teams on concrete and in 1930–31 played in the Country Colts XI that soundly beat Brisbane Metropolitan Colts. He took 6 for 29 off 14 overs. The other four wickets went to Jack Pizzey, later a Queensland cabinet minister. Fieldsmen complained as hard as batsmen about Gilbert's bowling, claiming they had extreme difficulty following the ball from bat to hand. When Gilbert took 6 for 82 off 20 overs for Queensland Colts against NSW Colts, he was picked for his first match in the Queensland senior side against South Australia. He took 2 for 22 from 11 overs, with several catches spilled, in SA's first innings of 72, and 2 for 76 from 19 overs in the second innings. In the following match against NSW (without Bradman), he had 4 for 118 from 25 overs in a total of 566.

He had moderate success on the southern tour and finished

the summer with 15 Shield wickets for 502 runs. He had a spectacular match against the West Indies, taking 5 for 65 and 2 for 26 before retiring injured. Learie Constantine hit Gilbert for a mighty six over square leg and Gilbert walked down the pitch to congratulate him. Later Gilbert retaliated by hitting Constantine high over the fine leg fence.

At Brisbane in 1931–32 NSW dismissed Queensland for 109 on a soft wicket. Then followed the period of play in which Gilbert had Bill and Bradman out with the score at 2 for 0. A short time later Kippax was taken to hospital after being struck by Thurlow, but Fingleton and McCabe held out until stumps. Next day Fingleton made 93, McCabe 229 not out. McCabe hit Gilbert audaciously at times without completely mastering him and Gilbert finished with 4 for 74 off 21 overs. In the second innings for Queensland against South Africa soon afterwards he took the first four wickets for 42.

Umpire Andy Barlow no-balled Gilbert 11 times in three overs in the 1931–32 match at Melbourne between Queensland and Victoria, during which spell Gilbert dismissed Jack Ryder. Gilbert took no further part in the match, but in the Adelaide match against South Australia Test umpire George Hele did not call him. Gilbert finished that season with 21 Shield wickets.

In 1932–33, he began to have problems with his shoulder and did not go south with the Queensland side, taking 4 for 140 in his only two Shield matches. He gave Jardine's English XI batsmen plenty of trouble in the Brisbane match but poor catching saw him finish with 2 for 93. But he did hit Jardine a fearful blow on the hip. He did not appear at all in the 1933–34 season because of his shoulder troubles and in 1934–35 played in only two games, taking 9 for 178 (6-64 and 3-114) against NSW in one of his best efforts and 5 wickets for 77 runs in the match with Victoria. He played his final Shield season in 1935–36 when he had 19 wickets for 700.

Slow motion photographs of his action were inconclusive about whether Gilbert threw. But they did stress that he had an exceptionally long bone formation in the area where the forearm joins the wrist. After his retirement Gilbert's pace bowling became a Queensland legend, much of it fanciful. One account had him performing a tribal dance when he got Bradman. Others depicted him as a physical giant. In fact he was a small, modest fellow. He was the inspiration for David Forrest's noted short story *That Barambah Mob*, in which one of Gilbert's victims proudly displayed words from a cricket ball imprinted in reverse on his biceps "When that ball hit the concrete", said the narrator, "you'd see this little wisp of smoke when she come at yer like the hammers of hell".

When Eddie Gilbert was discovered in the mental hospital at Cherbourg in 1972, having spent 23 years there, he was incapable of speech. Attempts were made to move him to more comfortable quarters but the Protector of Aborigines said in Brisbane that he could only agree to a move if Gilbert were placed in suitable employment with a responsible person. No job and no guardian could be found.

A multi-talented, left-arm fast-medium bowler and hard-hitting batsman whose first-class career was interrupted when he joined World Series Cricket. When the dispute between WSC and the Australian Cricket Board was settled, he chose to return to the Newcastle district where he had been born and drift out of big cricket. He performed with sporadic brilliance in a career that covered 75 first-class matches and tours to England and New Zealand (twice).

Gilmour, born at Waratah and bred in the Hunter Valley wine-growing district of New South Wales, moved to Sydney to develop his natural skills as a bowler, batsman and fieldsman. He joined the Western Suburbs club and for years benefited from advice of club captain Bob Simpson. In the first grade final against Balmain in 1972–73 he took four wickets in four balls and had Balmain out for 67, but Dave Renneberg then got busy for Balmain who had Wests out for the same score.

Gilmour first appeared for NSW in 1971–72 at the age of 20, scoring 122 in the second innings against South Australia. He was always a dangerous cricketer for the opposition, for he could swing a match in a few overs with his swinging left-arm deliveries, in a few blows of powerful hitting, or by dragging in spectacular catches. He made his Test debut against New Zealand in Melbourne in 1973–74 and over the next four seasons appeared in 15 Tests. He toured England with the Australian team in 1975 and in a typical display bowled Australia into the World Cup final against West Indies with a devastating spell of swing bowling against England at Headingley in humid conditions.

He faced consistent competition from Lillee, Thomson, Dymock and Max Walker for the Australian opening bowling role and he did not often get the new ball. But he was a very strong first change bowler who could sustain pressure on batsmen who survived the Lillee-Thomson onslaught. A nagging foot injury sometimes upset his bowling rhythm but could not stop the huge hits from his bat.

He toured New Zealand in 1976–77 for the second time but was a surprise omission from the 1977 Australian team that toured England, where conditions favoured his swing and ability to move the ball off the seam. After two seasons with World Series cricket, he returned to NSW in 1979–80 but was not selected again for Australia. At the start of the 1980–81 summer he returned to the Newcastle competition where he

GILMOUR, Gary John, 1951–

First-Class Averages: Batting, 3,126 runs at 30.64; Bowling, 233 wickets at 31.52.

Tests (15): 483 runs at 23.00; 54 wickets at 26.03.

435

had started by joining the Belmont club. He has made five first-class centuries, highest score 122, six times took five wickets or more in an innings, best figures 6 for 85 against England at Leeds in 1975, and took 68 first-class catches. Only when he was with WSC did he give his cricket the hard work his exceptional natural talents deserved.

GLEESON, John William ("Cho"), 1938–

First-Class Averages: Batting, 1,095 runs at 11.06; Bowling, 430 wickets at 24.95.

Tests (29, plus 1 abandoned): 395 runs at 10.39; 93 wickets at 36.20.

One of the most captivating personalities in the history of Australian cricket, a humorist of quality, whose unorthodox spinners puzzled the best batsmen of his period. He came into Test cricket late, at 29, and by tucking the middle finger of his bowling hand behind the ball had batsmen misreading his breaks wherever he played. He was an average fieldsman and could, mainly through deflections, score handy runs. He was on the original governing committee for World Series Cricket, serving in an honorary capacity as did Bob Cowper because he wanted to work towards a better deal for the players.

Gleeson, born in the New South Wales country town of Wingaree, near Kyogle, always remained a countryman in his happy, homespun attitude to cricket. He twice went round the world with the Emus, a group of bush cricket addicts who put up their own money to pay all costs, and dabbled with the Western Suburbs club before he joined Sydney's Balmain club in 1965–66 on condition Balmain—who got the money from the local Leagues Club—paid his weekly air fares to and from Tamworth. He couldn't afford it on a postal technician's pay. He had kept wicket for the Emus originally but developed his "mystery" ball because of his interest in Victorian Jack Iverson's bent finger grip.

Iverson perfected his unique grip after experiments flicking ping pong balls down a table. Gleeson learnt it by bowling at gum trees in Tamworth, starting a few metres out and moving to cricket pitch length as his control improved. He was the first to concede that the grip required long, strong fingers and could not be effective in bowlers with small hands. His fingers could handle the job because they were used to unscrambling telephone wires. He never turned the ball as sharply as Iverson (5 Tests) had done, but he used the bent-finger grip with far more subtlety.

Gleeson topped the Balmain bowling figures in 1966–67 with a strike rate of a wicket every five overs, taking 40 wickets at 17.03. His 6 for 55 against Randwick, included a hat-trick. In only his second season with the club he won State selection, topping the Shield averages with 23 wickets at 18.22. These were the best figures by any bowler in the competition and earned him a place in the Australian team that toured New Zealand that year. In eight matches in New Zealand, he took 26 wickets at 28.61, and scored 144 runs at 24. By now

436

John Gleeson shows his bent finger grip. Only bowlers with long fingers can manage it.

every cricket club bar in Australia buzzed with theories about how to read Gleeson's breaks.

Gleeson made his Test debut against India in 1967–68 and did well enough to be chosen at the end of that summer for the 1968 Australian team's English tour under Lawry. He topped our wicket-takers with 58 wickets on that English tour, although some critics thought he was used injudiciously. Alan Connolly was the next best wicket-taker with 55. Gleeson played all five Tests, taking 12 wickets at 34.75.

At home in the 1968–69 summer, he took five wickets in an innings twice against West Indies in playing five more Tests—5 for 122 in the First Test and 5 for 61 in the Second. By now it had become apparent that although Gleeson's spin was difficult to pick on pitches that offered him any assistance, his lack of deception and flight through the air placed him well below Mailey and Grimmett, O'Reilly and Benaud, among our great spinners. He went off on tour with the Australian team to Sri Lanka, India and South Africa in 1969–70 with less of an air of mystery about him but still a fine cricketer.

Indian batsmen prodded, pushed and groped against him without making contact. When he found the edges, catches went down or were denied by local umpires. Finally in a match against North Zone Brian Taber held an edged catch. The entire Australian side appealed. The umpire remained motionless. Two fieldsmen ran in from mid-off and covers and put the question again. Up went the umpire's finger. Thereupon the umpire apologised, saying that with such a strong wind blowing it had taken some time for the sound of the snick to carry to his end. On the South African part of the

437

tour Gleeson took 19 Test wickets in a soundly beaten Australian team.

Gleeson played 30 Tests according to the Australian Board of Control, but 29 according to the sanctuary at Lord's. He was chosen for the 1970–71 Test at Melbourne against England, when the toss was made and both teams nominated. Rain fell before a ball was bowled and after further rain the match was called off on the third day. The Australian Cricket Board ruled that the selected players could count this as a Test in their personal records, but Lord's ruled that as no play occurred it did not count. The ABC's ruling was important to Gleeson as he qualified for the Test Players' Superannuation Fund after 30 Tests. Nobody would begrudge such a likeable character whatever money this meant to him. He finished his career in South Africa, where he played for Eastern Province in the 1974–75 Currie Cup competition.

He played five years of Test cricket, topscore 45. His real joy, however, came from bowling, best effort 5 for 61. He also took 17 Test catches. Not bad figures for a cricketer who began his Test career in his 30th year.

GOODEN, THE FAMILY A splendid family of cricketers who helped pioneer the game in their part of South Australia. Three members of the family played for the State and all of them appeared for the Norwood club when it was first formed. **Charles Christopher Gooden** (1840–1913), the eldest in the family, introduced George Giffen to the Norwood club before it became East Torrens. **George W. Gooden**, who had been a good cricketer in England, was the first paid curator of Adelaide Oval, taking over in November, 1871. George played originally with Adelaide's Eastern Suburban club and joined Norwood with his family in 1865. He was later Town Clerk of Kensington and Norwood and was responsible for planting the trees around Adelaide Oval and improving the centre wicket.

James Edward Gooden (1845–1913), was a capital right-hand batsman and medium-pace round-arm bowler who was in the Norwood first grade team with George Giffen, J. J. Lyons, and H. Blinman when it won nine premierships in 12 years. He played for Kadinia against W. G. Grace's team in 1874, and captained South Australia in 1880–81 when it met Victoria for the first time on level terms. He was one of six batsmen who made ducks when SA were dismissed for 23, the lowest score in Australian first-class cricket in 1882–83 by Victoria. He played for Combined Australia v. Victoria in 1872–73. His 89 not out for British-born (he came from Brentford, Middlesex) players against Colonial-born players was the highest score in SA for more than three years. Jim Gooden made 172 runs at 11.46 in 16 innings for SA.

Henry Alfred Gooden (1858–1904) was a member of SA's first 11-a-side team captained by his brother Jim. He made 66 runs for SA at 16.50, topscore 49. **Norman Leslie Gooden** (1889–1966) was the only family member to score a first-class century. He did it in his first-class debut in 1912–13 against WA, scoring 102 in the second innings. This was the game in which Johnnie Moyes also made a century (104) in his first-class debut. Norman played only four innings for SA, scoring 196 runs at 65.33.

GOODMAN, Thomas Lyall, 1902–

One of Australia's most widely respected cricket writers who between 1920–21 and his retirement in 1967 covered 128 Test matches, including four series in England. He spent half a century in newspapers, starting as a copy boy with the *Evening News*. He worked as an assistant to the *News'* cricket reporter on England's 1920–21 tour of Australia, phoning in copy from the games, and in 1924–25 took over as the paper's cricket writer. After the *News* closed (with 60 years up), in 1932, he joined the *Sydney Morning Herald* as cricket and Rugby (both codes) writer. During World War II he had two years in southeast Asia as a Herald war correspondent. Only Ray Robinson among Australian cricket writers can challenge his record.

Tom Goodman, born at Parramatta, was accurate, fair and trusted with confidential information by players and officials. He helped many of them with advice on their careers, just as he calmed down hot-headed young reporters eager to break flimsily-based stories harmful to cricket. He was the Australian correspondent for *Wisden* for many years, and when Johnnie Moyes died he stepped in and finished Johnnie's book on the 1962–63 tour of Australia. He will always be remembered in the pressboxes of Australian cricket grounds.

GOONESENA, Gamini, 1931–

First-Class Averages: Batting, 5,751 runs at 21.53; Bowling, 674 wickets at 24.37.

A Sri Lankan-born right-arm leg spin bowler and right-hand batsman who completed a varied first-class career in the New South Wales team. At his prime he was a penetrative spinner who took five wickets or more in an innings 41 times and eight times had 10 wickets in a match. He could also bat splendidly and scored three first-class centuries. To complete his allround value to all the sides in which he played he held 108 first-class catches.

Goonesena was a small man, just over 5 ft in height and well under 10 stone, but he bounded to the stumps, each springy stride expressing his enthusiasm, and he gave the ball plenty of air. The leg-break was his stock delivery but he had a good wrong-un and topspinner.

He first played for Sri Lanka, then Ceylon, in 1947–48 before he went to Cambridge University. He got his Blue four years in a row and was captain in 1957. He joined the Nottinghamshire county club while he was at the university and played for Notts between 1952 and 1959 and in 1964. He recalls walking all the way out to bat against Australia at Trent Bridge, losing his wicket first ball to Ron Archer, and walking all the way back again, the whole thing taking five minutes of his cricket life. There were happier times in the West Indies with E. W. Swanton's team in 1955–56, with the Cavaliers in 1964–65 in the West Indies, and with an International XI in India, Pakistan and Ceylon in 1967–68. He settled in Sydney in 1960 and played his first match for NSW in 1960–61. He still appears in Sydney social matches.

GORRINGE, Harrison Reginald, 1928–

First-Class Averages: Batting, 228 runs at 6.91; Bowling, 89 wickets at 34.88.

An enthusiastic right-arm fast-medium bowler for Western Australia in the 1950s. His moment of glory came in the 1952–53 game at Perth against Queensland when he took 11 for 138, including 8 for 56 in the second innings. Perth cricket fans still refer to this as "Gorringe's match." His other notable performance was his 5 for 92 in 1954–55 against South Australia in Adelaide. He was a rank tailender with the bat both for WA and the East Perth and Perth clubs, but he stirred up plenty of opening batsmen, swinging the ball appreciably.

GOUGH, Francis Joseph, 1898–1980

First-Class Averages: Batting, 1,779 runs at 24.70; Bowling, 10 wickets at 92.30.

A reliable right-handed batsman in 40 matches for Queensland with a first-class career covering eight seasons. He was an efficient fieldsman who bowled occasional leg-spinners. He captained Queensland 15 times, and gave outstanding service in Brisbane grade cricket to the Toombul and Northern Suburbs clubs. His highest score in first-class cricket, 137, was scored in 1930–31, when Queensland made its highest ever first-class total of 687 in reply to NSW's 566 at Brisbane. Gough had scored 104 against England at Brisbane the previous summer. Gough clean bowled Bradman for his first duck in first-class cricket in December, 1927—the first of several leg-spinners to upset the great man.

GOULD, William John, 1872–1908
First-Class Averages: Batting, 346 runs at 18.21; Bowling, 24 wickets at 25.45.

A wonderful schoolboy cricketer who played later for New South Wales. In 1893–94 he toured New Zealand with the New South Wales team, headed the batting averages with 337 runs in 12 completed innings and was second best bowler with 33 wickets at 12.93 apiece. He played for NSW against Lord Sheffield's team in 1892.

The English right-hand master batsman, gamesman extraordinary, right-arm round-arm bowler and guileful captain whose lusty approach to all his cricket fired Australians' ambition on his two tours of Australia and in dozens of tense matches in England. He was the best known Englishman of his time, a symbol of the British Empire with his bushy black beard and imperious manner. Many of the legendary tales about Dr Grace's tough-minded approach to the game involve Australians. When he died of a heart attack following a zeppelin raid over London in 1915, *Wisden* said that he dominated cricket in a manner unmatched by any other cricketer, and that certainly remained true until Bradman came along.

GRACE, Dr William Gilbert, 1848–1915

Grace came to Australia in 1873–74 with the Third English team and in 1891–92 captained the Twelfth English team sponsored by Lord Sheffield. On both of those tours he lorded it over the cricket fields that were sprouting in major centres, a mesmerising combination of superb stroke player and tactician, with an insatiable appetite for the game. The Melbourne Cricket Club paid W. G. £1,500 plus extras to visit in 1873–74 and £170 to each of the professionals he brought with him, which in itself was an eye-opener to those who regarded him as the purest of amateurs. Hardly a match passed without him raising a point of procedure on the field and the lessons he taught were avidly absorbed.

Grace took the primitive conditions in which he was asked to play and travel in good part and in doing so helped create a public demand for the game that endures. When Australia's first teams went to England, he helped them get matches and played in a lot of them himself. Billy Murdoch was among his closest friends and he was instrumental in organising the first of all Tests in England after the Australians encountered an understandable backlash to the 1880 Sydney riot and larrikin behaviour of Australian spectators. Sydney Pardon said in *Wisden* that W. G. had intended to retire to the life of a general practitioner until the success of the 1878 Australians revived his ambitions as a cricketer. The most brilliant part of his career was over but for the next 20 years the Australians found him their most formidable opponent. He played his last match for England in 1899 at Trent Bridge against Australia, aged 51. He scored 54,896 runs at 39.55 in first-class cricket, took 2,876 wickets at 17.92, and made 877 catches. In 22 Tests he scored 1,098 runs at 32.29 and took 9 wickets at 26.22. In all first-class matches he made 126 centuries.

An ambidextrous young Victorian whom some southern experts believe could develop into a top-class allrounder in the Alan Davidson-Keith Miller mould. Graf bowls right-arm fast medium pacers to a consistent length but needs to achieve

GRAF, Shaun Francis, 1957–

more movement off the seam. He bats left-hand, driving powerfully in front of the stumps, and is a fine field. He was given an extended trial in the Australian team in one-day matches in 1980–81 after a summer with the Hampshire County club in 1980, but missed out on a place in the 1981 Australian side in England. He was twice twelfth-man for the 1980–81 Tests against India following his innings of 100 not out against WA at Melbourne, but since then has disappointed. He was dropped from the Victorian team at one stage of the 1981–82 summer.

GRAHAM, Henry ("The Little Dasher"), 1870–1911

One of the few Australians to score a century in his first Test, a dashing Victorian right-handed batsman who relished hitting hard and always played with crowd-pleasing vigour. He had the good fortune to have a headmaster at Berwick Grammar School who advocated all-out attack. All his career Graham tried to follow that advice. He was a quite brilliant runner between wickets and when he made his maiden Test century at Lord's in 1893 he figured in a partnership of 142 in 100 minutes with Syd Gregory that rattled English fieldsmen. He had a great aptitude for all phases of cricket, was a superb fieldsman, and an occasional bowler of very good leg-breaks.

Harry Graham made such a fine impression in his first appearance for Victoria in 1892–93, that nobody was surprised when he was included in the 1893 team to tour England at the age of 22. He justified his selection by scoring 1,435 runs on the tour at 28.70, heading the averages for all matches. He scored 219 against Derbyshire at Derby (not then first-class), and in the first Test of the tour played the innings of his life, scoring the first Test century by an Australian at Lord's. He went to the crease with Australia at 5 for 75, and with a mixture of audacious driving and swings to leg flayed the bowling. He was missed three times.

George Giffen wrote that it was never easy to set a field for Harry Graham. "Unlike many Australians, when he went to the pitch of the ball, you could not tell whether he was to make a straight drive, chop the ball past cover, or swing it to leg," said Giffen. Graham returned home a celebrity and immediately justified this status with an innings of 105 against the hostile fast-rising bounce of England's Tom Richardson in the Fourth Test at Sydney in 1894–95. This brilliant hand gave him a century in his first Tests in both England and Australia, and helped Australia to a win by an innings and 147 runs.

Graham made five centuries for Victoria in an era when it was the right thing to throw in your hand after you reached the century. He began in 1895–96 with 103 against NSW, and made his last century for the State in 1902–03, when he scored

First-Class Averages:
Batting, 5,054 runs at
26.32; Bowling, 6
wickets at 39.16.

Tests (6): 301 runs at
30.10.

442

101 against Queensland. He was disappointing on his second tour of England in 1896, largely because ill health restricted him to only 30 innings. At Trent Bridge against Nottinghamshire, however, he showed glimpses of his best form in a dazzling innings of 96.

He made 169 for Melbourne CC against Canterbury at Christchurch in 1899–1900 (not first-class), 124 for Victoria v. NSW at Sydney in 1898–99; 120 for Victoria v. South Australia at Melbourne in 1900–01, 118 for Victoria v. South Australia at Adelaide in 1899–1900, 103 for Victoria v. NSW at Melbourne in 1895–96, and 101 for Victoria against Queensland at Brisbane in 1902–03. In 1903 he accepted an appointment as coach to High School boys at Dunedin, New Zealand and while he was in that job he played for Otago (1903–04 to 1906–07) and for the South Island (1903–04). He had some outstanding innings for South Melbourne in club cricket, scoring 202 against South Melbourne in 1892 and 201 against Carlton in 1898. In 1898 he and Hugh Trumble added 325 for the third wicket for Melbourne against North Melbourne. In all first-class matches between 1892 and 1906, Harry Graham scored seven centuries, two of them in Tests.

GRANT, John William, 1941–

First-Class Averages: Batting, 1,172 runs at 22.53; Bowling 110 wickets at 31.53.

A right-hand batsman and right-arm fast-medium bowler who achieved the double by scoring more than 1,000 runs and taking more than 100 wickets for Victoria in the late 1960s. He made his debut for Victoria in 1964–65 after impressive performances for the Essendon club, and in 43 games for his State had a topscore of 70. Bowling was his strength, however, and he had some exciting figures, with 5 for 79 against NSW in 1965–66, 5 for 89 against NSW in 1966–67, 6 for 37 against NSW in the same season and 5 for 25 against Queensland in 1968–69. For Victoria he took five wickets or more in an innings four times and he held 25 catches. Grant played for Rawenstall in the Lancashire League in 1967.

GRAVENEY, Thomas William, 1927–

An outstanding English-born right-handed stroke-maker who coached and played for Queensland from 1969 to 1971. He was one of the most attractive batsmen of his time and the fourth cricketer after World War II to score 100 centuries. He played for Gloucestershire from 1948 to 1960 and was captain in 1959 and 1960. He played for Worcestershire from 1961 to 1970 and was captain from 1968 to 1970. Graveney played 79 Tests for England, touring Australia three times, the West Indies twice, New Zealand twice and India and Pakistan once each. He nade 11 Test centuries, but only one in Australia—at

Sydney in 1954 when he compiled an exhilarating 111 in 120 minutes. In his 732 first-class matches he made 47,793 runs at 44.91, with 122 centuries, took 549 catches, and 80 wickets. He often had trouble coping with the higher bounce batting on Australian pitches and in his seven appearances for Queensland scored only 138 runs at 17.25, topscore 56.

GREGORY, The Family   The most celebrated family in the history of Australian cricket. The family has produced more outstanding players than such families an the Harveys, the Bannermans, Trotts, Benauds, Trumbles or the McLeods, though their contribution has recently been forgotten due to the success of the Chappells and the passage of time.

Australia's Gregory clan stem from a man and wife who migrated from London to Australia in 1814. The wife died five years later and the husband returned to England, leaving their three sons in Sydney's Male Orphanage. The sons were discharged from the orphanage only when they found jobs with tradesmen. One of them, Edward William Gregory, later became a schoolteacher and played cricket on Sydney's Hyde Park when it was a far larger playing area than it is now.

E. W. Gregory married the daughter of a politician and one-time Mayor of Melbourne, Mary Ann Smith, and they had 13 children, including seven sons, five of whom played cricket for New South Wales. Twenty of E. W. Gregory's grandsons represented New South Wales at football, sailing, athletics or cricket, and the entire family became widely known for their fertility.

Two of E. W. Gregory's five cricketing sons graduated from the New South Wales to the Australian team, Ned and Dave. A third, Arthur, wrote cricket reports for the *Sydney Morning Herald* under the name of *Short Slip*. Ned had a son, Syd, who played for Australia for almost 20 years until 1912, and another son, Charles William, who scored a triple century for the State. Arthur (1861–1929) died of injuries sustained when he fell from a tram car returning from Syd's funeral. A fourth of E. W. Gregory's sons, Charles Smith, was the father of Jack Morrison Gregory, thrilling Australian allrounder just after World War I. The complete family record in cricket shows four Test players, two Australian captains, and seven New South Wales players, but it should also be remembered that the family has made major contributions in other sports and in other fields of endeavour. Justice Rae Else-Mitchell, for example, is the son of Pearl Gregory, whose father was Australia's first Test captain, Handsome Dave. Rae Else-Mitchell was at one time president of the Royal Australian Historical Society, and has held a number of important legal posts.

444

A right-hand batsman who built an impressive record in first-class matches for New South Wales before his death from blood poisoning at the age of 32. He was the son of E. J. ("Ned") Gregory and the brother of Sydney Gregory, and was the first batsman to score a triple century in Australia. Members of the Gregory family considered him a more talented batsman than Syd, who played 58 Tests, but he had scored only two centuries in big cricket on his premature death.

Charles Gregory played for the South Sydney club for four years and then for five seasons with Waverley. At 14, he visited Brisbane with a Sydney Junior XI. In one summer with Waverley he scored 828 runs in 10 innings at an average of 103.50. He made a sound 45 against New Zealand in his first major match.

On the first day of the NSW v. Queensland match in Brisbane in November, 1906, Queensland were dismissed for 145 and Gregory had made 48 not out at stumps. On the second day he took his score to 366 not out with an exciting display of strokemaking. On the third day he was out for 383, NSW finishing with 763 and winning by an innings, when Queensland made 316 in their second knock. Charles Gregory had made 102 against Queensland on the same ground in a NSW total of 692 only a year earlier, so they had good cause to remember him in Brisbane!

GREGORY, Charles William, 1878–1910

First-Class Averages: Batting, 1,546 runs at 32.89.

Australia's first cricket captain, a right-handed New South Wales batsman with a vast, distinguished beard who was appointed for the first Test at Melbourne in 1877 by a team that included six Victorians. He was a man of commanding presence, much sought after by the ladies, who was a keen student of the tactics advocated by the famous ex-Surrey player, William Caffyn. He was known throughout the colonies as "Handsome Dave." He was unanimously elected by his fellow players without assistance from selectors, committees, or using his own vote.

Dave Gregory looked a leader players would follow, 6 ft 2 in, 14 st 4 lb, erect in bearing, and confident in his decision-making. He enjoyed the company of cricketers, drank and smoked freely with them but was never seen the worse for it. His batting was safe and unhurried, with little style or polish but he could hit powerfully to the off. He set an example to team-mates in the slips at a time when this position was comparatively new to them, and he showed plenty of initiative in off the field organising.

He was born at Fairy Meadow, south of Sydney, while his father was teaching at Wollongong school, one of 13 children, seven of them boys. He went to St James' Church of England school in Sydney, where he won a medal for a good pass that

GREGORY, David William, 1845–1919

First-Class Averages: Batting, 889 runs at 14.57; Bowling, 29 wickets at 19.06.

Tests (3): 60 runs at 20.00.

earned him a job in the accounts section at Government House. He played cricket in Sydney's Domain with his brothers Ned, Walter, Charlie and Arthur on a pitch laid out with a spirit-level by members of the National Club, who played matches against hotel sides or teams of garrison soldiers.

At the time Victoria dominated Australian cricket, largely through the efforts of John Conway, Sam Cosstick and Thomas Wills, who had carried off the prizemoney in single wicket matches against New South Wales opponents. Sydney supporters of the game decided to back Ned, Dave and Charlie Gregory to beat the Victorians and for weeks they practised daily for their clash with the Victorians. A crowd estimated at 5,000 turned up to the Albert ground at Redfern to watch the Gregorys win the match after a row about a Victorian umpire no-balling Dave which led to an English-born umpire, William Caffyn, taking over.

This success established the family reputation and no doubt assisted Dave some years later when an All-Australian XI met the All-England team led by William Lillywhite at Melbourne in what later became recognised as the First Test. Dave was 31. He won the toss as the democratically elected captain of a team comprising six Victorians and five New South Welshmen. England were expecting to win comfortably but an innings of 165 by opening batsman Charles Bannerman gave Dave Gregory an edge he held to the end, Australia winning by 45 runs.

Dave did nothing extraordinary in this Test, but he learned quickly from England's field placements. Casting State loyalties aside, he gave Victorians most of the bowling. He now had a great respect for Conway and in the final innings accepted his advice to give left-hander Tom Kendall most of the bowling. All the winning team were presented with medals commemorating their win, but Dave Gregory's was bigger than the rest.

A fortnight later in the return match that became recognised as the Second Test Dave Gregory batted at No. 10 in Australia's first innings of 122. With his team trailing by 139 runs on the first innings, he promoted himself to open the second innings with Nat Thompson. They put on 88, with Gregory scoring 43, Thompson 41. It was Dave's highest Test score but it did not prevent England winning by four wickets.

Success of the two international matches in Melbourne convinced John Conway that an Australian team should go to England. Dave Gregory backed him in his efforts to get a team away despite opposition from the Victorian and New South Wales associations. Between them they picked a side of five New South Welshmen, four Victorians and one Tasmanian, George Bailey. Conway was appointed manager, Dave Gregory captain and each man agreed to contribute £50 towards

446

tour expenses. They further boosted tour funds by playing 16 matches against the odds in Queensland, NSW, South Australia, Victoria and New Zealand on their way to England in 1878. They had no baggageman and drew lots to carry the team's cricket gear. Dave Gregory was 33, most of his players under 25, but he played in 38 of the 41 matches on the tour.

Largely because of Dave Gregory's astute captaincy the world tour by that first Australian side—they came home through America—produced £750 for each player and established international cricket. The profit was enough to set up the players for life and the knowledge of it was to rankle Australia's touring players for many years. Dave Gregory played in his third and last Test at Melbourne in 1879, and did not go to England with the second Australian touring team in 1880, which was led by Murdoch. He retained his interest in cricket, however, turning out regularly for the Albert club and continuing in inter-Colonial matches until he was 37. For five years, he was honorary secretary of the New South Wales Cricket Association.

He married three times and was the father of 16 children, 13 by his first wife, Mary Ann Hitchings, who died in 1890, and three by his second wife, Lily Leslie MacMillan, whom he married in 1892. When Lily died in 1911, he married Ellen Hillier. He was in turn Inspector of Accounts and Paymaster to the Treasury and lived in the Sydney suburbs of Paddington, Neutral Bay and finally, Turramurra. He died at 74, with all his teeth intact, never having worn glasses in his life, carriage upright to the last.

He won two and lost one of his three Tests, in all of which he was captain, but probably his finest feat was in leading Australia at Lord's in 1878 when they overwhelmed a powerful MCC side in one afternoon. Above all, he set an example in thoughtfulness and tact for all the captains who have followed him.

A leading right-hand batsman and right-hand fast medium bowler in the early days of Australian cricket, brother of Dave Gregory who captained Australia in the first ever Test, and father of Sydney Edward Gregory, who played in 58 Tests. He was born in the Sydney suburb of Waverley and for over 30 years was curator at Sydney Cricket Ground. One of his daughters married Harry Donnan.

"Ned" Gregory was the first man to make a Test duck, which he recorded in the first ever Test in 1877. He held his place in the NSW team for 15 years after his debut against Victoria in 1863. The *Sydney Mail* described him as a first-class batsman, who was also a fair bowler when on the wicket. As a fieldsman he had no equal in the colony. In one match one of his

GREGORY, Edward James ("Ned"), 1839–1899

First-Class Averages: Batting, 470 runs at 17.40; Bowling, 5 wickets at 21.20.

Tests (1): 11 runs at 5.50.

deliveries flew off the shoulder of Victorian Tom Wills' bat and Ned ran the full length of the pitch to catch it. His batting improved with age, and he was one of the few men to score freely off Spofforth. In Sydney in 1877 when the players chosen for the first Australian trip to England played a Combined XV at the Albert ground, Ned made 41 and hit Spofforth out of the attack. The *Sydney Mail* said he provided plenty of employment for fieldsmen and scored fours rapidly.

Brought up in Paddington, Ned Gregory was a professional cricketer after he left school until he took over as curator at the SCG. He worked for a spell for the Bathurst Club and made occasional appearances for the Military and Civil Club on what became the Sydney Cricket Ground. He looked after the ground for the East Sydney Club, then for the Civil Service Club, and was retained when the newly formed NSW Cricket Association took over, living in the stone house built beside the ground by soldiers from Victoria Barracks. He was well known for his jolly manner and developed a fondness for spinning yarns about old cricketers as he matured.

Ned Gregory laid out and levelled the field that became the SCG playing area, and his house was the marker between No 1 and No 2 ovals. He once wrote to newspapers advocating the establishment of a special mill to produce timber for cricket bats. He realised the inadequacy of scoreboards in use at the time and in a fortnight built one to his own design that became the forerunner of scoreboards all around the world. The boards carried figures two feet high that could be read from the remotest corners of the ground, and had dozens of places for name plates, bowlers' figures, sundries and the fall of wickets. He was a proud man when his son Syd's name went up on the board.

Ned Gregory was often in line for trips to England but lacked keenness to go because of his family obligations. He frequently took visiting English cricketers fishing on Sydney Harbour. He died in his cottage at Sydney Cricket Ground.

GREGORY, John Morrison ("Jack"), 1875–1973

First-Class Averages: Batting, 5,661 runs at 36.52; Bowling, 504 wickets at 20.99.

Tests (24): 1,146 runs at 36.96; 85 wickets at 31.15.

One of Australia's greatest all-rounders and, with Keith Miller, the most spectacular. He bowled very fast with a right-hand action that ended with a three metre leap, swinging the ball away or bouncing it high into the batsman's body from a good length. He batted left-handed, usually without gloves, swinging the bat lustily, and hit a Test 100 in 70 minutes. He was also a brilliant slips fieldsman capable of leaping either way to bring in catches, with his long arms, that other men could not get near.

There was a gusto in all he did on a cricket field that made him the biggest crowd pleaser in cricket in the years immediately after World War I. He formed with E. A. McDonald

448

one of the most hostile opening attacks of all time. Heavy-footed Gregory, all leaps and bounds, 6 ft 3½ ins tall, 14 stone, with a run up of only 14 yards, McDonald, lithe and controlled with a classic high action and an approach run that barely marked the turf.

Gregory, son of Charles Smith Gregory who played for New South Wales in the early 1870s, nephew of Dave Gregory, Australia's first Test captain, and a cousin of Syd Gregory, who played 58 Tests for Australia, attended Sydney Church of England Grammar School (Shore) on Sydney's north shore. He was born in North Sydney and captained Shore's First XI in 1911 and 1912, when he was in the GPS side. He played Rugby for the First XV, and was the school's athletics champion in 1910–11–12. Then he went into grade cricket for North Sydney but had not progressed beyond third grade when he joined the first AIF.

He served in England and France with artillery units and while stationed at Salisbury won the AIF 100 yard sprint, 120 yard hurdles, and the tennis cup for his squadron. New South Wales batsman Frank Buckle, who was in the same unit, recommended him to the selectors of the first AIF team. Thus Gregory make his first-class debut in England without ever playing first grade in his native State, taking over the role of the AIF's main pace bowler when Cyril Docker hurt his back. In one match Gregory damaged a finger in a fall in the outfield and Herbie Collins sent him into the slips, reasoning that it was the best place for a man with a bad hand. Gregory never moved from the position, taking 195 catches there in his first-class career.

Gregory remains the only Australian to take 100 first-class wickets in his debut season (1919). He took six wickets in an innings six times for the AIF, with 7 for 56 against Worcestershire, 7 for 83 against C. I. Thornton's England XI, and 7 for 100 against Kent his best figures in England, where he also made 115 against Northants. On the South African part of the tour he had 9 for 32 against Natal at Durban and 7 for 21 against Natal at Pietermaritzburg. When the AIF side arrived home, he had innings of 122 and 102 in the match against New South Wales at Sydney. On the entire AIF tour through three countries he made 1,727 runs and took 198 wickets in first-class matches, a truly remarkable debut in big cricket.

But it was not until the first Test series after World War I, in 1920–21 against England, that Gregory confirmed his place among Test cricket's great all-rounders. He was third in the Australian batting averages with 442 runs at 73.66, third in the bowling averages with 23 wickets at 24.17, and took 15 catches, which in 1982 was still a series record for a fieldsman. He hit 100 in the Second Test, 93 in the Fifth and had three innings in the 70s. In the Third Test of that series he bowled with McDonald as his partner for the first time.

Jack Gregory's spectacular kangaroo hop in the delivery stride.

McDonald was not a big success at home in 1920–21 but when the Australians moved to England the following summer under Armstrong's captaincy McDonald flowered. Between them Gregory and McDonald took 46 Test wickets.

They peppered English batsmen in almost every match and the cream of England's batting talent reeled under an onslaught that produced bruised fingers and ribs, nasty blows to the chest and some around the heart. They won the First Test in two days by 10 wickets, the Second by eight wickets, and the Third by 219 runs. When he wasn't enthusiastically batting or bowling, the bareheaded, sun-tanned Gregory leapt yards to drag in slips catches off Mailey. England used 30 players in the series but some were dismissed by simply losing their nerve against the Australian pace attack. On the entire tour Gregory and McDonald took 270 wickets between them in all matches.

On the way home they carried on their mayhem in South Africa, with Gregory scoring a century in 70 minutes in the Johannesburg Test, still the fastest Test century. David Frith has recorded how McDonald shattered South African opener Jack Zulch's bat in this match, sending a fragment into the stumps. By the time they returned home Gregory's furious bowling speed was waning. He played in the 1924–25 series against England but his 22 wickets were costly. On his second tour of England in 1926 he managed only 36 wickets on the entire trip, with only three in five Tests for 298 runs. The curtain finally came down at Brisbane in the Fifth Test of the 1928–29 season when Gregory at the age of 32 broke down with torn knee ligaments.

Jack Gregory took 37 Test catches. In all first-class cricket he scored 13 centuries in 129 first-class games, holding 195 catches, and taking five wickets in an innings 33 times. He spent his final years in seclusion in a cottage at Bega, on the New South Wales south coast, hobbling about on busted knees, playing bowls and fishing, and occasionally returning to Sydney for reunions with his old AIF team-mates.

GREGORY, Ross Gerald, 1916–1942

First-Class Averages: Batting, 1,874 runs at 38.24; Bowling, 50 wickets at 35.34.

Tests (2): 153 runs at 51.00.

A brilliant shot-maker who, in 1936–37, helped Australia recover from the loss of the first two Tests against England to win the next three and retain The Ashes. Gregory's 80 in the decisive Fifth Test overshadowed even the batting of Bradman (169), McCabe (112) and Badcock (118) in an Australian total of 604. "Heaven bless us," Neville Cardus wrote of Gregory's innings, "We have again witnessed strokes in a Test match, gay and handsome and cultured strokes."

This was Ross Gregory's second Test and his exhilarating 80 came on the day before his 21st birthday. It was also his last Test, for he was killed at Ghafargon in Assam while serving

The late Ross Gregory, left, going out to bat with Don Bradman during the Fifth Test against England at Melbourne in 1936–37.

with the RAAF, aged 26. His omission from the 1938 tour of England had caused some surprise and his tragic premature death was a great loss to cricket.

For Victoria, for whom he made his debut in 1933–34 while still at school, his highest score was 128 against England in 1936–37 at the MCG. For St Kilda, where he had Ernie Bromley, Hec Oakley, Stuart King, Bill Newton and Bill Pearson as team-mates, he scored 1,357 runs in five seasons at 30.10, best score 155 not out.

A copybook, fast-scoring right-hand batsman and brilliant cover-point fieldsman whose fast footwork carried him through 58 Tests, eight tours of England, three to America, and one each to South Africa and New Zealand. He made only four centuries in 100 Test innings but scored well enough to hold his place in the Australian side for 22 years. At the age of 42, he was recalled to captain Australia on a 37–match tour of England. He was also one of the smallest Test batsmen at 5 ft 4 ins, but he was also one of the most venturesome runners between wickets.

Syd Gregory was born to play big cricket in a cottage on the present site of Sydney Cricket Ground which his father Ned Gregory, the ground's curator, built and maintained. Ned played for Australia in the first ever Test when Syd was six. Syd was the nephew of D. W., C. S., and A. H. Gregory, brother of C. W. Gregory, cousin of J. M. Gregory, and brother-in-law of Harry Donnan, all of whom played for New South Wales. Syd began his cricket education with the Sydney club but when the metropolitan clubs adopted electoral boundaries

GREGORY, Sydney Edward ("Little Tich"), 1870–1929

First-Class Averages: Batting, 15,192 runs at 28.55; Bowling, 2 wickets at 197.00.

Tests (58): 2,282 runs at 24.53.

451

Syd Gregory favoured open-slatted pads, a glove on only one hand and a high grip on the bat handle.

he played for Waverley. He first appeared for New South Wales at 19 and held his place in the State side until he was 43.

He made his first tour of England in 1890 at the age of 20, scoring 568 runs at 12.62, best score 59 not out, but he did a lot better on the seven English tours that followed, establishing himself as a brave batsman in a crisis, and saving countless runs in the field. He was the first Australian to follow his father into the Test side when he played in the 1890 series. He grew a moustache on that tour which he waxed and curled into points at the ends. He normally batted in open-slatted pads, with only his bottom hand gloved, and a sash as a waistband.

He showed a profit of around £400 on his first trip to England, far more than he earned as a post office clerk, but the second tour in 1893 was a financial flop. On that trip, however, he made his highest score in seven Test innings, 57 out of a partnership of 142 with Harry Graham that saved the Lord's Test for Australia. He made 1,162 runs on the 1893 tour at 23.71, 1,464 at 31.82 in 1896 when he topped the tour averages, 1,181 at 27.46 in 1899, 999 at 21.71 in 1902, 717 at 25.60 in 1905 when he played in only 18 of the 38 tour matches, 684 at 19.54 in 1909, and 1,055 at 23.44 in 1912. These figures covered all tour matches.

In a Test career that produced eight scores over fifty, the highlight was his 201 in December, 1894, at Sydney. This was the first double century in a Test in Australia and took him only 270 minutes. He added 139 with Giffen, and 154 in 73 minutes in a spectacular ninth wicket stand with Blackham that remains the Australian record. Australia scored 586 in that innings but lost the match by 10 runs when caught on a saturated pitch chasing 177 in the final innings. A collection at the ground for Gregory yielded £103/10/-. He also scored 103 at Lord's in 1896 when he and G. H. S. Trott (143) put on 221 for the fourth wicket, 117 at The Oval in 1899 and 112 at Adelaide in 1903–04.

For New South Wales, Syd Gregory made eleven entertaining centuries, 171, 147 and 186 not out in matches against England, 176, 168, 182 and 152 against South Australia, 101, 201, 179, and 169 not out against Victoria. Most of these knocks were full of hefty drives and splendid hooks, but he could stonewall with the best of them when necessary, batting with a grip high on the handle and an upright stance. For Australia in matches against the Rest Of Australia, he also had innings of 106 and 126 not out. Altogether he made 25 centuries in first-class cricket, 10 of them in England. At Trent Bridge in 1890 he once batted for 50 minutes without scoring when Australia was in a critical position against Nottinghamshire. Against Gloucestershire at Cheltenham in 1896, he went in with Australia 6 for 54 and produced an aggressive 71

452

Syd Gregory, right, with fellow captains C. B. Fry, centre, and Frank Mitchell, during the Triangular Tests in England in 1912.

not out. He was repeatedly at his best when his team were in difficulties on wet or damaged pitches.

His running between wickets frequently disorganised fielding sides and occasionally brought his own dismissal. At The Oval in 1909 he was run out for 74 after an opening partnership of 180 with Bardsley, but the stand remained the Australian record until Simpson and Lawry beat it in 1964. The footwork and powerful wrists and forearms that characterised his batting were also evident when he fielded and he pulled off many amazing saves. At the age of 40 he ran out Edgar Mayne and C. E. Simpson off successive balls, returning the ball to the bowler's end in C. T. B. Turner's benefit match. He took 25 Test catches and 174 in his first-class career.

Syd Gregory was so often absent overseas he lacked the time to consolidate himself in business, though most of his tours yielded useful sums. Ray Robinson reported that he spent £280 out of the £400 profit from one tour buying a house at Bondi Junction. But the fact that he had to leave people running his Sydney shop who turned out to be unreliable in Australia led to bankruptcy in 1903. He was discharged two years later, and in 1906–07 was given a Testimonial that brought in £630, in which he scored 94. This innings led to his recall to the NSW team and he made 201 in a 317 stand with Monty Noble against Victoria. This in turn brought his return to the Australian side.

When six famous players refused to tour under the Board of Control's terms in 1912, Syd Gregory was brought in to lead the weakest side Australia has sent overseas. A dismal tour nobody watched ended with the manager, G. S. Crouch, submitting a report strongly criticising the behaviour of some players. Thereafter the Board reserved the right to exclude players from Australian touring teams for reasons other than cricket. Syd captained his team shrewdly on the field but was too easy-going to discipline players who let him down off the field, an unfortunate end to a marvellous career.

In building up an Australian appearance record of 58 Tests that lasted 40 years before Ray Lindwall passed it, he played in seven series in Australia, eight in England and one (1902–03) in South Africa. In all of that time he was an inspiration to his colleagues in the field and a joy to spectators, clever in anticipation, quick to move and fielding the hardest hits cleanly and returning the ball with deadly accuracy. "While some have beaten his achievements as a run-getter," said *Wisden*, "the cricket field has seen no more brilliant cover point."

Syd Gregory was a prolific scorer in Sydney club matches. In 1891, he made 235 for Sydney against Warwick, adding 442 with E. G. Noble (227) for the eighth. For South Sydney against East Sydney in 1895, he made 253 not out. In an innings of 219 for Waverley against Redfern in 1907, he hit six sixes and 31 fours. For a Sydney Metropolitan XI against Combined Country in 1894, he and his brother-in-law, Harry Donnan both made 201 before they retired, their partnership reaching 309 for the fifth wicket. Syd's son Leo proved an attractive shotmaker for Randwick in Sydney club cricket but he was inhibited by people who expected him to be as good and successful as his dad, the first cricketer to pass the 50-Tests mark.

GREIG, Anthony William, 1946– The most controversial figure in world cricket, who migrated to Australia after helping to mastermind the World Series Cricket breakaway. He was a colourful player whose talents blossomed on big occasions but he would be remembered if he had never scored a run or taken a wicket for the manner in which he recruited players to join WSC and then assisted in the promotion of WSC in opposition to traditional matches.

Grieg, 6ft 7in, blond and handsome, was born in South Africa, son of a Scottish father with an outstanding record in the RAF and a South African mother. He moved to Sussex at the age of 20, a fine batsman with a flair for driving dramatically to the off and high over mid-on, and a bowler who could take wickets by digging his medium-pacers or off-spinners sharply into the pitch. From the time he won a place in the Sussex side he proved he was a bold fighter who relished the challenge when his team were in trouble.

He played in 58 Test matches and scored 3,599 runs at 40.43 and took 141 wickets at 32.20, but the figures do not convey the many thrilling fight-backs. In all first-class matches he made 16,660 runs at 31.19, with 26 centuries and took 856 wickets at 28.85, holding 345 catches, mostly in the slips. At the age of 30 he was given responsibility of the England captaincy and over the next two years helped recover England's lost prestige, largely through his own personality. His innings of 110 against Lillee and Thomson at their best in Brisbane in 1974–75 was only one of many memorable achievements.

Highly paid, occupying a position of great prestige, he chose to negotiate contracts with WSC players even while traditional matches were in progress. He was dismissed from the England captaincy and banned for a time from playing for Sussex, before settling in the Sydney suburb of Vaucluse and becoming a full-time executive with the Packer organisation. His brother Ian has recently turned in some outstanding figures for Sussex, whereas Tony is restricted to occasional appearances for the Waverley district club in between television commitments. In 1982 Greig became an Australian citizen.

GRIEVES, Kenneth James, 1925–

First-Class Averages: Batting, 22,454 runs at 33.66; Bowling, 242 wickets at 29.78.

A splendid right-hand batsman, leg spin bowler and slips fieldsman developed in Sydney, who after two seasons for New South Wales, went to England where he played League cricket and had a distinguished career in County cricket. He played for Lancashire from 1949 to 1961, and was later the County captain, as a professional, for the 1963 and 1964 seasons. He was also an outstanding soccer goalkeeper who played First Division League football in England with Bolton Wanderers, a tall, dark haired wiry man with rare dexterity.

Grieves scored 29 first-class centuries, including 102 not out for New South Wales against Lindsay Hassett's Australian Services team at Sydney in 1945–46, the year he made his debut for the State. He was a fine driver all around the wicket and could pull and cut with authority. He was among the best fieldsmen in Australia when he played with the Petersham club in Sydney and took eleven catches in his initial first-class season for New South Wales. His opportunities with the ball were limited but he could turn his leg-break sharply and had a useful top-spinner.

He played League cricket in England in 1947 and 1948 with Rawtensall and in his first season with Lancashire in 1949 scored 1,407 runs at 38.02, topscore 128 and took 63 wickets at 27.06. In all, he scored more than 1,000 runs in a season 14 times for Lancashire, with 2,253 runs at 41.72 his best season in 1959, when he made four centuries. He made three double centuries for the County, 224 in 1957, 202 not out in 1959, and 216 in 1960. He toured India with the Commonwealth side in

Australian Ken Grieves hits Johnny Wardle to leg for four in a Yorkshire v. Lancashire match at Leeds.

1950–51, taking two wickets at 69.50 apiece and scoring 1,193 runs at 42.60 with two centuries, topscore 155.

Grieves played 490 first-class matches and took a remarkable 610 catches. He also stumped four batsmen when he filled in as a 'keeper. Apart from his impressive 29 centuries, he made more than 50 runs in an innings 138 times—or 50 in every third match. His bowling fell away as his batting flowered, but he took five wickets or more in an innings eight times. He is now a member of the Lancashire committee. He was one of a select group who have represented New South Wales in three sports, soccer, baseball and cricket.

GRIMMETT, Clarence Victor ("Scarlet"), 1891–1980

First-Class Averages: Batting, 4,720 runs at 17.67; Bowling, 1,424 wickets at 22.28.

Tests (37): 557 runs at 13.92; 216 wickets at 24.21.

A wizened little gnome of a man born on Christmas Day, not much of a present for batsmen, although as Robertson-Glasgow suggested, a wonderful gift for cricket. There has never been a leg-spinner of greater subtlety in Australian cricket, and there probably has never been a more diligent student of the reasons why a cricket ball spins. Bowling in his backyard in his eighties, Grimmett complained that he had lost some of his zip off the pitch, but he still loved to skip those few steps up to the stumps and curl the ball up at the batsman, arm at 45 degrees from the shoulder.

This was the New Zealand-born bowler who conferred with Mailey about how to bowl the wrong-'un and listened to Mailey's advice. They did not meet for 10 years but when they did, Grimmett blurted out: "Hey, Arthur, you told me wrong about the bosey". As Robertson-Glasgow commented, "It was

456

rather like Virgil had tricked Horace on the number of feet in a hexameter".

Grimmett's parents had a house close to the Basin Reserve in Wellington, New Zealand, where he grew up (he was born in Dunedin). He went to Mt Cook Boy's School and after school played cricket for hours at a time with four neighbours' sons, three of whom were aspiring spinners. He began in matches, however, as a fast bowler because he feared he would be punished bowling breaks. A teacher saw him bowling spin one day when he felt too tired for pace and was so impressed he told Grimmett never again to bowl fast. Clarrie bowled fast after that only when the teacher was not looking, but fortunately the teacher umpired most of his matches. From the start, Grimmett understood why a ball gripped in a certain way, veered in the air in a certain way, and then behaved in a predictable way when it hit the pitch.

He could bowl a good over–spinner or top-spinner before he was ten and adults he deceived with it were highly impressed when they asked him how he did it and discovered the ball was no fluke. He played for Wellington East club and then for Wellington Province in Plunket Shield matches and against visiting Australian teams, but when he finished his apprenticeship as a signwriter, migrated to Australia at the age of 23. He had been chosen as a reserve bowler for a New Zealand side to tour Australia but when nobody dropped out he missed the trip.

He joined the Sydney district club in 1914 and despite captains who were apprehensive about risking his spin, played his way from third grade to the firsts in his first season, taking 76 wickets. His 28 wickets in first grade cost only 10 runs each. In 1917, he settled in Melbourne and joined the South Melbourne club. He received much valuable advice from J. V. Saunders. The Victorian selectors were inconsistent in their attitudes to his spin and he alternated between the State Second XI and the State senior side, but he picked up valuable experience in matches against New South Wales in Sydney and against Johnny Douglas' 1920–21 MCC side.

Grimmett married at the end of his third season in Melbourne and settled in Prahran, where he took 67 wickets, 39, 68 and 54 in four seasons for the district club. In Prahran, too, he trained his famous fox terrier to retrieve balls he bowled on a backyard pitch. The dog would wait until he bowled an over and then carry all the balls back to the bowling crease. Convinced his opportunities in Victoria would remain limited, Grimmett moved to South Australia at the end of the 1924 season, just after taking 8 for 86 for Victoria against South Australia in the Shield.

Bowling in a cap, prematurely bald, he first played for South Australia in 1924–25, aged 34, and that year won selection in the Australian Test Team, taking 11 wickets for 82 runs

457

New Zealand-born Clarrie Grimmett at the completion of the low arm-action from which he produced sharp spin.

against England at Sydney. In the next 11 years he took 216 Test wickets at 24.21 each, and over the next 15 years 668 wickets for South Australia. In 1982 his total of wickets for South Australia was almost 350 wickets more than any other bowler.

Remarkably, he hardly ever bowled a loose ball in big matches although he continued to experiment with new tricks for hours at a time in the practice nets. He never tried a new trick until he had perfected it and thought about how a batsman would react to it psychologically. When the word went round that you could expect a wrong-un from him when you heard his fingers click, he mastered clicking his fingers with his free hand. He knew where he wanted every fieldsman and he watched everything that happened on the field, alert for a chance to fool the batsman. If he overheard an outgoing batsman tell the incoming team-mate to watch for his sharp-turning googly, he gave the newcomer a straight topspinner.

In England in 1926, he and Mailey took 27 of the 41 wickets that fell in the Tests and both finished the tour with more than 100 wickets each, Grimmett 116, Mailey 141. Grimmett was Australia's spearhead against England in Australia in 1928–29, taking 23 wickets in the five Tests, and returned to England in 1930 a superb bowler, better on soft pitches than on the hard strips at home. This time he headed the tour averages with 142 wickets at 16.79—49 wickets more than any team-mate. Against Yorkshire, he took all 10 wickets for 37 runs off 22.3 overs. When he arrived late for the game at Oxford and found that Australia had taken 5 for 15, he said: "This would never have happened had I been here."

Grimmett, New Zealand origins forgotten, sustained Australia's reputation for producing champion tea-drinkers and clever wrist spinners in 1934 when he partnered Bill O'Reilly and took 25 Test wickets against England in a tour bag of 109 wickets. He proved a handful to all cricket countries, taking 33 Test wickets in the 1930–31 series against West Indies, 33 against South Africa in 1931–32 and 44 in South Africa in 1935–36 at a cost of only 14.59 apiece. He was very cranky about missing selection for the 1936–37 series in Australia against England and the 1938 series in England and nobody who saw him bowl in 1940 could blame him. He may have been 49 but his control, his nip off the pitch, and his variety remained a sight to behold. He never forgave the selectors for dropping him when he said he was at his peak.

In all first-class matches between 1911 and 1941, this astonishing, leathery little man, with the Groucho Marx walk, took five wickets in an innings 127 times, 10 wickets in a match 33 times, and held 139 catches. Sadly, the cricket scene may never see his like again while the present emphasis on speed persists.

458

A New Zealand-born all rounder who played for Australia in the first Test on English soil. He was a last-minute replacement for the 1880 Australian team's tour of England, joining the team when Charles Bannerman became ill during the preliminary tour of Australia. He won his place because of his high scoring for East Melbourne, for whom he had an average of 155.33 in the 1879–80 season, and nobody worried too much that he was not Australian-born.

Groube, a right-hander, was born at Taranaki, but was educated in Melbourne. He first played for Victoris in matches against the odds in 1878, when he made 173 runs at 15.72 in 11 innings, topscore 36. He had only played two 11-a-side matches for Victoria in 1879–80 prior to the English tour. He was 5 ft 11 in and weighed 10 st 10 lb, bowled medium-pacers, and fielded efficiently at cover point or long-on.

On tour in England in 1880, Groube made 210 runs in all matches at 13.12, topscore 61 against Yorkshire at Huddersfield, but did not bowl. In the only Test on that tour he scored 11 and 0 at The Oval, going in first wicket down. That was the Test in which Billy Murdoch surpassed W. G. Grace's 152 with an innings of 153 not out. England won by five wickets, largely because of the absence through injury of Spofforth. Groube dropped out of first-class cricket after that tour but in 1884 scored 101 and 98 for East Melbourne against South Melbourne, adding 174 in the second innings for the last wicket with G. Gordon (80 not out).

GROUBE, Thomas Underwood, 1857–1927

First-Class Averages:
Batting, 179 runs at 8.52.

Tests (1): 11 runs at 5.50.

A high-roller among wicket-keepers, who chanced his skill and his health against a few years of enjoyment from international cricket. When he died in a Brisbane hospital at 41, it was revealed that he had suffered a heart attack a few months before the Australian tour of the West Indies four years earlier. He had known he might collapse at any time, but his cheerfulness was unfailing and gave team-mates no inkling of his condition.

In life he was far from a weakling, a warm-hearted, generous character who savoured the big moments in a fine career. He came from the Brisbane State High School, and after making his debut for Queensland in 1946–47 came to prominence with a style remarkably similar to his idol, Don Tallon. He kept wicket for Queensland for 12 years. At his best he was unsurpassed in the world. If records mean anything, I should record that Grout disposed of eight batsmen in an innings in 1959–60 playing for Queensland against Western Australia, a world record.

In the memorable 1960–61 series against the West Indies, he had 23 dismissals, and in Australia against England in 1958–59 he dismissed 20 batsmen. Twice he had eight victims

GROUT, Arthur Theodore Wallace ("The Griz"), 1927–1968

First-Class Averages:
Batting, 5,168 runs at 22.56. Bowling, 3 wickets at 38.33. Dismissals, 587 (473 catches, 114 stumpings).

Tests (51): 890 runs at 15.08. Dismissals, 187 (163 catches, 24 stumpings).

in a Test, and only 'keepers who played in a lot more Tests have had more victims than Grout. At Johannesburg in 1957–58 he took six catches in an innings. On five occasions he dismissed five batsmen in an innings.

Don Bradman said that up to the end of his playing career he was inclined to hand the laurel for finest 'keeper to Don Tallon, but Grout had not then emerged. "When he did, the resemblance in style and method was remarkable," Bradman wrote. "I don't know whether Tallon was an inspiration to Grout or a model which he copied, but without doubt their glove work was very similar. They had the same basic footwork, the same 'swoop' on the snick, the same inevitability on holding a chance, and even the same air of intent."

Grout, born at Mackay in north Queensland, first played for Queensland in 1946–47 when he visited Adelaide as a replacement for the injured Tallon, but he had to wait another seven years before Tallon retired and he got Tallon's job permanently. Wally received important grounding as a schoolboy in a combined primary schools team which played in the Brisbane "C" grade competition. He was a useful batsman as well as a budding 'keeper and in some of his occasional early appearances for Queensland played as an opening batsman, fielding at cover.

In Army service with the infantry he scored his first century as an opening bat in a Services match. He was a brash youngster, fond of a bet, who would chat up batsmen and shout the odds against fieldsmen taking a catch when he kept wicket for South Brisbane club after the war. At first State selectors preferred Doug Siggs, a future Australian hockey captain, to Grout when Tallon was away, but when Grout began to concentrate more on wicket-keeping than batting they gave him the role of Tallon's occasional deputy. When Tallon retired in the 1953–54 season Grout got the chance to press his Australian team claims. For a time Len Maddock and Barry Jarman kept him out but he finally won an Australian team berth when he was picked for the 1957–58 tour of South Africa, under Ian Craig's captaincy. It was the first of Grout's six overseas tours.

Grout squatted low behind the stumps as the Lindwalls, Benauds, McKenzies and Davidsons moved in to bowl. His diving legside catches were thrillers in four home series of Tests between 1958 and 1964, in England in 1961 and 1964, and in the West Indies, South Africa, India and Pakistan. With the bat he was skilful enough to open for Queensland and to make four first-class centuries. In 1957–58 at Johannesburg, he claimed six victims in an innings and figured in an eighth wicket partnership of 69 with Richie Benaud. He should be remembered, too, for refusing to take the bails off when Fred Titmus was stranded after colliding with Neil Hawke during a Test against England.

460

He played in some great Australian teams and his genial spirit and encouragement to team-mates helped make them great. He still holds the record for the most dismissals in a Test innings (six). His daughter became a registered umpire in Queensland men's matches.

GUEST, Colin Ernest James, 1937–

First-Class Averages: Batting, 922 runs at 19.20; Bowling, 115 wickets at 27.13.

Tests (1): 11 runs at 11.00; 0 wickets for 59.

A right-arm fast bowler for Victoria, Western Australia, and in one Test for Australia. He was a lively performer, tall and strong, with a cheerful disposition, who played in the Third Test at Sydney in 1962–63 against Ted Dexter's English team, sharing the opening attack with Alan Davidson and Graham McKenzie. "I think I got picked so 'Davo' could have a rest now and then," said Guest.

Guest, born in Melbourne, took 10 wickets (7 for 95 and 3 for 39) against Western Australia, 5 for 36 against Western Australia, and 6 for 100 against Queensland, all in 1962–63. He took five wickets or more in an innings five times. He moved to Western Australia in 1964 and represented that State at cricket and baseball. In a first-class career that ran from 1958 to 1967 his batting efforts for Western Australia, topscore 74, suggested he was a genuine allrounder, for he scored 328 runs at 32.80 in eight matches. He has been coach of the Western Australia Under-18 cricket side and in 1979 took the Australian Under-18 team to America.

GULLIVER, Kenneth Charles, 1913–

First-Class Averages: Batting, 451 runs at 34.69; Bowling, 22 wickets at 40.13.

A bounding, leg-spin bowler, handy middle order batsman, and dynamic fieldsman who played first grade for Sydney's Mosman club for 33 years. In 1982 he was still playing for the club after 56 years continuous service, captaining and coaching the sixth grade to bring promising youngsters along. "If there is anything better to do on Saturday afternoons than play cricket, I haven't heard about it," said Gulliver, who in the 1930s played for New South Colts, New South Wales Second XI and in 12 matches for the State, in one of which he was captain.

In 1935, he scored 129 as captain of New South Wales Colts v. Queensland. He was an outstanding baseballer with a legendary throwing arm who played first grade baseball for Mosman for 30 years, including a stretch of 27 years without missing a game. He represented New South Wales at baseball many times. For Mosman, he took 940 wickets and scored 8,427 runs in first grade.

H

HACK, Frederick Theodore ("Fred"), 1868–unknown

First-Class Averages: Batting, 2,138 runs at 30.11; Bowling, 5 wickets at 59.00.

A gangling 6 ft 5 in right-hand opening batsman with wide shoulders and very large feet who was extremely difficult to dislodge once he dug those well-booted feet in. He was never quite Test class but gave South Australia and the Sturt club exceptional service. He was a batsman of immense patience who waited for the right ball to hit and when he connected with a loose ball all the power of his vast frame went into the shot.

Hack first played for South Australia in 1898–1899 after impressive allround performances for Sturt. He topped the Australian batting averages in his next season, scoring 115 against Victoria at Adelaide in November and 158 not out against NSW at Sydney in January, 1900, and he finished the summer with 441 first-class runs, average 88.20. The previous season in South Australia's first visit to Queensland, he made 63 in a total of 582.

In 1900–01, he topped the Adelaide grade cricket averages for both batting and bowling, averaging 71.16 with the bat, and 14.10 with the ball. He made 110 for SA v. Victoria at Melbourne in 1901–02, and in 1902–03 played in a notable match at Unley, the Sturt club's home ground, against Lord Hawkes' team, which was on its way back to England from a New Zealand tour. Lord Hawke's XI made 553 to which SA replied with 304, following-on automatically as the laws then required. Lord Hawke's team, who would have batted if the law had been optional, then received a hammering that began with 90 from Hack. Hill made 73, Gehrs 100 for SA to reach 454, leaving the visitors 206 to win. But Hay took 9 for 67, including a hat-trick, and SA won by 97 runs.

Fred Hack was a member of the Sturt teams that won the Adelaide premiership in 1902–03 and 1904–05. His sons, **Alfred Thomas Hack** (1905–1933), a right-hand batsman and wicket-keeper, and **Reginald Norman Hack** (1907–1971), a left-hand bat and right-arm fast-medium bowler, followed him into the SA team. Alfred scored 1,081 runs for the State at 26.78, including 100 against Queensland at Adelaide in

462

1928–29, but Reginald played only one match for the State without success. Alf Hack was a noted stone-waller. At Sydney in 1929–30 he took 65 minutes to open his account and was out lbw to Chilvers for 12 after batting for 125 minutes.

A controversial fast bowler no-balled for alleged throwing in two first-class matches. He was called 20 times in those matches but in a career that saw him take 57 first-class wickets, 13 for South Australia and 37 for Western Australia, was not called in any of his other matches. He lost the top half of the third finger of his bowling hand at the age of two and from then on tried to compensate with special wrist exercises.

In his schooldays at St Peter's College, Adelaide, his unusual action caused masters to arrange a special trial. The famous Englishman Archie MacLaren, taking a private team through to New Zealand, attended the trial with Percy Chapman, George Giffen and Clem Hill. They were amazed at Halcombe's pace, and at one stage he put splints on his wrist and elbow. Hill considered his action illegal, MacLaren had doubts about it and the others considered it fair.

Halcombe played regularly for St Peter's after this test, and at 18 played first grade with North Adelaide. Two years later he was in the South Australian team, taking 2 for 26 off 18 overs in his debut against Queensland. He was exceptionally

HALCOMBE, Ronald Andrewes, 1906–

First-Class Averages: Batting, 108 runs at 4.91; Bowling, 57 wickets at 38.63.

fast but reacted sympathetically whenever he hit a batsman. Jack Gregory, Ted a'Beckett and Charles Kelleway had retired from first-class cricket and there was a big opening for a bowler of genuine pace in the Australian side. When Halcombe moved to Perth for business reasons he took 6 for 31 and 6 for 32 in 1928–29 for Western Australia against his old State and appeared a likely candidate for the Australian team to tour England in 1930. He broke English star George Geary's nose in a dramatic over at the start of the MCC's 1928–29 tour in Perth. There was no doubt that he was faster than other prospects like Laurie Nash, so the Melbourne match between WA and Victoria in January, 1930, became a virtual Test trial for him.

The day before the match umpire Andy Barlow took the unusual step of going to watch Halcombe bowl at practice. The next day WA batted first and were all out for less than 200. On the Saturday, WA captain Dick Bryant tossed Halcombe the ball and he moved in off a 15-stride run, tall, spindly and extremely long-legged. There was a sensation when Barlow at square leg called "no-ball" to the first ball and when Bryant enquired, said it was for "chucking". Barlow repeated the call three times in succession, with Halcombe whistling the ball past opening batsman Leo O'Brien. Spectators went wild when Barlow made the eighth "no-ball" call. With the crowd counting Barlow out, Halcombe completed the over bowling slows. He did not bowl again in the match. Barlow, a Melbourne railway worker, later in his career called Eddie Gilbert and the West Australian R. R. Frankish for alleged throwing.

The *Australasian* said: "Halcombe was heart-broken, and showed natural distress in the dressing-room and regarded it as the finish of his career. It was a cruel blow, for Halcombe had practically lived for his bowling and felt that he had a chance of getting into the Australian XI. The no-balling was something Halcombe had never even considered a remote possibility." Hoyt's theatre chain arranged a special magic eye filming of Halcombe's action, which proved indecisive. In Hobart a week later Halcombe was called again by umpires Buttersworth and Lonergan and one over took him 18 balls.

After the Hobart match Halcombe was not no-balled again for throwing, although he was called for dragging. He continued in first-class cricket until World War II and in one of his last matches took 5 for 30 for WA against Victoria at Perth. He was an ABC commentator in Perth for 21 years between 1946 and 1967, and one of the founders of competitive baseball in WA. He has not watched, listened to or read about cricket for years, and the events of the WSC rebellion merely increased his determination to turn his back on the game. "We were not paragons of virtue," he says of his playing days, "but we didn't cheat."

464

A right-arm medium pace bowler, useful batsman and out-standing fieldsman for Tasmania, Cambridge University and Gloucestershire. He was born in Perth, Western Australia, saw his first cricket match at St Peter's College, Adelaide, and learned to play the game at Hutchin's School, Hobart, where he was coached by Test bowler Tom Kendall. He won selection in the Tasmanian team to tour New Zealand while still at school and in the match against Canterbury took 7 for 42. Playing for the Stanley club while visiting his father in Brisbane in 1885, he took 33 wickets and was judged unlucky not to play for Queensland against the English side led by Shaw.

In his three appearances in the annual Oxford-Cambridge match (he was absent ill in 1888), Hale's best figures were 5 for 63 in 1887. After he matriculated at Trinity College, he went to Gloucestershire and presented a letter of introduction to W. G. Grace, who allowed him to practise in his back yard. The Hale family had lived at Alderly, near Badminton, for generations, so Hale was qualified to play for Gloucestershire. He replaced E. M. Grace in the Gloucestershire-Surrey match at the start of the 1886 season and a month later played for the Gentlemen. His bowling efforts were 7 for 90 against Middlesex and 4 for 13 against Yorkshire and he also scored 44 against Middlesex. He returned to Tasmania in 1899 and played several times for the state until 1911.

HALE, Harold
1867–1947

First-Class Averages: Batting, 1,067 runs at 12.12; Bowling, 99 wickets at 23.18.

A wicket-keeper turned fast right-arm bowler who thrilled Australian cricket fans on tour with two West Indies teams. He was spectacular, athletic, and good tempered, using all of his 6 ft 2 in to bowl for hours at a consistently fast pace and tidy length. He was an extremely powerful man with scarcely any excess weight on his muscular frame. For batsmen he was a frightening prospect and for spectators an awesome sight as he bounded in to bowl, teeth bared, lucky necklet swinging across his wide chest. He toured Australia in 1960–61 and 1968–69 and played 16 Shield matches for Queensland between 1961 and 1963, taking 76 wickets at 26.28 and scoring 409 runs at 17.78, best score 50.

Hall fitted in well with both the Queensland and Colts team in Brisbane grade cricket and was immensely popular wherever he went. Few imported stars have given such great value. In all first-class matches between 1955 and 1971, Wes Hall took 546 wickets at 26.14. In 48 Tests he seldom had a poor match, finishing with 192 wickets at 26.38. Considering the pleasure his fast bowling gave all around the cricket world, it's odd to recall that when he went on his first overseas tour—to England in 1957—he had not taken a first-class wicket. He has been a senator in the Barbados parliament for some years.

HALL, Wesley
Winfield, 1937–

465

HALLEBONE, Jeffrey, 1929–

First-Class Averages: Batting, 1,192 runs at 41.10.

A reliable right-hand batsman from the South Melbourne club who performed capably for Victoria in the early 1950s. He scored a double century against Tasmania in 1951–52 and scored centuries against South Australia and Queensland. In 1953–54 he figured in first wicket stands of 123 with Colin McDonald against South Australia, and 108 against Queensland. Hallebone usually went in first or second wicket down but Victoria also used him as an opener. He was a very sound fieldsman.

HAMENCE, Ronald Arthur, 1915–

First-Class Averages: Batting, 5,285 runs at 37.75; Bowling, 1 wicket at 37.00.

Tests (3): 81 runs at 27.00.

A dependable right-hand batsman who had limited opportunities in Tests but gave South Australia long service. He had an array of attractive back foot strokes and excelled at moving forward quickly to drive. He twice made a century in both innings of a match for his State and was a valuable reserve in the famous 1948 Australian team that toured England. He was an extremely capable outfield, with a strong throw.

Short, compact, always cheerful, he had a splendid tenor voice that contributed much to the good spirits of the 1948 team. At Taunton when the Australian players heard that he was approaching his first century of the tour against Somerset they downed their poker hands and went out of the dressing-room to applaud, only to see him dismissed on 99. He made 582 runs on the tour at 32.33, but did not get another chance for a century.

Hamence, a printer by trade, first played for South Australia in 1935–36, when he scored the first of his 11 centuries for SA with an innings of 121 against Tasmania at Adelaide. In 1936–37 he made 104 on the same ground against Queensland, and in December, 1940, he scored 130 and 103 not out against Victoria at Melbourne. He repeated this feat in 1946–47 against NSW in Adelaide, with 132 and 101 not out. This won him a place in the Australia team for the Fifth Test against Hammond's England side. He went to the wicket when spinner Doug Wright threatened to run through the Australian side and unveiled his customary smart footwork. His calm 30 not out lifted Australia to 253, Wright taking 7 for 105, and Australia finally winning the match. He was brought back for the Second Test against India in 1947–48 and topscored with 25 in Australia's innings of 107. He got another 25 in the Third Test but that proved to be his final Test appearance, Neil Harvey taking his place in the last two Tests.

Hamence kept scoring heavily for South Australia and in 1950–51 made 114 against Freddie Brown's MCC team. He retired at the end of that season, having made a century for SA against every Australian State, topscore 173 against NSW at Adelaide in 1948–49.

A resourceful right-arm fast-medium bowler whose bad luck with injuries has hampered his first-class career. He made his debut for South Australia in 1969–70 against Victoria and in only his second season for the State took 34 wickets at the comparatively low cost of 20.26 heading the Australian averages. At that stage he appeared an outstanding prospect and he was considered unlucky not to play for Australia in 1971–72 against the Rest Of The World. He toured England in Ian Chappell's 1972 Australian side when he was the youngest member of the team. He took 6 for 15 against Minor Counties but could not clinch a Test place largely because of a back strain.

In the West Indies in 1972–73 he played in all five Tests and showed rich potential but on his return home broke a foot. This and further back trouble has since restricted his first-class career, although he has helped South Australia occasionally in one-day matches. His best figures for SA were 6 for 54 against WA in 1970–71. He has occasionally scored useful runs, and his topscore was 53 against NSW in 1971–72.

HAMMOND, Jeffrey Robert, 1950–

First-Class Averages: Batting, 922 runs at 16.46; Bowling, 184 wickets at 28.88.

Tests (5): 28 runs at 9.33; 15 wickets at 32.53.

A powerfully-framed Yorkshire right-hand batsman who made a notable contribution to Tasmanian cricket over five seasons. Hampshire, a fine player who hit the ball extremely hard off the front foot, had played eight Tests in a first-class career that began in 1961 when he became the Tasmanian Cricket Association coach in 1966–67. He returned in 1967–68 and 1968–69 and later was a key batsman in Tasmania's first two seasons in the Sheffield Shield competition when he was engaged by the Tasmanian Cricket Council. In all first-class matches for Tasmania, Hampshire scored 1,200 runs at 48.00, with three centuries, helping to pave the way for Tasmania's acceptance as a full member of the Shield competition from the start of the 1982–83 season. His best innings for Tasmania was his 147 against South Australia at Hobart in 1977–78. He was a member of Ray Illingworth's team that toured Australia in 1970–71.

HAMPSHIRE, John Harry, 1941–

A valuable all-rounder who, unlucky to miss at least two trips to England, gave outstanding service to Victoria. He was the victim of the worst of all selection blunders, missing a place as second wicket-keeper to Blackham in the 1890 team for England. The selectors, after a deadlock, preferred Ken Burn, who when he joined the team confessed that he had never kept wicket in his life. In 1896, Harry was chosen for the team to go to England but had to drop out because of a knee injury. He turned up at Lords that summer and played three times for the MCC.

HARRY, John 1857–1919

First-Class Averages: Batting, 1,466 runs at 25.71; Bowling, 26 wickets at 23.76.

Tests (1): 8 runs at 4.00.

Harry was an all-rounder in the truest sense, as he could bowl with either hand, was a dangerous batsman, fielded at mid-off with brilliance, and was a classy wicket-keeper. He made his debut for Victoria in 1883–84, with his best knocks 114 against Western Australia at Melbourne in 1893–94, and 107 against South Australia at Adelaide in 1895–96. He made 21 dismissals (18 caught, three stumped). Loyal and remarkably versatile, he was a fine team man, rated far higher by the great players of his time than his figures indicate. He was a devastating club cricketer, scoring more than 11,000 runs for East Melbourne and Bendigo. He also played baseball for Victoria. He showed his extreme dexterity when he bowled both right and left handed in a South Australian innings for Victoria in 1891–92. One wonders if he conformed to the laws of the game by informing the umpires before he switched hands.

HARTIGAN, Roger Joseph, 1879–1958

The fourth Australian to score a century in his Test debut, a bright, attractive right-handed batsman who achieved the feat going in at No 8. He made 48 in his first Test knock in 1907–08 against England and scored 116 in the second innings. In both innings he was second top scorer. He put on 243 in even time with Clem Hill in the second innings, and in 1982 this stand, made in heat that reached 42 degrees Celsius, remained the best for the eighth wicket by Australians in Tests.

Hartigan's century was achieved despite an illness that compelled Clem Hill to leave the field several times and saw Hill vomiting on the grass beside the pitch. They came together with Australia leading by only 102 with three wickets left, and were not parted until Australia's score was 423. Other tailenders stretched the total to 506 and then O'Connor and Jack Saunders bowled out England to give Australia victory by 245 runs. Hill was too ill to field throughout the match. Hartigan, who worked for a Brisbane auctioneer, had leave for only four days but when that expired with them still batting he received a telegram from his boss which read: "Stay as long as you are making runs."

Hartigan, born in the Sydney suburb of Chatswood, played for New South Wales, but won his Test place after scoring 104 for Queensland against New South Wales in 1907–08. He also represented New South Wales and Queensland at baseball and Queensland at lacrosse. In 19 matches for Queensland before they were admitted to the Shield competition he captained the State 10 times. Playing for Woolloongabba against Nundah in 1905–06, he made 206 not out when he put on 339 unfinished for the first wicket with W. J. Lewis, 122 not out.

Despite his century in his first Test, Hartigan found it difficult to make the Test team in a period of outstanding Australian batsmen. His chances were not helped by living in Queensland, which was comparatively isolated from the main strength of Australian cricket in his playing years.

Hartigan, a brilliant slips field, won selection in the Australian team that toured England in 1909 but had limited opportunities. In a batting lineup that included some of the greatest players Australia has produced—Trumper, Macartney, Bardsley, Ransford, Armstrong, Noble—he played in 21 of the 39 matches, scoring 603 runs in all games at 18.84, topscore 115. Back home he continued to score well for Queensland. In 1910–11 he made 65 v. South Africa.

Hartigan worked hard in support of Queensland Cricket Association president Jack Hutcheon to win a Shield place for Queensland and a Test for Brisbane. He was on the Australian Board of Control for 35 years and while he lacked Hutcheon's flamboyance in debate he was an effective Board delegate faced with formidable opposition from southern States, who in the days before regular aircraft travel were apprehensive about the time and expense involved in playing regularly in Brisbane. For a long time the southern States were able to stall Queensland's entry into the Shield on the grounds that the QCA pitch at the Brisbane Exhibition Ground would not last four days. Queensland finally got into the Shield in 1926–27 and was given a Test for the first time in 1928, Hartigan and Hutcheon turning the trick.

First-Class Averages: Batting, 1,901 runs at 25.01; Bowling, 9 wickets at 40.11.

Tests (2): 170 runs at 42.50.

A unique mixture of furious hitter and leg-break bowler, both right-handed. He won his place in the Victorian side as a spinner and took plenty of wickets, but he also caused lots of problems for opposing teams with his no-nonsense batting. He played in his only Test in 1924–25 and hit 80 not out in an Australian total of 600. Hartkopf had a ninth wicket partnership of 100 with Oldfield, Australia winning by 81 runs in a high scoring match.

Hartkopf, born in Fitzroy, first appeared for Victoria in 1911–12 and hit two centuries, 126 and 111 not out, both against South Australia. He took five wickets or more for Victoria seven times, with his best figures in 1922–23 against England when he had 8 for 105 and 5 for 23, and also made 86 and 14 not out in a fine all-round performance. He toured New Zealand with a Victorian team in 1924–25. He was a medical practitioner.

HARTKOPF, Dr Albert Ernst Victor, 1889–1968

First-Class Averages: Batting, 1,758 runs at 34.47; Bowling, 121 wickets at 30.79.

Tests (1): 80 runs at 40.00; 1 wicket at 134.00

A right-hand batsman who, unlike his brothers, adopted a patient, dogged attitude towards bowlers. "Mick" wore the bowlers down, whereas his brothers preferred all out aggres-

HARVEY, Clarence Edgar ("Mick"), 1921–

469

First-Class Averages: Batting, 1,716 runs at 27.23.

sion. He had a very sound defence and limitless patience, biding his time to employ his restricted range of strokes. "Mick", like his brothers Mervyn, Harold and Ray, was born in New South Wales. He made a big reputation as an umpire after he retired from first-class cricket.

"Mick" Harvey was born at Newcastle on the NSW coalfields and brought up in the family house in Argyle Street, Fitzroy, in among the smoke stacks, shirt factories, shoe factories and gasometers. Like his brothers he learned his cricket in the lane that runs south from Argyle Street, using the tennis ball his mother insisted upon to protect her windows. He went through the grades with the Fitzroy club and made his debut for Victoria in 1948–49. He moved to Brisbane and played for Queensland from 1949–50 until 1956–57, appearing in 37 first-class matches. His three first-class centuries were made for Queensland.

He became a first-class umpire in 1974–75 and has frequently umpired first-class and one-day internationals. He umpired an Australia-Pakistan Test in 1978–79 and an Australia-West Indies Test in 1979–80.

HARVEY, Mervyn Roye, 1918–

First-Class Averages: Batting, 1,147 runs at 38.23.

Tests (1): 43 runs at 21.50.

The eldest. of the six Harvey brothers, a free-scoring right-hand batsman who usually opened. His career was badly upset by World War II, but he remained a happy, smiling, good-humoured character whose good looks delighted women spectators. He played in only one Test, opening for Australia in the Fourth Test at Sydney against Wally Hammond's English tourists in 1946–47, scoring 12 and 31, adding 116 in the second innings with Arthur Morris.

Merv Harvey, born at Broken Hill, NSW, was a vigorous shotmaker, fond of the hook. When his luck held he annihilated even topclass bowling and gave crowds plenty to cheer about. He was the first Harvey to win Test selection, but disappeared all too soon from big cricket in the hurly-burly chase for Test places. He was the first among the four Harveys who made Sheffield Shield centuries, and scored three in all, topscore 163 against South Australia in Adelaide in 1946–47. The Harvey boys who did not join Mervyn, "Mick," Ray and Neil in first-class cricket were Harold and Brian, who had consistent success and throughly enjoyed their cricket with Fitzroy.

HARVEY, Raymond 1926–

A right-hand batsman and occasional left-arm bowler with an easy, graceful style who played attacking or defensive cricket with equal proficiency. Smart footwork played an important part in his batting. He was born in NSW, grew up in

470

Fitzroy and his 19 centuries for the Fitzroy club remains a record for the club. He was a brilliant fieldsman.

Early in his career Ray Harvey showed tremendous promise. He played for an Australian XI against the MCC after making his debut for Victoria in 1947–48, but had too easy an approach to big cricket, lacking the ambition that drove his brother Neil. Percy Beames wrote in *The Age* that it was a case of drifting along. "But he never tried to get on in big cricket the way Neil did," said Beames. Ray Harvey scored 121 for Victoria against Western Australia in 1953–54, 110 against South Australia in 1954–55, and 106 not out against NSW the same season. He held 44 catches in 40 first-class games. He appeared with his brothers Neil and Mervyn in the Victorian team in January, 1947, when the three Harveys made 149 of Victoria's 331 total.

First-Class Averages: Batting, 1,970 runs at 30.78; Bowling, 5 wickets at 65.20.

HARVEY, Robert Neil 1928–

Star performer in a proud family from the Melbourne suburb of Fitzroy in which four of six brothers played State cricket, two played in Tests, and the other two appeared regularly in first grade. Neil was one of Australia's finest left-hand batsmen and, using a right-hand throw, was among the greatest fieldsmen of all time. He scored more runs in international cricket than any Australian apart from Bradman and Greg Chappell and more Test centuries than any Australian except Bradman. He said he was never interested in making 300 but he scored centuries 67 times in first-class matches.

Neil was the son of Horace Harvey, who left his native New South Wales to settle in Victoria in 1922. He reared his family in a two-storey house in Argyle Street, Fitzroy, an industrial suburb of shirt and shoe factories, gasometers and chimney stacks. Only Neil and his younger brother Brian were born at Argyle Street. His sister Rita (the only girl in the family), Mervyn, Clarrie, Harold and Ray were all born in New South Wales.

Melbourne sportswriter Percy Beames, in his definitive work on the Harvey family told how the residents of Fitzroy came to know Neil as a serious-minded, dark-haired boy smiting a ball into their backyards or on to the roof of a woolshed. They admired the way he defended his kerosene tin wicket against long hops, half volleys and balls that turned mischievously on loose road metal in the back lane. His father Horace had rattled up his fifties, sixties, and an occasional eighty in Newcastle, New South Wales, and later at Broken Hill, and at an age when most men turned to bowls still played social cricket in Melbourne's Prince's Park, with daughter Rita keeping score.

From the age of seven, Neil often heard of his dad's record score of 198 in Newcastle. "When are you gonna beat that

First-Class Averages:
Batting, 21,699 runs at
50.93; Bowling, 30
wickets at 36.86.

Tests (79): 6,149 runs at
48.41; 3 wickets at 40.

198?" Horace would ask his sons, good-humoredly. The boys soon realised that nothing would give Horace greater pleasure than if they did beat 198. It was a family in which any success on the field by one member brought pleasure to the rest. In 1945–46 Mervyn scored 163 for Victoria against South Australia, followed by 136 against New South Wales in 1946–47. Old Horace's 198 looked a formidable target until one afternoon when Ray Harvey reached 205 not out for Fitzroy against University in a district match. As Ray came off the field, there was Horace ready to congratulate him.

Neil's elder brothers worked hard at teaching him the rudiments of the game, and they taught him well and they insisted that he hit the ball hard. In 1937 when Bradman was fighting hard to save the Third Test for Australia after "Gubby" Allen's team had won the first two Tests, Percy Beames has recorded that Neil Harvey was fighting just as hard to save a match in Argyle Street at the age of eight. Eleven years later that boy made the winning hit in an historic match at Leeds, with Bradman at the other end.

Neil played his initial first grade game in 1942 at 14, the sole left-hander in his family. He got his first chance in big

The Harvey brothers, Ray, Mervyn and Neil, taking the field for Victoria against New South Wales in 1947–48.

cricket in 1946–47 when he was picked to play for The Rest against Victoria, and after he scored 154 for Victoria's Second XI at Hobart against Tasmania, he made his debut for Victoria against New South Wales. He was out second ball for a duck, but made 49 in the second innings. He heard during the match that his brother Mervyn had been chosen to play for Australia against England in the Fourth Test at Adelaide.

In the return match between Victoria and MCC, Harvey scored a splendid 69, with spinner Douglas Wright bowling dangerously. His poise and calmness—he went to the crease with Victoria 3 for 32—established him in the Victorian team. At Sydney in 1947–48 Mervyn, Ray and Neil all played for Victoria against New South Wales, contributing 149 out of Victoria's total of 331.

When India toured Australia in 1947–48, Harvey went to the wicket in the India-Victoria match with his side 3 for 11. There was a jaunty air of confidence about him as he came through the gate which bowlers all around the world later learned to worry about. He made a hard-hitting 87, attacking from the first over in an innings that won him selection in the Australia XI v. India at Sydney, where he made 32 and 56 not out.

Neil was in Perth playing for Victoria against Western Australia when he heard he had been picked for his first Test. In Argyle Street Horace Harvey and his wife danced for joy, but it was short-lived when Neil was made 12th man for the Test and then dropped from the Australian 12 for the next Test. Finally Neil won selection in the Fourth and Fifth Tests. He failed in the Fourth but made a glorious 153 in the Fifth. His Test career was underway, his 1948 English tour spot secure.

Neil Harvey was still a virtually unknown figure in big cricket as he stepped nervously towards fame when Australia was in danger of defeat against Yorkshire at Bradford. With Sam Loxton unable to bat through injury, Australia lost 6 for 31 in the final innings, needing 63 to win. Harvey offered a chance at short leg but survived to score 18 runs that were as valuable as most centuries, hitting the winning runs with a huge straight drive for six.

At Leeds a few weeks later Harvey walked through the gate to play his first Test innings against England with Australia at 3 for 68 chasing 496 in the Fourth Test. He failed to make contact with the first three balls he played at and Miller, batting strongly at the other end, called him down for a chat. Neil took block again and proceeded to play glorious strokes all round the wicket, cutting surely, hooking and pulling powerfully, and as always, driving on either side of the stumps with computer precision. He finished with 112, a memorable innings notable for Miller's steadying influence early on and for Harvey's brilliant shotmaking with Sam Loxton later. Harvey, 19, was the only player in the 1948 side under 26, but only Bradman, Barnes and Morris finished ahead of his average of 66 in Tests. He made four centuries on the tour in scoring 1,129 runs at 53.76.

Strangely, for such a sweet timer of the ball, Neil's eyesight was judged unsound by oculists during tests on Australia's 1949–50 tour of South Africa. It never showed on the field. He picked up swing and spin, cut and pace variations with such consummate ease, clipping the ball away without risk on the legside, driving and cutting in the middle of the bat, even the most partisan South African had to concede his greatness. He made eight centuries on that trip in scoring 1,526 runs, equalling Bradman's record of four hundreds in a series.

Harvey played superbly for 178 in the Second Test at Cape Town, and in the Third Test at Durban produced one of the finest of all innings by an Australian batsman. South Africa scored 2 for 240 on the first day and when rain turned the pitch into a sticky on the second day Australia's crafty captain Hassett kept the South Africans in without trying to dismiss them. Our bowlers were instructed to bowl straight outside the off stump without trying to turn the ball. Finally South Africa's skipper, Dudley Nourse, realised what was happening and his batsmen hit out to be dismissed for 311. Australia was out for 75 in two hours, Tayfield 7 for 23.

Nourse declined to enforce the follow-on and batted again, with South Africa all out for 99. Australia had to score 336 to win on a pitch that had dried out into a patchwork quilt of small holes and divot-pocked spots. Harvey overcame all these problems despite Tayfield's vast turn to score a match-winning 151 not out, picking the balls to hit with clockwork ease in an innings of a master cricketer.

Neil Harvey toured England three times more after his marvellous 1948 tour, in 1953, 1956 and 1961, when he won the only Test in which he ever captained Australia. When South Africa toured Australia in 1952–53, he made 834 runs in the Tests with four more centuries including 205 at Melbourne. He returned to South Africa in 1957–58 for a second tour and went to the West Indies in 1955, when he made 204 at Kingston. He made ten overseas Test tours in 14 years and scored Test centuries in 15 different cities. His modesty remained constant and only left him once—in 1979 when he was sacked after fine service as an Australian selector and had some harsh words to say about the shabby manner of it.

His first-class career covered 306 matches, with 67 centuries. In 79 Tests he had a highest score of 205, with 21 Test 100s. For Victoria he made 12 centuries and for NSW seven with a topscore of 231 for NSW against South Australia at Sydney in 1962–63. He scored seven double centuries. He took 228 catches in first-class cricket, including 64 in Tests, and whatever he scored his fielding was worth 30 to 40 runs in every match he played.

A cricketer of immense cunning who drilled his small frame to perform exhilarating feats of daring or steamrolling defence as Australia or Victoria's cause required. He was perhaps the supreme team player, fashioning all he did for the good of his side. Few cricketers have done as much to boost Australia's reputation for sportsmanship and he has an astonishing collection of friends from every corner of the cricket world to show for it. He batted right-handed, usually first wicket down, and fielded brilliantly in the deep. He captained Australia 24 times, for 14 wins, four losses and six draws.

He was the most under-rated of all Australian captains particularly early in his career when officials simply did not understand him. He was a marvellous blend of impish prankster, skilled batsman, clever tactician, and sparkling speaker. He could deflate the pompous, encourage good fellowship, and build confidence in his players as enthusiastically as he waltzed with a duchess or conducted a mass rendition of the *Desert Song* for a titled group of singers. In the art of making friends for Australian cricket, there has never been anybody like him. Bradman could not go out and joke with people like Hassett; it was not in his nature. Benaud was always a little shy in groups he did not know; Chappell's behaviour had limited acceptance. Hassett was impeccable and witty when his team was on show, but was never afraid to discipline a player who wavered socially.

This was the man who installed a muddied goat in the bedroom shared by McCabe and O'Reilly and chatted confidently with royalty, but who received only one vote when the Board of Control picked a captain for the first postwar Australian side to New Zealand. Ray Robinson, unfailingly accurate in these things, wrote that when the Board had a telegram vote among its 13 members for the captaincy of Australia to South Africa in 1949, Hassett scraped in thanks to the last telegram. Yet when Hassett led Australia in England in 1953 his team, the first Australian side seen there since Bradman's great 1948 lineup, attracted more gatemoney (£200,428) than any touring side had ever done, and broke the Lord's record by attracting 137,915 spectators.

A dapper, cheerful sun-loving man, standing 5 ft 6 ins and weighing just over 10 st, he surprised every country he played against with the power of his strokes. Few Australians have batted as well as Hassett on wet wickets and fewer still have scored 16,890 runs in first-class cricket under all conditions. His success stemmed from superb technique. He was always extremely straight, with the bat close to the ball, and his nimble footwork enabled him to get well over the ball despite his size. He could hook, cut, glance and drive in front of the wicket with such ease he made scoring 100s look easy.

Hassett was born in Geelong, and learned to play in the

HASSETT, Arthur Lindsay, 1913–

First-Class Averages: Batting, 16,890 runs at 58.24; Bowling, 18 wickets at 39.05.

Tests (43): 3,073 runs at 46.56.

Lindsay Hassett, one of the smallest of Australia's master cricketers, but a giant among tacticians.

family backyard with his five elder brothers. From the age of nine to 19, he attended Geelong College, and played in the First XI for five seasons. His coach at Geelong College was P. L. Williams, who also coached Ross Gregory and Ian Johnson. In the school holidays Hassett played grade cricket for South Melbourne, where he was coached by Hughie Carroll, the former Victorian batsman. Carroll strongly advocated lofting the ball over close in fieldsmen, and stressed the need for setting targets in every innings. "Just set yourself to get 10 runs, and when you get 10, go after 20, and that way you build up good scores", said Carroll. Following the Carroll method, Hassett made 59 first-class centuries which, when he retired, had only been exceeded among Australians by Bradman.

Hassett glides a ball to the fine leg fence against England at Manchester in 1953, eluding Godfrey Evans's gloves.

A month after his debut for South Melbourne Hassett scored 147 not out for a Combined Victorian Country team against the touring West Indies. At school, he had a record batting aggregate, won the Victorian Public Schools tennis championship, and captained Geelong College at cricket, ten-

nis and football. "I still lost a few of our three-a-side backyard 'Tests' with my brothers", he said.

He was picked for Victoria shortly after leaving school but scored only 4 and 9 and was not picked again for the State for three years. His big chance came in the 1935–36 season when several of the Victorian team touring New South Wales and Queensland fell ill on the night before the first match. Hassett was one of the replacements rushed to the match and he produced scores of 21, 51, 49 and 73. The following season he sealed his State team spot by heading Victoria's batting averages with 74.83. He had made only one century for the State when he was chosen for his first tour of England in 1938.

Few players have begun an England tour so well. He made 43 in the opening match at Worcester, followed by 146, 148 and 220 not out and his tour average of 53.16 was only surpassed by Bradman and Brown. His Test scores were not outstanding but they were valuable. At Leeds when Australia needed 105 to win with rain threatening, we lost 4 for 61 but Hassett's 33 won the match and retained the Ashes only minutes before the ground was flooded. Back in Australia he batted brilliantly in Shield matches, scoring four centuries in 1938–39. At Sydney in the following season he made 122 in each innings, hitting O'Reilly back over his head as he had never been hit before, the lofted drive played to perfection, but New South Wales still won the match and the Shield.

Hassett at his prewar prime was a superlative attacking batsman, but war cut it all off. For five years he played very little cricket during service with the AIF in the middle East and Palestine. In 1945, he was appointed captain of the Second AIF side and in a packed schedule played a major role in reviving big cricket. The services matches provided entertainment for hundreds of thousands whose morale had been shattered by the war, and Hassett made sure they were played in a cheerful spirit. England was a triumph, India, where Hassett made 187 and 124 not out in the match against the Princes' XI, even better, and then, despite the players' weariness, came a triumphant swing round the Australian States in matches that put cricket back in business.

Hassett, who married Tessie Davis at 28 just before his unit was sent to New Guinea, led the Services side as a Warrant Officer, rejecting suggestions that he should accept a commission. His rate of pay was 12 shillings a day. His players received only their normal service pay and had no share in gate takings that earned thousands of pounds for British charities and vast piles of rupees for Indian hospitals. John McMahon, the Australian spinner who later played for Surrey and Somerset, recalls a match at High Wycombe when Hassett refused to pay the players their money until they challenged him at poker. When the team got back to London he led them past crowds of thirsty people to the cellar of *Ye Old Mitre* in

Leicester Square, run by a Kiwi mate, where he sat on a barrel like Buddha and worked on the ale.

On a hot day at Portsmouth the Services team were held up by Commander Mike Ainsworth, Commander R. J. L. Hammond and Lieutenant of Marines, T. E. Bailey. One of the bowlers left the field, returning hours later when the tailenders were in. He strolled through the gate asking where Hassett wanted him. Lindsay signalled him back a little, over a little, and right through the gate from whence he came. Hassett played most of his international cricket after his discharge as W/O Hassett, when he had turned 33, but his batting record stands second only to Bradman's among Australians.

Here the dashing brilliance of prewar years left Hassett's batting and he became much more defensive but just as dangerous in securing the required result for his side. He led Victoria to the Shield in 1946–47 with an average of 141.75, and in the first of the five Tests against Hammond's English team created a third wicket record of 276 with Bradman. The next season he averaged 110.66, highest score 198 not out, in Tests against India.

In England in 1948, he completed 10,000 runs in first-class cricket and after a moderate start scored seven centuries, finishing with 200 not out, 103 and 151. He made 1,563 runs on that tour at 74.42 and returned as Australian captain in 1953 to score a further 1,236 at 44.14. He had taken over as Australian captain when Bradman retired after the Fifth Test in 1948, taken a successful side to South Africa in 1949–50, and won four of the five Tests against Freddie Brown's MCC team in Australia in 1951. In South Africa he performed a brilliant feat of captaincy that gave Australia a win after scoring only 75 in the first innings, 236 behind. Hassett schemed to keep the South Africans in without conceding too many runs while the pitch dried out, a strategy that worked so well Australia won by five wickets.

Nothing in his outstanding record as a captain compares, however, with the Brisbane Test against Freddie Brown's MCC team. With England 160 behind, Brown declared his first innings closed at 7 for 68 to catch Australia on a sticky wicket. When Australia reached 7 for 32, Hassett declared, leaving England to get 192 to win. There had been two declarations in 79 minutes but the last one by Hassett enabled Australia to win the first of four Tests it took from Brown's side that summer.

When Hassett led Australia in Australia in 1952–53 and in England in 1953, the great postwar side was declining. He lost one Test to Freddie Brown's team in Australia and seemed to have The Ashes safe in 1953 until Watson and Bailey batted for most of the final day in the Second Test to salvage a draw. Hassett had to bear widespread criticism from Australians

478

unaccustomed to losing gracefully when England won the series by taking the Fifth Test at The Oval. Australia had held The Ashes since 1934. Hassett, who had made two centuries in the 1953 series, declined to be drawn publicly on the legality of Lock's action, though he was known to be unhappy about it. He retired immediately afterwards.

After his retirement Hassett continued his sports goods store business, with visitors from overseas constantly dropping in. He joined the ABC commentary teams in broadcasts that gave pleasure to all cricket lovers and finally, to give his wife some relief from the perpetual influx of friends at their Melbourne home, sold up and settled at Batehaven, New South Wales, a coastal town difficult for even the most dedicated Hassett worshippers to get to. He declined to join the ABC commentators in 1981–82 because he said he was fed up with the misbehaviour of the players.

Hassett had 216 first-class games, made 59 centuries, 23 of them for Victoria, and held 170 catches. In Tests he made 10 100s, and held 30 catches. His brother, **Richard Joseph Hassett** (1908–) scored two centuries for Victoria, 114 not out and 102, both against Tasmania in scoring 397 runs for the State at 56.71 "Dick" Hassett was the leg-spinner with whom Jack Hobbs was highly impressed when Percy Chapman's team toured in 1928–29.

HAT-TRICKS

The taking of three wickets with successive balls, not necessarily in the same innings, but in the same match. It is possible to take a hat-trick in three separate overs by taking a wicket with the last ball of one over and with the first ball of the next over to finish the innings, opening up in the second innings and taking a wicket first ball. Hat-tricks can be all stumped, all lbw, or all caught and it is quite allowable—as well as darned lucky—to take more than one hat-trick in an innings.

Probably the leading exponent of the hat-trick was the Sydney left-arm bowler Bill Hunt who performed the feat 11 times at various levels of cricket. In 1933, he did it five times, twice for the Balmain club in Sydney in social matches and three times for Rishton in the Lancashire League. Frank Tarrant took most hat-tricks in first-class cricket by an Australian—five—but he achieved all of them in England.

The most extraordinary hat-tricks by an Australian were both taken on the same day by off-spinner T. J. ("Jack") Matthews, from Williamstown, Victoria. Matthews took a hat-trick in each innings against South Africa at Manchester in the 1912 triangular tournament in England but took no other wickets in the match, finishing with 3 for 16 and 3 for 38. The South African tailender T. A. Ward bagged a "king pair," as the third victim in both Matthews' hat-tricks. Australian Albert Trott ruined his own benefit match by taking four wickets in four balls and a hat-trick in the same innings. The most recent Australian hat-trick in Tests was by left-arm spinner Lindsay Kline against South Africa at Cape Town in 1957–58.

HAT-TRICKS BY AUSTRALIANS IN FIRST-CLASS CRICKET

Bowler	Opponents	Venue	Date
W. W. Armstrong	(1) Victoria v. NSW	Melbourne	1902–03
R. H. Bettington	(1) Oxford University v. Essex	Oxford	1920
J. A. Cuffe	(1) Worcestershire v. Hampshire	Bournemouth	1910
A. K. Davidson	(1) NSW v. Western Australia	Perth	1962–63
K. R. Dollery	(2) Warwickshire v. Gloucestershire	Bristol	1953
	Warwickshire v. Kent	Coventry	1956
B. Dooland	(1) South Australia v. Victoria	Melbourne	1945–46
H. I. Ebeling	(1) Victoria v. Queensland	Melbourne	1928–29
G. Giffen	(3) Australia v. Lancashire	Manchester	1884
	South Australia v. Vernon's XI	Adelaide	1887–88
	Australia v. England XI	Wembley	1896
G. H. Gilbert	(1) NSW v. Victoria	Melbourne	1857–58
C. V. Grimmett	(1) South Australia v. Queensland	Brisbane	1928–29
H. P. Hay	(1) South Australia v. Lord Hawke's XI (1st-class debut)	Adelaide	1902–03
H. E. J. Hooker	(1) NSW v. Victoria (4 in 4)	Sydney	1928–29
A. J. Y. Hopkins	(2) Australia v. Cambridge University	Cambridge	1902
	NSW v. South Australia	Sydney	1903–04
T. H. Howard	(1) NSW v. Queensland (4 in 5)	Sydney	1902–03
W. P. Howell	(2) Australia v. Western Province (4 in 5)	Cape Town	1902–03
	Australia v. New Zealand XI	Wellington	1904–05
H. Ironmonger	(1) Victoria v. England	Melbourne	1924–25
V. E. Jackson	(2) Leicestershire v. Derbyshire	Derby	1946
	Leicestershire v. Surrey	Leicester	1950
C. Kelleway	(1) Australian XI v. WA	Perth	1911–12
A. Kermode	(1) Lancashire v. Leicestershire	Leicester	1906
L. F. Kline	(1) Australia v. South Africa	Cape Town	1957–58
E. A. McDonald	(3) Lancashire v. Sussex	Hove	1925
	Lancashire v. Kent	Dover	1926
	Lancashire v. Warwickshire	Birmingham	1930
T. R. McKibbin	(1) Australia v. Lancashire	Liverpool	1896
T. J. Matthews	(4) Victoria v. Tasmania	Launceston	1908–09
	Australia v. South Africa (1st Inn)	Manchester	1912
	Australia v. South Africa (2nd Inn)	Manchester	1912
	Australia v. Philadelphians	Germantown	1912–13
F. L. Morton	(1) Victoria v. Tasmania	Melbourne	1931–32
M. A. Noble	(1) NSW v. Tasmania	Sydney	1898–99
R. K. Oxenham	(1) Australia v. Ceylon	Colombo	1935–36
G. E. Palmer	(2) Australia v. Sussex	Hove	1882
	Victoria v. South Australia	Melbourne	1882–83
L. S. Pascoe	(1) NSW v. South Australia	Adelaide	1980–81
C. G. Pepper	(1) Commonwealth XI v. Holkar	Indore	1949–50
W. Prior	(1) South Australia v. NSW	Adelaide	1975–76
D. Robins	(1) South Australia v. NSW	Adelaide	1965–66
G. F. Rorke	(1) NSW v. Queensland	Sydney	1958–59
A. T. Sincock	(1) South Australia v. India	Adelaide	1977–78

480

F. R. Spofforth	(4)	Australia v. MCC	Lord's	1878
		Australia v. Players	The Oval	1878
		Australia v. England	Melbourne	1878–79
		Australia v. South of England	The Oval	1884
F. A. Tarrant	(5)	Middlesex v. Gloucestershire (4 in 4)	Bristol	1907
		MCC v. Cambridge University	Cambridge	1908
		Middlesex v. Surrey	Lord's	1909
		Middlesex v. Gloucestershire	Bristol	1909
		Middlesex v. Somerset	Bath	1911
J. Treanor	(1)	NSW v. Queensland	Brisbane	1954–55
A. E. Trott	(2)	Middlesex v. Somerset (4 in 4)	Lord's	1907
		Middlesex v. Somerset	Lord's	1907
H. Trumble	(3)	Australia v. Gloucestershire	Cheltenham	1896
		Australia v. England	Melbourne	1901–02
		Australia v. England	Melbourne	1903–04
C. T. B. Turner	(1)	NSW v. Victoria	Melbourne	1886–87
M. G. Waite	(1)	South Australia v. MCC	Adelaide	1935–36
A. K. Walker	(2)	NSW v. Queensland	Sydney	1948–49
		Nottinghamshire v. Leicestershire (4 in 4)	Leicester	1956
J. E. Walsh	(1)	Leicestershire v. Nottinghamshire	Loughborough	1949
S. M. J. Woods	(1)	Cambridge University v. Thorton's XI	Cambridge	1888

Notes: In the above list, only those by Kline, Matthews (twice), Spofforth and Trumble were achieved in Tests. Indian-born Rusi Surti performed the hat-trick for Queensland against Western Australia at Perth in 1968–69.

A big, powerful, right-arm medium-pace bowler with a chest-on delivery who cut the ball off the pitch and made it swing late in towards the batsman. He was a successful all-rounder for three States, South Australia, West Australia, and Tasmania, supporting his accurate bowling with handy late order batting and efficient fielding. After 27 Tests, two tours of England, and one to West Indies, he quit international cricket to play in the Lancashire League because he said he could no longer accept Bill Lawry's dictatorial captaincy of the Australian team. He was an outstanding Australian Rules footballer.

Hawke, born at Cheltenham, South Australia, first played State cricket for Western Australia in 1959–60 and played for South Australia in 1960–61. After two disappointing seasons he took 7 for 38 and 5 for 44 in a fine double against Western Australia in January, 1962, followed by 5 for 71 against New Zealand in 1961–62 and 6 for 130 against England in 1962–63, and at the end of the 1962–63 summer made his Test debut in the final Test of the series against England. He went into the Australian team in place of Ian Meckiff when Meckiff was called for allegedly throwing in the First Test at Brisbane against South Africa in 1963–64, and took 14 wickets in the series.

He toured England in 1964 under Simpson, heading the

HAWKE, Neil James Napier, 1939–

First-Class Averages: Batting, 3,210 runs at 24.32; Bowling, 441 wickets at 26.55.

Tests (27): 365 runs at 16.59; 91 wickets at 29.41.

Australian bowling averages with 83 wickets at 19.86, taking 5 for 75 in the Third Test at Headingley and 6 for 47 in the Fifth Test at The Oval. He gave the finest performance of his career in the West Indies in 1964–65, finishing as top wicket-taker in the Tests with 24 at 21.83 despite the presence of bowlers like Hall and Griffiths. At home he took 7 for 105 in the Third Test at Sydney in an England score of 488, and 5 for 54 in the Fourth Test at Adelaide in the 1965–66 series, bowling cleverly but not moving the ball as much as he did in England.

But in England in 1968 under Lawry's captaincy he had a most unhappy tour and was discarded after two Tests. "I found it impossible to play under Lawry," said Hawke. "I could never play under a dictator and that's what Lawry was. There was no give and take with the man—I found it impossible to communicate with him. You either bowled to his method, or you did not bowl at all. I was used to captains who respected your opinions. I couldn't enjoy my cricket under Lawry, so I got out." In all first-class cricket his best performance was 8 for 61 for South Australia v. New South Wales in 1967–68.

Hawke, who finished with 35 wickets at 21.40 on the 1968 tour of England, pulled up stakes and headed for the Lancashire League where he joined Nelson in 1967. He had seven seasons in the League, three with Nelson and four with East Lancashire, scoring more than 3,384 runs and taking over 528 wickets. He rejected frequent offers to play County cricket preferring just to play at weekends. He returned to Australia in 1980 and after a bowel operation in Adelaide complications set in that had him on the critically ill list for weeks. But after a series of operations and repeated crises he married the girl who helped nurse him during his recovery.

HAWKSBURN CLUB An important club in the early history of Melbourne district cricket which showed other clubs how to cheerfully survive financial crises. It was formed in 1879 at a meeting of locals under a tree on what is now Hawksburn Railway Station when the locals agreed to play cricket in the paddock where they were meeting. In 1889 a new pitch was found near Albert Lagoon and this was used for four years until the club moved to Toorak Park. Hawksburn were involved in an area that included too many clubs but they produced some useful players including the highly influential Rush family. They had some particularly tense matches against the South Yarra Union, St Kilda Juniors, and Prahran. After one match against South Yarra Union, an emotional Hawksburn supporter wrote to the *Prahran Telegraph* alleging South Yarra's supporters used language for which they would have been arrested outside a cricket field. By the time the Hawksburn club changed

482

its name to Prahran CC at the end of 1901–02 had built a proud record in 27 years and produced many outstanding cricketers, including Barlow Carkeek, who kept for Victoria and Australia.

HAWSON, Reginald James, 1880–1928

First-Class Averages: Batting, 1,705 runs at 37.06.

A skilful right-hand opening batsman for Tasmania in the first decade of this century. Against Victoria he made 139 at Hobart in 1908–09 and 199 not out at Melbourne in 1912–13. He also had an innings of 96 against Victoria. In 1898–99, he made 76 for South Tasmania against New Zealand, and in 1911–12 hit 82 v. South Africa. In 1904, he made 135 and 121 not out for Derwent in a match against Wellington at Hobart. His brother Stanley also played for Tasmania. In 1907–08, he scored 143 for Tasmania against the first Fijian team to visit Australia, and in 1910–11 he made 238 not out for Southern Tasmania against the North.

HAZLITT, Gervys Rignold ("Gerry") 1888–1915

A tragic, almost forgotten Australian Test star whose death at 27 paralleled that of Archie Jackson and Victor Trumper and was just as harrowing to his fans. He played for Victoria at 17 while still at school and was a Test player at 19 and in those years seemed likely to become the finest cricketer Australia had produced.

Hazlitt was born at Enfield, New South Wales, but spent his childhood in Melbourne, where he was a student at Haileybury College. He performed so excitingly for Haileybury, the Melbourne Cricket Club gave him one of their scholarships. He made his debut for Victoria in 1905–06, though even then it was known he had a weak heart.

He was a talented batsman who could hit freely, but it was his right-arm medium-pace bowling that was so exceptional, for he could make the ball cut about sharply and had a useful off-break. He played his first Test in 1907–08 against England, missed selection in the 1909 Australian team in England, but regained his Test spot in 1911–12. Many considered his action suspicious but he was not called.

In 1912, he won a place in the Australian team for England when Armstrong, Trumper, Cotter, Ransford, Carter and Hill objected to the Board's conditions. With Bardsley, Whitty, and Macartney, he was the only Australian to shine on the tour. A tall, angular, handsome character with unusually long arms, he fully exploited a drying pitch in the Third Test at Lord's, taking 7 for 25, including the last five English wickets for one run. But England also had bowlers to exploit the turning pitch in Woolley and Dean and Australia were bundled out for 65 in their second innings to lose by 244 runs.

First-Class Averages:
Batting, 876 runs at
12.69; Bowling, 188
wickets at 26.09.

Tests (9): 89 runs at 11.12;
23 wickets at 27.08.

Hazlitt took 101 wickets on the English tour at 18.96 in all matches, a remarkable result for a frail 24-year-old on his first overseas tour. He bowled 805 overs on the tour, and only Bill Whitty, 866, bowled more. He played his last first-class match at 25 in 1913–14. He was a master at King's School, Parramatta, where he died, four months after Victor Trumper's death.

HEALYS, THE, OF PRAHRAN

A notable father and son combination whose right-hand batting earned them a big reputation in the Prahran district of Melbourne over a 30-year period starting in the 1890s.

John Joseph Healy (1851–1916) was one of East Melbourne's most consistent batsmen and played one match for Victoria in 1880–81, scoring 16 runs at 8.00. He was secretary of the Victorian Cricket Association from 1911 to 1916.

Gerald Edward James Healy (1885–1946) won the Prahran club's batting average a record 13 times. Between 1906–29, he made 7,527 runs at 45.89 for Prahran and played in five premiership teams. He was a copybook right-hander, a brilliant cover and outfieldsman, and made 21 centuries for Prahran, as well as one double century. For Victoria, he made 301 runs at 30.10, including 218 in a Victorian total of 660 against Tasmania in 1909–10.

HENDRY, Hunter Scott Thomas Laurie ("Stork"), 1895–

First-Class Averages:
Batting, 6,799 runs at
37.56; Bowling, 229
wickets at 29.02.

Tests (11): 335 runs at
20.93, 16 wickets at
40.00.

A long-legged Sydney-born all-rounder who played in some of Australia's finest cricket teams during a 17-year career in first-class cricket. He was a right-hand first wicket batsman who used his height and long reach to hammer away cuts, drives and hooks, a right-arm fast-medium swing bowler of rare accuracy who dismissed the best batsmen of his time, and an outstanding fieldsman in the slips or in the outfield. He was a strong advocate of disciplined, ethical behaviour and a bitter, outspoken critic of the poor sportsmanship and moneygrabbing attitude of players in the 1970s. He also castigated the Australian Cricket Board for handing promotion of the game to World Series Cricket.

Hendry, born in the Sydney suburb of Woollahra, went straight from Sydney Grammar School to first grade with the Paddington club during World War I. Monty Noble took one look at his exceptional length of leg and nicknamed him "Stork." Noble became his special cricket tutor. Hendry made his debut for New South Wales in 1918 after a sequence of impressive all-round performances. He exploited his 6 ft 2 ins to get right over the top of the ball in shot-making, and used his long arms to impart disconcerting late swing when bowling.

He made two tours of England in Australian sides. On the

first under Warwick Armstrong he brilliantly caught Frank Woolley in his Test debut at Nottingham, but disappointed with the bat and ball. On the second in 1926 under Herbie Collins he was ill with scarlet fever from May until August. His luck and his form was much more impressive at home. He made his initial first-class century for New South Wales by scoring 146 against South Australia in 1922–23 at Adelaide.

Shortly afterwards he took over from Warwick Armstrong as pavilion clerk at the Melbourne Cricket Ground with the role of assisting members of the Melbourne club, a job that helped improve his consistency because of the daily practice it provided.

Hendry played some sparkling innings for Victoria between 1924 and 1932, including 325 not out against New Zealand at Melbourne in 1925–26, 177 against South Australia in 1926–27 and 168 against South Australia in 1927–28. His best bowling performance for Victoria was his 6 for 30 against South Australia in 1925–26. In the Second Test at Sydney in 1928–29 against England, when Bradman was Australia's twelfth man, he scored 37 and 112, adding 215 for the second wicket with Woodfull. This was his sole Test century. By the end of the series he had lost his Test place. He returned to Sydney and to grade cricket in 1932–33.

In all first-class matches, Hendry scored 14 centuries, and held 152 catches. He made 10 centuries for Victoria and three for NSW. Apart from his two tours to England, he also had trips to South Africa in 1921–22 and to India in 1935–36.

A fiery, unpredictable Aboriginal fast bowler who played seven first-class games for Queensland in the seasons 1901–02 to 1904–05. Henry was only slightly built but could bowl at exceptional pace. He was a genuine character, subject to moodiness. For the South Brisbane Club, he bowled in bare feet, and one way of taking his mind off the match was to refer to the snakes allegedly seen in the long grass, especially at his home ground, Davies Park. Henry played for Queensland against NSW in 1901–02 when Jack Marsh was in the NSW team, the first time Aboriginals opposed each other in Australian first-class cricket. Henry took 2 for 59 and 1 for 38, Marsh 2 for 64 and 3 for 67. In the following season, Henry took 5 for 40 in NSW's second innings. In a Brisbane club match in 1904, well known umpire A. L. Cossart no-balled Henry on several occasions from square leg, considering Henry's delivery action doubtful. The official report to the QCA on the incident recorded that at the end of the over Henry went up to umpire Cossart and said, "You bastard! You no ball my good balls but those I do throw, you never. You know nothing about cricket," shaking his fist at Cossart's face.

HENRY, Albert ("Alec"), 1880–1909

First-Class Averages:
Batting, 36 runs at 6.00;
Bowling, 21 wickets at 32.04.

HIBBERT, Paul Anthony, 1952–

First-Class Averages: Batting, 2,214 runs at 32.56; Bowling 15 wickets at 15.07.

Tests (1): 15 runs at 7.50.

A left-handed batsman and left-arm medium-pace bowler who has not fulfilled his early promise. He came into the Victorian team in 1974–75 after four years in the Colts. He made a century for Victoria without hitting a boundary in 1977–78 against India, an innings that earned him a place in the First Test at Brisbane. He lost his place as the team's opener after only one match.

In 1980–81, he made 153 not out, his highest first-class score, for Victoria against South Australia at Geelong, but he has since struggled to find form. He played for Burnmoor in the Durham League in 1977 to gain experience, which appeared to improve his bowling without doing much for his batting.

HIDE, Jesse Bollard, 1857–1924

An English (born at Eastbourne) all-rounder who had a big influence in lifting the standards of South Australian cricket. He was a fast bowler, steady batsman, and good field at point or long stop. He played for Sussex in 1876 and 1877 but in 1878 switched to Adelaide, where he played until 1883. For Fifteen of South Australia he bowled 64 deliveries in 1882 against the Australian XI for only one run.

Jesse Hide's five years as coach to the South Australian Cricket Association cost the association £200-a-year and laid the foundation for future development. He had been appointed at the suggestion of James Lillywhite. He was in the first South Australian XI in 1880–81 and sometimes played for South Adelaide. Hide is given the credit for introducing expertise into the preparation of Australian pitches.

The noted English cricket historian Harry Altham found frequent references to Hide's skill in persuading groundsmen that they would not bruise the turf by rolling it. On the 1876–77 tour by Shaw's team, Altham recorded that the roller at Ararat was made of wood and only 10 inches in diameter. At Sydney the English team batted on a roughly prepared strip and then saw their opposition bat on another strip. "Jesse Hide had not yet initiated our kinsmen into the art of wicket preparation in which they were to become pastmasters," Altham wrote.

HIGGS, James Donald, 1950–

A long-serving Victorian right-arm leg-spinner whose sense of fun has won him many fans and helped him accept the selectors' whims that have been part of his career. At his best he has been the best Australian leg-spinner since Richie Benaud and a world leader in the art. He has seldom had responsive pitches on which to bowl and often does not get a long bowl until the last day of a match. His batting has been as cheerful as his personality but despite all efforts to improve he has still taken more first-class wickets than he has made runs.

Higgs is a small man, with a short approach run, but he has a good high, easy action that imparts plenty of leg-spin. His googly is a useful diversion that achieves a high bounce. For a bowler of his type, he is extremely economical and even the most powerful hitters seldom try to cut loose against him. He has had the bad luck to play in the days of covered pitches, for he would have been quite devastating in the years when wickets were left to the elements once a game began.

He was born at Kyabram, Victoria and has played for University and Richmond in Melbourne grade cricket on pitches that sometimes allow more turn than the rock-solid Australian first-class strips. He made his debut for Victoria in 1970–71 and has been an automatic selection ever since. When Victoria won their 24th Sheffield Shield in 1979–80, it was Higgs' legspin that brought success on the last day in the vital match against South Australia. With Ian Chappell in a threatening mood at lunch, SA looked likely winners but Higgs had Chappell out quickly and finished with 6 for 57 off 20.1 overs to wrap up the Shield.

Higgs has made three overseas tours with Australian teams, in 1975 to England when 11 for 118 against WA just before the side was announced probably clinched a tour spot, in 1978 with Bob Simpson's team to the West Indies and in 1979 to India. He took 27 wickets in England in 1975 at 32.96 but did not play in a Test. That was the tour on which he received much publicity by failing to score a single run. He batted only twice on the tour and the only ball he had to face bowled him. World Series Cricket gave him his Test chance and he played in four Tests in the West Indies in 1978, taking 15 wickets at 25.60 and 42 wickets at 22.21 on the tour. At home against England in 1978–79 he took 19 wickets at 24.63 on dead wickets. In view of the outstanding record of Australian leg-spinners in England, the selectors preference for Bright ahead of Higgs for the 1981 tour of England was a sorry reflection on the precedence given to one-day matches in which leg-spinners have no place.

First-Class Averages: Batting, 383 runs at 5.72; Bowling, 397 wickets at 29.12.

Tests (22): 115 runs at 5.75; 66 wickets at 31.16.

A right-hand opening batsman who captained New South Wales at the age of 21, when he appeared a likely Test captain. Only Ian Craig was younger when he captained New South Wales. The Gods of Cricket have not smiled on Hilditch since the Second Test against Pakistan at Perth in 1979, when as the non-striker, he picked up a gentle return from a fieldsman and tossed the ball to Sarfraz Nawaz, who immediately appealed. Hilditch was given out "handled the ball." Australian selector Neil Harvey deplored Sarfraz's action. Umpires

HILDITCH, Andrew Mark Jefferson, 1956–

First-Class Averages: Batting, 1,998 runs at 32.75.

Tests (9): 452 runs at 25.11.

should not have to give batsmen out on appeals that are to the detriment of cricket, Harvey said. Several of the Pakistani players also condemned Sarfraz but it did not help Hilditch (although Australia won the Test), who had put on 96 and 87 in opening stands in the match with Darling.

Hilditch, born in North Adelaide, attended Sydney University, and played cricket for the Sutherland club while studying law. He was virtually unknown when he was appointed New South Wales captain 1978–79 after only two first-class matches. His name became better known when he scored 93 against England in Sydney, an innings that helped win him a berth as opening batsman in the Sixth Test against England and in two Tests against Pakistan, in the second of which he was made vice-captain to new captain Kim Hughes. He went to England for the Prudential Cup in 1979 as Australia's vice-captain and played responsibly but without luck. After the return of the WSC players, he was unable to find a place in the New South Wales State team. He married a daughter of Bobby Simpson and they moved to South Australia in 1981 to further his careers in cricket and law.

HILL, Clement
1877–1945

First-Class Averages: Batting, 17,216 runs at 43,47; Bowling, 10 wickets at 32.30.

Tests (49): 3,412 runs at 39.21.

One of the most distinguished of all Australian left-handed batsmen. In various parts of the world, he made 45 first-class centuries, 13 of them in England, and he played four innings in his career of more than 200 runs. He saved many lost causes but was also Australia's worst "Nervous Nineties" victim, with scores of 96, 97, 98, 98 and 99 in Tests against England. In the 1901–02 series in Australia he had a sequence of 99, 98 and 97 in the Second and Third Tests—and Australia won both matches. At Adelaide in front of his home crowd he made 98 and 97, following his 99 in the last innings of the previous Test at Melbourne.

Hill had a fabulous eye that enabled him to pull a lot of balls to leg from outside the off stump, but he could be a tremendously unlucky batsman. When he was out for the third time in the 90s at Adelaide, he chopped down on a ball from Gilbert Jessop that swung late. He middled it but then realised the ball was rolling back towards the stumps. Swinging round to stop it, he knocked off the leg bail.

From an awkward, crouched stance, hands choked low on the handle, he watched the ball carefully on to the bat, moving his feet quickly and freely. Short and stocky, his hitting on the legside was powerful and safe and he was merciless on anything short. He cut cleanly and confidently and drove straight and to the off efficiently, and he despatched pace bowling with an ease unequalled in what has been called the Golden Age of cricket. But it was the variety of his shotmaking and the power of his bottom hand that stamped him as a batsman of the highest class.

Hill was born in Adelaide, the son of the first player to score a century on Adelaide Oval, H. J. Hill, who made 102 not out against the visiting Kent CC on January 26, 1878, for North Adelaide. Clem was educated at Prince Alfred College, Adelaide and at 16 scored 360 retired for his school against St Peter's College. He made 214 on the first day and a further 146 on the second, his team scoring 621.

Seven Hill brothers played first-class cricket for South Australia, **Percival** ("Peter"), 1867–1950, **Roland James**, 1868–1929, **Arthur**, 1871–1936, **Clem**, **Henry John**, 1878–1906, **Leslie Roy**, 1883–1952, and **Stanley**, ("Solly") 1885–1970. There were eight sons and eight daughters in the family. Clem was the sole left hander. Leslie, with 123 against NSW at Sydney in 1910–11, was the family's other century-maker for the State apart from Clem. Leslie also had the family's best first-class bowling figures, with 5 for 82 against NSW at Sydney in 1907–08. Stanley also played one match for NSW. In 1912–13, there were several instances of three Hill brothers playing together for SA.

At 18, Clem topped the South Australian batting averages for the 1895–96 first-class season by scoring 371 runs in seven innings, including 206 not out against New South Wales at Sydney. In all he headed the South Australian first-class averages 10 times between then and the 1910–11 season, and scored 24 centuries for his State. He batted eight hours 35 minutes for his highest first-class score of 365 not out against New South Wales at Adelaide in 1900–01, hitting an eight and 35 fours. He was in two stands of more than 200 in that knock, adding 206 for the fifth wicket with J. C. Reedman (71) and 234 for the ninth wicket with E. Walkley (53). He made a double century (200) against England at Adelaide in 1897–98, and in the 1909–10 season scored 176 against Victoria at Adelaide, 205 against New South Wales at Adelaide and 185 against Victoria at Melbourne in successive innings.

Clem was a promising wicket-keeper in his youth, particularly smart at stumping, but gave it up rather than risk injury to his hands. He captained Australia 10 times, for five wins and five losses. A man of high ideals, popular with his fellow players, he had a 20 minute fist fight in the Board of Control's Sydney office with fellow selector Peter McAlister after a disagreement over the selection of an Australian team in 1911. Frank Iredale, one of the witnesses of the fight, said they both were game and determined. A blow-by-blow account of the brawl appeared in *The Australasian* in 1911, which said they fought fiercely, and, locked in each other's arms, swayed around the room, crashing against the table and walls. The table pinned Iredale in a corner when it was upset. "They went at it hammer and tongs," Iredale said.

Hill toured England four times, in 1896, 1899, 1902 and 1905,

Clem Hill had an awkward, choked grip on the handle but when he swung the bat he was all rhythm and power.

and South Africa in 1902–03. He made more than 1,000 runs in all but one of his trips to England—in 1899, when because of illness he only batted 23 times for 879 runs, delighting English fans with his aggressiveness and stubborn fighting, normally going in first wicket down. He twice declined tours of England on questions of principle, in 1909 when he said he distrusted the Board of Control's terms, and in 1912, when he was one of the six players who refused to tour unless they could appoint their own manager.

Hill was not among the team originally chosen to visit England in 1896, but immediately after the side was named he scored 206 not out for South Australia against NSW at Sydney, including 154 of his team's last 197 runs. The NSW captain who tried to curb his scoring was Tom Garrett, a Test selector. Hill's performance created a public outcry for his inclusion in the touring side and at 19 he was added to it.

Hill made his first Test century in his seventh Test, when he made 100 of Australia's first 142 runs and put on 165 for the seventh wicket with Hugh Trumble. His 188 in that knock remains the highest score in England-Australia Tests by a batsman under 21. He preferred pace bowling to slows and medium-pacers and hooked with such fearlessness even the greatest fast bowlers felt frustrated bowling to him.

Hill was the cause of one of the angriest demonstrations known to Australian cricket when he was given run out in the Sydney Test against England in 1903. He and Trumper ran four from a Trumper drive off Braund, with Hill running well past the stumps at the bowler's end. When overthrows resulted, he had to turn and again run the length of the pitch. The mid-on fieldsman, Relf, threw to wicket-keeper Lilley and umpire Crockett gave Hill out as he passed the stumps. Hill could not believe the decision, as the ball had to pass from behind him before his bat slid in. Spectators threw bottles on to the cycle track that encircled the ground, and amid the uproar that followed Crockett had to be escorted from the field by police. "English captain 'Plum' Warner threatened to take his team off as cries of 'Crock, Crock, Crock,'" echoed around the ground.

Curiously it was on the 1899 tour that he made his biggest impression, playing five Test innings for 60.20 per innings. "What Hill did up to the time of his illness showed without doubt he was the best bat in the Australian team," wrote *Wisden's* Sydney Pardon. "The way in which, on a hard wicket, he can turn balls to leg has to be seen to be believed. No left hander has ever depended so much on skill and so little on punishing power in front of the wicket." Hill has the honour of being the only Test century-maker at Bramall Lane in Sheffield. He scored 119 in 1902 in the only Test ever played there.

Hill was one of the great fieldsmen in the deep, with a tre-

490

mendous throwing arm. At Leeds in 1902 he threw in a ball from near the boundary that knocked down the stumps at one end and then hit the stumps at the other end. He was Australia's most prolific Test batsman in the years before Bradman and Ponsford, with 19 scores over 50 and seven over 100, top score 191. Against South Africa he made 142 at Johannesburg in 1902–03, 191 at Sydney, and 100 at Melbourne in 1910–11. Playing for Australia against New Zealand at Wellington in 1904–05, he made 26 from an over from K. M. Ollivier, with hits of 6, 6, 6, 4, 4.

In pennant matches in Adelaide he was for years a remarkable scorer. For North Adelaide, he had scores of 217 not out against Hindmarsh in 1895, and 241 against Adelaide in 1897. For North Adelaide, he averaged 111.33 in 1894–95 and 113.50 two seasons later, and for Sturt in 1906–07 he averaged 108. He disappeared from the game far too early because of his duties as a steward with the Adelaide Racing Club but did valuable work as a selector and coach. Clem one of three Hill brothers who also played inter-State Australian Rules football. At the age of 60, Clem was appointed handicapper to the Victoria Amateur Turf Club, which runs the Caulfield Cup. He held the job for six years before ill health forced him to switch to the less demanding job of handicapping for the Geelong Racing Club. He died of injuries sustained when he was thrown from a tram in a Melbourne traffic accident in 1945, and his body was taken to Adelaide for burial.

A smart, awkward spinner of brisk pace for Victoria and Australia in the 1950s. His leg break hardly turned at all and his top-spinner bounced uncomfortably high. He toured England in 1953 under Hassett and the West Indies in 1955 under Johnson, playing in three Tests in all. He did not play in a Test in Australia.

Jack Hill first played for Victoria in 1945–46 and he kept his place in the State side until 1955–56. His 69 first-class matches produced a best analysis 7 for 51 against South Australia in 1952–53.

His figures are not all that impressive but seven of his eight Test victims were class players. In England he took 63 wickets at 21.07 and in the West Indies he finished on top of the bowling averages with 18 wickets at 21.11. He was a star amateur Australian Rules footballer whose career was cut short when he twice fractured his skull. He headed the St Kilda club's bowling averages six times and captained the club for seven years.

HILL, John Charles, 1923–1974

First-Class Averages: Batting, 867 runs at 16.05; Bowling, 218 wickets at 23.11.

Tests (3): 21 runs at 7.00; 8 wickets at 34.12.

491

HIRD, Sydney Francis, 1910–1980

First-Class Averages: Batting, 1,453 runs at 33.02; Bowling, 59 wickets at 28.54.

An outstanding all-rounder for Sydney's Balmain club, for New South Wales, Ramsbottom in the Lancashire League, and Orange Free State and Eastern Province in South Africa. He was one of five brothers who excelled at various levels in the Balmain district, and a team-mate of Archie Jackson and Bill Hunt. He left for the Lancashire League on the fringe of Test selection because he could not find a job in Sydney, and never returned.

Originally, Hird bowled leg-spinners and googlies but when he went to England he was persuaded to switch to off-spin. Bill O'Reilly has recorded his great displeasure that Hird made the change, testimony of the low regard English coaches have for leg spin. Hird was a brilliant hitter and hit at least one six on every Australian ground on which he played. Some of his hits at Sydney Cricket Ground are still discussed with awe by oldtimers. He was a superb fieldsman.

At 13 he batted throughout an innings in short pants for Balmain in a lower grades match on a bad wicket at Redfern Oval. At 15, he created a Balmain third grade record by taking 84 wickets and in a Poidevin-Gray Shield final hooked a Randwick bowler on to the roof of the SCG Eastern Stand, from which it bounced on to a Showground cattle pen. He was picked for New South Wales as a bowler and made his first-class debut at Brisbane in the match in which Eddie Gilbert

The Hird brothers, who all appeared for Sydney's Balmain club (L to R): Syd, Jack, Bill, Harry and Lew.

492

had Wendell Bill and Bradman out for ducks in his first seven balls.

Hird made a century in his third first-class match, 101 against South Africa at Sydney in 1931–32. He followed the next season with 106 against Queensland in Brisbane, with nine fours and a six, cutting and driving stylishly. He was made 12th man for the First Test of the 1932–33 Bodyline series after taking 6 for 135 against England for NSW. Then, with Australia desperately short of all-rounders, he left for the Lancashire League.

Hird hit swashbuckling centuries twice in his first fortnight in England. Takings for the Ramsbottom club doubled. He was hailed as the greatest attraction in the League, and his income from crowd collections soared. He appeared in only one match for the Lancashire County team in 1939 but did not bowl or bat because of rain. In 1935, bowling off-spin, he took 100 wickets for Ramsbottom, and in 1937 he pushed his Ramsbottom record from 821 to 920 runs in the season. Five summers with Ramsbottom yielded 389 wickets and 4,136 runs at averages of more than 40 each year.

After World War II Hird moved to South Africa, where he became a respected coach. At 36, he made 130 in 1945–46 in his first match in South Africa, for Eastern Province against Griqualand West. In 1946–47, Hird had match figures of 9 for 39, for Eastern Province v. Border. He made 697 first-class runs in Australia at 33.19 and took 31 wickets at 30.58.

A strapping 6 ft. 3 in. Western Australian right-arm fast bowler who turned in some outstanding figures in 10 seasons of first-class cricket, playing in one Test. He let the ball go from quite high up and achieved swing and lift, digging the ball hard into the pitch. He played initially for Fremantle in the Perth grade competition and made his debut for WA in 1955–56. He had 63 first-class matches, taking five wickets or more in an innings 12 times and once taking 10 wickets in a match. His best figures were 8 for 98 against New South Wales at Perth in 1964–65.

Hoare played in the Adelaide Test in the exciting 1960–61 series against the West Indies, beginning dramatically by taking Conrad Hunte's wicket in his second over and contributing a handy 35 batting at No 10 in Australia's first innings. He finished with only two wickets in the match, however, and was not given another Test chance. He finished his grade career with Subiaco-Floreat, for whom he bowled off-spinners. One of the highlights of a career that produced three scores over 50 was his innings of 133 against the Australian XI at Perth in 1960–61 when he opened the batting for WA.

HOARE, Desmond Edward, 1934–

First-Class Averages: Batting, 1,276 runs at 18.49; Bowling, 225 wickets at 26.91.

Tests (1): 35 runs at 17.50; 2 wickets at 78.00.

HODGES, John Henry, 1856–1933

First-Class Averages: Batting, 75 runs at 12.50; Bowling, 12 wickets at 16.50.

Tests(2): 10 runs at 3.30; 6 wickets at 14.00.

A Victorian fast medium left-arm bowler who played in the first of all Tests at Melbourne in 1877 when more widely known Frank Allan declined to play. Allan said he could not spare the time, and Hodges went into the Australian side in his place without ever having played for Victoria.

Hodges, born in the Collingwood district, began his career in a junior competition with the Capulet side that included three of his brothers. After showing outstanding form he moved up to senior club cricket in 1876–77 with Richmond and played all his district cricket for that club. He quickly won a reputation for bowling straight and for an ability to move an occasional ball sharply but when he got his chance thanks to Allan he showed a tendency to bowl too short, a weakness that could not be persevered with in low scoring matches.

He took 1 for 27 off nine overs in the first innings of the first Test after England's Charlwood hit him about in scoring 36 out of England's total of 196. In the second innings he did better, taking 2 for 7 off seven overs. He retained his place for the second Test about a fortnight later but disappointed and disappeared from Tests. He batted like a bowler in both his Tests and was a slipshod field.

Hodges, a bootmaker by trade, played two matches in 1877–78 for Victoria against NSW, but his form deserted him and within two seasons he was back in the Capulet side. He is believed to have been the J. Hodges who umpired the Fifth Test in 1884–85.

HOGG, James Edgar Phipps, 1906–1975

First-Class Averages: Batting, 427 runs at 28.26.

A right-hand batsman who represented New South Wales and Queensland. In the second of his four matches for New South Wales in 1926–27, he was one of those who fielded for almost two days while Victoria made the world record score of 1,107. He played for New South Wales until 1929–30 and in 1931–32 won selection in the Queensland side from the Valley club. He was twice captain of Queensland. His best score was 71 for Queensland against South Australia in 1931–32. His brother, G. C. H. Hogg, represented New South Wales, in one match in 1928–29.

HOGG, Rodney Malcolm, 1951–

A spectacular right-arm fast bowler who made the finest debut of any bowler in Test history by taking 51 wickets in his first season as Australia's opening bowler. He bowled at the stumps and he bowled extremely fast, progressing from a dramatic 6 for 74 debut against England at Brisbane in 1978–79 to a sequence of superb performances, interspersed

494

by arguments with his captain Graham Yallop and big match walk-offs that raised doubts about his fitness and temperament.

Hogg took 41 wickets in the six Tests against England, five more than the record for an Australian bowler in Tests against England—by Arthur Mailey in 1920–21 when Mailey bowled in only four Tests. Hogg added ten more wickets to his total that season in two Tests against Pakistan. His 51 Test wickets cost 784 runs, average 15.37. With the bat, he contributed an invaluable 36 in his first Test at Brisbane.

Hogg made his grade cricket debut with Northcote club in Melbourne, bowling his first ball wide of the leg stump. "If you don't bowl four of the next seven deliveries at the stumps, you're off," bellowed Northcote captain Bill Lawry, a lesson in the need for accuracy Hogg never forgot. Rejected by the Victorian team selectors, Hogg considered moving to New South Wales but when that State picked West Indian Andy Roberts in its Shield team he decided to go to South Australia.

He made his debut for South Australia in 1975–76 against Victoria, taking 3 for 56 and 4 for 57. An outstanding perfor-

First-Class Averages: Batting, 737 runs at 9.32; Bowling, 219 wickets at 22.88.

Tests (22): 246 runs at 7.69; 82 wickets at 23.62.

Australian team-mates jubilantly congratulate Rodney Hogg after he dismissed Geoff Boycott at Sydney in 1978–79.

mance for South Australia against Queensland in 1977–78 when he took 6 for 80, lifted him into consideration as a Test bowler. With Lillee, Malone and Pascoe contracted to World Series Cricket and Thomson unavailable, Hogg went into the Australian Test side. Tall, wide-shouldered, with fair, curly hair he was seldom out of the headlines, often leaving the field because of apparent breathing problems. Doctors reported that he was not asthmatic but Hogg continued to go off when he chose. His captain, Yallop, repeatedly queried him about it and on Hogg's habit of changing his field placements without consultation. At one stage during the Adelaide Test against England, Yallop wrote, Hogg suggested that they survey the back of Adelaide Oval—"and I don't think Hogg had a tennis match in mind."

The return of the WSC pace men gave Hogg a big task to retain his place in the Australian team but to his credit he managed it and in a three-pronged Australian pace attack during the 1980–81 Australian summer against New Zealand and India he shared the job with Lillee and Pascoe, and often looked faster and straighter than either of them. He remained something of an enigma, however, for few Australian Test speedsters have shown Hogg's inability to swing the ball. He does so little in the air he wastes the shine of the new ball. Often he bowls with greater hostility with third use of the ball after other bowlers have had their chance at exploiting the shine.

Hogg visited England with Australia's 1979 World Cup team, and represented Australia that year in England in an international double wicket competition, partnering Peter Toohey. He returned to England with the Australian team in 1981, but he was probably fortunate not to be sent home after complaining of injuries doctors could not diagnose. He took the 1981–82 off from first-class cricket working on a back problem. In 1982–83 he may return with a more mature approach to the game.

HOGUE, Clarence Robert, 1879–1969

Son of an MLA for the Sydney electorate of Glebe who played district cricket for 72 years and asked for a new bat as his 90th birthday present. He claimed he was never out lbw in a career that began in 1887 and lasted until 1959. Hogue played for North Sydney first grade from 1915 until 1926, taking 384 wickets with his right-arm spinners at 18.19. He then took charge of North's Shire XI until 1941 when he switched to North's City and Suburban team, for whom he took more than 50 wickets in a season three times. He oozed advice in these matches for young players on either side, and was often seen in the gathering darkness on otherwise deserted grounds explaining grips and stance to teenagers.

496

Right: David Hookes hammers a ball past point.

Below: Bruce Laird driving through mid-off.

Below: Rick Darling, one of the finest runners in Australian cricket, moves off as he turns a ball to leg.

Above: Alan Border dives wide to reach a slips catch off Thomson. Below: A jubilant moment for the Australian fieldsman as Ashley Mallet claims a victim against England in Sydney.

A handy left-handed all-rounder for the Queensland team for 10 seasons who has never challenged for a Test place. He has repeatedly made a good start with the bat without moving on to a century and has scored 50 or more 17 times, with a highest score of 90 against Victoria in 1978–79. He has taken valuable wickets with his right-arm legspinners, best figures 6 for 56 against NSW in 1978–79. He has twice taken five wickets in an innings and has held 43 catches in first-class games. He set a Queensland eighth wicket partnership record of 146 with Geoff Dymock against Victoria in 1978–79.

HOHNS, Trevor Victor, 1954–

First-Class Averages: Batting, 2,470 runs at 27.75; Bowling, 90 wickets at 42.11.

A tall right-hand middle order batsman for New South Wales, South Australia and Australia. He was given frequent chances in Tests but never made the runs expected of a batsman who scored heavily in inter-State matches. He crouched awkwardly as he faced the bowling but drove splendidly, scoring a lot of runs with the sweep shot and cuts behind point. He was a brilliant slips field who twice caught four batsmen in a Test and a useful change bowler.

Hole, born at Concord West in Sydney, played in the New South Wales Colts team with Richie Benaud and Jimmy Burke and went into the State team in 1949–50, but after one season moved to South Australia, where he played for the next eight seasons and scored nine of his 11 first-class centuries. He made his debut for Australia in the Fifth Test against England at Melbourne in 1950–51, topscoring in the second innings with 63, England winning for the first time since 1938. He failed the following summer against John Goddard's West Indian tourists, scoring only 192 runs in nine innings. When South Australia beat the West Indies by 227 runs that season, Hole took four wickets for six runs off 30 balls. In 1952–53 against South Africa, he made only 158 runs in four Tests and was dropped in the Fifth.

With the outstanding Australian team of the immediate post World War II years declining, he had a golden opportunity to take a permenant Test spot in England in 1953 and he began with 112 in the first match against Worcester. He was a major disappointment in the Tests, however, scoring only 273 runs in 10 innings, falling five times to Bedser. He completed the tour with 1,118 runs at 33.87, but what mattered was that England had regained The Ashes after almost 19 years.

Despite his failures in three successive Test series, Hole continued to score heavily in inter-State matches. He made 226, his career best, in December, 1953 against Queensland for SA but found Tyson too much for him in the 1954–55 Tests against England. Tyson ran him out at 57 with a brilliant throw in the First Test and then clean bowled him three innings in a row to virtually end Hole's Test career. He was

HOLE, Graeme Blake, 1931–

First-Class Averages: Batting, 5,647 runs at 36.66; Bowling, 61 wickets at 44.03.

Tests (18): 789 runs at 25.45; 3 wickets at 42.00.

dropped from the last two Tests of the series. Hole scored further centuries for SA in 1956–57 and 1957–58 but did not play again for Australia. He had 33 Test innings in all for a topscore of 66, unfortunate figures for a likeable, good-looking young man for whom a brilliant Test career had been forecast.

HOLROYD, Henry North, 1832–1909

The third Earl of Sheffield, Viscount Pevensey, Baron Sheffield of Dunsmore, Meath, Baron Sheffield of Roscommon, Ireland, and Baron Sheffield of Sheffield, and the donor of the Sheffield Shield, symbol of cricket supremacy among the Australian States. The shield bears the Australian and Sheffield coats of arms, and various allegorical figures. He was not a great player but good enough to play for the Gentlemen of Sussex against the Gentlemen of Kent in 1856 when he was Viscount Pevensey. He was president of the Sussex County Cricket Club from 1879 to 1897 and again in 1904. In 1891–92 he financed and accompanied an English team captained by W. G. Grace to Australia and during the tour presented £150 to the Australasian Cricket Council for use in developing cricket. The Council wisely invested the money in the Sheffield Shield for competition between the States. Five Australian teams began their tours of England by playing on Baron Sheffield's private ground at Sheffield Park.

HONE, Sir Brian William, 1908–1978

First-Class Averages:
Batting, 2,790 runs at 39.29.

A splendid Adelaide-born right-hand batsman whose cricket career was severely restricted by his dedication to education. From 1928–29 to 1930–31 when he came a Rhodes scholar, he scored three fine centuries for South Australia—137 in 1928–29 against Victoria at Adelaide, 126 in 1929–30 against New South Wales at Adelaide, and 106 the same season against Victoria at Melbourne. When he made his 126 against NSW he made 67 in the second innings and his 193 runs in the match had a large bearing on SA's five wickets win. At Oxford University he won Blues for cricket in 1931–32 and 1933, when he was captain. He joined Marlborough College on graduation as head of the English department and played impressively for Wiltshire in the English Minor Counties competition, heading the batting averages between 1937 and 1939. He was noted for his stout defence and seldom missed a chance to punish bad balls. In 1940, he became headmaster of Cranbrook School in Sydney and 10 years later took over as headmaster of Melbourne Grammar School, a post he held for 20 years. He was later Deputy Chancellor of Monash University. He played 71 innings in first-class cricket, scoring nine centuries, highest score 170 in 1933 for Oxford.

498

A spritely right-arm medium pace bowler whose batting improved with age. He represented New South Wales from 1924 until 1932 and played against four successive English touring teams, the last in 1936. He did not play in a Test but he will be remembered long after many who did for two performances in the 1928–29 season. In the first he and Alan Kippax added a world record 307 for the tenth wicket against Victoria, and in the second a few weeks later he took four wickets in four balls, the only instance of this feat in an Australian first-class match. He was for years an ABC cricket commentator.

Hooker, a slender thin-faced figure with a pencil moustache, stood 6 ft 2 in, and was the first player from the Mosman club to appear against England. He was the baby in a family of seven children, and learned the game from his brother George, who was 20 years older and a noted authority on cricket theory. George took the first wicket ever on Mosman Oval. Hal went to Fort Street High School at the same time as "Doc" Evatt and Garfield Barwick and represented Combined High Schools at cricket. He joined Mosman in 1914–15 just before he went to Palestine as a trooper with the Seventh Light Horse.

Hooker was in a NSW Colts team to play England in 1924–25 and was heart-broken when the match was rained off. He played for an Australian XI and for NSW against England in 1928–29, for NSW against England in 1932–33, and in 1936–37 came out of retirement to captain Northern NSW against England at Newcastle. He also captained country teams against South Africa.

Although he batted at No. 11 for NSW in the innings that included his famous partnership in 1928–29 with Kippax, Hooker had won the Mosman club's batting as well as the bowling averages. He and Kippax came together with the score at 9 for 157, chasing Victoria's 376. They batted all Christmas Day 1928, keeping the Victorians from Christmas feasts, but finished the day still nine runs behind. Next day they continued to 464. "I reached 62 with two fours off Ted a'Beckett and then tried to hit him right out of the ground," said Hooker. "Jack Ryder, never a great fieldsman, reached out and caught it. 'Kipper' was furious and as we walked off told me he had been riding me for a century. I hadn't missed a ball in two days and I went and did a silly thing like that. More than 50 years later I still regret it. It'd make you cry."

Hooker worked for Kippax in his Sydney sports store so they had a good understanding. In 1932 Kippax sent Hooker to Newcastle to open another store for him. Ray Robinson, the Test batsman, was one of his discoveries in Newcastle. He headed the NSW bowling averages in 1924–25 and the Australian first-class averages in 1928–29. His four wickets in four balls came in the return match against Victoria at Sydney in 1928–29 when he took the last three wickets in the first in-

HOOKER, John Edward Halford ("Hal"), 1898–1982

First-Class Averages: Batting, 421 runs at 20.04; Bowling, 78 wickets at 28.50.

499

nings and had another with his first ball in the second innings. Three were bowled and the fourth caught and bowled. Until his death in 1982, he had a 68-year link with Mosman.

HOOKES, David William, 1955–

First-Class Averages: Batting, 3,503 runs at 38.00; Bowling, 6 wickets at 62.00.

Tests (8): 436 runs at 29.07.

A tall, fair-haired left-handed batsman who has never quite lived up to the exciting promise he showed in his second season in big cricket in 1976–77 when he was 21. In that summer Hookes forced his way into the Australian team with innings of 163, 9, 185, 101, 135 and 156 for South Australia (four centuries in 11 days) and then played an unforgettable innings of 56 in the Centenary Test at Melbourne during which he hit Tony Greig for five successive fours. He was only the second player in the history of cricket to score centuries in each innings of successive first-class games—Englishman Tom Hayward in 1906 was the first. Hookes is a batsman who loves to attack and his eagerness to get after bowlers has sometimes caused his dismissal. Since his return from WSC he has developed into a useful bowler of medium-pace swing, and in 1981–82 captained South Australia with flair and undoubted inspiration to win the Sheffield Shield.

Hookes' five superlative drives off Greig will remain one of the triumphant events of Australian cricket, each of them masterly in the timing of bat on ball and in their placement between fieldsmen, and the innings itself triggering an Australian revival after three wickets had fallen for 53 runs in the second innings. The combination in Hookes of courage and brilliant strokeplay caused Don Bradman in the stands to say, "I thought Frank Woolley had been born again." Greig's resentment increased with each stroke, conveying itself to the crowd who went wild at the end of the over. Cricket writers who dug into Hookes' past as the result of this marvellous display discovered that in a club match in England he had hit six sixes in a six-ball over for Dulwich.

A hero overnight, Hookes failed to follow up this dramatic start on tour in England with Greg Chappell's 1977 side. He made only 804 runs on the tour, highest score 108, frequently showing unnecessary temper. He made 283 runs in nine Test innings, and only his 85 in the Fifth Test had any of the magic of Melbourne. He joined WSC at the end of that tour and was promoted as an heroic figure, a status he had trouble justifying after he broke his jaw trying to hook Andy Roberts, though he did play a few fine innings for WSC.

Hookes, born at Mile End, SA, seemed to lack the application essential in playing long innings when WSC players returned to traditional cricket and was dropped from the Australian team after knocks of 43 and 37 in the Brisbane Test against the West Indies in 1979–80. He got another chance when he visited Pakistan at the end of that season but achieved spectacles in the only Test in which he appeared. His failures in one-day matches was equally inexplicable, for his bold shot-making looked ideally suited to this form of cricket.

He missed Australia's 1981 tour of England but his appointment as South Australian captain for the 1981–82 season had splendid results, settling him as a resourceful all-round cricketer. South Australia had finished in sixth position in the 1980–81 Shield competition and on the surface lacked the depth to do better but Hookes shrugged off his own poor form and led an enthusiastic young side to a remarkable Shield victory. Time is on his side and there is no doubting his talent and all lovers of crisp, authoritative stroke play no doubt hope he will soon return to the Australian team.

An almost forgotten all-rounder of outstanding merit who played for New South Wales for almost 20 years and for Australia in 20 Tests. He had a career studded with remarkable performances but such was the brilliance of the players with whom he appeared his name seldom is recalled in discussions on the Golden Age of Australian cricket.

Hopkins, born in Sydney, was a forceful batsman capable of thrilling hitting, a right-arm slow medium bowler with sharp swerve and cut from the off, and a brilliant fieldsman wherever he was placed. In a first-class career that began in 1896 and continued until the start of World War I, he made five overseas tours with Australian teams and appeared in two Test series at home.

He made his debut at 20 for New South Wales and at the age of 24 in 1901–02 scored 117 against Victoria at Sydney, the first of six centuries for the State and one of eight in first-class matches. He went to England with Joe Darling's team in 1902 and in the Second Test at Lord's distinguished himself by dismissing Ranjitsinhji and Fry before they had scored. He did not get another Test wicket in the series but ended the tour with 1,192 runs at 25.91 in all matches, topscore 105 not out against Gloucester at Bristol, and 38 wickets at 17.60. He toured South Africa with Australia in 1902–03 with little success. In 1902–03 against MCC at Sydney he went to the wicket with New South Wales 7 for 175 in their second innings, a lead of only 37. He and Duff then put on 236 for the eighth wicket, Hopkins scoring 133, Duff 194. MCC still needed 293 with 10 wickets left when the match was drawn.

Hopkins visited New Zealand with an Australian side in 1905 and that year went back to England again under Darling, this time scoring 1,094 runs in all matches, topscore 154 against Northants, average 29.56 and taking 27 wickets at

HOPKINS, Albert John Young ("Bert"), 1876–1931

First-Class Averages: Batting, 5,563 runs at 25.40; Bowling, 271 wickets at 24.40.

Tests (20): 509 runs at 16.42; 26 wickets at 26.76.

501

30.55. In 1906–07 at Sydney he made 171 for New South Wales v. Queensland at Sydney, and later that season, added 193 for the second wicket against South Australia at Sydney with Austin Diamond, finishing on 108. In 1908–09, he produced more of the same against South Australia at Sydney, adding 283 in 170 minutes for the second wicket with Monty Noble, finishing with his career best score of 218 after being dropped first ball.

Back in England in 1909 his form fell away and he made only 432 runs on the tour at 15.42, best score 56 not out, but took 58 wickets at 20.53. He played his last Test on that tour but continued to play for New South Wales until 1915. His best bowling analysis was 7 for 10 for Australia v. Cambridge University in 1902 (six bowled, one lbw). He took a hat-trick against South Australia in 1903–04, and took five wickets or more in an innings ten times. He also held 87 catches.

HORAN, Thomas Patrick ("Felix"), 1854–1916

First-Class Averages: Batting, 4,027 runs at 23.27; Bowling, 35 wickets at 23.68.

Tests (15): 471 runs at 18.84; 11 wickets at 13.00.

A hard-hitting right-hand batsman and round-arm medium-pace bowler. He was born in Middleton, Country Cork, and brought to Australia as a child. He played 15 times for Australia, captaining his adopted country twice against England. Horan wore black pads and a beard 100 years before WSC players adopted them but the luck of the Irish ran out and Australia was thrashed each time he was captain in 1884–85.

He gave Victoria notable service and in his last 10 years was rated the finest batsman in that State. He was very severe on the legside and could clump the ball powerfully through mid-off and the covers, as his eight first-class centuries in a low-scoring era indicate. He was particularly proud of the fact that in the first match between Victoria and South Australia in 1874–75 he took 11 for 29 in the 18 of South Australia's second innings and thus prevented a shock SA victory.

Horan, a heavy-shouldered, thick-set figure with enormous forearms, first played for Victoria in 1874–75. He played in the first ever Test at Melbourne in 1876 and in 1878 toured England with the first official Australian touring team under Dave Gregory's captaincy. He made a creditable 377 runs at 13.46 on the tour, despite many ill-prepared pitches and took 8 wickets at 17.87. He was one of a generation that believed batting without gloves was proof of manhood, dour and unflappable in defence but no stylist. In the First Test at Melbourne in 1881–82 he made 124 and added 124 with Giffen, the first century stand in Tests in Australia.

Horan batted well on damp pitches, unperturbed by the extra movement of the ball off the pitch, and on his second tour of England in 1882 under Murdoch played in the historic Ashes match at The Oval. He scored 1,175 runs on the tour at 25.00, including his career topscore of 141 not out against

Gloucestershire and 112 against a United XI. In his 15 Tests between 1877 and 1885 his highest score was 124, and his best bowling figures 6 for 40.

Horan had 13 innings for Victoria in matches with or against the odds in which he made 310 runs at 28.18 and took 13 wickets at 4.61. One of his sons, **Thomas Ignatius Bernard Horan** (1887–1952) played five times for Victoria from 1906–07, scoring 210 runs at 21.00. Another son, **James Francis Horan** (1880–1945), scored 820 runs at 24.11 for Victoria in 20 games from 1900–01.

Horan's strong personality undoubtedly played an important role when Australia first appeared in international cricket, but as a writer under the pen-name *Felix* after his playing days ended, he made an even more lasting contribution in his comments on the game for *The Australasian*. He had a wide and appreciative audience among his contemporaries and his work has proved invaluable to cricket historians both here and overseas.

HORDERN, Dr Herbert Vivian ("Ranji"), 1884–1938

Australia's first outstanding bowler of the googly and arguably our best. He was a dentist who could not afford to have his fingers hurt playing cricket and played only 33 first-class matches, including two Tests against South Africa and five against England, one of those with more Tests to his name than Shield matches, but during his short career he took 217 wickets and left many experts ranking him ahead of Mailey and Grimmett. He made no overseas tours with Australian teams.

"The comparison between Hordern, Mailey and Grimmett is of more than academic interest," wrote Johnny Moyes. "Two became world figures in cricket and the third rarely comes into discussion because he played so little. I'm inclined to place Hordern ahead of the others. He was as good as Mailey on hard Australian wickets and better than Grimmett; in England he would have been as outstanding as Grimmett. With his control of length, his disguised deliveries, his ability to flight the ball, and his clever fingers, I don't see how he could have failed."

Hordern took a longer run than most spinners, but it was smooth, not jerky like Grimmett, nor bounding like Wright, nor casual like Mailey's approach. He was taller than either Mailey or Grimmett and this gave him an advantage in flight and control. He never bowled loose balls like Mailey and he turned both leg break and googly about as much as Grimmett. His disguise was subtle, with no indication of the googly such as Grimmett's dropped shoulder. The only visible sign of his googly was the tip of his little finger pointing skyward as he dropped his wrist to bowl—and only alert bats-

First-Class Averages: Batting, 721 runs at 16.38; Bowling, 217 wickets at 16.79.

Tests (7): 254 runs at 23.09; 46 wickets at 23.36.

men with outstanding eyesight could pick that up. The English critics C. B. Fry and Pelham Warner rated him the best googly bowler they encountered.

Hordern, born in North Sydney where he played for the district club, first played for NSW in 1905–06, and spent several of his early years studying dentistry in America. He visited England in 1907 as a member of the Pennsylvania University team that played English public schools; in 1908 toured England with the Philadelphians' team that played 10 first-class matches. On these trips he developed a googly of exceptional accuracy and variable flight. He returned home from America before the 1910–11 matches against South Africa.

Despite his limited big cricket experience, he was chosen for the Tests, a tough challenge as the South Africans had shown themselves masters of the googly and had in Schwartz, a former team-mate of Bosanquet, one of the foremost exponents of the ball. In the two Tests he played, Hordern took 14 wickets at 21.07 and Australia won the series 4–1. Playing for New South Wales that summer against Tasmania, Hordern took 7 for 31 in a total of 49, and in 1912–13 against Tasmania he took 6 for 67.

Apart from Hordern, Australia's bowling lacked hostility for the 1911–12 series in Australia against England. He began by completely bamboozling the Englishmen in the First Test at Sydney, taking 5 for 85 and 7 for 90, a match-winning effort. In the Second Test, Australia were bundled out for 184 and England at 3 for 211 appeared certain of a huge lead. Hordern then took four of the last seven wickets for 50 runs to restrict the lead to 80. In the final innings, with England needing 219 to win, one of Test cricket's great duels developed between Hordern and Hobbs. Hobbs emerged the victor and his century won the match but Hordern was far from disgraced.

In the last Test of the series, Hordern took 5 for 95 and 5 for 66, thus achieving the remarkable record of dismissing five batsmen in an innings four times in his first full Test series in which he collected 32 wickets. "Tibby" Cotter was the next best Australian bowler with 12 wickets.

Hordern, nicknamed "Ranji" because of his swarthy complexion, was unavailable for the 1912 Australian tour of England and played no further first-class cricket after appearing for New South Wales in 1912–13. He later wrote a humorous book about cricket called *Googly* which contains a memorable account of a country cricket match and provides an enlightening insight into his light-hearted approach to his cricket.

Hordern was the bowler who hoodwinked the rising young batsman from South Australia, Johnny Moyes, in Victor Trumper's Benefit match in 1912–13 at Sydney. Trumper explained to Moyes that he must watch for the little finger lifting in the air before Hordern let go his googly. "I lost sight of the little finger, the ball broke the wrong way for me, but not for Sammy Carter the wicket-keeper," said Moyes. "Sammy simply said, 'Beat you, son,' and out I went, stumped."

HORNIBROOK, Percival Mitchell, 1899–1976

A high-actioned loosely-built left-arm spin bowler over a long period for Queensland and all too belatedly for Australia. Hornibrook played an important role in the development of Queensland cricket after World War I but despite consistently good figures did not get his chance in Tests until he was way past his best. Born at Obi Obi, Queensland, he made his first grade cricket debut for Toombul in 1919–20, taking 66 wickets at only 7.10 apiece and forcing his way into the State side. In 20 seasons with Toombul between 1919 and 1939 he took 833 wickets at 12.70. With Ironmonger and "Chilla" Christ, he built a big reputation for Queensland left-arm bowlers recently carried on by Geoff Dymock.

Hornibrook bowled fast or fast-medium early in an innings, pushing them through for five overs before he reverted to spin. In 1921 he had a high action that exploited his 6 ft 3 ins, but by 1930 his arm had dropped. He bowled the left-hander's natural leg-break with topspin at a pace that prevented batsmen moving out to him. Not long before his death he regretted that nobody had pointed out to him that his arm had dropped too low and that his left foot was pointing towards point. "I can see now that I was overbowled in club and State cricket and became too mechanical," he said.

Hornibrook toured New Zealand with Vernon Ransford's Australian XI in 1920–21, taking an impressive 81 wickets at 8.91 in all matches. He played two matches for an Australian XI against England in Brisbane, played for The Rest against Australia in Frank Iredale's benefit match, and for Australia v. New South Wales in the Howell benefit match. He also played for Australia v. The Rest at Sydney in 1925–26 and for Woodfull's XI v. Ryder's XI in 1929–30.

Many experts considered he was unlucky not to tour England in the 1921 and 1926 Australian teams before he won selection in the 1930 team. Hornibrook bowled more overs (779.2) on that English tour than any Australian bowler except Grimmett, who led the wicket-takers with 142 compared with Hornibrook's 93 wickets. He took 7 for 92 in The Oval Test, England losing the match and The Ashes as a result. He started bowling spinners but they were too slow so he changed to one-finger "slices," bowling round the wicket at the leg stump, moving the ball away to the slips. When he came on England had two men out, and apart from a run out he got the rest: Sutcliffe, Duleepsinhji, Hammond, Leyland, Wyatt, Larwood and Duckworth. Grimmett dropped Hammond off his bowling when Hammond, who made 60, was 16.

First-Class Averages: Batting, 754 runs at 10.77; Bowling, 279 wickets at 23.82.

Tests (6): 60 runs at 10.00; 17 wickets at 39.05.

Hornibrook retired from big cricket soon after he returned home from the 1930 tour, but kept going in grade until 1939.

Hornibrook was not an accomplished batsman, with 59 not out his highest score for Australia and 36 his best for Queensland. Some English Test players argued that he would have been even a more effective bowler had he been blooded in either the 1921 or 1926 Australian teams in England and if his slips fieldsmen had held their catches. Hornibrook's ability to beat famous batsmen from Australia's southern States improved Queensland's case for inclusion in the Sheffield Shield, which came in the 1926–27 season.

Hornibrook and Ron Oxenham carried the Queensland attack for years, but in Queensland's first Shield season Hornibrook was unavailable for the southern tour and played in only one State match—when Queensland dismissed a Victorian side that included Ponsford, Hendry and Rigg for only 86 to win by 234 runs outright. Hornibrook excelled in the slips, taking many fine catches (66 in all), but was slack in other fielding positions. He took five wickets or more in an innings 17 times and six times took 10 wickets in a match.

HORROCKS, William John, 1905–

First-Class Averages: Batting, 1,472 runs at 38.73.

A Western Australian right-hand batsman who showed outstanding promise early in his career for the State but preferred to go to England and play for Lancashire, where he was born. He made 148 not out for WA against Tasmania at Hobart in 1929–30 in an innings full of style and good strokes. But he disappointed for Lancashire, scoring 371 runs in 17 matches at 23.18, topscore 100 not out. He did not bowl, but was a very efficient field. On his return to the west he scored 140 not out against "Gubby" Allen's England team at Perth in 1936–37. Apart from his two centuries, he made five scores over 50 for WA.

HOUGH, Kenneth William, 1928–

A Sydney-born cricketer renowned in New Zealand for his powerhouse hitting. He was a New South Wales Colts and NSW Country XI cricketer who shared the new ball with Alan Davidson when NSW Colts played Queensland Colts. He also played as a goalkeeper for Australian and New Zealand soccer teams. One winter he played first grade Rugby League in Sydney and Rugby Union for the RAAF in the services competition, representing in the United Services XI.

Hough, 6 ft. 2 in., 17 stone, went to New Zealand in 1956–57 to work in the paper pulp business at Kawerau, but he lived in Gisborne for two years and while he was there played firstly for Northern Districts and then for Auckland in the Plunket Shield. An immensely strong character whose bulk belied his

506

agility, he bowled fast-medium, moving the ball either way. His big season was 1958–59 when he took 36 Plunket Shield wickets and appeared for New Zealand against Peter May's England team.

He went to the wicket with New Zealand 9 for 102. "When Hough took guard with a bat that was clearly the largest available but several sizes too small, he found Freddie Trueman regarding him," wrote New Zealand critic R. T. Brittenden. "Out of respect for Trueman's England cap and colourful turn of phrase, Hough played the first ball as if it was likely to explode. That was the end of formalities. Trueman was no-balled off the next delivery and Hough hit it for four. The next one went to the mid-wicket boundary. Trueman came in again with a ball of appalling velocity, but he made the mistake of bowling a length. With majestic calm Hough hit it back over the bowler's head, over the boundary, over the sightscreen, as good a blow as a batsman has ever struck. There was another two off the over and 16 in all, and before it was done the partnership produced 40 exciting runs."

In this, his only Test series, Hough headed the New Zealand batting averages with 62.00. But the innings of his life came in 1959–60 for Auckland against Otago at Carisbrook when he took the score from 7 for 129 to 246 in an hour of great ballooning hits which brought five sixes and seven fours. He had 44 first-class innings in New Zealand but could not win selection for NSW when he returned to Sydney, though he did make the NSW practice squad. New Zealanders remain puzzled why selectors did not risk him for he was one of the greatest entertainers New Zealand cricket has seen. Anybody who could hit F. S. Trueman back over his head out of the ground would have been worth a gamble.

A Bondi-born left-arm wrist spinner and right-hand batsman of unusual temperament who has had some devastating spells for Waverley and New South Wales without achieving the Australian team place his talents deserve. Hourn has bowled occasional deliveries that made great players look inept, and even when it became well known among first-class cricketers that he had an unusual bag of tricks he kept producing spin that had Test batsmen playing the wrong way. In the end, a frustrating inability to overcome a no-ball problem cost him his State team berth.

Hourn took five wickets in an innings 11 times for NSW and twice took 10 wickets in a match. His best figures were 9 for 77 against Victoria at Sydney in 1978–79, when he narrowly missed taking all 10 wickets and finished with match figures of 11 for 172. He also had 12 for 113 against South Australia in 1977–78. Later his failure to cure his over-stepping problems

HOURN, David William, 1949–

First-Class Averages: Batting, 220 runs at 6.67; Bowling, 164 wickets at 28.71.

507

caused a loss in confidence that saw him bowling to such a wayward length even his most ardent supporters despaired.

In one Sydney first-grade match Hourn bowled 26 no-balls for Waverley, an absurb count for a spinner. His wrist spin is admittedly harder to control than, say, Ray Bright's finger-spin, but the chances of Hourn beating a good batsman more frequently than Bright are obvious. Hourn has not helped his cause with poor batting and because of a touch football injury he is an immobile field, with a poor percentage of catches for the first-class games he has played. With the years running out, he seems likely to prove a wasted talent.

HOWARD, Roy, 1922–

First-Class Averages: Batting, 1,564 runs at 37.23.

A right-hand batsman from South Melbourne whose dependable scoring helped Victoria in the first few years after World War II. He went to New Zealand with an Australian side captained by Bill Brown in 1949–50, when he was one of only three batsmen to hit a first-class century, finishing with 246 tour runs from five innings at 49.20. He made 141 against Otago and figured in a third wicket stand of 141 with Brown. He also scored 91 against Wellington, dominating an Australian innings of 270. His best scores for Victoria were 132 against Tasmania at Launceston in 1948–49, 131 against South Australia at Melbourne in 1949–50, and 139 against Freddie Brown's England side in 1950–51.

HOWELL, William Peter ("Farmer Bill"), 1869–1940

First-Class Averages: Batting, 2,228 runs at 14.85; Bowling, 520 wickets at 21.45.

Tests (18): 158 runs at 7.52; 49 wickets at 28.71.

A fast right-arm medium bowler who turned the ball both ways and varied his flight skilfully enough to worry the finest batsmen of his period. He was a powerful country boy of striking physique and easy-going disposition who played many swashbuckling left-handed innings. He did not emerge as a potential international until he left his bee farm at Penrith, New South Wales, to visit Sydney at the age of 25 with a team of country cricketers, but in 12 years of big cricket he left a reputation as an all-rounder of the highest class.

Howell, who was a nephew of Edwin Evans, impressed with some lusty hitting on his first visit to Sydney in 1894 and was chosen for the State side to play Stoddart's visiting English team. The selectors thought he might prove to be a successor to the big-hitting Massie and McDonnell. When the Englishmen batted and were well set, Howell remarked to his captain that he thought he could get them out. As a last resort, he was given a bowl. He clean bowled both Stoddart and Brown and three others as well for only 44 runs. After that dramatic debut, his batting took second place to his bowling, but he remained a fine entertainer whatever he was doing.

He could turn the ball either way on the hardest pitches,

508

and had a ball that he let go from one or two paces behind the bowling crease which repeatedly puzzled batsmen in its flight. His off-break could be devastating. He was accurate and determined and withstood punishment well.

He made his Test debut at Adelaide in the Third Test against England in 1897–98, taking 4 for 70 in England's first innings. In the match between New South Wales and the touring Englishmen that season he helped New South Wales win by 239 runs in a match which saw 1,739 runs scored. Howell hit 95 in 66 minutes after Syd Gregory and Mackenzie had scored centuries for New South Wales. He took part in a memorable Australian win by six wickets in the Fifth Test after England had scored 335 in the first innings, forming a match-winning attack with Trumble and Jones that saw England dismissed for 178 in the second innings. Few batsmen have hit the ball as hard as Howell when he was in full flight.

In his first match in England in 1899, Howell took all ten Surrey wickets for 28 runs in 23.2 overs, and in the second innings took 5 for 29. He finished that tour with 117 wickets in all matches at 20.35. On the 1902 Australian tour of England, he took 68 wickets at 17.86 in all matches, and on his third trip to England in 1905, he had 71 wickets at 19.39 in all matches. In the match against The Gentlemen in 1905 he had 3 for 1. With the bat, his three trips to England were disappointing, with 49 not out his best score.

In the 1903–04 series against England in Australia he took 14 wickets, including 4 for 43 off 34.5 overs when England scored 315 in the Second Test. On matting wickets in South Africa in 1902–03 he took 14 wickets at 12.42 in two Tests, opening the bowling at Cape Town and finishing with 4 for 18 and 5 for 81. Australia won the series comfortably, thanks to his bowling.

For Australia in his 18 Tests between 1897 and 1904, his best analysis was 5 for 81, his highest score 35, and he held 12 catches. For New South Wales, his best effort was 9 for 52 against Victoria at Melbourne in 1902–03, with a spectacular big-hitting innings of 128 against South Australia in 1904–05, his sole first-class century. In all first-class cricket he took five wickets in an innings 30 times and caught 124 batsmen. What a shame he did not discover the game years earlier! His son, Bill Howell jnr, played 14 matches for New South Wales, scoring 100 runs at 6.66 and taking 32 wickets at 38.00.

HUGHES, The Reverend Canon Ernest Selwyn, 1860–1942

A Melbourne cricket-lover widely known and respected as "the sporting parson." He played for East Melbourne and was president of the club from 1911, before it became Hawthorn-East Melbourne. He was a vice president of the Victorian Cricket Association for many years. He was Canon of St Paul's

Cathedral, Melbourne, and conducted the marriages and funerals of many prominent Australian cricketers. He was president of the VCA during the 1932–33 Bodyline tour and was one of many deeply hurt by the incidents of the tour, and with his treatment by Jardine. In an interview soon after a confrontation he said: "I saw more of Jardine than most people and I do not like the gentleman. He does not like me and publicly insulted me in Sydney."

HUGHES, Kimberley John, 1954–

First-Class Averages: Batting, 7,158 runs at 36.89.

Tests (48): 3,121 runs at 38.53.

A talented, erratic, fair curly-haired West Australian right-hand batsman, brilliant fieldsman in any position, traditional cricket loyalist, and sometimes Australian cricket captain. His inconsistency has made it easier for Greg Chappell to discard and take up again the biggest job in Australian sport, the national cricket team captaincy, whenever Chappell's business affairs permit. Very few batsmen can match Hughes' exciting strokeplay when he compiles big scores, but he often gives his wicket away to impulsive lapses in technique. He is one of the most hestitant starters in Test cricket, given to producing the wrong shots for the first over or two, but once the anxiety goes his batting can be exhilarating.

The story is told that when Hughes first came into first-class cricket the senior members of the Western Australian team tried to persuade him to curb his explosive shotmaking and stressed the value of carefully building an innings. "Okay, so you've been batting for 240 minutes," said Rod Marsh. "How many are you?" Hughes looked about him in the manner of a man who had enjoyed a long innings. "Eight hundred," he said, confidently.

Hughes was born at Margaret River, WA, eldest son of a headmaster who starred for Subiaco Australian Rules football team. At 15, Kim scored 112 in a first grade match for Subiaco and at 18 he was in the State Colts, but at 20 left Perth for half a season in Adelaide. He trained as a physical education instructor at Graylands Teachers' College in Perth, and in 1976 played club cricket for a season in Scotland. He married Jenny Davidson, his schooldays girlfriend, when he moved from North Perth to take a job in promotions with a Fremantle building society.

He made a brilliant debut in first-class cricket, with scores of 119 and 60 against New South Wales in 1975–76 at Perth, sharing in stands of 205 for the third wicket in the first innings and 104 in the second innings, both with Rob Langer. He followed with another elegant knock for 102 that season against the West Indies. He was immediately talked about as a potential Test star but he took some time to make the jump from inter-State cricket to Tests, although he did make a dashing 137 not out against Pakistan at Perth in 1976–77. At

510

the end of that summer he went to New Zealand with Greg Chappell's Australian team but did not play in either of the two Tests, scoring 106 runs at 17.66 on the trip.

He made his Test debut in 1977 on tour with Greg Chappell's team in England, an unhappy trip on which 13 of the 17 Australians were known to have signed with WSC. Hughes made one run in his only innings in the Fifth Test at The Oval and completed the tour with 540 runs at 28.42, top-score 95. He has since toured the West Indies in 1978, England and India in 1979, England and Pakistan in 1980, England in 1981, and New Zealand in 1981–82. He confirmed his Test place in 1978–79 against England with an innings of 129 in the second innings of the First Test at Brisbane, when he shared a stand of 170 with Graham Yallop. This innings lasted 7 hours 56 minutes and showed for the first time that Hughes could control his instinct for all-out aggression.

Indeed Hughes' show of self-discipline persuaded the Australian Cricket Board to hand him the Australian captaincy when Yallop was injured after losing six out of seven Tests to England and Pakistan that season. Hughes achieved a remarkable transformation in the Australian team's morale and led the side in a recovery to square the series against Pakistan at a win each. He was rewarded with the Australian captaincy for the World Cup matches in England in 1979 and on the 1979 11-match tour of India. To cricket writers on these tours Hughes' candour and refusal to excuse Australian failures were a refreshing reminder of Richie Benaud's old realism. Hughes brought a new-found dedication to his own batting in India, scoring 594 runs in six Tests at 59.40. He also helped calm excitable players in matches before volatile crowds when umpires' decisions upset them. When Rodney Hogg bowled a wide high over a batsman's head at Bangalore in protest at being repeatedly no-balled, Hughes sent him from the field.

Hughes did so well there was speculation on the return of the WSC players at the start of the 1979–80 season over whether the Australian Cricket Board should reappoint Greg Chappell or stick with Hughes as captain. The Board picked Chappell but made Hughes his deputy ahead of long-serving Rodney Marsh and Dennis Lillee. The West Australian selectors also made Hughes their captain. In England in 1980, Hughes produced a magnificent display of fine strokes and spectacular hitting to win the Man of the Match award in the Centenary Test at Lords', with innings of 117 and 84. Two of his blows were among the longest hits seen at Lord's, striking the pavilion high up close to the TV commentators.

Back home Hughes made a dazzling 149 for WA against Queensland in Brisbane and 97 at Perth against South Australia. Then in January, 1981, he celebrated the birth of twin sons, Sean and Shane, by scoring a superb 213 in the Second Test

against India at Adelaide. His footwork in this, his first double century, was dazzling as he attacked Kapil Dev with fierce off-drives. Equally brilliant was his 100 not out in 1981–82 against the West Indies at Melbourne when Michael Holding threatened to blast Australia's batsmen out of the match.

Indeed the sight of Hughes charging down the track to hammer bowlers has become familiar in Australian cricket seasons. The old inconsistency remains, with the rush of blood particularly likely after an interval or when he first comes in to bat, but most cricket followers are prepared to allow Kim Hughes his failures in return for the awesome spectacle of him blitzing great bowlers. To date he has made 14 centuries and 37 other scores over 50, plus the one double century. Many of his 93 first-class catches have been gems. Such is the crammed life of an international batsman these days his club, Fremantle, sees less of him than big match spectators.

512

A friendly, warm–hearted, reformed cricket rebel, a left–arm medium–pace or slow bowler who grew up with Archie Jackson in the back streets and parks of Balmain, came under the sponsorship of H. V. ("Doc") Evatt, played for New South Wales, in one Test for Australia, and then quit Australian cricket for the Lancashire League, convinced he had no future in Tests while gentleman Bill Woodfull was captain. Hunt's career was full of incident, not the least his five hat-tricks in one year (1933), two for Balmain in social matches and three for Rishton in Lancashire. He took 11 hat-tricks in his career at various levels of the game and is one of three bowlers to take all 10 wickets in a Sydney first grade match. The others: Vic Jackson and Maurice Sievers.

Of his sole Test appearance, Hunt says: "Woodfull was a champion captain and a gentleman, and I was a fair cow to get on with. I did my kindergarten act when Herbie Taylor the South African was missed by Oldfield and Woodfull wouldn't bowl me after that. I deserved all that was meted out to me." Hunt believes the Board of Control considered his bad behaviour but, of course, the Board would never comment on that. He recalls Woodfull reprimanding him for being out of his position close in at silly leg when he chased a ball to the boundary. Hunt was one of the few bowlers Bert Oldfield had difficulty taking, particularly with the ball Hunt drifted in from outside the right-hander's legs.

HUNT, William Alfred, 1908–

First-Class Averages: Batting, 301 runs at 14.33; Bowling, 62 wickets at 23.00.

Tests (1): 0 runs; 0 for 39.

Bill Hunt, left, chatting with Learie Constantine, who hit him on to the roof of the "hill" stand.

513

Hunt came out of the tenements of Balmain, unable to pay his club and match fees or his fares to various grade grounds. "Doc" Evatt, who held regular meetings in front of the old wooden dressing rooms at Birchgrove Park with Dr "Fuzz" Porter and Dr Sam Gentle, freely offering advice to players on either side, paid Hunt's bills. Arthur Mailey as club captain made sure the money was well spent.

In his sole Test Hunt had 0 for 39 and was out for a duck, but held one catch, a poor result for such an obviously gifted cricketer. When Archie Jackson died in Brisbane in 1933, "Doc" Evatt paid Hunt's fare to go and bring Jackson's body back to Sydney.

After his stint with Rishton, Hunt continued to make headlines in Sydney grade cricket. In the 1936–37 season he took two hat-tricks in one over for Balmain against Rydalmere Hospital in a social match in the hospital grounds, and finished with 6 wickets for seven runs. In 19 seasons with Balmain between 1923 and 1948—he missed six—Hunt took 509 first grade wickets, and was the club's highest wicket-taker four times. Over the last few years he has given unlimited energy and time to establishing at Sydney Cricket Ground a world-class cricket museum.

HUNTINGTON, Ian Ross, 1931–

First-Class Averages: Batting, 2,233 runs at 34.35; Bowling, 16 wickets at 41.93.

A left-hand batsman and right-arm medium pace bowler for Melbourne and University clubs and over nine seasons for Victoria. He was an extremely versatile and enthusiastic cricketer who made five first-class centuries, took handy wickets and filled in at wicket-keeping. He made 35 catches and one stumping in 46 first-class games. He first appeared for Victoria in 1953–54, but did not reach his best form until the 1960s, scoring 163 against Western Australia at Melbourne in 1959–60, 117 not out against Queensland at Brisbane in 1962–63, and 130 against WA in Melbourne in 1963–64. He made his career highest score of 164 against New South Wales at Sydney in 1963–64.

HURST, Alan George, 1950–

First-Class Averages: Batting, 504 runs at 8.68; Bowling, 280 wickets at 26.28.

Tests (12): 102 runs at 6.00; 43 wickets at 27.90.

A tall, broad-shouldered, dark-thatched Victorian fast bowler whose back injuries and a tendency to lower his bowling arm have restricted his Test results. He was one of the few top-class Australian players to reject an offer from World Series Cricket. Hurst had an ideal side-on action but for some reason frequently let the ball go from around his ear instead of high up—the puny jab instead of the knockout punch. He was a slipshod fieldsman who had to be hidden in the field by his captains, and an outstanding exponent of batting at No. 11, having set all sorts of records for scoring ducks.

Hurst, a school teacher born at Altona, Victoria, bowled as fast as Lillee and Thomson at times but strayed down the leg-side a lot and in between spells when he swung the ball either way had periods when he did not move it at all. When he came into first-class cricket in 1972 the times when he strayed outnumbered the times when he got it all together. But he was a highly impressive bowler when he shrugged off his injuries and really let go, unlucky perhaps that in his prime years Thomson, Lillee and Walker prevented him securing a permanent spot in the Test side.

He made his Test debut against New Zealand in 1973–74. England critics considered Hurst almost as fast as Lillee when he made his first English visit in 1975. He was deputy to Lillee and took 21 wickets at 33.09. A bad back injury curbed his progress until 1978–79 when he had a golden season in the

Alan Hurst shows his elation after dismissing Derek Randall in the 1978–79 series against England.

absence of Lillee, Thomson, Pascoe, Walker, Malone and Prior. He took 40 wickets in eight Tests, six against England and two against Pakistan, a bag only slightly inferior to that of Rodney Hogg. In 14 matches during that summer, with appearances for Victoria thrown in, he took 65 wickets. He bowled enthusiastically, cheeks puffing, swinging the ball, sustaining his accuracy and introducing a superb leg-cutter he had only just taught himself. With Hogg, he formed a fine opening attack, and it is doubtful if the WSC players could have done any better. To cap it all he took a hat-trick in the Gillette Cup match at Perth for Victoria against Western Australia, and in the match that decided the Shield nine wickets against Queensland. He was among the first chosen for the World Cup in England in 1979 but after that trip he was unable to challenge Lillee, Hogg, Pascoe and Lawson for a Test place because of back injuries, and he finally announced his retirement from big cricket at the start of the 1980–81 season.

HURWOOD, Alexander, 1902–

First-Class Averages: Batting, 575 runs at 11.27; Bowling, 113 wickets at 27.62.

Tests (2): 5 runs at 2.50; 11 wickets at 15.45.

A right-arm medium pace bowler with nip from the pitch who kept a good length and varied his pace and flight. He moved the new ball off the seam and later turned it from the off, from a five pace approach, and was a useful tailend batsman, but on his sole tour of England in 1930 could not take wickets quickly enough for his captain, Bill Woodfull, to keep him on. He had to be taken off and replaced by bowlers who could get the batsmen out, even if they conceded more runs, with time a vital factor in three-day games against County sides.

Hurwood, who came from Redland Bay, Queensland, played for the Valley club, and made his debut for Queensland in 1925–26, an unfortunate period for an aspiring young bowler, with Queensland still struggling for Shield status. He clinched a tour place by taking 39 wickets in the summer before the 1930 tour. He bowled well in England for poor results, taking 28 wickets on the tour at 26.28, and scoring 188 runs at 10.44.

In the Queensland versus New South Wales match at Sydney in 1930–31 Hurwood hit Bradman's stumps after Bradman had made 80. The bails did not fall off, and at stumps that Saturday night Bradman was 205 not out. With no Sunday play, Bradman had a day's rest. On the Monday he added 105 before lunch and a further 142 before Kippax declared. Bradman's 452 not out in a total of 761 was a world record.

Hurwood, a tall, unlucky cricketer played in two Tests against West Indies in 1930–31, and was dropped after taking 4 for 22 in a West Indies' score of 90. He was an outstanding slips fieldsman with 29 first-class catches.

516

Influential Queensland brothers who gave a lifetime of service to the game in the north. **John Silvester Hutcheon** (1882–1957) was a right-hand batsman who played 11 matches for Queensland between 1905 and 1910, scoring 599 first-class runs at 24.95, topscore 73. He represented Queensland on the Australian Board of Control from 1919 until his death and with Roger Hartigan was responsible for Queensland's entry into the Sheffield Shield competition. He was a powerful debater, autocratic but fair in his dealings with QCA staff and president of the QCA from 1926 to 1957. **Ernest Henry Hutcheon** (1889–1937), also a right-hander, made 188 at 17.09 for Queensland between 1919 and 1925, and was co-author of A History Of Queensland Cricket. Jack and Ernie Hutcheon were the sons of J. M. Hutcheon who was a diligent worker for cricket at Warwick.

HUTCHEON, THE BROTHERS

E. H. Hutcheon.

A family of four who represented South Australia in first-class cricket. **William Frederick Percival Hutton** (1876–1951), known as "Percy", a wicket-keeper who began the family's representation by playing two matches for SA, averaging 30.00 in two matches. His sons **Maurice Percival** ("Moggy") **Hutton** (1902–1940), 20 runs at 5.00 in four innings, **Mervyn Douglas Hutton** (1911–   ), 20 runs at 20.00 in two innings, and **Norman Harvey Hutton** (1913–1980), 16 runs at 5.33 in three innings, all followed him into the SA team. The sons did a little bowling that took wickets in club cricket but was of no account in first-class matches.

HUTTON, THE FAMILY

A fast left-arm bowler, and one of the few men to dismiss Bradman for a duck. He was useful with the bat, scoring much needed runs for New South Wales and the Gordon club towards the tail. In first-class matches he had a topscore of 63 not out. He was one of many cricketers who have given distinguished service to charity, and was knighted in 1971 for his work in charities, broadcasting and hospitals.

When he was managing director of Radio Station 2UW in Sydney, Hynes appointed ex-Test player Ron Archer as Advertising Manager. On his first day, Archer was late back from lunch and Bob Hynes, a little put out, asked where he had been. "I met a chap at the Cricketers' Club who held me up and claims he knows you", said Archer. "What's his name?" said Hynes. "I think it was Little", said Archer. "Bowled Hynes, caught Ray Little", said Hynes curtly "And you don't know his name!" It was Little who had taken the catch off Hynes' bowling that put Hynes into cricket history as one of the select bowlers who got Bradman for a blob.

HYNES, Sir Lincoln Carruthers ("Bob"), 1912–1977

First-Class Averages: Batting, 436 runs at 17.44; Bowling, 48 wickets at 28.31.

I

IBADULLA, Khalid ("Billy"), 1935–

An extremely useful right-hand batsman and medium-pace change bowler for Lahore, Warwickshire, Pakistan, Tasmania and Otago. He is regarded as among the best coaches produced in Pakistan and was player-coach to the Devonport club in 1970–71 and 1971–72 when he appeared in four first-class matches for Tasmania, averaging 41.83 with the bat. He toured New Zealand with Pakistan in 1964–65, England in 1967, and played against Australia at home in 1964–65.

His all-round ability was such that he could fill in as a wicket-keeper without any loss in his team's efficiency. He was called from duties with Warwickshire in England in 1964–65 to play for Pakistan against Australia at Karachi, where in his Test debut he scored 166 and had a record opening partnership of 249 with Abdul Kadir. He scored 1,000 runs in a season six times for Warwickshire, sharing in record stands of 377 unbroken for the first wicket with N. F. Horner against Surrey in 1960 and 402 for the fourth wicket with Rohan Kanhai in 1968 against Nottinghamshire. His best bowling figures were 7 for 22 against Derbyshire in 1967. He settled in New Zealand and coaches in Otago.

INDIA VERSUS AUSTRALIA

Australians played in India as members of privately sponsored teams between World War I and World War II, and in 1935–36 an unofficial Australian team managed by Frank Tarrant and captained by Jack Ryder toured India. After their splendid tour of England the Australian Services team played several matches in India on their way home in 1945–46. The first official Test between the two countries was played at The 'Gabba in November, 1947, however, when the Indians were caught on a vicious sticky wicket. Since then Australia and India have met in 39 Tests, Australia winning 20, India 8, with 11 drawn. India did not win a Test until the tenth meeting of the two countries by which time Australia had had seven wins, with two drawn. Since then the matches in

Australia have generally favoured Australia but Australia has found it desperately hard to win in India on pitches unsuitable for pace bowling. The most striking features of the India–Australia matches since World War II has been the dramatic improvement in Indian batsmanship, with Sunil Gavaskar and Gundappa Vishwanath recent outstanding examples, and the ability of the Indians to keep producing clever exponents of flight and spin such as Bishen Bedi, Bhagwat Chandrasekhar and Dilip Doshi. Indian fielding has improved, though their throwing is still not comparable with that of the best Australian sides. Here is a summary of the matches between the two countries:

TARRANT'S TEAM IN INDIA, 1935–36

This team, universally referred to by the name of the manager who gathered the players together rather than by the captain's name, played 22 matches in India, winning 10, losing three, with nine left unfinished. Several members of the team came out of retirement to make the tour and towards the end found the heat and incessant travelling wearisome. They were a good colourful group of cricketers who attracted big crowds. The team comprised: J. Ryder (capt), H. H. Alexander, A. H. Allsopp, J. L. Ellis, H. S. Love, T. W. Leather, L. E. Nagel, H. Ironmonger, C. G. Macartney, O. W. Bill, H. L. Hendry, R. K. Oxenham, F. J. Bryant, R. O. Morrisby, F. Mair. On the journey to India they beat an All-Ceylon XI by an innings, scoring 334 and dismissing the home team for 96 and 111, Wendell Bill scoring 101 and Oxenham taking 9 for 18 in Ceylon's first innings. The Australians defeated All India by nine wickets and then by eight wickets, lost the third match by 68 runs and the fourth by 33 runs. Ryder made 1,121 runs at 48.7 on the tour, Bill 740 at 43.5, Morrisby 958 at 36.8 and Bryant 743 at 27.5. Of the Australian bowlers Oxenham was the most successful with 101 wickets at 8.19 each. Mair took 71 at 17.8, Leather 56 at 16.7 and Macartney 34 at 16.2.

AUSTRALIAN SERVICES IN INDIA, 1945

Lindsay Hassett's Services side scored 531 in the first match against All India, Pettiford making 124, Carmody 113, Hassett 53, and Pepper 95. India fought back strongly with Hazare, 75, and Amarnath, 64, scoring well in the first innings. In the follow-on All India made 304 with Merchant scoring 69, and Amarnath 50. The Services were 1 for 31 when the match was drawn. In the second match All India began with 386, Mankad scoring 78 and Modi 75 and Hazare 65, but the Services responded with 472 through fine knocks by Whitington, 155, Pettiford, 101, and Miller, 82. All India declared their second innings at 4 for 350, Merchant scoring 155 not out, but the result was a second draw. All India won the third match by six wickets after the Australian Services scored 339 in the first innings, with Hassett 143 and Pepper 87. All India made 525 in reply, Amarnath 113 and Modi 203 not

Frank Tarrant's Australian team
that toured India in 1935–36 (L to
R): Standing, Umpire, H. Alexander,
H. Hendry, J. Ellis, B. Tarrant,
L. Nagle, F. Tarrant, R. O. G.
Morrisby, F. Warne, Umpire;
Sitting, F. Bryant, R. Oxenham,
J. Leather, C. Macartney,
Maharajah of Patiala, J. Ryder
(capt.), H. Love, F. Mair, O. W. Bill.

out. The Services second innings began well with Carmody and Whitington adding 129 for the first wicket, but the innings faded out to reach only 275. All India knocked off the required runs without difficulty. Hassett, who scored a century in each innings—187 and 124 not out—against the Princes' XI at New Delhi, was the outstanding Services batsman on the tour, although Whitington, Carmody and Pettiford impressed. With the ball Price and Pepper were the best of the Services.

INDIA IN AUSTRALIA, 1947–48

L. Amarnath

The first official visit to Australia by an Indian team began with an unhappy decision by the Indian captain Lala Amarnath not to cover the Test pitches. The Australian Board of Control suggested that the pitches be covered but Amarnath apparently reasoned that his bowlers were more likely to benefit from damp or damaged pitches than Australia's predominantly pace attack. Amarnath had taken over the captaincy when the originally appointed skipper Vijay Merchant withdrew for health reasons, and the Indian side was further weakened by the withdrawal of the brilliant Rusi Modi, Mushtaq Ali and Fazal Mahmood (the team was picked before partition from Pakistan became official). On uncovered pitches, India needed some luck with the toss and they lost it four times and twice had the worst of the pitch after rain. In the First Test Australia made 8 for 382, thanks to 185 by Bradman and when rain interrupted play Bradman declared and put the Indians in on a vicious sticky. Under coaching from Bradman on precisely where to land his left-arm deliveries, Toshack took five wickets from 19 deliveries

520

for two runs and India were all out for 58. Further rain then interrupted play with India 4 for 41 in their second innings, Australia finally winning by an innings and 226 runs on the sixth day. Toshack's second innings bag of 6 for 29 gave him 11 for 31 for the match. The Second Test at Sydney was drawn because of rain, Australia batting no better than India on a rain-affected pitch. This was the match in which Mankad made Test history by running out Bill Brown at the non-striker's end. Brown accepted it as his fault in leaving his crease as he backed-up. Mankad had run him out in the same way in the India v. an Australia XI match earlier on the tour. Bradman hit a century in each innings for the first time in a Test, with innings of 132 and 127 not out in the Third Test at Melbourne. India declared at 9 for 291 in reply to Australia's 394 to catch Australia on a drying pitch in the second innings. Bradman replied by sending in three tail-enders. With Australia 4 for 32, the pitch dried enough for Bradman and Morris to put on 223 unfinished. That night further rain fell and next day Bradman immediately declared, sending India in to bat on a wet pitch. They managed only 125, Australia winning by 233 runs. Australia made a record 674 in the Fourth Test, still the highest total for any Test in Australia, to win by an innings and 16 runs despite a century in each innings (116 and 145) by Hazare, the first time this had been accomplished by an Indian in Tests. Australia won the series 4–0 by winning the Fifth Test by an innings and 177 runs, Harvey scoring 153 in only his second Test, and Australia taking 16 wickets for 147 runs on the fourth day. Amarnath, with 1,162 runs in all first-class matches at 58.10, was the most successful Indian batsman, Hazare a more pleasing stylist with 1,056 runs at 48.00, including four centuries. Mankad was the best Indian bowler with 61 wickets at 26.14. He also made 889 runs, with three centuries, an admirable allround effort. Bradman made four centuries in six Test innings for Australia, 156 against India for South Australia, and 172 for an Australian XI, his 100th first-class century.

AUSTRALIA IN INDIA, 1956

I. W. Johnson

Ian Johnson's 1956 Australian team, the 22nd to tour England, played three Tests against India on the way home, winning the first and third, with the second drawn. These were pleasing successes for the Australians who had just lost the series in England and had also lost their first-ever Test against Pakistan on a matting wicket at Karachi before they got to India. Richie Benaud's 7 for 72 in India's first innings and Lindwall's 7 for 43 in the second innings set up the Australia victory by an innings and five runs in the First Test at Madras. Harvey (140) and Burke (161) helped Australia to a total of 523 in the Second Test at Bombay when Lindwall captained Australia but India were saved by Umrigar's 78 in six hours. Benaud's match figures of 11 for 105 (6 for 52 and 5 for 53) gave

521

Australia a 94 runs win in the Third Test at Calcutta in a low scoring match. Lindwall's 12 wickets in this series took his tally of Test victims to 212.

AUSTRALIA IN INDIA, 1959–60

R. Benaud

Richie Benaud led Australia on its first full official tour of India, after playing first in Pakistan. Australia won the First Test at Delhi by an innings and 127 runs, the spin of Kline and Benaud forcing home the advantage created by a brilliant 114 by Harvey and a stubborn 78 by Mackay. Kline had match figures of 5 for 57, Benaud 8 for 76, including the unique analysis of 3 for 0 in the first innings. Spectators were upset that Australia cut short their viewing by a day and invaded the pitch throwing bottles and jostling the umpires. India struck back in the Second Test at Kanpur by bringing in the off-spinner Jasu Patel, who took 9 for 69 and 5 for 55, to give India her first win against Australia by 119 runs. Patel bowled on a freshly-laid turf pitch. Umrigar played a vital role in Australia's defeat by dismissing star batsmen Harvey, O'Neill and Mackay in Australia's second innings of 105. The Third Test at Bombay was drawn despite a third wicket stand of 207 by Harvey (102) and O'Neill (163). Alan Davidson took his 100th Test wicket during Australia's win by an innings and 55 runs in the Fourth Test at Madras, but again it was Benaud's legspin that did the damage. Benaud had match figures of 8 for 86, and bowled over 30 overs in each innings, a fine effort in the heat. Left to make 203 runs in the Fifth Test at Calcutta, Australia settled for a draw, taking the rubber 2–1, with 2 draws. One of the strange events of the tour came when Kenny left the field to have a tooth out midway through his long stand with Jaisimba in the Fifth Test. On balance Australia's batting was too strong and the bowling too resourceful, with Davidson able to switch to spin and Mackay bowling economically for long spells.

AUSTRALIA IN INDIA, 1964

R. B. Simpson

The 24th Australian team to tour England played three Tests in India on the way home, sharing the rubber with a win each and a draw in the last Test when there was no play on two days. Australia had their third consecutive win at Madras in the First Test by setting India to score 332 in 390 minutes in the final innings. McKenzie, who had taken 6 for 58 in the Indian first innings, took 4 for 33 in the second when he and Hawke each clean bowled an opener and had India at 2 for 0. Pataudi had made 128 not out in India's first innings but in the second McKenzie bowled him for 1. Australia had key batsman O'Neill absent ill for almost all the second Test in which Pataudi helped India to victory with innings of 86 and 53. Set to score 254 to win India got them with only two wickets and 30 minutes left. Simpson was seldom out of action in the Third Test, scoring 67 and 71 and taking 4 for 45 with his leg-spinners but rain prevented a result.

Australia won all four Tests in this series handsomely against basically the same Indian team that had given them such a tough battle in India in ˙964. India were handicapped by a hamstring injury to their captain, the Nawab of Pataudi, who did not play in a first-class match until the Second Test, when he played two notable innings. Prasanna took 25 wickets at 27.44, best figures 6 for 104, and Surti took 15 wickets in the Tests by bowling left-arm seamers and spinners, but Australia scored heavily in all four Tests. Australia won the First Test by 146 after centuries by Simpson (103) and Cowper (108) and second innings figures of 5 for 39 by Renneberg. The Nawab of Pataudi made 75 and 85 in the Second Test, remarkable for a batsman with restricted vision and hamstring trouble, but could not prevent an Australian win by an innings and four runs after Simpson made 109, Lawry 100 and Ian Chappell 151 in a total of 529. Australia took the Third Test by 39 runs. Freeman, in his Test debut, hit the first ball he received for six and took two wickets in his first 10 balls. Walters made 93 and 62 not out in the Third Test, followed by 94 not out in the Fourth Test, which Australia won by 144 runs, Cowper scoring 165 in Australia's second innings. A curious feature of a one-sided series was the Australian selectors' omission of McKenzie after the first two Tests. He had been a match-winner in the Second Test in taking 7 for 66 and 3 for 85. Simpson retired for the first time at the end of this series after his best Test bowling effort, 5 for 59. He had then held 99 Test catches.

This was a troublesome series for Lawry although Australia won 3–1, with 1 draw, because of disagreements over umpires' decisions, noisy crowd reactions to Australian behaviour, and an unfortunate incident involving an Indian cameraman. It was a struggle between outstanding spin bowlers, with Mallett emerging on top for Australia with 28 victims in the five Tests, Prasanna taking 26 and Bedi 21. Australia's superior batting strength proved the difference. The First Test at Bombay brought a public outcry before a ball was bowled when selectors omitted Venkataraghavan. Indian cricket fans could not believe it and finally S. Guha agreed to stand down and let Venkat play. Mankad and Pataudi put on a then record fourth wicket stand of 146 to lift India to 271, but Australia replied with 345, Stackpole making 103, Redpath 77. In the Indian second innings, Connolly, Gleeson and Mallett combined to get them out for 137, leaving Australia to score 64 to win. Play continued despite a riot in the last hour of the fourth day after Venkat was given out caught behind. Australia lost two wickets to Surti before scoring the winning runs. The Second Test at Kanpur was drawn after centuries by Sheahan (114) and Vishwanath, who made 137 in his Test debut. India won the Third Test at Delhi—and only her third

INDIA IN AUSTRALIA, 1967–68

Nawab of Pataudi

AUSTRALIA IN INDIA, 1969–70

W. M. Lawry

success ever against Australia—with a day to spare by seven wickets when Bedi, 5 for 37, and Prasanna, 5 for 42, found just the right pitch for their spin. Lawry batted right through the second Australian innings of 107 for 49 runs in 195 minutes. Ian Chappell had made 138 in Australia's first innings. With the series level, Australia made the rubber secure after another riot by winning the Fourth Test at Calcutta by 10 wickets, Ian Chappell batting beautifully for 99 and giving Prasanna a hiding (0 for 116) in the process. The Australians then confirmed their superiority by winning the Fifth Test at Madras by 77 runs, Mallett's 5 for 91 and 5 for 53 backing up a splendid innings of 102 by Walters.

INDIA IN AUSTRALIA, 1977–78

B. S. Bedi

This was one of the most eventful seasons in Australian cricket history, with WSC launching their matches in opposition to the India-Australia series staged by the Australian Cricket Board. Forced to rebuild their team the ACB persuaded Bob Simpson to come back from retirement and from the First Test at Brisbane it became clear the ACB had a colourful, closely-contested series on its hands which WSC would be hard-pressed to match in the battle for TV viewers. With a team that included six players making their Test debuts, Australia won by 16 runs, Simpson scoring a plucky 89 in his first Test since 1967–68. Bedi, colourfully turbaned, and Gavaskar, with a second innings of 113, were India's stars, Thomson and Clark taking 15 Indian wickets between them. The Second Test was equally tense. Simpson made 176, a record for a Test at Perth, and took his 100th Test catch. Gavaskar got 127 for India and Mohindar Amarnath 90 and 100 and Australia had to make 338 in the final innings to win. They did it with only

Bhagwat Chandrasekar, a match-winning leg-spinner against Australia in an era of dominance by pace bowlers.

two wickets left, after Mann, sent in as a night-watchman, made 105. With Australia 2–0 up, India fought back superbly to level the series at 2–2 by winning the Third Test at Melbourne by 222 runs at the Fourth Test at Sydney by an innings and two runs. In the Third Test Chandrasekhar paved the way to India's first-ever Test win in Australia by taking 6 for 52 in both innings. Chandra also made two ducks in this match to become the first player in Test cricket history to record a pair four times. Chandra followed with 4 for 30 and 2 for 85 in the Fourth Test. Australia won the rubber 3–2 by winning the Fifth Test at Adelaide by 47 runs after a magnificent fight by India. After Yallop made 121 and Simpson 100 in Australia's first innings of 505, India needed 493 to win in the final innings and reached 445, the second highest fourth-innings score in Test history and the highest by any side to lose a Test. Bedi took 31 wickets in the rubber, Chandra 28. Simpson swung the series with his captaincy and strong batting, scoring 539 runs at 53.90, a marvellous effort considering his long absence from big cricket. Wayne Clark, took 28 wickets at 25.03. Jeff Thomson, who had reversed his earlier decision to join WSC because of his contract with a Queensland radio network, took 22 wickets at 23.45.

Bishen Bedi, a popular captain among Australians.

With the WSC players unavailable, Kim Hughes captained this Australian team, on the third full tour of India. There were many disappointments in the Australian line-up, with Hilditch, Wood and Hogg struggling for form. When Hurst broke down in the Second Test at Bangalore he was flown home but his replacement, Geoff Lawson, did not play in a Test. Yardley and Higgs were fairly costly spinners, Sleep failed to develop as hoped. Dymock bowled manfully throughout and deservedly topped both the first-class and Test bowling averages. Only Hughes, 594 runs at 59.40, Border, 521 runs at 43.41, and Yallop, 423 at 38.45, performed capably among the batsmen in the Tests. The team played 11 matches, without a win, with eight draws and three losses. India won the six-Test series 2–0. Hughes made 100 in the drawn First Test at Madras and 86 in the drawn Second Test at Bangalore, where Vengsarkar, 112, and Vishwanath, 161, lifted India's total to 5 for 457 declared. India won the Third Test at Kanpur by 153 runs when Kapil Dev took 4 for 30 in Australia's second innings of 125. The Fourth Test at New Delhi was drawn following long innings by Gavaskar (115), Vishwanath (131) and Yapal Sharma (100 not out). Yallop made 167 in the Fifth Test at Calcutta, the fourth draw of the series, and in the Fifth Test at Bombay centuries by Gavaskar (123) and Kirmani (101 not out) paved the way to India's win by an innings and 100 runs, with Doshi (5 for 43 and 3 for 60) again getting most wickets. Kapil Dev proved a classy all-rounder for India.

AUSTRALIA IN INDIA, 1979

K. J. Hughes

INDIA IN AUSTRALIA, 1980–81

S. Gavaskar

Sunil Gavaskar.

India staged a splendid recovery against a full-strength Australian team to tie the three Test series at one-all with one draw. In the other first-class matches India drew with WA, lost to SA by 43 runs, drew with Tasmania and Queensland, and defeated Victoria by 10 wickets. India's captain, Gavaskar, did not add to his then 23 Test centuries during the tour, and his brother-in-law Gundappa Vishwanath failed to reproduce his outstanding home form. Australian spectators welcomed Doshi's lengthy spells of spin bowling, although he took only 11 wickets in the three Tests at 40.00, best figures 3 for 49. India lacked a capable pace bowler to support Kapil Dev, who disappointed with the bat but had some hostile periods with the ball. Greg Chappell played one of his finest innings to reach 204 in the First Test at Sydney after Lillee and Pascoe had bundled India out for 201 with a mixture of bouncers and real pace. Higgs chimed in with 4 for 45 in the second innings when 10 Indians wore helmets, but the additional protection could not save India from defeat by an innings and four runs. The drawn Second Test at Adelaide produced another Australian double century, 213 this time from Hughes who found bowling subdued by Woods 125 to his liking. Australia made 528, India 419 after a fighting 174 by Patil in only his fifth Test. Chappell declared at 7 for 221 in the second innings but India did not try for the 340 needed to win after losing Gavaskar cheaply. Chappell won the toss and asked India to bat in the Third Test at Melbourne and with India 3 for 43 and then 5 for 99, appeared to have been justified. But Vishwanath hung on to lift India to 237 and his own score to 114. Australia appeared in no danger when they replied with 419, Border contributing 124, Walters 78, Chappell 76. India came back with a second innings score of 324 marred by Gavaskar's "walk off" in protest at being given out lbw. Gavaskar tried to take opening partner Chauhan with him from the MCG but was stopped by Indian manager S. K. Durrani who waved Chauhan back to the wicket. Chasing only 143 to win in the last innings, Australia were in trouble at 2 for 11 but should have had plenty of batting strength left to do the job provided there was no panic. But only Walters batted calmly and Kapil Dev, who had missed two days play with a thigh injury, took 5 for 28 in an astounding recovery to have Australia out for 83, India winning by 59 runs.

INTERNATIONAL CRICKET CONFERENCE

The London-based organisation through which cricket-playing nations express their views on the conduct and administration of the game. The ICC is virtually only a consultative body and meets once a year. The Marylebone Cricket Club remains the arbiter of the Laws of Cricket and continues its traditional role as guide, counsellor and helpmate to cricket by providing offices and staff at Lord's for the ICC, and the president of the MCC automatically becomes chairman of the ICC.

Australia has been a member since its formation in July, 1909, as the Imperial Cricket Conference. The original invitations to the foundation meeting had called it the "British Colonial Cricket Conference," but this title was quickly discarded. The ICC originally was based on the old British Empire titles because it was in the Empire countries that cricket's strength lay. As the Empire broke up and other nations developed their cricket strength, the need for a more representative body with a more appropriate title became obvious. The name Imperial Cricket Conference was dropped in 1965, when associate memberships for non-Test playing countries were introduced, but not before South Africa, an original member, had ceased to be an ICC member because of the decision of the South African government to leave the Commonwealth.

The associate memberships opened the way for countries like Denmark, Argentina, Bangladesh and the Netherlands to play international matches, and pointed the way for the ICC to become cricket's world consultative body. This was fully put to the test when the attitude of the ICC resulted in court action in 1977 wherein the London judge ruled against the ICC and others imposing a ban on WSC players on the grounds of "restraint of trade." This court action forced the ICC and its members to pay heavy costs but over the following two years the ICC chairman, David Clark in 1977–78 and Charles Palmer in 1978–79, established a relationship with WSC that eventually led to a settlement.

The WSC affair was by far the most explosive issue the ICC has had to deal with but over the years there have been plenty of other controversial problems. Australia's delegates at the very first meeting, Peter McAlister and L. O. S. Poidevin, strongly supported the staging of triangular Test series, but then opposed the continuation of Triangular Tests at the ICC meeting in 1912. It was 50 years before Triangular Tests were again considered. But one of the good things to come out of the 1912 meeting was the agreement on qualifications for Test players whereby it was agreed a player had to be resident in a country for four years before he could represent it, a decision that stopped the practice perfected by Billy Midwinter of touring for two countries.

The ICC had many debates on the number of balls that should comprise an over and when agreement could not be reached gave Australia permission in 1921 to use an eight-ball over, the only country to do so. A more contentious problem came in 1934 when the ICC confronted the aftermath of Bodyline and after earnest debate passed a resolution which read in part: "That this conference affirms the principle laid down by the MCC that any form of bowling which is obviously a direct attack on the batsman would be an offence against the spirit of the game." In the 1940s the partition of India brought problems that were not resolved until Pakistan was granted ICC membership in 1952.

Through the 1960s the ICC applied itself to the problems of time wasting, over-use of the bouncer and whether it should have a junior section aimed at helping minor cricket countries. Frank Worrell showed up a major weakness in the ICC when he advocated limitation of the bowlers approach run at the 1963 ICC conference. It took until 1966 for the ICC to announce that there was no support for limiting the run-up but in 1967, after Worrell had died, the ICC agreed to urge young bowlers to limit their approach runs. A motion from Fiji that slow bowlers be brought back into the game by limiting each team to one new ball per innings remained on the agenda for 13 years! The time it takes for member countries to formulate their policy on matters such as dragging, intimidatory bowling, polishing the ball and the most contentious of all, throwing, appears to be extended beyond practical limits by the system of appointing observers rather than sending delegates to ICC meetings. This is why the Australian Cricket Board has recently taken to sending its chairman or his deputy to ICC meetings.

The 1960 meeting of the ICC which faced the dilemma of curbing the upsurge in throwing without unjustly penalising some bowlers, attracted the presidents of all the major controlling bodies. Bill Dowling and Sir Donald Bradman flew in from Australia. The conference agreed on a definition of the throw which is discussed under *Throwing*. It did not please everybody but it succeeded in diffusing the throwing controversy which had received such sensationalist treatment during the 1958–59 tour of Australia by Peter May's MCC team.

The evolution of the ICC towards a position of the controlling body for world cricket, took a major step with the decision in 1971 to give associate members one vote each, compared with two votes for Test nations. At last count there were 17 associate members and they have moved quickly to build their strength since they came into the ICC in 1965. When the ICC allotted two places in the draw for the first World Cup in 1975, the non-Test countries staged their own competition in the English midlands to decide on the two teams. Since then the associate members have made extensive plans to try and win one of the two places in the 1983 World Cup draw. All those who enjoy an underdog succeeding in sport would be captivated if Australia had to play Bermuda, Israel or Canada in a World Cup final.

Sri Lanka is the most recent admission to full membership. They played their inaugural Test against England in Colombo in February 1982 when England won by seven wickets. Sri Lanka will visit Australia for a short tour in February 1983.

528

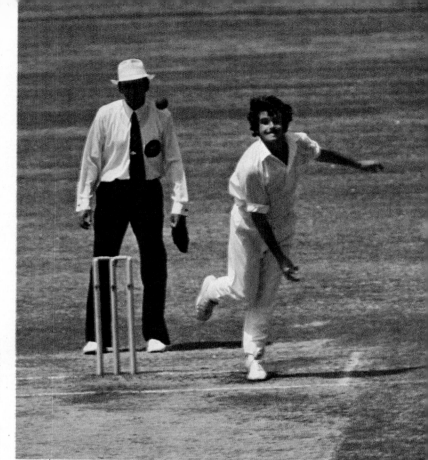

Right: Leg-spinner Jim Higgs in action during the Fourth Test against England at Sydney in 1979.

Below: Tony Greig under fire from Jeff Thomson at Sydney in 1975.

Right: Martin Kent glides a ball down to deep fine leg against the West Indies.

Below: The only Australian 'keeper to score a Test century, Rodney Marsh, clubbing a ball to the leg boundary.

Australian cricket received its first major impetus from matches between the colonies, which were held 50 years before Australia was federated and the States officially designated. These matches were played solely for recreation long before the formation of State Associations. They began with almost no publicity and only minor sponsorship from a few publicans, motivated by the desire of cricketers in each of the colonies to outdo each other. Here is a review of the matches between the colonies up to the introduction of the Sheffield Shield in 1892–93:

Matches between Victoria and Tasmania began at Launceston in February, 1851, with Tasmania winning by three wickets. The return match took place in Melbourne the following year and over the next 21 years to 1873 a further six games were held. The games between the States stopped for 16 years but Tasmania's splendid effort in 1888 against Vernon's English team when XIV of Tasmania made 405 prompted Tasmania to challenge Victoria and the next match between these States began on New Year's Day, 1889, at Melbourne. Victoria played their strongest side and won by nine wickets after Tasmania had batted on a difficult pitch in their first innings. Victoria made 230 and 1 for 33, Tasmania 67 and 195, with former Cambridge University player Claude Rock contributing 102. The States have since met annually except for the years of World War I and II and in 1891–92 when Victoria could not send a team because of the Australian tour by Lord Sheffield's team. Victoria won all three matches before the start of the Shield competition, from which Tasmania was excluded until 1977–78. The Tasmanians' batting in these inter-Colonial matches often was first-rate, with Rock, Burn, Eady, Gatehouse and the Savignys playing some lovely strokes, but the bowling was markedly inferior. For Victoria in 1890, Harry Trott took 6 for 10, and in 1891, J. Carlton took 12 for 79 at Melbourne. For Tasmania, N. Rock took 5 for 21 in 1891.

New South Wales responded to an advertisement inserted in the Melbourne *Argus* challenging any team in the Australian colonies to play the Melbourne Cricket Club. In taking up the challenge, the NSW team spurned the offer of £200-a-side, preferring to play for the honour of the game, and the first inter-colonial match began on Melbourne Cricket Ground on March 26, 1856. Both teams fielded with their boots off, some in bare feet or in their stockings, for the ground was devoid of grass. The first day's play was summarised in two sentences in the *Argus* which said betting was 3 to 2 on Victoria before play began. The scores were given with "Mr" before each player's name.

The batting surface was so rough anyone who made double figures was a hero. There was argument about procedure, such as who should bat first, what the umpires should wear, whether different pitches should be used for each innings, whether the scorers should sit together, but finally these were settled. Sargeant and Mather went to the wicket for Victoria and Gilbert sent down the first ball for NSW. Sargeant drove it for two, the first runs between Victoria and NSW.

Victoria's poor fielding allowed NSW to score 76 in reply to their own first innings total of 63. Gatemoney on the first day was £60/5/–. McKone took 5 for 11 off 52 balls in Victoria's second innings, which ended at 28. Set to make 15 to win NSW lost seven wickets before they made it. For the return match at Sydney in January, 1857, Victoria introduced Tom Wills and NSW brought in Captain Ward, who ran the Sydney Mint. This match attracted tremendous interest and the governor was among the 15,000 spectators on the second day. NSW won this second match by 65 runs, chiefly because of Ward's round-armers.

Victoria won five matches in a row, thanks to a three-pronged attack comprising Gideon Elliott, Wills and Sam Costick, with crowd support increasing for every match. In 1863 at Sydney the Victorian umpire declared NSW batsman Jones runout, but the NSW umpire said he had called over and that some fieldsmen were changing places when the bails were removed. Intense arguments ensued and the Victorian players left the ground and drove to their hotel. Next day the Victorians waived their claim that Jones had been runout but two of their players refused to agree and returned to Melbourne. This prevented any match being played in 1864 but when the MCC at Lord's ruled that the Victorians were

The annual inter-Colonial match between New South Wales and Victoria, January, 1867, at Melbourne.

wrong and the 1863 match awarded to NSW the series resumed. Meanwhile the visit of the second English team in 1864 taught Australians to pay more attention to preparation of pitches and as the series progressed the standard of pitches rapidly improved. The change from underarm to roundarm bowling and then to overarm brought many accusations of throwing. The Victorian star Wills was adept at confusing umpires with his expertise and deliberately throwing the odd ball to remove obstinate batsmen. Dick Wardill made 110 for Victoria, the first first-class century, in 1867 at Melbourne, with Frank Allan taking 8 for 102 (match figures) in his debut. With improved wickets, both sides produced some excellent batsmen but after a series of Victorian wins NSW turned the tide by selecting "a dodgy left-hander" called Coates. In 1874, when NSW had won only 4 times against 12 by Victoria, Coates found support in Fred Spofforth to finally give NSW a win.

In 1875 at Sydney the heroes were all bowlers, with Coates and Evans excelling for NSW and Midwinter and Cosstick for Victoria. Evans indeed took over from Wills as Australia's best allround man, but he got strong support from Ned Gregory and the rapidly emerging Charlie Bannerman. Evans' pinpoint accuracy helped NSW to seven wins in a row to take the tally at Victoria 12, NSW 11.

In 1879 a fine all-round display of batting, in which Alexander made 75, Horan and Kendall 43 each, Blackham 41 not out, Boyle 36 and Allan 34, took the Victorian total to 338, enough for Alexander and Allan to bowl out NSW twice and give Victoria victory by an innings and 96. At Sydney in February 1882, NSW had their revenge, however, when Victoria made 315 and 322 and lost by an innings and 138 runs! Murdoch made 321, S. P. Jones 109 and T. W. Garrett 163 in a NSW first innings score of 775. Victoria used 10 bowlers and in the end it was Horan who "fiddled" Murdoch out. There were many tense, close matches with the winners aware they had improved their prospects of a trip to England with an Australian team.

Between March, 1856, and the start of the Sheffield Shield competition in the 1892–93 season, NSW and Victoria played 48 11-a-side matches, Victoria winning 25, NSW 23. Victoria scored 14,356 runs at an average cost per wicket of 16.94 runs. NSW made 14,476 runs at an average cost per wicket of 16.83. Victoria's highest innings was 482, NSW's 775. Victoria's lowest score was 28, NSW's 37.

VICTORIA v. SOUTH AUSTRALIA

The first two English touring teams ignored South Australia. W. G. Grace's team in 1873–74 was the first to play in SA when they played in the memorable match at Kadinia. Soon afterwards Adelaide Oval was improved and in 1874 and 1876 Victoria played matches there against 18 of South Australia, Victoria winning the first by 15 runs and SA the second by an innings and 70 runs. South Australia graduated to 11-a-side matches in November, 1880, when they played Victoria on the East Melbourne ground. SA made a nervous start with 77 in the first innings but settled down to make 314 in the second innings. Victoria made 329 and 3 for 64 to win by seven wickets. The following April a strong Victoria side played SA on level terms in the first inter-Colonial match on Adelaide Oval and won again. The Victorian bowlers found Adelaide Oval to their liking, dismissing SA for 163 and 51. Despite the rough outfield, Victoria scored 191 and 174 to win by 151 runs. From then on SA made quick improvement and in only their third first-class encounter defeated Victoria by scoring 119 and 200 against Victoria's 105 and 182. This set the stage for regular matches between the States.

After SA won by 31 runs at Adelaide in March, 1882, with Affie Jarvis playing two good hands of 33 each, and a left-arm bowler named Quilty taking 9 for 55 in Victoria's first innings, Victoria fielded their strongest team for the following match at Melbourne in March, 1883. Sent in to bat on a mud heap the visitors were helpless against Palmer and Boyle and were dismissed for the lowest score ever in inter-Colonial matches. When the news was flashed across the telegraph wires and announced on a board outside the *Register's* office in Adelaide, large crowds challenged the total of 23 on the board. Boyle had taken 4 for 6, Palmer 5 for 16. One of SA's finest wins came in March, 1886, when George Giffen took 17 wickets for 201 runs and scored 20 and 82. In between these matches between the State sides, there were numerous games between Victorian and SA club sides. Among the most popular in Adelaide were the Jolimonters, an East Melbourne outfit that always played in striped shirts.

In February, 1888, when the Victorians visited Adelaide, Giffen began a series of annual all-round performances unsurpassed in inter-Colonial cricket when he scored 166 runs and took 14 wickets for 125 runs. For five seasons South Australia depended on Giffen who seldom faltered, delivering with bat and ball but erring occasionally as a captain. In December, 1888, for example he scored 135 and 19 and took 13 wickets for 157 but SA lost because of his poor tactical leadership. Victoria began their second innings 89 in arrears and their eighth wicket fell with the scores level. Horan then skied a ball very high which any number of fieldsmen could have caught but it fell harmlessly to the feet of a fieldsman who lost his nerve. Horan then set about scoring while his partners defended and SA were set 104 to win. SA reached 1 for 30 by six o'clock but Giffen them made the tactical error of playing on in poor light, trying to finish the game. At 5 for 50 bad light stopped play. Next day Victoria had SA all out for 88 to win by 15 runs.

532

This remarkable match paled into insignificance, however, compared with the SA v. Victoria match in Adelaide in December, 1889, when Giffen refused to leave the field after being given out. SA lost two wickets cheaply chasing Victoria's 320. Then Giffen fell as an lbw appeal against him was disallowed. As he rose, he dislodged a bail. The Victorians appealed again and the umpire at the bowler's end gave him out hit wicket but Giffen refused to go, claiming that the ball was dead once the lbw appeal was disallowed. Even Giffen's team-mates disagreed with him, but after much argument the Victorians generously allowed him to continue. Giffen added a further 76 runs but Victoria won the match by 18 runs despite a fine century from Lyons. Giffen and Lyons continued to inspire SA's performance and in Adelaide in November, 1891, Giffen made 271 in SA's score of 562 and had match figures of 16 for 166. SA won by an innings and 164 in one of the worst defeats ever inflicted on a colony. Altogether SA and Victoria played 13 inter-Colonial matches before the Shield competition began, Victoria winning seven and SA six. Victoria scored 4,961 runs at an average cost of 20.84 per wicket, SA 4,995 runs at an average cost of 22.00 per wicket.

South Australia versus Victoria in an 1876 inter-Colonial match at Adelaide. Victoria's defeat enabled South Australia to play thereafter on level terms.

533

NEW SOUTH WALES v.
SOUTH AUSTRALIA

South Australian cricket officials experienced difficulty persuading NSW administrators to inaugurate regular matches between the States. Only the brilliant form of Lyons, Giffen, the Jarvis brothers and to a lesser extent by the Goodens influenced Sydney officials to agree to play South Australia in Sydney in February, 1890, on the proviso that if SA did well NSW would return the compliment by playing in Adelaide the following season. SA began well when they had NSW out for 240, but they could only manage 155 and 148 on a Sydney pitch that was far slower than that at Adelaide Oval and lost by nine wickets. Only Lyons, with innings of 19 and 63, and Giffen, with 52 and 32 handled Charlton's bowling and in the second SA innings he finished with 7 for 44. In the return match at Adelaide in December, 1890, conditions suited the South Australians but they could not handle the bowling of Ferris who had a match analysis of 14 for 192. SA made 241 and 191, NSW 406 and 4 for 27, NSW winning by six wickets.

SA cast these disappointments aside with a brilliant win in the third meeting between the States at Sydney in January, 1892. On the first day SA dismissed NSW for 215. Rain began to fall soon after play started on the second day and, with the fieldsmen slithering about and the bowlers unable to grip the ball properly, Giffen and Lyons hammered the NSW attack all round the field. The NSW captain "Alick" Bannerman finally persuaded the umpires to adjourn, but the spectators kept up noisy jeering until the players returned. Lyons went on to 145 and Giffen ended the day on 95, which he took to 120 when play resumed. Lyons' hitting was a revelation to Sydney fans and one report said he broke a fence paling bludgeoning a delivery for four. SA made 330 and then routed NSW for 62 to win by an innings and 53 runs. This performance clinched a place in the Sheffield Shield competition for SA. In the three matches played before the Shield began, NSW won 2, SA won, NSW scoring 1,016 runs at an average cost per wicket of 22.57, highest score 406, SA scoring 1,065 runs at an average cost per wicket of 21.30, highest score 330.

NEW SOUTH WALES v.
QUEENSLAND

Queensland played matches with NSW against the odds from 1865, and in the 1880s J. V. Francis continually urged good cricketers from Sydney and Melbourne to play or settle in Brisbane. Finally, in April, 1893, the Queenslanders considered they were ready to test their strength by playing NSW on level terms. Some leading NSW players could not make the trip but a strong side still faced Queensland, who to the amazement of the cricket world won by 14 runs. NSW scored 64 and 100, with Hoare taking 6 for 12 in NSW's first innings. Queensland made 100 and 78, Newell taking 10 for 52 in the match for NSW. For the return match at Sydney, in March, 1894, NSW fielded their most powerful side with Turner the only notable absentee. Trailing by 47 runs on the first innings

534

the Queenslanders reached 246 at the second attempt. Queensland took several early wickets but with NSW in trouble a drizzle enabled Garrett and Newell to knock off the required runs.

Apart from the matches reviewed, several inter-Colonial matches were staged before the Sheffield Shield competition began that were not considered first-class, though they did have an influence in developing cricket in Australia. In the first of these Western Australia played South Australia at Adelaide in March, 1893. This was a bold venture by WA cricket lovers, but they were convincingly beaten, scoring 111 and 131 to SA's 236 and 0 for 11. North (25 and 5) Duffy (14 and 42) and Orr (9 and 44) batted well for WA, while Duffy (3 for 55) and Bishop (5 for 60) bowled splendidly for WA. In the second big match on that trip WA were heavily defeated by Victoria, scoring 38 and 130 to Victoria's 411, with John Harry scoring 114 for Victoria. A similar match that cannot be considered first-class had earlier been played at Adelaide in November, 1877, between South Australia and Tasmania. The scores were: South Australia 182, Tasmania 72 and 97.

The three colonies (later States) who contested the Sheffield Shield from the start of the 1892–93 season—South Australia, Victoria and New South Wales—all had regular experience in inter-Colonial cricket, which provided a colourful and at times argumentative period in Australian cricket when rivalries were honed and procedures worked out. The competitive spirit inter-Colonial cricket engendered has endured and, if anything, increased through the delay in admitting Queensland (1926), Western Australia (1947) and Tasmania (1977) to the Shield competition.

MINOR INTER-COLONIAL MATCHES

A dour right-hand batsman and left-arm slow bowler for Western Australia, Australia, and South Australia. He has had a distinguished career in Shield cricket, but has such a consistent record of occupying the crease for lengthy periods of dogged, strokeless defence it is probably just as well for spectators that he has played only six Tests. English critic Jim Swanton called him "Inforeverity". His caution sometimes carries over to his captaincy and captains from other states consider he has closed up many games that could have produced exciting finishes, but they forget the times his captaincy has been creative and imaginative. He has often been quite brilliant fielding in the "silly" positions and at slip.

Inverarity, tall, dark, personable, is the Perth-born son of former Western Australian representative **Merv Inverarity** (1907–1979), who scored 748 runs at 17.00 and took 50 wickets at 35.88 in 15 years in the State side, and captained the Fre-

INVERARITY, Robert John, 1944–

First-Class Averages: Batting, 10,307 runs at 35.70; Bowling, 141 wickets at 29.30.

Tests (6): 174 runs at 17.40; 4 wickets at 23.25.

mantle club for more than 15 years. John graduated from the first XI at Scotch College in 1957–58 to Claremont-Cottesloe first grade team and then to the Western Australian side in 1962–63. In all of these teams he had Ian Brayshaw as a team-mate and they practised together for hours at a time on Claremont oval.

He made his Test debut on tour in England in 1968, scoring 645 runs on the trip at 24.80. He played in three further Tests on the 1972 English tour on which he scored 453 runs at 21.57 and was used far more as a bowler of drifting slows, taking 35 wickets at 27.25. His best Test score was 56 against England in 1968 in the Fifth Test at The Oval. He also played in two international matches for Australia against the World XI in 1971–72, and in one Test against the West Indies in 1968–69. He captained Western Australia astutely but without adventure in six Shield campaigns and won four of them.

He was such a master of defensive batting there was unanimous surprise among the players when he appeared to miss a simple half volley from Greg Chappell and was bowled playing for Western Australia against South Australia at Adelaide in 1969. After Inverarity reached the gate the body of a swallow, freshly dead, was found on the pitch near the batting end. The umpires agreed the ball had struck the swallow before it reached Inverarity and he was recalled. The swallow was subsequently stuffed and mounted in a glass case that is on display in the committee room at Adelaide Oval. The only similar instance in cricket history occurred at Lord's when Majid Khan's father, M. Jahangir Khan, was bowling to T. N. Pearce for Cambridge against MCC in 1936. The dead bird fell against the stumps without removing the bails and the batsman played the ball. The bird was preserved and is in the Long Room at Lord's.

Inverarity transferred to Adelaide as a deputy headmaster in 1979–80 and commenced playing for his new State sometimes captaining the side. His highest score in first-class cricket is 187 for Western Australia against New South Wales in 1978–79, his best bowling figures 5 for 28 for Australia against Otago in 1969–70.

IREDALE, Francis Adams, 1867–1926

First-Class Averages: Batting, 6,794 runs at 33.63; Bowling, 6 wickets at 35.16.

Tests (14): 807 runs at 36.68.

A cool, resourceful right-hand batsman who combined watchful defence with punishing hitting. He could cut stylishly and drive gracefully but it was his big blows that roused the crowds. He was one of the finest outfielders of his period, moving very quickly to the ball and catching safely. He toured England in two Australian teams, in 1896 and 1899, after narrowly missing out in 1893.

His problem was that he invariably started shakily and it was unusual for him to reach 20 without playing streaky shots close to the slips or the 'keeper. Once into his stride, however, he was a commanding figure and treated bowling that had been troublesome for him early in his innings with disdain.

Iredale, born in Surry Hills, first played for New South Wales in 1888–89 but did not establish himself as a batsman of top class until 1894–95 when he excelled himself against Andrew Stoddart's English team. He was run out for 133 in his first knock against them, followed with 81 in his first Test, and later played splendidly for 140 in Australia's second innings of 411 in the Third Test at Adelaide. Australia won that match but lost the series 3–2, Iredale finishing with an impressive 337 runs at 37.44.

Just before he left for England with the 1896 Australians, he made 187 and 80 not out against South Australia, arriving in England as one of Australia's major hopes. He began badly but recovered to score 1,328 runs at 27.66 in all matches. His best efforts included 94 not out against Nottinghamshire, 114 against Yorkshire, 106 against Hampshire, 171 against The Players, and 108 in the Test at Manchester. He headed the Australian Test averages with 38.00.

At home he averaged 43.20 in the 1897–98 series against England, twice being dismissed before he reached a century that had seemed certain. In the Second Test at Melbourne he made 89 in a total of 520, Australia winning by an innings and 55 runs, and in the Third Test at Adelaide he scored 84 in a total of 573, Australia winning by an innings and 13 runs.

On his second tour of England in 1899 Frank Iredale scored 1,039 runs at 29.68 in all matches, with two centuries, 115 against W. G. Grace's XI and 111 against Middlesex at Lord's. He was not the dominating figure in the Tests that he had been in preceding series.

At home he made five centuries in State matches, with 196 for New South Wales against Tasmania in 1898–99 and 187 for New South Wales against South Australia in 1895–96 his highest scores. He retired from first-class cricket in 1902, with 12 centuries and 111 catches in first-class cricket. In his 14 Tests he made two centuries and four scores over 50. He was a journalist for some years and wrote a book, *Thirty-Three Years Of Cricket*. He was appointed secretary of the NSWCA in 1922. His uncle, **Francis Adams** (1835–1911), also played for New South Wales.

One of the most amazing characters in the history of Australian cricket, a left-arm spin bowler with half of two fingers missing from his bowling hand who made his Test debut in 1928–29 claiming he was 41 when he was in fact 46. Legend had it that after he lost part of his finger in a timber mill at Ipswich, Queensland, he was explaining the accident to his

IRONMONGER, Herbert ("Dainty"), 1882–1971

First-Class Averages:
Batting, 476 runs at 5.95;
Bowling, 464 wickets at
21.50.

Tests (14): 42 runs at 2.62;
74 wickets at 17.97.

foreman and lost half the middle finger in the demonstration. He was a bowler of infinite patience and of exceptional accuracy, who, despite his antiquity, tied down England and Australia's finest batsmen on good pitches, and made them look foolish on worn or wet pitches.

As a fieldsman, he was unbending, consistently clumsy, which brought him his nickname, but he took one of the most famous catches in Test history, one of only 30 he held in his entire career. When Larwood was on 98 in the Fifth Test at Sydney in 1932–33 he hit a ball hard and low and Ironmonger caught it at the level of his shin, denying the great bowler a Test 100. It was one of only three catches Ironmonger held in 14 Tests and he spilt plenty. In fact he was so bulky and awkward of movement he did not get near catches other fieldsmen could have reached with ease.

With the bat "Dainty" was quite hilarious. His Test average in 14 matches was an elegant 2.62, every run hard-earned, and he batted 21 times to get it. "Ironmonger went to the wicket mostly as a gesture to convention," Johnnie Moyes wrote. Ironmonger's wife is said to have rung the dressing-room at Melbourne Cricket Ground, only to be informed that he had just gone in to bat. "Oh, then, I'd better hold on," she said. When Ironmonger went in to bat, the horse that pulled the roller on to the MCG between innings moved round into the shafts. "Dainty" did much better batting for other teams than for Australia, and had a topscore in first-class cricket of 36 not out, most of them edges, in his 127 innings.

Some players—but not Bradman—claimed he was a thrower, but in a first-class career that began in 1909 and ended in 1935 when he toured India with F. A. Tarrant's team, he was never called, though he came under scrutiny from some of Australia's finest umpires. Ironmonger's fans said it was the lost finger tops that caused cross-grained people like Douglas Jardine and "Plum" Warner to doubt the fairness of his delivery. The fear that his action would be questioned may have cost him at least one trip to England with an Australian team.

As a lad in Ipswich, Ironmonger played for the Albert club, which claimed him as "District Champion". Born at Pine Mountain, Ipswich, he played several times in Queensland Country Week, and in the summer of 1909–10 was chosen for Queensland against Victoria. He took only 3 for 124 but Victorian batsmen must have been impressed because they told him during the game that he was wasting his time in Queensland and should go south. The primitive conditions under which Queensland cricket was conducted at the time certainly justified this advice.

Ironmonger was uncertain about where he should move, though he became more and more convinced that he had to quit Queensland. Just before leaving for Victoria in 1913–14,

538

he starred for Queensland against NSW, who made 571 and won by an innings. He got the wickets of Victor Trumper, Collins, Andrews, Kelleway and Folkard, bowling 38 overs to finish with 5 for 158. Telling his brother he would be back if he did not get wickets, he headed for Melbourne. While he qualified for Victoria, he took 20 wickets in four innings at 12.85 runs apiece against Tasmania. In the 1914–15 season he had match figures of 5 for 91 for Victoria against NSW and in the return 8 for 137. In his first match against South Australia, he took 13 wickets for 181 and 6 for 139 in the return. Although he was then 32, the annual report of the VCA called him a bowler of immense potential.

In 1920–21 he went to New Zealand (having played that season with Victoria) with an Australian team, taking 5 for 60 v. Hawkes Bay, 10 for 111 in two innings against Canterbury, 6 for 34 v. Otago and 9 for 127 (match figures) against the top New Zealand side. In 1921–22 he bobbed up in Sydney with the Balmain club, where he took a job with the waterfront firm, Poole & Steele. In 12 games for Balmain he took 51 wickets at 12.80.

Hugh Trumble, secretary of the Melbourne Cricket Club, who had always been impressed by Ironmonger's bowling, arranged a job for him in Melbourne in the 1924–25 season when "Dainty" was 42, by seconding him to the MCC ground

"Dainty" Ironmonger at the nets—holding the ball in a battered hand, but still deadly accurate.

staff. He played occasionally for Victoria after his return but did not become a permanent member of the State side until 1927–28, though he did sneak in a hat-trick against Gilligan's England side in 1924–25.

Working as a gardener for St Kilda Corporation between matches, he had match figures of 11 for 79 in the Fourth Test against the West Indies in 1930–31 and a few days later a match bag of 12 for 195 against South Australia. In the First Test against South Africa in 1931–32, he took 9 for 86 and 11 for 24 in the last of the five Tests of that series. In 1932–33 against England he missed the first of the five Tests, but played in the last four, taking 15 wickets in all and helping to win the Second Test. His best bowling performance for Australia was 7 for 23 against the West Indies in 1930–31 and for Victoria, 8 for 31 against the West Indies in the same season. Selectors no doubt kept picking him because they lost track of his age amid all the moves made by this remarkable cricketer through three Australian States.

IVERSON, John Brian, 1915–1973

First-Class Averages: Batting, 277 runs at 14.57; Bowling, 157 wickets at 19.22.

Tests (5): 3 runs at .75; 21 wickets at 15.23.

A bowler who shook the cricket world by inventing a new delivery. He had a ball that fooled great batsmen but he had insufficient background in cricket to cope when shrewdies like Keith Miller and Arthur Morris decided on a plan of attack against him. He just could not take a hammering, which all sophisticated spinners learn to accept, declared himself unavailable for first-class cricket and virtually ended his career. He said he wanted time to practise some more on his unique delivery.

Iverson's special was the ball he let go with the middle finger of his bowling hand tucked in behind the ball. He had begun experiments with it by flicking table tennis balls down the table at fellow servicemen in New Guinea. He was blessed with very strong and long fingers and found he could control the bent-finger ball at cricket pitch length. He held the ball between his right thumb and the middle finger, which was used to propel the ball. By changing the position of his thumb he could deliver a leg-break, off-break or a googly with little discernible change of action.

He entered first class cricket in the 1949–50 Australian season, a big, innocent cricketer of 6 ft 2 ins and 15 stone, and with all the star batsmen away in South Africa took 46 wickets at 16.60 for Victoria. At the end of that season he toured New Zealand with an Australian XI. He then made a remarkable Test debut against Brown's MCC side in 1950–51, taking 21 wickets at 15.23, best effort 6 for 27, and on the way to those figures frequently made even the best Englishmen play the wrong way. Even the great Hutton was befuddled by him.

At the practice nets before the Brisbane Test against Eng-

540

land that summer Miller and Morris, New South Wales stalwarts, objected when Hassett refused to bowl Iverson when they batted. "What is this, Lindsay, an Australian team practice or New South Wales versus Victoria?" said Miller, who was so annoyed that he got together with Morris to plan how to play Iverson. Later that season in Sydney, Miller stood half a metre outside the legside stump when Iverson bowled. Morris did the same. Instead of sticking to his line, Iverson did not know where to bowl. Confidence gone, he took a fearful hammering and at the end of season, walked into the VCA office in Melbourne, declared himself unavailable, and asked for more time to rehearse.

Iverson's best effort in his short Test career was 6 for 27 in the Third Test at the SCG against England in 1950–51. In the view of many experts who covered his matches he was the greenest of raw recruits ever to play big cricket. Hassett was probably right in trying to protect him.

George F. Evans, a Sydney lawyer, conceived the idea of a new cricket club in 1886 and presented his case to a small gathering at his father's residence, "Springfield", in Darlinghurst Road, Sydney. Those present were J. F. Jennings, R. Fitz-Evans, H. W. Radford and K. L. Street. They decided to call the new club the Iona Cricket Club. The Governor of NSW, the Right Honourable C. R. B. Carrington, became its patron, and Sir Patrick Jennings, a former premier of NSW, its first president. The new club lost its first match by 9 wickets and 4 runs. Permission then was sought to adopt the name of the famous English club, I Zingari, which had been founded in 1845, and this was given provided the word "Australia" was added. Approval was also given to use the black, red and gold as the

**I ZINGARI,
AUSTRALIA**

541

club colours. The colours symbolise "out of darkness, through fire, into light", and the gold, which must be worn on top, depicts "fair play".

In its early years the club fielded up to five teams and its home ground was a concrete wicket at Rushcutter's Bay. By 1982 the club's performances were good enough for it to enter the senior competition conducted by the NSWCA. When Electorate (now grade) cricket was introduced two years later, the senior clubs were disbanded and IZ reverted to purely social cricket.

Matches were played against the Army, the Navy and the GPS Schools, associations which continue to the present day. In the mid-week "Society" matches, bands were hired to provide musical relief during the intervals. The 1890s also saw the club venturing to country centres like Mudgee, Mittagong, Newcastle and Camden in search of games. Having lost its home ground with the advent of Grade cricket, IZ played wherever grounds were available. The lack of an association directly interested in social clubs led to the formation in 1903 of the City & Suburban Cricket Association of which IZ became a foundation member.

With no home ground, but in keeping with its name, which in Italian, means "the Wanderers" or "the Gypsies", the Club at various times in its history leased the Sydney Sports Ground, Lyne Park, Cranbrook playing fields and Concord Oval. The club in 1969 built its own oval some 50 kilometres from Sydney among the gum trees on historic Camden Park, birthplace of the Australian wool industry. The club had first played at Camden Park in 1895, when they were invited there by Messrs Onslow. The present owner of Camden Park, Mr R. Q. Macarthur Stanham, is an active member of the club. Although regular weekly fixtures are played by two teams in the Sydney Metropolitan area, it is to Camden Park that the club invites the growing number of visiting teams from overseas. These have included teams from the UK, Canada, India, Hong Kong, Sri Lanka, Malaysia, and New Zealand.

In addition to regular tours to NSW country centres, Melbourne and Brisbane, the club has toured New Zealand on three occasions. In 1977—its 90th year—the club sent a team to England, one of the highlights of which was the first cricketing encounter with the original I Zingari Club.

Members of I Zingari Australia are drawn from many walks of life and include a sprinkling of former international, State and first grade players as well as a much larger number whose main attributes are the enjoyment of good cricket and good companionship. Among international cricketers who have been members are Dr P. C. Charlton (Patron in Perpetuity), H. H. Massie, Dr H. V. Hordern, E. C. S. White, J. W. Burke, I. D. Craig, G. Goonesena, R. G. Archer, and the 1981 president of the club, M. P. Donnelly.

542

An astute manager of Australian teams in South Africa in 1966–67 and in the West Indies in 1973, who also managed the Rest Of The World team that toured Australia in 1971–72 when the tour by South Africa had to be cancelled. Jacobs had the repect of players and sportswriters and brought to his administrative work in Victorian cricket a long history of club cricket. Before World War II he was long regarded as the second best wicket-keeper in Victoria and played for the State seconds while Ben Barnett held the top job. Jacobs played 266 consecutive games as 'keeper for the Fitzroy club, claiming 448 victims. With the bat, he had a topscore of 100 not out. He captained Fitzroy for nine seasons, and played in three premiership sides. Later he was a Victorian selector for 14 years and became a wellknown broadcaster on cricket. He was conspicuous during the legendary Centenary Test at Melbourne as the TV interviewer during breaks in play. His son Ken is secretary of the VCA.

JACOBS, William Lawson ("Bill") 1918–

An artistic right-hand batsman who died at the age of 23 after delighting Balmain, New South Wales and Australian team followers for just a few seasons. His innings were invariably brief gems of style and elegance. Fifty years later people who saw them still mention his name with awe.

Jackson, born at Rutherglen, Scotland, was the son of impoverished migrants who settled in the Balmain district of Sydney. He was always a sickly figure but had a flair for inventive shot-making probably only Victor Trumper has matched. H. V. ("Doc") Evatt paid his fees and fares to Balmain's matches when he first entered grade cricket, a pale-skinned urchin in short pants who played in the streets of Balmain with Bill Hunt. Arthur Mailey nurtured them as Balmain's first grade captain. Jackson fell under the spell of State captain Alan Kippax and many saw in his batting touches of Kippax's effortless style.

JACKSON, Archibald, 1909–1933

First-Class Averages: Batting, 4,383 runs at 45.65.

Tests (8): 474 runs at 47.40.

He made 500 runs at 50.00 at the age of 17 in first-class cricket in his first season for New South Wales, with two centuries, and the following season, 1927–28 at the age of 18 years 125 days, had scores of 131 and 122 against South Australia when he was promoted to open. He then toured New Zealand with an Australian side. He went into the Australian team for the Fourth Test against England at Adelaide in 1928–29, a frail-looking 19-year-old who stood up straight at the crease, hands very high on the bat handle. Opening Australia's innings with Woodfull he saw three wickets fall for 19, but staunchly resisted the bowling of Larwood, Tate and J. C. ("Farmer") White. He cut and pulled superbly and danced metres down the pitch to loft White into the outfield. He was slow early, partly because of nervousness but as his innings blossomed, scored freely. His century came in 250 minutes and he added a further 64 at a run a minute. In that hour his batting made even Bradman look pedestrian.

Jackson remains the youngest player to make a century in his initial Test in England-Australia matches. His 164 did not prevent an England victory by 12 runs but it will always remain one of cricket's most stirring knocks, ending when he was lbw to White although metres down the pitch. He followed with a splendid 46 in the next Test at Melbourne, Australia winning by five wickets after eight days' play.

After scoring 182—his career best—in a Test trial at Melbourne in 1929–30 Jackson went to England scoring 1,097 runs, average 34.28, best score 118, with Woodfull's 1930 Australian team. His stamina was poor and although encouraged by his mate Alan Fairfax he showed only patches of his Australian form, but in the Fifth Test at The Oval he shared a match-winning stand with Bradman. Jackson made a lovely 73, Bradman 232 and Australia won back The Ashes on their captain Woodfull's 33rd birthday.

On his return to Sydney he suffered recurring bouts of influenza and inertia. Just before NSW took the field in Brisbane to play Queensland in the 1931–32 season he coughed up blood in his hotel room, collapsed, and had to be rushed to hospital, missing the match in which Eddie Gilbert bowled with such blistering pace and had 2 for 0 after one over. Jackson's replacement, Jack Fingleton, made a dour 93. Archie thought he had influenza again but within a week the Australian Board of Control arranged for him to go to a sanatorium at Wentworth Falls west of Sydney. He became restless with sanatorium life, occasionally slipping away to visit friends in Sydney, and in the spring of 1932 decided to go and live in Brisbane to be near his girlfriend, Phyllis Thomas, a black-haired dancer from Clayfield. He mistakenly believed the hotter Brisbane climate would improve his health.

In February, 1933, he collapsed after playing cricket for the Northern Suburbs club in Brisbane and was taken to Ingar-

A superb study of Jackson cover driving with his feet in perfect position.

field Private Hospital. He had batted with Queensland star "Cassie" Andrews as his runner in his last innings. He had tuberculosis in both lungs and faded quickly. Between shows at the Regent Theatre, Phyllis Thomas went to his bedside, and on her 21st birthday she and Archie became engaged.

"Doc" Evatt paid for Archie's parents to go north and for his mate Bill Hunt to fly to Brisbane with the famous aviator P. G. Taylor, but he had a severe haemorrhage just before they arrived. As English and Australian players assembled in Brisbane for the Fourth Test, his room filled with famous cricketers anxious about his health. Just after midnight on February 16, 1933, he asked for the Test score, and then died on the day England regained The Ashes. Hunt took his body back to Sydney on the train, all costs paid by "Doc" Evatt. A brief service was conducted at the Jackson home in Drummoyne. At the Field of Mars cemetery Bill Woodfull, Vic Richardson, Don Bradman, Bert Oldfield, Stan McCabe and Bill Ponsford were Jackson's pall-bearers. McCabe became ill and was re-

545

placed by Alan Kippax. A vast crowd filled the cemetery and surrounding streets.

In his brief career Archie Jackson made 11 first-class centuries, highest score 182. He had a particular liking for South Australian bowlers, against whom he made five of his centuries. His figures do not convey the fighting spirit of the man, the manner in which he took heavy blows without flinching and accepted them as part of the game. Many record books give his initials as "A. A." but his birth certificate shows that he had no second Christian name. His surviving sister Peggy explained in 1982 that when Archie was first chosen to play representative cricket he felt out of things with only one initial when his team-mates were people like "D. G." Bradman, "S. J." McCabe and "J. H." Fingleton, so "on a teenage whim" he asked his father if he could use his name, "Alexander." His dad agreed and Archie added Alexander thereafter when he filled in official forms.

JACKSON, Victor Edward, 1916–1965

First-Class Averages: Batting, 15,698 runs at 28.43; Bowling, 965 wickets at 24.73.

One of the best all-round cricketers developed in the Waverley district of Sydney, a slim, upright bowler of right-arm off-spin and a splendid middle-order right-hand batsman. He enjoyed every match he played in, and was killed in a level crossing smash travelling to a country game he could easily have missed, aged 48. As a professional cricketer in England he became a supreme craftsman, adaptable, shrewd, contributing to his team effort in every facet of the game.

He first played for NSW at the age of 20 and in 1938 at 22 decided he had little chance of selection in the Australian team and accepted an offer from Alan Fairfax, agent for Sir Julien Cahn, to join Sir Julien's team in Nottingham. He lived in Leicestershire with fellow Australian Jack Walsh so that he could qualify for the County team. He played one match as an amateur for Leicestershire in 1938 and one in 1939 and returned in 1946 as a professional, receiving his County cap on the same day as Jack Walsh. Between them they kept Leicestershire going for years.

Jackson scored 14,379 runs for the County at 28.53, highest score 170, and took 930 wickets at 24.15, with two hat-tricks. In all first-class matches, he scored 21 centuries and held 250 catches. He took five wickets or more in an innings 43 times and six times took 10 wickets in a match. He achieved the double of 1,000 runs and 100 wickets only once in an English season, in 1955, when he made 1,582 runs and took 112 wickets but several times missed by one or two wickets or a few runs; he was not a cricketer who cared much about such milestones.

Jackson left Leicestershire at the end of the 1956 season and in 1957 and 1958 played for Rawtenstall in the Lancashire League. He returned to his old club, Waverley, and played club cricket for several years. He died in the car smash with Peter Fingleton and Jim Webb when a train hit their car near Parkes. His son Keith, an all-rounder, continued with Waverley. Vic Jackson was one of three to have taken all 10 wickets in a Sydney first grade match.

JAMES, Ronald Victor, 1920–

A plucky, fair-skinned, ambidextrous all-rounder for New South Wales and South Australia whose talents were not fully exploited because of World War II. He was a hard-hitting right-hand batsman with strokes all round the wicket, a left-arm slow bowler of orthodox finger spin who occasionally bowled medium-pace away swingers, and an amazing fieldsman. He wrote and played golf left-handed but took brilliant catches with equal dexterity on both sides of the body.

James went to Paddington Technical and Ultimo Technical schools in Sydney, and learned cricket at the classes conducted by the Sydney *Sun* newspaper and the F. J. Palmer department stores, known as *Sun-Palmer* clinics. Bradman was one of the coaches. James joined Paddington, in 1935–36, the same year as Colin McCool, Tom Moore, the wide-bottomed opening bowler, and Albie Stone, the Wallaby Rugby hooker who kept wicket during the summer. Ronnie caught the eye of Paddington's State Selector Billy Wells and was in first grade at 15 and played his first match for NSW in 1938–39 at 18.

After service with the Army he went to South Australia for two seasons from 1946–47, and made a fine 85 in Adelaide against Hammond's England side. In 1947–48, he scored 531 runs in first-class cricket, including 210 against Queensland at Adelaide, his highest first-class score. After his return to Sydney he scored two centuries for NSW, best effort 111 not out against South Australia at Adelaide in 1950–51. In 1949–50 he had taken over the NSW captaincy when Keith Miller was hurriedly called to South Africa, leading the side to success in the Sheffield Shield.

In the match against South Australia at Sydney Alan Davidson objected when James ordered him to bowl down the legside to Hamence. Davidson said he would do better bowling on the off stump. "Do as I say," said James, who proceeded to dismiss Hamence with one of his freakish catches at leg-slip. "Ron James was an excellent skipper and an inspiration with his gifted fielding and resolute batting," Davidson wrote in his book *Fifteen Paces*, "Courage was his emblem, a fact he demonstrated against Victoria when he played on with one leg almost completely blue from bruising after a muscle tear. When we lost our wicket-keeper midway through the game, he took over the strenuous 'keeping duties although he must have been in agony."

First-Class Averages: Batting, 2,582 runs at 40.34; Bowling, 1 wicket at 199.00.

Many of James's 23 catches remain etched in the memory 35 years later. He scored hundreds of runs for both Paddington and Cumberland in Sydney grade cricket, and in many matches was almost a team on his own, so diverse were his skills.

JARMAN, Barrington Noel ("Barry"), 1936–

First-Class Averages: Batting, 5,615 runs at 22.00; Dismissals, 560 (431 catches, 129 stumpings).

Tests (19): 400 runs at 14.81; Dismissals 54 (50 catches, 4 stumpings).

A burly wicket-keeper from South Australia who was understudy to the great Wally Grout on five overseas tours and went as first wicket-keeper on four tours. When Grout was absent injured and after Grout retired, he established himself as a 'keeper of the highest class. Only Rodney Marsh, Bert Oldfield and Grout among Australian 'keepers have exceeded Jarman's total of 560 dismissals in first-class cricket. Jarman captained South Australia for several years and led Australia in one Test.

Wide in shoulders and chest, he kept himself extremely nimble for a man of 13 st 7 lb, partly by playing Australian Rules football or acting as a field umpire each winter. He was a very strong hitter and made five centuries in first-class cricket, topscore 196 for SA v. NSW in 1965–66. At the Scarborough Festival at the end of Australia's English tour in 1961, he scored 26 off an over bowled by David Allen for T. N. Pearce's XI.

Barry Jarman dives headlong during a practice workout.

Jarman was born at Hindmarsh, South Australia, and first played for his State in 1955–56. He dismissed six batsmen in an innings, five caught, one stumped, in his second season with South Australia. He made his Test debut against India at Kanpur in 1959–60 and then had to wait 13 Tests spread over three series as Grout's deputy before he got another chance. In 1961–62 he dismissed 10 New South Wales batsmen at Adelaide. In 1963–64, he played a major role in South Australia winning the Shield, by dismissing 45 batsmen in 11 first-class matches and scoring 118 against Western Australia at Perth.

He toured England three times, in 1961, 1964 and 1968, when he was vice-captain, visited India, Pakistan and New Zealand twice each, and went to South Africa and West Indies once each. At Lord's in 1968 he broke a finger in three places taking a delivery from McKenzie, but pluckily went in to bat, only to take a fast ball from David Brown on the damaged finger. A month later he got some compensation when Lawry was hurt and he took over as Australia's captain. He caught Keith Fletcher brilliantly down the legside in this Test at Headingley, with Australia retaining The Ashes by forcing a draw. But the catch of his life was undoubtedly the diving one-hander he took at Melbourne in 1962–63 to dismiss Geoff Pullar. Coming into the Australian side when Grout broke his jaw, Jarman found his catch compared with Oldfield's to dismiss Hobbs and a similar effort to dismiss Hobbs by Carter.

Jarman was unavailable for the 1967–68 Australian tour of South Africa and though he played a couple more seasons for South Australia, he finally dropped out of big cricket to concentrate on his sports goods business in Adelaide.

JARVIS, Alfred ("Fred"), 1869–1938

First-Class Averages: Batting, 1,767 runs at 19.85; Bowling, 107 wickets at 37.76.

A handy all-rounder who played with his elder brother "Affie" in South Australian teams but unlike his brother did not win Test selection. He was christened Alfred but to overcome confusion for scorers who had two A. Jarvises on their sheets, he was always referred to as Fred. He was one of the best cricketers in Australia in his time, batting soundly and troubling all batsmen with his lively medium-pacers. He was among the first to achieve the double of 1,000 runs and 100 wickets for his State.

Fred Jarvis bowled unchanged with George Giffen to give South Australia a surprise win over New South Wales at Sydney in 1891–92, Jarvis taking 5 for 33, Giffen 5 for 28. Fred played in Adelaide in Western Australia's first inter-Colonial match, topscoring with 69 not out and taking seven wickets. In February 1898, he figured in a stand of 193 with Clem Hill against NSW at Sydney, Hill scoring 170, Fred Jarvis 154, his career best. The next season Fred took 6 for 114 against WA in Perth.

JARVIS, Arthur Harwood ("Affie") 1860–1933

First-Class Averages: Batting, 3,234 runs at 15.79; Dismissals, 198 (115 catches, 83 stumpings).

Tests (11): 303 runs at 16.83; 18 Dismissals (9 catches, 9 stumpings).

One of Australia's finest wicket-keepers, unlucky to be a contemporary of Blackham, and a brave, talented batsman whose figures did not reveal his ability. He toured England in four Australian teams, in 1880, 1886, 1888 and 1893, played in 11 Tests, four in England and seven in Australia. Among South Australian wicket-keeper-batsmen, he was supreme, noted for his pluck in standing up to pace bowlers like Ernie Jones when "Jonah" first entered first-class cricket.

Jarvis, a coach-builder, came from the once-famous Hindmarsh club in Adelaide, and kept wicket at the age of 17 for South Australia in the first intercolonial matches against Queensland and Tasmania and against England. He was only kept out of the first South Australia v. Victoria match by his absence in England with the Australia 1880 team. The nickname "Affie" which stuck with him through a long career came from a lisping nephew who could not pronounce Arthur, but it was also indicative of Jarvis' affable nature. On or off the field, he was a smiling, unassuming cricketer.

George Giffen, who fought many battles for South Australia with Jarvis, wrote in his book that Jarvis "could do a day's work behind the wickets quite as brilliantly as anything ever seen". Giffen also noted that whereas the great Blackham scarcely had a sound finger on either hand because of the knocks he had received, Jarvis, 5 ft 11 ins, 12 st, did not have a single unsound finger. Certainly Jarvis was unrivalled in his taking of express bowling and his 'keeping on the legside to Ernie Jones was unrivalled.

Giffen also described Jarvis as "the best batsman in South Australia when I first came into first-class cricket". This was true, but Jarvis disappointed his admirers by his lack of success in England, where his habit of playing to the pitch of the ball was not as fruitful as on hard, true Australian pitches. Though he never made a first-class century, Jarvis made many valuable scores when batsmen of higher reputations had failed. He made 98 not out for South Australia v. New South Wales in 1894–95. In his first Test match, Jarvis made 82 for Australia against Shaw's England side at Melbourne in 1884–85.

That Australian team was weakened by the refusal of regulars such as Blackham to play, and it faced a large English total of 401. Horan, 63, J. W. Trumble, 59, and Jarvis fought hard to avoid the follow-on but the later batsmen, with the exception of Worrall, failed. Jarvis won £10 for the highest score by an Australian in the match. In the next Test Australia pulled off a surprise victory, attributable according to England captain Shaw, to Jarvis' outstanding 'keeping (5 catches, 1 stumping). At a critical stage in the last innings Jarvis caught Barnes and Bates, and finished by taking the catch that gave Australia victory.

For the fifth Australian team against Victoria at Melbourne

in 1885–86, he stumped 4 and caught 2 in an innings, and for the same team v. Eighteen Of Canterbury at Christchurch, New Zealand, he stumped 5 and caught 12. His topscore for Australia was 96 not out for the 1886 Australian team against Cambridge University. In December, 1886, against Twenty Two Of Wellington at Wellington, New Zealand, he achieved the unique feat of scoring 27 consecutive singles in an innings of 60. Playing for Australia v. MCC at Lord's in 1893 he was bowled by the first ball he received from C. J. Kortright in each innings.

A slow right-arm leg-spin bowler for Western Australia, South Australia, Cambridgeshire and Australia. He played in nine Tests, toured New Zealand with an Australian team in 1969–70 and the West Indies in 1972–73. He played for Australian teams against England in Australia in 1970–71 and in 1974–75, but missed selection for an English tour. He was always chosen primarily as a bowler but had claims to be considered a genuine all-rounder. In the Fifth Test at Adelaide against England in 1974–75 he played an aggressive innings of 74 (his topscore in Tests), that enabled Australia to recover and win the match after losing 5 for 84. He was a happy, smiling personality who enjoyed a leg-pull, and always had an uplifting effect on team morale.

Jenner, who played for Mount Lawley club in Perth with Ashley Mallett, found it hard to get a bowl when he first broke into the Western Australian team in 1963–64, largely because of the presence of the outstanding English spinner Tony Lock. He made centuries with the bat in district cricket and played some useful innings in State matches but found it difficult to get the long spells of bowling essential to an aspiring spinner. When Tony Mann emerged as a highly promising leg-spinner, Jenner moved to South Australia with Mallett in 1967–68. By then he had learned to flight his leg-break well, if not turn it sharply, and he had developed a good googly. In 1969–70, he was the best bowler on an Australian "B" team's New Zealand tour, with 32 wickets at 19.53.

He made his Test debut against England in 1970–71 in Brisbane and later in Sydney was the centre of one of cricket's most sensational incidents. The series saw repeated use of the bouncer, with Australian batsmen taking a hammering. When John Snow bowled two short-pitched balls at Jenner, batting at No. 9, Jenner squirmed awkwardly away from both deliveries and Snow's field was immediately changed to bring in four leg-trap fieldsmen. Snow's next ball struck Jenner a sickening blow on the head, knocking him out. He was led off on shaky legs, blood oozing from his head. This

JENNER, Terence James ("T. J."), 1944–

First-Class Averages: Batting, 3,580 runs at 22.23; Bowling, 389 wickets at 32.18.

Tests (9): 208 runs at 23.11; 24 wickets at 31.20.

551

delivery by Snow was followed by the England team walking off the field after beer cans bounced close to Snow and a spectator pulled Snow against the fence. Many believed England forfeited the match, but the umpires allowed play to resume.

Jenner resumed batting the following day with his head wound stitched and lasted another 32 balls, adding 22 runs before Lever bowled him off his thigh. It was an innings destined to give him more notoriety in big cricket than any of his bowling feats. Jenner's two Tests in that seven Test series yielded six wickets at 29.33, and he went off on tour to the West Indies in 1972–73 to take a further 13 Test wickets at 26.69. His West Indian tour figures were impressive, for in only 10 matches he took a total of 36 wickets at 28.50. In the Fifth Test at Port Of Spain he took 5 for 90, his best performance in Tests, in conditions suited to batting.

JENNINGS, Claude Burrows, 1884–1950

First-Class Averages: Batting, 2,452 runs at 25.54; Dismissals, 41 (38 catches, 3 stumpings).

Tests (6): 107 runs at 17.83.

A tidy right-hand opening batsman for South Australia, Australia and Queensland who was hampered by his inability to hit the ball hard. He was chosen as a replacement for the 1912 Australian team for England on the strength of an innings of 123 for Queensland against New South Wales at Sydney in 1911. Withdrawal of six star players from the English tour after a row with the Australian Board of Control gave him his chance. He opened in all six Tests and proved short of Test standard, though he did manage 1,060 runs at 22.55 on a rain-affected tour, topscore 82.

Jennings, born at East St Kilda, Melbourne, settled in South Australia on his return from England but did not get another Test chance. The century he scored for Queensland against New South Wales at Sydney remained his sole three figure score in a 10-year first-class career. He was prominent in Adelaide business circles after his retirement, representing the British Department of Overseas Trade in South Australia, and later serving as secretary to the Adelaide Chamber of Commerce. He was for a time a South Australian representative on the Australian Board of Control.

JOHNS, Alfred Ernest, 1868–1934

First-Class Averages: Batting, 429 runs at 11.28; Dismissals 84 (58 catches, 26 stumpings).

A highly capable wicket-keeper who had the misfortune to be a contemporary of the legendary Blackham. Johns became captain of Melbourne University after playing for Wesley College, Melbourne, Horton College, Tasmania, and Richmond, but did not get a chance of playing for Victoria until Blackham hurt a thumb and had to stand down. He did well enough to become a controversial selection in the Australian

552

teams that toured England in 1896 and 1899. "Johns undoubtedly has some genius for wicket-keeping but not having had continuous practice at it since his younger days, his hands are soft and easily knocked about," wrote Giffen.

He was discounted as a batsman but his left-handed style was good enough to help the 1896 Australian team get out of trouble and beat the Rest Of Australia at Sydney by two wickets, Johns batting for 90 minutes for 15 not out with Syd Gregory (75 not out). In 1896–97 for Victoria v. South Australia at Melbourne he scored 57 in a last wicket partnership of 136 with J. O'Halloran (128 not out). He later gave good service as a committeeman of the Melbourne CC. His 20 innings for two Australian touring teams in England brought him only 134 runs. He did not play in a Test as Blackham and later J. J. Kelly kept him out.

JOHNSON, Ian William, 1918–

One of the few successful off-spinners Australia has produced, and the slowest in pace to take 100 Test wickets. He was not quick enough to take advantage of wet pitches but on hard, fast or crumbling pitches his bounce and mastery of flight troubled even the most skilful batsmen. He preferred to bowl into the wind, to assist with flight. He was a dour middle order batsman and brilliant slips field.

Johnson, son of prominent administrator, State and Australian selector Bill Johnson, who played a match for Victoria in 1923–24, inherited his dad's cheerfulness and sound judgement. Dr Roy Park was his father-in-law. Ian's keenness showed in his resonant appeals. After leaving Wesley College, he first came into the Victorian side in 1935 and over the next 22 years took 270 wickets for his State at 24.29. He took five wickets or more in an innings 14 times for Victoria. His career was interrupted by World War II, in which he was an RAAF Beaufighter pilot.

He made his debut for Australia against New Zealand in 1945–46 and at Brisbane the following season he proved his worth as a slips fieldsman and scored 47 of Australia's total of 645. He did not get a bowl in that match, though England was caught on a sticky wicket. In the next Test at Sydney, however, conditions were ideal for him and he took 6 for 42 off 30.1 overs, with 12 maidens and 2 for 92 in the second innings off 29 overs. His first 88 balls in this match produced 1 for 3. He ended that series established as an ideal partner for leg-spinner Colin McCool, but in England in 1948 Bradman had little need for spinners as Lindwall, Miller, Johnston and Toshack helped Australia go unbeaten through a triumphant tour, Johnson still took 85 wickets on the tour at 18.38, and only Bill Johnston (102) and Ray Lindwall (86) took more. He had his career best figures of 7 for 42 against Leicestershire.

First-Class Averages: Batting, 4,905 runs at 22.92; Bowling, 619 wickets at 23.30.

Tests (45): 1,000 runs at 18.51; 109 wickets at 29.19.

Ian Johnson's characteristic delivery stride hop.

Johnson was leading wicket-taker with 79 wickets—18 in the Tests—for Hassett's 1949–50 side in South Africa, swinging the Third Test at Durban Australia's way with 5 for 34, but was left at home when Australia visited England in 1953. After losing the 1954–55 series in Australia 3–1 to Hutton's side, he returned to England in 1956 as captain. This followed a highly successful tour of West Indies in 1954–55 in which Johnson led the first Australian side to tour the islands to some thrilling wins. He took 7 for 44 against the West Indies at Georgetown to clinch his team's Test win, and handled a happy side shrewdly. On the flight from Trinidad to Tobago, Johnson and Keith Miller took over the controls and flew the aeroplane. This persuaded the Australian Board of Control to insert a clause in players' contracts forbidding them to take over the controls of any aircraft in which the Australian team travels.

With several of his players past their best, Johnson suffered sharp reversals in the English summer of 1956, both as a bowler and captain. His teasing flight, looped high into the breeze, was no match for the faster, high-actioned off-spin of Jim Laker and he could not coax big efforts from key players like Miller, whom many thought should have been captain. Johnson accepted his problems with good humour and retained a sportsmanlike front when his team had to bat on dusty, ill-prepared wickets ideal for Laker and Lock.

At lunchtime on the first day of the Manchester Test, for example, the ground staff drew clouds of dust when they swept the pitch. Laker took 19 wickets for the match on that pitch, which the Australians believed offended against all known standards of fair play. Frustrated over not being able to take advantage of the pitch with his own bowling, Johnson retained his cool in dealing with the media. That was the tour on which Keith Miller failed to show up for the start of play in the Hampshire match, when Miller was skipper.

In sum, Johnson was victorious as Australian captain seven times against the West Indies, Pakistan and India and was twice leader of losing sides against England. He had much to endure, not the least of it the jibes from commentators like former team-mate Sid Barnes, who referred to Johnson as Australia's "non-playing captain." It was significant of Johnson's methods that only 13 of his 109 Test wickets (he played 45 Tests to get them) were taken in England.

Some international players claimed Johnson's action was suspect but he was never called by umpires in Australia, England, South Africa, West Indies, India, New Zealand or Pakistan. Johnson scored two first-class centuries, took five wickets in an innings 27 times and 10 wickets in a match four times. He had a highest first-class score of 132 not out and held 138 first-class catches.

In 1957, Johnson was chosen from 45 applicants to become

secretary of the Melbourne Cricket Club, where he has continued his reputation for diplomacy and unfailing generosity. He played a leading role in the highly successful Centenary Test organisation. He was an Australian Rules footballer of skill, who played centre for the Victorian Amateur team in inter-State matches.

JOHNSON, Keith Ormond Edley, 1895–1972

Manager of the Australian Services team which played Victory Test matches in England in 1945 and helped revive big cricket, and manager of the famous 1948 Australian team in England. He was a man of immense tact who served as a Flight-Lieutenant in the RAAF, a stalwart of Sydney's Mosman club, and served on the Australian Board of Control for 17 years. He was a key figure in the unfortunate defamation case in Sydney in 1952 launched by Test opener Sid Barnes.

JOHNSON, Leonard Joseph, 1919–1977

First-Class Averages: Batting, 1,139 runs at 16.75; Bowling, 218 wickets at 23.17.

Tests (1): 25 runs, NA; 6 wickets at 12.33.

A lively fast-medium bowler who set records for Queensland but could not find a regular place in the Australian team just after the war because of the brilliance of Lindwall, Bill Johnston and Miller. He played in only one Test, against India at Melbourne in 1947–48, taking 3 for 66 and 3 for 8, which certainly could not be rated failure, scoring 25 not out and catching star batsman Lala Amarnath.

Johnson, born at Ipswich, Queensland, toured New Zealand in 1949–50 with what was virtually Australia's second team, under the captaincy of Billy Brown, while the first team players were in South Africa. He swung the match against Canterbury with a knock of 61 in an hour, hitting four sixes and four fours, adding 62 for the last wicket with Iverson. Then he took 5 for 22, Australia winning by 10 wickets. Against Wellington he had 3 for 38 and 6 for 20.

Johnson carried the Queensland pace attack virtually single-handed from the 1946–47 season to 1952–53. He had success against each touring team, in minor representative games, and in Shield cricket, taking five wickets or more in an innings 16 times.

JOHNSTON, William Arras, 1922–

A tall (6 ft 2½ in), loose-jointed, left-arm fast-medium or slow bowler who was a vital part of Australia's Test attack for seven years, a noted humorist of sunny disposition, who had the good fortune to head the 1953 Australian team's batting averages with 102. He batted 17 times to get the 102 and was once out, topscore 28 not out. He was Australia's leading wicket-taker in three series against England and the only

555

First-Class Averages:
Batting, 1,129 runs at
12.68; Bowling, 554
wickets at 23.35.

Tests (40): 273 runs at
11.37; 160 wickets
at 23.91.

bowler in the great 1948 side to take 100 tour wickets—but heading a tour's batting averages with 102 was the feat that really made him happy.

For Johnston's opponents in 40 Tests, his bowling was far from a laughing matter, however. From a seven-stride approach, he bowled fast-medium deliveries that swung late and lifted nastily, and from the same run he bowled leg-spinners that also kicked alarmingly, mixed with the odd faster ball that snapped up from the pitch and into the batsman. He was all arms and elbows as he ran into bowl, letting the ball go with a long swing of the arm that started behind his knees. He cocked his wrist markedly as it went in behind his back but it came out way above his head as the coaching manuals advocated. His fingers and arms were exceptionally long and there was enough strength in his wrist to have once propelled a baseball 132 yards before it bounced in a contest against American baseballers.

Johnston began as a slow-medium over-the-wicket spinner, playing with his brother for Beeac in the Colac competition in western Victoria. His wrist strength began through milking cows on his father's farm at Ondit. After representing Colac in Country Week tournaments, he moved to Melbourne to play for Richmond, working his way up from the thirds to the firsts by the time he was 17. He changed to bowling round the wicket on the advice of former Victorian and Middlesex left-hander Frank Tarrant. When Johnston turned out for the Army in a services match, Tarrant promptly no-balled him six times for "dragging".

He was picked for Victoria immediately after the war but for two seasons took so few wickets he was dropped to the State Seconds. He was lean and bony, with fleshless shoulders that did not fit his role as a pace bowler, and he failed to play in a Test against Hammond's 1946 side in Australia. The following season, 1947–48, he did well enough against India to earn selection in the 1948 side in England. In one spell for Victoria he gave a hint of what was to come by dismissing three Indian batsmen, Mankad, Rangnekar and Hazare, in 12 balls without conceding a run. In his four Tests against India, he took 16 wickets at 11.37.

The team management did not have him in the Test team when the 1948 tour began but by the time the first Test was played at Nottingham, he had bowled so well and with such versatility he forced his way into the side. Australia's attack was depleted when Lindwall tore a leg muscle and could not bowl in England's second innings but Johnston followed his first innings 5 for 36 with a marathon effort, sending down a match total of 84 overs in taking a total of 9 for 183. Here under the intense pressure of a Test he had shown he could do things on the damper pitches and in the heavier atmosphere of England that he could not do consistently at home. In fact, many star English batsmen said during that tour that they found Johnston more difficult because of his sharp, late swing and awkward bounce than Lindwall or Miller. He finished with 102 tour wickets, 16 more than Lindwall and matched Lindwall's 27 Test victims.

Johnston's value as an entertainer did not end with his bowling. He came out to bat, usually last man in, with a gangling lope that radiated fun. In the field he ran after the ball, head down on the turf, strides bruising the grass with a gait that compelled Sydney columnist Jim Macdougall to call him "the galloping hat-rack". He chortled wisecracks to teammates on and off the field, invented gremlins called Fred and Plushy with such realism many Englishmen thought they did exist. A great team man and the most successful left arm

Bill Johnston shows the wrist flick that brought plenty of trouble for batsmen.

bowler Australia had ever sent to England. "As a bowler, he has one failing—he hasn't a temper", quipped "Tiger" O'Reilly.

On tour in South Africa with Lindsay Hassett's 1949–50 Australian side, Johnston had his best ever Test match figures when he took 6 for 44 in the First Test at Johannesburg. He missed several matches following a car accident but still took 23 Test wickets and topped the bowling averages with 56 wickets at 13.75. His heavy work load was a strain on his knee and contributed to Australia's Ashes defeat in England in 1953. He recovered to again become Australia's leading wicket-taker in Australia in 1954–55 but in Frank Tyson England produced a bowler to match him. Johnston's last tour was to the West Indies in 1954–55.

In all first-class matches Johnston took five wickets in an innings 29 times, with 8 for 52 against Queensland in 1952–53 his best figures. With the bat, he never quite lived up to the promise of his 1953 English tour average of 102.

JONES, Ernest, ("Jonah"), 1869–1943

First-Class Averages: Batting, 2,405 runs at 13.07; Bowling, 645 wickets at 22.75.

Tests (19): 126 runs at 5.04; 64 wickets at 29.01.

A fine fast bowler for South Australia and Australia, as colourful as he was successful, who, after his retirement, rowed out in a dinghy to heckle English teams arriving at Fremantle. At dawn as the ship carrying the Englishmen anchored in the stream, "Jonah" would row round and round the liner, dropping his oars every now and then to shout, "Hundred to one England for the Tests". One English team really got fed up with "Jonah's" heckling as they were quarantined for a week and every morning he rowed close to their ship and through his megaphone related tales of the amazing skills of Australians the Englishmen were due to meet.

Years later when "Jonah" was asked his opinion of Larwood, he said, "Fast? Him fast? So help me, he wouldn't knock a dint in a pound of butter on a hot day. Don't tell me he's fast!" On Jonah's first tour in 1896 he was reported to have bowled a ball through Dr W. G. Grace's beard. When Grace asked what he was up to Jones replied; "Sorry, doctor, she slipped".

He really showed batsmen what fast bowling was all about. In one Adelaide Club match, he bowled 48 byes and his wicket-keeper failed to lay a glove on any of them. In desperation, his captain, one of the best fieldsmen in Australia, fielded at long-stop, and twice had to let the ball go to the chains, although each time he tried hard to prevent this. Once the force of the ball knocked the fieldsman over. Famous English cricketer the Hon F. S. Jackson said once that he wondered whether the cracked rib "Jonah" gave him with a fast delivery, or the handshake of apology, was the more painful experience.

"Whatever Jonah is doing on the field, he is a dasher", wrote George Giffen. "His mission seems to be to make things hum.

558

He is therefore a punishing batsman who makes no pretension to being a scientific player. When he has been hard put to it, he has often batted really well, and once for South Australia in 1895–96 scored 66 out of 89 for the last wicket against Victoria. In the field he is brilliant, especially at mid-off, and I have seen him bring off some extraordinary catches."

Jones, a former miner with big, heavy chest and shoulders, was hailed as Australia's answer when England produced the great fast bowler Tom Richardson. He was given long tuition and developed from a rough and ready terror whose pace left him after a few overs into a well co-ordinated fastie with a fairly short approach who could keep going for long sessions. Fellow Australian "Dimboola Jim" Phillips no-balled him for throwing in 1897–98 Test series against England, but "Jonah" recovered from this setback and with more concentration on control played a major role in later series when his delivery was not questioned.

Between 1894 and 1903, he played in 19 Tests, with a best performance of 7 for 88, and he held 21 catches, a colourful figure who aroused spectators and opponents alike.

He toured England three times, taking 121 wickets in 1896, 135 in 1899 and 71 in 1902, the cost of these wickets averaging 19.10 runs. His best figures included 7 for 36 against Yorkshire at Leeds, 6 for 74 against Yorkshire at Sheffield and 8 for 39 against C. E. de Trafford's XI at Crystal Palace, when he took the last four wickets for no runs, all in 1896. In all first-class matches he took five wickets or more a remarkable 46 times, with 7 for 80 and 7 for 157 as his match bag against England in 1897–98. On tour in New Zealand in 1896 with the Australia side he took 26 wickets at only 8.1 runs each. And he only ran second in the New Zealand tour averages, Hugh Trumble finishing on top with 34 wickets at 6.2 each. Playing against New Jersey on an American jaunt with the same team Jones took 8 for 6.

He was an enormous hitter in district cricket. For North Adelaide v. Sturt at Adelaide in 1888–89, he made 70 out of 80 in 35 minutes, the first 50 runs in 20 minutes. Playing for Queenstown Church of Christ in his 55th year, he took 8 for 38 runs in the match and cracked 116 of the 123 runs scored by his side in 35 minutes without loss, hitting 11 sixes and 11 fours. He scored all the first 52 runs made by his side and 80 of the first 84. This was the man who in 1902, playing for Australia v. an Eleven of Scotland at Edinburgh had a hit measured that covered 152 3/4 yards. At the end of his career he played a number of games for WA.

Christopher Martin-Jenkins recalled that when Jones was introduced to the Prince of Wales, later Edward VII, the Prince asked him if he had attended St Peter's College, Adelaide, to which "Jonah" replied: "Yes, I take the dust cart there regularly."

**JONES, Samuel Percy,
1861–1951**

First-Class Averages:
Batting, 5,193 runs at
21.10; Bowling, 55
wickets at 33.52.

Tests (12): 432 runs at
21.60; 6 wickets at 18.66.

One of the early heroes of Australian cricket, a right-hand batsman who played in The Ashes Test in 1882 and survived longer than anyone in the match. He was a watchful batsman with a strong defence, a useful change bowler, and a brilliant fieldsman. He could hit the ball very hard when he attacked. Few players of his era could so efficiently handle wet or worn pitches.

Jones, educated at Sydney Grammar School and Sydney University, was a splendid specimen, 5 ft 11 ins, 12 st 7 lb. He made a century in first-class cricket when he was 20—109 for New South Wales in 1881–82 against Victoria in a New South Wales total of 775 (Murdoch 321, Garrett 163). He went to England four times, in 1882, 1886, 1888 and 1890. He was only moderately successful on the first trip, scoring 370 runs at 11.93. After missing the 1884 tour, he was at his very best in 1886, finishing second on the tour averages to Giffen in compiling 1,498 runs at 24.16, which included a fine 87 in the Test at Manchester and 151 against The Gentlemen at The Oval. Australian friends who watched his great knock at The Oval later presented him with a gold watch and chain in the committee room at Lord's to commemorate his feat.

In 1888 he began splendidly and appeared set for big scores when he was stricken with smallpox. He was on the dangerously ill list for weeks but the team manager concealed the nature of his illness. He bounced back to win selection again for the 1890 English tour but was again taken ill and spent weeks in a London hospital. He made 303 runs at 16.83 on the 1888 tour and 400 at 12.12 in 1890. After playing in the first two Shield games for New South Wales he settled in Queensland. Among many fine innings at home, Jones made 134 not out against Shrewsbury's touring England side in 1887–88.

Jones is remembered for his unusual dismissal at The Oval in 1882 in the Test that began The Ashes legend. He was a fairly innocent 21-year-old, batting well with Billy Murdoch, who took a single to leg. After the run had been completed Jones went down the pitch to pat down a divot and the wily W. G. Grace threw down his stumps. Jones was furious when umpire Robert Thoms ruled him run out, a decision which intensified the Australians' desire to win the match. Thanks to Spofforth, who took 14 wickets in the match, and to brilliant fielding by players like Jones, they triumphed by just seven runs, dismissing England, who needed 85, for 77 in the final innings.

Jones made two trips to New Zealand with Australian teams. In 1886 he made 159 against Wellington, the only century of the New Zealand tour, and in 1896–97 he went back with a Queensland side. He took a job as a master at Auckland Grammar School in 1904 and played regularly for Auckland from 1904 to 1909, living in New Zealand for the last 47 years of his life.

A case-hardened Victorian wicket-keeper between 1959–60 and 1970–71. He was known as a tough competitor and astute gamesman. He appeared in 90 first-class matches, and toured Sri Lanka, India and South Africa with Lawry's unhappy side in 1969–70, deputising for Test 'keeper Brian Taber in 11 matches without threatening Taber's place.

Jordon began in Melbourne district cricket with Carlton but later moved to Fitzroy. He was a useful inter-State batsman with a highest score of 134 against South Australia in Adelaide in 1963–64 when he added 131 with Ian Huntingdon for the sixth wicket. The next season he also put on 123 with Bill Lawry for the sixth wicket against South Australia.

On the tour of Sri Lanka, India and South Africa, Jordon took 11 catches and made 11 stumpings but scored only 177 runs at 25.28. Against South Zone at Bangalore he was given out off Prasanna's bowling while fighting to save defeat with Lawry. On his way to the pavilion he asked the umpire how he was out. When the umpire said "caught," Jordon laughed and said he did not hit the ball. "Well if you did not hit it, you were out lbw," said the umpire. "Take your pick." Since he quit big cricket Jordon has had outstanding success as a coach of Victorian Football League Reserves and Under 19 sides.

JORDON, Raymond Clarence ("The Slug"), 1937–

First-Class Averages: Batting, 2,414 runs at 25.95; Dismissals, 283 (238 catches, 45 stumpings).

A left-handed batsman who figured in some important partnerships for Victoria but failed to fulfil the exciting promise he showed when he first broke into big cricket.

Joslin scored 7 and 2 in his only Test for Australia, the fourth against India in 1967–68. He toured England with the 1968 Australian team but scored only 344 runs at 21.50 with a topscore of 61.

Joslin, born at Yarraville, made his debut for Victoria in 1966–67, when he put on 107 for the fourth wicket with Jack Potter against Western Australia. In 1967–68 he was again associated with Potter in a big partnership, 177 unfinished for the fourth wicket against New South Wales, and in 1968–69, he added 103 with Keith Stackpole for the third wicket against South Australia. He dropped out of first-class cricket in 1968–69 having scored two centuries—126 against Western Australia at Melbourne in 1966–67 and 121 not out against New South Wales at Melbourne in 1967–68.

After Joslin missed selection in one Australian touring team, Board of Control secretary Alan Barnes asked national selector Jack Ryder what he would like to drink. Ryder, who had fought hard for Joslin's inclusion but failed to convince his co-selectors of Joslin's worth, simply said, "Arsenic".

JOSLIN, Leslie Ronald, 1947–

First-Class Averages: Batting, 1,816 runs at 29.77; Bowling, 1 wicket at 73.00.

Tests (1): 9 runs at 4.50.

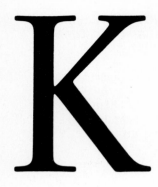

KALLICHARAN, Alvin Isaac, 1949–

A classy Guyanese left-handed batsman whose career with Queensland was cut short by the WSC affair. He signed with WSC only to find this contravened a contract he already had with a Queensland radio station to play Shield cricket. He took over the West Indian captaincy after Clive Lloyd resigned over the WSC issue but lost it when a settlement was negotiated between WSC and traditional cricket. Kallicharan came into first-class cricket in 1966, and had his Test debut in 1971–72 when he made a century against New Zealand. In 66 Tests, he has become a crowd-pleasing craftsman who can play all the shots with grace and effortless timing. He has made 47 first-class centuries in compiling 20,177 runs, and has scored 12 Test centuries. He plays county cricket for Warwickshire. For Queensland in seven matches in 1977–78, Kallicharan made 402 runs at 30.92, topscore 129 not out.

KANHAI, Rohan Babulal, 1935–

One of cricket's most brilliant right-hand batsman who twice toured Australia (1960–61, 1968–69) in West Indies teams and captained West Indies against Australia in the West Indies (1973). He coached and played for one season in Western Australia (1961–62) and for one season in Tasmania (1969–70). Short, compact, with a steely resolve to score runs, he probably did more than any batsman to dispel the notion—widely believed at one time—that West Indians were flamboyant batsmen who refused to graft and build an innings against persistently accurate bowling. He scored 28,639 runs at 49.29 in first-class cricket, including 83 centuries, best score 256. He could defend stubbornly but never hestitated to almost arrogantly despatch bad balls. In the 1960–61 Test at Adelaide he became the first West Indian to score a century in each innings of a Test, with 117 and 115, hitting the first ball of the third day for six, sometimes swinging himself off his feet. He was not a good captain because of his volatile makeup, nor an outstanding coach through his modesty in conveying the urges that motivate a great batsman, but he inspired all who watched by what he could do both in WA and Tasmania. He played eight matches for WA, scoring 533 runs at 41.00. While coaching at Devonport he played two matches for Tasmania, scoring 200 not against Victoria and 100 not out against New Zealand.

One of Australia's most reliable all-rounders in a long Test career. As a bowler, fieldsman and stonewalling batsman, he was a model of dependability for grade, State and Australian teams. "He was often a weariness of the flesh to spectators," said *Wisden* in 1913. "But his value to his side was very great indeed. One Kelleway in a side is enough. Two or three would be intolerable."

Kelleway was a right-arm medium-pace stock bowler who could keep an end going for hours without faltering in length or pace. He kept the runs down and he could be hostile. Some experts rated him the best of Australia's medium-pacers after World War I. He brought his arm over at peak height and had the ability to use even a slight breeze. He could swing and swerve on plumb pitches and at times ran through strong batting lineups.

As a batsman, he was deficient in strokes, destined to play long, defensive innings to rescue his team. When a good start was achieved, it was best to get him out of the way to allow strokemakers in his side to do the scoring. His reliability in the field was shown by his 24 Test catches, and he had a splendid throw. He was one of the few men to open both batting and bowling for New South Wales and Australia.

"Awkward but indomitable, deaf of opinion, contemptuous of style except as the servant of effect, Kelleway will stand as one of the most individual and formidable cricketers ever seen," wrote R. C. Robertson-Glasgow. "His runs were made and for the most part received, without observable emotion. He was not interested in spectators. If they were mute, so was he; if abusive, let them waste their breath; and their winged facetiousness bounced off the granite and teak that fused in his making."

Kelleway, born at Lismore, NSW, joined the Glebe club in Sydney in 1906–07, and made his debut for NSW in 1907–08 at Sydney, aged 18. After scoring 108 against South Australia in 1909–10 he began his Test career the following season against the touring South Africans. He scored 295 runs in the five Tests at 42.14 an innings and took seven wickets at 55.71 apiece, but this was impressive enough to show a new all-round star had arrived. He played against Douglas's MCC team in 1911–12, but like all Australian batsmen succumbed to the brilliant bowling of Barnes and Foster, who caused unprecedented havoc.

KELLEWAY, Charles, 1889–1944

First-Class Averages: Batting, 6,389 runs at 35.10; Bowling, 339 wickets at 26.32.

Tests (26): 1,422 runs at 37.42; 52 wickets at 32.36.

From the wreckage caused when Armstrong, Hill, Trumper,
Cotter, Ransford and Carter declared themselves unavailable,
Australia put together a team for the 1912 Triangular tournament in England. The Australians disappointed but the tournament was a personal triumph for Kelleway, who averaged
60 runs an innings in the six Tests, an effort inferior only to
that by Bardsley. He scored two centuries against South Afri-

564

ca and had innings of 61—in 4 hours 30 minutes—and 43 against England when the bowlers were on top. He was used as an opening bat throughout the tour.

In 1913–14, Macartney's brilliant batting, R. J. Massie's exceptional left-arm bowling, and Kelleway's all-round consistency, were the main reasons NSW recaptured the Sheffield Shield from SA. Kelleway took 4 for 34 and 7 for 48 against Queensland at Brisbane, and 1 for 68 and 7 for 35 in the return match at Sydney. In the final match of the summer v. Victoria, Kelleway and Collins added 136 for the first wicket before Collins was out. Macartney joined Kelleway and they hit 221 runs in two hours, NSW reaching 675 in eight hours. Kelleway made 138. Victoria's aggregate score in two innings was 32 short of the NSW total, Massie taking 10 wickets, Kelleway three.

Kelleway served in France as a captain in the Army in World War I, and immediately war ended was made captain of the first AIF team in England. After six matches he was replaced by Collins, apparently on the orders of Field Marshal Birdwood, GOC Australian forces. Collins said Birdwood told him Kelleway was a fine player but inclined to be quarrelsome. Kelleway attempted to take the field in the next match but team-mates refused to join him, and he went home on the next boat. In his six matches with the AIF Kelleway, who was recovering from a nasty leg wound, scored 505 runs, with two 100s, average 56.11, and took 18 wickets for 30.44 each.

A year later he was among the first chosen for Australia against Douglas' MCC side in Australia. He headed the bowling averages with 15 wickets at 21 runs apiece and averaged 47.14 runs an innings with the bat. He made his only century against England in that series, 147 at Adelaide, batting just under seven hours for it. Dropped before he scored, he had one session between lunch and tea on the third day in which he scored only 24, and he made only 96 in the entire day. In a partnership of 126 with Pellew, he made 42.

Kelleway was unavailable through business reasons for the 1921 Australian tour in England, but in 1924–25 in Australia played in all five Tests against Gilligan's MCC tourists, averaging 28 with the bat, taking 14 wickets. Although he was in peak form, he was overlooked for the 1926 tour of England. He did not play first-class cricket for the next two Australian seasons but won back his Test spot for the First Test against Chapman's team in 1928–29. He became ill during the match and took no further part in Test cricket.

Kelleway made 15 centuries in first-class cricket, with 168, which he reached twice, his best score. He played 18 of his 26 Tests against England, eight v. South Africa. To his credit he never gave Collins a moment's trouble after his sacking as First AIF team skipper, playing under Collins for NSW and Australia on the happiest of terms.

KELLY, James Joseph, 1867–1938

First Class Averages: Batting, 4,108 runs at 19.94; Dismissals, 355 (243 catches, 112 stumped).

Tests (36): 664 runs at 17.02; Dismissals 63 (43 caught, 20 stumped).

One of the distinguished line of Australian Test wicket-keepers, a Victorian who had to migrate to New South Wales to win recognition. He was a sure catcher of the ball, as good at the end of a long day as at the start, and although he lacked the flair for stumping of his great contemporary Blackham, he matched Blackham statistically by the end of his career. Kelly was a cricketer of great nerve and pluck, the first to 'keep in an innings of more than 500 runs without conceding a bye—at Sydney in 1897–98 when England made 551. Like Blackham, he stood right up on the stumps for all but the fastest bowling. When he went back he was especially skilful in taking Ernie Jones and "Tibby" Cotter at their fastest.

Kelly, born in Port Melbourne, made his big step towards fame when he decided Blackham's form gave him little hope of playing for Victoria and joined the Paddington club in Sydney. Within two seasons he had taken over from Blackham for Australia. He was always unshaken by hard knocks when 'keeping or by desperate situations when batting. His eight catches in the 1901–02 Test at Sydney v. England will always command a place in the record books.

He toured England with the teams of 1896, 1899, 1902 and 1905. In his first appearance at Lord's in 1896 against the MCC he made the topscore of eight in an historic Australian total of 18. Kelly and Hugh Trumble won the Second Test on that

tour by adding 25 for the eighth wicket at Old Trafford. They took an hour to get them. Australian captain Harry Trott left the ground and took a ride in a hansom cab to save himself from nervous collapse while Kelly and Trumble edged towards their target.

Kelly lacked grace as a batsman but always made bowlers work hard for his wicket. He played 185 first-class matches, with his best innings 108 for New South Wales v. South Australia at Sydney in 1896–97, 103 for Australia v. Warwickshire at Edgbaston in 1899, and 102 not out for Australia v. Rest Of Australia at Sydney in 1898–99. In 1899, he was in a partnership of 69 runs in 22 minutes with Ernie Jones for Australia v. Somersetshire, and when he made an unbeaten 74 against Gloucestershire in 1905, he and Frank Laver added 112 for the last wicket. In October, 1904, Kelly and Trumper put on 219 for the fifth wicket for Paddington against Waverley, Kelly scoring 98, Trumper 189 not out, including 51 from three overs by T. H. Howard. He was compelled to retire after taking a blow over the heart while batting against Walter Brearley at Old Trafford, his fingers already badly damaged by Australia's speedsters. He died on the same day as his old tour mate, Hugh Trumble.

KELLY, Peter Charles, 1942–

First-Class Averages: Batting, 1,611 runs at 40.27.

A right-hand opening batsman from the Sydney suburb of Mosman who transferred to Western Australia after one match for New South Wales in 1962–63. He played for WA from 1964–65 to 1966–67 and in that period scored four centuries, all of them in the 1965–66 season. He had shown the right temperament for first-class cricket in 1964–65 when he scored 72 in 270 minutes to set up WA's win on the first innings against Victoria at Melbourne, and batted through the WA innings for 82 not out in a total of 147 against South Australia at Perth, but his success the following summer was unexpected.

KELLY, Thomas Joseph Dart, 1844–1893

First-Class Averages: Batting, 543 runs at 20.11.

Tests (2): 64 runs at 21.33.

A successful Irish-born batsman in early Colonial matches who played in two Tests for Australia before Shield cricket began. He was a splendid free hitter and admirable fieldsman at point whose parents took him to Bristol, Gloucestershire, from his birthplace in County Waterford when he was a few weeks old. There on Durdham Downs he learned to play cricket along with the brothers Grace. He migrated to Australia in 1863, aged 19, and two years later made his debut for Victoria. In 16 first-class matches his best performance was 86 against NSW. In the Second Test in 1876–77 Kelly made eight successive scoring shots for four in the second innings, scoring 35. Kelly's main claim to fame, however, was that he was the first Australian cricketer to wear a blazer, a patriotic red, white and blue creation with a sash to match, which in the early 1870s caused a sensation at the MCG.

KENDALL, Thomas, 1851–1924

First-Class Averages: Batting, 141 runs at 12.81; Bowling, 40 wickets at 16.65.

Tests (2): 39 runs at 13.00; 14 wickets at 15.35.

A slow left-arm English-born bowler who was one of Australia's heroes in the first Test matches and was rated the best Australian bowler never to tour England. He was probably the first Australian cricketer disciplined for reasons other than cricket ability and this cost him a trip back to England, and his birthplace in Bedfordshire. He was sluggish in the field.

In the first Test ever at Melbourne in March, 1877, Kendall's contribution was second in importance only to Charles Bannerman's century in Australia's win by 45 runs. In Australia's second innings, when England appeared likely to have a simple task in the final innings, Kendall and Hodges put on 29 for the last wicket, leaving England 154 to score for victory. Kendall then proceeded to take 7 for 55, to complete the match with 8 for 109. In the second Test two weeks later he took 6 for 106.

Kendall ranked with the great Frank Allan as our finest left-arm bowler in the early days of big cricket in Australia, and it was regarded as a major coup for Tasmanian cricket when J. G. Davies lured him to Hobart in 1880. In 1878, Kendall had accompanied the Australian team that was to tour England as far as Perth but was sent back to Melbourne for "reasons other than cricket."

Kendall had impressive control of length, flighted the ball well, and could turn it either way. He lived in Hobart for 43 years and in all those years was employed by the Hobart *Mercury*. English cricket masters like W. G. Grace and James Southerton praised him highly, as did A. G. Steel. Grace's praise was soundly based as Kendall had him caught for eight off his bowling in 1873–74, playing for Fifteen of Victoria and in March, 1892 when Lord Sheffield's team visited Hobart, Kendall bowled Grace for 27. Perhaps Kendall's most important contribution to Tasmanian cricket, however, was in providing batsmen like Ken Burn, Claude Rock, Harold Hale, Edward Windsor, John Savigny and Charles Eady with regular practice against quality bowling. His presence enabled them to overcome their island's isolation and develop into quality batsmen.

Kendall appeared in five first-class matches for Tasmania between 1881 and 1889. In the 1883–84 season he took 150 wickets in club matches, including 50 when a team from the south toured New Zealand. He is still regarded as one of the best coaches ever in Tasmania.

A tall strongly-built Queensland right-hand batsman who made an impressive debut in three Tests for Australia in England in 1981 but then had to drop out of big cricket for a spell because of back problems. He hits the ball hard all around the wicket and gets into position quickly to play his drives, pulls and cuts. He has been a consistent run-getter for Queensland since he made 140 against New South Wales in his debut in 1974–75. He has probably been unsettled by repeated changes in his place in the batting order, and has batted everywhere from No 1 to No 6.

Kent has made seven first-class centuries and has a highest score of 171 against Tasmania in 1980–81. His Test debut was delayed by his period with WSC. He was one of the few players to emerge from Australia's 1981 tour of England with his reputation enhanced for he improved with every innings after making his Test debut at Edgbaston in the Fourth Test, but again his captain could not decide where he should bat. Kent went in fifth wicket down and made 46 and 10, switched to third wicket down and made 52 and 2 and opened in the last Test to score 54 and 7, adding 120 for the first wicket with Wood. He made 345 runs on the tour at 23.13, highest score 92 against Worcestershire when he put on 167 with Alan Border.

Kent showed glimpses of genuine class in his three Tests in England but injury interrupted his developing career in 1981–82.

KENT, Martin Francis, 1953–

First-Class Averages: Batting, 3,567 runs at 36.03.

Tests (3): 171 runs at 28.50.

A tall, lantern-jawed right-arm medium-pace bowler who was chosen to play for New South Wales by sole selector "Monty" Noble on his form in Moore Park juniors. He played in only two matches for NSW, taking nine wickets at 29. In the match between NSW and Archie MacLaren's MCC team at Sydney in 1901–02, he took 4 for 162 which impressed MacLaren who advised him to go and play for Lancashire. While he was qualifying, he played for Enfield, and is believed to be the first Australian to appear in the Lancashire League. Kermode played in non-championship games for Lancashire and also for London County in 1902 and 1903 while qualifying. From 1904 to 1908 he played in 76 matches for Lancashire, taking 321 wickets at 22.61, and scoring 631 runs at 7.88. Later played for Bacup in the League. After World War I, Kermode returned to Australia and played grade cricket for Balmain, finishing second to Lyall Wall in the Club's bowling averages in 1918–19, with 31 wickets.

KERMODE, Alexander ("Alex"), 1876–1934

First-Class Averages: Batting, 680 runs at 8.00; Bowling, 340 wickets at 23.01.

A fast-scoring Pakistani opening batsman who played for Queensland in 1973–74. He is the only non-Australian to score a century before lunch on the first day of a Test. He joined

KHAN, Majid Jehangir, 1946–

Trumper, Macartney and Bradman in the select group that have performed this feat by scoring 108 not out for Pakistan against New Zealand at Karachi in 1976–77, finishing with 112. Majid has played for Punjab, Cambridge University, Glamorgan and eight matches for Queensland in a career that has produced more than 25,000 in all first-class matches, with more than 70 centuries. In 61 Tests he has scored 3,900 runs at 39.79, including eight centuries. For Queensland he showed his customary facility for pushing the score along, punishing bad deliveries even when they were bowled in the first over. He made 496 highly attractive runs for the State at 31.00, top-score 107.

KIMPTON, Roger Charles McDonald 1916–

First-Class Averages: Batting, 4,166 runs at 33.59; Bowling, 26 wickets at 54.12; Dismissals 89 (69 catches, 20 stumpings).

A Victorian right-hand batsman who made four centuries in three seasons playing for Oxford University and Worcestershire just before World War II. "He is a cricketer of high promise," said *Wisden*. "His wristy defence and quickness in stroke-play were reminiscent of the great C. G. Macartney when he was at the crease." Unhappily, the war ruined Kimpton's cricket career, though he played one match with Worcestershire after the war and toured the West Indies with Jim Swanston's XI in 1956. Kimpton played for Prahran first grade side in 1933–34 when he was 17 and still at school. He went to Oxford with his brother Stephen in 1935. He kept wicket and bowled right-arm leg-spinners.

Between 1935 and 1956 Roger Kimpton played 75 first-class matches, with nine centuries. His highest score was 160 for Oxford against Gloucestershire in 1935. He was an outstanding fighter pilot during the war and commanded Australia's 75 Squadron. His brother, **Stephen Michael Kimpton**, a left-hander (1914–), made 112 runs for Oxford at 18.66 and took 9 wickets at 42.66 but failed to win his Blue. Stephen Kimpton took 90 wickets at around 20 a piece in four seasons for Prahran, heading the first grade bowling averages in each season.

KING, Ian Harold, 1943–

First-Class Averages: Batting, 65 runs at 8.12; Bowling, 30 wickets at 28.36.

An exuberant right-arm fast bowler who in 1969–70 became the first Aboriginal since Eddie Gilbert to play for Queensland. Like Gilbert, he was a non-conformist. He went into first-class cricket after four seasons in grade with the Toombul club. Unlike Gilbert, Jack Marsh, and Alec Henry, the other Aboriginal fast bowlers to play for their States, his action was as smooth as silk, though he was the fastest bowler to play for Queensland since Wes Hall.

King, one of a Brisbane family of 10, graduated to first-class cricket after brief tilts at hockey, basketball and professional boxing. On Brisbane's south side he was known as "Rainbow" because of his passion for brightly-coloured clothes. Later he was nicknamed "Sammy" because of his resemblance to Sammy Davis, Jnr. On a visit to Sydney he played for Bankstown fourth grade in 1964–65 and the following year played first grade. Bob Madden, then Bankstown's first grade captain, took over his instruction and that season King took 41 first grade wickets. In 1966–67 he improved that to 49 first grade wickets. He was fast and bounced the ball high into batsmen's shoulders, but he was also homesick. He returned to Brisbane and joined Toombul, for whom he took 50 wickets in his first season.

There was keen competition at the time for fast bowling places in the Queensland side, with Tony Dell, Peter Allan, Ross Duncan, Sandy Morgan and "Wild Bill" Albury competing for places. King got his chance in the 1969–70 season, taking 3 for 86 against Western Australia. He fell in love with Perth and after troubles in Brisbane settled in WA, disappearing from first-class cricket after only eight matches and content just to play club cricket in the west. He played only eight first-class matches but gave glimpses of rare talent, exceptional pace and splendid fielding ability.

One of Australia's great right-handed batting stylists, and a cricketer of great personal charm. Spectators enjoyed him defending as much as they did his attacking strokes. He had a way of diverting the direction of the ball, caressing rather than bludgeoning it, yet onlookers were still surprised by the speed at which his strokes hit the fence. He was one of the finest of all exponents of the cut and leg glance, and Bradman considered he played the hook better than anyone else he had seen. Wicket-keepers often claimed Kippax cut the ball right out of their gloves.

"Kippax's batting had a silken quality not seen in any player of his time or since," wrote Ray Robinson. "His leg-glancing, forward or back, was so delicate that it had a kind of moonbeam beauty. In square-cutting he stood erect, but when he cut late—the shot which captivated crowds most—he made a lissom bow over the ball and stroked it away with the bat face downwards as if to squeeze the ball into the ground. His advance down the wicket was a glide, with the right foot passing smoothly behind the left. In driving from the crease, a lift and downthrust of his left foot toward the ball brought his weight effortlessly into the stroke."

Sydney-born Kippax was a teenaged grade cricket sensation who took an unnecessarily long time to get his chance in big cricket. He began at Bondi Public School and spent much of his childhood watching Victor Trumper. At 16, in 1913, he appeared in the Waverley district first grade team captained

KIPPAX, Alan Falconer ("Kipper"), 1897–1972

First-Class Averages: Batting, 12,762 runs at 57.22; Bowling, 21 wickets at 52.33.

Tests (22): 1,192 runs at 36.12.

by Syd Gregory in a match against Glebe. "Tibby" Cotter knocked the bat from his hand with the first ball he faced, but he took the bat back from first slip and went on to make the first 100 of the 7,114 runs he scored over 23 years with Waverley.

Kippax, 5 ft 11 in, played his first State match in 1918–19 but he had to wait in a country brimming with talent until 1924–25 to make his Test debut. In the 1925–26 season, he made 271 not out against Victoria and averaged 112 in Shield matches, but he was omitted from the 1926 Australian team to England. Many had thought him good enough to go in 1921 but his exclusion in 1926 ranks as one of the worst of all selection blunders, made by Herbie Collins, Clem Hill and Jack Ryder, who selected the team in batches and allowed their expertise to desert them in their assessment of Kippax.

In 1926, at 29, he was at his absolute peak, defensively foolproof, bat straight, head over the ball, footwork perfect. Monty Noble described his omission for the trip to England as "a crime against the cricketing youth of Australia". New South Wales players won nine of the 16 places in that side, so it seems obvious inter-State jealousies caused Kippax to be dropped. In Victoria, which gained five places in the touring party, it was said Kippax's batting lacked the guts and brimstone needed to win Tests.

Even at the nets Kippax was all style and graceful movement.

Kippax, who took over the New South Wales captaincy when Herbie Collins retired in 1926, emphasised the selectors' poor judgment after a well beaten Australian side came home from England. The next summer in Australia he scored 315 not out, a chanceless innings that included 41 fours against Queensland, joining a select group who have made 300 in Australia. Over the next two summers he scored 1,846 first-class runs at an average of 83.91.

In 1928–29, he won a regular place in the Australian side in the series against Chapman's English team. At Melbourne he made 100 out of 161 for the fourth wicket with Ryder, an innings that broke the stranglehold Larwood had over Australian batsmen. That summer he also played one of the finest Shield innings of all time, again at Melbourne. New South Wales were 9 for 113, chasing Victoria's 376, when the last man, Halford Hooker, joined Kippax. They batted for a whole day, with Kippax scoring at the rate of 48 runs an hour, and carried on into the next day when Hooker was finally out for 62. Their last wicket partnership of 307, a world record, had seen a glorious display of Kippax stroke-making for more than five hours as he lifted his score by 238 runs to 260 not out.

Kippax finally won a place in an Australian side to tour England in 1930, aged 33. He quickly proved himself a master at batting on bad pitches. In his first Test knock in England he made 64 not out in an Australian score of 144 on a sticky wicket at Nottingham. Against Sussex on a fast pitch, seven Australian wickets fell for 79 before Kippax rescued the innings with 158. He followed with 102 not out in the second innings to become the first Australian since Bardsley in 1909 to make a century in each innings of a match on his first trip to England.

He made 83 in the Second Test, which Australia won by seven wickets, hit 77 in the Third Test when Australia had a draw and Bradman scored 334, and 51 in the drawn Fourth Test. Only in the Fifth Test did he fail and Australia won this match by an innings and 39 runs. In all matches on the tour Kippax finished second to Bradman among Australia's batsmen, scoring 1,451 runs at 58.04. His scoring was achieved with a calm elegance but the real surprise was the assurance with which Kippax batted on wet pitches that had all the other Australian batsmen floundering. In fact, many English experts rated Kippax ahead of Bradman on all wickets.

Although Kippax had a masterly hook shot that had at times made even Larwood look pedestrian, he kept playing the shot like a teenager as he moved into his thirties. At Brisbane in 1931–32, he hooked Eddie Gilbert at his fastest for several fours after Gilbert had dismissed Wendell Bill and Bradman in one over. Then he mistimed a hook at a bouncer from the slower H. M. Thurlow at the other end, and the ball thudded into his temple. Kippax spent three days in hospital after they stitched up the gash. He was almost 35, and although he played many appealing hands after that he never again had the same confidence when hooking. On the way to Brisbane for that match Kippax had his nose broken in a matting wicket innings at Parkes in western NSW. A large spike was later found under the mat. Bradman wrote that the blow at Parkes followed by the Brisbane injury ruined Kippax's confidence in hooking.

He went back to England for a second tour in 1934, scoring 961 runs at 50.57, topscore 250. The golden years were behind him, though he continued to make big scores for New South Wales, for whom he hit 32 centuries, and played many thrilling innings under 100. In all first-class matches (175), he hit 43 centuries, twice scoring two centuries in a match. In 1982 Kippax remains the record run-scorer for NSW, with 8,005 runs at 67.26. He did valuable development work by touring country areas in teams sprinkled with big names, companionable, serene and with a flair for giving baritone solos that enlivened many trips. He ran a successful sporting goods business in partnership with Herb Geldard and became a splendid lawn bowler.

The artistry he brought to batting will be remembered long after modern batsmen surpass his feats, for as Ray Robinson so aptly put it, Alan Kippax's batting should have been weighed in carats, not runs.

Kippax's stance was relaxed, his concentration on the bowling intense.

KLINE, Lindsay Francis, 1934–

First-Class Averages:
Batting, 559 runs at 8.60;
Bowling, 276 wickets at
27.39.

Tests (13): 58 runs at 8.28;
34 wickets at 22.82.

An acrobatic left-arm off-break and googly bowler and with one exception a duffer of a tailend batsman. He approached the stumps with a bound that carried him about 18 inches off the ground at the moment of delivery. Between 1955 and 1962 he had some outstanding coups for Victoria that won him selection in Tests for Australia and earned him trips to England, New Zealand, South Africa, India and Pakistan, but it will be for his one show of batting defiance that he will always be remembered.

Kline went to the wicket in the Fourth Test at Adelaide in 1960–61 against West Indies, with Australia apparently beaten. He was the last man in, with almost two hours left to play and Australia was more than 200 runs behind. He went straight from the practice nets to the middle. For 20 minutes Johnny Martin and Norm O'Neill had been embarrassed at how often they had got Kline out. In the dressing-room most of the Australian players started to pack their bags.

One of cricket's notable match-saving stands unfolded, with Kline and Ken Mackay defying the West Indian attack. Frank Worrell changed his bowlers frequently and they got through their overs at an almost furious rate. Kline was unruffled. For over after over he dead-batted the ball a few inches in front of him, with all the West Indian fieldsmen clustered around the bat. The nation stopped to listen to the

Lindsay Kline batting against the West Indies at Adelaide in 1960–61 when he and "Slasher" Mackay defied bowlers for almost two hours to gain a memorable draw.

574

broadcast of every ball, not daring to think that Kline could last until six o'clock. Finally the clock crept to within a minute of six o'clock. Worrell tossed the ball to Wes Hall and Mackay faced the last over. The tension was such that some of the Australian players could not watch the game as Mackay blocked only the balls he had to play and let the last delivery hit him a stunning blow in the ribs rather than play it. Australia had held out. Kline had made 15 in the unbroken stand of 66.

Kline, born in the Melbourne suburb of Camberwell, joined the Melbourne club after leaving school and first played for Victoria in 1955–56. In his second season in the State side he took 37 wickets at 24.89, including 3 for 6 against South Australia, 6 for 57 against NSW, and 5 for 65 against South Australia. This won him a tour of New Zealand with an Australian "A" team. In 1957–58 he went to South Africa with the Australian senior side and at Cape Town in the second Test took a hat-trick, finishing the tour at the top of the Test bowling averages with 15 wickets at 16.33. He again headed the Test bowling averages in India and Pakistan in 1959–60, with 16 wickets in four Tests at 14.43, including 7 for 75 at Lahore which clinched Australia's victory over Pakistan.

He continued to get wickets for Victoria at home, with 5 for 46 against NSW in 1959, a gem of a performance. He played in two Tests against England in 1958–59 and after his famous innings at Adelaide against the West Indies went to England in 1961 under Benaud, but was not used in a Test. He still managed to take 54 wickets on the tour at 28.14.

KORTLANG, Henry Frederick Lorenz ("Bert"), 1880–1961

First-Class Averages: Batting, 2,688 runs at 49.77; Bowling, 2 wickets at 42.00.

A Carlton-born right-hand batsman who played some big innings for Essendon and Victoria before settling in New Zealand. He first played for Victoria against New South Wales at Sydney in 1909–10 when he scored 34 not out and 15. In the match against Queensland that summer he made an attractive 116 at Brisbane and shortly afterwards played a long innings of 197 against Western Australia at Perth. In 1910–11 he made 69 against South Australia at Adelaide and then batted for two hours 30 minutes to score 94 out of 190 added with Warwick Armstrong in the return match in Melbourne. He followed with scores of 58 and 34 in Melbourne and 41 and 30 in Sydney, all against NSW. After World War I he had five seasons with Wellington and in 1923–24 appeared for New Zealand at the age of 44. In March, 1924, he had a partnership of 118 for the second wicket with W. A. Baker for Wellington against the NSW team, and in 1926–27 he made 100 for Wellington against a touring Melbourne CC side. He made six first-class centuries, topscore 214 not out for Wellington v. Auckland in 1925–26.

L

LAIRD, Bruce Malcolm ("Stumpy"), 1950–

First-Class Averages: Batting, 4,489 runs at 32.76.

Tests (18): 1,204 runs at 37.62.

A plucky right-hand West Australian opening batsman who has been battered by the world's fastest bowlers without any lessening of his dependable run-scoring. He has made 11 centuries and 17 other scores over 50 in a career that has been full of setbacks and bruises. A Test century continues to elude him although he has made 10 half centuries. He has made three overseas tours with Australian teams and was one of those whose careers were most affected when he joined WSC.

Laird, born at Mt Lawley, went from the South Perth club to the State side in 1972–73. He made his career highest score of 171 against Queensland in 1976–77 and appeared in his initial Test in 1979–80 against the West Indies, starting impressively with 92 and 75. An achilles tendon injury kept him out of most of the 1980–81 season and probably caused him to miss the 1981 tour of England.

In Tests his role has been to resist the onslaughts of pace attacks, grafting his way to good starts with his front-arm well

Bruce Laird looks with satisfaction on a square cut.

up, backlift minimal, and it is only when Australia has begun to score freely that he has unveiled an attractive array of drives, pulls, backcuts and glances. His century at Sydney in the limited over match against the West Indies in 1981–82 was one of the few occasions when he has attacked from the start and it proved a gem of an innings. He has become an outstanding player of class swing bowling and of the bouncer, but he still needs to show more authority in his running between wickets and in his judgement of when to glance and sweep. A great favourite with crowds because of his calm acceptance of the knocks his job demands, he is a specialist close-in field.

LAMBERT, Henry Francis ("Harry"), 1918–

First-Class Averages: Batting, 577 runs at 15.18; Bowling, 76 wickets at 28.72.

A useful ambidextrous all-rounder from the Collingwood club who played in the Lancashire League after a brief period in the Victorian team and was a member of the Commonwealth team that toured India in 1949–50. Lambert, born at Bairnsdale, batted right-handed in the late order and bowled a lively left-arm fast-medium. He made his debut for Victoria in 1946–47 and in 1948–49 took 5 for 64 against NSW. He went to the Lancashire League in 1949. In India with the Commonwealth XI he made 137 runs at 11.41 and took 29 wickets at 31.89, best effort 4 for 76 in the Second unofficial Test.

LAMPARD, Albert Wallis ("Allie"), 1885–

First-Class Averages: Batting, 2,597 runs at 30.91; Bowling, 134 wickets at 26.05.

A right-hand batsman and right-arm leg-break bowler for Victoria and the first AIF team who started his career as a wicket-keeper but gave this up in favour of spin bowling when his batting improved. He started his career with the Richmond club in Melbourne and played for the Victorian Second XI in 1908–09 as wicket-keeper. He made his debut for Victoria in 1908–09, often getting a start without scoring heavily and 1913–14 played his first Shield match in what was Victor Trumper's last Shield game.

Lampard served in England as a sergeant with the Australian Army Service Corps and was among the 14 players chosen after trials for the first AIF side. He made 112 for the AIF against Surrey, when he and "Nip" Pellew put on 170 for the seventh wicket. On the South African part of the AIF team's tour, he had a partnership of 153 for the sixth wicket with Herbie Collins against South Africa at Johannesburg, and took 7 for 71 (12 for 100 in the match) against Western Province at Cape Town. On the Australian part of the AIF tour, he took 7 for 99 against Victoria.

After his discharge Lampard represented Victoria for two more seasons, playing 63 first-class games in all, scoring three first-class centuries, highest score 111 against England at

Melbourne in 1920–21. He took five wickets or more in an innings seven times and once took ten wickets in a match. In 1920–21, he toured New Zealand with an Australian team captained by Vernon Ransford, scoring 556 runs at 42.76 in all matches.

LANGDON, Christopher Walter, 1922–

First-Class Averages: Batting, 2,529 runs at 35.62; Bowling, 27 wickets at 41.33.

A classy left-hand batsman who lacked opportunities to impress Test selectors at a time when Australia boasted an exceptionally powerful side. He batted skilfully enough to score five centuries and 15 fifties for WA although his formative years had been wasted in World War II. His left-arm spinners brought handy wickets. His international experience was restricted to a tour of India with the 1949–50 Commonwealth team led by Jock Livingston.

Langdon, born in the mining town of Boulder, played club cricket with Claremont-Cottesloe. He first played for WA when that State entered the Sheffield Shield in 1947–48. He made his initial first-class century, 112, for WA against an Australia XI in 1947–48 at Perth and added scores of 138 against Queensland at Perth in 1948–49, 131 against South Australia at Adelaide in 1950–51, 120 against South Africa at Perth in 1952–53, and 118 against Queensland at Perth in 1952–53.

He headed the Perth first grade 1950–51 averages with 1,020 runs at an impressive 145.70 and repeated it again the next season (1951–52), with 781 runs at 52.00. His average of 145.70 is the highest in Perth district cricket since the end of World War I. Langdon captained WA in 1952–53. He later became a wellknown cricket commentator.

LANGER, Robert Samuel (''Robbie''), 1948–

First-Class Averages: Batting, 2,769 runs at 41.33.

A hard-hitting Western Australian left-handed batsman who has made five centuries for Western Australia since his debut in 1973–74 against New Zealand. He is one of the most powerful strikers of the ball in inter-State cricket, a brawny, big-shouldered character who appreciates fast pitches, and excels in one-day matches. He made 99 not out in typical fashion in the 1981–82 MacDonald's Cup match against Tasmania, giving several chances in the innings that were just too fiercely hit for the fieldsmen to hold.

Langer, who plays for the Scarborough club in Perth, has been a model of consistency for WA, with 12 fifties to his credit apart from his centuries. His career best score of 150 for WA against Victoria at Perth in 1974–75 was brimful of power. His ability to make crowd-pleasing big hits was one of the reasons he was signed by WSC, but he appeared in only two matches.

A thickset South Australian with an ample midriff and an unsurpassed safety record as a wicket-keeper. Langley in the 1950s built a reputation for accepting chances that *Wisden* said made him the greatest ally Australian bowlers had ever had. He lacked Tallon's whip-like stumping speed and Oldfield's polish but he averaged four wickets per Test.

Langley had a ruddy, jowly, fair-topped face, an ability to concentrate for hours without lapsing, dexterity that stemmed from a background as an Australian Rules rover, patience that prevented him snatching at the ball, and the gift for social enjoyment off the field that immediately transmitted itself to his hosts. He looked like an apple orchardist who had somehow strayed on to Lords, The Oval, Sydney Cricket Ground and the other famous fields. But it is doubtful if Australia ever produced a more popular Test player. He became Speaker of the South Australian House of Assembly and has been a member for 20 years.

Langley took to wicket-keeping at school in Adelaide at the age of 12 with no family background in the job except that one grandfather had once umpired in a match between Fiji and South Australia. He was self-taught, beginning at Colonel Light Gardens for his school, ready to accept any hints that came his way from Vic Richardson after Gil joined the Sturt CC. Sturt nominated him for the South Australian Colts. Later he became Sturt's captain, learning to bat handily from the club's coach, Alfred Hodder. In 1945–46, South Australia chose Langley as a batsman against New South Wales and in 1947–48 he succeeded Roley Vaughton as the State's 'keeper. When Tallon withdrew from the Australian team to tour South Africa in 1949–50, Langley got the job of touring as deputy to Ron Saggers. Although a ball from Alan Walker broke a finger on that trip, he made 22 dismissals in six matches.

He was chosen as a stopgap in Saggers' absence in 1951 to play in the First Test at Brisbane against West Indies, and in this match he set a record for a newcomer of seven dismissals. He finished that five-Test series with 21 victims, a total that only Herbert Strudwick had achieved before him—for England against South Africa in 1913–14. Apart from absences through injuries and Tallon's reappearance for a Test at Nottingham in 1953, Langley remained Australia's 'keeper until he retired.

At initial inspection, Langley appeared to be one of those 'keepers who took whatever chances came his way but did not create chances, but when you talked to his bowlers they all enthused about the great threat he posed for batsmen by converting half-chances into dismissals. He had Tallon's facility to reach wide, swinging deliveries or edged catches without turning himself into a tumbler—two or three well-anticipated steps and he took the ball without falling in a heap. No doubt his 11 seasons with Sturt Australian Rules

LANGLEY, Gilbert Roche Andrews, 1919–

First-Class Averages: Batting, 3,236 runs at 25.68; Dismissals, 369 (293 catches, 76 stumpings).

Tests (26): 374 runs at 14.96; Dismissals 98 (83 catches, 15 stumpings).

helped. He represented SA 15 times in football.

Behind the stumps he watched his bowlers arms carefully, both gloves in front of his knees and not touching the ground as many modern 'keepers prefer. His shirt-tail usually was hanging out and a little of his tummy drooped over his waist-band. He waited with the right foot flat and the left heel raised. He was seldon given to flamboyance but when he had to reach low catches he was known to go down on the point of one shoulder to do so.

When a ball from left-arm bowler Jack Wilson hit Ron Archer's stumps and then cut into Langley's forehead in an inter-State game, Langley had to be replaced in the next Test against Len Hutton's 1954–55 side. Maddocks batted bravely and held the job for four Tests but finally Langley's deep appreciation of his bowler's skills prevailed and he returned in the Tests against West Indies. Although he missed a Test, Langley still achieved a record 20 dismissals against the West Indies.

Until 1955 he shared the record of eight victims in a Test but against England at Lord's in 1956 he became the first 'keeper to dismiss nine batsmen in a Test. His 19 dismissals from 44 wickets lost in his three matches that series gave him an unprecedented percentage of success for a 'keeper, and to the end of his career he carried through an average of around four dismissals for every Test he played—98 victims, 83 caught and 15 stumped, in 26 Tests spread over six years. His career highest score was 160 not out for SA versus New Zealand in 1953–54.

Langley's nephew **Jeffrey Noel Langley** (1948–) has played for South Australia and for Queensland, for whom he scored two centuries batting right-handed.

LAUGHLIN, Trevor John, 1951–

First-Class Averages: Batting, 2,770 runs at 32.58; Bowling, 99 wickets at 31.92.

Tests (3): 87 runs at 17.40; 6 wickets at 43.66.

A burly Melbourne sports store proprietor who has some of the biggest hits seen on Melbourne Cricket Ground to his cre-dit and has put together a respectable record as an all-rounder through a mixture of brawn and enthusiasm. He bats left-handed in the middle of the order and bowls right-arm medium pace. His big-hitting has won him an army of young fans at the Collingwood club where he is captain-coach.

Laughlin, born at Nyah West, Victoria, first played for Vic-toria in 1974–75 against South Australia when he had match figures of 5 for 62. He made his career highest score and his only first-class century with a swashbuckling innings of 113 against Western Australia at Perth in 1975–76. He played in the Scottish League in 1976 to gain experience, and went to the West Indies in 1977–78 with Bob Simpson's team. He made his Test debut in the Third Test at Georgetown, scoring 21 and 24 and taking 1 for 77. In the Fifth Test of that series, he helped give Australia a chance for victory by scoring 35 and taking 5 for 101 off 25.4 overs, but spectators rioted with Australia one wicket away from victory and the umpires refused to complete the match the following day.

Laughlin went to England in 1979 for the second World Cup in the team captained by Kim Hughes but failed to produce any of the big-hitting his supporters expected. On his return home he was tried several times in one-day matches for Australia in the hope that his hitting would prove valuable but his form fell away and he lost his place in the Victoria team in 1980–81, appearing in only five first-class matches.

LAVER, Frank, 1869–1919

First-Class Averages: Batting, 5,431 runs at 25.02; Bowling, 404 wickets at 24.72.

Tests (15): 196 runs at 11.52; 37 wickets at 26.05.

An ungainly right-hand batsman who was one of the most controversial figures in Australian cricket in the first decade of this century, thanks mainly to his popularity among his fellow players. His run-scoring and medium pace bowling success was a triumph of character. He was a smart judge of a players' capabilities and probably was our first outstanding local-bred coach. He toured England three times, twice as player-manager.

Laver, crude and unorthodox, could thrash even classy attacks. He was a plucky fieldsman whose bowling was highly suited to the heavy atmosphere and damp pitches of England. In district and Shield matches, his batting frequently won matches, but in Tests it was his bowling that most helped Australia's cause. Victor Trumper said he disliked batting with Laver because it made him nervous batting with a man who acted as if every ball might get him out.

Laver, born at Castlemaine, Victoria, turned up at East Melbourne's Jolimont ground at the age of 18 looking for a game, a gangling, heavy-legged six footer lacking in style, but he was so effective he went straight into the first grade side. He took 94 wickets and made three centuries in his first season with the club and held his position for the next 25 years. One of his early team-mates at East Melbourne was Percy McAlister, a stylish batsman. They became close friends and for years were the backbone of East Melbourne and Victorian team performances.

When Laver first joined East Melbourne, the club captain was Harry Boyle, who had virtually created the silly mid-on position by moving "in on the batsman's corns". Laver emulated Boyle by moving in very close at point and in grade matches the pair of them bluffed plenty of batsmen into indiscretions. Despite his own shortcomings in style, Laver developed into a deep thinker on the game, widely respected for his tactical acumen.

Laver had a remarkable summer in 1892–93, scoring more than 1,000 runs for East Melbourne, including a record 352 not

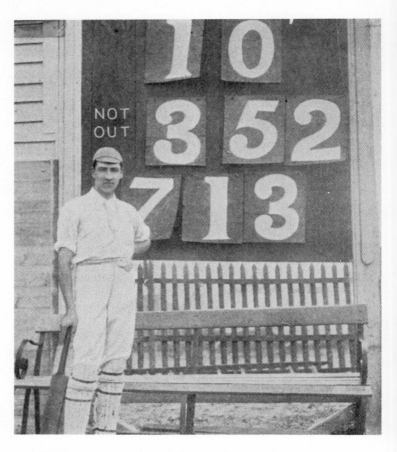

Frank Laver in front of the scoreboard showing his 352 in the 1892–93 season.

out. His heavy scoring won him a place in the Victorian team. He made 104 against South Australia at Adelaide in 1892–93, but he missed selection in the 1893 and 1896 teams to England. He finally won a trip to England in 1899, when his batting disappointed but his bowling justified his selection. At Lord's, in what proved to be the decisive Test of the tour, he dismissed Hayward, Tyldesley and Jessop to clinch an Australian win by 10 wickets. His 23 wickets on the trip cost 26.91 each and he had a score of 143 among his 859 runs at 30.67.

He retained his Test place at home in 1901–02 but missed a place in the 1902 side to England. Undaunted he returned to the Test side in 1903–04, the year in which his friend McAlister first won Test selection at 35. In one afternoon's batting for East Melbourne Laver made 341 against Fitzroy, opening the innings with McAlister, who made 173. The innings reached a Melbourne club cricket record of 2 for 744.

These were the days before the Australian Board of Control had full authority over players, and when the 1905 team for England was chosen, Laver was included and McAlister omit-

582

ted. Some of the star players in the team, Trumper, Noble, Darling, Iredale, Hill, Syd Gregory, Armstrong and Duff, were reported to have used their influence behind the scenes to have Laver appointed player-manager. Whatever the truth of this charge, McAlister blamed Laver for his omission and their friendship ended after 14 years.

The Australian Board of Control had been formed in 1905 and recognised by the Marylebone Cricket Club at Lord's, but it did not take part in selection of the 1905 side. Apart from the annoyance in Victoria over McAlister's omission there was dismay in New South Wales over the exclusion of Waddy, Carter and Mackay. Laver finished second on the 1905 tour bowling averages by taking 115 wickets at 18.19 but did little of value with the bat.

By 1909 when the next touring team for England was chosen the new Board's position had improved but the Board's growing strength was resented by established stars. Warwick Armstrong, who represented the Melbourne Cricket Club, who had organised early tours by overseas teams, also resented the Board's strong showing as it endangered the MCC's influence. McAlister, by then a powerful influence in Victorian cricket, strongly supported the Board.

For the first time the Board appointed the selectors of the 1909 team, organised the tour itinerary, and nominated the captain, Monty Noble. When the team requested that Laver be included as player-manager, the Board agreed but sent McAlister as treasurer and vice-captain and to act as Australia's delegate to the Imperial Cricket Conference in London. McAlister was 40 by then and could not get going with the bat, but Laver topped the bowling averages with 70 wickets at 14.97. In the Manchester Test Laver dismissed eight leading English batsmen for 31, and this, plus the all-round batting skill of Ransford, Bardsley and Macartney enabled Australia to come home with The Ashes.

When McAlister was asked for his books on the tour, he said his role as treasurer had not been defined before the team left and that he had kept no records. Laver refused to produce his records of the trip, insisting that he kept books merely for the players' benefit. The climax came in 1911–12 when the Board appointed Queenslander G. S. Crouch to manage the side to England and said he would have the power to suspend any player.

Hill, Trumper, Carter, Cotter, Ransford and Armstrong then announced that unless Crouch was replaced and Laver appointed manager, they were unavailable to tour. Laver offered to withdraw, but amid fervent public debate the Board picked six players to replace the six defectors. The Governor of New South Wales, Lord Chelmsford, got into the row and the State Premier, J. S. T. McGowan, said he would have the six players reinstated, but the Board remained unmoved.

When the Australian selectors met in Sydney to pick the team for the fourth Test against the visiting English side, Hill struck McAlister and an amazing 20-minute fist fight ensued before they could be separated. At the end of that summer Crouch took the team to England. Laver dropped out of international cricket but continued to play for East Melbourne until a few years before his death in north Australia, aged 50. He wrote *An Australian Cricketer On Tour*, which touched on everything from players' superstitions to captaincy and sportsmanship and is a valuable record of those early tours. Laver scored six centuries, with a topscore of 164 for Victoria against SA in Adelaide in 1904–05 and held 148 catches.

THE LAWS OF CRICKET (1980 Code)

PREFACE

During the last two hundred years the conduct of the game of Cricket has been governed by a series of Codes of Laws. These Codes were established as indicated below, and were subject to additions and alterations ordained by the governing authorities of the time. Since its formation in 1787 the Marylebone Cricket Club has been recognised as the sole authority for drawing up the code and for all subsequent alterations. It is of interest that the development and revision of the Laws was essential as a method of settling debts resulting from gambling associated with the more important cricket matches. The Club also holds the World Copyright.

There is little doubt that Cricket was subject to recognised rules as early as 1700, though the earliest known Code is that drawn up in 1744 by certain Noblemen and Gentlemen who used the Artillery Ground in London. These Laws were revised in 1755 by "Several Cricket Clubs, particularly that of the Star and Garter in Pall Mall."

The next arrangement was produced by "a Committee of Noblemen and Gentlemen of Kent, Hampshire, Surrey, Sussex, Middlesex and London," at the Star and Garter on February 25th, 1774, and this in turn was revised by a similar body in February, 1786.

On May 30th, 1788 the first MCC Code was adopted, and remained in force until May 20th, 1835, when a new Code of Laws was approved by the Committee. The Laws appear to have been first numbered in 1823.

The 1835 Code, amended in detail from time to time, stood until April 21st, 1884, when, after consultation with cricket clubs both at home ahd overseas, important alterations were incorporated in a new version adopted at a Special General Meeting of the MCC.

By 1939, these Laws supplemented as they had been by the inclusion of many definitions and interpretations in the form of notes, were in need of revision, and immediately on the conclusion of the World War II the opinions of controlling

584

Bodies and Clubs throughout the world were sought, with the result that the present code was adopted at a Special General Meeting of the MCC on May 7th, 1947.

The revision in the main aimed at the clarification and better arrangement of the previous Laws and their interpretations, but did not exclude certain definite alterations designed firstly to provide greater latitude in the conduct of the game as required by the widely differing conditions in which it is played, and secondly to eliminate certain umpiring difficulties.

During the last thirty years, however, changes and Notes have been included requiring the publication of five editions of the 1947 Code. At the International Cricket Conference of 1972, MCC suggested that the stage had been reached where, for the purposes of removing anomalies, consolidating various Amendments and Notes, and of achieving greater clarity and simplicity, the 1947 Code of the Laws of Cricket should be revised and rewritten. As a result of this suggestion, MCC were asked to undertake the task beginning in the autumn of 1974 following a period of consultation throughout the cricket-playing world.

After initial consideration, MCC decided that the original point of the Notes to the Laws—that of providing interpretations of difficulties arising from the Laws—had to some extent been lost. Many notes were, in themselves, Laws, and, as such should be included in the Laws. In addition to the object of re-codification, MCC have attempted to make this important change.

The Laws of Cricket apply equally to women's cricket as to mens'. As in the past however, this New Code refers to the male person only, for convenience and brevity.

Many queries on the Laws are sent to MCC for decision every year, and it is from these sources that the chief difficulties arising from the laws have become manifest. MCC as the accepted makers of the Laws, which can only be changed by the vote of two-thirds of the members present and voting at a Special General Meeting of the Club, have always been prepared to answer these queries and to give interpretations on certain conditions which will be readily understood, i.e.:

(a) In the case of League or Competition cricket, the enquiry must come from the Committee responsible for organising the league or competition. In other cases, enquiries should be initiated by a representative officer of a Club, or of an Umpires' Association of behalf of his or her Committee, or by a master or mistress in charge of school cricket.

(b) The incident on which a ruling is required must not be merely invented for disputation, but must have actually occurred in play.

(c) The enquiry must not be connected in any way with a bet or wager.

The basic Laws of Cricket have stood remarkably well the test of well over two hundred years of playing the game; and it is thought that the real reason for this is that cricketers have traditionally been prepared to play in the spirit of the game, as well as in accordance with the Laws. The unique character and enjoyment of cricket depends upon all cricketers, at whatever level, continuing to preserve this spirit.

Lord's Cricket Ground,   J. A. BAILEY,
London, NW8 8QN   Secretary, MCC

LAW 1
THE PLAYERS

1. Number of Players and Captain
A match is played between two sides each of eleven Players, one of whom shall be Captain. In the event of the Captain not being available at any time a Deputy shall act for him.
2. Nomination of Players
Before the toss for innings, the Captain shall nominate his Players who may not thereafter be changed without the consent of the opposing Captain.
NOTE
(a) More or Less than Eleven Players a Side
     A match may be played by agreement between sides of more or less than eleven players but not more than eleven players may field.

LAW 2
SUBSTITUTES AND
RUNNERS: BATSMAN
OR FIELDSMAN
LEAVING THE FIELD:
BATSMAN RETIRING:
BATSMAN
COMMENCING
INNINGS

1. Substitutes
Substitutes shall be allowed by right to field for any player who during the match is incapacitated by illness or injury. The consent of the opposing Captain must be obtained for the use of a Substitute if any player is prevented from fielding for any other reason.
2. Objection to Substitutes
The opposing Captain shall have no right of objection to player acting as Substitute in the field, nor as to where he shall field, although he may object to the Substitute acting as Wicket-Keeper.
3. Substitute Not to Bat or Bowl
A Substitute shall not be allowed to bat or bowl.
4. A Player for whom a Substitute has acted
A player may bat, bowl or field even though a Substitute has acted for him.
5. Runner
A Runner shall be allowed for a Batsman who during the match is incapacitated by illness or injury. The player acting as Runner shall be a member of the batting side and shall, if possible, have already batted in that innings.
6. Runner's Equipment
The player acting as Runner for an injured Batsman shall wear batting gloves and pads if the injured Batsman is so equipped.

586

7. Transgression of the Laws by an Injured Batsman or Runner

An injured Batsman may be out should his Runner break any one of Laws 33 (Handled the Ball), 37 (Obstructing the Field) or 38 (Run Out). As Striker he remains himself subject to the Laws. Furthermore, should he be out of his ground for any purpose and the wicket at the Wicket-Keeper's end be put down he shall be out under Law 38 (Run Out) or Law 39 (Stumped) irrespective of the position of the other Batsman or the Runner and no runs shall be scored.

When not the Striker, the injured Batsman is out of the game and shall stand where he does not interfere with the play. Should he bring himself into the game in any way then he shall suffer the penalties that any transgression of the Laws demands.

8. Fieldsman Leaving the Field

No Fieldsman shall leave the field or return during a session of play without the consent of the Umpire at the Bowler's end. The Umpire's consent is also necessary if a Substitute is required for a Fieldsman, when his side returns to the field after an interval. If a member of the fielding side leaves the field or fails to return after an interval and is absent from the field for longer than 15 minutes, he shall not be permitted to bowl after his return until he has been on the field for at least that length of playing time for which he was absent. This restriction shall not apply at the start of a new day's play.

9. Batsman Leaving the Field or Retiring

A Batsman may leave the field or retire at any time owing to illness, injury or other unavoidable cause, having previously notified the Umpire at the Bowler's end. He may resume his innings at the fall of a wicket, which for the purposes of this Law shall include the retirement of another Batsman.

If he leaves the field or retires for any other reason he may only resume his innings with the consent of the opposing Captain.

When a Batsman has left the field or retired and is unable to return owing to illness, injury or other unavoidable cause, his innings is to be recorded as "retired, not out". Otherwise it is to be recorded as "retired, out".

10. Commencement of a Batsman's Innings

A Batsman shall be considered to have commenced his innings once he has stepped on to the field of play.

NOTE

(a) Substitutes and Runners

For the purpose of these Laws allowable illnesses or injuries are those which occur at any time after the nomination by the Captains of their teams.

1. Appointment

Before the toss for innings two Umpires shall be appointed, one for each end, to control the game with absolute impartiality as required by the Laws.

2. Change of Umpires

No Umpire shall be changed during a match without the consent of both Captains.

3. Special Conditions

Before the toss for innings, the Umpires shall agree with both Captains on any special conditions affecting the conduct of the match.

4. The Wickets

The Umpires shall satisfy themselves before the start of the match that the wickets are properly pitched.

5. Clock or Watch

The Umpires shall agree between themselves and inform both Captains before the start of the match on the watch or clock to be followed during the match.

6. Conduct and Implements

Before and during a match the Umpires shall ensure that the conduct of the game and the implements used are strictly in accordance with the Laws.

7. Fair and Unfair Play

The Umpires shall be the sole judges of fair and unfair play.

8. Fitness of Ground, Weather and Light

(a) The Umpires shall be the sole judges of the fitness of the ground, weather and light for play.

(i) However, before deciding to suspend play or not to start play or not to resume play after an interval or stoppage, the Umpires shall establish whether both Captains (the Batsmen at the wicket may deputise for their Captain) wish to commence or to continue in the prevailing conditions; if so, their wishes shall be met.

(ii) In addition, if during play, the Umpires decide that the light is unfit, only the batting side shall have the option of continuing play. After agreeing to continue to play in unfit light conditions, the Captain of the batting side (or a Batsman at the wicket) may appeal against the light to the Umpires, who shall uphold the appeal only if, in their opinion, the light has deteriorated since the agreement to continue was made.

(b) After any suspension of play, the Umpires, unaccompanied by any of the Players or Officials shall, on their own initiative, carry out an inspection immediately the conditions improve and shall continue to inspect at intervals. Immediately the Umpires decide that play is possible they shall call upon the Players to resume the game.

9. Exceptional Circumstances

In exceptional circumstances, other than those of weather, ground or light, the Umpires may decide to suspend or aban-

588

don play. Before making such a decision the Umpires shall establish, if the circumstances allow, whether both Captains (the Batsmen at the wicket may deputise for their Captain) wish to continue in the prevailing conditions: if so, their wishes shall be met.

10. Position of Umpires

The Umpires shall stand where they can best see any act upon which their decision may be required.

Subject to this over-riding consideration the Umpire at the Bowler's end shall stand where he does not interfere with either the Bowler's run up or the Striker's view.

The Umpire at the Striker's end may elect to stand on the off instead of the leg side of the pitch, provided he informs the Captain of the fielding side and the Striker of his intention to do so.

11. Umpires Changing Ends

The Umpires shall change ends after each side has had one innings.

12. Disputes

All disputes shall be determined by the Umpires and if they disagree the actual state of things shall continue.

13. Signals

The following code of signals shall be used by Umpires who will wait until a signal has been answered by a Scorer before allowing the game to proceed.

This umpire's signal left no doubt that Peter Trethewey had dismissed Bob Simpson lbw in a West Australia v South Australia match.

Boundary	— by waving the arm from side to side.
Boundary 6	— by raising both arms above the head.
Bye	— by raising an open hand above the head.
Dead ball	— by crossing and re-crossing the wrists below the waist.
Leg Bye	— by touching a raised knee with the hand.
No Ball	— by extending one arm horizontally.
Out	— by raising the index finger above the head. If not out the Umpire shall call "not out".
Short Run	— by bending the arm upwards and by touching the nearer shoulder with the tips of the fingers.
Wide	— by extending both arms horizontally.

14. Correctness of Scores

The Umpires shall be responsible for satisfying themselves on the correctness of the scores throughout and at the conclusion of the match. See Law 21.6 (Correctness of Result).

NOTES

(a) Attendance of Umpires
   The Umpires should be present on the ground and report to the Ground Executive or the equivalent at least 30 minutes before the start of a day's play.

(b) Consultation Between Umpires and Scorers
   Consultation between Umpires and Scorers over doubtful points is essential.

589

(c) Fitness of Ground

The Umpires shall consider the ground as unfit for play when it is so wet or slippery as to deprive the Bowlers of a reasonable foothold, the Fieldsmen, other than the deep-fielders, of the power of free movement, or the Batsmen the ability to play their strokes or to run between the wickets. Play should not be suspended merely because the grass and the ball are wet and slippery.

(d) Fitness of Weather and Light

The Umpires should only suspend play when they consider that the conditions are so bad that it is unreasonable or dangerous to continue.

LAW 4
THE SCORERS

1. Recording Runs

All runs scored shall be recorded by Scorers appointed for the purpose. Where there are two Scorers they shall frequently check to ensure that the score sheets agree.

2. Acknowledging Signals

The Scorers shall accept and immediately acknowledge all instructions and signals given to them by the Umpires.

LAW 5
THE BALL

1. Weight and Size

The ball, when new, shall weigh not less than $5\frac{1}{2}$ ounces/155.9 g, nor more than $5\frac{3}{4}$ ounces/163 g: and shall measure not less than 8.13/16 inches/22.4 cm, nor more than 9 inches/22.9 cm in circumference.

2. Approval of Balls

All balls used in matches shall be approved by the Umpires and Captains before the start of the match.

3. New Ball

Subject to agreement to the contrary, having been made before the toss, either Captain may demand a new ball at the start of each innings.

4. New Ball in Match of 3 or more Days Duration

In a match of 3 or more days duration, the Captain of the fielding side may demand a new ball after the prescribed number of overs has been bowled with the old one. The Governing Body for cricket in the country concerned shall decide the number of overs applicable in that country which shall be not less than 75 six-ball overs (55 eight-ball overs).

5. Ball Lost or Becoming Unfit for Play

In the event of a ball during play being lost or, in the opinion of the Umpires, becoming unfit for play, the Umpires shall allow it to be replaced by one that in their opinion has had a similar amount of wear. If a ball is to be replaced, the Umpires shall inform the Batsmen.

NOTES

(a) Specifications

The specifications, as described in 1. above shall apply to top-grade balls only. The following degrees of tolerance will be acceptable for other grades of ball.

    (i) *Men's Grades 2-4*
         Weight: 5.5/16 ounces/150 g to 5.13/16 ounces/165 g.
         Size: 8.11/16 inches/22 cm to 9.1/16 inches/23 cm.
   (ii) *Women's*
         Weight: 4.15/16 ounces/140 g to 5.5/16 ounces/150 g.
         Size: 8.¼ inches/21 cm to 8.78 inches/22.5 cm.
  (iii) *Junior*
         Weight: 4.5/16 ounces/133 g to 5.1/16 ounces/143 g.
         Size: 8.1/16 inches/20.5 cm to 8.11/16 inches/22 cm.

1. Width and Length

LAW 6
THE BAT

The bat overall shall not be more than 38 inches/96.5 cm in length; the blade of the bat shall be made of wood and shall not exceed 4¼ inches/10.8 cm at the widest part.

NOTE

(a) *The blade of the bat may be covered with material for protection, strengthening or repair. Such material shall not exceed 1/16 inches/1.56 mm in thickness.*

1. Area of Pitch

LAW 7
THE PITCH

The pitch is the area between the bowling creases—see Law 9 (The Bowling, Popping and Return Creases). It shall measure 5 ft/1.52 m in width on either side of a line joining the centre of the middle stumps of the wickets—see Law 8 (The Wickets).

2. Selection and Preparation

Before the toss for innings, the Executive of the Ground shall be responsible for the selection and preparation of the pitch; thereafter the Umpires shall control its use and maintenance.

3. Changing Pitch

The pitch shall not be changed during a match unless it becomes unfit for play, and then only with the consent of both Captains.

4. Non-Turf Pitches

In the event of a non-turf pitch being used, the following shall apply:

(a) Length: That of the playing surface to a minimum of 58 ft (17.68 m).

(b) Width: That of the playing surface to a minimum of 6 ft (1.83 m).

See Law 10 (Rolling, Sweeping, Mowing, Watering the Pitch and Re-marking of Creases) Note (a).

1. Width and Pitching

LAW 8
THE WICKETS

Two sets of wickets, each 9 inches/22.86 cm wide, and consisting of three wooden stumps with two wooden bails upon the top, shall be pitched opposite and parallel to each other at a distance of 22 yards/20.12 m between the centres of the two middle stumps.

2. Size of Stumps

The stumps shall be of equal and sufficient size to prevent the ball from passing between them. Their tops shall be 28 inches/71.1 cm above the ground, and shall be dome-shaped except for the bail grooves.

3. Size of Bails

The bails shall be each 4³/₄ inches/11.1 cm in length and when in position on the top of the stumps shall not project more than ¹/₂ inch/1.3 cm above them.

NOTES

(a) Dispensing with Bails

In a high wind the Umpires may decide to dispense with the use of bails.

(b) Junior Cricket

For Junior Cricket, as defined by the local Governing Body, the following measurements for the Wickets shall apply:

Width   — 8 inches/20.32 cm.
Pitched — 21 yards/19.20 cm.
Height   — 27 inches/68.58 cm.
Bails   — each 3⁷/₈ inches/9.84 cm in length and should not project more than ¹/₂ inch/1.3 cm above them.

**LAW 9
THE BOWLING,
POPPING AND
RETURN
CREASES**

1. The Bowling Crease

The bowling crease shall be marked in line with the stumps at each end and shall be 8 ft 8 inches/2.64 m in length, with the stumps in the centre.

2. The Popping Crease

The popping crease, which is the back edge of the crease marking, shall be in front of and parallel with the bowling crease. It shall have the back edge of the crease marking 4 ft/1.22 m from the centre of the stumps and shall extend to a minimum of 6 ft/1.83 m on either side of the line of the wicket.

The popping crease shall be considered to be unlimited in length.

3. The Return Crease

The return crease marking, of which the inside edge is the crease, shall be at each end of the bowling crease and at right angles to it. The return crease shall be marked to a minimum of 4 ft/1.22 m behind the wicket and shall be considered to be unlimited in length. A forward extension shall be marked to the popping crease.

**LAW 10
ROLLING, SWEEPING,
MOWING, WATERING
THE PITCH AND
RE-MARKING OF
CREASES**

1. Rolling

During the match the pitch may be rolled at the request of the Captain of the batting side, for a period of not more than seven minutes before the start of each innings, other than the first innings of the match, and before the start of each day's play. In addition, if, after the toss and before the first innings of the match, the start is delayed, the Captain of the batting side shall have the right to have the pitch rolled for not more than seven minutes.

The pitch shall not otherwise be rolled during the match.

The seven minutes' rolling permitted before the start of a day's play shall take place not earlier than half an hour before the start of play and the Captain of the batting side may delay such rolling until 10 minutes before the start of play should he so desire.

If a Captain declares an innings closed less than 15 minutes before the resumption of play, and the other Captain is thereby prevented from exercising his option of seven minutes' rolling or if he is so prevented for any other reason the time for rolling shall be taken out of the normal playing time.

2. Sweeping

Such sweeping of the pitch as is necessary during the match shall be done so that the seven minutes allowed for rolling the pitch provided for in 1 above, is not affected.

3. Mowing

(a) Responsibilities of Ground Authorities and of Umpires

All mowings which are carried out before the toss for innings shall be the responsibility of the Ground Authority. Thereafter they shall be carried out under the supervision of the Umpires, see Law 7.2 (Selection and Preparation).

(b) Initial Mowing

The pitch shall be mown before play begins on the day the match is scheduled to start or in the case of a delayed start on the day the match is expected to start. See 3 (a)

Groundsmen sweeping a pitch on the first day of a match in England in 1956 when Australia found Laker and Lock so difficult.

above. (Responsibilities of Ground Authority and of Umpires).

(c) Subsequent Mowings in a Match of Two or More Days' Duration

In a match of two or more days' duration, the pitch shall be mown daily before play begins. Should this mowing not take place because of weather conditions, rest days or other reasons the pitch shall be mown on the first day on which the match is resumed.

(d) Mowing of the Outfield in a Match of Two or More Days' Duration

In order to ensure that conditions are as similar as possible for both sides, the outfield shall normally be mown before the commencement of play on each day of the match, if ground and weather conditions allow. See Note (b) to this Law.

4. Watering

The pitch shall not be watered during a match.

5. Re-Marking Creases

Whenever possible the creases shall be re-marked.

6. Maintenance of Foot Holes

In wet weather, the Umpires shall ensure that the holes made by the Bowlers and Batsmen are cleaned out and dried whenever necessary to facilitate play. In matches of two or more days' duration, the Umpires shall allow, if necessary, the re-turfing of foot holes made by the Bowler in his delivery stride, or the use of quick-setting fillings for the same purpose, before the start of each day's play.

7. Securing of Footholds and Maintenance of Pitch

During play, the Umpires shall allow either Batsman to beat the pitch with his bat and players to secure their footholds by the use of sawdust, provided that no damage to the pitch is so caused, and Law 42 (Unfair Play) is not contravened.

NOTES

(a) Non-Turf Pitches

The above Law 10 applies to turf pitches.

The game is played on non-turf pitches in many countries at various levels. Whilst the conduct of the game on these surfaces should always be in accordance with the Laws of Cricket, it is recognised that it may sometimes be necessary for Governing Bodies to lay down special playing conditions to suit the type of non-turf pitch used in their country.

In matches played against Touring Teams, any special playing conditions should be agreed in advance by both parties.

(b) Mowing of the Outfield in a Match of Two or more Days' Duration

If, for reasons other than ground and weather condi-

594

tions, *daily and complete mowing is not possible, the Ground Authority shall notify the Captains and Umpires, before the toss for innings, of the procedure to be adopted for such mowing during the match.*

(c) Choice of Roller
If there is more than one roller available the Captain of the batting side shall have a choice.

1. Before the Start of a Match
Before the start of a match complete covering of the pitch shall be allowed.

2. During a Match
The pitch shall not be completely covered during a match unless prior arrangement or regulations so provide.

3. Covering Bowlers' Run-Up
Whenever possible, the Bowlers' run-up shall be covered, but the covers so used shall not extend further than 4 ft / 1.22 m in front of the popping crease.

NOTE

(a) Removal of Covers
The covers should be removed as promptly as possible whenever the weather permits.

1. Number of Innings
A match shall be of one or two innings of each side according to agreement reached before the start of play.

2. Alternate Innings
In a two innings match each side shall take their innings alternately except in the case provided for in Law 13 (The Follow-On).

3. The Toss
The Captains shall toss for the choice of innings on the field of play not later than 15 minutes before the time scheduled for the match to start, or before the time agreed upon for play to start.

4. Choice of Innings
The winner of the toss shall notify his decision to bat or to field to the opposing Captain not later than 10 minutes before the time scheduled for the match to start, or before the time agreed upon for play to start. The decision shall not thereafter be altered.

5. Continuation After One Innings of Each Side
Despite the terms of 1 above, in a one innings match, when a result has been reached on the first innings the Captains may agree to the continuation of play if, in their opinion, there is a prospect of carrying the game to a further issue in the time left. See Law 21 (Result).

NOTES

(a) Limited Innings—One Innings Match
In a one innings match, each innings may, by agreement, be limited by a number of overs or by a period of time.

England captain C. B. Fry tosses and Australia's Syd. Gregory calls before the Triangular Test at Old Trafford, Manchester, in 1912.

(b) Limited Innings—Two Innings Match
In a two innings match, the first innings of each side may, by agreement, be limited to a number of overs or by a period of time.

**LAW 13
THE FOLLOW-ON**

1. Lead on First Innings
In a two innings match the side which bats first and leads by 200 runs in a match of five days or more, by 150 runs in a three-day or four-day match, by 100 runs in a two-day match, or by 75 runs in a one-day match, shall have the option of requiring the other side to follow their innings.

2. Day's Play Lost
If no play takes place on the first day of a match of two or more days' duration, 1 above shall apply in accordance with the number of days' play remaining from the actual start of the match.

596

1. Time of Declaration

The Captain of the batting side may declare an innings closed at any time during a match irrespective of its duration.

2. Forfeiture of Second Innings

A Captain may forfeit his second innings, provided his decision to do so is notified to the opposing Captain and Umpires in sufficient time to allow seven minutes' rolling of the pitch. See Law 10 (Rolling, Sweeping, Mowing, Watering the Pitch and Re-Marking of Creases). The normal 10 minute interval between innings shall be applied.

1. Call of Play

At the start of each innings and of each day's play and on the resumption of play after any interval or interruption the Umpire at the Bowlers' end shall call "play".

2. Practice on the Field

At no time on any day of the match shall there be any bowling or batting practice on the pitch.

No practice may take place on the field if, in the opinion of the Umpires, it could result in a waste of time.

3. Trial Run-Up

No Bowler shall have a trial run-up after "play" has been called in any session of play, except at the fall of a wicket when an Umpire may allow such a trial run-up if he is satisfied that it will not cause any waste of time.

1. Length

The Umpire shall allow such intervals as have been agreed upon for meals, and 10 minutes between each innings.

2. Luncheon Interval—Innings Ending or Stoppage within 10 Minutes of Interval

If an innings ends or there is a stoppage caused by weather or bad light within 10 minutes of the agreed time for the luncheon interval, the interval shall be taken immediately.

The time remaining in the session of play shall be added to the agreed length interval but no extra allowance shall be made for the 10 minutes interval between innings.

3. Tea Interval—Innings Ending or Stoppage within 30 Minutes of Interval

If an innings ends or there is a stoppage caused by weather or bad light within 30 minutes of the agreed time for the tea interval, the interval shall be taken immediately.

The interval shall be of the agreed length and, if applicable, shall include the 10 minute interval between innings.

4. Tea Interval—Continuation of Play

If at the agreed time for the tea interval, nine wickets are down, play shall continue for a period not exceeding 30 minutes or until the innings is concluded.

5. Tea Interval—Agreement to Forego

At any time during the match, the Captains may agree to forego a tea interval.

597

Don Bradman performing the unaccustomed duties of 12th man in 1928–29.

6. Intervals for Drinks

If both Captains agree before the start of a match that intervals for drinks may be taken, the option to take such intervals shall be available to either side. These intervals shall be restricted to one per session, shall be kept as short as possible, shall not be taken in the last hour of the match and in any case shall not exceed five minutes.

The agreed times for these intervals shall be strictly adhered to except that if a wicket falls within five minutes of the agreed time then drinks shall be taken out immediately.

If an innings ends or there is a stoppage caused by weather or bad light within 30 minutes of the agreed time for a drinks interval, there will be no interval for drinks in that session.

At any time during the match the Captains may agree to forego any such drinks interval.

NOTES

(a) Tea Interval—One-Day Match

In a one-day match, a specific time for the tea interval need not necessarily be arranged, and it may be agreed to take this interval between the innings of a one-innings match.

(b) Changing the Agreed Time of Intervals

In the event of the ground, weather or light conditions causing a suspension of play, the Umpires, after consultation with the Captains, may decide in the interests of time-saving, to bring forward the time of the luncheon or tea interval.

LAW 17
CESSATION OF PLAY

1. Call of Time

The Umpire at the Bowler's end shall call "time" on the cessation of play before any interval or interruption of play, at the end of each day's play, and at the conclusion of the match. See Law 27 (Appeals).

2. Removal of Bails

After the call of "time", the Umpires shall remove the bails from both wickets.

3. Starting a Last Over

The last over before an interval or the close of play shall be started provided the Umpire, after walking at his normal pace, has arrived at his position behind the stumps at the Bowler's end before time has been reached.

4. Completion of the Last Over of a Session

The last over before an interval or the close of play shall be completed unless a Batsman is out or retires during that over within two minutes of the interval or the close of play or unless the Players have occasion to leave the field.

5. Completion of the Last Over of a Match

An over in progress at the close of play on the final day of a match shall be completed at the request of either Captain even if a wicket falls after time has been reached.

598

If during the last over the Players have occasion to leave the field the Umpires shall call "time" and there shall be no resumption of play and the match shall be at an end.

6. Last Hour of Match—Number of Overs

The Umpires shall indicate when one hour of playing time of the match remains according to the agreed hours of play. The next over after that moment shall be the first of a minimum of 20 six-ball overs (15 eight-ball overs), provided a result is not reached earlier or there is no interval or interruption of play.

7. Last Hour of Match—Intervals Between Innings and Interruptions of Play

If, at the commencement of the last hour of the match, an interval or interruption of play is in progress or if, during the last hour there is an interval between innings or an interruption of play, the minimum number of overs to be bowled on the resumption of play shall be reduced in proportion to the duration, within the last hour of the match, of any such interval or interruption.

The minimum number of overs to be bowled after a resumption of play shall be calculated as follows:

(a) In the case of an interval or interruption of play being in progress at the commencement of the last hour of the match, or in the case of a first interval or interruption a deduction shall be made from the minimum of 20 six-ball overs (or 15 eight-ball overs).

(b) If there is a later interval or interruption a further deduction shall be made from the minimum number of overs which should have been bowled following the last resumption of play.

(c) These deductions shall be based on the following factors:
  (i) the number of overs already bowled in the last hour of the match or, in the case of a later interval or interruption, in the last session of play.
  (ii) the number of overs lost as a result of the interval or interruption allowing one six-ball over for every full three minutes (or one eight-ball over for every full four minutes) of interval or interruption.
  (iii) any over left uncompleted at the end of an innings to be excluded from these calculations.
  (iv) any over left uncompleted at the start of an interruption of play to be completed when play is resumed and to count as one over bowled.
  (v) an interval to start with the end of an innings and to end 10 minutes later; an interruption to start on the call of "time" and to end on the call of "play".

(d) In the event of an innings being completed and a new innings commencing during the last hour of the match, the number of overs to be bowled in the new innings shall be calculated on the basis of one six-ball over for every three minutes or part thereof remaining for play (or one eight-ball over for every four minutes or part thereof remaining for play); or alternatively on the basis that sufficient overs be bowled to enable the full minimum quota of overs to be completed under circumstances governed by (a), (b) and (c) above. In all such cases the alternative which allows the greater number of overs shall be employed.

8. Bowler Unable to Complete an Over During Last Hour of the Match

If, for any reason, a Bowler is unable to complete an over during the period of play referred to in 6 above, Law 22.7 (Bowler Incapacitated or Suspended during an Over) shall apply.

LAW 18
SCORING

1. A Run

The score shall be reckoned by runs. A run is scored:
- (a) So often as the Batsmen, after a hit or at any time while the ball is in play, shall have crossed and made good their ground from end to end.
- (b) When a boundary is scored. See Law 19 (Boundaries).
- (c) When penalty runs are awarded. See 6 below.

2. Short Runs

- (a) If either Batsman runs a short run, the Umpire shall call and signal "one short" as soon as the ball becomes dead and that run shall not be scored. A run is short if a Batsman fails to make good his ground on turning for a further run.
- (b) Although a short run shortens the succeeding one, the latter, if completed, shall count.
- (c) If either or both Batsmen deliberately run short the Umpire shall, as soon as he sees that the fielding side have no chance of dismissing either Batsman, call and signal "dead ball" and disallow any runs attempted or previously scored. The Batsmen shall return to their original ends.
- (d) If both Batsmen run short in one and the same run, only one run shall be deducted.
- (e) Only if three or more runs are attempted can more than one be short and then, subject to (c) and (d) above, all runs so called shall be disallowed. If there has been more than one short run the Umpires shall instruct the Scorers as to the number of runs disallowed.

3. Striker Caught

If the Striker is caught, no run shall be scored.

4. Batsman Run Out

If a Batsman is Run Out, only that run which was being attempted shall be scored. If, however, an injured Striker himself is run out, no runs shall be scored. See Law 2.7 (Transgression of the Laws by an Injured Batsman or Runner).

5. Batsman Obstructing the Field

If a Batsman is out Obstructing the Field, any runs completed before the obstruction occurs shall be scored unless such ob-

600

struction prevents a catch being made in which case no runs shall be scored.

6. Runs Scored for Penalties

Runs shall be scored for penalties under Laws 20 (Lost Ball), 24 (No Ball), 25 (Wide Ball), 41.1 (Fielding the Ball) and for boundary allowances under Law 19 (Boundaries).

7. Batsman Returning to Wicket he has Left

If, while the ball is in play, the Batsmen have crossed in running, neither shall return to the wicket he has left even though a short run has been called or no run has been scored as in the case of a catch. Batsmen, however, shall return to the wickets they originally left, in the cases of a boundary and of any disallowance of runs and of an injured Batsman being, himself, run out. See Law 2.7 (Transgression of the Laws by an Injured Batsman or Runner).

NOTE
(a) Short Run

A Striker taking stance in front of his popping crease may run from that point without penalty.

1. The Boundary of the Playing Area

LAW 19
BOUNDARIES

Before the toss for innings, the Umpires shall agree with both Captains on the boundary of the playing area. The boundary shall, if possible, be marked by a white line, a rope laid on the ground, or a fence. If flags or posts only are used to mark a boundary, the imaginary line joining such points shall be regarded as the boundary. An obstacle, or person, within the playing area shall not be regarded as a boundary unless so decided by the Umpires before the toss for innings. Sightscreens within, or partially within, the playing area shall be regarded as the boundary and when the ball strikes or passes within or under or directly over any part of the screen, a boundary shall be scored.

2. Runs Scored for Boundaries

Before the toss for innings, the Umpires shall agree with both Captains the runs to be allowed for boundaries, and in deciding the allowance for them, the Umpires and Captains shall be guided by the prevailing custom of the ground. The allowance for a boundary shall normally be four runs, and six runs for all hits pitching over and clear of the boundary line or fence, even though the ball has been previously touched by a Fieldsman. Six runs shall also be scored if a fieldsman, after catching a ball, carries it over the boundary. See Law 32 (Caught) Note (a). Six runs shall not be scored when a ball struck by the Striker hits a sightscreen full pitch if the screen is within, or partially within, the playing area, but if the ball is struck directly over a sightscreen so situated, six runs shall be scored.

3. A Boundary

A boundary shall be scored and signalled by the Umpire at

601

the Bowler's end whenever, in his opinion:

(a) A ball in play touches or crosses the boundary, however marked.

(b) A Fieldsman with ball in hand touches or grounds any part of his person on or over a boundary line.

(c) A Fieldsman with ball in hand grounds any part of his person over a boundary fence or board. This allows the Fieldsman to touch or lean on or over a boundary fence or board in preventing a boundary.

4. Runs Exceeding Boundary Allowance

The runs completed at the instant the ball reaches the boundary shall count if they exceed the boundary allowance.

5. Overthrows or Wilful Act of a Fieldsman

If the boundary results from an overthrow or from the wilful act of a Fieldsman, any runs already completed and the allowance shall be added to the score. The run in progress shall count provided that the Batsmen have crossed at the instant of the throw or act.

NOTE

(a) Position of Sightscreens

Sightscreens should, if possible, be positioned wholly outside the playing area or as near as possible to the boundary line.

**LAW 20
LOST BALL**

1. Runs Scored

If a ball in play cannot be found or recovered any fieldsman may then call "lost ball" when six runs shall be added to the score; but if more than six have been run before "lost ball" is called, as many runs as have been completed shall be scored. The run in progress shall count provided that the Batsmen have crossed at the instant of the call of "lost ball".

2. How Scored

The runs shall be added to the score of the Striker if the ball has been struck, but otherwise to the score of byes, leg-byes, no-balls or wides as the case may be.

**LAW 21
THE RESULT**

1. A Win—Two Innings Matches

The side which has scored a total of runs in excess of that scored by the opposing side in its two completed innings shall be the winners.

2. A Win—One Innings Matches

(a) One innings matches, unless played out as in 1 above, shall be decided on the first innings, but see Law 12.5 (Continuation After One Innings of Each Side).

(b) If the Captains agree to continue play after the completion of one innings of each side in accordance with Law 12.5 (Continuation After One Innings of Each Side) and a result is not achieved on the second innings, the first innings result shall stand.

3. Umpires Awarding a Match

(a) A match shall be lost by a side which, during the match,
  (i) refuses to play, or
  (ii) concedes defeat,
  and the Umpires shall award the match to the other side.
(b) Should both Batsmen at the wickets or the fielding side leave the field at any time without the agreement of the Umpires, this shall constitute a refusal to play and, on appeal the Umpires shall award the match to the other side in accordance with (a) above.

4. A Tie

The result of a match shall be a tie when the scores are equal at the conclusion of play, but only if the side batting last has completed its innings.

If the scores of the completed first innings of a one-day match are equal, it shall be a tie but only if the match has not been played out to further conclusion.

5. A Draw

A match not determined in any of the ways as in 1, 2, 3 and 4 above shall count as a draw.

6. Correctness of Result

Any decision as to the correctness of the scores shall be the responsibility of the Umpires. See Law 3.14 (Correctness of Scores).

If, after the Umpires and Players have left the field, in the belief that the match has been concluded, the Umpires decide that a mistake in scoring has occurred, which affects the result, and provided time has not been reached, they shall order play to resume and to continue until the agreed finishing time unless a result is reached earlier.

If the Umpires decide that a mistake has occurred and time has been reached, the Umpires shall immediately inform both Captains of the necessary corrections to the scores and, if applicable, to the result.

7. Acceptance of Result

In accepting the scores as notified by the scorers and agreed by the Umpires, the Captains of both sides thereby accept the result.

NOTES

(a) Statement of Results
   The result of a finished match is stated as a win by runs, except in the case of a win by the side batting last when it is by the number of wickets still then to fall.

(b) Winning Hit or Extras
   As soon as the side has won, see 1 and 2 above, the Umpire shall call "time", the match is finished, and nothing that happens thereafter other than as a result of a mistake in scoring, see 6 above, shall be regarded as part of the match.

However, if a boundary constitutes the winning hit—or extras—and the boundary allowance exceeds the number of runs required to win the match, such runs shall be credited to the side's total and, in the case of a hit, to the Striker's score.

LAW 22
THE OVER

1. Number of Balls
The ball shall be bowled from each wicket alternately in overs of either six or eight balls according to agreement before the match.

2. Call of "Over"
When the agreed number of balls has been bowled, and as the ball becomes dead or when it becomes clear to the Umpire at the Bowler's end that both the fielding side and the Batsmen at the wicket have ceased to regard the ball as in play, the Umpire shall call "over" before leaving the wicket.

3. No Ball or Wide Ball
Neither a No Ball nor a Wide Ball shall be reckoned as one of the over.

4. Umpire Miscounting
If an Umpire miscounts the number of balls, the over as counted by the Umpire shall stand.

5. Bowler Changing Ends
A Bowler shall be allowed to change ends as often as desired, provided only that he does not bowl two overs consecutively in an innings.

6. The Bowler Finishing an Over
A Bowler shall finish an over in progress unless he be incapacitated or be suspended under Law 42.8 (The Bowling of Fast Short Pitched Balls), 42.9(The Bowling of Fast High Full Pitches), 42.10 (Time Wasting) and 42.11 (Players Damaging the Pitch). If an over is left incomplete for any reason at the start of an interval or interruption of play, it shall be finished on the resumption of play.

7. Bowler Incapacitated or Suspended During an Over
If, for any reason, a Bowler is incapacitated while running up to bowl the first ball of an over, or is incapacitated or suspended during an over, the Umpire shall call and signal "dead ball" and another Bowler shall be allowed to bowl or complete the over from the same end, provided only that he shall not bowl two overs, or part thereof, consecutively in one innings.

8. Position of Non-Striker
The Batsman at the Bowler's end shall normally stand on the opposite side of the wicket to that from which the ball is being delivered, unless a request to do otherwise is granted by the Umpire.

LAW 23
DEAD BALL

1. The Ball Becomes Dead, when:
(a) It is finally settled in the hands of the Wicket Keeper or the Bowler.

604

(b) It reaches or pitches over the boundary.
(c) A Batsman is out.
(d) Whether played or not, it lodges in the clothing or equipment of a Batsman or the clothing of an Umpire.
(e) A ball lodges in a protective helmet worn by a member of the fielding side.
(f) A penalty is awarded under Law 20 (Lost Ball) or Law 41.1 (Fielding the Ball).
(g) The Umpire calls "over" or "time".

2. Either Umpire Shall Call and Signal "Dead Ball", when:
(a) He intervenes in a case of unfair play.
(b) A serious injury to a Player or Umpire occurs.
(c) He is satisfied that, for an adequate reason, the Striker is not ready to receive the ball and makes no attempt to play it.
(d) The Bowler drops the ball accidentally before delivery, or the ball does not leave his hand for any reason.
(e) One or both bails fall from the Striker's wicket before he receives delivery.
(f) He leaves his normal position for consultation.
(g) He is required to do so under Laws 26.3 (Disallowance of Leg-Byes), etc.

3. The Ball Ceases to be Dead, when:
(a) The Bowler starts his run up or bowling action.

4. The Ball is not Dead, when:
(a) It strikes an Umpire (unless it lodges in his dress).
(b) The wicket is broken or struck down (unless a Batsman is out thereby).
(c) An unsuccessful appeal is made.
(d) The wicket is broken accidentally either by the Bowler during his delivery or by a Batsman in running.
(e) The Umpire has called "no ball" or "wide".

NOTES
(a) Ball Finally Settled
  Whether the ball is finally settled or not—see 1(a) above—must be a question for the Umpires alone to decide.
(b) Action on Call of "Dead Ball"
  (i) If "dead ball" is called prior to the Striker receiving a delivery the Bowler shall be allowed an additional ball.
  (ii) If "dead ball" is called after the Striker receives a delivery the Bowler shall not be allowed an additional ball, unless a "no-ball" or "wide" has been called.

The famous Gordon Rorke drag that caused the introduction of the "front foot" law on the bowling of no-balls.

1. Mode of Delivery

LAW 24
NO BALL

The Umpire shall indicate to the Striker whether the Bowler intends to bowl over or round the wicket, overarm or underarm, or right or left-handed. Failure on the part of the Bowler to indicate in advance a change in his mode of delivery is unfair and the Umpire shall call and signal "no ball".

The difficulty facing umpires in calling no-balls is clearly shown in this shot of Alan Thomson bowling against England in 1970–71. The ball has left his hand but the front foot is still in the air.

2. Fair Delivery—The Arm

For a delivery to be fair the ball must be bowled not thrown—see Note (a) below. If either Umpire is not entirely satisfied with the absolute fairness of a delivery in this respect he shall call and signal "no ball" instantly upon delivery.

3. Fair Delivery—The Feet

The Umpire at the Bowler's wicket shall call and signal "no ball" if he is not satisfied that in the delivery stride:

(a) The Bowler's back foot has landed within and not touching the return crease or its forward extension

or

(b) some part of the front foot whether grounded or raised was behind the popping crease.

4. Bowler Throwing at Striker's Wicket Before Delivery

If the Bowler, before delivering the ball, throws it at the Striker's wicket in an attempt to run him out, the Umpire shall call and signal "no ball". See Law 42.12 (Batsman Unfairly Stealing a Run) and Law 38 (Run Out).

5. Bowler Attempting to Run Out Non-Striker Before Delivery

If the Bowler, before delivering the ball, attempts to run out the non-Striker, any runs which result shall be allowed and shall be scored as no balls. Such an attempt shall not count as a ball in the over. The Umpire shall not call "no ball". See Law 24.12 (Batsman Unfairly Stealing a Run).

6. Infringement of Laws by a Wicket-Keeper or a Fieldsman

The Umpire shall call and signal "no ball" in the event of the Wicket-Keeper infringing Law 40.1 (position of Wicket-Keeper) or a Fieldsman infringing Law 41.2 (Limitation of On-side Fieldsmen) or Law 41.3 (Position of Fieldsmen).

7. Revoking a Call

An Umpire shall revoke the call "no ball" if the ball does not leave the Bowler's hand for any reason. See Law 23.2 (Either Umpire Shall Call and Signal "Dead Ball").

8. Penalty

A Penalty of one run for a no ball shall be scored if no runs are made otherwise.

9. Runs From a No Ball

The Striker may hit a no ball and whatever runs result shall be added to his score. Runs made otherwise from a no ball shall be scored no balls.

10. Out From a No Ball

The Striker shall be out from a no ball if he breaks Law 34 (Hit the Ball Twice) and either Batsman may be Run Out or shall be given out if either breaks Law 33 (Handled the Ball) or Law 37 (Obstructing the Field).

11. Batsman Given Out Off a No Ball

Should a Batsman be given out off a no ball the penalty for

bowling it shall stand unless runs are otherwise scored.

NOTES

(a) Definition of a Throw

A ball shall be deemed to have been thrown if, in the opinion of either Umpire, the process of straightening the bowling arm, whether it be partial or complete, takes place during that part of the delivery swing which directly precedes the ball leaving the hand. This definition shall not debar a Bowler from the use of the wrist in the delivery swing.

(b) No Ball not Counting in Over

A no ball shall not be reckoned as one of the over. See Law 22.3 (No Ball or Wide Ball).

1. Judging a Wide

If the Bowler bowls the ball so high over or so wide of the wicket that, in the opinion of the Umpire, it passes out of reach of the Striker, standing in a normal guard position, the Umpire shall call and signal "wide ball" as soon as it has pased the line of the Striker's wicket.

The Umpire shall not adjudge a ball as being wide if:

(a) The Striker, by moving from his guard position, causes the ball to pass out of his reach.

(b) The Striker moves and thus brings the ball within his reach.

2. Penalty

A penalty of one run for a wide shall be scored if no runs are made otherwise.

3. Ball Coming to Rest in Front of the Striker

If a ball which the Umpire considers to have been delivered comes to rest in front of the line of the Striker's wicket, "wide" shall not be called. The Striker has a right, without interference from the fielding side, to make one attempt to hit the ball. If the fielding side interfere, the Umpire shall replace the ball where it came to rest and shall order the Fieldsmen to resume the places they occupied in the field before the ball was delivered.

The Umpire shall call and signal "dead ball" as soon as it is clear that the Striker does not intend to hit the ball, or after the Striker has made one unsuccessful attempt to hit the ball.

4. Revoking a Call

The Umpire shall revoke the call if the Striker hits a ball which has been called "wide".

5. Ball Not Dead

The ball does not become dead on the call of "wide ball"—see Law 23.4 (The Ball is Not Dead).

6. Runs Resulting from a Wide

All runs which are run or result from a wide ball which is not a no ball shall be scored wide balls, or if no runs are made one shall be scored.

7. Out from a Wide

The Striker shall be out from a wide ball if he breaks Law 35 (Hit Wicket) or Law 39 (Stumped). Either Batsman may be Run Out and shall be out if he breaks Law 33 (Handled the Ball) or Law 37 (Obstructing the Field).

8. Batsman Given Out Off a Wide

Should a Batsman be given out off a wide, the penalty for bowling it shall stand unless runs are otherwise made.

NOTE

(a) Wide Ball not Counting in Over

A wide ball shall not be reckoned as one of the over—see Law 22.3 (No Ball or Wide Ball).

LAW 26
BYE AND LEG-BYE

1. Byes

If the ball, not having been called "wide" or "no ball" passes the Striker without touching his bat or person, and any runs are obtained, the Umpire shall signal "bye" and the run or runs shall be credited as such to the batting side.

2. Leg-Byes

If the ball, not having been called "wide" or "no ball" is unintentionally deflected by the Striker's dress or person, except a hand holding the bat, and any runs are obtained the Umpire shall signal "leg-bye" and the run or runs so scored shall be credited as such to the batting side.

Such leg-byes shall only be scored if, in the opinion of the Umpire, the Striker has:

(a) attempted to play the ball with his bat, or

(b) tried to avoid being hit by the ball.

3. Disallowance of Leg-Byes

In the case of a deflection by the Striker's person, other than in 2(a) and (b) above, the Umpire shall call and signal "dead ball" as soon as one run has been completed or when it is clear that a run is not being attempted or the ball has reached the boundary.

On the call and signal of "dead ball" the Batsmen shall return to their original ends and no runs shall be allowed.

LAW 27
APPEALS

1. Time of Appeals

The Umpires shall not give a Batsman out unless appealed to by the other side which shall be done prior to the Bowler beginning his run-up or bowling action to deliver the next ball. Under Law 23.1 (g) (The Ball Becomes Dead) the ball is dead on "over" being called; this does not, however, invalidate an appeal made prior to the first ball of the following over provided "time" has not been called. See Law 17.1 (Call of Time).

2. An Appeal "How's That?"

An appeal "How's That?" shall cover all ways of being out.

3. Answering Appeals

The Umpire at the Bowler's wicket shall answer appeals before the other Umpire in all cases except those arising out of

Law 35 (Hit Wicket) or Law 39 (Stumped) or Law 38 (Run Out) when this occurs at the Striker's wicket.

When either Umpire has given a Batsman not out, the other Umpire shall, within his jurisdiction, answer the appeal on a further appeal, provided it is made in time in accordance with 1. above (Time of Appeals).

4. Consultation by Umpires
An Umpire may consult with the other Umpire on a point of fact which the latter may have been in a better position to see and shall then give his decision. If, after consultation, there is still doubt remaining the decision shall be in favour of the Batsman.

5. Batsman Leaving his Wicket under a Misapprehension
The Umpires shall intervene if satisfied that a Batsman, not having been given out, has left his wicket under a misapprehension that he has been dismissed.

6. Umpire's Decision
The Umpire's decision is final. He may alter his decision, provided that such alteration is made promptly.

7. Withdrawal of an Appeal
In exceptional circumstances the Captain of the fielding side may seek permission of the Umpire to withdraw an appeal providing the outgoing Batsman has not left the playing area. If this is allowed, the Umpire shall cancel his decision.

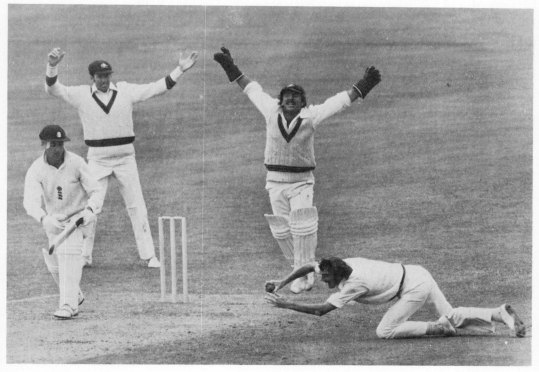

Australia's Rick McCosker and Rodney Marsh appeal as Richie Robinson catches England captain Mike Brearley.

The famous incident at Melbourne in 1960–61 when Joe Solomon was given out hit wicket bowled Benaud after his cap dislodged a bail.

LAW 28
THE WICKET IS DOWN

1. Wicket Down

The wicket is down if:

(a) Either the ball or the Striker's bat or person completely removes either bail from the top of the stumps. A disturbance of a bail, whether temporary or not, shall not constitute a complete removal, but the wicket is down if a bail in falling lodges between two of the stumps.

(b) Any player completely removes with his hand or arm a bail from the top of the stumps, providing that the ball is held in that hand or in the hand of the arm so used.

(c) When both bails are off, a stump is struck out of the ground by the ball, or a player strikes or pulls a stump out of the ground, providing that the ball is held in the hand(s) or in the hand of the arm so used.

2. One Bail Off

If one bail is off, it shall be sufficient for the purpose of putting the wicket down to remove the remaining bail, or to strike or pull any of the three stumps out of the ground in any of the ways stated in 1 above.

3. All the Stumps out of the Ground

If all the stumps are out of the ground, the fielding side shall be allowed to put back one or more stumps in order to have an opportunity of putting the wicket down.

4. Dispensing with Bails

If owing to the strength of the wind, it has been agreed to dispense with the bails in accordance with Law 8 Note (a) (Dispensing with Bails) the decision as to when the wicket is down is one for the Umpires to decide on the facts before them. In such circumstances and if the Umpires so decide the wicket shall be held to be down even though a stump has not been struck out of the ground.

NOTE

(a) Remaking the Wicket

If the wicket is broken while the ball is in play, it is not the Umpire's duty to remake the wicket until the ball has become dead—see Law 23 (Dead Ball). A member of the fielding side, however, may remake the wicket in such circumstances.

LAW 29
BATSMAN OUT OF HIS GROUND

1. When out of his Ground

A Batsman shall be considered to be out of his ground unless some part of his bat in his hand or of his person is grounded behind the line of the popping crease.

LAW 30
BOWLED

1. Out Bowled

The Striker shall be out bowled if:

(a) His wicket is bowled down, even if the ball first touches his bat or person.

(b) He breaks his wicket by hitting or kicking the ball on to it

610

before the completion of a stroke, or as a result of attempting to guard his wicket. See Law 34.1 (Out—Hit the Ball Twice).

NOTE

(a) Out Bowled—Not LBW

The Striker is out Bowled if the ball is deflected on to his wicket even though a decision against him would be justified under Law 36 (Leg Before Wicket).

1. Out Timed Out

An incoming Batsman shall be out Timed Out if he wilfully takes more than two minutes to come in—the two minutes being timed from the moment a wicket falls until the new Batsman steps on to the field of play.

If this is not complied with and if the Umpire is satisfied that the delay was wilful and if an appeal is made, the new Batsman shall be given out by the Umpire at the Bowler's end.

2. Time to be Added

The time taken by the Umpires to investigate the cause of the delay shall be added at the normal close of play.

NOTES

(a) Entry in Score Book

The correct entry in the score book when a Batsman is given out under this Law is "timed out", and the Bowler does not get credit for the wicket.

(b) Batsmen Crossing on the Field of Play

It is an essential duty of the Captains to ensure that the in-going Batsman passes the out-going one before the latter leaves the field of play.

1. Out Caught

The Striker shall be out Caught if the ball touches his bat or if it touches below the wrist his hand or glove, holding the bat, and is subsequently held by a Fieldsman before it touches the ground.

2. A Fair Catch

A Catch shall be considered to have been fairly made if:

(a) The Fieldsman is within the field of play throughout the act of making the catch.

(i) The act of making the catch shall start from the time when the Fieldsman first handles the ball and shall end when he both retains complete control over the further disposal of the ball and remains within the field of play.

(ii) In order to be within the field of play, the Fieldsman may not touch or ground any part of his person on or over a boundary line. When the boundary is marked by a fence or board the Fieldsman may not ground any part of his person over the boundary fence or board, but may touch or lean over the boundary fence or board in completing the catch.

One of three astounding catches Len Darling took in a single innings for Australia v. England in 1936–37 at Melbourne.

(b) The ball is hugged to the body of the catcher or accidentally lodges in his dress or, in the case of the Wicket-Keeper, in his pads. However, a Striker may not be caught if a ball lodges in a protective helmet worn by a Fieldsman, in which case the Umpire shall call and signal "dead ball". See Law 23 (Dead Ball).

(c) The ball does not touch the ground even though a hand holding it does so in effecting the catch.

(d) A Fieldsman catches the ball, after it has been lawfully played a second time by the Striker, but only if the ball has not touched the ground since being first struck.

(e) A Fieldsman catches the ball after it has touched an Umpire, another Fieldsman or the other Batsman. However a Striker may not be caught if a ball has touched a protective helmet worn by a Fieldsman.

(f) The ball is caught off an obstruction within the boundary provided it has not previously been agreed to regard the obstruction as a boundary.

3. Scoring of Runs

If a Striker is caught, no run shall be scored.

NOTES

(a) Scoring from an Attempted Catch

When a Fieldsman carrying the ball touches or grounds any part of his person on or over a boundary marked by a line, six runs shall be scored.

(b) Ball Still in Play

If a Fieldsman releases the ball before he crosses the boundary, the ball will be considered to be still in play

612

and it may be caught by another Fieldsman. However, if the original Fieldsman returns to the field of play and handles the ball, a catch may not be made.

1. Out Handled the Ball

Either Batsman on appeal shall be out Handled the Ball if he wilfully touches the ball while in play with the hand not holding the bat unless he does so with the consent of the opposite side.

NOTE

(a) Entry in Score Book

The correct entry in the score book when a Batsman is given out under this Law is "handled the ball", and the Bowler does not get credit for the wicket.

1. Out Hit the Ball Twice

The Striker, on appeal, shall be out Hit the Ball Twice if, after the ball is struck or is stopped by any part of his person, he wilfully strikes it again with his bat or person except for the sole purpose of guarding his wicket: this he may do with his bat or any part of his person other than his hands, but see Law 37.2 (Obstructing a Ball From Being Caught).

For the purpose of this Law, a hand holding the bat shall be regarded as part of the bat.

2. Returning the Ball to a Fieldsman

The Striker, on appeal, shall be out under this Law, if, without the consent of the opposite side, he uses his bat or person to return the ball to any of the fielding side.

3. Runs from Ball Lawfully Struck Twice

No runs except those which result from an overthrow or penalty, see Law 41 (The Fieldsman), shall be scored from a ball lawfully struck twice.

NOTES

(a) Entry in Score Book

The correct entry in the score book when the Striker is given out under this Law is "hit the ball twice", and the Bowler does not get credit for the wicket.

(b) Runs Credited to the Batsman

Any runs awarded under 3 above as a result of an overthrow or penalty shall be credited to the Striker, provided the ball in the first instance has touched the bat, or, if otherwise as extras.

1. Out Hit Wicket

The Striker shall be out Hit Wicket if, while the ball is in play:

(a) His wicket is broken with any part of his person, dress, or equipment as a result of any action taken by him in preparing to receive or in receiving a delivery, or in setting off for his first run, immediately after playing, or playing at, the ball.

(b) He hits down his wicket whilst lawfully making a second stroke for the purpose of guarding his wicket within the provisions of Law 34.1 (Out Hit the Ball Twice).

NOTES

(a) Not Out Hit Wicket

A Batsman is not out under this Law should his wicket be broken in any of the ways referred to in 1(a) above if:

(i) It occurs while he is in the act of running, other than in setting off for his first run immediately after playing at the ball, or while he is avoiding being run out or stumped.

(ii) The Bowler after starting his run-up or bowling action does not deliver the ball; in which case the Umpire shall immediately call and signal "dead ball".

(iii) It occurs whilst he is avoiding a throw-in at any time.

LAW 36
LEG BEFORE
WICKET

1. Out LBW

The Striker shall be out LBW in the circumstances set out below:

(a) Striker Attempting to Play the Ball

The Striker shall be out LBW if he first intercepts with any part on his person, dress or equipment a fair ball which would have hit the wicket and which has not previously touched his bat or a hand holding the bat, provided that:

(i) The ball pitched, in a straight line between wicket and wicket or on the off side of the Striker's wicket, or in the case of a ball intercepted full pitch would have pitched in a straight line between wicket and wicket.

and

(ii) the point of impact is in a straight line between wicket and wicket, even if above the level of the bails.

(b) Striker Making No Attempt to Play the Ball

The Striker shall be out LBW even if the ball is intercepted outside the line of the off-stump, if, in the opinion of the Umpire, he has made no genuine attempt to play the ball with his bat, but has intercepted the ball with some part of his person and if the circumstances set out in (a) above apply.

LAW 37
OBSTRUCTING THE
FIELD

1. Wilful Obstruction

Either Batsman, on appeal, shall be out Obstructing the Field if he wilfully obstructs the opposite side by word or action.

2. Obstructing a Ball from Being Caught

The Striker, on appeal, shall be out should wilful obstruction by either Batsman prevent a catch being made.

This shall apply even though the Striker causes the obstruction in lawfully guarding his wicket under the provi-

614

sions of Law 34. See Law 34.1 (Out Hit the Ball Twice).
NOTES
(a) Accidental Obstruction
The Umpires must decide whether the obstruction was wilful or not. The accidental interception of a throw-in by a Batsman while running does not break this law.
(b) Entry in Score Book
The correct entry in the score book when a Batsman is given out under this Law is "obstructing the field", and the Bowler does not get credit for the wicket.

1. Out Run Out

Either Batsman shall be Run Out if in running or at any time while the ball is in play—except in the circumstances described in Law 39 (Stumped)—he is out of his ground and his wicket is put down by the opposite side. If, however, a Batsman in running makes good his ground he shall not be out Run Out, if he subsequently leaves his ground, in order to avoid injury, and the wicket is put down.

2. "No Ball" Called

If a no ball has been called, the Striker shall not be given Run Out unless he attempts to run.

3. Which Batsman is Out

If the Batsmen have crossed in running, he who runs for the wicket which is put down shall be out; if they have not crossed, he who has left the wicket which is put down shall be out. If a Batsman remains in his ground or returns to his ground and the other Batsman joins him there, the latter shall be out if his wicket is put down.

4. Scoring of Runs

If a Batsman is run out, only that run which is being attempted shall not be scored. If however an injured Striker himself is run out, no runs shall be scored. See Law 2.7 (Transgression of the Laws by an Injured Batsman or Runner).

NOTES
(a) Ball Played on to Opposite Wicket
If the ball is played on to the opposite wicket neither Batsman is liable to be run out unless the ball has been touched by a Fieldsman before the wicket is broken.
(b) Entry in Score Book
The correct entry in the score book when the Striker is given out under this Law is "run out", and the Bowler does not get credit for the Wicket.

1. Out Stumped

The Striker shall be out Stumped if, in receiving a ball, not being a no-ball, he is out of his ground otherwise than in attempting a run and the wicket is put down by the Wicket-Keeper without the intervention of another Fieldsman.

2. Action by the Wicket-Keeper

The Wicket-Keeper may take the ball in front of the wicket in an attempt to Stump the Striker only if the ball has touched the bat or the person of the Striker.

NOTE

(a) Ball Rebounding from Wicket-Keeper's Person

The Striker may be out Stumped if in the circumstances stated in 1 above, the wicket is broken by a ball rebounding from the Wicket-Keeper's person or equipment or is kicked or thrown by the Wicket-Keeper on to the wicket.

LAW 40
THE WICKET-KEEPER

1. Position of Wicket-Keeper

The Wicket-Keeper shall remain wholly behind the wicket until a ball delivered by the Bowler touches the bat or person of the Striker, or passes the wicket, or until the Striker attempts a run.

In the event of the Wicket-keeper contravening this Law, the Umpire at the Striker's end shall signal "no ball" at the instant of delivery or as soon as possible thereafter.

2. Restriction on Actions of the Wicket-Keeper

If the Wicket-Keeper interferes with the Striker's right to play the ball and to guard his wicket, the Striker shall not be out, except under Laws 33 (Handled the Ball), 34 (Hit the Ball Twice), 37 (Obstructing the Field) and 38 (Run Out).

3. Interference with the Wicket-Keeper by the Striker

If in the legitimate defence of his wicket, the Striker interferes with the Wicket-Keeper, he shall not be out, except as provided for in Law 37.2 (Obstructing a Ball From Being Caught).

LAW 41
THE FIELDSMAN

1. Fielding the Ball

The Fieldsman may stop the ball with any part of his person, but if he wilfully stops it otherwise, five runs shall be added to the run or runs already scored; if no run has been scored five penalty runs shall be awarded. The run in progress shall count provided that the Batsmen have crossed at the instant of the act. If the ball has been struck, the penalty shall be added to the score of the Striker, but otherwise to the score of the byes, leg-byes, no balls or wides as the case may be.

2. Limitation of On-Side Fieldsmen

The number of on-side Fieldsmen behind the popping crease at the instant of the Bowler's delivery shall not exceed two. In the event of infringememt by the fielding side the Umpire at the Striker's end shall call and signal "no ball" at the instant of delivery or as soon as possible thereafter.

3. Position of Fieldsmen

Whilst the ball is in play and until the ball has made contact with the bat or the Striker's person or has passed his bat, no Fieldsman other than the Bowler, may stand on or have any part of his person extended over the pitch (measuring

22 yards/20.12 m × 10 ft/3.05 m). In the event of a Fieldsman contravening this Law, the Umpire at the Bowler's end shall call and signal "no ball" at the instant of delivery or as soon as possible thereafter. See Law 40.1 (Position of Wicket-Keeper).

NOTE

(a) Batsmen Changing Ends
   The five runs referred to in 1 above are a penalty and the Batsmen do not change ends solely by reason of this penalty.

1. Responsibility of Captains

The Captains are responsible at all times for ensuring that play is conducted within the spirit of the game as well as within the Laws.

2. Responsibility of Umpires

The Umpires are the sole judges of fair and unfair play.

3. Intervention by the Umpire

The Umpires shall intervene without appeal by calling and signalling "dead ball" in the case of unfair play, but should not otherwise interfere with the progress of the game except as required to do so by the Laws.

4. Lifting the Seam

A Player shall not lift the seam of the ball for any reason. Should this be done, the Umpires shall change the ball for one of similar condition to that in use prior to the contravention. See Note (a).

5. Changing the Condition of the Ball

Any member of the fielding side may polish the ball provided that such polishing wastes no time and that no artificial substance is used. No-one shall rub the ball on the ground or use any artificial substance or take any other action to alter the condition of the ball.

In the event of a contravention of this Law, the Umpires, after consultation, shall change the ball for one of similar condition to that in use prior to the contravention.

This Law does not prevent a member of the fielding side from drying a wet ball, or removing mud from the ball. See Note (b).

6. Incommoding the Striker

An Umpire is justified in intervening under this Law and shall call and signal "dead ball" if, in his opinion, any Player of the fielding side incommodes the Striker by any noise or action while he is receiving a ball.

7. Obstruction of a Batsman in Running

It shall be considered unfair if any Fieldsman wilfully obstructs a Batsman in running. In these circumstances the Umpire shall call and signal "dead ball" and allow any completed runs and the run in progress or alternatively any boundary scored.

8. The Bowling of Fast Short Pitched Balls

The Bowling of fast short pitched balls is unfair if, in the opinion of the Umpire at the Bowler's end, it constitutes an attempt to intimidate the Striker. See Note (d).

Umpires shall consider intimidation to be the deliberate bowling of fast short pitched balls which by their length, height and direction are intended or likely to inflict physical injury on the Striker. The relative skill of the Striker shall also be taken into consideration.

In the event of such unfair bowling, the Umpire at the Bowler's end shall adopt the following procedure:

(a) In the first instance the Umpire shall call and signal "no ball", caution the Bowler and inform the other Umpire, the Captain of the fielding side and the Batsmen of what has occurred.

(b) If this caution is ineffective, he shall repeat the above procedure and indicate to the Bowler that this is a final warning.

(c) Both the above caution and final warning shall continue to apply even though the Bowler may later change ends.

(d) Should the above warnings prove ineffective the Umpire at the Bowler's end shall:

(i) At the first repetition call and signal "no ball" and when the ball is dead direct the Captain to take the Bowler off forthwith and to complete the over with another Bowler, provided that the Bowler does not bowl two overs or part thereof consecutively. See Law 22.7 (Bowler Incapacitated or Suspended during an Over).

(ii) Not allow the Bowler, thus taken off, to bowl again in the same innings.

(iii) Report the occurrence to the Captain of the batting side as soon as the Players leave the field for an interval.

(iv) Report the occurrence to the Executive of the fielding side and to any governing body responsible for the match who shall take any further action which is considered to be appropriate against the Bowler concerned.

9. The Bowling of Fast High Full Pitches

The bowling of fast high full pitches is unfair. See Note (e). In the event of such unfair bowling the Umpire at the bowler's end shall adopt the procedures of caution, final warning, action against the Bowler and reporting as set out in 8 above.

10. Time Wasting

Any form of time wasting is unfair.

(a) In the event of the Captain of the fielding side wasting time or allowing any member of his side to waste time, the Umpire at the Bowler's end shall adopt the following procedure:

(i) In the first instance he shall caution the Captain of the fielding side and inform the other Umpire of what has occurred.

618

(ii) If this caution is ineffective he shall repeat the above procedure and indicate to the Captain that this is a final warning.

(iii) The Umpire shall report the occurrence to the Captain of the batting side as soon as the Players leave the field for an interval.

(iv) Should the above procedure prove ineffective the Umpire shall report the occurrence to the Executive of the fielding side and to any governing body responsible for that match who shall take appropriate action against the Captain and the Players concerned.

(b) In the event of a Bowler taking unnecessarily long to bowl an over the Umpire at the Bowler's end shall adopt the procedures, other than the calling of "no ball", of caution, final warning, action against the Bowler and reporting.

(c) In the event of a Batsman wasting time (See Note (f)) other than in the manner described in Law 31 (Timed Out), the Umpire at the Bowler's end shall adopt the following procedure:

(i) In the first instance he shall caution the Batsman and inform the other Umpire at once, and the Captain of the Batting side, as soon as the players leave the field for an interval, of what has occurred.

(ii) If this proves ineffective, he shall repeat the caution, indicate to the Batsman that this is a final warning and inform the other Umpire.

(iii) The Umpire shall report the occurrence to both Captains as soon as the Players leave the field for an interval.

(iv) Should the above procedure prove ineffective, the Umpire shall report the occurrence to the Executive of the batting side and to any governing body responsible for that match who shall take appropriate action against the Player concerned.

11.   Players Damaging the Pitch

The Umpires shall intervene and prevent Players from causing damage to the pitch which may assist the Bowlers of either side. See Note (c).

(a) In the event of any member of the fielding side damaging the pitch the Umpire shall follow the procedure of caution, final warning and reporting as set out in 10 (a) above.

(b) In the event of a Bowler contravening this Law by running down the pitch after delivering the ball, the Umpire at the Bowler's end shall first caution the Bowler. If this caution is ineffective the Umpire shall adopt the procedures, other than the calling of "no ball", of final warning, action against the Bowler and reporting.

(c) In the event of a Batsman damaging the pitch the Umpire at the Bowler's end shall follow the procedures of caution, final warning and reporting as set out in 10 (c) above.

12.　Batsman Unfairly Stealing a Run

Any attempt by the Batsman to steal a run during the Bowler's run-up is unfair. Unless the bowler attempts to run out either Batsman—see Law 24.4 (Bowler Throwing at Striker's Wicket Before Delivery) and Law 24.5 (Bowler Attempting to Run Out Non-Striker Before Delivery)—the Umpire shall call and signal "dead ball" as soon as the Batsmen cross in any attempt to run. The Batsmen shall then return to their original wickets.

13.　Player's Conduct

In the event of a player failing to comply with the instructions of an Umpire, criticising his decisions by word or action, or showing dissent, or generally behaving in a manner which might bring the game into disrepute, the Umpire concerned shall, in the first place report the matter to the other Umpire and to the Player's Captain requesting the latter to take action. If this proves ineffective, the Umpire shall report the incident as soon as possible to the Executive of the Player's team and to any Governing Body responsible for the match, who shall take any further action which is considered appropriate against the Player or Players concerned.

NOTES

(a)　The Condition of the Ball

Umpires shall make frequent and irregular inspections of the condition of the ball.

(b)　Drying a Wet Ball

A wet ball may be dried on a towel or with sawdust.

(c)　Danger Area

The danger area on the pitch, which must be protected from damage by a Bowler, shall be regarded by the Umpires as the area contained by an imaginary line 4 ft/1.22 m from the popping crease, and parallel to it, and within two imaginary and parallel lines drawn down the pitch from points on that line 1 ft/30.48 cm on either side of the middle stump.

(d)　Fast Short Pitched Balls

As a guide, a fast short pitched ball is one which pitches short and passes, or would have passed, above the shoulder height of the Striker standing in a normal batting stance at the crease.

(e)　The Bowling of Fast Full Pitches

The bowling of one fast, high full pitch shall be considered to be unfair if, in the opinion of the Umpire, it is deliberate, bowled at the Striker, and if it passed or would have passed above the shoulder height of the Striker when standing in a normal batting stance at the crease.

(f)　Time Wasting by Batsmen

Other than in exceptional circumstances, the Batsman should always be ready to take strike when the Bowler is ready to start his run-up.

Rodney Hogg shows his disgust after being given run out when he went down the pitch to do some gardening.

620

A right-hand batsman and right-arm medium-pace round-arm bowler who came to Australia with the first English team in 1862 and stayed to play an important part in the early development of Australian cricket. He became Australia's first paid cricket coach, accepting an offer from the Albert club in Sydney and was largely responsible for a dramatic improvement in playing standards. He captained New South Wales in some of the first inter-Colonial matches. His success as a coach persuaded William Caffyn to stay in Australia in a similar role after the 1864 English team toured Australia. Between them they laid the foundation for Australia's success in international cricket.

Lawrence, born in the London suburb of Hoxton, played for Surrey in 1854 and 1857 and for Middlesex in 1861. He took 46 wickets at 5.28 in all matches for Stephenson's team in Australia in 1862 and scored 99 runs at 6.60. In all first-class matches his highest score was 78. He took five wickets in an innings four times and twice took 10 wickets in a match, best figures 7 for 25. His gifts as a communicator were clearly demonstrated by his success with the Aboriginal cricketers whom he prepared and accompanied on their tour of England in 1868.

LAWRENCE, Charles, 1828–1916

First-Class Averages: Batting, 212 runs at 16.31; Bowling, 37 wickets at 10.32.

A pugnacious left-handed opening batsman, self-opinionated, as befitted the stubborn character of his batting, who took over the Australian captaincy after a string of brave innings and lost it because of his well-documented bad behaviour. Lawry performed with a dourness bordering on heroism in many big matches but to many cricket buffs at the end of his career he typified the loss of decorum among Australia's top players.

As a captain, Lawry led with unrelaxed intensity. He was unable to hide his annoyance when one of his bowlers was hit hard. Lou Rowan* said Lawry stifled his bowlers. In cities where previous Australian captains were popular, he repeatedly clashed with spectators. In India photographers turned up for an Australian team's game wearing black armbands, after Lawry had prodded one of their colleagues on the backside with his bat. Lawry remains the only Australian captain dismissed in the course of a Test series.

Lawry, born at Thornbury, Victoria, was 6 ft 2 ins tall, long-nosed and as alert as a pecking bird, a beguiling figure who studied plumbing at Preston Technical Institute and raced pigeons in his spare time. He was predominantly an on-side player when he made his debut for Victoria in 1955–56 but later developed strokes all around the wicket, batting with uncommon patience and an ability to concentrate for long pe-

*In his book, *The Umpire's Story*.

LAWRY, William Morris ("The Phantom"), 1937–

First-Class Averages: Batting, 18,734 runs at 50.90; Bowling, 5 wickets at 37.60.

Tests (67, plus 1 abandoned): 5,234 runs at 47.15.

riods. He fielded splendidly in the outfield and had a fine left-arm throw. He was heavily addicted to the comic strip hero that provided his nickname.

He played for the Northcote club in Melbourne and from a slightly crouched stance used his long reach to stifle the uncertain bounce of district cricket pitches. He was eager to hit loose deliveries and from an early age was adept in placing his shots. He had come from a family without any background in cricket, working his way through three years of church cricket with Thornbury Presbyterian teams. Northcote played him in the fourths at the age of 12 and within four years he was a regular first grader.

Lawry made his debut for Victoria a few weeks before his 19th birthday. He played in all Victoria's matches in 1956–57 after his debut the previous summer, but was dropped for all of the 1957–58 season, and for most of the 1958–59 season. He finally got back into the Victorian side for the match against MCC, and although he made only 24 and 22 he made them well enough to hold his place. He scored the first of his 20 centuries for Victoria in 1959–60, with an innings of 127 against Western Australia at Melbourne. Just before the selectors picked the Australian team to tour England in 1961 under Benaud's leadership, he made 266 against New South Wales at Sydney—he was dropped at 12—and that knock won him a place among the 11 newcomers to England in the Australian party.

Few Australians have made such an impact as Lawry did on that first visit to England; he proved staunch and reliable under intense pressure, at this time a modest, likeable character. His extremely short backlift suited pitches with marked spin and cut. He topped Australia's batting averages with 2,019 runs at 61.18 in all first-class matches, scoring 420 runs at 52.50 in the five Tests. He made nine centuries. Only Bradman (2,428) in 1948, and Harvey (2,040) in 1953, had made more than 2,000 runs for Australia on a post-World War II tour of England.

O'Neill, Harvey and Burge all scored centuries before Lawry got his first on that tour, a dominating innings against Surrey at The Oval which veteran reporter Tom Goodman described as "a flowering of technique and temperament that opened many English eyes and many Australian eyes, too." Lawry batted four and a half hours for 165 out of Australia's 341, hooking and pulling hard, driving powerfully, repeatedly finding the gaps. He followed with 104 and 84 not out on his first appearance at Lord's, against MCC. Clearly, a new Australian batting star had arrived.

In his Test debut he made a solid 57 at Edgbaston, and to fit him in as opener for the Tests, the selectors had to split an established opening pair, Colin McDonald and Bob Simpson. In the famous "Ridge Test" at Lord's which saw the ball rocketing

622

about as Trueman and Statham at their fiery best bounced the ball off a nasty patch that rose imperceptibly above the rest of the batting strip, Lawry was calm and defiant for 370 minutes, taking heavy knocks calmly, striking the loose balls cleanly between fieldsmen. His 130 remains one of the classic knocks in Australia–England Tests, and it gave Lawry 1,000 runs in two months.

Australia won the "Battle of the Ridge" thanks to Lawry and also won the Test at Old Trafford, which decided The Ashes. This time Lawry's contribution was 74 in the first innings and 102 in the second innings, a performance which induced former England Test bowler Bill Bowes to write: "Lawry is one of the best players of fast bowling I have ever seen." Bowes, of course, had seen McCabe in full flight against Larwood, Voce and Allen.

Lawry misses with a legside swing against Surrey at The Oval in 1961.

623

A Lawry pull shot that connected brings four in the Surrey match during his triumphant 1961 English tour.

Back home Lawry was made Victoria's captain in place of McDonald and scored centuries regularly in inter-State cricket. His bat was ideally straight, his stroke range continually expanding. He was devastating against pace, a superb runner between wickets, who formed with Bob Simpson one of the finest of Australian opening pairs, our equivalent of Hobbs and Sutcliffe in their judgment of a run. Under Lawry's captaincy, Victoria regained the Shield in 1962–63 after a gap of 12 seasons.

He returned to England in 1964 under Simpson as one of the world's finest batsmen, and certainly the most difficult Australian to dismiss. This time he made 1,601 runs at 42.13, contributing 78 in the Third Test, won by Australia, 106 in the drawn Fourth Test, and 94 in the drawn Fifth Test. Back home in 1965–66, he made 979 runs against Mike Smith's touring England side, with 166 in the First Test, 88 and 78 in the Second Test, 119 in the Fourth Test when he and Simpson added a record 244 for the first wicket, and 108 in the Fifth Test when he batted over six hours, bringing his batting time against England that summer to more than 41 hours.

Lawry took over the Australian captaincy on Simpson's first retirement in 1967–68, having won the Shield again with Victoria in 1966–67. He held the job for three years, starting with a disappointing tour of England in 1968 when rain ruined many matches and Lawry had a finger broken in the Third Test by a ball from Snow. He made 906 runs at 45.30 this time on tour, with only two of the five Tests providing a result, but he was cheerful and popular, determined to set an example for his team.

In Australia the following season, Lawry led Australia to a marvellous win in a splendid series against West Indies. Wisden reporter Henry Blofield said Australia's success was a major shift in the balance of power in world cricket. "The famous West Indies side of the last decade finally disintegrated against the young and highly efficient Australian team which itself was nearing greatness by the end of the series," Blofield wrote. "The West Indies won the First Test at Brisbane mostly as a result of winning the toss on a wicket which broke up, but from then on were systematically destroyed by a side which outplayed them at all points and went on to win the series 3–1."

Lawry's captaincy played as important a part in that series as his batting, which saw him add three more big scores to his record, 205 in the Second Test at Melbourne, 151 in the Fifth Test at Sydney, and 105 in the First Test at Brisbane. A new era seemed about to begin, with Australia splendidly balanced in attack, brimful of batting talent, assisted by Taber's classy wicket-keeping, ably led, and morale high.

Here the strain of 15 years in first-class cricket caught up with Lawry on the long tour of India and South Africa in

Left: David Ogilvie shows the aggression that brought him six first-class centuries for Queensland in 1977–78.

Right: Ian Redpath drives through the covers during the 1974–75 series against England.

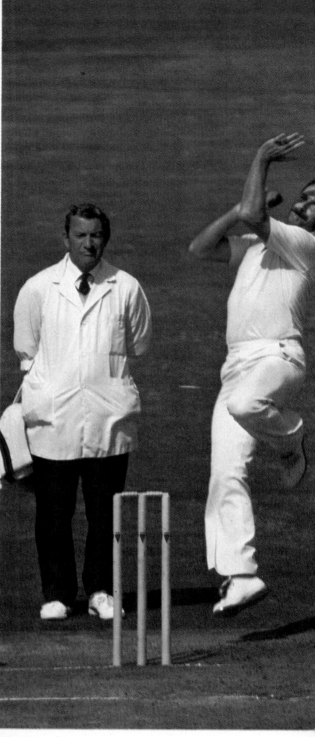

Right: Dennis Lillee in action against England at Edgbaston in 1981.

Below: The well known Lillee appeal on view in a Sydney one-day match.

1969–70. He became persistently petulant over umpires' decisions, aloof from his team. He had always been a non-drinking, non-smoking loner who disliked official functions but now he became a virtual recluse, disappearing after each day's play, seldom meeting opponents socially. There was a famous curry plate-throwing incident on the train from Delhi to Jullundur. In South Africa, the heckling of umpires continued and vulgar hand signs to spectators were added. Successful despite the heat and unaccustomed food in India, Australia took a 4-nil drubbing in South Africa, with some players avoiding each other.

The Board of Control took some time to consider manager Fred Bennett's report of that disastrous India-South Africa tour and one can only sympathise with the manager who had to report on the conduct of such a fine servant of Australian cricket. Finally, during the Sixth Test in Adelaide in 1970–71, Lawry lost the captaincy to Ian Chappell. Since then the Lawry junta in Victoria has continually returned to the injustice that was done when he was sacked as captain, with Paul Sheahan particularly vocal. Despite the unusual manner of his sacking, the facts suggest they would be better to remember him as he was in his prime, a gritty fighter and one of Australia's finest Test batsmen. Lawry captained his country 25 times for nine wins, eight draws and eight losses. In 67 Tests, he had a highest score of 210, with 13 centuries and 27 fifties, a proud record. In 249 first-class matches he scored 50 centuries with a topscore of 266 and took 121 catches. In all matches for Victoria, he scored 7,618 runs, a total no other batsman has reached.

LAWSON, Geoffrey Francis ("Henry"), 1957–

A tall, hard-working New South Wales fast bowler with an unusual delivery stride who came into prominence when he dismissed master batsman Geoff Boycott on Sydney Cricket Ground in 1979–80 and was warned for bowling too many bouncers at Boycott in the next innings. Lawson has visited India, Pakistan and England with Australian teams but has been unable to confirm his Test place because of injuries. He was very impressive in his best Test performance in the Second Test against England at Lord's in 1981, when he won the Man-of-the-Match award by taking 7 for 81.

Lawson, a raw-boned optometrist from Wagga Wagga, produced some fiery spells in grade matches for the University of NSW in between studying for his degree. He made his debut for NSW in 1977–78 against Western Australia. He has built up his physique since then but continues to lose pace because of his curious habit of throwing his front leg sideways just as he reaches the crease. This flick of the leg probably also accounts for some of his injury problems. He has proved a

First-Class Averages: Batting 568 runs at 12.09; Bowling, 176 wickets at 24.21.

Tests (5): 56 runs at 9.33; 16 wickets at 25.88.

whole-hearted trier, however, and a right-hand late order batsman who can occasionally make valuable runs. He is an efficient outfield with a power arm.

Lawson went to the Central Lancashire League club Heywood to gain experience in 1979 and played one match for Lancashire against Cambridge University. This tuned him up for a splendid season in Australia in 1979–80, during which he took five wickets in an innings twice and helped lift NSW up the Shield ladder, and finished with 34 wickets at 20.97. He had limited opportunities on dead pitches in Pakistan and India in 1979–80, and made his Test debut at Brisbane in 1980–81 against New Zealand. After only one Test appearance he was dropped but he came back strongly in England in 1981 and when Rodney Hogg was injured went into the Australian team. He took his chance admirably, taking 2 for 2 off his first 16 deliveries, dismissing the first four English batsmen and the last three. He took four more wickets in the following Test but lost his place through injury in the Fourth Test. His 25 wickets on the tour cost 26.08. Injuries continued to worry him in the 1981–82 Australian season and he missed the Australian tour of New Zealand.

Geoff Lawson bowling against England at Leeds in 1981.

An Australian right-arm leg-break and googly bowler who gave the finest allround performance in the 155-year history of the annual Oxford versus Cambridge Universities cricket match. He took five wickets in an innings 10 times and four times took 10 wickets in a match, in a first-class career that was confined almost entirely to England. He was a useful batsman in the bottom of the order and a fine field. When his spinners found a length, his bowling could be devastating but his performance depended on how much time he could spare from his studies to practise.

Le Couteur was born at Kyneton, Victoria, and was educated at the Warrnambool Academy and Melbourne University. He went to Oxford as a Rhodes scholar and won Blues in three successive years, 1909, 1910 and 1911. He played for the Gentlemen against The Players six times in 1910 and 1911. In 1910 he distinguished himself with an innings of 70 at Scarborough that enabled the Gentlemen to salvage a draw, and in 1911 he paved the way to a win by the Gentlemen at The Oval in taking 5 for 98 in the Players' second innings, all the best professionals in England except Jack Hobbs appearing helpless against his wide breaks.

His finest triumph came in the Oxford-Cambridge match at Lord's in 1910, however, when he made 160 and took 11 wickets for 66 runs (6 for 20 and 5 for 46), an unsurpassed allround effort. In this match he proved a brilliant hitter on the on-side and a superb exponent of spin. He took 108 wickets in three seasons for Oxford. His 59 wickets at 14.32 in 1910, compares with 70 wickets by Ian Peebles, at 18.15 in 1930, and with 61 wickets at 16.55 in 1923, by Australian Reg Bettington.

After World War I when Le Couteur made his debut for Victoria in the 1918–19 season against New South Wales at Melbourne, he took 2 for 59. In his second game against South Australia he had nine overs that yielded 1 for 41 in the match, and in his only other game for Victoria he took 1 for 0 and 0 for 48 against NSW at Sydney. He then dropped out of first-class cricket, and died at Gunnedah, NSW, four days after his 73rd birthday, a cricketer whose achievements were virtually unknown to his countrymen.

LE COUTEUR, Philip Ridgeway, 1885–1958

First-Class Averages: Batting, 982 runs at 21.34; Bowling, 138 wickets at 19.07.

A right-hand batsman and right-arm medium-pace bowler whose experience as a first-class player with two centuries to his credit proved invaluable during his period as secretary of the Victorian Cricket Association and of the Australian Board of Control. Ha had 21 matches for Victoria between 1934 and 1938, topscore 154.

Ledward, born at East Melbourne, played for the Richmond club and took over as VCA secretary in 1951 after working with a bank. He took over from Bill Jeanes as the Board of

LEDWARD, John Allan, 1909–

First-Class Averages: Batting, 1,252 runs at 39.12.

Control secretary, relinquishing the VCA position in 1973 to concentrate on Board problems. He was a diligent and courteous servant of Australian cricket whose long hours forced his retirement through ill-health in 1976, when he handed over to Alan Barnes.

LEE, Ian Somerville ("Meggsy"), 1914–1976

First-Class Averages: Batting, 3,481 runs at 38.25.

One of a talented group of Victorian left-handed batsmen that included Leo O'Brien, Len Darling, Ernie Bromley, Ben Barnett, George Newstead, Joe Thomas and Frank Sides. In an era in which more than half the Victorian team batted left-handed, Lee made six centuries and one double century. He still holds the Victorian record with Stan Quin of 424 runs for the fourth wicket, in 1933–34 against Tasmania. Lee, who made his debut for Victoria in 1931–32, built this record stand with an innings of 258, while at the other end Quin made 210. Victoria had been dismissed for 68 and conceded Tasmania a first innings lead of 320. The Lee-Quin stand saved the game. In 1936–37, Lee scored 160 against England at Melbourne. For South Melbourne between 1930–31 and 1938–39, Lee scored 3,002 runs at 40.56, topscore 146.

LEE, Phillip Keith, 1904–1980

First-Class Averages: Batting, 1,669 runs at 18.54, Bowling, 152 wickets at 30.16.

Tests (2): 57 runs at 19.00; 5 wickets at 42.40.

A leading South Australian allrounder of the late 1920s and early 1930s. He was an aggressive batsman and efficient spin bowler, mainly of off breaks, with excellent control and subtle flight. He achieved the double of 1,000 runs and 100 wickets for his State and played in two Tests, one against South Africa and one against England.

Lee, born at Gladstone, South Australia, first achieved prominence when he took 5 for 36 against a strong New South Wales side at Sydney in January, 1927. He took five wickets in an innings six times for his State, with 5 for 23 against Victoria at Melbourne in 1932–33, his best performance. In 1929–30, he made 100 against Western Australia at Adelaide in 73 minutes and had match figures of 9 for 105, and in 1930–31 had a splendid match against the first West Indies team to visit Australia, taking 5 for 57 and scoring 106, his highest first-class score. He was an outstanding allround sportsman, a champion athlete at St Peter's College, excelling at cricket, baseball and football.

LIDDICUT, Arthur Edward ("Lid"), 1891–

A splendid allrounder for Victoria for 17 years. He usually opened the bowling with his lively right-arm fast-medium pacers, moving the ball about by exploiting his 6 ft 1 in. He batted at No. 9 in a very strong batting lineup, mainly so that he could be rested for bowling. But he was good enough to score three first-class centuries and achieve a topscore of 152. He was often mentioned as a Test possible without winning the selectors' approval but twice toured New Zealand, in 1920–21 with an Australian team captained by Vernon Ransford and in 1924–25 in a Victorian side led by E. R. Mayne.

Liddicut, born in the Melbourne suburb of Fitzroy, played for Geelong, St Kilda and Fitzroy. He made his debut for Victoria in 1911–12 and played his last game for the State in 1932, an admirable span, interrupted by World War I, which saw him play 62 first-class games. He twice took five wickets in an innings but it was the practice in his time to take off the opening bowlers once they had broken through the early batting. His figures for Victoria repeatedly showed him taking three or four wickets without getting a second bowl. His best figures for the State were 6 for 65 against South Australia in 1923–24 and 7 for 40 against Tasmania in 1929–30 when he was in his 40th year. One of this finest efforts was in 1922–23 against Maclaren's MCC team when he took 4 for 16 and then scored 102.

Liddicut's form on two tours of New Zealand suggested that he would have been ideally suited to English conditions, for he handled the damp pitches and heavier atmosphere well. In 1920–21 he scored 727 runs at 60.58 and consistently broke through the opening batting with the ball. He was one of the most successful players in Mayne's side two seasons later. Liddicut later represented the Fitzroy club on the VCA for many years serving on a series of important committees. His Fitzroy club record of 13 first grade centuries was unapproached for many years and then Ray Harvey broke it and took the record to 19 first grade centuries. Liddicut played in Fitzroy firsts until he was past 50 and at 56 was still active in the club's seconds. In his 91st year he was still eager to discuss cricket's finer points.

First-Class Averages: Batting, 2,503 runs at 31.28; Bowling, 133 wickets at 27.56.

Arthur Liddicut at the age of 90 shows one of his treasured souvenirs.

An orthodox right-hand batsman who built an impressive record for South Australia despite interruptions caused by university studies. He fashioned his scores calmly but confidently, punishing bad deliveries and remaining watchful for good deliveries. He had some of the biggest hits in Australian cricket to his credit when he retired to concentrate on his work with a giant chemical engineering firm. He made eight first-class centuries for South Australia, highest score 176 against Victoria at Melbourne in January, 1960. He toured New Zealand in 1959–60 with Ian Craig's Australian side.

Lill, 6 ft 1 in, brown-haired, was the son of Alec Lill, who won the Magarey medal for South Australia's most brilliant Australian footballer in the 1925 season. John went to Prince

LILL, John Charles, 1933–

First-Class Averages: Batting, 4,109 runs at 36.36; Bowling, 1 wicket at 47.00.

Alfred College, Adelaide, but gave credit for his cricket education to his father. He won Blues for football and cricket at Adelaide University and played district cricket with the University before transferring to Kensington and finally to Sturt. He became a doctor of philosophy, metallurgy and chemical engineering. He played 78 successive games for the Norwood Australian Rules club but confessed he did not enjoy training for either cricket or football. These days John Lill, who has three sons playing cricket, coaches one of the Melbourne CC teams.

LILLE, Dennis Keith ("Fot"), 1949–

First-Class Averages: Batting, 2,038 runs at 14.25; Bowling, 758 wickets at 22.08.

Tests (63): 872 runs at 13.62; 328 wickets at 23.07.

A magnificent right-arm fast bowler who has taken more wickets than any bowler in the history of Test cricket. He became the highest wicket-taker for Australia in the summer of 1980–81 in the Third Test against India at Melbourne, and the highest wicket-taker in all Test cricket at Melbourne against the West Indies in 1981–82. He achieved these milestones after overcoming a back injury earlier in his career and after missing two years of first-class cricket while he was with WSC. Tireless, resourceful, fiercely competitive, he was still discussing ways of improving his technique with former pace bowling master Ray Lindwall after he had passed Benaud's Australian Test record.

In 1982 he was nowhere near as fast as in his earlier tearaway days, but he bowled with sustained control, every delivery planned. He mixed leg-cutters with a near perfect out-swinger and bounced the ball awkwardly. His great friend Rodney Marsh considers the only weaknesses in Lillee's repertoire are his lack of a good yorker and his inability to bowl as well to left-handers as he does to right-handers.

Cricket has given Lillee the prestige of a matinee idol and financial security for life, and he has had to work tremendously hard for them. The sight of him running in to bowl has been one of the most exciting things in Test cricket for ten years, and he still keeps charging in eager for wickets at the end of the most arduous day. And it is this unrelenting determination that has conveyed itself to hundreds of thousands of small boys and made Lillee one of cricket's genuine superstars. Television has done a lot for modern cricketers, but nobody has benefited more from it than Lillee.

He has perfect equipment for TV stardom. He is big, dark, with a face that is all menace, if not as satanic as Spofforth's. Even when he is walking back to his mark, husbanding his strength for another delivery, rubbing the ball determinedly, he gives spectators their money's worth, flicking sweat from his brow with an index finger on to the ball. He turns and gallops back to the bowling crease with long, co-ordinated strides, black hair and lucky gold necklace flopping up and down. When he finds an edge or hits a pad, there are few more enthusiastic appealers in cricket.

He was born in the Perth suburb of Subiaco and attended Belmay Primary School and Belmont Secondary School, joining Perth grade club at 15. All he wanted to do then was bowl fast, and he wasted his abundant energy in furious, wild spells that at the end of a long run-up sprayed the ball all around the striker but not often enough at the stumps. He was raw but he was strong and immediately likeable and coaches were eager to help him.

Mick Basile coached him in the Under 16s and Perth Seniors, then Bert Rigg, an ex-State player and Hugh Bevan, the West Australian opening bowler continued the instruction. He was helped, too, by the fast pitches of Perth, particularly the strip at the State's main ground, the WACA, where a succession of pace bowlers such as Harry Gorringe, Des Hoare, Ron Gaunt and Graeme McKenzie had given outstanding displays. He made his debut in first-class cricket in 1969–70 in Brisbane, however, taking 2 for 60 and 1 for 16. Test opener Sam Trimble was his first victim in big cricket.

Lillee took 32 Shield wickets that season and at the end of the summer went to New Zealand with an Australian B team, that included Dave Renneberg and Alan Thomson, Test pace men. He headed the averages on the trip with 16 wickets at 18.00 and always seemed the bowler most likely to break through. He was one of the bowlers punished when Barry Richards scored 356 for South Australia against Western Australia the following season 1970–71. Lillee bowled 18 overs, finishing with 0 for 117. Australian batsmen took a hammering that summer from English fast bowlers Snow, Lever and Willis and by the Sixth Test Australia's selectors decided to gamble with a bowler who could retaliate, Lillee. On the splendid batting strip at Adelaide he took five wickets, and was impressive enough for Ray Lindwall to offer him advice on sorting out his approach run. He worked hard in the nets and in mid-1971 went off for a season with Haslingden in the Lancashire League.

Despite his fearsome pace he was not immediately successful at Haslingden, but then he discovered that the team's off-spinner Jack Ingham was filling up the curator of the Haslingden ground, Ben Gate, with pints of beer to prepare wickets that suited off-spin. He got together with Ingham and the curator and henceforth one end was left well grassed for Lillee's benefit. It was at Haslingden that Lillee hit a young batsman on the pad, plumb in front. When the batsman didn't move after being given out, Lillee yelled at him to go. Lillee had broken the batsman's foot and he couldn't move. Haslingden players carried the poor batsman from the crease.

By the time the Rest Of The World arrived in Australia for the 1971–72 summer, Lillee had matured markedly. In the

A fascinating shot of Lillee's grip as he starts to roll his fingers over the ball.

Perth match Australia defeated the Rest Of The World by an innings and 11 runs, Lillee taking 8 for 29 and 4 for 63. Lillee, who had a virus, asked Ian Chappell to take him off after dismissing Gavaskar and Engineer in the first innings but Chappell persuaded him to continue, and by the end of the match it was clear Australia had found the fast bowler it had been looking for since Davidson retired. He took 24 wickets in four matches of the series.

At this time he was ferociously fast, finishing his approach with a spectacular final leap and in five Tests in 1972 he took 31 wickets, then a record for an Australian bowler in England. When Massie took 16 wickets in the Lord's Test, Lillee took the other four wickets and in the Fifth Test at The Oval he took 5 for 58 and 5 for 123, Australia winning a splendid match by five wickets to square the series.

He went off to the West Indies with the Australian team early in 1973 at his peak but broke down with stress fractures in the back. He spent a long time in plaster, with most critics saying he was finished in big cricket. He solved his back problems with rare intelligence, consulting a Perth doctor and then following a herculean programme of exercises which the doctor said was the only way the injury could be cured. There was intense pain in the exercises which included running on a treadmill and lifting weights with pulleys but he stuck at it.

Miraculously, he returned to international cricket and in 1974–75 formed with Jeff Thomson in Australia one of the most devastating opening combinations in cricket history. Thomson took 33 wickets in the Tests, Lillee 25, Australia winning the six-Test series 4–1. Lillee indicated what was to come on the 1975 Australian tour of England by taking 5 for 15 in England's first innings in the First Test at Edgbaston. Both he and Thomson made demoralising use of the bouncer. Lillee finished the tour with 41 wickets compared with 53 wickets three years before in England. In the Lord's Test Lillee scored 73 not out in his best batting display.

Lillee's success continued in 1975–76 in Australia, a season highlighted by his sensational dismissal of the great Vivian Richards at Perth in the Gillette Cup match between Western Australia and Queensland, who had Richards in their side. Bowling at a ferocious pace, Lillee gave Richards four successive bouncers that had the great man ducking and weaving and then scattered Richards' stumps with a half volley.

By now the innate showmanship in Lillee's makeup had emerged and in the Centenary Test at Melbourne in March, 1977, he played with the crowd's emotions with every ball he bowled. When England were dismissed for 95 in the first innings he took 6 for 26 and in the second innings he bowled tirelessly for 34.4 overs to take 5 for 139. In a match of many heroes, his performance got Australia home by 45 runs.

632

He missed the Australian tour of England in mid-1977, saying he wanted to rest his still suspect back. But such was his public following that when official cricket banned him from representative cricket, the WACA dared not bar him from grade matches, and Lillee opened the batting for his grade club in Perth. He gave tremendous service to WSC and was a major reason for their success after shaky beginnings. Nothing on Australian television could match his appeal or appeals.

After normal first-class cricket returned, Lillee came back a different bowler. The ferocious pace and the high bound had gone, but in its place there was great subtlety, every ball planned, more thought in his attack, more cunning. On tour with the Australian team in Pakistan in 1979–80, he made little impression and found the heavily doped pitches innocuous to pace—so he started bowling fast-medium legbreaks. In one Test he had the indignity of not taking a wicket. But back in Australia against England in 1979–80 he was back in business, with 4 for 73 in the First Test, 4 for 40 in the Second, and 6 for 60 and 5 for 78 in the Third. His performance was marred only by his attempts to use an aluminium bat in Perth.

Umpire Crafter gamely steps between Lillee and Miandad during their notorious Perth confrontation.

633

At this point Lillee had played 41 Tests and taken 209 wickets—a strike rate of just over five wickets per Test. Since then Lillee has played a further 22 Tests and taken a further 119 wickets, so his strike rate has improved as he has aged. He took five wickets in the Centenary Test at Lord's, 16 in the three Tests against New Zealand in 1980–81, 21 in the three Tests against India the same season, 39 in the six Tests in England in 1981, 15 in the three Tests against Pakistan in 1981–82, 16 against the three Tests against the West Indies in 1981–82 and 7 in the three Tests against New Zealand in 1982. He has taken five wickets or more in an innings 46 times and 10 wickets in a match 13 times, best figures 8 for 29 for Australia v. Rest Of The World in 1970–71.

He continues to be controversial and provocative and it is rare for a Test to pass without his involvement in some incident. In England in 1981 there was a problem over some of his headbands carrying advertising and he played out the series in a striped version with no logo. At Perth in 1981–82 against Pakistan he appeared to bump Javed Miandad during a run and after he had made good his ground Miandad turned and shaped to swing the bat at Lillee, umpire Crafter bravely intervening. For all the argument, however, Dennis Lillee's performances place him indisputably among the great bowlers in cricket history.

LIMITED OVER CRICKET, IN AUSTRALIA

A hectic, energetic type of cricket in which technique is often thrust aside as each team takes wild risks to try and score more runs than the opposition in an agreed number of overs. A result is guaranteed within the space of one bustling day, and although there is little subtlety or artistry in it, limited over cricket produces dramatic events ideal for television. Much of it has outraged lovers of traditional cricket, and a lot of former Australian Test players are on record as saying they never watch it. Noisy, boisterous crowds averaging more than 20,000 have attended limited over "international" matches in Australia for the past two summers. Limited over cricket has, however, widened the circle of people interested in the game. Australians are not particularly good at it, but sponsorship money from limited over matches has eased the worries of cricket associations suffering from financial stress. For this reason programmes for Australia's first-class players have become heavily over-loaded with one-day games, mostly of 50 overs a side.

Limited over cricket often shows even the most stylish batsmen in grotesque attitudes as they slash wildly or swing themselves off their feet. Spin bowlers have no place under rules that enable selectors to fill their teams with pace bowlers. Containment has become more important than taking wickets. Batsmen prepared to wear down an attack are unwanted. Fielding alone has benefited and is far more proficient than before limited over cricket was introduced. At a Test level this had worked to Australia's disadvantage, for it has brought improvement in the fielding of English teams over whom Australian sides always had a marked superiority in the past.

Spectacular catching has become a regular feature of limited over cricket as has the sight of fieldsmen sliding to cut off boundaries with their bodies. Run-outs have become more frequent as the strain to sustain high scoring rates erodes the good judgment essential in skilful running between wickets. Technical faults developed in limited over cricket later embarrass players in Tests.

The unique feature of limited over cricket in Australia is the Sydney Cricket Ground lights, ugly monuments to the holy dollar at a famous cricket venue. The SCG lights provide Australia with a strange but compelling spectacle unmatched anywhere in the cricket world, a night-time setting that is a huge television success. Cricket played there after dark with a white ball on a dewy field, has a breathless quality as matches reach a climax in the last few hectic overs, the players in coloured clothing dripping with perspiration invisible by day, the big prizemoney just a few runs or a couple of quick wickets away. A visit to the dressing-rooms immediately after one of these SCG contests is a memorable experience, for night-time cricket leaves the players absolutely spent. The fielding side just slump on the benches utterly drained, reliving the decisive moments while outside the big trucks stand empty ready to take away the beer cans.

"One day cricket is injecting a dementia into the souls of those who play it," former Test bowler Bill O'Reilly said in the *Sydney Morning Herald*. "The whole thing is cancerous. For men to whom money is god, there is no time to be concerned about what is happening to the proper game. People seem prepared to watch batsmen get out in strange ways. It's sad to see a player like Kim Hughes dance down the wicket and get stumped having a wild swing. It's character assassination. Even Dennis Lillee does not try to bowl fast in this ridiculous game that seems to be all about containment rather than taking wickets. The bowling is boof-headed rubbish."

Various forms of shortened cricket have been played since the game was first introduced in Australia. Single wicket cricket was fairly common in the 1850s and 1860s, and in the 1880s the three Gregory brothers, Dave, Charles and Ned, won a thrilling restricted wicket match for New South Wales against a Victoria team comprising Conway, Cosstick and Wills. The Gregorys made 24 and 30, the Victorians 21 and 28 giving the Gregorys victory by five runs. Bob Simpson was involved in promoting Double Wicket Cricket after his first retirement in the late 1960s. But the big breakthrough in crowd appeal did not come in Australia until WSC introduced white balls, black sightboards, coloured clothing, field restricting circles, embellishing the game that had revived struggling clubs in England in 1963. Just as England's Gillette Cup success caused a rapid spread in limited over cricket and the introduction of the Prudential Cup international limited over competition in 1975, so, too, did the WSC one day games achieve a crowd acceptance that was remarkable.

Australia reached the final of the first Prudential World Cup in 1975 against the West Indies, defeating Pakistan by 73 runs (Ross Edwards 80 not out; Lillee 5 for 34) and England by four wickets (Gilmour 6 for 14) on the way. The final was full of drama from the time Fredericks was out hitting Lillee for six when his foot dislodged a bail. At 3 for 50, West Indies appeared to be in trouble, but then Lloyd played a spectacular innings, reaching 102 in only 82 balls, and assuring a big score. Only brilliant fielding prevented Australia getting closer than 17 runs from the West Indies total. Richards twice hit the stumps from side-on and then ran Ian Chappell out with a throw to Lloyd, Australia losing five batsmen to run outs.

One-day internationals had been part of every touring team's programme since 1970–71, but the success of the World Cup in 1975 and 1979 really gave international one-day matches its big impetus. Australia was weakened in 1979 by the absence of WSC players and in the first match went down to Engand by six wickets. Australia were 1 for 97 at lunch in this match but indiscreet batting saw a collapse that left England only 160 to win. Australia followed with a further loss to Pakistan, which virtually cost them a place in the semi-finals. Without Hogg, who was injured, Australia were reduced to bowling Border and Yallop. In the final the West Indies started badly as they had in 1975, losing 4 for 99, but from that point Richards and King added 139 in 21 overs, setting up a comfortable 92 runs win over England.

Since the World Cup flop in 1979 Australia has seen a series of dramatic events at home in one day cricket. Before 52,990 spectators on February 1, 1981, Trevor Chappell, on the instructions of his brother Greg, bowled an under-arm last ball to complete the match against New Zealand, with New Zealand needing seven to win or six to tie. This incident caused such a storm of criticism that Chappell's Test captaincy was at one stage in jeopardy. One-day crowds in Melbourne in 1980–81 were 52,990, 31,882, 30,590 and 23,601, and in Sydney 29,171, 28,555, 27,662, while the best Test crowd during the season was 28,671 for the first day of the Australia v. New Zealand Test in Melbourne.

This trend of bigger attendances for one-day cricket continued in 1981-82 when a world record 78,142 people watched

636

the one-day match at Melbourne on January 11, 1982, between Australia and West Indies at Melbourne. This was followed by a record attendance for a night match when 52,053 saw West Indies v. Australia in Sydney on January 19, 1982. But the players were clearly showing the strain of switching from Tests to one-day cricket and back again, and it showed in their performances. Wisely, the Australia Cricket Board arranged the 1982–83 programme so that all the one-day games are played after the Test series has been completed.

Australia has had a domestic limited over competition between the States since 1969–70, with a variety of sponsors. New Zealand has entered this competition several times. In the 13 years to the end of the 1981–82 season, Western Australia has won four times, Queensland and New Zealand three each, Victoria two and Tasmania one. New South Wales has yet to be successful although they have reached the final on many occasions.

A great fast-bowler, whose exceptional pace and exciting delivery style inspired an entire generation of young fast bowlers. Lindwall opening a Test match to Len Hutton has seldom been equalled as a sporting spectacle. Every stride Lindwall put in as he moved in to bowl toyed with the emotions of the crowd and by the time he swung his footballer's shoulders into the delivery you could almost touch the tension. Power, rhythm, balance, and aggression went into every one of the 13 strides Lindwall took to cover his 18-metre approach. He was a Test century-maker with a fierce drive, and an efficient field.

Lindwall, born in the Sydney suburb of Mascot, had uncommon control of length and direction, swung the ball sharply and late, and varied his speed and direction with extreme cunning. His bowling was all planned, from the moment he began his limbering-up exercises in the dressing room. He took only four minutes to bowl an eight-ball over. On the field he went through a sequence of stretching and bending exercises and removed his sweaters only when he was properly warmed up. His action at the instant of delivery was not as high as purists require but he preferred to retain a smooth arm action backed by strong body swing. He was 5 ft 11 ins tall and weighed around 12 stone but such was his pace spectators argued that he was well above 6 ft tall. He seldom let go his fastest ball until his third over.

When he came into the St George club's first grade team, aged 16, from Darlinghurst Marist Brothers College in Sydney, a magic eye camera was used to slow his bowling action and disclose faults and then Bill O'Reilly, his club captain showed him how to correct his faults. In Australia in the first Test se-

LINDWALL, Raymond Russell, 1921–

First-Class Averages: Batting, 5,042 runs at 21.82; Bowling, 794 wickets at 21.35.

Tests (61): 1,502 runs at 21.15; 228 wickets at 23.03.

637

ries after World War II against Hammond's MCC team, there was clear evidence that Lindwall dragged his back foot almost a metre before releasing the ball and the question of whether he should be no-balled arose. He watched a film of his drag, decided to increase his approach run by a pace and on the English tour in 1948 was seldom no-balled.

Indeed the 1948 tour was all triumph for Lindwall as well as for the Australian team and he came out of it established as one of the finest fast bowlers of all time. He was fortunate to have in Bradman a captain who used him shrewdly. Bradman let him work up to his peak in the early weeks of the tour and did not let him go until about a fortnight before the First Test at Nottingham. From then on Bradman used Lindwall in five and six over spells and only in Tests did spectators see Lindwall bowl more than 20 overs in an innings.

One abiding memory of Lindwall was his dedication to practice. He worked hard to master accuracy that seldom gave batsmen any respite. Even great players like Hutton, Compton and Washbrook found they had to play at almost every ball, and for a bowler who moved the ball a lot in the air Lindwall was on the stumps for over after over. Of the 86 wickets he took on the 1948 English tour, 43 were bowled, 11 leg-before-wicket, and 14 caught by the wicket-keeper.

Lindwall bowled with greater variety than Larwood and perfected an outstanding slower ball. He could bowl an over with every delivery of a different type but his faster ball and bouncer were so fiery at throat level batsmen always felt they were going backwards against him. It was extremely difficult to play forward to him such was the effect he had on the senses with his extra fast one. Len Hutton said the fact that Lindwall's arm was slightly low made the ball harder to sight.

Lindwall learned his cricket in the paddocks and back streets of the Sydney suburbs of Bexley and Mascot, often playing in games with wickets chalked out on a wall or when a kerosene tin served for a wicket. He once joked that the best innings he ever played was his 75 not out in a Bexley street with 120 boys fielding and hits over the fence on either side of the street were "six and out". The ball had to be very sharply driven to score runs and a lot of the innings was played in the dark. He hit his first formal century for Hurstville Convent in Sydney. He was always thankful for the guidance given by the brothers. At 15, he scored a double century and a century in one day, scoring 219 for Oatley Juniors in the morning and 110 for Carlton Waratahs in the adults competition in the afternoon.

Like his brother Jack, Ray developed into a first-class surf swimmer and rugby league player. Ray played full-back, Jack at outside centre. Both had exceptional pace and Ray was clocked to run 100 yards in 10.6 secs. Ray won a place in the

New South Wales team in 1941–42 against Queensland at 20.

He returned from service with the Army in New Guinea and the Solomon Islands in poor physical shape. Doctors thought he had malaria but tests disproved this. For weeks he needed injections and doses of atebrin tablets to overcome debilitating illnesses. He resumed playing football with St George and the regular training helped bring him back to full fitness, but after kicking a memorable goal in the 1946 Sydney League final against Canterbury he had to decide between concentrating on football or cricket. Experts have no doubt that he would have been a noted Test full-back had he not chosen cricket.

He resumed cricket for New South Wales in 1945–46 and scored 134 not out against Queensland, excelling on the drive. Regaining his bowling skills took a little longer, but he managed 9 for 80 against South Australia and was picked for the trip to New Zealand by Bill Brown's Australian side. Back in Australia he was selected for the first Test against Wally Hammond's side in Brisbane but after bowling in the first innings an attack of chicken pox prevented him taking further part in that match or in the Second Test.

Lindwall returned for the Third Test and showed his all-round value by dismissing Hutton and then combining with Tallon to score 154 runs in 87 minutes in a partnership that

Lindwall shows his value as a batsman with a strong pull shot for four.

639

Lindwall bowling against England at The Oval in 1953.

swung the match. Lindwall completed an exhilarating century in only 115 minutes but Tallon was out in the nineties. In the Fourth Test, Ray took three wickets in four deliveries, the closest he ever came to a Test hat-trick. The ball that cost him this rare feat missed Wright's stumps by a millimetre. Lindwall took the last four wickets in two overs for two runs.

In the Fifth Test, Lindwall took 7 for 63, ending the series with the best bowling average on either side, 18 wickets at 20.38 each. Such was Australia's bowling strength, however, he had to do well in the following summer's five Tests against India to make certain of his 1948 tour spot to England. He clinched the English trip with 7 for 38 in the Fourth Test. In an Australian side that included Lindwall, Miller and Bill Johnston, there were many who still considered Fred Freer unlucky to miss selection for the English tour.

With Miller, the black-haired extrovert of flamboyant manner, the quiet, fair-haired, modest Lindwall formed a thrilling opening attack, Bill Johnston filling in splendidly, if either was unfit or taking a rest. Lindwall and Miller were room-mates who wore each other's shirts, calmed each other down on the field, and pooled their small change on a dressing table without ever bothering to count it. Lindwall took 6 for 14 to rout Notts at Trent Bridge, twice ran through Sussex to finish with 11 for 59, took 8 for 131 in the Lord's Test, and at The Oval had 6 for 20 (5 for 8 before lunch) as England were tumbled out for 52, her lowest ever score in England.

In South Africa in 1949–50, Lindwall took 49 wickets for Lindsay Hassett's Australian team, setting up a win in the Second Test at Cape Town with 5 for 32 in South Africa's second innings. He returned to England in 1953 and 1956 in teams captained by Hassett and Ian Johnson but was not the same force he had been in 1948. In 1954–55, he made his highest Test score, 118 in the Barbados Test against the West Indies, and had some tremendous duels with Walcott, Worrell and Weekes.

Lindwall left New South Wales to play in Brisbane in 1954–55, and played for Queensland until he retired at the end of the 1959–60 season, the last five years as captain. Though his pace had slowed, he worked out a highly effective style of medium-pace swing bowling. One year when his outswinger failed, he discovered that his left arm was not being thrown as high as it should, causing him to bowl front-on instead of side-on to the batsman. He devised a contraption like a wall pulley and worked on it all winter, hauling his arm back high above his head as it should have been in his bowling action. Next summer his out-swinger was as deadly as ever, front arm up high.

In 61 Tests, Lindwall 12 times took five wickets in an innings. With the bat, he hit two centuries, five times making more than 50 and held 26 catches. In a career that saw him bowl out batsmen in all the cricket-playing nations, and took him into the Lancashire League for Nelson in 1952 (where fieldsmen couldn't hold the catches he provided and he had to hit the stumps to get batsmen out), Lindwall scored five first-class centuries and 34 times took five wickets in an innings. He took 123 catches. He captained Australia in one Test in 1956–57 in India for a draw.

LIVINGSTON, Leonard ("Jock"), 1920–

First-Class Averages: Batting, 15,269 runs at 45.04; Bowling, 4 wickets at 12.50.

An aggressive left-handed batsman and occasional wicket-keeper for New South Wales and Northamptonshire, with whom he played most of his first-class cricket. He made four double centuries for Northants in a county career that saw him score 13,165 runs at an average of 45.55. He also made 23 stumpings and held 149 catches in his career.

Livingston, a sprightly, bubbling character who gave some outstanding Rugby League football displays for South Sydney club just before World War II, played cricket for North Sydney and Randwick clubs and in five matches for New South Wales before he went overseas, scoring 100 not out against Queensland at Sydney in 1946–47. He pulled and hooked strongly and enjoyed getting on to the front foot to drive on either side of the stumps.

He played for Northants from 1950 to 1957. He made 210 against Somerset in 1951, 200 against Kent in 1954, and 207 not out against Nottinghamshire in 1954. He figured in a then record Northants' second wicket partnership of 299 unfinished in 1953 with D. Barrick against Sussex, and in 1951 put on 320 for the third wicket with F. Jakeman against South Africa, scoring 201 not out. A knee injury caused his early retirement.

Livingston, who had been playing in the Lancashire League, captained a Commonwealth team on a tour of India in 1949–50, India winning an unofficial Test series with a thrilling victory in the Fifth Test. The two Tests lost were the Commonwealth side's only defeats on a tour in which Livingston's sound captaincy did much to sustain interest in cricket in India. He made three centuries scoring 1,020 runs on the tour at 51.00, including 123 in the unofficial Test at New Delhi. Only Frank Worrell and Bill Alley scored more runs on that tour. He was among the first paid players to be admitted to membership of the MCC when it opened its ranks to professionals in 1961. In 1964, seven years after he retired he was invited to represent Australia in the MCC team that played Lancashire in the Lancashire Centenary match.

A top-rank right-arm fast bowler who with Alec Bedser formed the opening attack that enabled Surrey to win seven

LOADER, Peter James, 1929–

consecutive English County championships between 1952 and 1958. From a vigorous, high-stepping run, Loader swung the ball appreciably and when the shine left the ball varied his pace cleverly. He played 13 Tests for England and at Leeds in 1957 took the first post-war Test hat-trick against the West Indies. In all, he took 39 Test wickets at 22.51 and scored 76 Test runs at 5.84. In all first-class matches, he took 1,326 wickets at 19.04, including 9 for 17 for Surrey against Warwickshire at The Oval in 1958 and 9 for 28 against Kent at Blackheath in 1953. He took 100 wickets in a season four times in his years with Surrey. He toured Australia in 1958–59 and South Africa in 1956–57, but his chances in Tests were restricted in a period when England had a surfeit of quality pace bowlers. He migrated to Western Australia in 1964, and retired after only one appearance for the State to concentrate on his business life. He is a regular cricket broadcaster now in Perth.

LOCK, Graham Anthony Richard, 1929–

A multi-talented cricket prankster who in nine seasons for Western Australia proved the most successful left-arm spinner to play in Australia, a batsman with a surprising array of strokes, one of the most brilliant of all close to the wicket fieldsmen, and an imaginative inspiring captain. He is one of a select band of nine bowlers to take more than 300 wickets for their State.

Lock began at 17 with the Surrey County club as a bowler of generous flight, but in an era of over-prepared pitches did not become a match-winner until he changed his technique and bowled faster. He went to Surrey Colts in 1944 from Limpsfield School, and in 1946 with The Oval still scarred by the direct hits it had sustained from German bombs, he signed as a professional with the county. He won his county cap in 1950 and from 1952 played in Surrey teams that carried off the county championship seven years in succession. He swung many tense matches in that period with his bowling and superb catching close in on the leg side. In 1956 took all 10 Kent wickets in an innings at Blackheath, match bag 16 wickets. He was in the Surrey team which in May, 1956, became the first English county in 44 years to defeat Australia.

Twice he changed his action after being called for throwing, a staggering feat that could only have been attempted by a great bowler. He bowled the left-arm spinner's natural leg-break and one that went straight on with the arm, and never stopped experimenting to find ways of getting the ball past the bat. With Jim Laker he formed one of cricket's greatest slow bowling combinations.

Lock first altered his technique to suit slow turning pitches at The Oval, fizzing his faster ball at the batsman with what appeared a suspect action. When English officials congratulated Australian captain Lindsay Hassett on the grace with

642

which he congratulated Hutton's England side that had just won The Ashes at The Oval in 1953, Hassett said,"Not bad, I guess, seeing how we've been thrown out by Lock all summer." After watching films of his action Lock dropped the faster ball and gave the ball more air. This certainly helped on hard pitches during his seven overseas trips with English teams, only one of them to Australia.

Fun-loving Lock left Surrey to play for Western Australia after the 1963 English summer and played in the west from 1962–63 until 1970–71, taking over as captain in 1963–64, and leading Western Australia to the Shield in 1967–68. He played or coached for four district clubs in Perth, Claremont-Cottesloe, Subiaco, Midland-Guildford, and Bassendean-Bayswater and his coaching helped lay the foundation for Western Australia's strong showing in later Shield seasons.

He was colourful and foxy in all he did, arousing spectators with raucous appeals, continually plotting the downfall of the opposition, but always uncompromisingly fair. There was uproar at Sydney when umpires ordered him to remove ointment he had pasted over a hole in his spinning finger worn away by 20 years of trundling. At Melbourne when he was given out twice against Victoria in decisions that were plainly wrong, team-mates found him in the dressing-room with a powerful gas lighter setting fire to his bat.

Lock played for England in 49 Tests from 1952 to 1968, taking 174 wickets at 25.58, best figures 7 for 35. He made 742 Test runs at 13.74 and took 59 Test catches. He played for Leicestershire from 1965 until 1967 and was county captain in his last two years. He finished a first-class career that lasted from 1946 to 1971 with 2,844 wickets at 19.24, 10,336 runs at 15.90 and 827 catches. He took 100 wickets or more in a season 14 times and on four occasions took a hat-trick. Right to the end his fiery nature and exuberance enlivened every feature of his cricket. He broke all wicket-taking records in 74 matches for Western Australia, for whom he took 316 wickets at 24.50, held 85 catches, and scored 1,467 runs at 16.30, highest score 66. He became a naturalised Australian citizen early in 1982, aged 52.

A stalwart South Australian batsman between 1929–30 and 1934–35, scoring consistently despite a frail physique. In 1935–36 he played three times for New South Wales. In 1931–32, he made 586 runs at an average of 48.83 and was twice out within sight of a century against Queensland, with innings of 95 and 97. In 1933–34, against Victoria he made amends with knocks of 115 and 100 at Melbourne. Lonergan was deeply involved during the Bodyline tour by Jardine's team, batting six times against the MCC for 105 runs. Loner-

LONERGAN, Albert Roy, 1909–1956

First-Class Averages: Batting, 3,137 runs at 41.27.

gan hit nine centuries in his career, highest score 159 v. Victoria in 1930–31. He was involved in cricket administration for many years after his retirement.

LOVE, Hampden Stanley Bray ("Hammy"), 1895–1969

First-Class Averages: Batting, 2,906 runs at 35.01; Dismissals, 102 (73 catches, 29 stumpings).

Tests (1): 8 runs at 4.00; 3 catches.

A craftsmanlike wicket-keeper who had the misfortune to play at the same time as Bert Oldfield—which prevented Love's selection in many Tests. A popular, jovial figure, "Hammy" Love played for Victoria and New South Wales, and in one Test against England in 1932–33. He was Oldfield's replacement when Oldfield was struck on the head by Larwood in the Third Test of that "Bodyline" tour, taking over for the Fourth Test in Brisbane, scoring five and three, and taking three catches.

Love attended St Andrew's Cathedral School in Sydney, where he captained the First XI in 1911–12. He joined the Balmain club in Sydney after leaving school and built a reputation as a free-scoring wicket-keeper-batsman. He served as a corporal with the AIF in England in World War I and was one of three 'keepers chosen for the First AIF side, but had to return home for family reasons after the first match of the AIF tour.

He made 91 against Queensland in his debut for New South Wales in 1920–21, but then decided his opportunities in first-class cricket would be improved by moving to Victoria. He played for Carlton and later for St Kilda and in 1922–23 began five years as Victoria's 'keeper. He met with a lot of success with the bat, hitting six centuries at 56.70 but ironically the talents of Jack Ellis restricted his chances behind the stumps. He always joked about scoring only six when Victoria made the world record score of 1,107 in 1926–27 v. New South Wales. The next week he scored 188 against South Australia.

Love returned to New South Wales in 1927 and was Oldfield's deputy from 1927–28 to 1932–33. He toured India in 1935–36 with an Australian side led by Jack Ryder. He was a member of eight first grade premiership teams, four times with St Kilda, four with Mosman. In 54 first-class matches, he scored seven centuries.

LOXTON, Samuel John Everett, 1921–

A popular, genial, belligerent Victorian all-rounder whose all-out aggression more than compensated for his lack of style. He played some of the most entertaining knocks by an Australian in the years just after World War II, a born swashbuckler who loudly threatened to hit bowlers who bounced the ball at him over the fence. He bowled fast medium for long periods, moving the ball in the air, bustling the batsman as he got through his overs in smart times. He could field any-

644

where with distinction, for he moved quickly and had a strong throw—Don Tallon once complained about him pelting the ball in at him with unnecessary force when the batsmen were home, but that was the style of the man.

Loxton, born at Albert Park, Melbourne, went to Wesley College where one of his team-mates was Ian Johnson. Years later they played together for Victoria and Australia. Even at school Sam was all gusto, chin jutting out as he strode to the wicket. He first played for Victoria in 1946–47 and quickly established himself as an Australian team candidate by scoring 232 not out in his debut against Queensland at Melbourne. He was chosen as a player who could fill any number of roles if any of the brilliant specialists in the 1948 side for England was hurt.

Even in that team of brilliant cricketers, he established himself as a star in his own right when he hit five sixes in a glorious innings of 93 in the Fourth Test at Leeds. He was bowled when he swung and missed, trying for a sixth six, with Australia needing quick runs; lesser men would have closed up shop and prodded to 100. He played in three Tests, scoring 973 runs at 57.23 on the tour. At Essex when Australia made 721 in a day, he scored the third century of the innings with a dazzling 120 in 88 minutes. He also made 159 not out against Gloucester at Bristol and 123 against Middlesex at Lord's.

In his first Test against South Africa at Johannesburg in

First-Class Averages: Batting, 6,249 runs at 36.97; Bowling, 232 wickets at 25.73.

Tests (12): 554 runs at 36.93; 8 wickets at 43.62.

A characteristic shot of Sam Loxton swinging the ball to the leg fence.

1949–50, he scored 101 in 135 minutes, again when Australia desperately needed runs. It was his sole Test century, though he had three Test scores over 50. He made seven centuries for Victoria, and 13 in all first-class games, and three times took five wickets in an innings, best figures 6 for 49 against WA in 1956–57.

Loxton, 60, stood up at a Victorian Cricket Association in April, 1981, and announced that he was severing all connections with cricket, an association which had begun almost 50 years previously when he played for Prahran in the lower grades at the age of 12. He had lost the art of communicating with the players despite his years as a State and Australian selector since 1972, he said, and he was disenchanted with some aspects of the game. Loxton was a capable full forward with St Kilda from 1942–46 before he gave up football to concentrate on cricket. He scored 5,243 runs for Prahran at 32.36 and took 323 wickets for the club at 17.99. He was the Liberal party Whip in the Bolte and Hamer governments and the MLA for Prahran for a quarter of a century. He retired to live on Queensland's Gold Coast.

LUSH, John Grantley ("Ginty"), 1913–

First-Class Averages: Batting, 554 runs at 19.78; Bowling, 50 wickets at 26.92.

A colourful allrounder whose best years were lost to Australian cricket, firstly by his two years with Sir Julien Cahn's team in England and then by World War II. He was a fast bowler of tearaway pace, a splendidly aggressive middle order batsman, and a brilliant fieldsman. He was 6 ft tall, with dark curly hair, always well groomed, an Errol Flynn of Australian cricket.

Lush, born in the Melbourne suburb of Prahran, grew up in the Mosman district of Sydney. He played several seasons of first grade with Mosman "as a batsman who bowled like greased lightning but all over the place." When he moved one street out of the Mosman district, he played one season for North Sydney, changing his residence to go back to Mosman the next summer.

Despite outstanding performances in first grade he did not get his chance to play regularly for New South Wales until the latter half of the 1936–37 season. He was an immediate sensation. In February, 1937, against England at the SCG he bowled with fire and stamina to take 6 for 43 and 7 for 72. His 13 wickets in the match was still a record by a New South Wales bowler against England in 1982 and included three wickets in four balls. He topscored in the same match with a knock of 49 out of a New South Wales total of 231, going to the crease as Chipperfield left it with his jaw smashed by Ken Farnes. Lush was widely praised by his captain in that match, Alan McGilvray, and by critics who hailed him as a strong prospect for the Australian team to England in 1938.

646

Although Lush topped the Australian first-class bowling averages that season he was not chosen for the Fifth Test at Melbourne, for which selectors recalled Tasmanian Laurie Nash, who had not played in a first-class match that summer. Browned off at this treatment and at missing a berth in the team for England he was a willing victim when ex-Test player Alan Fairfax approached him to join Sir Julien Cahn's famous team at £600-a-year. At the time Lush earned £4.10.0 for a Shield match and £5 a week as a fourth year cadet journalist with a Sydney paper. Harold Mudge, Jack Walsh and Vic Jackson, similarly frustrated in their Australian careers, joined Lush in Cahn's side, along with Test players from New Zealand, South Africa and England. They lived in luxury but played cricket hard for a boss determined to win. Lush said playing for Cahn gave him more satisfaction than his Test contemporaries got touring England.

Lush toured New Zealand with Cahn's team in 1939. Then war began and he returned to Australia, his contract terminated. He joined the Gordon club, won back his State team place and, in 1946–47 found himself captain of New South Wales against England, sole survivor of the New South Wales side that had played the previous England team.

He led Gordon to the first grade premiership in 1945–46 and in 1947–48 when he made 201 not out in 164 minutes against University. In nine seasons with Gordon he made 3,119 runs at 31.83. He has long been one of the most popular characters in Australian journalism, cheery, genial, ageless.

LYONS, John James, 1863–1927

First-Class Averages: Batting, 6,751 runs at 25.57; Bowling, 107 wickets at 30.04.

Tests (14): 731 runs at 27.07; 6 wickets at 24.83.

One of the most spectacular hitters in the history of Australian cricket, a South Australian right-hander who played several daring innings in the early years of Test and inter-Colonial matches. He bowled effective fast-medium pacers early in his career but concentrated on his batting towards the end. He was a safe but unenthusiastic field.

Lyons was born at Gawler, South Australia, and moved with his family to Adelaide as a small child. He played his early cricket with Royal Park and later joined Norwood. Unlike other noted big hitters such as Bonnor, Massie and McDonell, whose heaviest blows were confined to drives, he could hit with exceptional power all around the wicket. His timing was so good he often appeared to just block shots that cleared the fieldsman. His footwork was quick and confident and he often left good fast and medium-pace bowlers frustrated over where to pitch them. Only top quality leg-break bowlers worried him.

He first played for South Australia in 1884–85 at the age of 21, and he toured England three times, in 1888, 1890 and 1893, when he was in his prime. He made 489 runs at 13.21 on his

first trip, 1,142 at 17.84 on the second, and 1,527 at 28.27 on the third in all matches. At Lord's in the 1890 Test he hit 55 out of 66 in 45 minutes and later took 5 for 30. On the same ground he made 99 out of 117 in 75 minutes against MCC in 1890.

He played the innings of his life in 1893 at Lord's. Australia followed-on 181 runs in arrears, and in 90 minutes Lyons and A. C. Bannerman made exactly that number for the first wicket. Lyons reached his century in an hour and when he was out for 149 he had hit 22 fours. Haygarth records that during this innings Lyons hit the ball on the roof of a temporary stand, over the awning in front of the grandstand, over the spectators in front of the old tennis court, and into the enclosure in front of the player's room. On the same tour he made 75 out of 102 in 70 minutes against the North at Manchester.

In Australia, Lyons played in Tests between 1887 and 1897, heading the Australian averages in 1891–92 with 287 runs at 47.83 in three matches, including a daring, match-winning innings against England at Sydney. Australia, 162 behind on the first innings, lost G. H. S. Trott for one and were in a desperate position when Lyons went in. He scored 134 of the 174 runs added for the second wicket with A. C. Bannerman in 165 minutes, and Australia eventually won the match by 72 runs.

Apart from his two memorable centuries against England, Lyons scored 101 for Australia's 1888 team against New South Wales, 134, 104, 101, 135, 110 and 113 for South Australia against Victoria, and 145 and 124 for South Australia against New South Wales. Batting for South Australia in Sydney in 1891–92 he hit a ball with such force it broke an iron paling in front of the pavilion. For Norwood against North Adelaide in 1891, he took all ten wickets in an innings. After his retirement from cricket he became a stockbroker.

M

A right-hand opening batsman who scored eight centuries and a double century for Victoria and thousands of runs for the East Melbourne club but disappointed in his eight appearances for Australia. He was the centre of a dispute between the Board of Control and the manager of the 1909 Australian team to England, Frank Laver, and in 1911–12 was involved in a protracted fist fight with fellow selector Clem Hill in the Sydney offices of the NSWCA. He was a spare, wiry six-footer, so gentle of manner in later years that it was difficult to believe he had been involved in such a brawl.

McAlister, born at Williamstown, first played for Victoria in 1898–99, when he made 224 for the State against New Zealand at Melbourne. He was befriended by the Victorian secretary of the Board of Control, Ernie Bean, and thereafter became active in administration. He made his Test debut in the Fourth Test against England at Sydney in 1903–04, scoring 2 and 1. He made 36 and 9 in the Fifth Test of that series but missed a place in the Australian team that toured England in 1905. Following Reg Duff's retirement he was tried as an opener with Trumper in the First Test in 1907–08 when he made his highest Test score, 41, in the second innings. Despite this effort he could not retain a regular Test place.

The Board annoyed all Australia's leading players by appointing McAlister vice-captain and treasurer of the 1909 side in England. He scored 816 runs at 29.14 on the tour but failed in the two Tests in which he was tried again as an opener. The players returned home adamant that he was below Test class. When the Board asked for his books on the tour finances, he confessed he had not kept any as he had received no clear-cut instructions as treasurer. He continued in first-class cricket until the end of the following season, 1909–10 but remained active as a selector and administrator. There is a touch of irony in the fact that such a pleasant, well-meaning character should be remembered more for his fisticuffs than his batting or hard-work behind the scenes.

McALISTER, Peter Alexander, 1869–1938

First-Class Averages: Batting, 4,552 runs at 32.74; Bowling, 3 wickets at 18.66.

Tests (8): 252 runs at 16.80.

649

MACARTNEY, Charles George ("The Governor-General"), 1886–1958

First-Class Averages: Batting, 15,019 runs at 45.78; Bowling, 419 wickets at 20.95.

Tests (35): 2,131 runs at 41.78; 45 wickets at 27.55.

An all-rounder of rich gifts who matured late in a Test career that spanned 19 years. He was at his best at 40, a mercurial right-handed batsman who played some of big cricket's finest innings, a left-arm slow bowler who clean bowled all the great batsmen of his time off a five-metre run, and a fieldsman of rare talent with safe hands, powerful forearms and a superb flicked throw. At his peak he was a great entertainer, commanding the crease as if it was his personal stage.

Macartney with a bat in his hands could be brilliantly unorthodox and yet profoundly safe. He had the great batsman's gift of being able to change his mind in mid-stroke, hitting the ball over mid-on which he had originally intended to crash through the covers. Few players have so effectively blasted out of the attack bowlers who posed a threat to Australia's winning chances. He did not try to hide his annoyance when he played a maiden over.

He was supreme in assessing the imminent danger from a bowler of skill who ruined his team's innings. "Don't worry", he would say to a batsman just dismissed, as he went to bat. "I'll fix him". The great English cricket writer R. C. Robertson-Glasgow, wrote: "Macartney's batting suggested a racket player who hits winners from any position. Length could not curb him, and his defence was lost and included in his attack. No Australian batsman, not even Bradman, has approached him for insolence of attack. He made slaves of bowlers."

Macartney worked as a junior clerk for a produce store in Sussex Street, Sydney in 1902. At lunchtime the staff played cricket on a nearby wharf, using a bag of chaff as a wicket, a lump of packing case for a bat and potatoes as a ball. Charlie had gone to this job after schooling at Woollahra Public School and Fort Street High School, when it was near Circular Quay, and finally at Chatswood.

He had no coaching as a boy but went on to make 49 first-class centuries. He was born at West Maitland but made Chatswood Oval his spiritual home, practising there each morning as a schoolboy and even after he became a Test player. He played three seasons for North Sydney but was a foundation member when the Gordon club was formed in 1905. He learned by careful study of the great players of his time but had the confidence to bring his own special brand of audacity to his batting. He always considered that some of the easiest balls he would face came in the first over he received and whether he opened or went in first wicket down he relished hitting one of those first few balls straight back past the bowler.

From the start of his career in big cricket in 1905–06, Macartney had a curious air of ascendancy at the crease but in the beginning he did not make the scores to back it up. Incredibly, considering his later success, his batting was brand-

650

ed as awkward and crude by critics who found more merit in his bowling. The sceptics appeared to be right when, after a moderate debut in Tests with the bat in Australia, Macartney averaged only 18.50 in Tests on his initial English tour in 1909. In all games on that tour he made 638 runs at 19.33, but he finished third in the tour bowling averages with 71 wickets at 17.46. In the Leeds Test he took 7 for 58 and 4 for 27. He actually went in last in matches on that trip.

Australia's opening pair Duff and Trumper had been broken after Duff played his last Test in England in 1905, Macartney was promoted to open with Trumper in 1907–08. What in retrospect looks a dynamic pairing, was not particularly successful, however. When he was chosen for the unhappy tour of England in 1912, Macartney went in first wicket down. He made an outstanding 99 at Lord's, but in missing a full toss he tried to hit for six, and finished second on the tour averages to Bardsley, with 2,207 runs at 45.04 and heading the bowling averages with 43 at 16.34.

By the end of World War I Macartney's batting overshadowed his bowling. He played in only two Tests v. Johnny Douglas' MCC side in 1920–21 because of illness and injury but made a thrilling 170 at Sydney. He returned to England in 1921 in triumphant form. Against Nottinghamshire at Trent Bridge he made 345 in 233 minutes after being missed in the slips at nine. He hit 47 fours and four sixes, Australia scored 675, and won the match by an innings and 517 runs. After an innings like that his captains made less use of him as a bowler, but to many English critics Macartney remains one of the best left-arm bowlers Australia ever sent to England, though he bowled only 153 overs on the 1921 tour.

At Leeds in 1926 Macartney played another superfine innings. Going in after Bardsley had been dismissed off the first ball of the match, he survived a catch to first slip, which Carr spilt with the score at two, to score 112 before lunch. He was out after 180 minutes batting for 151, with Australia's score on 235. In 1982, Macartney, Trumper and Bradman remain the only Australians to have scored 100 before lunch on the first day in a Test against England.

Macartney's 151, one of the most praised innings in cricket, came when he was 40, and was preceded by 133 at Lords and followed by 109 at Manchester. But none of these knocks matched his 160 on the tour against Lancashire, at Manchester. It was a fitting climax to a remarkable career. In his 35 Tests Macartney scored seven centuries and nine times exceeded 50. As well as touring England four times he also visited South Africa (1921–22), North America (1913), New Zealand (with NSW in 1923–24), India (with Tarrant in 1935–36). Macartney played the 1909–10 season with Otago.

"When Macartney drove, it was as though he had been wound up like a spring and someone had released the coil," wrote Johnny Moyes. "Attack was his motto, and he believed that once you got on top, the bowler did not come back. I recall a club match with Gordon in which we got the opposition out for something just over 100, with not much more than an hour left for play on the first day. Charlie said, 'We'd better get them tonight—it might rain next Saturday.' And Gordon had a lead by six o'clock."

After his retirement from big cricket, Macartney went on playing for Gordon in Sydney grade matches, as perky as ever, peppering buildings adjacent to Chatswood Oval with his sixers. Between 1905 and 1934, he played 158 innings for Gordon, scoring 7,638 runs at 48.34 and took 547 wickets at 14.46. He scored more runs, 824, in a first grade season (1914–15) than any Gordon batsman and in 1982 still held the record for the club's highest first grade score—227 in 1913–14.

Sydney Cricket Ground members applaud as Charles Macartney, one of Australia's greatest batsmen, goes confidently out to the crease.

McCABE, Stanley Joseph ("Napper"), 1910–1968

First-Class Averages: Batting, 11,951 runs at 49.38; Bowling, 159 wickets at 33.72.

Tests (39): 2,748 runs at 48.21; 36 wickets at 42.86.

A courageous and stylish right-hand batsman, a virtuoso who played three historic innings. Spread over six years, all three knocks were produced in adversity, with powerful yet artistic strokes that uplifted the senses of all who saw them. McCabe scored 26 other centuries in big cricket, but in these three innings, each in a different country, he gave Australian batsmanship some of its finest moments.

McCabe, son of a barber from the New South Wales country town of Grenfell, played all bowling skilfully, but pace drew from him a daring array of hooks, drives and cuts. From a beautifully balanced stance, he scored with a freedom that made other batsmen look hacks. He was a splendid fieldsman in any position, and bowled a brisk medium pace accurately enough to worry the best batsmen of his time, occasionally producing a googly of surprising nip.

In his first match for St Joseph's College, Sydney, McCabe made a duck. In his first match for New South Wales Seconds, he made a duck. Chosen for New South Wales as a Country Week player, he got another duck in 1928–29 in his first first-class match. In his first Test innings in 1930, he hit a four off the first ball and was out off the second. He was able to dismiss these failures because of a fluent, copybook technique. He took the bat straight back over the middle stump and brought it back as straight as a rifle barrel, a short, stocky figure with powerful arms and flexible wrists, always immaculate in appearance.

He was chosen in St Joseph's first XI at 14 and held his place for three years. After leaving school he played for Grenfell Juniors. He first played for New South Wales at 18 and for Australia at 20, when he toured England with Woodfull's team in 1930, with a single first-class century against Tasmania in 1929–30 to his credit. He made 1,012 runs on that first overseas tour at 32.66, but he looked so promising he was included in all five Tests. He made 49 in the First Test, 44 in the Second, 54 in the Fifth, and took 4 for 41 in the Fourth Test, returning home a seasoned international.

In 1931–32 he made 229 not out for New South Wales against Queensland at Brisbane, 106 and 103 not out against Victoria, for a Shield average that summer of 438. He also averaged 33.50 in five Tests against South Africa. He was just past his 21st birthday, had 15 Tests behind him, but his parents had never seen him play in a big match so he decided to invite them down from Grenfell for the first match at Sydney against England in 1932–33.

McCabe had to go to the wicket with Australia 3 for 82, after weeks of newspaper criticism of England's bodyline tactics. His main worry was his mother, an excitable woman. "Dad, if I get hit out there today, you keep Mum from jumping the fence," he told his father. Then he went out and played one of cricket's great knocks, hooking the first ball he received from Larwood to the fence in front of deep square leg. He kept hooking balls off his eyebrows as if the bat was a magic wand, casting an occasional glance at where his mother was sitting.

"The crowd really shaped the innings." McCabe wrote years later. "With them yelling and cheering, my reaction was to hit at almost every ball. It was really an impulsive, senseless innings, a gamble that should not have been made but came off against all the odds. Vic Richardson helped me add 129 but when he was out Australia was in trouble again. I was hit once or twice about the shoulders by bouncers but not painfully or hard enough to bring Mum in over the fence."

653

England's captain Jardine brought "Gubby" Allen on and McCabe struck him for three handsome fours in a row. Jardine demanded that Allen bowl to his packed legside field but Allen refused. "You can take me off," Allen said. In the end Jardine dropped the leg-side attack and brought on Hammond, Verity and the other English bowlers to bowl orthodox stuff. Not out on 130 that night, McCabe scored a further 57 next morning, 49 of them for the tenth wicket in a partnership of 55 with Tim Wall. McCabe's 187 not out took 240 minutes but Australia lost the match by 10 wickets. "Larwood took 5 for 96 and 5 for 28, with Australia all out for 164 in our second innings, so it was really Larwood's match not mine," McCabe said.

McCabe scored 385 runs in the five Tests against Jardine's team, average 42.77, but he could not recapture in the other Tests the form of his 187 not out innings. But he returned to form in England in 1934, scoring eight centuries, more than any team-mate, including 240, the highest score of his career, against Surrey at The Oval, and 137 in the Third Test at Old Trafford, blossoming, as *Wisden* said, as a complete batsman of the forcing type.

In 1935–36 on tour in South Africa he hit 149 in the First Test at Durban, adding 161 with Billy Brown, and a memorable 189 not out in the Second Test at Johannesburg, where he put on 177 with Fingleton. Many regard this as his finest knock. After Dudley Nourse had scored a magnificent 231, Australia were set 399 to win on a turning pitch in the last innings when McCabe began, dark clouds gathering, Australia 1 for 17.

In his first 40 minutes he made 50, 40 of them from boundaries, with Fingleton struggling at the other end to keep out shooters and unexpected breaks. Australia appealed against the light and won the appeal to go off at 1 for 85, with a day to play. Next day McCabe thrashed the South African bowlers in a seemingly endless flow of boundaries. Fingleton went for a plucky 40 and Len Darling joined McCabe, who completed his 100 runs before lunch. With both batsmen hard pressed to sight the ball in appalling light, McCabe rushed the Australian score to 2 for 274—only 125 away from victory with 180 minutes left—and his own score to 189, with 29 fours.

Then came a moment in cricket history, with South African captain Herbie Wade appealing against the light, grumbling that there was danger to his players the way McCabe was hitting. The umpires agreed and the players left the field. Further rain fell and the match ended in a draw. McCabe headed our Test batting on that tour with 420 runs at an average of 84.00.

McCabe's third classic innings came in 1938 in the First Test at Trent Bridge where England batted first and scored 8 for 658 declared. Fighting for a draw, Australia lost 6 for 194. Then Mccabe set about the bowling, scoring 232 out of the 300 added while he was at the crease. At the end Hassett was out for 1, Badcock 9, Barnett 22, O'Reilly 9, Ward 2, McCormick 2 and Fleetwood-Smith 5. McCabe made 44 off three overs from Wright and finished by adding 72 out of 77 runs in 28 minutes with Fleetwood-Smith for the last wicket.

"When Stan returned to the dressing-room at the conclusion of this epic performance," Don Bradman wrote in his book *Farewell to Cricket*, "I was so moved by the superb majesty of his performance that I could scarcely speak. I gripped his hand, wet with perspiration. He was trembling like a thoroughbred racehorse. I recall expressing my congratulations and saying 'I would give a great deal to be able to play an innings like that.'"

Ironically in a batsman with such quicksilver footwork, McCabe suffered from foot trouble and this shortened his career. Even when he could not run the length of the pitch, however, he still gave some superfine displays of stroke-making, timing so sweet he almost caressed the ball to the fence. He captained New South Wales from 1936–37 until his retirement in 1941–42. In 182 first-class games, he hit 29 centuries, 68 half centuries. His highest score was 240 versus Surrey in 1934.

For Australia in his 39 Tests spread over eight years, he had 13 innings over 50 as well as the six centuries, topscore 232. His medium pacers brought handy wickets but only once did he take five wickets in an innings, results which disguise events such as his dismissal of Hammond at The Oval in 1930, which probably decided the series. He made 139 first-class catches, 41 in Tests.

McCabe died in a fall from a cliff at the rear of his home in the Sydney suburb of Mosman. He had for many years run a sports store in Sydney. He was Mosman district club's first international player. The NSWCA awarded him and Bill O'Reilly a Testimonial match at Sydney in 1956–57 from which they each received £3,570.

McCabe went bald in his early twenties, but that was not the source of his nickname. This came about when he appeared suddenly through a disused door while an Australian team was inspecting Napoleonic heirlooms at Fontainebleau, near Paris. Surprised team-mates said he looked like Napoleon's ghost and thereafter called him "Napper."

McCOOL, Colin Leslie, 1915–

One of Australia's best all-rounders immediately after World War II. He could field at first slip better than anyone of his era, bat well enough to score a Test 100, and as a leg-spin bowler produced a spectacle for connoisseurs by defying purists with an almost round-arm action to dismiss master batsmen. McCool, a short, powerful man of studious manner,

First-Class Averages:
Batting, 12,420 runs at
32.85; Bowling, 602
wickets at 27.47.

Tests (14): 459 runs at
35.30; 36 wickets at
26.61.

played in 14 Tests and would have played in a lot more but for the introduction of a law that enabled captains to take a new ball every 65 overs, discarding their spinners for continual pace.

Playing for Paddington in Sydney grade matches he was almost unplayable on badly prepared pitches, so wide and sharp was the turn of his leg-breaks. If "Paddy" Ryan, the horny-handed curator at Trumper Park, neglected to water the practice pitches, McCool made even State batsmen look inept. McCool would then walk away to a roller in the corner of the ground and spend an hour taking catches from balls thrown into the side of the roller—and my, how he could catch!

He bowled with a curious round-arm action, flipping the ball at the batsman from an arm almost parallel with the pitch. Famous bowlers tried to alter his action when he first came to the notice of State selectors. He tried alternative methods briefly but always returned to his natural style. He got a wicket with only his second ball in Tests to dismiss the last New Zealand batsman at Wellington in 1945–46 and clinch victory for Bill O'Reilly's Australian team. Just before the first international series against England after the war he left Paddington to play in Queensland, where he formed a formidable partnership with Tallon. McCool's spin and Tallon's stumping speed put enormous pressure on batsmen.

Both were chosen for the first series after World War II against Hammond's team after McCool had made the best score of his career, 172, for Queensland against SA at Adelaide the previous season. McCool opened his career against England with 95 at Brisbane, took eight wickets in the Second Test at Sydney, hit 104 not out to save the Third Test at Melbourne, and took 5 for 44 to bring victory in the Fifth Test at Sydney. He finished that series against Hammond's team with 18 wickets in five matches at 27.27 and 272 runs at 54.40. But spinning his leg breaks tore a callous off his third finger whenever he bowled lengthy spells in England in 1948, and he did not play in a Test though he took 57 wickets. For the rest of his career McCool, an extremely fair man with soft skin, was troubled by the skin rubbing off his spinning finger.

McCool's leg-breaks proved extremely useful to Lindsay Hassett's side in South Africa in 1949–50. He took 51 wickets on tour, including 5 for 41 off 11.4 overs in the Second Test at Cape Town, and played in all five Tests. His catching remained a joy, and he contributed several fine innings with the bat. He hit 100 not out v. Western Province and in the Third Test at Durban helped Australia to an exciting victory with 39 not out in an unfinished stand of 106 with Harvey. This enabled Australia to win after being dismissed for 75 in the first innings.

Before the 1953 Australian side for England was named,

Rod Marsh taking a catch to dismiss Gooch off Jeff Thomson in the First Test at Edgbaston in 1975.

Right: Jeff Thomson's famous delivery stride, with the front-arm well up as he prepares to power the ball into the pitch.

Left: Len Pascoe's powerful arm action in closeup.

McCool joined East Lancashire, and in 1956, aged 40, qualified for Somerset where he scored 1,000 runs in each of his five years with the County, distinguishing himself as one of the best Australian cricketers Somerset has had since the legendary Sammy Woods. His best season was in 1956 when he made 1,967 runs at 37.80, and the best of many fine bowling feats was his 8 for 74 against Nottinghamshire in 1958.

In 251 first-class matches he made 18 centuries and took five wickets in an innings 34 times, twice taking 10 wickets in a match. He held 261 catches as a fieldsman and made one catch and two stumpings as a substitute 'keeper. When he returned from England after finishing his professional career, he became a market gardener at Umina, near Gosford, NSW, growing rare blooms. His son Russell, one of the best prospects among Australia's young leg-spinners, delivering the ball from far higher up than his dad, but turning it almost as sharply, signed a contract in 1982 to play for Somerset. Russell was born at Taunton, when his father was with Somerset.

McCORMICK, Ernest Leslie ("Goldie"), 1906–

A dark-thatched, Melbourne jeweller ("I'm one of Cupid's best friends") who bowled off probably the longest run (31 paces) used by an Australian fast-bowler, and turned in some of the funniest gags and most ferocious bowling in the decade before World War II. McCormick marked out his run as though he needed engineers to help him, beginning with a series of skips, followed by around 20 running strides, arms stiff at his sides, but when his run-in got him to the stumps on line, his pace on to the bat was hair-raising. He once bounced the ball off the head of his club captain at Richmond, Les Keating, and on successive Saturdays broke the jaws of North Melbourne's Roy Watters and Essendon's Ian Leembruggen.

McCormick was born at North Carlton and learned his cricket at Yarra Park School, Punt Road, Richmond, and with the Richmond district club. His father, J. L. McCormick, was one of the founders of La Mascotte Club, parent body of the Collingwood Club. Ernie began as a wicket-keeper but he was so fast and fiery at the practice nets Les Keating persuaded him to switch to pace bowling. He batted left-handed and bowled right-handed like Jack Gregory. He suffered from chronic lumbago for most of his career. He had extremely long arms and finished with fingertips near the ground after following through.

He moved in to bowl without swinging his arms. When his action worked, he let the ball go from a fluent high arm swing with enough of his 6 foot tall frame behind it to produce pace that had the finest batsmen in the world flinching. He operated mostly in the years after the Bodyline tour and when he hit a batsman spectators often heckled him for trying to

First-Class Averages: Batting, 582 runs at 8.68; Bowling, 241 wickets at 27.74.

Tests (12): 54 runs at 6.00; 36 wickets at 29.97.

maim them, ignorant of the fact that he bowled only with two short legs.

McCormick played his first match for Victoria in 1929–30, consistently heading the Melbourne grade competition averages. Team-mates like Bill Woodfull saw in him a bowler who could return some of the hidings they were taking from overseas fast bowlers, but Ernie did not win selection for a Test until 1935–36 when at the age of 29 he was picked for the Australian tour of South Africa. He took a wicket with his first ball in South Africa, and took 15 wickets in the Test series at 27.86. At Johannesburg he had a spell of 3 for 9 in the second innings of the Fourth Test finishing with 3 for 28. "I did so little bowling in South Africa it was only like normal exercise", he said. "I'd bowl the shine off the ball and then those vultures who feed off the bones of fast-bowlers, the spinners, would grab it."

In his first Test against England at Brisbane in 1936–37 he took a wicket with the first ball of the match for the second time in an international series, dismissing Worthington. He followed by taking the wickets of Hammond and Fagg and after four overs had 3 for 16. His fastest spell came in 1936–37 when he took 9 for 40 off 11 overs for Victoria against South Australia at Adelaide. Bradman gave two chances before he was out and Maurice Seivers was most upset when he took the last wicket at the other end and deprived McCormick of all 10 wickets. In 1938–39, he took 5 for 62 against New South Wales. There were only six occasions in a long career that he took five wickets or more in an innings but he dismissed the first two or three batsmen dozens of times.

Umpire Harry Baldwin no-balled McCormick eight times for over-stepping in the first over of his first match in England in 1938 and 35 times in 20 overs during the match. Ernie told team-mates not to worry. "I'll be right after lunch", he said. "The umpire's hoarse." McCormick sent down 54 no-balls in his first 48 overs on that tour and achieved a century of no-balls by the tenth match. He tried everything to correct the problem, practising with caps and handkerchiefs to mark key spots on his run-up, working off a six-pace run, slowing his pace to slow-medium. With plenty of time to swing the bat under the old back foot rule, batsmen scored off 49 of his century no-balls.

Before the Lord's Test, McCormick studied a film of the team's matches taken by Billy Brown and reasoned that he had lost his bowling rhythm because of his characteristic stiff-armed approach. He started to pump his arms as he ran in and took 3 for 14 in his first spell with scarcely any no-balls. That most diligent of researchers, Ray Robinson, recorded that McCormick dismissed nine opening batsmen in the 11 innings in which he bowled against England, and averaged a wicket every 59 balls through his Test career.

658

Playing golf in Ireland McCormick hit his ball into high grass and disappeared into the grass to look for it. After a long search Ernie called, "Have you found it?" The caddy replied that he had just stepped on the ball. "Then come and look for me", hollered McCormick, whose career ended when he joined the RAAF in 1939. His State and grade appearances were invariably amusing romps. One of his best was when he and Fleetwood-Smith swung at every ball to add 90 for the tenth wicket for Victoria against Queensland at Melbourne in 1934–35. Ernie was dropped 13 times, Fleetwood-Smith 11, but Ernie made 77, his topscore in first-class cricket.

A right-handed batsman who won an international reputation as an opener after struggling for years for recognition in the middle of the batting order. A neat, tidy strokemaker with a solid defence, he proved a superb timer of the ball in many valuable knocks for New South Wales and Australia after making a hard-won debut in first-class cricket at the age of 26. His courage became a cricket legend when he returned to bat in Australia's second innings in the Centenary Test at Melbourne after having his jaw and his stumps broken by a Willis bouncer in the first innings.

McCOSKER, Richard Bede ("Rick"), 1946–

First-Class Averages: Batting, 7,107 runs at 43.34.

Tests (25): 1,622 runs at 39.56.

Rick McCosker hammers the ball away behind point.

McCosker drives through the covers, feet perfectly positioned.

McCosker, born in the New South Wales country town of Inverell 674 kilometres from Sydney, did not move south until he was twenty. He joined the Sydney club as a third grader, pushed his way into first grade in his first season, but took a further five seasons to impress the New South Wales selectors. In the 1972–73 season, he made 48 for New South Wales Colts against Victoria and finished second in the Sydney grade averages with 565 runs at 40.36. He was within a fortnight of his 27th birthday when he first played for New South Wales in November, 1973. He made only 13 against South Australia in his first knock and did not bat in the second innings, but the selectors gave him a further chance a week later against Western Australia. This time he made an impressive 71 not out, and he finished that summer a confirmed member of the State side after scoring 346 runs at 49.43 an innings.

In 1974–75, he failed in the first State match at Brisbane and was dropped by Inverarity before he had scored in the second match against Western Australia, with New South Wales chasing 422. From there he scored 138, followed by 136 not out in the second innings, New South Wales escaping with a draw. Wally Edwards, who had made a century in that fateful Western Australia v. New South Wales match, was tried as an Australian opener in the first three Tests that summer against Mike Denness's Englishmen but when Edwards flopped the selectors gambled with McCosker in the Fourth Test. He capped his rise from an obscure No. 6 to Test opener, by making a fine 80.

At the end of that triumphant Australian season he went to England in 1975 for the Prudential Cup series and four Tests against England. Again his sound, thoughtful methods paid off and he finished second only to Doug Walters on the Australian averages for the trip, with 1,078 runs at 59.88, topscore 127 in the Fourth Test at The Oval, after innings of 59 in the First Test at Birmingham, 79 in the Second Test at Lord's and 95 not out in the abandoned Third Test at Leeds. Against Sussex he had innings of 111 and 115.

Then followed his plucky knock in March 1977, in the Centenary Test at Melbourne, broken jaw strapped, every movement painful as he helped add valuable runs. That year he also toured New Zealand and made a second tour of England, this time scoring 737 runs at 23.77. He joined World Series Cricket in 1977–78. He appeared in seven Super Tests with WSC, scoring 306 runs at 21.85, with one century—129 v. The World in 1977–78.

When a settlement was negotiated between WSC and traditional cricket in 1979–80, McCosker returned as New South Wales captain, and immediately added to his fine record with centuries against Western Australia (123) at Perth and against Tasmania (115 not out) at Launceston. In 1980–81 he led New

660

South Wales in a determined but vain bid to regain the Sheffield Shield. He made 168 that season against WA—his highest score. He moved to Newcastle to further his career in law at the end of that summer but was able to continue in first-class cricket. In the 1981–82 season he scored two centuries in a match for the third time in his career when he made 123 and 118—both unbeaten—against Victoria in Sydney, and finished the season with four centuries, taking his career total to 23. McCosker and John Dyson continued their splendid record of good opening stands—they hold the NSW record of 319 for the first wicket, which they established in 1980–81 against WA—with a stand of 253 in a limited over game against SA in 1981–82, a record for this style of cricket.

McDONALD, Colin Campbell, 1928–

A plucky right-hand opening batsman for Australia between 1952 and 1961 who turned back many hostile attacks. He used little backlift and was very forceful off the back foot when bowlers gave him the chance to cut or pull. His cut behind point was a memorable stroke, hit crisply and along the turf with power. Going in first, he took many painful blows from pace bowlers like Wes Hall.

McDonald, born at Glen Iris, Victoria, came up through Scotch College and Melbourne University, where he formed a fine opening pairing with George Thoms. He played in an era when pace bowlers were just starting to bowl two or three bouncers an over and umpires were looking for official guidance on this habit. He first played for Victoria in 1947–48, when Australia had a surfeit of outstanding players, and made his first century for Victoria in 1949–50 with 186 against South Australia at Adelaide.

He made his debut for Australia in 1951–52 against the West Indies after an innings of 207 against New South Wales at Sydney. He played in five series in Australia, toured England three times (1953, 1956 and 1961), twice toured India and Pakistan (1956–57, 1959–60), toured the West Indies in 1954–55 and South Africa in 1957–58. He captained Victoria from 1958 until 1963, taking over from Neil Harvey.

In the 1952–53 series in Australia against South Africa, McDonald scored 437 runs, including a splendid 154 in the Fourth Test at Adelaide. At Lord's in 1956, he put on 137 for the first wicket with Jim Burke in an innings of 78. He was Australia's leading batsman in the 1958–59 series in Australia against England, scoring 519 runs at 64.87, including 170 in the Fourth Test at Adelaide and 133 in the Fifth Test at Melbourne.

His 170 at Adelaide featured an opening stand of 171 with Burke and controversy after McDonald was hurt and returned with a runner. Umpire Mal McInnes looked the wrong way

First-Class Averages: Batting, 11,375 runs at 40.48; Bowling, 3 wickets at 64.00.

Tests (47): 3,106 runs at 39.32.

and gave McDonald not out to a confident appeal, with McDonald's runner Jimmy Burke behind him. McDonald then took things into his own hands by swinging wildly until he was bowled by Trueman.

McDonald retired soon after the end of the memorable 1960–61 series in Australia against the West Indies after facing Wes Hall with determination that was a model for opening batsmen. His 91 in front of 90,800 people at Melbourne helped swing the rubber Australia's way. In 47 Tests he made five centuries and 17 scores over 50, a tribute to his toughness and 24 centuries in all first-class matches, topscore 229. He made 53 catches and two stumpings. After his retirement, he worked for a time in insurance, then he formed his own insurance broking firm, which he sold in 1977 when he became Executive Director of the Lawn Tennis Association of Australia. The finest tribute to McDonald's tenacity was his batting at Manchester in 1956 when Jim Laker took 19 wickets for England. McDonald made 32 and 89 after leaving the field with a leg injury in the second innings.

McDONALD, Edgar Arthur ("Ted"), 1891–1937

First-Class Averages: Batting, 2,663 runs at 10.44; Bowling, 1,395 wickets at 20.76.

Tests (11): 116 runs at 16.57; 43 wickets at 33.27.

One of the best fast bowlers of all time, who played in only 11 Test matches for Australia—three against South Africa and eight against England. He had a splendid physique, tall and heavy-shouldered but had a temperament which prevented him exerting himself against lesser batsmen. Bowling against great players, however, he was a sight for connoisseurs, moving through his 15-pace approach run with high, superbly balanced steps and into a delivery action that was smooth and without strain. Ian Peebles, respected English critic, noted that McDonald left no mark on the softest of ground so well co-ordinated was his approach.

He was a very difficult bowler to face at his best, for he could move the ball either way and vary his pace subtly through his controlled arm swing. "His greatest performances were when his side was in most urgent need," wrote Peebles. "This was typical of a curiously detached and somewhat taciturn nature. He had no interest in bowling out batsmen for the sake of compiling records. When catches went astray, which they were inclined to do in abundance, he was never heard to say an impatient word, nor betray a flicker of expression on a face cast in Red Indian mould."

McDonald went to Charles Street School in his native Launceston, Tasmania, and played for Tasmania at the age of 17 in 1909–10. After two seasons with Tasmania he went to Victoria, where he was regarded chiefly as a batsman at first. In 1914–15, he took 5 for 33 and 5 for 22 against Queensland, and in 1918–19 took 8 for 42 against New South Wales, and 6 for 111 and 6 for 69 against South Australia, but such was the ca-

662

libre of the available Australian pace bowlers he did not win a Test place until the last three Tests of the 1920–21 series in Australia against J. W. H. T. Douglas's England side. McDonald took only six costly wickets but his talent was obvious as he repeatedly beat the bat, and he was chosen to tour England in 1921 to open the attack with Jack Gregory in Armstrong's famous side.

McDonald and Gregory formed one of Australia's greatest opening attacks, comparable with Lindwall and Miller and Lillee and Thomson in their prime. McDonald's graceful, rhythmical bowling was the perfect foil to the high-leaping tempestuous Gregory whose tactics were to make an all-out frontal assault, without McDonald's each-way swing or clever changes in pace. McDonald's wickets came from controlled speed—Gregory got wickets with long hops delivered from that intimidating final bound. McDonald was Australia's leading wicket-taker on the 1921 tour, with 150 wickets—four more than Mailey and 30 more than Gregory. In the Trent Bridge Test against England, McDonald took 5 for 32, his best Test performance. McDonald took 27 wickets at 24.74, Gregory 19 at 29.05 in the five Tests.

McDonald toured South Africa in 1921–22 with the Australian side, but had an unhappy trip, taking only 10 wickets in three Tests. After a superlative performance in 1921–22 in which he took 8 for 84 against the powerful New South Wales team, McDonald joined the Nelson club in the Lancashire League and was lost to Australian cricket, fulfilling a contract he had signed two years earlier in England, when English critics objected to the importation of such a fine player at the expense of locals. He qualified for Lancashire's County side in 1924 and in his halcyon years with the County made important contributions to its remarkable success.

McDonald took 205 wickets in the 1925 English summer and more than 150 wickets in each of the next three county seasons. He began with Lancashire as the opening bowling partner to Durham-born Cecil Parkin and then shared the new ball with Richard Tyldesley. In the seasons 1926, 1927 and 1928 McDonald took 484 wickets in County championship matches, Tyldesley 303. In all he took three hat-tricks and more than 100 wickets in a season seven times in his career, and 1,053 wickets for Lancashire between 1924 and 1931. In 1981 he still held the Lancashire record for most wickets in a season—198 in 1925.

Right to the end of his fine career he was able to produce the odd ball of tremendous pace, but often as he aged he reverted to medium-paced off-breaks, particularly when the pitches were soft. Altogether he was an invaluable member of four champion Lancashire sides, and at the age of 38 he bowled Bradman for nine. He remained a moody character, fired only by the challenge of opposing batsmen who had scored heavily from him in the past or players like Hobbs or Gunn whose reputations he was always keen to dent. When H. J. Enthoven faced him at Old Trafford after scoring a century against him at Lord's, McDonald greeted him with a burst considered the fastest bowling ever seen in England.

In 1937, McDonald died tragically when his car was forced off the road after colliding with another car at Bolton, England. McDonald, who was unhurt, climbed back on to the road to help the other motorist and was hit and killed by a passing car. His career had yielded 119 instances of five wickets in an innings and 31 of 10 wickets in a match, and strangely for one whom Victorian officials originally rated as a batsman, only one first-class century—100 not out for Lancashire v. Middlesex in 1926.

McDONALD, Dr Ian Hamilton, 1923–

First-Class Averages: Batting, 843 runs at 16.86; Dismissals 131 (79 catches, 52 stumpings).

A right-hand batsman and wicket-keeper for Melbourne and Victoria between 1948 and 1952, who often played in the same teams as his younger brother, the Test opening batsman Colin Campbell McDonald. He was a very reliable inter-State 'keeper who never aspired to Test status, and occasionally contributed valuable runs batting near the bottom of the order. He made his debut for Victoria in 1948–49 and was at his best the following season 'keeping to the mystery spinner, Jack Iverson, who provided him with numerous stumping chances. Against WA at Perth he made three stumpings and three catches, and against SA at Adelaide he stumped the first three batsmen off Doug Ring in SA's second innings. In the return match that season at Melbourne he also had three stumpings in SA's second innings.

MACDONALD, Dr Robert (''Robbie''), 1870–1945

First-Class Averages: Batting, 2,068 runs at 31.81; Bowling, 3 wickets at 60.33.

A dour, stonewalling doctor of dentistry, born in Melbourne and developed in Queensland club cricket, who inflicted his ultra-defensive batting on Leicestershire in his mature years. He batted with tiresome caution from a right-handed stance and was an occasional slow bowler. In 1895–96 at Sydney, he made a laborious 77 not out for Queensland against NSW. Two years later he visited New Zealand with the Queensland team, heading the tour averages with 50.30, and scoring the only century of the tour. He and O. Cowley put on a Queensland record of 238 for the sixth wicket against Hawke's Bay at Napier. He played two notable innings for Queensland against NSW at Sydney in 1902–03, scoring 51 and 61 not out while occupying the crease for 6 hours 15 minutes. In 1903–04, he played another marathon innings of 62 not out for Queensland against NSW at Sydney.

Macdonald first played for Leicestershire in 1899 and con-

664

tinued in the County team until 1902, scoring 1,300 runs in 33 matches at 30.95, with three centuries. His highest score was the 147 not out he made in a then record fifth wicket stand of 226 with F. Gleeson (104) against Derbyshire at Glossop in 1901. In all first-class matches he made four centuries and took 34 catches. He was a prominent figure in Leicester where he practised dentistry. From 1922 to 1929 he was the County's honorary secretary. For many years he watched over Australia's interests in big cricket administration and he represented Australia at the Imperial Cricket Conference at Lord's in 1929. He played for Stanley, Oakfield, Brisbane, Valley, South Brisbane and Rockhampton clubs at various stages of his career, spending the summers in England and the northern winters in Australia.

McDONNELL, Percy Stanislaus ("Greatheart"), 1858–1896

A Greek scholar who played for three States—Victoria, New South Wales and Queensland—and captained Australia six times, but could not get his on field studies right as Australia lost five matches under his leadership. He was a right-handed batsman with a splendid defence who performed so well on wet pitches many considered him our finest ever player on rain-affected pitches. Something motivated him to play better on damp pitches than on hard, true strips.

He was born in Kensington, London, and went back to England four times in Australian teams, the first three trips as an ordinary tourist and on the last trip as captain. He was a medical student who adored Greek mythology and often was unavailable for home matches before he graduated. He led Australia in 1886–87, 1887–88 and in 1888, and in all of those years England had first-rate teams that were tremendously difficult to defeat. His hitting when Australia was in difficulty was so enterprising and fearless, however, that he sometimes swung games back Australia's way.

McDonnell first toured England in 1880, when he scored 418 runs at 23.22, topscore 79. Only Murdoch did better. He went again in 1882, when he scored 900 runs at 17.30, topscore 82, and 1884, when he made 1,225 runs, topscore 103, average 23.55, a performance that again was only surpassed by Murdoch. He missed the 1886 tour of England because of his studies but returned as the captain in 1888, when he headed the batting averages with 1,393 runs at 22.83, topscore 105.

He was a batsman of character, blessed with fine footwork and a big heart. "Percy Greatheart," one paper called him. Perhaps his finest achievement was a knock of 82 against the North of England at Old Trafford in 1888, which won the match for Australia. His highest score in Tests, 147, was made in a low-scoring match at Sydney in 1881–82, and gave Australia victory by six wickets. In this match England batted

First-Class Averages: Batting, 6,470 runs at 23.52; Bowling, 2 wickets at 123.50.

Tests (19): 950 runs at 28.78.

first on a damaged pitch and after being 5 for 56 got to 188 thanks to a skilful innings by Shrewsbury. Australia were then allowed to bat on a fresh pitch but were still 3 for 24 at the end of the first day. Australia struggled to 3 for 146 on a rain-shortened second day. McDonnell, then 24, hit all the England bowlers powerfully on the third day, once lifting Bates over the stand and his partnership with Bannerman yielded a match-winning 199. Bannerman made 70, but nobody else in the Australian team reached double figures.

McDonnell's century meant that in eight successive Test innings he had a Test average that was remarkable for those days of 44.57. He made seven first-class centuries, three in Tests. For New South Wales, his highest score was 239 against Victoria at Melbourne in 1886–87. Sadly considering his nickname, he died of a heart attack eight weeks short of his 38th birthday, leaving a widow and three children, one of whom was born six months after his death.

"Percy Greatheart's" eldest son Stan played cricket for Sydney University while studying medicine and after becoming a doctor practised at St George, 520 kilometres west of Brisbane, for almost forty years. He built a fine reputation as a hospital superintendent who could be relied on to provide fireworks with his big-hitting in outback cricket matches. He was president of the Queensland branch of the Australian Medical Association and chairman of the Red Cross. McDonnell airfield at St George was named after him. Stan McDonnell died in 1970, aged 77. His son, Dr Michael McDonnell now practises at St George.

Percy's second son, Whit McDonnell (christened Wilfred Francis) was a professional soldier who kept wicket for Randwick and once stumped seven of the ten batsmen playing for a North Coast team in a Country Week match against a combined North Sydney and Balmain team. Whit played cricket regularly for Victoria Barracks teams while serving with the Army Service Corps.

McELHONE, William Percy, 1870–1932

One of Australian cricket's outstanding personalities, a Sydney solicitor who conducted debates with rare skill. He first became a member of the New South Wales Cricket Association as a delegate for the East Sydney club in 1896 and represented that club for four years. From 1900 to 1914, he was a delegate to the NSWCA for the Sydney club. He was on the NSWCA's executive from 1904 to 1914, and was chairman from 1906 to 1914 when he was appointed a vice-president of the association. In 1920, he succeeded J. H. Clayton as president, holding that office until ill-health forced his retirement in 1931. He was made a Life Member of the NSWCA in 1927. While president he was a member of the Sydney Cricket

Ground Trust. He was one of the founders of the Australian Board of Control and a member of the Board from 1905 until 1914, strongly influencing Board policy in its early years. He was the first secretary of the Board, holding that position for one year. In the three succeeding years, he held the dual roles of secretary and treasurer. He was chairman of the Board in 1911–12 when the famous revolt by six star players occurred. He was Lord Mayor of Sydney in 1922.

McGILVRAY, Alan David, 1910–

First-Class Averages: Batting, 684 runs at 24.42; Bowling, 20 wickets at 56.75.

The authentic voice of Australian cricket in his Australian Broadcasting Commission broadcasts of big matches. Although he played 20 matches for New South Wales, some of them as captain, he had to take a minor role in some of his years as a commentator to men like Victor Richardson and Johnny Moyes, but once appointed to the big job he gave it distinction it had never had before. He has been paid the supreme compliment on overseas tours when Australian captains and team managers have sought his advice on tactics and the conduct of matches.

For many Australians their cricket education began with McGilvray and the standards he upholds in the behaviour of players and ethics of the game are widely accepted. It would be hard for administrators of the Australian game to find a better advocate of sportsmanship and playing to the spirit of cricket. McGilvray is no snob despite a certain stuffiness but he is a staunch believer in good manners and high standards of decorum on and off the field.

He was educated at Sydney Grammar School, one of four children of Tom McGilvray, a Sydney shoemaker. When he and his brother Norman finished school they went to work in the family's Belmore factory. Alan was an outstanding close to the wicket fieldsman, left-hand opening batsman and right-arm medium pace bowler, playing with Waverley Poidevin-Gray team and later for Paddington club. He was most annoyed when Waverley claimed him for a season under the residential qualification rule as he said he did not live within the Waverley district. In 1936, he married Gwendolyn Griffith. They had a son, Ross, and a daughter, Carolyn.

In between making shoes, he took over the captaincy of the New South Wales side when Alan Kippax retired. He had made 66 in one of his first matches for New South Wales in 1935–36 against E. R. Holmes' English team. His scores in grade cricket were impressive. He put on 300 odd in one partnership for Paddington with Harold Mudge and in 1936–37 headed the Sydney first grade batting averages.

When he was given the captaincy of New South Wales, McGilvray was impressed at the nets by the extreme pace of

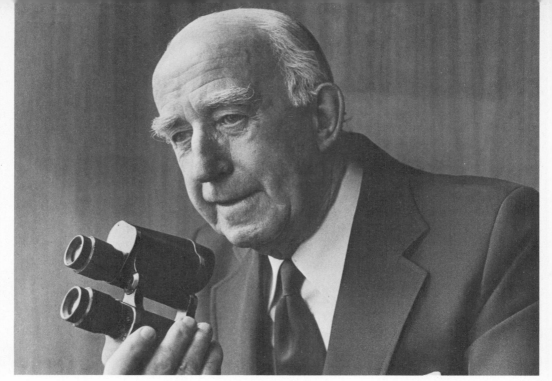

an untried bowler named "Ginty" Lush. Much to everybody's surprise he handed Lush the ball and asked him to open in 1936–37 against England at the SCG. Lush took 6 for 43 and 7 for 72, and his 13 wickets remains the finest debut by a New South Wales bowler against England. McGilvray was also given credit for setting the trap that saw Ray Little catch Bradman for a duck in the South Australia v. New South Wales match in 1935–36.

McGilvray lost the New South Wales captaincy when officials objected to him commenting on the radio on the matches in which he played. He preferred his radio work to cricket when compelled to make a choice.

Before World War II he was involved in both ABC broadcasts and broadcasts for a commercial station, for whom he made two overseas trips. He served with the First Armoured Division in Western Australia ("Curtin's Koalas"), 20,000 men who never got to fight. After discharge he returned to the family shoe business and when this was sold became a full-time broadcaster. His influence has grown steadily ever since and with it his mastery of all the skills of broadcasting. He has seen cricket commentaries develop from synthetic affairs in which studio announcers were handed short coded cables from Test grounds which they built into descriptions of play, faking the sounds of ball hitting the bat, to satellite programmes with 40 million listeners annually.

He says he learnt a lot from former Prime Minister, Sir Robert Menzies, who with his wife Dame Pattie, was a keen critic of McGilvray's broadcasts. "Menzies kept stressing the art of the pause, and the art of using the crowd to give excitement to the comnmentaries," McGilvray said. Today his broadcasts are smooth, measured, with his words just a little ahead of the play. The drama comes when he corrects his description of an incident, when the listener hears that the ball has not reached the boundary as McGilvray said but has been brilliantly caught by a fieldsman.

He has seen three great captains of Australian teams since the war, Bradman, Benaud and Ian Chappell, and he leans towards Chappell when asked to nominate the best skipper. "The reason I say Ian Chappell is because he made fine teams out of nothing", he says. "Chappell went to England in 1972 with three bowlers who had never been to England before, Lillee, Massie and Colley. And yet he drew the rubber, a tremendous triumph for Chappell. In 1972–73 he won the series in the West Indies against a very strong side, and he did it with unknowns."

Chappell himself admires McGilvray tremendously. "The thing I like about Mac is that he is so loyal to Australia", Chappell said. "He was tremendously inspiring. If he thought I'd had a bad day as captain, he'd tell me. He's a man's man." Another of McGilvray's close friends, Keith Miller, said: "Mac has it all. He knows more about cricket than anyone in the game."

McGLINCHY, Walter William, 1866–1946

First-Class Averages: Batting, 476 runs at 14.00; Bowling, 71 wickets at 18.95.

An all-rounder from Newcastle, NSW, who in the days before Sheffield Shield cricket achieved impressive results in inter-Colonial matches and made two tours of New Zealand with representative teams. He played for NSW from 1885–86 to 1892–93, touring New Zealand with NSW in 1889–90. He switched to Queensland in 1893–94 and had seven seasons with that State, touring New Zealand in the Queensland team in 1896–97. He played in Brisbane for the Graziers club which made many tours of Queensland country centres as well as touring New Zealand. In all first-class matches, McGlinchy had a topscore of 45, and with the ball had best figures of 6 for 62. He twice took ten wickets in a match and four times took more than five wickets in an innings. He ended his career with the Nundah club, and later became a well known character as dressing-room attendant at major grounds.

McGUIRK, Harold Vincent, 1906–

A right-arm fast-medium bowler chosen to play for New South Wales in 1926–27 after sensational performances in bush cricket. He had no experience whatsoever in big cricket.

First-Class Averages:
Batting, 0 runs, NA;
Bowling, 4 wickets at
51.75

Half of Goulburn had a bob in to defray his expenses on the trip to Adelaide and Melbourne with the State team, and he was given a big send-off as the train departed. He had one pair of white pants for the entire trip. As he turned to begin his approach run, he shouted "Play" before every delivery. At Adelaide he took 3 for 20 in South Australia's second innings and this won him a hat donated by a local manufacturer. McGuirk chose a wide-brimmed ten gallon model which he wore for the rest of the trip. At Melbourne, Victoria made 1,107, with McGuirk taking 1 for 130, Victoria winning by an innings and 656. This experience was too much for him and he was not seen again in first-class cricket though he played grade cricket with Gordon. He did not score a run in three Shield innings and took 4 for 207 at 51.75. His brother, **Leo Daniel McGuirk** (1908–1974) played for NSW in one first-class match in 1930–31.

**McILWRAITH, John,
1857–1938**

First-Class Averages:
Batting, 1,468 runs at
24.06.

Tests (1): 9 runs at 4.50.

A hard-hitting Collingwood-born right-hand batsman who toured England with the Fifth Australian team. He did not take up the game until he was past 20. From the 1883–84 season, when he decided to concentrate on cricket, he progressed remarkably. In the 1883–84 season he scored more than 1,500 runs for Melbourne CC. In 1885–86, he scored 133 for Victoria against New South Wales, followed by 125 for the Australian team against Victoria after he had become a member of our 1886 side for England. His results on tour were disappointing. He scored 532 runs at 16.62, topscore 62 not out against the South of England at Hastings.

**MACKAY, John Robert
Edward, 1937–**

First-Class Averages:
Batting, 1,148 runs at
19.79; Bowling, 115
wickets at 31.82.

A right-handed batsman and right-arm fast medium bowler from Rockhampton who played 47 matches for Queensland between 1959 and 1966. Enthusiastic and reliable, he performed creditably as a late order batsman, with 77 his highest first-class score, and he took five wickets in an innings three times. He also made 28 catches. Mackay graduated from country carnivals to the South Brisbane club and brought a powerful physique to the task of pounding the ball down on flint-hard pitches, with 5 for 56 against Pakistan in 1964–65 his best bowling figures.

**MACKAY, James
Rainey Munro ("Sunny
Jim") 1881–1953**

A right-handed batsman of such brilliance he was hailed as a successor to Victor Trumper. He came down in 1902–03 from the New England district of New South Wales where he was reared from tough Scottish stock, and in three years he had

Australian cricket at his feet. Week after week he batted with power and elegance for Western Suburbs in district cricket.

" 'Sunny Jim' Mackay electrified Sydney cricket lovers with the forcefulness and rugged power of his batsmanship," said former Western Suburbs team-mate, George Garnsey. "Six feet in height with a well proportioned frame that was all wire and whipcord, he was a teetotaller and non-smoker like most country-bred boys, and very observant. He also had the great asset of visual memory and it was a standing joke among cricketers that there was no need to consult averages, statistics or 'phone numbers when Jim was around. This visual gift enabled him to learn quickly by watching the great players and give his batting polish and versatility to go with his sound defence and great hitting power. He seemed to gain greater ease and fluidity with each succeeding innings."

First-Class Averages: Batting, 1,556 runs at 50.19.

His season of magic was 1905–06. In successive matches he scored 90 v. South Australia, 194 v. Victoria, 105 and 102 not out v. South Australia, 18 and 50 v. Victoria, all for NSW, and finally 136 against the 1905 Australian XI. Earlier in the season Mackay had scored 203 v. Queensland. In all he made 902 runs at 112.75 in eight completed innings. But "Sunny Jim" had missed selection in the 1905 Australian team to tour England, and after the 1905–06 season migrated to South Africa. He played for Transvaal in 1906–07 and was unlucky not to tour England with the 1907 South African team. He was involved in a near fatal motor accident that affected his sight, and returned to Sydney but played in only one more club game. A ball which, in his halcyon days, he would have despatched for four, bowled him. For a second his body drooped, then up came his head with the sunny smile for which he was known. "He walked off proudly erect," said Garnsey, "as if to say 'I might have lost my sight, but never my courage.' The crowd cheered him to the echo for making a duck."

His cricket career finished, "Sunny Jim" went back to the land that spawned him and years later Garnsey, by then State coach, found him coaching kids in Armidale. He worked every day on a property and he still told the kids about the joy of making a century. When he could get away he played for country teams, and he did so without a hint of animosity about the way the fates had treated him.

MACKAY, Kenneth Donald ("Slasher"), 1925–1982

One of the most beguiling cricketers ever to wear an Australian cap, a left-handed batsman with a slightly withered arm, who specialised more in deflections than full-face shot-making. Late in his career he developed into a valuable bowler of right-arm seamers at Test level. He irritated spectators who then grew to love him. From Brisbane to Cardiff, his incessant and vigorous gum-chewing, his stubborn faith in

671

First-Class Averages:
Batting, 10,823 runs at
43.64; Bowling, 251
wickets at 33.31.

Tests (37): 1,507 runs at
33.48; 50 wickets at
34.42.

his own unorthodoxy became legendary. "Mackay does not hit the ball, he squirts it," said England's captain Peter May. It was always a mesmerising experience for young English bowlers on their first tour to encounter "Slasher" in Brisbane.

He opened the batting for Queensland with a highly suspicious attitude towards the bowlers, and he bowled with the same nervous, furtive approach, moving to the crease as if stepping through a minefield. John Arlott called it Mackay's Groucho Marx walk. Despite his strange mannerisms and a lengthy list of superstitions, Mackay, born at Windsor, Queensland, had a superb big match temperament, amazing reflexes and eyesight that enabled him to produce weird strokes that were all his own invention with unflagging precision. He toured England twice, played in two series at home against England and once against West Indies and also visited South Africa, India and Pakistan in Australian sides.

"Slasher" Mackay provided double centuries for Queensland and innumerable rescue acts for Australia but he did not score the Test century he deserved. He came to the rescue so often between 1956 and 1963 that it became customary for Australian cricket devotees, when Australia was in trouble to say, "She's right—"Slasher's still there". Not many people understood how he survived, though.

His highest score, 223 for Queensland against Victoria at Brisbane in 1953–54, took nine hours and 45 minutes. Not the least of his rescue knocks was at Adelaide in 1960–61 when he and Lindsay Kline batted out time in a last wicket stand of 66 that frustrated all the West Indies attempts to dislodge them for 100 minutes, and enabled Australia to escape with a draw. "Slasher" said he was annoyed when the West Indians appealed for a catch off an obvious "bump ball" 75 minutes from the end, and this stirred him up and made him determined to resist to the last ball. He stayed to the end, bat and pad a long way apart, telling himself as big Wes Hall steamed in for the last over, "This is war and that big bloke pelting in is not going to beat you." Hall made three attempts to bowl the last ball before he finally let go a screamer. As soon as he saw it was short, "Slasher" decided to let it hit him. The ball crashed into his side, he staggered, but did not go down. Australia had drawn it!

The same year Mackay helped Australia to a marvellous win at Manchester by shutting up one end with his medium pacers. Few failed to enjoy the remarkable adaptability of this unique cricketer who in 1956 had attempted to counter Jim Laker's vicious off-breaks by not offering a shot, meeting each ball with his pads. "Mackay is like the common cold," said the *Manchester Guardian*. "There is no cure for either."

Noted English critic Ian Peebles had this to say of a Mackay innings at Lord's: "To describe his innings in any technical detail is difficult in the extreme. The striker lifted the bat no higher than is his habit, which is not very high at all, but the ball came forth with that velocity that caused John Nyren to exclaim: 'Egad, she went as though she had been fired.' "

"When Mackay cut, the effect was, in the words of the television copywriters, richer, creamier, delicious, refreshing. Most strokes were, however, largely of his own invention, one particularly fascinating, when the half volley is half cut, half trapped, so that it spurts past cover like an apple pip playfully squeezed from finger and thumb."

Mackay wrote one of the best books ever published on cricket, *Slasher Opens Up*, but got involved with poor marketing and although enthusiasts have been clamouring for it for years, the book remains a collector's item that has not been reprinted. Who could forget the slightly deaf batsman who mistook a bowler's grunts for a no-ball call and hit him for six! If, as the experts argue, the complete cricket book has not been written, then Mackay's book comes closest because it portrays all the off-beat characters and humour of big cricket with warmth and honesty. The record books can never convey the rare flavour of this astonishing cricketer, but they say that in 37 Tests he had a topscore of 89, and that he made 13 scores over 50 and held 16 catches. As a bowler he surprised everybody, with a best analysis of 6 for 42 in taking 50 Test wickets. In 201 first-class matches he made 23 centuries, topscore 223, seven times took five wickets in an innings. He took 84 catches. Sadly "Slasher" died in 1982 aged 56, but while cricket is played in Australia, he will be fondly remembered.

McKENZIE, Graham Douglas ("Garth"), 1941–

A West Australian fast-medium bowler who took 100 wickets in Tests faster than any other Australian bowler—three years, 165 days. At 23, he was also the youngest to achieve the feat. He was a bowler of immense strength who bowled from a nine pace approach run and used his height (6 ft 1 in) and weight (14 st 7 lb) in co-ordination with back and arm that were all muscle to produce remarkable whip. His bowling suffered in the transition to the front foot rule as did that of most pace bowlers but his persistence over long spells repeatedly boosted Australia's Test prospects.

Frank Worrell first drew attention to McKenzie's potential in 1960 after batting in the nets against him at Perth when McKenzie was approaching 19, and just out of John Curtin High School, Fremantle. He was a "baby" of the Australian team in England in 1961 and when Davidson retired at the end of the 1962–63 season became the spearhead of the Australian attack. With Davidson, McKenzie made a famous last wicket stand at Manchester in 1961, which took the score

Graham McKenzie's powerful physique in evidence at the moment of delivery.

from 334 to 432 when Australia appeared beaten. Those 98 runs proved vital, Australia winning the match by 54 runs. McKenzie made 32, Davidson 77 not out.

McKenzie, born at Cottesloe, Western Australia, toured England again in 1964 and 1968, India and Pakistan in 1964–65, the West Indies in 1965, and South Africa in 1966–67 and India and South Africa in 1969–70 where he was the sole Australian bowler capable of match-winning spells. Meanwhile he gave unflagging service to his home State, often labouring so long and so unselfishly for Western Australia that critics feared he would break down.

First-Class Averages: Batting, 5,653 runs at 15.57; Bowling, 1,204 wickets at 26.39.

Tests (60 plus one abandoned): 945 runs at 12.27; 246 wickets at 29.78.

Through all this he kept producing one of the best away swingers of all time, retaining the ability to upset batsmen when they appeared well set. In his 60 Test matches, McKenzie had a best score of 76 in the Third Test against South Africa in 1963–64. With the ball he took 246 Test wickets, just two short of Benaud's record at that time, but in three Tests fewer than Benaud. Ironically, McKenzie was denied the record when he was left out of the last two Tests of the 1967–68 series against India. He had taken 10 wickets in the

674

previous Test and most experts agreed he was omitted because his bowling threatened the success of the Indian tour. His best Test figures were 8 for 71 against the West Indies in 1968–69. He took five wickets in an innings 16 times and 10 wickets in a match three times.

McKenzie worked diligently on improving his batting and towards the end of his career was rated a genuine all-rounder. He had seven successful seasons (1969–1975) with Leicestershire after losing his Test place. His uncle, **Douglas Charles McKenzie** (1906–1979) captained Western Australia in 1945–46 and played some fine innings for the State before Western Australia won Shield status. Douglas McKenzie scored 214 runs at 42.80, topscore 88 against the Second AIF team in 1945–46 at Perth. Doug McKenzie played hockey for WA and was a vice-president of the WACA. Graham's father, **E. N. (Eric) McKenzie** also played once for Western Australia against South Africa in 1931–32.

McKIBBIN, Thomas Robert, 1870-1939

One of the most popular cricketers at the end of the last century and one of the most discussed. He bowled right-arm medium-paced off-breaks that turned sharply. Doubts arose about the validity of his action. He batted left-handed pluckily and efficiently and was a highly dexterous slips fieldsman. He was no-balled for throwing in both Australia and England but never in a first-class match. Three times in his career he took 14 wickets or more in a match.

McKibbin, who came from Bathurst like C. T. B. Turner and G. J. Bonnor, made some of the most famous batsmen look foolish with his sharp turn. "I shall remember for a long time the really ludicrous attempts of Walter Read to dispose of McKibbin's breaks at Kennington Oval," George Giffen wrote. "Fully a dozen balls Read received without playing one, and then he was bowled neck and crop." Giffen conceded that McKibbin bowled a lot of bad balls but added that he knew no bowler who had to be so closely watched. But McKibbin has always been one of the first bowlers mentioned in discussions about illegal actions.

He switched from Bathurst to further his cricket career in Sydney with the Glebe club and in 1894–95 played for New South Wales and for Australia in the Fifth Test against England. In 1896 he was in the Australian team that toured England, America and New Zealand, and in all matches on that trip in England took 101 wickets, at an average cost of 14.26 runs. His best efforts included 4 for 7 at Cheltenham against Gloucestershire, who were all out for 17, and a hat-trick at Liverpool where he had match figures of 13 for 38 against Lancashire. For Australia v. Fifteen Chicago Wanderers, he took four wickets in five balls.

First-Class Averages: Batting, 683 runs at 10.04; Bowling, 319 wickets at 19.73.

Tests (5): 88 runs at 14.66; 17 wickets at 29.17.

For New South Wales his most impressive figures were 14 for 87 (including 9 for 68) against Queensland at Brisbane in 1894–95, 14 for 189 (including 8 for 66) against South Australia at Sydney in 1894–95, 8 for 93 against Victoria at Melbourne in 1895–96, 15 for 125 (including 8 for 74) against South Australia at Adelaide in 1896–97, and 13 for 240 (including 8 for 111) against Victoria at Sydney in 1896–97.

He did not get a second trip to England. All around the cricket world the need to ban bowlers with suspect deliveries had strengthened, and when McKibbin was named as a chucker in a letter to the *Sporting Times* by fellow Australia tourist Fred Spofforth it virtually ended McKibbin's international career. His best Test figures were 3 for 35 so he really did not do much damage.

In first-class matches other than Tests he was a lot more impressive taking five wickets in an innings 28 times and 11 times taking 10 wickets in a match.

McLACHLAN, IAN, 1936–

First-Class Averages: Batting, 3,743 runs at 31.72; Bowling, 6 wickets at 63.66

A tall, fair-haired right-hand batsman who, after a successful career with Cambridge University (winning Blues in 1957 and 1958), returned to assist in a South Australian revival in the early 1960s. He was a crisp, hard driver with a powerful pull shot who could also cut strongly, and at his peak was rated an Australian XI prospect. He was educated at St. Peter's College, Adelaide, with his brother **A. A. McLachlan** (1944–) who followed him to Cambridge and also won his Blues in 1964–65. Between December, 1960, and November, 1963, Ian McLachlan scored eight centuries for South Australia, topscore 188 against Queensland at Adelaide in 1960–61. In 1961–62 he scored 576 runs at 38.40, finishing ahead of players like Booth, Cowper, and Trimble in the Australian first-class averages. In one golden period in 1961–62 he made 120 against Victoria, 109 against NSW, 35 and 71 against Queensland and 19 and 139 against Western Australia.

McLAREN, John William, 1887–1921

First-Class Averages: Batting, 564 runs at 12.53; Bowling, 107 wickets at 26.71.

Tests (1): 0 runs; 1 wicket at 70.00.

A right-hand fast bowler and right-handed batsman, who by playing in the Fifth Test at Sydney against England in February, 1912, became the first native-born Queenslander to play in a Test. McLaren did not score a run and took only one wicket, but he had one of the strangest entries of all times into Tests. Australian trade unions threatened industrial action when he was picked for the Fourth Test at Melbourne if McLaren played. He had acted as a special constable in a strike earlier that year. Although he was named in the twelve for the match, McLaren did not play, but appeared in the Fifth Test.

McLaren, born at Toowong, went to England a replacement

676

for Cotter as Australia's pace bowler for the 1912 triangular tournament, but did not play in any other Tests. His 27 tour wickets cost 22.96 each. But he was an impressive performer for Queensland, and captained the Valley team that won the Brisbane first grade premiership three years in succession.

He was lithe, well-built and full of life. *Felix*, after watching him bowl for Queensland against Victoria in 1910, said: "With a fairly long run, McLaren takes a sinuous course to the wicket and when his length is good his swing away is calculated to the downfall of batsmen unless they are wary and watchful, and fully realise how essential it is to get well over the ball in playing bowling of McLaren's class." McLaren, who died at 35 from diabetes, suffered all his career from dropped slips catches. He took 65 wickets in first-class matches for Queensland at 29.12 and contributed useful runs when he batted, topscore 43 not out. He took five wickets in an innings three times, best figures 5 for 55.

McLAUGHLIN, John Joseph, 1930–

First-Class Averages: Batting, 2,988 runs at 33.95; Bowling, 1 wicket at 130.00

A right-hand batsman who for several years was the most attractive player in the Queensland team. He was also one of the most brilliant cover fieldsmen produced in Queensland, a man who saved countless runs with his gathering and throwing and always had opposition batsmen watching him carefully. They had no trouble identifying him because he always played in a white hat. He played 59 first-class games in all spread over 12 seasons, starting as an opening bat and later batting at No 4 or No 5. He still holds the Queensland second wicket partnership record of 243 which he set in 1957–58 with Ray Reynolds at Adelaide against South Australia.

McLaughlin, born at Corinda in Brisbane's western suburbs, played in the Brisbane first grade competition as a teenager with Colts and later joined Western Suburbs. He first played for Queensland in 1949–50, aged 19. He scored 450 runs in nine completed innings for Queensland in 1956–57, and in 1957–58 scored 615 runs for 13 times out.

MACLEAN, John Alexander, 1946–

A long-serving Queensland wicket-keeper, who captained that State and also made many useful scores with the bat. In 96 matches for Queensland, he dismissed 346 batsmen—making him on figures at least a more successful 'keeper for Queensland than either Wally Grout or Don Tallon. He made two first-class centuries. Brisbane-born Maclean was unlucky not to be chosen for Australia until his final season, when he probably was past his prime. His two overseas trips were with an Australian team to New Zealand in 1969–70 and the International Wanderers to Rhodesia in 1972–73.

In four Tests, all against a strong England side in the

677

First-Class Averages:
Batting, 3,888 runs at
24.45; Dismissals, 385
(354 matches, 31
stumpings).

Tests (4): 79 runs at 11.28;
Dismissals, 18 (all
catches).

1978–79 summer, he was Australia's vice-captain. Selectors made him one of the scapegoats for miserable Australian performances, replacing him and Geoff Dymock for the remaining two Tests. Maclean, a civil engineer from Queensland University played for the South Brisbane club, and was a right-hand batsman who could cut well, and played many fruitful lofted drives. He kept splendidly to the predominantly fast bowling attacks that operated in his 10 years in first-class cricket. His shrewd leadership helped make Queensland a major Shield force between 1977 and 1979.

McLEOD, Charles Edward, 1869–1918

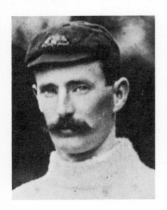

First-Class Averages:
Batting, 3,321 runs at
21.15; Bowling, 334
wickets at 24.32.

Tests (17): 573 runs at
23.87; 33 wickets
at 40.15.

A right-hand all-rounder who could drive effectively, had useful strokes to the leg, and an ultra-cautious defence. He bowled medium pace and on pitches that gave any assistance got a lot of work on the ball. He was one of a remarkable family of seven brothers, all of whom played cricket for Melbourne Cricket Club, three of them for Victoria, and two, Charles and Robert, for Australia.

Charles, born at Port Melbourne, made his debut for Victoria in 1893–94, and played his first Test against Stoddart's English team in 1894–95. The next season he made 100 and 50 for Victoria against New South Wales at Sydney. Playing against Stoddart's second English team in 1897–98, he scored an impressive 63 for Victoria at Melbourne and this clinched his place in all five Tests. He proved more than useful in scoring 50 not out and 26 at Sydney, 112 at Melbourne, 31 at Adelaide, 1 and 64 not out at Melbourne, and 64 and 4 at Sydney. In the second innings of the First Test at Sydney, McLeod, who was deaf, left his crease after being bowled, having not heard the umpire's call of no-ball, and the English wicket-keeper, W. Storer, ran him out.

McLeod toured England twice—in 1899 and 1905—and justified his selection without reproducing anything brilliant. On the 1899 trip, he scored 31 not out and 77 in The Oval Test, adding 116 with Jack Worrall for the first wicket in the second innings. He made 544 runs on the 1899 tour and took 81 wickets and in 1905 he scored 700 runs and took 80 wickets in all matches. His sole Test century (112) in 1897–98 was topscore in a match Australia won by an innings and 55 runs. He was one of the few batsmen to have both opened and gone in last for Australia.

Most of McLeod's best performances were in Australia, where the hard pitches suited him better, though he did bowl unchanged through an innings at Lord's with Ernie Jones against Middlesex in 1899, taking 10 for 125 in the match. He took 5 for 13 against Cambridge University in 1905. At Adelaide in 1897–98, he took 5 for 65 for Australia v. England.

Charles McLeod took five wickets in an innings 22 times

678

and four times took 10 wickets in a match. His brother, **Daniel Hutton McLeod** (1872–1901) played two matches for Victoria between 1892 and 1894, scoring 142 runs at 71.00, with a highest score of 107. Daniel also took 8 wickets at 26.62, best figures 6 for 95.

McLEOD, Robert William, 1868–1907

First-Class Averages: Batting, 1,701 runs at 22.38; Bowling, 141 wickets at 22.73.

Tests (6): 146 runs at 13.27; 12 wickets at 32.00.

One of the Melbourne Cricket Club's noted brotherhood of McLeods and with Charles the only one of the seven to play Test cricket. Robert was a left-handed batsman with strokes all around the wicket, and a right-handed medium-pace bowler who could move the ball both ways. He was a fine fieldsman and sure catch.

Robert, born at Port Melbourne, was educated at St James' Grammar School and Scotch College, where he was in the First XI for three years. At 15, he made 144 not out for the Grammar School against King's College. He made his debut for Victoria at 20 and did so well he was regarded as an automatic choice for the 1890 Australian team to England—but he could not spare the time.

In 1891–92 he figured in a remarkable incident in the Sydney Test against W. G. Grace's English team. Early on the Tuesday morning news arrived from Melbourne that Robert's brother Norman had died. Australia's captain, Blackham, had the delicate decision of whether to ask Robert to bat. His team-mates wore black crepe and Robert batted, scoring 18 runs before he caught the night train to Melbourne.

Robert McLeod's departure saw Blackham approach Grace and ask if the Melbourne University student, Hutton, could field in his place as twelfth man. Grace asked: "Is Hutton a better field than McLeod?" Blackham had to agree that Hutton was superior. "Then find someone else," said Grace. The Australians found Harry Donnan, a move that gave no cause for protest from the good doctor. After that incident it became virtually traditional in big cricket that the fielding side never replaced an absent player with one of superior fielding skill.

The McLeods figured in many eventful matches for Melbourne CC. Playing against North Melbourne in 1896, Robert was run out in both innings without facing a ball, the only case of this kind on record. In 1892 he scored 213 for the club against Williamstown in a partnership of 421 for the fourth wicket with C. H. Ross. The following month he made 324 against Essendon and followed that with 98 v. South Melbourne and 207 against Williamstown. He batted five and a half hours for his 324 and Melbourne reached 828. In March, 1893, he carried this form into the State match against South Australia at Adelaide, scoring 101 in an eighth wicket partnership of 198 with Frank Laver.

Robert McLeod toured England once, in 1893, scoring 633 runs at only 18.08, and taking 46 wickets at 24.60 runs apiece, but he played a creditable part in the match at Lord's in which MCC narrowly avoided defeat after Lyons made a superb 149 for Australia. MCC had to score 167 in the last innings to win but McLeod took 5 for 29 in 19 overs to almost bring off a dramatic Australian win. For Victoria Robert McLeod, 6 ft 1½ ins and 12 st 7 lb, made many contributions in his 10 year career towards Victoria winning the Sheffield Shield four times in seven seasons prior to his retirement. His highest Test score was 31, with 5 for 55 his best bowling effort. He made only one first-class century, but took five wickets in an innings seven times and twice took 10 wickets in a match.

McMAHON, John William Joseph, 1919–

One of the world's leading left-arm spinners for ten years after World War II. McMahon, son of "Big Jim" McMahon, a south-paw amateur boxing champion, from Balaklava, South Australia, took 590 first-class wickets at 27.60 playing County cricket for Surrey and Somerset, and spent a further ten years in Central Lancashire League cricket with clubs like Milnrow and Rochdale. He has never returned home after wartime service in the Middle East with the Australian Army as an artilleryman and with the RAAF in Britain.

He learned to play cricket at Balaklava High School and in Country Week carnivals in Adelaide. His first coach, Clarrie Grimmett, arranged for him to travel to Adelaide to play district cricket with Adelaide club. His first victim in grade was Vic Richardson. He received regular coaching from Grimmett, "Nip" Pellew, and J. F. Travers while he worked as a junior school teacher at Rostrevor College. He played Australian Rules for Norwood. In 1945, he played for the Australian Services in England under Hassett, a novel experience for any cricketer. While awaiting discharge in England he trialled for Surrey with a bowler called J. C. Laker.

In his first bowl for Surrey he deceived Lancashire's Malcolm Hilton with three successive Chinamen. Dick Pollard at the other end bellowed: "Can't you pick him? I'll show you." Next over Pollard swung confidently at what he thought was the off-break and had his stump removed by the Chinaman. Errol Holmes at mid-on laughed his head off. McMahon went on to take 234 wickets at 29.50 for Surrey between 1947 and 1953, best figures 8 for 46 against Northants in 1948. For Somerset, he took 349 wickets at 26.12, best analysis again 8 for 46, this time against Kent. He played 201 first-class matches in all, including two for the MCC. He was of little account with the bat, scoring 989 runs at 6.18. His best season was 1956, when he took 103 wickets at 25.57 for Somerset. In the 1980s John McMahon blossomed as the author of the whimsical memoirs for *Wisden Cricket Monthly*, and for the Manchester *Evening Chronicle*.

A left-arm bowler with exceptional control who also scored well as a left-handed batsman. He achieved a distinction rare in Test cricket when he umpired the Fourth Test at Sydney of the 1884–85 series, which Australia won and played in the Fifth Test at Melbourne, won by England. His Test career was cut short while he was curator of the St Kilda Club's ground in Melbourne and had to receive treatment at a mental home. McShane had a topscore in first-class matches of 88 and took 24 catches. With the ball he took five wickets in an innings four times. For Victoria his best performances were 5 for 19 against South Australia in 1880–81, 6 for 43 against South Australia in 1882–83. His best analysis was 9 for 45 for The Rest v. The Australian XI at Sydney in 1880–81.

McSHANE, Patrick George, 1857–1903

First-Class Averages: Batting, 1,117 runs at 18.31; Bowling, 72 wickets at 25.37.

Tests (3): 26 runs at 5.20; 1 wicket at 48.00.

A cheerful Victorian right-hand batsman and wicket-keeper in 21 years of first-class cricket, who, since his retirement, has built a reputation for administrative skill. He was the second best wicket-keeper in Australia for much of his playing career, touring England, the West Indies, New Zealand and India without winning a permanent Test place. He had the unhappy job of managing the Australian tour of England in 1977 knowing most of his players had contracted to play for WSC.

He was around the size of a bantamweight boxer, born at Beaconsfield, and a stalwart of the North Melbourne club. He first played for Victoria in 1946–47, two years ahead of his brother, **Richard Ivor Maddocks** (1928–), a right-hand batsman also from the North Melbourne club, who scored two centuries for Victoria, 271 against Tasmania in 1951–52 and 115 against South Australia in 1953–54, and totalled 1,227 runs at 40.90 in 21 first-class games. Len did not make the first of his five centuries for the State until 1955–56.

Len Maddocks topscored in his first innings against England, scoring 47 in the Third Test at Melbourne against Statham and Tyson at their fastest in 1954–55, in an innings that gave Australia an unexpected first innings lead. He also topscored in his second Test shortly afterwards at Adelaide, adding 92 in 95 minutes with Ian Johnson for the ninth wicket. Maddocks made 69, hitting strongly and running with great gusto in his sole Test knock over 50.

He toured the West Indies in Johnson's Australian side in

MADDOCKS, Leonard Victor, 1926–

First-Class Averages: Batting, 4,106 runs at 32.84; Dismissals, 277 (209 catches, 68 stumpings).

Tests (7): 177 runs at 17.70; Dismissals, 19 (18 catches, 1 stumping).

1954–55 and visited England and India in 1956 but could not clinch a regular Test place in a team that included Gil Langley. He made 201 runs in England at 14.35 in all matches, topscore 56. He visited New Zealand in an Australian team in 1959–60. In 1962–63 he moved to Tasmania and over the next six seasons helped lift the island's cricket standards, his experience and smart, efficient 'keeping proving invaluable to young players.

Len Maddocks's son **Ian Leonard** (1951–) made his debut for Victoria in 1977–78 and has since played a number of matches for the State. In his long first-class career, Len made six centuries, highest score 122 not out in 1960 for an Australian XI v. New Zealand in Auckland. He matured late as a batsman. He became an Australian selector in 1981–82.

MAILEY, Arthur Alfred, 1886–1967

First-Class Averages: Batting, 1,529 runs at 12.33; Bowling, 779 wickets at 24.10.

Tests (21): 222 runs at 11.10; 99 wickets at 33.91.

An impish, whimsical, sometimes inspired, leg-break and googly bowler for New South Wales, and Australia, various Sydney clubs and for numerous teams he took wherever he could get a game. He bowled in Moose Jaw, in Piccadilly Circus in a dinner jacket after midnight, and Temuka, and enjoyed being hit for six as much as he did fooling good players with his spin. He worked for almost 40 years as a cartoonist and commentator in a style that was as individual as his bowling.

Mailey came from the sandhills at the back of the Sydney suburb of Waterloo. His parents simply put up another room of hessian as each offspring arrived. Arthur had a lifesize portrait of Victor Trumper on the wall in front of his bed and when the wind blew across the sandhills at night it seemed that Trumper played his drives straight down the room in the moonlight. He started his working life as a glass blower which strengthened his fingers, then as a labourer with the Water Board and once flooded a department store (Farmers, now Myers) basement by turning on the wrong taps. From these humble beginnings, he wined and dined with kings, spreading the Mailey brand of bonhomie and rich fun. He was a perfectionist at heart, always seeking to bowl the unplayable ball, never worried about the loose ones batsmen hit out of the ground.

I remember him appearing unexpectedly in the London Office of the Sydney *Daily Telegraph* in the summer of 1956 in the midst of a Test that was being played hundreds of miles north at Leeds.

"Arthur, why aren't you at the Test?" I said, thinking of the sub-editors back in Sydney waiting for his daily copy.

"Jack," he said, "They are so bad I can't bear to watch them, so I thought I'd buy you a champagne lunch."

The previous day "Slasher" Mackay had attempted to solve

the problems of facing Laker and Lock on a turning wicket by not offering a stroke, offering instead his pads, elbows, knees and backside. The first time Mackay tried to make contact with the bat he was out. Mailey could not watch this capitulation by someone wearing an Australian cap. He did not find it amusing as Neville Cardus, John Arlott and the other critics had done. For him there was no joy in seeing even the most gifted of bowlers bamboozle a Test batsman who did not take up the challenge. He hated the solemnity that sometimes attacks the pressbox, and once asked colleagues in the box who were taking things very seriously to join in a hymn.

From his early years in the sandhills of Waterloo, he joined Redfern club and then Balmain, for whom he became the first Sydney first grader to take 100 wickets in a season. His 102 wickets in 13 matches in 1915–16 enabled Balmain to win its first premiership. Later he played for Waverley, Manly and Middle Harbour. Mailey graduated to the New South Wales team in the 1912–13 season. He came back from service in World War I, aged 32, the best googly bowler in the world, ahead of Bosanquet its inventor and capable of wider, sharper turn than Hordern. Trumper was always Mailey's idol and years later he described in touching words how in his initial first grade match he clean bowled Trumper with the googly. "I felt like a boy who had killed a dove," wrote Mailey.

At the age of 35, his Test career began dramatically in 1920–21 when he took 36 wickets, an Australian record, in four Tests against Johnny Douglas' English side. This record ran for 57 years till Rodney Hogg beat it in 1978–79. Australia's captain Warwick Armstrong did not bowl Mailey in the second Test, although he used seven bowlers. In the Fourth Test at Melbourne Mailey showed big Warwick what a mistake that had been by taking 9 for 121—and the tenth man was dropped from his bowling.

Mailey went to England for the first of his two tours there in 1921 taking 146 wickets in all games at 19.78. Four years later he topped the Australian bowling averages in England at the age of 40 with 141 wickets at 18.70, including 9 for 86 against Lancashire. He also toured South Africa with Australia in 1920–21. In his last Test for Australia against England at The Oval in 1926, Mailey bowled Jack Hobbs with a full toss. He also dismissed Sutcliffe, Woolley, Chapman, Stevens and Rhodes, but he liked that full toss best.

Mailey got more pleasure recalling the Shield match at Melbourne in 1926 against Victoria, however, than he did from his Test records. Victoria scored 1,107, a world record total for an innings in first-class matches, and Mailey finished with 4 for 362. "A chap in the crowd kept dropping his catches," Mailey said. "I was just finding a length when the innings finished."

He had exceptionally long and powerful fingers and when

Mailey delivering the ball with a copybook side-on action.

he wrapped them around a cricket ball it almost disappeared. He moved in to bowl off half a dozen, short, bouncy paces, with his bowling hand tucked down behind his buttocks, and as he reached the stumps he swung his arm high above his head and let the ball go with a neat movement of wrist and fingers. At the other end, batsmen could hear the ball buzzing, such was the remarkable amount of "work" he got on it. As the ball left Mailey's hand it appeared to be badly overpitched, but the spin cut the ball down in its flight in front of the batsman, leaving him with the problems of deciding which way it would turn and how fast. Mailey got along with an appeal Neville Cardus described as "an apologetic whimper."

On the 1921 trip to England he took all ten wickets for 66 against Gloucestershire. Team-mates joshed him by saying he could have got Gloucester out more cheaply. "Perhaps but I wanted a good title for my book," he said. Years later he published the book *Ten For 66—and All That*, an entertaining work that oozed with wry humour. Mailey said he got bored with writing it once he had the task beaten. He was a great beginner, but often didn't finish things too well. He organised a marvellous trip to America in 1932 for Australia's star cricketers, a joyous romp that was also Bradman's honeymoon trip, but frequently was missing when the side was asked to show all their passports or some other crisis occurred.

In South Africa in 1921–22, he was used by Herbie Collins mainly to mop up the tail-end of innings after the faster bowlers, Gregory, McDonald and Macartney had dismissed the top order batsmen, but he still took 13 wickets in the three Tests played. In the Third Test, after the first two had been drawn, Mailey scored the single required to give Australia victory in the fourth innings, a feat that gave him great glee.

Mailey retired from Tests after the 1926 English tour when the Australian Board of Control objected to him pursuing his profession in journalism and commenting on matches in which he often starred. He relieved the strain of his work as a cartoonist and commentator with landscape painting and by taking teams away to wherever he thought there would be a bit of fun. His rules on these trips were simple—nobody got a duck and the home team won if possible. Denzil Bachelor, the English critic, recalled umpiring for Mailey's side in a country match in which Mailey delivered a ball which removed the leg bail while the batsman chased it outside off stump. "Better call no ball," Mailey murmured. "Chap hasn't scored."

In his all too brief five years of Test cricket Mailey played for Australia 21 times, six times dismissing five batsmen or more in an innings and twice taking 10 wickets in a match. Having won a Test match with the required single and set a 10th wicket Australia-England partnership record of 127 in 1924–25 with Johnny Taylor (108), Mailey, who made 46 not out that day, was content to remain a comparative duffer with the bat. In all first-class matches he took five wickets or more in an innings 61 times and captured 10 wickets in a match 16 times. He summed up his bowling this way: "Sometimes I am attacked by waves of accuracy, and I don't trust them."

For New South Wales his best analysis was 8 for 81 against Victoria at Sydney in 1920-21 six years before conceding that memorable 4 for 362. Mailey's 102 wickets in a Sydney grade season was not repeated until Bill O'Reilly took 108 for St George in 1941–42 and Hughie Chilvers took 110 for Northern Districts, also in 1941–42. It was Mailey who, when rebuked by Australian team manager Syd Smith for offering some of his spin bowling secrets to England spinner Ian Peebles, replied: "Spin bowling is an art—and art is international."

In 1955–56, when the New South Wales Cricket Association gave Mailey and Johnny Taylor a testimonial match in Sydney, the two old men went out to the middle at the lunch interval, Mailey in an overcoat. Mailey delivered just one ball to Taylor—and to the crowd's immense glee, bowled him. Said Mailey afterwards: "Perhaps I should always have bowled with my coat on."

One of the best slow off-spin bowlers Australia has produced, and on figures the most successful. He is one of only three bowlers to take more than 300 wickets in Sheffield Shield matches, and the only spinner in the 1970s who could swing big matches for Australia. He sometimes suffered from the whims of selectors and was underbowled by Bill Lawry, but under Ian Chappell he enjoyed several notable successes for Australia and South Australia.

Mallett, 6 ft 3 ins, lean and wiry, was born in the Sydney suburb of Chatswood, an instinctively reticent character so quiet team-mates dubbed him "Rowdy." He once lost his way to a State team's net practice in Adelaide but was too shy to ask his way to the ground—an official found him wandering the streets. He spent his youth in Perth and was twice chosen for Western Australia while playing with the Mt Lawley club, but each time was made 12th man. With his friend, leg-spinner Terry Jenner, he reasoned that he would get more opportunities in South Australia than in Western Australia, where Tony Lock and Tony Mann held the spinning spots.

Mallett arrived in South Australia with a season's experience playing for Ayr in 1967 in the Scottish League behind him. A Scottish paper tabbed him "the best spin bowler in Scotland," which maybe is why he has continued to wear a vivid red-tartan jacket. After a couple of club matches in

MALLETT, Ashley Alexander ("Rowdy"), 1945–

First-Class Averages: Batting, 2,326 runs at 13.60; Bowling, 693 wickets at 26.27.

Tests (38 plus one abandoned): 430 runs at 11.62; 132 wickets at 29.84.

685

Ashley Mallett clean bowls Derek Underwood.

Adelaide he was named in the South Australian side soon after the start of the 1967–68 season. At his first South Australian practice, he kept bowling after a spinning finger was dislocated until Bradman took him to the doctor in his car.

In 1968, Mallett went to England with the Australians, playing in the final Test. He took 44 wickets on the trip at 28.36, chances limited by captain Lawry. But he developed into a real match-winner under Chappell for both South Australia and Australia, and his dynamic gully fielding to pace men Lillee and Thomson helped them enormously as they became a devastating opening pair. His catching was all the more surprising as he wore contact lenses.* Off the field, he was a scholarly-looking trained journalist, given to peering over the top of his spectacles. With the bat he occasionally hung around to add valuable runs. Long tours were not his strength because of a tendency towards homesickness but Ian Chappell knew how to get him right for big matches.

Faster through the air than Ian Johnson, he bowled tight for hours at a time. His persistence finally won him recognition. He visited England twice under Ian Chappell, playing a big role in important games despite comparatively small tour bags. In 1972 he took 37 wickets at 31.37, when Massie and Lillee took more than 50 wickets, and in 1975 took 31 wickets at 39.36. He retired in 1976, having played in 35 Tests over eight years, but in 1977 he returned to join WSC, and when the dispute was settled continued in first-class cricket until the end of 1980–81, and played in three more Tests, including the Centenary Test at Lord's in 1980. His 344 Shield wickets was second only to Clarrie Grimmett's 513 Shield victims, with Tony Lock on 302 the only other bowler to take more than 300.

MALONE, Michael Francis, 1950–

First-Class Averages: Batting, 914 runs at 17.24; Bowling, 260 wickets at 24.77.

Tests (1): 46 runs at 46.00; 6 wickets at 12.83.

A tall, dark West Australian right-arm medium-pace bowler of swing and cut who bowled an impeccable length and varied his pace cleverly. His skills deserved greater Test recognition but he joined WSC just as he reached his prime and the two-year break cost him many Test appearances. This was clearly demonstrated when he emerged from the obscurity WSC imposed on him to immediately achieve success with Lancashire. He was a workmanlike fieldsman and occasionally scored useful runs.

Malone, born in Perth, had a lovely high, fluent arm action and approached the bowling crease well-balanced up on his toes. He was seldom heavily punished such was his com-

*South Australia's Eric Freeman, Queensland's Geoff Dymock, New South Wales' David Hourn, England's Geoff Boycott, and South Africa's Eddie Barlow, are among those who played international cricket wearing contact lenses.

686

mand of length and even Clive Lloyd and Vivian Richards when well set found him difficult to despatch. He earned promotion from the Scarborough club's first XI into the WA side in 1974–75. Over the following six seasons he took five wickets in an innings 11 times and twice took 10 wickets in a match, with best figures of 6 for 63 against Victoria at Melbourne in 1976–77. His best analysis in two seasons with Lancashire was 7 for 88 against Nottinghamshire in 1979.

He made his Test debut in 1977 against England at The Oval and celebrated with 5 for 63 in England's first innings and his highest first-class score, 46. The match ended in a draw after almost 12 hours were lost to rain. Malone finished that tour of England with 32 wickets at 26.46. He also toured Pakistan in 1980 with the Australian team under Greg Chappell, but played only two matches, finishing with 1 wicket for 123 runs, scarcely a genuine guide to his skills. Right up to his retirement after the 1981–82 season Malone's accuracy was invaluable to his captains. He was chosen in the Australian teams for one day matches against the West Indies and Pakistan with the specific task of subduing the powerful stroke players for 10 overs and he achieved this in admirable style. Malone, whose son died in a swimming pool tragedy not long before his retirement, was an outstanding Australian Rules fullback with Subiaco who attracted offers from Melbourne clubs before he decided to concentrate on cricket.

MANN, Anthony Longford, 1945–

A cheery, long-serving Western Australian all-rounder who has made a major contribution to his State's rise to the top in inter-State cricket. Mann's left-handed batting and right-arm leg-spinners have been seen in only four Tests but his colourful personality and pugnacious approach to the game have delighted thousands for 20 Australian summers.

First-Class Averages: Batting, 2,397 runs at 24.27; Bowling, 188 wickets at 33.98.

Tests (4): 189 runs at 23.62; 4 wickets at 79.00.

Mann, the son of a wine-grower from the Swan Valley, learned his cricket on the side verandah of the family house in the heart of the Houghton vineyards. Elder brother Dorham was the batsman of the family, brother Bill the fieldsman, and Tony did the bowling. The verandah permitted only a short approach run so Tony bowled leg-spinners, flighting the ball on the high side, "sending them along the rafters and dropping them down from the dark". His father, Jack Mann, was a stalwart of the Middle Swan cricket club, renowned for his fast underarm spinners. His sons all played for the club.

Tony played "A" grade for Midland-Guilford at 14, and at 15 played for the Combined High Schools XI against the Governor's XI, which included Test players Richie Benaud and Neil Harvey. John Inverarity was captain of the school's side,

Rodney Marsh the wicket-keeper. Tony took 7 for 45 and had Harvey stumped down the legside by Marsh. In 1963–64 Tony Mann made his debut for WA but failed to take a wicket in 15 overs and went in last. He was not chosen for the State team again for a further two years.

Mann and Tony Jenner were rivals for the State team, and with Tony Lock already in the side it became obvious WA was not big enough for two spinners. Tony packed his bags to go to South Australia, but it was Jenner who went, taking Ashley Mallett with him. In 1969–70, Mann claimed five wickets in an innings against NSW. Victoria and Queensland, and with 25 wickets at 26.88 that season thought he would make the Australian Second XI's tour of New Zealand. The selectors preferred Jenner and Kerry O'Keeffe. The next summer Mann scored a century against England but the State selectors kept treating him solely as a bowler. Mann spent three winters playing Lancashire League cricket in England with Bacup and minor county cricket with Shropshire, and for the Cavaliers, a side that included Fred Trueman, Ted Dexter and Graeme Pollock. At Exmouth he made a century in 44 minutes for the Cavaliers, who were glad to regard him as an all-rounder. English pitches taught him to adjust his flight and vary his pace.

In 1977–78, with Australia's Test attack weakened by the loss of the Packer players, Mann was chosen at 32 for Australia. In his second Test, Bob Simpson sent him in as a nightwatchman against India at Perth. Mann hit 105 and this innings enabled Australia to win a close match by two wickets. His consistent all-round performances have been one of WA's strengths for many seasons. At the end of the 1981–82 Australian season he had made two first-class centuries, scored 50 or more 10 times, and five times taken five wickets or more in an innings—best figures 6 for 94 v. South Australia in 1974–75. He had also made 42 catches.

MANNING, John Stephen, 1924–

First-Class Averages: Batting, 2,747 runs at 15.60; Bowling, 513 wickets at 22.68.

An orthodox left-arm spin bowler and left-hand batsman who learned the game in Adelaide but played most of his first-class cricket for Northamptonshire for whom he produced many impressive performances. He took 116 wickets in the 1956 season for Northants, 104 in 1957, 111 in 1959. In 1956, he also had his career best figures of 7 for 68 against Surrey. He was awarded his County cap in 1956, and in 1957 was one of the players responsible for Northants finishing runners-up in the County championship.

A dark, curly-haired, lightly-framed figure, Manning could bowl long accurate spells without losing line or length. He was also a useful batsman who scored 132 for Northants against Yorkshire in 1957. He was on the County books as a full-time professional from 1956 to 1960 but played little in the 1960 season because of injury. Before he settled in England, he took 66 wickets at 29.98 in three seasons for South Australia and returned there after his career with Northants. Overall he took 428 wickets at 21.10 for Northants.

MARKS, THE FAMILY

A father and two sons who gave exceptional service to New South Wales cricket over a long period. Enthusiastic and efficient in all they tackled, the Marks family were all admirable inter-State cricketers who were occasionally mentioned as Test prospects. But through a mixture of strong competition and bad luck they did not make it.

Alexander Edward Marks (1910–) was a splendid left-hand batsman and left-arm slow bowler who forced his way into the NSW team in 1928–29 after a series of fine performances for the Randwick club. He was at his peak at a time of a very powerful Australian XI. In 35 first-class matches he scored 2,038 runs at 37.05. His three centuries included an innings of 201 against Queensland in 1935–36. He had little opportunity with the ball because of the presence of so many fine spinners, but took 5 wickets at 70.80.

His eldest son, **Neil Graham Marks** (1938–) played for the Northern Districts club, a punishing left-handed batsman who made 568 runs in 10 matches for NSW at 47.33, with two centuries, 180 not out on his debut, and 103 in his next match. His youngest son, **Lynn Alexander Marks** (1942–) played with Northern Districts and also made two first-class centuries. Lynn compiled 1873 first-class runs at 30.70. Lynn's top-score was 185 against South Australia at Adelaide in 1964–65 when he shared a record second wicket stand of 378 with Doug Walters. Neil's first-class career was cut short by an operation for a hole in his heart. All three Marks were splendid fieldsmen.

MARR, Alfred Percy 1862–1940

First-Class Averages: Batting, 304 runs at 11.25; Bowling, 14 wickets at 32.42.

Tests (1): 5 runs at 2.50.

A right-arm medium pace bowler and right-handed batsman, who played for New South Wales before the Sheffield Shield competition began, and in one Test for Australia. He was chosen three times to tour England with Australian teams on the strength of his achievements in Sydney grade cricket but each time had to declare himself unavailable. He left a record of great fitness and pluck when his teams were in trouble.

Typical of Marr's determination was his 8 for 28 in the second innings when Queensland beat New South Wales in an against the odds match in 1884. New South Wales scored 78 and 39, Queensland 122 and 68. Queensland seemed certain to win the match but he gave them a hard fight in a defiant second innings spell. In his only Test in 1884–85 at Melbourne Australia made 11 changes when its top side demanded 50 per cent of the gatemoney. England won the match by 10 wickets and Marr disappeared from Test cricket. Marr, who played for the old Carlton club in Sydney had a career top-score of 69 in first-class cricket but scored many centuries in grade cricket, one of them at the age of 67.

MARSH, Jack,
1874–1916

First-Class Averages:
Batting, 40 runs at 5.00;
Bowling, 34 wickets at
21.47.

A controversial right-arm fast bowler for New South Wales, who in only two seasons three times took five wickets in an innings and once took 10 wickets in a match. Marsh, born at Yugilbar in the Clarence River district, was a full-blood Aboriginal, with thick, wiry hair who came into first-class cricket at the turn of the century when a campaign to eliminate chucking was at its peak. He was discovered when an official of the old Sydney Cricket Club saw him throwing a boomerang for holidaymakers at La Perouse, on the outskirts of Sydney. The official was impressed with the remarkable whip in Marsh's arms and the lithe manner in which he moved.

Marsh was made a ground bowler at Rushcutter's Bay, and after a period of bowling to the Sydney club's best batsmen at practice was chosen in the club's first grade side. There was something in the flexibility of his bowling arm that enabled him to bowl very easily at exceptional speed. Sydney grade batsmen stamped him as a potential champion. In a trial match between the powerful New South Wales team and a State trial XI at Sydney Cricket Ground in November, 1900, Marsh clean bowled Victor Trumper. This success should have vindicated those who claimed Marsh was a world-beater, but instead it led to trouble. For the umpire at square leg who witnessed Trumper's dismissal, W. Curran, labelled Marsh a chucker and openly said he would no-ball Marsh for it when play resumed next day.

The secretary of the Sydney Club took Marsh to a doctor early the following morning and had Marsh's bowling arm encased in splints and bandages. Marsh arrived at the ground brandishing a medical certificate which said he could not throw the ball with his arm bound up in this way. Curran was at square-leg again when play continued, but despite the bandages and splints Marsh bowled just as fast and still with that easy, fluid hostility. Curran came off at the luncheon interval claiming he had been humiliated and all at the ground agreed that the chucking stigma had been quashed for good by Marsh and his advisors.

There were four interstate matches in the summer of 1900–01 and Marsh took 24 wickets at 22.37. In March, 1902, Jack Marsh opened the bowling in Brisbane for New South

690

Wales and Alex Henry for Queensland, the only time in first-class cricket that Aboriginals have been on opposing sides (Australian cricket historian Johnnie Moyes wrote that the only comparable event was when two Aboriginals played together in the Victorian side). The match was drawn, Henry taking 3 for 101, Marsh 5 for 131. In the next season Marsh played his last game for NSW, also against Queensland.

Frank Laver was batting for Victoria when Marsh was no-balled for chucking. Marsh lost his temper and as the ball was returned to him he rushed up the pitch, caught it, and threw it at Laver. Laver ducked and laughed. Marsh regained his composure and apologised to Laver, who said: "Don't worry any more about it, Jack. I've often felt like doing the same thing." Victoria won this match in Melbourne by five wickets but in the return at Sydney, New South Wales put up a much stronger showing. Dismissed for 170, they were 109 behind for the first innings, but then Trumper played a superlative innings of 230, batting four hours 35 minutes without a mistake. Victoria needed 344 to win and with Marsh to open the bowling New South Wales appeared to have a strong hold on the match. But Victoria, some of whose batsmen claimed Marsh was a chucker, had brought with them their own umpire, the controversial Bob Crockett, who had no-balled Marsh three times for throwing in Melbourne. Crockett proceeded to no-ball Marsh 19 times for throwing, including three times in his first over to Warwick Armstrong.

The crowd booed incessantly every time Marsh took the ball to bowl but the booing had no effect on Crockett's composure. The crowd apparently considered Marsh was being victimised because Crockett no-balled only Marsh's slower ball, whereas Curran and other umpires who called him no-balled his faster ball. After the splints incident with Curran in Sydney, Marsh had considerably reduced his pace, relying more on accuracy and swing than on sheer speed. His jerky wrist action was very hard to follow, and some experienced players claimed it was perfectly legal. Nobody in Sydney grade cricket objected to Marsh's action, and after he bowed out of the State side he continued to head the grade averages.

In 1903–04, against an English batting lineup which that season scored freely off Australian bowlers in winning three Tests, Marsh took 5 for 55 for a Bathurst XV. The English batsmen pronounced his action perfectly legal and named Marsh the best bowler they faced on that Australian tour.

Among New South Wales cricket fans there was a strong feeling that Marsh may have been the victim of the anti-throwing hysteria prevalent at the time. He retired from cricket not long afterwards and spent sometimes demonstrating his skill as a bowler in a travelling circus. He was not heard of again until his death at Orange in what was described as a drunken brawl.

MARSH, Rodney William ("Bacchus") 1947–

First-Class Averages: Batting, 11,257 runs at 36.66; Dismissals, 739 (681 catches, 58 stumpings).

Tests (83, plus one abandoned): 3,362 runs at 28.02; Dismissals, 302 (291 catches, 11 stumpings).

One of the phenomena of cricket, thickset yet agile wicket-keeper whose competitive makeup has enabled him to set records that may never be broken. When he first came into the Test team in 1970–71, some very sound judges considered him the worst wicket-keeper to represent Australia. He has confounded them by remaining in the job for a record number of Tests and by dismissing more batsmen than any 'keeper in the history of Test cricket. The derogatory labels such as "Iron Gloves," "Fat Rodney," and "slips fieldsman in pads," have long since been replaced by admiration for his record-breaking feats and the manner in which, week after week, he gives everything for his team.

There is probably no more popular cricketer in Australia, Dennis Lillee included. Together they have made a devastating combination, Lillee overcoming his serious back problems, Marsh ignoring an arthritic right knee that swells like a balloon at times. The sight of Marsh flinging his bulky frame sideways, both feet off the ground, to bring in another catch, has become familiar to thousands of small boys, just as his fierce clubbing of the ball has become so well known to opposing bowlers. Asked to pick between Marsh diving in front of the slips cordon to pick up a faint edge from a Lillee outswinger, and Marsh's powerhouse hitting, I'd settle for more of the treatment he handed to New Zealand's Lance Cairns in a one day match in 1980–81 when he hit 26 runs off five balls. One shot soared right out of Adelaide Oval and another landed on the bonnet of a car intended for a player's award.

This jowly, pugnacious father of three first donned his wicket-keeper's gear for the under 16s at Armadale, the Perth suburb where he was born. He was eight years old at the time. After school he and his brother Graham, now a world famous golfer, played mock "Tests." Rodney joined West Perth club as a teenager and progressed through the grades to the Western Australian team in 1968–69 when he scored 104 against the West Indies on his debut. He has always had weight problems, probably because of his liking for Swan Lager and Western Australian crayfish.

He made his debut for Australia at Brisbane against England in 1970–71. Veteran Test watchers who could recall the stylish 'keeping of Oldfield, Tallon and Grout could not believe selectors had preferred Marsh to Brian Taber when they saw Marsh in action, for he seemed so slow of reflex, and so ponderous of movement that it was to them an incomprehensible selection. But what Bradman and the other selectors who had a hand in Marsh's inclusion had realised was that the demands of wicket-keeping had changed dramatically since the days when a wicket-keeper stood up close and claimed numerous stumping victims. The emphasis on pace bowlers who were favoured by regular new balls meant that 'keepers spent most of each innings standing back.

Marsh catches Andy Roberts off the bowling of Max Walker without disturbing the seagulls.

Marsh's record since then shows how right the Australian selectors were, for he has made only 11 Test stumpings. Indeed he so rarely stands up on the stumps his stumping skill remains difficult to assess. Standing back his reflexes are less than automatic but he has time to judge how to use his remarkable skills as an acrobat and once he decides becomes totally committed. Not for Rodney the half-hearted dive—he goes for his catches like an Olympic swimmer on the starting platform. Significantly, when he equalled the record for most dismissals in a Test rubber in 1975–76 against the West Indies, all 26 victims were caught.

In his fourth Test appearance he had made 92 in an Australia score of 493 when Bill Lawry declared, depriving Marsh of possibly becoming the first Australian 'keeper to score a century. In the final Test of that series against Illingworth's English team, Marsh caught John Hampshire off the bowling of Dennis Lillee, who was also playing his first Test series. It was the start of a remarkable association that has seen Marsh dismiss almost a third of Lillee's record total of Test victims. Indeed he has developed a system of signals with Lillee that are immediately and often fruitfully acted on by the bowler.

On his first visit to England in 1972 Marsh equalled the record for an England-Australia Test by taking five catches in England's second innings in the First Test at Manchester. He followed with a spectacular knock of 91 in 123 minutes, add-

693

Marsh dives headlong towards the stumps to run out West Indian opener Roy Fredericks.

ing 104 in 82 minutes with Gleeson for the ninth wicket, 60 runs in boundaries from four sixes and nine fours. He ended that series with 23 victims, a record for Australia in a rubber against England. He earned his success by training very hard and by matching the fierce competitiveness of his captain, Ian Chappell. Often when he did his laps around cricket ovals to stay in trim Lillee ran with him, a friendship that dates back to 1966 when Marsh was a trainee teacher playing for the University club in Perth and Lillee was a tearaway opening bowler for the Perth club.

Marsh made his highest first–class score, 236, for Western Australia against Pakistan at Perth in 1972–73. He carried this form into Tests that summer and in the First Test against Pakistan at Adelaide became the first Australian 'keeper to make a Test century by scoring 118. He scored further Test centuries against New Zealand (132) at Adelaide in 1973–74 and against England in the Centenary Test at Melbourne in 1977, when his 110 not out probably swung a great match. On his third tour of England in 1977 there were stories about him smashing dressing-room fittings when he hurled a bat away in disgust at an umpire's decision but on the field he kept his combative urges within reason.

By signing with WSC Marsh was estimated to have more than doubled his income from cricket, which enabled him to become a full-time cricketer. He had always been at pains to

694

keep his wife Roslyn and sons out of the limelight but by joining WSC he put unexpected pressure on them. "During the
early days of WSC, it was really hard on the family," he said.
"There were some nasty telephone calls." The Marsh family
live in a house at Dalkeith, Perth, which Rodney bought from
his brother Graham.

He was one of the successes of the WSC matches and returned to traditional cricket after a two year break a complete
professional, determined to keep fit and hold off the challenges of young 'keepers for his Australian team place. His
appeals were just as raucous, his headlong dives to scoop up
snicks just as fearless. Only his batting appeared to have faded. He could still cut a short ball as ruthlessly and drive half
volleys back over the bowler's head just as boldly, but his co-
ordination appeared lacking on the legside swings that had
been so devastating. But as Lance Cairns discovered in
1980–81 it did not pay to consider this was permanent.

In the English summer of 1981 Marsh became the most successful 'keeper of all time when he passed Alan Knott's record
of 263 Test victims. In the Australian summer that followed
he broke Neil Harvey's Australian appearance record when
he played in his 80th Test, though there is doubt over
whether he achieved that record in the Second Test at Sydney
or the Third Test at Adelaide against the West Indies. At 35,
he seemed indestructible and enormously keen to go on. "I'll
give those young blokes something to chase," he said defiantly as he prepared for yet another season and his second tour
to Pakistan. At that stage of his career he had made 10 first-
class centuries, six of them for WA, was approaching 750
first-class dismissals and had won every honour open to a
Test cricketer, except the Australian captaincy.

MARSHAL, Allan, 1883–1915

First-Class Averages:
Batting, 5,177 runs at
27.98; Bowling, 119
wickets at 22.84.

One of the greatest Queensland batsmen of all time who in
England with the Surrey County side established himself as a
superlative hitter of the ball. He was also a remarkable
fieldsman and a versatile bowler of both pace and spin.

He was born at Warwick on the Darling Downs and went to
Brisbane with his parents at the age of four. He learned the
game with his brothers, Marcus and Isby, in the front of the
family house in Gladstone Road, South Brisbane. His first club
was the Brooksteads, named after the family house, but he
played with Franklins and Cliftons and before the electoral
system was introduced in Brisbane for the Graziers.

About this time he came under the guidance of Australian
players Percy McDonnell, Harry Boyle and Sam Jones. He
played for South Brisbane when the electoral system began,
but in the 1902–03 season he joined the Paddington club in
Sydney, especially to further his cricket education, and

played in one match in which Victor Trumper scored 324. He returned to Brisbane in 1903–04 and won selection in the Queensland side but then sailed to England for further experience in a game to which he was by now passionately devoted.

While he was qualifying for Surrey, he had the good luck to play for London County's side in 1905–06 captained by Dr W. G. Grace. In 1906 Marshal showed he was a hitter of extraordinary power. In all matches in 1906 he scored a remarkable 4,350 runs and made 14 centuries, topscore 300 not out. Surrey offered to pay him a winter allowance while he spent two years qualifying for their senior side, a move that was interpreted by some as poaching, although it lifted Marshal into a higher level of cricket.

He was a trifle disappointing in 1907, his first year with Surrey, partly because of a row over his right to play County cricket, but in 1908 his hitting brought comparisons with the heaviest strikers of the ball cricket had known. Sidney Pardon, editor of *Wisden*, wrote: "Some of Marshal's hits in the matches against Middlesex and Kent at The Oval were beyond the capacity of any other batsman now playing first-class cricket. He lacks Jessop's ability to score in all directions but with his immense advantages of height and reach—he stands 6 ft 3 ins—he certainly can send the ball further. In every way he is a thorough cricketer." He matched Tom Hayward almost run for run while also taking 55 wickets and proving a virtuoso in the field.

Marshal made 176 for Surrey against Worcestershire—the highest score of his career—in 200 minutes and followed with centuries against Northants, Philadelphia, Middlesex and Kent, the latter a superb 167 when he added 239 for the third wicket with Hobbs. He also made 12 scores over 50 and five times took five wickets in an innings. This plus his fielding made him an obvious choice as one of *Wisden*'s five Cricketers of The Year. Only five Queensland players have won this honour, Peter Burge, Don Tallon, Bill Brown, Alan Border and Marshal.

Pardon rated Marshal the finest fieldsman in England and the surest catch. Surrey terminated his engagement in unfortunate circumstances at the end of the 1910 season claiming Marshal was guilty of "insubordination." Marshal returned to Queensland, where he won back his place in the State side. In 1910–11, he scored 106 against South Africa for an Australian XI, and hit 50 and 34 for Queensland against the South Africans. He sustained his reputation for spectacular hitting in club cricket until World War I began. He joined the AIF and died of enteric fever in a hospital in Malta, without having played in a Test or a Shield match. In 198 first-class innings, he scored eight centuries. He took 114 first-class catches and took five wickets or more in an innings seven times.

A resolute, heavily-bearded allrounder who captained Tasmania in three matches against Victoria between February, 1851, and March, 1854, which are regarded as the first first-class matches played in Australia. The matches made Marshall Australia's oldest representative cricketer, as he was 55 when the first match was played and 58 when he retired after the third match. Although 1795 is accepted by cricket historians as the year of his birth, it has not been proved as it occurred in England before registration of births became compulsory.

Marshall or his father are believed to have been connected with one of the early garrison regiments after the Tasmanian colony was founded in 1804. He was involved in the creation of the Hobart Town Cricket Club in 1832, and in 1835 he proved the match-winner for the club in a game against a United Services side drawn from officers of the 21st Regiment and HMS *Hyacinth*. He batted 105 minutes for 13 in Hobart CC's first innings and made 10 out of 84 in the second. As a bowler and wicket-keeper, he had a hand in eight dismissals in the United Services' innings of 39 and 21. Shortly afterwards he joined those who left the Hobart Town CC to form the Derwent club and he was the main reason the Derwent club were seldom defeated over the next 20 years.

In 1837, Marshall captained a British-born team against a Tasmanian-born side in a match that aroused wide interest, the Tasmanians winning. In February, 1839, hundreds of people watched a "festival match" for a silver cup and 22 sovereigns, Marshall accepting the prize when his team won by an innings and 32 runs. *The Tasmanian*, in reporting this match, said, "Luncheon was supplied on the ground to upwards of 100 persons and the band of the 51st Regiment performed."

Marshall formed a closely knit cricketing group, according to Roger Page's *History of Tasmanian Cricket*, with talent counting less than social position. Marshall's clique was drawn from the wealthy aristocracy, landowners and professional men who were aloof from other free classes like shopkeepers, labourers and publicans. Marshall was employed by the Bank of Van Dieman's Land, rising from the office of collector to senior accountant on his retirement. He married a Miss Tabart, daughter of an Oatlands gentleman farmer, which Page said further strengthened his standing with the Derwent CC. He was a very strong manager with plenty of energy and slowly weeded out the older native-born aristocrats to give young men in the club a chance.

For many years Marshall owned Lyndhurst, a property on New Town Road that was later the home of the Lyons family of political renown. He was chosen to captain Tasmania against Victoria in February, 1851, his team comprising three players from Hobart one each from Longford, Perth and West-

MARSHALL, John, 1795–1876

First-Class Averages: Batting, 46 runs at 7.66; Dismissals 4 (1 catch, 3 stumpings).

bury, and five from Launceston. He won the toss in this and the two matches against Victoria that followed in March, 1852, at the South Yarra ground, and in March, 1854, when the players returned to Launceston for "the decider." In all three matches he kept a firm hold on field placements and team discipline. He was too old to bowl at 55 when the matches began but kept wicket with great skill and generally was accepted as the difference between the sides, Tasmania winning the first and third matches. One Victorian paper praised his 'keeping as "seldom surpassed in England; as sharp as a needle." Marshall retired after the last match and within a few years the Derwent club, deprived of his firm management, disappeared when it merged with the Young Derwent club.

Although the uncertainty over Marshall's birth remains, there is no doubt that he fully deserves the title "Father of Tasmanian cricket," for his name appears more often than any other in the accounts of early matches on the island. He was a successful bowler in his youth, an outstanding captain, resolute opening batsman, and in his late 50s alert enough to stump Victorian batsmen off the spinners. Only George Moore (born 1820), who played his last match for NSW in 1872–73 in his 53rd year approaches Marshall's record, but Moore did not match Marshall's versatility. Marshall died at Kent Town, Hobart, in September, 1876, when his age was given as 81.

MARTIN, John Wesley, 1931–

First-Class Averages: Batting, 3,970 runs at 23.77; Bowling, 445 wickets at 31.17.

Tests (8): 214 runs at 17.83; 17 wickets at 48.94.

A jaunty little allrounder whose big-hitting and unorthodox spin bowling, coupled with an enthusiastic approach, made him one of Australia's most entertaining cricketers for 11 years between 1956–57 and 1967–68. He hit some massive sixes batting near the tail and he hoodwinked plenty of famous batsmen bowling left-arm googlies, but it is for his smiling, enthusiastic demeanour that he is to be fondly remembered. He was too erratic to enjoy a long Test career but he toured England, India, South Africa and New Zealand with Australian teams.

Martin hailed from Burrell Creek, a small township not far from Taree, where the Martins gathered once a year to play a Burrell Creek XI. He learned to bowl at the Bo Bo school on a concrete pitch under the tuition of John Dennis, a master with a love for cricket. Johnnie was one of a family of 10 children—he had three brothers and six sisters—whose father ran the Burrell Creek Post Office and general store, and acted as agents for local dairymen. He made his first trip to Sydney at 15 to watch Bradman and Barnes make 234 runs each and Hutton hit a sparkling 39 and what he saw fired him with the urge to become a Test cricketer.

698

He practised every night until dark with his brothers and sisters and became a prolific scorer in the Taree district. He was approached in 1951 to play Rugby League for Newtown and cricket for Randwick, but he delayed his appearance in Sydney until 1953–54 when he joined the Petersham club as a batsman. For the next few years he paid for a season ticket that enabled him to leave Taree at 9.40 on Friday and arrive in Sydney at 6 a.m. on Saturday morning. After playing in a grade match he left Sydney at 7.45 p.m. on Saturday and arrived back in Taree at 2 a.m. on Sunday. Fed-up with all the travelling he lived for a time in a house at Marrickville but his father persuaded him to return to Burrell Creek to manage the Post Office.

Martin made his debut for NSW Colts as a batsman but when his form slumped he was dropped and Petersham relegated him to the seconds. He first played for the State senior side as a bowler in 1956–57. In 1958–59 he was offered a job in Adelaide, which he took in the hope of furthering his Test prospects. His ambition was to play in a Test against England and he appeared a strong chance when he took 7 for 110 in November, 1958, for South Australia against Peter May's English tourists. But until 1960–61 the selectors preferred to rely on pace and when they did use a left-arm spinner Lindsay Kline was preferred.

Johnny Martin clubs a ball behind point in typically belligerent style.

He made his Test debut at 29 in Melbourne in 1960–61 against the West Indies, starting in spectacular fashion by scoring 55 in a ninth wicket stand of 97 in 72 minutes with "Slasher" Mackay and taking the wickets of Rohan Kanhai, Gary Sobers and Frank Worrell in four deliveries. Kline displaced him after two Tests but Martin returned for the Fifth Test at Melbourne.

Most experts believed Martin's slow, lofted spinners—the "Chinaman" or left-arm googly was his stock ball—were more penetrative than Kline's left-arm off-breaks and googlies, but when the 1961 Australian team for England was picked Kline was again preferred to Martin. Johnnie spent the season playing Lancashire League cricket with Colne, taking 70 wickets at 12.04 and scoring 706 runs at 35.30.

He was by now a genuine allrounder, capable of a useful contribution with bat or ball. In grade cricket he continued to hit some enormous sixes and over the years is believed to have hit more than 200 sixes for Petersham. One or two of his blows in Sheffield Shield matches still bob up on diagrams of famous big-hits.

He went back to England in 1964 with Bob Simpson's Australian team and proved immensely popular. Simpson introduced him to guests at dinners as "the Mayor of Burrell Creek" and Englishmen loved it. But Martin was not used in Tests, scoring 362 runs at 19.05 and taking 35 wickets at 32.62 on the tour. He had better luck in South Africa in 1966–67, forcing his way into the Fifth Test with some outstanding figures in minor matches, including 7 for 30 against Griqualand West. But in this and in Tests against India and Pakistan he could never recapture the three wickets in four balls magic of his first Test.

Martin took 293 wickets in all for NSW at 30.67. In all first-class matches he took five wickets in an innings 17 times and once had 10 wickets in a match. He was a dependable fieldsman who held 114 first-class catches. With the bat he had a highest score of 101, his sole first-class century. When he had a heart attack in November, 1971, his former cricketer friends opened a testimonial fund for him and a benefit match was held at Wallsend, where he coached for several years after he retired from first-class cricket. He made a splendid recovery and remains as chirpy and enthusiastic as ever.

MASSIE, Hugh Hamon, 1854–1938

A hard-hitting right-hand batsman who played nine Tests and some historic innings for Australia between 1881 and 1885. He had a splendid physique at 6 ft 1 in and 12 st 7 lb and used his long reach admirably to build a reputation for savagely punishing anything loose in the early years of international matches. His off-driving, straight-driving and cutting were outstanding, and he was one of the best fieldsmen of his time.

Massie was born at Port Fairy, Victoria, but his parents moved to New South Wales when he was three. He was educated at Goulburn and later joined East Sydney CC and then the Albert CC. In full flight, Massie dominated the scoring. Playing for The Rest of Australia against Australia in 1881 at Sydney, he made 80 out of 118 runs put on for the first wicket with A. C. Bannerman. He had made his debut for New South Wales in the 1877–78 season and did well enough over the next three summers to be invited to tour England with the 1880 Australian team. He declined because of his work in banking.

He went to England with the Third Australian team in 1882, however, the last man chosen, and scored more runs on the trip (1,405) than anyone in the team except the captain Billy Murdoch. He opened the batting in the first match of the tour against Oxford, and for three hours thrashed the University attack to score 206, his only century in first-class cricket. He made his second 100 while 12 runs were added by batsmen at the other end.

First-Class Averages: Batting, 2,485 runs at 23.00; Bowling, 2 wickets at 30.00.

Tests (9): 249 runs at 15.56.

In the famous "Ashes" match at The Oval, he opened with Bannerman but by the end of the first morning's play Australia were 6 for 48 and when Garrett was brilliantly caught at long-off the innings folded for 63 runs, the lowest of the tour. Australia struck back by dismissing W. G. Grace for four but England still managed 101, a lead of 38 at the end of the first day.

Here Massie played the innings of his life, taking advantage of heavy overnight rain which made the ball slippery for the bowlers, while Bannerman defended grimly at the other end. In 45 minutes, Massie scored 55 out of 66, in a brave and lusty innings. England made frequent bowling changes but could not halt Massie's hitting. At point Grace was tugging on his beard as Australia cleared the arrears and then Lucas missed a catch from a fierce Massie drive to long-off.

After Massie hit over a half-volley and was bowled by Steel, England dismissed Bonnor, Horan, Bannerman and Giffen, but then a captain's knock by Murdoch saw Australia's lead stretched to 84 runs by the close. The scene that ensued in the Australian dressing-room as the players debated their chances was vividly described by Giffen. Spofforth was adamant they could get England out and this they did to win by seven runs. Australia had beaten England in England in an official Test for the first time, a result that would have been impossible without Massie's daring second innings.

Massie was a genial, companiable character, and it was no surprise when he was picked to captain Australia in the Third Test at Sydney against Shrewsbury's England side in 1884–85

(Australia winning by six runs) after playing in both the 1882–83 and 1884–85 series in Australia. Banking duties continued to interfere with his career but after he retired from first-class cricket in 1888 he gave many thrilling displays of big hitting in grade cricket. On a private visit to England in 1895 he played for MCC against Kent and Cambridge University and for the Gentlemen v. I Zingari in their Jubilee match. The MCC made him an honorary member. His son, **Robert John Allright Massie** (1890–1966) played 16 matches for New South Wales as a bowler, taking 99 wickets at 18.38 each. Unlike his father, R.J.A. was only fair with the bat, scoring just 199 runs at 10.47, best score 50 not out. His career was cut short tragically when he was wounded at Gallipoli.

MASSIE, Robert Arnold Lockeyer 1947–

First-Class Averages: Batting, 380 runs at 10.00; Bowling 178 wickets at 24.47.

Tests (6): 78 runs at 11.14; 31 wickets at 20.87.

A right-arm Perth medium-pacer who for six Tests swung the ball with magic power but lost his wizardry as dramatically as he had found it. Massie took 31 Test wickets in 1972 and 1973, including an amazing bag of 16 wickets in the Lord's Test in 1972 when he took 8 for 84 and 8 for 53, and beat the bat so often, some English batsmen refused to believe his methods were fair and complained about the shape of the balls used and Massie's alleged use of lip salve to retain shine on the new ball.

Massie, who made his debut for Western Australia in 1965–66 without taking a wicket, took seven years to find the chemistry that gave him 16 wickets at Lord's to beat the previous best by an Australian bowler in a Test—14 wickets for 90 by Spofforth in the 1882 Test at The Oval. Only Jim Laker (19 wickets) and Sydney Barnes (17) have taken more wickets in a Test. Two years before his dazzling debut at Lord's Massie had been rejected after a trial by Northamptonshire while he was playing for Kilmarnock in Scottish League cricket. And he had seldom looked a record-breaking bowler in grade matches for Perth's Bassendean-Bayswater club.

Most of the Australians who played in "Massie's match" agreed that conditions were absolutely perfect for swing bowling. There was a strong, low-hanging cloud cover, humidity was high. Indeed Massie swung the ball so much he frequently was frustrated in beating the bat but also missing the stumps. The strange aftermath was that Massie never again took five wickets in a Test innings. Within a year after his Lord's triumph, he could not find a place in the West Australian side. When he went without wickets in 1972–73 in the West Indies, Australians blamed the thin Caribbean atmosphere, but the truth was that he had lost his control of swing. Foolishly, he tried to increase his penetration by adding to his pace, digging the ball into the pitch instead of "giving it air." In the process he unconsciously altered his action, turning chest-on to the batsman. He tried everything to get back the knack of swinging the ball, trained vigorously, consulted experts, studied films of his bowling coups. Occasionally, the old ability to swing the ball sharply returned for a few minutes, but then it disappeared again.

Massie, son of a chiropodist, born in the Perth suburb of Subiaco, curved the ball extremely late on his great days, moving the ball in or away from the batsmen off a good length. He learned his cricket at Bedford Park Youth Club while attending Hillcrest Primary and Mount Lawley High School. Even Geoff Boycott, a master in handling swing, was bemused by Massie. When Lillee took the other four wickets at Lord's he and Massie ranked as a great new Australian opening pair, the long sought replacements for Lindwall and Miller. Massie took only seven wickets in the three Tests that followed his Lord's triumph and only eight in two Tests against a weak Pakistan outfit the following summer at home.

To the end of his career he remained an enigma, who never once took five wickets in an innings for WA, though he did it six times for Australia. Most bowlers would settle for one magical match when they got it all together as Massie did at Lord's, in his first Test, but he didn't even rate it his best performance, preferring his 7 for 76 against the Rest Of The World in 1971–72 at Sydney, a performance that won him the trip to England in the first place, when his victims included Sobers and Graham Pollock.

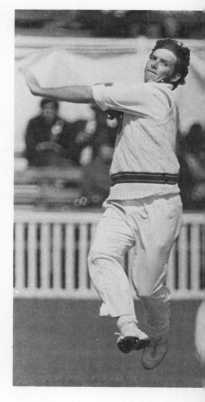

A tiny right-arm leg-break bowler and stubborn late order right-hand batsman who won a unique place in cricket history in one incredible day. He was tough and persistent, his skin darkened by a lifetime in the sun, overcoming his lack of height with sound technique. He kept his leg-breaks well up to the batsman, demanding that they play every ball. He was an efficient field and a sure catch.

Matthews learned his cricket at Williamstown, his birthplace, and spent his early years with the local club. Later he played with the Essendon, St Kilda and East Melbourne clubs to improve his job prospects as a groundsman and boost his chances of State selection. He played his first match for Victoria in 1906–07 against Tasmania when he had match figures of 5 for 93 and scored 20 in both innings. He won his place in the Victorian team by scoring 200 for Williamstown on their home ground against South Melbourne's second team, and in that season he took 60 wickets at 12.70 for Williamstown.

His opportunities were limited because of the presence in the Victorian team of spinners Armstrong, Hazlitt and Saunders and he had matches when he was not asked to bowl

MATTHEWS, Thomas James, 1884–1943

First-Class Averages: Batting, 2,149 runs at 24.98; Bowling, 177 wickets at 25.46.

Tests (8): 153 runs at 17.00; 16 wickets at 26.18.

at all. Playing for Victoria against the touring South Africans in November, 1910, he scored 51 and took 3 for 13 and 3 for 33, clearly troubling the South Africans with his spin. He made his debut for Australia at Adelaide against England in January, 1912, scoring 53 in Australia's second innings. His chances with the ball were restricted by Hordern's success, but when leading players declared themselves unavailable for the tour to England for the triangular tournament in 1912, Matthews was chosen to tour under Syd Gregory.

In the first Test of the 1912 tournament Matthews made 49 not out in Australia's total of 448 against South Africa. On the second day only Faulkner resisted strongly against the bowling of Emery, Whitty and Hazlitt. At 7 for 265 Matthews took the ball, bowling Beaumont with his first delivery, trapping Pegler lbw with the second and Ward lbw with the third. Following-on South Africa could not cope with the bowling of Kelleway. At 5 for 70, Matthews bowled Taylor, caught and bowled Schwartz with the next delivery, and then caught and bowled the unfortunate Ward with the following ball to complete his second hat-trick in the match. Two hat-tricks in a Test match on one day was sensational stuff, but they were the only wickets Matthews took in the match. His figures were 3 for 16 and 3 for 38.

Although he could not repeat the form shown in this famous double hat-trick, he proved a splendid leg-spinner while the pitches were hard, but lost hostility after rain. He finished the tour with 35 wickets at 19.37 and 584 runs at 18.25, top-score 93 against Sussex at Brighton, hitting very hard after Macartney had softened up the bowling. He continued in reliable all round form at home and in the 1912–13 season took 5 for 25 to help dismiss NSW for 84 and pave the way to Victoria's six wickets win. In all first-class matches he took five wickets in an innings eight times, best figures 7 for 46. His first-class career ended when World War I began. When the war ended he went back to Williamstown as curator at the ground where he had begun his career.

Matthews finished his career with a total of four hat-tricks. In addition to the two in 1912 for Australia against South Africa, he took one for Victoria against Tasmania in 1908–09, when he had match figures of 12 for 91, and one for the 1912 Australian team on the way back to Australia at Germanstown, Pennsylvania, USA.

MAYNE, Edgar Richard ("Ernie"), 1884–1961 A sound right-hand batsman who made 14 first-class centuries and figured in the highest partnership for any wicket in the history of Australian cricket. He had bad luck to reach his prime at a period when Australian batsmanship was immensely strong and he appeared in only four Tests. On hard

704

wickets, he could cut and drive with great fluency but he was an indifferent field and this contributed to his omission from other Tests. He played his cricket without histrionics, silent and avuncular, taking sharp knocks from pace bowlers in his role as opener without shirking or showing malice.

Mayne, born at Jamestown, South Australia, played his early cricket with East Torrens club in Adelaide. He first appeared for South Australia in 1906–07. In 1908–09, he hit 142 for South Australia against Victoria at Melbourne. He went to England for the first time for the Triangular series in 1912 when several stars defected and he did reasonably well scoring 877 runs at 21.39, topscore 111, appearing in all four Tests.

He went back to England in 1921 with Warwick Armstrong's crack side but took very little part in the tour, playing only 20 innings compared with 44 on his previous trip. He did not play in a Test but he did get 157 not out against Kent in scoring 654 runs at 36.33. Such was the batting strength of that side he appeared only in minor matches, a fate which caused his enthusiasm for fielding to slump further. The famous cricket writer R. C. Robertson-Glasgow, who played for Oxford against the Australians recorded Mayne's disinterest in the field and added: "Once or twice I saw Armstrong look at Mayne as if wondering why Edgar had not stayed at home in Australia."

The national selectors stuck with Mayne, however, and he went to South Africa at the end of 1921–22, but he could not win a Test place. He had made 124 for South Australia against New South Wales at Sydney in December 1912, and a month later got 106 against Victoria at Adelaide, but after World War I transferred to Victoria. He captained both South Australia and Victoria and led a strong Australian side that toured America in 1914.

Mayne's biggest triumph came in his 40th year when he scored 209 in a partnership of 456 with Bill Ponsford for Victoria against Queensland at Melbourne in 1923–24. This was the highest score of Mayne's long career and his sixth century for Victoria.

Mayne was Victoria's captain in 1925 when he gave expert comments on Radio 3AR of the Second Test between England and Australia at the MCG in one of the first radio descriptions of a cricket match. 3AR paid £75 for the radio rights to the MCG for the whole season.

First-Class Averages: Batting, 7,620 runs at 32.70; Bowling, 13 wickets at 33.84.

Tests (4): 64 runs at 21.33.

A right-arm fast-medium opening bowler from Western Australia who, in the days before Dennis Lillee, toured the West Indies (1965), South Africa and India (1969–70) in Australian sides, without showing the hostility the job demands at Test level. His first Test against the West Indies at Kingston in 1964–65 produced a fine match analysis of 8 for 99 from 41

MAYNE, Laurence Charles, 1942–

First-Class Averages:
Batting, 667 runs at
12.82; Bowling, 203
wickets at 30.12.

Tests (6): 76 runs at 9.50;
19 wickets at 33.05.

overs, but he was unable to repeat this effort. He had plenty of chances as Graham McKenzie's partner to confirm a permanent Test place, giving his work energy and enthusiasm without generating that tell-tale ability to regularly break through. He took 118 wickets at 31.21 for Western Australia and six times in his first-class career took five wickets or more in an innings. He twice reached 50 with the bat. He played for the Claremont-Cottesloe club.

MECKIFF, Ian, 1935–

First-Class Averages:
Batting, 778 runs at
11.27; Bowling, 269
wickets at 23.35.

Tests (18): 154 runs at
11.84; 45 wickets
at 31.62.

A controversial Victorian left-arm pace bowler who played his way from South Melbourne first grade into State and Australian teams, toured South Africa, India and Pakistan before he was branded a chucker and dismissed from the game. The insensitivity of some officials, umpires and fellow players towards Meckiff was appalling. They made him a social oddity, a man people pointed to as a rebel. Few of them knew him or understood what he was alleged to have done wrong or the law involved. Instead of trying to appreciate that Meckiff was the victim of what Sir Donald Bradman called the most complex problem cricket has known they joined in the Fleet Street witch-hunt.

Bill Dowling, chairman of the Australian Cricket Board and known for his fair-mindedness, said after he attended the Imperial Cricket Conference in London in 1960: "The attacks being made in England on the Australian fast bowlers Ian Meckiff and Gordon Rorke amounted to intimidation of umpires. They have been prejudged and condemned as throwers without ever being seen in England." Dowling said that he and Sir Donald had been shocked by the way press, radio and TV had aroused public opinion on Meckiff in particular, and Rorke to a lesser extent. "It is contrary to every principle of fair play that feeling should be whipped up and that sportsmen should be condemned out of hand before ever appearing in a country," said Dowling.

Meckiff was not called for throwing in Tests until his sixth Test series. He came into big cricket under one law and was outed after that law had been changed. Behind the scenes a truce had been agreed on by administrators worried about the harm the throwing controversy was doing to cricket generally. Because of injuries neither Meckiff nor Rorke was considered for what shaped as a showdown tour against England in 1961.

Meckiff bowled with a left arm that has a permanent bend in it and could not be fully straightened, letting the ball go from a bent elbow wind up. He achieved his pace from double-jointed shoulders and from extremely thin wrists. Originally he made very little use of his front arm but when the chucking controversy raged he started to use the front-arm more, throwing it up higher. The action of his bowling arm remained the same but the change in the use of his front-arm made some critics believe he had altered his bowling action. Ironically, Meckiff had a poor throwing arm when fielding.

When Meckiff was cheered from the field after taking 6 for 38 against England at Melbourne Cricket Ground in 1958–59, he celebrated his 24th birthday in perfect style. But before long he was sniped at by people who that day cheered him. His children were called "Chucker" by neighbourhood kids, and his relatives were repeatedly confronted by friends who asked, "Does Ian really throw?" Some of his closest friends addressed him sourly as "Chucker." When he bowled a few spinners to schoolboys one of them called, "No-ball!" If he landed in a bunker at golf, other players suggested he "Chuck it out." The strain of these jibes caused his health to crack and he had to undergo medical care.

Ian Johnson, secretary of the Melbourne Cricket Club, pointed out in an article in the Melbourne *Herald* that if Rorke and Meckiff were called under Law 26 relating to throwing then so too should Statham, Loader, Lock, Trueman and many others. He said both Rorke and Meckiff had whippy actions that jerked and had relaxed elbows at the moment of delivery because both were loose-limbed, but emphasised that these things were not apparent to umpires, and only showed on slow-motion films.

After Meckiff was no-balled for throwing in the First Test against South Africa at Brisbane in 1963–64, the Australian captain, Richie Benaud, surprised Meckiff's supporters by not bowling him at the other end. Col Egar called him for chucking at a time when Meckiff had only been called twice in Shield matches in the previous season but never been called in 17 previous Tests and his State selectors still supported him. Although it meant he was a bowler short for the rest of the match, Benaud refused to bowl Meckiff at umpire Lou Rowan's end. The witch-hunters had won by creating a row of such proprotions administrators felt they were justified in sacrificing at least one career for the future of the game.

In 18 Tests, Meckiff had best figures of 6 for 38. In all first-class matches, he took five wickets or more in an innings 12 times and once took 10 wickets in a match. Whatever the rights or wrongs of the Meckiff case, the circumstances surrounding his abrupt departure from the game were most unfortunate.

One of the no-balls that ended Meckiff's career at Brisbane in 1963.

Australia's oldest and most prestigious cricket club which helped pioneer international cricket and has provided it with the world's largest cricket ground. Some of Australia's first tours to England and several of the early visits to Australia by

MELBOURNE CRICKET CLUB

707

English teams were organised and sponsored by the Melbourne Cricket Club, which in the years before the formation of the Australian Board of Control, was closely involved in the affairs of all Australia's leading players, helping to plan itineraries and dividing tour profits with them. The club's position was so strong that when moves began to establish a governing body for Australian cricket the club was offered representation equal to that enjoyed by each of the State associations. When Australia's leading players rebelled against the Board of Control's authority in 1912, it was to the Melbourne Cricket Club they looked to take over control of the game.

The Melbourne Cricket Club no longer is represented on the Australian Cricket Board, though several of the Victorian delegates to the ACB have been MCC committeemen, but the club's prestige remains unchallenged. And there has been no diminishing in the club's desire to promote cricket at all levels.

The Melbourne Cricket Club was formed when Melbourne was three years old, when on November 15, 1838, five gentlemen met and agreed to join a village cricket club. The five signatories were: F. A. Powlett, R. Russell, Arthur Mundy, C. P. Mundy and George B. Smyth. They all paid a guinea for membership and on the same day the first secretary, D. G. McArthur, used some of the money to buy two bats, some balls and stumps. Horse racing had already begun in John Batman's village but the five foundation members of the MCC soon organised matches that won widespread attention. Powlett, the first president, was the Crown Land Commissioner of the Western District of the Port Phillip Settlement and the first Police Magistrate. He was also the first to make a century and the first to take a hat-trick in the settlement.

Among the early members the club attracted were Captain Bacchus, of the 18th Light Dragoons, who later founded Bacchus Marsh, D. C. McArthur, who came from Sydney to open the Bank of Australasia, and Peter Snodgrass, who fought the first duel in the colony. The club played its first matches in a paddock that is now the site of the Royal Mint in William Street, but later moved to a better ground in Spencer Street, where the railway station now stands. The club's first election of office-bearers on November 1, 1841, saw F. A. Powlett appointed President, with G. Cavenagh, Honorary Secretary. Cavenagh had been joint editor of the *Sydney Gazette*. He was President of the MCC from 1846–49 and from 1850–54 and won the club's batting average in 1846–47. By 1847 there were 127 members, including W. C. Haines, who in 1856 became Victoria's first premier.

In 1847 the club sent a team to play a match against Geelong, which took eight hours to reach by steamer. In 1851, they ventured a little further by sending a team to Launceston to play the Gentlemen of Van Dieman's Land. The Melbourne CC team practised diligently before they left but they found the captaincy of John Marshall too much to overcome and Van Dieman's Land won by three wickets. The return match at the MCC's ground on the south bank of the Yarra was delayed until 1852 following the discovery of gold which distracted even the cricketers. This game virtually established the club as a host for visiting teams, both sides toasting each other in champagne before play began. This time the MCC won comfortably by 61 runs.

When trains were introduced the first stretch of railway track went through the MCC's ground, so as compensation Governor La Trobe offered the club a plot of ground in Richmond Park, which is the site of the present Melbourne Cricket Ground. Permission to fence the site was given in September, 1853, when the Governor gave the club occupancy for five years and agreed to allow the erection of whatever buildings the club needed. From the start the MCC committee had the declared aim of making the MCG the best cricket arena in the Colony and better than anything in Sydney. The gold rush brought a rush for membership and in four months in 1855 the club gained 200 members.

F. A. Powlett. First known President of M.C.C. 1841–1843.

To entertain its growing membership, the MCC advertised in all newspapers that it was ready to play any eleven in the colonies for up to £1000-a-side. This challenge was accepted in March, 1856 by New South Wales, and was the start of inter-State cricket as we know it. These games were so successful, the MCC decided on the even more ambitious venture of bringing an English team to Australia but before it could finalise arrangements the club's caterers, Spiers & Pond, got in first and on New Year's Day, 1862, England appeared for the first time on the MCG.

The MCC watched Spiers & Pond profit from the visit of Stephenson's English team with great interest, and promptly began moves to ensure that the tours that followed were organised by the club. Similarly, after private entrepreneurs profited from the first Australian team's visit to England, the Melbourne Club took over the sponsorship of other early tours. Further prestige came to the club with the staging of the first of all Tests at the MCG in 1877.

Since then the Melbourne Cricket Club has expanded its interests into baseball, lacrosse, lawn tennis, hockey, lawn bowls, rifle shooting and Australian Rules football, which was invented by a member of the club to keep cricketers fit in winter. The Board of Control and later the Australian Cricket Board took away the Melbourne CC's management of tours, but the club continues to hold an important place in the life of Melbourne that has now lasted for 144 years.

MELBOURNE CRICKET GROUND

The world's largest cricket ground, with a history and tradition almost as long as the most famous overseas grounds. Although the trees and flower beds that once featured the ground have been replaced by massive concrete stands, the approaches to the MCG and the parkland in which the ground is set are pleasant and uncomplicated. It is one of the easiest of all sporting arenas to enter or leave and its amenities are of a very high standard. Altogether the MCG makes a major contribution to the life of Melbourne and because of its capacity and the gate money it attracts its value to Australian cricket is incalculable.

Melbourne was the venue for the first ever cricket Test and has retained a prestigious position second only to Lord's. Facilities at the ground have been steadily improved since the Melbourne Cricket Club began operations on the present site in 1853. A succession of thoughtful Melbourne club committees made membership of the club and ground among the most sought after of any sporting club, and it reputation for smooth management was further enhanced by the staging of

The Melbourne Cricket Ground scoreboard showing the world record score of 1,107 in 1926.

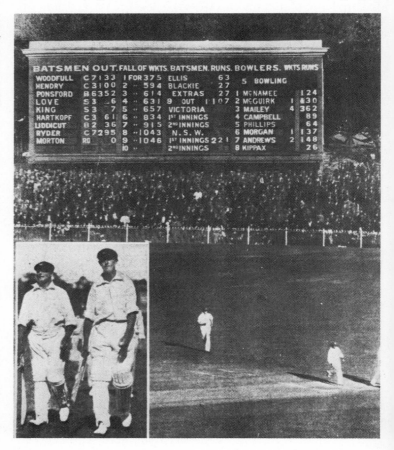

710

An aerial shot of Melbourne Cricket Ground on the day 90,800 attended the Australia versus West Indies match in 1961

the 1956 Olympic Games. The job of running the MCG carries more prestige than any other administrative role in Australian sport, and when the MCG develops problems such as the present crisis with its centre wicket it is the cause for national concern.

First International Match At The MCG: The Melbourne Cricket Club's caterers, Spiers & Pond, sponsored the first English team to Australia and the first international match was played on the MCG from January 1, 1862. The all-professional English team expressed amazement at the new stand, opened specially for the match.

First Test At The MCG: The first of all Tests was played at the MCG in March, 1877, Australia winning by 45 runs. Success of this venture persuaded the Melbourne club to sponsor four Australian teams to England and eight English teams to Australia, building up resources in the process that were invested in further ground improvements.

First Century And First Hat-Trick In Tests At The MCG: Charles Bannerman made the first century, 167 not out in the First Test, Fred Spofforth the first Test hat-trick in January, 1879, in the Third Test when he dismissed Royle, Mackinnon and Emmett in England's first innings.

Highest Ever Score At The MCG: 1,107 by Victoria against NSW in 1926–27, when Arthur Mailey had more runs hit off him than any other bowler in a first-class match, 362. A month later in Sydney NSW had Victoria out for 35.

711

The MCG "Sticky Wickets": In the years of uncovered pitches, the MCG had a reputation for providing the most spiteful of all "sticky wickets," surpassing even the gluepots of the Gabba. South Africa were bowled out on a vicious MCG sticky in 1931–32 for 36 and 45 and the match aggregate of 234 remains the lowest in all Test cricket.

MCG Attendance Records: More than 130,000 attended the MCG for a Billy Graham (with spectators inside the ground) Crusade, 121,696 for the 1970 Australian Rules grand final, but the record for cricket was 90,800 for the second day of the Fifth Test between West Indies and Australia in February, 1961. The world's record aggregate for a Test, 350,534, was established at the MCG for the six-days of the England-Australia Third Test in January, 1937. Close to two million people attend fixtures at the MCG each year.

MENZIES, Rt Hon Sir Robert Gordon, 1894–1978

A wholehearted patron of Australian cricket from the time he began the long public career that made him Prime Minister and one of the world's most distinguished statesmen. He played little cricket as a student but came to love the game and its players. His enjoyment was reflected in his contributions to *Wisden* and in his Forewords to a long list of cricket books. Many of Australia's finest players were among his closest friends.

He staged one of the notable events in the itineraries of visiting cricket teams, the match against the Prime Minister's XI in Canberra. Apart from bringing cricket's heroes to the nation's capital, this match produced some memorable social occasions, for Menzies was a generous host and a witty dinner companion. He made no secret of the fact that he tried to influence the dates for Prime Ministers' conferences in London so that they coincided with Tests at Lord's or The Oval. He was president of the Kent County club during his term as Lord Warden of Cinque Ports, and a frequent visitor to Canterbury Cricket Week.

Menzies loved the personalities and yarns cricket threw up, not the least his wife Dame Pattie's response when Arthur Mailey asked how she liked cricket. "Bob tried to get me interested in 1924," said Dame Pattie. "When I arrived Hobbs and Sutcliffe were batting, and after a couple of hours I became bored and left. Then when we were in England in 1926 I went to The Oval when England were playing Australia again. When I arrived, there they were again—Hobbs and Sutcliffe. They were still batting." Menzies always said the Bodyline crisis might not have developed if the Australian Board of Control, who sought his legal advice, had expressed its protest to MCC as he suggested.

A stubborn, accomplished Victorian-born right-hand batsman whose Test hopes were frustrated by the heavy run-scoring of Sid Barnes, Arthur Morris and to a lesser extent Billy Brown. Meuleman's only Test was the first after World War II against New Zealand, when he failed to score. Thereafter the brilliance of Barnes and Morris denied him another chance in his prime years, although he continued to score freely.

Meuleman, who opened for the Essendon club in Melbourne with his brother Ron, made his debut for Victoria in 1945–46, and in 39 matches for the State scored 2,614 runs at 43.56, with seven centuries, topscore 206 against Tasmania at Melbourne in 1947–48. He twice scored 150 against South Australia, in 1945–46 and 1949–50, and he made centuries for Victoria against every other State.

His bad luck came in 1946–47. He was twelfth man for Australia in the first three Tests against Wally Hammond's England team. In the first two Tests, Arthur Morris failed, and Meuleman, an opening batsman, appeared the logical replacement for Morris. But the selectors persevered with Morris and his century in the second innings of the third Test set up a series of superb innings and at the same time ruined Meuleman's Test chances. When the 1948 side to tour England was chosen, the selectors took Billy Brown as the third opening batsman. Brown, after all, had scored a magnificent double century at Lord's on the previous Australian tour of England.

Meuleman, always a fine striker of the ball, often seemed to stonewall unnecessarily after that. He was an outstanding batsman against spin but frequently he got into position to hit the ball hard but failed to do so. His footwork was so quick Arthur Mailey dubbed him "Pavlova Meuleman." He went back to New Zealand for the second time in 1949–50, and in the early 1950s moved to Western Australia, where he was for a long time the backbone of the Western Australian batting, usually in the middle of the order. He took over the Western Australian captaincy from Keith Carmody in 1956–57, and captained the State until 1959–60, occasionally filling in for Bob Simpson in 1960–61. In 48 matches for WA, he scored 3,398 runs at 51.48, topscore 234 not out against South Australia at Perth in 1956–57. He made 11 centuries in all for WA, and in four of them was undefeated.

Ken Meuleman hit 22 centuries, made 41 fifties, and held 35 catches in first-class matches. All he had to show for his one Test was one catch. He toured India with a Commonwealth team in 1953–54, scoring 1,158 runs at 52.63, with four centuries. His son **Ron Meuleman** had 18 matches for Western Australia for 545 runs at 28.68, best score 101 not out against New South Wales at Sydney in 1969–70.

MEULEMAN, Kenneth Douglas, 1923–

First-Class Averages: Batting, 7,855 runs at 47.60; Bowling 19 wickets at 50.31.

Tests (1): 0 runs.

MIDWINTER, William Evans, 1851–1890

First-Class Averages:
Batting, 4,493 runs at
19.11; Bowling, 418
wickets at 17.38.

Tests (8 for Australia):
174 runs at 13.38; 14
wickets at 23.78. (4 for
England): 95 runs at
13.57; 10 wickets at
27.20.

A hard-hitting right-hand batsman, medium-pace round arm spin bowler, outstanding outfielder with a powerful arm, splendid quarter mile runner, fine rifle shot and billiards player, variously known on the Victorian goldfields as the "Bendigo Giant" or the "Sandhurst Infant". He remains the only player to have appeared for and against Australia. He was an extremely steady batsman who could hold an innings together with resolute defence and occasional big hits. He is believed to have scored the first double century recorded in Australia, 256 for Bendigo against Sandhurst.

Midwinter was born at St Briavels, Forest of Dean, Gloucestershire, but spent his early years at Cirencester in the Cotswolds, 50 miles to the east of the Forest of Dean. His father, William John Midwinter, migrated to Australia in 1861 at 38 with his wife Rebecca, 36, William, 9, Jane, 7 and John, 5. The family were among the many unemployed from the Forest of Dean who opted to try their luck in the gold rushes. Midwinter, senior, worked as a goldminer and then as a butcher at Sandhurst, now Eaglehawk, on the Bendigo goldfields. At Sandhurst, William began his lifelong friendship with Harry Boyle, whom he helped clear and level a pitch from the bush at Sydney Flat. The Midwinters lived in a shack at California Gully and William practised cricket there with his father in between his butcher's rounds. In the 1864–65 season, William left the Sydney Flat CC to play for Bendigo United and although only 13 won a place in the senior XI.

Midwinter and Boyle made a big impression playing for Bendigo against the visiting Carlton club in 1870 and were invited to play in Melbourne. In 1871 Midwinter and Boyle were in the Bendigo VI that surprisingly beat Charles Bannerman's (NSW) IV. Midwinter was playing in Melbourne when he was invited to play in a match against W. G. Grace's visiting English team that attracted 40,000 spectators over three days. He was out for seven off the bowling of Grace, but in a second match in March, 1874, bowled W. G. Grace and his brother G. F. Grace. He was 6 ft 3 in and 14 stone when he played in his first inter-Colonial match in 1874–75.

Midwinter was one of the stars of the All Australia v. All England match at Melbourne in 1877, later recognised as the first Test. Australia defeated England for the first time in an even-handed game, Midwinter finishing with match figures of 6 for 101. He returned to England in 1877 and quickly joined W. G. Grace in South of England teams that played in Birmingham, Holbeck and Barrow-on-Furness. He played for a combined Yorkshire-Gloucestershire team against the Rest of England at Lord's but his first appearance for a full Gloucestershire side was at The Oval against England when, in a famous victory, Gloucestershire won by five wickets. Midwinter took 7 for 35 and 4 for 46. W. G. taught him to combine defence

714

with his powerful hitting and in the match against Yorkshire Midwinter saved Gloucestershire by batting four hours for 68.

When the first Australian team arrived to tour England in 1878, they had 11 players and, by arrangement, Midwinter joined them. He had played 10 innings for Australia, helping them to win their first-ever match at Lord's against the MCC by nine wickets, when he went to play against Middlesex at Lord's. With Bannerman and Midwinter padded up ready to open the innings, W. G. Grace burst into the dressing-room and grabbed Midwinter, persuading him that he should be across town at The Oval playing for his native Gloucestershire against Surrey.

W. G. bundled Midwinter into his carriage and took off for The Oval, but the Australian manager, John Conway, Midwinter's pal Harry Boyle, and the Australian captain Dave Gregory hired another carriage and chased the kidnappers. Outside The Oval gates a nasty altercation occurred during which W. G. called the Australians "a damn lot of sneaks." Letters of increasing bitterness were exchanged between the Australians and the Gloucestershire club, who claimed Midwinter as "a Gloucestershire man who had promised Mr Grace to play in all county matches." Gloucestershire claimed that W. G. Grace's "stormy language" was justified because the Australians had induced Midwinter to break his commitment to the county by offering a larger sum than Gloucestershire could afford. Finally W. G. apologised and the Australians agreed to play Gloucestershire at Bristol, where with Midwinter absent injured, and Spofforth at full cry, Gloucestershire were thrashed.

Midwinter commuted between England and Australia from 1880 to 1882. He joined the MCC staff of bowlers at Lord's in 1880, and in one of his last games in that job in 1882 played a remarkable knock for MCC in a two-day match against Leicestershire, taking the MCC score from 2 for 19 to 3 for 473 in five and a half hours. He made 187, Barnes 266. He was in Shaw's England team in Australia in 1881–82 and played in four Tests. When he arrived back in Australia after the English 1882 season he said he objected being called an Anglo-Australian and considered himself an Australian to the "heart's core." The *Sydney Mail* commented, "Are we to submit to another season of vagueness from this very slippery cricketer? One day he is an Australian and the next day an English player." But when Ivo Bligh's English team arrived in 1882–83, Midwinter was in the Australian team for one Test. He returned to England with the Australians in 1884 and played for them in all three Tests. He also played two Tests for Australia against Shrewsbury's team in 1886–87.

In all first-class matches this unique cricketer scored three centuries, took five wickets in an innings 26 times and held 123 catches. For Victoria he made 541 of his runs at 28.47, topscore 92 not out, and took 40 wickets at 16.45, including 7 for 54 in 1886–87 against England, 7 for 53 in 1883–84 against New South Wales and 5 for 22 against South Australia in 1886–87. In matches Against The Odds for Victoria, he scored 80 runs at 16.00 and took 12 wickets at 13.91. He died tragically in Melbourne's Kew asylum for the insane, aged only 39, following the tragic early death of his wife and two children. His ten months old daughter Elsie died of pneumonia in 1888, his wife of apoplexy in 1889 and his three year old son Albert three months later. He loved his family intensely and broke down in the face of these deaths. In one of his rare moments of consciousness at Kew Asylum he spoke with Harry Boyle. He was buried beside his family in the Roman Catholic section of Melbourne General Cemetery in grave No L286, which has recently been restored by the Australian Cricket Society.

MILBURN, Colin, 1941–
One of the most exciting cricketers to play in Australia, a right-hand batsman of forceful method with crowd-pleasing gusto who had two memorable seasons with Western Australia before he lost his left eye in a motor accident. Jovial and rotund, usually with shirt hanging out over his trouser top, he played one unforgettable innings of 243 at Brisbane, 181 of them in two hours between lunch and tea, and peppered the faces and grandstands of most Australian grounds with shots that are still discussed.

Milburn, son of a professional cricketer from the Tyneside Senior League, first played for Burnopfield Cricket Club, County Durham, at the age of 12. His father, an 18-stoner like Colin, once made 164 in 45 minutes. Colin played his first match for Northants in 1960, preceded by stories of his immense crowd appeal and high-scoring. He was fat because he liked eating and drinking but defied the odds by fielding nimbly at short leg. He became a master in mixing his uncomplicated big hits with finely executed square cuts, cover drives and glances, working his way up the Northants batting order to No. 3.

He first played for Western Australia in 1966–67 when he had already established his reputation by scoring 94 in 150 minutes for England against West Indies in his Test debut, and a thrilling 126 not out at Lord's. This was the Test in which Milburn struck 17 fours and sixes off David Holford, Wes Hall and Lance Gibbs, saving a match that England appeared likely to lose. When elated spectators tried to lift him to their shoulders his bulk was too much for them, and they tottered away.

In his first appearance on Adelaide Oval in November, 1966, Milburn made his first 50 in 44 minutes, 100 in 77 min-

716

utes and 129 in 95 minutes with two sixes and 20 fours. That same season he hammered 106 for WA against Queensland at Perth. Australians could not believe it when he was left out of the England team to tour South Africa soon after he hooked his way to 83 against Australia at Lord's in 1968, but this amazing omission opened the way for Milburn to return for a second season with WA. He did not disappoint, for he scored a WA record of 940 runs at 62.66, including eight fifties and the 243 at Brisbane that will be talked about forever by the 3,000 lucky to see it. He was 61 out of 92, with 10 fours, at lunch, and then set about the Queensland bowlers, rushing to 242 by tea. His 181 between lunch and tea came off 134 balls. He was out in the first over after tea having hit 38 fours and four sixes, some of them right out into the street. His partnership of 328 with Chadwick remains the highest for any wicket for WA. Peter Burge congratulated him in the dressing-room "on behalf of all fat men."

After Milburn lost his left eye and slightly damaged the right in the smash on the outskirts of Northampton, they put a black patch over his sightless eye for a time. To get rid of the patch they offered him a glass eye. Asked to pick from a box of 50 false eyes to match his good brown eye, he said, "Better find two. One to match it now, and a bloodshot one for the mornings." On another occasion he laughed so much sharing jokes with friends that tears came to his eyes. Trying to wipe them clear he dislodged the false eye which rolled across the floor. He got down on the floor calling, "Where's my eye? Where's my eye?" still laughing until his vast frame shook.

Milburn returned to play 25 more first-class matches for Northants following his accident but was never again the same devastating hitter. In 35 innings between 1973 and 1974, his best score was 57. In WA they thought so much of him they took him back for a season to help him recuperate on the beaches and the Swan beer. Everyone knew he would be unable to play. In a first-class career between 1960 and 1974, Milburn made 13,262 runs at 33.07, an average that was markedly reduced after the loss of his eye. He made 23 first-class centuries, two of them in his nine Tests. He also made 226 first-class catches and took 99 wickets with his medium pacers at 32.03. For WA, he made 1,414 runs at 52.37 and took five wickets at 60.40, with that epic 243 the highest score of his 14 years in big cricket.

A superbly co-ordinated all-rounder of classical style, with a matchless flair for exciting crowds, who could swing a game in a few overs of his right-arm fast bowling, right-hand batting or slips catching. His fame will endure as long as cricket, for when he took the field boundary fences or ropes disap-

MILLER, Keith Ross ("Nugget"), 1919–

717

First-Class Averages:
Batting, 14,183 runs at
48.90; Bowling, 497
wickets at 22.30.

Tests (55): 2,958 runs at
36.97; 170 wickets at
22.97.

peared and spectators virtually became part of the match, reacting to every switch of his mane of black hair. He was aggressive but casual, combining the aesthetic with red-blooded pleasure, proud of all the runs, wickets and catches he took, but disinterested in his averages or aggregates.

He played for Victoria, the Australian Services, NSW, Australia, Nottinghamshire, MCC, and for the South Melbourne, Manly and North Sydney clubs, borrowing bats or pads, bowling in odd shoes or without socks. His performance frequently depended on how he had spent the previous night, but he thought deeply about the individual skills and match tactics of the game, sometimes outwitting talented opponents with a bold, innovative approach. He often was an inspired cricketer, whether bowling, batting or fielding but he lost keenness when the going was easy.

As a batsman, Miller would annihilate difficult bowling. Few Australians have combined classy stroke play with big-hitting as he did in the years just after World War II. His front-foot play was devastating, his straight drive a rifle shot, his pull and sweep shots cool and effortless. Few could cut as elegantly. Yet he hit seven sixes in a Lord's century, twice hit sixes over square-leg with backhand tennis shots, and once began the day's play in a Test with a six.

With the ball, he formed one of cricket's finest opening combinations with Ray Lindwall, often bowling faster than his partner off a classically high arm action, but the demands of bowling dulled his batting wizardry towards the end of his career. He moved the ball sharply either way and bounced the ball up around the batsman's throat off a good length. When class batsmen were well set, he was always trying something new, bowling one ball off a five stride run, the next off 15 paces. He took many wickets through sheer surprise with his round-armer.

Fielding in the slips, he seemed to be forever lunging and diving and holding acrobatic catches. He would catch Len Hutton or Denis Compton with a typical leap, nonchalantly flip the ball back to the bowler, and immediately resume the discussion he had been having with second slip or the wicket-keeper. He was an incorrigible talker and on the rare occasions that he dropped a catch tossed the ball back with the same disdain he showed if he caught them, carrying on the discussion with those nearest him, usually about the prospects of racehorses.

Miller was born in Melbourne during the month the Melbourne Cup is run, when Keith and Ross Smith were near the end of their record-busting England-Australia flight, and because of this his engineer father Leslie Harold Miller christened him Keith Ross Miller. Leslie came from the Wimmera district of Victoria and played football for Ballarat Imperials. Keith became addicted to horse racing during infancy in the

Melbourne suburbs of Sunshine and Elsternwick, and could never understand why, when his sister Gladys and brothers Les and Ray were short, he grew to be too big (6 ft 2 ins, 13 st 7 lb) to become a race rider. The first time he cried was when his mother Edith took him to the Victoria Racing Club's Melbourne office and he found he was too big to become an apprentice jockey. He has always said he would rather have ridden a Melbourne Cup or English Derby winner than have scored a century at Lord's.

He went to Melbourne High School, where Bill Woodfull taught geometry, but he had little affinity with Woodfull's dour, stoical approach to cricket. Keith preferred to ride horses around Caulfield racecourse than attend cricket practice under Woodfull. A character more to Keith's liking was his boyhood mate, dashing Ross Gregory, who died in a wartime air crash.

Miller grew 12 inches between the ages of 16 and 18, and developed early into a champion Australian Rules footballer with a wonderful long kick. He played for St Kilda, Victoria and NSW at football. At South Melbourne he came under the influence of Hughie Carroll, the only cricket coach he ever listened to and a great advocate of hitting the ball hard and high. After he left school he found a job as a clerk with an oil company. He was an established first-class batsman when he went to Adelaide in 1938–39 with the Victorian team and Clarrie Grimmett persuaded him to take up bowling, reasoning that bowling was a more satisfying art form than batting. Miller went off to the war to train with RAAF aircrew mindful of Grimmett's words about bowling's great challenge.

Throughout his life Miller has pursued his love of classical music with a fervour matched only by his love for horse racing and handsome women. He hates pretentiousness but he wears a silk topper at the races or a dinner jacket at a symphony concert as easily as he mixes with racecourse toughs. After earning his wings under the Empire Air Training Scheme, he travelled across America to Boston and there he met brunette Margaret Lillian Wagner, a secretary who shared his taste in music. Then he went off to the war in England, a good pilot who did not take kindly to discipline imposed by chairbound officers. His closest mate was jockey-size Bill Young from Broken Hill.

Miller flew up the straight of Royal Ascot on one training flight and buzzed over the Goodwood track on another. On a flight over Germany, he detoured to take a peek at Bonn, Beethoven's birthplace. His friend Bill was killed on a mission over Berlin. At Great Missingham in Norfolk in 1945 Miller's Mosquito came in to land with the starboard engine spurting flame. Skilfully, in a variable wind, Keith crash-landed the Mosquito, which lost its tail. He was charged over the loss of the aircraft and although the charge was thrown out he later advised sportswriters not to take out policies with his former commanding officer, who in peacetime had become an insurance salesman. Miller later found the same ex-C.O. working as a car park attendant at Ascot races.

Miller was the dynamic hero of the Victory Tests which helped re-establish big cricket immediately war ended. At Lord's the famous pavilion came under a sustained barrage from his big hitting as he scored 185 in 165 minutes for a Dominions XI. He toured England with the Australian Services team led by W. O. II Lindsay Hassett and arrived home with cricket lovers desperate to catch a glimpse of him as the team moved round the States. On discharge he moved quickly, throwing in his job with the oil company in Melbourne, and putting all his cash into a boat ride to America, where he married Peggy Wagner. They settled in the Sydney suburb of Dee Why and later moved to a splendid house in Newport. Keith named the first of their four sons Bill, after his dead air force mate, and the third Denis as a way of showing respect for Denis Compton, whose prestige had slumped at the time.

In his first Test at Brisbane in 1946–47 against England, Miller scored 79, hitting the longest six ever at the ground, and took 7 for 60 in the first innings. He played in 55 Tests against all the cricket nations, but that remained his best bowling analysis. On tour in England in 1948, 1953 and 1956 he was seen frequently at the Royal Albert Hall, sometimes debating with Sir John Barbirolli or Neville Cardus the merits of a concerto, or at the races with friends like Edgar Britt and Scobie Breasley. One year when he captained NSW he arranged with Don Tallon to take the players from the field to

Miller caught in Jim Laker's leg trap in the Leeds Test against England in 1956.

720

hear the Melbourne Cup broadcast. The stoppage broke "Slasher" Mackay's concentration and Alan Davidson bowled Mackay first ball after the resumption to give Mackay a pair for the match.

He scored more than 200 seven times in a career that produced 41 first-class centuries. He had a topscore of 281 for Australia in 1956. He took five wickets in an innings 16 times, and took 136 catches. But he was never interested in scoring runs or taking wickets for the sake of his averages and the figures cannot convey his tremendous influence on the results of matches and indeed of entire series. Only in 1956 when his powers had begun to wane and he was somewhat despondent over Ian Johnson's appointment to captain Australia in England did he fail in the role of matchwinner.

In 18 matches for Victoria between 1938 and 1947, he scored 1,396 runs at 53.69, with 206 not out against NSW in 1946–47 the highest of five scores over 100. His 14 wickets for Victoria cost 21.35 each. For NSW he scored 10 centuries between 1947–48 and 1955–56, highest score 214 against the MCC in 1950–51. He was a forceful, at times unorthodox NSW captain in 26 matches. In 50 first-class matches, he made 3,538 runs at 57.06 and took 119 wickets at 25.36. Three years after he retired he was invited to play one match for Nottinghamshire in 1959 against Cambridge University. He scored 62 and 102 not out and although he was 40 this appears in the record books as "Century On First Appearance For County."

Since he retired Miller has moved from one newspaper job to another, tried his hand as a TV sports commentator, sponsored everything from hair oil to bats, and owned a few slow racehorses. Bookmakers have taken heaps of money from him. He works now as a public relations man for Robert Sangster's pools organisation in Sydney.

John Arlott, the distinguished English cricket writer and lover of good wine, said of Miller: "If I had my choice of a player to win a match off the last ball, whether it required a catch, a six or a wicket, I would pick only one player, Keith Ross Miller."

MINNETT, Roy Baldwin, 1888–1955

The most successful of three brothers who played for New South Wales, and the only member of the family to play for Australia. Roy was a right-hand batsman and a right-arm fast-medium bowler with a windmill action. He made 90 at Sydney in 1911–12 in his first Test innings and was considered unlucky to miss a century. His brothers Leslie and Rupert figured in first-class matches before distinguished professional careers cut short their cricket. Roy Minnett was one of the best performed of the disappointing Australian team that went to England for the Triangular series with England and

First-Class Averages:
Batting, 2,203 runs at
28.98; Bowling, 86
wickets at 25.02.

Tests (9): 391 runs at
26.06; 11 wickets at
26.36.

South Africa in 1912, scoring 734 runs, topscore 65 not out, and taking 41 wickets at 23.65. Roy's career topscore was 216 not out against Victoria at Sydney in 1911–12.

Leslie Alma Minnett (1883–1934) played 10 first-class matches, scoring 202 runs at 12.62 and taking 37 wickets at 29.91 and holding eight catches. **Rupert Villiers Minnett** (1884–1974) played five first-class matches and scored 270 runs at 38.57 and made three catches. Rupert did not bowl. Rupert scored 2,863 runs at 34.07 in first grade for North Sydney and Leslie took 139 first grade wickets at 21.26 for the same club. Rupert made 169 of his first-class runs for NSW v. Queensland in 1910–11.

MISSON, Francis Michael ("Tarzan"), 1938–

First-Class Averages:
Batting, 1,052 runs at
17.53; Bowling, 177
wickets at 31.13.

Tests (5): 38 runs at 19.00;
16 wickets at
38.50.

A Sydney physical fitness freak who figured in two of the most exciting Test series since World War II. He was a splendid team man who gave a whole-hearted effort that was repeatedly praised by his captain Richie Benaud, and he was rewarded with thrilling moments most cricketers go a lifetime without enjoying. His figures in five Tests give no indication of his contribution.

Misson was born in the Sydney suburb of Darlinghurst and went to Gardener's Road Public and Randwick Boys' High School. In 1950 he saw Ray Lindwall bowling in an inter-State match at Sydney Cricket Ground and immediately told himself that was how he wanted to bowl. From then on he lengthened his approach run by 20 paces, discarded the medium-pace stuff he had been bowling, and aimed for sheer speed. To help him he followed a physical fitness programme styled on Olympic swimmers, running four miles every morning before breakfast, hurdling park benches, and following a diet that included honey, nuts and lots of fruit.

He made his debut for NSW in 1958–59 and after two seasons in first-class cricket replaced the injured Ian Meckiff in the Australian team to play the West Indies. His selection ended a 34-year spell by his club Glebe-South Sydney without a Test player. Warren Bardsley, who had been the club's last Test representative in 1926, had died six years before Misson was selected.

Misson made an immediate contribution in the Second Test at Melbourne as Alan Davidson's new ball partner, clean bowling Conrad Hunte with only his second ball. At 6 ft 3 ins, 13 st 6 lb, he looked the answer to Australia's pace bowling problems, with Meckiff and Rorke suspect because of their delivery styles, and he went to England in Richie Benaud's 1961 team.

At Lord's in the Second Test he played a vital part in Australia's win, adding 49 for the 10th wicket in Australia's first innings with Mackay. This stretched Australia's lead to 134.

Then Misson, Davidson and McKenzie bounced England out for 202, leaving Australia to make only 68 runs to win. They lost five wickets scoring them. But McKenzie's continued success cost Misson his Test place and his international career ended after only five matches. Misson took 51 wickets at 25.37 on the tour despite a recurrent ankle injury, and seven wickets at 34.71 compared with McKenzie's 11 at 29.36 in the Tests.

On his return home he continued in the NSW team until 1963–64 without coming into consideration again for Tests. In 1965–66 he was appointed captain of the newly formed Sydney club when that club was formed by the amalgamation of Glebe and Paddington. Towards the end of his career he developed into a useful batsman and it was as an all-rounder that he went to play for Accrington in the Lancashire League where his English-born wife Carole gave birth to their first child.

MOORES, THE MIGHTY

The name given to a family from West Maitland, New South Wales, who all played first-class cricket for New South Wales. George Moore, born April 18, 1820, was Australia's oldest first-class player when he appeared for New South Wales against Victoria in 1872–73 at 52 years 325 days. His brother James, his son William Henry, and his nephew Leon all appeared for their State. George Moore's grandson was the famous Charlie Macartney whom George taught to play strokes by bowling green apples at him in West Maitland. George Moore scored 22 runs in three matches for New South Wales but took 15 wickets at 12.26. Leon Moore, in 11 matches for New South Wales, scored 292 runs at 17.17, and William Moore, in five matches for the State, scored 109 runs at 13.62. James Moore's grandson was Frank Cummins, who played 11 matches for New South Wales, scoring 264 runs at 16.50, topscore 78.

MORGAN, Oliver John ("Sandy"), 1945–

First-Class Averages: Batting, 1,410 runs at 25.17; Bowling, 113 wickets at 28.90.

A successful Queensland all-rounder in the late 1960s, an efficient blond-haired right-arm fast-medium bowler and a useful left-hand batsman. He held his place in the Queensland team from 1965 to 1969 largely because of his bowling, six times taking five wickets in an innings, best figures 6 for 42. But he scored runs regularly near the bottom of the order. Unfortunately, when he was promoted to No. 3 he suffered from runout problems. Morgan played for the University club in Brisbane and could feel well pleased with his 100 wickets and 1,000 runs double for Queensland, even though he seldom worried the Australian XI players of his period.

723

MORONEY, John Rodger ("Jack"), 1919–

First-Class Averages: Batting, 4,023 runs at 52.24.

Tests (7): 383 runs at 34.81.

A right-hand opening batsman of quality who hit a century in each innings of a Test and played for Australia against three countries. He could use his powerful arms and shoulders to hit enormously hard but had far too many spasms when timing and confidence appeared to desert him and he lapsed into painful defence. He was a batsman of intense concentration. "You can't get runs if you are not out in the middle" was his catch-phrase.

Moroney, born in the Sydney suburb of Randwick, was a prolific run-getter for Petersham-Marrickville in grade cricket. Week after week his achievements cried out for a chance in first-class matches. He made his first appearance for New South Wales in 1945–46 and scored his first Shield century for the State in 1948–49, 122 against Queensland at Brisbane. That same season he made 100 not out against Victoria at Melbourne, to finish with an aggregate of 655 Shield runs at 72.77. He clinched his place in the Australian team to tour South Africa in 1949–50 under Hassett by scoring 217 in a Testimonial match at Sydney for Kippax and Oldfield.

He was an outstanding success in South Africa, scoring six centuries in a tour total of 1,487 runs in 31 innings. At Johannesburg in the Fourth Test, he made 118 and 101 not out, the first time an Australian batsman had scored a century in each innings of a Test against South Africa. He returned home an automatic Test selection but in the first Test against England at Brisbane in 1950–51 was dismissed for a duck by Trevor Bailey in each innings, and was dropped from the Test team.

Moroney, who was a teacher at St Joseph's College in the Sydney suburb of Hunter's Hill, continued to score heavily for New South Wales. In 1950–51, he made 113 against Queensland at Brisbane and in 1951–52 he scored 106 against Victoria at Sydney, but his over-emphasis on defence and his shoddy fielding counted against him whenever the Test selectors picked a side. He played only one more Test, against West Indies in 1951–52, and then disappeared from the Australian team for good. In all first-class matches, he scored 12 centuries.

MORRIS, Arthur Robert, 1922–

A champion left-handed batsman who began in grade cricket bowling slow spinners and going in last. He opened for Australia 77 times in 46 Tests but bowled only 111 balls for two wickets and 50 runs. He is the only Australian to score a century in each innings of his initial first-class match. He rates with Hill, Darling, Ransford, Harvey and Lawry among our greatest left-handed batsmen, and was one of the few to go in first.

Morris, fair-skinned, curly-haired, unflappable, learned the basics of cricket from his schoolmaster father, who bowled fast for Sydney's Waverley club. Morris, snr, not only taught his son technique but how to adhere to the highest standards of sportsmanship. Arthur became cricket's equivalent of "Gentleman Jack" Crawford in tennis, the player about whom nobody had a critical word. He took his setbacks, few as they were, with unruffled calm, and was always full of praise for his opponents.

Morris was born at Bondi but learned to play cricket between the ages of five and 11 at Dungog while his school teacher father was posted there. He began as a spin bowler with the Newcastle High team at 13. He had three years in Canterbury High firsts in cricket and rugby when his family returned to Sydney. He gave up a promising future in rugby to concentrate on cricket.

He joined the St George club and came under the influence of Bill O'Reilly, who gave him valuable advice. He was then a bowler who went in last but club officials noticed his marked improvement with the bat and moved him up the order. At 16, he scored a first grade century against Sydney University. He was still at school when he appeared for New South Wales Seconds v. Victoria Seconds. Before his 19th birthday, he was chosen for New South Wales at Christmas, 1940, and in his first big match won world fame with a century in each innings, 148 and 111. In 1982, that feat was still unequalled. In the first innings he shared a second wicket stand of 261 with Sid Barnes, and in the second innings he opened with Mort Cohen (118) and figured in another major partnership. He ended the season with an average of 55.14 for the State.

When Keith Miller was 20 he bowled a bouncer at Morris in a Victoria-NSW match in Sydney. Morris hooked it for four. Stirred at this affrontery Miller proceeded to bowl a whole over of bouncers at Morris who hit four fours in a row and the next for three. It proved the costliest over Miller ever bowled, conceding 24 runs.

Morris seldom held a bat for the next six years, serving with the Australian Army's Movement Control Unit in New Guinea. He returned to big cricket in the 1946–47 season, scoring 27 and 98 in his first State match, combining with Keith Carmody to add 153 for the first wicket in the second innings against Queensland. He followed with 115 for an Australia XI against the MCC in a virtual Test trial and with 81 not out for New South Wales v. MCC Test selection was automatic.

At Melbourne in the Third Test of the series he made 21 and 155, and in the Fourth Test at Adelaide scored 122 and 124 not out in the match in which Compton also made a 100 in each innings. Morris had quickly formed with Barnes an opening pairing so strong that Bill Brown, who had hit 206 in his debut at Lord's, had to be discarded.

Morris played many majestic innings after that, but none

First-Class Averages: Batting, 12,614 runs at 53.67; Bowling, 12 wickets at 49.33.

Tests (46): 3,533 runs at 46.48; 2 wickets at 25.00.

better than his 182 in Australia's second innings at Leeds in 1948 and his 196 at The Oval on the same tour. He headed our Test batting in 1948, with 696 runs at 87, and in all matches on the trip scored 1,922 runs, best score 290. By now he was a superb player who got into position to hook, drive or cut so effortlessly his batting always appeared certain to bring big scores. He led a massive assault on Jim Laker at Leeds that led to Laker's omission from Tests for two years. At Bristol he hammered Tom Goddard's off-breaks in scoring 102 by lunch and 231 by tea. Goddard, who had been confident of ending Morris' big-scoring, had 186 taken off his bowling. Bedser interrupted Morris' run-getting spree for a time but by the end of the tour Arthur was hailed as the world's best left-hander.

Back in Australia controversy developed over whether the reserved, easy-going Morris or the flamboyant Miller should captain the sides they were in. They captained NSW 26 times each, but the national selectors preferred Morris as Lindsay Hassett's vice-captain. Morris lost both times he captained Australia in Tests, Miller never was Test captain.

Just as the war had carved a big gap in his career, the illness of his first wife, former Windmill Showgirl Valerie Hudson and her subsequent death from cancer at the age of 33 led to Morris' early retirement in 1955. He spent the money he got from Test reporting giving Valerie a trip back to her English homeland. She died five months later. Twelve years after Valerie's death he married Judith Appleton, a divorcee from Western Australia. He was 46. He made a brief comeback to big cricket in 1963. Such was his brilliance in one innings against India at Bombay for a Commonwealth side that Norm O'Neill rounded up Australians in the dressing-room to make sure they did not miss Morris' spectacular stroke play. He remained unsurpassed in hooking short balls, and immediately adaptable to strange conditions. This was the batsman who had made a century in his first innings in four countries. Indian spectators gave him a standing ovation.

Morris made 12 centuries in Tests, eight of them against England. Among Australians only Bradman (19) has scored more centuries against England. In all first-class matches Morris scored 46 centuries. He has been a member of the Sydney Cricket Ground Trust since 1965, helping to run the ground where he first found fame.

MORRIS, Samuel
1855–1931

The first coloured man to represent Australia in Test cricket, a right-hand opening batsman and medium pace bowler selected on merit in the 1884–85 season when notable players often were reticent about playing for their country because of the fees offered. He was born in Tasmania of West Indian parents, who had been lured to Hobart by the gold-rush.

726

Morris learnt cricket at Daylesford, north-west of Melbourne, and the local association still competes for the "Sam Morris" Cup.

An easy-going character with a flair for ball games, he first played representative cricket for Tasmania against an Australian XI in 1880, making an immediate impact with his wicket-keeping. Not long afterwards he was appointed curator of Richmond Cricket ground in Melbourne. In January 1885, he played in the Test against England at Melbourne, scoring 4 and 10 not out and taking 2 wickets for 75 runs.

Morris' 280 for Richmond against St Kilda remained a Melbourne club cricket record for many years. After making his debut for Victoria in 1881–82, he played 19 times for the State, scoring 577 runs at 18.03, topscore 64 not out, and took 29 wickets at 25.37. He was appointed groundsman at South Melbourne in 1887 and held the job until he went blind before World War I. For 30 years he attended representative matches to chat with old friends, although he was totally blind.

First-Class Averages: Batting, 623 runs at 18.32; Bowling, 31 wickets at 26.09.

Tests (1): 14 runs at 14.00; 2 wickets at 36.50.

A sound, elegant right-hand Tasmanian batsman who refused good offers from mainland clubs and with them possible Test selection. Over a long period he batted with an ease and style few batsmen could match and had a career total of 74 centuries at all levels, the highest by any Tasmanian. He captained Tasmania 21 times between 1938 and 1952 and made 37 appearances for the State, not all of them in first-class matches. He was in six century partnerships in first-class matches for Tasmania and scored three first-class centuries, topscore 145 for Tarrant's XI v. Patiala.

Morrisby made his debut for Tasmania at 16. He was recommended to Frank Tarrant for the team that toured India in 1935–36 for the Maharajah of Patiala by J. A. ("Snowy") Atkinson. He made 958 runs at 36.80 on the Indian tour, almost as many as the tourists' leading run-scorer, Jack Ryder, a splendid achievement for a 20-year-old. The St Kilda and Prospect clubs both made him tempting offers on his return but he declined. He scored 2 and 57 in the Bardsley-Gregory testimonial match at Sydney in 1936–37 and never made the huge scores needed to compel the Test selectors to acknowledge his talents.

To Tasmanian oldtimers, however, there was in his batting a hint of Ken Burns' ease of strokeplay and some of Badcock's assured competence. In 1947–48 he made a spendid 130 for Tasmania against India at Launceston. Morrisby scored 1,000 runs in all games four times in a Tasmanian season, 1,133 at 50.21 in 1937–38, 1,081 at 72.21 in 1940–41, 1,000 at 52.63 in 1945–46 and 1,099 at 57.84 in 1951–52.

MORRISBY, Ronald Orlando George, 1915–

First-Class Averages: Batting, 2,596 runs at 32.45.

MORTON, Francis Lonsdale, 1901–1971

First-Class Averages: Batting, 204 runs at 7.84; Bowling, 94 wickets at 32.75.

A right-hand batsman and right-arm fast-medium bowler for South Australia and Victoria in the 1920s who toured New Zealand with the Australian team in 1927–28. He was born at Rose Park, SA, and played nine matches for his native State in 1921–22 and 1922–23. He joined the South Melbourne club when he moved to Victoria and in 1926–27 went into the Victorian team. He had a most unhappy match against NSW that season despite the Victorian total of 1,107 and their outright victory. Morton failed to score and failed to take a wicket.

On tour in New Zealand with Vic Richardson's Australian team, he took 31 wickets at 15.00. He was of little account with the bat and had a best score of only 23 in 28 first-class games, but he was an extremely useful opening bowler who could be relied on to break through the early batting. He took a hat-trick for Victoria v. Tasmania in 1931–32 in his last first class game, and three times took five wickets in an innings. He captained Victoria four times.

MOSES, Henry ("Harry"), 1858–1938

First-Class Averages: Batting, 2,898 runs at 35.77; Bowling, 1 wicket at 52.00.

Tests (6): 198 runs at 19.80.

One of the best left-handed batsmen Australia has produced. He took heavy toll of visiting English bowlers and was a prolific scorer in matches for New South Wales, but declined numerous invitations to tour England with Australian teams because of commitments in his job with a Sydney wine merchant. Many thought he would have challenged Murdoch as the No 1 Australian batsman of his era had he gone to England.

Moses, born at Windsor, New South Wales, was educated at Dr Sly's School, Calder House, Sydney. He was a noted dog lover and at one time was president of the New South Wales Kennel Club. He played grade cricket with Albert and Belvidere clubs and was one of the first trustees of the Sydney Cricket Ground, a happy dark-haired man with laughing eyes, and a big, wavy moustache.

He had a remarkable defence that was seldom bested and he waited with unwearying patience for deliveries to hit. He could hit brilliantly all round the wicket and was brutally efficient in despatching short deliveries to the mid-off boundary. His special joy was the leg glance, which he sometimes played while almost down on his knees. He was an outstanding deep field, safe in catching and throwing.

Early in 1884, Moses played a masterly hand of 149 for Fifteen of New South Wales against the Australia team at Sydney. In 1886–87, he made his debut for Australia at Sydney and in a low-scoring match topscored in both innings with 31 and 34. On wickets helpful to bowlers, he was superior to any batsman on either side in this series. In 1887–88 he made 109 against Shrewsbury's English team at Sydney, and 297 not out

728

for New South Wales against Victoria, both at Sydney. After the match against England the NSWCA presented him with a 50 guinea trophy and his Sydney club gave him a diamond pin.

In 1890–91, he made 147 against Victoria , and in 1893–94 104 against South Australia. In a match against South Australia 1892–93 at Adelaide, he tried his pet leg glance after scoring 99, missed, and was bowled by George Giffen. During the Australian tour by Lord Sheffield's English team in 1891–92, he damaged a tendon in his left leg and as a result faded out of Test cricket.

MOSS, Jeffrey Kenneth, 1947–

A hard-hitting, no-nonsense Victorian left-hander whose aggression has proved invaluable to Victoria. He was a key figure in teams that won the Sheffield Shield in the 1978–79 and 1979–80 seasons. He scored 881 runs at 67.77 in 1978–79 and critics called for his inclusion in our Test team long before he was finally chosen for the final Test of the season against Pakistan. Moss made 22 and 38 not out, with Australia winning by seven wickets. He was included in the Australian World Cup squad in England in 1979, but missed out on later tours when the WSC players returned to the national team. Moss has scored nine centuries, highest score 220 for Victoria against South Australia in 1978–79. Moss and Julien Wiener set an Australian third wicket record of 390 for Victoria v. WA in 1981–82 at Geelong. His bat is always straight and he hits loose deliveries very hard. Even our best bowlers find his defence difficult to penetrate.

First-Class Averages: Batting, 3,416 runs at 43.79.

Tests (1): 60 runs at 60.00.

MOULE, William Henry, 1858–1939

A useful right-hand batsman and medium pace bowler, and fine fieldsman with a powerful throw and safe hands. He played his sole Test at The Oval for the 1880 Australian team, scoring 6 and 34, and taking 3 for 23 in an England innings of 420. He bowled in place of Spofforth, who was ill. As Australia's No 11 batsman, he stuck with his captain Billy Murdoch in a last-wicket partnership of 88 when Australia followed-on. This saved an innings defeat and forced England to bat again. He was the last survivor of the first Test in England when he died in 1939.

Moule, educated at Melbourne Grammar and Melbourne University, was 6 ft tall, 11 st 6 lb. He was a barrister and principal partner in one of Melbourne's largest law firms and later a Judge. He first played for Victoria in matches Against The Odds in 1878, scoring 15 runs at 7.50 without taking a wicket.

First-Class Averages: Batting, 137 runs at 11.41; Bowling, 5 wickets at 21.20.

Tests (1): 40 runs at 20.00; 3 wickets at 7.66

MOYES, Alban George ("Johnnie"), 1893–1963

First-Class Averages: Batting, 883 runs at 29.43; Bowling, 5 wickets at 53.60.

A prominent writer and commentator on cricket who played for South Australia and Victoria and was selected in the Australian team whose tour of South Africa had to be cancelled because of World War I. He was a useful seam bowler, but it was his aggressive right-hand batting that stamped him as a cricketer of uncommon ability.

He was born at Gladstone, South Australia, and played for South Australia while studying at Adelaide University. In his first match for South Australia, he scored 104 in 103 minutes, with a six and 17 fours, against Western Australia in 1912–13. In the decisive Shield match that season against New South Wales at Adelaide, South Australia made 569, Mayne 124, Chamberlain 103, Steele 113 not out and Moyes 64. New South Wales made 276 and 240 and lost by an innings. That summer he played for the Rest of Australia against New South Wales in the Victor Trumper Testimonial match at Sydney, top-scoring with 76. Trumper invited Moyes to play as a guest for Gordon against North Sydney but Moyes was out first ball for a duck.

In 1913–14 Moyes was in the SA Shield team that narrowly lost the competition to New South Wales, distinguishing himself with a fighting 50 against the bowling of Ryder and Armstrong at Melbourne. After army service in England and France and playing in services matches at Lord's and The Oval, he joined Victoria for two matches in 1919–20 scoring 74 runs at 24.66, best score 55.

He was at various times news editor and sports editor of leading Australian papers and when he moved to Sydney to work in 1921–22 he joined the Gordon club, immediately showing that his duck on his debut for the club was a poor guide to his quality. At Chatswood Oval he caused a sensation by scoring 218 runs in 83 minutes. He made 50 in 20 minutes, 100 in 40 minutes, 150 in 62 minutes, 200 in 72 minutes and when he was out 11 minutes later on 218 had hit seven sixes and 36 fours. This rapid scoring remains without parallel in the history of the Gordon club. In 1923–24 he captained the Gordon team that won the Sydney premiership, scoring 174 in another big hitting knock. His captaincy and the good fellowship he inspired caused fellow players to present him with an engraved silver ball.

However, it was as cricket commentator for the Australian Broadcasting Commission between 1950 and 1963 that "Johnnie" Moyes achieved widest fame. He was always bright and informative, a cheery character respected by players and listeners. In this period, too, he was at his most productive, writing nine books on cricket, including the first definitive history of Australian cricket published 1959, *Bradman* (1948), *Australian Bowlers*, and *Australian Batsmen*. He had two sons, one of whom became head of IBM in Australia, and the other editor of one of our biggest Sunday newspapers. One of

Johnnie Moyes's brothers, the Rt Rev. **John Stoward Moyes**, was Bishop of Armidale, NSW and Deputy Chancellor of the University of New England. Another brother, Captain **Morton Henry Moyes**, was a member of the Shackleton Relief Expedition in the Antarctic and the RAN's Chief Rehabilitation Officer.

MUDGE, Harold, 1914–

First-Class Averages: Batting, 1,060 runs at 33.12; Bowling, 25 wickets at 44.24.

A delightful right-hand batsman and occasional slow leg-break bowler for NSW, Sir Julien Cahn's team, and for Leicestershire in two matches. Mudge was short-sighted and could not read scoreboards but there was nothing wrong with his sight in the centre. He made his debut for NSW in 1935–36 after impressive displays with the Glebe club. That season he reached 94 for NSW against Queensland before Geoff Cook had him caught off the new ball. In 1936–37 he took eight wickets with his spinners against Allen's MCC team at Sydney, including 6 for 42 in the first innings when Wally Hammond was among his victims. He signed with Sir Julien Cahn's troupe in 1937. He did not want to play County cricket but played for Leicester against Oxford University. When he returned to Sydney he opened the batting for NSW in 1939–40 with "Mort" Cohen figuring in some splendid stands characterised by his running between wickets and skillful shot placement. In 18 first-class matches, Mudge had a highest score of 118 for Sir Julien Cahn's XI v. New Zealand in 1938–39 and twice took five wickets in an innings.

MURDOCH, William Lloyd, 1854–1911

First-Class Averages: Batting, 16,953 runs at 26.86; Bowling, 10 wickets at 43.00; Dismissals, 243 (218 catches, 25 stumpings).

Tests: (18 for Australia) 896 runs at 32.00; Dismissals, 14—(13 catches, 1 stumping); (1 for England) 12 runs at 12.00. Dismissals, 1—(1 stumping).

The first great Australian batsman, the first to match the highest English batting skills, and the first player from any country to score a double century in Tests. Only W. G. Grace ranked ahead of him, when Murdoch was in his prime. He was a small, very straight right-hander who made up for his limited reach with speedy footwork, essentially a front foot batsman who skipped well down the pitch to drive, mainly on the offside. He could cut handsomely, and according to English historian Harry Altham was the last regular exponent of the under the leg stroke behind square leg.

In a long career he went to England with five Australian teams (1878, 1880, 1882, 1884 and 1890), and topped the batting averages on all bar the first trip. He captained four of those teams. He led Australia in the very first Test in England, scoring 153 not out in the second innings, led Australia to victory on his second trip at The Oval in 1882, and after he finished playing in Australia captained Sussex in the English County championship for seven years. He was a firm friend of W. G. Grace, one of his great admirers, and contemporary critics said their rivalry spurred both men to bigger things.

Murdoch, born at Sandhurst, Victoria, began at Sydney University as a wicket-keeper while living in the Balmain district where his brother, G. C. Murdoch, was Mayor. Billy and Gilbert played on the old Pigeon Ground (Gladstone Park), many times when the ground was not required for pigeon shooting contests. He was good enough as a 'keeper for demon bowler Fred Spofforth to refuse to play in the first of all Tests at Melbourne in March, 1877, because Murdoch was not the 'keeper. In the face of Blackham's success behind the stumps, Billy concentrated on his batting but often on tour he would 'keep while Blackham fielded.

Murdoch's batting flowered as his 'keeping skill fell away and on his last English tour in 1890 he said he found 'keeping distasteful. But after he finished his Australian career he kept wicket for England in a Test at Cape Town in 1891–92 against South Africa. After he finished his stint with Sussex, he played for London County until that club's dissolution in 1904, the year he made 140 for The Gentlemen against The Players at The Oval, his eighth appearance for The Gentlemen.

On his first tour of England in 1878 Murdoch made only 319 runs at 13.29 in a very wet English summer on pitches that did not suit him. When the sun shone on following tours, however, his mastery emerged. He headed the Australian averages in 1880 with 465 runs at 25.83, and in 1884 made 1,378 runs at 30.62, topscore a memorable 211 at The Oval, international cricket's first double century. Back in Australia he scored 321 for New South Wales v. Victoria at Sydney in 1881–82, for many years the best score in Australian cricket.

Murdoch's tact and personal charm were almost as valuable to those early Australian touring teams as his batting. The teams often arrived with very few fixtures arranged for them, but thanks to Murdoch's reputation and contacts ended up with busy programmes. He captained Australia in 16 Tests, for five wins, seven losses, and four draws.

Murdoch was a New South Wales hero when the crowd at Sydney rioted because he was given run-out in a match against Lord Harris' visiting English team in February 1879. Lord Harris was hit on the back with a stick by a larrikin in a shameful day for Australian cricket, with demonstators preventing play from continuing over the last three hours on the second day. Harris said he would block any future matches between Australian and English teams. When the 1880 Australians arrived in England, they found that the MCC had instructed the Counties not to play them. Murdoch advertised for matches and finally Yorkshire agreed to play his team. The Australians created such a good impression in that match, there was widespread approval when Murdoch shrewdly offered to play a representative English XI for the Cricketers' Benefit Fund. Lord Harris still refused but

Murdoch and Victorian George Alexander persuaded him to agree to the match and lead England. This was the match in which W. G. Grace scored 152 and Murdoch went one run better with 153 not out.

Murdoch was dropped from the Australian team after the 1890 tour of England on the grounds that he was too old at 36. He made fools of the people who came to this decision by migrating to England and taking over the Sussex XI and playing for England. There he became a famous captain, a noted wit about whom C. B. Fry said it was not easy to avoid becoming epic. Every dressing-room he entered was relaxed and full of fun.

"Murdoch does not commit puns, of course, nor sputter epigrams: he is simply, genuinely, and unaffectedly amusing," wrote Fry. "It's the way, not the words. Mark him even now as he leads his adopted sons of Sussex into the field. He has lost the toss easily; he has suggested to ten sad pals that 'Now, boys, the white coats are out.' How well they know the sound of that cheerful, well-fed voice making that remark! And three or four of them were waiting, padded and gloved, silently jostling to go in first. 'Not again, Billy, splendid sunshine, too, and a real Brighton wicket.' But who would have expected so experienced a captain to have so little control over a shilling.

"But mark him. A square-round—the double term applies—powerful, well-knit figure, as active as most men half his age and every bit as keen; a man who would enjoy a Klon-

The 1890 Australian team to England. Back row—H. Trumble, J. McC. Blackham, K. E. Burn, Dr J. E. Barrett, H. F. Boyle (manager); seated—F. H. Walters, G. H. S. Trott, W. L. Murdoch (captain), J. J. Lyons, C. T. B. Turner; front—S. E. Gregory, J. J. Ferris, P. C. Charlton, S. P. Jones.

dyke or a Mansion House dinner. His company will help a digger down on his luck no less than an alderman with an appetite. His spirit would refuse to be unfortunate, his body scorn incapacity for meat and drink. No wonder he led Australia well in the old days—a fit Odysseus to meet our mighty bearded Ajax."

Murdoch always had a whimsical suspicion about the six martlets that embroidered Sussex caps and sweaters. He claimed they were crows. He shared the Sussex captaincy sometimes with Ranji, the great exponent of the leg glance, reviving his under the leg shot when Ranji nicked one away around his legs. As Fry remarked, nothing about Murdoch was commonplace. He ate, drank, smoked, talked and wore a hat distinctively, and did nothing by formula.

Despite his individuality, Murdoch's methods were so sound he was able to make big scores when past his physical peak, and scored his last first-class century at 49. He was of such sound constitution, it was a shock when he was seized by a fatal heart attack at 56 while watching Australia play South Africa at Melbourne.

In all first-class matches, Billy Murdoch made a prodigious 19 centuries, two in Tests, topscore 321.

MURRAY, John Tinline ("Jack"), 1892–1974

First-Class Averages: Batting, 1,926 runs at 26.75; Bowling, 11 wickets at 58.63.

A South Australian grazier renowned for his lusty right-hand hitting. He was a man of powerful physique, 6 ft 3 in tall, with wide shoulders, who was among the most exciting batsmen in Adelaide club cricket before and after World War I. He was a useful medium-pace bowler and dependable fieldsman. In England just after serving as a gunner with the AIF, he made three centuries for the first AIF team captained by Herbie Collins, two of them in minor matches but one gem of heavy hitting for 133 against Oxford University.

Murray made his first grade debut for East Torrens in 1911–12 and later that season had an impressive debut for SA, scoring 48 and 36 against NSW at Adelaide. His agricultural studies prevented any further first-class appearances until after World War I. He made 793 runs in all matches in England for the AIF at 24.03, 72 runs at 12.00 in South Africa, and 57 runs at 19.00 in Australia.

For SA, he scored 152 v. Victoria at Adelaide in 1922–23, 113 v. Queensland in 1923–24 at Adelaide when he shared a stand of 229 with E. L. Bowley, and 126 v. Victoria at Adelaide in 1924–25. His exciting hitting brought him 3,310 runs at 56.20 in only seven seasons for East Torrens. In the Adelaide district A Grade final in 1923–24, he made 248 for East Torrens against Sturt, and finished with 869 runs at 66.84 for the season. All his big scores were studded with clean, long blows. He retired to his property at Woodside, SA.

A gentlemanly right-handed batsman who got his chance to represent Australia when Australia's leading players objected to their cash rewards. He went into the Australian side for the Second Test at Melbourne as a late replacement against Shrewsbury's 1884–85 English team. Twelve years later Musgrove, who was born at Surbiton in Surrey, managed the 1896 Australian team in England and proved a tactful, courteous handler of cricketers and their problems.

Musgrove won his chance for a brief Test career when Murdoch's Australian team returned home after their 1884 trip to England intent on getting more money for playing in big games. For the First Test at Adelaide Murdoch's players demanded 30 per cent of the takings. They refused an offer from the English management of 20 per cent of the takings and when public opinion showed to be strongly opposed to their demands—they were amateurs—they agreed to play for 40 per cent of the profits. This was also rejected and finally the SACA paid each team £450 for the Test, a decision which disgusted the Englishmen.

After the Adelaide Test the Englishmen played several country matches and in one of these at Ballarat, Musgrove and Jack Worrall had a partnership of 151, Musgrove scoring 109, Worrall 67. When the dispute with players continued over terms for the Second Test at Melbourne, all Murdoch's team declined to play and the VCA suspended all the Victorians in Murdoch's side, selecting a completely new XI, which included Musgrove and Worrall.

Worrall went on to a successful international career, while Musgrove played three matches for Victoria. The century at Ballarat had been a once in a lifetime effort. He showed skill as a manager, however, in England in 1896, when Australia did well despite the lack of a really hostile bowler. Under the guidance of Musgrove and captain Harry Trott new players like Clem Hill, Joe Darling, Ernie Jones and J. J. Kelly were blooded for performances later that were of immense value to Australian cricket. Musgrove was a member of the famous Australian theatrical partnership of Williamson, Garner and Musgrove, which later evolved into J. C. Williamson Theatres Limited.

MUSGROVE, Henry, 1860–1931

First-Class Averages: Batting, 99 runs at 8.25.

Tests (1): 13 runs at 6.50.

N

NAGEL, Lisle Ernest, 1905–1971

First-Class Averages: Batting, 407 runs at 12.33; Bowling, 67 wickets at 28.35.

Tests (1): 21 runs, NA; 2 wickets at 55.00.

A remarkable right-arm medium-pace swing bowler whose first-class career was upset by a ricked neck. "I was standing beside him in the slips during the Blackie-Ironmonger Testimonial match in 1933–34 in Melbourne, when he turned to tell me something and ricked his neck", said Bill O'Reilly. "I never saw him play again." Lisle Nagel, whose twin brother also played for Victoria, was 6 ft 6 ins tall, and swung the ball so disconcertingly some batsmen appeared powerless against him.

Nagel, born at Bendigo, first played for Victoria in 1927–28, five years ahead of his twin. Both gave stalwart service to the Melbourne CC and both were all-action cricketers. Lisle took 8 for 32 in 10 overs for an Australian XI against the MCC in Melbourne with a bandage around his elbow to protect an injury sustained while he was cranking a car. MCC were all out for 60. Lisle's performance earned him a Test against England in the 1932–33 Bodyline series in which he failed to consolidate his place. In 1939–40, Lisle Nagel set a Melbourne district cricket record by taking 86 wickets at 13.45.

Lisle Nagel toured India with Frank Tarrant's Australian side in 1934–35, shrugging off his neck problems to take 5 for 24 against Sind and 7 for 53 against Maharashtra. For Victoria, his best figures in 10 matches were 6 for 35 against South Australia in 1931–32. **Vernon George Nagel** (1905–1974) made four appearances for Victoria that produced 29 runs at 5.80 and three wickets at 94.33.

NASH, Laurence John, 1910–

A brilliant Australian Rules footballer who had an unusual career in international cricket as a tearaway fast bowler. Nash never played in Shield cricket, but played 17 times for Tasmania and once for Victoria.* He let the ball go with a fur-

*Among other Australians who played more Tests than Shield matches were: Stan McCabe, 39 Tests, 37 Shield matches; Victor Trumper, 48, 46; Keith Miller, 55, 44; Syd Gregory, 58, 53; Herbert Hordern, 7, 2; and Jack Gregory, 24, 11.

ious arm action, as if a fortune depended on every ball. He had a storybook debut for Australia in 1931–32, taking 4 for 18 against South Africa while Bert Ironmonger took 5 for 6 at the other end and South Africa were bundled out for 36.

Nash was born in Melbourne but brought up in Tasmania, a chunky 5 ft 9 in, 13 st bundle of sporting mayhem who really made the ball fizz as he charged through the crease at a speed that always appeared likely to topple him over. He could bat effectively. He was the son of Bob Nash, a star Collingwood footballer, and found his football and cricket interests conflicted. His father wanted him to concentrate on cricket but Laurie opted for football and became one of the finest Australian Rules players of all time. He was twice winner of the Hardenty Cup for the best and fairest player in northern Tasmania, and at centre half forward excelled for many years with South Melbourne.

After his debut in 1931–32, aged 21, Nash did not get another chance in big cricket until the last Test of the 1936–37 season when most critics believed "Ginty" Lush should have got the opening bowler's job. His selection caused grumbles among the MCC tourists who objected to the number of bouncers Nash, nothing if not a fierce competitor, had bowled at them in the Victoria v. England match.

Nash took 4 for 70 in the second innings, bowing out of Test cricket with handsome figures. He also took six catches. His sole match for Victoria—against MCC—produced 4 for 37 off 96 balls, and 29 runs in his only innings.

First-Class Averages: Batting, 953 runs at 28.02; Bowling, 69 wickets at 28.33.

Tests (2): 30 runs at 15.00; 10 wickets at 12.60.

NETHERLANDS VERSUS AUSTRALIA

Australia has played two matches, both of one-day at The Hague, against official All-Holland teams, winning one and losing one. Other matches have been played in Holland between teams that included Australian Test players such as Rod Marsh and Greg Chappell, but these were not part of the official itinerary of Australian touring sides.

According to the Archives Committee of the Royal Netherlands Cricket Association, the first match between Australia and Holland took place on July 16, 1953, when the Australian side comprised Hassett, Morris, McDonald, Harvey, Miller, de Courcy, Benaud, Archer, Davidson, Tallon and Ring. Australia batted first and reached 279, mainly through a second wicket stand by Morris (70) and McDonald (66). Holland struggled for three hours against Australia's varied attack to score 122 in reply. The Archives Committee says this was the first-ever appearance by an Australian Test side on the European Continent.

The second match on August 29, 1964, saw Australia's shock defeat. The Australian side that suffered this ignominy

AUSTRALIA v. THE NETHERLANDS
Played at The Hague, 29 August 1964

AUSTRALIA

W. Lawry, c van Weelde, b Trijzelaar	5
W. Grout, b Trijzelaar	20
N. O'Neill, st Schoonheim, b Pierhagen	87
P. Burge, c Trijzelaar, b Pierhagen	22
B. Booth (Capt.), c Bouwman, b Vriens	13
J. Potter, retired hurt	7
R. Cowper, c and b Trijzealar	2
T. Veivers, run out	12
J. Martin, lbw, b Pierhagen	12
G. McKenzie, not out	8
A. Connolly, b Vriens	1
L.B. 6, N.B. 2	8
Total (nine wickets)	197

THE NETHERLANDS—BOWLING

	O.	M.	R.	W.
Trijzelaar	11	2	41	3
van Arkel	4	—	20	—
Pierhagen	21	6	75	3
Vriens	14.1	—	53	2

Trijzelar, 2 no-balls.

THE NETHERLANDS

P. Marseille, lbw, b. Cowper	77
W. van de Vegt, b McKenzie	33
P. van Arkel (Capt.), c and b Cowper	45
W. van Weelde, b McKenzie	8
P. Bouwman, c. Veivers, b Cowper	1
R. Onstein, not out	24
E. Vriens, lbw, b Cowper	3
H. Trijzelar, b. McKenzie	0
H. Wijkhuizen, not out	2
B. 4, L.B. 4	8
Seven wickets for	201

R. Schoonheim and W. Pierhagen did not bat.

AUSTRALIA—BOWLING

	O.	M.	R.	W.
McKenzie	19	4	48	3
Connolly	4	—	11	—
Veivers	6	1	13	—
Martin	10	—	46	—
O'Neill	6	2	6	—
Cowper	12.4	1	69	4

Umpires: W. Amons and G. Stallman.

The Netherlands won by 3 wickets

had just defeated England for The Ashes but could score only 197 against All-Holland's XI, O'Neill topscoring with 87. Potter was struck by a fast rising ball trying to hook and was taken to hospital with a skull fracture. Holland started well with Marseille (77) and Vandervegt (33) adding 99 for the first wicket. Holland reached 3 for 160, and scored the 20 runs needed to win off the last two overs through some spirited hitting by the tailender, Onstein, who clubbed two straight sixes and a four in a knock of 24 not out. All-Holland won with four balls left. Efforts to get more recent Australian teams to visit Holland at the end of their English tours have failed. A crowd of 3,000 saw Holland achieve her first win over a touring international team. Jim Manning, noted English sportswriter, said Australia's 1964 defeat was the most staggering sporting message he had had to handle, with the possible exception of America's one-nil defeat of England at soccer in 1950.

New South Wales cricketers played their initial first-class match on March 26 and 27, 1856, against Victoria at Melbourne. An "Intercolonial Committee" comprised of keen Sydney cricket fans made arrangements for this match. They quickly became aware of animosity about their work among players and clubs in the Sydney area. To prevent a recurrence of this in organising a return match with Victoria, the New South Wales Cricket Association was formed in 1857 at a meeting at Cunningham's Hotel on the corner of King and Castlereagh Streets, Sydney, which was attended by officials from the Albert, Union, Royal Victoria, Australian, the National and Marylebone clubs. The governor, Sir William Denison, was appointed president, J. R. Clayton secretary, and John Fairfax, Richard Jones, William Tunks and Captain Ward vice-presidents.

NEW SOUTH WALES, CRICKET IN

The association used the only available public park, the Domain, for its early matches. For events such as inter-Colonial games against Victoria an application was made to the Government for permission to board up the ground and charge admission. The usual price for standing room was one shilling, which was increased to two shillings and sixpence when the English team played. Early matches on the Domain were marred by hooliganism and the papers printed letters calling for reforms to rescue Sydney cricket "from its present degraded position."

The only competitive matches in Sydney at the time were for challenge cups and they were dominated by the Albert club. The Leigh Challenge Cup was won outright by the Alberts in January, 1867, and was replaced by the Challenge Cup two years later. Then it was discovered that as the Domain was public property, the teams who played there had no right to charge for admission. There was a lot of unpleasantness when many people refused to pay and at the last inter-Colonial match on the ground no attempt was made to enforce payment.

"Everyone came to practice in his ordinary clothes, cricket boots were seldom worn, and flannels were unknown," wrote the fast bowler Fred Spofforth in an account of the period. "There was no place of shelter to change in, and even in a match, more than half the players would turn out with no alteration to their costume. I remember that as boys we used to think a great deal of a man who appeared in flannels; it was a sure sign that big things were expected of him. There was no such thing as a professional cricketer in Australia. Artisans and gentlemen played together in all the clubs, and if the ordinary boots got slippery, off they came; even socks were discarded by the artisans. Very few players had bats of their own: a stock of materials were kept in a huge canvas bag at the house of the secretary of the club or at some member's house near the ground."

After the visit of the second English team in 1864, roundarm bowling began to be used and some bowlers sent down a mixture of underarm and roundarm deliveries in the same over. The first State captain was G. H. Gilbert, who had played for the Gentlemen against The Players in England in 1851. One critic said Gilbert's batting was "very effective but wanting in finish, and he would do more if he was not so fond of hitting to leg. His fielding is good but would be rendered more elegant if he curbed his sometimes exuberant spirits." The same critic said Gilbert placed his men well but "we consider it throwing away a chance not to have a wicket-keeper."

High scores were unusual, but in 1866–67 George Gordon hit 112 not out for the Alberts against the Australian club, and in 1868–69 Nat Thompson made 125 not out for the Alberts against the Surrey club. In the 1869–70 season during a match between the Albert and Warwick clubs Charles Oliver and Alfred Park had a punch-up in the middle of the pitch.

To solve the problems caused by using the Domain, a group of gentlemen, who included P. C. and G. Curtis, W. Alderson and A. L. Park, bought a piece of boggy ground in the suburb of Redfern where they started the first club cricket ground. This ground in Elizabeth Street, Redfern, built as a private speculation, was known as the Albert Ground after the club who were its main tenants. It had a pavilion and between 1864 and 1876 all inter-Colonial and international matches in Sydney were played there.

One of the stars of Sydney cricket was Captain Ward, deputy master of the Mint, later Major-General Wolstenholme Ward, who batted with his backside facing the bowler and peered at him over his left shoulder, leaving the bowler utterly confused about when he was ready. Ward was among the colony's first exponents of roundarm bowling, a style which aroused great suspicion. Another identity was J. McKone, an underarm bowler of "Sydney grubbers," who as a batsman unnerved bowlers by playing forward to every ball. Another character was Tom Lewis, a batsman who hated to let a ball

740

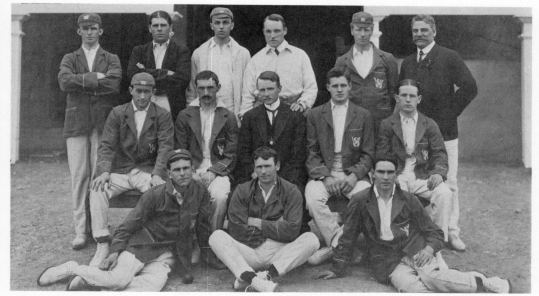

get past him and chased every delivery wherever it was pitched. He even threw his bat at a ball that was too wide on the legside to reach.

Curiously, two distinct styles of batting developed in the Sydney area because of the varying methods of Charles Lawrence and William Caffyn, the two imported English coaches. Lawrence stressed the value of playing back, while Caffyn was all for playing forward. In the inter-Colonial matches Victorians whom Caffyn had coached played forward, and Lawrence's Sydney pupils played back. Members of W. G. Grace's English team in 1873–74 said the difference in technique in the two colonies was quite marked. In both colonies the bowlers were confused over which style to follow as under-hand bowling evolved into over-arm. Spofforth confessed to throwing a lot of deliveries in his struggle to find a style that suited him.

Higher scores came with improved pitches. In 1866–67, Oliver and David Gregory had an opening stand of 155 for the Alberts against University. This remained the highest Sydney partnership until 1876–77 when "Alick" and Charles Bannerman scored 258 for the Warwick club off the East Sydney bowling before they were separated, "Alick" scoring 154, Charles 140. On Moore Park in March, 1878, Harry Moses made 136 and a batsman named Cape hit 139 in a total of 500 for the Commercial Bank, who thereupon routed the Australian Joint Stock Bank for 65. Three weeks later the King's School scored 532 against Oaklands, who managed only 66 in reply. J. Hillas, E. Pell and W. S. Brown scored centuries for King's.

New South Wales team v. Queensland, Brisbane, 1910 (L to R): Standing, H. Cranney, C. R. Gorry, Dr H. V. Hordern, A. J. Hopkins, E. L. Waddy, G. H. Power; Seated, C. E. Simpson, A. Diamond (Captain), A. M. Jones (Manager), C. Kelleway, H. L. Collins; Front, J. Scott, R. B. Minnett, F. Gow.

741

The NSWCA became increasingly unhappy over charges set by the company that controlled the Albert Ground, and began to look at the area behind Victoria Barracks known as the Garrison Ground. Back in 1812 Governor Lachlan Macquarie had established a "town common", but this was forgotten until the Mayor of Sydney, John Sutherland, took possession of the marshy town common land in 1860 in the name of the City Corporation. A new Lord Mayor, Charles Moore, spent around £42,000 in 1867 and 1868 having the sandhills of the common levelled and grass planted. As Moore Park, the so-called common became an important part of the Sydney cricket scene, and has remained so for more than a century. Surrey United was the first club to play cricket on Moore Park, but dozens of other teams quickly followed. Then the government was induced to allocate part of Moore Park to the NSWCA, and the first inter-Colonial match was played on the Association Ground in February, 1878.

Meanwhile cricket had spread to country areas of NSW, with Maitland and Canberra particularly active. A team from the Canberra district captained by William Davis played matches at Braidwood, Yass, Gunning and Collector in 1861, using Goulburn as their base. In 1871, a strong Melbourne Cricket Club team played against Northern NSW. Sydney defeated a Combined Country XI by an innings in 1873.

New South Wales team southern tour, 1921 (L to R): Standing, J. Bogle, H. S. T. L. Hendry, J. M. Gregory, C. Kelleway, A. F. Kippax; Seated, W. A. Oldfield, J. M. Taylor, H. L. Collins (Captain), E. L. Waddy (Manager), W. Bardsley, A. A. Mailey, T. J. E. Andrews.

English teams who had played most matches against the odds on their early visits encountered a different quality of opposition on later tours. The Albert Ground company had been sold up and the land went for building lots. On the Association Ground the wickets and amenities were of a high standard. A Fifteen of NSW beat Lillywhite's team very easily in 1876–77, and from this came the desire among NSW and Victorian players to meet England on level terms. From this in turn Test matches and overseas tours developed, with NSW players consistently prominent.

When John Conway wrote to Australia's leading players asking if they were interested in a tour of England after the two Tests against Lillywhite's team, he included the New South Welshmen Dave Gregory, Charles Bannerman, Billy Murdoch and Fred Spofforth among his original list of possibles. When the Victorian Tom Kendall was omitted he invited Nat Thompson, NSW, to join the team, but he declined and A. C. Bannerman went in his place. Even in that first Australian overseas touring team, however, the rivalry between the colonies of NSW and Victoria ran high. "The rivalry is not limited to the field," wrote Spofforth, "it extends from politics to society, to every side of life. In the matter of the selection of the first team, the press and the public were widely at variance. One felt Victoria had been slighted, the other NSW, and even on the tour itself the players were seen separating themselves as far as possible from compatriots of the other colony."

District cricket began in Sydney in 1893–94 when East Sydney were premiers. The Paddington, Glebe, Waverley and Cumberland clubs were all prominent, and North Sydney had an impressive array of talented players before its resources were reduced by the formation of the Gordon club. The NSWCA's first trophy for first grade premiers, the Hordern Shield, was played between 1893–94 and 1901–02 when it was discovered that as Paddington had won it three times they should keep it under the terms of the original donation. The Rawson Cup became the symbol of Sydney first grade supremacy in 1902–03 and was competed for until 1912–13 when North Sydney won it for the third time and with that won the right to keep the Cup.

Club cricketers developed great camaraderie travelling to matches together by tram, carriage or train. A trip to play Manly before the Harbour Bridge was built involved players from, say, the Burwood or Cumberland clubs, in long hours of travelling by tram and ferry but there was a spirit among the players seldom enjoyed by teams nowadays who travel individually to matches by car.

Originally the district clubs concentrated on running five or six teams graded according to playing ability, relying on new settlers and schools for players, conducting cricket as a

743

game for adults with little effort given to junior development.

The leading schools did not let the district clubs down, providing an endless stream of talent, already soundly coached by masters. *Crown Street* Superior Public School developed Monty Noble and Victor Trumper but they had to play their way through matches on Moore Park before they joined the Paddington club. "Tibby" Cotter, Charles Kelleway, Bert Oldfield and Warren Bardsley all came from the *Forest Lodge* Public School, where Bardsley's father was headmaster.

The *King's School*, founded in 1831, was playing cricket in 1832 and by the 1840s was strong enough to play regularly against Cumberland's first grade team. King's subsequently produced players like E. L. and E. F. Waddy, Reg Bettington and his brother Jack, and H. O. Rock, who all played for NSW. *Sydney Grammar School*, founded in 1859, played the first inter-schools match against King's in 1875 and the first inter-State schools match against Melbourne Grammar in 1876, playing an annual match that is now in its 106th year. In 1909, Grammar made 916, believed to be the highest total by an Australian schoolboy side, against Shore at North Sydney. Grammar has produced 10 Test players, F. R. Spofforth, S. P. Jones, H. Donnan, S. M. J. Woods, P. C. Charlton, A. Cotter, F. Iredale, H. S. T. L. Hendry, A. K. Walker and J. W. Burke.

Sydney *Church of England Grammar School* ("Shore"), founded in 1889, produced noted players like Jack Gregory, A. J. Hopkins, "Ranji" Hordern, R. J. A. Massie, the Minett brothers and later E. C. S. White. Opening for Shore against Newington in 1904, O. H. Dean made 412, then the highest score by a schoolboy. *St Ignatius College*, founded in 1880, developed eight cricket fields on the school's 110 acres at Lane Cove, and in 1885 Patrick Clifford made 212 on the main ground against Newington College. On the same ground in 1895, Walter Fraser took 12 for 23 in the match against Grammar.

At the beginning of grade or electorate cricket in Sydney, matches were conducted over three Saturdays. Many of the original clubs went through rapid transformations. The Canterbury club, for example, had no home ground when it was formed in 1892–93, and this proved too big a handicap and its members joined certain residents of Burwood who had arranged a lease on what was known as Burwood Recreation Ground to form the Burwood club in August, 1895, continuing strongly as Burwood with players like G. P. Barbour, G. L. Garnsey, A. Diamond and C. Docker until 1913–14 when it became the Western Suburbs District CC. Paddington club was originally known as Sydney, changed to Paddington and then in the 1960s reverted to Sydney when the NSWCA merged it with Glebe. North Sydney club, founded in 1893, lost a lot of its players when the Gordon club was formed in 1905.

A typical example of how Sydney district cricket has

744

grown with the city is the St George club. Founded in 1910–11, St George was admitted to first grade in 1921–22, and produced its first Test players in 1928–29 when D. G. Bradman and A. G. Fairfax played for Australia. It had built an impressive record through players like W. J. O'Reilly, R. R. Lindwall, W. Watson, N. C. O'Neill, and B. C. Booth, and then lost some of its territory when the Sutherland club came into first grade in 1964–65.

Balmain, formed as a second grade electorate club in 1897, became Leichhardt-Balmain in 1900 and from 1904 was known simply as Balmain. The club's first committee met in the funeral parlours of the club's embalmer-treasurer A. C. Wood and there were many eerie gaslight discussions recorded. The Mosman club, founded in 1908–9 when it entered teams in the second and third grade competitions, had receipts and expenditures for the whole of its first season of

New South Wales team, 1929–30 (L to R): Standing, A. E. Marks, N. O. Morris, B. A. Cooper, C. O. Nicholls, F. M. Cush (Manager), A. G. Fairfax, D. C. Seddon, D. G. Bradman; Seated, W. C. Andrews, A. Jackson, A. F. Kippax, T. J. E. Andrews, W. A. Oldfield.

745

£92-7-9. Mosman were admitted to first grade in 1921–22 together with Randwick and Marrickville.

There were dozens of colourful grade players who never aspired to State or Test places. Balmain had a left-arm "tweaker" named "Magic" Sullivan who played for them for more than 20 seasons. Paddington stalwart, gravel-voiced Billy Wells, always referred to opening bowler Tom Moore as "the chamberpot man," a reference to the occasion when a Moore delivery was hit into a house near Trumper Park and the owner refused to return it until she was paid for her broken chamber pot. From the time he started with Glebe spinner Fred Mair trusted nobody with his possessions and took all his small change, rings, watches with him on to the field. When opponents complained about the rattling noises as he ran in to bowl, Fred refused to trust the umpires but built his loot up in a pile behind the stumps. Not the least of cricket's characters were the curators, usually council employees, who prepared grade wickets.

Only at centres like Moore Park, with its matting on concrete, did criticism of playing surfaces not exist. Indeed there is valid reason for the argument that concrete pitches have been a major strength of Australian cricket by offering young players true surfaces on which to develop their strokes. Most country towns boast several concrete pitches. Parks in major NSW cities invariably contain concrete strips and that great cauldron of cricket activity, Sydney's Centennial Park, has so many concrete pitches that boundaries for most matches played there overlap and involve chasing boundary hits into somebody else's match.

The showplace of NSW cricket remains the Sydney Cricket Ground, on one side of Moore Park. The doyen of Australian administrators, Syd Smith, considered the atmosphere for Test cricket generated at the SCG was unmatched in the world and SCG trustee Arthur Morris shares that view. It is the ground on which all NSW cricketers seek to play at least once in their lives, whether it is in a social match or a first-class game, and many of the legends of Australian cricket concern the long walk out to the SCG centre wicket. But the State has harvested a great deal of its cricket strength and subsequently its cricket prestige from the country areas. An extraordinary number of famous players have been produced in remote areas which lack the sophisticated organisation and practice facilities offered in the State's big cities. They have come from outlying towns where cricketers are left to themselves to dream about playing in country carnivals, the first step to following Bill O'Reilly, Stan McCabe, Doug Walters, Brian Booth, Johnny Gleeson, Charlie Macartney, Don Bradman, Arthur Chipperfield, Ray Robinson and the others who came from the bush to play for NSW and Australia.

746

Over 125 years of committee meetings and prolonged debate the NSWCA has built a comprehensive administrative structure that now controls cricket for all age groups through its network of district clubs. It is unlikely that any player of talent would not be quickly spotted by someone in this organisation and given a chance to go on and play for the State or for Australia. Vast sums are now spent on junior development and there are national Under-16 and Under-19 competitions designed to help promising colts. There is, however, a noticeable absence of Test players standing for club and NSWCA committees, possibly because Test players have used up all their spare time when they retire and have to concentrate on catching up on business and family life.

For more than 100 years the NSWCA had priority rights over the use of the State's major ground, the SCG, under the State government's Sydney Cricket & Sports Ground Act. In 1977–78, when the Sydney Cricket Ground Trust agreed to let WSC use the SCG, the NSWCA took the Trust to court and won a ruling that the NSWCA had sole right to the ground for the playing of cricket from October to March each season. The State Government promptly changed the Act and in March, 1978, deprived the NSWCA of its priority use of the SCG. One can only wonder at how strongly the ex-cricketers on the Trust fought to preserve the NSWCA's traditional rights!

The administration of NSW cricket has always depended heavily on the acumen of the secretaries, who administer the policies thrashed out by delegates from the grade clubs and from country associations. The first secretary, Joe Clayton, had the task of re-establishing inter-Colonial cricket after two Victorian players objected to an umpire's decision and went home midway through the 1863 match with NSW. Australia's first Test captain, Dave Gregory, did the job for eight seasons in addition to helping to run the State's treasury. John Portus, who held the post after Gregory, had represented NSW on the defunct Australasian Cricket Council, and was one of the founders of the famous Paddington club. Percy Bowden, who took over from Portus, was a brother of Montague Bowden, the prominent Surrey cricketer who toured Australia in Vernon's team in 1887–88. Frank Iredale ("The Apostle of Pessimism") had 12 years as secretary but was always happier practising in the nets with the State team than in his office. Harold ("The Fuhrer") Heydon was the complete secretary, trained to a life with ledgers and filing systems. Alan ("Justa") Barnes had to handle both NSWCA and Board of Control affairs. Bob Radford, who played in the Shore School firsts for three years, had to deal with WSC and the loss of his association's privileged position at the SCG. They were all different in their approach to the job and like most other State secretaries they have helped produce a cricket system that is envied around the world.

NEW SOUTH WALES CRICKET ASSOCIATION

Presidents

1857–60	Sir W. Denison	1907–14	J. H. Carruthers
1860–65	Hon J. B. Darvall	1914–20	J. R. Clayton
1866–67	R. M. Isaacs	1921–31	W. P. McElhone
1868–70	Hon. R. Jones	1931–35	A. W. Green
1870–71	M. Fitzpatrick	1936–66	S. Smith
1871–80	R. Driver	1966–70	E. G. McMillan
1881–1904	Hon. G. H. Reid	1970–	A. K. Davidson
1904–06	W. J. Trickett		

Secretaries

1857–65	J. R. Clayton	1891–92	J. Portus
1865–67	R. Driver	1893–1914	P. K. Bowden
1867–70	R. Teece	1914–26	F. A. Iredale
1870–74	W. Clarke	1926–50	H. Heydon
1874–82	J. M. Gibson	1950–75	A. R. Barnes
1883–91	D. W. Gregory	1975–	R. M. Radford

RECORD PARTNERSHIPS FOR NEW SOUTH WALES

Wkt

1st	319	J. Dyson and R. B. McCosker v WA (Syd), 1980–81.
2nd	378	K. D. Walters and L. Marks v SA (Adel), 1964–65.
3rd	363	D. G. Bradman and A. F. Kippax v Qld (Syd), 1933–34.
4th	325	N. C. O'Neill and B. C. Booth v Vic (Syd), 1957–58.
5th	397	W. Bardsley and C. Kelleway v SA (Syd), 1920–21.
6th	332	N. Marks and G. Thomas v SA (Syd), 1958–59.
7th	255	G. Thomas and R. Benaud v Vic (Melb), 1961–62.
8th	270	V. T. Trumper and E. P. Barbour v Vic (Syd), 1912–13.
9th	226	C. Kelleway and W. A. S. Oldfield v Vic (Melb), 1925–26.
10th	307	A. F. Kippax and J. E. H. Hooker v Vic (Melb), 1928–29.

Note: J. H. Fingleton, W. A. Brown and D. G. Bradman shared a three-way opening partnership of 340 v Victoria (Sydney), 1933–34, in which Fingleton retired hurt.

OUTSTANDING NEW SOUTH WALES BATSMEN

Batsman	Career	Matches	Innings	Not Out	H. Score	Runs	Average	100s
A. F. Kippax	1918–1936	87	135	16	315*	8005	67.26	32
K. D. Walters	1962–1981	103	179	21	253	6612	41.84	19
W. Bardsley	1903–1926	83	132	11	235	6419	53.04	20
V. T. Trumper	1894–1914	73	123	9	292*	5823	51.07	15
D. G. Bradman	1927–1934	41	69	10	452*	5813	98.52	21
M. A. Noble	1893–1920	77	124	10	281	5653	49.58	19
C. G. Macartney	1905–1927	81	123	12	221	5581	50.73	22
B. C. Booth	1954–1969	93	146	18	177	5577	43.57	11
N. C. O'Neill	1955–1967	70	115	12	233	5419	52.61	18
S. E. Gregory	1889–1912	80	136	8	201	5340	41.71	11
R. B. Simpson	1952–1956 1961–1968 1977–1978	67	116	16	359	5317	53.17	15
T. J. E. Andrews	1912–1929	74	115	6	247*	4869	44.66	11
S. G. Barnes	1936–1953	56	91	4	200	4773	54.40	19
A. R. Morris	1940–1955	50	77	4	253	4660	63.83	17
S. J. McCabe	1928–1942	55	89	5	229*	4556	54.23	9
G. Thomas	1957–1966	68	105	7	229	4351	44.39	15
A. Turner	1968–1978	76	142	8	127	4171	31.12	4
R. Benaud	1948–1964	86	121	10	158	4116	37.08	9
R. B. McCosker	1973–1982	54	94	13	168	4035	49.81	15

OUTSTANDING NEW SOUTH WALES BOWLERS

Bowler	Career	Matches	Runs	Wickets	Average	B.B.	5W	10W
A. A. Mailey	1912–1930	67	9246	334	27.68	8/81	28	6
W. J. O'Reilly	1927–1946	54	5369	325	16.52	9/41	26	7
R. Benaud	1948–1964	86	8376	322	26.01	7/18	17	4
J. W. Martin	1956–1968	78	8987	293	30.67	8/97	12	—
A. K. Davidson	1949–1963	72	5858	273	21.45	7/31	10	—
C. T. B. Turner	1882–1910	43	4256	263	16.18	8/32	29	11
M. A. Noble	1893–1920	77	5379	230	28.38	7/44	13	2
C. Kelleway	1907–1929	57	5137	215	23.89	7/35	7	1
K. J. O'Keeffe	1968–1980	65	5708	211	27.05	6/49	12	1
D. J. Colley	1969–1978	71	6513	203	32.08	6/30	6	—
R. R. Lindwall	1941–1954	50	4451	196	22.70	7/45	7	1
W. P. Howell	1894–1905	48	4698	196	23.96	9/52	11	1
D. A. Renneberg	1964–1971	54	5793	190	30.48	7/33	8	1
T. R. McKibbin	1894–1899	25	3822	181	21.11	9/68	17	7
A. Cotter	1901–1914	38	4005	171	23.42	7/77	10	1
D. W. Hourn	1970–1982	44	4708	164	28.71	9/77	11	2
P. I. Philpott	1954–1967	52	4755	153	31.07	7/53	7	2
J. D. Scott	1908–1925	35	3364	150	22.42	6/48	9	1

NEW ZEALAND VERSUS AUSTRALIA

Australian cricketers have visited New Zealand since 1878, but there has been only a spasmodic exchange of visits until recently. The countries have played only 15 official Tests, Australia winning eight, New Zealand two, with five drawn. Six of those Tests have been played in the last two seasons. For until Geoff Howarth's team toured Australia in 1980–81 there was a curious spectator and administrative indifference towards Australia-New Zealand matches. Howarth's team changed all that, although they lost two of their three Tests in Australia. They won crowd support undreamed of a few years ago, and they showed up as well as any of the major cricket nations on television.

Australia has rarely done much to foster cricket in New Zealand, using matches there as a reward for long-serving players or to test aspiring youngsters. The events of the tour by Howarth's team provided the essential "needle" in matches between the countries. The notorious underarm ball at Melbourne, some disputed umpiring decisions, and the spirited, attractive displays of Geoff Howarth, John Wright, Brian Edgar and that superb TV scene-stealer, Richard Hadlee, have brought tension and keen disputation into matches Australian officials long considered lacked attraction.

The history of cricket matches involving Australians and New Zealanders dates back to the first Australian international team in 1878. To prepare for the first ever tour of England, the Australians went to New Zealand to sharpen their team-work and played seven matches against the odds.

The pill-box hats and sashes of the 1878 Australian team

749

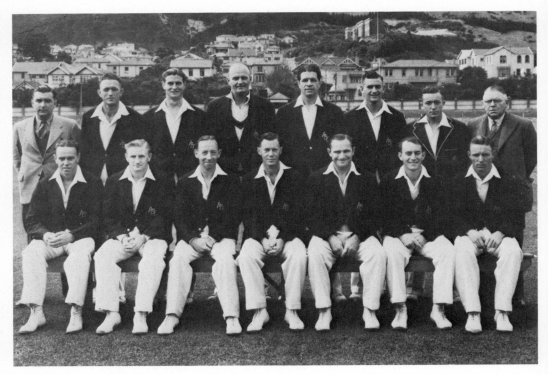

were first seen at Invercargill, when Charles Bannerman made the first century in New Zealand by an Australian. The Australians had already played nine warm-up matches around Australia and they scored 267, to which XXII Of Invercargill replied with innings of 89 and 39, giving Australia victory by an innings and 139 runs.

The Canterbury team wanted to play the Australians on level terms and when the visitors would not agree to this said the match would be abandoned if Australia asked for more than 15 opponents. They fielded a dozen players more than 6 ft in height and dismissed Australia for only 46. A fast bowler named E. Fuller took 8 for 35 in Australia's second innings of 143, Horan batting for four hours for 58. Canterbury, having led by 89 on the first innings, needed only 56 to win in the second innings and lost eight wickets scoring them. More than 5,000 spectators watched the final day, an astounding crowd considering that New Zealand had been a crown colony for less than 20 years. Canterbury were so encouraged by their win they sent a team to tour Victoria in 1878–79, but the trip was a financial disaster and money had to be sent from Christchurch to get the players home.

Charles Bannerman averaged 36.00 on that first Australian tour of New Zealand, remarkably high considering the poor pitches. Spofforth took 102 wickets at less than 4 runs each.

The Bannermans were missing from the second Australian team, the 1880 team to England returning home, to visit New Zealand in January, 1881, but Spofforth again took most wickets, finishing with 148 at 3.70. 'Joey Palmer took 141 wickets at 3.30. The Australians were desperately keen to avenge their loss to Canterbury three years earlier and their captain, Billy Murdoch, backed himself successfully to score more runs than the entire Canterbury team. Australia won by an innings and 100 runs, with a first innings score of 323. The only Australian loss on this 10-match tour was to XXII Of Wanganui, a team handpicked for their fielding skill. Wanganui won by 10 wickets, Australia scoring 49 and 83 against 48 and 11 for 86. Australia won 6, drew 3 and lost 1 match on the tour.

A series of visits to New Zealand by Australian State teams followed, starting with Tasmania in 1883–84. Playing on level terms Canterbury beat Tasmania twice and Otago also defeated them. The 1886 Australian team, watched by 3,000 spectators, made a large score of 475 against Wellington in one of the matches they played in New Zealand on the way home from England. S. P. Jones made 159 for Australia, but the match was drawn. The Australians won 2 and drew 3 of their five matches.

Among the early visits to New Zealand by Australian State teams was that by New South Wales in January, 1890. This side, captained by J. Davis, played seven matches, won 6 and drew 1. The NSW team's star was S. T. Callaway, a pace bowler of military bearing who moved the ball off the pitch. Callaway played three Tests for Australia without conspicuous success, but found the pitches in New Zealand to his liking, taking 54 wickets on that first trip at only 7.07 each. NSW won 6 and drew 1 of their seven games. Callaway later took a job in Christchurch as a clerk in a railways workshop and settled in New Zealand, where in 24 first-class matches he took 167 wickets. On the second tour by a NSW side in the 1894–95 season, New Zealand assembled a fully representative team for the first time, but NSW defeated them by 160 runs.

In December, 1895, a NSW team, backed for the first time by the NSWCA, played five matches in New Zealand, winning 3, with 1 drawn and 1 lost. These games were played on level terms for the first time. At Christchurch, New Zealand made 187 and NSW replied with 198. The home team then made 254, leaving NSW to score 244 to win. They were routed for 101. A. H. Fisher, one of the early stars of New Zealand cricket, took 5 for 20 in NSW's second innings and had match figures of 7 for 73 as well as scoring 59 runs for once out. The best players for NSW were L. O. S. Poidevin, who made 54 and 38 and S. T. Callaway, who had match figures of 15 for 175. Poidevin and Callaway were the stars of the tour. The 1896 Australian team to England played five matches against the odds in

New Zealand on their way home. They won 3 and lost 2, and were followed in New Zealand by a team from Queensland who lost only one of their eight games. This tour was a financial disaster.

The New Zealand Cricket Council was formed in 1894 and sent its first team overseas in 1898–99. The team played two matches in Tasmania, opening with a draw against Southern Tasmania at Hobart and a win over Northern Tasmania in Launceston. New Zealand started the match against Victoria at Melbourne by scoring a creditable 317, but Victoria responded with 602, of which Percy McAlister made 224. Victoria won by an innings and 132 runs. NSW batsmen then had their turn and ran up a score of 558 (Trumper 253) to win by an innings and 388 runs.

The Melbourne Cricket Club sent a team to New Zealand at short notice in 1899–1900 for six matches. The Melbourne CC team won five matches, with the sixth drawn. Hugh Trumble and Harry Graham were outstanding in the Melbourne CC team.

By far the biggest attraction seen in New Zealand cricket to that time was the Twelfth Australian team that visited New Zealand prior to touring England in 1905, a side with drawcards like Trumper, Noble, Armstrong, Hill, Duff and Cotter. They drew 8,000 on the second day for the match at Auckland and an amazing 10,000 on the first day at Wellington. The Australians made 442 at Auckland , 433 at Wellington, 533 and 9 for 593 in the two matches against New Zealand. Armstrong averaged 100.00 for the tour, Trumper 90.30, Hill 69.00. Armstrong went back to New Zealand at the end of the 1905–06 Australian summer with a Melbourne Cricket Club team and scored 956 runs in 10 completed innings, as well as taking 104 wickets at 9.80. He made 335 against Southland.

By 1909–10 New Zealand standards had improved enough for most of the nine games played by an Australian side to be on level terms. The Australians won seven games, with two drawn. The fine New Zealand allrounder D. Reese scored 108 for Canterbury, whom Australia trailed by 81 on the first innings. Set to score 340 to win Australia reached 8 for 307 by stumps, E. R. Mayne and Armstrong adding 176 after half the Australian side were out for 39.

In the 1912–13 season Harry Trott took a South Melbourne club side on a short New Zealand tour and that summer also saw the first of the tours by Australian social teams when the NSW Teachers side made a short visit. Early in 1913–14 a New Zealand team visited Australia, beating Queensland but being destroyed by both NSW and Victoria. A splendid match with South Australia ended in a draw, and a number of matches against country sides were all won. That fine New Zealand cricketer D. Reese was the star of the tour.

In February and March, 1914, Arthur Sims, a former Canterbury and New Zealand player, took a marvellous Australian team to New Zealand that included Trumper, Armstrong, Noble, Ransford, Collins, Mailey and the distinguished Englishman J. N. Crawford. The Australians began by scoring 658 against Auckland.

At Lancaster Park in Christchurch, a little more than a year before his tragic death, Trumper went to the wicket with Australia 7 for 209. He played what most New Zealand experts regard as the greatest innings seen in New Zealand, reaching 50 in 26 minutes, and in just three hours scored 293. He made his third 50 in 19 minutes, his fifth in 21, and at one stage 50 runs were added by Trumper and Sims in just 12 minutes. Sims went on to 184 not out and the partnership was worth 433 in 180 minutes. At Temuka the Australians made 9 for 922 against Fifteen of South Canterbury. J. N. Crawford shared stands of 298 in 69 minutes with Trumper and 213 with Noble in scoring 354, the last 200 in 60 minutes. The innings included 45 fours and 14 sixes—264 in boundaries.

Australian teams visited New Zealand frequently between the two world wars. In 1920–21 an Australian side attracted big crowds, with Ransford, Liddicut, Bogle, Lampard and Waddy scoring consistently and Ironmonger and Hornibrook taking most of the wickets. The team played crowd-pleasing cricket under Ransford's captaincy but the New Zealand newspapers' labelling of the main matches as Tests certainly did not have the blessing of the Australian Board. NSW had a successful tour early in 1924, and Victoria followed in 1925.

New Zealand made their third tour of Australia in 1925–26 but their players found the hard, dry pitches difficult. Queensland beat New Zealand by an innings thanks to a century from captain Leo O'Connor, and Victoria, South Australia and NSW all headed the New Zealanders on the first innings. The Melbourne Cricket Club arranged a tour at short notice in 1926–27, and New Zealand returning from its first tour of England in 1927, were soundly beaten by NSW. The differences in the two countries' standards was just as evident when Victor Richardson took an Australian team to New Zealand in 1927–28 that made some huge totals despite the fact that several of their New Zealand opponents had just returned from New Zealand's first tour of England. The next contact was not until the 1937 New Zealand side to England arrived, losing to South Australia, Victoria and NSW on the way home.

Up to the end of World War II Australian officials felt justified in not playing official Tests against New Zealand because of one-sided results by Australian club, State and National teams over more than 60 years. Thus it was a surprise when the Australian Board of Control decided to include one official Test in the New Zealand tour by an Australian side at the end of the 1945–46 home season.

AUSTRALIAN TEAMS IN NEW ZEALAND SINCE WORLD WAR II

1946 AUSTRALIAN TEAM IN NEW ZEALAND

W. A. Brown

Brown's team was enormously strong, comprising ambitious young players eager to improve their English tour chances in 1948 and old hands determined to hold their Test status. The Australians made 579 against Auckland, Miller scoring 139, Hassett 121, Barnes 107. O'Reilly and Toshack then bundled Auckland out twice to seal an innings win. At Christchurch against Canterbury Brown closed Australia's innings at 8 for 415, enough for another innings win. Otago fought hard in their second innings after a first innings failure, Wally Hadlee's 198 taking them to 347, but Australia hit off the runs to win by eight wickets. Hassett made 114 out of 415 and Toshack took 6 for 40 in Australia's innings defeat of Wellington. The Test saw O'Reilly and Toshack at their best on an uneven pitch, O'Reilly taking 5 for 14, Toshack 4 for 12, to dismiss New Zealand for 42. Cowie, the pace bowler who before World War II had dismissed Bradman and McCabe in Australia, bowled splendidly to take 6 for 40 and restrict Australia to 8 for 199 declared. The Australian bowlers then dismissed New Zealand for 54, giving Australia victory by an innings and 103 runs. This was a tragic result for New Zealand, for it gave Australia reason to delay the staging of a second official Test for another 27 years.

1950 AUSTRALIAN TEAM IN NEW ZEALAND

W. A. Brown

The 1950 Australian team to New Zealand was virtually a second team, with the first team players touring South Africa. Bill Brown had veterans such as Tallon and Ring to help guide a group of aspiring players that included Jack Iverson and Alan Davidson. Phil Ridings was vice-captain. The team played five first-class matches, winning three and two draws, plus several minor games. At Wairarapa Davidson achieved his fabled double of 10 for 29 and 159 not out. The Otago game saw the emergence of a young New Zealand left-hander, Bert Sutcliffe, who made 43 out of 116 and 44 out of 96 as his side lost by an innings. The match against New Zealand, "an unofficial" Test, was drawn, New Zealand made 231, Ring taking 7 for 88. Australia were in trouble until Tallon hit 116 in three hours, a strange innings that included dogged defence, seven sixes and eight fours. New Zealand were 9 for 76 in their second innings when time ran out.

1957 AUSTRALIAN TEAM IN NEW ZEALAND

I. D. Craig

Ian Craig's team won five of their seven first-class matches. The team played three unofficial Tests, with the first two drawn and Australia winning the third. In the First "Test," Craig made 123 not out and O'Neill 102 not out, and Johnny Martin took 6 for 46 in the New Zealand second innings. Harvey hit a brilliant 161 in around even time against Otago. Meckiff took 4 for 28 and 2 for 17 in the Second "Test." Harry Cave was the most impressive of the New Zealanders in taking 17 wickets in the three "Tests" and Bert Sutcliffe made an attractive 107 in the Second "Test." The financial results

754

from this and the previous tour were far from encouraging for the Australian Board of Control.

Ian Craig took his second team to New Zealand early in 1960 for nine matches, with the Australians winning four and playing five draws. The tour included four representative matches. Australia won one of these and the others were drawn. Bob Simpson led the Australian batting aggregates and spinner Ian Quick took most wickets. Frank Misson topped the bowling averages. Bert Sutcliffe scored the only century against the Australians on the tour, but John Reid also batted impressively.

1960 AUSTRALIAN TEAM IN NEW ZEALAND

I. D. Craig

Les Favell's 1967 team in New Zealand played 10 first-class matches for two wins, two losses and six draws. They played four representative matches. New Zealand won the first and the others were drawn. The Australian loss came against Canterbury at Christchurch, where the fast bowler Dick Motz took 3 for 72 and 7 for 56. Bruce Taylor, who took 3 for 56 and 1 for 38 in this match also hit the winning run and made 106 not out. Johnny Gleeson puzzled most New Zealand batsmen on the tour and ended as the leading Australian wicket-taker.

1967 AUSTRALIAN TEAM IN NEW ZEALAND

L. E. Favell

Sam Trimble captained an Australian team to New Zealand early in 1970 in eight matches. The side won only two of these and played six draws. All three representative matches were drawn. Trimble and Greg Chappell were the outstanding Australian batsmen on this tour and Terry Jenner took most wickets with his leg-spinners. This was Dennis Lillee's first overseas trip and he finished at the top of the Australian tour bowling averages. The top Australian team was on tour in South Africa at the time.

1970 AUSTRALIAN TEAM IN NEW ZEALAND

S. C. Trimble

Ian Chappell captained an Australian team in New Zealand in March, 1974, when the old labels about second-string teams were forgotten. This was the full-strength Australian senior side. The First Test of the three-Test series produced records galore at Wellington. Greg Chappell set a record for most runs (380) in a Test by scoring 247 not out and 133. The Chappell brothers, Ian and Greg, both scored centuries in each innings, and in the first innings their 264-run stand was the highest in Australia v. New Zealand Tests. Despite the Chappells' brilliance, however, the Test was drawn. New Zealand made 484 in their first innings of a match that produced 1,455 runs.

New Zealand won for the first time ever against Australia at Christchurch in the Second Test. It was only New Zealand's eighth win in 113 official Tests against all countries. New Zealand's victory by five wickets on the fifth morning was due to fine bowling by Richard and Dayle Hadlee, supported by R. O.

1974 AUSTRALIAN TEAM IN NEW ZEALAND

I. M. Chappell

Collinge, and to a century in each innings (101 and 110 not out) by Glenn Turner. This win, hailed throughout the Dominion as New Zealand cricket's finest achievement, meant that New Zealand had beaten every cricket nation except England. New Zealand's win also guaranteed big crowds for the Third Test in the series at Auckland, where a record Eden Park attendance of 35,000 saw Australia win with two days to spare despite a nine-wicket haul by Collinge. Centuries by Walters and Redpath and hostile bowling by Gilmour, Walker and Mallett gave Australia a win by 297 runs.

1977 AUSTRALIAN TEAM IN NEW ZEALAND

G. S. Chappell

Australia returned to New Zealand under Greg Chappell's captaincy for a two-Test series in February, 1977. Walters produced the record score in Tests against New Zealand by hitting two sixes and 30 fours in an innings of 250 during the First Test at Christchurch. Gilmour (101) had a stand of 217 in 187 minutes for the seventh wicket with Walters but it was not enough to produce a result. Congdon hit 107 in a solid New Zealand response. New Zealand began the final hour on 8 for 260 but Congdon and Richard Hadlee batted on to stumps. The Second Test of that series gave Australia their fifth win in nine official Tests against New Zealand and was achieved by a brilliant display from Lillee (5 for 51 and 6 for 72), who passed 150 wickets in only his 31st Test.

1982 AUSTRALIAN TEAM IN NEW ZEALAND

G. S. Chappell

The furore created by the underarm delivery in the limited over game between the countries at Melbourne in 1980–81 had barely faded when Greg Chappell took the Australians to New Zealand early in 1982. The one-day games attracted vast audiences in both countries, with boisterous crowds overflowing the grounds to see matches that were packed with incidents—one spectator rolled a lawn bowl on to the field while Chappell was batting, a reminder of the delivery he had ordered in Melbourne. The First Test at Wellington was drawn, rain preventing any chance of a result. The Second Test at Auckland produced New Zealand's second win in the matches between the countries. A magnificent 161 by opener Bruce Edgar enabled New Zealand to score 387 in their first innings and lead Australia by 177 runs. When Richard Hadlee bowled superbly in Australia's second innings to take 5 for 63, Australia reached only 280, despite a century by Wood. Set to score 104 to win New Zealand lost five wickets in doing so, with Lillee, Alderman and Yardley bowling defiantly. In the Third Test at Christchurch, Greg Chappell played one of his best innings after a summer of unprecedented failures, scoring 176 out of Australia's 353. Lillee, Thomson and Alderman then bowled Australia to an eight wickets victory, dismissing New Zealand for 149, and when New Zealand followed-on for 272.

After their unhappy defeat by Australia in 1946, New Zealand faced a long, hard build-up to justify Test recognition. Improvement came slowly and invitations to make long tours scarce, and the New Zealanders had to be content with playing a few matches in Australia on their way to tours further afield or on their way home. A New Zealand team played three Australian States on the way home from South Africa in 1954, they defeated Western Australia convincingly when Sutcliffe made 142, and at Adelaide won with 10 minutes to spare against South Australia, Sutcliffe scoring 149. The game against Victoria was drawn. This time Sutcliffe made 117.

New Zealand played three matches against State teams on the way home from South Africa in 1961–62, but the results were disappointing for a team that had just squared a Test series against the strong South African lineup by winning two Tests. They were beaten by South Australia and New South Wales and drew with Western Australia.

In 1967–68 a New Zealand team led by B. W. Sinclair played four matches against the States. They were beaten by South Australia and New South Wales and drew with Queensland and Victoria. Vic Pollard made the only century on this visit for New Zealand, and Dick Motz turned on a memorable big-hitting display in scoring 94 at Adelaide. Sheahan and Simpson made centuries against New Zealand.

In 1969–70 G. T. Dowling's New Zealand team played three matches against the States on a short tour. Their main mission was to compete in the first Limited Over competition in Australia and they won this handsomely by beating Victoria in the final by six wickets.

New Zealand were now beginning to record a number of wins in Tests, but these victories were hard-won by a country whose teams were often weakened by the loss of star players to English counties, and by the failure of players to get leave. Australia finally agreed to play official Tests against New Zealand with a rubber of three in Australia.

The first official Test between the countries in Australia went to Australia by an innings and 25 runs, with Stackpole (122) scoring the first century in Australia-New Zealand Tests. Australia made 462, New Zealand 237 and 200. In the Second Test at Sydney Australia were 425 runs behind with eight second innings left when rain prevented play on the fifth day. J. M. Parker (108) and J. F. M. Morrison (117) became the first New Zealand century-makers in official Tests against Australia. In the Third Test at Adelaide Rod Marsh set up Australia's win by an innings and 57 runs with an innings of 132. Although Australia won the series 2–0, New Zealand has shown enough to remove all Australia's objections to meeting her in Test cricket.

NEW ZEALAND TEAMS IN AUSTRALIA SINCE WORLD WAR II

1973–74 NEW ZEALAND TEAM IN AUSTRALIA

B. E. Congdon

1980–81 NEW ZEALAND TEAM IN AUSTRALIA

G. P. Howarth

New Zealand played 29 matches in Australia in 1980–81 over a period of 96 days in which they were asked to switch repeatedly between one-day matches and Tests, hardly an ideal preparation for Test cricket. In the Tests, lapses in concentration sometimes caused silly mistakes. In the First Test at Brisbane, for example, Parker dragged a ball from outside the off on to his stumps and started a slump that saw New Zealand lose seven wickets for 32 runs after looking set for a big score at 3 for 193. Graeme Wood made a fine 111 to seal Australia's win by 10 wickets, Lillee having match figures of 8 for 89. Australia took the series by winning the Second Test at Perth by eight wickets. On a perfect batting strip pace bowlers Lillee, Pascoe and Hogg had New Zealand out for 196 and 121.

The Third Test at Melbourne attracted big crowds to see an absorbing draw. With Walters on 77, Australia's last man, Jim Higgs, touched a ball to the New Zealand 'keeper. The New Zealanders began to leave the field but the umpire explained he had no-balled bowler Lance Cairns for excessive use of the bouncer against Higgs. Walters and Higgs remained together while Walters moved to 107 and Australia's total to 321. Rejection of the appeal against Higgs had cost New Zealand 42 runs and 69 minutes. Set to score 193 in 145 minutes to win, New Zealand made 6 for 128 on the last day, losing a golden chance when three wickets fell cheaply with the score at 2 for 95. New Zealand played in the final series of the World Series Cup against Australia—amid widespread controversy.

NEWELL, Andrew Livingston, 1870–1915

First-Class Averages: Batting, 477 runs at 15.90; Bowling, 82 wickets at 20.26.

A useful all-rounder for the Glebe club and New South Wales who disappeared while walking on the cliffs near Ben Buckler, off Bondi, Sydney, when recuperating from a serious illness. Fears that he had met a tragic end proved unfounded, and he died some years later at Heron's Creek, near Wauchope. Newell toured New Zealand with a NSW team in 1889–90. His best effort with the bat was a not out innings of 68 against Stoddart's English team in 1897–98. He added 169 for the eighth wicket with Syd Gregory (171) and 109 for the last wicket in 66 minutes with Howell, who scored 95 of those 109 runs. This astounding recovery enabled NSW, who scored 415 runs in the first innings, to score 574 in the second and win by 239 runs. Newell bowled medium-pace off-breaks. In 1893–94 he had match figures of 10 for 52 against Queensland, and in the same season he took 10 for 233 in the match against SA. His best analysis was 8 for 56 v. Victoria in 1897–98.

NEWLAND, Philip Mesner, 1876–1916

A South Australian wicket-keeper considered fortunate to have been chosen to tour England with the 1905 Australian team after missing several chances just before the side was picked for South Australia v. New South Wales. His poor form on the tour threw an added burden on the team's No. 1 'keeper, J. J. Kelly, who fortunately performed admirably. Newland batted 16 times on the tour for 95 runs, lowest aggregate in the side, average 10.55. For SA, Newland had a topscore of 77 in 1903–04 at Adelaide against NSW. His most notable effort came in the last match of the 1903–04 English team's Australian tour when he scored 50 in 35 minutes for SA.

First-Class Averages: Batting, 556 runs at 16.35; Dismissals 48 (30 catches, 18 stumpings).

NICKNAMES, OF AUSTRALIAN CRICKETERS

One of the characteristics of Australian cricketers has been the passion for nicknames. Indeed it has been said of Australian Test sides that they could conduct conversations on the field without opposing players becoming remotely aware to whom they were referring. Since the first settlers arrived Australians have shown a flair for inventing nicknames. Australian cricketers are among the leaders in continuing this national skill, their nicknames reflecting the popularity and mien of fellow players and even their approach to personal hygiene.

Origin of some of the nicknames is obscure and even the players who bear them cannot recall how they began. "Fot" stuck with Dennis Lillee from the day his Western Australian captain Tony Lock accused him of bowling like "a Flipping Old Tart." Spofforth's legendary tag, "The Demon" stemmed from his satanic countenance, Bill Lawry's "The Phantom" from his addiction to the comic strip hero of that name, Herbie Collins became "Horseshoe" because of his luck at cards and at winning tosses. Ashley Mallett became "Rowdy" because he was so quiet and studious, Graeme McKenzie "Garth" because his strength compared with the comic strip figure with that name who pushed over houses. Don Tallon was "Deafy" from the day his team-mates realised he was hard of hearing and could not hear snicks, and Ian Chappell was "Chappelli" because that is how his name looked on the scoreboard. From a long list, here is a selection:

H. H. Alexander	Bull	N. H. Dansie	Nodder
W. A. Armstrong	The Big Ship	J. L. Ellis	Nana
G. R. Beard	Agatha	A. G. Fairfax	Noodles
D. D. Blackie	Rock	L. O'B. Fleetwood-Smith	Chuck
R. Briggs	Biggles	H. Graham	The Little Dasher
R. J. Bright	Candles	S. G. Gregory	Little Tich
H. Carter	Sammy	C. V. Grimmett	Scarlet
I. M. Chappell	Chappelli	A. T. W. Grout	The Griz
H. L. Collins	Horseshoe	H. S. T. L. Hendry	Stork
A. Cotter	Tibby	H. V. Hordern	Ranji
R. M. Cowper	Wallaby	W. P. Howell	Farmer Bill

759

W. A. Hunt   The Count
H. Ironmonger   Dainty
A. Jackson   The Champ
E. Jones   Jonah
R. C. Jordan   The Slug
B. M. Laird   Stumpy
W. M. Lawry   The Phantom
G. Lawson   Henry
I. S. Lee   Meggsy
D. K. Lillee   F.O.T.
R. R. Lindwall   Jackson
C. G. Macartney   The Governor-General
J. R. Mackay   Sunny Jim
K. D. Mackay   Slasher
A. A. Mallett   Rowdy
S. J. McCabe   Napper
E. L. McCormick   Goldie
P. S. McDonnell   Percy Greatheart
G. D. McKenzie   Garth
K. R. Miller   Nugget

F. M. Misson   Tarzan
M. A. Noble   Mary Ann
W. A. S. Oldfield   Cracker
W. J. O'Reilly   Tiger
C. E. Pellew   Nip
W. H. Ponsford   Puddin
V. N. Raymer   Possum
J. W. Rutherford   Pythagorus
R. A. Saggers   Big Chief Paleface
F. R. Spofforth   The Demon
D. Tallon   Deafy
A. L. Thomson   Froggy
C. T. B. Turner   The Terror
M. N. H. Walker   Tangles
K. D. Walters   Freddie
D. M. Wellham   Smirk
W. M. Woodfull   The Wormkiller
E. L. Wyeth   Boxer
B. Yardley   Roo

NITSCHKE, Homesdale Charles ("Slinger"), 1906–

First-Class Averages:
Batting, 3,320 runs at 42.03.

Tests (2): 53 runs at 26.50.

A plucky, big-hitting left-handed batsman, who opened for South Australia for seven seasons and for Australia in two Tests. Nitschke spent half of each year managing his family's station property "Hiltaba", 400 miles north-west of Adelaide, but gave cricket his undivided attention each summer, going to the crease "breathing fire and slaughter", eager for a chance to hit the bowling into the stands. After he retired from cricket he became a successful racehorse breeder, and in 1972 his horse Dayana made history by winning the Derbies of four States, followed by the $100,000 Perth Cup on New Year's Day, 1973.

Born in Adelaide, Nitschke went to St Peter's College, where so many fine cricketers were developed, and from the time he joined the East Torrens club in 1924 showed great promise. After he hit 105 against Victorian Colts at Melbourne, he was promoted to the South Australian side in 1929–30 taking the place of Brian Hone when Hone went to England as South Australia's Rhodes scholar.

His defence was extremely sound, and he played the left-hander's onside shots with great gusto. He was particularly adept in despatching anything short, and if he timed it right his straight drive was a dazzling blow. When he first appeared in first-class cricket his fielding was poor but he worked hard at it and became a smart and reliable outfield. He could alternate stubborn defence with hurricane hitting, but was sometimes dismissed trying for six when he would have survived had he been content with fours.

Nitschke topped the South Australian batting averages in 1930–31 with 830 runs at 55.33, including an innings of 142 against Queensland at Adelaide. He followed with 695 runs at 46.33 in 1932–33, to top the State's batting aggregates. He was chosen in two Tests against South Africa in 1931–32, falling twice to Bell, but he did not get another Test chance.

In all first-class matches he had commendable figures considering he was often in well beaten teams. He scored nine centuries, including 141 against New South Wales in 1930–31, 172 against Western Australia in 1929–30 and 120 against Tasmania in 1930–31. In 1933–34 he batted throughout SA's innings v. NSW, scoring 130 not out of 246.

A master cricketer whose sportsmanship and devotion to the game's ethics over 27 years of big cricket put to shame some Australian Test players who followed him. As Australia's captain in 15 Tests, he ranks with our best exponents of that job. He was an accomplished bowler of peculiar flight and mixed sharp off-spin with clever flight at medium pace. He hit the ball hard with the bat, but could stonewall for hours when required and he played some of cricket's notable innings. Most of all, he had character.

Noble was a cricketer of unwavering confidence in his own ability to provide whatever was needed to win or save a game. When he told team-mates at lunch time as he went in to bat that he would see them at stumps, he meant it. He disliked team-mates appealing unless they were certain opposing batsmen were out. He once chastised Oram Cohen for jumping the fence at Mosman Oval to go in to bat with Paddington needing only a few runs to win. "Mosman are giving us every chance to get these runs—go back and come through the gate," he said. In State matches he reprimanded New South Wales players for paying more attention to girls in the crowd than to the play.

Ray Robinson, who wrote the definitive piece on Noble in his book on Australian captains, discovered that Noble wore size 10½ boots. This was surprising as cartoonists made great play with Noble's boots. He was certainly a big man at 6 ft 1 in or 185 cm and 13 stone or 83 kg, but he was agile and unsurpassed in his time fielding at point. His habit of lifting his front toe as he took his stance to face bowlers is perhaps why caricaturists gave him boots like banquet salvers.

Noble's parents migrated from Egham in Surrey and his eldest brother was born on the ship bringing them from England to a new home in Sydney's Haymarket. Monty was born at home in Chinatown's Dixon Street and learned his cricket playing with his brothers in the streets of Paddington, where his father managed a pub. He grew into a tall, gangling lad

NOBLE, Montague Alfred ("Mary Ann"), 1873–1940

First-Class Averages: Batting, 13,975 runs at 40.74; Bowling, 625 wickets at 23.11.

Tests (42): 1,997 runs at 30.25; 121 wickets at 25.00.

761

who much impressed clubmate Victor Trumper at Paddington. At 20, he made 152 not out for 18 Colts of New South
Wales against England and this won him a place in the State
senior team. Montague was his first name, and he often was
spoken of as Monty, besides answering to Alf.

He worked initially with a bank but resigned when the
bank refused him time off to play inter-State cricket. He decided on a career in dentistry, confident as ever that he could
pass his exams between matches. He became a regular in the
New South Wales side in 1896–97 and played in four Tests
against England in 1897–98. Between then and his retirement
from first-class cricket in 1919–20, he made 37 centuries in big
matches, 14 of them in England. He toured England four
times, in 1899, 1902, 1905 and 1909, when he was Australia's
captain. He also toured South Africa in 1902–03 and New Zealand in 1904–05 and 1913–14.

762

He had very lean, bony fingers and he learned a bowling grip that was all his own from American baseballers who toured Australia to boost their sport. Holding the ball between his thumb and forefinger, he could impart what baseball pitchers call curve, cricketers swing. After the ball landed it spun or swung late and if the wicket was damp or worn Noble's medium-pacers were devastating. In his first two Tests he took 15 wickets, most of them by surprise. His accuracy with longer throws was evident as the team's ship passed through the Suez Canal. Objectional gestures by a canal-side Arab were disgusting many passengers until an apple flung by Noble hit the performer behind the ear.

Both as a bowler and as a batsman he had great adaptability, and on each of his overseas trips he understood the need to change the methods that brought success in Australia.

In his first innings in England he made 116 not out against the South of England at Crystal Palace. On that trip Australia got into awful trouble in the Manchester Test, on a pitch that assisted bowlers after England had scored 372 in its first innings. Noble's response, with Australia 7 for 57, was to bat for 190 minutes for 60 not out in Australia's first innings of 196 and then for a monumental 320 minutes for 89 in the second innings, at one state batting for 45 minutes without a run, a feat which saved Australia. It was one of the finest rescue acts in big cricket.

The Noble who had held back the English bowling in that epic made four centuries in succession for New South Wales between 1898 and 1900 and hit 19 centuries altogether for New South Wales. Perhaps the best proof that he could score quickly came at Hove in 1902 when he made 284 in adding 428 for the sixth wicket for Australia against Sussex with Warwick Armstrong. Haygarth's *Scores & Biographies* lists these as Noble's highest innings:

- 284 Australia v. Sussex, 1902 at Hove
- 281 NSW v. Victoria, 1905–06 at Melbourne
- 267 Australia v. Sussex, 1905 at Hove
- 230 NSW v. SA, 1903–04 at Adelaide
- 213 NSW v. SA, 1908–09 at Adelaide
- 213 NSW v. Vic., 1908–09 at Sydney
- 200 NSW v. SA, 1899–1900 at Adelaide.

Noble was a great exponent of team batting, the art of keeping the score mounting steadily without taking unnecessary risks or worrying about your own score. He was a superb judge of a run. "Stork" Hendry told the story of batting with Noble in a State game when Noble hit a shot and called "Two." Hendry had to look after the first run and yelled "No" to the second. Nothing was said on the field but that night Noble idled over to Hendry at a team get-together, and said: "When I say 'two' I mean 'two'."

For Australia against Oxford University at Oxford in 1899,

Noble made 86 and 100 not out. When he made 127 for Australia against Somerset in 1905 at Bath, he and Armstrong (303 not out) put on 320 for the third wicket. When he made 176 for New South Wales v. Victoria in 1907–08 at Sydney he put on 315 with Syd Gregory (201) for the fourth and scored a further 123 in the second innings. He made one Test century but he helped save or win several with his batting. When he hit his sole Test century, 133 at Sydney v. England, in 1903–04, Australia lost. There was more value in his 16 other Test scores over 50.

With the ball, he was often quite destructive. For Australia v. Leicestershire in 1899, he took 7 for 15, and in the corresponding match in 1902 he took 8 for 48. In the 1901–02 Test against England at Melbourne, he took 7 for 17 in England's first innings of 66, and finished the match with 13 for 77. For New South Wales against Tasmania in 1898–99 he took a hattrick and in the New South Wales v. Victoria match in 1908–09 he bowled his first ten overs without conceding a run, but it was also off Noble's bowling that A. E. Trott batting for MCC v. Australia in 1899 made his historic hit right over the pavilion at Lord's.

Noble was given a dinner by the Paddington club in 1924 at which it was said that he had scored more than 10,000 runs and taken more than 600 wickets for the club in first grade. He had averaged 273.00 for the club in 1888–89, 128.80 in 1910–11, with a highest score for the club of 267 not out against East Sydney in December, 1898. He liked to keep young cricketers in order in his later days and warned them against late nights during matches or drinking during the day. No wonder a fine grandstand at SCG was named after him, for martinet or shrewd psychologist, he was dedicated to Australian cricket in a manner few Australians have ever been. Even in a grade match, he felt an obligation to ask the opposing captain, "What's wrong with him?" when asked for a substitute fielder, and he would never agree unless he was satisfied the man going off was genuinely indisposed.

Noble wrote a number of highly regarded books on cricket and was involved in the early "ghost" broadcasts of the Tests from England. One of his patients as a dentist was the legendary scorer, Bill Ferguson, and when "Fergie" sent his sister Ellen to Noble for treatment, a romance developed which ended with Noble at 40 marrying Ellen Ferguson, aged 24. They had a very happy marriage that produced four children, Noble dying at 67, his widow 23 years later.

NOBLET, Geoffrey, 1916– A lean, clean-cut Adelaide-born right-hand batsman and right-arm medium-pace off-spinner and swing bowler who had a brief Test career for Australia in the 1950s. He had a most unusual action that started with a barn-dance hop and ended with a flick as he went through with a long delivery stride. Some observers claimed he threw and there was no denying that he got exceptional "work" on the ball, but he was never called in eight years in first-class cricket. He toured South Africa with the 1949–50 Australian team and played in Australia against the West Indies and against South Africa.

Noblet, 6 ft 3 in, could move the new ball either way and was very accurate. When the ball had lost its shine, he bowled off-spinners that turned quite sharply if the pitch was worn or wet. He recorded some outstanding performances for South Australia, 13 times taking five wickets in an innings and his 236 wickets for the State cost only 18.92 apiece. Only the presence of Keith Miller, Bill Johnston and Ray Lindwall prevented him achieving a far more imposing Test record. His best figures were 7 for 29 against Victoria in 1951–52 at Adelaide, where he took all bar one of his five wicket hauls.

In South Africa with Lindsay Hassett's team he took 38 wickets at 14.65 and scored 138 runs at 23.00, making his Test debut in the Fifth Test when he took 3 for 21 in South Africa's first innings. He appeared in the Third Test at Adelaide against the West Indies in 1951–52, taking 2 for seven and in the Fifth Test against South Africa at Melbourne in 1952–53, taking 2 for 109 in the match. He is currently a vice-president of the SACA.

First-Class Averages: Batting, 975 runs at 13.92; Bowling, 282 wickets at 19.26.

Tests (3): 22 runs at 7.33; 7 wickets at 26.14.

A distinguished all-round sportsman who gave Australian cricket important service as a player and administrator. He was a very large, powerful man who bowled a zestful medium pace and feared no bowler with a bat in his hand in a Golden Age of Australian cricket. His strong personality helped Queensland enormously in its early years in the Sheffield Shield competition.

At Sydney University he won a big reputation as an athlete, and he played for Australia at Rugby Union against New Zealand. He played cricket 13 times for Queensland, taking 27 wickets at 38.33 and scoring 650 runs at 27.08. In 1928–29, he played for an Australian XI against Percy Chapman's touring MCC side, led Queensland against the same side, and scored 52 runs in his sole Test appearance at an average of 26 (top-score 44), and took 0 for 72.

He captained Queensland in three of his 13 matches for the State. For Queensland v. NSW at Sydney in 1929–30, he hit his sole first-class century, 121, but it was in the conference rooms that he excelled. He was born in Teutoburg, Queensland, and it was fitting that when he died he was president of the QCA. He was always a man more interested in character than statistics, and there was a rich, infectious air about him.

NOTHLING, Dr Otto Ernst, 1900–1965

First-Class Averages: Batting, 882 runs at 24.50; Bowling, 36 wickets at 41.05.

Tests (1): 52 runs at 26.00; 0 wickets for 72.

765

O

OAKLEY, Hector Herbert, 1909–

First-Class Averages: Batting, 1,605 runs at 43.37.

A dependable right-hand batsman from the St Kilda club who gave Victoria consistent service between 1929 and 1938, scoring four first-class centuries. He was a splendid field and a pugnacious fighter when Victoria needed runs. He made three of his centuries against South Australia, all in Melbourne and his career highest score, 162, at Hobart against Tasmania.

O'BRIEN, Leo Patrick Joseph, 1907–

First-Class Averages: Batting, 3,303 runs at 36.70; Bowling, 3 wickets at 42.33.

Tests (5): 211 runs at 26.37.

A short, wiry, conspicuously neat left-hand opening batsman of exemplary courage in the most argumentative years of big cricket between 1932 and 1936. He watched the high kicking ball with great care and his concentration was such that many rated him a better player on damaged pitches than any batsman of his time. He was also a fine fieldsman, but against the skill of England's Larwood, Voce, Bowes and Tate was unable to consolidate his place in the Australian team.

O'Brien, born in West Melbourne, travelled around Victoria as a boy when his father, a Police Superintendant, was moved to new posts. He learned his cricket at St Patrick's, Ballarat, and at Melbourne's Xavier College, where Fleetwood-Smith was a class-mate. He played for Richmond and then for Melbourne clubs and made his debut for Victoria in 1929–30. Over the next eight years he made five centuries for the State and seven centuries in all, topscore 173 against New South Wales at Sydney in 1934–35 when he defied Bill O'Reilly.

He first appeared for Australia in 1932–33 in the Bodyline series, playing the innings of his life in the Fifth Test on the first morning, when he made 61, adding 99 with Stan McCabe for the fourth wicket after Richardson, Woodfull and Bradman had gone cheaply.

He missed the 1934 tour of England but returned to the Australian side for the 1935–36 visit to South Africa, his only overseas tour. He pitched for the Richmond club and for Australia in the initial cricketers' international baseball match

766

against Transvaal at Johannesburg and was a leading amateur boxer. In all he appeared in five Tests, two in the Bodyline series against England, two in South Africa, and one at home against England in 1936–37. In 1959, at the age of 52, he toured the world with the Australian Old Collegians.

A tall, shrewd right-arm fast-medium bowler for New South Wales and South Australia between 1904 and 1910. He had some great days in inter-State cricket and against county teams in England in 1909, but after an impressive debut against England at Adelaide in 1907–08 failed to win a regular Test place. He varied his flight and pace cleverly, moving the ball in from outside the off-stump, but contributed little with his left-handed batting, and was undistinguished in the field.

O'Connor, born in Sydney, played for NSW at the age of 29 but did not reach his best until he moved with his family to South Australia. He headed the South Australian bowling averages two seasons in a row in 1907–08 and 1908–09, getting through a lot of overs in both summers. In 1907–08 he bowled 1,509 balls for 16 wickets at 45.25 and in 1908–09 bowled 1,338 balls for 26 wickets at 26.34. He took five wickets or more five times in an innings for South Australia.

He made a fine Test debut in taking 8 for 150 in 1907–08 against England, including 5 for 40 in England's second innings in a performance that helped Australia to a handsome win by 245 runs. This proved to be the high point of his Test career and he played in only three further Tests.

On tour in England with the 1909 Australian team he found the pitches too slow, though he bowled subtly, taking 85 wickets at 19.04. He took 5 for 51 and 5 for 56 against Warwickshire, 7 for 40 and 3 for 85 against Derbyshire, and 7 for 71 against Essex. He played in only the First Test, taking 1 for 40. With the bat, he scored 295 runs on the tour at 13.40 with the ball, best performance was 7 for 36 at Melbourne in 1908–09 when he bowled South Australia to an unexpected win against Victoria.

O'CONNOR, John Denis Alphonsus, 1875–1941

First-Class Averages: Batting, 695 runs at 11.77; Bowling, 224 wickets at 23.45.

Tests (4): 86 runs at 12.28; 13 wickets at 26.15.

A wicket-keeper batsman who captained Queensland in 31 of the 43 matches he played for that State. O'Connor gave Queensland impressive service, scoring eight centuries. He made his debut for Queensland in 1912–13 and scored his initial first-class century in 1923–24 against South Australia at Adelaide, where he made 184. In 1927–28 he had an innings of 133 not out against South Australia. He also scored four centuries against New South Wales (196, 141, 103, and 143 not out), one century against Victoria (160), and one against New Zealand (103).

O'CONNOR, Leo Patrick Devereaux, 1890–

First-Class Averages: Batting, 3,311 runs at 39.89. Dismissals, 103 (82 catches, 21 stumpings).

His innings 103 and 143 not out against New South Wales in 1926–27 at Brisbane made him one of the few batsmen to score a hundred in each innings of a first-class match. Behind the stumps he took five catches in the first innings against Victoria in 1928–29 and three catches in each innings against New South Wales at Sydney in 1927–28.

O'Connor's all-round skill and his fighting spirit as a captain were largely responsible for Queensland justifying her inclusion in the Sheffield Shield in her very first season in the competition, 1926–27. Queensland lost her first Shield match to New South Wales in Brisbane by only eight runs but reversed that result in Sydney by scoring 300 runs in the fourth innings, with O'Connor contributing a match total of 246 runs. Sydney papers called O'Connor "an inspiring captain and a great fighter". Queensland followed this great victory by beating Victoria outright by 234 runs and thus defeated the two glamour sides of the Shield competition in her first season.

O'Connor's efforts that summer earned him selection for the Charlie Macartney benefit match at Sydney in February, 1927, and he vindicated the selectors' wisdom by making a fine 101. O'Connor was one of four Queenslanders who played in the Test trial at Melbourne in the 1928–29 season but despite a strong all-round performance he missed selection. At 38, his last chance of an Australian cap had gone. Leo O'Connor was born at Murtoa, Victoria. His son **Brian Redmond Devereaux O'Connor** (1913-1963), born at South Brisbane, played for Valley club like his dad and played five matches for Queensland, scoring 83 runs at 11.85 and taking 6 wickets at 75.00.

OGILVIE, Alan David, 1951–

First-Class Averages: Batting, 2,959 runs at 34.40.

Tests (5): 178 runs at 17.80.

A tall, red-haired schoolmaster with an appropriate academic beard whose confidence and Test aspirations were badly dented when he was hit on the head by Bob Willis during the 1978–79 season. Ogilvie had impressed all the experts to that point with his straight, upright style. He had played in five Tests, highest score 47, but he had always looked a player who would develop into an exciting acquisition to the Australian team. He went from the Brisbane University team into the State side in 1974–75. In 1977–78 he scored 1,215 first-class runs at 50.62, including six centuries, a performance seldom matched by even the finest batsmen. He made his Test debut against India in Australia during the absence of the WSC players and went to the West Indies with Bob Simpson's side in 1977–78. In all first-class matches, Ogilvie scored eight centuries.

Queenslander David Ogilvie, one of the few batsmen to score 1,000 runs in a Sheffield Shield season. ▶

769

O'KEEFFE, Frank Aloysius, 1896–1924

First-Class Averages: Batting, 926 runs at 71.23; Bowling, 12 wickets at 19.16.

An outstanding right-hand batsman, exceptional field, and useful right-arm off-break bowler for New South Wales, Victoria and for the Church Club in the Lancashire League, who died in London from peritonitis, aged 27, just three months before he would have qualified for Lancashire. He was a man of great personal charm, born in the Sydney suburb of Waverley, and was widely mourned.

He began with Waverley club before switching to Paddington for two seasons under Monty Noble's captaincy. He made his first-class debut for New South Wales in 1919–20, and in 1920–21 scored 83, 4 and 72 in three knocks for New South Wales against Queensland. The next summer, 1921–22, he settled in Melbourne, where he played for Carlton. In successive innings he made 87 and 79 for Victoria against New South Wales, 177 and 141 for the Rest Of Australia against the Australian XI, and 180 for Victoria against South Australia, when he and E. R. Mayne, 85, had an opening stand of 144.

O'Keeffe seemed destined for big things when he moved to the Lancashire League in 1922 but the damper, colder English weather did not suit him and gradually his strength weakened. In 1923, however, he managed 650 runs for Church at 40.62 apiece, and took 50 wickets at 14.38.

O'KEEFFE, Kerry James, 1949–

First-Class Averages: Batting, 4,169 runs at 26.05; Bowling, 476 wickets at 28.11.

Tests (24): 644 runs at 25.76; 53 wickets at 38.07.

A right-hand leg-break bowler who struggled manfully for turn in 24 Tests on over-prepared pitches and proved a useful right-hand middle order batsman. He ran up to the stumps with an unusual hand action, massaging the ball into his bowling hand as if he was trying to wind up a spring. He bowled as many topspinners and off-breaks as he did leg-breaks in some spells as he sought spin on flint-hard pitches ideally suited to the fast bowlers who dominated his era. He had a long record as Australia's twelfth man in big matches.

O'Keeffe, born in the Sydney suburb of Hurstville and developed by the St George district club, looked enormously promising when he came into the New South Wales team in 1968–69 against Queensland, a tall, fair-haired spinner with a high action who bowled at a slightly faster pace than most leg-break bowlers. In 169 first-class matches he never quite lived up to that promise, though he did turn in handy performances with ball and bat and proved one of the best gully fieldsmen in the world.

He played two seasons with Somerset to widen his experience in 1971 and 1972 and took 93 wickets for the County, including 5 for 41 and 7 for 38 against Sussex at Taunton in 1971. He broke into the Australian team in 1970–71 against England at Melbourne and made his sole official tour of England with the 1977 Australian team under Greg Chappell. He took 36 wickets at 29.27 on the trip and scored 355 runs at 50.71, finishing second on the batting averages to Chappell in a very disappointing side. He toured New Zealand with Australian teams three times and the West Indies in 1973 with Ian Chappell's team. In 1975, he scored 1,000 runs and took 68 wickets for the East Lancashire League club.

He had lost his Test place when he joined WSC and he spent most of his time with WSC in country town matches. He settled in Newcastle when peace was achieved but returned to Sydney early in 1981 when he declared himself unavailable for first-class cricket. In all first class matches, O'Keeffe took five wickets in an innings 24 times, and 10 wickets in a match five times and had a highest score of 99 not out for Australia v. Auckland at Eden Park in 1973–74. He was New South Wales' captain in one match in 1975–76.

Kerry O'Keeffe bowling his leg-spinners in 1977 in England.

OLDFIELD, William Albert Stanley ("Cracker") 1894–1976

First-Class Averages: Batting, 6,135 runs at 23.77; Dismissals, 661 (399 catches, 262 stumpings).

Tests (54): 1,427 runs at 22.65; Dismissals 130 (78 catches, 52 stumpings).

One of cricket's great wicket-keepers, a dapper little fellow whose work behind the stumps was all polish and style. He helped make wicket-keeping a sophisticated part of cricket devoid of crudities. All his movements were neat and controlled, his appearance was always impeccable. He did not fall down or somersault and batsmen knew that when he appealed they were out.

Oldfield, born in Alexandria, Sydney, was educated at Cleveland Street and Forest Lodge schools, and began keeping wicket with Glebe third grade team. His captain asked him if he would take over when the regular 'keeper did not turn up. From this almost accidental start, he went on to delight cricket lovers throughout the world, taking some of the greatest catches and making some of cricket's most dramatic stumpings. He had an extraordinary safety rate, allowing a bye for every 68 runs scored by England, for example, and his missed catches or stumpings were so rare they made headlines.

He had played only two matches with the Glebe first grade team that included express bowler "Tibby" Cotter when he enlisted in the first AIF. A corporal in the 15th Field Ambulance Brigade, he was buried for several hours during the heavy bombardment of Polygon Wood in 1917 in France and was close to death when they dug him out. He recovered to play a leading role in the success of the first AIF team. Pace bowler Jack Gregory had gashed the face of the AIF side's sole 'keeper, Ted Long, when skipper Herbie Collins found Oldfield living in a dingy apartment near the team's headquarters in Horseferry Road, London. Collins, who did not know his name, asked Oldfield if he was the chap who kept wicket and offered him the job of 'keeping for the AIF team.

Oldfield protested that he was not in that class but when Collins said he had heard praiseworthy reports on Oldfield's skill from fellow soldiers, Oldfield agreed to join the team that night on the train to Oxford. But he had no flannels and he boarded the train with an assortment of cricket gear tied in a bundle. By the end of the first over, Collins knew the reports on Oldfield were true and by the end of the first innings in which he kept for the AIF it was clear a new Australian cricket star had arrived. Ted Long expressed it all when he told Collins he would no longer be needed, but he stayed with the team as second 'keeper.

For a cricketer of such humble beginnings, Oldfield was remarkably subtle in all his tasks on the field, and well-groomed in his appearances at social events. He took catches with effortless ease, moving to positions later Australian 'keepers had to dive headlong to reach. He could stump a batsman by flicking off a single bail, but when he went through his stumping action and left the bails intact, the batsmen invariably were still inches inside the crease. He did

772

not believe in bashing down all the stumps, and looked apologetic as his victims departed.

The entire Australian slips cordon sometimes appealed vociferously. Umpires learned to look at Oldfield, who was invariably silent if he believed the batsman was not out. He could make Mailey's most erratic deliveries look tidy, he was not deceived by Fleetwood-Smith's "Chinaman", and he stood right up on the stumps to all but the fastest bowlers.

After serving an apprenticeship as second 'keeper to Hanson Carter on the 1921 Australian team's tour of England, Oldfield reigned supreme as Australia No. 1 'keeper for 17 years, and in that time only Englishman Les Ames approached his standard. At Melbourne in February 1925, he stumped Hobbs, Woolley, Chapman and Whysall and caught Gilligan in a single innings of the Fourth Test against England.

When England got to within 12 runs of victory in the Third Test, Oldfield caught Freeman off Mailey, and The Ashes remained in Australia. In the Fifth Test of that series, Oldfield caught Hobbs in the first innings and stumped him in the second. He moved five or six yards towards square leg to take the catch, and later flicked off a bail when Hobbs missed a leg glance and momentarily raised his toe, to make the stumping. In 1926 when England regained The Ashes after 15 years, the Australian captain, Herbie Collins, said he could not recall Oldfield making a mistake on the entire tour. Oldfield never read newspapers or books or went to the movies for fear of straining his eyes.

Oldfield's value should be measured by his effect on the entire performance of the teams in which he played, not just in his own statistics. When Jack Gregory became lethargic, for example, he stood right up on the stumps, which made Gregory feel insulted. Gregory would then develop new hostility. Oldfield wore two pairs of inner gloves and had thick finger stalls but his hands were still gnarled and twisted from years of taking Gregory and McDonald.

Oldfield's 56 Tests were spread over four tours of England (1921, 1926, 1930, 1934), and two to South Africa. He batted in the same elegant style that he kept wicket and four times scored more than 50 runs in Tests, with 65 not out his best score. His 52 stumpings is still a record for Test cricket. Once in a Test, English 'keeper Strudwick appealed for a caught behind. The umpire said not out, but Oldfield, who knew he had hit it, walked.

In all first-class matches, he made six centuries with 137 for the Australian XI v. Canterbury at Christchurch in 1927–28 his highest score. He was the centre of perhaps the ugliest incident in England-Australia Tests, when, after Woodfull and Fingleton had been knocked about, he was hit on the head by Larwood at Adelaide and was taken to hospital with concussion. Typically, Oldfield explained that the injury was his own fault and that he had ducked into the ball.

In his heyday Oldfield always insisted that the staff of his sports store in Hunter Street, Sydney, should throw things to him, not pass them. Customers would enter amid a hail of hockey, golf, tennis balls, cricket bats and golf clubs. It was his way of keeping his eye in. He also wrote two highly regarded books on cricket. Towards the end of his busy life in sporting goods, Oldfield took several Australian schoolboys teams overseas. Included in the itineraries were matches in, of all places, Ethiopia, where Bert Oldfield from the backstreets of Sydney was a great favourite with Emperor Haile Selassie. He was a man whose religion helped shape a clean-living life-style, and he served as a vestryman at St Andrew's Cathedral in Sydney for several decades.

Australia's most stylish wicket-keeper, Bert Oldfield.

A right-hand batsman of matinee idol appeal who because of nervous starting had 12 fluctuating years in big cricket. He was a brilliant, powerful shotmaker, dark-haired and handsome, with a daring sweep shot, who thrilled spectators by the manner in which he rushed the score along. Off the back foot, he was dynamic, but he played full-blooded strokes all around the wicket, and supported it with twinkle-toed running between wickets. His fielding in the covers matched the excitement of his batting.

He was 6 ft tall, tough and agreeable, but he had the bad luck to play just before television discovered the enormous appeal of cricket super-stars. He was labelled another "Bradman" after he scored 1,005 runs in his third first-class season in 1957–58, having just turned 21. In Melbourne against Victoria, he made 175 in around three hours and in the return match against Victoria at Sydney made 233 in four hours.

O'Neill, born in the Sydney suburb of Carlton, was a punishing hitter from the time he began in grade cricket with the St George club, sometimes practising by smacking a ball hanging from a backyard clothesline. He had five first-class centuries behind him when, amid nationwide publicity, he was thrown into the first big match of the 1958–59 MCC tour of Australia by being included in a Combined XI to play the tourists at Perth. His presence and the Englishmen's eagerness to test him fully attracted a huge crowd. O'Neill got a methodical, if slow 104 in as nerve-tingling a challenge of his craft as any young batsman is likely to face.

Later, as the responsibility he carried in the Australian batting lineup became burdensome, he developed increasing nervousness at the start of important innings. In this period, he was known as "Nervous Norm" to the headline writers. He reacted badly to the label, choking low on the bat handle, scratching and fidgeting as no batsman of his gifts should have done. He was always more successful against other countries than against England, whose teams pressured his weakness in temperament consistently and cleverly.

O'Neill toured England twice, in 1961 and 1964, scoring 1,981 runs at 60.03 on the first trip, with seven centuries, and 1,369 runs at 45.63 on the second tour. He also toured New Zealand and India twice and went to the West Indies, South Africa and Pakistan. He made his highest Test score in the tied Test at Brisbane against West Indies in 1960–61, and his first century (117) against England in his tenth Test against them at The Oval in the Fifth Test in 1961.

He made a glorious 163 at Bombay and a hard-driving 113 at Calcutta against India in 1959–60, and 134 (his first Test century) against Pakistan on the same trip. He also scored his career highest of 284 against the Indian President's XI on the visit.

O'NEILL, NORMAN Clifford, 1937–

First-Class Averages: Batting, 13,859 runs at 50.95; Bowling, 99 wickets at 41.01.

Tests (42): 2,779 runs at 45.55; 17 wickets at 39.23.

Despite his jitters, O'Neill averaged 45.55 in his 42 Tests, more than some critics would have you believe. He scored a century against every cricket playing nation except South Africa, and was one of the most spectacular fieldsmen of his era, with a brilliant, long and accurate baseballer's throw to the stumps.

After the 1965 Australian tour of the West Indies he put his name to an article written for him by the Sydney journalist Robert Gray in which he told London newspaper readers that Charlie Griffiths was a chucker and bitterly attacked Keith Miller. The article appeared the day after the Australian tour to the West Indies ended, but the Australian Board of Control claimed that the tour did not end until the team landed back in Australia. Cricket was the loser over the article to which Miller trenchantly responded with phrases like "O'Neill's 20-odd Test innings without a century".

O'Neill continued to play first-class cricket and was the highest run-scorer in the 1966–67 Australian season, with 741 runs at 74.10. Australia's selectors omitted him from the team for South Africa, which on form was puzzling. He went away to New Zealand with an Australian "A" team, but at thirty the spark that had made him a hero had left him, and he retired soon afterwards, saying his knees would not stand further big cricket, a sad end to a career that promised so much more, although O'Neill's achievements were better than most.

O'Neill's son Mark has played for WA for the past few seasons, and has also had experience in Lancashire League cricket.

ONYONS, Basil Austin, 1887–1967

First-Class Averages: Batting, 997 runs at 62.31.

A right-hand batsman from the powerful Melbourne club who made six first-class centuries for Victoria. He made three centuries for the Melbourne Cricket Club in 1926–27 in New Zealand. He made a further century, 152 for Victoria against Fiji in a match that was not considered first-class. In the 1928–29 season he made three successive first-class centuries, and at Brisbane against Queensland had scores of 105 and 127, opening the innings each time. This followed his 131 in his previous knock against NSW at Sydney.

O'REILLY, William Joseph ("Tiger"), 1905–

A masterly unorthodox right-hand medium-pace spin bowler for NSW from 1927 to 1946 and for Australia from 1932 to 1946. On the field he hated all batsmen and considered bowlers to be cricket's persecuted. He bowled some of the longest spells in Test cricket history on some of the most unresponsive, controversial pitches the game has known, but he never gave up the struggle to outwit the batsmen.

776

O'Reilly was an ungainly 6 ft 3 ins, thinly-thatched, subtle, remarkably accurate and absolutely tireless. He loped to the wicket, wrist cocked, arms flailing, face strained with emotion, but such was his command of length and the cleverness with which he varied his pace and spin even top-class batsmen sometimes looked to the wrong part of the field when they were caught off O'Reilly's bowling. With his first and second fingers wrapped around the ball and the other fingers folded on to the palm of his vast hand, he bowled a leg break, a bosey and a top-spinner at disconcerting pace, turning the ball enough to find an edge or beat the bat, bouncing some deliveries like a tennis ball. He had an awkward stoop at the moment of delivery caused by bending his right knee. But there was a remarkable rhythm in all the grotesque aspects of O'Reilly's delivery.

O'Reilly was at his exciting best when he was angry. At Leeds in 1938 in one of the most dramatic Tests ever played he was no-balled when bowling to Hardstaff. Livid with rage, O'Reilly thundered up to the wicket and let go a vicious fast legbreak that removed Hardstaff's off bail. Next ball he had Hammond caught by Brown. Those two balls virtually clinched the Test and The Ashes for Australia. O'Reilly took 5 for 66 and 5 for 56 in that match, breaking the back of England's batting in each innings.

O'Reilly came from Wingello, a small country town about 100 miles south of Sydney, where his father was the local schoolmaster. He learned to bowl with a ball he and his brothers fashioned from a banksia tree root with a chisel. He frequently bowled against Bradman, who played for the nearby Bowral team. From St Patrick's College, Goulburn, O'Reilly followed his father into teaching and this took him to Sydney where he played for North Sydney and St George while he trained with the NSW Education Department. But the Department gave him country postings "out where the crows fly backwards" that upset his cricket career and delayed his entry into big cricket.

When O'Reilly first appeared at the Sydney Cricket Ground nets, Arthur Mailey and others suggested he change his grip and eliminate the stoop. O'Reilly politely declined, a wise move for a bowler with such an individual action. Bradman rated O'Reilly the best bowler he ever faced, and figures support that view. O'Reilly took more than 20 wickets in each of his four successive series against England—a feat unmatched by any other bowler—averaging a wicket every 77 balls despite having to play on wickets prepared to last a fortnight.

O'Reilly was written off as a failure in 1930 by Don Bradman, one of the great man's few errors of judgement. "He was a medium-pace bowler," Bradman wrote, "who could turn the ball both ways, but never achieved outstanding success on turf wickets." O'Reilly had been tried in two matches for

First-Class Averages: Batting, 1,655 runs at 13.13; Bowling, 774 wickets at 16.60.

Tests (27): 410 runs at 12.81; 144 wickets at 22.59.

New South Wales in 1927–28 with little success and it was not until 1931–32 after recovering his NSW place and taking 5 for 22 that he won a place in the Australian team. He won a place in the team for the Fourth and Fifth Tests against South Africa but did not establish himself as a Test player until the Bodyline series against England in 1932–33. He took 27 wickets at 26.81, and in the only Test Australia won, the Second at Melbourne, he took 5 for 63 and 5 for 66. He was as big a success for Australia in that series as Larwood was for England.

In England in 1934, O'Reilly took 28 Test wickets at 24.92 and 109 wickets on the tour at 17.15, which put him ahead of Grimmett in both sets of averages. On the first morning of the Old Trafford Test on that tour he bowled one of the most sensational overs in cricket history after the ball had lost its shape and been replaced. He had Walters caught at forward short leg from the first ball, knocked back Wyatt's middle stump with the second, watched Hammond edge the third through Oldfield's outstretched gloves for four, and bowled him with the fourth. From 0 for 68, England had slumped to 3 for 72. English reporters, irritated over the delay in changing the ball, slipped out for a drink and missed O'Reilly's over.

He was Australia's leading bowler for the third successive series in 1936–37 against "Gubby" Allen's English team, taking 25 wickets at 22.20, to bring his bag from three Test series against England to 80. It was in the Tests against Allen's team that O'Reilly was criticised for bowling leg theory, concentrating his attack for hour after hour on the leg stump, mixing googlies, topspinners and leg-breaks to pin down England's strokemakers. O'Reilly replied that on over-prepared wickets that nullified a bowler's skills, pitching the ball on the leg stump with two short legs could hardly be called defensive bowling.

After two Tests were drawn and the third washed out in England in 1938, critics were writing that O'Reilly was a has-been. "He has been played this season almost with ease," commented Neville Cardus. But in one of the finest Tests ever played O'Reilly swung the match Australia's way in the third innings by dismissing Hardstuff and Hammond with successive balls, Eddie Paynter scraping away the hat-trick ball. Set to get 105 to win, Australia struggled desperately in failing light, until Hassett made 33. With nine runs needed and five wickets in hand, down came the rain.

But the storm cleared and Australia rushed to a win that ensured Australia retained The Ashes. O'Reilly took his Test bag to 99 in that game, and a month later at The Oval became the sixth Australian to take 100 wickets in Anglo-Australian Tests. After having written O'Reilly off as a failure, Bradman later said that big Bill was the greatest bowler he ever batted against.

778

In all first class matches, he took five wickets in an innings 63 times and 10 wickets in a match 17 times. In 15 seasons of Sydney grade cricket from 1931 to 1946, he took an amazing 921 wickets for under 10 runs each, heading the first grade averages 12 times. No other bowler has averaged under 10 runs per wicket more than once in Sydney grade matches.

As a batsman, O'Reilly swung lustily from a left-handed stance sometimes lifting bowlers into the stands. He was a master at Sydney Grammar School for years, then dabbled in sporting goods before becoming secretary to a large brick-making and tile company. For some years he has been a prominent cricket commentator and is the author of books on the game. He ranks with Spofforth and C. T. B. Turner as the finest Australian bowler of his type and certainly one of the great characters of the game.

OXENHAM, Ronald Keven, 1891–1939

Queensland's best all-rounder. A right-hand medium pace bowler with a jerky action who turned from the off, noted for accuracy of length and direction and skilful flight. He was a resourceful batsman who could hit powerfully, and a splendid slips field. He bowled a fine slower ball that dipped into the batsman and produced a lot of nicks and lbws. Percy Hornibrook fielding to him in the slips could pick it by watching for when Ron spread his fingers. His weakness was that he disliked punishment and was prone to fall back on negative bowling.

Ron Oxenham began with the Noondah club and after taking 277 wickets in 11 seasons switched to Toombul for whom he became a remarkably consistent wicket-taker (479 victims) and run-getter in Brisbane first grade matches. In 1929–30, he took all 10 wickets for Toombul for 32 runs against Northern Suburbs, a feat that has only been accomplished by two other Queensland bowlers, C. B. Barstow in 1909–10 and G. G. Hardcastle in 1934–35.

He made his debut for Queensland in 1911–12 but despite many outstanding performances in first-class matches was not chosen for Australia until 1928. Overcoming this late entry into international cricket at 37, he did well enough to appear certain of selection for the 1930 Australian tour of England, but was overlooked in favour of Ted a'Beckett—a selection that angered those aware of Victoria's strength around selectors' tables.

Consistently impressive performances from the Oxenhams, F. C. Thompson, Andrews, Bensted, Hurwood, Les O'Connor and Percy Hornibrook finally won Queensland admission to the Sheffield Shield competition in 1926–27. For an Australian XI in 1924–25 against England, for example, Oxenham took the wickets of Hendren, Sandham, Kilner and

First-Class Averages: Batting, 3,693 runs at 25.64; Bowling, 369 wickets at 18.67.

Tests (7): 151 runs at 15.10, 14 wickets at 37.28.

779

Howell for 25 runs. Oxenham's prime years were lost, however, before Queensland won Shield membership and he didn't play Test cricket until his skill was declining.

In Queensland's first Shield season, Oxenham made 134 not out at Sydney in a Queensland total of 577 against New South Wales. Left to score 300 runs to win in the last innings, Queensland got them in an historic victory. At the Brisbane Exhibition Ground in February 1927, Oxenham took 4 for 18 as Queensland dismissed a Victorian side that included Ponsford, Hendry, Rigg and Baring for only 86. He then scored 104 and 73 with the bat to complete a splendid double and assist Queensland to victory by 234 runs. He made his highest first-class score, 162 not out, against Victoria at Brisbane in 1931–32.

Oxenham, a lean, dark-complexioned figure with a prominent part in a thatch of well-brushed black hair, played three Tests against Percy Chapman's English team in 1928–29 in Australia and took 4 for 67 in the Fourth Test. He also played for Australia against South Africa and West Indies, against whom he opened the bowling at Brisbane in 1930–31, taking 4 for 39, off 30 overs. In 1932–33 at Melbourne, he took 5 for 53 and 2 for 4 for an Australian XI against Jardine's English tourists.

In all first-class matches for Queensland, he scored 3,082 runs at 27.27, and took 231 wickets at 22.66 each. He captained Queensland eight times and had 70 matches for the State. He toured New Zealand with an Australian XI in 1927–28 and visited India with F. A. Tarrant in 1935–36, enjoying rare success with the ball, taking 101 wickets at 8.19. He was always a keen student of cricket's finer points and kept experimenting with grips for spin and arm swing for flight right up until his death at 48. Fairly late in his career he perfected a marvellous slower ball that drifted from the off towards leg stump. He suffered a serious injury in a car accident in 1937 and never fully recovered. His brother **Lionel Emmanuel Oxenham** (1888–1970), from the Toombul club, scored 1,055 runs for Queensland at 24.53, topscore 119, as a right-hand batsman, and took 1 for 88.

P

Pakistan, created by the partition of British India on August 14, 1947, first put a national cricket team into a Test in October, 1952, and first played a Test against Australia in October, 1956, on the mat at Karachi. Australia fielded the same team they had used six weeks earlier in the Fifth Test of the series they had played in England. Pakistan had won only four of 17 Tests before that game, fielding teams that often included players who had formerly appeared for India. The inspiration of the Pakistan team was Abdul Hafeez Kardar, who had played for India before going to Oxford University, the team captain and the man regarded as the founder of Pakistan cricket. The star of the Pakistan team was a tall, teak-tough fast-medium bowler, Fazal Mahmood, who had been included in the original Indian team to tour Australia in 1947–48 but left out when partition became a reality. Between them, Kardar and Fazal produced one of the most notable victories in cricket—and one of Australia's most surprising setbacks—in that first Test between the full strength of both countries.

PAKISTAN VERSUS AUSTRALIA

Australia batted first and soon found Fazal's cut off the mat as vicious as the spin they had just had to deal with from Laker and Lock. Fazal dismissed the first three batsmen before Keith Miller made a fast 21. Miller played at and missed five successive balls that came off the mat like fast leg-breaks and was caught when the sixth came back sharply into him. Australia were out for 80, with only four batsmen reaching double figures. Fazal, 6 for 34, and Khan Mohammad, 4 for 43, bowled unchanged. By stumps on the first day Pakistan were 2 for 15. The Australians who played in that match still regard the first day as one of the most fascinating they ever encountered although only 95 runs were scored.

1956 AUSTRALIAN TEAM IN PAKISTAN

I. W. Johnson

Pakistan were made to struggle for every run but they made 199 in their first innings thanks to Kardar's topscore of 69. Only Ian Johnson among the Australian bowlers got any sharp movement from the mat, and he finished with 4 for 50. Fazal took 7 for 80 in Australia's second innings for a match bag of 13 for 114, Kardar sustaining the pressure with shrewd field placements and all his fieldsmen responded with athletic saves and smart throwing. At the end of the third day Pakistan, needing 67 runs to win, were only nine runs short with all wickets intact. To the amazement of the Australians the ground was packed next morning and when they were scored—Pakistan winning by nine wickets—the Pakistan nation, the two parts separated by the width of India, celebrated as one.

1959–60 AUSTRALIAN TEAM IN PAKISTAN

R. Benaud

Despite further Test successes by the Pakistanis, three years elapsed before the second meeting with Australia. Thrown straight into a Test at Dacca without any warm-up games, Richie Benaud decided the wisest course was to send Pakistan in when he won the toss so that he could study the behaviour of the mat. Here the unlikely talents of "Slasher" Mackay as a bowler proved ideal for the surface. He did not cut the ball as far or as sharply as Fazal but he made the ball deviate enough to worry all batsmen. Pakistan made 200 in their first innings, with Hanif Mohammad, who in 1958–59 had made the world record first-class score of 499 for Karachi against Bahawalpur, was clean bowled by Mackay for 66. Australia replied with 225, Harvey contributing a glorious 96, Grout an aggressive 66. Then Mackay bowled at his finest to take 6 for 42 off 45 overs (with 27 maidens) to set up an Australian win. With Pakistan all out in their second innings for 134, Australia won by eight wickets. Pakistan had just started to replace its matting pitches with grass but this game was on mats following heavy rain. Almost as big a loss as the mats was the loss of Kardar's calm leadership. Back on turf for the Second Test at Lahore, Australia won comfortably by seven wickets. Norm O'Neill made 134 in Australia's first innings of 391 and a long knock of 166 by Saeed Ahmed could not save Pakistan. Left to score 122 in two hours to win, Australia got home with 12 minutes to spare to become the first country to win a rubber in Pakistan. American president Dwight Eisenhower attended the drawn Third Test at Karachi, but picked a bad day for it. Pakistan batted all day to score 5 for 104, the second slowest day's play in Test history. Intikhab became the first Pakistani bowler to take a wicket with his first ball in Tests when he bowled Colin McDonald, but on the mat again neither side could score quickly enough to gain an advantage.

1964 AUSTRALIAN TEAM IN PAKISTAN

R. B. Simpson

Australia played two Tests against Pakistan in 1964, the first at Karachi when the Australian team were on their way home from England, and the second at Melbourne when Pakistan were on their way to their tour of New Zealand. The first was distinguished by Bob Simpson's centuries in each innings (153 and 115), and by a record Pakistan first wicket partnership of 249 by Khalid Ibadulla (166) and Abdul Kadir (95). Set to score

782

342 runs to win in 290 minutes, Australia made 2 for 227 before time ran out, Pakistan using nine bowlers in this innings.

Two months later in Melbourne Hanif, captaining Pakistan in their first Test in Australia, topscored in both innings (104 and 93) and kept wicket throughout in the place of the injured Abdul Kadir. Ian Chappell made his Test debut in this game, scoring 11 runs and conceding 80 runs off 26 overs without taking a wicket. The game petered out in a draw.

New stars had arisen from the Pakistan nation of 112 million people when a balding Intikhab Alam captained them on their first full Australian tour. The batting responsibilities carried for so long by the Mohammad family was lightened by Majid Khan, Zaheer Abbas, and Asif Iqbal, all of them delightful stroke players. The Mohammad family were still represented by Sadiq and the ever popular Mushtaq, whose talents as a leg-spinner backed his attractive batting. In the First Test at Adelaide Australia had her first win at home against Pakistan due to Ian Chappell and Ashley Mallett. In Australia's first innings Ian scored 196 out of 585. After Rod Marsh chimed in with the first Test century (118) by an Australian 'keeper, Mallett took 8 for 59 in Pakistan's second innings. Australia also won the Second Test at Melbourne, this time by 92 runs. Redpath (135) and Greg Chappell (116) made centuries in Australia's first innings score of 441, but Pakistan headed that with 574, Majid making 158 and Sadiq Mohammad 137. Paul Sheahan (127) and John Benaud (142) then got hundreds for Australia, and three run outs helped bring defeat for Pakistan who were chasing 293 to win. Australia took the series 3–0 when Max Walker produced a spell of five wickets in 30 balls for three runs in Pakistan's second innings of the Third Test at Sydney. Walker's 6 for 15 denied Pakistan the chance Mushtaq had provided with a lovely 121 in Pakistan's first innings.

Mushtaq returned to Australia four seasons later as Pakistan's captain following a dispute at home over terms that ended with the resignation of Kardar, for so long the guiding force in Pakistan cricket. Before he went Kardar opened up membership of the Pakistan Cricket Board to banks, railways and other institutions so providing Pakistani cricketers with job security. At Adelaide in the first Test of the 1976–77 series, Australia wanted 56 to win when the mandatory last 15 overs began but the batsmen declined the challenge and the match was drawn. But it seemed Pakistan did not have the bowling strength to twice dismiss Australia cheaply. Davis (105) and Walters (107) made centuries for Australia. In the Second Test at Melbourne, Greg Chappell (121) and Cosier (168) both made centuries in Australia's total of 517. Sadiq made 105 in Pakis-

1964 PAKISTAN TEAM IN AUSTRALIA

H. Mohammad

1972–73 PAKISTAN TEAM IN AUSTRALIA

I. Alam

1976–77 PAKISTAN TEAM IN AUSTRALIA

M. Mohammad

tan's reply of 333, but Lillee's match bag of 10 for 135 was more than the Pakistani batsmen could overcome and Australia won by 348 runs. Pakistan pulled off a major upset by winning their first Test in Australia when Sarfraz Nawaz and Imran Khan combined to blast out the Australians for 211 and 180. Imran set a record for Pakistan in Australia with his 12 for 165 in the match, and Asif Iqbal scored 120 to make the victory possible.

1978–79 PAKISTAN TEAM IN AUSTRALIA

M. Mohammad

Pakistan had another remarkable win over Australia in the First Test of this two-Test series when the medium-pace bowler Sarfraz took 7 for 1 in 33 balls to give his side a 71-run win at Melbourne. Australia needed 382 to win the Test and appeared the winners when Alan Border (105) and Kim Hughes (84) added 177 runs for the fourth wicket. At one stage Australia were 3 for 305. Sarfraz then bowled Border and 40 minutes later Pakistan had won, Sarfraz finishing with his career-best figures of 9 for 86. The Pakistan captain Mushtaq Mohammad described this as "a miracle win." The final scenes were memorable as the stunned Australian batsmen succumbed to fine bowling and dazzling fielding. The Second Test at Perth saw Hughes replace the injured Yallop as Australia's captain. But Hughes, the first West Australian to captain Australia, was injured when he stepped on a ball at practice and had to be replaced as captain on the last three days by Andrew Hilditch. Australia won by seven wickets but not before two unsportsmanlike incidents marred the match. Fast bowler Alan Hurst ran out tailender Sikander Bakht at the bowler's end to end Pakistan's second innings—without giving Sikander the customary warning for backing up too far. Sarfraz successfully appealed for "handled the ball" when Hilditch picked up the ball and passed it innocently to Sarfraz. Umpire Tony Crafter was obliged to uphold the appeal. Border was the Australian batting hero with innings of 85 and 66 not out while Javed Miandad made a dashing 129 not out in Pakistan's first innings.

1980 AUSTRALIAN TEAM IN PAKISTAN

G. S. Chappell

Australia's first tour of Pakistan in 15 years brought charges of doctored pitches from the Australians, but strangely no accusations against the Pakistani umpires who had to deal with a constant barrage of appeals by the Pakistani players. "Pakistan is an interesting place but I don't want to hurry back," said star batsman Alan Border who despite these misgivings scored 674 runs on the tour at an average of 112.33. Australia lost the First Test at Karachi and then played draws in Tests at Faisalabad and Lahore, giving Pakistan the rubber 1–0. The First Test defeat was due to Australia's collapse in the second innings for 140, Iqbal Qasim taking 7 for 49. The Australians turned the Second Test into a farce by batting for almost three of the scheduled four days. Greg Chappell made 235, Yallop

784

172 in an Austalian total of 617 to which Pakistan replied with 2 for 382 before time ran out, Taslim Arif making 210 not out and Javed 106 not out, in an unbroken third wicket stand of 223. Border made 150 not out and 153 in the drawn Third Test in which Australia lost all chance of forcing a win when Majid made 110 not out. Pakistani newspapers blamed Australia's loss in the series to an over-cautious approach after they had lost the initial Test. Javed captained Pakistan for the first time while Majid and Taslim averaged over 100 in the Tests. The tour was played against a background of an unsettled cricket board suffering severe financial restraint.

1981–82 PAKISTAN TEAM IN AUSTRALIA

J. Miandad

Australia won this three-Test series 2–1 against a Pakistani team that failed to exploit the full potential of its highly talented members. The series had an unhappy start at Perth with the much-discussed Lillee-Miandad clash. Australia started with a modest 182, but then shocked Pakistan by dismissing them for 82. Lillee took 5 for 18 and Alderman 4 for 36. Kim Hughes made 106 in the Australian second innings of 424, leaving Pakistan to score 543 to win. Faced with this monumental task, Pakistan made only 256. Bruce Yardley took 6 for 84. Australia clinched the rubber by taking the Second Test by 10 wickets after further splendid bowling by Lillee, who took 9 for 132 in the match, and a superb 201 by Greg Chappell. Some controversial umpiring decisions and the generally slow over rates spoiled this and other matches in the series as a spectacle. Pakistan came back to win the Third Test by an innings and 82 runs with some excellent batting and despite fine bowling by Yardley, who took 7 for 187 off 66 overs and was alone among the Australian bowlers in challenging the batsmen. Wood was the sole Australian batsman to play up to Test standard, although Laird scraped together 35 and 52. The Pakistani bowlers used the conditions splendidly, with Imran and Sarfraz both taking five wickets in the match and Iqbal Qasim 7.

In September, 1982, the keen contest between the two countries resumes in Pakistan.

PALMER, George Eugene ("Joey"), 1860–1910

A prominent all-rounder for Victoria, Tasmania and Australia in the early years of big cricket. He bowled right-arm medium pace spin and when he first came into first-class cricket had impressive command of length, direction and of the off-break. Later he tried to develop a leg-break and his control fell away. His yorker was always his outstanding wicket-taker. When his powers as a bowler faded he improved his batting to a stage where this alone won him selection in representative teams, for he had a stout defence, could hit strongly all around the wicket, and did it with style.

785

First-Class Averages: Batting, 2,728 runs at 17.71, Bowling, 594 wickets at 17.71.

Tests (17): 296 runs at 14.09; 78 wickets at 21.51.

Palmer, born at Mulwala, New South Wales, got his chance when Frank Allen missed a train to the match against Lord Harris' team in Melbourne in 1878–79. As a late substitute, Palmer, then only 18, had match figures of 9 for 94. This feat greatly impressed the visitors and earned Palmer a trip to England a few months later with the 1880 team. He played in the first Test ever in England at The Oval, when Australia could not overcome the absence through injury of Spofforth and lost by five wickets.

Palmer, who married Jack Blackham's sister, was regarded as the finest bowler in Australia in the early 1880s. At Sydney in the Second Test in 1881–82 he took 7 for 68 and 4 for 97, Australia winning by five wickets, and at Sydney in the Third Test that summer he took 5 for 46 and 4 for 44, Australia winning by six wickets. Both wickets were said to favour the batsmen but there was a touch of genius in Palmer's bowling. He returned to England in 1882 but missed selection in the famous Ashes Test at The Oval. He took 138 wickets at 12.54 on the tour, and only Boyle (144) and Spofforth (188) did better.

Back home he turned in a match-winning effort in the First Test at Melbourne in 1882–83, taking 7 for 65, Australia winning by nine wickets. Two years later he was again a match-winner at Sydney, taking 4 for 32 to help Spofforth dismiss England for 77 in the second innings of the Fourth Test at Sydney. They bowled unchanged.

Palmer made his highest Test score at Lord's in the Second Test in 1886, batting for two and a half hours for 48 in a plucky but vain attempt to save the match. He badly injured his knee that year and could never again use his leg properly, finishing his career in Tasmania some ten years later. In all first-class matches, he took five wickets in an innings 54 times and 10 wickets in a match 16 times and held 108 catches. He took five wickets or more six times in a Test innings and twice took ten wickets in a Test. On the last of his four tours of England in 1886 he became the first Australian to achieve the double in England scoring 1,028 runs and taking 106 wickets.

PARISH, Robert John, 1916–

A tireless Melbourne cricket administrator who has had two terms as Chairman of the Australian Cricket Board. He was more closely involved than other officials in the WSC negotiations. He played grade cricket for Prahran from 1935–36 to 1948–49 and was respected in all Melbourne clubs for his accurate medium-pace bowling. He was appointed to the Prahran committee in 1936–37 and became the club's delegate to the VCA in 1950–51. At Prahran he has done everything from sweeping floors to marking out pitches, painting scoreboards and broadcasting scores to spectators. He became Prahran's fourth president in 1954–55 and was made chairman of the

ACB from 1966–69 and from 1976–79. He managed the Australian teams to the West Indies in 1965 and to England in 1968. His son, Bob Parish, jnr, also bowled medium-pace swing, headed the Prahran bowling averages in 1969–70, and was Prahran secretary between 1963 and 1971.

An outstanding right-hand batsman of stubborn defence who scored nine centuries for Victoria just before and just after World War I. He lost all chance of building an impressive Test record because of his medical studies and through matches lost during the war. In his sole test for Australia he was bowled first ball at Melbourne in the Second Test in 1920–21 and he did not get another chance. His daughter married Australian Test captain Ian Johnson.

Park, born at Ballarat, Victoria, was a small man with a keen cricket brain. He made his debut at the age of 20 for Victoria in 1912–13, and made the first of his handy list of centuries for the State in 1913–14—104 against South Australia. He was picked in the Australian team to tour South Africa in 1914–15, that had to be abandoned because of World War I. At the end of the war he was prominent in services matches in England but did not play for the first AIF side because of his studies. He had made 134 for Victoria against South Australia at Melbourne in 1914–15.

When Victoria recovered from a poor start against New South Wales at Melbourne in 1919–1920, his 92 helped them reach 464. In a period in which the triumphant Australian side brimmed with batting talent, he kept scoring well for his State. He made his highest score, 228, against South Australia in 1919–20 at Melbourne and the next year scored 152 against South Australia at Adelaide, plus 111 against New South Wales at Melbourne, and 100 against NSW at Sydney. In 1921–22 he made 122 against NSW at Melbourne, and his last century for his State in 1922–23 when he made 101 against England at Melbourne. Park was a leading Australian Rules footballer for several years, playing with University, Melbourne and Footscray.

A right-handed batsman who performed impressively for Western Australia in the years before World War I. He was killed in action in France in the last year of the war. He was a superb batsman in his youth despite the lack of first-class opportunities caused by living in Perth, and even when he made only a handful of runs there was a touch of class in all he did. In 12 first-class matches he scored two centuries and five fifties.

Parker played with the Corinthians, Wanderers and East

PARK, Dr Roy Lindsay, 1892–1947

First-Class Averages: Batting, 2,514 runs at 39.28; Bowling, 3 wickets at 46.33.

Tests (1): 0 runs; NA.

PARKER, Ernest Frederick, 1883–1918

First-Class Averages, Batting, 834 runs at 34.75.

787

Perth clubs, and made his debut for WA in 1905–06. He played twice for the Rest of Australia versus the Australian XI in 1908–09, and in the Melbourne game hit an attractive 65. He scored 116 in 1905–06 for WA against SA at Fremantle in the match in which Algy Gehrs scored a century in each innings. He made his highest score, 117 against Victoria at Perth in 1909–10. In 1902–03 he scored 1,003 for East Perth at 71.64, top-score 246. During his grade career he made many centuries and was regarded as the leading batsman in the State. Parker was also an outstanding tennis player who won the Western Australian singles championship eight times.

PASCOE, Leonard Stephen (formerly Durtanovich), 1950–

First-Class Averages: Batting, 430 runs at 9.35; Bowling, 262 wickets at 24.56.

Tests (14): 106 runs at 10.60; 64 wickets at 26.06.

A crowd-pleasing right-arm fast bowler of awesome strength who powered the ball down at such a pace he rivalled the great Dennis Lillee as Australia's top pace bowler before he dropped out of the 1981 tour of England for an operation on his knees. There is little subtlety in Pascoe's bowling but he has such power in his wide, heavily-muscled chest and broad shoulders, he can sustain true pace for long periods. He is a poor batsman but fields well in the deep, using his big arm to fire in heavy, accurate returns.

Pascoe in full flight is tremendous entertainment for cricket lovers, for he gives everything as he lets them go. Television coverage of cricket may have made Lillee into a super star, but Pascoe loses little by comparison. A more whole-hearted trier would be hard to find and woe betide the opposition who make him as angry as Ian Chappell did in February 1980, at Sydney Cricket Ground. Pascoe, on the boil after a first innings run-in with Chappell, produced tremendous bursts of speed in the second innings to blast South Australia out for 69, New South Wales winning by 98 runs a match they could easily have lost. Pascoe took 7 for 18.

"I felt Chappell went too far", said Pascoe. "It was a premeditated personal attack—very intense. I don't think I got in the last word but I got the last laugh. Granted, I get emotionally involved out there. If they want to knock me off my length that's okay. If they want to play silly buggers, I'll accommodate them."

Pascoe, born at Bridgetown, Western Australia, the son of Yugoslav migrants, grew up in the Bankstown area of Sydney and played for the same school as Jeff Thomson, Punchbowl High. He says Thommo showed him the way; if one kid from Bankstown could make it, so could he. When he was in Primary School, he recalls a woman teacher going into the nets and attempting to explain the finer points of cricket to his class. She stood at the crease and invited her 10-year-olds to send down a few at her. Pascoe obliged, knocking the bat sideways and leaving the teacher in a very undignified position.

788

He was one of the wildest bowlers ever to play grade cricket in Sydney when he first appeared for Bankstown and word spread through the grade clubs that he was part animal. "When I was 21 or 22, I'd run through a brick wall", he said. "One of the things that has dawned on me now that I am 30 is that you have to control yourself. You have to keep your composure if you want to succeed."

Marriage to a handsome woman, a change of name, and family responsibility have brought out the best in Lennie. He realised midway through the 1980–81 season he could not go to England with an Australian side without risking his physical future and he told the selectors. There was no crying over a tour missed, nor was there any the following Australian summer when he became the first player suspended by his team-mates after a clash in Perth with Kim Hughes. Pascoe's NSW team-mates suspended him for one match after he

English umpire Dickie Bird watches Pascoe deliver a ball for Australia.

bowled a head high ball and exchanged words heatedly with Hughes. His suspension was the first after the introduction of the code of behaviour suggested by players.

He made his debut for New South Wales in 1974–75 after dramatic grade performances, against Queensland at Brisbane. He made his Test debut against England at Lord's in 1977 while on tour with Greg Chappell's team. He joined WSC when it began and performed creditably through its two year existence, forming a splendid opening pair with Lillee. After peace was declared, he was among the first chosen for the Australian team. During the 1981–82 season in Australia, big Lennie had his career best figures of 8 for 41 against Tasmania at Hobart. He went to New Zealand with the Australian team in 1981–82, having played one Test against West Indies in Australia, still struggling to regain the form shown before his knee operation.

PELLEW, Clarence Everard ("Nip"), 1893–1981

First-Class Averages: Batting, 4,531 runs at 33.56; Bowling, 12 wickets at 72.23.

Tests (10): 484 runs at 37.23.

The most successful of four Pellews who played for South Australia and the only one in the family to play Test cricket. He was a right-hand middle order batsman who could flay tiring attacks, and a brilliant outfieldsman with a pick up and throw of such vigour that he ripped the heels off several pairs of boots as he stopped and turned. Sir Pelham Warner, the noted English critic, called Pellew the finest outfielder he ever saw. Pellew was often referred to as the D'Artagnan of cricket, so charming was his batting.

Clarence was a cousin of John H. Pellew, and the elder brother—by six years—of Lance V. Pellew. All three, plus A. H. Pellew, played for South Australia. Clarence played for University after graduating from St Peter's College, Adelaide, in 1910–11, and made his debut for South Australia in 1913–14. The story goes that at St Peters' College a master on hearing his name said, "What have we here—another 'Nip'?" The original Nip had been his cousin Jack. Somehow the name suited the dashing University cricketer, fine swimmer, and champion inter-Varsity quarter miler that Clarence became.

At St Peters' and in the State XI he opened the batting with Johnny Moyes, later an outstanding critic. Moyes wrote that Pellew was always a sound player and that he had a big occasion temperament, ideally suited to the stress of Test cricket. As a fieldsman, said Moyes, Pellew was superb, bringing off many runouts with his baseballer's retrieve and throw. None who saw him patrolling the boundary ever forgot his skills.

"Nip" matured into a slim-waisted figure, with a trim dark moustache and big blue eyes. He joined the AIF at the outbreak of World War I and served with the 27th Battalion in the Middle East, France and Belgium. In a soldier's match at

Cairo he and Johnny Moyes scored the 85 needed to win in 38 minutes after Moyes began with three sixes off the first over. "Nip" played for the Dominions XI against England at Lord's and then joined the first AIF team. He was so fit he gave the two stone heavier Jack Gregory close contests in knock about wrestling matches.

"Nip" scored 1,260 in 40 innings for the AIF at 38.18, including four centuries, highest score 195 not out against Worcestershire when he and Carl Willis put on an unbeaten 301 for the fifth wicket. He also made 106, retired hurt, in a seventh wicket stand of 170 with Allie Lampard against Surrey. He joined the North Adelaide club on his return home and regained his place in the State team. In March, 1920, at the age of 26, he scored his only century for South Australia in a truly extraordinary knock that saw him break three bats and end up with one borrowed from his brother Lance. Resuming at 26, he scored his first 100 on the third day in 66 minutes and 200 in even time. He was 219 at tea after scoring a century in the lunch-to-tea sesssion, and he went on to a chanceless 271, which equalled the highest score for the State set by George Giffen.

"Nip" made his Test debut at Sydney in 1920–21 against England and in his second Test at Melbourne scored 116 in three hours, adding 173 with Jack Gregory for the eighth wicket. He made 104 in his third Test at Adelaide. Batting at No. 7 he hit 13 fours in two hours of dashing shotmaking, reaching his 100 with 16 runs off an over. He had a high grip and a very high backlift and hit towering sixes on most Australian first-class grounds.

He went to England with Armstrong's team in 1921 and toured South Africa in 1921–22. His English tour produced 848 runs at 24.94, including 146 against Cambridge University and 100 against Nottinghamshire. When he dropped a catch against Middlesex, it was the first team-mates had ever seen him spill. His run-getting may have been disappointing in a team of brilliant stroke players, but his speed around the boundary saved countless runs.

He retired from first-class cricket in 1923 to become a farmer at Saddleworth but returned to district cricket in 1928–29 as the Prospect club's first captain. After four successive club centuries, he was recalled at 35 for four matches in the State side in which he made 484 runs. In 1930, he was appointed State coach, a job he held for nine years. He played for RSL teams for many years and for the Commercial Travellers' Association until he was 63. He was reappointed as State coach in 1958 and kept going until he was 77. He was Australia's oldest Test cricketer when he died in 1981 at 87.

"Nip" Pellew's 10 Tests produced two centuries. In all first-class matches he hit nine centuries. High kicking balls broke both his hands. For South Australia, these are the figures

achieved by the four Pellews in their 56 matches for the State:

BATTING

	Inn	N.O.	H.S.	Agg.	Av.
A. H. Pellew (2)	4	—	14	32	8.00
C. E. Pellew (23)	43	2	271	1611	39.29
J. H. Pellew (21)	40	1	87	893	22.89
L. V. Pellew (10)	19	—	81	604	31.78

BOWLING

	Balls	Mdns	Runs	Wkts.	Av.
A. H. Pellew			Did not bowl		
C. E. Pellew	1373	18	724	10	72.40
J. H. Pellew	575	7	439	3	146.33
L. V. Pellew	128	—	90	—	—

PEPPER, Cecil George, 1916–

First-Class Averages: Batting, 1,927 runs at 29.64; Bowling, 171 wickets at 29.35.

A burly, outspoken Australian all-rounder whose big-hitting, right-arm spin bowling and clashes with umpires and opponents enlivened English League cricket for almost 20 years but were seen only briefly in Australia. Few Australians have hit a ball as far, fewer still have bowled the googly and flipper with such effectiveness. Only Freddie Truman and Bill Alley among modern cricketers matched his flair for shearers repartee. One way or another he spiced every match in which he appeared and this continued when he became a first-class umpire.

Watching a timid batsman grope at his spinners, Pepper came to the end of an over and said, "All right, lad, you can open your eyes now—it's over." Asked how he would like his field positioned, he said: "Tell 'em to walk about—I'll bowl this bloody lot out." When his slips fieldsmen retreated, he shouted, "Come back—I don't go that far on my holidays." Bruce Francis informed Pepper before one of his county matches for Essex that he had been out 16 times leg-before that summer. Soon after play began Francis was hit on the pad amid loud appeals. "That's 17, Bruce," said Pepper, raising his finger.

Eric Denison wrote in the Manchester *Evening News* that he could not imagine any match in which Pepper played pursuing a peaceful course. "Something is bound to erupt and it's usually Cecil George," said Denison. "He is mustard on a cricket field, inclined to let his emotions get the better of him. Because of his habit of abusing players in choice terms, he has made quite a few enemies, but if you realise this is his safety valve, he is easier to get on with."

Pepper was a right-hand batsman with huge forearms and vast hands, surprisingly quick on his feet for a heavy six-footer, and prepared to get down the pitch to create half-volleys. He could pull and cut with power, but driving was his strength. His defence produced a straight, full-faced bat which he loudly explained was wider than bats others used. He bowled his spinners at a brisk pace, starting with his arm down behind his back, relying on leg-breaks, occasional googlies and his notable flipper. His manner suggested that he expected to get a wicket from every ball. He bowled too many bad balls to be ranked with the great bowlers, but he deceived the finest players in England and regularly took 100 League wickets in a season.

Pepper was born in the NSW country town of Forbes, 240 miles west of Sydney, but spent his boyhood at Parkes 50 miles away. He was a promising schoolboy tennis player. At 16 he had won several country tennis tournaments and highly impressed Davis Cup stars John Bromwich and Adrian Quist, who advised him to move to Sydney and concentrate on tennis. But he could get no assistance from NSW tennis officials, and, after scoring 2,834 runs (topscore 251) and taking 116 wickets in the 1934–35 season for Parkes, went to play cricket for the Petersham club in Sydney. For a time he lived at Sid Barnes' home. Each morning at six he went to the nets with Barnes and Ken Grieves. At night they practised on the road, using the space between tram lines as their pitch. When the trams drove them away at peak periods, they found back lanes where they could chalk wickets on a wall.

Pepper received helpful coaching from Petersham stalwart Tommy Andrews, who urged him never to curb his natural hitting. He was a natural games player who took easily to roller skating and got his golf handicap down to two, playing matches with Norman von Nida. At squash, he was one of the few who could extend Lindsay Hassett. He made his debut for NSW in 1938–39 and played in 16 first-class matches before he joined the AIF in 1940, established as a spectacular hitter and an outstanding spin-bowling prospect.

He served in the Middle East and New Guinea and at the end of the war was in England, playing occasionally at Eastbourne and for a camp side at High Wycombe, where he hit a century in 23 minutes in a services match. When the Australian Services XI was formed, he became the nucleus of an entertaining team with Hassett, Cheetham, Sismey, Bob Cristofani, Miller and Carmody. In the Victory Test at Lord's Pepper's all-round performance helped clinch victory over an England side that included Hutton, Washbrook, Hammond, Robins, Gover, Wright and Griffith. Pepper made the winning hit in the last over in compiling a fast 54.

Before he left England Pepper played a few times for Nelson in Lancashire League matches and was impressed by his match fees and the system of cash collections for outstanding feats. Pepper and Miller were the outstanding all-rounders as the Services team drew the five Test series with England—two wins each and a draw—and played its way through India and each of the Australian States. At Adelaide he had an lbw

appeal disallowed by umpire Jack Scott during Bradman's knock of 112 for South Australia, and had some pointed words to say about the impossibility of dismissing Bradman on his home pitch. The umpire complained and later Pepper was asked to apologise. Cricket writer Dick Whitington helped him compose an apology to the Board of Control, but the Board said it was never received. Some writers have since argued—Whitington among them—that this clash with Bradman caused Pepper to forsake Australian cricket for a career in the Lancashire League.

Pepper was discharged from the Army in Sydney and after missing selection in the 1946 Australian side to New Zealand, returned to England with his new wife. He became Rochdale's professional in 1946 and in the next three seasons scored 3,137 runs at 52.28 and took 297 wickets at 10.56, rounding off his efforts for Rochdale with 1,083 runs and 102 wickets in 1948. At Stockport in 1946 he hit six sixes and 17 fours in an innings of 148, scoring the last 98 in 44 minutes. For five years he played for Burnley, helping them to the League championship in 1952. He switched to Radcliffe for two seasons in 1954 and then went to Oldham, then to Royton, and finally to North Staffordshire. He was the biggest drawcard in the League, and could be counted on for 100 wickets each season. His batting efforts became more modest as he aged, but his tongue remained sharp. League officials became accustomed to complaints about his behaviour.

Periodically there were pleas for Pepper's inclusion in the Australian Test side but the Australian Cricket Board never took them seriously while Pepper remained in England. Pepper showed what he could do when he visited India with a strong Commonwealth side in 1949–50. Early in the tour he formed a formidable spin bowling combination with George Tribe. But umpiring decisions, notoriously biased in India, continued to receive his noisy protests and after discussing the problem with his captain "Jock" Livingston, Pepper agreed to return to England. He played in only six of the 21 matches on the tour but headed the bowling averages with 34 wickets at 15.94. At Indore he took a hat-trick against Holkar. With the bat, he averaged 24.00, topscore 95.

After he retired as a player in 1964 Pepper became a first-class umpire but was removed from the Test panel after uttering a few typical expletives. In this period he umpired several times with old pal Bill Alley in matches that reached the highest standards of colourful rhetoric. He retired from umpiring at the end of the 1978 season to concentrate on his prospering packaging business in Rochdale. In his 16 matches for NSW, Pepper scored 648 runs at 27.00, topscore a blazing 81 against Queensland at The Gabba in 1939–40 when he hit seven sixes and eight fours. He took 57 wickets for NSW at 33.89. For the Australian Services, he scored 249 runs at 31.12 and

794

took 14 wickets at 35.14 in the five Victory Tests against England. In the three matches against India, he made 214 runs at 53.00 (topscore 95) and took 16 wickets at 33.75. He failed to shine as a bowler in the matches against the Australian States, but scored 63 against South Australia and 63 against NSW. His absence from the Australian scene when he was at his prime was a tragedy for all lovers of the game.

PETTIFORD, Jack, 1919–1964

A useful all-rounder for New South Wales, Kent and the second Australian Services team. He was an attractive, reliable right-hand batsman and spin bowler, with a keen sense of fun, and played in two "Victory Tests" which did much to revive cricket in England after World War II. He was then a Flying Officer with the RAAF. When the Services team toured India on the way home, he scored centuries in each of the first two representative matches and topped the batting averages with 67.25. After his discharge he played 16 matches for NSW, scoring 738 runs at 28.38 and taking 40 wickets at 38.95 with his leg-breaks.

Pettiford returned to England, where he played League cricket for Oldham and Nelson, and in 1954 joined Kent as a professional, heading the County's batting averages in his first season and continuing in County cricket until 1959, twice scoring more than 1,000 runs in a season. His best score was 133 against Essex at Blackheath in 1954. In his six years with Kent he scored 5,103 runs at 23.85 and took 194 wickets at 29.79. He also toured India and Pakistan in 1949–50 with the Commonwealth team.

First-Class Averages: Batting, 7,077 runs at 25.64; Bowling, 295 wickets at 31.38.

Pettiford learned his cricket with the Gordon club in Sydney. He took 41 wickets for Gordon in 1942–43 and in 1943–44 he headed the first grade batting averages with 320 runs at 45.71, including 154 in 122 minutes against Randwick. After his return from war service he was a member of the Gordon side captained by "Ginty" Lush that won the 1945–46 first grade premiership.

PHILLIPS, James, ("Dimboola Jim"), 1851–1930

First-Class Averages: Batting, 1,826 runs at 12.59; Bowling, 355 wickets at 20.00.

A South Australian allrounder whose first-class figures would have been far more impressive had he not lived in an outback town until he was nearing his 35th year. He was a very useful right-hand batsman on occasions, a splendid field at cover, and a capital medium-pace bowler. He is best remembered, however, as a fearless umpire who was largely responsible for stamping out throwing around the turn of the century. He stood as an umpire in 29 Tests (13 in Australia, 11 in England, 5 in South Africa), establishing an international reputation for acumen and honesty.

795

Phillips, born at Pleasant Creek near Port Adelaide, lived in the town that provided his famous nickname until a time when most cricketers feel their careers are virtually over. He had moved to Dimboola in the western districts of Victoria early in the 1880s, and first played for the State in 1885–86. In 1893, he made 165 for Players of Melbourne against Melbourne. For a number of years he travelled between England and Australia following the cricket seasons.

He played for Middlesex from 1890 to 1898, scoring 1,152 runs at 11.29 and taking 211 wickets at 22.28. His best score for the County was 67 was not out against Surrey at The Oval in 1894. In 1895, he took 13 for 117 for Middlesex against Surrey at Lord's, 8 for 69 the same year for Middlesex v. Kent at Lord's, and in 1896 he took 13 for 187 for Middlesex v. Gloucestershire at Lord's. In a minor match at Lord's in 1888 between MCC and Scarborough, he took 16 of the 20 wickets Scarborough lost, and later the same week took four wickets in four balls against Notts Castle on the same ground. He was given a benefit match, Australia v. Middlesex, in 1899.

Phillips scored 316 runs in 17 first-class matches for Victoria at 15.04, topscore 85 against NSW at Melbourne in 1891–92. He also took 62 wickets for Victoria at 17.82, best analysis 7 for 20 v. NSW in 1890–91, with match figures of 10 for 44. He was a coach for a time at Christchurch, New Zealand, and made 110 not out, his only century, for Canterbury v. Wellington in 1898–99.

Phillips accompanied the 1896 Australian team to England and umpired their three Tests. *Wisden* was highly critical of the bowling actions of Ernie Jones and Tom McKibbin on that tour and branded both as throwers. At Adelaide in the first match by Stoddart's team in 1897–98, Phillips no-balled Jones for throwing and he repeated the call in Melbourne during the Second Test when Jones became the first bowler no-balled for throwing in a Test. The following year *Wisden* applauded Phillips for those calls.

"No-one who knows James Phillips can think it possible that he would have no-balled Jones without adequate cause," *Wisden* said. "Nothing but good can come from what Phillips has done. If years ago any representative umpire had shown the same good sense many scandals would have been avoided. As regards both McKibbin and Jones, the point to bear in mind is that the fault rests primarily with English bowlers and England umpires. Australian bowlers never threw in England until we had shown them over and over again that Law 10 could be broken with impunity."

The throwing that apparently had been allowed to go unchecked on English grounds now became the object of a full-scale offensive by umpires as the result of the stand taken by Phillips. Reviewing the 1898 season, *Wisden* said, "For the first time within my experience—with some trifling excep-

796

tions—bowlers were no balled for throwing in first-class matches in England, C. B. Fry being no-balled by West at Trent Bridge, by Phillips at Brighton and by Sherwin at Lord's. More than that there were, I believe, one or two cases of no-balling for throwing in matches played by smaller counties". *Wisden* was particularly delighted at the no-balling of C. B. Fry, a pillar of fair play and true-blue amateurism, who among other things, wrote Latin verses, held the world long jump record for 21 years, was offered the throne of Albania, commanded the naval training ship *The Mercury*, stood for Parliament and represented India at the League of Nations. "The no-balling of Mr. Fry was only a case of long-delayed justice," said *Wisden*.

With Phillips in the centre of it, a conference of County captains was called at Lord's in December, 1900, when it was recommended that nine regular bowlers should not be used by their captains the following season. Fry, finding himself declared a chucker by 11 votes to one, gave up plans to specialise in bowling lobs and seldom bowled again. The following season, 1901, Phillips no-balled Lancashire pace bowler Arthur Mold 16 times in 10 overs for throwing against Somerset. That ended Mold's first-class career.

After he finished his Test umpiring career in 1906, Phillips became a mining engineer, and was said to have made a fortune in North America. He died at Burnaby, Vancouver, Canada, in 1930.

PHILLIPS, Wayne Bentley, 1958–

First-Class Averages: Batting, 1,123 runs at 44.92.

One of the successes in South Australia's surprise Sheffield Shield win in 1981–82, a young lantern-jawed left-handed batsman with a mop of unruly fair hair who is a useful substitute wicket-keeper. He first played for South Australia in 1977–78 against Victoria at the age of 19, but was given time to mature. In 1980–81, he scored 111 against Victoria and scored 91 in the second innings. Phillips, who plays for Sturt, scored 260 for South Australia against Queensland in 1981–82 and 104 against Pakistan, taking his total of first-class runs past 1,000 in only 14 matches, with three centuries, a performance that earned him a place in the Australian team to tour Pakistan. He had not kept wicket in a first-class match at that stage of his career. Phillips was a member of the Australian Under-19 team that played 12 matches in England in 1977 under management of former NSW player Warren Saunders.

PHILPOTT, Peter Ian ("Percy"), 1934–

A successful all-rounder for Manly, New South Wales, Australia and Lancashire League teams who later became an outstanding coach. He was a brilliant slips and gully fieldsman,

First-Class Averages:
Batting, 2,886 runs at
31.36; Bowling, 245
wickets at 30.31.

Tests (8): 93 runs at 10.33;
26 wickets at
38.46.

a first-class cricket century-maker, but at the Test level he owed his selection to his clever leg-spin. Few Australians have played cricket in as many places as Philpott, one of the game's most travelled players.

He was in the Manly first grade team at 15, while still at North Sydney Boy's High school where he captained the First XI and had Ian Craig as his vice-captain. He had played grade cricket for three years by then—from the age of 12!—but it was still a big jump to a first grade side that included Keith Miller, Alan Walker, Tom Brooks and Jimmy Burke, all successful first-class players. He made his debut for New South Wales in 1954–55 while still in his teens. Philpott and Ron Briggs rescued NSW after they had lost six wickets cheaply, and their partnership led to NSW winning the match.

For the next 13 years Philpott—"Percy" to team-mates—played all over the cricket world, scoring a century and taking six wickets or more in an innings against each Australian State. He played Lancashire League cricket with great success for four seasons (1955, 1959, 1960 and 1962) and during the English winters went off coaching in South Africa. When the Australian summers ended, he coached in New Zealand, or south-east Asia.

Philpott has always thought deeply about his cricket, and was much taken by the Jack Iverson method of bowling with a finger bent back behind the ball, and in experimenting with this grip badly damaged the tendons of his bowling hand. He retired at 29 without having played in a Test, but made a remarkable comeback soon after to win Australian selection.

"My selection came at an age when I thought I had missed my chance," he said. "The 10 p.m. news in Sydney was to include the names of the Australian team to tour West Indies in 1964–65. Tension. The announcer's calm disciplined voice. One by one the names were read but mine did not come in alphabetical order as it should had I been chosen. I told myself I had missed. A crushing disappointment. And then on the end of the tour names that marvellous announcer's voice apologised and added, 'Peter Philpott, New South Wales.' That moment, that wonderful, blissful fraction of time was worth every sacrifice, every day of hard practice, all the concentration on correcting faults and learning tactics."

Philpott played in all five Tests on that tour of West Indies, where his 49 wickets remains the highest total any Australian bowler has taken there. In his eight Tests his best figures were 5 for 90 against England at Brisbane in 1965–66. He made four first-class centuries, all for NSW, with a highest score of 156 in 1963–64 against Queensland at Sydney. He headed the Sydney first grade bowling averages in 1950–51 with 38 wickets at 12.28.

Since his retirement he has had remarkable success as a coach, and this could earn him a bigger place in the history of

798

Australian cricket than any of his playing feats. An English and History master firstly at Shore and now at Kings, he has shown himself a born communicator conveying his love for the game to hundreds of boys. Sydney grade clubs who asked him to lecture the best youngsters in their districts were amazed by the clarity of his talks, commonsense instruction which is conveyed in his book for young players. He took over as New South Wales coach in 1978–79 and brought a new spirit to the New South Wales side.

In 1980, when Philpott had successful open heart surgery, it was revealed that he had played with a weak heart, the result of rheumatic fever when he was a child. He recovered through a disciplined therapy and in 1981 was named cricket manager of the Australian team that toured England.

PINCH, Colin John, 1921–

First-Class Averages: Batting, 4,206 runs at 39.67; Bowling, 8 wickets at 30.25.

A nuggety, determined right-hand batsman and left-arm medium pace bowler who also played quality Rugby League football and baseball. He made his debut in first-class cricket for NSW in 1949–50 after serving his formative years with Glebe and Paddington clubs. His prospects appeared limited because of the great strength of the NSW side, so after scoring 116 runs in two Shield matches, topscore 54, he moved to South Australia. He made 11 centuries for SA, nine in Shield matches and one each against Tasmania and New Zealand. From the time he scored 146 not out in a total of 259 for SA against Victoria in 1950–51, when he carried his bat, he was an automatic choice in the SA team. He captained SA from 1957 to 1960.

Pinch was a dour character, ideal for middle order batting. He had nine years with the Adelaide club, with whom he twice topped the A grade club averages and aggregates, and one season with Sturt. He had a fine throwing arm, a legacy of his days with the Marrickville baseball club in Sydney as a pitcher. He is best remembered for twice scoring a century in each innings of a first-class match. He did it first in Perth against WA in 1956–57 when he scored 110 and 100, and a year later repeated the feat for SA against Victoria at Melbourne by scoring 102 in each innings.

PLAYLE, William Rodger, 1938–

A New Zealand Test batsman who settled in Western Australia, playing some fine innings for the State team in Sheffield Shield matches. Playle, a right-hander with a wide array of strokes, toured England with New Zealand in 1958 but disappointed in a wet summer. He made only 414 runs in 23 matches, topscore 96 at Leicester. He also represented New Zealand in the 1962–63 series at home against England, scoring 65 at Wellington, his highest Test score. He made 18 appearances for WA in first-class matches, scoring 802 runs at 25.87. He was at his best on hard pitches and scored 122, his career best, at Perth against Queensland in 1965–66. In all first-class matches, Playle scored 2,888 runs at 21.87, with four centuries. His eight Tests brought 151 runs at 10.06. He was a safe, craftsmanlike fieldsman but seldom bowled.

POIDEVIN, Dr Leslie Oswald Sheridan, 1876–1931

First-Class Averages: Batting; 7,022 runs at 32.96; Bowling, 46 wickets at 41.89.

A prominent administrator, player and writer on Australian cricket, who also represented Australia in Davis Cup tennis. He first came to notice as a schoolboy with the Sydney club in the days before district cricket began. In 1887–88, he scored 231 and took all 19 wickets that fell to his side in a school match. He was a punishing right-hand batsman who, in 1894–95, played for New South Wales Colts against Stoddart's English touring side, alongside Victor Trumper and Monty Noble. In the 1918–19 season he became the first Australian to score a hundred centuries at all levels of cricket.

In 1895–96, while he was playing with the Glebe club, he was chosen at 19 for the official New South Wales team's tour of New Zealand, and headed the tour averages with 40.80 per innings. He also proved difficult for the New Zealanders to shift when they visited Sydney in 1899 and played New South Wales.

Poidevin made 140 not out in 1900–01 in New South Wales then world record first-class score of 918 in a Shield match against South Australia. Other scores in the New South Wales total included 168 by Sid Gregory, 153 by Noble, 119 by Reg Duff and 118 by Frank Iredale. South Australia lost by an innings and 605 runs, one of the worst defeats in first-class cricket. In 1901–02, Poidevin made 151 not out for New South Wales against McLaren's MCC side, New South Wales winning after trailing by 44 on the first innings, thanks to his match-winning effort in the second innings, when New South Wales reached 422. MCC managed 325 in reply.

Poidevin graduated in Arts from Sydney University and went to Edinburgh University to graduate in medicine, returning home occasionally to play cricket or tennis. In April, 1904, he scored 179 in a New South Wales total of 686 against Queensland at Sydney. From 1902 to 1908, he played County cricket with London County and Lancashire scoring 5,784 runs in seven seasons, hitting 11 of his 14 first-class centuries. He headed the Lancashire batting averages in 1905 with 1,376 runs at 44.38 despite the presence in the team of such noted players as J. T. Tyldesley, Archie McLaren and Reggie Spooner. In 1906 he played Davis Cup tennis for Australasia at Newport, Wales, and then dashed back to Lancashire to score a century for the County.

Kim Hughes drives a ball for four at Birmingham in 1981 when he captained Australia in Greg Chappell's absence.

The 1979 World Cup finalists at Lord's, with the team captains in front. L to R: Sri Lanka, Pakistan, the West Indies, England, Australia, New Zealand, India and Canada.

Above: Bob Simpson, seen square cutting in Sydney during his marvellous comeback in 1977–78.

Right: Max Walker, delivers a ball in his unique style.

For a number of years while he played London club cricket he represented the Australian Board of Control in England. Back in Sydney he played grade cricket for Glebe, North Sydney and Waverley, which he captained to three successive premierships in 1920–21, 1921–22, and 1922–23. He then joined the Waverley president, the well known industrial chemist F. P. Gray, in presenting a shield for competition among the best colts from Sydney district clubs. The Poidevin-Gray competition, originally an event in which other clubs had to challenge Waverley, became a mandatory annual contest for all district clubs and an invaluable proving ground for young cricketers.

PONSFORD, William Harold ("Puddin"), 1900–

A thickset, taciturn, camera-shy right-handed batsman who regarded scoring a 100 as a warm-up for his full assault on the bowling. He had a few years start on Bradman in big cricket and during those years was considered the heaviest scorer cricket has known. When Bradman arrived Ponsford was the only batsman who could bat with him without being outshone. Their partnerships were a duet of almost impregnable batsmanship.

Ponsford was the first batsman to score 400 in a first-class match outside England. He scored centuries in his first innings against four Australian States. He was the first batsman to score six centuries in an Australian season. He made 110 in his first Test innings and 110 in his first innings at Lord's. He is still the only batsman to score more than 400 in an innings twice. In 18 first-class innings in Australia between 1925 and 1928, he had 11 centuries. With E. R. Mayne, he set an Australian first wicket record of 456, with Bradman second and fourth wicket Test records of 451 and 388, and with McCabe, an Australian third wicket record of 389.

He was born in North Fitzroy, eight years before Bradman's birth at Cootamundra, and at Alfred Crescent School, Melbourne, grew into a powerful youth with a bulky backside, enormous calf muscles, and a shy, almost suspicious disposition. He played district cricket for St Kilda first grade at 16, but after making his debut in 1920 when Victoria had an enormously strong side found it difficult to win regular State selection. He had to break the world record for a first-class knock against Tasmania to win a spot in Victoria's Shield team. In his third first-class innings, he made 429 in 477 minutes, with 42 fours in February, 1923. Only Englishman Archie McLaren, with 424 for Lancashire against Somerset in 1895, had previously scored more than 400 in a first-class match. Ponsford repeated the feat in 1927–28 when he made 437 against Queensland.

In his first nine first-class matches, Ponsford scored 1,580

First-Class Averages: Batting, 13,819 runs at 65.18.

Tests (29): 2,122 runs at 48.22.

runs at an average of 121.54, and after that held his place in Victoria and State teams for the next 11 years, retiring early at the age of 34, satiated with run-getting. Critics such as Jack Fingleton said he quit because of the strain of the run-scoring standards he had set himself. In 1982, he remained the only batsman to have scored 300 in a day's play in Australia—he did it when he was 26 by making 334 in 5 hours 22 minutes against New South Wales, scored out of 573 runs.

Ponsford was so reserved even team-mates who remained close for months at a time on English tours found it hard to get to know him. He had a way of pulling his cap down over his eyes to thwart photographers after shots of his face as he went out the gate to bat. That cap peak went further round his head towards his left ear as his innings progressed. Ray Robinson said it was better than a bookmark. "If you saw the peak at a rakish angle close to his left ear, you knew he was heading for his second 100", said Robinson.

Ponsford's footwork was always precise, certain, but he was so bulky England captain Jardine once made the mistake of calling him slow-footed. This was nonsense as in 48 Test innings Ponsford was never out lbw and was only once out stumped, and he got down the pitch to drive half volleys with such certainty the ball really hammered into boundary fences. He was the world's finest player of spin bowling, and all the spinners of his period agreed that they preferred to bowl to Bradman than to Ponsford. Bradman gave you some chance, they said, Ponsford none.

When Ponsford's left hand was broken by a flyer from Larwood in the Second Test at Sydney in 1928–29, his substitute on the field was Bradman, who had been dropped for the only time in his career. Larwood undoubtedly curbed Ponsford's prolific scoring but in the Adelaide Test of the Bodyline series in 1932, Ponsford bravely took the fast stuff on his backside. His career ended in a spectacular flourish with innings of 181 in the Fourth Test at Leeds in 1934, and 266 in a stand of 451 with Bradman in the Fifth Test at The Oval. Ponsford was out hit wicket at The Oval after being missed six times in an innings of 455 minutes that included a five and 27 fours.

His record shows that he was vulnerable only to pace bowling of the highest quality such as Larwood provided and occasionally to wet pitches. His dislike of damp pitches was so strong he was said to wake in the night the moment even a few drops of rain fell. More than any batsman up to his time, he spurned the satisfaction of a century or a double-century, ferreting about furtively at the crease as he set out after more runs as he reached these marks.

When Ponsford volunteered for the RAAF in World War II, doctors discovered that he was colour blind and could not tell red from green. To a doctor who asked him how he had sight-

Bill Ponsford's stance was relaxed but alert with both eyes on the bowler.

W. F. Ponsford (295) and F. Yeomans (186) after they created an Australian record of 472 in a second wicket stand for Carlton against South Melbourne in 1926–27.

ed a cricket ball when batting, Ponsford said, "I never noticed its colour, only its size".

There was no showmanship in Ponsford's batting and he appeared to give no thought to the scoring rate, only to his job of subduing and carving up the bowling. He did it with such effectiveness rivals sometimes joked that his bat was wider than the legal limit. In fact, an umpire who measured his bat in a Sydney match found that Ponsford had hit his drives in the meat of the bat so often the edges had spread wider than the allowed $4\frac{1}{4}$ ins. The bat was scraped back to the lawful width with bottle tops, amid uproarious dressing-room laughter. Few noticed that there was hardly a mark on the edges of the bat, only on that tell-tale spot a few inches from the bottom where Ponsford pounded his cuts and drives.

"When Bradman and Ponsford batted together you saw no lopsided partnership of the kind in which the spotlight followed one batsman and the other was in the shadows, like a stage magician and his table shifting offsider", wrote Ray Robinson. "Bradman usually outshone his batting companions so much that sometimes you were barely conscious of their presence. But not Bill Ponsford. He was the only one who could play in Bradman's company and make it a duet, match-

804

ing Bradman in invincibility, concentration and endurance, keeping close to him in output of runs, and even surpassing him in some ways."

With Woodfull, Ponsford put together a remarkable 22 century partnerships and five stands over 200. One of the most notable paved the way to the highest total ever recorded in first-class cricket, 1,107 by Victoria against New South Wales in 1926. At the end of the first day, Victoria was 1 for 573, Ponsford 334 not out, Woodfull 133. Next day Ponsford reached 352 and then played a ball on to his stumps. He turned and looked mournfully at the wreckage and said, "Cripes, I am unlucky". Here is a list of the major Woodfull-Ponsford partnerships, which clearly shows that Ponsford invariably was the dominant scorer:

WOODFULL AND PONSFORD
THEIR CENTURY PARTNERSHIPS

FIRST WICKET	375	W. M. Woodfull (133) and W. H. Ponsford (352), Victoria v. New South Wales at Melbourne, Dec. 1926.
	236	W. M. Woodfull (106) and W. H. Ponsford (336), Victoria v. South Australia at Melbourne, Dec. 1927.
	227	W. M. Woodfull (99) and W. H. Ponsford (202), Victoria v. New South Wales at Melbourne, Dec. 1927.
	223	W. M. Woodfull (140) and W. H. Ponsford (131), Australia v. Rest (Macartney Benefit), Sydney, Feb. 1927.
	214*	W. M. Woodfull (107) and W. H. Ponsford (148), Australia v. Otago, at Dunedin, Feb. 1928.
	184	W. M. Woodfull (284*) and W. H. Ponsford (86), Australia v. New Zealand, at Auckland, March 1928.
	162	W. M. Woodfull (155) and W. H. Ponsford (81), Australia v. England (2nd Test), at Lords, June 1930.
	159	W. M. Woodfull (54) and W. H. Ponsford (110), Australia v. England (5th Test), at the Oval, Aug. 1930
	158†	W. M. Woodfull (73*) and W. H. Ponsford (84*), Victoria v. South Africa, at Melbourne, Feb. 1932.
	138	W. M. Woodfull (78) and W. H. Ponsford (200), Victoria v. New South Wales, at Sydney, Nov. 1932.
	122**	W. M. Woodfull (165) and W. H. Ponsford (58), Australia v. Wellington, at Wellington, Feb. 1928.
	118	W. M. Woodfull (34) and W. H. Ponsford (76), Australia v. an England XI, at Folkestone, Sep. 1930.
	117	W. M. Woodfull (51) and W. H. Ponsford (144), Australia v. Warwickshire, at Birmingham, Aug. 1926.
	115	W. M. Woodfull (56) and W. H. Ponsford (151), Victoria v. Queensland, at Melbourne, Dec. 1926.
	106	W. M. Woodfull (54) and W. H. Ponsford (83), Australia v. England (4th Test), at Manchester, July 1930.
	104	W. M. Woodfull (34) and W. H. Ponsford (84), Victoria v. South Australia, at Melbourne, Jan. 1927.
OTHER WICKETS	109	Second. W. M. Woodfull (67) and W. H. Ponsford (77), Victoria v. South Australia at Adelaide, Oct. 1924.
	178	Fourth. W. M. Woodfull (126) and W. H. Ponsford (138), Victoria v. New South Wales, at Sydney, Jan. 1926.
	133	Fourth. W. M. Woodfull (123) and W. H. Ponsford (108), Victoria v. South Australia, at Adelaide, Feb. 1923.
	183	Fifth. W. M. Woodfull (58) and W. H. Ponsford (183), Australia v. West Indies (2nd Test, Sydney), Jan. 1931.

*Not out.   †Unfinished.   **Recognised as First Class In New Zealand.

The great Yorkshire left-arm bowler Hedley Verity dismissed Bradman eight times in Tests but only got Ponsford once—and then when Ponsford's foot touched the stumps after hooking the ball to the fence and dislodged a bail. Bill O'Reilly has always said Ponsford's ability to concentrate made him the greatest batsman he ever bowled against. Ponsford concentrated so fiercely he sometimes lost track of where his stumps were and was bowled around his legs.

Ponsford toured England three times, in 1926, 1930 and 1934 and scored a total of 4,273 runs on these trips at 55.49. He made 110 in his Test debut at Sydney in 1924–25 and 128 in his second Test appearance at Melbourne the same summer. This wonderful start caused people to consider he had failed when he did not make a century but many of his best innings were for scores below 100. At Adelaide in 1932–33, he played a marvellous hand in scoring 85 in perhaps the most acrimonious match of all time, turning his back to take England's Bodyline stuff on his backside or upper back.

Ponsford was contemptuous of Bodyline. He had learned to play cricket under a code of ethics which suddenly had been changed. He was not frightened of Larwood and Voce, merely irked by their methods, which he believed were outside the bounds of fair play. At a time when newspapers were suggesting that he was afraid of Larwood, Ponsford went into the 1930 Test at The Oval and made 100 in 135 minutes and 110 of Australia's first 159 runs. Larwood let him have a surfeit of fast rising balls and positioned a fieldsman close in on the legside, but Ponsford came out clearly on top. For the rest, he was content to stick his ample backside at the English bowlers who tried to intimidate him.

After averaging 94.83 in the 1934 Test series in England, he retired to forego his job as a bank clerk for a post in journalism. Later he became assistant secretary of the Melbourne Cricket Club. It was noteworthy that at both the Centenary Test in Melbourne and later in its counterpart at Lord's he was apprehensive of interviewing journalists. Ponsford's cricket remains a game for deeds, not cameras.

"I always thought that Ponsford's premature retirement was due to his over-sensitivity to criticism," wrote Arthur Mailey. "This complex character harboured what seems to most of us an unwarranted suspicion that the Press were his mortal enemies. Off the field he was extremely modest, undemonstrative and congenial company, but on the field, with that heavy bat in his hand, he was tough and relentless to the point of being vindictive. I don't think it was the rungetting Ponny enjoyed so much as the bowlers' discomfort, especially when those bowlers came from New South Wales."

In all first-class cricket, he scored 47 centuries, with 13 innings over 200. In 29 Tests, he scored seven centuries. For Victoria in 55 matches, he scored 6,902 runs at 86.27, topscore 437.

Australian cricket's most dedicated "camp follower", notorious for the 40 or more pieces of luggage he took on trips with Australian teams that he made at his own expense. In those bags he stored everything he thought a touring cricket team might need. He was a doctor and a handy player, neat and correct in his batting style, an enthusiastic bowler of lobs, who fielded actively with a quick return.

He was born in Sydney, educated at Hutchin's School, Hobart, and was coached by the famous Tom Kendall. Later he played for Sydney University. In 1884–85, he scored 170 for Melbourne I Zingari against Richmond, and this innings won him invitations to play for New South Wales and Australia. With Australia's best team depleted by disagreements over match fees, he was called on to play in the Second Test at Melbourne in January, 1885. He made 0 and 3 and did not bowl.

Rowley Pope played regularly for Sydney University while he studied medicine and later while he was at Edinburgh University played first-class cricket for Scotland. After he had established a good practice in Sydney he went to England frequently with Australian teams. He was never an official member of a touring team but helped them out often when they were short. He made his debut at Lord's with the fifth Australian team in 1886, and played several games.

After World War I he went to England in 1921 and 1926 with the Australian sides and started to pack his bags with items he felt Australian players would need. When an Australian player went to his room in 1926 and asked for a button hook, Rowley was undismayed and dug into his bags and came up with a button hook, although the last Australian player to wear button up boots was Monty Noble back on the 1902 trip. The only player to get the better of Pope's gear was Edgar Mayne, who on the voyage home from England in 1921 asked for a bicycle pump. Pope could not produce one but thereafter always packed a bicycle pump in his luggage.

On the private tour of America in 1932, Arthur Mailey restricted Pope for the 100-day trip to 36 bags. On the voyage to America Vic Richardson realised that as the team's captain he would have to make around 30 speeches, so he visited Pope's cabin and sure enough was handed a three-volume history of the United States, a history of Canada, and a book on cricket in Philadelphia. In every town the team visited, Pope patiently unpacked all his bags and on the day of departure repacked the whole 36 bags. Team-members who fell ill usually ignored the ship's doctor and went to Pope's cabin for a dose of whatever he thought would fix them. Mailey, an ex-glassblower and water board labourer, said Pope was the man who taught him the difference between a fish knife and an ordinary one, and how to tie a bow tie.

POPE, Dr Roland James ("Rowley"), 1864–1952

First-Class Averages: Batting, 318 runs at 12.23.

Tests (1): 3 runs at 1.50.

PORTER, Graeme David, 1955–

First-Class Averages: Batting, 663 runs at 21.38; Bowling, 52 wickets at 31.51.

A steady right-arm medium-pace bowler and right-hand batsman who toured England and India with the Australian team soon after making his first-class debut in 1977–78. He had shown an ability to swing the ball either way in his few matches with WA but on tour with the national team disappointed, scoring only 63 runs in nine innings and taking only nine wickets. He has since shown sound form for Subiaco-Floreat and more recently for Fremantle without showing any of the form that made Australian team selectors pluck him from obscurity. He has batted everywhere from No. 1 to No. 8 for his grade clubs and usually struggles to make the ball wobble about as he did so strikingly early in his career.

POTTER, Jack, 1938–

First-Class Averages: Batting, 6,142 runs at 41.22; Bowling, 31 wickets at 41.51.

One of the best performed right-hand batsmen never to win Test selection. Potter, who scored one double century and 12 centuries for Victoria in compiling 5,101 runs at 42.50, scored 751 runs at 31.29 on tour in England with Bob Simpson's 1964 team, without making a century. At the end of the English part of the tour he suffered a skull fracture in a one-day match against Holland at The Hague and had to be sent home without accompanying the team in India and Pakistan.

He was an extremely handsome, dark-haired, splendidly built (5 ft 10 in, 12 st 4 lb), physical education teacher who played for Fitzroy. He made his debut for Victoria in 1956–57. Within a year he scored 115 against South Australia in a partnership of 221 for the fifth wicket with Sam Loxton, and scored a fine 110 against South Australia. He went to New Zealand with an Australia side in 1959–60.

In 1960–61 he put on 252 with Bill Lawry for Victoria against NSW, and 237 with Lawry against Queensland, second wicket stands that still rate among Victoria's highest. He made his highest score, 221, against NSW in 1965–66 at Melbourne. He was a firm believer in gaining pyschological advantages and when he was captain of Victoria instructed his fieldsmen not to talk to incoming batsmen and to turn their backs if the batsman spoke. He did not want batsmen to relax in the exchange of greetings. He stepped down from the State side at 29, asking selectors not to consider him for the 1967–68 side because he wanted a young player to be given a chance. In 104 first-class matches he held 85 catches. He was invariably entertaining, scoring his runs quickly.

PRICE, Reuben Henry, 1923–

A left-handed batsman and left-arm fast medium bowler from the East Perth and Fremantle clubs, a product of good pitches and sunshine, who was part of a hostile Western Australian attack in the early 1950s. The success of the Puckett,

Price and Dunn combination helped WA enormously in her first years in the Sheffield Shield competition. London-born Price, who played with East Perth and Fremantle, made his debut for WA in 1949–50 and in 26 first-class matches held 11 catches, four times took five wickets in an innings and once took 10 wickets in a match, best figures 5 for 49 against Queensland at Perth in 1950–51.

First-Class Averages: Batting, 378 runs at 13.50; Bowling, 93 wickets at 27.39.

PRIOR, Wayne, 1952–

A South Australian right-arm fast bowler and right-hand batsman who played with World Series Cricket but has not represented Australia. At his peak experts have rated him faster than Rodney Hogg. He is a placid, easy-going character until he gets a ball in his hand and sees a batsman at the other end. Apart from his success with the new ball, he has been effective in taking wickets late in an innings.

First-Class Averages: Batting, 185 runs at 8.04; Bowling, 136 wickets at 32.67.

Prior first played for South Australia in 1974–75. He was given special coaching before the start of his next season by SA coach Ernie Clifton aimed at building up his strength and accuracy. He took 6 for 41 against the West Indies at Adelaide and then had match figures of 10 for 168 against New South Wales, a match-winning effort including a hat-trick. With the match due to end at 5.30 p.m., Prior took the ball at 5.11 p.m. He dismissed Peter Toohey, Len Pascoe and David Hourn with successive balls. It was the first hat-trick for SA since Don Robins did it against NSW in 1965–66. Early in that innings a ball from Prior flattened NSW captain Doug Walters who fell on to his stumps and was out hit wicket. Prior took 42 wickets that season at 18.71.

When Prior signed to play with WSC in 1977, he lost his job. The SACA had got him the job with a motoring company who sacked him for signing an employment contract with another company. Since the settlement Prior has been involved on a farm he bought at Lobethal, SA, the demands of which forced him to make himself unavailable for the State side early in 1981–82. When he returned he was suspended for a month by the SACA for disputing an umpire's decision playing for his club, Salisbury, in district cricket. This forced him to miss the rest of the first-class season.

PRITCHARD, David Edward, 1893–

A dashing South Australian left-hander who produced a string of high scores in inter-State and club cricket in the decade after World War I. He hit the ball extremely hard and only the most accurate bowling could contain him when he was set. His pulls and hooks were hit with such force he was devastating on Adelaide Oval with its short boundaries square of the wicket. He bowled occasional medium-pacers.

First-Class Averages: Batting, 2,958 runs at 34.00; Bowling, 3 wickets at 34.06.

Pritchard headed the Adelaide district batting aggregates

in 1919–20 for Port Adelaide when he scored 846 runs at an average of 94.00, including a score of 203. This was enough to take him into the State team that year and he showed what was to come by scoring 91 in a stand of 200 for the third wicket at Melbourne against Victoria. He made the first of his five centuries on Adelaide Oval, 100, in 1921–22 against NSW. In 1924–25 he made 115 out of 288 for SA versus Victoria.

Perhaps his best first-class knock was his 167 against Western Australia at Adelaide in 1925–26, when he hit a six and 17 fours. In 1928–29 he hit 119 against Percy Chapman's England team. This was the season he scored 1,023 runs for Port Adelaide in district cricket at an average of 102.30, which included 327 not out. Merv Waite later played a bigger innings—339 in 1935–36—but Pritchard's 1,023 were the most runs in an Adelaide club season until 1976–77 when Barry Causby scored one run more. In December, 1929, he had scores of 148 and 75 against NSW at Adelaide and in 1929–30 made 80 against WA. He played in three successive Port Adelaide premiership teams, 1927–28, 1928–29, and 1929–30, and was a member of the South Australian side that won the Sheffield Shield in 1926–27.

PROVIDENT FUNDS FOR AUSTRALIAN CRICKETERS

Australian first-class cricketers now benefit from generous retirement funds designed to reward long service to the game. These schemes have replaced the old system of granting players benefit matches, and have the added advantage of safeguarding the Australian and State controlling bodies against misbehaviour, breach of contract or disloyalty to the game. Big sums are involved for players who have long Test careers, with lesser amounts payable to those who have long records in inter-State cricket.

All of the money due to players under these provident schemes are payable two years after the players retire and at the discretion of the Australian or State authorities. A player who contracted to appear in matches outside the Australian authorities jurisdiction would certainly jeopardise his payment from the funds as would a player who unfairly criticised the control bodies in the media. The amount paid players under the provident schemes are all in addition to their match payments, in 1981–82 standing at $1800 for a Test and $130 for a State game. States with sponsors add sponsorship money to these match fees. New South Wales players, for example, received $230 a match from brewery sponsors in 1981–82. All these amounts are in addition to their expenses.

The Australian Cricket Board conducts the most remunerative of the provident funds under which Test players have fixed amounts set aside for them after they have played the qualifying 20 Tests. One-day matches for Australia count as a quarter of a Test, so that a player with 10 Tests and 40 one-day matches to his credit would reach the qualifying mark.

At present the ACB credits Test players on the following scale in assessing their provident fund entitlements: For 1 to 20 Tests, $300; for 21 to 30 Tests, $500; for 31 to 40 Tests, $700; for 41 to 50 Tests, $800; for 51 Tests and over, $900. Thus Rodney Marsh, who is currently credited with 84 Tests will be entitled to $75,600 plus credit for one day matches under the scheme two years after he retires, a major consideration if, say, he was offered a contract to play in South Africa. Other players with long service entitlements to come from State and Test appearances would think carefully if contracts such as those offered in the WSC years were again available.

The ACB has already paid useful sums to long-serving Test players like Bob Simpson, Ian Redpath and Terry Jenner under the scheme and expects to pay out to a lot more in the next few years as long-serving players come up for payment. The Board has revised the scheme repeatedly since it began in 1974 and has the schedule under regular review. Players who appeared in Tests before 1974 can count the Tests in which they appeared towards the minimum qualifying mark but are not paid for those Tests.

Apart from the ACB scheme each State now controls a provident or retirement fund for long-serving State players. The amounts the States credit to each player after they reach the qualifying number of appearances depends on the affluence of the States concerned—but they still guarantee valuable rewards. As with ACB's fund for Test players, no payments are made until two years after players retire and all payments are at the discretion of the State associations. The associations are under no legal compulsion to settle with individual players.

Victoria's scheme provides for a credit of $50 for every match after players qualify by making 40 first-class appearances with Victorian teams. The VCA also credits Victorian players in the scheme with $50 for every Test and $12.50 for each one-day match. The Victorian plan provides for payments to a player's widow or dependants in the event of the player's death.

South Australia also has a qualifying proviso of 40 matches but credits players with $40 for every match once they reach that qualifying mark. But South Australia does not credit players with any match in which they have been found guilty of an offence by the Australian Cricket Board or by the Players Cricket Committee. South Australia also refuses payment to any player who transfers to another State to play Sheffield Shield cricket unless the SACA recommends payment by a two-thirds majority.

New South Wales and South Australia make no additional credits for Test appearances or for one-day matches. NSW credits players with $40 a match once they have played 40 matches, but in Western Australia, the only State where Sheffield Shield crowds have been consistently high in recent years, the WACA retirement fund credits players with $100 a match once they have played 40 qualifying matches.

All of the schemes have been regularly revised since the States introduced them after the last official benefit matches were played for Test stars. In all States payments per match have increased since the funds began. Experience had shown that some benefit matches were poor drawcards and they became extremely difficult to fit into packed first-class itineraries. The existence of the provident funds is clear evidence that administrators acknowledge their debt to long-serving players. Equally there is no doubt that efforts to improve the provident schemes were accelerated by the advent of WSC. From the players' standpoint the major anomaly that remains is that of Brian Booth, one of the most admired players in the history of Australian cricket, received nothing from the ACB for playing 29 Tests. Had he played one more Test under the scheme that operated in his time he would have qualified and had he played today he would have played nine Tests more than the present qualifying mark.

PUCKETT, Charles William, 1911–

First-Class Averages: Batting, 643 runs at 14.95; Bowling, 158 wickets at 25.58.

The "iron man" of Western Australian cricket whose stamina and versatility proved invaluable to his adopted State. Puckett, born at Beddington Corner, Surrey, played for West Perth, for whom he topped the Perth first grade bowling averages five times between 1940–41 and 1952–53. He first played for WA in 1939–40 and in 37 first-class matches took five wickets in an innings 14 times and twice took 10 wickets in a match. He often opened the bowling with his right-arm fast medium-pacers and returned later for a long session of off-breaks. He was an authentic tailender who made only one first-class fifty. His allround fielding was brilliant, as expected from an inter-State baseballer.

Puckett, the first West Australian to take 100 wickets in Sheffield Shield matches, kept going for hour after hour but still chased the ball enthusiastically at the end of the day. He never seemed to tire. He had his first big success in 1946–47 when he took 5 for 126 in a long bowl for WA against England at Perth. In 1947–48 he took 5 for 56 and 6 for 78 against India at Perth and 24 wickets at 24.79 in Shield matches to help WA win the Shield at its first attempt. In 1949–50 he had a spell of 32 wickets at 18.87 each in only four games. This won him a trip to New Zealand with Bill Brown's Australian team at the age of 39. He took 5 for 24 against Otago to set up Australia's win by an innings and 356 runs.

He continued to bowl long spells for WA after his 40th

birthday, and had his career best figures of 6 for 35 against South Australia at Perth in 1951–52. That was the season he also took 5 for 45 against the crack West Indies side at Perth, combining with Henry Price and Peter Dunn in a pace attack that helped WA to a commendable victory. He kept going until the 1952–53 season when his best effort was 5 for 119 against South Africa at Perth. He was unfortunate that in his prime years great bowlers Lindwall, Miller and Johnston held the Australian team places his whole-hearted efforts deserved.

PUNCH, Austin Thomas Eugene, 1894–

A right-hand batsman and right-arm leg-break bowler who played played ten seasons of first-class cricket immediately after World War I. He played 31 matches for New South Wales between the 1919–20 and 1928–29 seasons and toured New Zealand with the New South Wales team in 1923–24. He also played one match for Tasmania in 1927–28. He made one first-class century, 176, against Otago in 1923–24, and captained NSW in one match in 1923–24. He took five wickets in a match only once. Although his figures were not spectacular he generally contributed useful runs and wickets and was a fine field. He was a stalwart of the North Sydney club from the time he headed the Sydney first grade batting aggregates in 1917–18 with 750 runs at 57.69 and he remains the club's highest scoring batsman with a career total of 8,682 runs in first grade at 36.78. He also took 192 wickets for the club in first grade at 27.72. In 1911–12, he took five wickets in five balls for the club's third grade at the age of 17.

First-Class Averages: Batting, 1,717 runs at 35.04; Bowling, 35 wickets at 29.82.

**QUEENSLAND,
CRICKET IN**

Cricket began in Queensland, Australia's youngest State, as a relaxation for the tough and hardy pioneers who moved into virgin country after Brisbane was established as a convict settlement in 1823. The early games were played barefoot with primitive equipment in areas lacking passable roads. Enthusiasm was high, the standards low. Unlike England, where cricket developed in an already civilised and long established community, Queensland cricket was pioneered by settlers as they carved out a completely new State.

The first recorded reference to cricket in Queensland appeared in the second issue of the *Moreton Bay Courier* on June 27, 1846, 13 years before Queensland was separated from New South Wales and given its own identity. Under the heading "Cricket," the *Moreton Bay Courier* said, "As a finale to the amusement of Race Week, a challenge from eleven of the working men of Brisbane to play an equal number of gentlemen for five pounds ten shillings a side, was accepted by the latter, and the match came off on the terrace leading to the government gardens. The gentlemen were successful, beating their opponents easily. The stakes were generously handed over by the losing party. Arrangements were made for another match to come off in the next year's Race Week."

The *Moreton Bay Courier* on August 26, 1847, under the heading "Hints For Cricketers," showed there was interest in the game by publishing some extremely basic laws of the game: "The stumps must be three in number; twenty seven inches out of the ground; the bails eight inches in length; the stumps of equal and sufficient thickness to prevent the ball passing through."

The colony which was then part of New South Wales was divided into two administrative districts, Brisbane and the Darling Downs, the best of which had all been claimed by 1842. On October 18, 1848, the *Moreton Bay Courier* reported that a cricket club had been established at Ipswich and the first game played on October 13. The club had 20 members, who, when sufficiently practised, intended to challenge the

Brisbane club. "Such a pastime as this ought to meet with encouragement, as it certainly tends to the preservation of health," the paper said.

The same paper ended its report on the races at Drayton, later an outer suburb of Toowoomba, with the news that as the races had ended early on the first day (May 14, 1850), a cricket match "was got up on the afternoon of the two following days between eleven squatters and eleven Draytonians. The Squatters XI 40 (Bell 7) and 48 (Wiggins 13) defeated the Drayton XI 24 and 21. Knights took 12 wickets for Drayton. As a result the Ipswich Cricket Club challenged the Squatters XI to a match at Ipswich on June 14. Ipswich won by scoring 66 (Goode 14, Byrnes 11) and 68 (Wilkinson 12, Warren 20 not out) against the Squatters XI 69 (Thelwell 16, Burgoyne 23) and 59 (Burgoyne 25, Walker 11). Cricket was played at Drayton over the Christmas period in 1850 and at Ipswich over the Christmas-New Year holidays in 1854–55.

When Brisbane played Ipswich at North Quay, Brisbane, in 1859, the home team made 322, with Joseph Bolger one of the first Queensland cricket heroes "standing for three and a half hours under a hot sun" to score 118. According to Hutcheon's *History of Queensland Cricket*, this was almost certainly the first century scored in Queensland. By now clubs were regularly founded, and in 1860, two matches were played between Toowoomba and Dalby. The powerful Albert club was formed in 1861 and the same year the South Brisbane club met the United (or North) Brisbane Club. Joseph Bolger and George Cowlishaw did well for the Southern team but Hall led North Brisbane to victory by scoring 55 not out. South Brisbane won the return match by seven wickets, Bolger taking 10 for 51. Attempts were made at this time to entice visiting English teams to Brisbane but the Brisbane organisers were unable to agree on terms with either H. H. Stephenson's 1861–62 side or George Parr's 1863–64 side.

At a meeting on December 23, 1861, called to form a cricket authority, it was agreed to set up the Brisbane Cricket Club, with the officers to be named after a grand challenge single wicket match on January 11, 1862. Originally stakes for this match were £10 a side but when it was found that Joe Bolger had included in his side George Cowlishaw "a crack from Sydney," and brother of the Brisbane Cowlishaw, the stake was waived and the teams played "for love." Plank's team, comprising G. Plank, D. Jacobs and J. Meades made 9 for 5, Joe Bolger's team, comprising J. Birley, J. Bolger and G. Cowlishaw made 46. Cowlishaw took two wickets and made 27. The governor, Sir George Bowen, was patron when officers of the Brisbane Club were announced, and the Colonial Secretary, the Honourable R. G. W. Herbert, president.

The Brisbane club began by staging a match between Marrieds and Singles, which the Singles won by 10 wickets. Next

Queensland XI, 1907. (L to R) Standing, W. A. Armstrong, C. B. Barstow, S. J. Whittred, M. M. F. Dunn, G. F. Martin, Seated, W. B. Hayes, E. R. Crouch, W. T. Evans, R. J. Hartigan, S. J. Redgrave, (In front) J. W. McLaren, J. Thomson.

a single wicket match was held between a Mr Launder and a Mr Putman, but this came to an abrupt end when Mr Putman was given out for handling the ball. The high percentage of byes was a problem in these early matches and a reliable long-stop was a big advantage.

One of the most publicised matches in the formative years was between an All Brisbane team and "a hot eleven" from the migrant ship *Flying Cloud*, supposedly made up of strong Kentish players. Reporting this match at Greenhills on January 22, 1863, the *Courier Mail* said: "The Oval was properly marked out, and tents were pitched for the competitors and scorers. Mrs Ahern, of St Patrick's Tavern, had a large marquee erected . . . there was a good attendance of spectators . . . the play on both sides was remarkably good." The *Courier* praised the batting of the men from the *Flying Cloud* and added that the fielding of the Brisbane side was "very superior." All Brisbane scored 93 and 1 for 19, the *Flying Cloud* side

62 and 47, the Cowlishaw brothers bowling well, and All Brisbane won by nine wickets.

Up country cricket included a match between Dalby and Toowoomba in April, 1864. Toowoomba could only make 21, but star bowlers Hull and Crane then routed Dalby for nine. Toowoomba replied with a second innings of 37, but after a tense struggle Dalby reached 9 for 50 and victory. There were a lot of squabbles during the game and at the dinner after the match a lot of bitterness, culminating in the Dalby side walking out after a tirade of abuse from some of the Toowoomba players. The next season a Brisbane team played the passengers of the *Golden City*, "Jem" Moore and Joe Cowlishaw bowling them out for 31 and 21 to give Brisbane a win by an innings.

In other matches, the Banks played the Civil Service and a team from *The Guardian* newspaper played the Government Printing Office. Then a series of matches were played to prepare players for the first inter-Colonial match. One of them was a complete disaster against Sixteen of Ipswich, who made only 56 but then dismissed the cream of Brisbane's cricketers for only four runs. George Cowlishaw scored two, there were two byes and 10 batsmen had ducks. T. B. Foden, who took 4 for 2 for Ipswich, was included in Queensland's team that played NSW.

Foden bowled admirably in the first innings of the big match, taking 6 for 6 against the NSW team led by Charles Lawrence, and there was not a double figure score in NSW's total of 32. Queensland, who batted XXII against NSW XI, lost 8 for 16 on the first day but scraped into the lead with a total of 45, in which sundries topscored with 11. The bowling of Lawrence and Nat Thompson, who bowled unchanged was highly praised, as was the NSW wicket-keeper J. Foulis, later a doctor in Edinburgh. NSW's second innings began with seven wides in his first 11 balls from Shaw and thanks to 42 from Clarke and 28 from Lawrence, NSW made 145. The XXII of Queensland could only manage 49 in their second innings, Thompson taking 7 for 25 to go with his 7 for 9 in the first innings. Joe Bolger topscored for Queensland with 26. The scorecard of this first encounter between the States credited runouts to the bowlers. In Queensland's first innings, for example, Deedes played a ball from Lawrence, left his crease, and was run out by Neale, but the wicket was given to Lawrence.

The *Courier Mail* criticised the players for starting play late, condemned people who preferred to stay outside the fence rather than pay the shilling entrance fee, and complained that the ground was damp and spongy with plenty of sawdust required. The Courier added, however, that the "state of the ground could not militate against the display of first-class cricket, but in spite of frequent slips and capsizes, jumping after the ball into waterholes and other unavoidable mishaps, an amount of good play was exhibited by both sides." NSW won by 163 runs, leaving Queenslanders with the uncomfortable feeling that they had failed to include in their team many of the first-class cricketers from English universities and county teams who were scattered over a large area of the State.

In tropical Queensland clubs had been formed at Maryborough (1860), Gladstone (1868), Rockhampton (1862), and at Clermont a local side backed by the town's publican played frequent matches. In towns that could only be reached by ship before the railways went in, there were plenty of players worth considering for the State teams. In Bowen, which is credited with staging the first match in North Queensland, the Bowen CC played the crew of the survey vessel Pioneer in 1862, and the Port Denison Times in November, 1863, reported a further match between the locals and the crew of the survey ship Salamander. Conway's Australian Cricketer's Annual for 1876–1877 claimed there were no less than seven sugar planters around Mackay who had played in Oxford or Cambridge Elevens.

While Queensland was having difficulty picking her best players, NSW had no such problem. On Queensland's first visit to Sydney for an inter-Colonial match in April, 1865, NSW included William Caffyn, whom the Queenslanders considered to be a Melbourne man. Caffyn made 55 in NSW's first innings of 198. The Queenslanders were appeased by promises that Caffyn, Lawrence and Nat Thompson would go to Brisbane for future inter-Colonial games. Indeed it became the custom for NSW to send her best players to help improve Queensland's standards. In 1875, the NSW team that went north included "Alick" Bannerman, then only 16, and Tom Garrett, 17. Batting XVIII against NSW's XI, Queensland that year had her first win over NSW, with the Queenslander W. Sheehan winning a cup for the highest scorer by making 20.

Before it wound up, the Brisbane committee that organised this inter-Colonial match instructed its secretary to call a meeting of cricketers interested in forming a Cricket Association. On April 5, 1876, at the Australian Hotel the first meeting of delegates from clubs elected officers for the new association and set up a committee to frame the association's rules. Sir Maurice O'Connell became the first president. Clubs represented at the association's first meeting were the Albert, Stanley, Milton, GPO, Police, Eagle Farm and Shaws. Country clubs soon joined and within two years delegates from Toowoomba and Warwick clubs attended association meetings.

In 1887 at Eagle Farm racecourse, the first Australian XI played a Queensland XVIII. Queensland scored 58 and 68, the Australian XI 149, with Charles Bannerman scoring 74. In 1884, two matches were played at Eagle Farm between a NSW

XI and XVIII of Queensland, and Queensland won them both, the first by 73 runs and the second by an innings and 17 runs. These results delighted the Queensland officials who within a few days arranged the first 11-a-side match against NSW. This match was left unfinished after Queensland scored 58 and NSW 8 for 164.

After further wins over NSW, Queensland graduated in 1893 to permanent 11-a-side matches, and from that date all Queensland matches were ranked as first-class. A setback came for the QCA between 1895 and 1899 when an opposition body, the National Cricket Union, conducted a competition and played annual matches against NSW, the Union's strength was its Wednesday competition. The NCU had W. Welsby as its chairman and W. S. Cowell as secretary and many of its best players were former QCA club players. Finally when South Australia played Queensland for the first time in a visit to Brisbane in 1899 and defeated the Queensland side by an innings and 284 runs—Joe Darling made 210, George Giffen 115—this unhappy result had the effect of bringing the rival controlling bodies together and an amalgamation was arranged that brought all NCU players under the Association's control.

Victoria paid her first visit to Brisbane in 1903 and gave Queensland a hiding, with Warwick Armstrong scoring 145, Harry Graham 101 and Tuckwell 93 in the Victorian total of 490. Then Queensland could not handle Saunders (6 for 57)

Queensland XI v New South Wales, 1908, (L to R) Standing, G. White, W. B. Hayes, G. F. Martin, J. S. Hutcheon, W. T. Evans, G. A. L. Brown, E. R. Crouch, Seated, G. M. Colledge (Hon. Sec.), J. Thomson, S. J. Redgrave, R. J. Hartigan (Capt.), C. E. Simpson, J. W. McLaren, W. B. Hill (Scorer).

Queensland Sheffield Shield Team, 1930. Standing, H. Leeson, G. Amos, E. Gilbert, E. Bensted, K. Mossop. Sitting, H. M. Thurlow, R. K. Oxenham, P. M. Hornibrook, F. J. Gough, F. C. Thompson, A. Hurwood, M. Biggs.

and Laver (6 for 17) and were dismissed for 123 and 40. An encouraging aspect of the game for Queensland was the brilliance of W. T. Evans, one of the State's long list of distinguished wicket-keepers.

A feature of these years were the tours organised by Victor Trumper and Roger Hartigan to take teams sprinkled with star players into the remote areas of Queensland, centres that could only be reached by boat. Hartigan had a special joy in promoting these tours, when entire towns stopped work to watch the play, and the local inhabitants all came down to the boat to greet the visitors. At Cairns, Charters Towers, Townsville and Cooktown matches were played in temperatures over 120 degrees Fahrenheit. The strong Brisbane Graziers club sent one team north under the captaincy of P. S. McDonnell in 1894 that defeated Eighteen of Townsville, Eighteen of Charters Towers, a Combined Townsville-Charters Towers XI, Eighteen of Mackay and drew with a North Queensland side. In 1906 Trumper's team played matches against the odds in Charters Towers, Townsville, Rockhampton, Mt Morgan, Bundaberg, Maryborough, and Gympie, winding up the tour with two matches against strong Brisbane sides. In each centre all business stopped

820

while the population went to the cricket to watch Trumper bat.

One of the early delegates to the QCA was J. M. Hutcheon, who represented the Warwick district. His sons, E. H. and J. S. Hutcheon, became strongmen of the QCA after enjoyable careers as players devoting themselves to securing regular visits to Queensland by English teams and to the inclusion of Queensland in the Sheffield Shield competition. Every big defeat suffered by Queensland—and there were plenty of them in the early years of this century—added to the Hutcheons resolve to build up Queensland's strength by importing top-class coaches, improving wickets and whatever else was needed.

Queensland cricketers were elated in February, 1883, to receive a visit from the Hon. Ivo Bligh's English team, and the Shaw and Shrewsbury team included Brisbane on their itinerary in 1885. Two years later the Shaw and Lillywhite team played at Maryborough and Gympie. A sad feature for Queensland was the reluctance of outstanding players developed in the State to remain once they had made their names. J. A. Cuffe went off to Worcestershire, Alan Marshal to Surrey, Dr R. MacDonald to Leicestershire, and without them successes were hard-won.

After World War I a strong State team was built around O'Connor, Thompson, Hornibrook and the Oxenhams, and at every meeting of the Australian Board of Control delegates Roger Hartigan and Jack Hutcheon pushed Queensland's case for recognition as a Shield State and for Brisbane to be given a Test match. They were both outstanding debaters and exploited every win on the field by Queensland but they had to convince the other Board delegates that Queensland's pitches were of first-class standards and that the cost of sending first-class players all the way to Queensland was justified.

A public meeting was held in Brisbane to try and have a Test played in Brisbane during England's tour in 1924–25, but without success. The break-through finally came in 1926–27 when Queensland was included in the Shield competition. The first match was a thriller against NSW, with only a fighting 127 by Kippax enabling NSW to reach 280 in the first innings. Queensland replied with 356 to establish a useful lead. NSW then recovered to make 475 in their second knock. Set to score 400 to win, Queensland started badly losing three batsmen cheaply, including first innings century-maker F. C. Thompson. Then great efforts by O'Connor and R. K. Oxenham gave the Exhibition Ground crowd a hint of victory. With eight runs needed, Gordon Amos ran out O'Connor with a lightning throw.

The second major landmark for Queensland came with the staging of the first Test in Brisbane in November and December, 1928. Bradman in his first Test made only 18 as Australia

Alan Marshal

821

chased England's first innings score of 521. The match was a disaster for Australia with Jack Gregory's knee finally giving way and Kelleway retiring with food poisoning. Larwood took 6 for 32 in Australia's first innings of 122 and J. C. ('Farmer') White 4 for 7 in Australia's second innings of 66 and Australia lost by a massive 675 runs. But Brisbane had shown she could efficiently stage a Test match. The venue for this match, the Brisbane Exhibition Ground, was a fine natural amphitheatre but too many spectators were admitted free by using their Agricultural Society membership badges. To ensure bigger returns through the gate the QCA later switched to the ground at Woollongabba.

Although Queensland teams had some notable successes before World War II the State did not often figure high on the Sheffield Shield table. But Queensland did produce some great players, notably Don Tallon, Wally Grout, Ron Oxenham, Billy Brown, Peter Burge, Geoff Dymock, and Percy Hornibrook. But the old problems of trying to develop youngsters in a State of such vast distances have not been solved with the railways or the aeroplanes. Queensland schools do not have the impressive lists of Test players among their former pupils boasted by schools in the south, though Brisbane Grammar School did produce Otto Nothling, Alec Hurwood, H. M. Thurlow, Ross Duncan and David Ogilvie.

This is why Queensland was wise to import so many of their star players after World War II, names who could inspire the State's youth, ranging from Ray Lindwall, Colin McCool, Alan Border, Jeff Thomson, and the magnificent Greg Chappell. With these players Queensland has played a far more prominent role in the Sheffield Shield, but the packed schedule undertaken by today's cricket stars means they are often absent when Queensland needs them most. The Sheffield Shield victory Queensland cricket fans crave may still elude the State but recent impressive performances by native Queenslanders and wins in limited over competitions demonstrates there is plenty of talent in the sunshine State, and that their first Shield win may not be far away. As in the early days of Queensland cricket, the problem is to get all the State's best players on to the field at the same time.

QUEENSLAND CRICKET ASSOCIATION
Presidents

1867–79	Sir Maurice O'Connell	1922–24	Mr Justice McNaughton
1880–82	Hon. J. P. Bell	1924–26	J. N. Horton
1883–94	B. D. Morehead	1926–57	J. S. Hutcheon
1895–99	Hon. T. J. Byrnes	1957–64	Arthur C. Dibdin
1899–91	Hon. E. J. Stevens	1964–65	Dr Otto Nothling
1901–02	George Down	1965–69	Hon. Sir T. Hiley
1902–16	Col. The Hon. J. F. G. Foxton	1969–78	D. G. Murphy
1916–21	T. M. W. McWilliam	1978–	H. R. Tanner
1921–22	Mr Justice Blair		

822

Secretaries

1876–77	J. Gaul	1910–11	J. Ashton*
1878	G. Down	1911–14	A. Brazil
1879	H. W. Banbury	1914–19	R. A. Alexander
1880	C. Gardiner,	1919–21	H. Sunderland
	W. D. Armstrong	1921–22	G. Ward
1881–83	G. Down, J. C. Bourne	1922–23	G. Brown
1884–86	S. Wearne	1923–42	R. T. Stephens
1887–88	G. Prentice	1942–60	T. E. Williams
1889	J. J. Taylor	1961–66	B. M. Gibbs
1890	J. Parlane	1966–69	L. A. Nash
1891	J. J. Taylor	1969–71	L. D. Cooper
1892	R. Doran	1972–73	Mrs F. Harvey
1892–93	F. Bone	1974–75	M. L. Robins
1894	Dr R. McDonald, H. V. Hewitt	1975–77	T. R. Veivers
1895	W. H. Beattie	1977–80	W. P. McCarthy
1895–96	F. R. Smith	1980–	G. H. Evans
1896–97	W. H. Sayer, G. M. College	*First Paid Secretary	
1897–08	G. M. Colledge	Alderman C. Jones acted as secretary from	
1908–10	S. C. Whittred	October, 1971, to June, 1972.	

RECORD PARTNERSHIPS FOR QUEENSLAND

Wkt		
1st	265	G. G. Cook and W. A. Brown v NSW (Syd), 1938–39.
2nd	243	R. Reynolds and J. McLaughlin v SA (Adel), 1957–58.
3rd	304	G. M. Ritchie and K. C. Wessels v Tas (Dev), 1981–82.
4th	295	P. J. Burge and T. Veivers v SA (Bris), 1962–63.
5th	231	K. D. Mackay and R. G. Archer v Vic (Bris), 1953–54.
6th	238	R. McDonald and O. Cowley v Hawke's Bay (Napier), 1896–97.
7th	335	C. W. Andrews and E. Bensted v NSW (Syd), 1934–35.
8th	146	T. V. Hohns and G. Dymock v Vic (Melb), 1978–79.
9th	152*	A. T. W. Grout and W. Walmsley v NSW (Syd), 1956–57.
10th	105*	W. Walmsley and J. Freeman v NSW, (Bris) 1957–58.

*Denotes unbeaten partnership.
Note: The sixth wicket record was on a tour of New Zealand by the Queensland side. The sixth wicket record in Australia is 211, shared by J. Bratchford and T. R. Veivers against South Australia (Brisbane), 1959–60.

OUTSTANDING QUEENSLAND BATSMEN

Batsman	Career	Matches	Innings	Not out	H. Score	Runs	Average	Centuries
S. C. Trimble	1959–1976	133	246	14	252*	9465	40.79	24
P. J. Burge	1952–1968	91	150	14	283	7627	56.08	24
K. D. Mackay	1946–1964	109	175	26	223	6875	46.14	16
G. S. Chappell	1973–1982	45	73	10	194	5001	79.38	19
W. A. Brown	1936–1950	50	90	4	215	4567	53.10	9
D. Tallon	1933–1954	86	153	8	193	4355	30.03	6
P. H. Carlson	1969–1981	89	157	14	110*	4144	28.97	5
F. C. Thompson	1912–1934	54	99	9	275*	3966	44.06	10
J. A. Maclean	1968–1979	96	166	20	156	3652	25.01	2
G. R. Reynolds	1955–1964	53	87	9	203*	3626	46.48	12
G. G. Cook	1931–1948	67	123	9	169*	3426	30.05	3
R. E. Rogers	1935–1949	51	95	1	181	3382	35.97	8
A. T. W. Grout	1946–1966	94	147	9	119	3351	24.28	3
D. F. E. Bull	1956–1968	67	116	7	167*	3292	30.20	5
T. R. Veivers	1958–1968	55	92	12	137	3092	38.65	3
L. P. D. O'Connor	1912–1930	43	82	5	196	3084	40.05	8
R. K. Oxenham	1911–1937	70	129	16	162*	3082	27.27	4

OUTSTANDING QUEENSLAND BOWLERS

Bowler	Career	Matches	Runs	Wickets	Average	B.B.	5W	10W
G. Dymock	1971–1982	87	8533	309	27.61	6/79	8	—
R. K. Oxenham	1911–1937	70	5236	231	22.66	6/45	10	2
J. R. Thomson	1974–1982	46	4852	209	23.21	7/33	13	2
P. J. Allan	1959–1969	52	5085	199	25.55	10/61	11	3
L. J. Johnson	1946–1953	48	4613	191	24.15	7/43	14	1
V. N. Raymer	1940–1957	71	6131	191	32.09	7/100	6	1
C. L. McCool	1945–1953	47	5984	189	31.66	7/74	15	1
J. R. F. Duncan	1964–1971	58	5856	186	31.48	8/55	7	1
F. M. Francke	1971–1980	52	4932	161	30.63	6/62	7	1
K. D. MacKay	1946–1964	109	4787	134	35.72	5/15	5	—
A. R. Dell	1970–1975	39	3498	131	26.70	6/17	6	1
G. G. Cook	1931–1948	67	4392	124	35.41	6/94	2	—
P. H. Carlson	1969–1981	89	3006	122	24.64	7/42	5	1
J. R. Bratchford	1952–1960	53	3537	120	29.47	6/57	3	—
B. Fisher	1954–1968	50	3668	116	31.62	6/41	4	—
R. G. Paulsen	1966–1972	44	4407	116	37.99	7/73	4	—
R. R. Lindwall	1954–1960	34	2732	115	23.75	7/92	6	—
J. R. E. MacKay	1959–1967	47	3660	115	31.82	5/56	3	—
O. J. Morgan	1965–1970	37	3266	113	28.90	6/42	6	—
T. R. Veivers	1958–1968	55	3785	104	36.39	5/63	2	—
W. T. Walmsley	1954–1959	28	3073	102	30.12	6/56	3	—

QUICK, Ian William, 1933–

First-Class Averages: Batting, 816 runs at 14.06; Bowling, 195 wickets at 30.36.

A right-handed batsman and slow left-arm bowler who toured England with the 1961 Australian team. The selectors gambled that he would be assisted by English pitches but Quick never appeared likely to force his way into the Test side. He took 50 wickets on the tour at 34.02. The selectors could not be blamed for his failure to progress to the Test team for the other three players they introduced to international cricket on that tour, Bill Lawry, Graham McKenzie and Brian Booth, were outstanding successes.

Quick, who came from Geelong and played for the South Melbourne club, proved a shy, reserved character on tour, preferring to sit in his hotel room listening to music than get out and see the sights. Team-mates nicknamed him "Cure 'em" and were mesmerised during the Manchester Test when Australian captain Richie Benaud called for drinks with Ted Dexter 76 not out and really punishing the bowling. Spectators thought it was a stalling tactic and heckled the Australians and poor "Cure 'em" Quick, as twelfth man, was obliged to carry the drinks out with the crowd calling for blood. Dexter was out soon after the resumption and Australia pulled off a dramatic win.

Quick first won selection in the Victorian team in 1956–57 and took 6 for 65 that season against Western Australia. He took five wickets in an innings seven times and 10 wickets in a match once in a first-class career that spanned five seasons. His best figures were 7 for 47 against Western Australia in 1958–59. He toured New Zealand with the Australian team in 1959–60 after taking 7 for 64.

R

A powerful, big, blond Queensland right-arm fast bowler and tailend right-hand batsman from Brisbane's Wynnum-Manly club. Since his first-class debut in 1979–80 he has had matches when he looked the best of Australia's aspiring young pace bowlers, but he has been dogged by injuries and has never produced the figures that would have won him Australian team selection. His 5 for 25 in his first season of big cricket remains his best effort, although he has shown consistent ability to dismiss opening batsmen.

Rackemann, born at Kingaroy, the son of a farmer, was one of the Esso company's three scholarship-winners in England in 1981. This enabled him to play for 12 weeks in England during which he assisted the Australian touring team in a minor match. But for injury he would have been recruited to the Australian team ahead of Michael Whitney, who played for Australia in the last two Tests of that tour. When he returned home, Rackemann tried to return to first-class cricket before he was fully fit and his back problems compelled him to miss the rest of the 1981–82 Australian season after only two matches.

RACKEMANN, Carl Grey, 1960–

First-Class Averages: Batting, 55 runs at 3.92; Bowling, 48 wickets at 37.66.

A family of four brothers brought up on a Queensland sheep farm who played a prominent role in the early development of Australian cricket. The family migrated from Gloucestershire and resided at Cambooya on the Darling Downs. At least two of the boys were born at Eton Vale, Queensland. The family's significance is that they were among the first settlers to return to England from the new colony to play cricket. They all played in early matches in Queensland.

Marmaduke Francis Ramsay (1860–1947) was born in Gloucestershire and played at Lord's in 1878 and 1879 but by 1887 was living at Cambooya. He played regularly in Queensland, usually in the Darling Downs district, and was in the

RAMSAY, THE FAMILY

Queensland XI in 1892. He also played for Queensland against Shaw's English team in 1885. The *Toowoomba Chronicle* reported in July 1894 that he had played in the MCC v. Leicestershire match at Lord's in May that year, scoring 17 and 58. He played again in Toowoomba in the 1895–96 season.

Robert Christian Ramsay (1861–1957) was born at Cheltenham, Gloucestershire, played cricket at Elstree School and at Harrow, where he was in the XI in 1879 and 1880. He was a useful slow bowler and effective batsman and won his Blue at Cambridge but disappointed in the University match. He took 12 wickets for 179 against Murdoch's 1882 Australian team, however, and 13 for 49 against MCC. He was known as "Twisting Tommy" because of "his curly leg-break". He played for Somerset after leaving Cambridge but after a short first-class career settled in Bourke, NSW, and later at Cambooya, Qld. He played for a Darling Downs XI in Brisbane and for I Zingari in Warwick.

Arthur Douglas Ramsay, born at Eton Vale, Qld, in 1868, played for Harrow against Eton at Lord's in 1884. He was an average batsman and a good field at mid-on, but excelled mainly as a pace bowler. He played occasionally in Queensland after returning to the family sheep farm.

Norman Ramsay (1869–1916) born at Eton Vale, was the youngest of the four Ramsay brothers and played for Harrow against Eton in 1887 and 1888. He was a very useful medium pace bowler of off-breaks who fielded well in the slips but was of little account with the bat. He headed the Harrow bowling averages in 1887, and played soccer for the Harrow XI in 1886–87. He was killed in World War I while serving in the Rifle Brigade.

Two other Ramsays, J. M. and R. O., the sons of M. F. Ramsay, also played for Harrow.

RANSFORD, Vernon Seymour, 1885–1958

First-Class Averages: Batting, 8,268 runs at 42.40; Bowling, 29 wickets at 30.62.

Tests (20): 1,211 runs at 37.84; 1 wicket at 28.00.

An outstanding left-handed batsman and brilliant fieldsman whose international career was upset by the 1912 dispute between players and the Australian Board of Control but who played for Victoria for 20 years. He was a mixture of stubborn defence and an impatient surge of brilliance with a great flair for driving. Ransford was at his peak on the 1909 Australian tour of England, scoring 1,783 runs in one of the wettest northern summers on record, topscore 190. He made 143 not out in the Second Test at Lord's his sole Test century, taking four hours to do it, but in the process he helped begin an Australian revival in big cricket that lasted into the 1920s.

Ransford, born at South Yarra, worked hard at his cricket at Hawthorn College under the coaching of the English professional Harry Carpenter, and in his last year at the College scored 1,000 runs. In his debut in big cricket in February, 1904, he was in the Victorian XI dismissed for 15 by England—still the lowest total on record in an Australian first-class match. Despite this horrendous beginning Ransford made 152 the following season for Victoria against Queensland, the first of his 13 centuries for the State, and he also made an impressive 80 not out against South Australia. After missing selection in the 1905 Australian side for England, he suffered a disheartening lapse in form in 1905–06, but kept working hard on his game at the nets, and in February, 1907 reasserted himself with an innings of 136 in Gregory's Benefit match at Sydney. The next summer he made 102 not out for Victoria against England at Melbourne, 109 for Victoria against South Australia at Melbourne, and 129 v. NSW in Sydney.

By now Ransford was established as one of Australia's finest left-handed batsmen, a run-getter bracketed with his contemporaries Bardsley and Hill. He was also a fieldsman without peer, saving countless runs with his splendid running and safe hands in the deep. He played in the five Tests against England in Australia in 1907–08, averaging 32 runs an innings, topscore 54. The English tourists returned home at the end of the Australian summer unanimous in the view that he would be one of the first picked for the next Australian tour of England in 1909.

Ransford made sure of it with innings of 171 not out against South Australia at Melbourne and two centuries, 182 and 110 in the match between Victoria and New South Wales at Sydney in 1908–09. He ended the season with a better average than Bardsley or Noble. In England he was a model of consistency despite the damp pitches and if his strokemaking did not thrill spectators his fielding certainly did. Only Bardsley (2,180) scored more than Ransford (1,783) on that tour. They made a fascinating contrast, with Ransford stronger on the drive but Bardsley a powerful hitter to leg and past point. At Leeds when Hirst was making the ball swerve sharply at the start of Australia's second innings, Ransford held him out in a desperate duel.

In the five years to 1912 Ransford played in 20 Tests for Australia, seven times scoring more than 50 as well as his sole Test century. His Test career ended when the showdown occurred between the Australian Board and disgruntled leading players in the 1911–12 season. He was one of the six Test players who signed a letter to the Board saying they would not tour England that year unless Frank Laver was manager. The Board, having already said that Queenslander G. S. Crouch would manage the side, stood firm and none of the six went to England.

Ransford continued to play for Victoria until 1927, and finished his career with 25 first-class centuries, the last at Christchurch in 1924–25 on his third tour of New Zealand. He was an occasional bowler of left-arm spin.

In 1938, Ransford defeated Don Bradman in a ballot for the position of secretary to the Melbourne Cricket Club. He succeeded Major Ben Wardill and Hugh Trumble. He sustained the distinction the job had always had until his retirement in 1957 through ill-health. He died within a year, never regretting his decision to stand down from the 1912 tour of England when he was at the height of his power.

RATCLIFFE, Andrew Thomas, 1891–1974

First-Class Averages: Batting, 1,899 runs at 32.18; Dismissals 75 (45 catches, 30 stumpings).

A quality wicket-keeper and splendid left-hand batsman whose opportunities in big cricket were restricted by the presence of Hanson Carter and Bert Oldfield. He had one of the hardest-hit straight drives in Australian cricket. He spent 16 years as reserve wicket-keeper for New South Wales, turning in outstanding performances week after week for Glebe and Balmain. When he did play in the State side, it was often for his batting. Among his many accomplishments in 26 years of first grade cricket was a remarkable 27 stumpings for Balmain in the 1915–16 season, when he topped the club's batting averages with 584 runs at 34.35. The following season he made 566 runs at 47.16, with two centuries. Between 1925–26 and 1935–36, he scored 3,104 runs for Glebe first grade at 30.73, with five centuries.

Ratcliffe toured New Zealand with an Australian XI in 1920–21 and a second time with a New South Wales side in 1923–24. He played in 43 first-class matches, scoring four centuries. His highest score was 161 in a Test trial in 1924–25 for "Farmer Bill" Howell's benefit. He represented New South Wales at cricket, Australian Rules football and lawn bowls.

RAYMER, Vincent Norman ("Possum"), 1918–

A colourful left-handed hitter and versatile left-arm bowler of medium-pace or spin, deaf as a post, who played his way through 15 seasons and 71 matches for Queensland. He was one of the most popular players in Australian first-class cricket, and the opposition relished his natural humour as much as his team-mates. He was never a possibility for Tests but was a great stalwart for Queensland XI. Tales about his deafness are part of Australian cricket legend.

Raymer, born and developed as a cricketer in Toowoomba, joined the Toombul club in Brisbane after he became a regular State player. He was an exceptionally accurate left-arm bowler who could drop the ball on a good length for hours on end without turning dangerously. He would have been better suited to pitches in England or New Zealand than he was on hard, dry Australian strips.

On one occasion when he hammered New South Wales bowlers all over Sydney Cricket Ground, his captain, Bill

Brown, told him to "Have a go for the light," but Raymer did not hear the last three words and swished at every ball. It was at the SCG, too, that he made a whirlwind half-century thinking the umpire was calling no-ball when it was really fast bowler Tom Brooks grunting.

Raymer took five wickets in an innings six times in his long career and once took 10 wickets in a match. He held 64 catches in first-class matches, evidence of his reliable fielding. His hitting was always entertaining, especially when he lay back and clubbed short balls, but he was never able to sustain it long enough to make a century, and had a highest score of 85. He always thought he deserved a trip to New Zealand with Bill Brown's Australian team at the end of the 1949–50 Australian season during which he took 34 first-class wickets, but the selectors preferred Doug Ring and Jack Iverson. Raymer's deafness was due to an infection he picked up in the tropics during World War II.

First-Class Averages: Batting, 2,262 runs at 22.84; Bowling, 201 wickets at 32.34.

A resolute, dependable, bandy-legged Victorian right-hand batsman who played for Australia against all the cricket nations over a ten year period that produced 32 first-class centuries. He established himself in the Test team batting down the order but assumed the key role of opener on Bob Simpson's initial retirement. He had exceptional powers of concentration ideally suited to matches that lasted for several days but he was only a moderate runner between wickets. He was a fine player of bouncers, a fine judge of when to duck, and remained alert for half volleys that he could drive on either side of the wicket. He was a superb fieldsman, particularly at short leg, holding 83 Test catches—an outstanding total for a player who seldom stood at first slip.

Redpath was born at Geelong and went to Geelong College. He joined South Melbourne after leaving school, a tall, long-necked youngster with a prominent adam's apple and a sallow complexion. He replaced Colin McDonald as Victoria's opening batsman in 1962–63 and formed a notable partnership with Bill Lawry. They shared 10 stands of more than 100 runs for Victoria, with 204 against South Australia in 1965–66 the highest.

He opened with Lawry in his Test debut in the Second Test against South Africa at Melbourne in 1963–64, Simpson going in first wicket down, and figured in an opening stand of 219. But he was out at 97, and did not play in another Test until the First Test against England at Nottingham on the 1964 Australian tour. In the Third Test of that series, Redpath hit the winning runs, his 58 not out in the second innings giving Australia victory and ultimately The Ashes by seven wickets. Redpath scored 1,075 runs at 32.57 on that tour.

REDPATH, Ian Ritchie ("Redders"), 1941–

First-Class Averages: Batting, 14,993 runs at 41.99; Bowling, 13 wickets at 35.84.

Tests (66 plus one abandoned): 4,737 runs at 43.45.

829

He opened in the First Test against England in Australia in 1965–66 but scored only 17 and did not play another Test in the series. Despite high scoring for Victoria—including 261 against Queensland in 1963–64 and 180 against Queensland in 1965–66, both in Melbourne—he could not confirm his Test place until the 1966–67 Australian tour of South Africa, when he batted first or second wicket down in all five Tests.

He returned to England in Lawry's team in 1968, scoring 1,474 runs at 43.35, including 92 in the Fourth Test at Headingley. He made his first Test century the following summer,

Ian Redpath and Bill Lawry opening at Lord's during the 1968 tour of England.

1968–69, in Sydney in the Fifth Test against the West Indies, with a fine innings of 132, during which he added 210 with Walters. He was a much more positive batsman by then and one of the world's best players of spin bowling. He toured India and South Africa with Lawry's side in 1969–70, scoring well without making a Test century. He made his highest Test score, 171, in 1970–71 in Perth against England, but missed selection in the 1972 team to England. While the Australians struggled to square the rubber 2–2 in the final Test, Redpath taught cricket at Charterhouse School in Surrey. At Melbourne in December, 1972, he made a splendid 135 in the Second Test against Pakistan.

Throughout the Australian tour of the West Indies in 1972–73 he had a tense battle with Lance Gibbs, with honours even. He missed the series against New Zealand in Australia in 1973–74 but in the three-Test series against New Zealand in New Zealand the same season made history. At Auckland in the Third Test he became the first player to bat through a complete innings in New Zealand by scoring 159 not out. At Sydney the next summer against England he made further headlines by scoring 105 in a stand of 220 with Greg Chappell, a record for the second wicket against England in Australia, finishing the series with 472 runs at 42.90.

His consistency was again demonstrated in 1975–76 against the West Indies when he scored 575 runs at 52.27, scoring 102 and 101 in the Melbourne Tests and 103 at Adelaide, plus a further century against the tourists for Victoria. He came out of retirement in 1977 to join WSC but tore an achilles tendon in a warm-up game as he leapt high in celebration of taking a wicket as a bowler. He was paid his full contracted amount, underlining one of the players' reasons for joining WSC—agreements that protected them against injury—and retired to his antique shop in Geelong.

REEDMAN, John Cole ("Dinny"), 1867–1924

A tough South Australian postman whose batting lacked any pretensions to style or polish but was all heart and heavy knocks. He was prepared to stand and be hit rather than be dismissed and in 141 innings for South Australia stood and took it long enough to score more than 3,000 runs. In a career that stretched from 1887 to 1909 he had a topscore of 113 against Victoria in 1893–94 at Adelaide, where he was a favoured son. His second first-class century was for The Rest against an Australian XI in March, 1899, when he made 51 and 108. With the ball his best performance was 13 for 149 (7 for 54 and 6 for 95) against Victoria in 1904–05.

Reedman, born in Adelaide, scored 17 and 4 in his only Test in 1894–95, took 1 for 24, and held one catch. This was the Test that England won by 10 runs after Australia scored 586. It was

First-Class Averages: Batting, 3,337 runs at 23.24; Bowling, 118 wickets at 32.10.

Tests (1): 21 runs at 10.50; 1 wicket at 24.00.

the first time a team followed-on and won, and the first Test to extend to six days. Reedman must have enjoyed that struggle, for he was a tough customer who was once reputed to have misjudged a rising ball and driven a fast bowler to the fence after making contact with his knuckles.

Tall and slim, he bowled accurate right-arm medium-pacers and spun the ball from the off when pitches suited him. He was captain of South Australia several times and captained North Adelaide club. He was an exceptionally good field with a fine arm, and a sure catch. He coached at St Peter's College for some years and was a prominent footballer, but in this, too, his play lacked artistry. "Dinny" Reedman's stubborn persistency aroused wide admiration and made him extremely valuable in teams that included attractive dashers in both sports. He carried his resolution into every game and in 1907–08 topped the Adelaide A grade bowling averages at the age of 40.

REES, William Gilbert, 1827–1898

First-Class Averages: Batting, 31 runs at 15.50.

The first outstanding player from the Moreton Bay district of New South Wales, before it became a part of Queensland. Rees, a cousin of the legendary W. G. Grace, travelled from the Darling Downs area to Sydney to play in the NSW v. Victoria inter-Colonial match in January, 1857, and has been described as "Queensland's first representative player". Rees managed a station at Stonehenge on the Darling Downs and was one of the many ex-Public School and University men who migrated from England in search of Colonial wealth and experience. Rees later played for the Moreton Bay Cricket Club, formed in 1859. Rees had distinguished himself soon after his arrival in Australia by topscoring for the Garrison club in Sydney in each innings of a match against a composite team from the Australian, Marylebone and Union clubs. He performed well in every match in which he appeared in Australia but after playing one inter-Colonial match for NSW against Victoria returned to England. He later settled in New Zealand, and died at Marlborough, aged 71.

RENNEBERG, David Alexander, 1942

First-Class Averages: Batting, 466 runs at 7.06; Bowling, 291 wickets at 29.30.

Tests (8): 22 runs at 3.66; 23 wickets at 36.08.

A right-hand fast bowler in eight Tests for Australia and in 54 matches for New South Wales. A big, strong, lantern-jawed character from Sydney's Balmain club, he toured South Africa in 1966–67, England in 1968 and New Zealand in 1969–70 with the Australian teams. He played in all five Tests in South Africa, taking 11 wickets at 48.00 each, but did not play in a Test on his English tour. His best effort was in the first of three Tests he played in Australia against India in 1967–68, when he took 5 for 39 at Adelaide.

Renneberg took five wickets in an innings 13 times in first-class matches and once took 10 wickets in a match. For New South Wales, he took 190 wickets at 30.48 and scored 380 runs at 8.44. A sometimes formidable proposition on the uneven pitches provided for grade matches, he fell just below top-class when given his chance in first-class cricket, mainly because he bowled without shoulder or body action supporting his strong right-arm. He had one spectacular coup against Queensland in 1967–68 with a 40 mile-an-hour gale behind him when his pace got him through Peter Burge's defence while Burge's bat was still halfway through its backlift. He finished with 7 for 33. He took most wickets in a season three times for Balmain, for whom he captured 383 wickets in all grades between 1955 and 1974.

REYNOLDS, George Raymond, 1936–

First-Class Averages: Batting, 3,693 runs at 46.16.

A hard-hitting right-hand opening batsman who went straight from Brisbane Church of England Grammar School's First XI into the Queensland team in 1955–56. He scored 371 runs at 53.00 the next year in his first full season and did even better in 1957–58, scoring 698 with three centuries, including one of 203 not out, showing excellent defence and unlimited patience. Over the next few seasons he shared some big opening stands with Sam Trimble and scored a career total of 12 centuries, but he could not win Test selection.

Reynolds, who played for the Western Suburbs club in Brisbane, had two seasons in the Lancashire League for Royton in 1962 and 1963. He returned home to regain his State team place, but retired to run a sugar farm he bought in Bundaberg, where he was born. Later he sold the farm and he now runs a shop close to the Woolloongabba ground.

RICHARDS, Barry Anderson, 1945–

One of the brilliant batsmen in the history of cricket forced to display his talents in England and Australia outside of Tests because of government policies in his native South Africa. He scored his first Test century against Australia at Durban in 1969–70, taking 116 balls to pass 100 on his way to 140. This score set up South Africa's first Test victory by an innings over Australia. Richards made 508 runs in that four-Test series at 72.57. He played for South Australia in 1970–71 and at Perth played one of the greatest innings known to Australian cricket, scoring 325 on the first day and reaching 356 on the second. He also appeared in Australia for WSC in 1977–78 and 1978–79. He uses a high backlift against even the fastest bowlers, giving all his shots the full face of the bat thanks to easy, graceful footwork. In his sole first-class season in Australia he averaged 109.86 in scoring 1,538 runs. He has since coached in Western Australia, but tragically appears unlikely to be seen again in the Test arena.

833

RICHARDS, Isaac Vivian Alexander, 1952–

One of the greatest West Indian batsmen, a cricketer of marvellous, effervescent talent whether he is batting, bowling or fielding. He can destroy even the finest bowlers with his imperious driving, fearless hooking and full-faced cutting. He is among the best on-side players cricket has known, capable of hitting anything that strays off a length between mid-on and square-leg to the fence with almost nonchalant ease. He played the 1976–77 season with Queensland and in five matches scored 349 runs at 43.62, including a blazing 143 against Pakistan. Since he has been in Australia so often on visits with West Indian teams or with WSC he is almost regarded as a local.

Richards, born in Antigua, son of Malcolm Richards, for years Antigua's best fast bowler, represented the island at cricket and football, like his two brothers, while he was still at school. He joined Somerset in 1974 and in 1974–75 he was picked as a promising recruit who could be blooded on the West Indies' tour of Pakistan. But Lawrence Rowe was injured and Richards had to be thrown into the Tests, a raw youngster. In his third Test innings he made 192 not out at Delhi and he has been an automatic selection in the West Indian team ever since. He first toured Australia in 1975–76 and Australian spectators quickly recognised him as a player of unusual talents.

Few cricketers have given Australian audiences as much pleasure. He is a model of relaxation on the field, chewing his gum aggressively like the late "Slasher" Mackay, but always ready to clap an opponent's successes. To the end of the 1981–82 season which saw him in action again on Australian grounds, Richards had scored almost 20,000 first-class runs at just over 50 an innings with 59 centuries. In 47 Tests he had made 4,129 runs at 58.98 with 13 centuries. These figures undoubtedly would be better but for his efforts in one-day games in which he is a match winner.

RICHARDSON, Arthur John, 1888–1973

First-Class Averages: Batting, 5,277 runs at 41.55; Bowling, 212 wickets at 30.69.

Tests (9): 403 runs at 31.00; 12 wickets at 43.41.

An outstanding South Australian all-rounder not related to Victor. He matched his namesake in achievement in two fine seasons of Test cricket and gave notable service for eight years to his home State. Arthur was a right-hand batsman and right-hand off-break bowler, born at Seven Hills, South Australia, who arrived for the State practice at the Adelaide nets with a heavy bat bound in greenhide which few players would care to use. With such a bat he made a century before lunch on his way to 280 in the return against MCC at Adelaide in 1922–23. He had scored 150 in the first game.

Richardson played in spectacles and could really flay the ball when in the mood, unleashing fierce drives. At other times he simply resisted without scoring. He made 11 centur-

834

ies for South Australia including 200 not out against MCC in 1926 as well as the 280 three years earlier.

He was a handy off-spinner and a cricketer whose enthusiasm for the game conveyed itself to all those he played with, and he travelled the world looking at cricket and coaching. On one sojourn in the West Indies he coached future Test stars Stollmeyer and Gomez. After he finished playing he became an outstanding first-class umpire and officiated in Tests in the West Indies in 1934–35.

Richardson scored one Test century (100) at Leeds against England in 1926 and remains the oldest Australian at 37 years 351 days to hit a maiden Test century. On his sole tour of England in 1926 he had some good days with his slowish off-spinners but was too inclined to indulge in a modified brand of leg theory that did not test top-class batsmen. He took 63 wickets on the tour at 17.66, and scored 766 runs at 31.91. He later played Lancashire League cricket with Bacup and finally for WA where he coached for some years. He made 101 not out for WA against England at Perth in 1928–29.

A remarkable all-round South Australian sportsman who scored 27 centuries in first-class cricket, represented Australia at baseball, South Australia at golf and tennis, was a prominent lacrosse and basketball player and a topclass swimmer. He captained South Australia and Australia at cricket, was the star of three Sturt premiership Australian Rules sides, South Australian captain of football, an outstanding gymnast and athlete, and a first grade hockey player. He was also one of our greatest fieldsmen, absolutely fearless close to the stumps and a spectacular saver of runs, and nobody could remember ever seeing him drop a catch. He took a career total of 211 catches.

He was born in the heart of the Sturt district, which comprises Unley and parts or the whole of other suburbs. His father, Valentine Yaxley Richardson, was a member of a firm of house decorators. There had always been a "V. Y." Richardson in the family so they christened him Victor York, partly because they did not want to brand him with Yaxley and partly because the Duke of York was born in the same year, 1894. The family moved into a house in Malvern when Vic was six and there he and his brother, Osma Voy, who was killed at Pozieres in 1916, grew to robust manhood. Joe Darling, who captained South Australia and Australia and Sturt, lived opposite and he coached Vic and Osma on a lawn at the side of his house.

Vic went to Kyre College (now Scotch College), Unley Park, where he was coached by Davis Cup star Adrian Quist's father, Karl Quist, who represented New South Wales, South

RICHARDSON, Victor York, 1894–1969

First-Class Averages: Batting, 10,727 runs at 37.63; Bowling, 8 wickets at 66.50.

Tests (19): 706 runs at 23.53.

Australia and Western Australia at cricket. He first played cricket for Sturt, the club to which he gave more than 30 years' service, in 1912–13. He worked in the Government Produce Department in Adelaide, where one of his workmates was Sir Charles McCann, the man who bowled Dr W. G. Grace first ball at Adelaide Oval in 1891. On Monday nights he went to gymnastics training, Tuesday football practice and later a basketball match with the Mitcham team, Wednesdays another basketball match, Thursdays football practice, Fridays gymnastics at Unley Park Boys club, where he was secretary.

On Saturday afternoons he played league football or, in the years he dropped out of football, baseball and lacrosse matches on the same afternoon. He was acknowledged one of the great Aussie Rules centremen of all time. In 1920, his first year at centre, he tied for the Magarey medal with Dan Moriarty, but lost on a revote.

Richardson captained the Sturt cricket team from 1921 until 1942, and led South Australia from 1921 until 1935, when Bradman took over. In 1924–25 he scored a century in each innings (100 and 125) for South Australia against New South Wales at Sydney, a feat he failed to repeat by only four runs five years later against Queensland at Brisbane when he made 112 and 96. At Melbourne in 1924–25 he made 138 in his Second Test and 83 in the fourth at Brisbane. His career highest score of 231 against the MCC at Adelaide in 1928–29 included a six off Larwood into the pavilion.

He was an imposing figure, tall, straight-backed, with a pencil-moustache and the carriage of a great general. Neville Cardus called him "The Guardsman". In 1928, he took an Australian team to New Zealand, with Woodfull as his vice-captain, and in December that year at Sydney gave one of the most astonishing displays of fielding seen in Australia. His work at silly point and cover to punishing batsmen like Hammond, Hendren and Chapman was so brilliant *The Sydney Morning Herald* led one of its leading articles next day with "Is Richardson Human?"

"If we were Greeks and permitted long Test matches as our Olympics, Richardson would be a demigod this morning with precedence over Satyrs and all other earth gods", said the *Herald*. "But the ancive gone, alas, and we do not deify our heroes now. So Richardson must be content with the thought that last night thousands of small boys slept with cigarette cards bearing his portrait under their pillows."

Richardson made his career highest score, 231, against Chapman's team at Adelaide in 1928–29, causing the crowd to go wild with glee when he hooked Larwood into the pavilion. Later they named the gates on the opposite side of the ground the "Victor York Richardson Gates", for he hit dozens of shots over that fence, too. He was at his best when forcing the pace, a splendid driver all round the stumps from an awkward stance in which he tucked the bat handle in between his thighs, a fierce puller and hooker who took heavy blows calmly and, during the Bodyline series, courageously.

He was involved in a last-minute switch in plans in 1930 when the Board of Control dropped Jack Ryder as captain of the team for England, replaced him with Woodfull, and made Richardson vice-captain. Richardson was so obviously a born leader, with qualities that inspired his players, that South Australians reacted angrily. He scored 832 runs at 26.83 on his sole tour of England, topscore 116. He suffered persistent attacks of hayfever that ruined his tour but not his good humour and did not win a permanent Test place until 1932-33 in Australia when it was felt that hookers like him and McCabe could provide the answer to Larwood's bouncers. Richardson was brave and determined but only in the Fourth Test at Brisbane, where he made 83 in an opening stand of 133 with Woodfull, did he make the runs expected.

Cartoonist-cricket writer Arthur Mailey organised a tour of North America by an Australian team in 1932 and asked Richardson to captain the side. Mailey had the backing of the Canadian Cricket Board of Control and Canadian Pacific Railways. Mailey suddenly realised that as the main bowler in the side he would, at the age of 44, have to dismiss 1,000 batsmen on the tour because most of the opposition teams would include 18 men in an innings. So he sent Vic a telegram which read, "If Fleetwood Smith any good invite him to America". Asked if he would like to go with the Australian team Fleetwood-Smith said, "My oath I would", and off the 12 Australians went to play in places like Moose Jaw, Medicine Hat, Kicking Horse Falls, with Fleetwood-Smith taking 249 wickets at eight runs a wicket. Mailey took 240 wickets at 6.5. Bradman chipped in with 3,779 runs and over 100 wickets, a fair contribution for someone on his honeymoon, and McCabe made 2,360 runs and took 187 wickets. The 100-day trip took in 51 matches in which the Australians made more than 10,000 runs, dismissed more than 1,000 batsmen, and travelled 16,000 miles with Richardson directing operations, Mailey frequently absent.

In 1935–36, Richardson captained Australia on tour in South Africa after Woodfull's retirement, winning four of the five Tests, with one draw. Players who made that tour remember it as the most enjoyable of their careers and attribute this to Richardson's handling of the team. He was a tough task master who did not mind his players' party-going until the small hours provided they did their job next day.

One player complained as they went on the field about his aching limbs. "And I suppose you have a searing headache, too?" said Richardson, and when the player nodded, Vic said, "I feel like that every morning—now get over there and field". It was Richardson who added menace to O'Reilly's bowling by

introducing the famous legtrap, standing a man close in to worry the batsmen and make O'Reilly more economical. Often he filled the spot himself to set an example.

In the Fifth Test at Durban when O'Reilly lacked his usual fire and could not get his legbreak or wrong'un to turn, Richardson stood him out near the fence and instructed Stan McCabe and Len Darling to keep baiting him. "Aren't you playing in this match, Tiger", they would say. At lunch they kept up the baiting, while Richardson deliberately ate alone. When he threw the ball to O'Reilly for the first over after lunch, the big man was fuming, and in less than two hours took six wickets to finish off the match by tea. In this Test Richardson set a record still unbeaten after 46 years by taking five catches in a Test innings.

Typical of the fun the Australians had on the South African trip was the baseball match at Johannesburg. A cricket match had been scheduled to raise funds for the estate of the late Springbok Test hero Jock Cameron, but Richardson suggested that as the Australians had already played four cricket matches on the ground more spectators might attend if Australia played Transvaal at baseball. Len Darling and Richardson had represented Australia, Leo O'Brien was a noted pitcher in Victorian baseball and Ernie McCormick a "first base ace", but the star of the match turned out to be "Grum" Grimmett, who staggered back in the outfield, raising first one hand then the other and finally held a dramatic catch in the hand without the glove, with the bases loaded, giving Australia a one-run win. That victory in "Clarrie Grimmett's game" began a tradition which sees every Australian cricket team in South Africa play a big baseball match.

On his return from South Africa Richardson played under Bradman's captaincy for South Australia, with Grimmett in the same side. Bradman continually urged Grimmett to concentrate on his legbreak and only use the flipper and top-spinner as surprise balls, but Grimmett was so happy with his invention of the flipper he kept bowling it. Finally Bradman said, "I don't think you *can* bowl a leg-break any-more". When Richardson and Grimmett were given a joint Testimonial match in 1937–38, Bradman came in to bat before a big crowd just before lunch and Grimmett bowled him with a huge leg break. "There y'are, I told him I could still bowl me leg break", said Grimmett. Richardson, who knew that Bradman's dismissal would reduce the crowd after lunch said, "Maybe, Grum, but you've cost a couple of thousand pounds each with that leggie."

He was married twice, firstly to Vida Knapman and then to Peggy Chandler. One of his daughters became the mother of the Chappell clan. They played backyard cricket when the Chappells were small but thereafter Vic left them alone, a grandad who preferred to let his record inspire the boys.

After his retirement Richardson became an internationally known broadcaster on big matches for the ABC. Nobody could challenge his knowledge of sport, for there was hardly a game the ABC covered that he had not played with distinction. He will be remembered as long as cricket broadcasts are made for his partnership with English captain Arthur Gilligan and the phrase: "And what do you think, Arthur?"

RIDINGS, Kenneth Lovett, 1921–1944

A right-hand opening batsman who appeared certain to win Test selection when he was killed piloting a Sunderland on patrol over the Bay of Biscay during World War II. He appeared in 19 first-class matches and made two centuries, 122 against Queensland at Brisbane in 1938–39 and 151 against Queensland 11 months later in Adelaide. Ken Ridings was Keith Miller's first victim as a bowler in first-class cricket. Ken Ridings, 5 ft 11 ins, bowled useful right-arm leg breaks. He had outstanding qualities of leadership which many believe would have earned him the Australian captaincy had he lived.

First-Class Averages: Batting, 919 runs at 32.82; Bowling 7 wickets at 26.00.

RIDINGS, Philip Lovett, 1917–

One of four brothers who played for the West Torrens club in Adelaide, a proficient right-hand batsman and right-arm medium-pace bowler. He played for the West Torrens club for 27 years and for South Australia for 17 years between the 1936–37 and 1956–57 seasons. He was South Australia's captain for 12 years from 1946, controlling the team initially when Bradman was absent and then permanently when the great man retired. South Australia won the Sheffield Shield in 1952–53 under his captaincy without losing a match.

Phil Ridings did not appear in a Test, but he had an unusual near-miss in the Adelaide Test against West Indies in 1951–52. He was selected to replace the injured Lindsay Hassett, but Board of Control approval could not be obtained before the match began. Hassett had to act as twelfth man. Ridings toured New Zealand with Bill Brown's Australian side in February 1950 while the senior Australian side was in South Africa. He was made an Australian selector in 1952–53 and to avoid embarrassment made himself unavailable for the national side. He was elected chairman of the Australian Cricket Board in the 1980–81 season after representing South Australia on the Board for many years.

The Ridings brothers, **Sydney Bradshaw Ridings, Roley Lovett Ridings,** and **Kenneth Lovett Ridings,·** and Phil learned to play cricket at Henley Beach Private School. The West Torrens club each year took the school's two most

First-Class Averages: Batting, 5,653 runs at 36.23; Bowling, 61 wickets at 46.95.

promising players into grade cricket and Phil was recruited into the club with the late Charlie Walker, who toured England as Australia's reserve wicket-keeper in 1938. Phil and Ken Ridings, the family's right-handers, played together in the South Australian team before World War II. Sid and Roley, both left-handers, had to be content with playing in West Torrens premiership sides. The West Torrens club won nine Adelaide premierships with at least one Ridings in the side.

Phil Ridings served as a Warrant Officer with the Fourth Armoured Brigade during World War II. He had a flair for mathematics and made a close study of the money market and was one of seven men who started the Custom Credit operation in Australia. When he retired from the company in 1980 as South Australian manager, Custom Credit assets topped $100 million. He made nine centuries, highest score 186 not out for South Australia against Victoria in 1947–48 at Melbourne. He had made 151 against Victoria three months earlier in Adelaide.

RIGG, Keith Edward, 1906–

First-Class Averages: Batting, 5,544 runs at 42.00.

Tests (8): 401 runs at 33.41.

A tall, angular Victorian right-hand batsman who, in a 12-year first-class career of reliable, attractive run-getting, was unlucky to play in only eight Tests. He scored more than 5,000 first-class runs, figured in some exhilarating partnerships, captained Victoria, hit 14 centuries and was several times out in the nineties—but in a period of outstanding Australian batsmanship could not hold a regular Test place.

He began as a middle order batsman but later opened. He was a splendid exponent of the hook, drove handsomely on both sides of the pitch, and excelled with cuts behind point down to the third-man fence. He was a brilliant fieldsman and a sure catch, and a splendid runner between wickets.

Rigg, born at Malvern, Victoria, went to Tooronga Road Public School and Wesley College, where he captained the First XI. He hero-worshipped Edgar Mayne whose style influenced his batting. He played for Prahran, University, Hawthorn-East Melbourne and finally Melbourne, which in 1981 awarded him the rare honour of life membership. At 20, he made 62 against New South Wales in his first match for Victoria in 1926–27, but his score lacked significance in the Victorian total of 1,107, including 352 from Ponsford. He was dropped for the next match but was re-instated for the return match against New South Wales in Sydney. Victoria were all out for 35.

Rigg made his initial first-class century against New South Wales in Sydney in 1928–29, scoring 110 not out in Jack Gregory's last Shield match. Jack Ellis lent Rigg a brand new bat for luck and when Rigg scored a century let him keep it. In 1930–31, he won Test selection by scoring 126 in a partnership of 200 with Ponsford against the West Indies in Melbourne, but he was twelfth man for the first four Tests. In his Test debut in the Fifth Test, he scored 14 and 16. Australia, winners of the first four Tests, lost the Fifth.

The next season Rigg was twelfth man in the First Test against South Africa and grabbed his chance by making 127 in the Second Test, sharing a smart partnership of 111 with Bradman for the third wicket. He had an aggregate of 253 runs at 50.60 in his four Tests in that series. He missed selection in the Bodyline series in 1932–33 but scored 88 for Victoria against an England XI captained by Bob Wyatt after the Tests. This was probably his finest innings. Wyatt set the Victorians 178 to win in two hours. Batting with Ernie Bromley, Rigg faced the last ball with the scores level. Bill Bowes bowled a short one and Rigg mis-hit his favourite hook shot and was caught, the match ending in a tie.

Rigg's career for Victoria was studded with big partnerships. He added 249 in a third wicket stand with Bill Ponsford in 1928–29 against South Australia. He and Jack Ryder added 219 for the third wicket in 1930–31 against Queensland. Rigg and Len Darling put on 281 for the third wicket in 1932–33 against South Australia, and with Leo O'Brien added 234 for the first wicket in 1934–35 against NSW. Rigg and J. W. Scaife put on 201 in 1935–36 in a third wicket stand against Queensland.

He played his first Test against England in 1936–37 when O'Brien and Chipperfield dropped out of the side for the Third Test. He made 16 and 47 in the second innings on a sticky wicket. Australia virtually reversed the batting order in the second innings to allow the pitch to dry. Fingleton batted at No. 6, Bradman at No. 7. Batsmen like Rigg who went in ahead of Bradman handled their delaying role well enough for Bradman to make 270. In the Fifth Test, Rigg opened the batting with Fingleton. It was his last Test.

Rigg was unfortunate that at a formative stage of his career he missed the 1930 Australian tour of England. Only 15 players toured, and a selector later told him he was No. 16. On the tour before (1926), and after (1934), 16 players went.

In 1935–36, Rigg shared in a Melbourne grade cricket record opening stand of 331 with Ponsford for the Melbourne club against University. Rigg made 158 not out, Ponsford 165 not out. The following summer (1936–37), he scored 100 and 167 not out in Melbourne against NSW, and 97 and 105 in Melbourne against South Australia—all before New Year. His 167 against NSW was the highest innings of his career.

After Keith Rigg retired he served with the RAAF in New Guinea. He was on the Melbourne club's committee for 25 years and was a State selector for 12 years.

841

RING, Douglas Thomas, 1918–

First-Class Averages: Batting, 3,418 runs at 23.25; Bowling, 451 wickets at 28.48.

Tests (13): 426 runs at 22.42; 35 wickets at 37.28.

A large, sandy-haired, philosophic right-arm leg-spinner and big-hitting right-hand batsman whose skills and laughter graced Australian cricket fields for 15 summers. He was always picked as a bowler, but deserves to be considered historically as a genuine allrounder, for he could bat and field (93 career catches) efficiently. Only his enjoyment in lifting the ball out of the ground prevented him scoring more than one first-class century. His Test record would have been more impressive had he played in an era when pace bowling had not dominated the game's tactics.

Ring, born in Hobart, is claimed as a Tasmanian Test representative but he moved to Victoria at an early age, played district cricket with Richmond and inter-State cricket for Victoria. He was 6ft tall and caused an English umpire to ask if he was Lindwall when he came on to bowl during the 1948 tour. The ball looked small in his big hands but he got plenty of work on it, though he did perhaps push it through a little too fast at times on the slower English pitches whereas giving it air had paid off for Mailey, Grimmett and O'Reilly.

Ring first played for Victorian in 1938–39 in his 20th year, and took 6 for 97 in his first season against Western Australia. He made his Test debut against India in 1947–48 in the same match as Sam Loxton, taking 3 for 103 off 36 overs and 3 for 17. It was enough, coupled with an 11-wicket haul against Tasmania, to win him selection in the famous 1948 Australian side in England. He led the Australian reserves in rehearsing the ditty "Ground staff bowling is our game," sung to the tune of Champagne Charlie. With captains able to call for a new ball after only 65 overs there was no reason to use spinners as Australia had done so well between the two world wars.

In the match against Derbyshire Ring hit "Dusty" Rhodes on the toe and immediately appealed. The umpire said, "Not out." Ring asked: "Why not?" Umpire: "He hit it." Ring said, "He never touched it." By then Rhodes was near the bowling end, completing a leg bye. "Did you hit it?" the umpire asked Rhodes. "Never touched it," Rhodes said. Umpire: "Aye, then, you're out." Rhodes walked off glowering at Ring. In his only Test appearance on the tour Ring took 1 for 44, finishing the tour with 60 wickets at 22.13 and 150 runs at 16.66.

Ring's biggest Test coups came in 1951–52 at Brisbane against the West Indies when he took 6 for 80, and 1952–53 on the same ground when he took 6 for 72 against South Africa. He had innings of 65, 67 and 32 not out against the West Indies, exploiting his pulls and lofted on-drives to boost Australia's totals against tired bowlers. He returned to England in 1953 but played in only one Test, this time taking 68 tour wickets at 19.98, and scoring 252 runs at 15.75. Ring took five wickets in an innings 21 times and 10 wickets in a match twice, best analysis 7 for 88. His sole first-class century, 145, was scored for Victoria v. Queensland in 1946–47.

A tall, energetic wicket-keeper for New South Wales since 1974–75 who played 10 successive Tests for Australia during Rodney Marsh's absence with WSC. His batting has provided many invaluable runs from the time he scored 115 against Queensland at Sydney in his initial first-class season. He is somewhat slack in his dress, with shirt-tails and pad straps much in evidence, but his enthusiasm behind the stumps lifts the performance of all his fieldsmen. He has taken many outstanding catches standing back but like most modern 'keepers has a low percentage of stumpings.

Rixon, born in the border town of Albury, played originally for the Waverley club in Sydney, later with Western Suburbs, and more recently with Sutherland. He first appeared for New South Wales in 1974–75 following the retirement of Brian Taber. He was picked solely as a 'keeper and it was a bonus for selectors that he turned out such a handy batsman. He has twice scored first-class centuries as a nightwatchman.

He went into the Australian team with Western Suburbs team-mate Bob Simpson when Simpson came out of retire-

RIXON, Stephen John, 1954–

First-Class Averages: Batting, 2,502 runs at 21.57; Dismissals, 287 (251 caught, 36 stumped).

Tests (10): 341 runs at 21.31; Dismissals, 35 (31 caught, 4 stumped).

Steve Rixon keeping wicket for Australia against India in 1977–78 at Sydney.

ment for the series against India in 1977–78. He made a valuable 50 in the Second Test at Perth in the first innings and when Australia were set 341 to win in the second innings steadied things when Bedi looked threatening to help Australia to a two wickets win. He finished the five-Test rubber with 22 victims, a fine start, which earned him a trip to the West Indies in 1977–78. He made 54 and 39 not out when Australia won the Third Test at Georgetown and had 13 victims in the five Tests. He was dropped for the following Tests in 1978–79 at home against England, a setback that was compounded when he broke his arm batting for NSW at Perth.

After the return of WSC players Marsh regained the Australian 'keeper's job but Rixon has remained his deputy, slightly ahead of an array of aspiring 'keepers like Kevin Wright (SA) and Ray Phillips (Qld). He went to Sri Lanka and England as the No 2 Australian 'keeper but with Marsh setting further records had limited opportunities, even though his 'keeping had improved considerably. In nine matches on the tour he scored 164 runs at 18.22, making 22 catches and three stumpings. At the end of the 1981–82 Australian season in which his high calibre 'keeping helped NSW press strongly in both the McDonald's Cup and Sheffield Shield he had lifted his total of first-class centuries to four, scoring his second "night-watchman's hundred" against Victoria with 124.

ROBERTSON, William Roderick ("Digger"), 1861–1938

First-Class Averages: Batting, 109 runs at 13.62; Bowling 15 wickets at 31.06.

Tests (1): 2 runs at 1.00; 0 wickets for 24.00.

A leg-break bowler who sometimes scored handy runs, executing both functions right-handed and with considerable zeal. He took eight wickets for Victoria in the tied match against Alfred Shaw's England team in 1884–85 and as a reward was asked to play in the Second Test at Melbourne when a group of better players dropped out unwilling to accept the pay offered. He played only seven first-class matches, topscore 33. He was born in Deniliquin, NSW, and played for East Melbourne and South Melbourne clubs.

ROBINSON, Rayford Harold, 1914–1965

First-Class Averages: Batting, 2,441 runs at 31.70; Bowling, 44 wickets at 37.59.

Tests (1): 5 runs at 2.50.

An outstanding right-hand batting stylist whose lack of judgement off the field ruined a career rich in promise. Yet only a handful of Australians have handled a cricket bat with such culture. His timing and elegance of stroke-play were comparable only to that of Trumper, Jackson and Kippax. Often when you watched him in the nets you felt he was a class above the others.

Robinson learned his cricket in Newcastle and the Gordon club brought him to Sydney in 1934–35 on the basis of reports they had had on his strokeplay, finding him a job as a caretaker. At 21, he scored 613 runs in his second season with the

844

New South Wales team, for ten times out, with centuries against Queensland (103) in Brisbane and against South Australia (102) in Adelaide. He could play every shot in the coaching manuals and had a few of his own but did not always keep the ball down.

In 1936–37 when New South Wales beat "Gubby" Allen's England team by 135 runs in Sydney, Robinson scored 91 in NSW's first innings. This innings won him a place in the first Test at Brisbane, but he was caught in both innings by Walter Hammond off Bill Voce for two and three. He had caught Hammond first ball off McCormick. He did not get another Test chance. At the end of that season he went to South Australia, but in 12 innings for that State scored only 259 runs at 21.58, topscore 62. He fought his way back into the NSW side on his return to Sydney with a sequence of fine scores despite opposition from selectors aware of his social problems.

He served with the 24th Battalion AIF and in the Sixth Division during World War II. After discharge he drifted from jobs on the wharves to labouring in warehouses and on the roads, but could not get back into the State team. He scored 404 runs for the Gordon side that won the 1945–46 Sydney premiership, turning in some brilliant knocks. He and Sid Carroll added 194 in 114 minutes against Paddington, and in the last round against Balmain in what was a virtual final batted splendidly. He had blossomed as a bowler and took 33 wickets at 16.21 in first grade that summer. In all first-class matches Ray Robinson—no relation to the famous cricket writer—scored four centuries. He played in New Zealand for Otago from 1946–47 for three years and eventually returned to Newcastle where he died, aged 51.

ROBINSON, Raymond John, 1905–1982

The most widely read Australian cricket writer, who reported major matches for more than half a century. His Test match comments appeared in up to 20 cities around the world, but it was through his six books that he was best known. He died only three days short of his 77th birthday after carrying on courageously for more than a decade despite the loss of one eye, partial sight in the other, a major stomach operation, the tragic death of his daughter, and the loss of his wife. For years he was forced to watch cricket through binoculars, producing material unmatched by any Australian. It was in this period of adversity that he wrote his finest work, his book on Australian captains, and some sparkling magazine articles.

Robinson was a fully trained journalist, with a background in police rounds, foreign news, industrial work and on sub-editing tables. He served his cadetship with the Melbourne *Herald-Sun* group and began writing cricket in 1930 for the Melbourne *Star*, one of Australia's first tabloids. He first toured England in 1934 with Woodfull's team. He was not a flamboyant phrase-turner in the style of Cardus or Robertson-Glasgow, but he stayed a long course, always searching for the precise word or phrase to describe events. He was an astonishing fact-finder. Years after votes had been counted behind closed doors he continued probing until he knew how each man voted and whether it was for personal gain or the good of Australian cricket.

His first book, *Between Wickets* (1946) was also one of his best and gave Australians a stake in a field dominated by English writers. It was followed by *From The Boundary* (1951), *Green Sprigs* (1954), the title of which was changed to *The Glad Season* in some countries, *The Wit of Sir Robert Menzies* (1966), *The Wildest Tests* (1972), and the oddly titled *On Top Down Under* (1975), a classic in painstaking research and pithy commentary. He was the Australian cricket writer for the London *Daily Telegraph* for 30 years, and contributed to *The Cricketer* magazine, England, for around the same period. He wrote regularly for *Wisden*, and for papers as widespread as the *Jamaica Gleaner*, *Trinidad Guardian*, *The Times of India*, and the *Argus*, South Africa. After he died a half-finished obituary on his friend "Slasher" Mackay was found in his typewriter.

Ray Robinson was respected by cricketers everywhere for his tact in deciding what to print, and for the trust he gave confidential information. When he originally developed retina trouble he was flown to America for an operation by surgeons at the Boston Retina Clinic. The night after the operation he developed agonising abdominal pains from a twisted bowel. Transfusion of 17 pints of blood were needed at a cost Robinson could not immediately meet. Australian journalists in New York gave their blood to be offset against that supplied to him in Boston, and within a fortnight he was back at the retina clinic. Cricket lovers throughout Australia should be grateful to those blood donors, for they kept alive a man who gave them untold pleasure. To watch him at the cricket it seemed fitting that his bearded son, Dr Brian Robinson, is one of the world's leading authorities on radio telescopes and the study of life in the outer galaxy.

ROBINSON, Richard Daryl, 1948–   A tall, combative Victorian wicket-keeper batsman whose enthusiasm has overcome glaring technical frailties. He was remarkably fortunate to play three Tests as a batsman and specialist close-in fieldsman on Australia's 1977 tour of England while Rodney Marsh kept wicket. His entire record is a testimony to the rewards cricket can provide for one who is prepared to adopt a buccaneering approach.

Robinson joined the Carlton district club at 13 as a skinny

846

Richie Robinson leaps high when keeping wicket for Victoria against NSW in Sydney in 1981–82, as batsman Steve Smith cuts the ball for four.

medium-pace bowler. He switched to keeping wicket at 16 and made his first grade debut at 20, when Ray Jordon, Carlton's No. 1 'keeper was away with the State team. When Jordon returned, Robinson retained his place as a specialist batsman. After 11 years with Carlton he transferred to Northcote as coach in 1971–72 convinced his efforts were not being pressed when State teams were chosen. The change worked wonders and he played for Victoria in his first season at Northcote.

He made his first tour of England in 1975 as Marsh's deputy but did not play in a Test. He took over as Victorian captain in 1975–76 when Ian Redpath retired and held the job in 1976–77 and again in 1979–80 after two seasons with World Series Cricket. Tall for a 'keeper at 6 ft, he has outstanding reflexes, which showed when he kept to spinners like Jim Higgs or fielded at silly leg. He made his highest score, 185, in a total of more than 4,500 first-class runs for Victoria against South Australia in 1976–77, the season in which he scored four centuries in four consecutive matches. He made seven first-class centuries but had a topscore in Tests of only 34. He retired during the 1981–82 season to concentrate on life as a publican at Bonnie Doon, 180 kilometres north-east of Melbourne.

First-Class Averages: Batting, 4,776 runs at 39.86; Dismissals 329 (289 catches, 40 stumpings).

Tests (3): 100 runs at 16.66; Dismissals (4 catches).

ROCHE, William ("Micky"), 1871–1950

First-Class Averages: Batting, 924 runs at 14.66; Bowling, 181 wickets at 24.97.

A right-arm off-break bowler of wide turn who appeared a few times for Victoria in the 1890s but played most of his first-class cricket with Middlesex, where Albert Trott was one of his fellow professionals. He played for the MCC in 1897 and 1898 and for A. J. Webbe's XI. Roche, born in South Australia, played for the Melbourne club, and went in to the Victorian side in 1894–95. He took 6 for 63 against NSW at Sydney in January, 1897, his best figures for Victoria. But his best season for the State was 1897–98 when he took 33 wickets, including 5 for 51 against NSW at Melbourne, 6 for 88 v. NSW at Sydney, 5 for 58 v. South Australia at Melbourne, and 5 for 77 against England in Melbourne. As a result of these impressive performances he was advised to go to England.

While he qualified he made regular appearances at Lord's with MCC sides. He joined Middlesex as a professional in 1899 and in two seasons took 49 wickets for the County. His best performance was in May, 1899, when he bowled superbly against the powerful Yorkshire lineup and clinched Middlesex's win by an innings and two runs by taking 5 for 93. Albert Trott, who had made 164 in Middlesex's innings, bowled at the other end with Roche, the two Australians proving too much for batsmen like F. S. Jackson, Frank Mitchell, E. Wainwright, George Hirst and David Denton. That same season Roche clean bowled the last four Gloucestershire batsmen in taking 6 for 28 and clinching a Middlesex win by seven wickets. Roche took five wickets in an innings 13 times and once for the MCC against Kent in 1898, took 12 for 145 including his best figures of 8 for 72.

ROCK, Claude William, 1863–1950

First-Class Averages: Batting, 809 runs at 16.18; Bowling, 142 wickets at 16.54.

An outstanding Tasmanian-born all-rounder who turned in remarkable performances for Cambridge University, Warwickshire and Tasmania. He was selected to play for Australia in the Test in 1888 at Sydney but could not play through illness. He was a slow-medium round-arm bowler with a long arm and a "majestic swing like a fly wheel." He broke back from the off and was particularly hostile on a wet or sticky pitch. As a batsman, he was stiff-wristed, inelegant, lacked strength on the legside, but his bat was straight and he was difficult to dislodge in a crisis. In 1886, he batted all day—5 hours 20 minutes—for Cambridge against the touring Australians, scoring 75 and defying George Giffen at his best.

Rock was born at Deloraine, son of a Warwickshire-born doctor who had a large country practice that demanded much travelling. He learned to play cricket in neighbourhood paddocks while his dad was away. At 13, he was sent to Launceston Grammar, where he immediately won a place in the First XI because of his large break back. At 15, he took 6 for 39 for Northern Tasmania against Southern Tasmania at Hobart.

In Launceston club cricket he was often irresistible with figures like 8 for 5 and 8 for 7. He was a brilliant student and in 1881 headed the Tasmanian scholarship list with the best pass in mathematics ever recorded in Tasmania.

At Cambridge University he had difficulty winning a place in the senior XI but when he was finally chosen in the senior's trial in 1884 he took 5 for 16 and thereafter was a valuable member of the Cambridge XI for three seasons. In the University match of 1884, Rock's 56 runs in 200 minutes is still rated one of the most notable examples of defensive batting in the long history of these matches. He followed by taking wickets with his second and third balls and Lillywhite's Annual judged him the best University bowler of the year. In 1885, he took 10 for 108 against Surrey.

In 1886, he seldom failed, and was possibly the best slow-medium bowler in England. In the match against C. I. Thornton's XI, he bowled 85 overs for 87 runs and 11 wickets. In the MCC and Ground match he took 11 for 103. Playing for the Gentlemen against the visiting Australians, he took 5 for 51 off 44 overs, Dr W. G. Grace allowing him to take the first ball of the innings against his countrymen. In the match between Cambridge and the Australians, he gave a remarkable display of stamina, bowling 59 overs in each innings. He then saved the follow-on and the match, making a painstaking 38.

Rock declined an invitation to play for Surrey but turned out for Warwickshire, his father's native County, before he returned to become a master at Launceston Grammar School. This appointment restricted his first-class appearances but he scored one century for Tasmania against Victoria and once took 8 for 25 against the strong Melbourne club. He moved to New South Wales in 1894. His brother Norman, a skilful off-break bowler of slightly faster pace than Claude, made several appearances for Tasmania.

An opening batsman who scored at a brisk pace, a master on the drive with a rare skill in finding gaps in the field with all his shots. His career is probably without parallel in Australian cricket, for he played only five first-class matches for NSW over two seasons, 1924 to 1926, for an aggregate of 711 runs at an average of 118.50. Rock, the son of Cambridge Blue and Warwickshire County player C. W. Rock, was lost to Australian cricket when he qualified as a doctor.

Many felt he would have ranked among our great players had he continued in the game. In his first match for New South Wales, Rock scored 127 and 27 not out, and in his second 235 and 51. Despite these outstanding figures, he was dropped from the State side when Collins, Bardsley, Taylor, Andrews and Kelleway returned from Test duties. He played

ROCK, Dr Harry Owen, 1896–1978

First-Class Averages: Batting, 758 runs at 94.75.

in two further Shield games and one against Western Australia in which he made 151. He also played in a Test trial in 1925–26. He was a slightly-built figure with a stiff, upright stance but had such splendid basic technique and timing he kept scorers busy.

ROGERS, Rex Ernest, 1916–

First-Class Averages: Batting, 3,600 runs at 34.95; Bowling, 1 wicket at 157.00.

A burly, fair-skinned Queensland left-hander renowned for his forceful hitting just before and just after World War II. He had enormous forearms, developed in his youth at Cairns, and the power of his square cut matched his full blooded pull shot. At the Sydney Cricket Ground he hit one shot with such power it smashed a fence paling. He bowled right-arm medium-pace and was a capable fieldsman in the deep.

Rogers played his way into the Queensland team in 1935–36 after some impressive performances for the State Colts. He hit the first of his eight centuries for Queensland, 113, at Adelaide against South Australia in December, 1936, and one year later on the same ground made his career highest score, 181. He joined the Colts team in Brisbane during this period and later played for the Eastern Suburbs and South Brisbane clubs. He was always a no-nonsense batsman who kept scorers and fieldsmen busy.

He made 104 against Victoria at Melbourne in 1938–39, 114 against NSW at Sydney in 1940–41 and 103 against Victoria at Brisbane in the same year before World War II interrupted him in his prime. He made a whirlwind 138 for Queensland against South Australia at Brisbane in 1945–46 and a splendid 66 against Wally Hammond's MCC team at Brisbane the same summer. He kept going in the State team until 1948 with only occasional flashes of the fierce hitting for which he had been known before the war. His brother **Noel Thomas Rogers** (1923–) played three matches for Queensland as a right-handed batsman in 1947–48, scoring 50 runs at 10.00.

RORKE, Gordon Frederick, 1938–

First-Class Averages: Batting, 248 runs at 10.78; Bowling, 88 wickets at 24.60.

Tests (4): 9 runs at 4.50; 10 wickets at 20.30.

One of the most controversial fast bowlers of all time, a good-looking, easy-going blonde giant whom I feel sure history will find was misjudged by the game's administrators. More than anyone else, Rorke was responsible for the introduction of the front foot law that has afflicted international cricket for several seasons now. He did this without intent and despite diligent work at the nets, simply because he had an action in which he could take the weight of his entire body on the outside edge of his left-foot, dragging for several strides through the bowling crease and up the pitch. It was a unique delivery stride but it should never had caused law changes to the detriment of the overwhelming mass of cricketers who could never drag like Rorke.

The pity of it all is that Rorke is among the most genial of men, a highly intelligent figure, and certainly no miscreant. At 18, he stood 6 ft 5 ins. One of his uncles, Jack Ford, was among Australia's greatest Rugby forwards, but Gordon gave up Rugby after several games for Mosman in the Whiddon Cup to concentrate on cricket. Miller, Lindwall, Crawford and Walker had just retired so it seemed a sound decision.

Rorke had been no sensation at school with St Aloysius College and did not make the Combined Associated Schools XI, but playing for St Aloysius Old Boys he impressed former cricket star Austin Punch, who recommended him to Mosman club. He played his way through third and reserve grade into Mosman firsts and Poidevin-Gray matches. In his initial season in Mosman first grade, he was chosen in the New South Wales squad, a big lad who had filled out to 16 stone since his schooldays and had the help at Mosman of coaching from Halford Hooker, Stan McCabe and Ken Gulliver.

He was exceptionally fast from his early days in grade cricket but he had a short, awkward run up, with his pace stemming from his vast shoulders. He had bowled spinners for several seasons until his last year at school when he was pushed into the gap when St Aloysius lacked an opening bowler. Unfortunately, nobody ever quite worked out his approach run. If they had Gordon Rorke would have been one of the great fast bowlers.

Rorke first played for New South Wales in 1957–58 and was an immediate success, invariably crashing through the early batting, but he could not sustain his pace through a whole day and finished the season with 19 wickets at 26.89 in seven inter-State matches. In the following winter, he went through a physical build up to assist his control and also to enable him to sustain his pace for longer periods. In his second encounter with English cricketers he took 4 for 57 off 21 overs, startling the members of Peter May's side with sheer speed. When May looked set for a big score, Rorke bowled him with a real fire ball.

English cricket writers attributed Rorke's pace to a jerky action and Brian Chapman wrote in the London *Daily Mirror* that Rorke was "a honey of a chucker". In fact, Rorke's drag was more of a problem to English batsmen than his arm action, for he appeared to get unusually close to them before he let the ball go. He made his Test debut at Adelaide in the Fourth Test that summer, replacing an injured Ian Meckiff. When NSW team-mate Jim Burke was asked how Rorke would handle Test cricket he said, "He seems to have gone off his food since they picked him. He had only three steaks and three eggs for breakfast". Rorke turned in a marathon performance in the Test, bowling 52 overs in extreme heat, and dismissed Cowdrey, May, Graveney, Watson and Lock for 101 runs.

At the end of the 1958–59 season new laws were introduced

on throwing and dragging. Rorke said he was unconcerned about the throwing laws but was worried about his dragging. He was also worried by stomach trouble, which caused him to miss big games at the end of the 1958–59 season. He went off on a tour of Pakistan and India with the Australian team as one of the most controversial bowlers in the game but stomach ailments, which doctors diagnosed as hepatitis, caused a dramatic collapse and he had to be sent home before the tour ended, two and a half stone lighter than when he left. He was never quite the same speedster again and when the Australian team went to England in 1961 Frank Misson had the fast bowling spot many thought Rorke would get. He kept losing his rhythm and with it his blistering pace and in 1964 was dropped from the State squad.

Rorke's seven year career in first-class cricket, dogged by injuries and that horrendous trip to India and Pakistan, left cricket with a front foot law even the experts agree cannot be fairly applied. Famous umpire Lou Rowan, a bitter opponent of the law, said: "I believe the front foot law is difficult to apply because it demands the umpire's attention at the critical moment when he should be watching the ball in flight on its way to the striker. By the time the umpire transfers his attention from the bowler's front foot to the action at the striker's end the ball has already arrived there. Application of the front foot law is defeatist and it is wrong to adopt it simply because some countries do not have umpires capable of reaching uniformity in restricting the advantage gained through dragging, of which Rorke was a prize example."

ROSE, Robert Peter, 1952–

First-Class Averages: Batting, 981 runs at 30.65.

One of the most promising right-hand young batsmen in Australian cricket when he was tragically crippled in a motor accident in 1974. After his debut in 1971–72 Rose, son of a famous footballer, played 19 matches for Victoria, showing the highest promise. In 1973–74 he and Alan Sieler put on 271 for the fifth wicket against Queensland, a record in matches between these States. Rose scored 118 not out and Sieler 157. Rose, who came from the Collingwood club, was popular with players, sportswriters and officials and his accident stunned the sporting world.

ROTHWELL, Barry Alan, 1939–

First-Class Averages: Batting, 1,685 runs at 31.20; Bowling, 2 wickets at 19.50.

A chunky, pugnacious right-hand batsman who in a six year career in the New South Wales team proved himself a Sheffield Shield stalwart. He came into the New South Wales side when Richie Benaud retired in 1963 and retained his place until 1969, captaining the State in 1964–65 and 1965–66, the last season that New South Wales won the Shield. He batted anywhere from opener to No 6, gregarious on tour, tenacious when New South Wales was in trouble. Of his 36 matches for the State, he played 31 of them in Shield cricket. In club cricket for Manly and Northern Districts he scored almost 10,000 runs.

Rothwell was batting cautiously to try and retrieve a poor position for New South Wales at the SCG when a voice on The Hill called, "You must be on the pill, Rothwell, you're taking so few chances". He did not play in a Test but he gave cricket exceptional dedication. Since he retired to concentrate on his job as personnel manager of a heavy engineering conglomerate, he has been a diligent State selector.

ROWE, William Denis, 1892–1972

First-Class Averages: Batting, 2,022 runs at 25.59; Bowling, 53 wickets at 39.92.

A fine allrounder for Queensland between 1911–12 and 1929–30. He made a splendid start as a slow left-arm spin bowler in November, 1912, at Brisbane when he took 6 for 15 against New South Wales, hitting the stumps five times with flighty deliveries that nipped off the pitch. Despite these remarkable figures, NSW won the match by eight wickets. This was the only time in 47 matches that Rowe took five wickets in an innings, but he developed into an attractive left-hand batsman eager to play strokes. His finest season came in 1927–28 in Queensland's second year of Sheffield Shield competition. He made 128 not out in November, 1927, against NSW at Brisbane, 147 in January, 1928, against NSW at Sydney, and 134 against Victoria in Brisbane the following month. Rowe, who played with the Woolloongabba, South Brisbane and Eastern Suburbs clubs in Brisbane district cricket, kept picking up useful wickets and runs and figured in several big partnerships. In 1921–22 at Toowoomba, Rowe (175) and S. J. Fenelly (168 not out) scored 288 runs for the third wicket for a Queensland XI against Toowoomba.

RUNDELL, Percy Davies, 1890–1979

First-Class Averages: Batting, 1,722 runs at 31.88; Bowling, 25 wickets at 67.84.

A steady, capable right-handed batsman who played regularly for South Australia just before and just after World War I. He had a gift for timing the ball so well he made scoring runs look simple, using his slender, 6 ft frame to run the ball off the bat down to the leg or third man boundaries, or moving back to square cut powerfully. He could also drive through the covers efficiently. He was an outstanding close-in fieldsman who bowled leg-breaks and bosies successfully early in his career but an operation later curtailed his bowling.

Rundell played for Port Adelaide club when he first entered inter-State cricket in 1912–13 but later his work as a bank manager sent him into country areas and he had to play wherever he was posted. He played for Glenelg when he was at Victor Harbour, driving up for Saturday matches, batting quietly for an hour for practice and then hitting out. In his initial first-class match at Adelaide in December, 1912, he made 36 in a South Australian total of 569 and took 3 for 34, South Australia defeating a side that included Trumper, Waddy, Collins and Minnett by an innings and 53 runs.

He made his first century (100) for South Australia in January, 1919, at Melbourne, and had centuries on the same ground against Victoria in January, 1920 (122 not out), and November, 1920 (116). But probably the best knock of his career was his 121 against England at Adelaide in March, 1921, England winning by an innings and 63 runs after scoring 627. Rundell's father, **Joshua Upcott Rundell** (1861–1922), a North Adelaide postman who was later secretary of Port Adelaide club, had a remarkable coup for South Australia at Melbourne against Victoria in 1884–85. Victoria made 189 and 82, Rundell, senr., bowled South Australia to victory by taking 5 for 31 in Victoria's second innings. Joshua took eight wickets altogether in first-class cricket at 15.00 and made 27 runs at 6.75. He was a familiar figure at Adelaide district games when his son was playing but he died two years before the 1924–25 season when Percy Rundell topped the district competition averages with 134.66.

RUSH, THE FAMILY A Melbourne family who made a major contribution to Victorian cricket both on the field through their skills as players and in the committee meetings that shaped the present conduct of the game. They were all educated at Wesley College.

Henry Reynolds ("Harry") **Rush** (1858–1928) began the family association with the Hawksburn-Prahran club that lasted through four generations. He retired from Hawksburn at the end of the 1897–98 season after 18 years as a player, many of them as a highly competent first grade captain, to concentrate on his work as treasurer of the Victorian Cricket Association. He also gave 21 years service to the Australian Board of Control.

Edward Reynolds ("Eddie") **Rush** (1868–1936) captained Wesley College in the 1880s and became Hawksburn's finest-ever batsman. He won the Club's batting average seven times between 1885 and 1901 and twice headed the bowling averages. He still holds the Hawksburn-Prahran record of 293 not out, which he made against Carlton in 1897–98, when he also hit 187 against North Melbourne. Eddie Rush played three times for Victoria, scoring 75 runs at 12.50, but could not carry his prolific run-scoring in grade into first-class matches. Eddie Rush made two ducks for Victoria against Stoddart's MCC team.

Thomas Reynolds Rush (1876–1926) played with his

brother Eddie in the Hawksburn side that won the VCA premiership in 1899–1900 and topped the Hawksburn batting averages several times. Tom Rush played eight matches for Victoria from 1906–07 for 197 runs at 13.13.

John Rush (1910–), one of Eddie Rush's seven sons, three of whom played for Prahran, took over from Jack Ellis as Prahran's wicket-keeper in 1930–31 and played for Victoria twice that season against Tasmania, scoring 116 runs at 29.00. He taught at Wesley College for 40 years, much of it as cricket coach, his star pupils including Sam Loxton and Ian Johnson.

The Rush family association with Prahran ended in the 1970's when Trevor Rush, a grand-nephew of H.R.Rush, left the club to play with Hawthorn. The Hawthorn-Prahran Rushes were not related to W. L. ("Leo") Rush, a prominent Board of Control member.

RUTHERFORD, John Walter ("Pythagorus"), 1929–

A Perth mathematics master who became the first West Australian selected for a major overseas tour and the first to play in a Test. He was a right-hand opening batsman who took extreme care with his defence, driving strongly and placing his cuts and glances well. He earned his selection in the 1956 Australian team to England by scoring four splendid centuries for Western Australia between 1953–54 and 1955–56, including a topscore of 167 against South Australia at Adelaide Oval. He further enhanced his tour claims with an innings of 113 in the England tour trial at Sydney in January, 1956.

He proved an excellent tourist, but in a highly disappointing Australian batting lineup, could not find a Test place, possibly because the selectors were not prepared to risk him against the turning ball in a summer in which the major matches were dominated by the spin of Laker and Lock. Against the MCC he and "Slasher" Mackay, new chums to Lord's, got lost on their way to the field to open the Australian innings. They left the Australians' first floor dressing-room and wandered around corridors, poking their heads in doors hoping to find an exit to the field. "There must be a way out of here," said Rutherford. "The other mob's been out there for ages." They finally sighted the field in front and jumped the fence about 30 yards upfield from the player's gate. Rutherford was led back along the correct route to the dressing-room at lunch by Neil Harvey. They put on 282 for the second wicket, Harvey scoring 225, Rutherford 98 in a first look at Lord's he will never forget.

That turned out to be Rutherford's highest score on the tour and he finished with 640 runs at 22.86. Keith Miller nicknamed Rutherford "Pythagorus" after giving him mathematical exercises to solve in the slips such as the speed over the ground of passing planes. Rutherford always answered dead-

First-Class Averages: Batting, 3,367 runs at 31.79; Bowling, 22 wickets at 53.95.

Tests (1): 30 runs at 15.00; 1 wicket at 15.00.

pan with what sounded like a logical solution. On the way home Rutherford played in his only Test against India at Bombay, putting on a 57-run opening stand with Jimmy Burke. There was great joy among the Australians when he bowled Manjrekar in India's second innings for his only Test wicket. He made his sixth first-class century, 160, for WA against NSW at Perth in 1957–58 and dropped out of cricket soon afterwards.

RYAN, Albert James ("Bulla"), 1904–

First-Class Averages: Batting, 1,453 runs at 29.65; Bowling, 19 wickets at 43.31.

An outstanding Australian Rules footballer who played frequently for South Australia between 1927–28 and 1936–37. He was a sound but slow right-hand batsman who could be relied on dig in and never give his wicket away carelessly, and he bowled handy right-arm slow-medium off-breaks. He played for the Adelaide club and then Sturt, always attracting barracking from the crowd because of his fame as half-forward for South Adelaide. He hit 86 out of a South Australian total of 471 in his debut against Queensland at Adelaide in 1927–28. He made an impressive 61 against England at Adelaide in 1932–33 and four years later made 71 against England on the same ground. He scored his initial first-class century (124) against Queensland at Adelaide in 1933–34 and his topscore (144) against Queensland at Brisbane in 1935–36. Ryan headed both the averages and aggregate in Adelaide club cricket in 1931–32, with 615 runs at 61.50.

RYDER, John, 1889–1977

A tall, big-hitting right-handed Victorian batsman who made a valuable contribution to Australian cricket, although he was never in the class of many of his contemporaries. He was a plucky, competent player who made up for technical deficiencies with an indomitable spirit but in a period of master cricketers his position in the Australian side often was insecure. He enjoyed wide popularity because of his pugnacity and eagerness to hit hard, particularly in his birthplace, Collingwood. He captained Australia five times for four losses and a win.

Ryder's ability to get runs stemmed from his ability to get his powerful front-foot drives flowing. He was an adequate but not outstanding field, and bowled useful right-arm medium-to-fast away swingers, occasionally making the ball lift disconcertingly. He was unpretentious and honest but suffered several setbacks from selectors in his prime. In a record run as an Australian selector he handed out plenty of shocks himself.

Ryder was always a tremendously enthusiastic cricketer of abundant energy and in a first-class career that spread from

856

1912 to 1935 he enjoyed every moment. In his initial season for Victoria he took 30 wickets, bowling vigorous stuff that brought him 6 for 44 and 1 for 17 in a match against New South Wales, and 7 for 53 and 6 for 102 against South Australia. In this year he also scored 38 and 71 and had match figures of 8 for 88 in Victor Trumper's benefit match. In 1913–14, he took 7 for 88 against South Australia, scoring 36 not out and 105 in the same match. Three centuries before the World War I established him as an exceptional hitter.

After the war he was used mainly as a change bowler and a middle order batsman who could thrash tiring attacks. He made 127 against South Australia in 1920–21, and produced an outstanding performance against the touring England side, scoring 54 and 108 for Victoria. He made his Test debut in that series and after innings of 44 in the Third Test and 52 not out in the Fourth won a place in the famous 1921 side in England. In a brilliant lineup, he finished fourth in the batting averages with 1,032 runs at 38.22 and took 24 wickets at 24.41, but did not play in a Test. Against South Africa in 1921 he made 334 runs in the three Tests at an average of 111.33, including 142 in the Third Test at Cape Town.

Back in Australia he missed selection in the first two Tests against Gilligan's MCC side in 1924–25 because of a back injury but returned triumphantly in the Third Test, going in at 6 for 119 to score 201 in 390 minutes, disciplining his attacking urges to get Australia out of trouble. His second innings brought 88, one of his drives sending "Tich" Freeman from the field with a painful wrist injury.

Over Christmas 1926 Ryder played an innings for Victoria against New South Wales that is recalled whenever big-hitting arises. Going in after Woodfull had made 133, Ponsford 352 and Hendry 100, Ryder hit 295, the first 100 in 115 minutes, the second in 74 and his last 95 in 56 minutes, six times hitting the ball out of the field. He moved from 275 to 295 in four strokes and was out trying for another six.

On his second tour of England in 1926 Ryder again scored more than 1,000 runs—1,145 at 35.78. By now his bowling had fallen away but he managed 27 wickets at 33.59. He did very little in the Tests with 42 out of 494 in the Third Test his best effort, and it surprised most critics when he took over as Australian captain after Herbie Collins retired. An extraordinary run of big scores by Hammond brought about Australia's downfall in the 1928–29 series against Chapman's England side. Ryder scored more runs than anyone in his team, 492 at 54.66, including 112 in the Third Test when he put on 161 with Kippax. Woodfull was Victorian captain when Ryder was appointed Test Captain, and Woodfull gracefully stepped down as State skipper so that Ryder's national standing could be confirmed at State level.

Ryder was at his shrewdest when England played Victoria

First-Class Averages: Batting, 10,499 at 44.29; Bowling, 238 wickets at 29.68.

Tests (20): 1,394 runs at 51.62; 17 wickets at 43.70.

that summer. Victoria were on 9 for 572, the State's highest score ever against England, when Larwood was given the ball against tailender Bert Ironmonger. Twice Ironmonger delicately cut Larwood's fastest balls for two. Spectators, who could not believe it as Ironmonger was a renowned duffer with the bat, heckled Larwood as he moved in to bowl. Larwood stopped and all the English players sat on the grass waiting for the crowd's jeers to stop. Larwood threw the ball to his captain, Chapman, who tossed it back. Three times the England players stood to continue, each time sitting down again as the crowd's abuse continued. Ryder promptly closed the Victorian innings, an action which was hailed as a fine piece of diplomacy but which possibly deprived Woodfull (275 not out) of the chance of the only 300 of his career.

Although he was one of the selectors, Ryder missed a place in the 1930 team to England, his co-selectors believing he was too old for the trip at 41. They preferred Woodfull. His omission sparked angry protests. In Collingwood, hundreds of protesters attended a meeting urging his inclusion. Pentridge Gaol prisoners wrote to the Chief secretary threatening to break out unless Ryder made the trip. Ryder refused to comp-

Jack Ryder moves down the pitch to drive against England.

858

lain publicly and continued to captain Victoria. In 1935–36, he captained a side organised by Frank Tarrant to India.

Jack Ryder played in 20 Test matches, scoring three centuries, and nine fifties. In all first-class matches, he hit 24 centuries, and also held 132 catches.

After his retirement from first-class cricket in 1935, he had a long career as a selector, continuing after a break until he was 84, using binoculars to help his view of the play towards the end. There was widespread criticism of his appointment after 80 but he could be seen in the nets bowling a few down or telling Test players with problems on certain shots that he would help them, a shrewd old rooster who warned Keith Stackpole before the John Snow bouncer barrage began in 1970–71 to get his hook shot in order. Until he died at 87 he was always ready to help youngsters. For years after he quit first-class cricket he got plenty of wickets for Collingwood with slow leg-breaks.

Known as the "King of Collingwood," he led the parade of old Australian Test players at the Centenary Test in March, 1977, but died shortly afterwards.

RYMILL, Jack Westall, 1901–1976

First-Class Averages: Batting, 1,260 runs at 35.00.

A forceful left-handed batsman whose hard-hitting and brilliant outfielding frequently thrilled Adelaide cricket followers in the 1920s. He used all his strong, 6 ft physique to power the ball away with hooks and cuts, and his speed across the field as he chased balls right to the boundary fence regularly aroused applause. He learned his cricket at St Peter's College, Adelaide, and later played for East Torrens and Kensington. He made 110 for South Australia against New South Wales in January, 1925, and two months later scored a brilliant 146 to set up an unexpected South Australian win by 10 wickets over England, adding 151 with Rundell. South Australia made 443 after losing 2 for 12. Rymill scored two centuries against Victoria, 124 in January, 1926, at Melbourne and 142 the following December at Adelaide. In 1924–25, he scored most runs in Adelaide district cricket for Kensington, 820 at 74.54. Rymill played in a Test trial at Sydney in December, 1925, scoring 13 and 5 for The Rest versus Australia. He still holds the South Australian seventh wicket partnership record of 183, set in 1925–26 with W. C. Alexander, the Adelaide batsman who went to New Zealand with an Australian team in 1927–28 after scoring three centuries for SA.

S

SAGGERS, Ronald Arthur, 1917–

First-Class Averages: Batting, 1,888 runs at 23.89; Dismissals 221 (147 catches, 74 stumpings).

Tests (6): 30 at 10.00; 24 dismissals (16 catches, 8 stumpings).

A smart, polished wicket-keeper of exceptional stumping skill in the international matches just after World War II. On the tour of England by Bradman's famous 1948 team, Saggers replaced the injured Tallon for the Leeds Test. He missed no chances and Australia lost nothing by playing Saggers, who, however, lacked the exceptional speed and agility of Tallon. They were both tall, lean men who seldom conceded a bye and they had an equal number of dismissals for the tour, 43 (Tallon caught 29, stumped 14. Saggers caught 23, stumped 20).

Saggers, born in the Sydney suburb of Sydenham, worked extremely hard in the practice nets immediately war ended, standing behind the stumps at the Marrickville club's practice sessions for hours at a time perfecting his skills. He remains one of the few batsmen to score more than 1,000 runs in a Sydney first grade season. In the match against Essex at Southend when the 1948 Australians made history by scoring 721 in a six-hour day, Saggers was one of our four century-makers, adding 166 in 65 minutes with Loxton on his way to 104 not out.

He took over as Australia's top 'keeper on the 1949–50 tour of South Africa, when Tallon was unavailable, playing in all five Tests. He was particularly effective in the Second Test at Cape Town, where his stumping swiftness added to the threat of McCool's legspin. He stumped three of McCool's first innings bag of 5 for 41. He retired from big cricket after that series to concentrate on his career in insurance.

SAUNDERS, John Victor, 1876–1927

A tall, heavily-moustached Victorian left-arm bowler who approached the stumps in a curving run from mid-on and bowled at variable pace, mostly medium. For a long time he was the best left-arm spinner in Australia, a spare, energetic cricketer who turned the ball disconcertingly. He was almost unplayable on sticky or wet pitches even for the outstanding

860

batsmen of his period. He was a genuine tailender with the bat and never made 50 in his life, but he was a tidy, reliable fieldsman.

Saunders played district cricket early in his career with Carlton but later switched to North Melbourne. He made his first-class debut in 1899–1900 but did not develop into a match-winning bowler for two seasons. In 1901–02, he took 6 for 57 and 5 for 73 for Victoria against New South Wales, and this outstanding effort won him a place in the Fourth Test against England at Sydney. He had match figures of 9 for 162, including 5 for 43 when he and Noble (5 for 54) bowled unchanged through England's second innings of 99. Despite this outstanding debut—Australia won by seven wickets—he was dropped for the Fifth Test by selectors who wanted to have a look at South Australian left-hander J. F. Travers before naming the team for England.

On tour of England in 1902 with the Australian team led by Joe Darling, Saunders took 127 wickets at 17.07, and only Trumble (140 at 14.27) did better. He emerged as a topline Test bowler in the Third Test at Bramall Lane, where both sides struggled against bad light caused by smoke from factories. He took 5 for 50 in England's first innings of 145. In the Fourth Test at Old Trafford, England were set to score 124 to win in the final innings. With eight runs needed and the last pair at the wicket, rain forced the players from the field. Forty-five minutes later they returned and Darling threw Saunders the ball. Fred Tate prodded Saunders away for four, but when another four would have given England victory, Saunders clean bowled Tate. Saunders always claimed that it was his batting as much as his bowling that brought Australia the win, for he made three, the margin of victory. On the whole tour he made only 84 runs in 34 innings! Saunders took six more wickets in the Fifth Test at The Oval to finish the series with 18 at 26.27. In South Africa in 1902–03, he took 15 wickets in two Tests at 11.73 including 7 for 34 at Johannesburg.

Between 1899 and 1910 Saunders took five wickets or more in an innings 24 times for Victoria and 48 times in all. In 1902–03, he took 8 for 106 and 5 for 88 in one match against South Australia, and the same summer he took 6 for 118 against England. In 14 Tests he six times took five wickets or more an innings, best effort 7 for 34. His best Test series was his last, in 1907–08 against England. He had match figures of 9 for 104 in the Fourth Test at Melbourne and 8 for 196 in the Fifth at Sydney, completing the series with 31 wickets at 23.09.

Saunders settled in New Zealand after the 1909–10 Australian season and appeared in representative matches for Wellington and New Zealand between 1910 and 1914. He was the man who persuaded Clarrie Grimmett to further his cricket ambitions by migrating to Australia.

First-Class Averages: Batting, 586 runs at 4.76; Bowling, 553 wickets at 21.81.

Tests (14): 39 runs at 2.29; 79 wickets at 22.73.

SAUNDERS, Warren Joseph, 1934–

First-Class Averages: Batting, 1,701 runs at 32.71.

An attractive right–hand batsman who performed efficiently for New South Wales between 1955–56 and 1964–65, but frequently had to stand down when Test stars like Norm O'Neill, Bob Simpson and Brian Booth returned to the State side. He was unfortunate not to score a first-class century. In January, 1964, for example, he topscored for NSW in both innings against Victoria with 87 and 98, but two days later had to drop out of the match against South Australia. In both the innings against Victoria Saunders, a great team man, sacrificed his century in the interest of his team, which needed quick runs, continuing to hit out instead of playing safe.

Saunders captained NSW twice in 1964–65 and had just been appointed captain of the NSW team to play South Australia and Western Australia when he announced his retirement because of urgent commitments in his insurance business. He continued to play for St George, however, and in January, 1972, scored his 10,000th run for the club he had joined as a small boy from Arncliffe. Recently he has become devoted to developing young cricketers and in 1977 took the Australian Under-19 team on a 12-match tour of England. He has been a St George delegate to the NSWCA and a State selector for several years.

SAVIGNY, John Horatio, 1867–1923

First-Class Averages: Batting, 648 runs at 29.45; Bowling, 5 wickets at 30.60.

For 30 years the most gifted batsman in Tasmania who played an innings of what Roger Page called "heroic grandeur" against England in 1904 at Hobart. Savigny hit 21 fours and a five in a graceful five hour innings of 164 not out, adding 202 for the first wicket with O. H. Douglas. This marvellous innings, highly praised for its style by MCC players, was the last of Savigny's 17 appearances for Tasmania.

Refusing repeated inducements to play again for his State, he was content to turn his back on possible Test selection and became the island's prince of coaches. An impressive number of fine cricketers were coached by him in his Launceston backyard (where he demonstrated strokes with an axe handle), at the Launceston Grammar School, or at the West Launceston club where even in his late forties he remained a prolific scorer. He figured in some huge partnerships with his elder brother **William H. ("Beau") Savigny** (1864–1922) including 334 in 1893 and 250 for North v. South in 1895. W. H. Savigny was for 26 years a master at Sydney Grammar School where there is a memorial tablet to his memory.

J. H. Savigny overcame a childhood plagued with sickness to score more than fifty centuries at all levels of cricket. His health meant he could not withstand a long sea voyage such as would have been involved in pursuing a career in Australian first-class cricket and he was content to play club cricket and help build the game in Launceston. He owed a lot to coaching he received as a boy from C. W. Rock, when his parents sent him to Deloraine for his health. He became a master of batting and in the 1901–02 summer became the first Tasmanian to score 1,000 runs in a season—1,020 runs at an average of 78.46. He loved fishing as passionately as he did cricket and was found dead on the banks of the Lefroy after setting out alone on a fishing trip.

SAWLE, Lawrence Michael, 1925–

First-Class Averages: Batting, 1,669 runs at 29.28.

A dour right-hand opening batsman who played many long innings for Western Australia between 1954 and 1960. He scored 109 not out, his sole first-class century, against New South Wales at Perth in 1955–56, and the same season created a record first wicket partnership for WA of 124 with John Rutherford against South Australia. Sawle also made nine fifties during his career for WA. After he retired he turned to cricket administration and after service on a number of committees now represents WA on the Australian Cricket Board.

SCAIFE, John Willie, 1909–

First-Class Averages: Batting, 2,206 runs at 33.93; Bowling, 1 wicket at 68.00.

A right–hand batsman from Melbourne's Fitzroy Club who was one of Australia's youngest ever first–class players when he first played for Victoria in 1926–27 a few days short of his 17th birthday. Others such as Victoria's Len Junor, Tasmania's Cyril Badcock and New South Wales' Ian Craig have since appeared in inter–State matches at a younger age than did Scaife but Melbourne newspapers at the time treated him as a prodigy.

Scaife held his place in the Victorian side with frequent good scores, batting after stars like Woodfull, Ponsford, Hendry and Ryder. He made his highest score, 120, against NSW at Sydney in January, 1934, and also made 100 runs against Queensland in Melbourne in 1935–36. He was a diminutive figure, who scampered through quickly for his runs, and played 46 first-class matches in 10 seasons, ending in 1935–36.

SCHNEIDER, Karl Joseph, 1905–1928

First-Class Averages: Batting, 1,509 runs at 48.67; Bowling, 10 wickets at 35.50.

A tragic Victorian-born left-hander who died of tuberculosis three weeks after his 23rd birthday after a brilliant summer of run-making in which he made five first-class centuries. Although he was only 5 ft 2 in tall and lacked power because of his short reach, he was regarded as a potential champion.

Schneider was born in the Melbourne suburb of Hawthorn and a big reputation preceded him to the Melbourne Cricket Club, where he proceeded to shock experts with his skill despite his tiny physique. He made his debut for Victoria in

1922–23 but played only two games for the State over the next two seasons. When he moved to Adelaide, the noted English Test batsman, Patsy Hendren, who was coaching in South Australia called him "the coming Warren Bardsley." Schneider played his first game for South Australia in 1926–27 and scored his initial first-class century that season in Sydney against New South Wales, a dour knock of 146 that contained only three fours.

His success in 1927–28 was remarkable, for he scored 108 v. NSW at Adelaide in December, 1927, 143 v. Victoria in 315 minutes at Melbourne in January, 1928, 114 out of 505 v. Queensland at Brisbane in January, 1928, and 107 v. Western Australia at Perth in March, 1928. This fine performance earned him a trip to New Zealand at the end of the Australian season with the Australian side captained by Vic. Richardson. There he scored another 547 first-class runs in only 12 completed innings, including 138 against Canterbury at Auckland, where he was in a stand of 218 with Woodfull.

Towards the end of the New Zealand visit he was horse-riding on the slopes of Mount Cook with Archie Jackson and several other players when he began to haemorrhage. Jackson was among those who carried him to a hut, and Jackson's family always suspected that this was where Archie contracted the contagious tuberculosis that killed him. Schneider died on September 5, 1928, Archie Jackson's 19th birthday, only six months after he collapsed on Mount Cook.

SCHOLES, Walter John, 1950–

First-Class Averages: Batting, 3,201 runs at 30.78; Bowling, 1 wicket at 140.00.

A pugnacious right-hand batsman and leg-break bowler who took over the Victorian captaincy from Richie Robinson in 1981–82. A resolute, intelligent cricketer who went into the Victorian team from the Carlton Club in 1968–69, Scholes faced a tough job, with Victoria in one of their worst slumps for years. Inconsistent form by star batsmen Yallop, Moss and Weiner, coupled with his own failure to produce big scores, gave him a difficult task. Scholes has made three first-class centuries in a career of fairly handy run-scoring, the highest, 156 in 1980–81 against Tasmania at Hobart, which followed immediately on his two ducks at Sydney against NSW. This 156 enabled Victoria to reach their highest total in 16 years, 9 for 543 and top the Tasmanian first innings total of 425, and ultimately win the game by six wickets.

SCORERS, FOR AUSTRALIAN TEAMS

Australia's official records of Test matches have been kept by a succession of specially appointed scorer's since 1905, when W. H. Ferguson virtually created the job. Before then Australian teams on tour had kept their own scorebooks, players or

864

managers taking a turn, or had simply accepted the score-cards of scorers in the host countries. Under Ferguson, the scorer's job evolved to include supervising all the teams' laundry and caring for their luggage. Today he is a key man in the success of any Australian overseas tour, on call to answer media queries. The scores of every match in which an Australian team plays are sent back to the Australian Cricket Board immediately a match ends and at the end of a tour a complete scorebook of the tour matches is sent to the ACB. These become the official tour records.

When "Fergie" presented himself for one of the first matches of his initial tour in 1905 he found resentment over his presence among English scorers, who at first refused to make room for him in the scorer's seats. "We have enough scorers and don't require any more," he was told. At first he had to eat in a basement with local professionals but when manager Frank Laver heard of this he invited him to eat with the Australian players, a move that immediately raised his status with local scorers. He had never scored before but as the tour progressed he improved his methods, and from this came his famous charts that showed where every ball in a batsman's innings had been played. One of his jobs on that first trip—for which he was paid £2 per week and met all his own travel and accommodation expenses—was to check figures for Mrs Clem Hill, who insisted on keeping her own scorecards.

"Fergie" made his last tour with John Goddard's West Indian team in England in 1957. Norm Gorman, scorer for the Mosman club in Sydney and for NSW matches, took over the Australian team job with Ian Johnson's 1956 team in England. Jack Cameron, from the Australian Broadcasting Commission's Melbourne office, toured as scorer for Richie Benaud's team in England in 1961, and since then Dave Sherwood, formerly a caterer and office manager, has filled the job with Australian touring teams. Sherwood, a genial, lean figure of impeccable neatness, learned the job as scorer for the Randwick club in Sydney and by studying Ferguson's scorebooks in the archives of the ACB. He has been scoring since 1936, and has seen scoring evolve to include instant answers of queries from commentators. Apart from the runs scored, the scorer has to be able to provide a player's career record, confirm the manner of dismissal and even the direction of a stroke. They do this by dividing the field into sections and using symbols such as "E" for an edged stroke, "X" for played and missed. Every ball is plotted and even no-balls are clearly shown. A circled figure 4 in a scorebook, for example, means a no-ball went for four, whereas a circled dot means no runs came from the no-ball. It's a complex and demanding science, with concentration essential throughout each match, but an important public relations exercise in Australian cricket.

Dave Sherwood.

SCOTT, Dr Henry James Herbert ("Tup"), 1858–1910

First-Class Averages: Batting, 2,863 runs at 22.72; Bowling, 18 wickets at 27.44.

Tests (8): 359 runs at 27.61.

The first Victorian to captain an Australian team on tour in England. He was a right-hand batsman with a sound defence who could hit powerfully on occasions, though he tended to be over-cautious. He was a good fieldsman and a useful right-arm medium-pace change bowler. His tour as Australian captain was marred by quarrels among his players which his easy-going approach failed to heal, and he lost all his three Tests as Australia's captain.

He was born at Toorak and educated at Wesley College and Melbourne University and won the St Kilda club's first grade average while still at school. At 19, he took 6 for 33 for Victoria against NSW at Sydney, winning a trophy for the best bowling performance in the match. Initially he studied engineering but he changed to medicine after two years. At 23, he switched to East Melbourne club for whom he scored several centuries and starred as an all-rounder.

In December, 1883, Scott made 114 not out for Victoria against New South Wales at Melbourne. This innings won him a handsome album from the Victoria Cricket Association and a place in the 1884 Australian team to England as a last-minute replacement when Evans, Garrett and Horan dropped out. He quickly became a valuable member of the side and only Murdoch, Giffen, and McDonnell made more than his 973 runs at 22.62. After scoring 106 for once out in the Lord's Test (he was caught in the first innings by W. L. Murdoch, fielding as a substitute) he was promoted in the order for The Oval Test, going in at No 4. Here he played the innings of his life, scoring 102 in 210 minutes while adding 207 for the third wicket with Murdoch (211). He made a habit while he was in London of taking two-penny bus rides and because of this team-mates nicknamed him "Twopence" and later simply "Tup".

His splendid form in inter-Colonial matches continued and in 1885–86 he made 111 for Victoria against New South Wales at Melbourne. He returned to England in 1886 as Australia's captain but was handicapped throughout the tour by squabbles within the team and by injuries to key players. "There is no doubt that the cares of leadership affected his run-getting," wrote Frederick Lillywhite in his *Scores And Biographies*. "For quarrels among the players were many, and he had not sufficient strength of character to cope with the situation." *Wisden* in its review of the Australians' tour regretted the absence of authority and experience in the captain.

Scott played several fine innings on the tour, including 123 against Middlesex at Lord's where he and S. P. Jones put on 155 for the first wicket. In the match against Yorkshire at Sheffield he gave Australia a spectacular victory by hitting the last four balls of the match for 22 runs, with 6,4,6,6. The umpire called "over" after Scott had despatched the first three balls and had to be corrected by scorers in the pavilion.

Scott's 22 remains the best scoring off a four-ball over by an Australian batsman, beating George Bonnor's 20 in a match at Scarborough four years earlier. No wonder critics lamented that Scott did not attack more often.

The injury problem was so bad during this tour that Scott had to get manager Major Ben Wardill to play in one match. Dr Rowley Pope, who was not an official member of the team, had eight innings for 31 runs. Scott and 'keeper Affie Jarvis both batted in tour games despite painful leg injuries. At The Oval, where Scott had had such a fine Test two years earlier, the Australians dropped Dr Grace four times before he scored 100, Grace going on to 170 in a knock which saw him hit the great Spofforth into the crowd. Australia were then caught on a sticky wicket and lost by an innings and 217 runs.

At the end of this disastrous tour in which eight matches were lost and only nine won, Scott stayed in England to complete his medical studies. He dropped out of first-class cricket on his return home but became a pioneer country doctor who appeared regularly in bush cricket matches. He practised at Bathurst and later at Scone, where he was Mayor and later Chief Magistrate. In areas where rough bush tracks served as roads, he travelled vast distances to reach patients on remote farms. Scone's Scott Memorial Hospital was named after him. In all first-class matches, "Tup" Scott scored four centuries. For Victoria against the odds he scored 32 runs at 8.00 and took three wickets at 24.00. He died of typhoid fever, complicated by pneumonia at 51. Among the mourners was his close friend Banjo Paterson, noted Australian poet.

SCOTT, John Drake, 1888–1964

First-Class Averages: Batting, 1,113 runs at 14.64; Bowling, 227 wickets at 28.31.

A right-arm fast bowler of surprising pace for a man of average height, whose well-coordinated action made the ball fly awkwardly. He had the bad luck in the years of his best chance for a Test place that some of Australia's finest opening bowlers were in action, but he took more than 200 first-class wickets for New South Wales and South Australia, and contributed useful runs as a right-hand batsman. After his retirement he became a famous umpire. Most of all he was noted for his outspoken manner and firm opinions.

"Tibby" Cotter kept Scott out of Tests before World War I, but they formed a fearsome opening attack for NSW, inflicting many painful bruises and breaking more than their quota of stumps. After the war which saw Cotter killed at Beersheba, the emergence of Gregory and McDonald spoiled Scott's Test hopes, although Scott was rated one of the fastest bowlers in Australian cricket.

Scott was the bowler when Bert Oldfield made one of cricket's greatest catches from a leg glance by Bill Woodfull in the NSW-Victoria Shield match at Sydney in 1922–23. Scott was a

memorable legside field, who could cover the area from square leg to mid-on by himself. Hal Hooker regarded him as one of cricket's likeable larrikins. Scott jumped the fence during a grade match at Petersham Oval in Sydney to deal with a spectator who heckled him. "Let's see if your courage is as big as your mouth," he hollered. Team-mates restrained him.

On the 1928–29 tour of Australia by Chapman's English team Phil Mead captivated crowds with his drill before facing every ball. Mead took four steps forward, four steps back, and then turned towards the square leg umpire and touched the peak of his cap. Playing for an Australian XI, Scott responded at short leg by doffing his own cap every time Mead touched his cap. When his captain, Vic Richardson, admonished him for making fun of Mead, Scott said, "If he's respectful to me, I'm going to be respectful to him." The exchange of cap salutes went on for the 130 minutes Mead batted.

After he moved to South Australia in 1925–26 Scott took 6 for 58 against Victoria at Adelaide, and 5 for 117 against NSW at Adelaide. In 1927–28 he took 5 for 108 against NSW at Adelaide.

As an umpire he was the centre of many controversies in 10 Tests between 1936 and 1947, usually standing with George Borwick. He built a reputation for disciplining fast bowlers for bowling short rising deliveries—the type of bowling for which he had been known. He was also a Rugby League player of note and scored the first try for the Newtown club in premiership football in 1908. One day he visited the press box at Melbourne to study the angle from which commentators were criticising his decisions. "Bloody well worse than I thought," he said, looking down on the pitch 150 yards away. The London *Star's* L. N. Bailey said, "If you have any doubts about a decision Jack, just look up here and we'll give you the sign."

SCOTT, Robert Barrington ("Barry"), 1916–

First-Class Averages: Batting, 318 runs at 13.82; Bowling, 59 wickets at 36.22.

An enormously powerful Victorian fast bowler who was probably deprived of Test selection by World War II. He was ideally built for pace bowling, with heavily-muscled wide shoulders, stout legs and long, sinewy arms. He was over 6 ft tall. He broke into the Victorian side in 1935–36 in his 20th year after some outstanding performances for Wesley College, where he was a class-mate of Ian Johnson, Sam Loxton and Ross Gregory, and for the Melbourne Colts and University clubs. He had a curious action in which he seemed to tie his arms in knots and he jumped high in his final delivery stride but there was no doubting his pace.

Scott was regarded as the fastest bowler in Australia in the summer of 1939–40 and three times took five wickets or more in an innings—5 for 62 against Tasmania, 7 for 33 and 5 for 46 against NSW. He seemed the logical successor in the Australian team to Ernie McCormick as war began, but he had days when he could match McCormick in bowling no-balls. He usually went in last as a batsman and in 33 first-class innings had a topscore of 49. He was a well-known Melbourne advertising executive after World War II.

SEDDON, Cecil Dudley, 1902–1978

A right-hand batsman with a peculiar two-eyed stance who played for New South Wales between 1926 and 1929. He was better known, however, for his services as an administrator, acting as a New South Wales selector for 20 years from 1947, and as an Australian selector from 1954 until he was replaced by Neil Harvey in 1967. He hated his first christian name, Cecil, and always signed himself as "Dudley", but he was affectionately known by cricketers at all levels as "Snow."

Seddon travelled vast distances to watch and coach junior cricketers, and always stressed that the boys watching his unorthodox square-on-to-the-bowler stance should "do as I say—not as I do". He was captain of the Petersham district club for many years and devoted almost 60 years to the club's affairs. He played six times for NSW, with one century, 134 v. Tasmania in February, 1929. He was one of an exclusive group to represent New South Wales in two sports, as he played for the State as a centre-threequarter in his days with Newtown Rugby League club.

First-Class Averages: Batting, 361 runs at 36.10.

SEITZ, John Arnold, 1883–1963

A right-hand batsman for East Melbourne, Oxford University and Victoria whose first-class career was upset by his work as an educationalist. He was a Carlton-born Rhodes scholar who proved his value as a cricketer with Oxford in 1909. On his return home he made his debut for Victoria against South Africa in November, 1910, when the Sheffield Shield programme was curtailed because of the presence of the South African team. The following season Seitz helped Victoria defeat South Australia at Adelaide with scores of 75 and 107. In the next match against South Australia at Melbourne, he made 101. Thereafter he concentrated on his academic career.

Seitz was one of those who temporarily displaced Warwick Armstrong as State captain. He later became Victorian Director of Education and was president of the Victorian Cricket Association from 1947 to 1963. In this role he was at the centre of the notorious watered pitch affair at the Melbourne Cricket Ground during the Third England-Australia Test in 1954–55. The MCG pitch was worn and pitted when play ended on Saturday night but when play resumed on Monday morning, was firm and even. Amid charges that the pitch had been wa-

First-Class Averages: Batting, 981 runs at 28.85; Bowling, 1 wicket at 12.00.

tered during the Sunday rest day, Seitz produced a statutory declaration denying this from the MCG groundsman. Seitz made three centuries, one for Oxford University (120 v. Surrey in 1909 at Reigate) and two for Victoria.

SELECTORS   Cricket teams—and the men who select them—have caused controversy since the game had its beginnings among early settlers in Sydney's Hyde Park, van Dieman's Land, the village John Batman called Melbourne, Adelaide, Moreton Bay, and later among the builders of Perth's Government House. Before Tests were introduced there were disputes about the inter-Colonial teams. International matches simply added national pride to the fervour of these debates.

The first teams in Australia were chosen by the publicans who sponsored them, by the officers of convict garrisons, and when trips overseas began, by the men who sponsored the teams and their senior players. John Conway wrote to the players he wanted for the first Australian team to England in 1878 and asked if they were available and if they could put up the share of expenses expected from each player. The first men he contacted helped pick the rest.

Later the Melbourne Cricket Club, the Australasian Cricket Council and the Australian Board of International Cricket Control in turn appointed selectors. Today the appointment of selection committees is the right of the district clubs, the State associations, and the Australian Cricket Board. The right to democratically elect their own captains was lost by players in Australian and State teams 50 years ago, and today is held by only some district first grade teams. Sometimes today Australian captains are being named and then invited to help the selectors pick the team, but we have not so far followed the frequent English habit of appointing captains who are perhaps not worth their place in the side if judged solely on Test performances.

The 19th century super-star Fred Spofforth disagreed so strongly with Spiers & Pond in the selection of the team for the first Test in 1877, he refused to play. Spofforth wanted Murdoch as 'keeper instead of Blackham. Albert Trott was so annoyed about missing selection in the 1896 Australian team to England when he was 23 he forsook Melbourne for Middlesex, where he demonstrated the error of his omission over the next decade as a match-winning allrounder. Victor Trumper was excluded at the age of 21 from the 1899 Australian team to England until public outcry forced his addition to the team. Trumper was paid only half the other players' allowance until halfway throught the tour, when he was raised to full pay.

It is easy to condemn the non-selection of Trott and Trump-

870

er knowing how superbly they subsequently performed, but their exclusion was the result of honest mistakes in the hazardous task of national team selection—and one of those responsible, Joe Darling, admitted this. No such excuse could be raised to justify the inclusion of Tasmanian Ken Burn as one of the 1890 team 'keepers when he had never kept wicket in his life. A little later there was the sorry spectacle of the great George Giffen refusing to tour England unless his brother Walter also was selected.

Friction over selections reached an all-time low, however, with the notorious fist fight between Clem Hill and Peter McAlister in the board room of the NSWCA in 1912. No gentle scuffle this, but a full-blooded fight that went on for an amazing 20 minutes. Warwick Armstrong, one of those who dropped out of the 1912 tour with Hill, had troubles of a different kind when attempts were made to depose him as captain of Victoria. His autocratic captaincy made enemies, and when the Victorian players were about to meet and elect their captain, bowler James Kyle disclosed that two VCA members had urged him to propose another skipper instead of Armstrong. Kyle said Armstrong had always handled him well as a bowler and led the side satisfactorily. "If this is the sort of thing that's going on in big cricket, I don't care whether I ever play for Victoria again," said Kyle. Armstrong was replaced for a time as captain by Arnold Seitz but he was back as captain when Dr A. E. V. Hartkopf was told he could not vote for Armstrong on the grounds that he was 12th man!

Armstrong got the job of captaining Australia to England in 1921 by only one vote, according to the late Ray Robinson. One of the disappointing omissions from the 1921 side and the one that followed in 1926 was Alan Kippax. "Because of maladroit selectorship this batsman of rare talent was 33 before he represented Australia in England," wrote Robinson in *Between Wickets*. "If that recognition and experience had come to him in his twenties, I believe he would have soared to even greater heights. If the selectors descended to the level of inter-State bargaining, Kippax was not the batsman who should have been sqeezed out." Monty Noble called Kippax's omission in 1926 a "crime against the cricketing youth of Australia."

The perils of Australian team selection were shown when Jack Ryder, who had captained his country through the previous Tests against England in 1928–29, sat down with Richard Llewellyn Jones and Dr Dolling to pick the 1930 team for England. In their early discussions they each made a provisional list and Ryder was on all three, but when the final team was announced Ryder was excluded. To his undying credit, Ryder shrugged off his disappointment and went on to a record term as an Australian selector. He was still selecting Test teams at 84, though he had to use binoculars to follow

871

the play. Ryder always denied that he was responsible for one of Australia's most discussed selection mistakes—the omission of Bradman after only one Test in 1928–29. One of the selectors that season, Warren Bardsley, said he was outvoted by fellow selectors Dr Dolling, Jack Hutcheon and Ernie Bean when Bradman was made 12th man for the second Test.

An Australian star in the 1928–29 rubber was Clarrie Grimmett, who after frustrating failures to win selectors' approval of his leg-breaks and googlies in Wellington, Sydney, Melbourne and Adelaide, appeared in his first Test, aged 36. He was virtually as successful in England in 1930 with the ball as Bradman was with the bat, but he lacked support and had to do it alone. O'Reilly's skill had not yet been recognised by the selectors.

Understandably, selectors keep secret the reasons for their various choices, and any instructions they receive from the Board remain confidential. The Board did instruct the selectors in 1932, however, not to pick left-arm googly bowler Fleetwood-Smith in any of the preliminary games against Jardine's England team, allowing him only to play for Victoria against England before the First Test. The instructions apparently leaked to master batsman Wally Hammond, who made 203 against Victoria. Fleetwood-Smith finished with 2 for 124 and went another four years before he bowled in a Test against England.

872

In 1937, the Australian selectors, E. A. Dwyer, W. J. Johnson and Bradman, named a provisional team of 13 for the Fifth Test at Melbourne against "Gubby" Allen's team. The Board told them to reduce the squad to 12, apparently thinking the fast bowler Laurie Nash would miss out. The selectors said they would rather resign than unfairly omit any player before conditions for the match were known. The Board backed down. The following season saw another selection dispute when Queensland's brilliant Don Tallon was excluded from the 1938 team for England. One report said that each of the three selectors had Tallon's name among the two wicket-keepers they preferred. Bradman (South Australia) is said to have named Walker and Tallon, Dwyer (NSW) Oldfield and Tallon and Johnson (Victoria) Barnett and Tallon. But Walker and Barnett went, much to the chagrin of Queensland cricket lovers.

After World War II came the shock omission of Keith Miller from the original team to tour South Africa in 1949–50, a selection blunder that could easily have sent Miller off to the Lancashire League for the rest of his career. Since then we have had an occasional selection shock—the choice of leg-spinner John Watkins to tour the West Indies in 1973 or Ian Quick for England in 1961, for example—but there have been suprisingly few failures in recent overseas touring teams. The selectors are not only watching more big matches but they have television to guide them on matches they cannot attend. They appear to be relying more on their visual assessment of players and less on the notebooks full of statistics that intruded into selection meetings in the old days.

And while Australian captains like Greg Chappell and Kim Hughes are included in selection discussions they can never blame the sides they are given for Australian defeats as the famous England captain Archie McLaren frequently did. During the 1902 series against Australia in England he was said to have thrown open the dressing-room door on the day a Test began and called: "My God, look at the lot they've given me this time!"

A slowish, pint-sized right-arm off-spinner in the C. T. B. Turner mould who was starved of first-class opportunities but had some remarkable figures for Western Australia in the first decade of this century. He bowled with his sleeves buttoned in the Sonny Ramadhin style. Selk, who was born at Omeo, Victoria, made his debut for WA in 1898–99 and turned in some devastating performances when pitches assisted him for the South Fremantle, Fremantle and Claremont clubs, often taking 100 wickets in a season. His frail build made him a popular figure with spectators.

SELK, Rudolph Albert ("Bobby"), 1871–1940

First-Class Averages: Batting, 192 runs at 11.29; Bowling, 75 wickets at 26.33.

In the 1905–06 season, he took 7 for 108 and 5 for 19 in the match against South Australia at Perth, and 5 for 103 in the return match at Fremantle. He also had 8 for 28 that season against Victoria at Fremantle. When NSW went west for the first time in 1906–07, Selk took 7 for 45 as NSW were bundled out for 95, only second innings centuries by E. L. Waddy and Hopkins saving NSW. He had an outstanding double in 1909–10 against Victoria, taking 5 for 49 at Fremantle and 5 for 73 at Perth. In 1911–12 he took more than five wickets in an innings for the eighth time, finishing with 7 for 46 against an Australian XI at Perth. His first-class career ended more than 30 years before WA won Shield status but Selk was truly a giant in the early years of West Australian cricket.

SELLERS, Reginald Hugh Durning, 1940–

First-Class Averages: Batting, 993 runs at 17.12; Bowling, 121 wickets at 38.26.

Tests (1): 0 runs; 0 for 17.

A tall, loose-limbed Indian-born leg-spinner who played for five seasons for South Australia between 1959 and 1964 and won a place in the 1964 Australian team that toured England and India. He flighted the ball cleverly and achieved genuine spin on worn pitches on the last day of Australian first-class matches, and was a handy late order batsman. His career was upset and finally ended by an injury to his spinning finger.

Sellers was born at Bulsar, a tiny siding on the Bombay coast of India, while his father worked there on the railways. When the partition of India occured in 1947 his parents, both British citizens, judged that opportunities might be limited in the new India and migrated to Australia. Sellers, then seven-years-old, became a boarder at King's College (now Pembroke College) in the Adelaide suburb of Kensington and when he finished school joined the Kensington club.

He first played for South Australia in 1959 but his results were modest until the 1963–64 season when he took 48 first-class wickets, including five wickets in an innings three times. This earned him selection in Simpson's team to tour England. Just before he left Australia with the team he received a letter from Prime Minister Sir Robert Menzies, bestowing on him Australian citizenship, a generous gesture that ended any doubts English journalists may have had about his eligibility to play for Australia.

In the cold English weather Sellers found he could not properly grip the ball and had to have an operation in which a cyst on the tendon of his spinning finger—the third finger of his right-hand—was removed. Back in action he took 30 wickets at 37.66 in the last weeks of the English part of the tour. On the way home he played his sole Test against India at Calcutta, but bowled only five overs. The operation on his hand had not been completely successful and he retired from big cricket when he arrived home. For the past four years he has been a South Australian selector.

A modest, reserved Perth pharmacist who had an extended trial in the Australian team after scoring consistently for Western Australia. Despite his extremely determined efforts, his right-hand batting has failed to fulfil its early promise, though he remains a valued member of his State team. He is a tall, clean cut figure who hits the ball powerfully on the onside and has a sound range of drives and cuts. He began wearing glasses following a series of big match failures but the big scores he needs to regain a Test place have not come.

Serjeant, born in Perth, began in Perth district cricket with Nedlands but later switched to South Perth. He made his debut for WA in 1976–77 and in eight Shield matches that season scored 496 runs at 49.60, including 140 against Queensland at Perth. He also made 101 not out against England in Perth and after only 10 first-class matches was chosen in the Australian team that toured England in 1977 under Greg Chappell. His batting was unpretentious but he hit the ball crisply from an upright stance and after only 18 first-class innings forced his way into the Australian team for the First Test at Lord's. He topscored in his initial Test innings with 81, repeatedly lifting the ball high to the leg boundary, but he played in only three Tests in the series.

He appeared in the first four India-Australia matches in Australia in 1977–78, but apart from a hard-hitting 85 in the Third Test at Melbourne badly disappointed. He played in all five Tests for Bob Simpson's Australian side in the West Indies in 1977–78 scoring his maiden Test century (124) in the Third Test at Georgetown. This innings appeared to have confirmed his place in the Australian team but his form slumped and he was not used against England in Australia in 1978–79.

Problems with his eyes and the return of the WSC players have since made it difficult for Serjeant to rise above the status of a very useful State player. He was Western Australia's captain in 1981–82 in the absence of Hughes, Marsh and Lillee and did the job well in a quiet, studious manner that characterises all his cricket. His eight centuries and aggregate of almost 4,000 runs in six years of first-class cricket have all been hard-earned since his initial scoring flourish.

SERJEANT, Craig Stanton, 1951–

First-Class Averages: Batting, 3,994 runs at 35.65.

Tests (12): 522 runs at 23.72.

Australia has had two outstanding cricket teams picked from men who served in the first and second world wars. These teams played attractive cricket that brought crowds back to some of the world's most famous grounds immediately the wars ended. The players in these teams provided a nucleus for strong Australian teams when Tests began again, but they also did an invaluable job for international cricket.

The best cricket in Australia in World War I came from the matches organised by the Melbourne Cricket Club and the

SERVICES CRICKET TEAMS

Victorian Cricket Association to help the wounded soldiers' appeal. The New South Wales Cricket Association refused to join in because it claimed the matches interfered with recruiting, so the VCA went it alone, but included NSW stars like Monty Noble and Charlie Macartney. The first match on Boxing Day, 1915, was labelled "Fifteen Of Victoria v. the Sheffield Shield XI" and the second match on New Year's Day, 1916, was "Victoria versus Warwick Armstrong's Eighteen."

The matches were lavishly staged. Three bands attended, a biplane performed acrobatics over the MCG, and later there was an auction of cricket relics to benefit the wounded. There were some fine performances on the field. Bert Ironmonger took 5 for 74 and 7 for 59 in one match, Warwick Armstrong made 102 for his Eighteen, Jack Ryder 83, Dr Roy Park 96. The major feature of the auction was the cricket ball souvenired by Jack Blackham when Australia won the 1882 Test at The Oval and The Ashes legend began. In the excitement that followed Australia's win Blackham had had the presence of mind to pocket the ball.

The VCA secretary Hugh Trumble initiated the plan whereby every person who subscribed £1 would have his name recorded in an album that would be displayed at the MCG with the ball. Trumble set a minimum price of £500 on the ball but subscriptions reached £617, making it the most expensive cricket ball in history. It is now in the VCA offices.

Other features at the auction were the scorebook of the 1882 tour, which went for 33 guineas; Billy Murdoch's bat, which brought 70 guineas, Clem Hill's bat, 20 guineas; a bat signed by the 1909 team, 24 guineas; a handwritten letter home by Spofforth; and an autographed Victor Trumper bat, 55 guineas. Trumper had died only a few months before his bat was auctioned.

THE FIRST AIF TEAM IN ENGLAND, 1919

To Australians serving in Europe, the cricket fields of England were a major attraction and many big matches were played at Lord's, Crystal Palace, Honor Oak and other famous grounds in aid of services' charities. Out of these games came the idea of forming an AIF team, and when peace came the Australian commander, Field Marshal Birdwood, agreed to set up an AIF Sports Board to supervise the selection of representative teams. At a meeting of the Australian Board of Control in Sydney on December 6, 1918, the following cable from the Marylebone Cricket Club at Lord's was discussed:

"Would you favour the idea of a tour in England in 1919 of an Australian team composed of those serving? If so, could you nominate a representative here to negotiate with the Marylebone Cricket Club."

The Australian Board decided it supported the idea and named Major Gordon Campbell, a former South Australian player to represent it in London. The Board retained "sovereignty over the constitution of the touring side," which meant they wanted to approve of the side chosen. The Board set the number of players to make up the touring team as 15, nominated Bill Ferguson to act as scorer-baggage master if he paid his own fare, set aside £200 for Campbell to act as treasurer, and decided to pay each player £150. Campbell joined Dr Roy Park and Dr Eric Barbour in London as the selectors of the team.

After a number of trial matches and problems with the withdrawal of leading players (Jack Massie was wounded; Dr Park and Dr Barbour wanted to get home quickly to re-establish their medical practices; Charlie Macartney returned home following the death of his father) the tour party was announced as: NSW, C. Kelleway, E. A. Bull, H. L. Collins, C. T. Docker, J. M. Gregory, E. J. Long, W. L. Trenerry, J. M. Taylor, H. S. B. Love; Victoria, A. W. Lampard, C. B. Willis; South Australia, J. T. Murray, C. E. Pellew, W. S. Stirling. Love played in only one game and when he pulled out Bert Oldfield joined the team.

At that stage only Herbie Collins and Charlie Kelleway had established themselves in first-class cricket. From the start the team deleted all reference to a man's rank, and they quickly developed into a happy combination whose attractive cricket soon won headlines. This reputation for sparkling cricket increased when Kelleway, an imperturbable stone-waller, left the team and Collins took over as captain, a Lance-Corporal running a team that included seven officers.

The MCC withdrew its offer of financial support when the list of unavailable players was announced, leaving the AIF Sports Board in control of the team. The proposed "Test" matches were cancelled because of the MCC's withdrawal but the Surrey club, whose links with Australian cricket went back to William Caffyn, stepped in and helped organise matches. The Australian Board of Control appointed a 65-year-old Irishman, Howard Lacy, from the Mitcham Club, who had arranged several wartime matches for AIF players, to manage the team.

The team played 34 matches in England, 28 of them first-class and won 15, with 15 draws and four losses. The first match at Attleborough, Norfolk, was played at the private ground of Lionel Robinson, son of the former financial editor of the Melbourne *Age*. Set to score 283 to win in the final innings against a strong lineup of English County players, the AIF had made 8 for 274 when play stopped because they had to catch a train back to Leyton. Even in this light-hearted affair, however, it became clear that a great fast bowler in Jack Gregory had arrived, for he really made the ball whistle past the batsmen's tentative bats. As the tour developed his batting also blossomed and he was found to be a superlative slips field.

877

In the third game, against Cambridge at Fenners', the AIF scored 8 for 650, with Kelleway and Collins adding 165 for the first wicket. Kelleway made 168, Pellew 105 not out. Cambridge replied with 293, Gregory taking 6 for 68, and twice knocked the stumps of batsmen yards out of the ground. Following-on, Cambridge made only 118, Docker taking 5 for 41, giving the AIF its second first-class win by an innings and 239 runs. This was to prove the most convincing win on the English tour.

Enthralling draws followed against Middlesex, Oxford University and Surrey. Against Middlesex Gregory knocked M. H. C. Doll off his feet with a fast rising ball and the bails were dislodged as Doll went down. But the AIF could not remove Hendren cheaply and he made 135 and 63 not out. At Oxford Kelleway had 7 for 47 and Taylor, 104, and Murray, 133, made centuries. At The Oval Jack Hobbs made 205 not out despite tight bowling and brilliant AIF fielding. With Surrey leading by 114 on the first innings, the AIF appeared to be in trouble when they lost 6 for 292 in the second innings but a fine stand of 170 for the seventh wicket by Pellew (106) and Lampard (112) helped take Australia to 8 for 554 and save the game. In their sixth match the AIF defeated the MCC And Ground by 10 wickets. By then it was clear that the AIF were such a splendid side that the MCC had erred in withdrawing their support.

This was underlined when the AIF defeated the powerful Lancashire and Yorkshire teams in successive matches. Lancashire had to follow-on when they made only 125 in reply to Australia's 418, but they managed only 136 in their second innings, giving the AIF victory by an innings and 157 runs. Lampard's 9 for 42 were the best figures of his career. Against Yorkshire Gregory took three wickets in one over to finish with 6 for 91 in a Yorkshire total of 224. The AIF led by 41 runs and with Gregory bowling at frightening speed in the second innings Yorkshire were always struggling. Gregory dismissed Wilfred Rhodes, Roy Kilner, Robinson, Sutcliffe and then hit the Yorkshire captain Burton in the face to end his part in the match. Chasing 170 runs to win the AIF slumped to 9 for 116, when Long joined Gregory. Slowly they edged towards the Yorkshire total, defending desperately but picking up singles with deft dabs into spaces left by substitute captain George Hirst. They added 37 runs in an hour when Gregory decided to hit out.

Gregory's power hitting brought victory that made headlines all round England, for Yorkshire had been the best County team in England before World War I and were to win the 1919 County Championship. The last wicket partnership had added 54 in 80 minutes and snatched the game from Yorkshire. George Hirst was the first man into the Australian dressing-room to congratulate them.

Charles Kelleway, original captain of the first AIF cricket team.

The elation of this win had barely ebbed when the AIF were thoroughly beaten by the Gentlemen of England at Lord's, showing all the well-known Australian weakness for adapting to the demands of a wet pitch. The Gentlemen scored 402 against spiritless bowling with superb fielding preventing an even higher total. Michael Falcon, an MP whose parliamentary duties kept him out of big cricket, took 6 for 41 in an AIF first innings of 85 and when they followed-on removed star batsman Johnny Taylor. The AIF scored 184 this time, losing by an innings and 133 runs. Jack Gregory scored 115 and took 4 for 74 in the second innings in the AIF's win by 196 runs over Northants that provided the needed boost in morale after the Lord's debacle.

After a tame draw against Leicestershire, the AIF suffered a humiliating loss to Derbyshire, who won only four of their 15 matches in 1919. Derbyshire were the only English County to beat a representative Australian team between the wars. They did it by dismissing the AIF for 125 and 132 and scoring 181 and 112. Set to score 165 to win in the last innings, the AIF lost 5 for 26, and despite strong resistance from Murray (54) and Oldfield (26 not out), the AIF were all out 36 runs short of their target. Horsley took 12 for 117 in the match.

The drawn match with Surrey saw the return to English first-class cricket of J. N. Crawford, who lived in Adelaide after he quarrelled with the Surrey committee in 1909. Crawford celebrated with a superb rescue innings of 144 not out after Surrey had lost 5 for 26 chasing the AIF 436. Johnny Taylor played one of the finest innings of the season in scoring 146 in 150 minutes to set up Australia's win over Essex. Collins paved the way to victory over Somerset by taking 8 for 31 off 14 overs.

Collins's team played 10 matches on their way home in South Africa, eight of them first-class, and remained undefeated on this section of the tour. The Australian Minister for Defence, Senator Pearce, gave permission for the six weeks tour after the AIF Sports Board received a cabled request from the South African Government. Ernest Jones Cameron, a former rover with the Essendon Australian Rules club, managed this tour, which was guaranteed by Sir Abe Bailey, a vice-president of the South African Cricket Association. Cameron had helped Howard Lacy with the team's affairs in London.

FIRST AIF TEAM IN SOUTH AFRICA, 1919

Gregory relished the hard, sun-baked South African pitches, scoring heavily and taking wickets in spectacular fashion. After a fast 50 against Transvaal, he took three wickets in an over and then made 86. At Durban against Natal he took 9 for 32 and then ruined his prospects of taking all 10 by running out the last batsman. In the return match against Natal at Maritzburg he had 7 for 21. When he couldn't get a wicket against Transvaal at Johannesburg he made 73. Despite

Gregory's success, however, South African papers acclaimed Collins as the finest player in the AIF side. At Johannesburg against a South African XI Collins made a masterly 235 out of the AIF's 441 and he took wickets regularly throughout the tour, bowling with variety and great shrewdness.

The *Cape Times* said of the AIF tour, "The South African team was well beaten and while one believes the South African side has not reflected its true worth, the superiority of their opponents has been emphatically demonstrated. The Australian team has given us good, honest, clean cricket and has revealed our weaknesses. The AIF team was hard to beat due to their skill, their keenness, their combination and their batting."

FIRST AIF TEAM IN AUSTRALIA, 1919

The AIF team played three matches in Australia after they arrived home, all of them first-class, with the team receiving half the takings, plus hotel expenses and an allowance of £1-a-day. They defeated Victoria at Melbourne by six wickets, played a draw with Queensland at Brisbane when rain ended a match they had had the best of, and wound up their long tour by beating NSW by 203 runs—an indication of their strength because NSW won the Sheffield Shield in 1919–20. Collins and Gregory both scored two centuries in Australia and Willis made a fifth.

Collins shocked Victoria by winning the toss and sending them in to bat against Gregory, who made a sensational debut for a bowler who was completely unknown at home by taking 7 for 22. Only four Victorians reached double figures and they were all out for 116. The AIF then scored 311, with Willis making 111 of them. Victoria scored 270 in their second innings, Lampard taking 7 for 99, and the AIF had no difficulty scoring the 76 runs needed to win.

At Brisbane Taylor made 60 and Gregory 45 in the AIF's first innings of 215, but Queensland reached only 146 in reply. Collins then produced some of the finest strokes of the tour to make 135 in around even time, Taylor completing a good double with 67. Collins declared at 5 for 319 but when Queensland had lost 6 for 144 in the chase for 389, a typical Brisbane storm flooded the ground and the match was left unfinished. Oldfield impressed with six dismissals in the match.

Gregory dominated the match against his home State, scoring 122 and 102 and taking 8 for 130 in the match, as well as holding three brilliant catches. The AIF scored 265 and NSW took a 14-run lead by making 279. Collins, out for a duck in the first innings, then produced a superb 129 in his last tour innings in helping his team to 395. Arthur Mailey, often mistakenly described as an AIF team member, gave all the AIF batsmen but Collins and Gregory difficulty in taking 7 for 122. Ronald Cardwell in his book on the AIF team, pointed out that in this match Cyril Docker's brother, Keith and Bill Trenerry's

AIF skipper Herbie Collins going out to bat in England.

880

brother, Ted, represented NSW. In the AIF's second innings, Ted bowled Bill, and in the NSW second innings Cyril dismissed Keith.

Sixty-two years after they walked from the field in Sydney at the end of their last match the reputation of the First AIF cricket team remains a source of wonderment. Fielding a team comprising players who had just survived an arduous war, they played the game with an animated sparkle that endures, winning 20 of their 39 first-class matches in three countries, and losing only four. They made a major contribution to Australian cricket, with big crowds attending wherever they played. Within a few months of their disbandment, their captain, Collins, their wicket-keeper, Oldfield, their pace bowler, Gregory, and two of their most entertaining batsmen, Johnny Taylor and "Nip" Pellew, took the field for Australia.

The First AIF team (L to R): Standing, C. W. Winning, C. T. Docker, J. M. Gregory, E. C. Bull, J. T. Murray, E. J. Long, A. W. Lampard; Seated, W. S. Sterling, C. E. Pellew, H. L. Collins, H. Lacy (manager), C. D. Willis, W. L. Trenerry; Front, W. A. Oldfield, J. M. Taylor.

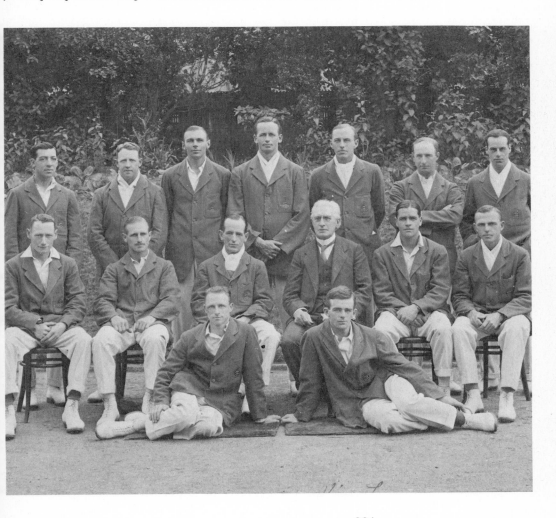

When war began in 1939, the Australian Board of Control decided to play out the rest of the 1939–40 season and then suspend the Sheffield Shield competition for the duration of the war. At the request of the Federal Government they organised several patriotic matches in aid of war charities. The best of these was the game that began in Melbourne on New Year's Day, 1941, between teams led by Don Bradman and Stan McCabe. On the first day McCabe's team scored 9 for 449, with Badcock making 105 and Sid Barnes 137. Bradman's team then were dismissed for 205 and had to follow-on.

McCabe and his opening bowler Maurice Sievers were both injured so Keith Miller, who had not bowled in the first innings, was asked to open the attack. He began with two balls that pitched no more than halfway down the wicket but then bowled accurate medium-pacers that bounced high in towards the batsmen's chest. Phil Riding's brother, Ken, touched one of these kicking deliveries into the slips to give Miller his initial first-class wicket and Miller finished with 1 for 24. Bill O'Reilly, 5 for 53, and Clarrie Grimmett, 4 for 46, and Bradman's side were dismissed for 141 to lose by an innings. Bradman was out first ball in the first innings and made only 12 in the second innings.

In the Middle East and in England during World War II cricket matches of a high standard involving Australian stars like Hassett, Pepper, Miller and Carmody, were played whenever possible. The Australians found themselves taking the field alongside first-class players from South Africa, New Zealand and India. Sometimes the opposition included English Test heroes. At the end of the war the MCC, mindful of their error in not arranging "Tests" after World War I, gave first-class status to matches between England and a Dominions XI, a Services XI against Leveson-Gower's XI at Scarborough, and also to five "Victory Tests" between England and the Australian Services XI captained by Lindsay Hassett. This team drew some of its players from the Middle East but, unfortunately, none from the Far East where players such as Arthur Morris, Ray Lindwall and Colin McCool had kept in trim with matches on crushed-coral pitches.

The Victory Tests produced some spectacular cricket, although the England team included Hutton, Washbrook, Hammond, Ames, Edrich, Wright, and Jack Robertson. England began the first Test at Lord's with 267, with the Services' bowling honours going to the fast-medium bowlers Albert Cheetham and R. G. Williams—who had been a prisoner of war—with good support from slow bowlers Price and Ellis. Miller then made 105 in 210 minutes, Hassett 77, and Williams a handy 53, as the Services went to a total of 455. Robertson made 84 and Edrich 50 in England's second innings of 294, but the Services had little difficulty knocking off the required runs for the loss of only four wickets. Whitington

882

made 37 of these and Pepper 54 not out in a whirlwind show of big-hitting.

At Bramall Lane, Sheffield, where bomb damage was still evident, Hammond made a delightful 100 but England scored a modest 286. The Services could not handle George Pope, the bald-headed Derbyshire swing bowler, and were dismissed for 147. England struggled in their second innings but an eighth wicket stand of 55 by Griffiths and Pollard gave the score respectability. The Services began well, Whitington and Workman sharing an opening stand of 108, but when they were separated Pope bowled Hassett with a superb delivery and Pollard dismissed Miller, England finally winning by 41 runs. More importantly, some 50,000 people in one of the most heavily bombed cities in the war watched the three days play.

Back at Lord's for the Third Test, Australia won by four wickets despite a superb innings by Hutton (104). This time Bob Cristofani, a quickish leg-spinner, and Miller were the Services penetrative bowlers, with four and three wickets each. The Services' first innings yielded 194, Hassett 68, but they swung the match by dismissing England for 164, Hutton scoring 69, Edrich 58, with Hammond unable to bat because of lumbago. Miller played exciting strokes to make 71 not out and with Sismey contributing 51, the Services made the required runs with four wickets to spare. The aggregate crowd for this match reached 84,000.

The Fourth Test was also at Lord's and ended in a draw after another impressive century (118 in 200 minutes) from Miller, who had a partnership of 121 with Sismey. The Services total of 388 was gradually overtaken by some fine batting by Fishlock, 69, Hammond, 83, and Washbrook, 112. Edrich was 73 not out and the score at 7 for 468 when Hammond declared. Australia only had time to score 4 for 140 in their second knock before time ran out.

England introduced a battery of fast bowlers for the Fifth Test at Old Trafford and the Services were 5 for 104 at lunch on the first day. Miller batted splendidly but ran out of partners and the Services were dismissed for 177. All the English batsmen had trouble against Cristofani, who took 5 for 55, but England went to the lead with a first innings of 243. The Services collapsed to 8 for 105 in their second innings. Then Cristofani attacked in thrilling style to add 95 with Williams, who defended stubbornly. Cristofani hooked Pope for a spectacular six and when he reached 101 out of the 126 scored while he was at the crease spectators stood and cheered for several minutes. But Cristofani's 110 not out was not enough to give England worries and they scored the 141 required with the loss of only four wickets.

At Scarborough Cec Pepper gave a remarkable display of big hitting in scoring 168 of the Services 506. One of his blows cleared the roofs of nearby houses. Pepper hit six sixers, Miller three, Pettiford and Hassett one each. Whitington made 79, Miller 71 and Sismey 78. Levenson-Gower XI replied with 258 and the Services forced the follow-on to win by an innings and 108 runs, a marvellous end to a triumphant series. Ellis took 10 for 67 in the match and Pepper 6 for 121.

Several of the leading Australian players had also played for a Dominions XI against England at Lord's. New Zealander Martin Donnelly played superbly for 133, with two sixes and 18 fours in the Dominions first innings of 307. Then Hammond made a stylish 121 in 160 minutes, adding 177 for the seventh wicket with Edrich, 78. At stumps at the end of the second day the Dominions were 3 for 145 in their second innings, with Miller on 61 not out. Next morning Miller scored 124 runs in 90 minutes of absolutely astounding batting with every stroke cleanly hit. One of his seven sixes landed on top of the broadcasting box above the England dressing-room. Some said it went higher than Albert Trott's legendary blow. Miller's 185 took only 165 minutes. Constantine, who captained the Dominions in Hassett's absence, hit a glorious 40. England batted brightly in their second innings but the Dominions won by 45 runs eight minutes from stumps. Wright took 10 wickets in the match for England, Pepper seven and Cristofani five for the Dominions.

SERVICES TEAM IN INDIA, 1945

On the way home Hassett led the Services on a 10-games tour of India, but without Cheetham and Williams, two useful opening bowlers. They played three representative matches (see India) losing one and drawing 2, and winning 2 of the 7 other first-class games.

SERVICES TEAM IN AUSTRALIA, 1945–46

By now very weary after months of cricket, the Services were asked for a final fling, taking on each of the States in turn after they arrived home. They drew with Western Australia and South Australia, Bradman scoring 112 at Adelaide. Victoria then defeated them in the absence of Hassett by an innings and 151 runs. Ian Johnson took 6 for 27 and 4 for 17. At Sydney Barnes made 102, Alley 119, Donaldson 99 and Grieves 102 not out in the NSW total of 7 for 551 declared. Against an attack that included Lindwall and O'Reilly, the Services managed only 204, Whitington again batting soundly for 49, in assisting Miller to give respectability the score. Miller's 105 not out was one of his finest centuries, played in adversity against clever bowling. The Services batting was more consistent in the second innings but NSW were easy winners.

At Brisbane against Queensland, Whitington scored 84, Sismey 60, Hassett 67 and Bill Morris 104 not out for Queensland, and the match ended in a draw. The last match of the tour in Hobart against Tasmania also ended in a draw, Ross Stanford scoring 153, Pepper taking 9 for 142 in the match. M. R. Thomas made 164 for Tasmania. Within a few months Hassett and Miller were in action again for Australia in Tests, but none of the other Services' side played any further international cricket. Pepper was perhaps the biggest loss when he decided to live in England. But the Services had emulated the First AIF side by re-establishing cricket as a crowd-pleasing game in three countries, and as the AIF had done with Gregory, had produced a match-winning fast bowler, brilliant fieldsman and big-hitting batsman in Keith Miller.

SHARPE, Duncan, 1937–

An Anglo-Pakistani Test cricketer who migrated to South Australia in 1960 and played 14 matches for the State between 1961–62 and 1965–66. He was a right-hand middle order batsman, and also a handy wicket-keeper. He batted well in his first Test at Dacca in 1959–60 against Australia, scoring 56 out of 200 and 35 out of 134. His three Tests for Pakistan brought 134 runs at 22.33. For South Australia, he scored 515 runs at 22.39, topscore 72.

SHAW, John Hilary, 1932–

A right-hand batsman for Victoria between 1953 and 1960. He was a very strong driver of the ball and a splendid fieldsman who held some exciting catches. He was born at Geelong, hometown of his uncle, Lindsay Hassett, and went to Hassett's old club, South Melbourne. He made his debut for Victoria in 1953–54 and made his initial first-class century in 1956–57, 114 against South Australia in Adelaide. He made 167 against NSW at Sydney in 1957–58, and 107 against South Australia at Adelaide in 1959–60, performances that earned him a tour of New Zealand. In New Zealand he hit his fourth first-class century, 120 for an Australian XI against Auckland.

First-Class Averages: Batting, 3,276 runs at 40.44; Bowling, 1 wicket at 55.00.

SHEAHAN, Andrew Paul, 1946–

A handsome, intellectual right-handed batsman from the Victorian town of Werribee whose eight year career produced many classic strokes and disappointingly few splendid innings. He failed to fill the gap left by Norm O'Neill as a batsman. He is something of a novelty as a broadcaster beguiling many devotees with an educated delivery that probably was refined by his two years as a master at Winchester, England.

Sheahan was a naturally good player, with everything going for him, a family rich in the game's history, Prime Minister R. G. Menzies as a sponsor, and so much coaching from big names that he can only have been bewildered by it all. Fellow grade players were heard to say he would have been better off left to play his own game. Sheahan rose above all

First-Class Averages: Batting, 7,987 runs at 46.16; Bowling, 1 wicket at 66.00.

Tests (31): 1,594 runs at 33.91.

885

Bob Willis takes cover as Paul Sheahan sweeps a ball to the square leg boundary.

the jibes by getting into the Australian team. But unhappily, after devoting much of his formative years to cricket and developing his batsmanship, he retired from first-class cricket when he married, disappointing all those who had supported him in his years as an erratic Test batsman.

Sheahan first attracted the admiration of R. G. Menzies while he was still at Geelong College. Paul's father had played district cricket in Melbourne for 17 years, and his great-grandfather, William Cooper, went to England with the Fourth Australian team in 1884. The Sheahans laid out a splendid turf wicket in the backyard of their home in Geelong and many stirring father and son duels occurred on that pitch. Paul played for Geelong College at Australian Rules as well as cricket before he moved to Melbourne University and took up basketball to improve his fielding. Watching Paul on the backyard pitch not long before he got into Test cricket one could not help being impressed by his driving.

In his second season with Victoria, 1966–67, he was second in the Shield averages with 66.00, which was helped by his career best score of 202 against South Australia at Melbourne. He first appeared for Australia in the Adelaide Test against India in 1967–68, scoring 81 and 35, and over the next four years appeared in 25 consecutive Tests. He scored 817 runs at 28.17, topscore 137, on his first tour of England in 1968 and made 721 runs at 40.05, topscore 135 not out, on his second trip in 1972.

886

He scored his first Test century against India at Kanpur, 114 in 1969–70, and his second, 127, in the second Test against Pakistan at Melbourne in 1972–73. His two best Test innings, however, were 88 against England at Old Trafford in 1968, and 44 not out at The Oval in 1972, an innings which clinched an Australian win. He played against all the cricket-playing nations, visiting South Africa in 1970 and New Zealand in 1973–74. But he may best be remembered for his stylish and magnificent fielding in the covers. In all first-class matches, Sheahan made 19 centuries. He is now a master specialising in mathematics at his old school, Geelong College.

SHEFFIELD SHIELD, THE

The Sheffield Shield competition was the Australasian Cricket Council's sole significant contribution to Australian cricket in the few argumentative years of its existence. The Council spent the £150 the Earl of Sheffield donated to the furtherance of Australian cricket by having the 46 ins × 30 ins Shield made, and in 1892–93 competition for the Shield began between New South Wales, Victoria and South Australia. The winner earned the right to retain the Shield for one year as the leading cricket State, each team playing the others twice, once at home and once away. The Shield has remained the symbol of supremacy among the States for 90 years, with interruptions during World War I and World War II and until the introduction of one-day matches remained the chief attraction when there were no Tests. Here is a summary of the Sheffield Shield competition:

1892–93 TO WORLD WAR I

Victoria won the first Shield competition by winning four matches. NSW had one win and South Australia one. Victoria defeated NSW by eight wickets and by 232 runs and South Australia by six wickets and then by five wickets. The left-handers William Bruce, Bob McLeod and Frank Laver hit centuries for Victoria but Harry Donnan was the first of all Shield century makers with a knock of 120 against South Australia at Adelaide in December, 1892. Frank Iredale made 101 for NSW at Melbourne in the same month. Victoria's success stemmed from its allround strength, with Jim Phillips impressive among the bowlers. Lyons hit a brilliant century (124) against NSW at Adelaide but Giffen was the South Australian star.

South Australia, who had only been admitted to the competition because of their defeat of NSW by an innings and 53 in 1891–92, caused a major surprise by winning the Shield in its second season, 1893–94. They beat Victoria by 74 runs at Melbourne, where Giffen made 103 and repeated the win in Adelaide, where Reedman made 113, Lyons 101 and Lyons took three wickets in four balls on the final morning. Against

The Sheffield Shield.

NSW at Adelaide Giffen scored 205 out of 483. Set to score 478 to win, NSW were all out for 234, Andy Newell taking 10 wickets in the match and Ernie Jones 5 for 50 in NSW's second innings. South Australia had to wait 16 years before she won the Shield again.

Victoria won for the second time in 1894–95, thanks to the allround skills of Harry and Albert Trott, and Charles McLeod, who all took wickets and made big scores. McKibbin took 14 for 189 against South Australia. But Giffen remained the finest allrounder in the competition, with 12 wickets and a score of 94 against Victoria, 16 for 186 against NSW at Adelaide and 65 and 10 wickets against NSW in Sydney. NSW won two seasons in a row, 1895–96 and 1896–97, when Noble

888

came in to the team to support Turner, Howell and McKibbin. In all three States new stars were rising and the Shield was already established as the ideal proving ground for Test aspirants.

This was a golden period of Australian cricket, with the three Shield States brimful of talent. Clem Hill, Joe Darling, George Giffen, Affie Jarvis, Dinny Reedman and Joe Travers all did some brilliant things for South Australia but they far from overshadowed a Victorian team that included both Trotts, Harry Graham, Charlie and Bob McLeod, Jack Worrall, Frank Laver, Alf Johns and the rising Hugh Trumble. NSW had Syd Gregory, Harry Donnan, Frank Iredale, Bill Howell, Tom Garrett and J. J. Kelly in outstanding form. And then came Trumper.

Clem Hill and Harry Graham reigned as the most dashing batsmen in Australia at the turn of the century, but between 1901–02 and 1906–07 as NSW won the Shield six times in a row, Trumper played some majestic innings. At Sydney in 1900–01 he batted without error for 275 minutes and hit 31 fours in compiling 230. Hill made 365 not out against NSW at Adelaide but in the return match in Sydney Trumper started the scoring orgy that took NSW to 918 in 560 minutes. Iredale made 118, Noble 153, Syd Gregory 168, Duff 119 and Poidevin, in his first Shield game, 140 not out, but Trumper's 70 was the innings of sheer genius. The next season he began his remarkable partnership with Duff.

At Sydney in 1902–03 Trumper and Duff opened the NSW innings against Victoria with 267 in 135 minutes, Trumper scoring 130, Duff 132. A week later they reduced the South Australian bowlers to impotency with a stand of 298 in 150 minutes, Trumper scoring 178, Duff 132. South Australia made 412 in their first innings but lost by 10 wickets. In 1903–04, Duff made 271 in 280 minutes and Noble 230 in 300 minutes in a NSW total of 681 against South Australia at Sydney. In the Adelaide match NSW scored 624, including 152 by Syd Gregory, 97 by Charles Gregory and 147 by Noble. "Tibby" Cotter emerged in 1904–05 season, along with the first of the outstanding Waddy brothers, the Rev. E. F. Waddy. Cotter took 7 for 76 against South Australia and Waddy made 129 in his first Shield game against South Australia.

The Board of Control took over the administration of Australian cricket in this period, originally to arrange overseas tours and pass profits back to the States, and eventually to organise all cricket within Australia. One of their first moves was to introduce a rule preventing Shield players from representing two States during the one year. English Counties were regarded as equivalent to States. This prevented Frank Tarrant, who played for Middlesex and The Players, from displacing locals in the Victorian team during the English winters. The Shield competition was hard-fought, sportsmanlike, tense, and occasionally argumentative, but from the Shield ranks Australia picked some fine sides. NSW's dominance was largely due to the strength of her reserves when Test stars were absent. Groundsmen at the capital city grounds developed new skills that made lumpy, dusty pitches painful memories, though Australia continued to leave pitches uncovered. The Australian "sticky" became world renowned and no batsman was rated complete until he proved he could bat reasonably well on one.

Charlie Macartney, Vernon Ransford, Charles Kelleway, and "Ranji" Hordern and his novel new-fangled delivery, the googly, appeared to challenge Trumper, Duff, Noble, Hill, Darling, Cotter and Armstrong for headlines. In 1906–07, Charles Gregory lifted Clem Hill's Australian record first-class score from 365 not out to 383 but this came in a non-Shield match against Queensland and such was the competition for team places Charles Gregory was dropped from the NSW side after a couple of failures the following season. In 1906–07 two splendid bowlers, Jack O'Connor and Andrew McBeth bobbed up in the South Australian team after transferring from Sydney. Another outstanding bowler, Bill Whitty, followed them in 1908–09, knowing he could be more certain of a place in the South Australian side than in the all-conquering NSW XI.

Victoria finally ended NSW's run of Shield success in 1907–08 when the competition was shortened because of the English team's visit. Armstrong and Ransford were the batting heroes, Saunders and Hazlitt a formidable bowling duo. At Sydney that season Clem Hill made two more of his famous nervous nineties, 92 and 94. He was caught by a fieldsman standing on the SCG cycling track on the outside edge of the ground in the second knock. The fieldsman did not believe Hill was out and urged him to go back to the crease but Hill explained that the captains had agreed the boundary was the fence not the cycling track, and kept walking. NSW needed 593 to win the match and got to within 20 of the target, a wonderful effort. Hanson Carter was one of NSW's stars, with his brilliant wicket-keeping and a knock of 125 when the final innings chase was on.

South Australia finally broke through to win the Shield for the second time in 1909–10, thanks mainly to Clem Hill who made two centuries against Victoria and 205 out of 397 against NSW, and to the allround skill of J. N. Crawford, who went to South Australia after a dispute with the Surrey County club. NSW introduced the eccentric Sid Emery for the match against Victoria in Melbourne and he had control of his fastish googlies for the entire match, taking 7 for 28 and 5 for 85 in a dramatic debut. Clem Hill's brothers Roy and "Solly" played important roles for SA in supporting Crawford and Whitty. SA made a determined effort to retain the Shield in 1910–11 but lost it on percentages to NSW. SA used medium-pacer Roy Hill and slow leg-spinner Alby Wright to open the attack and achieved excellent results.

NSW won all their matches to hold the Shield in 1911–12, when Warwick Armstrong made 250 and figured in three century stands against SA at Melbourne. Hazlitt started with the ball for NSW after transferring from Victoria and Barbour and Bardsley were the leading batsmen. For once NSW's reserves failed in 1912–13 and without Bardsley and Macartney they lost the Shield narrowly to South Australia. One of the headlined bowlers that season was Victoria's Jimmy Matthews who bundled NSW out for 84 by taking 5 for 25 and proved his hat-tricks in England in 1912 were no flukes. Trumper played one of his last great innings, 201 not out, for NSW versus South Australia at Sydney, and when he batted with Macartney, who made 125, it was sheer magic. NSW edged out SA again in 1913–14, when the left-arm bowling of Jack Massie showed hints of greatness. But World War I began with Victoria in possession of the Shield, due to the wonderful bowling in 1914–15 of Bert Ironmonger, who took 32 wickets in the season at 17.15. Jack Ryder gave an indication of things to come with a whirlwind 151 for Victoria against SA.

The Shield was not at stake in the initial first-class season after World War I, 1918–19, but the inter-State matches that were played disclosed an encouraging sprinkling of new talent. Vic and Arthur Richardson made their first appearances for SA, for whom P. D. Rundell made 100. Baring and Mayne—who had moved from Adelaide—scored impressively for Victoria, who had a very fast new pace bowler, E. A. McDonald. Jim Bogle and Tommy Andrews joined Bardsley in a powerful NSW lineup that was strengthened even further when the First AIF team returned with Collins, Gregory and Oldfield established stars. The AIF players immediately showed their strength when the Shield competition resumed in 1919–20, Dr Roy Park scoring 228 for Victoria against SA and "Nip" Pellew making 271 in the return game. But NSW won the Shield for the first two competitions after World War I. In 1920–21 NSW made 802 against SA at Sydney, Bardsley 235, Kelleway 168, Bogle 103, but the game had to be abandoned through rain.

From the start of the Shield competition in 1919–20, Queensland began intensive efforts to be included in the competition. The Board of Control rejected the idea because of the costs involved for southern States in sending teams to Queensland by rail, and because of fears about the low standard of Queensland pitches. The competition continued through the 1920s with NSW and Victoria dominating it with some great teams. Covered wickets became optional because of worries about the loss of gatemoney if pitches were ex-

SHIELD CRICKET BETWEEN THE WARS

891

posed to rain, but matches continued to be played to a finish. This resulted in some enormous scores and saw batsmen ask for a fresh guard as they reached 100 and then set off after another. Few radio stations thought about broadcasting scores but the papers carried columns of detailed accounts of play.

There was little between the standards of NSW and Victorian teams throughout the 1920s. Ponsford's emergence gave Victoria an edge in 1923–24 when he hit 110 and 110 not out in the same match against NSW at Sydney. His 529 runs in seven innings enabled Victoria to remain unbeaten that season. Frank Tarrant reappeared in the Victorian team in 1924–25 after his long career with Middlesex. Victoria defeated NSW that summer in remarkable style after NSW had made 614 in the first innings. Rock made 235, Kippax 212. Victoria responded with 502, of which Liddicut scored 132, Willis 100, and Victoria then dismissed NSW for 152. Victoria then scored the 265 runs needed for the loss of only three wickets.

NSW stormed back to regain the Shield in 1925–26 with innings of 708, 705, 642, 593 and 554, with 11 of the 13 players used averaging over 40 runs an innings. Mailey always bowled with the knowledge that he had runs to spare. In the first game against Victoria that season NSW made 705 thanks to a ninth wicket stand of 226 by Oldfield and Kelleway. Victoria made 413 and 130 in reply. NSW scored 708 in the return match at Sydney, Kippax batting gracefully for seven hours for 271 not out.

Queensland played in the competition for the first time in 1926–27, when South Australia won the Shield on percentages, playing five matches compared with six by NSW and Victoria. Fine performances by Queensland players—and years of Board meeting debate—finally forced their entry, but NSW deserves credit in continually sending teams to Queensland to help lift standards in the 60 years before Queensland was admitted. Queensland were magnificent in defeat in their first Shield match, losing by only eight runs to NSW in Brisbane. Poor fielding and a superb 127 by Kippax gave NSW a chance to win which Amos, who later settled in Queensland, clinched by running out Queensland's last batsman, O'Connor. The return match at Sydney was just as absorbing, with O'Connor scoring 103 and 153 not out to give Queensland a win by five wickets. Kippax added 182 to his two centuries in the first game. Victoria scored the highest total in a Shield innings, 1,107, in this season against NSW at Sydney. Ponsford made 352, Ryder 295, Woodfull 133, Hendry 100, and the tail wagged vigorously. Naturally, NSW were beaten—by an innings and 655 runs.

The retirement of Collins, Taylor, Kelleway, Gregory and Bardsley forced NSW to bring in new players in a reconstructed side. One of the newcomers was Archie Jackson. Bill O'Reilly was also given a trial, and Bradman was brought up from Bowral for the selectors to watch him at the SCG nets. In 1926–27 Ponsford became the first batsman to score more than 1,000 runs in a Shield season—1,091 runs at 136.37—and the following season he beat this, making 1,217 runs at 152.12, including 437 against Queensland at Melbourne. This remains the record for most runs in a Shield season, but the highest score lasted only until 1929–30 when Bradman surpassed it with 452 not out against Queensland.

An important change to Shield rules occurred in 1930–31, when all matches were limited to four days, ending the enormous totals that had been achieved when matches were played to a finish. Four days remains the scheduled period of play for all Shield matches.

The New South Wales Shield team, southern tour, 1930 (L to R): Standing, S. J. McCabe, H. S. Love, J. E. H. Hooker, G. Stewart, O. W. Bill, J. H. W. Fingleton, W. A. Hunt; Seated, D. G. Bradman, A. Jackson, A. F. Kippax, F. Buckle (Manager), H. C. Chilvers, A G. Fairfax.

For the next decade big crowds regularly attended Shield games, with crowds of 20,000 customary for Victoria–NSW matches. If Bradman was not out at the luncheon interval one could look from the SCG and watch hordes of people swarming across Moore Park to see Bradman bat, deserting their homes and offices once they learned he was still in. On Australia Day, 1934, a crowd of 32,587 watched the first day of the NSW-Victoria match. Bradman made it a memorable holiday by hitting three sixes in one over from Fleetwood-Smith on his way to 128 in 96 minutes. Of the 21 Shield competitions between the wars, NSW won nine, Victoria nine and South Australia three. Two of South Australia's wins came in 1935–36 and 1938–39 after Bradman joined the team from NSW. Queensland was still without a win when the competition was suspended between 1940 and 1946.

SHIELD CRICKET SINCE WORLD WAR II

After the six-year break Victoria scored enough runs through the batting of Hassett, Loxton and Miller to regain the Shield from NSW. Miller then moved to NSW and immediately public discussion began on whether he or Arthur Morris should captain NSW, after O'Reilly retired. While the argument raged one of NSW's best batsmen, Keith Carmody left to become captain-coach of Western Australia, who pulled off a surprising coup by winning the Shield in their first season 1947–48. Western Australia played only four matches compared with seven by the other States and had to bear the expenses of States travelling to Perth. Some of their opponents had key players absent for the Tests against India, but it was still a remarkable effort for Western Australia to win the Shield. Carmody began with 198 in his first Shield match for WA and made 428 at 61.14 in the four games. Edwards and Puckett also made centuries for WA and Puckett took 24 wickets.

Miller scored 392 at 49.00 in his first season with NSW, but one of the stars of the season was South Australia's Phil Ridings who made three centuries in scoring 649 at 59.00. The struggle for Test places was intense and this heightened the desire of players to shine in Shield matches. Bradman retired in 1948–49 with an aggregate of 8,926 runs at 110.19 in the Shield competition and Arthur Morris took over for a time as the nation's highest scoring Shield batsman, scoring 858 runs in seven Shield matches that season, four of which NSW won outright.

The 1953–54 competition saw a close tussle for the Shield between NSW and traditional rivals, Victoria. The issue was not decided until the final day of the season when Victoria failed to achieve an outright win over South Australia, and the Shield went to NSW, with 26 points to Victoria's 24. This began a NSW sequence of nine successive Shield wins, a feat

894

without parallel in Shield history. Players like Jim Burke, Richie Benaud, Alan Davidson and Ian Craig kept NSW on top and were given great assistance when Neil Harvey transferred to the State from Victoria. In these golden years for NSW their fielding was always a powerful ally in their success, and this was improved even further when Norman O'Neill and Brian Booth joined the side.

Victoria finally ended NSW's run in 1962–63. Crowds were down to around 10,000 on important days but until television came to Australia in 1956 cricket administrators knew they could comfortably expect enough gatemoney to pay all team expenses. Sunday cricket was introduced for Shield matches in 1964–65, and from the 1960s each State was permitted to play one overseas star (Tasmania was later allowed two imports) in their sides. But with TV and the rise in playing standards of the West Indies, India and Pakistan and a dramatic increase in tours by overseas countries, the Shield was gradually overshadowed. By the time Tasmania was admitted to the Shield on a restricted basis in 1977–78, the Shield was no longer a paying proposition for most States. Only Western Australia has increased attendances at Shield matches over

Queensland's first Shield team, 1926 (L to R): Back, H. D. Noyes, E. C. Bensted, N. Beeston; Centre, F. J. Gough, F. M. Brew, R. Higgins, R. K. Oxenham; Front, W. D. Rowe, F. C. Thompson, L. P. D. O'Connor (captain), A. D. Mayes, L. Oxenham.

895

the past few years. The NSWCA in 1980–81 lost on every Shield match played at Sydney Cricket Ground. The losses ranged from $11,965 on the Tasmania-NSW match in Sydney to $2,788 on the match against Victoria.

The Shield remains the ideal and the only proving ground for aspiring Test players, however, and the ACB have adopted a schedule of matches in 1982–83 aimed at stimulating some of the old interest in the competition. Test players will be available for more Shield matches than over the past few seasons and there will be a final between the two leading teams after each State has met the others twice. The emergence of a new Trumper or Bradman would also help.

SHEFFIELD SHIELD CONDITIONS

From 1982–83 all six States will play 10 Shield matches. After a total of 30 matches the two leading teams on the Shield points table will play a final. All matches are of four days duration, played under the Laws of Cricket recognised by the Australian Cricket Board. Each State may include one overseas player in their team, with the exception of Tasmania which may include two overseas players. The residential qualification for all Australian-born players is three months.

When two States gain the same number of points and wins, their relative positions on the final Shield competition table will be obtained by averages—dividing runs for and against by wickets lost or taken. The pitch may be covered against rain up to the start of play and for the duration of matches. The bonus points system that operated for a few seasons no longer applies. New balls may now be taken by the fielding team after 85 six-ball overs have been bowled. A minimum of 100 overs must be bowled each day, less allowances for each fall of wicket, drink breaks, injuries, bad weather etc.

In all Shield matches points are scored as follows:

For an outright win if the winning team leads on the first innings	16 points
For an outright win where the first innings was a tie	14 points
For an outright win, if the winning team was behind on the first innings	12 points
For a tie where both teams have completed two innings (irrespective of the first innings result)	8 points each
For a win on first innings (these points to be retained even if beaten outright)	4 points
For a draw or tie on first innings	2 points
For an outright loss after tie on first innings	2 points
For a loss on first innings	Nil
For an outright loss where a losing team was behind on first innings	Nil

896

Abandoned match:

In the event of a match being abandoned without any play having taken place   2 points each

An observer is appointed by the Board to attend each Sheffield Shield match and, if in the opinion of the observer, a result has been contrived and he so reports to the Board, then the Board may amend points obtained in the match by either team.

SHEFFIELD SHIELD WINNERS
From 1892–93 to 1981–82

Season	First	Second	Third
1892–93	Victoria	New South Wales	South Australia
1893–94	South Australia	New South Wales	Victoria
1894–95	Victoria	South Australia	New South Wales
1895–96	New South Wales	Victoria	South Australia
1896–97	New South Wales	Victoria	South Australia
1897–98	Victoria	South Australia	New South Wales
1898–99	Victoria	New South Wales	South Australia
1899–1900	New South Wales	Victoria	South Australia
1900–01	Victoria	New South Wales	South Australia
1901–02	New South Wales	Victoria	South Australia
1902–03	New South Wales	Victoria	South Australia
1903–04	New South Wales	Victoria	South Australia
1904–05	New South Wales	Victoria	South Australia
1905–06	New South Wales	Victoria	South Australia
1906–07	New South Wales	Victoria	South Australia
1907–08	Victoria	New South Wales	South Australia
1908–09	New South Wales	South Australia	Victoria
1909–10	South Australia	New South Wales	Victoria
1910–11	New South Wales	South Australia	Victoria
1911–12	New South Wales	South Australia	Victoria
1912–13	South Australia	New South Wales	Victoria
1913–14	New South Wales	South Australia	Victoria
1914–15	Victoria	New South Wales	South Australia
1915–19	Matches were abandoned during World War I.		
1919–20	New South Wales	Victoria	South Australia
1920–21	New South Wales	Victoria	South Australia
1921–22	Victoria	New South Wales	South Australia
1922–23	New South Wales	Victoria	South Australia
1923–24	Victoria	New South Wales	South Australia
1924–25	Victoria	New South Wales	South Australia
1925–26	New South Wales	Victoria	South Australia
1926–27	South Australia	Victoria	New South Wales
1927–28	Victoria	South Australia	New South Wales
1928–29	New South Wales	Victoria	South Australia
1929–30	Victoria	New South Wales	South Australia
1930–31	Victoria	New South Wales	Queensland
1931–32	*New South Wales	South Australia	Victoria
1932–33	New South Wales	Victoria	South Australia
1933–34	Victoria	New South Wales	South Australia
1934–35	Victoria	New South Wales	South Australia
1935–36	South Australia	New South Wales	Victoria
1936–37	Victoria	South Australia	New South Wales
1937–38	New South Wales	*South Australia	Victoria
1938–39	South Australia	Victoria	Queensland

897

1939–40	New South Wales	*South Australia	Victoria
1940–46	Matches were abandoned during World War II.		
1946–47	Victoria	New South Wales	Queensland
1947–48	†Western Australia	New South Wales	South Australia
1948–49	New South Wales	Victoria	Qld. & Sth. Aus.
1949–50	New South Wales	Victoria	Western Australia
1950–51	Victoria	New South Wales	Western Australia
1951–52	New South Wales	Victoria	Queensland
1952–53	South Australia	New South Wales	Victoria
1953–54	New South Wales	Victoria	Queensland
1954–55	New South Wales	Victoria	Western Australia
1955–56	New South Wales	Victoria	Queensland
1956–57	New South Wales	Queensland	Victoria
1957–58	New South Wales	Victoria	Queensland
1958–59	New South Wales	Queensland	Victoria
1959–60	New South Wales	Victoria	Western Australia
1960–61	New South Wales	Victoria	Western Australia
1961–62	New South Wales	Queensland	South Australia
1962–63	Victoria	South Australia	New South Wales
1963–64	South Australia	Victoria	New South Wales
1964–65	New South Wales	Victoria	South Australia
1965–66	New South Wales	Western Australia	South Australia
1966–67	Victoria	South Australia	New South Wales
1967–68	Western Australia	Victoria	South Australia
1968–69	South Australia	Western Australia	Queensland
1969–70	Victoria	Western Australia	Queensland / New South Wales / South Australia
1970–71	South Australia	Victoria	Western Australia
1971–72	Western Australia	South Australia	New South Wales
1972–73	Western Australia	South Australia	New South Wales
1973–74	Victoria	Queensland	New South Wales
1974–75	Western Australia	Queensland	Victoria
1975–76	South Australia	Queensland	Western Australia
1976–77	Western Australia	Victoria	Queensland
1977–78	Western Australia	Queensland	Victoria
1978–79	Victoria	Western Australia	New South Wales
1979–80	Victoria	South Australia	New South Wales
1980–81	Western Australia	New South Wales	Queensland
1981–82	South Australia	New South Wales	Western Australia

*Gained position by averages.   †Gained position by percentages.

SUMMARY

NSW has held the Shield for 36 seasons, Victoria for 24 seasons, South Australia for 12 seasons and Western Australia for 8 seasons.

Queensland first competed in 1926–27; Western Australia in 1947–48; Tasmania in 1977–78.

HOW THE STATES HAVE FARED

States	First Season	Played	Won	Lost	Drawn	Ties	Abandoned
New South Wales	1892–93	481	231	124	125	1	—
Victoria	1892–93	479	206	143	126	1	3
South Australia	1892–93	477	143	230	103	1	—
Queensland	1926–27	361	81	148	128	1	3
Western Australia	1947–48	247	82	84	81	—	—
Tasmania	1977–78	25	2	16	7	—	—
		2070	745	745	570	4	6

HIGHEST INDIVIDUAL SHIELD SCORES

452*	D. G. Bradman, NSW v. Q'land (Sydney), 1929–30.
437	W. H. Ponsford, Vic. v. Q'land (Melb.), 1927–28.
365*	C. Hill, SA v. NSW (Adel.), 1900–01.
359	R. B. Simpson, NSW v. Q'land (Brisbane), 1963–64.
357	D. G. Bradman, SA v. Vic. (Melb.), 1935–36.
356	B. A. Richards, SA v. WA (Perth), 1970–71.
352	W. H. Ponsford, Vic. v. NSW (Melb.), 1926–27.
340*	D. G. Bradman, NSW v. Vic. (Sydney), 1928–29.
336	W. H. Ponsford, Vic. v. SA (Melb.), 1927–28.
325	C. L. Badcock, SA v. Vic. (Adel.), 1935–36.
315*	A. F. Kippax, NSW v. Q'land (Sydney), 1927–28.
295	J. Ryder, Vic. v. NSW (Melb.), 1926–27.
283	P. J. Burge, Q'land v. NSW (Brisbane), 1963–64.
281	M. A. Noble, NSW v. Vic. (Melb.), 1905–06.
277	R. B. Simpson, NSW v. Q'land (Sydney), 1967–68.

RECORD SHIELD PARTNERSHIPS

Wicket	Stand	Batsmen, State, Venue and Year
1st	375	W. H. Ponsford (352) and W. M. Woodfull (133), Vic. v. NSW, Melbourne, 1926–27.
2nd	378	L. A. Marks (185) and K. D. Walters (253), NSW v. SA, Adelaide, 1964–65.
3rd	390	J. K. Moss (220*) and J. M. Weiner (221*), Vic. v. WA, Melbourne, 1981–82.
4th	325	B. C. Booth (123) and N. C. O'Neill (253), NSW v. Vic., Sydney, 1957–58.
5th	397	W. Bardsley (235) and C. Kelleway (168), NSW v. SA, Sydney, 1920–21.
6th	332	N. Marks (180*) and G. Thomas (189), NSW v. SA, Sydney, 1958–59.
7th	335	E. C. Bensted (155) and C. W. Andrews (253), Qld v. NSW, Sydney, 1934–35.
8th	270	V. T. Trumper (138) and E. P. Barbour (146), NSW v. Vic., Sydney, 1912–13.
9th	232	C. Hill (365*) and E. Walkley (58), SA v. NSW, Adelaide, 1900–01.
10th	307	A. F. Kippax (260*) and J. E. H. Hooker (62), NSW v. Vic., Melbourne, 1928–29.

RECORD SHIELD TEAM SCORES

1107	Victoria v. New South Wales, Melbourne, 1926–27.
918	New South Wales v. South Australia, Sydney, 1900–01.
7–821	South Australia v. Queensland, Adelaide, 1939–40.
687	Queensland v. New South Wales, Brisbane, 1930–31.
5–615	Western Australia v. Queensland, Brisbane, 1968–69.
9–505	Tasmania v. Queensland, Hobart, 1979–80.

LOWEST SHIELD TEAM SCORES

27	South Australia v. New South Wales, Sydney, 1955–56.
31	Victoria v. New South Wales, Melbourne, 1906–07.
49	Queensland v. Victoria, Melbourne, 1936–37.
50	Western Australia v. New South Wales, Sydney, 1951–52.

LEADING SHIELD BATSMEN

	State	Inn	NO	HS	Runs	Ave
D. G. Bradman	NSW, SA	96	15	452*	8926	110.19
S. C. Trimble	Qld	230	13	252*	8647	39.85
L. E. Favell	SA	220	4	164	8269	38.28
G. S. Chappell	SA, Qld	151	18	194	8040	60.45
R. J. Inverarity	WA, SA	227	23	187	7918	38.81
I. M. Chappell	SA	157	13	205	7665	53.22
P. J. Burge	Qld	138	12	283	7084	56.22
H. N. Dansie	SA	196	6	185	6692	35.22
W. M. Lawry	Vic	139	14	266	6615	52.92
R. B. Simpson	NSW, WA	132	21	359	6471	58.29
K. D. Mackay	Qld	162	21	223	6341	44.97
C. Hill	SA	126	6	365*	6274	52.28
V. Y. Richardson	SA	148	7	203	6148	43.60
A. F. Kippax	NSW	95	9	315*	6096	70.88

MOST SHIELD RUNS FOR EACH STATE

New South Wales	A. F. Kippax	6,096 runs at 70.88
Victoria	W. M. Lawry	6,615 runs at 52.92
South Australia	L. E. Favell	8,269 runs at 38.28
Queensland	S. C. Trimble	8,647 runs at 39.85
Western Australia	R. J. Inverarity	6,888 runs at 40.04
Tasmania	B. F. Davison	1,335 runs at 47.68

MOST RUNS IN A SHIELD SEASON

Season	Player (team)	Match	Inn	NO	HS	Runs	Ave
1927–28	W. H. Ponsford (Vic.)	5	8	0	437	1217	152.12
1970–71	B. A. Richards (SA)	8	13	2	356	1145	104.09
1926–27	W. H. Ponsford (Vic.)	5	8	0	352	1091	136.37
1939–40	D. G. Bradman (SA)	6	10	2	267	1062	132.75
1977–78	A. D. Ogilvie (Q)	9	18	2	194	1060	66.25
1981–82	K. C. Wessels (Q)	9	15	0	220	1015	67.66
1973–74	G. S. Chappell (Q)	7	13	2	180	1013	92.05
1957–58	N. C. O'Neill (NSW)	8	14	2	233	1005	83.75
1938–39	W. A. Brown (Q)	6	10	1	215	990	110.00
1937–38	D. G. Bradman (SA)	6	12	2	246	983	98.30
1963–64	G. S. Sobers (SA)	8	13	0	195	973	74.84
1963–64	S. C. Trimble (Q)	8	13	2	252*	950	86.36
1933–34	D. G. Bradman (NSW)	5	7	2	253	922	184.40
1980–81	G. S. Chappell (Q)	7	10	2	194	906	113.25
1959–60	R. B. Simpson (WA)	5	6	3	236*	902	300.66

LEADING SHIELD BOWLERS

	State	Runs	Wkts	Ave
C. V. Grimmett	Vic/SA	12,976	513	25.29
A. A. Mallett	SA	8170	344	23.75
G. A. R. Lock	WA	7216	302	23.89
A. N. Connolly	Vic.	7908	297	26.62
D. K. Lillee	WA	6196	275	22.53
J. W. Martin	NSW/SA	8715	273	31.92
G. Dymock	Qld	7138	266	26.83
R. Benaud	NSW	7213	266	27.11
A. K. Davidson	NSW	5210	246	21.17

L. Fleetwood-Smith	Vic.	6040	246	24.56
R. Lindwall	NSW/Qld	5535	243	22.77
T. J. Jenner	WA/SA	8145	234	35.11
G. D. McKenzie	WA	7388	232	31.84

MOST SHIELD WICKETS FOR EACH STATE

New South Wales	R. Benaud	266 wickets
Victoria	A. N. Connolly	297 wickets
South Australia	C. V. Grimmett	504 wickets
Queensland	G. Dymock	266 wickets
Western Australia	G. A. R. Lock	302 wickets
Tasmania	F. Stephenson	30 wickets

MOST WICKETS IN A SHIELD SEASON

Season	Player (team)	Matches	Runs	Wickets	Ave	BB
1939–40	W. J. O'Reilly (NSW)	6	718	52	13.80	8-23
1966–67	G. A. R. Lock (WA)	8	1086	51	22.29	6-85
1934–35	C. V. Grimmett (SA)	6	1043	49	21.28	9-180
1939–40	C. V. Grimmett (SA)	6	1215	49	24.79	6-118
1969–70	A. L. Thomson (Vic.)	8	943	49	19.24	8-87
1972–73	A. A. Mallett (SA)	8	893	49	18.22	5-41
1977–78	D. W. Hourn (NSW)	9	995	48	20.72	7-71

An elated Victorian team in the dressing-room after winning the Shield by defeating South Australia at Adelaide in March 1980.

**SHEPHERD, Barry
Kenneth, 1938–**

First-Class Averages:
Batting, 6,558 runs at
41.50; Bowling, 3
wickets at 103.66.

Tests (9): 502 runs at
41.83.

A burly, consistent left-hand batsman from Donnybrook, Western Australia, whose batting was studded with brawny, enthusiastic hitting. The powerhouse treatment he gave some loose balls was still talked about in Perth 15 years after he retired, for he was a batsman who kept fieldsmen's hands warm. He was an intelligent cricketer, however, who knew how to use his big frame, and he captained Western Australia 39 times, a record that only John Inverarity has surpassed. He made all his three-figure scores for WA, 10 centuries and three double centuries.

Shepherd learned his cricket at Scotch College, Perth, where he was an outstanding student. He played for Claremont originally but later joined South Perth and then Mt Lawley. He went into the WA team in 1955–56, when he hit a valuable century (103 not out) at the age of 18 in his first game. The next season he made 173 against Queensland at Brisbane and 101 at Perth against Victoria. By 1961–62, when he made his first double century with an innings of 212 not out against Queensland at Perth, he was an established crowd-pleaser with seven centuries to his record. This double century was part of a record third wicket stand of 223 for the third wicket with Kanhai. Shepherd hit six sixes and 20 fours and made his last 112 runs in 68 minutes.

He made another double century (219) against Victoria at

Melbourne in 1962–63 and that season made his Test debut against England at Sydney, scoring 71 not out before he ran out of partners. But after two Tests he was dropped and for the rest of his career he became a batsman Australia called on to strengthen the middle order but did not use regularly.

Shepherd narrowly missed a place in the 1964 Australian side in England, an omission Western Australians were justifiably peeved about, but he toured the West Indies in 1964–65, and appeared in further Tests in Australia against England, South Africa and Pakistan. He made 96 at Melbourne in the Second Test against South Africa in 1963–64 and 70 and 78 in the Fourth Test of that series. At Melbourne in 1964–65 he scored 55 and 43 not out against Pakistan. The last big innings of his career was his 215 not out for WA against Victoria in Perth in 1964–65.

SHERIDAN, Edward Orwell ("Ned"), 1842–1923

First-Class Averages: Batting, 230 runs at 12.77; Bowling, 4 wickets at 20.50.

Hero of the first match in February, 1878, between Victoria and New South Wales on the Association Ground, later the Sydney Cricket Ground, and a prominent figure in the early development of batsmanship on the Australian east coast. He played all his first-class cricket for NSW, but did most of his coaching in Queensland. He was picked to tour England with the first Australian team in 1878 but declined because of the death of his mother. He is not to be confused with Philip Sheridan, the high-spirited Irishman who ran the SCG for many years.

Ned Sheridan was a tough, gnarled, heavily-moustached right-hander below medium height, who first played for NSW in 1867–68. He won the trophy for the best batting average in the strong Warwick club in successive seasons 1873–74 and 1874–75. He also won a trophy for outstanding batting against Victoria in March, 1869, but his day of glory came in 1878 at the SCG when he went out to bat with NSW on 5 for 18, chasing 119 to win in the final innings to beat Victoria. Mainly through singles, he confidently lifted the NSW score to within 15 runs of victory, when he was caught at short leg.

When NSW won with the last pair at the wicket, spectators rushed the pavilion shouting for Sheridan. Amid cheering, they had an immediate whip round for him, which yielded nearly £40, money he later used to set himself up in a barber shop-tobacconist business in Queen Street, Brisbane, where he contracted to play for The Stanleys club. One of the features of his Brisbane shop was a reading room for cricketers. He remained in Brisbane for 40 years, playing with several clubs, a veteran whose knowledge helped young Queenslanders wherever he played. He delighted in showing them the scars he had collected from his many encounters with the demon bowler Spofforth.

SHERIDAN, Philip
1833–1910

One of the first trustees of Sydney Cricket Ground, a good-humoured Irishman who migrated to Australia in 1849 at the age of 15. He formed the Sydney Club and was their delegate to the NSWCA when he was appointed a trustee in 1877 and ran the ground as secretary until his death the year after the stand named in his honour was opened. Cricketers regarded him as one of the game's staunchest friends. Ranjitsinhji described him as a vivacious, active man always full of fun and high spirits. "One can always tell when Philip Sheridan is in the room from the amount of talking and laughing that is going on," wrote Ranji. "His ready wit is indeed astonishing; he always turns everything into a joke. One cannot sit a few moments by his side without being convulsed with laughter. He is a firm and true friend." Sheridan was the man who asked Ned Gregory to build the scoreboard that revolutionised the concept of cricket scoreboards. The Sheridan stand replaced a smaller one known as the Smokers' Stand.

SHIELL, Alan
Bruce, 1945–

First-Class Averages:
Batting, 1,276 runs at
33.57.

A right-hand batsman who had three impressive seasons for South Australia before he concentrated on cricket writing. He scored 72 and 110 against New South Wales at Sydney in 1964–65 and 202 not out against England at Adelaide in 1965–66. Thereafter Shiell, son of a bus driver, preferred journalism. He succeeded Ray Barber as cricket writer at the Adelaide *News* and in 1982 transferred to the Adelaide *Advertiser* to take a similar role. Like his brother Colin, he played for East Torrens and the Australian Schoolboys XI. On May 9, 1977, Shiell and Peter McFarline, of the Melbourne *Age*, shared a world exclusive when they broke the news of WSC.

SHIPPERD, Gregory,
1956–

First-Class Averages:
Batting, 1,950 runs at
38.23.

A dependable and diminutive Perth right-hand batsman with an attractive array of strokes who has shown steady improvement in five seasons of first-class cricket. He has been especially valuable to Western Australia when their Test stars have been absent. He made his debut for Western Australia in 1977–78 while playing with the West Perth club but has since switched to Scarborough. He topped the Perth district batting averages in 1978–79 with 607 runs at 67.44, and in 1979–80 made two first-class centuries, 106 against Victoria at Melbourne and 104 against Queensland in Perth. He produced his highest score, 140, at Perth in 1980–81 against Queensland and scored 646 runs at 38.00 in the season. He was impressive in Western Australia's 115-run win over NSW at Perth, scoring 80 and 65. His driving through cover and mid-off was graceful and fluent, but his running between wickets was impetuous. In 1981–82 he had another splendid season, scoring 613 runs at 40.86.

A hard-hitting left-hander for Queensland and Victoria who scored more than 1,000 runs in first-class matches in a few seasons before World War II. Sides, born at Mackay, first played for Queensland in 1930–31 and scored 449 of his runs in first-class cricket with Queensland and 859 with Victoria. His best knock in first-class cricket was 121 for Victoria against WA at Perth.

Sides, an outstanding baseballer, scored 1,984 runs in four seasons for Essendon at 49.60, including three centuries in succession in the 1938–39 season. He was an extremely vocal cricketer, who enjoyed chatting up opponents and umpires. He was killed in action at Salamaua, in north-east New Guinea during World War II.

SIDES, Francis William, 1913–1943

First-Class Averages: Batting, 1,308 runs at 31.14.

A versatile Victorian allrounder who gave valuable assistance to Victoria in 39 matches between 1969 and 1976. He was often used as an opener when Lawry, Stackpole and Redpath were absent on Test duty, and scored four first-class centuries, topscore 157 against Queensland at Brisbane in 1973–74 when he added 271 for the fifth wicket with Robert Rose. He could bowl both left-arm medium pacers or orthodox left-arm spinners and was a craftsmanlike field. He played for Hawthorn, East Melbourne and St Kilda. Another of his best efforts was his first wicket stand of 145 with Robert Rose against New South Wales in December, 1972.

SIELER, Alan John, 1948–

First-Class Averages: Batting, 1,801 runs at 30.52; Bowling, 41 wickets at 35.39.

A rugged, resourceful 6 ft 4 ins medium pace to fast bowler of exceptional lift, and a useful right-hand batsman who played for Victoria from 1934 to 1945 and in three Tests for Australia. Sievers' Test career was brief but in his three appearances in the 1936–37 series against "Gubby" Allen's England team he helped Australia to retain The Ashes.

Sievers, born at Wonthaggi, Victoria, headed the Australian bowling averages for the series. He was almost unplayable on a Melbourne "glue pot" in the first innings of the Third Test when he took 5 for 21, using his great height to make the ball rise almost vertically. Australia won the match by 365 runs. Before this fine coup Sievers had toured South Africa with Australia in 1935–36 without being able to win a Test spot.

He was a bowler whose wicket-keepers said "always felt very heavy in the gloves". He took all 10 wickets for Cumberland in a Sydney grade match against Western Suburbs in 1943–44, and remains one of only three players, with Bill Hunt and Vic Jackson the only others, to have dismissed all 10.

Sievers took 92 wickets for Victoria with a best analysis of 6 for 43 against South Australia in 1937–38 and had a topscore of 76. He took five wickets or more in an innings four times and held 56 catches in 58 first-class games.

SIEVERS, Morris William, 1912–1968

First-Class Averages: Batting, 2,075 runs at 29.64; Bowling, 116 wickets at 33.36.

Tests (3): 67 runs at 13.40; 9 wickets at 17.88.

SIMMONS, Jack, 1941–

One of the most valuable of all the players Tasmania has imported in a bid to lift standards, a right-hand batsman and offspin bowler who coached in Launceston from 1972–73 to 1978–79. He played a major role in Tasmania's victory in the Gillette Cup in 1978–79 and in Tasmania's first win in a Sheffield Shield match—also against Western Australia. He had 30 first class games for Tasmania, scoring 589 runs at 21.03. He was associated in a memorable stand with L. J. Appleton in 1972–73 against Pakistan, adding 82 for the last wicket. Simmons ended with 77, Appleton 5 not out. Jack Simmons hails from Lancashire where he has taken almost 600 wickets since 1968. He took 46 wickets for Tasmania at 31.97, best figures 7 for 59 against Queensland at Brisbane in 1978–79. It was his canny leadership, however, which contributed most to Tasmanian cricket for he moulded a team of inexperienced players into a side that was seldom disgraced in inter-State matches even though they found the going hard. The work he began was carried on in grand style by Brian Davison. Simmons gave up the Tasmanian captaincy largely because he wanted to concentrate on assisting organisers of his benefit, which in 1981 yielded a record £128,000, a marvellous tribute to his popularity in Lancashire.

SIMPSON, Robert Baddeley, 1936–

First-Class Averages: Batting, 21,029 runs at 56.22; Bowling, 349 wickets at 38.07.

Tests (62): 4,869 runs at 46.81; 71 wickets at 42.26.

A right-hand opening batsman, slips fieldsman, and captain of uncommon skill. He had a successful 52-Test career, retired, and returned ten years later in the most astonishing comeback in Australian cricket history to captain Australia in 10 more Tests, taking over a team of raw recruits and helping them to perform creditably when WSC signed most of Australia's best players. Simpson risked missing out on business opportunities while he rescued established cricket, but his success ended up emphasising his loyalty and dependability in a crisis.

Simpson was born in the Sydney suburb of Marrickville, of Scottish migrant parents. His father "Jock", a former soccer professional with Stenhousemuir in the Scottish League, was a popular character on the printing floor of the Sydney *Daily Telegraph* who could strike with the best of them in the old days of hot metal setting when the editors Brian Penton, Lew McBride or King Watson poked their heads in the printing room door. Bobby, whose mother came from Falkirk in Stirlingshire, went to Tempe Boys' High, and began as a legspinner for St. Clements, an Anglican Church team in the under-16 competition. He was good enough to make Petersham-Marrickville first grade a week after his 15th birthday. His two brothers were with him in the church side and went on to play first grade with Western Suburbs and University.

He won selection for New South Wales in January, 1953

906

when he was only 16. He recalls running out on to the Sydney Cricket Ground as 12th man to deputise for a New South Wales fieldsman who had to go off for some reason. When he asked State Captain Keith Miller where he should field, Miller, who cared little for the refinements of positioning the 12th man where he had least chance of taking catches, pointed to the slips. Simpson caught Neil Harvey and Harry Lambert within a half hour and remained in the slips for the rest of his cricket career. Before Miller put him there he had fielded around the boundary. In the 1954–55 season, Simpson took 14 of the 15 chances that came his way in the slips for New South Wales against MCC and the States. He caught Len Hutton twice in the second MCC v. New South Wales match and years later Hutton confessed he was amazed by the second catch in which Simpson dived wide to the right to grasp a full-blooded back cut.

After four good seasons for New South Wales without gain-

One of the great Test catches: Bob Simpson dives wide and low to his right to dismiss Len Hutton, who talked about this for years afterwards. Alan Davidson was the lucky bowler.

Bob Simpson makes a majestic square cut against Bishen Bedi's Indian team during his amazing comeback.

ing a Test place, Simpson moved to Western Australia for five years in 1956, and in this period served a four year cadetship in journalism with a Perth paper. In 1959, he had a season with Accrington in the Lancashire League. Neil Harvey suggested to him after Jimmy Burke retired that he try opening as Australia clearly had an opening problem. He had batted No 3 or No 5. The move was a startling success. At one stage in the 1959–60 season in Australia, Simpson had an average of 300, with knocks of 230 not out against Queensland, and 236 not out against New South Wales, a total of 902 runs in six innings with three not outs. His thirst for runs continued in 1959–60 on a tour of New Zealand as an opener, and on his first tour of England in 1961, when he made 1,947 runs, with six centuries. But he could not get a century in Tests.

Apart from Tests he put together some remarkable scores, including 800 runs in four innings for New South Wales in 1963–64, throwing in a knock of 247 not out versus Western Australia and 359 against Queensland, his career highest score. He succeeded Benaud as Australia's captain during the series against South Africa in 1963–64.

Scores over 50 kept coming but he had to wait until his 30th Test to score a century. And what a feast he had when he broke through! At Manchester in 1964 he batted for more than two days to score 311. This innings, the longest ever played by an Australian in Tests against England, occupied 12 hours 42 minutes, most of it sheer tedium, but it made The Ashes safe for Australia. Simpson, whose previous topscore in Tests was 96, hit 23 fours and a six. He was 109 not out at the end of the first day, with Australia 2 for 253. His opening stand with Lawry realised 201, and he added 219 with Booth for the fifth wicket, hitting out unconcernedly on the third morning when he appeared to have· the individual scoring records (Bradman's 334 and Hutton's 364) within his sights.

To his undying credit, he said he cared little for the records once Australia was safe and The Ashes held. Despite a fractured thumb and later another chip from the same bone, he scored 458 runs in the five Tests in 1964 and 1,714 runs, with five centuries on the tour. At Karachi on the short tour of India and Pakistan which immediately followed the England tour, he hit two separate hundreds in a Test, the fifth Australian batsman to achieve this honour.

Simpson at the crease was a difficult batsman to summarise, for he changed from a front-on player to a side-on batsman in Western Australia. He found that the side-on stance made it far easier for him to combat balls that swung away from him late. His strokes are easy to describe, however, for he has always had one of the best square cuts in the game, and a devastating straight drive. He seldom hooked but pulled occasionally and he had an elegant ondrive.

In the 1965–66 series against England in Australia, Simpson

led Australia for three Tests and scored 225 in the Fourth Test
at Adelaide (after missing the First Test through a broken
wrist and the Third because of chickenpox). This time he batted for over nine hours, hitting 18 fours and a six, and set an
Australian first wicket partnership record against England of
244 with Lawry. In South Africa in 1966–67, Australia went
down 3–1 in the Tests but Simpson had a splendid tour, scoring 1,344 runs, including 243 against North Eastern Transvaal
at Pretoria and a marvellous 153 in the Second Test at Cape
Town. He retired at the end of the 1967–68 season after the
series against India with 4,131 Test runs to his name at an
average of 48.60.

Simpson continued to play grade cricket for Western
Suburbs after his first retirement from big cricket. He was involved in the promotion of Double Wicket Cricket in Australia. He was involved in a libel action in 1965 with Ian Meckiff,
whose writ was served on him on the morning of a Test
match. He had to make financial sacrifices, however, to accept an invitation from the Australian Cricket Board in 1977
to captain Australia against India. He was 41 and taking a big
risk with his reputation but was shrewd enough to realise
that India lacked express bowlers and that he could still
handle spin, even that of the Bedi-Chandrasekhar calibre.

With clever deflections, superb placements, dabbing the
ball rather than hitting it, he returned to Test cricket with an
eighty at Brisbane, a truly phenomenal effort. He got through
the five Tests against India remarkably well but had little
chance against the West Indies pace attack on their wickets,
though his brave captaincy made every game a true contest.
On his return to Australia, with 10 comeback Tests behind
him and his side starting to benefit from his careful tuition,
he asked the Board of Control for a guarantee that he would
be chosen for the First Test against England in 1978–79. The
Board declined to give this guarantee and Simpson retired
permanently, accepting lucrative newspaper and commentary jobs.

The Board appointed Graham Yallop to replace Simpson as
Australian captain, with unhappy results. The lack of character in the Australian batting under Yallop was in sharp
contrast to that which Simpson had encouraged throughout
his career, as an opener and as a captain, and we suffered
dearly from the lack of a class slips fieldsman such as
Simpson in Yallop's sides.

During Simpson's comeback he took his total of Test
catches beyond that of Ian Chappell, 110 against Chappell's
103, an Australian record, which gave him 383 first-class
catches in his career. He finished with a highest Test score of
311, with 10 centuries and 27 scores over 50. In all first-class
cricket he made 60 centuries, with a highest score of 359 for
New South Wales against Queensland in 1963–64 at Brisbane.

910

An erratic left-arm Adelaide googly bowler who for a time was Australia's most exciting wicket-taker. He bowled some unplayable deliveries but like most bowlers of his type he often lacked control. His talents deserved far more than the one overseas tour and three Tests they achieved. This was due in part to the selectors' emphasis on pace bowling but also to the hammering Sincock took when he was given his chance in Tests.

Sincock started playing cricket in the backyard of his parents house in the Adelaide suburb of Plympton, with his father, Harold Sincock, who had played a few games for South Australia in the 1930s, coaching him. Shy, red-haired, David was a natural ball player with a powerful arm. He won the prize for the outstanding player at the Australian Schoolboys' baseball carnival in 1959. He had a brilliant scholastic career at Glenelg Sacred Heart College. When he became a dental student at Adelaide University, fellow cricketers nicknamed him "Stumps," and spectators at Glenelg club matches soon took up the cry.

In 1961 he was invited to go to Adelaide Oval to act as a ground bowler when Frank Worrell's West Indian team were practising. He stunned the West Indians by clean bowling four of their best batsmen, Worrell, Rohan Kanhai, Conrad Hunte and Gary Sobers. "He's the best left-hand googly bowler we've seen in Australia," said Worrell. "We just could not pick him. If he's not playing for Australia within two years I'm a bad judge. I cannot understand why he had not been in the South Australian team."

A week later Sincock was in the State side against New South Wales and he shocked the cricket world by taking 6 for 52 off 13 overs, including the wickets of Richie Benaud, Brian Booth and Graeme Thomas. He was mentioned as a likely tourist in Richie Benaud's 1961 side for England but he was only 19 so the selectors decided to delay his Test debut. For a time studies and his dental exams interfered with his cricket but after he qualified he settled to regular Shield appearances, an easily-spotted fieldsman because of his marvellous throwing arm and the white ointment coated heavily on his nose and lips.

Sincock made his Test debut at Melbourne in the only Test against Pakistan in 1964–65. He took 3 for 67 in the first innings off 17.6 overs but took some punishment in the second innings when his 28 overs yielded 1 for 102. But he impressed by mixing bold flight with varied spin and it seemed that he only needed to improve his control to become a topflight bowler. He was given another Test in May, 1965, against the West Indies at Port-of-Spain, Trinidad, taking 2 for 79 and 2 for 64, clean bowling Sobers in the first innings. But he had a disappointing West Indies tour, finishing with 18 wickets at 31.55 and 68 runs at 17.00 from six matches.

SINCOCK, David John ("Stumps"), 1942–

First-Class Averages: Batting, 810 runs at 17.61; Bowling, 156 wickets at 36.25.

Tests (3): 80 runs at 26.66; 8 wickets at 51.25.

911

He played in his third and last Test against England in January, 1966. Bob Barber (185), John Edrich (103) and other English batsmen cracked 98 runs off his 20 overs in this Third Test at Sydney in compiling 488, England winning by an innings and 93 runs. Sincock later played for the Randwick and Northern Districts club in Sydney. He retired in 1973, aged 31. His brother **Peter Sincock** (1949–)played five games for South Australia without success. His cousin **Andrew Thomas Sincock** (1951–), a right-arm medium-pacer bowler, has often played for South Australia and in 1977–78 took a hat-trick against India at Adelaide. Andrew Sincock topped the Adelaide district wicket-takers in 1973–74 for Teachers' College with 62 wickets at 15.46, and has since done well with East Torrens and Adelaide clubs.

SISMEY, Stanley George, 1916–

First-Class Averages: Batting, 725 runs at 17.68; Dismissals, 106 (88 catches, 18 stumpings).

A skilful New South Wales wicket-keeper whose chances of Test selection were lost during a distinguished career in World War II. He played for Western Suburbs for 25 years and in 20 matches for NSW between 1938–39 and 1950–51. He was stylish and tidy in all his work behind the stumps, one of the last of Australia's first-class 'keepers to stand up on the stumps through most of the innings.

Sismey, born at Junee, took 20 catches and made seven stumpings for the Western Suburbs club in Sydney in 1938–39 and he did it with such impressive style he was chosen for the State team. After two seasons in the NSW side he joined the RAAF and left for Europe. He had a distinguished war record. In 1942, as a Squadron Leader, he was shot down in the Mediterranean while piloting a Catalina on a mission off Algiers. Eight hours later the RN fished him out of the water, unconscious, his back full of shrapnel. Sismey joked that he had so much shrapnel in his back it affected the compass needle when he resumed flying.

He captained RAAF teams in several matchs in England and after the war became the 'keeper for the Australian Services team that toured England, India and Ceylon, leaving the field several times to have pieces of shrapnel that had worked to the skin surface removed. He resumed as NSW's 'keeper in 1946–47 and went to New Zealand in 1950 under Bill Brown. He was a craftsmanlike 'keeper, who played cricket in an admirable sporting spirit. After he retired he gave meritorious service for several years as a NSW selector.

SLATER, Keith Nichol, 1935–

A happy, smiling allrounder from the Midland-Guildford club in Perth who was among the bowlers no-balled for throwing in the early 1960s. He started his career as a medium-pace bowler but reverted to off-spinners and it was

912

claimed that he chucked his faster ball when he bowled spinners. There was a pronounced wrist flick in Slater's action but camera evidence on whether he threw was inconclusive. He was a most unlikely target for all the publicity his jerky arm received and even those who cried the loudest that he was a chucker liked him.

Slater, born in Perth, never once took five wickets in an innings in 77 first-class matches, and in retrospect a calm study of his figures makes one wonder what the fuss was all about. His best figures were 4 for 33 at Perth against England in 1958–59, during which he had a spell of 4 for 8. As the English team continued round the States the throwing controversy became headline news, particularly after Ian Meckiff took 6 for 38 against England in the Second Test. Slater was one of those branded a thrower by the English pressmen—but not the English players—and the Australian selectors added to the controversy by picking Slater for the Third Test at Sydney. Slater had a non-productive match and was not picked again for Australia. He was not called in the Test for throwing but he was warned by umpire Col Hoy for running on the wicket in his follow-through.

Slater's value in WA's team was in his allround skills, rather than in his match-winning batting or bowling. He made 13 fifties for his state, but only one century—154 against Queensland at Brisbane in 1963–64. He could break threatening stands with the ball and held 50 first-class catches. He had one overseas tour for an Australian XI to New Zealand in 1959–60. Later he became a hard-working coach, his popularity with his pupils enhanced by his reputation as a baseballer and Australian Rules footballer.

First-Class Averages: Batting, 2,198 runs at 21.13; Bowling, 140 wickets at 42.15.

Tests (1): 1 run, N.A.; 2 wickets at 50.50.

Is this a throw? Some experts said that when Slater delivered his faster ball his action became an outright chuck (See right-hand photograph).

SLEEP, Peter Raymond ("Sounda"), 1957–

First-Class Averages: Batting, 2,899 runs at 32.21; Bowling, 149 wickets at 32.06.

Tests (3): 95 runs at 15.83; 2 wickets at 111.50.

A South Australian allrounder of rich promise whose perseverance paid off with his selection in the 1982 Australian team to tour Pakistan. Sleep has scored runs consistently with his right-hand middle order batting, and at 24 has five first-class centuries and numerous match-saving efforts to his credit. He plays shots all round the wicket, but is particularly partial to the drives. His fielding is sure, lively and skilful. But it is his right-arm leg-spin bowling that could turn out the most important of all his attributes, for he has an impressive high action that produces loop and spin off a full length from an ideal side-on delivery stride.

Sleep, born at Penola, South Australia, began in club cricket

with Kensington but switched to Salisbury after the 1979–80 season. He first played for South Australia in 1976–77 at 19 against Victoria. He made his Test debut at Melbourne in 1978–79 against Pakistan. He made 10 and 0, took 1 for 16 and 1 for 62 off only eight overs and looked very immature. He went off to play League cricket with East Lancashire but was fined for breaking his contract when he missed the last six games to join Kim Hughes' Australian team in India. His enthusiasm saw him practising alone at voluntary net sessions.

This dedication brought results at Nagpur where he bowled superbly to take 5 for 71 against the Indian Central Zone. At one stage he had 1 for 48, but he bounced back to take a further 4 for 23. In the Fourth Test his determined 64 helped save the game for Australia, but he did not take a wicket in either this Test or the Sixth Test, finishing the tour with 175 runs at 19.44 and 14 wickets at 31.57.

At this stage of his career he seriously considered forsaking leg-spin bowling to concentrate on his batting and bowling medium-pacers. South Australian selector Rex Sellers prevailed on him to persevere, however, and encouraged him to bowl less chest-on, with a little more arch in his back to give more control of his flight. With an attack comprised mainly of John Inverarity's left-arm drifters and the spin of Sleep and Malcolm Dolman South Australian captain David Hookes was compelled to give them all plenty of bowling. Fortunately, Hookes's batsmen gave the three slow bowlers plenty of runs to bowl at and they improved with work, South Australia jumping from near last to take the Shield. Devotees of leg-spin, disturbed by the predominance of pace bowling in recent years, are hoping Sleep continues to get similar hard work in big matches.

A Victorian right-hand batsman whose big chance on tour in England with the 1880 Australian team was unhappily marred by ill-health. He had a strong defence with a free and easy style and fielded well at long-on or at point, a wide-shouldered man of 5 ft 8 ins and 11 stone.

Slight, born at Ashby, near Geelong, went to South Melbourne Grammar School, and played many valuable innings for the South Melbourne club, including 205 not out against Williamstown in March, 1881, and 279 in early 1883 when he put on 395 for the first wicket against St Kilda with J. Rosser (192). He first played for Victoria in 1874–75.

He had only six innings with the 1880 Australian team in England and was operated on in London for a fistula. He played in the First Test at The Oval, the first ever Test on English soil, scoring 11 and 0, and made 41 runs on tour at 6.83.

SLIGHT, James, 1855–1930

First-Class Averages: Batting, 415 runs at 12.57; Bowling, 3 wickets at 12.33.

Tests (1): 11 runs at 5.50.

915

Australians like to think they have a reputation for dashing, fast-scoring batting, but the record of past first-class matches includes a liberal sprinkling of slow and low scoring. Indeed matches in which every run was hard to get often proved more absorbing than those that produced large, easily-made totals. Selectors of early Australian teams always recognised the great value of including defensive batsmen like "Alick" Bannerman or Harry Donnan in teams that included hitters like Massie, Bonnor and Lyons, for they could soften and frustrate the bowling for the hitters and hold together an innings when big-hitters failed. Later Charles Kelleway won an international reputation for stonewalling, and all the great teams that followed have had periods when staying in was more important than scoring runs.

Unquestionably the slowest Australian batsman was "Alick" Bannerman, who in an innings of 45 not out for New South Wales against Victoria in 1890–91 went 70 minutes without scoring. His 45 not out in that knock took 330 minutes. This was only slightly slower than his 91 in 448 minutes for Australia against England in Sydney in 1891–92. Bannerman's career was sprinkled with similar slow-scoring. Kelleway had one Test innings against England at Adelaide in 1920–21 when he batted 420 minutes for 147 runs, but there were not as many notable periods of slow-batting in his career as Bannerman provided. Here are some other outstandingly slow innings by Australians:

SLOWEST BATTING IN TESTS BY AUSTRALIANS

Runs	Minutes	Batsman	Match	Venue	Date
28*	250	J. Burke	Australia v. England	Brisbane	1958–59
31	264	K. Mackay	Australia v. England	Lord's	1956
40	289	H. Collins	Australia v. England	Manchester	1921
19*	150	W. Murdoch	Australia v. England	Melbourne	1882–83
57	275	W. M. Lawry	Australia v. England	Melbourne	1962–63

SLOWEST CENTURIES IN TESTS BY AUSTRALIANS

384 minutes	A. R. Border	115	v. England	Perth	1979–80
375 minutes	A. R. Border	123*	v. England	Manchester	1981
374 minutes	K. J. Hughes	129	v. England	Brisbane	1978–79
337 minutes	K. J. Hughes	130*	v. West Indies	Brisbane	1979–80

SLOWEST DOUBLE CENTURIES BY AUSTRALIANS IN TESTS

642 minutes	S. G. Barnes	234	v. England	Sydney	1946–47
608 minutes	R. B. Simpson	311	v. England	Manchester	1964

SLOWEST TRIPLE CENTURIES IN TESTS BY AUSTRALIANS

753 minutes	R. B. Simpson	311	v. England	Manchester	1964
727 minutes	R. M. Cowper	307	v. England	Melbourne	1965–66

At Adelaide in 1946–47 Godfrey Evans set the record for the longest innings without scoring when he batted for 95 minutes before he scored his first run in the England-Australia Test. Denis Compton took most of the Australian bowling in that period. Slow scoring like this is not quite the same, however, as low scoring in which a succession of batsmen arrive at and leave the crease in a short time. When Australia defeated the MCC at Lord's in 1878 31 wickets fell in a single afternoon for 105 runs. MCC made 33, Australia 41. Then MCC's second innings totalled only 19, leaving Australia to score the 12 runs needed to win with the loss of one wicket.

In Test Matches, South Africa had the lowest ever match aggregate when they were caught on a "sticky" at Melbourne in 1931–32. South Africa scored 81 runs, with completed in-

Alan Border drives hard during a slow period of play. He holds the record for the slowest Test century by an Australian.

nings of 36 and 45, Australia winning by an innings and 72 runs. Here are the lowest innings totals by Australia teams:

36	Australia v. England	Birmingham	1902
42	Australia v. England	Sydney	1887–88
44	Australia v. England	The Oval	1896
53	Australia v. England	Lord's	1896
58	Australia v. England	Brisbane	1936–37
60	Australia v. England	Lord's	1888

Australian teams have twice been dismissed for under 100 in both innings of a Test—in 1887–88 against England at Sydney, when Australia made 42 and 82, and in 1888 at Manchester, when Australia scored 81 and 70. Apart from these low scores, Australia has twice declared an innings closed under 50 runs. At Brisbane in 1950–51, Australia declared at 7 for 32 against England, and in 1953 at Manchester Australia declared at 8 for 35. Australia won the first match and drew the second.

For the States, Victoria holds the dubious honour of having made the lowest score—15, against England in 1903–04 at Melbourne. In matches between the States, Tasmania recorded the lowest total—18 against Victoria at Melbourne in 1868–69. Here are the lowest innings totals by each State:

Queensland

40	v. Victoria	Brisbane	1902–03
49	v. Victoria	Melbourne	1936–37
54	v. Victoria	Brisbane	1932–33

New South Wales

37	v. Victoria	Sydney	1868–69
42	v. Victoria	Melbourne	1859–60
44	v. Victoria	Melbourne	1859–60

Victoria

15	v. England	Melbourne	1903–04
28	v. New South Wales	Melbourne	1855–56
35	v. New South Wales	Melbourne	1887–88

South Australia

23	v. Victoria	Melbourne	1882–83
27	v. New South Wales	Sydney	1955–56
47	v. New South Wales	Sydney	1940–41

Western Australia

38	v. Victoria	Melbourne	1892–93
49	v. New South Wales	Perth	1922–23
50	v. New South Wales	Sydney	1951–52

Tasmania

18	v. Victoria	Melbourne	1868–69
25	v. Victoria	Hobart	1857–58
33	v. Victoria	Launceston	1857–58

The most recent of these debacles occurred in 1955–56 when Keith Miller took 7 for 12 in Sydney to dismiss South Australia for 27, the lowest total in an inter-State match for 72 years.

918

A rugged, fast-scoring Victorian right-hand batsman, born at Richmond, who toured New Zealand with the Australian team in 1909–10 and England in 1912 as a replacement when six star players declined to tour. At The Oval he scored 100 against Surrey in a stand of 176 in 118 minutes with Claude Jennings for the sixth wicket but was responsible for Jennings being run out.

A leg injury forced a premature retirement after the England tour. Smith made his debut for Victoria in 1908–09, and had a top score of 146 against South Australia at Melbourne in 1909–10. On his 1912 tour with Australia, he made 316 runs at 13.73.

SMITH, David Bertram Miller, 1884–1963

First-Class Averages: Batting, 1,764 runs at 23.83; Bowling, 1 wicket at 22.00.

Tests (2): 30 runs at 15.00.

David Smith, who was one of the players cited to appear before the Australian Board of Control to answer questions about behaviour on the disastrous 1912 tour of England.

SMITH, Sydney, 1880–1972

A Sydney merchant who spent much of his life in cricket administration and was secretary of the Australian Board of Control in the formative years between 1911 and 1926. He managed the 1921 and 1926 Australian teams in England and was president of the New South Wales Cricket Association from 1935 to 1966. He was a man who knew most of Australian cricket's secrets but he remained tight-lipped about them even among friends. He was originally chosen as secretary to the Board by W. P. McElhone and he did the job without payment for 15 years, with trips as manager his only reward. He sat continuously on the NSWCA for 61 years. He published a book, *History Of The Tests*, in 1946, which remains an invaluable account of the first 70 years of England-Australia Tests, and an account of the 1921 team's tour, *With The 15th Australian XI.*

SMOKERS VERSUS NON-SMOKERS

Leading Australian and English players combined on two occasions to play under first-class conditions matches that were labelled Smokers versus Non-Smokers. The scores have been included in the first-class records of the players who took part. The matches provided a unique opportunity for players who had strenuously countered each other's efforts through a hard season of matches to play alongside each other, with Australians playing in the same team as Englishmen and in opposition to other Australians.

Smokers and Non-Smokers at Lord's in 1884 (L to R): Back, T. Hearne (umpire), G. Alexander (Australian manager), A. Bannerman, T. C. O'Brien, F. R. Spofforth, C. I. Thornton, G. Giffen, G. Palmer, R. Pilling, E. Willsher (umpire): Centre, R. G. Barlow, S. Christopherson, H. J. Scott, W. L. Murdoch, W. G. Grace, Lord Harris, G. J. Bonnor, E. M. Grace, W. Wright; Front, W. Gunn, E. Peate, C. C. Clarke, P. S. McDonnell, M. P. Bowden, T. Emmett.

The first match was played at Lord's in September, 1884, with gate proceeds going to the Cricketers' Fund Friendly Society. The Non-Smokers made 250, with A. C. Bannerman scoring 22 and Bonnor 124. The Smokers made 111 and 152, with McDonnell scoring 7 and 14, Giffen 6 and 15. Palmer had match figures of 2 for 70, Spofforth 2 for 90, Bonnor 1 for 16.

The second match was played at the East Melbourne ground in March, 1887. Non-Smokers scored 803, then the highest score in a first-class match. Arthur Shrewsbury made 236 and William Gunn 150 and of the Australians Bruce made 131, Houston 57, Worrall 78, Cooper 46, and Musgrove 62. The Smokers responded with 356 and 5 for 135, with Palmer scoring 113 and 24. With the ball for the Non-Smokers Bruce had 2 for 107, Worrall 1 for 52, and for the Smokers Palmer 3 for 189, Boyle 1 for 60.

One of the greatest allrounders in the history of cricket, and the only player to score 1,000 runs and take 50 wickets in an Australian season, which he achieved twice during three wonderful summers for South Australia. He was one of the best left-handed batsmen of all time, a stylish stroke player or devastating hitter as the occasion required, and a fieldsman of cat-like reflexes who pulled in brilliant catches. He began as a slow left-arm orthodox spinner, later added back of the hand leg-breaks and Chinamen, and also opened the bowling with fast-medium left-arm swing of the highest quality.

Sobers was born in Barbados with an extra finger on each hand that had to be removed soon after his birth. His father died at sea during World War II when Sobers was five. He played golf, soccer and basketball for Barbados and was chosen for his initial first-class match as a spin bowler against India. He made his Test debut against England at Kingston in March, 1954, and in 1957–58 at Kingston made the highest score in Tests, 365 not out, with 38 fours, batting for 10 hours 14 minutes. He was 21 and this was his first three-figure score in Tests. Over the next 16 seasons he added a further 25 Test centuries.

The Sobers legend in Australia began long before he married an Australian girl and became a naturalised Australian. He was a hero of the magnificent 1960–61 series in Australia, scoring 132 in the tied First Test at Brisbane, 168 in the Third Test at Sydney and taking 5 for 120 in the Fifth Test when he bowled unchanged for 41 eight-ball overs. He returned the following season, 1961–62 to play for South Australia and did some wonderful things in his three seasons of Shield cricket. When he succeeded Worrell as captain he led the West Indies to their first ever series win against Australia in 1964–65

SOBERS, Sir Garfield St Aubrun, 1936–

921

against Simpson's team. His record run of 39 Tests as captain began with that series. He returned to Australia for the 1968–69 series, scoring 110 in the Fourth Test and 113 in the Fifth Test after taking 6 for 73 in the First Test. Throughout a career that brought him 28,315 runs at 54.87 including 86 centuries, 1,043 wickets at 27.74 and saw him take 407 catches in first-class matches his sportsmanship and modesty were exemplary. In 93 Tests he scored 8,032 runs at 57.78, took 235 wickets at 34.03, and held 109 catches. He remains the only batsmen to hit six sixes in a six-ball over, a feat he performed while captaining Nottinghamshire against Glamorgan at Swansea in 1968.

SOUTH AFRICA VERSUS AUSTRALIA

Australia was the first fully representative team from any country to visit South Africa, but the South Africans had to wait 64 years for their first win at home over Australia. Matches between the countries began in 1902, when Joe Darling's team, which had just won the series against England 2–1, stopped and played three Tests against South Africa on the way home. South Africa won matches in Australia, but it was not until 1966 that she won at home. Between 1902 and 1970 when Tests between the countries were suspended because of apartheid, Australia played 53 Tests against South Africa, winning 29, losing 11, with 13 drawn. South Africa's four wins in the last four Tests played against Australia included some of the heaviest defeats Australia has ever suffered. There seems little likelihood of the contests resuming soon, which is a tragedy for Australian cricket lovers and for the young men whose talents Australians will never see.

AUSTRALIA IN SOUTH AFRICA, 1902–03

J. Darling

The First Test between Australia and South Africa was played on matting at the Old Wanderers' ground, Johannesburg, at an altitude of almost 6,000 feet. The Australians were rushed to the game immediately their ship berthed. South Africa's L. J. Tancred got to 97 before he was caught by Duff off Trumper's bowling. Tancred added 173 in a second wicket stand with C. B. Llewellyn. South Africa were captained by H. M. Taberer in what proved to be his only Test. Clem Hill made 142 in Australia's second innings but the three days allotted to each of these Tests ran out with South Africa 114 short of victory with six wickets in hand. In between the Tests Trumper hit a classic 218 not out against XV of Transvaal. The Australians won the next two Tests convincingly. Warwick Armstrong opened with Syd Gregory in the second innings of the Second Test, also at Johannesburg, and batted right through the innings for 159 not out. Jack Saunders then took 7 for 34 to dismiss South Africa for 85 runs and give Australia victory by 159 runs. J. H. Sinclair made 101 to become the first

South African to score a Test century against Australia, and he repeated the feat in the Third Test at Cape Town, with 104. Saunders (6 for 110 in the match), and Howell (9 for 89) were too much for the South African batsmen, apart from Sinclair, and Australia won by 10 wickets. Sinclair's century in the Third Test included six sixes and eight fours, and took only 80 minutes—the fastest century ever by a South African in a Test match. The left-handed Llewellyn had a tremendous season for South Africa, with 25 wickets in three Tests at 17.92.

Warwick Armstrong handed over the captaincy of the 1921 team which had just beaten England 3–0 to Herbie Collins for the three Tests against South Africa on their way home. The Tests, still on matting pitches, were extended to four days. The First Test at Durban was drawn, despite the batting wizardry of Macartney (59 and 116). Collins made the first double century by an Australian against South Africa, 203, in the Second Test at Johannesburg and Jack Gregory made a century in 70 minutes on his way to 119, but this match too, was drawn. Gregory's knock is still the fastest century in Test cricket. Frail, slightly-built C. N. Frank, who had been badly gassed in World War I, took 518 minutes to score 152 for South Africa, and his fourth wicket stand of 206 with Nourse (111) remains the highest for South Africa against Australia. Australia won the Third Test at Cape Town by 10 wickets when Ryder made 142 and Macartney took 5 for 44 in the second innings, Ryder ending the series with the best batting average, 111.33.

AUSTRALIA IN SOUTH AFRICA, 1921–1922

H. L. Collins

For Australia's first full scale tour of South Africa and a five-Test series Vic Richardson took over the Australian captaincy vacated by Woodfull with Bradman unable to tour through illness. Australia won the series 4–0, thanks to the outstanding bowling of Grimmett, O'Reilly and McCormick and brilliant batting of McCabe, Brown, and Fingleton. Australia outplayed Natal, Western Province (Fleetwood-Smith 7 for 71 and 5 for 32), and Transvaal in the lead-up to the Tests. O'Reilly clinched Australia's nine-wicket win in the First Test at Durban by taking 5 for 49 in the second innings following centuries by McCabe (149) and Chipperfield (109). The Second Test at Johannesburg was drawn after a masterly 231 by Nourse, with Australia 125 runs from victory with eight wickets in hand. McCabe was then on 189 not out and hitting the ball so hard that the South African captain H. F. Wade had appealed to the umpires that his fieldsmen were in danger, when the storm that ended the game began. McCabe's score included a century before lunch. Fingleton started a marvellous sequence by scoring 112 in the Third Test at Cape Town, adding 233 for the first wicket with Brown (121). Grimmett

AUSTRALIA IN SOUTH AFRICA, 1935–1936

V. Y. Richardson

took 10 wickets in the match for only 88 runs, to give Australia victory by an innings and 78 runs. The Australians then outclassed Eastern Province, Border, Orange Free State and Basutoland, Transvaal, Griqualand West and drew with Rhodesia. Fingleton got another century (108) in the Fourth Test at Johannesburg and Grimmett a further 10 wickets for 110. Australia won by an innings and 184 runs. At Durban in the Fifth Test Fingleton made his third successive century (118) and Grimmett took 13 for 173. Australia won by an innings and six runs. Richardson set a Test record by taking five catches in South Africa's second innings. Fingleton made 1,192 runs at 79.16 on the tour and Grimmett took 92 wickets at 14.80, O'Reilly 95 wickets at 13.56. The tour saw Richardson introduce two "suicide" fieldsmen in the leg trap for O'Reilly.

The scoreboard at Melbourne in 1932, when Australia dismissed South Africa for 36 and 45.

AUSTRALIA IN SOUTH AFRICA, 1949–1950

A. L. Hassett

Australia won this rubber 4–0 with a team that was strong in all departments and brilliantly led by Hassett. Transvaal had a great chance to beat Australia before the Tests when they needed only 69 in the fourth innings, but they made only 53 (Ian Johnson 6 for 22). At Johannesburg in the First Test Hassett (112) and Loxton (101) made centuries. Miller took 5 for 40 in South Africa's first innings, Bill Johnston 6 for 44 in the second, Australia winning by an innings and 85 runs. Miller had been surprisingly omitted from the original Australian team but was rushed to join them when Johnston was hurt in a car crash. Australia won the Second Test at Cape Town by eight

924

wickets due to Harvey's 178 and the bowling of McCool (5 for 41) in the first innings and Lindwall's 5 for 32 in the second. Only Nourse (65 and 114) handled the Australian bowling well. Australia won the Third Test at Durban by five wickets after being dismissed in their first innings for 75, the lowest Australian total in Tests against South Africa. On the second day 18 wickets fell for 146 runs on a rain-affected pitch. Set to score 336 runs to win in 435 minutes Australia got them with 25 minutes to spare, because of a dazzling 151 not out by Harvey. Australia may not have escaped had Nourse enforced the follow-on. At Johannesburg in the drawn Fourth Test opener Jack Moroney scored two centuries—118 and 101 not out. Australia made their highest Test total in South Africa in the Fifth Test at Port Elizabeth, 7 for 549, with Morris (157), Harvey (116) and Hassett (167) scoring centuries. South Africa then succumbed twice to Australia's allround bowling strength to give Australia victory by an innings and 259. This was South Africa's sixth series against Australia without a win. Saggers kept wicket stylishly for Australia throughout the series. Harvey made 660 runs in the Tests at 132.00, with four centuries. Morris made nine of Australia's 33 centuries on the tour, Harvey eight and Moroney seven.

Splendidly captained by Ian Craig, Australia won an absorbing series 3–0. Australia's batting was attractive and productive throughout and the South Africans could not master the pace and swing of Davidson nor the spin of Benaud. South Africa began the First Test at Johannesburg with a record opening stand of 176 by McGlew (108) and Goddard (90). J. H. B. Waite also made a century (115), but Australia fought back strongly, helped by a fine 122 by Benaud. Grout, in his first Test, set a then Test record by taking six catches in an innings, but the match was drawn. Australia won the Second Test at Cape Town by an innings and 141 runs. Colin McDonald (99) and Jimmy Burke (189) put on 190 for the first wicket. Kline ended the match with a hat-trick and had match figures of 6 for 47 but Benaud was the match-winner with 9 for 144, including 5 for 49 in the second innings. The Third Test at Durban was drawn. McGlew made his second century of the series (105) in 545 minutes, and then Waite emulated him with 134 in 414 minutes. Adcock took 6 for 43 in Australia's first innings. Australia won the Fourth Test at Johannesburg by 10 wickets after Harvey scored 100 and Mackay 83 not out in a total of 401. Benaud took 4 for 70 and 5 for 84 in another outstanding display of leg-spin bowling. The Fifth Test at Port Elizabeth saw the Australian bowlers prevail again, Davidson taking 4 for 44 and 5 for 38, and Benaud chiming in with 5 for 82 in the second innings. Craig's captaincy made clever use of talent that did not match previous Australian sides in South Africa. Grout kept wicket superbly throughout a happy

AUSTRALIA IN SOUTH AFRICA, 1957–1958

I. D. Craig

tour. Australia won 11 of its 20 first-class games and drew the other nine. This was the fifth time an Australian team toured South Africa without suffering defeat.

AUSTRALIA IN SOUTH AFRICA, 1966–1967

R. B. Simpson

South Africa won their first Test at home against Australia after 64 years and 22 attempts by scoring 620 in the second innings of the First Test at Johannesburg. Lindsay took 274 minutes to score 182, which included five sixes. He had previously equalled the world record for wicket-keepers by dismissing six Australians in the first innings. Goddard followed his 2 for 39 in the first innings with a match-winning 6 for 53 in the second innings. Taber, who had never before attended a Test, made eight dismissals in his debut for Australia. At Cape Town in the Second Test Australia fought back strongly to level the series with a six-wicket win. Simpson (153) and Stackpole (134) scored centuries in Australia's first innings of 542, but South Africa replied with 353, of which 209 was made by Graeme Pollock. McKenzie's match figures of 8 for 132 were a major factor in the win. Simpson won the toss and put South Africa in at Durban in the Third Test. He looked to have acted wisely when Barlow was out to the first ball of the match, but South Africa reached 300, to which Australia could only reply with 147. Following-on Australia made 334, but South Africa scored the 185 needed to win for the loss of only two wickets. Rain prevented a result in the Fourth Test at Johannesburg after Lindsay's third century of the series (131) with South Africa well placed. South Africa then clinched their first win in a series against Australia by taking the Fifth Test at Port Elizabeth by seven wickets. Graeme Pollock made 105 and then his brother Peter became the fourth South African to take 100 Test wickets. Lindsay set a record for a five-Test series by catching 24 batsmen, although Rodney Marsh had 26 catches in a six-Test series against the West Indies in 1975–76. This was a fine South African side, well led by Peter van der Merwe, with strong batting and an outstanding set of bowlers in Peter Pollock, Mike Proctor, Goddard and Barlow. Only McKenzie among the Australian bowlers penetrated regularly.

AUSTRALIA IN SOUTH AFRICA, 1969–1970

W. M. Lawry

Australia took a sorry beating in this four-Test series, with morale at a low ebb and captain Bill Lawry unable to lift his team. Barlow made his fourth century against Australia in the First Test at Cape Town, which South Africa won by 170 runs. At Durban in the Second Test Barry Richards made a superb 140 but even this was overshadowed by Graeme Pollock's brilliant 274. South Africa made 622, with Pollock hitting 43 fours and a five. Richards needed only 116 balls for his century. South Africa won by an innings and 129, their biggest winning margin at home. South Africa also won the Third Test, with the margin this time 307 runs. Gleeson took 8 for

186 in the match but the Australian batting again failed. South Africa completed a memorable triumph by winning the Fourth Test at Port Elizabeth, by 323 runs, Richards (126) and Irvine (102) scoring centuries for South Africa. Connolly gave Australia some hope with 6 for 47 in South Africa's first innings but the Australian batsmen disappointed. Ian Chappell had his worst series, having been described by Lawry as the best batsman in the world before the rubber began. The South Africans were an ebullient team, who fielded brilliantly, and were splendidly led by Ali Bacher. Australia lacked the leadership and bowling to challenge one of the outstanding teams of modern times, lacking only a class spinner in an otherwise ideal combination.

SOUTH AFRICA IN AUSTRALIA

Four South African teams have toured Australia, without winning a series. The 1963–64 team may easily have done so, however, but for a last wicket partnership of 45 in 75 minutes by Tom Veivers and Neil Hawke in the Fifth Test. The South Africans were then set to score 171 in 85 minutes to win, a task that would have been far easier had they separated Veivers and Hawke quickly. The South Africans always played attractive, crowd-pleasing cricket and included some great players, but were frustrated by some outstanding Australian batting. Of the 20 Tests played between the countries in Australia, Australia has won 12, South Africa four, and four have been drawn. Only the 1931–32 series, which Australia won 5–0, was one-sided. All the rest have been fairly evenly fought. Indeed South Africa appeared to have the players that would enable her to get on top and avenge some of her past losses when the contests between the countries lapsed.

SOUTH AFRICA IN AUSTRALIA, 1910–11

P. W. Sherwell

Percy Sherwell's South African team included a great batsman in Aubrey Faulkner and some outstanding bowlers in Vogler, Schwartz and Llewellyn, but they encountered Trumper, Hill, Bardsley and Armstrong in superlative form for a team that could afford to bat Ransford at No. 6. They began with a big win over South Australia who could not handle Schwartz's googlies. Nourse made 201 not out and Schwartz took 6 for 66 and 5 for 64. Victorian and New South Wales batsmen decided the best method of countering the South Africans' spin attack was all-out aggression and in this way both States had good wins over the tourists. South Africa recovered to beat Queensland but were frustrated by a brilliant 106 by Alan Marshal when a win over an Australian XI appeared likely. The great strength of Australia's batting was shown in the First Test at Sydney when Trumper was run out for 27. Bardsley and Hill then added 224 for the second wicket, both batsmen attacking the spinners from the time they took guard. Hill, who captained Australia throughout this series, finished with 191, Bardsley 132, Australia totalling 528. Cotter

927

P. W. Sherwell

and Whitty then took eight wickets each to dismiss South Africa for 174 and 240, Australia winning by an innings and 114. The Second Test at Melbourne produced a dramatic Australian win by 89 runs after South Africa had led by 158 on the first innings. Faulkner scored a superb 204 in South Africa's total of 506. Trumper led Australia's recovery with 159 in under three hours. South Africa wanted only 170 to win but Cotter took 4 for 47 and Whitty 6 for 17 on a good batting pitch and only two South Africans reached double figures in a total of 80. South Africa won their first Test in Australia by taking the Third Test at Adelaide by 38 runs. Zulch made 105 and Snooke 103 in the South African first innings of 482. Australia responded with 465. Trumper batted brilliantly for 214 not out. In four hours batting he did not give a chance or make a false stroke. Faulkner batted for four hours for 115 as South Africa built up their lead in the second innings. Set to score 378 to win, the Australians batted well but Schwartz (4 for 48) just had enough runs to bowl at. This proved to be South Africa's sole win in Australia for 40 years, and was achieved in a match that produced a then record aggregate of 1,646 runs for 40 wickets. Australia dropped Macartney for googly specialist "Ranji" Hordern in the Fourth Test and the move worked splendidly. Hordern took 3 for 39 and 5 for 66 to seal Australia's win by 530 runs after centuries from Hill (100) and Armstrong (132). Macartney returned for the Fifth Test and made 137, overcoming an outstanding bowling display by Schwartz (6 for 47). The South Africans again struggled against Hordern's googlies, strange in a side that included its own distinguished exponents of this ball. Australia won by seven wickets to take the series 4–1 despite 150 in the final innings by Zulch. Although they won only one Test, the South Africans showed that in Faulkner they had a master batsman. He scored two centuries in the Tests, 204 and 115, in compiling 732 runs at 73.20, and in all first-class matches made 1,534 runs at 59.00, a record only Hammond among visitors has surpassed. Dave Nourse was not far behind him in scoring 1,454 runs at 60.58, with five centuries. Nourse's one-handed catch to dismiss Whitty in the Second Test at Melbourne was still recalled with awe half a century later. South Africa paid heavily for the lack of a pace bowler, for their spinners faltered badly when attacked.

SOUTH AFRICA IN AUSTRALIA, 1931–32

H. B. Cameron

South Africa's attack was based on pace bowlers but they lacked support from their fieldsmen and paid heavily for dropped catches in the Tests. Bradman was in tremendous form and Ironmonger and Grimmett were far too clever for a disappointing South African batting lineup. Cameron kept wicket impressively and some of the batsmen like Christy, Viljoen and Mitchell did well in matches against the States but a well-balanced Australian attack proved too much for them in the big matches. Grimmett foreshadowed what was to come when he took 6 for 50 in South Africa's first innings against South Australia. Ironmonger followed with 5 for 87 and 5 for 21 for Victoria as South Africa lost easily by 87 runs. At Sydney against NSW H. W. Taylor lived up to his reputation with 124 in a total of 425. South Africa then dismissed NSW for 168 and declared their second innings at 3 for 190. Here the might of NSW's batting emerged. Fingleton made 117 and Bradman and McCabe carried on in exciting fashion, time running out with NSW at 3 for 430 and only 18 runs short of winning. Bradman continued in this superb form in the First Test at Brisbane, scoring 226 in Australia's total of 450. Wall (2 for 39 and 5 for 14) and Ironmonger (5 for 42 and 4 for 44) were outstanding as South Africa were bundled out for 170 and 117 to give Australia victory by an innings and 163 runs. Bradman made 219 in the South Africans drawn return match against NSW, in which Hird hit 101. The Second Test at Sydney produced the inevitable Bradman century (112) and 127 from Rigg, Australia winning by an innings and 155 runs. Grimmett's match figures were 8 for 72 and McCabe had 4 for 13 in the first innings. South Africa did well to recover from such a beating to lead Australia by 160 runs on the first innings in the Third Test at Melbourne. Viljoen scored 111 out of 358 after Bell had taken 5 for 69 in Australia's first innings of 198. Woodfull and Bradman had a then record stand of 274 for the second wicket in Australia's second innings of 554, Woodfull scoring 161, Bradman 167. Grimmett then took 6 for 92 for Australia to win by 169 runs, with only Christy (63) passing 50. After fine wins against Tasmania and South Australia, the South Africans went into the Fourth Test at Adelaide determined to make a big showing against an Australian side that saw Bill Hunt, Bill O'Reilly and H. M. Thurlow make their Test debuts. But none of the new bowlers could surpass Grimmett's 7 for 116 and 7 for 83. Bradman ran out Thurlow off the last ball of an over when Bradman was on 299. Australia won by 10 wickets. The South Africans' vulnerability to spin showed in the return match against Victoria, when Fleetwood-Smith took 6 for 80 in his initial first-class game. Rain caused a draw. The Fifth Test at Melbourne produced a vicious sticky wicket and the lowest aggregate of runs in all Tests. South Africa were all out in 90 minutes for 36, with Ironmonger taking 5 for 6. Australia replied with 153, with Bradman absent hurt. South Africa's second innings reached only 45, Ironmonger finishing with 6 for 18 for match figures of 11 for 24. Grimmett did not get a bowl in this amazing match although he had dominated all the South African batsmen throughout the tour. Bradman made 805 runs in the series in four completed innings at 201.50. Ironmonger took 31 wickets at 9.67, Grimmett 33 wickets at 16.87. Christy headed the South African batting with 909 runs at 39.52.

SOUTH AFRICA IN AUSTRALIA, 1952–53

J. E. Cheetham

The South African team in Australia in 1952-53 (L to R): Back, H. J. Tayfield, J. C. Watkins, A. R. A. Murray, M. G. Melle; Centre, W. Ferguson (scorer), K. J. Funston, H. J. Keith, E. B. Norton, G. Innes, E.R. Fuller; Front, J. H. B. Waite, P. N. F. Mansell, J. E. Cheetham (captain), K. G. Viljoen (Manager), D. J. McGlew, W. R. Endean, R. A. McLean.

Cheetham proved an outstanding captain and Viljoen a fine manager and an entertaining series ended with two wins each and one draw. With the exception of Harvey and Endean, the batsmen on both sides found big scores difficult. The fielding on both sides was first-class, as was the wicket-keeping of Langley and Waite. Tayfield was the best bowler on either side and his off-spinners took vital wickets in both the Tests the South Africans won. South Africa might have won the rubber had they had just one outstanding batsman to match Harvey. McGlew began with 182 in his initial first-class game in Australia against Western Australia at Perth. The game was drawn, but Tayfield showed he would be a force on the tour with 5 for 98. South Africa batted poorly at Adelaide but revived with a strong showing against Victoria, who were dismissed for 159 when Tayfield took 7 for 71, including a hat-trick. But NSW beat them by five wickets and they had to struggle desperately to avoid outright defeat by Queensland. Australia won the First Test by 96 runs due to 109 from Harvey and intelligent bowling by Ring (6 for 72) and Lindwall (5 for 60). South Africa achieved their first win over Australia since 1910–11 at Melbourne in the Second Test. This win came from a wonderful effort with the bat by Endean, who batted 450 minutes for 162 not out in the second innings, some remarkable catching, and from Tayfield's match figures of 13 for 165 (6 for 84 and 7 for 81). Tayfield's catch off his own bowling to dismiss Morris was an astounding effort. A full-

blooded Morris drive bounced off Cheetham at silly-point toward mid-off, Tayfield turned, and took the ball inches from the turf as he skidded along the ground. Later Endean reached over the fence to bring in a right-hand catch to dismiss Miller. South Africa won by 82 runs. Australia won the Third Test at Sydney because of magnificent bowling by Miller and Lindwall and a splendid 190 by Harvey, who added 168 for the fourth wicket with Miller. "Toey" Tayfield, so-called because of his habit of stubbing his toe before he bowled or received a ball, broke a thumb fielding a drive from Miller. Lindwall and Miller took 13 South African wickets in totals of 173 and 232 and gave Australia victory by an innings and 38 runs. The Fourth Test at Adelaide was drawn after South Africa saved the follow-on by just seven runs, MacDonald scoring 154 and Hassett 163 for Australia in the first innings, and Harvey 116 in the second. Miller and Lindwall both broke down and were unable to bowl in South Africa's second innings. Needing a win to level the series, South Africa won the Fifth Test at Melbourne by six wickets despite an Australian first innings total of 520. Ian Craig, his Test debut at 17 years 239 days—the youngest Australian to appear in Tests—made 100 runs, with innings of 53 and 47. The Australian second innings folded up against accurate pace bowling from Fuller (5 for 66) and further brilliant catching in close-in positions. A dazzling 76 not out by Roy McLean, who was missed before he scored, clinched the match, and the rubber ended when Australian captain Lindsay Hassett came on and conceded three fours in five balls. Tayfield's 30 wickets in the Tests cost 28.10 and he took 70 wickets in all first-class matches on the tour.

SOUTH AFRICA IN AUSTRALIA, 1963–64

T. L. Goddard

Goddard's team arrived in the midst of a controversy over Meckiff's bowling which was speedily resolved in the First Test. Hassett, Miller, Johnston, Lindwall and other great players of the post-World War II era had departed, and several of the Australian players had yet to prove their value in Tests. Benaud relinquished the Australian captaincy to Simpson after one Test but played in the last three Tests. The South Africans shared the series, each side achieving a win, with three draws. The Pollock brothers, Graeme, the brilliant, forceful left-hand batsman, and Peter, who batted splendidly and bowled a lively fast-medium, were the South Africans' stars, but Eddie Barlow and Colin Bland were not far behind them. Bland justified his reputation as one of the finest fieldsmen of all-time with some magnificent displays and his throwing was a sight for connoisseurs. The First Test at Brisbane was full of sensations but ended in a tame draw when torrential rain fell after lunch on the last day. Meckiff retired from first-class cricket after being no-balled four times in his only over by umpire Col Egar. Barlow scored 114 in the South African first innings and remains the only South African batsman to make a century in his first Test against Australia. Brian Booth scored 169 in Australia's first innings of 435. Barlow sustained his splendid batting in the Second Test at Melbourne, scoring 109 but he was virtually alone in resisting a keen Australian attack. Lawry made 157, Redpath 97 and Shepherd 96 for Australia, who won by eight wickets. South Africa played two sets of brothers in this match, R. G. and P. M. Pollock and A. J. and D. B. Pithey. At Sydney in the Third Test Australia set South Africa to score 409 runs in 430 minutes in the last innings and time ran out with South Africa on 5 for 326. Graeme Pollock's 122 in this match made him the youngest South African at 19 years 318 days to score a Test century. Australia used eight bowlers in South Africa's second innings but could not get a winning breakthrough. The Fourth Test at Adelaide brought a convincing South African win by 10 wickets on the fifth day. The South Africans made their highest Test score in Australia, 595, in reply to Australia's 345. Barlow made 201 of these and Graeme Pollock 175 and their third wicket stand of 341 was a record for South Africa in all Test cricket. Australia batted solidly for 331 in the second innings but South Africa needed only 82 to win and they got them without loss. South Africa had a great chance to win their first series ever in the Fifth Test but were frustrated by a grim last-wicket partnership by Veivers and Hawke which had the Sydney Cricket Ground crowd spellbound. Time was as important as runs and the overs passed and when Barlow caught Veivers off Goddard to end it, there was just not enough time for South Africa to score the 171 required. Partridge, who bowled well throughout the tour, had 7 for 91 in Australia's first innings. Goddard's team won five of their 14 first-class matches, lost three and drew six. They were one of the few overseas teams to defeat NSW, they attracted bigger crowds than any previous South African team, and they scored more centuries (19) than any other Springbok side in Australia.

SOUTH AUSTRALIA, CRICKET IN   Only 23 months after South Australia was proclaimed on December 28, 1836, an advertisement in the *South Australian Gazette and Register* indicated that cricketers were already active in the colony. The advertisement was directed to gentlemen cricket players, and announced that a meeting "of the patrons of that old English and manly game of cricket will take place at the London Tavern, opposite Gilles Arcade" for the purpose of forming a club. Gentlemen wishing to join the club were urged to attend. Both the *Gazette and Register* and the opposition paper, *The Southern Australian*, published the advertisement in their editions of November 3, 1838. A further advertisement appeared on November 24, advising that two members of the London Tavern Club were open to play any two gentlemen a game of single wicket cricket for £10 or £20.

The initiative from publicans eager to attract business through cricket continued with a long advertisement boasting about the services of the Royal Admiral Hotel in Hindley Street, Adelaide. The owner of the Royal Admiral advised that he expected a supply of bats, bails and stumps of the very best quality to arrive any day in the *Prince George*, and that he proposed to form a club for lovers of cricket and for the promotion of that healthy game.

Other publicans saw the value of this venture. On October 19, 1839, John Bristow, proprietor of the Great Tom of Lincoln Hotel in the Adelaide suburb of Thebarton, inserted an advertisement in the *Gazette and Register* which announced that "a grand match will be played on Monday, October 28, on the Thebarton Cricket Ground between Eleven Gentlemen of the Royal Victoria Independent Club and Eleven Gentlemen of Adelaide, for 22 guineas a-side, with the wickets to be pitched at 10 o'clock." Bristow added, of course, that he would have refreshment available. On the day of this, the first recorded match in South Australia, he provided attractions such as climbing the greasy pole, juggling acts, and footraces. The Gentlemen of Adelaide lost by 11 runs.

Adelaide had been laid out to provide ample space for parks and gardens but the best of these areas were used as staging camps for new arrivals and later as grazing land for the colony's growing population of cows. The cricket gear used was as primitive as the grounds, with the bats carved from saplings and the balls made from cheap leather. Gloves and pads were unknown until the arrival in 1847 of a player named Smith who joined the Adelaide Club. He immediately became famous as the owner of the first pair of pads seen in

The South Australian side that played NSW at Sydney in January, 1892 (L to R): Standing, J. Noel, A. Wilkinson, W. F. Giffen, H. Haldane, J. Slight (umpire); On chairs, W. O. Whitridge (manager), C. W. Hayward; Kneeling, W. Delaney, J. J. Lyons, J. Reedman; Front, F. Jarvis, G. Giffen (captain), A. H. Jarvis, H. Blinman.

the colony. A large crowd gathered to watch Smith in his first appearance in these pads, plus his special batting gloves. Smith went to the wicket before a crowd expecting to watch a cultured exhibition of shot making, but he was bowled first ball.

A more talented cricketer was John Cocker, who had played for Kent and claimed to have been a team-mate of Alfred Mynn, James Lillywhite and Fuller Pilch. He proved a batsman of quality and the best under-arm bowler in the colony. Cocker lived at the Kentish Arms Hotel in North Adelaide, and he formed a club called the Kent and Sussex, which quickly proved strong enough to take on the Adelaide Club, which had its headquarters across the River Torrens. Cocker had in his team Bill and Tom Botten, the first round-arm bowler seen in South Australia. Tom Botten was viewed with great suspicion by players and spectators who considered his technique was unfair.

Clarence Moody in his book, *South Australian Cricket*, described the leading players of the Adelaide club and told how one of them, Colman of Strathalbyn, rode 48 miles to Adelaide to appear in a game, played all day, and then saddled his horse and rode the 48 miles home again. Moody also told of the sad fate of a sailor named Wilkins who challenged any player in South Australia to a single-wicket match. W. B. T. Andrews, then secretary of the Adelaide Cricket Club, took Cocker to the Halfway House Inn on the Port Road to meet Wilkins and a match was arranged for £10 a-side. Wilkins insisted that each man should do his own fielding. Cocker won the toss and selected his own pitch at the foot of Stanley Street, North Adelaide, where several hundred spectators gathered to watch the contest.

Cocker struck the first ball from Wilkins for four and proceeded to hit Wilkins all over the field. Spectators tired of the slaughter and called to Cocker to end it, but he carried on mercilessly until he had scored 109, when he allowed a ball from Wilkins to hit the stumps. Wilkins replied with seven runs from two innings and did not enforce the agreement which gave the loser the right to a return match. A contemporary wrote of Cocker: "He would play cricket nearly all day no matter how hot it was on the level ground in front of his hotel. If he could not get men to play with him, he would go out with the lads, and many a boy he taught to play cricket. Nothing delighted him more than to be bowled by one of his proteges. Then in the evening he would entertain us with his fiddle in the parlour of his hotel, and many's the pleasant evening we have spent there listening to his music and his yarns about Alfred Mynn, Fuller Pilch, and the other identities whom he played with in Old England." Cocker went off to the Victorian goldfields for a time but when he found no gold returned to found his own business in Adelaide.

934

Another early South Australian cricketer was Mr Justice Bundey, who as a boy at Woodside in the Adelaide Hills had made a century with a bat he fashioned from the limb of a cherry tree. In 1852, he called a meeting that formed the Union Cricket Club, taking the name from the hotel at Marryatville where the meeting was held. On January 11, 1854, this advertisement appeared in the *South Australian Register*:

I, on behalf of the Union Cricket Club, do hereby challenge the Province of South Australia to play a friendly match upon the Park Lands between North and South Adelaide. This challenge to remain open for ten days from the date hereof. The said game to be played from day to day until completed.

—W. H. Bundey, secretary.

The challenge was accepted and the Union CC heavily defeated the Rest of South Australia. The Union CC made 96 and 134, of which a player named Baker scored 51. The Rest of South Australia responded with 44 and 59, with Cocker (20 not out and 10) the only batsman to reach double figures in either innings. Later Judge Bundey said this win ruined the Union CC, for membership fell away through lack of opposition. Within a year the Adelaide Club defeated the badly depleted Union side by an innings, Tom Botten and Cocker bowling them out as they pleased.

In the 1860s, the newly formed South Australian club dominated cricket in the colony, partly because it had leased six acres of the north parklands where the Adelaide Oval is now, and had fenced the area. Another strong club was North Adelaide, known as the "Pig and Whistles" because they met at the hotel of that name. The Adelaide Club was referred to as the "Toffs" because their advertisements always mentioned "gentlemen players."

In 1862, after a bowler named Cox had taken 15 wickets to help the South Australian Club crush the Union, a match between British and Colonial-Born elevens was staged at Thebarton racecourse. The Colonials led by 22 runs on the first innings and left the British 146 to win. After the British reached 7 for 41, they claimed it was too dark to continue and that stumps should be drawn. The umpires ruled otherwise and when no further British batsmen went in awarded the match to the Colonials, a result that caused widespread bitterness.

Clubs sprang up in country areas throughout the 1860s, with players in action at Jamestown, Caltowie, Gladstone, Gawler, and author-cricketer Johnnie Moyes's favourite, Orroroo. Kadina played their first game in February, 1862, and the Mount Pleasant Club had their first fixture in March, 1862. Kapunda in their first match defeated Hamilton on Baker's Flat by an innings. A year later George Davey made 71 not out for Kapunda against Barossa. In 1864, matches were played at

Clare, Rapid Bay, Clarendon and Guichen Bay. Angaston lost their first two matches, both to Nuriootpa. Penola in their first match scored only eight runs, five of them byes, in the first innings against Mount Gambier.

On March 19 and 20, 1868, James Gooden from the Norwood club met Arthur Malcolm, of the South Australian Club, to decide who was the champion cricketer of Adelaide, with each having three men to field. Malcolm won by scoring 3 and 6 in his two innings against Gooden's 4 and 1. The Gooden family had begun playing cricket with the Eastern Suburban Club founded by a former Kapunda man, J. Scandrett, and in 1865 moved to the newly formed East Torrens Club.

Apart from Judge Bundey's reported century at Woodside around 1857, the first hundred in Adelaide was scored in February, 1870, by F. D. Harris for St Peter's College against the Young Australian Cricket Club. Harris knocked down his own wicket after making 101 out of the College's total of 163. Sir

The South Australian team that had a fine win over England in 1894-95 (L to R): Back, C. Hill, J. McKenzie, E. Jones, C. Hack, G. Giffen, E. H. Leak, P. Argall (umpire); Front, J. Matthews, J. Travers, J. Reedman (captain), F. Jarvis, B. T. Bailey.

Charles du Cane, Governor of Tasmania and a former well known cricketer in England, led a side against St Peter's later the same year. Harris made 82 this time and was presented with a bat. Harris appears to have been the first of the succession of outstanding players developed at St Peter's.

Aware that matches between colonies had begun in Hobart, Launceston, Melbourne and Sydney, South Australian cricket followers saw the need for both a control body for the whole colony and a central ground. One enthusiast, H. Yorke Sparks, went to Melbourne at his own expense to inspect the Melbourne Cricket Ground, how it was maintained, and to learn how the ground had been financed. Back in Adelaide he approached three clubs about forming a central cricket ground and finally persuaded the South Australian Club to sponsor the project. In November, 1869, he sent out a circular to all South Australian clubs which read:

"I beg to inform you that an effort is now being made to form a Central Cricket Ground similar to those in the sister colonies, the want of which has hitherto acted very prejudicially against the success of the game here, and as the Corporation has granted a suitable plot of ground, it is proposed to have it grassed, levelled, fenced and surrounded by a belt of shrubs, trees, etc., so as to render it both serviceable and ornamental and a place of pleasant resort."

Sparks's campaign for a first-class ground included letters to newspapers in which he emphasised the need for an arena suitable for all sporting purposes that "would encourage young men to partake in all forms of athletic exercise." His appeal raised around £150 and the South Australian Cricket Club began the preparation of the cricket pitch by planting couch grass in the centre and fencing the playing area. The cost of this was £50 more than Sparks had raised but the club bore the extra expense. The Corporation, in granting the South Australian club the lease on a peppercorn rental, had specified that no charge for admission be made at the ground, and this raised doubts about its suitability for inter-Colonial matches. Money to pay the expenses of visiting teams normally was raised from gate charges.

By early in 1871 the need for a body that could control the ground and cricket generally throughout the colony led to the Norwood Club instructing their secretary to secure the agreement of the South Australian, Kent, North Adelaide and Gawler Cricket Clubs in calling a meeting to discuss the formation of a South Australian Cricket Association. About 60 cricketers attended this meeting at the Prince Alfred Hotel, King William Street, Adelaide, on May 31, 1871. Formation of the "South Australian Cricketing Association" was agreed on. After further meetings the Governor, Sir James Ferguson, accepted the position of president. The South Australian Club offered the new Association its ground on the North Park

Lands, now the Adelaide Oval, on condition that the Association paid the club's debt of £50 on improvements to the ground. A tender from H. Copas to level, plough and plant fresh grass at the ground was accepted and because of his knowledge of cricket and gardening G. W. Gooden was appointed the first curator. Copas' quotation proved to be half right and he had to secure a judgment in the South Australian Supreme Court before he was paid what amounted to double his original tender.

John Darling, M.P., Joe Darling's father, introduced a Bill in the South Australian Parliament in September, 1871, empowering the Corporation of Adelaide to grant a lease on the ground to the Association. Not long afterwards the fence and grass inside the ground caught fire. The formation of the SACA and the formal establishment of its ground brought quick improvement in cricket standards throughout the colony. In 1873–74, W. G. Grace's team played a match at Kadina and then travelled to Adelaide to play Twenty Two of South Australia, the first appearance by an England team in Adelaide. Grace was caught on the boundary for six by Alexander Crooks, who had begun his career with North Adelaide Young Men. In 1882, Crooks became general manager of the Commercial Bank of South Australia, largely because of the fame his dismissal of Grace had earned him. The bank lost more than a million pounds because of Crooks' unconventional and irresponsible management and was wound-up, paying three shillings in the pound.

In 1873, H. Yorke Sparks succeeded the SACA's foundation secretary Joe Pickering, and immediately began a campaign to raise £1500 for assistance in preparing Adelaide Oval. But the public failed to support him and the Association had to borrow by issuing debentures to its own committeemen. Gooden was relieved of his duties as curator and put on a commission to collect subscriptions from member clubs. In the winter the SACA could not afford a curator at all and weeds and thistles grew on the oval undisturbed. Yorke remained enthusiastic and erected chains around the playing area at his own expense.

John Hill hit the first century on Adelaide Oval early in 1878 for North Adelaide against Kent. He was the father of Clem Hill and the owner of the coach that had driven W. G. Grace and his team to Kadina in 1874. The Association hired a different sort of coach, Harry Gay, a prominent Ballarat all-rounder, at £3 per week but he had to be sacked when he absented himself from work.

South Australia played their first inter-Colonial match against Victoria in 1874–75. The Victorian side was virtually only a Second XI, which met Eighteen of Adelaide, winning by 15 runs. Takings for the three days of the match were £285 and there was much grumbling among the citizens of Ade-

laide about the two shillings admission charge. Victoria made 92 and 98, with a bowler called Scott bowling unchanged for South Australia through both innings, for match figures of 10 for 72. The pitch was uneven and while the caterer was preparing lunch on the second day half a dozen of the more robust players got between the shafts of the roller and rolled out the bumps. But 38 matches were played on the ground in its first season, including matches against Kadina, Marrieds versus Singles and British against Colonial-born. J. E. Gooden took the trophy for the best batting average in the special games. His 89 not out remained the highest score in the colony for three years.

James Lillywhite's England team visited Adelaide in 1876–77 and before a crowd of 9,000 had no trouble easily defeating 22 opponents. Alfred Shaw took 14 for 12 in the first innings and 7 for 25 in the second. George Giffen and "Affie" Jarvis were brought in to strengthen the South Australian team for the return match but failed. Giffen, then 18, made a duck, Jarvis, aged 16, scored 8.

Conway, the Victorian captain, recommended that clover and rye form the basis of the outfield and to give this a good

South Australian team that played the Centenary match against Victoria at Adelaide Oval in October, 1971 (L to R): Back, G. St.A. Sobers, J. R. Hammond, G. S. Chappell, A. A. Mallett, A. J. Woodcock, T. J. Jenner; Front, D. J. Sutherland, K. J. McCarthy, K. G. Cunningham, D. L. Munn (SACA secretary), I. M. Chappell (captain), E. W. Freeman, M. Hendricks.

foundation the Adelaide Oval was dug up at the end of its first summer and a thick layer of rich loam from Athelstone laid below the turf. A second area known as the Neutral Ground was prepared next door and remains a useful adjunct to the main oval more than a century later. Jesse Hide, the coach Lillywhite selected, arrived in 1878 on a salary of £200 a year and doubled as a curator until the appointment of Charles Checkett.

South Australian cricket in the last 20 years of the 19th century was blessed by the publication of the always lively *South Australian Cricketers' Guide*, which became essential reading because of its pithy comments on players. On T. A. Reeves, of Norwood, the *Guide* said, "If ever he could bat, he doesn't show it now," and on J. Medhurst of Mt Gambier, "A light of other days; cricket has advanced too much for him." The *Guide* said W. L. Noon was "a moderate field; rather sleepy" and reprimanded A. M. Pettinger because he "shirks practice." Of W. J. Gardwood, of Norwood, the *Guide* said, "A fast bowler, occasionally straight. Wretched fieldsman."

One of the *Guide's* favourites was George Giffen, of Norwood, the "colt of the team and one of the best batsmen in the colony. Play too recklessly occasionally and treats bowlers with too much levity." When G. F. Vernon's team visited Adelaide in 1884 Giffen took a hat-trick but the Englishmen won as they had insisted on playing on level terms. The return match was marred by a vandal damaging the pitch during the night between the third and fourth days. The locals had followed-on and were in extreme difficulty and the culprit must have thought he would help them by watering and rolling the pitch in the dark. But he left deep footprints and a pitch that resembled glue. The Englishmen were upset about it but continued and Giffen made 203, and South Australia a record 493.

In the 1894–95 season South Australia had a great victory over Stoddart's team. England began with 477, but South Australia fought back with 383, Joe Darling scoring 117 in his first encounter with English bowlers. Giffen took 6 for 49 in England's second innings, which produced 130. Reedman and Darling then hammered the bowling to clinch the win. Women threw their bonnets and parasols in the air and small boys tried to carry Darling from the ground, and Adelaide rejoiced far into the night.

Test cricket came to South Australia in December, 1884, when Billy Murdoch led Australia against Arthur Shrewsbury's team. The Australians had just returned from an arduous tour of England and the prominent critic, Clarence Moody, condemned their failure to practise. P. S. McDonnell made 124 and 83 for Australia, the finest batting seen to that time in Adelaide. "I have never seen more charming batting and I shall never forget the disappointment which everyone felt when Giffen stupidly ran McDonnell out in the second innings when he seemed certain to make a century in each innings." England won by eight wickets. The Adelaide *Advertiser* said of Shrewsbury's dismissal in England's first innings: "A jump out, a miss, and a deadly rattle followed."

District cricket began in Adelaide in 1897–98 when a rule compelling players to play for the clubs in whose territory they resided was introduced. Norwood disappeared and became East Torrens, West Torrens took over the Hindmarsh area, and Port Adelaide began to win matches. South Adelaide had fast bowler Ernie Jones in their team and in that 1897–98 season umpire James Phillips caused a sensation by no-balling Jones for throwing for South Australia on Adelaide Oval against A. E. Stoddart's team. The incident had little effect on Jones, for he bowled 54 overs and took 7 for 189 in England's innings of 475.

Jones remained a hero in a State that produced a high number of great players considering its size. J. J. Lyons, George Giffen, Clem Hill and Affie Jarvis were followed by Arthur and Vic Richardson and then by the imports, Grimmett and Bradman. Between them they gave South Australia a prominent place in the Sheffield Shield competition right from its inception and a regular sprinkling of places in Australian Test teams. Later Les Favell and the incomparable Chappells gave South Australian teams star quality.

South Australia's on the field contribution to Australian cricket has been matched by intelligent administration. Since the days of the enterprising H. Yorke Sparks, strong, capable men have helped build the State's reputation. Hurtle Fisher, B. V. Scrymgour, Harry Blinman, Don Bradman and Phil Ridings have all been capable presidents and in Bill Jeanes, one-time secretary of the Australian Board of Control, South Australia produced a fine secretary. But the State's greatest cricket asset remains the most English of all Australian cricket fields and the ground where so much of Australia's cricket history occurred.

SACA PRESIDENTS		SACA SECRETARIES	
Governor(s) of S.A.	1871–1897	J. P. Pickering	1871–1873
Sir Edwin Smith	1897–1919	H. Y. Sparks	1873–1875
G. M. Evan	1919–1924	R. F. Burton	1875–1877
H. Fisher	1924–1929	C. S. Leader	1877–1878
B. V. Scrymgour	1929–1940	*C. S. Leader	1878–1883
H. Blinman	1940–1950	J. Creswell	1883–1909
R. F. Middleton	1950–1965	J. A. Riley	1909–1926
Sir Donald Bradman	1965–1973	W. H. Jeanes	1926–1955
P. L. Ridings	1973–	A. M. Lyon	1955–1959
		H. V. Millard	1959–1970
		D. L. Munn	1970–1978
		N. H. Blundell	1978–1980
		R. A. Watson	1980–

*C. S. Leader in his second term became the first paid secretary for the S.A.C.A. and from then on—1878—the secretaryship remained a paid position.

RECORD PARTNERSHIP FOR SOUTH AUSTRALIA

Wkt		
1st	313	L. T. Gun and A. J. Richardson v WA (Adel), 1925–26.
2nd	308	B. A. Richards and I. M. Chappell v WA (Perth), 1970–71.
3rd	356	D. G. Bradman and R. Hamence v Tas (Adel), 1935–36.
4th	253	I. McLachlan and G. Sobers v S. Africa (Adel), 1963–64.
5th	281	C. L. Badcock and M. Waite v Qld (Adel), 1939–40.
6th	255	G. Sobers and B. N. Jarman v WA (Perth), 1963–64.
7th	183	W. C. Alexander and J. Rymill v Vic (Melb), 1925–26.
8th	192	C. Hill and W. F. Giffen v Eng XI (Adel), 1894–95.
9th	232	C. Hill and E. Walkley v NSW (Adel), 1900–01.
10th	104	L. Michael and R. Pynor v Vic (Adel), 1949–50.

OUTSTANDING SOUTH AUSTRALIAN BATSMEN

Batsman	Career	Matches	Innings	Not Out	H. Score	Runs	Average	10
L. E. Favell	1951–1970	143	258	5	164	9656	38.16	23
I. M. Chappell	1961–1980	109	188	18	205*	8873	52.19	26
C. Hill	1892–1923	87	160	9	365*	8027	53.15	24
V. Y. Richardson	1918–1938	104	188	7	231	7698	42.53	21
H. N. Dansie	1949–1967	124	228	9	185	7543	34.44	18
D. G. Bradman	1935–1949	44	64	9	369	5753	104.60	25
P. L. Ridings	1937–1947	98	168	17	186*	5610	37.15	9
K. G. Cunningham	1960–1974	89	153	14	203	5144	37.00	9
G. Giffen	1877–1904	64	115	8	271	4699	43.91	11
A. J. Woodcock	1967–1979	81	143	4	141	4453	32.04	5
R. A. Hamence	1935–1951	68	116	7	173	4244	38.93	11
G. S. Chappell	1963–1973	57	100	10	156*	4133	45.92	11
C. Pinch	1950–1960	61	109	8	146*	4040	40.00	12
J. C. Lill	1955–1966	60	112	4	176	4087	37.84	8
A. J. Richardson	1918–1927	45	86	4	280	3755	46.79	11
B. N. Jarman	1955–1969	94	158	16	196	3447	24.20	3
G. B. Hole	1950–1958	51	94	10	226	3401	40.48	9
D. R. A. Gehrs	1902–1921	49	92	6	170	3387	39.38	13
C. L. Badcock	1935–1941	40	65	7	325	3282	56.58	12

OUTSTANDING SOUTH AUSTRALIAN BOWLERS

Bowler	Career	Matches	Runs	Wickets	Average	B.B.	5W	10
C. V. Grimmett	1924–1941	105	16567	668	24.80	9/180	62	17
G. Giffen	1877–1904	64	9719	419	23.21	9/91	47	18
A. A. Mallett	1967–1981	91	9534	386	24.70	7/57	20	2
T. J. Jenner	1963–1977	77	7733	259	29.85	7/127	12	1
E. Jones	1892–1903	47	6497	248	26.19	8/157	24	4
G. Noblet	1945–1953	49	4466	236	18.92	7/29	13	2
N. J. N. Hawke	1960–1968	60	5803	211	27.50	8/61	12	5
G. Attenborough	1972–1981	57	6160	193	31.92	7/90	8	1
F. A. Ward	1935–1941	38	5046	187	26.98	7/62	12	1
J. W. Wilson	1950–1958	55	5750	182	31.59	7/55	6	—
T. W. Wall	1924–1936	53	5257	178	29.53	10/36	3	1
W. J. Whitty	1908–1926	43	5677	178	31.89	7/66	8	1
E. W. Freeman	1964–1974	44	3932	150	26.22	8/47	5	2
P. K. Lee	1925–1935	50	4194	146	28.72	5/23	6	—
G. St. A. Sobers	1961–1964	26	3610	137	26.35	7/110	8	—
W. Prior	1974–1982	46	4443	136	32.67	6/41	6	1
D. J. Sincock	1960–1966	35	4793	134	35.76	7/48	10	—

942

Australian cricket's original demon bowler, lithe, sinewy, a man of satanic countenance who bowled fast-medium leg and off-breaks with a very high action, bounding up to the crease from an oblique approach. He was an accomplished gamesman, an intense student of ploys that produced batting weaknesses who is said to have frightened out some of his victims. He played with legendary success for New South Wales, Victoria, Australia and Derbyshire.

Spofforth was born in the Sydney suburb of Balmain, son of a Yorkshireman who migrated to Australia 25 years earlier. Spofforth's earliest memories, however, were of his childhood at Hokianga near Auckland, New Zealand, which often claims him. He was a bowler of such accuracy and nerve that in 1882 he bowled nine successive maidens against England at The Oval. Indeed he and Harry Boyle bowled 13 overs between them for one run!

The subtlety of his variations in pace was such that many of his contemporaries disagreed about his speed. The great Dr W. G. Grace described him as "terrifically fast" and bracketed him with Richardson, Kortright and other speedsters. Other English Test players variously tagged him as medium-pace or slow-medium. The truth is that he varied his pace according to the pitches on which he bowled and the importance of the occasion, for make no mistake, he was a man who relished big occasions. The greater the challenge the better he bowled.

Spofforth began by bowling fast underarm as a schoolboy but switched to overarm when he saw George Tarrant bowling for George Parr's visiting English team in 1863–64. At 20, while he worked as a clerk in a Sydney bank, he experimented with swing and breaks from the pitch, consulting a University professor about the reasons for a ball "curling" in the air. Spofforth wrote later that he had three kinds of break, right-to-left, left-to-right, and vertical but he did not explain how he obtained vertical spin. I am inclined to think he was describing what we know today as a top-spinner, the ball that gathers pace after it strikes the pitch.

He had another delivery which dropped far shorter than expected after looking like a full toss, causing batsmen to pop the ball in the air. He bowled with balls that had less polish than modern cricket balls and lacked today's raised seams, but on the under-prepared pitches of his time his high delivery enabled him to dig the ball into the turf and turn it with a variety of grips. His hand action was a poor guide to how the ball would eventually behave. He studied all the great bowlers of his time but what he produced was original and unexpected.

"What a sight it was to see Spofforth bowling when a game had to be pulled like a brand from the burning", wrote Giffen. "He looked the Demon every inch of him, and I verily believe he has frightened more batsmen out than many bowlers have

SPOFFORTH, Frederick Robert ("The Demon"), 1853–1926

First-Class Averages: Batting, 1,928 runs at 9.88; Bowling, 853 wickets at 14.95.

Tests (18): 217 runs at 9.43; 94 wickets at 18.41.

943

fairly and squarely beaten. When the Demon meant business, the batsmen had to look out for squalls. His pitch would be perfect, and it was almost impossible to get the ball away."

Spofforth first made a favourable impression playing for New South Wales against W. G. Grace's team in 1874 a long-legged man, over 6 ft tall who could run 100 yards inside 11 seconds. He was invited to play in the very first Test at Melbourne in 1877 but refused because Billy Murdoch was not chosen as wicket-keeper. He considered his combination with Murdoch vital to his success. The selectors had already chosen the Victorian Jack Blackham, so Spofforth did not play. It is intriguing that he later developed an ingenius signal system which informed Blackham when he was about to bowl fast, medium or slow, an important tactic for Blackham was the first 'keeper to discard backstops and had to know when he could stand right up on the stumps.

Spofforth toured England five times with Australian teams. By the time he reached London with the first Australian side in 1878 he had matured into a natural drawcard for the tour promoters, a swarthy, slim-waisted black-haired lady killer with long sideburns, a droopy moustache, surplus vitality, and a way of glaring at incoming batsmen as if their departure was imminent. He carried on this undisguised hostility towards batsmen on tour in England in 1880, 1882, 1884 and 1886, backing his contemptuous air with remarkable figures.

On May 27, 1878, Spofforth drove with the Australian team to Lord's, unrecognised by the 500 or so spectators. A few hours later England rang with the news that the flower of English cricket had been beaten in a single day and Spofforth, as the man most responsible, was famous. Forty minutes after the start, Australian captain Gregory, who had opened with Allan and Boyle, replaced Allan with Spofforth, who in 5.3 four-ball overs took 6 wickets for 4 runs, with three maidens. England were out for 33. When news of this collapse spread, spectators swarmed to the ground from all over London, and when Spofforth and Boyle opened the bowling in England's second innings—Australia had made only 41—more than 5,000 spectators were present.

Spofforth's first ball saw Blackham drop a catch from Grace at the stumps, and the second ball bowled him. This time it was Boyle, with 6 wickets for 3 runs off 8.1 overs, with six maidens, who did most damage but Spofforth took 4 for 16, for match figures of 10 for 20. Australia needed 12 runs to win and by 5.40 p.m. a match that began at noon was over. In five hours 40 minutes Australia's cricket reputation had been made.

On his first venture as an Australian team player, Spofforth took 107 wickets at 11.71 in first-class matches in England. On the entire tour in Australia, New Zealand, England, America and Canada he is said to have taken 764 wickets at 6.04 each,

944

Fred Spofforth bowling in England at the peak of his career.

while in 1880 for the entire tour his figures were 763 wickets at 5.49. It was said that he would lie awake at night turning over in his mind the best method of dismissing the batsmen to whom he was opposed.

By the time he went back to England for his second trip he had dropped his pace, reasoning that he lacked the physique of brute force bowlers like Tarrant and Jackson, but that he could exploit greater subtlety. His second tour began with matches against outclassed local clubs in northern England and the Midlands as nobody had known for certain if the Australians would arrive. W. G. Grace tried to organise a match between Australia and an England XI without success and finally, right at the end of the season Lord Harris agreed to captain England against Australia in the first of all Tests on English soil. England won by five wickets, with more than 20,000 spectators watching each of the first two days. Although he missed the Test Spofforth again proved he was in a class by himself and his 46 first-class wickets on the English part of the tour cost only 8.60 each.

At home Spofforth's figures were not as remarkable as on the soft pitches in England, but he still registered some excellent performances. Against Lord Harris's team in 1878–79 he took 13 wickets for 110, including the hat-trick. In the 1882–83 series in Australia, he took 18 wickets at 22.66, including 7 for 44 in the Third Test at Sydney, and 11 for 117 in the match. In 1884–85, his 4 for 54 and 6 for 90 in the Third Test brought Australia back into a series that seemed lost after two easy England victories, and he helped level the series with 5 for 30 in the Fourth Test. He put on 64 with Trumble in an innings of 50 as last man in during the Fifth Test but England again won comfortably.

Much of Spofforth's fame hangs on his performance in the Ashes Test at The Oval in 1882, when he took 7 for 46 and 7 for 44, causing the famous epitaph for English cricket in the *Sporting Times*. He bowled his last 11 overs for two runs and four wickets. He was carried shoulder-high from the field, having told the Australian team in the dressing-room that they could prevent England scoring the 84 needed to win. A turning point in Australia's seven runs win was Spofforth's advice to captain Murdoch after Lucas and Lyttleton had played 12 maidens in succession. Bannerman deliberately misfielded a hit from Lyttleton, allowing Spofforth to get a go at him and after two more maidens Spofforth knocked down Lyttleton's stumps.

Between 1877 and 1887 Spofforth played in 18 Tests, with best figures 7 for 44, seven times taking five wickets or more in an innings and four times taking ten wickets in a match. He moved from New South Wales to Victoria in 1885 and played there for two seasons. In all first-class cricket he took five wickets or more in an innings 84 times and ten in a match 32

Spy's caricature of Spofforth in Vanity Fair stressed his length of leg and neck.

times. One of his legendary performances was in a country match in Victoria in 1881–82 when he rode on horse back more than 400 miles in the return trip from New South Wales and twice bowled out all ten batsmen, all 20 clean-bowled.

Spofforth retired from Australian cricket in 1887 and moving to England eventually became a director of the Star Tea Company. He turned out occasionally for Derbyshire, then a "second-class County", between 1889 and 1891 and in 1889 he took 15 wickets for 81 runs against Yorkshire. Nine years after his retirement from big cricket he returned to dominate the Scarborough Festival by taking 9 for 82 and 8 for 74 in two matches against Yorkshire. He also took 11 for 100 in the game between Wembley Park and the 1896 Australian team. He was still topping the bowling averages for the Hampstead club when well past 50. He became managing director of his company and when he died at Long Ditton, Surrey at 73, left £164,000, a fortune in those days.

SRI LANKA VERSUS AUSTRALIA

Australia played a leading role in Sri Lanka's struggle to achieve Test match status, which was granted at the July, 1981, meeting of the International Cricket Conference in London. Frequent matches against Australian teams travelling to and from England by sea helped lift Sri Lankan enthusiasm for the game before air travel took over. Since then visits by private teams from Australia and the official schoolboys' sides further improved standards. In May, 1981, Sri Lanka dismissed a full-strength Australian team captained by Kim Hughes for 124 and 178 and was only deprived of outright victory in this four-day game by rain, a performance that undoubtedly boosted Sri Lanka's claims for Test status at the ICC meeting a few weeks later.

First Australian Team In Sri Lanka: The 1884 Australian team captained by Billy Murdoch played a match against Eighteen of Ceylon at Galle Face on their way to England. The Australians scored 75, with "Alick" Bannerman contributing 36, Palmer 18. F. L. Shand, the former Harrow school left-arm fast bowler, took 5 for 42. The All-Ceylon team, made up entirely of Englishmen living in Ceylon, replied with 49, Boyle taking 8 for 20, Palmer 7 for 20.

First Extended Sri Lankan Tour By Australians: The Rev. E. F. Waddy took a New South Wales team to Ceylon in 1914. The team played matches in Colombo, Galle, Kandy, Anuradhpura and Darrawella.

First Century By A Sri Lankan Against Australia: This honour went to F. C. ("Derrick") de Saram, who scored 128 for Oxford University against the touring Australian team in 1934 whose attack included Grimmett, Fleetwood-Smith and Ebeling. de Saram, the first Ceylonese to win a University

947

Blue, also scored 176 in the 1934 season for Oxford against Gloucestershire.

Sri Lankan Players In Australia: At least five Sri Lankan-born players have appeared in first-class cricket in Australia. The first was P. C. D. McCarthy who migrated to Western Australia in 1948 and played seven matches for WA, scoring 388 runs at 27.71, topscore 98. Malcolm Francke played regularly for Queensland between 1971 and 1978 and Sri Lanka's Gamini Goonesena had seven games for NSW in the early 1960s. George Henry Bailey, a member of the first Australian team to England in 1878, was born in Sri Lanka. He was the son of Archdeacon Bailey of Colombo. Dav Whatmore, who played seven Tests for Australia during the WSC years was also born in Sri Lanka.

Sri Lanka's Emergence As A Test Nation: Heavy, one-sided defeats became a thing of the past for Sri Lanka from the 1960s, and in 1975 a powerful West Indies team was held to a draw in two unofficial Tests. The Sri Lankans did well that year in the inaugural World Cup in England, defeating Canada for a place in the final draw, and scoring 4 for 276 against an Australian attack at The Oval that included Thomson, Lillee, Mallett, and Walker. This progress was sustained with victory in the ICC trophy in England in 1979 and a 47-run win over India in the main World Cup competition.

Australian Official Visits To Sri Lanka: From the "whistle stop" matches of pre-World War II days Sri Lanka graduated to official visits by Bill Lawry's Australian team in 1969 and in 1981 to a four-match tour by Kim Hughes' side on their way to England. The first three matches were one-day affairs, which Australia won 2–1 and the fourth a four-day match under first-class conditions billed as "an unofficial Test." Rain ended the match when Sri Lanka needed 127 runs with all their second innings wickets intact to record their first win over Australia. The Sri Lankan spinners, Lalith Kaluperuma, off spin, and Ajit de Silva and Anura Ranasinghe, both left-arm spinners, took the Australian wickets between them, de Silva finishing with 6 for 36 and 3 for 64, Kaluperuma with 3 for 35 and 5 for 74, Ranasinghe 2 for 7.

Sri Lanka's Test Future: Several grounds in Sri Lanka have been improved to Test match standard and big crowds are assured. In their first Test at Colombo against England in February, 1982 Sri Lanka lost a match of great interest by seven wickets, crumbling under pressure on the fourth day. They led by 147 runs with seven second innings wickets standing on a pitch assisting spin, but the last seven wickets fell for eight runs, leaving England to score 171 to win. The normally hostile Sri Lankan spinners, Kaluperuma and the de Silvas showed their inexperience by bowling far too many loose deliveries, but they showed that from here on the other Test nations will have to take them more seriously.

948

One of the great entertainers of postwar cricket, a right-hand batsman who attacked from the first ball he received. He became an opener as he matured but early in his career went in at No. 3. He was an outstanding close to the stumps fieldsman and a handy leg-spinner at the start of his 14 years in first-class cricket but towards the end seldom bowled. He built a big following among Australian cricket fans who knew they could rely on him cutting and hooking lustily. In Melbourne in the week of a Test he had a god-like status.

A big, powerful man, with heavy shoulders, he hit the ball so hard that even when he edged it, the ball frustrated fieldsmen, spurting to the fence as if fired from a rifle. Few events in Tests over the past 25 years have excited spectators as much as "Stackie" hooking John Snow to the fence in the first over of a Test. Predominantly a back foot player when he began with the Victorian team, he learned to go forward and drive straight or over mid on.

Stackpole's father, also Keith Stackpole, played for Victoria just after World War II and scored two good centuries in 20 matches for the State. His son went to St John's Primary School at Clifton Hill and then the Clifton Hill Christian Brothers' College, where he quickly showed all his father's eagerness to attack with the bat. He joined Collingwood, his father's old club, and there he was coached by the old fox, Jack Ryder. He played his first match for Victoria as an opener in 1962–63 in the absence of Lawry, facing a South Australian attack comprising Gary Sobers, Neil Hawke and David Sincock. When Lawry returned for the next game Stackpole was dropped to No. 3. He failed in both innings. It was the start of a long struggle to establish himself.

Two years elapsed before he started to make big scores regularly. In 1964–65 he made his first century for Victoria, 113 against New South Wales at Sydney, and the next season made his Test debut, batting down the order against England. He made 43 in Australia's only innings and took 2 for 33 with the ball, a promising enough start for the selectors to include him in the Australian team that toured South Africa in 1966–67. There he really started to get it all together and in the Test at Cape Town made 134, his first Test 100. Bowlers peppered him with bouncers on that tour and he was often out hooking but he worked hard at controlling the shot without eliminating it from his repertoire.

Setbacks followed when he was omitted from the Australian teams for the Tests against India and missed a place in the side for England in 1968, but he scored two excellent centuries for Victoria in 1968–69, 123 against Western Australia and 110 against West Indies, to win a place in the Tests and finally establish himself as an opening batsman, playing in 25 consecutive Tests.

Stackpole made the highest score of his career, 207, in the

STACKPOLE, Keith Raymond, 1940–

First-Class Averages: Batting, 10,100 runs at 39.29; Bowling, 148 wickets at 39.28.

Tests (43 plus one abandoned): 2,807 runs at 37.42; 15 wickets at 66.73.

First Test at Brisbane against England in 1970–71, surviving a run out decision early in the innings which photographs later showed was clearly out. He headed the Australian averages in that series with 627 runs at 52.25 and the following year went to England for the first time at the age of 32. He made more runs on the tour than any team-mate, 1,268, and headed the Test averages with 485 runs at 55.88, including a grand 114 at Trent Bridge where Snow bowled at his fiery best. He followed with 52 at Headingley and 79 in the final Test at The Oval which Australia won to square the series.

Stackpole scored the last of his seven Test centuries against New Zealand at Melbourne in 1973–74, and retired from Test cricket after playing against New Zealand at Auckland the same summer. He said he was browned off over the treatment of Test players by the Australian Board of Control and he wrote a fiery book *Off My Chest*, with prominent Melbourne journalist Alan Trengove, which in retrospect was a warning to the authorities about the trouble to come with the advent of World Series Cricket.

In his 43 Tests Stackpole held 47 catches, most of them in the slips. In all first-class matches, he took 166 catches and scored 22 centuries.

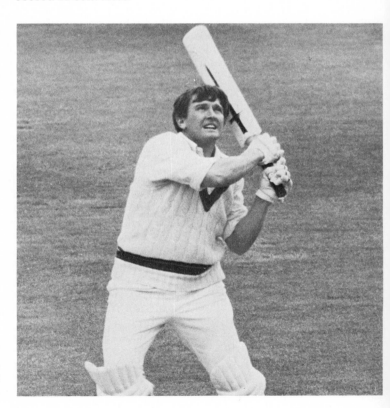

Stackpole hooks a ball from John Snow for four at Manchester in 1972.

950

One of the strongest clubs in Queensland in the last quarter of the 19th century. The Stanleys had their headquarters in Brisbane but were a nomadic outfit whose teams visited all the main country centres of Queensland and occasionally sent surprisingly strong teams to Sydney. The Stanleys were one of the foundation clubs when the Queensland Cricket Association was formed in 1876. They did invaluable developmental work and when the first annual inter-Colonial matches were played by Queensland sides in 1889 and 1890 Stanleys' players dominated the teams.

The Stanleys were first organised in 1873 by J. Fowles on the ruins of an old club called The Orwells. Among The Stanleys' main rivals were the Butterflies, the Albert and the Union clubs. In 1883, The Stanleys made the revolutionary move of engaging a coach from Sydney for a 12 month period. They selected Ned Sheridan, who became one of Queensland's most influential coaches.

THE STANLEYS CRICKET CLUB

A dependable right-hand batsman from Sydney's Balmain club who scored three first-class centuries and toured New Zealand with an Australian team in 1969–70. He had a lovely shot off the back foot in which he lay back and punched the ball hard forward or backward of point, and he could drive efficiently. All his big scores came in one season, 1969–70, when he made 158 against Queensland in Sydney, 152 against South Australia in Sydney, and 123 against Western Australia at Perth. He captained NSW twice after John Benaud was suspended over the boots incident. His form slumped after that and he disappeared from big cricket after the 1970–71 season, although he scored heavily in grade matches for some seasons.

STEELE, John Anthony ("Tony"), 1942–

First-Class Averages: Batting, 1,168 runs at 36.50.

A Melbourne solicitor who has held most of the important positions in Australian cricket, and has been at the centre of most of the controversies of the past decade. He is most outspoken in refuting the view of some officials overseas that they were let down in the settlement negotiated by the Australian Cricket Board with WSC. Steele was educated at Scotch College, and Melbourne University, where he won Blues for cricket and football. He was captain of the Hawthorn-East Melbourne Cricket Club in 1948–49 and president from 1957 to 1973. He captained the Victorian Amateur Australian Football team in 1939 and played VFL football for Richmond from 1940 to 1943. He has been a VCA delegate to the ACB since 1967 and treasurer since 1969, and has been president of the VCA since 1973. He also managed the Australian teams to England in 1961, 1964 and 1972.

STEELE, Raymond Charles, 1917–

951

STEVENS, Gavin Byron, 1932–

First-Class Averages: Batting, 3,061 runs at 38.26.

Tests (4): 112 runs at 16.00.

A proficient, dark-haired right-hand opening batsman whose career was cut short by an illness contracted while he was on tour in Pakistan and India with the Australian team in 1959–60. He was a strongly-built, broad-shouldered, 5 ft 11 in son of a champion snooker player who inherited his father's dexterity for ball games. He hit the ball exceptionally hard once he overcame early nervousness, and included a knock of 259 not out against New South Wales among his seven centuries.

Stevens, who played with the Glenelg club, appeared for South Australia between 1954 and 1960, retiring at 28 when he should have had several more years of big scoring ahead of him. He dehydrated so badly from the strain of hepatitis he picked up in Pakistan or India that he, like Gordon Rorke, lost around two stone in weight. They was both invalided home before the tour ended. Stevens could not shake off the affects of the illness and dropped out of big cricket the following summer, a tragic end to a career which appeared so promising when he made his Test debut at Lahore against Pakistan in November, 1959.

He made his first century for South Australia (125 not out) in November, 1956, against Western Australia in Adelaide, and in January, 1958 at Sydney became the ninth South Australian to score a century in each innings of a first-class match by scoring 164 and 111 against NSW in Sydney. He made his third century in successive innings by scoring 143 immediately afterwards in Brisbane against Queensland, and finished the 1957–58 season with an aggregate of 666 runs.

In December, 1958, he played the highest innings of his career against a second string NSW attack—the State's frontline bowlers were absent at a Test—at Sydney. He made 57 in the first innings total of 303. NSW replied with 7 for 554 and SA appeared to be in trouble until Stevens hammered out his 259 not out and took the SA score to 4 for 486 before time ran out. Stevens was particularly severe on the spinners Peter Philpott (1 for 128) and Hugh Marjoribanks (1 for 120). This match aggregate of 316 helped lift his total of runs for the 1958–59 season to 951 and clinched his selection for the tour of Pakistan and India. He opened with Colin McDonald in two Tests in Pakistan and two in India with modest results that were explained when he had to be sent home.

STILL, Robert Stewart, 1822–1907

A good all-round New South Wales cricketer who helped pioneer round-arm bowling in Australia. At Sydney in March, 1843, during a match between the Australian and Victoria clubs, Still, who was born at Bathurst, demonstrated the style in which bowlers—they had previously all bowled underarm—extended the arm from the body horizontally at the

952

moment of delivery. Still continued to use round-arm in Sydney matches and when he moved to Tasmania in 1854. He visited England in 1878, and was at Lord's to watch the historic win by the Australians—using over-arm, which was the natural development from round-arm.

Round-arm had been introduced in England by Kentish cricketer John Willes 21 years before Still first used it in Australia. Willes, who had been impressed watching his sister bowl round-arm to get around the hoops in her crinolines, disappeared from cricket when he was no-balled for bowling round-arm at Lord's, but others continued to practise the style. Traditionalists fought bitterly to prevent acceptance of round-arm but in 1828 the Laws of Cricket were changed to allow bowlers to raise their arms as high as the elbow. This proved virtually impossible to police. Bowlers kept raising their arms as high as the shoulder because they found they did not bowl as many wides using the higher arm action. Finally, in 1864 the diehards capitulated and in a meeting at Lord's all reference to the height of the arm on delivery was omitted. Over-arm bowling had begun.

First-Class Averages: Batting, 49 runs at 16.33; Bowling, 3 wickets at 7.00.

One of the exclusive group of Australian batsmen who have batted through an innings, an outstanding schoolboy cricketer who did not fulfil the promise shown in his teens. He captained Victorian Colts in 1973–74, when he scored 150 against Western Australian Colts at Melbourne. He represented Victoria in 18 first-class matches between 1970–71 and 1975–76, scoring 892 runs at 26.23, highest score 77 against South Australia at Melbourne in 1974–75. He played in the Scottish League in 1976 and made his debut for South Australia in 1977–78 against India. The highlight of his career came in 1977–78 when he opened for SA against his old State at Melbourne and finished unbeaten on 88 in a South Australian score of 211.

STILLMAN, Walter Leslie, 1949–

First-Class Averages: Batting, 1,299 runs at 24.98.

One of the finest exponents of swing bowling developed in Western Australia, a big, strong open-chested bowler who kept himself extremely fit. He frequently beat the bat with fairly quick deliveries that swung sharply. He played for WA from 1952 to 1960 and during that time was mentioned as a Test prospect. He did well in a Test trial in 1958–59 but found it impossible to displace bowlers like Lindwall, Davidson and Meckiff in the Test side. He took five wickets in an innings nine times, best performance 7 for 59 against South Australia at Adelaide in 1956–57.

STRAUSS, Raymond Bernard, 1927–

First-Class Averages: Batting, 805 runs at 16.42; Bowling, 139 wickets at 24.29.

STUCKEY, John Henry ("Harry"), 1869–1952

First-Class Averages: Batting, 2,514 runs at 29.92; Bowling, 2 wickets at 8.50.

A left-handed batsman who played for the North Melbourne club with his brother George and gave Victoria valuable service in 51 matches between 1891 and 1909. The Stuckey brothers were born at Walhalla in the Gippsland Mountains, scene of a goldmining boom in their childhood. Harry was an early order batsman who in the typical left-handers' style despatched anything loose on the leg side with great gusto. He forced his way into the Victorian side in 1891–92 but made infrequent appearances for the State until near the end of the century when his form was far more consistent. At Adelaide in 1898–99 he made a splendid 134 against South Australia, and in the 1900–01 season had scores of 130 against NSW at Sydney and 130 against South Australia at Melbourne. Near the end of his long career he made 129 in 1909–10 against Tasmania at Launceston. **George Stuckey** (1871–1932) could not repeat his splendid club form in first-class matches and scored just 89 runs at 14.83 in the three matches in which he was tried, topscore 51.

SURTI, Rusi Framroz, 1936–

An effervescent Indian allrounder whose wide range of skills served Queensland admirably in 35 matches. He was a free-scoring left-handed batsman who loved to hit the fast bowlers, a left-arm medium-pace or slow bowler who opened the attack for India, and an outstanding cover fieldsman renowned for his swift pickups and strong, accurate throwing. He had played in 26 Test matches, scoring 1,263 runs at 28.70 and taking 42 wickets at 46.71, when he settled in Queensland in 1969. In the 1959–60 Indian season he had made 246 not out for Rajasthan against Uttar Pradesh in the Ranji Shield, an innings that helped earn him tours of West Indies (1961–62), England (1967) and Australia (1967–68). In New Zealand in the Fourth Test at Auckland in March, 1968, he gave three chances with his score at 99. The first two were missed and the third taken and he never again got close to a Test century. He did make a first-class century (100) for Queensland, however, his best score in compiling 1,859 runs at 28.16. With the ball, he took 51 wickets for Queensland at 33.49.

SWANSON, John David, 1940–

First-Class Averages: Batting, 1,139 runs at 31.63; Bowling, 36 wickets at 35.63.

A left-handed batsman and slow left-arm bowler from the Essendon club who played 29 matches for Victoria between 1965–66 and 1969–70. He often made useful runs in the middle of the order, but had only one century, 156 against South Australia at Adelaide in 1966–67. His best figures with the ball were achieved at Sydney in 1968–69 after Alan Connolly injured a hand and could not bowl. Swanson took 6 for 71 to give Victoria first innings points and 3 for 31 in the second innings for a match bag of 9 for 102.

954

Australia's most famous cricket ground, but not the biggest, oldest or most attractive. Spectators and players always feel an indefinable sense of the great occasion when a Test match is staged there. Part of this atmosphere stems from the great traditions of a ground that has been the venue for so many historic events in Australian cricket since February, 1878. Billy Murdoch scored 321 at the SCG for New South Wales against Victoria in 1881–82, an undreamed of performance that remained unsurpassed for 47 years until Bradman lifted it to 340 not out. Victor Trumper played many of his masterly innings at the SCG, which was also the home ground of the remarkable Gregory family, of Spofforth, the original Demon bowler, and of C. T. B. Turner, The Terror.

Bradman has said that when he visited the SCG as a small boy with his carpenter father the atmosphere inspired him and he knew in the train returning to Bowral that what he wanted to be was a Test cricketer like the men he had watched. Bill O'Reilly, another man for the big occasion, always seemed to keep his best form for the SCG. Keith Miller made many of his biggest coups there with both bat and ball. Arthur Morris, Alan Davidson and Rodney Marsh all rate the SCG as their favourite among all the cricket grounds of the world. And it is true that even when the ground is empty on weekdays one senses that this is a place where historic events in cricket occur.

Origins Of The SCG: The ground grew up haphazardly without any architectural master plan after it was pegged out by British soldiers garrisoned at the nearby Victoria Barracks in 1852. The troops used it for their unit sports for about 20 years and then it was taken from them and turned into Sydney's main sporting venue. Although cricket enjoyed priority at the SCG during its season, the ground has also been the scene of Rugby League, Rugby Union, and Soccer Tests, the Empire Games, Australian Rules and historic cycle races.

The SCG Scoreboard: The first sizeable scoreboard at the ground, created by Ned Gregory when he was curator, was the father of cricket's comprehensive scoreboards. Gregory built the first board in a fortnight on top of a refreshment booth, where oysters were served at ninepence a dozen. Two men operated it by turning rollers which carried calico strips bearing numbers. They painted the players names on planks that hung on the board. First time the board was used, Victoria beat NSW by four wickets in January, 1896.

The SCG Hill: Although it has recently fallen into disrepute because of hooliganism, The Hill has been a world famous institution for almost a century. One of the reasons for this was the erudition of the cricket fans who gathered there. "Patsy" Hendren, the famous English batsman, always called the crowd on The Hill cricket's most knowledgeable spectators.

"Patsy" endeared himself to Hillites by jumping the fence and chatting with them when a wicket fell.

The SCG Trust: The first trustees, Richard Driver, W. W. Stephen, and Philip Sheridan, were appointed to run the ground for the NSW Government in 1877. The first secretary, J. Perry, began work in 1881. The SCG Trust was amalgamated with the Sports Ground Trust next door in 1952 and since then one body has controlled both grounds and the SCG No. 2. The last military custodian of the ground was Lieut-Colonel John Richardson, who took over command of NSW troops at Victoria Barracks when the last British garrison left in 1870. Richardson was an active polo player and cricketer. He was to have been appointed a trustee but instead went to the Sudan to command the NSW contingent in 1885. The soldiers who remained were out-manoeuvred in their attempts to retain control of the ground by Driver and Sheridan. The NSW Cricket Association spent comparatively big sums up-grading the ground for inter-Colonial matches and when the Army left it became known as the Association Ground.

The Sydney Cricket Ground scoreboard viewed from the back of The Hill in the 1901 England-Australia Test, and Opposite page, The Sydney Cricket Ground scoreboard and The Hill during the 1979 England-Australia Test.

956

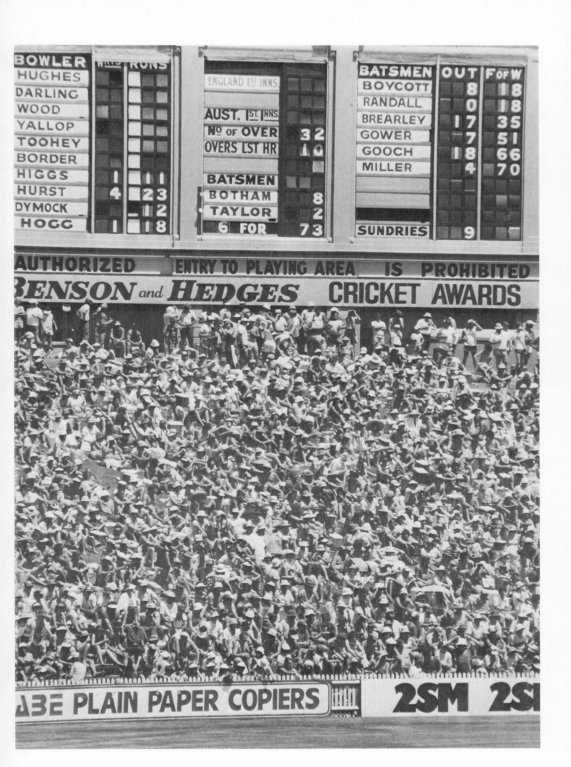

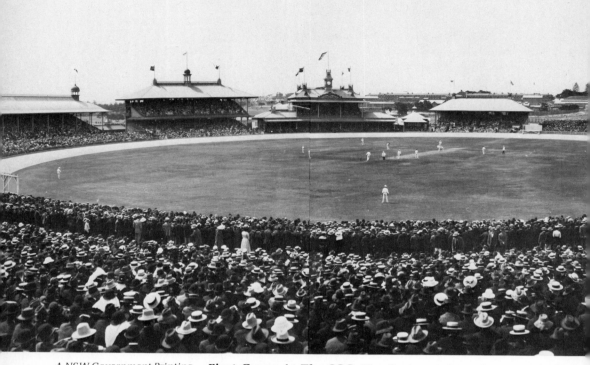

A NSW Government Printing Office shot of Sydney Cricket Ground during the 1901 Test between England and Australia, showing spectators in their Sunday best, the bicycle track inside the fence.

First Game At The SCG: The first match at the ground after the NSWCA took it over was in October, 1877, between the Government Printers, for whom "Alick" Bannerman scored 169 not out, and the Audit Office, captained by Dave Gregory. Ned Gregory prepared the pitch, Arthur Gregory played in the Audit Office team, and Charles Gregory umpired.

Tennis At The SCG: Australia's oldest tennis club, the Sydney Lawn Tennis Club, played its first matches on courts laid out at the northern end of the SCG in 1878. Inter-Colonial matches were played there when they began in 1885, and until the NSW Lawn Tennis Association took over in 1908, the Sydney LTC was the controlling body for tennis in NSW.

The SCG's Bike Track: A track for bicycle races was laid around the ground in 1896 and most of the world's top cyclists raced there until the track was torn up in 1920. There were frequent arguments among cricketers over whether catches taken on the sloping bike track were out. The rule was that the fence was the boundary but some captains agreed to call the edge of the grass the boundary.

The SCG Stands: The only buildings at the SCG when big cricket began there in 1878 were the original Brewongle Stand, known then simply as the Grand Stand, and a small pavilion where the Members' Stand now stands. The first improvements were to raise the level of the mounds on what be-

958

came The Hill and the Paddington Hill so that they sloped
and could hold more people. In 1886, the present Members'
Stand was built. The membership fee was then two guineas
which also entitled members to two ladies' tickets. The Paddington entrance to the ground was built in 1894 and in 1895
the Bob Stand was erected, separating the Paddington Hill
and The Hill. The Ladies Stand was opened in 1896 on the
same day as the bike track. The Northern Stand was built in
1897 and demolished to make way for the Noble Stand in
1935. In 1909 the Sheridan Stand replaced a small structure
known as the Smokers' Stand which was moved to the SCG
No. 2. The Noble Stand was always planned as the first stage
of a bigger development and when stage two was opened in
1973 it became the Bradman Stand. In June, 1980, the new Brewongle Stand, built at a cost of $8.7 million on the site of the
old Brewongle Stand, was opened.

The Private Box System: The new Brewongle Stand included
24 private boxes which in 1982 were leased for $15,000 a year
each. These boxes provide the SCG Trust with a large guaranteed annual income and have been so popular many big firms
have been frustrated in their attempts to secure one. Further,
the public has shown that it prefers to pay the higher prices
for a covered seat in the Brewongle Stand than sit on The Hill.
The system seems certain to lead to the building of new
stands and change the face of the old ground even further.

959

T

TAAFFE, Frederick Herbert, 1899–1964

First-Class Averages: Batting, 719 runs at 24.79; Bowling 7 wickets at 53.71.

A quiet accumulator of runs in Western Australian cricket between 1922 and 1936 whose talents were not developed because of the State's restricted first-class programme in those years. Taaffe, born at Deolali, India, had an almost impregnable defence and made dozens of big scores for West Perth, North Perth and Claremont in a long district cricket career. He had the unusual experience in a "Test Trial" against the MCC in 1924–25 when he batted on every day of a rain-interrupted match. He was not dismissed and made 86 not out and 10 not out in the game, but there were too many great players in the Australian team for him to progress beyond matches for his State.

TABER, Hedley Brian, 1940–

A small, dapper wicket-keeper of the highest quality. He gave some outstanding displays for New South Wales and Australia in 10 seasons of first-class cricket, sustaining the traditions of wicket-keeping excellence established by J. J. Kelly, Hanson Carter and Bert Oldfield decades before he learned the game on a Wollongong paddock. His work was always neat and unobtrusive, devoid of extravagant mannerisms or over-acted appeals. He took some fine catches standing back and supported the spinners well when he moved up on the stumps. His batting was calm and workmanlike, but did not produce the heavy scoring experts predicted.

Taber toured England in 1968 as Barry Jarman's deputy, and visited England in 1972, South Africa in 1966–67 and 1969–70, and India in 1969–70 as the No. 1 Australian 'keeper. A serious chest infection, and the consequent treatment, affected him on his last tour in India and South Africa and he retired after sustaining an eye injury in a Sydney grade match in 1974. He is now the Australian national coach.

Taber was born at Wagga Wagga, but he and his brother Ross were brought up in the family home in the Wollongong suburb of Fairy Meadow. They played cricket every afternoon

960

after school on a paddock beside their home, and their pitches became known to locals as "Tabers' wicket." The Taber brothers built an impressive record in matches for Country Schoolboys sides against representative A. W. Green Shield teams from Sydney. When they joined the Gordon club they had to make a round trip of 120 miles each Saturday to appear in grade matches. Ross Taber was a good first grader but did not graduate to the State side. Brian became Gordon's first grade 'keeper at 16, succeeding former Shield representative Bill Englefield.

Taber made his debut for NSW in 1964–65 in spectacular style, taking five catches in his first match, against Western Australia. He dismissed 31 batsmen in first-class matches that season, including eight in the match at Sydney against South Australia. The next season he made 35 dismissals and it became clear that as he was also a promising batsman that he would be the ideal replacement in the Australian team for Wally Grout or Barry Jarman.

First-Class Averages: Batting, 2,648 runs at 18.01; Dismissals, 395 (345 catches, 50 stumpings).

Tests (16): 353 runs at 16.04; Dismissals, 60 (56 catches, 4 stumpings).

Brian Taber throws the ball jubilantly in the air after running out a Hampshire batsman for Australia at Southampton in 1972.

His Test debut was just as impressive as his State baptism, for in his first Test at Johannesburg in 1966–67 he made eight dismissals, the most by an Australian 'keeper against South Africa. It was only when he was discussing this feat with reporters that it emerged that he had never been to a Test before. Jarman, who had been unavailable for the South African tour, returned as the Australian 'keeper for the tour of India in 1967–68.

Taber's sole first-class century, 109, came in the NSW–South Australia match in Adelaide in 1967–68, and he went to England at the end of that season as Jarman's deputy in the 1968 team captained by Lawry. His opportunities on that tour were limited, but he made 365 runs at 26.07. Back in Australia he equalled the world record for 12 dismissals in a match (nine caught, three stumped) against South Australia in the 1968–69 season. This feat had only been achieved by Pooley, Surrey, and Australian Don Tallon. He returned to the Australian team for his only Test at home in the 1968–69 Fifth Test against the West Indies, scoring 48 in Australia's first innings of 619 batting at No. 9, and taking six catches in the match. He started dramatically in the West Indian first innings by catching the first four batsmen.

He suffered a lung infection not long before the Australian team left to tour India and South Africa in 1969–70 but went on with the tour, a ruddy-faced figure because of the treatment. He was one of the selectors on that unhappy trip, 'keeping splendidly in the five Tests in India, which Australia won 3–1, and in the four Tests in South Africa, in which Australia were thrashed 4–0. Rodney Marsh took over as Australia's 'keeper the following Australian season against England.

A great wicket-keeper for Australia and Queensland, one of the fastest and most brilliant stumpers cricket has known, with superb anticipation for catches. His Test career began late—when he was 30—but in 21 Tests he gave a series of masterly displays that confirmed his place among the best 'keepers of all time. He was also a valuable middle-order right-hand batsman who made nine first-class centuries.

Tall, lean, skin burned brown by his long apprenticeship in the sun, Tallon was all style behind the stumps. There was grace in his movements. In footwork and anticipation, he had speed few 'keepers have matched. Bradman rated Tallon's all-round performance in 1948 in England superior to that of any Australian 'keeper in England. In 14 matches, Tallon stumped 14, caught 29. He only made 283 runs on the tour, with 53 his topscore, but Bradman ranked him inferior only to Les Ames, of Kent, as a wicket-keeper-batsman.

He received many tips from his predecessor, Bert Oldfield, and like Oldfield he eliminated flamboyance and flourish from his neat, clean glove work. He folded himself down on his haunches as the bowler approached, without moving until he judged the speed, flight and length of the ball. For over after over, he was completely unobtrusive and then suddenly the half chance would present itself and Tallon would whip the bails off in a twinkling or dive for a catch. His anticipation and agility in catching a well-hit leg glance by Len Hutton at The Oval in 1948 is regarded as one of the finest of all catches by a 'keeper. He also made a careful study of fielding after he had shed a glove and could scamper down to deep fine leg and throw the ball back with remarkable speed. So well did he time the ball behind the stumps his hands remained unmarked after 20 years of first-class cricket and could have been mistaken for a violinist's.

Tallon was born at Bundaberg, birthplace of pioneer aviator Bert Hinkler, and one of his earliest memories was helping to push Hinkler's plane down the main street after Hinkler landed in the town after a record England-Australia flight. Don was one of four brothers whose father had been a handy slow bowler in inter-city matches. The Tallon boys practised all day long in the backyard and on a pitch rolled by their dad, sometimes sneaking on to Hinkler Park, Bundaberg's main oval. Don's brother Les ("Bill") was a leg-break bowler, and Don developed his skill in taking spin by 'keeping to Bill's spinners. At North Bundaberg State school the boys were coached by a former wicket-keeper, Tom O'Shea.

Don was in the school team at seven, and at 13 captained Queensland Schoolboys. He played A grade cricket at 14, and at 16 kept wicket for Queensland Country against the 1932–33 MCC side, conceding only five byes in an MCC innings of 376 and stumping the legendary Herbert Sutcliffe. Playing in Country Week carnivals, he impressed with the ease in which

TALLON, Donald ("Deafy"), 1916–

First-Class Averages: Batting, 6,034 runs at 29.14; Dismissals, 432 (303 catches, 129 stumpings).

Tests (21): 394 runs at 17.13; Dismissals, 58 (50 catches, 8 stumpings).

he took the fierce pace of Eddie Gilbert. At 17, he made his debut for Queensland against Victoria, who made 542, including only six byes. But selectors rated him too young to take on the southern tour. He regained his State spot when the side returned home and held it for the next 20 years.

At 19 in 1935–36, Tallon played an innings of 193 against Victoria, the highest of his career, and then dismissed five Victorian batsmen in an innings. This followed innings of 58 and 86 against South Australia whose attack included Clarrie Grimmett. He appeared a certainty for the 1938 tour of England but to the dismay of Queenslanders the selectors preferred Barnett and Walker. Tallon showed how valid was the criticism of his omission by setting world records in the next Australian summer. He dismissed 12 New South Wales batsmen, six in each innings (nine caught, three stumped). A few weeks later he became the first of only four Australian 'keepers to dismiss seven batsmen (three caught, four stumped) in an innings against Victoria, when he did not concede a bye.

In 1942 he was discharged from the Army with a ruptured ulcer that worried him throughout his career until he had a large section of his stomach removed. But he won selection in the Australian side for New Zealand in 1945–46 and against Hammond's MCC team in Australia in 1946–47 when he broke all Australian records by dismissing 20 batsmen in his first Test series. He had developed a notable association with leg-spinner Colin McCool in the Queensland team and his 'keeping to McCool was a feature of the matches against England. He probably was still on trial as Test 'keeper when in the space of a few overs in the Second Test at Sydney he caught Hutton, spun round to take a spectacular rebound catch off Ian Johnson's chest to dismiss Compton, and then caught Hammond and Yardley. In the second innings he stumped Evans and caught Wright for a match haul of six, enough to establish a Test career that lasted seven years. At Melbourne he backed up his brilliant 'keeping with a thrilling display of power driving in an eighth wicket stand of 154 in only 87 minutes with Lindwall that ended with Tallon on 92.

Tallon finished that series ranked as the world's top 'keeper. He enhanced that reputation in five Tests against India in 1947–48 and four Tests in England in 1948 but Ron Saggers replaced him in the Leeds Test because of a finger injury. A slight deafness that prevented him hearing snicks, and an unheard-of tendency to fumble saw him retire after Australia's 1953 tour of England. He stands sixth on the list of Queensland batsmen, with 4,355 runs at 30.03.

A rare photograph of one of Australian cricket's noted funny men, leg-spinner Bill Tallon.

Leslie William Thomas Tallon (1914–1972) played nine games for Queensland, scoring 183 runs at 16.63, and taking 21 wickets at 41.85, and was one of Australian cricket's noted humourists.

A sound right-hand batsman whose best years were lost in World War II but still managed to average over 40 runs an innings in 21 matches for Victoria. Born at Wallaroo Mines, South Australia, he joined the St Kilda Club in 1936–37 and continued with that club until the end of the 1947–48 season. He made his debut for Victoria in 1938–39, when he made 100 against Western Australia at Perth. He made four centuries in all for the State, topscore 136 against Queensland at Brisbane in 1940–41. He set a St Kilda record of 19 centuries, highest score 201 not out in 1944–45 and altogether made 5,504 runs for the club at 47.80. He was secretary of St Kilda for many years. His son, **Geoffrey Leonard Tamblyn** (1949–   ), a right-hand batsman and wicket-keeper, also played for St Kilda and had one game for Victoria in 1974, scoring 32 runs.

TAMBLYN, Gordon Erle, 1918–

First-Class Averages: Batting, 1,324 runs at 40.12.

An all-rounder for Victoria and the Middlesex County team who for 10 years before World War I was ranked among the best players in the world. He was an opening batsman, sound if slow, but always a beautiful cutter, who as he matured developed scoring shots all around the wicket. He was particularly aggressive on the on side. He could attack or defend at will, with confidence that stamped him as a player of the highest class. He also bowled left-arm spinners at a pace just above slow, accurate on hard pitches and deadly on soft. He was a fine field close to the stumps but had a poor throw.

Tarrant, born in Fitzroy, made his debut for the State in 1898–99 at 18. He went to England in 1903 and joined the ground staff at Lord's to serve his two years qualifying period for Middlesex. By the time he qualified only George Hirst ranked ahead of him as an all-rounder in County cricket, for his batting had improved markedly and his bowling was ideally suited to damp English pitches. For 10 seasons he produced exceptional figures, and for eight years, 1907 to 1914, he obtained the double of 1,000 runs and 100 wickets. In 1911 he scored 2,000 runs as well as taking 100 wickets. Only four years after qualifying for Middlesex, he was named one of *Wisden's* Cricketers of The Year in 1908.

He returned home for the 1907–08 season, scoring 104 for Victoria against South Australia at Melbourne and 206 against New South Wales at Sydney. In the match between Victoria and the touring MCC team, he scored 81 and 65, and this caused the rule to be tightened to prevent players appearing for two counties or States in the one year, Tarrant having already appeared for that year for Middlesex.

In 1909, Tarrant batted through the Middlesex innings of 145 to score 55 against Gloucestershire at Bristol. He repeated the feat in 1910 against Sussex at Lord's with 140 out of 262,

TARRANT, Francis Alfred, 1880–1951

First-Class Averages: Batting, 17,857 runs at 36.37; Bowling, 1,489 wickets at 17.66.

against Yorkshire at Bradford in 1911 with 207 out of 378, and did it for the fourth time in 1913, when he made 81 out of 159 at Liverpool against Lancashire. He also achieved this feat twice when playing for the MCC.

By 1913 the all-round ability of Tarrant and J. W. Hearne had made Middlesex a dominant force in the County championship but they could not win despite all Tarrant's efforts. He took 15 wickets for 47 runs in the match against Hampshire at Lord's in 1913, and the following year took 16 for 176 against Lancashire. That summer of 1914 proved his finest season as he scored 250 not out against Essex at Leyton and put on 380 with Hearne for the second wicket against Lancashire at Lord's, a record which still stood in 1981. In this, his final season with Middlesex, Tarrant made 1,879 runs and took 138 wickets, but it was not enough to give Middlesex the championship. They won it after he had gone in 1920. In 1918, Tarrant took all 10 wickets in an innings and made 182 not out against Lord Willingdon's XI for the Maharajah of Cooch Behar's XI, one of the few occasions this has been done in first-class matches and the first time all ten wickets had been taken in an innings in India.

In his 13 games for Victoria between 1898 and 1925, Tarrant scored 1,020 runs at 60.00, best score 206. He took 28 wickets for the State at an average of 39.60. In all first-class matches, he scored 33 centuries and took five wickets in an innings 129 times, 10 wickets in a match 36 times and five hat-tricks. After World War I he became a dealer in high-priced racehorses in India and Australia. In 1935–36 he managed an unofficial Australian team's Indian tour.

TASMANIA, CRICKET IN

Adye Douglas, known as the "Father of Launceston Cricket".

Tasmania began as a gaol for surplus convicts from New South Wales, with the aim of forestalling French explorers who had landed on the island. There was no preliminary planning of recreational facilities, and among the first free settlers there developed an urgent desire to establish playing fields, if only to establish that they had rights the convicts did not enjoy.

Among the first to exploit the Hobart population's need for relaxation was Joseph Bowden, who built the Lamb Inn soon after he arrived in 1824 from Plymouth. Bowden organised the island's first cricket match early in 1825 between teams drawn from civilians and troops garrisoning the port. There are no scores in the accounts of the match that have survived but it was recorded that the military won by 15 runs. The match was so successful that Bowden staged another match at Easter, 1826, for a stake of 50 guineas.

Tasmania's first club, the Hobart Town Cricket Club, was formed on October 27, 1832, and granted tenancy of its own ground by Governor Arthur on the site of the present Hobart Railway Station. There were frequent matches each summer in Hobart and in Launceston, 150 miles to the north, but in the beginning contact was hampered by mountainous terrain and the lack of a regular coach service. A convict-built road existed but was used mainly for trade. The Launceston Cricket Club, founded in 1843, ranks third, however, behind only the Melbourne and the Brighton cricket clubs in terms of unbroken activity.

In the 1830s, a Launceston newspaper published a report from Sydney suggesting success in courtship could be improved by becoming a cricketer. "Let no adoring swain thereafter think to dangle at a lady's apron string, feast upon the smiles from partial beauty won, unless he can boast of excellence in handling a bat, or sending up a ball," said the report.

The North versus South matches began on April 20, 1850, when teams from Hobart and Launceston met at Oatlands about halfway between the two cities. The North won by 12 runs, but the South won the return match at Campbell Town by one wicket. North versus South matches continued for more than a century, with the longest break between 1852 and 1858. They were finally discontinued when Tasmania entered the Sheffield Shield in 1977–78 and replaced with an intra-State competition which officials believed would serve as a better preparation for Shield matches as well as a valuable pre-season guide for selectors.

The early matches between North and South were arranged by the Hobart Town CC, the Launceston or Derwent clubs, but in 1858 the Southern Tasmanian Cricket Club was formed and took over control of the game in the south. The foundation clubs were Derwent, Break-o'-Day and Wellington. To play against mainland teams in those days meant an often rough voyage across Bass Strait, but gradually the interchange of teams increased. After one heavy defeat in 1869 the Tasmanians said they were only prepared to meet Victoria again on level terms if the Victorians treated it as an amateurs only affair and left out their professionals. Even that did not adjust the playing strengths of the teams and the Victorian Amateurs twice beat the Tasmanians and the series lapsed for 16 years, from 1873.

In 1863, a year before over-arm bowling was formally accepted in the Laws Of Cricket, a leading Tasmanian bowler Tom Hogg was no-balled for bowling above the shoulder. Hogg took exception to this and after questioning the umpire's decision stormed from the field. The Southern Tasmanian Cricket Association was formed in 1866, with the Governor, Sir Charles du Cane, formerly a leading cricketer, as patron and Thomas Whitesides, another prominent player, as the first secretary. The meeting that formed the association was chaired by William Hogg. The Southern Tasmanian

Cricket Club, was absorbed into the STCA in October, 1867, while Whitesides was still struggling with the difficult task of securing a main ground for the STCA's feature matches.

In the 1870s, a few games were played against East Melbourne with the Tasmanians showing promising form, but in 1879–80, East Melbourne made 742 runs at home off the Tasmanian bowlers. The Albert Club, a strong Sydney outfit, won games in Hobart and Launceston in 1874. Tasmania repaid the Alberts with a visit to Sydney in November, 1875, but lost a match in Sydney. Next Tasmania won a two-day match at Bathurst after William Walker took 11 for 44. A hot wind blew across the drying pitch and kept dislodging the bails and the players had to tie on their hats.

John Arthur is credited with the first century in North versus South matches in 1875, while George Bailey, the first Tasmanian to tour with an Australian team in England, made a century the following year. John Arthur's form was consistent, for in February, 1867, he had hit 151 for Longford against Launceston, a feat improved on in February, 1876, when his brother George Arthur made 177 not out in a match between the same teams. Two years later this score was beaten by Charles Butler, who made 191 not out for Break-o'-Day against Wellington.

Towards the end of 1872 a match was staged in Melbourne between Victoria and the Rest Of Australia, and both the Southern Tasmanian Cricket Association and the Launceston Cricket Club nominated two players, John Arthur, George Davies, Thomas Hogg, and Richard Barnes. Davies was unable to appear through injury but the others performed splendidly. Barnes took four wickets, Hogg three, and Arthur scored 34 not out which won the match on the last day.

Tasmanian cricket, in common with that on the mainland, benefited from the support of large schools. **Hutchins School**, Hobart, founded in 1846, built an impressive record, with the Bailey, Butler, Barclay and Davies families all learning their cricket at the school. H. C. Smith and A. C. Newton played regularly for Tasmania after they left the school, and were followed by Doug Wardlaw, a fine pace bowler of the 1920s, Ron Morrisby, who toured India with Tarrant's team, and Emerson Rodwell, Tasmanian captain just after World War II, who were both Hutchins old boys. **Launceston Church Grammar School**, founded in 1846, won the Northern premiership in 1859, and has since won more premierships than any school in the State. Shield players David Boon and Peter Faulkner are both Launceston CGS oldboys. **Scotch Oakburn College**, formerly Scotch College, Launceston, founded in 1901, produced A. P. Finlay, J. N. Nicholson, P. Gatenby, David Smith and G. Whitney, who all represented the State.

When the first Test was played at Melbourne in 1876–77, there were no Tasmanians in the Australian team, although preliminary arrangements had provided for at least one Tasmanian, G. H. Bailey, to play in the side. Bailey received his compensation in a letter from organiser John Conway inviting him to join the first Australian team to tour England in 1878. Bailey was in fact the second-choice Tasmanian for this touring team. Conway had earlier asked his No. 1 choice, John Arthur, to join the team but Arthur had died suddenly in 1877.

When the Northern Tasmanian Cricket Association had been formed in 1886, Bailey quickly became the star cricketer in the Launceston district. He went in at No. 11 when he began with Launceston CC but in England batted effectively in the middle of the order for Australia. In the ninth match of the tour he defied the Middlesex attack which had dismissed six Australians for 45 by scoring 39, mostly from drives. From that innings, he became one of the most consistent batsmen in the side. He made a century against Eighteen of Hastings and finished fourth in the averages with 281 runs at 14.78 in the first-class games.

Through the final years of the 19th century Tasmanian cricket involved occasional appearances in inter-Colonial matches, matches against clubs from the closer mainland Colonies, and when finances permitted, an occasional trip by Tasmanian teams to Adelaide or Sydney. The major attraction, however, was the visit of an English team. Stephenson's team visited Tasmania in 1862 and there was great excitement among the locals when Tom Whiteside made 50 against them. W. G. Grace's team played Tasmania in March, 1874, with G. F. Grace scoring 154 out of 368, Tasmania replying with 195 and 198, to give England victory by eight wickets. Lord Harris' team beat XVIII of Tasmania by six wickets in 1878–79, and in the same season New Zealand visited Tasmania for the first time.

In 1882–83, the Hon. Ivo Bligh's side beat Southern Tasmania by seven wickets, and in 1887–88 Vernon's England team played two matches in Hobart and two in Launceston. After showing stage fright in the first match a Combined Tasmanian team made 405 against the Englishmen, with E. J. K. Burn scoring 100. Burn was the finest batsman in Tasmania at the time but he was soon challenged by the giant C. J. Eady. In 1894–95, Eady made 116 and 112 not out for Tasmania against Victoria, the first time a century was scored in each innings of an Australian first-class match. Not long after Burn made 365 not out for Wellington against Derwent in 1898–99, whilst in March, 1902, Eady scored 566 for Break-o'-Day against Wellington at Hobart.

Another landmark for Tasmanian cricket came in 1903–04 when Tasmania played England for the first time on level terms. "Plum" Warner's side scored 185 and 4 for 354, Tasmania 191 and 1 for 63. This historic Tasmanian team comprised R. J. Hawson, L. A. Cuff, O. H. Douglas, N. Dodds, E. A. Windsor,

C. J. Eady, E. J. K. Burn, H. Hale, D. R. Smith, D. G. Paton and G. K. B. Bailey. The following season, 1904–05, Tasmania defeated NSW, thanks to Eady, who took 6 for 58 and 5 for 41. On February 12, some of the oldest clubs in Australia, Derwent, Break-o'-Day, and Wellington disbanded because of the introduction of district cricket, and Hobart was divided into North, East, New Town, and South and West Hobart.

When the Australian Board of International Cricket Control was formed in 1905, Tasmania was invited to join, but declined because of disagreement between the North and South. Later a Tasmanian Cricket Council was formed, comprising three delegates from the North and three from the South. This body applied for and was granted Board of Control membership. In 1967, the Tasmanian Cricket Council was enlarged to include three delegates from the North-West Tasmanian Cricket Association, which has its headquarters at Devonport on the west coast of the island.

With Board of Control membership, Tasmania received regular visits from Australian teams on their way to England, ideal matches for measuring the standards Tasmanians had to reach if they were to compete nationally. Collins' 1926 team saw Woodfull make a century and Mailey take 10 wickets in the match at Launceston and Macartney make 163 not

The Tasmanian team that played South Africa at Hobart in 1932 (L to R) Standing, W. T. Longeran (umpire), G. H. J. James, R. C. Townley, A. O. Burrows, D. G. Hickman (manager), G. G. Gibson (12th man), L. W. Richardson, L. J. Nash, M. Leonard (umpire); Seated, C. L. Badcock, A. W. Rushforth, J. A. Atkinson (captain), D. C. Green, C. N. Parry, R. O. G. Morrisby.

out and Bardsley 124 at Hobart. The 1930 Australian side dismissed Tasmania for 157 and 158, and Stan McCabe hit his first century in first-class cricket in setting up a 10-wickets win. A problem for Tasmania has always been to keep her star players at home. Fast bowler E. A. McDonald and master batsman C. L. Badcock were two who would have enormously strengthened the Tasmanian side had they remained at home.

Entry into the Sheffield Shield competition was no easier for Tasmania than it was for Queensland and Western Australia. All three had to fight hard for recognition, but Tasmania had to wait the longest. Finally admission was granted on a restricted basis in 1977–78, with Tasmania playing each of the mainland States once, or five matches in all, compared with nine matches by the mainland States, each of whom played each other twice and Tasmania once. This was altered for the 1982–83 season when Tasmania was granted full Shield membership, a tribute to years of hard work by Bob Ingamells and other members of the TCC.

Tasmania had produced eight Test cricketers up to the 1981–82 season: Sam Morris, the Hobart-born all-rounder of West Indian descent who played all his cricket in Victoria, Ken Burn, Charles Eady, E. A. McDonald, C. L. Badcock, Max Walker, Laurie Nash and Doug Ring. McDonald, Badcock, Walker, Ring and Nash all won Test selection while playing for other States. Every Tasmanian cricket follower is eager to learn who will be the first Tasmanian player to appear for Australia direct from the Tasmanian Sheffield Shield team. Whoever it is will be only the third to play for Australia while representing Tasmania, with only Burn and Eady similarly honoured in the past.

Tasmanian players celebrate their surprise victory in the Gillette Cup of 1978–79 (L to R): T. Docking, R. Woolley, R. Knight, and S. Howard.

971

TASMANIAN CRICKET COUNCIL

Chairmen

1907–08	W. J. Campbell	1933–69	H. C. Smith
1908–28	C. J. Eady, F. C. Hobkirk (Alternatively)	1969–79	M. J. Jillett
1928–33	Col. L. M. Mullen	1979–	C. R. Ingamells

Secretaries

1907–23	P. Facy	1953–63	J. F. Farrell
1923–50	R. J. Shield	1963–64	F. J. E. Johnson
1951–53	N. J. Ruddock	1964–	P. G. Hadlow

Note: From its formation on June 14, 1907, until 1961, the Council was known as the Executive Cricket Council of Tasmania.

RECORD PARTNERSHIPS FOR TASMANIA

Wkt		
1st	182	R. F. Jeffrey and G. W. Goodman v Qld (Hob), 1979–80.
2nd	204	B. R. Doolan and G. R. Cass v Pakistan (Laun), 1972–73.
3rd	183	R. J. Hawson and D. G. Paton v Vic (Hob), 1908–09.
4th	174	D. C. Boon and B. F. Davison v Vic (Hob), 1980–81.
5th	158	D. C. Boon and D. Smith v SA (Dev), 1979–80.
6th	213	B. F. Davison and R. D. Wooley v SA (Adel), 1980–81.
7th	184	J. L. Hudson and F. Chancellor v Vic (Hob), 1908–09.
8th	121	B. Brownlow and M. R. Thomas v Vic (Hob), 1953–54.
9th	148	H. C. Smith and A. C. Newton v Vic (Laun), 1921–22.
10th	122	W. G. Ward and N. Dodds v Vic (Hob), 1898–99.

Note: The second wicket record was set in a match for a Tasmanian Combined XI.

OUTSTANDING TASMANIAN BATSMEN

Batsman	Career	Matches	Innings	Not Out	H. Score	Runs	Average	Centuries
R. O. Morrisby	1931–1952	33	62	6	130	1774	31.68	1
R. J. Hawson	1898–1914	27	54	8	199*	1726	37.52	2
B. F. Davison	1979–1982	21	37	2	173	1579	45.11	5
R. D. Woolley	1977–1982	24	45	4	116	1576	38.44	2
D. C. Boon	1978–1982	23	42	3	114	1429	36.64	1
E. J. K. Burn	1883–1910	25	49	4	119	1385	30.77	2
E. A. C. Windsor	1890–1912	24	44	2	90	1341	31.93	–
J. A. Atkinson	1926–1934	22	42	5	144	1273	34.41	2
R. V. Thomas	1933–1951	24	45	1	125	1268	28.81	1
C. L. Badcock	1929–1934	19	37	4	274	1267	38.39	4
D. C. Green	1924–1937	25	44	2	150*	1235	29.40	2
R. F. Jeffrey	1979–1982	20	37	3	198	1128	33.17	2
A. C. Newton	1911–1934	27	49	5	117	1117	25.38	1
C. J. Eady	1889–1908	19	35	2	116	1106	33.51	3
J. H. Hampshire	1967–1979	14	27	4	147	1079	46.91	3
A. O. Burrows	1923–1936	30	54	3	69	1043	20.45	–

972

OUTSTANDING TASMANIAN BOWLERS

Bowler	Career	Matches	Runs	Wkts	Average	B.B.	5W	10W
E. A. C. Windsor	1890–1912	24	3557	126	28.23	7–95	10	3
C. J. Eady	1889–1908	19	2241	109	20.56	8–34	12	5
G. H. J. James	1928–1946	35	3169	82	38.65	6–96	2	—
A. O. Burrows	1923–1936	30	2251	76	29.62	5–35	3	—
T. J. Cowley	1948–1962	24	2403	76	31.62	6–55	2	1
S. W. L. Putman	1930–1939	20	2138	62	34.48	7–102	3	—
A. C. Newton	1911–1934	27	2215	56	39.55	4–36	—	—
L. J. Nash	1929–1934	17	1630	51	31.96	7–50	3	—
J. Simmons	1972–1979	19	1407	46	30.58	7–59	1	—
W. Hird	1952–1961	14	1447	37	39.11	6–66	1	—
J. M. Walsh	1932–1936	14	1432	37	38.70	5–134	1	—
F. D. Stephenson	1981–1982	7	630	36	17.50	6–19	3	1
N. V. Diprose	1947–1957	15	1374	36	38.16	7–83	2	—
R. C. Townley	1926–1936	16	1279	36	35.53	4–111	—	—
G. D. Paton	1898–1914	21	1599	35	45.68	5–66	1	—

The Tasmanian team which played India at Launceston in 1948. Standing (L to R): D. C. Hickman (umpire), L. Alexander, C. G. Richardson, R. V. Thomas, N. V. Diprose (12th man), J. L. R. Laver, J. Watkins (umpire). sitting (L to R): A. E. Wilkes, M. R. Thomas, R. O. G. Morrisby (capt.), C. Thornbury, W. T. Walmsley, D. J. Jackman, J. I. Murfett. Absent: E. E. Rodwell. Note—No photograph was taken at Launceston, but the only team change from the Hobart match (pictured) was Rodwell for Diprose.

973

TAYLOR, John Morris, 1895–1971

First-Class Averages:
Batting, 6,274 runs at
33.37; Bowling, 1 wicket
at 53.00.

Tests (20): 997 runs at
35.60; 1 wicket at 45.00.

A dashing right-hand batsman who helped build Australia's reputation for producing attractive, fast-scoring stroke-makers in the years just after World War I. He was a brilliant schoolboy sportsman, probably the best that Newington College in Sydney has had, and played for New South Wales in 1913–14 while still at school. His 20 Tests yielded one century and eight scores over 50.

Taylor was picked for the Newington first XI in 1909, aged 14, and was in the Combined GPS side for five years, the final year as captain. He scored 15 centuries for Newington, top-score 295 against Sydney High in 1914–15, the season in which he totalled 989 runs in GPS matches at an average of 109.88. He was Newington's athletics age champion for five successive years, the school's rifle shooting champion five times, and played in the firsts' Rugby XV for five years.

In 1912–13 he played for New South Wales Colts against Victoria Colts at the age of 18 and scored 226. The following summer he appeared for the full New South Wales side against Tasmania and made 83, and in 1914–15, his final year at school, he was a regular member of the New South Wales team. He played a few matches for Petersham after he left school but went off to the war as a gunner with the 1st Field Artillery Brigade in England and France. In 1918 he played for the Dominions XI against England in three-day matches, and was one of the first chosen when the concept of forming an AIF side was proclaimed in Order No. 1539 on January 31 1919.

Ronald Cardwell in his book on the First AIF team and its performances described Taylor as an erratic performer, capable of bursts of sheer brilliance, happiest when chasing runs and giving full exposure to his array of strokes. Taylor suffered from knee injuries, a legacy of his war service in France but he scored centuries against Oxford University, H. K. Foster's XI, and against Essex.

Even when he did not make centuries, however, there was a distinction in this small man's batting that excited spectators. At Scarborough against an England XI, he made a lovely 71 and when the AIF returned home for the matches against State sides he had a delightful double, 60 and 67 against Queensland at Brisbane. When Mailey was on the rampage (7 wickets) in the AIF's second innings against New South Wales at Sydney, he came in and made a thrilling 32 that settled the AIF batting and helped them to victory by 112 runs.

These performances with the AIF side and recovery from his knee injuries made him an automatic selection against Douglas' visiting English team in 1920–21. He also toured England in 1921 and 1926, played against England at home in 1924–25, and toured South Africa in 1921–22. He was Australia's leading run-scorer in the 1924–25 series against England, with 541 runs at 54.10. His sole Test century, 108 against England at Sydney in 1924–25, was scored when he and Mailey (46 not out) added a record 127 for the last wicket. In all first-class matches he scored 11 centuries, hitting five for NSW. He retired from first-class cricket in 1927 to concentrate on his career as a dentist.

TERRY, Richard Benjamin (Dates Unknown)

First-Class Averages: Batting, 60 runs at 12.00; Bowling, 6 wickets at 15.66.

One of the umpires in the first Test in March, 1877, at Melbourne, who played three matches for Victoria during the next three Australian seasons. Terry, who came from Nottinghamshire, where he was said to have appeared in the County team, was a useful batsman and a "swerve bowler of note". He returned to England with the 1882 Australian team, umpiring some of their matches, and then remained in England. His six innings for Victoria produced a topscore of 30. His fellow umpire in the first of all Tests was Curtis A. Reid. Terry held his place for the second Test but Sam Cosstick was brought in to replace Reid.

THATCHER, Allen Norman, 1899–1932

First-Class Averages: Batting, 93 runs at 23.25; Bowling, 7 wickets at 45.42.

A gifted Sydney cricketer who showed in one appearance at Lord's how much he may have achieved but for wounds sustained in World War I. He played for Western Suburbs club in Sydney and enlisted at 17. A year later in France he was badly wounded and gassed. In 1918 at Lord's he took 13 wickets for 38 runs for Howard Lacy's team of overseas cricketers against a strong Public Schools XI. He played for NSW against Queensland in 1920–21, and 1923–24, and for Marrickville club from its formation in 1921. He took the wickets of Hobbs, Hendren and Hearne in one innings in the 1920–21 match between England and NSW Colts. He was the captain of Marrickville firsts when he died. His brother George, who lost a leg in World War I, was a prominent Sydney sportswriter for more than 40 years.

THOMAS, Grahame, 1938–

First-Class Averages: Batting, 5,726 runs at 40.32.

Tests (8): 325 runs at 29.54.

A graceful, powerful right-hand Sydney strokemaker who failed to win a permanent Test place in ten seasons of first-class cricket despite periodic displays of sheer brilliance. Few players have matched Thomas's elegance and versatility in shot production, and he must rank high among the great talents that failed to make a Test century. He suffered badly from homesickness, though he appeared in New Zealand, England, the West Indies and South Africa, and this undoubtedly upset his career.

Thomas, born in the Sydney suburb of Croydon Park, was the youngest of seven brothers. He topscored regularly for the

Belmore Technical College's team and this attracted officials
from the Bankstown district club to select him in first grade
at the age of only 16. He became an apprentice compositor
with a Sydney suburban newspaper. He had just turned 20
when he was picked for the NSW team against Western Australia after a string of impressive scores in first grade. He
made 19 and 6 and spent most of that 1957–58 season as the
State team's 12th man. His initial first-class century came in
1958–59, when he made 189 against South Australia.

He made 120 not out in 1959–60 against South Australia in
Sydney and at the end of that summer toured New Zealand
with an Australian Second XI. Experience of damp pitches
that gave bowlers plenty of cut tightened his defence, and in
1960–61 he made 103 against Victoria at Sydney and 113
against Western Australia in Perth. These scores lifted him to
the top among Shield batsmen but failed to gain him a berth
in the 1961 Australian side that toured England under
Benaud. The place he may have got went to Bill Lawry, and
when Lawry returned home a hero Thomas's job of winning
Test selection became far harder.

The centuries kept coming, most of them gems of controlled stroke play. At Sydney in 1963–64 he made 127 against
Western Australia in splendid fashion, starting with a spank-
ing square cut and a fierce hook off Graham McKenzie's opening over. Then he hooked Hugh Bevan clean over the fence in
the left-hander's first over. But he missed out again when the
1964 Australian team to England was named, the place he
might have got going this time to Ian Redpath. In 1964–65, he
hit four magnificent centuries for NSW which won him a
place in the Australian team to the West Indies captained by
Bob Simpson. He made his Test debut in the First Test at
Kingston, and held his place throughout the series. His 61 in
the Second Test was his best score in the Tests, and he finished the tour with 450 runs at 40.91, topscore 110 not out
against Barbados at Kingston.

On December 23, 1965, Thomas walked out to bat on the
Melbourne Cricket Ground in 100 degree heat after opener
Barry Rothwell had to leave with a cut cheekbone. All the
way on that long walk to the crease he kept telling himself
this was his big chance for a Test place in Australia. He proceeded to add 214 in 147 minutes with Bobby Simpson, and
when Simpson went carried on flawlessly with Norm O'Neil
"You must keep going, Graham" said O'Neil. "A century is no
good—you must make it 200." Thomas had the Victorian
fieldsmen spreadeagled as he cracked boundaries all over the
ground. By tea he was 158 not out, having made a century in
the session since lunch, but cramps weakened his legs. Salt
tablets kept him going past 200, and at 229 he was run out
when he failed to beat a hot return from the outfield. He had
made 136 of his 229 in boundaries in what Bob Simpson

Above: John Snow clashes with a spectator during the Sydney Test in 1970–71 just before Ray Illingworth took England from the field. Below: The Hill at Sydney during the Seventh Australia–England Test in 1970–71.

Cornhill Test

Above: Australian seamer
Terry Alderman makes
England 'keeper Paul
Downton one of his nine
victims in the First Test at
Nottingham in 1981.

Right: Geoff Lawson
throws his front arm and
leg high in an action shot
taken during the 1981
Australian tour of
England.

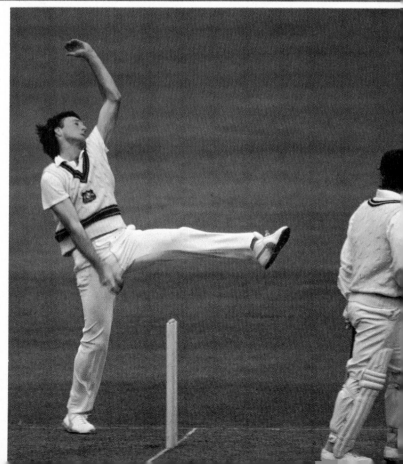

ranked as one of the finest displays he had seen of power batting. NSW finished the day on 3 for 464 and went on to beat Victoria by nine wickets.

Despite this incredible innings Thomas lost his Test place at the start of the 1965–66 series against England, but was brought back for the Third Test to open with Lawry. He made 51 in the Third Test, 52 in the Fourth and 19 in the Fifth Test, struggling against the wily Titmus in all these innings. He toured South Africa in 1966–67 in Simpson's Australian team but following unfortunate pre-tour publicity about his ancestry failed to settle down. His form fell away badly and he was never considered for any of the Tests, a chronic case of homesickness. He retired immediately he arrived home. He made 17 first-class centuries and took 92 catches and the memory of his stroke play lingers still.

THOMPSON, Francis Cecil, 1890–1963

First-Class Averages: Batting, 4,132 runs at 42.16; Bowling, 31 wickets at 40.93.

A solid, consistent right-hand batsman who was one of the mainstays of the Queensland team for 16 seasons. He scored eight centuries against New South Wales, two against Victoria and one for an Australian XI against England in Brisbane, but failed to win a Test place although he was given several Test trials. He was a brilliant fieldsman and a useful right-arm medium pace change bowler. His 275 not out against NSW at Brisbane in November, 1930, achieved in 626 minutes batting which kept him at the crease on three days, was the highest first-class score by a Queenslander until Peter Burge scored 283 in 1963–64.

Thompson, who played for the South Brisbane, University and Toombul clubs, was a prolific scorer in Brisbane grade cricket. He made his debut for Queensland in November, 1912, at the age of 22, and retired at the end of the 1932–33 season in his 43rd year. He made his first century (100) for Queensland in February, 1913, and built a record of heavy scoring against NSW bowlers. The next season he scored 242 not out for University against North Brisbane.

Thompson scored a typically stubborn 114 in an Australian XI total of 526 against England at Brisbane in 1924–25 but was not called on in the Tests. He had probably his finest season in 1925–26 when he had the remarkable average in club cricket of 279.66 for nine innings, six of them not out. In QCA matches, not necessarily first-class that season he scored 1,525 runs at 152.50, with nine centuries, including two against New South Wales. When Queensland entered the Sheffield Shield competition in 1926–27, he became Queensland's first Shield century-maker with an innings of 134 at Brisbane versus NSW. He played in Charlie Macartney's benefit match that season and was given another Test trial in 1928–29 but again failed to find a Test place.

He played the innings of his life at Brisbane early in the 1930–31 season when Queensland replied to a NSW first innings score of 566 with a total of 687. Hutcheon's *History of Queensland Cricket* said: "Thompson's innings was a masterpiece of patience and grit. It was played under circumstances which called for the best that our batsmen could give, for the New South Welshmen had amassed a huge total and believed their position was impregnable. As it turned out, their bowlers hammered in vain against the brick wall represented by the bat of Cecil Thompson, who completely mastered their attack and won the game for Queensland. It was fitting that a man who has been one of the mainstays of Queensland batting for many years should thus crown his cricketing career with a record score."

THOMPSON, Nathaniel ("Nat"), 1838–1896

First-Class Averages: Batting, 705 runs at 14.10; Bowling, 23 wickets at 22.26.

Tests (2): 67 runs at 16.75; 1 wicket at 31.00.

A right-hand batsman prominent in the first international matches in Australia, a useful right-arm round-arm medium pace bowler, and a handy reserve wicket-keeper. History remembers him not for the runs he scored or for the dismissals he made, however, but as the first player given out in a Test match—bowled by England's A. Hill at Melbourne in March, 1877, after he and opening partner Charles Bannerman had each taken singles.

Thompson's cricket flourished with Sydney's prestigious Albert Club and on tour with the Alberts in Hobart he took 6 for 41 and 6 for 50 against Tasmania in 1875–76. In his first big match he went to Brisbane with a New South Wales team in 1864 and took 7 for 9 and 7 for 25, bowling unchanged in both Queensland innings, spoiling his match record by recording two ducks.

Thompson, born at Birmingham in England, was a key figure in the famous riot at Sydney in 1878–79 which almost snuffed out big cricket before it began. Umpire George Coulthard from Melbourne gave local hero Billy Murdoch run out and spectators jumped the fence screaming for Murdoch to go back. "Not out!" and "Go back, go back," they cried. The New South Wales captain dashed off to confer with England captain Lord Harris, demanding that Coulthard be replaced but Harris refused. Looking out on to the ground, Harris saw that Coulthard was being attacked and he rushed out to defend the umpire, now hard-pressed by larrikins. A hoodlum with a stick hit Lord Harris on the back.

Thompson was next man in but before he could get to the wicket to join Bannerman the crowd over-ran the ground. English players who joined Lord Harris in defending Coulthard had shirts torn from their backs. All attempts to clear the field failed and Lord Harris resolutely stayed on the field until it was time for drawing stumps. Bannerman and

Thompson resumed batting first thing the following Monday. With this experience behind him, Thompson became an umpire himself when he stopped playing. He was also a successful coach.

In a first-class career that spanned 23 years—1857 to 1880—Thompson played 27 games and had a topscore of 73.

A right-hand opening batsman who partnered Colin McDonald in many big stands just after World War II. They were a splendid pair, with a fine understanding in running between wickets. Thoms, born at Footscray, made his debut for Victoria in 1946–47. His best score was 150 in 1951–52 against Western Australia, but he also made 120 against Queensland the same year and 140 against Tasmania in 1953–54. He played in only one Test, the Fifth against West Indies at Sydney in 1951–52 when he scored 16 and 28.

THOMS, George Ronald, 1927–

First-Class Averages: Batting, 1,137 runs at 35.53; Bowling, 1 wicket at 14.00.

Tests (1): 44 runs at 22.00.

A colourful, unorthodox right-hand fast-medium bowler who made a dramatic debut in big cricket, but failed to justify predictions of Test stardom through a lack of pace. He bowled with the wrong foot forward in the delivery stride, which gave him additional bounce, and coupled with a fiery attitude, delighted spectators. But he was not fast enough and lacked the swing or cut to deceive class batsmen.

Thomson, born at Reservoir, Victoria, bounced into the Victorian team in 1968–69 from successes with the Fitzroy club and in his first match for the State took 6 for 114 v NSW. His other success that year was 5 for 76 and 6 for 84 in the match against West Indies. In 1969–70 he took 5 for 42 and 4 for 47 against Queensland, and 5 for 54 and 8 for 87 against New South Wales. No bowler could have wished for a better start in big cricket and by the end of that summer Thomson had built up a considerable crowd following.

He was discussed as a new Test fast bowling hope when he took 6 for 80 and 3 for 101 against the MCC side in his second full season. By November, 1970, he had taken 101 wickets, a milestone he achieved by taking 7 for 115 against South Australia. In the Tests, however, it was a different story. This was the argumentative series, extended to seven Tests, that saw John Snow repeatedly hit Australian batsmen. Thomson matched the Englishmen in verbal clashes but could not match Snow in hostility. "A cannon against a pea-shooter," said one critic. Thomson's four Tests produced best figures of 3 for 79. He did not get another chance in the Australian team, though he continued to play for Victoria until 1974.

In all first-class matches, Thomson took 184 wickets, a fine

THOMSON, Alan Lloyd ("Froggy"), 1945–

First-Class Averages: Batting, 260 runs at 8.12; Bowling, 184 wickets at 26.72.

Tests (4): 22 runs at 22.00; 12 wickets at 54.50.

bag for six season's work, 12 times taking five or more in an innings. Selectors judged that the bounce from Australia's hard, dry pitches that provided most of his wickets would not worry batsmen overseas and he did not make a single tour, surprising for a cricketer who attracted so much publicity.

THOMSON, Jeffrey Robert ("Thommo"), 1950–

First-Class Averages: Batting, 1,600 runs at 13.79; Bowling, 481 wickets at 24.69.

Tests (42): 549 runs at 12.48; 172 wickets at 26.86.

An easy-going, uncomplicated big occasion cricketer whose immense physical strength enables him to bowl faster than any contemporary Australian. He is a shock bowler whose heavily-muscled right-arm delivers knock-out blows, aiming for dismissals with his sling-shot action but frequently inflicting other kinds of pain. He has a large and noisy following all over Australia. The sight of him jogging in to bowl always carries the threat that spectacular events are at hand.

Facing Thomson on a fast pitch that gives him bounce can be a shattering experience, not only through his extreme pace but because of his unique delivery. He holds the ball behind his body where it can't be seen until he whips it down with the action he used for throwing javelins in his youth. He seldom swings the ball. Refinements in grips are not for him and although he polishes the ball he has less movement in the air than many of the great pace bowlers. For him, bowling is all a co-ordination of muscles. And what muscles they are when he gets it all together!

Thomson in top gear is in fact such a difficult proposition that he cannot afford to let himself go in district cricket or in social matches on ill-prepared pitches. Even against batsmen of the highest quality he bounces the ball into the body off a full length, often striking the ribs or gloves. His career has been studded with deliveries that flattened batsmen who just did not have time to get out of the way.

He was born at Greenacre in Sydney's western suburbs, son of a good cricketer from Newtown who had been unable to pursue his ambitions in representative cricket because of a shortage of money. He was one of five boys, and says he learned his bowling action from his father. Punchbowl High School is proud to have "Thommo" and Len Pascoe among its oldboys but "Thommo" does not have the happiest memories of the school. He remains hostile about his omission from Punchbowl High's Sixth Grade team by a music master who doubled as cricket selector. "It was ridiculous," he told his biographer, David Frith. "This guy just did not like me. I had to go down and play what they call house cricket with all the other mugs who couldn't even hold a bat. I used to slog hundreds and take ten for nothing. I wasted a whole year that way." He has never since got on well with established authority.

After he left school Thomson joined the Bankstown club and word went round the Sydney clubs like a runaway bush-

980

Patrick Eagar's famous study of Thomson's action.

fire about the terrifying new pace man. He was wild and he was desperate to get out of the humble circumstances in which he had been brought up. Saturday afternoon grade matches provided the outlet. One Saturday he hit the son of former Test umpire Reg Ledwidge in the face. "It wasn't actually a bouncer, but it was bloody fast and it smashed him straight in the eye," said Thomson in his book. "It was frightening to see this bloke just screaming and shaking, and the pitch splattered with blood as it poured through his fingers. He was in the intensive care unit of a hospital for a week. Like so many blokes he just hadn't had time to move out of the way, even though the Bankstown pitch was pretty dead. I never let this sort of thing put me off. The batman's got the bat and he can hit the ball and do what he likes to me. I don't mean to hit him, even though I could if I wanted to. I'd rather bowl them out than knock 'em out."

Thomson played soccer in the winter and in one match showed his fast bowler's aggression. He was banned for life in 1972 for allegedly striking a referee in a Protestant Churches Soccer Association game while representing St Paul's Bankstown. The ban was lifted in February, 1978, on a request from the Queensland Soccer Federation, but new evidence from the Churches' Association led to the ban being reimposed in August, 1978. Thomson wanted to play for Trident, a Brisbane Second Division club, when the life ban was originally lifted.

He made his debut for New South Wales in the 1972–73 season against Queensland, bowling with such obvious hostility he was picked for his first Test against Pakistan at Melbourne in December that summer. He disappointed with match figures of 0 for 110. Later it was discovered that he had played with a broken bone in his foot. After seven matches for NSW he moved to Queensland and although he bowled extremely fast for the State team it was still a gamble when he was picked for the first Test against England in Brisbane in 1974–75. The result was remarkable, for in the first five Tests of that series he and Lillee bowled at a ferocious pace, forming one of the greatest opening attacks Australian cricket has produced. Thomson took 33 wickets at 17.93, starting with 3 for 59 and 6 for 46 at Brisbane. When he wasn't taking wickets he was inflicting painful blows and between them the Australian pace bowlers handed a frightful battering to the English batsmen.

Amiss and Edrich sustained hand fractures in the First Test and Cowdrey had to be flown from England to make his first Test appearance since 1971 four days after arrival in Australia. Lloyd had to retire in the second innings of the second Test at Perth after being hit in the stomach by a Thomson delivery. The English dressing-room bustled with masseurs tending bruises with ice packs and fitting special pads to forearms and rib cages. If it did nothing else, the Lillee-

982

Thomson onslaught made rival batsmen thoroughly re-examine their gear, and much of it was found wanting, especially the old style of batting gloves.

At Adelaide England's batsmen received a respite when Thomson tore fibres in his right shoulder playing tennis on the rest day. He was unable to bowl in the second innings and could not play in the Sixth Test, where England gained their solitary success of a rubber Australia won 4–1. Slow pitches in England in 1975 reduced their effectiveness (Thomson took 16 wickets at 28.56), but in Australia against the West Indies in 1975–76 Lillee and Thomson were back at their awesome best on hard, true pitches. Thomson took 29 wickets at 28.65,

Tony Greig and Alan Knott show their joy as Thomson's stumps are scattered by Derek Underwood during the Lord's Test in 1975.

983

including 5 for 62 in the Third Test at Melbourne and 6 for 50 in the Fourth Test at Sydney. Largely due to Thomson and Lillee's ability to subdue their great batsmen, the West Indies team that had been acclaimed the best in the world lost the series 5–1, the first time the West Indies had ever lost five matches in a series.

Now at the peak of his fame Thomson and his earnings dominated the sports pages, but a setback soon arrived. In the First Test of the 1976–77 series against Pakistan he collided with team-mate Alan Turner as they went for a catch and dislocated his right collarbone so badly he missed the rest of the series, and the Centenary Test in March 1977. He signed a contract with WSC at the Centenary Test but later had to withdraw from it when a Brisbane radio station showed it had prior right to his services.

Thomson recovered to tour England in 1977 when he took 23 wickets at 25.34 for Greg Chappell's team, played against India in Australia in 1977–78 (22 wickets at 23.45), and against the West Indies in 1977–78 under Bob Simpson (20 wickets at 28.85). By now he was in trouble with business ventures and he accepted another offer from WSC, playing for the WSC team in the West Indies in 1978–79 instead of in Australia against England and Pakistan. His business problems had a sobering effect and he gave his practice workouts an energy and enthusiasm previously unknown as he prepared for the resumption of his Test partnership with Lillee after the WSC settlement.

For a time, however, the old lift and spite disappeared from his bowling. He played in one Test against the West Indies and one against England in 1979–80 but was passed over for the others. In England in 1980 for the Centenary Test at Lord's he played in the preliminary games, but was omitted from the Test. When he was again overlooked for the 1981 Australian team in England, he signed with Middlesex. He appeared to have declined through years of heavy demands on his great physique, but in the match against Australia made a ball lift in the fashion of his best years and floored opener Graeme Wood, who was taken to hospital. Shortly afterwards he broke down again and a hernia operation prevented him completing his contract with Middlesex.

To his undying credit, Thomson came back in the 1981–82 Australian season and produced some of the best bowling of his career. The pitches he bowled on didn't help him ("green tops are a thing of the past"), and fieldsmen kept spilling catches from his bowling, but he bowled with fire and marvellous stamina. For Rodney Marsh, the signs were clear— "Thommo" had started to hurt his hands again. It hurt, but it was great. He played through the Tests against Pakistan and the West Indies and went to New Zealand, an important part of the Australian Test attack.

984

A problem that arises periodically in Australian cricket when somebody who bowls with a doubtful action takes a lot of wickets. Suspect bowlers who do not become a threat by taking wickets regularly usually are permitted to continue without protest. Australian cricket has known some memorable throwing disputes, and administrators have always strongly supported moves to outlaw the practice, but in common with overseas officials they have been unable to define a throw in terms acceptable and observable to all.

The problem of bowlers who throw has bedevilled cricket's law-makers for more than a century, and it remains the game's most complex problem, still unsolved. Players, umpires, spectators, sportswriters and officials all consider they know the differences between bowling and throwing, but nobody has been able to define them. No bowler who has had his career ruined by being called consistently for throwing has ever had a satisfactory explanation of how he broke the Laws of Cricket.

There are in fact a large number of ardent cricket fans who believe it is impossible to define a throw. The prize-winning English columnist Jim Manning expressed the views of this group when he called the 1965 Imperial Cricket Conference London meeting on throwing a waste of time. Manning quoted the MCC member, G. T. Knight, who wrote in 1828: "There is no need to define throwing; you might as well define the action of the horse trotting." Another noted London critic, John Arlott, said the job of explaining a throw for the law book was one for barristers, not cricket writers.

Sir Donald Bradman wrote after the throwing arguments on the 1958–59 Australian tour by Peter May's team that it was not necessary to define a throw. Sir Donald pointed out that a bowler must be no-balled if the umpire is not certain the ball is bowled. He also favoured the Oxford Dictionary definition of a throw in cricket: "To deliver the ball with a sudden straightening of the elbow."

Another Australian captain, Ian Johnson, offered this definition of a throw, which he claimed was clear and free of technicalities: "The action of stopping, bending the elbow sharply, and hurling the ball from you." Johnson stressed that every pace bowler of quality gives a violent jerk with his wrist and fingers. Leg-spinners who flicked their wrists and off-spinners who jerked their shoulders, wrists and fingers to impart spin also breached the law.

Law 24 had never been interpreted as written, according to Johnson, and if Gordon Rorke and Ian Meckiff were to be called for throwing under this law then so, too, should Brian Statham, Tony Lock, and Fred Trueman, for they all disobeyed Law 24 as it was written. Law 24 says: "For a delivery to be fair, the ball must be bowled, not thrown; if either umpire is not entirely satisfied of the absolute fairness of the delivery in

985

this respect, he shall call and signal no-ball instantly upon delivery." A note that defines a throw follows Law 24. See the *Laws of Cricket*.

The best thing to come out of the throwing controversy that began in the late 1950s was a clear indication from administrators of support for umpires who no-ball "chuckers." Umpires have always been reticent about calling bowlers for throwing because of the notoriety it brings and doubts that they would get official backing for their actions. *Wisden* claimed that Frank Chester, one of the finest English umpires, disapproved of South African Cuan McCarthy's action in a Test at Trent Bridge in 1951 but refrained from no-balling McCarthy because he could get no assurance of support from the MCC committee and was not prepared to stick his neck out.

The problems of legislating against chucking began when cricketers changed from under-arm and round-arm bowling to over-arm or over the shoulder bowling. Variations in flight and length immediately became easier to disguise but bowlers who wanted more spin or a little extra pace found the easiest way to achieve these objectives was by jerking the shoulders or wrists at the instant of delivery. Between 1882 and 1902 cricket went through a stormy period because of the throwing scandal. Only umpires at the bowler's end could then call bowlers for throwing and they found it impossible to watch the feet as well as the hands. After Australian Jim Phillips had shown the way by no-balling Ernie Jones and Tom McKibbin, a meeting of the English County captains in late 1901 agreed not to bowl 14 players they all agreed were throwers. The problem was temporarily solved.

One of the key figures in that particular throwing debate, Jim Phillips, wrote in a booklet published in 1899: "I am one of those who hold the opinion that to bowl a fair ball it is immaterial whether the arm be straight or at an angle so long as there is no perceptible movement in the elbow-joint at the precise moment the ball leaves the hand of the bowler. Just as one bowler, in his desire to make his delivery more difficult, gets as near the return crease as possible, and occasionally inadvertently oversteps the mark, thereby bowling a no-ball, so another bowler will, in attempting an increase in pace, use his elbow, especially if he is a bowler whose arm is not quite straight. In each of these instances it does not seem just to suppose that either bowler is unfair." Phillips made it clear that the all-important movement of the elbow joint was easy to detect when standing at square leg, whereas it was difficult to spot standing at the bowler's end.

Ian Peebles, the English Test player who wrote a book on the throwing problem, *Straight From The Shoulder*, explained how he once asked a friend to report to him in England on the fairness of "Dainty" Ironmonger's bowling in Aus-

Ron Halcombe demonstrating his bowling action for newsreel cameras at Melbourne in 1930.

tralia. The friend made a close study of Ironmonger's action and said, "Before lunch he threw two balls in every over. Between lunch and tea he threw four an over. After tea, when he was tired, he threw the lot." Like all the other alleged chuckers Ironmonger was convinced his delivery was legitimate and he certainly was never called in first-class matches.

The Queensland Aboriginal Eddie Gilbert complained when he was no-balled for throwing, but there was no doubt in the minds of most of his opponents about how he achieved his exceptional pace. One-time international Bill Hunt recalls how he dismissed Gilbert with an intentional throw. As he walked back to the pavilion, Gilbert said, "Good ball, Bill," proof to Hunt at least that Gilbert did not know the difference between a throw and a legitimate delivery.

A common plea among bowlers called for chucking is that they have a physical defect that gives the impression of a throw. Ron Halcombe, who was called for throwing while bowling for Western Australia in 1930, showed the stub of his middle finger to reporters who asked for an explanation. He had lost the top portion of the finger in a childhood accident and tried to compensate by using more wrist in his action. "Dainty" Ironmonger also blamed the loss of two finger tops on his bowling hand for the wrong impressions about his bowling. Ian Meckiff said he had a wrist that could not be straightened.

Undoubtedly the worst of all throwing disputes occurred on England's 1958–59 Australian tour when alleged chuckers appeared in every other game, all on the Australian teams. For weeks on end Australian umpires, administrators and selectors took heavy flack from English journalists, much of it unfounded. The most blatant of the chuckers, Jimmy Burke, was also the least dangerous to batsmen. Keith Slater was

987

branded at Perth, Gordon Rorke in Sydney, Ian Meckiff in Melbourne, and even before they got to Adelaide the English journalists discussed Hitchcox and Trethewey ("Pitchcox and Trethrowey") as if they were relatives. One English paper informed readers that spectators at Adelaide Oval regularly called out, "Strike One," after Hitchcox bowled the first ball of a match. Another had a spectator yelling: "Put Harvey on—he throws straighter."

It was all fairly harmless fun until Meckiff started to dismiss England's best batsmen. He took 14 wickets in the first two Tests and after his 6 for 38 set up an Australian win in the Second Test at Melbourne, the full wrath of Fleet Street descended on him. Meckiff, in fact, went to the crease with a beautifully relaxed approach, paused momentarily with his arm absolutely straight, and then let the ball go with a blurred swing of the arm that was impossible to follow from 60 yards away, even with the aid of good binoculars. Anyway, the English players said he threw although he had been officially accepted by his own team and by the selectors and umpires who had watched him throughout his career.

The furore that developed became so heated that many Australian officials felt that it bordered on character assassination. Meckiff was lampooned by critics, harrassed at his office and on the golf course by people who called him a cheat but had no idea of the complexity of the throwing problem. Bill Dowling, the Victorian former Board president made no attempt to hide his concern at the unfairness of the attacks on Meckiff when he went to London in 1960 for the discussion on unfair bowling at the Imperial Cricket Conference.

The conference agreed on this definition of a throw, which in effect was a combination of English and Australian drafts on the subject:

The ball shall be deemed to have been thrown if, in the opinion of either umpire, the bowling arm having been bent at the elbow (whether the wrist be backward of the elbow or not), is suddenly straightened immediately prior to the instant of delivery. The bowler shall, nevertheless, be at liberty to use the wrist freely in the delivery action."

The definition was immediately attacked for its lack of brevity and the complicated instruction it offered umpires. Ian Peebles called it a brave attempt, but inadequate for legal purposes, and he was proved right when the definition was tested. Meanwhile Meckiff changed his action and this proved so ineffective he was not chosen for the 1961 Australian tour of England. This diffused the issue and the MCC improved the situation even further by announcing that a truce had been agreed on for the 1961 Australian tour whereby any umpire that was not satisfied with the fairness of an Australian bowler's action would report this to the president of the MCC and not take any action on the field. None of these reports were needed because Australia did not select any of the suspect bowlers for the tour.

Australia had played a leading role in trying to solve the throwing problem and many of her leading players were far from happy when the West Indian Charlie Griffith was allowed to continue in Test cricket. They believed Griffith should have been treated like Meckiff whose career ended abruptly when he was no-balled for throwing in the Brisbane Test in 1963–64 against South Africa. Umpire Col Egar called his second, third, fifth and ninth balls and at the end of the over captain Richie Benaud took him off. The fuss over throwing ended then and has not been revived since, although six Australians, including Ian Redpath and Bruce Yardley, have been called since Meckiff. For the present at least the throwing argument has subsided, but most administrators would be happier if somebody could frame a more practical definition of the throw.

AUSTRALIANS NO-BALLED FOR THROWING IN FIRST-CLASS MATCHES

DAVE GREGORY, NSW v. Victoria; Sydney, 1870–71.
  No-balled four times in a row by N. Thompsom
TOM WILLS, Victoria v. NSW, Melbourne, 1871–72
ERNIE JONES, South Australia v. England; Adelaide, 1897–98
  No-balled once by J. Phillips
ERNIE JONES, Australia v. England; Melbourne, 1897–98
  No-balled once by J. Phillips
JACK MARSH, NSW v. Victoria; Melbourne, 1900–01
  No-balled three times by Bob Crockett
JACK MARSH, NSW v. Victoria; Sydney, 1900–01
  No-balled 19 times by Bob Crockett
FRANK PITCHER, Victoria v. South Africa; Melbourne, 1910–11
  No-balled once by Bob Crockett
RON HALCOMBE, West Australia v. Tasmania; Hobart, 1929–30
  No-balled twice by umpire Buttsworth on 24-1-30
RON HALCOMBE, West Australia v. Victoria; Melbourne, 1929–30
  No-balled eight times in a row by A. N. Barlow
RON HALCOMBE, West Australia v. Tasmania; Hobart, 1929–30
  No-balled 10 times by umpire Lonergan in his first over on 25–1–30
EDDIE GILBERT, Queensland v. Victoria; Melbourne, 1931–32
  No-balled eight times in two overs by A. N. Barlow
HAROLD COTTON, South Australia v. Victoria; Melbourne, 1936–37
  No-balled by umpire Barlow for the only time in Cotton's career
RON FRANKISH, West Australia v. Victoria; Melbourne, 1950–51
  No-balled once by A. N. Barlow
KEITH SLATER, West Australia v. Victoria; Melbourne, 1957–58
  No-balled
JACK McLAUGHLIN, Queensland v. New South Wales; Sydney, 1959–60
  No-balled once by J. Bowden.
BRIAN QUIGLEY, South Australia v. Victoria; Adelaide, 1960–61
  No-balled twice by C. J. Egar.
IAN MECKIFF, Victoria v. South Australia; Adelaide, 1962–63
  No-balled once by J. Kierse
IAN MECKIFF, Victoria v. Queensland; Brisbane, 1962–63
  No-balled once by W. Priem
IAN MECKIFF, Australia v. South Africa; Brisbane, 1963–64
  No-balled four times in his only over by C. J. Egar.

IAN REDPATH, Australia v. Glamorgan; Cardiff, 1964
   No-balled once by John Langridge
EDWARD ILLINGWORTH, Victoria v. South Australia; Adelaide, 1964–65
   No-balled twice by C. J. Egar and once by J. J. Ryan
KEITH SLATER, West Australia v. New South Wales; Sydney, 1964–65
   No-balled once by E. F. Wykes
BARRY FISHER, Queensland v. New South Wales; Sydney, 1967–68
   No-balled once by E. F. Wykes
JIM HIGGS, Australia v. Leicestershire, Leicester, 1975
   No-balled once
BRUCE YARDLEY, Australia v. Jamaica; Kingston, 1977–78
   No-balled twice by D. Sang Hue

South Australian Peter Trethewey a moment before releasing the ball against Barry Shepherd, of Western Australia.

THURLOW, Hugh Motley ("Pud"), 1903–1975

First-Class Averages: Batting, 202 runs at 5.31; Bowling, 80 wickets at 42.88.

Tests (1): 0 runs, NA; 0 wickets for 86.

A lively right-arm pace bowler who played 30 matches for Queensland and one Test for Australia and is best remembered for being run out. Thurlow went in to bat against South Africa at Adelaide in 1931–32 with Australia 9 for 499 and when he was run out at 513 Bradman was left on 299 not out. With the ball, Thurlow conceded 86 runs without taking a wicket.

Thurlow played cricket for Queensland from 1928–29 to 1934–35, and five times took five wickets in an innings. In the 1929–30 season, he distinguished himself by taking 6 for 60 for Queensland against Victoria at Melbourne, breaking the finger of Australia's future captain Bill Woodfull, an injury that put Woodfull out for the rest of the season. At Brisbane in 1931–32, Thurlow sent New South Wales captain Alan Kippax to hospital when Kippax hooked too early at his bouncer and was cut on the eyebrow.

TIED MATCHES

Australia first played in a tied match in 1930 against Gloucestershire at Bristol. Gloucester were out for 72 in their first innings and Australia replied with 157. Gloucester made 202 in their second innings, leaving Australia to score 118 to win. McCabe and Archie Jackson made half of them, 59, for the first wicket, but then Charlie Parker found a length and a worn spot on the pitch. Australia reached 115 when the ninth wicket fell, and with scores level Gloucester bowled three maidens. Then Hornibrook was out lbw and the match became a tie.

The most famous tie, however, was in the First Test between Australia and the West Indies at Brisbane in December, 1960. Australia needed six runs to win from the last eight-ball over with five minutes left. A single came from the first ball and Benaud was dismissed off the second ball. Needing five runs with two wickets left, Australia failed to score off the third ball but got a bye off the fourth. A single came from the fifth ball when Grout was dropped—three to win with three balls left.

The finish of the only tied Test, with Lindsay Kline turning to see Ian Meckiff run out by a one-handed throw from Joe Solomon off the seventh ball of the final over. Chronologically it was the 500th game of Test cricket.

991

THE ONLY TIED TEST—AUSTRALIA v. WEST INDIES

Played at Woolloongabba, Brisbane on December 9, 10, 12, 13, 14, 1960.

WEST INDIES

C. C. Hunte	c Benaud, b Davidson	24	c Simpson, b Mackay		39
C. W. Smith	c Grout, b Davidson	7	c O'Neill, b Davidson		6
R. B. Kanhai	c Grout, b Davidson	15	c Grout, b Davidson		54
G. St A. Sobers	c Kline, b Meckiff	132	b Davidson		14
F. M. M. Worrell*	c Grout, b Davidson	65	c Grout, b Davidson		65
J. S. Solomon	hit wkt, b Simpson	65	lbw, b Simpson		47
P. D. Lashley	c Grout, b Kline	19	b Davidson		0
F. C. M. Alexander†	c Davidson, b Kline	60	b Benaud		5
S. Ramadhin	c Harvey, b Davidson	12	c Harvey, b Simpson		6
W. W. Hall	st Grout, b Kline	50	b Davidson		18
A. L. Valentine	not out	0	not out		7
Extras	(LB 3, W 1)	4	(B 14, LB 7, W 2)		23
		453			**284**

	O	M	R	W	O	M	R	W
Davidson	30	2	135	5	24.6	4	87	6
Meckiff	18	0	129	1	4	1	19	0
Mackay	3	0	15	0	21	7	52	1
Benaud	24	3	93	0	31	6	69	1
Simpson	8	0	25	1	7	2	18	2
Kline	17.6	6	52	3	4	0	14	0
O'Neill					1	0	2	0

AUSTRALIA

C. C. McDonald	c Hunte, b Sobers	57	b Worrell		16
R. B. Simpson	b Ramadhin	92	c sub (L. R. Gibbs), b Hall		0
R. N. Harvey	b Valentine	15	c Sobers, b Hall		5
N. C. O'Neill	c Valentine, b Hall	181	c Alexander, b Hall		26
L. E. Favell	run out	45	c Solomon, b Hall		7
K. D. Mackay	b Sobers	35	b Ramadhin		28
A. K. Davidson	c Alexander, b Hall	44	run out		80
R. Benaud*	lbw, b Hall	10	c Alexander, b Hall		52
A. T. W. Grout†	lbw, b Hall	4	run out		2
I. Meckiff	run out	4	run out		2
L. F. Kline	not out	3	not out		0
Extras	(B 2, LB 8, W 1, NB 4)	15	(B 2, LB 9, NB 3)		14
		505			**232**

	O	M	R	W	O	M	R	W
Hall	29.3	1	140	4	17.7	3	63	5
Worrell	30	0	93	0	16	3	41	1
Sobers	32	0	115	2	8	0	30	0
Valentine	24	6	82	1	10	4	27	0
Ramadhin	15	1	60	1	17	3	57	1

FALL OF WICKETS

Wkt	WI 1st	A 1st	WI 2nd	A 2nd
1st	23	84	13	1
2nd	42	138	88	7
3rd	65	194	114	49
4th	239	278	127	49
5th	243	381	210	57
6th	283	469	210	92
7th	347	484	241	226
8th	366	489	250	228
9th	452	496	253	232
10th	453	505	284	232

Umpires: C. Hoy and C. J. Edgar.

In this match Alan Davidson became the first player to score 100 runs and take 10 wickets in a Test match. Australia lost her last four wickets for six runs. The match ended with a runout off the second last ball.

992

Meckiff hit Hall's sixth ball for two before Grout was run out attempting a third. Last man in was Kline, with Australia needing a run to win with two balls to go. Kline played the seventh ball away to square leg but as he and Meckiff attempted a run, Solomon scooped up the ball and, with only one stump to aim at, threw down the stumps at Meckiff's end. In 1982, that remained the only tie in Test cricket history, and photographs of the West Indian players leaping joyously in the air as they realised Solomon had hit the stumps continued to adorn dressing-room walls and appear in cricket books all over the world.

Two Sheffield Shield matches have also produced ties. At Christmas, 1956, Victoria (244 and 197) tied with New South Wales (281 and 160). New South Wales had Ian Craig ill and Jimmy Burke—who had made 132 not out in the first innings—injured. Both batted, but Ian Meckiff (4 for 56) and Lindsay Kline (6 for 57) bowled Victoria to the tie. At Adelaide in February, 1977, David Hookes hit 185 and 105 in South Australia's match aggregate of 602 runs. Queensland needed 262 to level the scores or 263 to win, and with four batsmen run out—including three in the last seven deliveries—finished in a tie.

Victoria and MCC played a tie under the "old" laws in 1932–33. However, Victoria were not all out, although the score finished level. The match was regarded as a tie, but under present laws would be a draw. The same applied to Sir Donald Bradman's benefit match at Melbourne in 1948–49.

TOOHEY, Peter Michael, 1954–

First-Class Averages: Batting, 4,909 runs at 39.27.

Tests (15): 893 runs at 31.89.

A crowd-pleasing right-hand batsman from the New South Wales country town of Blayney who received his education at St Stanislaus, Bathurst, and became one of Australia's most dashing batsmen. He hits with power that belies his slight frame and fields better than most of his contemporaries. He is one of those players who has not been handled with any guile by selectors.

Toohey left the bush to try his luck in Sydney cricket in 1972, joining the Western Suburbs club where Bob Simpson was captain. He made the State squad in his second season, scoring a lot of runs and earning comparison with another big-hitter from the bush, Doug Walters. He first appeared for New South Wales in 1974–75. He scored six centuries in his first 50 innings for the State but impetuousness cost him other centuries when he was well set.

He won the man-of-the-match award in his first Test, by scoring 82 and 57 in 1977–78 against India at Brisbane, and batted so entertainingly in all five Tests that Indian captain Bishen Bedi called him "The find of the series". He went to the

Peter Toohey in a typically aggressive mood as he pulls powerfully against India.

West Indies at the end of that series in the Australian side captained by Simpson but broke his thumb in the First Test and missed the next two Tests. He returned in the Fourth Test and in the Fifth Test at Kingston hit 122 and 97. He was in the Australian team in all five Tests against England in 1978–79 but disappointed in all but the Second Test at Perth, where he hit 81 not out.

In 1979, he took a job as a food technologist with Toohey's brewery in Sydney and switched to the Mosman club. He was rushed too quickly back into the Test team after missing matches through injury in 1979–80 and his form slumped, causing him to miss the tours of India and Pakistan. His potential remained high but he struggled to make 357 first-class runs in the 1980–81 Australian season, missing the 1981 tour of England. He had a happier season in 1981–82 scoring 511 runs, including a hard hitting 137 against Queensland—his eleventh first-class century.

TOOVEY, Ernest Albert, 1922–

First-Class Averages: Batting, 1,346 runs at 24.03.

One of the characters of Queensland cricket, a left-hand batsman who survived the sinking of HMAS Perth and years as a Japanese prisoner-of-war returned to play 37 inter-State matches. He claimed that left-handers are cricket's privileged class and no right-handers can match the enjoyment they get from it. Toovey, who played for Northern Suburbs club, became president of Western Suburbs after his retirement and has been a State selector for 20 years. He scored consistently for Queensland without achieving a century, a good team player in his State's lean years. He retained a keen sense of humour despite his time as a prisoner in Burma and Thailand and is recognised as an outstanding judge of youthful talent.

994

A unique New South Wales left-arm medium-pace and slow bowler who worried the world's finest batsmen just after World War II, and was a match-winner for Australia in a third of his 12 Tests. His exceptional talents were widely known to bush cricketers for 15 years before he played representative cricket and he had to tell fibs about his age to tour England. "I stayed on 35 a long time," he said.

Toshack bowled his stock delivery from over the wicket, cutting the ball across right-handed batsmen from the off stump to the leg stump. He could drift the ball either way, had a fine faster ball, and could occasionally spin one from the leg stump towards first slip. He was remarkably accurate and under Bradman's captaincy bowled superbly to his field in the first three Test series after World War II. Even brilliant stroke players had difficulty scoring against him, with four men, including a slip, on the off and five on the leg side. On pitches that were at all helpful, he had a leg slip and a forward short leg.

Toshack was born at Cobar, the mining town in western NSW, one of five children whose parents died before they reached their teens. He played a lot of cricket with Bert, Les and Stan McCabe at Grenfell and always says Les was a better batsman than Stan. He also played in the Maher Cup Rugby League competition with the famous Newtown winger, Edgar Newham. In 1934, he first came to Bradman's attention in a match at Cowra to open a new turf wicket that brought stars like Kippax, Dwyer, and McCabe from Sydney.

He knew he should play in Sydney to further his prospects in big cricket but like most bush folk just after the Depression he was too poor to make the switch. He won a place in the NSW Colts with Ray Robinson, another star of bush cricket, and played for NSW Seconds under Alan McGilvray's captaincy, but a ruptured appendix ruined his dreams of a tour of England in 1938 with the Australian side. He spent months in a wheelchair.

When he moved to the Sydney suburb of Stanmore after World War II, his local club, Petersham, refused him a trial. "They wouldn't even give me a form to fill in," said Toshack, who went next door to the Marrickville club. In his first match he took 7 for 28 and after a string of dramatic figures Petersham realised what a prize they had missed and protested that he was playing outside the district in which he lived. The NSWCA let him finish the season with Marrickville before he changed to Petersham. He practised every morning at 5 a.m. in the nets at Newington College across the road from his home, bowling for hours at a single stump to improve his accuracy.

Toshack made his first-class debut for NSW in the 1945–46 season when he bowled at a pace brisk enough for him to open the bowling with Lindwall. In his initial Test at Welling-

TOSHACK, Ernest Raymond Herbert, 1914–

First-Class Averages: Batting, 185 runs at 5.78; Bowling, 195 wickets at 20.37.

Tests (12): 73 runs at 14.60; 47 wickets at 21.04.

ton against New Zealand that summer he had match figures of 6 for 18 off 29 overs. At Brisbane the following season a shrewd piece of captaincy by Bradman helped him to a notable coup. After Australia had batted into the third day a tropical storm deluged the pitch and while it was drying Bradman took Toshack out on to the field and showed him the spot where he wanted him to pitch the ball. Bradman used his right to not having the pitch mown or rolled that day and England had to face Toshack on a strip that had not been shaved for three days. Toshack took 9 for 99 in the match and 17 wickets in the series. He had to have pain-killing needles so that he could bowl with torn ligaments in the third finger of his left hand.

In 1947–48 against India, he returned to Brisbane to take 5 for 2 off two overs and three balls, but this time required no instruction on where to pitch the ball. He also took 6 for 29 in the second innings for match figures of 11 for 31. When he was cutting batsmen down like that Bradman used only three fieldsmen on the entire offside, confident of Toshack's extreme accuracy. Keith Miller gave Toshack a hiding once by taking guard well outside the leg stump, but Ernie had learned to counter this ploy when Hutton and Compton tried it—by cutting the ball in at the leg stump. Compton said he could pick Toshack's leg cutter by the way he held his right-arm in his approach run, but there is no evidence of Compton profiting from it.

A panel of five doctors examined Toshack before he was allowed to go to England in the 1948 side. Two in Melbourne said his knee injury disqualified him but the three Sydney doctors took a more charitable view ("You wouldn't want to miss this trip, Tosh.") and he went by a medical margin of 3–2. Team-mates who enjoyed his homespun humour and easygoing approach were relieved. He was tall, with sleek black curly hair, nicknamed "The Black Prince," not very mobile in the field, and had reduced his pace since his days as an opening bowler to give his each-way spin more chance to work. Bradman prophesied that Toshack would be the team's most successful bowler in England but Toshack's dicky knee forced Bill Johnston to do much of the work planned for Toshack.

He finished the tour with 50 wickets at 21.38. In four Tests he took 11 wickets at 33.09 and had the handsome Test batting average of 51.00. It was not as impressive a performance as in the two previous series in Australia, but in a great team it was enough. Only Bill Edrich among English batsmen hammered him. When Essex replied to Australia's 721 at Southend, Toshack increased the country's agony by taking 5 for 31 and Essex were out for 83. He bowled 40 overs in a four-hour spell against Yorkshire at Sheffield to take 7 for 81. He helped swing the Second Test at Lord's by taking 5 for 40 in England's second innings.

Until he reached England for that trip he was considered an inept batsman, but proved difficult to dislodge. At Leeds when his legs finally gave up, he batted with a runner, Bill Johnston, but he managed to frustrate England by adding 55 for the last wicket with Lindwall, cutting England's first innings lead to 38. Johnston, ninth man out, provided an hilarious diversion by galloping up and down far out near the boundary as Toshack kept nudging the ball into the gaps. When the Fifth Test was played at The Oval a fortnight later Toshack was in a bed at Battersea Hospital, recovering from a cartilage operation.

In a first-class career of only five years, he took five wickets in an innings 12 times, but held only 10 catches, with his captains contriving to "hide" him in the field. After working as a railway gang labourer, he became a building company executive and moved to the fashionable suburb of Wahroonga on Sydney's North Shore. His hair went white and in 1979 at a reunion dinner for the 1948 side he had to be introduced to old team-mates.

THE TOSS

The practice of tossing for the right to bat first originated in England in 1744 where the winner of the toss originally also had the right to choose the pitch. After 1774 the visiting team always had the right to choose when it would bat and the toss was only used for matches played on neutral grounds. The practice of tossing for innings only was revived at the start of the 19th century by which time clubs had started to work on the preparation of pitches.

Australians have had mixed luck in tossing. Monty Noble was so good at it he won all five tosses in the five Tests against England in England in 1909. Lindsay Hassett repeated the feat by winning all five tosses for Australia in England in 1953.

Australian captain Jack McC. Blackham was reported in *The Argus* in 1892 to have used a battered old penny for tossing that drew comment from opposing captain W. G. Grace. Blackham spun the coin and Grace called "man", but the coin turned up "lady". Grace looked at the penny with disgust, said *The Argus*. "That's a pretty penny to toss with", said Grace. "You have to toss first and then take it into the light to see whether it's man or woman."

TRAVERS, Joseph Patrick Francis, 1871–1942

A South Australian slow left-arm bowler who took five wickets or more in an innings five times for his State. He was a cagey character, varying his flight and pace well and was renowned for his subtlety. His best performance was 9 for 30 against Victoria at Melbourne in 1900–01, when he took 28

First-Class Averages:
Batting, 760 runs at
16.52; Bowling, 116
wickets at 31.66.

Tests (1): 10 runs at 5.00;
1 wicket at 14.00.

wickets in the Shield. He played in only one Test, the Fifth against England at Melbourne in 1901–02 scoring 9 and 1 and taking 1 for 14, with Noble and Trumble doing most of the bowling in a tight match which Australia won by 32 runs. He took more wickets than any other South Australian bowler in three successive seasons, 1900–01 (28), 1901–02 (22) and 1902–03 (22) and again in 1905–06 (16). Despite the presence in the South Australian side of bowlers like Ernie Jones and George Giffen he also headed the South Australian bowling averages twice. He could make useful runs, too, and had a topscore of 77.

TRENERRY, William Leo, 1892–1975

First-Class Averages:
Batting, 1,547 runs at
26.67; Bowling, 10
wickets at 33.70

One of three brothers who played cricket well. A right-hand opening batsman, born in Queanbeyan, he went to school at Sydney Church of England Grammar School (Shore), where Jack Gregory was one of his class-mates. After he left school his family moved to Maitland and Bill went with them. In club cricket in Maitland in 1912–13, he averaged 102. In 1913–14 he won selection in the New South Wales team to play South Australia after scoring 130 for New South Wales Colts against Victorian Colts, but could not play in Adelaide for business reasons. He headed the Paddington club averages in 1914–15.

He served in the 19th Battalion at Gallipoli, in the Middle East and France. He married an American nurse in England and was one of the first picked when the First AIF side was assembled. Trenerry scored 961 runs at 28.26, topscore 82 against Lancashire, and made a century in a second-class game against a Scottish Western Districts side at Glasgow. He added a further 403 runs at 31.00, topscore 74, on the South African part of the AIF team's tour and 93 runs at 15.50 on the Australia part of the tour.

After discharge he played for Paddington, Glebe-South Sydney and Mosman, and in three matches for New South Wales between 1920–21 and 1924–25, all against Queensland, captaining the State in his last match. His best score for New South Wales was 70 against Queensland in 1920–21. His brother **Edwin** ("Ted") (1897–), a fast medium bowler, played five first-class matches, taking 18 wickets at 25.05.

TRETHEWEY, Peter Grant, 1935–

One of the most controversial fast bowlers in Australian cricket since World War II. He played for South Australia for five seasons and had one game with Queensland, completing his first-class career just short of 100 wickets. He was a poor batsman who often took more wickets in a season than he scored runs. Throughout his career he was accused of throw-

998

ing by spectators, writers and opponents but he was never called for chucking in 28 first-class matches.

Trethewey, tall and loose-limbed, learned his cricket at Adelaide Technical School and played for several Adelaide clubs. He took five wickets or more in an innings six times between 1957–58 and 1961–62. He often opened the bowling for South Australia with Alan Hitchcox, who was also accused of chucking, so they formed a well-discussed and controversial attack. Hitchcox was never called in first-class cricket, but was called in a grade match.

First-Class Averages: Batting, 79 runs at 3.43; Bowling, 92 wickets at 28.48.

An unorthodox left-arm spin bowler and hard-hitting batsman for Victoria, Australia, Lancashire League clubs, and Northamptonshire, with whom he performed the double of 100 wickets and 1,000 runs in a season seven times. A small man (5 ft 7 in), with an unusually wide hand, Tribe switched from orthodox left-arm finger spin at the age of 18 to become one of cricket's best exponents of left-arm wrist spin. After impressive performances with Victoria, Tribe missed selection in Bradman's 1948 Australian side for England, and was lost to Australian cricket, playing out a long, outstanding career in England.

Tribe was born in Yarraville to a family of Sussex origin. He began playing cricket with his brothers in the backyard of the family home. From matches on matting pitches for St Augustine's, Yarraville, he graduated to turf pitches for the Yarraville Seconds at the age of 14. He held his place for four years, occasionally playing for the Firsts.

In the 1938–39 season he changed from finger spin to bowling out of the back of his hand, reasoning that he would have more success under the amended lbw law with the ball that turned from the off to right-handed batsmen. He also felt that his big hand would get more turn from the wrist on hard Australian pitches than would his fingers. In his first match bowling wrist spin, he took 7 for 82 and at the end of that season played for Melbourne City Colts against Country Colts. At 19, he won permanent first grade selection.

The war interrupted his first-class cricket ambitions but enabled him to play seven years as a professional Australian Rules footballer. He served six months in the Army but was discharged to return to his work as an engineer, a reserved occupation. He made his debut for Victoria in 1945–46 and in his first match took 6 for 101 in Queensland's second innings. In 1946–47, he helped Victoria win the Sheffield Shield by taking 33 wickets at 17.54 each, and in the match between Victoria and England took 5 for 49.

Before Tribe's Test debut against England in 1946–47 Bradman asked wicket-keeper Don Tallon, a superb taker of spin,

TRIBE, George Edward, 1920–

First-Class Averages: Batting, 10,177 runs at 27.34; Bowling, 1,378 wickets at 20.55.

Test (3): 35 runs at 17.50; 2 wickets at 165.00.

to make sure he got some net practise in "reading" Tribe's wrong-un, the only time Tallon was ever advised in this way. Tribe's three Test performances that summer produced only two wickets at 165 runs each and gave no indication of his later brilliance.

After taking 86 wickets for Victoria at 19.25 (in only 13 games), he signed for three seasons with Milnrow in the Central Lancashire League, and in his first season (1947) took 136 wickets. He followed with a record 148 wickets and in his third season in England lifted that record to 150 wickets. He then played two seasons with Rawtenstall and could not accept invitations to play county cricket for Lancashire because of his League commitments. In 1949–50, he enhanced his reputation as the world's best left-arm spinner by taking 99 wickets—more than twice as many as any team-mate—at 17.22 on a tour of India with the high quality Commonwealth team. He paid a return visit to India in 1950–51 with another Commonwealth team.

Tribe worked each English winter as an engineer and when in 1952 he was hired by a prominent Northampton firm he joined the County side. In his first four matches for Northants he took 40 wickets and he finished the 1952 season with 126 wickets and 1,039 runs. He was now a superb tradesman with the ball, a master of flight and length, and he performed the double of 1,000 runs and 100 wickets in all bar one of his eight seasons before his retirement in 1959.

In 1955 he set a Northants season record by taking 175 wickets, and in 1958 he set a match record for the county by taking 15 for 31 against Yorkshire. His batting had steadily improved and for the second half of his 13 seasons in England he was a genuine all-rounder, playing many invaluable innings, defending stoutly and hitting very hard in front of the stumps.

In all first-class matches, George Tribe scored seven centuries. He took five wickets in an innings 93 times and 10 wickets in a match 23 times. His best bowling analysis was 9 for 43 for Northants v Worcestershire in 1958, and he held 239 catches. When he quit first-class cricket, he became a leading coach and at 60 he was still trundling up to the stumps and bowling them out of the back of his hand.

TRIMBLE, Samuel Christy, 1934–

First-Class Averages: Batting, 10,282 runs at 41.79; Bowling, 3 wickets at 59.00.

An irrepressible New South Wales-born right-hand opening batsman who made more runs than any other Australian without winning Test selection. He scored 22 centuries and two double centuries in 17 seasons with Queensland after failing to win a place in the NSW side. He sometimes refused to let spectators share his profound love for cricket as he batted ponderously on, each run only temporary relief from the overall agony. He toured the West Indies, New Zealand and New Guinea in Australian teams, scored more runs for Queensland than any other batsman, and was second only to Bradman among Sheffield Shield run-getters when he finally retired in his 42nd year.

Trimble made 8,647 runs in the Shield, but was not too depressed about missing Bradman's record of 8,926. "I'd be much happier if I can be like my father and still be playing at 72 and batting without glasses," Sam said. "I love the game and I'll never give it up. I'll always be playing some sort of cricket somewhere." Trimble played 230 Shield innings compared to Bradman's 95, continuing because he enjoyed it, not because he wanted the great man's record. His highest Shield score was 252 not out, Bradman's 452 not out, but there the comparison ends.

Trimble was born at Lismore in northern NSW and learned to play cricket on his father's dairy farm, progressing through school and district teams to the NSW Colts in 1958–59, when he made a century against Queensland Colts. He was chosen for NSW's Second XI but could not make the senior team at a time of abundant talent. He moved to the Western Suburbs club in Brisbane and made his debut for Queensland in 1959–60 against Victoria at Melbourne. His technique improved with experience and he became an extremely difficult opener to dislodge, picking up runs with safe deflections and nudges, and an occasional drive.

He scored 113 and 136 not out in 1963–64 against Victoria at Brisbane to become the first Queensland batsman since L. P. D. O'Connor in 1926–27 to score a century in each innings. He made his career highest score, 252 not out, against NSW at Sydney the same season. In 1964–65, he scored 220 against South Australia at Adelaide. This high scoring won him a trip to the West Indies in Bob Simpson's Australian team in 1965, but he played in only four of the 10 first-class matches, scoring 262 runs at 52.40, including 155 against the Windward Isles at Granada. He was 12th man for the First Test, the closest he ever got to Test selection.

Trimble toured New Zealand in 1969–70 as captain of the Australian Second XI, while the senior team toured India and South Africa. He scored 213 in the third international match against New Zealand at Wellington, leading the side cheerfully and shrewdly. His 555 runs at 55.50 made him the leading run-getter on the tour. At Brisbane in November, 1970, he batted for 539 minutes for 177 against England, an innings which the Sydney *Sun* called "the most boring, frustrating, utterly pointless effort on the ground since Trevor Bailey pulled a similar stunt in a Test match 12 years ago." With crowds dropping from Brisbane matches, Queensland officials were not pleased by Trimble's long occupancy of the crease, and shortly afterwards he lost the State captaincy.

1001

He was still going strong in the Queensland team soon after his 40th birthday in 1975, however, and in October that year won Queensland the match against NSW with a sparkling 66. As Trimble and his captain, Greg Chappell, plundered the NSW attack, the Gabba crowd called, "Sam, Sam, Sam," after every run scored. Later Sam attributed his longevity and sharp eyesight to his father, Christie Trimble, who was still playing cricket at the age of 71 after 60 years in the game. Trimble, senr, was an opening batsman and bowler for the Booyong Club in the Lismore area and scored most of his runs and took most of his wickets between 40 and 50 years of age.

Sam Trimble, co-proprietor of a Brisbane cricket coaching centre, was forced to retire for a time to concentrate on the business during the 1974–75 season but he returned to play a few more Shield matches and lift his aggregate of runs past the 8,269 scored by Les Favell. He couldn't get to Bradman's record before the rising group of talented young Queensland batsmen forced his final retirement. In 144 first-class matches he made 26 centuries and held 86 catches.

Trimble ducks under a bouncer from Eddie Barlow in a Queensland v. South Africa match at The Gabba.

A colourful, all-round cricketer who judged there was only suffering ahead following a series of illnesses and shot himself in his London lodgings, aged 41, leaving his wardrobe to his landlady and four pounds in cash. Trott, one of three Melbourne-born cricketing brothers, could bat, bowl and field with match-winning brilliance. He was responsible for some of the most spectacular hitting and bowling in the history of first-class cricket. If he had a weakness, it was that he developed a mania for attempting to repeat his legendary blows.

Albert Trott, a heavy tall man, had vast hands with which he imparted sharp off-spin, natural swerve from the leg, and cleverly concealed variations from his normal medium pace. He could bowl really fast from a fairly low action but at times reverted to slow breaks that turned appreciably. In his benefit match in 1907 against Somerset at Lord's he virtually ruined prospects of a big gate by taking four wickets in four balls and later in the same innings a hat-trick. "I've bowled myself to the work house," he said.

Trott, born at Abbotsford, Victoria, played for Victoria against Western Australia in the 1892–93 season and two seasons later he scored 38 n.o., 72 n.o. and 85 n.o. in successive Test innings against Stoddart's English team. In the Adelaide Test of that series he took 8 for 43. In all his matches against England that summer he took 19 wickets and made 331 runs. His form disappointed in the following first-class seasons and he was not picked in the 1896 Australian team that toured England. "Dimboola Jim" Phillips, the great Australian umpire, advised him to go to England, and he accompanied the Australian side, captained by his brother Harry, settling in London and securing a position on the Lord's ground staff. He took two years to qualify for Middlesex but in this period gave indications of what was to come with some impressive hitting and bowling in games for the MCC.

He played his first match for Middlesex in 1898 and continued with them for the next 12 seasons, but it was in the first six years with that County that he became one of the most spectacular cricketers of his time. He made 1,175 runs and took 239 wickets in 1899, and had 1,337 runs and 211 wickets in 1900. In all first-class cricket he hit eight centuries, and some of his innings were sprinkled with blows that remain part of cricket legend. Playing for MCC against Sussex at Lord's in 1899 he hit Fred Tate to the top of the pavilion, striking the MCC Coat of Arms. In 1899 at Lord's he struck a ball from Monty Noble right over the pavilion playing for MCC against Australia. Many thought that this was the hit that converted him into an unashamed slogger.

In five Tests, three for Australia and two for England v. South Africa, Albert Trott took 26 wickets at 15 runs apiece. On tour in South Africa with Lord Hawke's team in 1898–99,

TROTT, Albert Edwin ("Alberto"), 1873–1914

First-Class Averages: Batting, 10,696 runs at 19.48; Bowling, 1,674 wickets at 21.09.

Tests—Australia (3): 205 runs at 102.50; 9 wickets at 21.33.
England (2): 23 runs at 5.75; 17 wickets at 11.64.

1003

he hit 101 not out against Transvaal at Johannesburg and took 168 wickets at 9.67. He also played for Lord Hawke's team in Australia in 1902–03, after playing for Hawke's Bay in New Zealand. He took 100 wickets in a season seven times and his 10 for 42 for Middlesex v. Somerset at Taunton in 1900 remained his best career figures. During his career he took five wickets in an innings 132 times and 10 wickets in a match 41 times. He was easy-going, heavily moustached, mischievous, and loved a pint. His Test average is the best by an Australian batsman.

In the slips or fielding to his own bowling, he was superb and held 449 catches. From 1911 to 1913 he was a first-class umpire. The 15th Volume of *Scores & Biographies* published in 1928, included these highlights of Albert Trott's career:

Batting

At Lord's in 1899, he made 64 for MCC v. Sussex, when he and S. M. Tindall added 46 in 15 minutes.

At Lord's in 1899, in his highest first-class knock, 164 for Middlesex v. Yorkshire, he hit 26 in four minutes. One drive hit the pavilion seats with such force it rebounded to within a few yards of the wicket.

He and C. M. Wells put on 96 in 35 minutes for Middlesex v. Somerset at Taunton in 1899, including 21 off an over, Trott driving two balls into the river for six each.

At Leeds in 1900 for Middlesex v. Yorkshire, Trott made 50 in 22 minutes while G. MacGregor made two.

At Lord's in 1902 for Middlesex v. Somerset, he made 103 out of 136, in 70 minutes.

For MCC v. Leicestershire at Lord's in 1903 he and L. C. Braund made 60 in 20 minutes.

At Lord's in 1906 for Middlesex v. Nottinghamshire he made 84 out of 104 in 95 minutes with Frank Tarrant.

Bowling

10 for 42 Middlesex v. Somerset at Taunton, 1900.

8 for 43 Australia v. England at Adelaide, 1894–5.

8 for 47 Middlesex v. Gloucestershire at Clifton, 1900.

8 for 53 MCC v. Oxford University at Lord's, 1897.

8 for 54 Middlesex v. Essex at Lord's, 1901.

8 for 83 Middlesex v. Notts at Nottingham, 1898.

8 for 84 an England XI v. Yorkshire at Lord's, 1901.

8 for 91 Middlesex v. Lancashire at Lord's, 1899.

8 for 115 Middlesex v. Sussex at Lord's, 1901.

TROTT, George Henry Stevens, 1866–1917 A Victorian all-rounder of flair and quality, the elder brother of A. E. Trott and Fred Trott who played for Middlesex Second XI. Harry Trott captained Australia eight times between 1896 and 1898 for five wins, three losses, and was described by the great South Australian all-rounder George Giffen as the best all-round player Victoria ever sent to England. He was not as spectacular as his brother "Alberto" but he could bat well under all conditions.

"On a good wicket," wrote Giffen, "I have seen Harry Trott adopt forcing tactics worthy of the big hitter, and in the very next match play keeps on a difficult pitch with wonderful skill." Harry Trott bowled medium pace, breaking in from the leg, and became a noted fieldsman at point.

He began with the Capulet Cricket club in Melbourne and later played grade for South Melbourne, for whom his best knocks were 200 not out versus St Kilda in 1886–87 and 216 v. Melbourne in February, 1889. He played for Victoria from the summer of 1885–86 until 1897–98, when his health broke down and he went into a psychiatric institution. A public testimonial was then opened for his benefit and the Melbourne Club began with a donation of a hundred pounds. Miraculously, Harry Trott recovered and he played again for Victoria occasionally from 1903–04 until the 1907–08 season. At Melbourne in 1903–04 Harry Trott made top score of nine in Victoria's total of 15 (six ducks) against England. He was dropped twice. Victoria's 15, made in 45 minutes, remains the lowest score in a first-class match in Australia.

First-Class Averages: Batting, 8,804 runs at 23.54; Bowling, 386 wickets at 25.12.

Tests (24): 921 runs at 21.92; 29 wickets at 35.13.

He went to England four times with Australian teams in 1888, 1890, 1893 and 1896, captaining the team on the last trip, when among many fine achievements Australia beat Gloucestershire by an innings at Bristol and dismissed them for 17 at Cheltenham. He scored more than 1,000 runs on each tour and took a total of 175 wickets on those four tours. He made 143 in the Test match at Lord's in 1896 and his career best score of 186 v. Cambridge University in 1890.

For Victoria, he had 59 games, scoring 2,881 runs and averaged 26.92. He took 181 wickets for the State at an average of 24.97. In all first-class cricket he made nine centuries, took five wickets in an innings 17 times, and held 183 catches.

Trott was held by many opponents to be the finest of tacticians ever ready to change his policies to suit the state of a game. Prince Ranjitsinhji and Clem Hill both regarded him as the best Australian captain in their experience. It was said that he never made an enemy and was universally admired. Sadly, he like his two brothers, found an early grave.

Frederick Trott (unknown–1921), a younger brother of G. H. S. and A. E. Trott, died at Glasgow in March, 1921. For a period he was engaged at Lord's and played a few times for Middlesex Second XI, without achieving the efficiency of his brothers. He went to Scotland as a professional to the Peebles County CC in 1906 and remained there for eight years, two as a professional and six as an amateur. He was a useful allrounder. After World War I he was engaged by the Clydesdale C.C. as groundsman and coach.

1005

**TRUMBLE, Hugh,
1867–1938**

First-Class Averages:
Batting, 5,395 runs at
19.47; Bowling, 929
wickets at 18.44.

Tests (32): 851 runs at
19.79; 141 wickets at
21.78.

A bony, long-arm, lantern-jawed all-rounder of the highest class, who bounded in to bowl, leaping high to exploit his 6 ft 4 ins, releasing the ball with his long arms fully-stretched above his head. He gripped the ball with uncommonly long and strong fingers, a master of variations in pace. He made three first-class centuries and many other valuable scores and was a remarkable slips field.

"That great camel, Hughie Trumble," famous cricket-author Pelham ("Plum") Warner called him. Another England captain, Johnny Douglas, said Trumble should not be allowed on a cricket field. "His proper place is up trees in the bush," Douglas said. Trumble, who had prominent ears and a big nose, packaged his unusual physiognomy under wide-brimmed stetson hats which he imported especially from America and behind long bent-stemmed pipes. His scholarly appearance was backed by his cleverness on the field.

"I would prefer not to see Hughie Trumble against me in flannels," wrote English Test star C. B. Fry in 1904, "for the simple reason that he is the most long-headed, observant and acute judge of the game, a perfect master of the whole art of placing fieldsmen and changing bowlers. It is his head—that long, solemn head, I should fear this summer if I were England's captain "Plum" Warner, not his bowling arm, spinning fingers, deft as they are. It is the head, the best of the side, that makes Hugh Trumble the big difference to the Australians."

Most Test batsmen who confronted Trumble or played with him ranked him the finest bowler of his time. And nearly all of them agreed his batting suffered because of the demands made on him at the bowling crease. He bowled an impeccable length at right-arm medium, with a sharp break from the off, could swing the ball when it was new, and somehow always controlled his long arms and legs. Statistics do not do justice to his colourful personality, for such was his zest for cricket that he added flavour to every game he played. Monty Noble was captivated by Trumble's approach run—"sidelong and insinuating, with his neck craned like a gigantic bird." England's Sir Stanley Jackson was hoodwinked by his slower ball. "You old devil, Hughie," he used to say. "But I'll pick that slower one sooner or later."

Trumble, son of an Irishman and his Scottish wife, was born at Abbotsford, Melbourne, and educated at Hawthorn Grammar School. He worked initially in a bank. In 1911 he became secretary of the Melbourne Cricket Club, succeeding Major Ben Wardill, and he remained in the job for 27 years until his death from a heart attack. He administered major improvements at Melbourne Cricket Ground, including two new grandstands, and became an elder statesman of Australian cricket, conspicuous in his support for pressmen at whatever hour they called.

He was in five Australian teams in England, in 1890, 1893,

1006

1896, 1899 and 1902, and on those five tours took 603 wickets at 16.74 runs each. He scored 3,424 runs on his English trips at 19.56 an innings. After the 1902 trip, English critics wrote that Trumper was the best batsman in the world, Noble the best all-rounder and Trumble the best bowler.

Cagey in all he did, Trumble captained Australia twice in 1901–02 and won both Tests. He performed the hat-trick twice in Test matches at the Melbourne ground, in 1901–02 and in 1903–04, both against England and the second in his final Test when he took 7 for 28 to give Australia victory. After he retired he became a prominent writer on the game and the source of endless stories that kept cricket in the headlines. It was Trumble who, on a visit to Queensland spotted "Dainty" Ironmonger bowling in a match at Ipswich. He recommended to the MCC on his return that the club sign Ironmonger.

"Trumble was one of the great bowlers of history," Johnny Moyes summed up. "He had a flight which annoyed and often perplexed the batsman as the ball would drop a little shorter

Hugh Trumble, an uncommonly shrewd allrounder who performed two Test hat-tricks with off-breaks.

1007

than seemed probable. He would often attack the batsman's strength by feeding the cover drive until the strokemaker did not get quite to the pitch of the ball, and spooned up a catch to the cover fielders. Able to stand the strain of the longest day, imperturbable, resourceful, this giant ranks with the immortals of the bowling art."

In all first-class matches he took five wickets in an innings 69 times and 10 wickets in a match 25 times. He made three centuries and held 329 catches. His best bowling figures for his State were:

7 for 52 v. New South Wales, 1887–88
7 for 89, 8 for 113 v. South Australia, 1889–90
8 for 129, 3 for 36 v. South Australia, 1898–99
8 for 58, 3 for 45 v. New South Wales, 1898–99
8 for 39, 3 for 57 v. South Australia, 1898–99
7 for 54 v. New South Wales, 1900–01

Right to the end he was a remarkable storehouse of cricket legends. When Jack Ryder crashed a mass of sixes into the MCG stands on his way to 295 in 1926 against New South Wales, one paper wrote that Ryder had missed a crate of champagne by not hitting the MCG clock. Next day reporters rushed to Trumble to ask about the champagne. "Break the clock? Nobody has ever done it," Trumble said. "Champagne? I've never heard of champagne being offered. If it had been I would have had a go myself."

TRUMBLE, John William, 1863–1944

First-Class Averages: Batting, 1,761 runs at 18.93; Bowling 109 wickets at 24.10.

Tests (7): 243 runs at 20.25; 10 wickets at 22.20.

The elder Trumble, a splendid allrounder for Victoria who made a big impression at an early age and was chosen for the 1886 Australian tour of England at 23. He was not the success his admirers expected, scoring 823 runs at an average of 18.70, highest score 56 not out and taking 30 wickets at 26.76.

In January, 1890, he made 116 for Melbourne University against Sydney University. Thereafter his work as a solicitor restricted his first-class appearances. As a batsman, he had a very strong defence and could hit hard when required. He was a very smart fieldsman and bowled with accuracy, but he lacked hostility. He bowled 19 maidens in 20 overs playing for the Australian XI against Victoria at Melbourne early in 1886. For Victoria, in eleven-a-side matches, he played 18 times for 508 runs, average 16.38, and captured 54 wickets at 23.59.

In 1926, J. W. Trumble suggested a public subscription for the famous Australian umpire, Bob Crockett, who had built a considerable reputation for fairness in 33 Tests but had never been to England. The fund raised enough to send Crockett and his wife to England for the 1926 Test series. J. W. Trumble was one of the few Australian cricket experts to defend Larwood's bowling as fair during the 1932 Bodyline debates.

Right: Bruce Laird, one of the hardest-hitting batsmen in Australian cricket pulls a ball to the leg boundary.

Below: Rick McCosker cuts a ball down to the third man fence.

Rodney Hogg, one of Australia's fastest bowlers in recent years.

A right-hand opening batsmen whose stroke play had a magic all its own. Others have scored more runs and more centuries, but for all who saw him he was the most brilliant of all Australian batsmen. He was a useful right-arm medium pace bowler, and a magnificent field with a powerful throwing arm, but it was the artistry of his batting that produced a legend as strong today as when he died 67 years ago.

For all that he was a scruffy genius, batting in crumpled shirts and baggy pants. His cricket bag was a mess of dirty clothes, mud-spattered bats and pads and grubby socks. He was a soft touch for cadgers and those down on their luck, a teetotaller and non-smoker who never kept late hours, worshipped his wife and family, but died in great pain from Bright's disease, aged 37. He was such a man that on the rare occasions that he was bowled he would stop before he left and apologetically replace the bails.

On tour in England with an Australian team he emerged from a music hall and spotted a boy shivering in the rain selling sheet music. He went over and bought the boy's entire stock. He hated self-promotion, cared little about his appearance, and often chastised team-mates who, having scored a century, tried for another. He once ran out Warren Bardsley deliberately. When Bardsley complained, he said that having scored one century Bardsley had had enough and it was time to give others a knock. Monty Noble said, "It did not worry Trumper in the slightest that his cricket gear was disgracefully creased, nor did the jocular epithets about owning a cricket bag that was so untidy it was the only one in the Australian team nobody could close."

Ever since Trumper died people who knew him have tried to explain the curious mystique Trumper conveyed, aware that he was a most uncommon man. Of his personality, his one-time team-mate Frank Iredale wrote in *33 Years Of Cricket*, "To be near him seemed to me to be an honour. His was one of those natures which called to you, in whose presence you felt it good to live. I never knew anybody who practised self-effacement as much as he did." Of his batting C. B. Fry wrote: "He had no style and yet he was all style."

The famous English cricket historian Harry Altham said in *The World of Cricket*, "The measure of Trumper's genius is not to be found in any figures: it was essentially qualitative rather than quantitative, revealed in terms of spontaneous art rather than in any acquired technique. He had the lissom and co-ordinated body of a natural athlete; like all great batsmen he seemed to sight the ball as soon as it left the bowler's hand, and he moved into his strokes with effortless and perfectly balanced ease. There was no limit to his range, or flaw in their fluency or timing; the better the bowling, the more difficult the wicket, the more likely was his genius to rise to the challenge."

TRUMPER, Victor Thomas, 1877–1915

First-Class Averages: Batting, 16,939 runs at 44.57; Bowling, 64 wickets at 31.73.

Tests (48): 3,163 runs at 39.04; 8 wickets at 37.62.

Trumper was born in the Sydney suburb of Darlinghurst, the first son of a London-born migrant who had tried life in New Zealand before settling in Sydney. His father was a short man with a goatee beard and keen sense of fun. His mother, the former Louise Coughlan, was three years older than her husband. There were eight children in the family the Trumpers brought up in a terrace house at 112 Paddington Street, Paddington, where Trumper senr. taught his eldest son the piano.

Victor went to Crown Street, a government school in an underprivileged suburb, where Monty Noble was a school-mate but a few years ahead. At lunchtime and before and after school, the boys played cricket, with the boy who dismissed the batsman next man in. Trumper once batted for six weeks. When his father asked him how he was going at school, he simply said, "I'm still in." He played Rugby each winter and joined the South Sydney Rugby Club after he left school. He played, too, for South Sydney Cricket Club before joining Paddington.

When Victor's father realised his son had special talent for cricket, he began taking him to a concrete pitch on Moore Park for two hours each morning before he went to work and Victor had to go to school. Trumper's skill was so pronounced at school he was barred from some matches by opponents who could not get him out. He went to the South Sydney Cricket Club at 17, and although he did not make big scores in his two seasons with that club he was invited to play for NSW Colts against Stoddart's England XI in December, 1894. He was ill on the morning of the match but scored an impressive 67. Then he went home to bed for some days.

Trumper's stance was easy, relaxed. He stood up straight at the crease, preferring open-slatted pads, but scorning gloves, which he said cost him a loss of touch with the bat. He disliked grips on his bat handles and preferred to rough up the corn binding on his bats by using glass or resin. He wanted the weight of the bat to be in the centre, not the bottom, and frequently shaved off thick portions at the bottom of his bats. His brothers, Sid and Charlie, were educated at Sydney Grammar School and because he sometimes practised with them at their school's nets people mistakenly thought he went to Grammar.

After he left Crown Street, he was a teacher for a short time, then a storeman for the NSW Government, a clerk in the Government Printing Office, and next a clerk with Tom Garrett, the former Australian bowler who was Registrar of Probates and Curator of Intestate Estates. Then he opened a sports store in partnership with Hanson Carter, but delayed the opening of this venture until Syd Gregory, whom he did not want to hurt, closed down his sports shop. He had three sports stores altogether. Later he joined J. J.Giltinan in a shirt

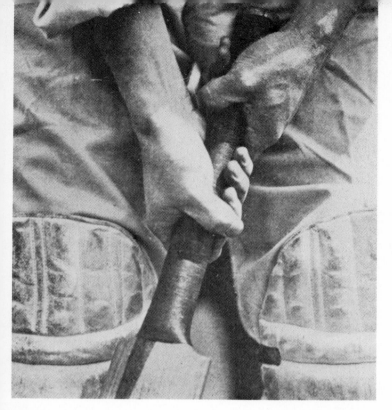

and tie shop, and during this period he became the first secretary of the Australian Rugby Football League, with Giltinan a foundation member. The meetings that founded Rugby League in Australia were held in Trumper's shop.

When he had the sports stores, Trumper entertained newsboys when they came to buy their cricket gear, helped them select their pads and bats, and then handed them back their money. His father tried his hand at running a slipper factory but like Victor he had little business acumen. There was the time when Victor was late for a match and without a bat, so he grabbed one from stock, went and made a century with it, and returned it to stock—marked at half-price because it was second-hand.

The Sydney Cricket Ground Trust gave membership to all schoolboys and students at a special rate of half a guinea. This gave the boys use of all practice wickets and admission to pavilions. Schools were offered a special net for £7 10s for the summer, but Sydney Grammar was the only school to take this offer. Charles Bannerman coached at the nets and gave Victor special advice on defence, but gave up the tuition when Trumper insisted on chasing balls wide of the stumps to cut and drive or pull. The critics claimed Victor was too flashy and they appeared to be right when he failed on his first appearance for NSW in 1894–95 against South Australia at Adelaide, and against Queensland in Sydney.

After these failures Trumper was omitted from the State side for two years, but in November, 1896, he made 113 for the next XV against NSW on the SCG. It was at this time that Noble induced him to transfer to Paddington, where Noble was captain. Noble could see that the South Sydney club would disappear with the introduction of electorate cricket, and he knew that at Paddington's Hampden Oval Trumper would have a first-class turf pitch on which to bat. In the 1897–98 season Trumper had scores of 82 against North Sydney, 123 against Central Cumberland, 125 against his old club, South Sydney, 85 against Waverley, 120 not out against Glebe, 191 not out against Burwood, 133 against Redfern, and 162 not out against Leichhardt, finishing the season with 1,021 runs at 204.20.

For a gentle man, there was a defiance in his batting that expressed itself well in grade cricket. When a young bowler bragged that he could get Trumper out any time, Trumper hit 32 runs off his first over. He blocked the first ball, and then destroyed the braggart by hitting 50 off the next 10 balls he received from him.

Monty Noble, an ardent Trumper fan, argued for Trumper's inclusion in the 1899 Australian team to England. Hugh Trumble, of Victoria, Joe Darling, of South Australia, and Syd Gregory, NSW, were the selectors and of these only Gregory

Victor Trumper driving a goat cart during the 1902 Australian tour of England.

agreed with Noble that Trumper should tour. Trumble and Darling argued that Trumper had failed in most of his appearances for NSW and there were plenty of young players with far better figures to support their inclusion in the Australian team. Two notable successes with the bat in 1898–99 were 292 not out for NSW v Tasmania and 253 for NSW v New Zealand, both in Sydney. Noble tried hard to persuade Trumble to pick Trumper but the team was announced without him. Then a vice-president of the Melbourne Cricket Club, J. McLauchlin, saw Trumper make 260 not out for Paddington in Sydney, and returned to Melbourne to inform the cricket fraternity that he had seen a genius bat.

Before the Australian team sailed to England three warm-up matches were played against the Rest Of Australia, one in Sydney, one in Melbourne and the final one in Adelaide. Joe Darling described in his son's book *Test Tussles On And Off The Field* how Trumper played only fairly in the first two matches and then played a magnificent innings of 75 in Adelaide. "Trumble and I were then convinced that Trumper was a coming champion and we realised we had made a mistake in not selecting him, owing to the chance that we had never seen him at his best," said Darling. The team organisers decided to take an extra player, at a reduced fee, with the extra man acting as an assistant to the manager, Major Ben Wardill, and assisting with team autographs, laundry and letters. Trumper went on an agreed bonus of £200, the rest of the team on £700.

He was clean bowled in five of his first seven innings in England, but impressed Darling and Trumble enough at the nets to win selection for his First Test at Trent Bridge. Hearne bowled him for a duck in the first innings, and Jackson bowled him for 11 in the second innings. The Australian selectors boldly stuck with what they saw in the nets and picked him again for the Second Test at Lord's. Here at the age of 21 Trumper made a chanceless 135 not out to give Australia victory by 10 wickets. Ernie Jones had match figures of 10 for 164 and Clem Hill made 135, but these efforts were completely overshadowed by the artistry of Trumper's batting. For the rest of the tour Joe Darling always asked if Trumper was aboard before he let the Australians' coach leave for the grounds.

Against Sussex at Brighton Australia scored 4 for 624, Trumper batting brilliantly for 300 not out, the first triple century by an Australian in England. But this innings noticeably sapped his strength and for weeks Darling seldom used him as a bowler. But because of the triple century against Sussex a team meeting decided to put Trumper on the same financial terms as his team-mates. He finished the tour in fifth place in the Australian averages, with 1,556 runs from 32 matches at 34.57. Noble predicted then that he would become an even greater batsman than Ranjitsinhji. At home in 1899–1900 he made 644 runs in eight innings at 80.50, including 165 against South Australia at Adelaide. In 1900–01, he made 230 against Victoria at Sydney, finishing with 458 runs at 65.43.

In 1901–02 he took an office job involving night work which affected his eyesight and he was a major disappointment against McLaren's England team, with a topscore of only 65 in the Tests. Back in England in 1902 the Trumper wizardry blossomed again and he carried all before him, scoring 11 centuries and playing innings of 92 against Gloucestershire and 96 against The Players despite a wet and miserable summer. Many of his big innings that season were played on "sticky" wickets and he came to be regarded as the best of all Australia's great batsmen on rain-affected pitches. At Old Trafford he opened for Australia with Reg Duff in the Fourth Test, and in 108 minutes before lunch made 103, taking Australia's score to 1 for 173. This feat has only been equalled three times since in Tests (by Macartney, Bradman and Majid Khan), and it proved to be decisive in a match that Australia won by only three runs, the closest runs margin in Tests.

He batted throughout that English season with a carefree spirit that infected all his team-mates, defying testing conditions and performing just as brilliantly after a night's rain as he did on hard dry pitches. "All bowling came alike to him, and he reduced our best bowling for the time being to the level of the village green," said *Wisden*. "They were simply incapable of checking his wonderful hitting. The way in which he took good length balls and sent them to the boundary had to be seen to be believed. His cutting and off-driving approaches perfection, and he did everything with such a grace of style that his batting was always a delight to the eye." Trumper made 2,570 runs at 48.49 on the tour, without showing the slightest interest in ever going on to a double century. His aggregate easily surpassed Joe Darling's previous tour record of 1,941 runs set in 1899. Of his 11 innings over 100, his topscore was only 128.

Trumper returned to England in 1905 and 1909 but he was never again so pre-eminent. He was fifth in the averages in 1905 with 1,754 runs at 36.54 and in 1909 was overshadowed by Bardsley, Armstrong and Ransford, finishing with 1,435 runs at 33.37. But he continued to produce innings of sheer magic, notably against England at The Oval in 1909 when he treated the googlies of D. W. Carr with nonchalant ease as he breezed to 73. He appeared in South Africa with the 1902 team and in New Zealand with the 1905 side.

Among his finest performances at home were his 178 in a first wicket stand of 298 with Duff against South Australia in 1902–03, a 267-run stand with Duff for the first wicket against Victoria in the same season, and 101 out of 139 in 57 minutes on a wicket favouring the bowlers for NSW against Victoria

Trumper preferred open-slatted pads and bats without grips.

A series of George Beldam photographs of Victor Trumper on driving.

at Sydney in 1905–06. For NSW against Victoria in 1903–04, Trumper and Duff made 113 for the first wicket in the first innings, and 119 without being separated in the second innings, NSW winning the match by 10 wickets. Trumper's scores were 53 and 53 not out, Duff's 67 and 62 not out. In 1906–07, Trumper made 119 out of 150 in 101 minutes for NSW against Victoria. He scored 62 out of 81 runs, and completed his 100 out of 124 in 90 minutes. He scored 20 runs (five fours) off an over from Gervys Hazlitt for NSW v. Victoria in 1907–08.

In grade cricket, Trumper built an enormous following. Cricket lovers flocked to Sydney's suburban grounds to see him do great things and were seldom disappointed. For in 19 consecutive seasons he made 8,946 runs at an average of 69.34, including 28 centuries for Paddington and eight for Gordon. A striking example of his hitting powers was his knock of 335 at Redfern Oval in January, 1903, when he and Dan Gee put on 423 for the first wicket in 135 minutes. Trumper hit 22 fives, 39 fours, no threes, 16 twos and 37 singles and gave chances at 195, 287 and 310 in an innings that progressed this way:

```
 50 in  20 minutes (Trumper,  45; Gee,    5).
100 in  45 minutes (Trumper,  80; Gee,   20).
198 in  75 minutes (Trumper, 103; Gee,   95).
300 in 100 minutes (Trumper, 166; Gee,  125).
352 in 120 minutes (Trumper, 200; Gee,  143).
402 in 127 minutes (Trumper, 234; Gee,  159).
423 in 135 minutes (Trumper, 242; Gee   172).
501 in 167 minutes (Trumper, 301).
558 in 180 minutes (Trumper, 335).
```

Paddington declared at 9 for 618 and won by an innings and 443 runs.

When Trumper scored 189 not out for Paddington against Waverley in October, 1904, he hit 15 fives, 22 fours or 163 in boundaries. The following season he made 215 out of 330 in 110 minutes for Paddington against Redfern, in an opening stand that went this way:

```
 50 in  25 minutes (Trumper,  35; Chapman,  15).
 79 in  32 minutes (Trumper,  53; Chapman,  26).
100 in  38 minutes (Trumper,  68; Chapman,  32).
131 in  52 minutes (Trumper,  81; Chapman,  50).
150 in  60 minutes (Trumper,  94; Chapman,  56).
157 in  63 minutes (Trumper, 100; Chapman,  57).
200 in  80 minutes (Trumper, 135; Chapman,  64).
303 in 102 minutes (Trumper, 198; Chapman, 104).
330 in 110 minutes (Trumper, 215; Chapman, 110).
```

1016

The Off Drive

The Late Cut

The Straight Drive

The Pull

1017

Small wonder that cartoonists had a field day with feats of this brilliance or that his Testimonial match between NSW and the Rest of Australia at Sydney in February, 1913, produced the handsome sum—for that time—of £2,950. He even figured in Australian ballads, which saw this tribute by Guy Eden in his *Bush Ballads And Other Verses*:

"Oh! he's just a dandy batsman, he's a rajah, he's a toff,
Widout any fancy feelin' for the 'on' or for the 'off,'
He just takes his bat, and thin, wid one apologetic cough,
Sets to work to play the divil wid the bowlin'."

Trumper's parents moved from Paddington to a new home in Help Street, Chatswood, on the western side of Chatswood station, in 1908. They bought a large stone house that stood on a large block of land and then built several cottages around it. Victor married Sarah Ann Briggs on June 7, 1904. She was a sister of the wife of J. J. Kelly, the Australian wicket-keeper, and Victor first met her during one of his visits to Melbourne when he stayed with the Kellys. Trumper had two children, Ann Louise, who died of leukemia at 50, and **Victor Trumper junior** (1913–1981), who played six matches for NSW in 1940–41. His son was a left-handed batsman and right-arm fast medium bowler who played for the Manly club. Trumper, jnr, scored 74 runs at 7.40 in first-class cricket and took 12 wickets at 36.08. Trumper jnr, always delighted in playing at Trumper Park, the new name for Hampden Oval, Paddington. Trumper, senr, always lived with his parents, probably because he wanted his wife to have friends near when he was away on cricket tours. Charlie Macartney lived nearby and sometimes practised on Trumper's backyard pitch.

Neville Cardus said that when Victor Trumper was out the light seemed to go out for a time on an Australian innings. "Imagine Spooner's cover drive, Hirst's pull, MacLaren's hook, J. T. Tyldesley's square cut, Macartney's late cut through the slips—imagine a mingling of all these attributes of five great and wholly different batsmen, and perhaps some notion of Trumper will emerge in the mind," Cardus wrote. "The grand manner of MacLaren, the lyrical grace of Spooner, the lion energy of Jessop, the swift opportunist spirit of Tyldesley—all these excellences were compounded proportionately in Trumper."

Trumper toured New Zealand with an Australian team in 1913–14, although his health was beginning to break down. In one brilliant innings against Canterbury at Christchurch, he and Arthur Sims scored 433 for the eighth wicket at 144 runs an hour, Trumper contributing 293. It was his last great effort. In the 19 seasons between 1894–95 and 1913–14, Trumper scored 42 centuries, took 171 catches and twice took five wickets in an innings with his medium-pacers, best figures 5 for 19 against Cambridge University in 1902. He had nine innings over 200, and a topscore of 300 not out.

A swarthy left-hand opening batsman whose consistent success in Sheffield Shield cricket made him a regular contender for a Test place in the mid-1970s. He hit the ball hard and had a splendid temperament but failed to make the big scores required to make his Test place automatic. He showed his best form in 1975–76 as a member of the Australian team that outplayed the then world champion West Indian team. He had scores of 81, 53, and 136 in helping Australia win the rubber 5–1.

TURNER, Alan, 1950–

Turner played first grade for the Randwick club in Sydney at 17. He made his debut for New South Wales in 1968–69, scoring 89 in the second innings against Victoria. He toured New Zealand in 1969–70 in the side captained by Sam Trimble, scoring 117 runs at 19.50 in four first-class matches. He made his initial first-class century, 110 against Queensland in Sydney in 1971–72 and 127 against Western Australia at Perth in the same season. In 1973–74 he got another century (100) against Queensland in Brisbane. In 1974–75, he scored 578 at 32.11 for NSW and his consistency earned him a place in the 1975 Australian team in England.

First-Class Averages: Batting, 5,744 runs at 30.88; Bowling, 1 wicket at 10.00.

Tests (14): 768 runs at 29.54.

He made 156 against Kent at Canterbury, an innings sprinkled with full-blooded square cuts and powerful leg-side pulls and sweeps. This won him a place in the First Test at Birmingham, which Australia won by an innings and 85 runs

after being sent in to bat. Turner made 37 in an 80-run opening stand with Rick McCosker that put Australia on the path to victory. Another highspot of that tour was Turner's century before lunch in the World Cup match against Sri Lanka at The Oval.

The climax of his career came at Adelaide in the Fifth Test against the West Indies, when he put on 148 for the first wicket with Ian Redpath in Australia's second innings. Turner made 136, Redpath 65, to set up a win that clinched the series for Australia. They were particularly severe on Lance Gibbs, who during this match dismissed Ashley Mallett to take his 307th Test wicket and equal Fred Trueman's world record. This was Turner's sole Test century in a career that yielded seven first-class hundreds. He toured New Zealand for the second time in 1976–77, scoring 184 runs at 20.44 in five first-class matches for the team captained by Greg Chappell. He retired at the end of the following Australian season from first-class cricket but continued to play grade cricket for Randwick. He was in the Randwick team that won the Sydney premiership in 1981–82 for the third time since Turner joined the club in 1967.

TURNER, Charles Thomas Biass ("The Terror"), 1862–1944

First-Class Averages: Batting, 3,856 runs at 15.54; Bowling, 993 wickets at 14.24.

Tests (17): 323 runs at 11.53; 101 wickets at 16.53.

A right-hand, front-on medium pace bowler of the highest class who turned the ball viciously from the off. Turner was the successor to Spofforth as the second great Australian bowler. He delivered the ball from a low arm action, his whole body facing the batsman. He was a forceful batsman who probably would have won a big reputation for run-scoring had he not devoted so much energy to bowling. On the 1888 Australian tour of England Turner bowled an astonishing 2,589.3 overs, with 1,222 maidens, taking 314 tour wickets at 11.12 each!

Turner was born at Bathurst in the New South Wales midwest and was educated at Bathurst Grammar but he was not in the First XI. But he had the country boy's great strength of limb and wind and enormous hands. Late in his life Arthur Mailey visited him at his home and asked how Turner had produced such sharp turn. Turner went to a dish full of oranges on his mantlepiece and crushed an orange to pulp in his fingers.

In 1881–82, Turner was chosen for Twenty Two of Bathurst against Alfred Shaw's English Team. He took 7 for 33 in the first innings and all 10 for 36 in the second innings. Despite this prodigious feat it still took another year for him to get an invitation to play for New South Wales. He made his debut for the State in 1882–83. Country cricketers have taken some fearful blows at the hands of capital city selectors but surely

1020

this has to be the worst of all. Fancy rolling over all ten Englishmen in an innings and having to wait another year to play for your State!

Turner's big chance came with his selection for the first of his three tours of England in 1888. With left-armer Ferris at the other end, he had the top English batsmen almost in a state of terror. Haygarth's authoritative *Scores And Biographies* described the condition of English batsmen facing Turner and Ferris as "one of near panic". W. G. Grace said Turner came off the pitch faster than any bowler he had faced except George Freeman. Sir Stanley Jackson, great English captain, rated Turner the best medium pacer he ever had to face. The famous English cricket historian Harry Altham, gave this account of the 1888 feats of stamina by Turner and Ferris: "It is usual today to suggest that a bowler who approaches 1,000 overs in a season has endured more than flesh and blood can stand, so the record of Turner and Ferris in the tour of '88 may come as something of a revelation. Necessity, it is said, knows no law, and there was certainly necessity enough, for with the exception of Harry Trott's leg-spinners there was no other bowling of merit in the side. Turner and Ferris knew that until and unless they got the other side out, their fellows would continue in the field. Bowl they had to, and bowl they did.

"Together they took 534 wickets or just 405 more than the rest of the Australian team put together, and this against the flower of English batting, with hardly a rest in 20 weeks. Admittedly, the season was one of the wettest on record, but even so their performances were really astonishing." Note that these were four ball overs.

So stunned were English cricketers by Turner's bowling that they wheeled him off for special tests at Woolwich Observatory, near London. Woolwich chronographs established that the pace of a Turner delivery midway between the bowler's crease and the batting end was 81 ft per second or 55 miles an hour. This is not a frightening speed when compared with the pace, say, of Larwood, Lindwall, Thomson or Ted McDonald, but the secret of Turner's success was in what happened to the ball after it bounced. He could break it both ways but from the off he was quite deadly and he mixed up his breaks and his bowling speed with devilish cunning, letting the ball go from the curious front-on action no coach would recommend.

On his three tours of England, Turner's results were 314 wickets at 11.12 in 1888 , 215 wickets at 12.67 in 1890, and 149 for 14.25 each in 1893. He bowled so long, usually with maiden overs galore, even his 5 ft 8 in, 12 stone frame did not have much spark left for batting. But he still managed 103 for Australia against Surrey at The Oval in 1888 and 102 for Australia v. The Rest at Sydney not long afterwards, on this occasion scoring his 102 while A. C. Bannerman collected 32 in a first wicket partnership of 144. For New South Wales in 1890–91, he scored 70 of the 92 runs put on for the first wicket in 72 minutes against Victoria.

No other Australian bowler has taken 100 wickets in an Australian first-class season as Turner did in 1887–88, 106 wickets at 13.59. In first-class matches between October, 1886, and September, 1888, Turner took 492 wickets at 11.12 apiece. For New South Wales against Victoria in Melbourne in 1886–87, he performed the hat-trick, and in a match between the same States three years later in Sydney a bail landed 41 yards from the wicket after he had hit the stumps. In 1888 he took 17 wickets, with 8 for 13 and 9 for 37, against an England XI at Hastings, having earlier in the same season taken 9 for 15 in an innings against an England XI at Stoke—the other man was run out. Bowling against the North of England at Manchester in 1888, he took three wickets in four balls, finishing with 12 for 64. For New South Wales v. Victoria at Sydney in 1891–92, he took 15 wickets for 174 runs.

In among all these phenomenal feats, Turner prized his 6 wickets for 35 runs in a total of 200 for New South Wales against South Australia at Sydney in 1895–96. Only one ball of the 261 he delivered in that innings reached the boundary. He bowled unchanged through many innings. With Ferris in 1888 against Middlesex at Lord's, against Derbyshire at Derby, against an English XI at Stoke, they bowled unchanged through both innings of the match. Two years later this remarkable twosome did it again v. Warwickshire at Edgbaston and v. Staffordshire at Stoke.

In all first-class matches Turner took five wickets in an innings 102 times and 10 wickets in a match 35 times. He held 85 catches. Turner finished his Test career in 1894–95 and 87 years later, in 1982, his bowling average of 16.53 (101 Test wickets) is still unchallenged by any bowler for Australia.

TYSON, Frank Holmes ("Typhoon"), 1930– A Lancashire-born pace bowler who, after a brief but spectacular career with Northants and England, settled in Australia where he became a successful schoolmaster, author, broadcaster and coach. He has had a strong influence on the Victorian team for more than 10 years, and has been the Victorian Cricket Association's Director of Coaching since 1975, a post which enabled him to give up teaching after 13 years at Carey, a leading Melbourne Grammar School.

Tyson trialled with Lancashire but for some reason did not find a place in the County team. To play first-class cricket, he had to move to Northampton, where England captain Freddie Brown groomed him. Brown, who had watched Lindwall and Miller give English batsmen a battering for years, kept Tyson in wraps until the 1953 Australian team's match against Northants. Brown's delight was unrestrained as Tyson gave the cream of Australian batsmanship a dusting. He was fearsomely fast as he let the ball go at the end of an approach of some 50 paces and even full tosses and half-volleys found their way past the bat through sheer pace.

In Australia in 1954–55 Tyson formed a devasting partnership with Brian Statham. His action demanded a lot from even his immensely strong frame, particularly on the final jarring delivery stride. It seemed obvious he could not last on very hard pitches but he virtually traded a longer career for one season of glory. At Brisbane he took 1 for 160. At Sydney he cut down his run and took 4 for 45 and 6 for 85. At Melbourne he bowled as fast as anyone has ever done in Australia, skittling Australia out for 111 by taking 7 for 27 after Australia needed 165 to win on the final day with eight wickets in hand. He took 28 wickets at 20.82 in the series.

The injuries started to come and he played only a few Tests between 1954 and his last Test in 1959, but he gave a superb performance on a fast Trent Bridge strip against South Africa in 1955, taking 6 for 28. He toured Australia and New Zealand for a second time in 1958–59, and South Africa in 1956–57 but never again recaptured the pace of the last four Tests of the 1954–55 series in Australia when he throughly earned the "Typhoon Tyson" tag.

Tyson married an Australian girl, Ursula Miels, of Melbourne, and they have a son and and two daughters. As a graduate of Durham University he was well qualified to take senior teaching jobs in Australia, though parents of his pupils sometimes felt their offspring were neglected because of his pre-occupation with cricket. As a coach, his Victorian teams have had only limited success. He is perhaps the only great pace bowler who can quote Keats and Shakespeare. In a career that lasted only from 1952 to 1960, Tyson scored 4,103 runs at 17.09 and took 766 wickets at 20.92. In 17 Tests for England he scored 230 runs at 10.95 and took 76 wickets at 18.56.

"Typhoon" Tyson used all the power of his immense physique to produce extreme pace.

U

UMPIRES

From the time the game began in Australia, cricketers have always adhered to the Laws of Cricket laid down by the MCC and have accepted that the umpire's duties should be carried out as those laws dictate. Periodically local laws have been tried. In the late 1920s the New South Wales Cricket Association allowed eight runs for hits over the fence to try and foster brighter Sydney club cricket. The experiment lasted only one season. Nobody has ever suggested an Australian set of cricket laws. This has not prevented the umpires who have interpreted and arbitrated on the MCC's laws from doing so in a highly individual manner. Some of the most colourful personalities in Australian cricket have been umpires. Here is a review of some of the most striking incidents involving those umpires and how they were handled:

PRE-WORLD WAR I UMPIRES

The first of all Tests at Melbourne in 1877 was umpired by C. A. Reid and R. B. Terry, who were kept busy until the fourth day. Dave Gregory ran himself out in the first innings of the match but walked off before an umpiring decision was made. The rest of the innings proceeded without incident, each dismissed batsman leaving as he was caught or bowled. In England's first innings, opener H. Jupp had reached 54 when he played back. The Australians appealed, believing Jupp had broken his own wicket, but umpire Reid had missed it, and gave Jupp not out. This could be counted the first controversial umpiring decision in Test cricket, except that the players accepted the decision without the slightest argument. Jupp was out (after adding nine runs) for 63. In the whole match Reid and Terry gave three lbw decisions in Australia's favour and one in England's favour. Each time the batsmen walked without argument when the decision was given. For the return match a fortnight later, Terry, who had played first-class cricket with Nottingham before migrating to Australia, was joined by Sam Cosstick, who worked as a ground bowler for Melbourne Cricket Club members. Again all the umpires' decisions were accepted without a murmur although this time

1024

they had a tricky stumping by Blackham off Spofforth to dismiss Shaw to arbitrate on and later the run out of Hill for 49 was a near thing.

The Third England v. Australia Test at Melbourne in January, 1879, was umpired by George Coulthard, a Victorian who accompanied the England team throughout the tour, and P. Coady and this, too, went off without incident. On February 7, at Sydney, the same England team played New South Wales on what was then called the Association Ground. Several of the NSW players had been in the first Australian team to tour England under Dave Gregory and had complained about the umpires in England, whom they claimed were a bunch of professionals in the pay of wealthy amateur players, and against decisions in Philadelphia, where they had walked off the ground. Now in NSW's second innings against Lord Harris' team local hero Billy Murdoch, who had made 82 not out in the first innings, was given run out by umpire Coulthard. There was immediate uproar in the crowd and the NSW captain, Dave Gregory, refused to play until Coulthard was replaced. Lord Harris refused and an angry mob invaded the field. Mounted police tried to restore order and at one stage Lord Harris was struck by a larrikin, who was immediately bundled from the field by A. N. Hornby. Play was then abandoned but continued next day. Recriminations over the Murdoch run out and the resultant riot continued for months. Lord Harris claimed that the other umpire, Edmund Barton, later Prime Minister of Australia, was prepared to award England the match if a NSW batsman did not appear to replace

The contents of umpire Tom Brooks' pockets for a Test match: 1, carry-all purse; 2, spare bail; 3, insect repellant; 4, salt tablets; 5, towel; 6, ball counter; 7, over counter; 8, sticking plaster; 9, bootlaces; 10, band aids; 11, boot scraper; 12, safety pins; 13, sprig spanners; 14, pocket knife; 15, aspirin; 16, chewing-gum; 17, nail file; 18, scissors; 19, bowler's mark. Umpires also carry a ball-sizing ring and a spare ball.

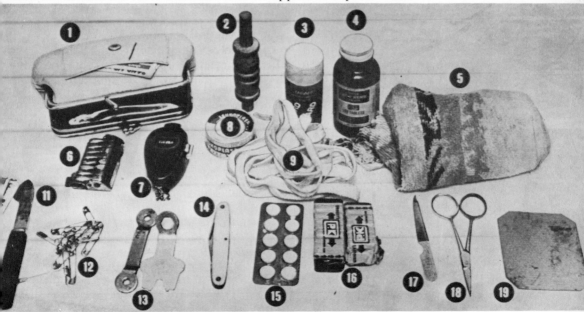

Murdoch, but the crowd had rioted before that was possible. Anyway the Australian team that toured England the following year found matches hard to get because of Lord Harris' displeasure over the Sydney riot.

There was no organisation for training and appointing umpires in those early years and the teams usually agreed on the appointments in pre-match discussions. James Lillywhite umpired the four Tests in Australia in 1881–82 (and one three years later), local man John Swift joining him in the first three Tests, and George Coulthard in the fourth. Swift, a wicketkeeper in three games for Victoria, continued in the job in 1882–83, and when he retired in 1887 had eight Tests to his credit. He helped set the trend of former players taking over as umpires when big matches came round. P. G. McShane, J. J. Hodges, and Charles Bannerman were among the Test players who later stood as umpires. McShane, in fact, umpired a Test before he played in one, in 1884–85. Bannerman umpired 12 Tests but was generally agreed to be a better batsman than umpire. The first great Australian umpire was James Phillips, whose no-balling of chuckers in Australia and England was universally applauded and led to a campaign that cleared them from the game, for a time at least. Phillips umpired 13 Tests in Australia between 1885 and 1898, 29 Tests in all. Another great Australian umpire, Bob Crockett, took over when Phillips went off to make his fortune mining in North America. Crockett still holds the record for most Test appearances by an Australian umpire, 32. He began in December, 1901 at Sydney and umpired his last Test in February, 1925 at Sydney. A stony-faced, meticulous man, renowned for his fairness, he made many controversial decisions but always tried to uphold the spirit of the game. Once when a fieldsman anxious to prevent another over kicked a ball to the boundary to waste time, Crockett refused to allow four. They called him the "Chief Justice," an umpire without mannerisms who never played up to the crowd or moved to distract a bowler or batsman. Every night after stumps he discussed the day's play in his room at the Melbourne Cricket Ground with friends over drinks. You knew you had "arrived" when Crockett invited you to one of these sessions.

UMPIRES BETWEEN THE WARS

Crockett retired before the biggest of all umpiring crises in Australia, the Bodyline series, but he set standards that helped guide George Borwick and George Hele in handling that series. Borwick and Hele umpired throughout that summer without having to rule the main issue—intimidation—as no law existed then on the excessive use of bouncers. To their credit, they finished the most argumentative rubber on record well liked by the players because of their equable temperaments. Borwick umpired 84 first-class matches in all, 24 of them Tests between 1931 and 1948. He saw umpires change

from obscure sporting figures whose names were seldom mentioned in match reports to headline personalities whose decisions were debated for days. In December, 1936, Borwick was at square leg when he no-balled Queensland Aboriginal Eddie Gilbert for throwing after rearing balls caused three NSW batsmen, Harold Mudge, R. H. Robinson, and Bob Hynes to retire hurt. In January, 1937, he was at the centre of a dispute in the Melbourne Test against England when "Gubby" Allen walked off with last man Bill Voce, saying "I've had it." England were 9 for 76, batting on a wet pitch. Don Bradman asked Borwick if Allen had announced what he was doing. Borwick said, "We take it he's declared." When Bradman stressed that he hadn't heard Allen declare, Borwick ran off the ground, but four minutes were wasted before he confirmed the England declaration. Reversing his batting order to waste further time, Bradman ended up winning the match handsomely and saving the series. Borwick umpired in a high-scoring era, standing while seven of the 46 centuries scored in his 24 Tests went past 200. But he always said Bradman's 103 not out in the Second Test of the Bodyline series was the best innings Bradman ever played. Bradman had been out first ball in the first innings and was still in the 90s with last man, Bert Ironmonger, managing to stay with him while he completed his 100. Another outstanding umpire of the 1930s was Andy Barlow, who stood in 11 Tests between 1931 and 1951. This was the period that saw the start of dramatic appeals by the fielding side. Queenslanders blamed Don Tallon's spectacular appeals after he made catches or stumpings on his absence from the 1938 Australian team in England.

UMPIRES SINCE WORLD WAR II

Umpiring became a major issue immediately Tests resumed in Australia with the England-Australia Test at Brisbane in 1946–47. Bradman was given not out in response to an appeal for a catch in slips by Ikin, and proceeded to add a match-winning 276 with Hassett for the third wicket. After almost daily criticism of his decisions in that rubber umpire Jack Scott visited the press box before the start of a day's play in Melbourne to see how the angle 150 yards away compared with his own from 22-yard range. The London Star's L. N. Bailey told Scott: "If you're in the slightest doubt about an lbw decision, Jack, just look up here, and we'll give you the sign." Scott retired at the end of that series and George Borwick was paired with Andy Barlow for the India-Australia Tests the next summer. In the Second Test at Sydney there was a furore when Vinoo Mankad made Test history by running out Bill Brown for backing up too far at the bowler's end. Mankad had run out Brown in the same manner in the match between India and an Australian XI.

Above: (L to R) Colin Egar, Mel McInnes, Lou Rowan.

In the 1950s another outstanding umpire appeared, Mel McInnes, who was to stand in 16 Tests and win admiration from Test players throughout the world for his judgment and impartiality. But McInnes doubted that he would progress beyond his first international match when, in 1950–51, he no-balled Englishman Doug Wright three balls in succession for over-stepping. He was wondering if Wright would ever speak to him again and turning over the no-ball law in his mind when Wright approached and said jocularly, "Can't we be friends?" The tension faded immediately. McInnes was the umpire in the Fourth Test between England and Australia at Adelaide in 1958–59 when Colin McDonald, who was using a runner, hit a ball into the covers. Instead of moving to keep both runners, Lindwall and Burke, who was running for McDonald, in view, McInnes moved to the normal viewing side. Statham returned the ball to Tyson, who broke the wicket and appealed. McInnes signalled "out" but then realised that Burke was behind him and that he could not give a run out against a runner he had not seen. He reversed his decision, a courageous thing in a Test. McInnes was also the umpire in a grade match between Glenelg and West Torrens when Phil Ridings told Bruce Stanford, a noted trencherman, to bowl immediately after the tea interval. Stanford was reluctant to take the ball but Ridings insisted, so Stanford approached McInnes and carefully handed him his cap. Inside the cap was a huge cream cake.

Col Egar and Col Hoy, one of many famous Australian umpiring partnerships, were on duty in the Second Test at Melbourne in 1960–61 between Australia and the West Indies when Joe Solomon dislodged a bail when his cap fell off and had to be given out hit wicket. Egar later paired with the Queensland policeman Lou Rowan and they umpired through the midst of the throwing, dragging and bouncing disputes of the 1960s. They were the umpires at Brisbane when Ian Meckiff was no-balled for throwing against South Africa and vir-

At Melbourne in the Centenary Test 1977 a ball from Underwood touched the top edge of O'Keefe's bat, popped over the 'keeper's head, and was caught behind the 'keeper by Brearley diving to his left. Umpire Max O'Connell correctly ruled a fair catch.

AUSTRALIAN TEST UMPIRES
1877–1982

Umpire	Span	Tests	Umpire	Span	Tests
R. W. Crockett	1901–1925	32	W. Curran	1910–1911	2
C. J. Egar	1960–1969	29	G. A. Watson	1912	2
L. Rowan	1963–1971	26*	W. French	1930–1931	2
G. Borwick	1932–1948	24	G. Cooper	1948–1950	2
T. F. Brooks	1970–1979	24*	C. E. Harvey	1979–1980	2
R. C. Bailhache	1974–1982	23	S. Cosstick	1877	1
M. G. O'Connell	1970–1980	19	C. A. Reid	1877	1
G. Hele	1928–1933	16	P. Coady	1879	1
M. J. McInnes	1952–1959	16	I. Fisher	1884	1
D. Elder	1912–1929	14	J. Travers	1884	1
J. Phillips	1885–1898	13	J. Bryant	1885	1
R. Wright	1947–1959	13	J. Hodges	1885	1
C. Bannerman	1887–1902	12	P. G. McShane	1885	1
A. N. Barlow	1931–1951	11	E. Payne	1885	1
J. Scott	1936–1947	10	W. Gunn	1887	1+
H. Elphinston	1948–1953	10	H. Rawlinson	1887	1
A. R. Crafter	1978–1982	10	G. Downes	1892	1
C. Hoy	1954–1961	9	J. Tooher	1892	1
J. Swift	1881–1887	8	W. Whitridge	1892	1
R. A. French	1977–1982	8	G. Seracy	1895	1
M. W. Johnson	1979–1982	8	T. Laing	1908	1
P. Argall	1902–1908	7	W. Young	1912	1
E. H. Elliot	1882–1885	6	A. P. Williams	1924	1
A. C. Jones	1903–1929	6	C. Garing	1925	1
J. Lillywhite	1881–1885	5	G. Armstrong	1930	1
J. R. Collins	1972–1976	5	J. Jenkins	1930	1
T. Flynn	1892–1895	4	A. Orr	1930	1
W. Smyth	1962–1966	4	R. Richards	1930	1
R. Callaway	1901–1902	3	A. Wyeth	1930	1
W. Hannah	1907–1911	3	A. F. Cocks	1951	1
P. R. Enright	1972–1974	3	L. Townsend	1959	1
R. A. Ledwidge	1975–1977	3	E. Wykes	1962	1
D. G. Weser	1979–1981	3	A. Mackley	1963	1
R. Whitehead	1980–1981	3	N. Townsend	1972–1973	1
R. B. Terry	1877	2	W. Copeland	1979–1980	1
G. Coulthard	1879–1882	2	P. M. Cronin	1979–1980	1

*L. P. Rowan and T. F. Brooks are credited with the abandoned Test match at Melbourne in 1970–1971. A toss had been made, and although a ball was not bowled, the match was drawn.
+W. Gunn acted as a replacement umpire in the Second Test at the Sydney Cricket Ground in 1886–1887.

tually dismissed from the game. Rowan was also one of the umpires at Sydney in 1970–71 when England walked off the field after the crowd's demonstration against excessive bouncers during which John Snow clashed with a spectator. Tom Brooks, who umpired that day with Rowan in Sydney, later had to retire when he said his nerve cracked during the Perth Test against England in 1978–79. It was in Perth, too, that the notorious dismissal of Australian opener Andrew Hilditch occurred for "handling the ball." Hilditch picked up the ball and flipped it to the bowler but the umpire had to give him out when Sarfraz Nawaz appealed. Television and the injustice of the instant replay has brought added pressure for umpires, as has limited over cricket. Umpires had to adju-

1030

dicate on the legality of Trevor Chappell's underarm delivery at Melbourne in 1980–81 against New Zealand and correctly allowed it as the laws at the time permitted it. Just as dramatic was umpire Tony Crafter's action in stepping between Javed Miandad and Dennis Lillee during their Perth encounter during the 1981–82 tour by Pakistan. First-class careers of Australian umpires certainly are more strenuous these days than in Bob Crockett's time and it will take a mighty effort to surpass his Australian record of 32 Test matches.

Many Australian cricket clubs and societies have gone to America to play cricket, but only one team has done so with the involvement of the Australian Board of Control in matters of tour profits, payments to players and team personnel. The Board, mindful of profits paid to Test players who organised their own overseas tours before the Board gained control of Australian cricket, laid down the conditions when Arthur Mailey organised a 51-match tour of America in 1932. Mailey arranged the tour with the help of the Canadian Pacific Railway, shipping lines, various American government offices, and the Canadian Cricket Board of Control.

UNITED STATES, AUSTRALIAN TOURS OF

The Board acted under a resolution it passed in 1927 which said that no team of first-class cricketers who came under the jurisidiction of a State association could privately visit any country outside Australia without Board approval. The Board informed Mailey that (a) it must approve of the team chosen and the conditions under which the players toured, (b) the Board must be given detailed and complete accounts of all receipts and expenditure, and (c) that none of the players should receive more than £100 from tour profits, with all profits above this amount to be distributed by the Board as it thought fit. The team comprised: A. A. Mailey (player-manager), V. Y. Richardson (captain), D. G. Bradman, P. H. Carney, H. Carter, L. O'B. Fleetwood-Smith, W. F. Ives, A. F. Kippax, S. J. McCabe, R. N. Nutt, E. F. Rofe, E. K. Tolhurst, with Dr. Rowley Pope baggage-master and able to fill in for injured players. C. V. Grimmett was originally named in the side but did not go. Fleetwood-Smith was hurriedly included in the team when Mailey realised that with 51 matches to be played in 100 days the Australians would have to dismiss 1,000 batsmen on strange pitches in places like Moose Jaw, Medicine Hat, Kicking Horse Falls, Saskatoon and Calgary.

The Board lifted its ban on wives accompanying Australian teams to allow Bradman's wife Jessie to go on what was virtually a honeymoon trip. They had been married only 26 days before the American trip began and the Board realised that Bradman's absence from the team might cause cancellation of the entire tour. Jessie Bradman acted as the team's hostess when it entertained, attended all the team functions, and occasionally helped the captain, Vic Richardson, with his speeches. Richardson made 30 speeches in 100 days. Three of the team paid their own expenses, but all the leading players and the Bradmans had their expenses paid. All except Rofe, a club cricketer from the Manly club in Sydney, and Carney, a Melbourne district player, were Sheffield Shield players. Hanson Carter at 54 was the oldest and smallest player in the side. None of the team's matches were first-class and more than 25 were against the odds. The pitches, the outfields, and the umpiring often were ludicrous but the tourists laughed off all handicaps and everyone had a marvellous time.

Bradman was the star of the tour, the player Americans and Canadians most wanted to see. He played in 49 of the 51 matches, and although he was on his honeymoon had only one day off when the team played 26 matches in 32 days. In 51 innings on the tour, Bradman made 18 centuries, which his biographer, Irving Rosenwater, has calculated was almost precisely the ratio of centuries he scored in first-class cricket. Bradman also took 26 wickets from 52 overs on the tour. Rosenwater says Bradman's 260 against XVIII of Western Ontario at Guelph remains the highest score ever made in Canada. When Bradman made 159 not out against an Edmonton XVIII he put on 50 in seven minutes at one stage. Bradman's partnership with E. K. Tolhurst in San Francisco yielded 168 in 34 minutes.

The Australians learned that cricket had been played in Philadelphia, Georgia, the Carolinas and throughout Canada long before Captain Cook sailed into Botany Bay. They were entertained in Hollywood by film stars and played a match against a team that included C. Aubrey Smith, the former English Test player who was then in his 70th year, and Boris Karloff, who had to be hidden in the slips. Apart from Bradman, stars of the tour were Stan McCabe, who scored 2,361 runs at 54.90 and took 189 wickets at 6.00, W. F. Ives ("Big Bill") who took 92 wickets at 7.51, and the spin bowlers Fleetwood-Smith and Mailey. Fleetwood-Smith, then 22, took 249 wickets, including two hat-tricks, at 8.00 each and Mailey, aged 42, took 240 wickets at 6.5. Some of the matches were so one-sided once the spinners were brought on, keeping opposing batsmen at the wicket long enough to avoid embarrassment proved fairly difficult.

OTHER US TOURS BY AUSTRALIAN TEAMS

Dave Gregory took the first Australian team to tour England to play in America on their way home in 1878. In Philadelphia, where local teams had played international sides from England as far back as 1859, the Australian 'keeper Jack McBlackham hurled the ball to Dave Gregory in annoyance when an umpire disallowed his stumping appeal. Gregory led his players from the field. In the dressing-room Philadelphian cricket officials told the Australians that unless they returned to the field payment for a cheque for their guaranteed expenses that had been handed to them that morning would be stopped, and they would not be paid their share of that day's gate. Gregory took the Australians back to finish the match.

Dave Gregory's team had beaten MCC at Lord's in one day but in the three-day match at Philadelphia they earned only a draw after being led on the first innings by 46 runs. This was the first match in which an American team met an international side on level terms and the result established the reputation of Philadelphia cricket.

Blackham took the 1893 Australian team to Philadelphia for two matches on the way home from their English tour. In the first match Philadelphia scored 525, the highest innings total by an American team in first-class cricket, and dismissed the Australians for 199 and 258 to win by an innings and 68 runs. The Australians made no excuses for their defeat, although they had been rushed straight to the match in a private railway car as soon as their ship, the *Germanic*, arrived in New York.

Three years later G. H. S. Trott's Australian team played three matches on level terms in Philadelphia. Australia won the first two easily but Philadelphia won the third by an innings and 99 runs. The successes against the Australians encouraged the Philadelphians to send a team on a tour of England in 1897, a tour that was accepted as entirely first-class. The hero of the victories over Australia and of the English tour was J. Barton King, an outstanding inswing bowler. From 1893 to 1912, King was one of the most feared bowlers in the world. He took 7 for 13 against Sussex on a good pitch at Brighton and in 1908 headed the English first-class bowling averages.

The Australian team of 1912, weakened by the loss of six leading players, lost an exciting match to Philadelphia by two runs. In 1914, an Australian team that toured America and Canada, playing 53 matches, winning 49, drawing 3 and losing to XII of Germantown by two wickets, in what is now considered the last important match played in the US. This 1914 Australian side also played three matches in Chicago, winning them all handsomely.

Since World War II the Australian Old Collegians, the Emus, and the Australia House Cricket Club from London, have all played matches in the United States. The Southern California Cricket Association defeated the Old Collegians in 1959 on the C. Aubrey Smith Field in the first victory by a local side over foreign opponents since 1913. Southern California made 6 for 160 in three hours and then dismissed the Old Collegians who at one time were 4 for 112, for 126. The Old Collegians' side included ex-Test player Leo O'Brien, and players rich in first grade experience at home.

1033

V

VEIVERS, Thomas Robert, 1937–

First-Class Averages: Batting, 5,100 runs at 36.95; Bowling, 191 wickets at 38.70.

Tests (21): 813 runs at 31.26; 33 wickets at 41.66.

A burly, dark-haired Brisbane radio station executive, who was Australia's best right-hand off-spin bowler in the 1960 and among the best of this type Australia has produced. He played in 21 tests and toured all the major cricketing nation except the West Indies. He was unavailable, through family reasons, for the 1965 Australian tour of West Indies when he would have been a certain selection.

Veivers was an ambidextrous cricketer, born at Beenleigh Queensland. He bowled right-hand, batted left-hand and fielded with equal dexterity with either hand. He first played for Queensland in 1958–59 and developed into a dependable hard-hitting batsman who hit many spectacular sixes Veivers' first game against England was for an Australian XI in 1962–63, when Ted Dexter delighted the crowd by hitting his off-breaks for consecutive sixes. He finished his first bowl against England with 0 for 146. His start in Test cricket came in the following season against South Africa but his bowling was disappointing in three tests. But Veivers was a stalwart character who worked hard in the nets, and in 1964 he was outstanding in England when he was only the second off spinner Australia had sent there since World War II—Ian Johnson was the first.

One London cricket writer likened him to a koala bear which had just emerged from sleeping upside-down in a gum tree. Another said he looked like an Italian tenor, but his appearance wasn't all they had to write about. He took wickets he was most economical, and he had guts. In the Manchester Test in which England answered Australia's first innings total of 8 for 656 declared with 611, Veivers bowled 95 six-ball overs. He took 3 for 155, with 36 maidens. The 571 balls Veivers delivered in that innings was only 17 balls short of the alltime Test record set by Sonny Ramadhin, of the West Indies.

Veivers' was by far the longest spell by an Australian in Test cricket—Fleetwood-Smith came next with 87 six-ball overs (522 balls). They showed that while genial, teak-tough

Veivers could bowl tidily and economically he was unable to penetrate at the highest level. Veivers followed that epic bowling effort by scoring a splendid 67 not-out in the next Test at The Oval. In 22 matches on that tour, Veivers took 52 wickets at 36.17 and scored 725 runs at 34.52.

In his 21 Tests Veivers had a highest score of 88, with seven half-centuries and best bowling figures of 4 for 68. He was widely tipped as Queensland's next captain when he retired early in the 1967–68 season. For Queensland he played 55 matches, taking 104 wickets at 36.39 and scoring 3,092 runs at an average of 38.65. He hit four first-class centuries, with a topscore of 137 for Queensland against South Australia in 1962–63.

Many considered he was just approaching his best when he retired, aged 30. "The successful off-spinner needs the dedication of a hot gospeller, the physical endurance of a long-distance runner and the hide of a rhinoceros," Veivers once wrote. "If punishment makes you panic, your spinbowling career will be brief."

VERNON, Murray Trevor, 1937–

First-Class Averages: Batting, 4,184 runs at 34.86; Bowling, 10 wickets at 23.10.

A left-handed batsman who captained Western Australia in 10 matches and was a consistent scorer for the State with a career total of eight centuries and 22 scores over 50. He played for South Perth and Nedlands and made his debut for the State in 1955–56. He made his initial first-class century, 128, against Queensland at Brisbane in 1958–59, and made his highest score, 173, against New South Wales at Perth in 1965–66. But perhaps his most impressive knock was his 118 for WA against England at Perth in 1965–66. He captained WA a few times in 1962–63 and for all of the 1966–67 season. He twice headed the Perth first grade batting aggregates, in 1963–64 (956 at 63.73) and in 1964–65 (821 at 68.42), also topping the averages in 1964–65.

VICTORIA, CRICKET IN

The start of cricket in Victoria came shortly after the birth of the game in New South Wales and Tasmania. The first settlements were on Batman's Hill, where Spencer Street station now stands, and three years later—on November 15, 1838—the most prestigious of Australia's cricket clubs, the Melbourne Cricket Club, was formed. The club played its first game against The Military on November 17, 1838, on a ground almost certainly located where the Royal Mint now stands in William Street, between Latrobe and Little Lonsdale Streets. Later the club moved to a ground now replaced by the No 1 platform at Spencer Street Railway Station, where interstate trains start and finish.

The *Port Phillip Gazette* in its report on the Melbourne CC versus Military match said it was played on one of the beautiful fields in the fast-rising new town, grounds where "this most elegant and manly of sports can be enjoyed in". The *Gazette* said: "During the week arrangements had been made by the gentlemen civilians of the district to play a match of cricket against the Military . . . It was a heart-enlivening sight to witness from an adjacent hill the ground as it was laid out Camps pitched, banners tastefully arranged, and the all-enlivening smiles of beauty that would have graced a far-famed tournament of the olden times. At 12 precisely a signal called the players to their post, when the game commenced, the Military taking first innings. We have not the particulars of the game before us and can therefore but briefly notice those who particularly distinguished themselves. After a duration of some hours, the match concluded by a triumph on the part of the civilians. Mr Powlett's and Mr Macarthur's bowling and Mr Russell's batting attracted universal applause."

David Charteris Macarthur (1808–87), pioneer banker, son of Donald Macarthur, born at Gloucester, England, and educated in Scotland, had such a marked effect in popularising the game even while the settlement was still part of New South Wales that he has been called the "father of Victorian cricket". He was not on the early Melbourne Cricket Club committees but always figured prominently in the club's matches. Outside the Melbourne club, a group of tradesmen and retailers formed the Melbourne Union Cricket Club and on January 12, 1839, the "Gentlemen of the District" played the "Tradesmen of the Town", the tradesmen winning easily. A week later the Gentlemen reversed this result. Matches between "Marrieds" and "Singles" were frequent and in one of these F. A. Powlett, already a power at the Melbourne Cricket Club, scored 101. Powlett was a descendant of the Rev. Charles ("Squire") Powlett, a founder of the famous Hambledon Club in England.

Among other early Victorian clubs was Brighton, founded in 1842, which used a piece of ground for matches that only a few years earlier had been an Aboriginal camping area. Brighton had two fine round-arm bowlers, Coldham and Brown, whose presence helped give the club an influential bearing on cricket. Brighton played their first match against the Melbourne club on Easter Monday, 1845. Melbourne opened the match before "a great turn-out of the fashionable world," and made 70. Brighton replied with 62. The teams then had a half hour spell and when they resumed Melbourne were unable to cope with the Brighton bowling and Brighton won with ease. But Melbourne won a match in April the same year against Geelong, by scoring 55 and 91 compared with Geelong's 121 and 13.

Williamstown, founded in 1852, was another active early club, with Sir John Taverner, Sir George Verdon and Richard Seddon, later Prime Minister of New Zealand, among the founders. The club's funds were low and every member was required to do half an hour's rolling each week to overcome the lack of a groundsman. The settlement at Gellibrand Point received the official name "Williams Town" in 1837 and the Williamstown club's ground was on a site ajoining Fort Gellibrand, with a basalt road built by convicts passing the rear of the ground.

In the early 1850s gold fever virtually emptied Melbourne, Geelong and Williamstown. On the goldfields some former Oxford and Cambridge men debated on the standards at the two Universities. The outcome was a challenge match in 1853 between teams called the "Light Blues" and the "Dark Blues". Boyle and Scott's *Cricket Annual* (1880–81) included an article on the match signed "Old Fogey" which described how the bats were made out of ironbark and an india rubber ball used that belonged to one of the miners. The Dark Blues batted first and lost two wickets without scoring but then came a stand of 20 runs. "One of them, a fellow named Barney," Old Fogey wrote, "looked more like a bandit than a cricketer in his huge boots, broad-brimmed hat, and jet-black flowing beard,

An artist's sketch of a fieldsman chasing a ball in a match between Sydney and Melbourne teams on the Richmond Ground, Melbourne, in 1856.

1037

but was a tremendous slogger and created quite a sensation. Our innings closed for 43, a fellow named Johnson heading the list with 19. During lunch the wagering was heavy. The Light Blues soon had 10 on the score sheet, and they went to 15 without loss. I tried underhand lobs, and the first was hit for five, but then a wicket fell, and indeed two more at the same score.

"An old Cantab, by as correct play as could be shown on the peculiar pitch, increased the score to 35, and then the other batsman—not the Cantab—overshot the mark in backing up before the ball was delivered, and I turned and knocked the stumps flying. The umpire gave him out, and the batsman made tracks for the tent, but the crowd shouted 'Swindle', and told him to go back. The hum of voices swelled into a deafening roar, but after a long argument it was admitted that he was out and harmony was restored. The last two were now in and when only three short of our score, one of the batsmen made a good hit. They ran one and the fielder fumbled the ball. 'Go again,' yelled the crowd, which they did, and the fielder, recovering the ball, took a shot at the wicket and knocked a stump out of the ground. He was carried from the field in triumph." The "Dark Blues" had beaten the "Light Blues" by two runs.

In 1852, *The Argus* reported that a match between 11 Melbourne gentlemen and 11 gentlemen from Adelaide was held at South Yarra. "That the match was not finished when time was called was a godsend to the Adelaidians, who would in all probability have been soundly beaten had it been played out," said *The Argus*, "the scores of the Melbournites for two innings being so large as almost to preclude hope for the other side, even had they played their second innings. We may mention that Mr Fook's wicket-keeping was very clever and that the fielding of Messrs Cary and Dicker was very much admired".

An Australian Cricket Club was formed in Melbourne in October, 1850. Another club was established at nearby Emerald Hill, South Melbourne, in December, 1853. A month later Bendigo Cricket Club was founded. Richmond, the oldest of Melbourne's present district clubs, began in 1854, but most of the colony's exciting cricket was then played at the goldfields in rough conditions before crowds that bet heavily on the outcome. One of the fields used, Wood's Point, near Ballarat, had hardly any level ground on it, but that did not lessen the players' enthusiasm.

Members of the Melbourne Cricket Club were horrified in 1853 when it was announced that the new Hobson's Bay railway line from Melbourne to Sandridge (Port Melbourne), would cut right through the club's ground. The new track, the first public steam railway in Australia, was laid and the club moved to an area of five acres in Yarra Park known as "Rich-

1038

THE VICTORIAN EIGHTEEN.

The Victorian Eighteen who defeated W. G. Grace's English Team of 1873–74 by an innings and 21 runs. Top (L to R): B. B. Cooper, S. Costick, G. Gibson, H. G. Wyndham. Second Row (L to R): B. McGan, G. Hedley, G. P. Robertson (captain), J. Conway. Third Row (L to R): L. Goldsmith, J. Coates, H. F. Boyle, C. Carr. Fourth Row (L to R): W. Midwinter, F. Allan, T. J. D. Kelly, T. Horan. Bottom: W. W. Gaggin, Colonel Ward (umpire), H. Bishop.

mond Paddock", the site of the now world famous Melbourne Cricket Ground. The club first used the site in November, 1854, and quickly put up an iron fence around the ground. Later a wooden pavilion and a nine-foot high fence to keep out non-playing spectators were erected.

The Sydney Cricket Club challenged the cricketers of Geelong to a match for a £20 bat in January, 1854. The challenge, issued to Geelong as the port for voyagers bound for the goldfields, caused wide speculation. The Sydney club offered to pay £75 towards the visitors' expenses, but the members of the Geelong team were not willing to give up all the time needed to sail round to Sydney, play the match, and sail home. Then the Melbourne Cricket Club inserted an advertisement in *The Argus* challenging any team in the colony to a match, and this led to the first match between Victoria and New South Wales at Melbourne in March, 1856. A charge for admission was made for the first time at an Australian match, but the conditions were very primitive. Victoria, who had beaten Tasmania in the first inter-Colonial match in 1850–51 at Launceston, lost this time to NSW by three wickets.

There was keen competition at the time in Melbourne for the title "champion cricketer of Victoria". The Victorian cricket historian David Roylance says that Jerry Bryant, who had played first for Surrey in England and then for Victoria, challenged any man in the colony to a game of single wicket cricket. A little known player named John Mace took Bryant on and beat him by 24 runs. Mace, who had played for Bedale in Yorkshire with Roger Iddison and George Anderson of the All England XI, emigrated in the early 1850s to search for gold with his brothers. Both **John Mace** (1828–1905) and **Christopher Mace** (1830–1907) later played for Victoria before moving on to the Otago goldfields in 1862. After defeating Bryant, Mace was challenged by Thomas Wentworth Wills, but the match before "an immense crowd of spectators," was a disaster for Mace, who was out for four after 25 balls. Wills then scored 57 runs off 258 deliveries. This was the start of the career that established Wills as the first outstanding Australian-born cricketer.

Mace was a member of the Richmond club who won the first Melbourne cricket competition in the 1860–61 season. The city's clubs at that time included Collingwood, East Melbourne, South Melbourne, an offshoot of Emerald Hill, and St Kilda, but it is not known how many of them played in the first competition or how it was controlled. St Kilda had staggered what Roylance calls "the most glacial upholders of royal protocol," by applying in 1857–58 to Queen Victoria for royal patronage. The club's petition, headed by Sir George Stephen, requested the right to use the title, "The Royal Cricket Club of Victoria". But Queen Victoria's private secretary, Sir

1040

The Melbourne Cricket Ground, c. 1890.

C. Phipps, considered the application "entirely inadmissible". Lord Carnarvon, as Colonial Secretary, asked Sir Edward Lytton to reply, saying: "I think a civil letter must be drafted declining". A year later Sir George Stephen represented St Kilda at a meeting of the city's cricket clubs called by Melbourne. He tried to introduce the question of "a cricket congress of the Australian colonies" but was ruled out of order.

A Victorian Cricketers' Association was first formed in 1864 but was dissolved before 1875, reformed in that year, dissolved in 1879, reformed the same year, dissolved in 1895 and reformed again that year in its present form as the Victorian Cricket Association. But the VCA annual reports list premiership records from 1860–61. One of the surprising aspects of these early years was the frequent appearance of cricket magazines. They usually lasted only a couple of summers but they left a vivid picture of Victorian cricket in the 19th century. William Fairfax, who acted as secretary to the meeting of clubs called by the Melbourne club, edited the first one, which disappeared after three issues. This *Australian Cricketer's Guide* was replaced four years later by Hammersley's *Victorian Cricketer's Guide*, which referred to the five matches between Victoria and NSW as "Test" matches. A

1041

hundred years later the noted English cricket historian, Major Rowland Bowen, said this was the first known use of the words.

Apart from the Melbourne club, the most powerful team in Victoria towards the end of the 19th century was East Melbourne, founded by Tom and Charley Dight with Fred and Joseph Moody. This club practised and played at a variety of grounds, including one in Clarendon Street, East Melbourne, and changed its name from the original Abbotsford Cricket Club in 1860, when permission was sought to create a cricket field on what was then known as Captain Lonsdale's cow paddock. East Melbourne and Melbourne shared the honours in the Melbourne premiership until 1872–73 when South Melbourne took first place. There was also a Challenge Cup, the Coppin Trophy, presented by the Hon. G. S. Coppin, president of Richmond Club. The Trophy had to be held for two years without defeat before it became the permanent property of any club. Richmond at one stage held it for a year and 10 months and seemed certain to take permanent possession when they were beaten by East Melbourne. *The Argus* commented sourly, "The glittering illusion, always to be played for but never won. From the little differences the Trophy has already given rise to, it promises to be the very apple of discord among cricketers".

A lot of clubs in this period ceased to function during the winter and reformed the following summer. The Victorian Cricket Association at one of its first meetings brought in a rule prohibiting all play for the Challenge Cup for four weeks prior to the inter-Colonial match between NSW and Victoria. The VCA met then in Oliver's Cafe, and were offered the Melbourne Cricket Ground for the inter-Colonial match in return for 12½ per cent of the gross receipts. Reluctantly the VCA accepted but decided it could not afford a band at the game. When it sent a Victorian team to Sydney in February, 1876, in the steamer *Macedon*, the VCA had £540 in the bank and £220 of that went in boat fares. Another cost met by the VCA was the £9 it paid to the Lands Department so that star bowler Frank Allan could get leave to go to Sydney.

The Fourth England team played its Melbourne matches in December, 1876, under the auspices of the VCA, and in March, 1877, the VCA voted £30 to buying a gold medal for each of the players in the first Australian XI as a souvenir of the first victory by an Australian team over England on level terms. The Australian captain, Dave Gregory, got a slightly bigger medal than his players. In December, 1879, the VCA delighted all players in the State by staging a benefit match for Sam Cosstick, which raised £140. But funds remained short, and when E. D. Heather was appointed Hon. Sececretary of the VCA in May, 1882, the VCA could allocate only £20 towards his clerical expenses.

At Colac, some 100 miles south-west of Melbourne, the first game was played in 1853. Isaac Hebb in *The History of Colac and District*, writes: "Having agreed to get up a match amongst the local players we were in a great fix for the necessary materials, having neither bat nor ball to make a start with. However, after sundry consultations with our mates, we went to Rymer, the wheelright, and got him to make two bats, and we made the stumps ourselves. Then we hied to a shoemaker, who supplied us with a ball, his own handicraft, for 10 shillings. Having got this far, we ordered a large supply of bottled beer and porter, and did our best, in the absence of a local paper, to circulate the news that a grand cricket match was coming off on a certain date and invited everybody to favour us with their presence. A large crowd gathered on a vacant piece of ground on the south side of Lempster's blacksmith's shop, and here we wielded the willow and trundled the leather to the wonder and astonishment of all. At intervals we relaxed the sterner business of the game, and started the fiddlers to work, dancing on the green being vigorously indulged in by numbers of the ladies and gentlemen present".

The difficulty experienced in Colac in finding bats was largely overcome when deciduous, moisture-loving trees of the genus *Salix* were introduced by early colonists along streams in various parts of temperate Victoria. The willow, as it was commonly known, proved ideal for bat-making. Cricket-bat willow has been grown for the manufacture of cricket bats of high quality at Shepherd's Flat, near Daylesford, Vic., for more than 100 years.

As in other States, Victoria's new cricket clubs looked to the schools for talent and regular replenishment of their membership. **Scotch College**, founded in 1851, played the State's first recorded schools match in 1858, against Geelong Grammar. Scotch has since produced seven Test players, W. Bruce, C. E. and R. McLeod, A. E. V. Hartkopf, B. A. Barnett, C. C. McDonald, R. M. Cowper, 18 State players, and two VCA presidents, J. A. Seitz and R. C. Steele. Scotch's highest score was 646 against Wesley in 1898. **Geelong Grammar**, founded in 1855, produced State players Arthur Liddicutt and Nigel Murch. **Geelong College**, founded in 1861, produced four Australian players, A. L. Hassett, J. B. Iverson, I. R. Redpath and A. P. Sheahan, and prominent State players J. L. Chambers and J. Hallebone. **Wesley College**, founded in 1866, also became a rich cricket nursery, producing two Australian captains, Henry ("Tup") Scott and Ian Johnson, and eight Test players in all, Scott, Johnson, S. J. E. Loxton, J. E. Barratt, J. D. Edwards, R. Gregory, R. L. Park, and K. E. Rigg. Among Wesley's long list of State players was J. A. Prout, who made 459 in an innings total of 710 against Geelong Grammar in 1909, and later played for Queensland.

Australia's first inter-State schools match was played in

Bill Johnston and Doug Ring with souvenir stumps after their match winning last wicket stand in the 4th Test against the West Indies at Melbourne in January 1952.

1876 between Melbourne Grammar (founded in 1858) and Sydney Grammar, when R. C. Allen enabled Sydney Grammar to win the match with an innings of 145. In 1887, the Melbourne Grammar scorer gave his school victory by one run and the Sydney Grammar scorer said his team won by the same margin. It was decided to call the game a tie. The schools began their second century of annual rivalry in 1977, when Melbourne Grammar won in Melbourne.

Country cricketers also contributed to Victoria's growing cricket strength. W. E. Midwinter first came to notice when he made 256 for Bendigo v. Sandhurst at Bendigo in 1869–70. Peter McAlister, later an Australian batsman and national selector, came to attention by heading the batting averages for Williamstown for three straight seasons, 1886–87. Indeed Williamstown cricket was so strong that Lord Sheffield's England team, captained by W. G. Grace, played there in January, 1892, on a guarantee of £70. The gate fell £5.9.4. short but Lord Sheffield waived this. Williamstown batted 22 men and scored 154. W. G. Grace took 11 for 58 and G. A. Lohmann 8 for 89. The Englishmen had scored 1 for 43 when rain prevented further play and gave Williamstown a draw.

Between 1860–61 and 1905–06 East Melbourne won the premiership outright 18 times, Melbourne 14 times. South Melbourne, North Melbourne, Hawksburn and Richmond enjoyed their good years, but in an era of extremely heavy scoring East Melbourne ranked supreme, producing players like Horan, Boyle, Laver, McAlister and Seitz. East Melbourne was the venue of the historic match between Smokers and Non-Smokers, when the then world record score of 9 for 803 was made in 1886–87. In 1897–98 in a district match, University made 1,094 against Essendon.

In the VCA's formative years the stronger clubs had more delegates to meetings than the weaker clubs. Melbourne had three, East and South Melbourne two, and the rest one each. But in 1905–06 all member clubs were given equal voting strength with two delegates each. The Association took control of the Melbourne competition from 1889–90, but at the end of the 1904–05 season had a bank balance of only £14. Formation of the Australian Board of Control in 1905 in turn strengthened the control of the State Associations and over the next two decades the VCA disbursed more than £20,000 to member clubs and added a fine building in Melbourne to its assets. Two officials who did as much as anyone to achieve this were the much discussed Ernie Bean and Harry Rush, tough, strong-willed administrators who fought desperately hard around countless committee tables for the rights of Victorian cricket.

Popularity of Australian Rules Football meant that almost from their inception Melbourne cricket clubs had to struggle with football clubs over the occupancy of their grounds. The VCA made it a prerequisite for member clubs to have an enclosed ground, not just a boundary fence. This compelled the cricket clubs to share their grounds with football clubs who left the playing area badly churned up for the start of each summer season. The secret has been to build harmonious relations between football and cricket officials, and hopefully develop a strong licensed club from which both sports could derive benefit.

The Melbourne Cricket Ground remains the showpiece of Victorian cricket but it is on the 16 grounds used by district clubs that players who eventually perform for Australia and Victoria are developed. Victoria has won the Sheffield Shield 24 times since it was first staged, a record second only to NSW. There has been a steady flow of Victorian players into Australian teams for more than 100 years and the State's appetite for cricket remains unsated. The world's highest first-class total was compiled in Melbourne, 1,107 by Victoria against NSW in 1926–27, surpassing the 1,059 Victoria made there in 1922–23 against Tasmania. The world's biggest crowd for a day's Test cricket, 90,800, was achieved at Melbourne in 1960–61 for the West Indies-Australia Test.

Bill Ponsford made the world's first quadruple century in Melbourne and had scores of 437, 429, 352, 336 and 275 not out there, and when he made his 352 he made 334 of them in a single day that produced 573 runs in 322 minutes, against NSW in 1926–27. Victoria's oldest first-class player, Bert Ironmonger, kept going until he was 53 years and 305 days in 1935–36, and the youngest-ever Australian first-class player, L. J. Junor, was only 15 years and 265 days old when he played for Victoria in 1929–30 against WA. The first of all Tests and the most magnificently staged Australian cricket match, the Centenary Test, were also set in Melbourne.

Victoria probably suffered more than other States when Sheffield Shield matches were restricted to four days instead of being played to a finish. Victorian batsmen were adept at wearing down opposing bowlers and going on to huge scores. Six of the States' partnership records were set when first-class matches were played to a finish. One wonders if a batsman like Woodfull would have been so successful had all his cricket been played in a time of four-day Shield games.

Victoria's contribution to Australian cricket in the 144 years since it began in an organised form in that State has been vital in building Australia's international reputation. One can only agree with the Melbourne *Sun-Pictorial's* writer Tom Prior who lamented during the 1981–82 Tests against the West Indies that it just does not seem right that there was no Victorian in Australia's team.

VCA PRESIDENTS

F. G. Smith	1896
A. E. Clarke	1896–1898
Jas. Aitken	1898–1906
L. A. Adamson	1906
Hon. D. MacKinnon	1906–1932
Canon E. S. Hughes	1932–1942
Dr R. L. Morton	1942–1947
J. A. Seitz	1947–1963
W. J. Dowling	1963–1973
R. C. Steele	1973–

VCA SECRETARIES

E. D. Heather	1896–1911
J. Healey	1911–1917
E. E. Bean	1917–1925
H. E. Brereton	1925–1950
J. A. Ledward	1951–1971
D. L. Richards	1973–1980
K. W. Jacobs	1980–

RECORD PARTNERSHIPS FOR VICTORIA

Wkt		
1st	456	E. R. Mayne and W. H. Ponsford v Qld (Melb), 1923–24.
2nd	358	C. H. McKenzie and H. F. L. Kortlang v WA (Perth), 1909–10.
3rd	390	J. Moss and J. Weiner v WA (Melb), 1981–82.
4th	424	I. S. Lee and S. O. Quin v Tas (Melb), 1933–34.
5th	343	R. I. Maddocks and J. Hallebone v Tas (Melb), 1951–52.
6th	289	S. J. Loxton and D. Ring v Qld (Melb), 1946–47.
7th	187	P. McAlister and W. Murray v NZ (Melb), 1898–99.
8th	215	W. W. Armstrong and R. L. Park v SA (Melb), 1919–20.
9th	146	T. S. Warne and A. C. Facy v Tas (Laun), 1911–12.
10th	211	M. Ellis and T. Hastings v SA (Melb), 1902–03.

OUTSTANDING VICTORIAN BATSMEN

Batsman	Career	Matches	Innings	Not Out	H. Score	Runs	Average	Centuries
W. M. Lawry	1955–1972	99	164	16	266	7618	51.47	20
W. H. Ponsford	1920–1934	55	87	7	437	6902	86.27	26
A. L. Hassett	1932–1953	73	121	13	232	6825	63.19	23
W. W. Armstrong	1898–1922	83	143	14	250	6732	52.18	23
I. R. Redpath	1961–1976	92	159	12	261	6103	41.51	13
J. Ryder	1912–1932	80	137	13	295	5674	45.75	14
W. M. Woodfull	1921–1934	59	94	21	275*	5488	75.17	17
J. Potter	1956–1968	81	135	15	221	5101	42.50	13
R. N. Harvey	1946–1957	64	103	5	209	4914	50.14	12
R. M. Cowper	1959–1970	66	101	14	195*	4611	53.00	10
K. E. Rigg	1926–1939	71	116	10	167*	4582	43.22	13
V. S. Ransford	1903–1928	76	123	13	182	4536	41.23	13
K. R. Stackpole	1959–1974	75	122	8	145	4483	39.32	8
G. N. Yallop	1972–1982	65	116	11	134*	4340	41.33	11
A. P. Sheahan	1965–1974	47	78	11	202	3988	59.52	12
C. C. McDonald	1947–1963	60	101	8	229	3919	42.13	8
R. D. Robinson	1971–1982	76	121	26	185	3838	40.40	6

OUTSTANDING VICTORIAN BOWLERS

Bowler	Career	Matches	Runs	Wkts	Average	B.B.	5W	10W
A. N. Connolly	1959–1971	83	8925	330	27.04	9/67	12	4
H. Ironmonger	1913–1934	61	6964	313	22.24	8/31	26	7
L. O. B. Fleetwood-Smith	1931–1940	51	7194	295	24.38	9/36	31	10
J. D. Higgs	1970–1982	80	8112	274	29.60	8/66	13	2
I. W. Johnson	1935–1956	77	6560	270	24.29	6/27	14	3
J. V. Saunders	1899–1910	51	6475	264	24.52	8/106	24	4
W. W. Armstrong	1898–1922	83	5587	248	22.52	6/66	7	—
M. N. H. Walker	1968–1982	70	6999	248	28.22	6/49	11	—
D. T. Ring	1938–1953	67	7362	236	31.19	6/41	8	2
H. Trumble	1887–1904	47	4832	229	21.10	8/39	15	6
A. G. Hurst	1972–1981	50	5003	197	25.39	8/84	7	1
W. A. Johnston	1945–1955	56	5496	192	28.62	8/52	9	3
G. H. S. Trott	1885–1908	59	4520	181	24.97	8/36	12	2
I. Meckiff	1956–1964	37	3802	164	23.18	5/41	7	1
A. L. Thomson	1968–1975	35	3906	160	24.41	8/87	12	3
D. D. J. Blackie	1924–1933	33	3705	158	23.44	7/25	10	2
F. Laver	1891–1912	78	5087	154	33.03	6/17	3	—
J. Ryder	1912–1932	80	4454	150	29.69	7/53	7	1

W

WADDY, THE FAMILY

E. L. ("Gar") Waddy.

Three big-hitting brothers, sons of Colonel R. A. Waddy and grandsons of General Sir Richard Waddy, who built a reputation for their family's prowess as cricketers, wits and academics that has lasted for more than half a century. None of them played in Tests, but two played for NSW and two appeared in English first-class cricket.

Canon **Percival Stacey Waddy** (1875–1937), eldest of the family, played for a Parramatta District Twenty in 1891–92 against Lord Sheffield's XI, while still at King's School. He was out for 34 in the second innings, caught W. G. Grace bowled Stoddart. In 1896 he scored 107 not out for Oxford University against Surrey to win his Blue, which he also won in 1897. In 1903–04 he made 92 and 102 for Eighteen of Northern District at Maitland against "Plum" Warner's England team while he was rector at Stockton. He was headmaster at King's from 1906–16, when he joined the Army. He became Canon of Jerusalem and never returned to Australia.

The Reverend **Ernest Frederick** ("Mick") **Waddy** (1880–1958) made his debut for NSW in 1902–03. He set an inter-Varsity record of 308 for Sydney University against Melbourne University in 1904. He made 129 not out in 1904–05 in his first Shield match for NSW against South Australia, the first of his four first-class centuries. He finished the season at the head of the Australian first-class batting averages with 351 runs at 70.20. In 1907–08 he made 107 not out and 54 for NSW v. England. He was Australia's 12th man in the final Test of the 1907–08 series. After a spell teaching at King's School, he became a master at Rugby School from 1915 to 1940. In four seasons for Warwickshire between 1919 and 1922, he made 955 runs at 23.87, topscore 109 not out. For NSW, he made 1,359 runs at 33.14. He was a bee-keeper, member of the Magic Circle, a brilliant after dinner speaker, and excelled at boxing, rowing and Rugby football.

Edgar Lloyd ("Gar") **Waddy** (1878–1963) scored 2,031 runs for NSW at 30.77. His best score was 140 against New Zealand at Auckland in 1913–14 for an Australian XI. In a career that

1048

lasted from 1896 to 1921, he was in four teams that won the Sheffield Shield, and played first grade for Cumberland Club until 1931, when he was 53. He toured New Zealand in Australian teams in 1913–14 and 1920–21. He spent much time and effort taking teams of prominent Sydney players into country areas.

"Mick" was regarded as the best cricketer of the three. "Gar" occasionally kept wicket, while Stacey was a better than average medium-pace bowler. A fourth brother, Dr Richard Granville Waddy, did not play cricket but made up for it by becoming a Rhodes scholar and rowing for Oxford. There were also two sisters in the family, Florence and Catherine. E. L. ("Gar") Waddy's son, John Lloyd Waddy, played cricket for Paddington and I Zingari. He was a distinguished air ace in World War II (15½ kills) and later as a Liberal MP was Minister for Health and Police in the NSW government.

WAITE, Mervyn George, 1911–

First-Class Averages: Batting, 3,888 runs at 27.77; Bowling, 192 wickets at 31.62.

Tests (2): 11 runs at 3.66; 1 wicket at 190.00

A workmanlike right-hand South Australian allrounder in the decade before World War II. He batted efficiently enough in the lower order to take heavy toll of any loose or tired bowling and often took valuable wickets with his medium-pacers and off-breaks. He made one tour of England with the Australian team performing splendidly against the Counties without carrying this form into his only Test appearances.

Waite was born in the Adelaide suburb of Kent Town and played all his early cricket with West Torrens club. He first appeared for South Australia in 1930–31 against the West Indies at Adelaide, aged 19. In November, 1935, he took 5 for 42 for South Australia against England at Adelaide. He toured England in 1938 with Bradman's team, performing solidly against the Counties in scoring 760 runs at 25.33, topscore 77, and taking 57 wickets at 26.03, including 5 for 23 against Cambridge and 8 for 90 (match figures) against Derbyshire.

He made his Test debut in the Fourth Test at Leeds, when Bradman won a notable tactical battle by protecting him from the strike. In one five over period Waite faced only five balls and he made only three runs in a 37 run partnership that helped towards Australia's exciting five wickets victory. Waite opened the bowling with McCabe in the Fifth Test at The Oval in the absence of the injured McCormick. England made 7 for 903. Waite bowled 72 overs to take 1 for 150.

The experience improved his cricket and in the 1939–40 Australian season he shared a record South Australian fifth wicket stand that remains unbeaten of 281 with Cyril Badcock against Queensland. Waite made 137, his only century in first-class cricket, Badcock 236 in a total of 7 for 821. In all first-class matches for South Australia he scored 3,011 runs at 28.95 and took 120 wickets at 35.41.

Waite has some notable triumphs in Adelaide district cricket. He twice topped the first grade batting averages for West Torrens, in 1932–33 (68.12) and 1935–36 (73.54) and in each season West Torrens were premiers. In the 1935–36 season he played an innings of 339, which is still the Adelaide first grade record score. Waite bowled against Bradman for Glenelg in 1939–40 when Bradman made 303 in 220 minutes for Kensington and gave Waite's record a shake. Waite took most wickets in Adelaide district cricket that year, 49 at 16.18.

WALKER, Alan Keith, 1925–

First-Class Averages: Batting, 1,603 runs at 17.42; Bowling, 221 wickets at 27.47.

One of the many versatile sportsmen produced in the Sydney seaside suburb of Manly. As a fast left-arm bowler, he played cricket for Australia, New South Wales, Nottinghamshire and in the Lancashire and the East Staffordshire Leagues. As a Rugby centre, he played for Australia against the All-Blacks in 1947, toured Britain, France and the United States with the 1947–48 Wallabies, scoring one of the finest tries ever seen at Twickenham, and in two Tests against the 1950 British Lions. A shoulder injury sustained while he was playing Rugby League for Leigh in the English League championship forced his retirement from cricket in 1958, but not before he left some interesting landmarks.

Walker's cricket began in coaching classes conducted on Saturday mornings at Manly Oval by Les Gwynne and George Lowe, to whom he attributes his success. Walker used to polish one side of the ball with boot polish and scruff the other side to help produce swingers that bewildered other boys in the coaching class. At Sydney Grammar he was undecided whether to concentrate on left-arm spin or pace until the school's fast bowler broke down and he was asked to relieve him. He enjoyed the experience and stuck to pace from then on. He represented Grammar at rugby and cricket and played for the Combined GPS in 1943 in both sports. In first grade cricket for Manly, he took 7 for 8 and 7 for 6 in one outstanding game against Cumberland.

He played five seasons for New South Wales in the Shield competition between 1948–1953. In his first season, he headed the Australian bowling averages and took a hat-trick against Queensland. He took five wickets in an innings five times for NSW. He was in Lindsay Hassett's Australian team in South Africa in 1949–50 but did not play in a Test. His tour total of 25 wickets included 4 for 22 against a South African XI. He was an extremely wristy bowler who approached the crease with his left-arm cocked behind his left ear and there was frequent discussion about the fairness of his delivery, but he was not called.

With bowlers like Miller, Lindwall and Johnston ahead of him in the Australian side, he went off to play three seasons for Rawtenstall (1953, 1954, 1955) in the Lancashire League, and in 1954 joined Nottinghamshire. The following season against Leicestershire he performed one of cricket's legendary feats, taking a wicket with the last ball of the first innings and wickets with the first three balls of the second innings—the first bowler to take four wickets in that manner. Between 1954 and 1958 he took 93 wickets for Nottinghamshire at 32.78, four times taking five wickets in an innings, best effort 7 for 56 against Middlesex in 1957 at Lord's. In 1956 he and Bruce Dooland added 123 for the 10th wicket against Somerset at Trent Bridge.

WALKER, Charles William ("Chilla"), 1909–1942

First-Class Averages: Batting, 1,754 runs at 14.99; Dismissals, 319 (171 catches, 148 stumpings).

Australia's cheerful deputy wicket-keeper on two tours of England, a smiling, curly-headed cricketer everybody liked. He kept wicket for South Australia for 12 seasons, and scored more than 1,000 runs for that State. He died in an air battle over Germany while serving as a Flying Officer with the RAAF, aged 33, without having played in a Test.

Charlie Walker first won a place in the South Australian team at the end of the 1928–29 season and dismissed eight batsmen on his debut, five stumped and three caught. The following summer he had an outstanding match against Arthur Gilligan's England team in Adelaide, with seven victims (four stumped, three caught). This effort won him a place as deputy to Oldfield on the 1930 tour of England. He showed uncommon promise but a succession of injuries to his fingers hampered him and sapped his confidence. He made only 43 runs at 4.77, and in 16 tour games made 25 dismissals from 11 catches and 14 stumpings.

There was always keen debate about the merits of Walker and Victorian Ben Barnett. In 1934 Barnett was preferred for the trip to England as Oldfield's deputy. In 1938, Barnett and Walker both toured, following the retirement of Oldfield. Walker broke a finger before the first team was picked in England and missed so many matches that when he took the field against Somerset team-mates asked who was the stranger. To support his fragile left forefinger Walker wore a three-fingered glove: he put the first two fingers for half their length into a wide leather stall containing sponge-rubber and jammed the lot into one enlarged compartment in his left glove.

Barnett played in all the Tests in 1938 and Walker played in only nine matches. He scored 198 runs at 24.75 and made 14 dismissals from seven catches and seven stumpings. Despite his injured fingers Walker dismissed six NSW batsmen in an innings at Sydney in 1939–40 and nine in the match, thereby equalling the South Australian record set by Gordon Inkster, at 6 ft 3 in perhaps the largest Australian ever to stoop to wicket-keeping.

WALKER, Maxwell Henry Norman ("Tangles"), 1948–

First-Class Averages: Batting, 2,014 runs at 15.49; Bowling, 499 wickets at 21.66

Tests (34): 586 runs at 19.53; 138 wickets at 27.47.

An instantly likeable right-arm medium-pace bowler of profound eneavour and uncomfortable technique who gave great pleasure throughout the cricket world. He did what coaches advise their classes not to do. His arms, legs and body weight were all in the wrong place but produced deliveries that swung and cut quite sharply. He bowled off the wrong foot, turned chest-on instead of side-on, and crossed his feet in the delivery stride, but in his halcyon days gave batsmen little respite if they survived Lillee and Thomson. He played several important innings, had safe hands befitting a star Australian Rules footballer, but was slow of foot.

Walker was born at West Hobart, and educated at The Friends' School Hobart. He moved to the mainland in his teens, primarily to further his career as a footballer while he studied architecture at the Royal Melbourne Institute of Technology. Bowling off a 13-stride run, he used all of his 6 ft 4 in rawboned physique to propel the ball at a brisk medium-pace, digging the ball into the pitch in a flurry of arms and legs and achieving high bounce. The inswinger was his stock delivery but he could also make it swing away and had a handy leg-cutter when he rolled his big fingers over the ball.

He forced his way into the Victorian side in 1968–69 with a series of fine performances in district games for the Melbourne club. In 1972–73 he took 39 first-class wickets and made his Test debut against Pakistan at Melbourne, taking 2 for 112 and 3 for 39. He was responsible for a remarkable Australian victory in only his second Test when Pakistan required only 159 runs to win at Sydney. Taking the ball with Lillee, he took 6 for 15, including five wickets for three runs off his last 30 deliveries, and Pakistan were out for 106.

This display earned Walker a trip to the West Indies at the end of that season in the team managed by Bill Jacobs, who, realising Walker was innocent to the international scene, gave him the job of minding the Australian flag. Big Max promised he would protect it with his life, but the first time the flag was raised on a West Indian ground a coloured lad shinned up the flagpole and souvenired it. This loss did not upset Walker's on-the-field efforts, however, and when Lillee broke down he took over as the mainstay of the Australian attack. He captured 26 Test wickets at 20.73, an astounding effort for a bowler on his first tour. The English critic John Thicknesse said, "The magnificence of Walker's performance is best shown by comparing his figures with those of the West Indies' most successful fast bowler, Keith Boyce, whose nine wickets cost nearly 40 runs each, in a series Australia won 2–0."

Despite this success Walker did not enjoy first use of the new ball for long. When Lillee's back mended, Walker took the ball as first change, hardly a fair test of his capacity to swing the ball, but he did so manfully and enthusiastically.

Max Walker's rich appeal to spectators is clear in this shot of his reaction to a miscued stroke.

In the six Tests against England in 1974–75, he took 23 wickets at 29.73, including 8 for 143 in England's first innings of 529 in the Sixth Test when he held the stage without Lillee and Thomson. Through all these endeavours the big man built up a large and noisy following, particularly the occupants of Bay 13 at the Melbourne Cricket Ground.

On tour in New Zealand in 1973–74 and 1976–77, in England in 1975 and 1977, and at home until 1976–77, when he joined WSC, Max Walker was always looking for work, a stock bowler who could prove hostile, always ready to back up his captains with a few more accurate overs. Popular wherever he played he gave it his all, although in England he bowled too short and did not give his powers of swing a full chance. In 1975 in England, he took 14 Test wickets at 34.71 and in 1977 he had 14 Test wickets at 39.35.

He was a most valuable WSC player because of his great appeal to fans at the grounds and on TV. He continued in first-class cricket for Victoria after the settlement, but moving that vast frame around became increasingly arduous and when he found it was not fun anymore he stepped down from the Victorian team in 1981–82. He has written two books, *Tangles* and *Back to Bay 13*, and has already built a following as a TV commentator on the game.

Walker removes Ian Davis's leg stump with a ball that swung in from wide of the off stump.

A right-hand fast bowler short of express speed but of exceptional accuracy for South Australia and Australia. He toured England twice and played in four Test series at home. He is one of only three bowlers to take all ten wickets in an innings in Sheffield Shield matches (the others: Peter Allen, Ian Brayshaw). He was a great favourite with spectators who enjoyed heckling him as he took what was probably cricket's slowest walk back to his bowling mark. When he was taking wickets the walk seemed to get even slower. Ray Robinson called him the most gentlemanly of all fast bowlers.

Wall, a tall, dark, sharp-featured figure, delivered the ball off a 27 pace run after a fairly graceful approach, punctuated in the middle by a scissor-like movement of the legs, throwing his head back as he shot out his left leg in the delivery stride, and following through enthusiastically. He was a bowler of stamina as befitted one who bowled for 12 years in first-class matches but gave the impression as he took that long, tortured walk back that he was near collapse.

His big moment came at Sydney in 1932–33 when he took 10 for 36 for South Australia against a New South Wales side that included some of Australia's greatest batsmen. On a normal wicket, Wall at one stage took four wickets for none in one over, and he took the last nine wickets for five runs, six of them bowled. This is how he did it:

WALL, Thomas Wellbourne ("Tim"), 1904–1981

First-Class Averages: Batting, 1,063 runs at 10.52; Bowling, 328 wickets at 29.83.

Tests (18): 121 runs at 6.36; 56 wickets at 35.89.

Fingleton, b Wall	43
Brown, c Whitington, b Wall	0
Bradman, c Ryan, b Wall	56
McCabe, c Walker, b Wall	0
Rowe, b Wall	0
Cummins, c Walker, b Wall	0
Love, b Wall	1
Hill, b Wall	0
Howell, b Wall	0
O'Reilly, b Wall	4
Stewart, not out	2
Sundries	7
	113

Wall bowled at the stumps on a good length, seldom straying down the legside or outside the off stump, and he had a good bouncer off which he had Herbert Sutcliffe caught a few times at square leg. He was an erratic point or square leg fieldsman, capable of inspired spells in which he stopped everything and took brilliant catches, sometimes becoming leaden-footed and listless. As a tail-end batsman, he frequently stayed long enough for the batsman at the other end to score useful runs.

He made his debut for Australia in 1928–29 against England in the Fifth Test at Melbourne, taking 3 for 123 and 5 for 66. In

18 Tests over the next five years he took five wickets in an innings three times. In the infamous Adelaide Test during the 1932–33 Bodyline series, he took 5 for 72 and he headed Australia's bowling in that series with 16 victims at 25.56. His Test career included 13 wickets against South Africa in the 1931–32 series, against whom he had his career best of 5 for 14.

Wall first toured England in 1930 and was the third most successful Australian bowler with 56 wickets, behind Grimmett (142) and Hornibrook (93), but he was fairly expensive at 29.71 per wicket. He had one innings of 40 not out on that tour but finished with a mere 107 runs, average 8.23. He went back to England in 1934 and took 42 wickets at 31.02, finishing ahead of only Fleetwood-Smith in the batting averages, with 84 runs at 9.33. For South Australia, he had impressive figures with 10 for 36 against NSW, 5 for 92 against Queensland in 1928–29 at Adelaide, and 6 for 40 against West Australia in 1925–26 at Adelaide his best analyses.

WALMSLEY, Walter Thomas, 1917–1978

First-Class Averages: Batting, 1,064 runs at 27.28; Bowling, 122 wickets at 31.64.

An allrounder who sprung from Sydney's Western Suburbs club but performed best in first-class cricket for Tasmania and Queensland, for Northern Districts in New Zealand and in the Lancashire League.

Walmsley, a right-arm leg-spinner who flighted the ball effectively, brought rare application to his batting and fielding, and travelled the world polishing his skills. After limited opportunities in New South Wales, where the State had a crack eleven just after World War II, Walmsley took over as coach to the Northern Tasmanian Cricket Association and in 1947–48 scored 180 against the touring Indian side. Two months later he helped the Tasmanian side avoid defeat by scoring 41 in Hobart against the legendary 1948 Australian team, then on its way to England. Walmsley had four seasons coaching in Tasmania and in the English summers played League cricket for Stockport and then Oldham, until 1953.

Walmsley switched to Queensland at that start of the 1953–54 season as an official QCA coach and became an automatic choice for Queensland sides from 1954–55. In all, he took 102 wickets for Queensland with his spinners. With the bat, he helped set Queensland ninth and tenth partnership records, scoring 152 with Wally Grout against New South Wales in 1956–57 for the ninth wicket, and 105 with fellow spinner John Freeman against New South Wales in 1957–58 for the tenth wicket. He had a way of conveying his great enthusiasm for the game to all he coached. Finally, he went coaching in New Zealand, playing for Northern Districts from 1958 to 1960, often returning to watch Tests in Australia.

1056

Doug Walters driving during a one-day game in Sydney against the West Indies. Below: Graeme Wood, talented left-handed opener, turns a ball to leg.

A lithograph by Charles Troedel of the Melbourne Cricket Ground on January 1, 1864, when George Parr's English team played XXII of Victoria.

Steve Rixon and slips fieldsman Bob Simpson alert for the next ball during a match in Sydney.

A practitioner of all of cricket's infinite skills, who for want of classification has to go in under all-rounders. As a left-arm spin bowler, he could get exceptional turn on the ball, frequently beating the batsman, stumps and wicket-keeper. With the bat he made 1,062 runs in a season at the age of 40 for Leicestershire. He spent a lifetime experimenting with spin and never regretted not playing for Australia, though he was far superior to many who have been honoured.

He began playing cricket with the Glebe club in Sydney in the 1930s as an orthodox left-arm finger spinner, but rejected this and turned to back-of-the-wrist spin, fascinated by the feats of Fleetwood-Smith. He developed a "Chinaman" ball that was to have devastating effect on batsmen in seven countries. He played for New South Wales Colts and New South Wales Seconds and in 1937 signed for two years with Sir Julien Cahn's team. He had a season in grade for Petersham when he returned in 1939 and played for New South Wales in two matches. When the war began, he joined the RAAF and for five years his bowling was confined to ground-coral pitches in the South Pacific.

On discharge in 1946 he went straight to Leicestershire, where with fellow-Australian Vic Jackson, he formed the spearhead of the attack for many years. He was a loveable man, who just enjoyed playing cricket every day. When the batsman played the wrong way and the ball missed everything and ran away for byes, he would look at the batsman he had just fooled and laugh, "That had you—didn't it?" Young bowlers went to him from all over England for advice.

Probably no left-arm spinner has had the mastery of the left-arm wrist-spinner's wrong-un or "Chinaman" that Walsh perfected over years of diligent practice. And few bowlers have been so consistently difficult to "read" as was Walsh at his prime. He could make the best of them from Len Hutton down through the Dennis Comptons and Bill Edrichs look quite foolish. He was one of the few Australians I have ever met who was happy in his life as a professional cricketer, despite the low pay, constant travelling, constantly changing conditions. "I love it", he said. "Fancy being paid for doing what you love."

He did not mind the English attitude to professionals or playing in teams led by amateur captains. In 1952 he did the "double" by scoring 1,106 runs and taking 122 wickets, but he always said his best performance was in taking 148 wickets in 1946, having come straight from the war in Dutch New Guinea and Borneo to a completely different English climate. He coached after he left Leicestershire in South Africa, Pakistan, Tasmania and died at Wallsend, where he had taught small boys about wrist spin before the war. In 279 games for Leicestershire he scored 6,892 runs at 17.63 and took 1,127 wickets at 24.25. He took five wickets in an innings 98 times

WALSH, John Edward ("Jack"), 1912–1980

First-Class Averages: Batting, 7,247 runs at 17.76; Bowling, 1,190 wickets at 24.56.

Jack Walsh, master left-arm spinner, unveils the action that brought more than 1,000 first-class wickets.

and ten wickets in a match 26 times. In two matches for New South Wales, he took 2 wickets at 65.50, and scored 11 runs, average 11, figures that in no way convey the craftmanship of this immensely likeable cricketer.

A sound, free-scoring right-hand batsman for Victoria and New South Wales, a useful medium-pacer, and a reliable fieldsman who wasted his chance for Australia by becoming over cautious. He played in one Test at Melbourne in 1884–85 against Shrewsbury's English team, and toured England with the 1890 Australian side but the splendid range of shots that featured in his displays for State teams disappeared when he played in the national team.

Walters, born in East Melbourne of parents who migrated from Gloucestershire, played his early grade cricket for Carlton, but later transferred to South Melbourne. He scored two centuries for Victoria, 106 in January, 1891 and 112 in 1891–92 both in Sydney against New South Wales, where the hard pitch suited his stroke play. It was at Sydney that he scored 122 for Combined Australia in 1888–89 against the 1888 Australian team, and it was at Sydney that he made 150 for New South Wales against Queensland in 1895–96 after he changed States.

In England he was unsettled by the slower, damper pitches, and he made only 402 runs at 10.05. The one bright spot of his tour was a plucky innings at 53 not out against Surrey at The Oval. In his sole Test, he scored 7 and 5 for an average of six. Walters, originally an ironmonger, was a very powerful hitter when set. He later became a hotel owner and died at sea off Bombay.

WALTERS, Francis Henry, 1860–1922

First-Class Averages: Batting, 1,755 runs at 20.17; Bowling, 1 wicket at 81.00.

Tests (1): 12 runs at 6.00.

One of four children brought up on a Dungog dairy farm 240 kilometres from Sydney, and one of the most popular of all Australian cricketers. Even after 74 Tests and 15 Test centuries he still approached his cricket as naturally as when he batted on the antbed wicket he and his family, mother included, used in between milking 150 cows a day. He was always eager to attack with the bat and hit some of the longest sixes seen on Australian grounds.

Walters was the first player for whom fans made a banner on the Sydney Hill—"The Duggie Walters Stand." When he was omitted from the Australian team to tour England in 1981, his followers organised protest marches, questions were asked about it in parliament, and one selector received a death threat. He had started the 1980–81 Australian summer with good scores, but had disappointed towards the end.

His fielding and his bustling medium-pace bowling added to the big contributions he made to whatever team he was in, but the appeal of the man remained in his laconic acceptance of success or failure. He was the relaxed Australian, just as happy with a beer in his hand or playing a game of cribbage as in acknowledging the crowd's applause for a century or another big six. He is said to have frequently gone in to bat not

WALTERS, Kevin Douglas ("Freddie"), 1945–

First-Class Averages: Batting, 16,180 runs at 43.84; Bowling, 190 wickets at 35.69.

Tests (74 plus 1 abandoned): 5,357 runs at 48.26; 49 wickets at 29.08.

Doug Walters faces a hat-trick ball from Phil Edmonds in the Third Test at Leeds in 1975. This was the match ruined by vandals who damaged the pitch with knives and oil.

knowing his team's score, dropping his cards to grab his bat and cap. Team-mates joked about him warming up by throwing a single dart into the dart board. He was no joke, however, to a long list of batsmen he dislodged when they were well set. He had a rare talent as a partnership-breaking bowler.

Walters began his competitive cricket at 11, in the Dungog school team. His love for kids communicated itself to youngsters in the crowd even after he turned 35. After playing for his school on Saturday mornings he played for Dungog Colts on Saturday afternoons. Then he started journeying 50 kilometres into Maitland for grade matches. State selector Jack Chegwyn saw him in Maitland in 1963–64 and picked him in the State Colts. Doug made 140 not out against Queensland Colts, hitting one six right out of Sydney Cricket Ground No 2 into Kippax Lake 60 metres from the ground. That innings earned him a place in the State side, and 18 months later he moved to Sydney to play for Cumberland, where he believed he could get wise counsel from Richie Benaud. In 1964–65, he got 100 in his first State game at Melbourne (one six) and 235 (two sixes) at Adelaide in a record second wicket partnership of 378 with Lyn Marks. In 1965–66, two centuries and an 80 in State matches won him a Test berth against England. He started gloriously with an innings of 155 in his first Test at Brisbane, followed by a century in his next Test at Melbourne, and a fine all-round effort in the Fifth Test at Melbourne, where he made 60 and took 4 for 53. Then, at a crucial time in

1060

his cricket career, he was lost to the game while he did two years Army service. He won many admirers by the manner in which he accepted Army service without complaint, and returned full of runs, as determined as ever to attack the bowling.

Some observers believe that Walters' technique slipped during his two years out of the game. On hard, fast pitches his crisp driving, bold cutting and quite devastating hooking, combined with speedy running between wickets made him a match-winner. But when the ball turned on wet or damaged pitches or moved in the air a lot as it does on hazy days in England he began to fan at the ball with a bat that was less than straight. Smart bowlers like John Snow and later Bob Willis exploited this weakness.

The end of Walters' last Test innings in England in 1977, with Bob Willis removing his off stump.

Walters candidly admitted to a fault that often had him caught in the gully. "I think it's because I see the ball too well," he said. "Most batsmen play straight through the ball moving away from them and miss it completely. I tend to follow the ball, with the result that I get an edge to those that swing." He was not helped by the umpires' acceptance of two or three bouncers an over, nor the selection of four fast bowlers in teams like the West Indies, who virtually discarded slow bowlers, for Walters has been one of the greatest players of slow bowling Australian cricket has produced.

Ian Chappell rated Walters in his prime as a match-winner, reasoning that in a six-Test series Walters would have a possible 12 innings and only had to get two or three big scores in his peculiarly daring style to swing the series. Walters' high average for New South Wales (41.84) and Australia (48.26) certainly did not make him a passenger, and he scored 19 centuries for New South Wales in a career total of 45 centuries.

Few innings in modern times have matched Walters' 103 against England at Perth in 1974–75 when he scored a century between tea and stumps, hooking the last ball of the day from

The Walters pull shot was characteristic of his crowd-pleasing aggression and brought him countless runs.

1062

Walters, on 100, nonchalantly lets a wide delivery pass at the Sydney Cricket Ground.

Bob Willis for six. That innings played just as big a part in the ultimate Australian victory by nine wickets as did the pace bowling of Thomson and Lillee and the outstanding catching that saw Australia hold 17 of the 18 catches offered.

Walters did not fare well in World Series Cricket but he was loyal to Kerry Packer's operation and took his relegation to matches in the bush without irritation. Came the settlement and he was recalled to boost Australia's chances in 1979–80 one-day games and then got back into the Test side in 1980–81, when he headed the Australian batting averages.

He had become a highly efficient No 6 batsman, able to push the score along with smart dabs and the occasional brave pull shot, as always a superb driver and runner between wickets. Not many of his shots went over the fence anymore but only the finest bowling could restrict his scoring. When he missed a place in the Australian side for England in 1981 he took it like the good sport he is, praising the selectors for choosing youngsters like Dirk Wellham and stressing that the death-threat to selector Alan Davidson was taking things too far.

The selectors had based their decision to drop him on his past performances in England, Walters said. For the record, he made 933 runs at 31.10 on his first tour of England in 1968, scoring 343 in the five Tests at 38.11. In 1972 he made only 54 in seven Test innings, making 935 runs on the tour at 38.95. In 1975 he topped the Australian averages with 784 runs at 60.30 but made only 125 at 31.25 in Tests. In 1977, he made only 663 runs on the English tour at 26.52, scoring 223 runs in five Tests, best score a dashing 88 at Old Trafford.

Thus in four tours of England he failed to score 1,000 runs in a season and failed to score a Test century. Most who saw him bat through the 1980–81 Australian season believed he deserved a fifth crack at the only real blemish in his record, a Test 100 in England. He had scored four centuries in Tests against England at home, and his overall performance in 37 Tests against England had not been all that bad—1,961 runs at 35.02.

Up to his retirement at the start of the 1981–82 season, Doug Walters had made 103 appearances for New South Wales, ten more than the previous record of 93 by Brian Booth. For his State, he hit 6,612 runs, topscore 253 against South Australia in 1964–65. He passed 200 for NSW a second time with 201 not out against England in 1970–71. The New South Wales Cricket Association in a move unprecedented in the 123 years of the Association's existence, decided in 1980–81 to give Walters a benefit season. The Association had staged testimonial matches for top players but this was the first time it had given a player a benefit year. Not that it meant as much as it should to Walters, who stood to lose a substantial proportion of his benefit year income to taxation.

A right-arm leg-break and googly bowler who had to compete for a Test place against Clarrie Grimmett, Bill O'Reilly and Fleetwood-Smith, a sad misfortune of birth for any bowler to have to bear. He deserves to be considered individually, however, for he was a degree graduate leg-spinner on unresponsive pitches even if he did not go on to his masters. On a pitch that gave even the slightest help he could really turn the ball and was one of the select group whose spin could be heard as well as seen. He was one of the honest toilers Arthur Mailey had in mind when he condemned the awarding of honours only to batsmen ("The last bowler knighted was Sir Francis Drake").

Ward, born in Sydney and developed in the St George area, could baffle the finest batsmen though he lacked the inspiration of Mailey or Grimmett. By following these great bowlers so closely he was often unfairly compared with them. He was a rank tailender with the bat but had the courage to stick around when required. His fielding was adequate but looked pedestrian in such a brilliant fielding side as Australia boasted between 1936 and 1938.

Ward took 121 wickets at 21.23 in first grade for St George before he moved to Adelaide to qualify for South Australia. He made his first-class debut for SA in 1935–36 while Grimmett was absent with the Australian team in South Africa, and in his first season took 33 wickets at 23.51. When Grimmett returned they provided SA with a splendid spin attack, and when the Australian team was chosen for the First Test against England at Brisbane in 1936–37 Ward was preferred to Grimmett. He did reasonably well, bowling long stints in both innings to take 2 for 138 and 6 for 102. In the Third Test at Melbourne when Australia was asked to bat on a rain-affected pitch in the second innings Bradman sent in O'Reilly and Fleetwood-Smith and when O'Reilly went quickly replaced him with Ward. With a lot of pluck and some luck they batted out time, giving the pitch time to dry out. Ward was finally out for 18, his highest Test score, having done a grand job in holding up the England attack. Bradman, batting at No 7, made 270, Fingleton, batting at No 6 scored 136 and Australia won the match by 365 runs. Dropped from the Fourth and Fifth Test of that series, Ward watched Australia win the series 3–2.

Ward was again chosen ahead of Grimmett for Australia's 1938 tour of England, a highly controversial selection in view of Grimmett's brilliant record in England. He did well in the matches against the Counties and took 96 wickets at 18.98, including match figures of 9 for 142 against Leicestershire, 8 for 53 v. Derbyshire, 6 for 64 v. Cambridge, and 11 for 77 v. Essex. But he appeared in only one Test, the first at Trent Bridge, where England made 658 and Ward had 0 for 142.

At home in 1938–39 he teamed with Grimmett to help win

WARD, Francis Anthony, 1909–1974

First-Class Averages: Batting, 871 runs at 13.83; Bowling, 320 wickets at 24.68.

Tests (4): 36 runs at 6.00; 11 wickets at 52.18.

the Sheffield Shield for SA, taking 24 wickets at 35.20 apiece, compared with Grimmett's 27. His first-class career ended with World War II with 6 for 105 v. WA at Perth in February 1940 his last big coup. But he did appear in a few Sydney grade games during the war. He took 187 wickets in all for SA at 26.98, 10 times taking five wickets in an innings for the State, best figures 7 for 62 against New Zealand in November, 1937, a performance that undoubtedly boosted his 1938 English tour selection.

WARDILL, Benjamin Johnson ("Major"), 1842–1917.

First-Class Averages: Batting, 21 runs at 10.50.

A skilful and popular administrator, who played a vital role in establishing international cricket when it first began. He took three Australian teams to England (1886, 1899, and 1902) at the invitation of the MCC, and accompanied MCC teams around Australia. He was known as "The Galloping Major" and when he settled in Melbourne not much happened in that city in which he did not figure.

He was born at Everton, near Liverpool, England, but came to Australia in 1861. He took a job with the Victorian Sugar Company and later joined the Garrison Artillery, where he won his rank. He was a good cricketer who kept wicket for Victoria and Melbourne Cricket Club. He was also a fine rifle shot who did much to popularise this sport, and toured America with a team of Australian marksmen who shot at the first international rifle competition held as part of the Philadelphia Exhibition in 1876.

Wardill became secretary of the Melbourne Cricket Club in 1879, when it had 572 members, and when he retired in 1911 the club had 5,353 members. He was much loved by players in the teams he managed and the Governor-General, Lord Dudley, presided over his testimonial day when he retired. He played for Australia at Hastings in 1886, scoring 17. In two first-class innings for Victoria he made four runs, average four, but in matches with or against the odds he did better, averaging 5.66. His brother, **Richard Wilson Wardill** (1835–1873), played 10 first-class matches, scoring 383 runs at 31.63 and taking 8 wickets at 10.50. He scored the initial century in Australian first class cricket, 110, for Victoria v. NSW at Melbourne in 1867–68. Dick Wardill died tragically when he threw himself into the Yarra River.

WARNES, THE

Father and son from the Melbourne suburb of Carlton who had impressive careers in first-class cricket.

Thomas Summerhayes Warne (1870–1944), a Life Member of Carlton Football Club, was a right-hand batsman of quality who made his debut for Victoria in 1894–95, and in 46 first-class matches for the State scored 2,148 runs at 31.58, with two centuries, topscore 153 against Tasmania at Hobart in 1911–12. He toured New Zealand with a Victorian team in 1909–10 and in 1906–07 took 6 for 50 with his left-arm wrist spinners against New South Wales.

Tom Warne, a little man of stern will, scored 402 for Carlton against Richmond in 1888–89, which was the club's record score until Jack Worrall made 417 not out against Melbourne University in 1895–96. Tom Warne began work at Carlton Oval as a groundsman in 1885, and was appointed curator in 1895. On his death the job passed to his son, H. C. J. Warne—who played for Carlton between 1927 and 1939—and for some 80 years until 1964 the Warne family were responsible for one of the finest grounds in Australia.

Tom's other son, **Frank Belmont Warne** (1906–   ), a left-hand batsman and left-arm googly bowler who, like his father, played for Carlton district club, played two games for Victoria in 1926-27, scoring 54 runs at 27.00. Frank played county cricket for Worcestershire from 1934 to 1938, and in 78 matches scored 2,670 runs at 20.69, with two centuries, top-score 115. He also took 96 wickets for Worcestershire at 26.26, best figures 6 for 51. He appeared in 10 matches in India between 1934–35 and 1937–38, and in 1935–36 played for the Australian team in India. After he settled in Johannesburg he played for Transvaal in 1941–42 and for the Rest of South Africa in 1942–43.

T. S. Warne, whose family had an 80-year association with Melbourne Carlton CC.

WARWICK CLUB

An important Sydney cricket club in the three decades before district cricket was introduced. The Warwick club hired William Caffyn at £300-a-year to coach in Sydney before he transferred to the Warwick CC's great rivals, the Albert CC. The Warwick had some enthralling matches against the Albert, Australian, National, Belvidere and Carlton. The Bannerman brothers, Charles and "Alick," John Cottam, Edwin Evans, and Fred Spofforth all began the careers that led to Test status with the Warwick club, which also developed an extensive list of State players. Ned Sheridan, Nat Thompson and the Gregory brothers, Arthur and Charles, all played for Warwick at a time when there was keen competition for their services. Like most of their colourful rival clubs, the Warwick disappeared when Sydney district cricket began in 1893–94.

WATKINS, John Russell, 1943–

One of the strangest of all Test selections, a right-arm leg break bowler of extremely wayward length. He was so nervous it was difficult to assess if he could really spin the ball and he gave Australia's top wicket-keepers a dreadful time in

1067

First-Class Averages:
Batting, 71 runs at 10.14;
Bowling, 20 wickets at
36.30.

Tests(1): 39 runs at 19.50;
0 wickets for 21.

his brief period in big cricket. But he had such a happy nature all his team-mates liked him and felt sorry that he could not settle down and bowl to a length.

Playing for Northern New South Wales against Pakistan at Newcastle, his birthplace, he took 6 for 38 in 1972–73. He had played only five first-class games and taken only 10 wickets at 36.90 when he was chosen for the Third Test at Sydney against Pakistan. A week before the Test he went on to bowl for NSW in a Shield match played on a strip adjoining the Test pitch. His first few overs were studded with wides and full tosses. David Colley asked wicket-keeper Brian Taber who had been jumping and sprawling trying to put a glove to Watkins' deliveries if the pitch was taking spin. "Don't know about the one we're playing on, but Watkins should be right for the Test—he's getting turn out of *that* wicket."

Watkins appeared completely overawed in the Test when he was given the ball and had several wides in his six overs. But with the bat he played a notable role in Australia's 52 runs win, scoring 36 not out in an 83-run ninth wicket stand with Massie. This gave Max Walker just enough runs to bowl at and his 6 for 15 when Pakistan required only 159 to win clinched an astounding victory, Watkins taking the catch that ended Pakistan's innings.

The selectors apparently believed nerves had produced the wides and high full tosses in that Sydney Test, for they persisted with Watkins for the team that toured the West Indies immediately the Australian season ended. He played in four matches on tour, taking 10 wickets at 33.60 and scored 20 runs at 10.00, and disappeared from first-class cricket on his return.

WATSON, Graeme Donald, 1945–

First-Class Averages:
Batting, 4,674 runs at 32.68; Bowling, 186 wickets at 25.31.

Tests (5): 97 runs at 10.77; 6 wickets at 42.33.

One of the select group who have represented three Australian States, a durable all-rounder of Victorian origin whose right-hand batting and right-arm medium pace bowling was seen all over the cricket world. His record is a tribute to his enthusiasm and resilience as midway through his career he took a ball in the face from Tony Greig which smashed his nose and cheekbone and had him in a serious condition in a Melbourne hospital during which he was given 40 pints of blood in transfusions. At one point he stopped breathing and doctors gave him heart massage and mouth-to-mouth resuscitation.

Watson, born in the Melbourne suburb of Kew, was a cricketer who deserved his triumphs. His versatility and sunny disposition made him invaluable to the three States for whom he played, for Australia in England, South Africa and New Zealand and finally for WSC. He bowled brisk medium-pacers, cutting the ball sharply when the pitch was damp, fielded splendidly and could open the batting or go in in the middle of the order. He was in Victorian and Western Australian teams that won the Shield.

When Watson first appeared in first-class cricket in 1964–65 he was an opening batsman, and the job was firmly held for his home State by Lawry and Redpath. He was dropped after two games and went back to opening for the Melbourne club in grade cricket. He was laid up with a broken wrist in 1965–66 but returned to win a place in the Australian team that toured South Africa in 1966–67. His selection followed an impressive burst of form in which he scored 109 against Queensland and took 6 for 61 against South Australia. He had his National Service call-up papers at home but was able to have this deferred because of his studies in architecture and made the tour as a replacement

Graeme Watson pulls a ball for four in a typically pugnacious innings for WA against NSW.

for Doug Walters, whose call-up was not deferred. But the tour did cost his place in the Melbourne Australian Rules team as a wingman.

Neil Hawke broke down in the First Test in South Africa and Watson was rushed in as his replacement. He batted soundly for 50 but did little bowling. In his next Test appearance he suffered a pinched nerve in the spine at Johannesburg but recovered to bowl a further 19 overs and take 2 for 67. The tour brought a big improvement and in his first match in the 1969–70 Australian season he shared a stand of 263 in 205 minutes with Peter Bedford for the fifth wicket against Western Australia in Melbourne. Watson's 150 in that partnership was his highest score for Victoria and he finished that season with 533 runs at 38.07. His reward was a tour of New Zealand at the end of that season in the Australian team captained by Sam Trimble.

He moved to Perth in 1971–72 and became a valuable player for the Western Australian team with his forceful driving, superb fielding and vigorous medium-pace bowling. Having played in the Victorian team that won the Shield in 1966–67 he proceeded to play in the WA teams that won in 1971–72, 1972–73, and 1974–75. He hit two centuries in 1971–72, 122 against Queensland in Brisbane and 145 in the return game at Perth. On January 5, 1972, he was hit on the face by that ball from Greig which almost ended his career. After he recovered doctors advised him to retire but he declined. Two months later he was chosen in the Australian team to tour England under Ian Chappell.

Watson's dramatic recovery was completed when he made 176 in a stand of 301 with Keith Stackpole against Hampshire. This was the highest opening partnership by an Australian pair in England and a record for the fourth innings of a first-class match in England. Watson hit 26 fours and five sixes and was out when he mishit another huge blow. This remarkable knock won him a place in the First Test at Manchester in that series but he made only 2 and 0 and was dropped from a defeated side. He had other triumphs on the tour, such as his double against Middlesex at Lord's when he took 4 for 23 and then opened the Australian innings with 84 in 97 minutes but was not picked again until the Fifth Test, which Australia won to square the series.

At the age of 31 he was transferred in his job as marketing executive for a construction group in Sydney and soon won a place in the NSW Shield team. In five games for his third State he had a topscore of 70 in compiling 188 runs at 28.85 and took 8 wickets at 22.50. The following season, 1977–78 he signed to play for WSC and in his first match took 7 for 26, including the wickets of Barry Richards, Asif Iqbal and Mike Proctor. His colourful career finally ended with the settlement between WSC and the ACB.

A powerful right-arm fast bowler and right-hand batsman from the Mudgee district of New South Wales who showed rich promise for the University of NSW and briefly for the NSW and Worcestershire County teams. He also played a match for Western Australia, but five years of non-stop cricket and marriage to an English girl saw him forsake Test ambitions for life in the Birmingham League. He made his debut for NSW in 1977–78, appeared for Worcestershire in 1978 and 1979 and for WA in 1979–80. He toured England in 1977 with the Old Collegians. He reached 100 first-class wickets so quickly a big future seemed ahead of him.

WATSON, Gregory George ("Gulgong"), 1955–

First-Class Averages: Batting, 552 runs at 12.83; Bowling, 102 wickets at 37.56.

A sound, painstaking right-hand opening batsman who made two overseas tours with Australian teams but failed to grasp his chance when tried in Tests. He had a pleasing array of drives and cuts, glanced splendidly and had a particularly effective sweep shot. He went into the NSW side from the St George club in 1953–54 and in only his second first-class match batted 375 minutes for 155 against Len Hutton's England team. This won him a place in the Australian team for the Fifth Test of that series but he made only 18 and 3.

Watson, born at Randwick, NSW, went to the West Indies under Ian Johnson's captaincy in 1954–55, but was overshadowed by some prodigious scoring by his team-mates. He was tried at second wicket down but in five Test innings on superb batting strips had a best score of 30. The tour experience did wonders for his batting and although he could not regain his Test place he became a valued member of the NSW team until a family bereavement ended his career. He made six first-class centuries, including 206 for NSW against Western Australia at Perth and 198 against Queensland in 1956–57. He was still turning out regularly in his 40's for the NSW Cricketers' Club, companionable and likeable as ever, thoroughly enjoying the relaxed atmosphere of City & Suburban cricket.

WATSON, William James ("Willie"), 1931–

First-Class Averages: Batting, 1,958 runs at 32.09.

Tests (4): 106 runs at 17.66.

The reserve wicket-keeper for the 1912 Australian team in England and one of the least known of all Australian first-class cricketers. He played only six matches for South Australia in the 1910–11 and 1911–12 seasons during which he caught five and stumped two batsmen. When Australia's No 1 'keeper Hanson Carter refused to visit England under the Board's terms, Victorian Barlow Carkeek replaced him as the Test 'keeper, with Webster as his deputy. Webster, who came from North Adelaide club, did not appear in any of the six Tests of the Triangular series although Carkeek was below

WEBSTER, Harold, 1889–1949

First-Class Averages: Batting, 275 runs at 13.09; Dismissals 23 (20 catches, 3 stumpings).

top-class. In all matches on the tour Webster, then 23, made 15 catches and one stumping and scored 139 runs at 15.44, top-score 26 against Worcestershire. He was not seen in first-class cricket again after the Australian team returned home. His six matches for SA had produced a topscore of 39. He was born and died in Sydney.

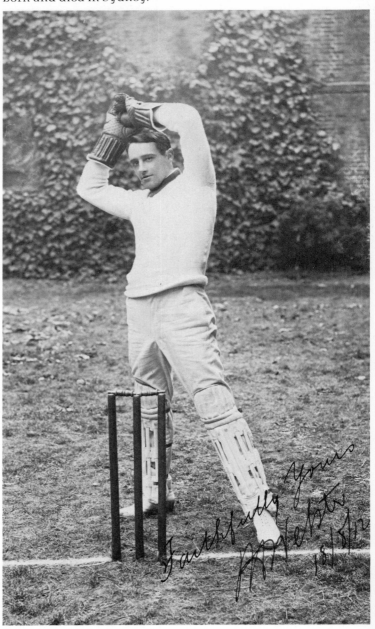

Slightly-built Harold Webster, one of the least known of all Australia's first-class players.

A solid, determined right-hand batsman who played 23 matches for New South Wales between 1972–73 and 1977–78. He was a dour competitor, capable of holding out even the most talented bowling but he lacked the shot-making skill to punish the occasional loose ball. His runs came mainly from dabbing the ball into the gaps rather than from full-blooded drives and cuts. He was born at Orange in the NSW mid-west and was a promising Rugby Union player until he damaged a cartilage playing for NSW Country against Queensland in 1971. He was in the Western Suburbs team that won two Sydney grade premierships and captained Wests when Bob Simpson was absent. Later he played for Balmain and then Waratah-Mayfield in the Newcastle competition. Highspot of his first-class career was his 112 not out for NSW against Victoria at Melbourne in 1972–73.

WEBSTER, Stuart Edward, 1946–

First-Class Averages: Batting, 1,215 runs at 28.92.

A studious right-handed batsman who won a place in the 1981 Australian team for England after only five Shield matches. He scored two centuries in those matches at an average of 68 and probably won a tour spot in front of the public's idol Doug Walters. He is the son of Charlie Wellham, who played first grade with Western Suburbs club in Sydney, and the nephew of Wally Wellham, who played for New South Wales. Dirk captained the NSW Colts in Perth only a few weeks before he won Australian selection on the day before his 22nd birthday. He has shown fine temperament and intense application to the task of scoring runs despite a limited range of strokes on the offside. His brother Greg plays in Wests firsts and a cousin, Dale, in lower grades. Wellham, a diabetic, is a university graduate and qualified teacher. He justified the Australian selectors faith in him by scoring a splendid century in his first Test, just as he had done in his first Shield match.

WELLHAM, Dirk ("Smirk"), 1959–

Wellham showed such dedication to adjusting his technique to meet unusual English conditions—the pitches were covered for the first time on an Australian tour of England—that cricket writers with the team urged his inclusion in Tests long before he appeared in the Sixth Test at The Oval. Wellham did not let his admirers down, playing a glorious range of strokes that quickly carried his score past fifty and on into the nineties. There he suddenly succumbed to nerves and shots that had been easy for him only a few minutes before became difficult.

England's captain Mike Brearley cleverly blocked chances of singles, with Wellham on 99. Finally he punched the ball fiercely through the covers to take his score to 103. He was bowled soon afterwards. This outstanding innings enabled him to head both Test and tour batting averages, a fine

First-Class Averages: Batting, 1,058 runs at 42.35; Bowling, 1 wicket at 11.00.

Tests (4): 221 runs at 31.57.

Dirk Wellham with NSW team-mates Steve Rixon and John Dyson after their selection for the 1981 tour of England.

achievement on his first overseas trip with the Australian senior side (he had been to Sri Lanka with an Australian schoolboys team). He scored 497 runs at 55.22 on tour, top-score 135 not out, and in his sole Test scored 127 runs at 63.50, topscore that memorable 103. The 1981–82 season was a disappointment for Wellham and he lost his place firstly in the Australian team and then in the NSW team. There is no doubt he has the class to come back, as his four first-class centuries have shown.

WESSELS, Kepler Christoffel, 1957–

First-Class Averages: Batting, 8,618 runs at 49.25; Bowling, 3 wickets at 37.33.

A tough, skilful, consistent South African-born left-hander whose tenacious opening batting is expected to take him into the Australian Test team. He played for WSC in Australia in 1978–79 and has had three outstanding seasons with Queensland. He lives in Brisbane, where he owns a newsagency, and is a naturalised Australian. At the end of the 1981–82 season, when he was 24, he had scored 19 first-class centuries and taken two of these past 200 runs. He is a brilliant fieldsman, but has bowled only a few overs in six seasons of first-class cricket.

1074

Wessels, born in Bloemfontein in the Orange Free State, made his first-class debut for Orange Free State in 1973–74 against Northern Transvaal. Outstanding performances as a youth earned him selection in the Currie Cup competition at the age of only 16 years four months. He joined the Sussex County team in 1976 and was capped the following season, aged 20, but South Africa's sporting isolation induced him to forsake his homeland in 1978 and migrate to Australia in the hope of playing Test cricket.

He joined Ian Chappell's WSC ranks soon after his arrival and was an immediate success, challenging the recognised Test batsmen by scoring 291 runs at 41.57 in four matches. He moved to the Queensland team when the settlement with WSC was achieved and in his first season, 1979–80, he made five half centuries in scoring 623 runs at 36.67 topscore 93, but did not bat with his expected authority. Since then he has been the most consistent high-scoring batsman in the Shield competition, showing an off-side mastery unusual in a left-hander and an ability to fight his way out of trouble when confronted by hostile pace bowling.

Wessels made two centuries in 1980–81—134 against Victoria in Brisbane and 160 against NSW at Sydney—in scoring 814 runs at 50.88. In 1981–82 he improved further by becoming the seventh batsman to score more than 1,000 runs in a Shield season, 1,015 runs at 67.66. This performance included 220, the second highest score in his career, in a stand of 304 for the third wicket with Greg Ritchie, nine runs more than the previous best by Ken Mackay and Peter Burge in 1960–61. Only Wessel's 254 for Sussex against Middlesex in 1980 was higher. Not long after that innings the Australian Cricket Board ruled that he would be eligible to play for Australia after September, 1982.

WEST INDIES VERSUS AUSTRALIA

The record of wins and losses in matches between Australia and the West Indies strongly favours Australia, but most Australian cricket lovers are more mindful of the spectacular entertainment the West Indians have provided. There is always plenty of attractive cricket when the two countries meet, a tradition that dates back to the first Tests they played in 1930–31. To the end of the 1981–82 Australian season, Australia had won 26 of the 52 Tests between the countries, the West Indies 13, with 12 draws and one memorable tie, the only one in the history of Tests.

The Australian experience of West Indian cricketers has been as exciting as it has been remunerative for administrators who handle the gatemoney. In the early years, there was a tendency for the West Indians to squander advantages won by their marvellous flair for the game. Lately there has been a hardening in their approach, and their teams no longer are upset by pressure. They have learned to discipline their talents, and in achieving this over the past two decades owe a tremendous debt to two wonderful captains, Frank Worrell and Clive Lloyd, and to a lesser extent to Garfield Sobers.

The most enthralling Test series in modern times was played between Australia and the West Indies in 1960–61. Crowd records set during that series still stand, as does that tour's legacy of sportsmanship combined with whole-hearted endeavour. Matches against the old enemy, England, may provide more tension and more "needle" between the players, but for exuberant, joyful cricket the Australia v. West Indies matches stand alone.

WEST INDIES IN AUSTRALIA, 1930–31

G. C. Grant

The West Indies first played Test cricket in 1928, when they were defeated by an innings and 58 runs by England at Lord's, and lost all three Tests in the series. In 1929–30, England and the West Indies played a four Test series in the West Indies, each side winning a Test, with two drawn. The West Indies had only these seven Tests behind them when they undertook their first Australian tour in 1930–31. The touring party was badly chosen for Australian conditions at the time, with an attack based on fast bowling and spinners who could have been invaluable left at home. Many of the team met for the first time on the voyage to Australia. Worst of all, the captain, Jack Grant, was completely inexperienced in big cricket, although he had won Blues at Cambridge in 1929 and 1930, and his deputy, L. S. Birkett, had similarly played no Test cricket. The team ended with a disappointing record but with a big reputation as entertainers. Learie Constantine's big-hitting, acrobatic fielding and pace bowling is still discussed with awe by those who saw him. George Headley's batting skill remains a piquant memory, and the fast bowling of Griffith and Francis had character as well as genuine pace.

The tour began disastrously with a four wickets defeat by NSW at Sydney. Chilvers took 4 for 84 and 5 for 73 with his leg-spinners. In the second match at Melbourne against Victoria, Ironmonger took 5 for 87 and 8 for 31 after Ponsford had made 187 and Rigg 126 in a Victorian total of 594. The West Indies made only 212 and 128. At Adelaide in the third match Grimmett took 4 for 71 and 5 for 43 to set up a 10 wickets win for South Australia. Jack Grant batted bravely in the First Test at Adelaide but again Grimmett's spin was too much for the West Indies, who were beaten by 10 wickets. Grimmett had 7 for 87 and 4 for 96. Kippax's 146 included a stand of 182 for the fourth wicket with McCabe, who was brilliantly caught and bowled for 90 by Constantine. Ponsford made 183 in the Second Test at Sydney, where the West Indians again failed badly against Grimmett, Hurwood and Ironmonger and lost by an innings and 172 runs. Australian sealed the rubber by winning the Third Test at Brisbane by an innings and 217 runs. Bradman, missed in the slips at 4, scored 223 in 300 minutes, Ponsford 109, and the sole consolation for the West Indies was Headley's 102 not out, the first West Indian Test century against Australia. Australia went 4–0 in the series by taking the Fourth Test at Melbourne by another wide margin—an innings and 122 runs, with Bradman scoring another century (152). Ironmonger took 7 for 23 and 4 for 56 in West Indies' two batting collapses (99 and 107).

With the tour an apparent shambles, the West Indies then staged a dramatic revival. They defeated the powerful NSW side at Sydney by 86 runs, with Constantine having a splendid double by scoring 41 and 93 and taking seven wickets. The Fifth Test also provided an upset, with the West Indies winning their first Test against Australia by 30 runs. Their win was built on first innings centuries from F. R. Martin (123 not out) and Headley (105), and probably was clinched when Griffith bowled Bradman before he had scored in Australia's second innings. Griffith's jubilant reaction to this feat delighted spectators who gave him a standing ovation. He kept leaping and dancing well after the next man, Oldfield, had taken his guard. Grant headed the Test batting averages with 255 runs for six times out, but Headley was the star batsman, with four centuries on the tour and two in the Tests. Grimmett, with 33 wickets in the Tests at 17.96, and Ironmonger with 22 at 14.68 set problems the West Indies could not solve. Australia's Fifth Test defeat was helped by Grant's well timed declarations to allow his bowlers maximum use of a wet pitch.

George Headley

WEST INDIES IN AUSTRALIA, 1951–52

J. D. C. Goddard

John Goddard's team arrived in Australia after a triumphant tour of England in 1950, where they won a four Test series 3–1 thanks to memorable performances by Worrell, Weekes and Walcott and some superb spin bowling by Ramadhin and Valentine. Australia had defeated England and South Africa and the series looked to be a close tussle for world leadership. The First Test at Brisbane was an even contest, Australia winning by three wickets after Ring took 6 for 80 in the West Indies' second innings. Ramadhin bowled 64 overs in the match for 6 for 165, Valentine 65.7 overs for 6 for 216.

Thereafter the star West Indian batsman struggled against the pace bowling of Miller, Lindwall and Johnston and the Australian batsmen, helped by hard, fast pitches, solved the problems posed by Ramadhin and Valentine. Australia won the Second Test by seven wickets, West Indies the Third by six wickets, Australia the Fourth by one wicket and the Fifth by 202 runs to take the series 4–1. The failure of Weekes and Walcott was a mystery. Worrell made a good century (108) in the Fourth Test and Stollmeyer (104) in the Fifth but for the rest the West Indian batting crumbled against the Australian

pace attack. Worrell alone of the much publicised West Indian stars performed up to his reputation. His 6 for 38 in the Third Test saw Australia dismissed for 82, and his cricket throughout was skilful and versatile. Lindwall took 21 wickets in the series at 23.04, Miller 20 at 19.20.

The West Indies undoubtedly suffered from accepting an itinerary which gave them only one first-class match before the First Test. Gerry Gomez was the surprise of the West Indian lineup, establishing himself as a sheet anchor in a team that became accustomed to batting failures. A major cause of Australia's one-sided win in this rubber was the judicious use of the short ball by Australia's pace attack. Back in the West Indies George Headley was highly critical of his countrymen's failure against the bouncers sent down by Miller and Lindwall. All the Australian teams the West Indians encountered played it hard and they were never given a chance to settle down to confidence-building displays.

WEST INDIES IN AUSTRALIA, 1960–61

F. M. M. Worrell

At a time when Test cricket was stagnating through the overuse of defensive tactics that characterised Len Hutton's period as England's captain, Australia and the West Indies played an historic series. Before the First Test Kanhai made a chanceless 252 as the West Indies crushed Victoria, setting the pattern of spectacular batting that the tourists followed throughout. At Brisbane in the First Test, West Indies made 453 in the first innings when Sobers produced a masterly 132.

Australia responded with 505, O'Neill contributing 181, Simpson 92. The West Indies second innings yielded 284, leaving Australia to score 233 to win. Wes Hall, a fearsome figure with chest and lucky charm necklet exposed as he came tearing in, ripped through the early Australian batting. At 6 for 92, Australia could have settled for a draw. Instead Benaud and Davidson went fearlessly for the runs. Half an hour from stumps, Australia needed 27, but at 226, with only seven runs needed, Solomon ran out Davidson for 80.

When the last over began, Australia wanted six runs with three wickets in hand. Benaud, trying to win the match with one blow, was caught behind off Hall by Alexander off the second ball. Hunte then made a marvellous save to reduce a shot from Meckiff to two, running Grout out with a throw to Alexander as they attempted a third run. With Meckiff on two, Kline came in with two balls remaining, the scores level. Kline nudged what appeared to be the winning run but Solomon gathered it at square leg and with only one stump to aim at, hit the wicket. Three wickets in the final over of an enthralling match had produced cricket's first tied Test, Australia's second innings reaching 232. It was a match of records, with Davidson (44 and 80 with the bat, 5 for 135 and 6 for 87 with the ball), becoming the first to make 100 runs and take 10 wickets in a Test, and Sobers completing his 3,000th Test run.

From then on the captains, Benaud and Worrell, appeared to sense they had an obligation to play attractive cricket, and they allowed their talented players the widest scope. Australia won the Second Test at Melbourne by seven wickets despite a century from Hunte (110), Davidson taking a further eight wickets. West Indies won the Third Test at Sydney by 222 runs when Sobers hit another marvellous century (168) and Gerry Alexander produced a surprising and chanceless 108. Gibbs and Valentine both took eight wickets in this victory, with Gibbs the match-winner by dismissing Mackay, Martin and Grout in four balls. The Fourth Test at Adelaide was a thriller. Kanhai became the first West Indian to score a century (117 and 115) in each innings of a Test in Australia, and Gibbs took the first hat-trick in Tests between the countries. Typical of the cricket was Kanhai's six off the first ball of the third day from Benaud. Kline and Mackay finally staged a 100-minute partnership for a draw, Mackay taking the last ball of the match in the ribs rather than risk using the bat.

This sent the teams to Melbourne for the Fifth Test with a wonderful series level at a win each. Melbourne virtually stopped work for the five days the match lasted, and all around Australia offices and desks were deserted as people crowded to watch TV coverage of the play. The West Indies began with 292, Australia responding with 356, the difference being Colin McDonald's 91. Sobers bowled unchanged for 41 overs in Australia's first innings to secure 5 for 120. Davidson kept Australia in the match with 5 for 84 in the West Indies' second innings of 321. Set to score 258 in the final innings, Australia got them with only two wickets to spare. On the second day a world record 90,800 had attended and the following week when they left for home the West Indies were given a ticker tape send-off by the people of Melbourne. The result of the series had been in doubt when Valentine bowled with Australia at 7 for 254 in the last hour of the fifth day. The players noticed a bail on the ground at the striker's end but after consultation the umpires decided in Australia's favour, leaving the cause of the bail falling unexplained.

WEST INDIES IN AUSTRALIA, 1968–69

G. St. A. Sobers

Just as the failure of the legendary three Ws, Walcott, Weekes and Worrell had been inexplicable in 1950–51, the 3–1 defeat of Sobers' side was difficult to understand. They arrived in Australia with a glamorous reputation but were comprehensively outplayed by a young, enthusiastic Australian side. The answer once again was probably that the West Indies were given no easy games, even the State teams extending them with keen, competitive cricket. At Brisbane in the first Test Ian Chappell (117) and captain Bill Lawry (105) scored centuries for Australia, and Clive Lloyd got one (129) for the West Indies. Carew and Kanhai made a record second wicket stand of 165 for the West Indies, who won by 125 runs when Sobers had a second innings bag of 6 for 73. Ian Chappell (165) and Lawry (205) had a partnership of 298 in 310 minutes for the second wicket in the Second Test at Melbourne to pave the way to victory by an innings and 30 runs, which McKenzie sealed with 10 for 159 in the match. The Third Test at Sydney went to Australia by 10 wickets, Doug Walters scoring a lovely 118 in Australia's first innings of 547. The Fourth Test at Adelaide was drawn after centuries by Sobers (110), Butcher (118) abnd Walters (110) and some clever bowling by Alan Connolly. Australia decisively won the Fifth Test in Sydney when Walters made 242 in the first innings and 103 in the second. This gave him four centuries in the rubber. His stand of 336 in the first innings with Lawry remains the highest fourth wicket stand by Australia against the West Indies.

In beating this hitherto invincible West Indian side so convincingly, many young Australians created their reputations. From the West Indian standpoint, it was clear the selectors had gone a series too long with some of the older players, especially the pace bowlers Hall and Griffith. Sobers calculated that his team dropped 30 catches in the five Tests.

WEST INDIES IN AUSTRALIA, 1975–76

C. H. Lloyd

This was one of the most eagerly-awaited Test series of modern times between the two teams recognised as the strongest in world cricket. The outcome was an anti-climactic 5–1 win in the series to Australia, with the great fast bowling partnership Lillee and Thomson giving the West Indies a

1080

caning. Not only did they take wickets consistently, but they also gave the West Indian batsmen a battering, with batsmen frequently retiring hurt. The West Indies had only one opening stand of more than 50 runs in the six Tests. Between them Lillee, Thomson and the left-handed pace bowler Gary Gilmour took 76 of the 110 West Indian wickets to fall, Marsh enjoying a feast with 26 catches. A feature of the West Indian failure was how frequently star batsmen fell to the hook shot.

Australia won the First Test in Brisbane by eight wickets despite innings of 107 by Rowe and 101 by Kallicharan, Greg Chappell producing knocks of 123 and 109 not out. The Second Test at Perth produced 156 from Ian Chappell, but the West Indies won by an innings and 87 runs thanks to 169 by Fredericks and 149 by Lloyd in a total of 585. Fredericks scored his century off only 71 deliveries. Roberts was the destroyer for the West Indies with 7 for 54 in Australia's second innings. From then on Australia gained complete ascendancy, winning the last four Tests easily. The Australians supported fiery pace bowling with some splendid batting, Redpath scoring 102 in the Third Test, 103 and 65 in the Fifth, and 101 and 70 in the Sixth. Ian Chappell became the first Australian to take 100 Test catches during the Third Test, and his brother Greg contributed three centuries. But the series belonged to Lillee and Thomson. Vivian Richards made 1,107 runs at 58.26 on his first Australian tour, an indication of things to come.

A three Test series in Australia in 1979–80 saw a strong West Indian side triumph by two Tests to nil after a drawn First Test. Lloyd won the toss in the First Test at Brisbane and took the unusual step of asking Australia to bat. The combination of Vivian Richard's batting, Lloyd's generalship and the pace bowling of Garner, Holding, Roberts and Croft proved too much for Australia. Richards made a delightful 140 in the drawn First Test at Brisbane, where centuries by Greg Chappell (124) and Kim Hughes (130) on the last day saved Australia. The West Indies made 441 and 3 for 40, Australia 268 and 6 for 448 declared. Richards made 96 in the Second Test at Melbourne in a West Indian total of 397. Then the West Indian pace attack dismissed Australia for 259 in the second innings, leaving Haynes and Greenidge to score the 22 required for victory. Holding's pace in this match approached the fastest ever seen in Australia. Lloyd made 121 in the West Indies' first innings and Kallicharan 106 in the second innings during the Third Test in Adelaide. Australia folded up again against the four-man pace attack and the West Indies won by 408 runs, their highest winning margin against Australia.

WEST INDIES IN AUSTRALIA, 1979–80

C. H. Lloyd

The West Indies shared the Australian summer of 1981–82 with the Pakistan touring team, and the results were a tribute to their popularity. More than 355,000 watched the three

WEST INDIES IN AUSTRALIA, 1981–82

C. H. Lloyd

Tests played by Lloyd's men, compared with 90,000 for the three Australia v. Pakistan Tests. For most of the short series, the West Indians were on top but they were only able to draw the series because of their poor batting in one innings—the final innings of the First Test at Melbourne. Australia were probably fortunate to square the series. Larry Gomes was the surprise of the rubber, scoring 393 runs in six Test innings at 78.60, finishing ahead of Lloyd and other more publicised players. Gomes was the sole West Indian century-maker during the series, which was again dominated by the fast bowlers. Holding bowled at searing pace and on pitches that had the slightest bounce in them was a frightening proposition. Alan Border, John Dyson and Kim Hughes made centuries for Australia. After Australia won the First Test in Melbourne a brave rearguard action by Yardley helped save the Second Test at Sydney, which was drawn. In Adelaide Australia had chances to win until Lloyd strode to the crease on the fifth afternoon and proceeded to play a masterly innings of 77 not out that was brimful of thrilling square cuts and powerful drives. Yardley was Australia's potential match-winner but he failed to take a wicket as the West Indies comfortably scored the 239 runs needed to win with five wickets to spare. Gomes' calm, resourceful 124 in the West Indies first innings was probably the turning point, Australia fighting all the way to keep the result in doubt until only 17 balls were left.

AUSTRALIA IN THE WEST INDIES, 1954–55

I. W. Johnson

Australia's first tour of the West Indies produced some amazing scoring and records galore. There were 21 centuries in the five Tests, Australia scoring 12 of them, with the West Indies' Clive Walcott, who had failed so lamentably in Australia in 1951–52, taking the individual batting honours with five Test centuries. Twice in a series that produced Australia's highest ever Test total of 8 for 758 declared, Walcott scored a century in each innings of a Test. But perhaps the most notable feat of all was the seventh wicket stand of 347 by Atkinson and Depeiza in the Fourth Test which surpassed all other stands for that wicket in first-class cricket anywhere in the world. For many of the great Australian players, this West Indian tour was a last show of their quality, and they were never the same again once it was over. The Australians had only one warm-up match before the First Test at Kingston but prepared themselves well with a programme of calisthenics.

Australia's first Test in the Caribbean began with some accomplished batting by Harvey and Miller who, after a sound start by McDonald and Morris, added 224 for the third wicket to help Australia to a total of 515. Collie Smith, then only 20, made 44 in his first Test innings and 104 in the second. Despite this fine effort and 108 from Walcott, Australia won by nine wickets, the Australians revelling in the bright sunlight

1082

and all the bowlers adhering to a tight line and length. The Second Test at Port-of-Spain, Trinidad, the first played there on turf, saw some tremendous batting from Walcott (126 and 110) and Weekes (139 and 87 not out), but Australia matched them, McDonald (110), Morris (111) and Harvey (133) all making centuries in an Australian first innings of 600. The Third Test on the Bourda ground at Georgetown proved a triumph for Australian bowlers Benaud and Johnson in a spinners' match. In a low-scoring game that was quite different from others in the series, the West Indies managed only 182 and 207, Australia scoring 257 and 2 for 133 to win by eight wickets. Benaud took 5 for 58 in the match, Johnson 8 for 86.

With Australia leading 2–0, the teams went to the Fourth Test at Bridgetown tuned for a grim tussle but probably not for the flood of runs that ensued. Australia scored 668 in the first innings, Miller 137, Archer 98, and Lindwall 118, showing that pace bowlers can bat. The West Indies were in big trouble at 6 for 147 in reply when Atkinson and Depeiza came together. Cautiously, they put on 41 before stumps, giving no hint that they would bat all the next day and take the score to 494 before they were separated. Atkinson made 219, Depeiza, the team's wicket-keeper 122, and the West Indies reached 510. The match ended in a draw after six days.

The Fifth Test at Kingston yielded a duck for Les Favell and joy for most of the other Australian batsmen. The West Indies did not bat badly, with totals of 357 and 319, Walcott (155 and 110) again scoring a century in each innings, but Australia's record total of 8 declared for 758 gave them victory by an innings and 82 runs. McDonald (127), Harvey (204), Miller (109), Archer (128) and Benaud (121) were the five Australian century-makers in this amazing score. Miller completed a wonderful match with 6 for 107 and 2 for 58. The series was a personal success for Ian Johnson whose bowling was suited to pitches with plenty of bounce. Big crowds crammed the grounds wherever Australia played and much of this enthusiasm followed them even to their hotels. The first tour to a new place probably is always the best.

AUSTRALIA IN THE WEST INDIES, 1964–65

R. B. Simpson

Most of the outstanding players involved in the great series in 1954–55 had retired when Australia returned ten years later under Bob Simpson's leadership. The West Indies had built up their strength and their best players had a tougher, more seasoned outlook. Sobers had developed from a youngster of promise to a great cricketer and in Kanhai and Butcher the West Indies boasted two exciting stroke players. But the balance probably rested with the West Indies' more penetrative bowling. MacKenzie and Hawke had their moments and Mayne had one big match, but far too many Australians failed to bat sensibly against Charlie Griffith whose action was claimed to be suspect. Indeed at the end of the tour Norman O'Neill produced a series of articles condemning Griffith's delivery style and the umpires who sanctioned it. Bob Simpson was diplomatic about Griffith at the time, but has since been outspoken in his belief that Griffith should have been no-balled. But Griffith's figures were not as damaging as the Australians would have had you believe. He may have demoralised the Australians during the series but only in the Fifth Test, when he took 6 for 46 in Australia's first innings, did his figures influence the outcome.

Griffith's partnership with Hall gave big Wes the support he had lacked in the previous series against Australia, and they were admirably backed up by Sobers' left-arm swing and the off-spin of Lance Gibbs. With Sobers and Kanhai in their prime with the bat and Hendriks to keep wicket, the West Indian team was ideally balanced. Australia failed to get a good start in either innings of the First Test in which Hall took 5 for 60 and 4 for 45 and Griffith clean bowled four key batsmen. The West Indies won by 179 runs, their first success at home against Australia. The Griffith issue became highly emotional in the Second Test when O'Neill had to retire hurt after being hit by a Griffith bouncer. Cowper (143) and Booth (117) made centuries in an Australian first innings total of 516 but the match fizzled out in a draw. The West Indies went to a 2–0 lead and virtually wrapped up the rubber by winning the Third Test at Georgetown by 212 runs. Hawke had match figures of 10 for 115, but Gibbs was the match-winner with his 6 for 29 in Australia's second innings of 144.

Set to score 253 in 270 minutes to win the Fourth Test at Bridgetown, the West Indies finished only 11 runs short with five wickets in hand. This match produced double centuries by Lawry (210) and Simpson (201) whose 382 remains Australia's highest Test opening stand. Cowper made 102 in Australia's first innings of 6 for 650 declared. The West Indies came back strongly, with Kanhai, 129, and Nurse, 201, helping the total to 573. The draw gave the West Indies their first series win over Australia, who revived to win the Fifth Test at Port-of-Spain by 10 wickets inside three days. McKenzie clinched the match by taking 5 for 33 in the West Indies' second innings, including the last three wickets in four deliveries. Kanhai made 121 in the West Indies first innings of 224 and Hunte batted through the second innings of 131 for 60 not out.

AUSTRALIA IN THE WEST INDIES, 1972–73

I. M. Chappell

When Ian Chappell's team arrived in the West Indies, their batting strength was well known. The Chappell brothers, Walters, Redpath and Stackpole formed a powerful array of run-getters. The bowling appeared to depend on Lillee and Massie repeating their triumphs against England. Sobers had retired to have a cartilage operation and the West Indian captaincy had gone to the greying Kanhai. Sobers missed the First Test but declared himself fit for the Second Test. The selectors refused to pick him, however, without a doctor's certificate proving his fitness. Sobers was indignant at this request and refused to produce a doctor or a certificate. The issue enraged cricket lovers throughout the Caribbean, most of whom agreed with the parliamentarian who declared that Sobers on one leg was preferable to most players on two legs.

Australia, too, had problems. Lillee broke down with a serious back injury and played in only one Test without taking a wicket and Massie completely lost his ability to swing the ball and had to be dropped. Manager Bill Jacobs and captain Ian Chappell turned to the then-inexperienced Tasmanian-born medium-pacer Max Walker. Walker bowled 100 more overs in the Tests than any of his team-mates and took 26 wickets at 20.73 apiece, a remarkable effort. The first two Tests were drawn, M. L. C. Foster scoring 125 and Keith Stackpole 142 in the first, and Greg Chappell (106), Ian Chappell (106 not out) and Kanhai (105) all making centuries in the second. Walters swung the Third Test at Port-of-Spain Australia's way with a century between lunch and tea on the first day, scoring 112 of Australia total of 332. Rowe damaged his right ankle on the first day and took no further part in the series. Batting a man short, the West Indies lost by 44 runs.

Australia won the rubber by taking the Fourth Test at Georgetown by 10 wickets, Ian Chappell contributing 109. Lloyd made a heavy-hitting 178 in the West Indies' first innings but his side then collapsed for only 109 due to excellent pace bowling by Walker and Hammond. The Fifth Test was drawn after rain curtailed play on the second day. Walker was the hero of the series for Australia and Walters played the innings of the series in the memorable Third Test, swinging a vital, fluctuating match with a blaze of magnificent strokes. The Third Test attracted 90,000 spectators but with the series decided some days of the Fifth Test were played before audiences of little more than 1,000 people.

AUSTRALIA IN THE WEST INDIES, 1977–78

R. B. Simpson

This was a tough, exhausting trip that fully tested the patience of Bob Simpson's mainly inexperienced players long before the 12 weeks of the tour was up. The Australians quickly realised that the Caribbean is not the island paradise of the tourist brochures, but an oppressively hot and primitive place of unfamiliar food, and matches played before crowds that are crammed behind barbed wire. Even at practice armed guards with dogs patrolled the grounds on which they appeared. Mix all this with outrageous prices for even incidental items, endless bouncers, poor umpiring, crowd riots, hotel rooms without power or water, and dressing-room break-ins that had players fishing their bats out of toilets, and you have a tour that proved a disillusionment to the young men on their first overseas trip.

The Tests fell into two parts. In the first two Tests Clive

Lloyd's professionals defeated Simpson's raw youngsters twice within three days. Simpson's batsmen were no match for the West Indian barrage of bouncers. Australia made 90 and 209 in the First Test at Port-of-Spain, where Kallicharan made 127 as the West Indies coasted to victory by an innings and 106 runs. In the Second Test at Bridgetown, Australia made 250 and 178 and the West Indies won by nine wickets. Mercifully, the predictable slaughter ended when a dispute between the West Indies Board of Control and their WSC players resulted in Clive Lloyd resigning as captain. All the WSC players withdrew from the Third Test leaving the West Indies with a team that included six new caps. The second part of the tour against Kallicharan's new team then began. Australia won the Third Test at Georgetown by three wickets, thanks to centuries by Wood (126) and Serjeant (124), which enabled Australia to make 7 for 362 in the fourth innings. The Fourth Test at Port-of-Spain went to the West Indies who clinched the rubber when they bundled Australia out for only 94 in their second innings to win by 198 runs. Parry's 5 for 15 was achieved when he clean bowled the last four Australian batsmen.

1086

Australia were robbed of a likely win in the Fifth Test at Kingston when spectators invaded the field after Holder was given out near the end of the fifth day. The West Indies then had only one wicket left with 38 deliveries of the mandatory final 20 overs remaining. All attempts to persuade umpire Ralph Gosein to continue the match on the scheduled sixth day failed, and the match was declared a draw. Peter Toohey headed the Australian Test batting averages with 296 runs at 59.20 but missed two Tests through injury. Graeme Wood scored 474 runs at 47.40. Thomson took most Test wickets with 20 at 28.85, but Yardley headed the bowling averages with 15 wickets at 25.13. The brick-throwing rioters at the final Test soured all the Australian players and correspondents, and it was sad to hear commentators like Alan McGilvray vowing never to return.

British settlement in Western Australia started with the establishment of a military base at Albany in 1826 and cricket followed soon afterwards. On instructions from London the Governor of New South Wales, Sir Ralph Darling, had sent a small contingent of soldiers and convicts to garrison King George Sound and forestall French attempts to claim the area. Three years later, after Captain Charles Fremantle had landed at the mouth of the Swan River and confirmed British claims to the Australian west coast, the first settlers arrived from England, and Perth was founded. On April 5, 1835, an advertisement in a Perth newspaper challenged the mechanics erecting Government House to play one or more cricket matches against their counterparts building the Commissariat Store. No details of the first match survive, but the Perth *Gazette and Western Australian Journal* on April 13, 1835, noted the progress of cricket with approval.

"This manly exercise has been started with some spirit within the last fortnight in Perth, and we understand a club is likely also to be formed at Guildford," said the *Gazette*. "The Perth club consists at present of about 22 members. They meet each Saturday afternoon at the Flats. The ground is not well adapted for the purpose, but it is expected that His Excellency the Governor will grant a suitable piece of ground adjacent to the town for the purpose, from which opinion we are reluctantly compelled to dissent. The revival of the sports of our native country in a distant land, forms a link of connection which it should be our pride to encourage.

"The Perth Club does not number very many efficient hands. There are, however, some gentlemen among whom are two men of Kent who play an excellent game both in batting and bowling. An amusing private match at single wicket came off on Wednesday last between Mr L. Samson and Mr J.

WESTERN AUSTRALIA, CRICKET IN

1087

Leake. The former beat the latter by one run. A very handsome *dejeuner* was provided on the ground, of which several ladies and gentlemen partook. The day passed off with great glee."

The first match for which scores were kept was played in mid-May, 1846 between a team called the Tradesmen Of Perth and the Perth Club. The *Journal* said it had seldom seen a public amusement so well attended, although the ground was horribly dusty and a brisk breeze prevailed from the north-west. "Throughout the innings the bowling was admirable, chiefly being of the slow school, but not less dangerous than the rapid play of some modern artists," said *The Gazette*. "As the scores show the incautious or hasty player had no chance, but so wary were the strikers in most cases that some three overs were called without a notch. In general the batting was good. There was a visible want of practice in most of the men on both sides, but there was occasionally some exquisite play. In short on reconsidering the whole matter, we think the Tradesmen showed the best bowlers, the Perth Club the best fielders, and if there be any difference in the batting we think it in favour of the Club. It is worthy of note that throughout the whole match not a wide ball was bowled."

The scorecard for the match showed that The Tradesmen had scored 38 and 26, the Perth Club 45 and 5 for 21, giving the Perth Club victory by five wickets. Several batsmen made a duck in both innings. In the Tradesmen's second innings a batsman named Hall was given out "touched the ball," for two runs. Only dismissals which are clean bowled were credited to the bowlers. Fieldsmen who took the catches were credited with the dismissal of all those caught.

By the late 1840s and early 1850s cricket had spread to country areas of Western Australia, and matches were reported at Bunbury, Bussel Town (now Busselton), Toodyay and Northam, but development of the game was restricted by the State's non participation in early inter-Colonial matches. Geraldton and Beverley formed clubs in about 1866 and began regular matches between Beverley and York. Although it was unable to sustain more than one club for long, Perth played matches against Fremantle, York and Northam. The 51st Regiment also fielded a team. The outstanding players of the colony were all in the Perth CC or Fremantle CC sides and between them these clubs helped promote the game.

In 1862, there was great excitement in the colony when a team from Fremantle sailed to Bunbury in a vessel called the *West Wave* to play a match. The voyage took two and a half days and although many of the Fremantle team were badly seasick they recovered to beat the Bunbury side by an innings in a low-scoring game. On New Year's Day, 1863, Perth played Fremantle and *The Gazette* reported that "as usual the Perth players were defeated." A couple of months later Bunbury travelled to Fremantle for a return match but were beaten again, this time by 115 runs. Cooper's 52 in Fremantle's second innings was the highest individual score in the colony to that time. In March, 1863, the Perth club was "remodelled" and to everyone's surprise defeated Fremantle. The margin was only two runs but it reversed an established trend. George Knight was Perth's hero with 29 runs.

The Perth club appeared to have made a break-through when it secured Government permission to use convict labour to clear a swamp area and establish a cricket ground, but the arrangement ended abruptly when one convict attacked another with a pick axe. The swamp area was left undrained. In the 1865 match between Perth and Fremantle, Edward Ashton made 79 not out for Fremantle, who won by an innings. In 1867, after Fremantle had inflicted another defeat on Perth, the Perth papers criticised the "Fremantle larrikins" for showering the Perth players with stones as they departed. The Fremantle papers, however, called it "a rather amusing scene". Perth produced a trump in 1869 in one Robert Sholl, a government official who took 14 Fremantle wickets for only 34 runs and set up a crushing win for Perth.

Soon after this defeat the Fremantle club took on a team from *HMS Galatea*, in which players from the Perth club were invited to play in the Fremantle lineup. The *Fremantle Herald* said: "The ground was well prepared and in fair order; tents were erected for the cricketers and for the ladies, and additional seats were placed on the ground for the benefit of all. There was a large attendance, amongst whom was HRH Prince Alfred, who drove from Perth, and stayed for some time watching the game." The home team won by 10 wickets, with the *Galatea's* players showing themselves to be ill-prepared.

The 1872–73 season in Western Australia ended with Newcastle defeating a combined York and Beverley team in a low-scoring match. "This match," said the Perth *Gazette*, "terminates the work for the season, quoits and other winter games now taking the place of cricket." In November, 1874, when officers of *HMS Barracouta* played Perth, George Parker hit 91 for Perth, the highest score to that time in the colony, helping Perth to an unprecedented 238. Joe Hillman and Fred Hare then bundled out the *Barracouta* team for 13 in each innings. Parker was later chairman of the first WACA committee and his son, Ernest, achieved wide fame as a tennis player and cricketer. Parker, senr, was a versatile cricketer, for in a match between Perth and *HMS Sappho*, he took 10 wickets. In January, 1876, Parker scored the first century recorded in Western Australia with an innings of 106 against a side from *HMS Sapphire*. Charles Hanham made 102 later in the same innings to take Perth to 260. The *Sapphire* were then dismissed for 24 and 50.

Perth cricket was starting to advance but was far behind developments in the eastern Colonies, where Test cricket had already begun. When it became known that the first Australian team to England would pass through Perth on the way efforts were made to stage a match, but this fell through because of the lack of a suitable ground. In February, 1879, an Aboriginal team arrived in Perth from the New Norcia Mission, coached and captained by H. B. Lefroy, a former Perth cricketer. They were beaten by the Metropolitan Club in their first match, but two days later defeated Fremantle, captained by George Parker, by eight runs. Wanola, who had been the best bowler in the Perth match against Metropolitan, top-scored with 29 runs. Metropolitan agreed to send a team to New Norcia, about 75 miles north of Perth, to play a return. The journey took two days by coach. Metropolitan won a thrilling game by 24 runs. Jackimarra took six wickets in Metropolitan's second innings, but George Randell was the star with 6 for 23 and 8 for 20 for Metropolitan. In the 1879–80 season the New Norcia Aboriginal side returned to Perth and defeated Metropolitan by 10 runs in another exciting match on the Perth Club's old ground. Jackimarra took nine wickets in this match.

Until then there had been no organised competitive cricket, and all matches had been played on a challenge basis. At the annual general meeting of the Metropolitan Club on October 2, 1885, George Parker formally moved that steps be taken to combine the clubs in Perth and those in nearby districts into a cricket association. The four main Perth clubs then held a meeting at the United Services Hotel on November 12, 1885, at which a committee was formed. J. C. H. James, president of the Metropolitan Club was elected President and George Fruin as secretary-treasurer. Within a year the English club, the Port and the Fremantle clubs were added to give the Association seven member clubs, and then in 1894 Karrakatta CC was admitted.

The new Association quickly formed a deputation to send to the Perth City Council to urge the setting aside of what was known as the Recreation Ground for exclusive use by the Association. As a result of this meeting the Council granted the Association a lease. But footballers who used the ground in winter asked that it not be fenced. The Association laid down a concrete pitch which was first used in March, 1886, in a match between I Zingari and Perth.

The Association's first President, J. C. H. James invited subscriptions to pay the cost of sending a team to play in the eastern colonies, and in October, 1887, the *West Australian* announced that on the advice of the famous cricketers Boyle and Scott in Melbourne a professional named Duffy had been engaged to come to Perth as the Association's first coach at a salary of £100 for the season. Duffy arrived to find the Asso-

J. C. H. James, first president of the WACA.

ciation concentrating its efforts on solving the problem of securing a central ground. Temporarily the sending of a team to the east was forgotten and Derby, a township on the north-west coast in the West Kimberley district, had the first team to travel out of the Colony. Derby's team went to Darwin, at that time part of South Australia, with Darwin winning easily by an innings and 223 runs.

On December 9, 1889, a deputation from the Association conferred with the Governor, Sir Frederick Broome, and asked him to set aside a plot of land on which they could feel justified in outlaying the money involved in establishing a first-class ground. Sir Frederick arranged this in one of his last official acts before retiring, setting aside 28 acres of swampland on a 999-year lease. "I am glad as almost the last official act of my long administration of this Colony's Government, to serve so good a cause as cricket," Sir Frederick said. The Trustees went to work, issued debentures which they personally guaranteed, erected a fence, contracted to raise the level of the whole ground, planted trees, and imported Merri Creek soil for turf pitches. In a Colony where all cricket had been played on coconut matting pitches, a turf wicket appeared.

The first Western Australian team to the eastern Colonies played seven matches on their pioneering trip in 1893, losing both the inter-Colonial games with South Australia and Victoria. They had had no preparation on turf as the Association's ground was not then ready in Perth, and found the pace of the eastern States' pitches troublesome. In the first match the Adelaide Club scored 211, to which Western Australia re-

Western Australia's first inter-Colonial team, 1893 (L to R): Back, R. E. Bush, E. Wilson, W. V. Duffy, W. Bateman, A. Moffatt, J. W. C. Bird, T. Brown; Centre, P. L. Hussey, E. Bishop, H. R. Orr (captain), F. D. North, W. Back; Front, F. Bennett, H. Wilson, E. Randell.

F. D. North, hit the initial century for WA.

plied with 232. They then played their first inter-Colonial match against South Australia. Clem Hill played in this game and was bowled by Batemen for a duck. A press report said, "The diminutive Hill could not make up his mind quickly enough as to how he should meet the ball and as a result had to retire." South Australia made 236, Bishop taking 5 for 60 for WA. North topscored with 25 in WA's first innings of 111. When they followed-on, Duffy made 42 before Ernie Jones bowled him, and Orr 44 before he was bowled by Fred Jarvis, WA reaching 131. South Australia then knocked off the 11 runs needed without loss.

Victoria defeated Western Australia comfortably in Melbourne in the next game, John Harry scoring 114, but North again batted well for the Western Australians with 77 in the second innings. The Melbourne Cricket Club then defeated the Western Australians, with North scoring 102 and thus becoming the first West Australian to make a century in another colony. Matches against local sides in Melbourne, Geelong and Ballarat followed, with Orr scoring 107 against Geelong.

The turf pitches of the new Association ground in Perth were first used on February 3, 1894, and were so successful that the trustees were immediately authorised to spend a further £3000 improving the ground. New clubs began to appear, with migrants attracted by the gold discoveries pouring into the State, and despite a short-lived feud with the Fremantle club the new Association's influence spread rapidly. Harry Brown was appointed the Association's first paid secretary in 1896, defeating 21 applicants for the job, which carried a salary of £100-a-year. Ten years later a South Australian team visited Perth for the first time and found unexpectedly tough opposition. Fremantle defeated South Australia by an innings, scoring 220 against 76 and 121. Right-hand off-spinner Bobby Selk paved the way to the win with 6 for 39 and 5 for 50. L. Herring made 69 for Fremantle and Karl Quist, father of David Cup tennis star Adrian Quist, made 34. South Australia then played the Western Australian team and were beaten again, WA scoring 198. South Australia were routed by Selk and Coyne for 54 and reached 230 in their second knock, Gehrs scoring 84. Selk's figures this time were 5 for 19 and 7 for 108.

The next match was drawn, Gehrs scoring 100 and Fred Hack 152 not out in South Australia's 6 for 451. The home side replied with 234. In the third match between the Colonies, Gehrs made history by becoming the first Australian batsman to score a century in each innings of a first-class match, with 148 out of 235 and 100 out of 4 for 259. But it was not enough to give South Australia victory, for Western Australia made 202 and had lost 5 for 252 when time ran out, Parker scoring a splendid 116.

1092

New South Wales made their first trip to the west in 1906–07. The Western Australian team captained by Harold Evers made 307 and 238. NSW scored 310 and then won the match by a wicket in a thrilling finish. NSW were badly shaken against Fremantle, where Bobby Selk took 7 for 45 and had them out for 95 but in the second innings E. L. Waddy, 111, and Hopkins, 126 not out, regained lost prestige by adding 200 in 90 minutes. In 1907–08, came the long awaited first visit by an English team. A. O. Jones's MCC side played WA, winning by an innings and 134 runs.

For years after that Western Australia had to struggle hard for its first-class cricket. The eastern States occasionally sent teams to the west and sometimes Australian sides on the way to England popped in for games that were mainly designed to build team work for the matches in England. In 1912, a Western Australian team made their second trip east and played in Sydney for the first time. They sent NSW in on a bad pitch and had them out for 95, but could only manage 105 in reply. Batting again, NSW made 348 and the match petered out in a draw with WA on 2 for 83. Mailey proved too much for the westerners in the return match, taking 7 for 105 and 6 for 47.

A major problem for WA in this period was that their most promising players tended to migrate to eastern States to further their careers in big cricket. Fremantle-born Ernie Bromley did this after making his debut for WA in 1929–30, moving to Victoria to play against England in 1932–33 and in 1934 in England. While they were not able to play in the Sheffield Shield competition nobody could blame the WA stars for leaving.

Western Australia's team that toured the eastern States in 1956 (L to R): Back, M. T. Vernon, B. K. Shepherd, D. E. Hoare, K. N. Slater, R. A. Gaunt, A. T. Preen; Front, R. B. Strauss, B. A. Rigg, K. D. Meuleman (captain), A. R. Edwards, L. M. Sawle, B. L. Buggins.

For years before World War II the Western Australian delegates pressed for inclusion in the Shield without success. Securing further experience for Western Australian players was a costly exercise involving long rail journeys The breakthrough came soon after World War II ended when a group of young, energetic administrators voted out long standing officials. This led to an all-out effort on winning admission to the Shield, which succeeded when WA was admitted on a restricted basis for the 1947–48 Shield competition. Keith Carmody was engaged as State coach and led WA in their first Shield matches. At the end of their first day in Shield cricket WA was 5 for 375, with Carmody on 166 not out. Next day he took his score to 198 and WA reached 444. They then bundled South Australia out for 109, and went on to a remarkable three-day victory by an innings and 124 runs.

For the first decade of its Shield appearances, WA had to pay the expenses of teams from other States travelling to Perth. Some States did not always insist on this but paying the fares for inter-State teams cost the WACA more than $30,000 before the Australian Cricket Board agreed in 1956–57 that each State should pay its own fares to Perth. The fares burden kept the WACA poor for years despite help from the Perth City Council in granting them free use of the Association's ground without paying rates. But the WACA persisted in its efforts to build an outstanding team and did a little poaching of its own. Bobby Simpson was brought from NSW

Champagne flows in the Western Australian dressing-room after John Inverarity led the team to another Sheffield Shield win in 1977–78.

1094

and played his first Test cricket while representing WA. Then Tony Lock was imported after his long association with Surrey in 1962–63, a move which *Wisden* said resulted in a shift of the balance of power in Australian cricket.

Lock was just the man to end the Western Australians' inferiority complex about their Shield chances and he instilled in them a will to win which in 1982 had seen them sweep to five Shield victories in 10 years. In 1972, Western Australia had six players in the Australian team that toured England, Lillee, Marsh, Watson, Massie, Ross Edwards and Inverarity. In 1981–82, there were seven West Australians in the national side.

Part of this phenomenal rise is attributable to Lock and to the fine job John Inverarity did as State captain, but it is also due in part to the failure of eastern State selectors to recognise the special problems involved in winning in Perth. For example, it is essential to have a good into-the-wind bowler in Perth. Western Australia has had Charlie Puckett, Ron Gaunt, Des Hoare, and now Terry Alderman to do this job but visiting States often lack such a bowler. Another reason is that pitches in WA are generally of a higher standard than in the east and young stroke players there can rely on playing every week on strips of fast, consistent pace. The WACA does not even allow footballers on the ground and only permits football umpires to train there. The light in Perth is always crystal-clear and there is so little rain a young player can usually count on a whole season without losing a day's play. Most of all, though, the west has some outstanding officials, as it showed when it restructured the WACA management setup and brought John Rogers from Sydney to become General Manager of the Association. With enterprising characters in charge, WA's recent record in first-class cricket can only improve.

WACA PRESIDENTS

J. C. H. James	1885–1897
James Gardiner	1897–1899
R. H. Kelsey	1899–1900
S. H. Parker	1900–1901
W. J. Kingsmill	1901–1906
James Gardiner	1906–1915
W. J. Farley	1915–1917
James Gardiner	1917–1924
T. P. Draper	1924–1938
S. H. D. Rowe	1938–1939
G. W. Miles	1939–1951
H. L. Jackson	1951–1963
C. R. Bunning	1963–1980
B. F. Prindiville	1980–

WACA SECRETARIES

G. Fruin	1885–1887
A. Woodbridge	1887–1889
H. H. Sherlock	1889–1890
F. D. North	1890–1896
H. Brown	1896–1900
J. Rushton	1900–1906
L. Gouly	1906–1907
A. W. B. Mather	1907–1909
J. Rushton	1909–1917
R. W. Thompson (act.)	1916–1917
*W. J. Farley	1917–1927
R. G. Heath (acting)	1927–1929
C. H. Guy	1928–1948
L. E. Truman	1948–1973
R. Miller (acting)	1972–1973
B. Bellon	1973–1980
K. R. Preston	1980–

In 1980–81 the newly created position of WACA General Manager was filled by W. J. Rogers.
*First paid secretary.

RECORD PARTNERSHIPS FOR WESTERN AUSTRALIA

Wkt

1st	328	C. Milburn and D. Chadwick v Qld (Bris), 1968–69.
2nd	238	F. J. Bryant and W. McRae v Vic (Perth), 1927–28.
3rd	223	B. Shepherd and R. Kanhai v SA (Adel), 1961–62.
4th	262	G. R. Marsh and C. S. Serjeant v NSW (Syd), 1981–82.
5th	301*	R. B. Simpson and K. Meuleman v NSW (Perth), 1959–60.
6th	244	J. T. Irvine and R. Edwards v NSW (Syd), 1968–69.
7th	156	D. K. Carmody and B. Shepherd v Qld (Perth), 1955–56
8th	108	R. W. Marsh and L. Varis v Qld (Bris), 1972–73.
9th	111	J. T. Irvine and L. C. Mayne v West Ind. (Perth), 1968–69.
10th	154	F. Buttsworth and J. Lanigan v Vic (Perth), 1921–22.

*Denotes not out.

Note: R. W. Marsh, R. J. Inverarity and L. Varis shared a three-way fifth wicket partnership of 301 v Pakistan (Perth), 1972–73, in which Inverarity retired hurt.

OUTSTANDING WESTERN AUSTRALIAN BATSMEN

Batsman	Career	Matches	Innings	Not Out	H. Score	Runs	Average	Centuries
R. J. Inverarity	1962–79	121	211	21	187	7643	40.22	20
B. K. Shepherd	1955–66	85	143	15	219	5382	42.04	12
R. Edwards	1964–75	70	122	15	158	4481	41.87	11
R. W. Marsh	1968–82	82	134	20	236	4398	38.57	6
I. J. Brayshaw	1960–78	101	161	25	160	4325	31.80	3
M. T. Vernon	1955–68	73	125	5	173	4069	33.90	8
D. Chadwick	1963–72	65	118	10	137	3886	35.98	9
K. D. Meuleman	1952–61	47	75	9	234*	3398	51.48	11
R. S. Langer	1973–82	44	64	11	150*	2756	52.00	5
C. S. Serjeant	1976–82	49	83	16	144*	2595	38.73	6
K. J. Hughes	1975–82	37	57	2	149	2497	45.40	6
B. M. Laird	1972–82	41	75	4	171	2496	35.15	7
J. W. Rutherford	1952–61	40	73	4	167	2456	35.59	5
A. R. Edwards	1946–57	45	78	5	105	2370	32.46	3
R. I. Charlesworth	1972–82	47	82	5	101*	2327	30.22	1
A. L. Mann	1963–82	69	106	15	110	2208	24.26	1
K. N. Slater	1955–68	69	113	11	154	2162	21.19	1
G. M. Wood	1976–82	32	57	4	151	2069	39.03	5
G. C. Becker	1963–69	42	69	2	195	2005	29.92	3

OUTSTANDING WESTERN AUSTRALIAN BOWLERS

Bowler	Career	Matches	Runs	Wkts	Average	B.B.	5W	10W
G. A. R. Lock	1962–71	74	8075	326	24.76	7/53	16	2
D. K. Lillee	1969–82	61	6478	284	22.80	7/36	17	4
G. D. McKenzie	1959–74	85	8706	271	32.12	6/100	7	—
D. E. Hoare	1955–66	57	5362	204	26.28	8/98	11	1
T. M. Alderman	1974–82	49	4382	195	22.47	7/28	8	2
A. L. Mann	1963–82	69	6074	184	33.01	6/94	5	—
I. J. Brayshaw	1960–78	101	4465	178	25.08	10/44	7	2
M. F. Malone	1974–82	42	4060	163	24.90	6/33	6	—
C. W. Puckett	1939–53	34	3873	150	25.82	6/48	13	2
L. C. Mayne	1961–70	34	4369	134	32.60	7/75	5	—
R. B. Strauss	1952–60	34	3159	134	23.57	7/59	9	—
B. Yardley	1966–82	45	3181	126	25.42	7/44	9	1
K. N. Slater	1955–68	69	5497	124	44.33	4/33	—	—
H. G. Bevan	1956–64	42	4175	121	34.50	6/65	7	—
R. A. Gaunt	1955–60	29	2894	109	26.55	7/104	5	—
J. B. Gannon	1966–79	37	3204	106	30.22	6/107	2	—

A former swampland in Perth that is now the only privately owned venue for international cricket in Australia. The ground had undergone a series of remarkable changes since it was an eyesore and today is among Australian cricket fans' favourite cricket arenas because its fast, bouncy pitches invariably produce exciting matches. Accommodation at the ground is now tested during major matches and each season brings marked improvement in facilities. The WACA perhaps lacks the big occasion atmosphere of Sydney Cricket Ground, does not have the charm of Adelaide Oval, and can comfortably seat only about as many as fit in one of Melbourne's main stands, but it is the most spacious ground in Australia, with crystal-clear light and a welcome change as a cricket setting from the grandstand-dominated major grounds in the eastern States.

The Perth pitch is unanimously rated the fastest and truest in the world, with bad bounces virtually unknown and plenty of lift and pace for the fast bowlers. The ball comes on to the bat at consistent speeds, which makes it ideal for stroke-making. Few grounds as vast are as close to the centre of the city and on Test match days there is a steady build-up of people walking to the ground.

Origin Of The WACA: The Governor of Western Australia, Sir Frederick Broome, granted the WACA a 999-year lease on the site where the ground now stands in 1889. A Certificate of

WESTERN AUSTRALIAN CRICKET GROUND ("The WACA")

A section of the WACA ground at Perth during a Test against the West Indies in 1975.

Title was issued in the name of the Association in 1923. The area was developed from swampy terrain covered by salt bush with funds raised by the WACA and a government grant of £500. The Mayor of Perth, Alexander Forest, officially opened the ground in 1893 and to mark the occasion his daughter, Sylvia, was made the Association's first life member.

Introduction Of Turf Pitches: Turf pitches were first used at the WACA on February 3, 1894. Soil for the pitches was brought from New South Wales. Later a cycling and trotting track was added, along with grass tennis courts and a bowling green.

Members' Stand Opened: The Members' Stand, named after a former president of the WACA, W. J. Farley, was opened in 1931.

Ground Sold To Trotting Club: World War I severely strained the WACA's finances and in 1918 it sold 14 acres of its land to the Western Australian Trotting Association to clear a debt due to the Colonial Treasurer.

Coaching At The WACA: In the late 1920s the WACA brought Test allrounder Arthur Richardson to Perth to become State coach. He coached on the ground and among his pupils were Ernie Bromley, Frank Alexander and Eric McKenzie, father of Test fast bowler Graham McKenzie.

The WACA As A Sheffield Shield Ground: When Western Australia was admitted to the Sheffield Shield on a restricted basis in 1947–48, two matches were played in Perth. Western Australia won the first against South Australia by an innings and 124 runs, and won the second against Victoria by 59 runs on the first innings. Team captain Keith Carmody made 198 in the first match, George Robinson 134 and Alan Edwards 104 in the second.

Test Cricket Begins At The WACA: Following intensive efforts by WACA delegates to the Board of Control, the WACA was granted an England versus Australia Test on December 11 to 16, 1970. Almost 85,000 spectators saw the five days play.

The WACA Exempted From Rates: Following representations from the WACA president, C. W. Bunning, the Perth City Council declared the WACA ground exempt from rates in May, 1973, and supported a WACA application to the Governor to exempt the ground from rates while cricket is played there.

The Fremantle Doctor: The name given to the cooling breeze that blows up after lunch at the WACA. The wind springs off the nearby Swan River from the direction of the port of Fremantle. Opinions differ over how much help it gives off-spinners and swing bowlers and this has changed a lot since the erection of new buildings near the ground. But on a ground that can become fiercely hot the arrival of "the doctor" is unanimously welcomed.

The second Sri Lanka-born cricketer to play for Australia, a powerful right-hand striker of the ball with a flair for driving on either side of the stumps. He captained Victoria occasionally in 1977–78 and 1978–79, but has not produced scores that would have enabled him to retain his place in the Australian side since the return of WSC players. He was a brilliant schoolboy cricketer who was carefully nurtured by Prahran stalwart Sam Loxton. He won the Prahran batting average in his second season in the firsts, played club cricket in England to develop his skills in 1975 and 1977 and played for D. H. Robin's side in South Africa in 1975–76. He has always been a brilliant gully fieldsman and has a superb throw.

Whatmore, born in Colombo, made his debut for Victoria in 1975–76 and from the start of his first-class career showed commendable fighting spirit. He made 113 against Tasmania and 108 against Queensland to win his place in the two Tests against Pakistan in 1978–79, scoring 43 and 15 in the first. He helped clinch the Shield for Victoria that year with consistent displays. He went to England with the 1979 Australian World Cup team but did not play in a major match, and toured India with Kim Hughes' 1979 Australian team, where he played in five of his seven Tests. His value as a fieldsman was emphasised on this tour as he took 20 catches in nine games, and in the Third Test at Kanpur he held six catches.

WHATMORE, Davenell Frederick, 1954–

First-Class Averages: Batting, 2,773 runs at 31.15; Bowling, 3 wickets at 9.66.

Tests (7): 293 runs at 22.53.

Sri-Lankan born Dav Whatmore plays a handsome drive.

WHITE, Edward Clive Stewart, 1913–

First-Class Averages: Batting, 1,316 runs at 22.30; Bowling, 115 wickets at 26.71.

A tall, fast-medium left-arm bowler and right-hand batsman whose solid all-round performances won him a trip to England with the 1938 Australian team. He was a disappointment on tour, scoring only 318 runs at 22.71 and taking 32 wickets at 23.06, missing a big opportunity to win a Test place at a time when O'Reilly was badly in need of support following the breakdown of McCormick.

White was educated at the Sydney Church of England Grammar School, and followed his father **Alfred Becher Stewart White** (1879–1962) into the North Sydney district club and the New South Wales team. Father and son both topped the North Sydney first grade batting averages in two successive seasons, A. B. S. White in 1905–06 and 1906–07, and E. C. S. White in 1933–34 and 1934–35. A. B. S. White played for NSW between 1905–06 and 1908–09 and his son from 1934–35 to 1938–39.

E. C. S. White's masters at Shore always considered his bowling had greater potential than his batting and so it proved in first-class cricket. He scored 108 not out against South Australia at Sydney in 1936–37, but his bowling had more distinction. He varied his pace subtly, made occasional deliveries nip unexpectedly off the pitch and was extremely accurate. Against South Australia at Sydney in 1935–36 he cleverly exploited a wet patch at one end of the pitch to take 8 for 31, his career best figures. He remained a stalwart of the North Sydney club, for whom he had a total of 182 wickets at 14.67, for more than 50 years.

WHITINGTON, Richard Smallpiece, 1912–

First-Class Averages: Batting, 2,781 runs at 32.33.

A former lawyer who played Sheffield Shield cricket for South Australia before World War II, and for the Services XI at the end of the war. He was persuaded by Eric Kennedy, then Chief Executive of the *Sydney Sun* newspaper group, to turn to cricket writing. He has since written 23 books on cricket and worked as a cricket writer in all the cricket nations.

Whitington, a tall, willowy right-hand opening batsman played for the University and Sturt clubs in Adelaide after captaining Scotch College. He first played for South Australia under Vic Richardson in 1932–33 and at the start of World War II had scored 1,728 runs for his State at 30.86 with three centuries and a topscore of 125 against Queensland in 1936–37 and in 1938–39. He served as an Army captain in the Middle East and played for Lindsay Hassett's Services side in all the Victory Tests in England after the war, scoring 215 runs at 21.50. He also scored 263 in five innings for the Services XI in India, including 155 in the Calcutta "Test." On the tour around the Australian States he made a further 363 in eight innings at 45.37.

He has covered over 100 Tests and was for a period with the

Rand Daily Mail. He has had four wives, and two sons, one of whom bought a village in Italy, where Whitington stays while working on cricket books. One has to admire the manner in which he has sustained a high life style despite his divorces. Several of his books were produced in collaboration with Keith Miller and one with South African Test star John Waite.

WHITNEY, Michael Roy, 1959–

A left-arm Sydney-born fast bowler called into the Australian team for two Tests in England in 1981 because of injuries to bowlers in the official touring party. Whitney, an ex-surfie with a Afro hairdo, proved a highly promising bowler of lively pace and stout heart who could get the ball to lift, but he needed an inswinger to go with his natural outswinger to reach the highest class. He was a novice with the bat, but showed plenty of spirit in defying guileful fast bowlers like Bob Willis and Mike Hendricks.

Whitney, a qualified ground engineer with Qantas, entered the NSW team from the Randwick club in the 1980–81 season. The Randwick secretary said he had settled down after sometimes failing to turn up on the second day of matches when he was in the minor grades and good surf beckoned. He went to England to gain experience with Fleetwood in League cricket, and after several impressive performances played for Gloucestershire against Sri Lanka, Worcestershire and Lancashire taking 13 wickets at 30.69. He was about to travel to Cheltenham to play for Gloucestershire against Hampshire when he got the dramatic call to go to Manchester instead and join the Australian Test team. The Australians initially wanted Carl Rackemann who was in England on an Esso scholarship, but he was injured, a piece of luck that could turn out to be important to Whitney's career. In 1981–82 Whitney played six first-class matches for NSW before losing his place in the State team following injury, taking only nine wickets and failing to fulfil the promise of his appearances in England.

First-Class Averages: Batting, 13 runs at 1.08; Bowling, 44 wickets at 34.95.

Tests (2): 4 runs at 1.00; 5 wickets at 49.20.

A dramatic illustration of Michael Whitney's follow-through.

WHITRIDGE, William Oswald, 1853–1919

A star bowler in the early days of cricket in South Australia and a noted administrator when the first controlling bodies were established for both South Australian and Australian cricket. He played for the Stepney club, which he represented at the foundation meeting of the South Australian Cricket Association in May, 1871. He played for South Australia in 1874–75 in the first inter-Colonial match (against odds) against Victoria, who won by 15 runs. In the second match between these States in 1875–76, he took 8 for 10 off 20.5 overs and 3 for 14 off 21.1 overs, enabling South Australia to win by 77 runs. His club later merged with Norwood, for whom he became a forceful committee room debater. He topped the Adelaide district bowling averages for Norwood in 1877–78 and 1878–79. He was a South Australian delegate to the Australasian Cricket Council and was president of the Council for one year. He was also chairman of the South Australian Cricket Association at many meetings during which he had some keen debates with Joe Darling, Clem Hill and Ernie Jones. He umpired the Adelaide Test in the 1891–92 England-Australia series.

WHITTY, William James, 1886–1974

First-Class Averages: Batting, 1,464 runs at 11.52; Bowling, 491 wickets at 23.39.

Tests (14): 161 runs at 13.41; 65 wickets at 21.12.

A left-hand fast medium bowler who orginated in New South Wales but played almost all of his first-class cricket with South Australia. He had a lovely fluent action and a strike rate that won him a trip to England at the age of 23 in 1909. He went back again with the 1912 team. He had trouble holding his Test place when he first was chosen but had some magical moments later on, finishing with an impressive 65 Test victims.

Six feet tall, with a high arm action, he swung the ball appreciably when it was new, and when the shine had gone settled to left-arm orthodox deliveries at a brisk pace. He was sharp-tongued, known for his debates with umpires. There was a time when he was refused a caught behind and deliberately bowled the next one well wide of the batsman, appealing noisily. When the umpire remonstrated with him, Whitty said, "Just thought you might make two mistakes in the same day."

Whitty, born in Sydney moved to South Australia in 1908, and in 1909–10 took 5 for 43 in Sydney against his former New South Wales team-mates. He had returned from England after the 1909 tour a much improved bowler, having taken 77 wickets on his first trip away at 20.42 and played in one Test. Many saw a pace bowler of his type as the ideal partner for speedster "Tibby" Cotter and they opened Australia's bowling against South Africa at home in 1910–11. Whitty took 37 wickets in the five Test series beginning with eight wickets in the First Test, and following with 6 for 17 in the second innings of the Second Test when South Africa were out for 80, needing

1102

only 170 to win, and a further eight wickets in the Third Test. When South Africa played South Australia at Adelaide, he took 5 for 79.

In England in the Triangular Tests of 1912 he took 25 wickets, including seven wickets in the Third Test against England at The Oval, and 5 for 55 against South Africa at Old Trafford. He took more wickets than any Australian bowler on the tour, 109 at 18.08, finishing second in the bowling averages to Macartney. He was in full flight when World War I interrupted his career and prevented him accompanying the Australian team to South Africa in 1914–15. He had taken 5 for 65 against Victoria at Melbourne and 5 for 90 against New South Wales at Sydney in 1912–13.

His Test career was finished when the war ended, but he was still good enough to take 7 for 66 against New South Wales at Sydney in 1921–22, 5 for 82 against Victoria at Melbourne in 1922–23, and 5 for 49 at Melbourne in 1923–24 at the age of 38. Whitty played for East Torrens club in Adelaide from 1908 to 1915, and consistently took 50 wickets in a season for the club, heading the district club bowling averages for four years in succession from 1911. He played for Glenelg from 1920 to 1927, and was still playing cricket in the Mount Gambier area in 1937, repeatedly producing fine figures.

With the bat his highest score in Tests was 39 not out, and for South Australia 81. With the ball he took five wickets in an innings 26 times and four times took ten wickets in a match. Whitty lived from 1938 on his property Tantanoola, in the south-east of the State.

WICKET-KEEPERS

The wicket-keeper's job is historically the hardest to win when Australian Test teams are picked. Only 21 men have had the job since Test cricket began. It has also proved a difficult spot to win back once it has been lost, for Australia's 'keepers have a habit of staying put. Selectors encourge lengthy tenure and dislike upsetting carefully nurtured teamwork by making changes to such a key position. Only ten of Australia's Test 'keepers have done the job for less than 15 Tests.

The small number of Australian cricketers who have become Test 'keepers is all the more surprising considering the keen competition that usually occurs for the job. Only three Australian 'keepers—Jack Blackham, who held his place for 19 years, Bert Oldfield, who did it for 54 Tests, and Rodney Marsh, who has re-written the 'keepers record book—have held the position unchallenged.

"The first thing, highly important, for a cricketer to do towards becoming Australia's wicket-keeper is to be born at an appropriate time," wrote the late Ray Robinson. "The saying about plenty of room at the top is meant for batsmen and bowlers, but not for wicket-keepers. For a 'keeper to be born about the same time as an Oldfield is to have entered the world in vain."

Since Blackham was appointed to keep wicket for Australia in the First Test in 1877, there has invariably been a queue for the job. Strangely, very few have faltered once selected. Blackham held off the challenge of Billy Murdoch and played a profound part in the development of wicket-keeping as an art, but all the time he reigned there were good 'keepers challenging for his position in the Victorian team. J. J. Kelly followed him into the Test team and sustained Australia's reputation for 'keeping excellence, and when he departed Hanson Carter took over to add further distinction to the role.

Oldfield tidies up after the batsman missed with a lusty swing.

Oldfield and Carter shared a tour to England with the 1921 Australian side and on the long voyage from Australia Carter gave Oldfield daily advice on everything from stumping technique to oiling his gloves with eucalyptus oil. Carter stood a yard back from the stumps and had to make a big step forward before he executed a stumping, which Oldfield reasoned was time wasted. Oldfield also argued that the further he stood back the wider the angle of deflection of the snicked ball and the further he would have to reach for it. The former English captain C. B. Fry told Oldfield he was the greatest 'keeper of all time and when Oldfield thanked him said: "When a man goes about his job without being noticed that is the greatest test of quality."

Oldfield belonged to a select school of 'keepers who believed they should only appeal if the batsman was out. Jack Hobbs said he could not recall Oldfield having a bad match. "His timing was perfect," said Hobbs. "Those big gloves he wore always seemed to be in the right place to receive the ball, leg-side or off-side alike, never slack or relaxed." Oldtimers argue that Oldfield made the greatest stumping in the history of Australian cricket in 1924–25 in the Fourth England-Australia Test at Melbourne. Hobbs failed with an attempted leg glance off Jack Ryder, missed and momentarily lifted his foot. "Although I swear I wasn't out of my crease more than an split second, the bails were off and I knew what the answer would be to the confident 'How's that?' from the man behind me," said Hobbs. Two weeks later in the Fifth Test at Sydney, Hobbs glided a ball from Gregory down the legside and started to run. Oldfield covered almost six yards towards square leg to take the ball in his outstretched hand without losing his feet or diving.

Oldfield had his failures, however, and on the South African tour by Vic Richardson's team repeatedly went the wrong way to take Fleetwood-Smith's wide breaks. Ben Barnett, who had a big range of tricks with ribbons, flags and cards as an amateur conjurer, learned to read Fleetwood-Smith better than anybody. Fleetwood-Smith used to signal Barnett before bowling his googly but stopped this when he realised Barnett had learned to detect the slight change in his wrist action. When Barnett introduced gloves with webbed fingers in Australia, the Queensland delegate, J. S. Hutcheon, tried to get the Inter-State Cricket Conference in 1937 to declare them illegal and unfair. Queensland barred them for their 'keepers but the other States took no action.

Australia has boasted two very large wicket-keepers, Harold Evers, who kept for NSW and Western Australia and was 22 stone, and **Gordon Brewster Inkster**, the 6 ft 3 in, 18 st 3 lb South Australian 'keeper who had a long way to go when he lowered himself behind the bails. Inkster was the first Australian 'keeper to dismiss six batsmen in an innings, a feat

Agile NSW 'keeper Steve Rixon leaps high to bring in a wild return.

he achieved against Victoria in the 1927 New Year match. Like most big men, he was a happy, jolly fellow, a commercial traveller quick with the wisecracks. Probably the smallest Australian first-class 'keeper was **Cyril Norman Parry**, who kept for both Tasmania and South Australia between 1925 and 1934. Parry was a fraction over 5 ft tall and weighted 8 st 7 lb, a cabinet-maker who could have passed for a jockey. He had to have special finger stalls made to fit his hands. In 1931–32, Parry conceded only 18 byes while 2,063 runs were scored, a record second only to Oldfield's that year. Cyril Badcock always reckoned Parry's brilliance as a 'keeper was matched only by Don Tallon among Australians.

When Oldfield was injured and could not play in the Fourth Test against England at Brisbane in 1932–33, many critics believed Parry should have got the job, but it went to "Hammy" Love, probably because of his superior batting skill. Parry left for Melbourne when he missed out but could not displace Jack Ellis or Ben Barnett from the Victorian team, although he played for the South Melbourne first grade team until 1939, when he retired, aged 39. Apart from Parry, Barnett had two outstanding 'keepers pressing him for his place in the State side, **Henry Jack ("Harry") Kroger (1906–)** and **Stanley Oldfield Quin** (1908–). Kroger played only two matches for Victoria but his form for Prahran in district cricket was outstanding. Quin, 5 ft 8 in tall, and broad in the chest, played in 24 first-class matches but such was the competition in his period that he only had one full season of Shield cricket—in 1935–36 when Barnett was away in South Africa. Quin dismissed four South Australian batsmen in an innings and in 1937–38 dismissed five in an innings when captain against Western Australia. He had 59 first-class victims in all, 34 caught and 25 stumped. He also had a topscore of 210, made in 1933–34 against Tasmania in the Victorian record fourth wicket stand of 424 with I. S. Lee.

In NSW in the 1930s there was similar keen competition for the State 'keeper's job. **Hugh Lavery Davidson** (1907–1960), a red-haired 'keeper from the Waverley club, dismissed nine South Australian batsmen on one of his 11 appearances for NSW in Oldfield's absence. Davidson had 40 first-class victims from 32 catches and eight stumpings. Another topclass Sydney 'keeper was **Frank Alexander Easton** (1910–), who played for Glebe and Petersham. He was so thorough in his approach to his cricket he passed the umpire's course. Easton has 44 victims in first-class matches, 28 caught and 16 stumped. He had to give up 'keeping because a war injury to his left thigh upset his balance behind the stumps.

Queensland built a similar tradition for wicket-keeping excellence through the work of Leo O'Connor, and later Tallon, Grout and Maclean. O'Connor had an amazing span in the job,

1107

starting in 1912 and carrying on until 1929. He had 103 first-class victims in all (82 caught, 21 stumped) despite limited opportunities in the years before Queensland played in the Shield competition. O'Connor, of course, took over from one of the rich personalities of early Queensland cricket, **William Thomas ("Poley") Evans** (1876–1964), who had 40 first-class victims (24 caught, 16 stumped) between 1898 and 1913. Evans once dropped his gloves during the match between Queensland and South Australia, when Joe Darling, Giffen and Clem Hill were hammering his bowlers, and took 7 for 70 with his slow bowling, South Australia scoring 582. Evans was quite a handy batsman and in 1907–08 when Queensland defeated NSW by 171 runs he reached his century with a hit for six, finishing with 103 not out. Evans had a career total of 1,132 first-class runs at 22.64, extremely good figures for a 'keeper in a low-scoring era.

Challenging O'Connor for the Queensland 'keeper's job was **John Farquhar** (1887–1977), from the Goodna and Western Suburbs clubs. He had seven dismissals in one match against NSW, and in 16 first-class games for Queensland had 29 dismissals (13 caught, 16 stumped). But he could not match O'Connor's skill with the bat and in 28 innings had a topscore of only 46.

Brian Taber stood right up to the stumps for spin bowling.

Two 'keepers with a single thought. Rodney Marsh and Richie Robinson appeal for a catch during Australia's 1977 tour of England. Robinson was a superb close in fieldsman.

Since World War II some magnificent 'keepers have done the job. Don Tallon brought unrivalled stumping speed to the role and seldom missed a catch during the first Test series after the war. Ron Saggers deputised splendidly for Tallon in South Africa and then Gil Langley maintained the high standard. In the Second Test at Lord's in 1956 Langley established a then world record when he dismissed nine batsmen, eight caught and one stumped. At 37, Langley was three years younger than Oldfield when he retired and left the stage to Wally Grout.

Grout was warned when he took the job to make it hard for his rivals from the start, and he did just that. Grout had had to wait until he was 30 to get the big job. In South Africa in 1957–58 he made up for it by dismissing 46 batsmen on the whole tour and 19 in Tests. In 1958–59 he equalled Tallon's series record by making 20 dismissals in the five Tests against England, and in February, 1960, he dismissed eight West Australians in a Brisbane Shield match. In the 1960–61 series against the West Indies he dismissed 23 batsmen, 20 caught, three stumped. Grout equalled and passed Oldfield's record of 130 Test victims during the South Africans' visit in 1963–64.

Barry Jarman waited in the wings for nine years for Grout to vacate the job but when he took over made a great successs of it before NSW's Brian Taber moved in behind the stumps in the big green cap. Taber had bad luck through illness but he, too, performed admirably before he retired and Rodney Marsh took the job. Marsh has been there for a record 83 Tests and has passed the world record for most Test dismissals set by England's Alan Knott. Everything Marsh achieves from now on is for the wicket-keeping record books.

AUSTRALIAN TEST WICKET-KEEPERS
(To 1981-82)

	Tests	Caught	Stumped	Dismissals	First-Class Total	Caught	Stumped
R. W Marsh (WA)	83	291	11	302	739	681	58
A. T. W. Grout (Qld)	51	163	24	187	587	473	114
W. A. S. Oldfield (NSW)	54	78	52	130	661	399	262
G. R. A. Langley (SA)	26	83	15	98	369	293	76
H. Carter (NSW)	28	44	21	65	271	182	89
J. J. Kelly (NSW)	36	43	20	63	355	243	112
H. B. Taber (NSW)	16	56	4	60	395	345	50
J. M. Blackham (Vic)	35	36	24	60	451	272	179
D. Tallon (Qld)	21	50	8	58	432	303	129
B. N. Jarman (SA)	19	50	4	54	560	431	129
S. J. Rixon (NSW)	10	31	4	35	287	251	36
K. J. Wright (WA, SA)	10	31	4	35	231	210	21
R. A. Saggers (NSW)	6	16	8	24	221	147	74
L. B. Maddocks (Vic, Tas)	7	18	1	19	277	209	68
A. H. Jarvis (SA)	11	9	9	18	198	115	83
J. A. Maclean (Qld)	4	18	—	18	385	354	31
W. L. Murdoch (NSW)	18	13	1	14	243	218	25
W. Carkeek (Vic)	6	6	—	6	159	114	45
B. A. Barnett (Vic)	4	3	2	5	358	216	142
H. S. Love (Vic, NSW)	1	3	—	3	102	73	29
F. J. Burton (NSW, Vic)	2	1	1	2	29	23	6

Notes:
Blackham and Murdoch often swapped duties in the field (17 Tests).
In 1886, Blackham, and in 1888, Jarvis, fielded while the other kept wicket (4 Tests).
In 1887–88, Burton fielded while Blackham kept wicket.
Only Marsh and Oldfield have scored 1000 Test runs, and Marsh is Australia's only Test 'keeper who has also made Test century.
Marsh was selected and is credited with one abandoned Test.

OTHER FIRST-CLASS WICKET-KEEPERS

	Caught	Stumped	Total Dismissals
G. C. Becker (WA)	116	22	138
B. L. Buggins (WA)	144	20	164
J. L. Ellis (Vic)	186	107	293
D. A. Ford (NSW)	122	57	179
R. C. Jordon (Vic)	238	45	283
I. H. McDonald (Vic)	79	52	131
P. M. Newland (SA)	30	18	48
L. P. D. O'Connor (Qld)	82	21	103
A. T. Ratcliffe (NSW)	45	30	75
R. D. Robinson (Vic)	289	40	329
S. G. Sismey (NSW)	88	18	106
C. W. Walker (SA)	171	148	319
H. Webster (SA)	20	3	23
R. D. Woolley (Tas)	35	10	45

1110

The powerful, blond-haired, Melbourne-born son of Austrian migrants whose childhood dream of playing for Australia came true. He is a right-hand opening batsman with strong drives, a productive cut stroke, a well-executed pull shot, and no fears about using any of them. He was the best batsman in Victoria in 1981–82 and scored so consistenly he cannot be far from regaining a Test spot should either Graeme Wood or Bruce Laird falter. He is a fine fieldsman in any position but appears to have forsaken his right-arm off-breaks to concentrate on his heavy responsibilities as a batsman.

Wiener was born at Melbourne's Queen Victoria Hospital to parents to whom cricket was a mystery. He joined the Prahran club as a teenager and was strongly influenced by the aggressive approach of the club's former Test all-rounder Sam Loxton. He worked his way through the grades to the firsts in 1975–76 and improved dramatically in only a few seasons. In 1977 he played with Kent's Second XI in England to gain experience, and in 1977–78 he became one of the select few to score a century in their first match for Victoria by scoring 31 and 106 against Queensland in Brisbane. He topped 500 runs in each of his first two seasons and hit four centuries.

There was an exciting belligerence about his batting for he was eager to hit loose balls hard even early in his innings but he lacked judgment in running. In his Test debut against Eng-

WIENER, Julien Mark, 1955–

First–Class Averages: Batting, 2,920 runs at 33.18; Bowling, 10 wickets at 76.90.

Tests (6): 281 runs at 25.54.

Weiner lifts a ball high over long-on for six in a one-day match against England.

land at Perth in 1979–80 he was run out for 11 in the first innings by Graham Dilley, with whom he had stayed while he was in England with Kent. In the second innings he made an impressive 58. Then followed a plucky 40 against a fiery West Indian pace attack in Melbourne. He toured Pakistan in Greg Chappell's Australian team in 1980 and returned to the Test side for the last two Tests, scoring 93 in the Third Test at Lahore, his highest Test score.

Wiener made his career best score of 221 not out in his record third wicket stand of 390 for Victoria against Western Australia at Melbourne in 1981–82. With Victoria struggling because of poor batting, he was notably consistent, scoring 847 runs in the season at 52.93, with his droopy blond moustache and handsome driving familiar to all Australian cricket watchers.

Weiner back cuts superbly in 1980 against England in Sydney.

A short, bald-headed Adelaide dentist who mixed right-arm leg-breaks and googlies with a sunny disposition. He was one of South Australia's most popular cricketers and in the opinion of many who watched him in his prime in the 1920s the finest locally-born spinner. He had some triumphant days for South Australia, eight times taking five wickets in an innings and twice taking 12 wickets in a match but he was never tried in Tests because of the presence of Mailey and Grimmett.

Williams went bald while still in his teens and always bowled in a cap. When caps were barred in team photographs, he would expose his head until the cameraman was about to take the picture and then slip his cap back on. Rivals and team-mates enjoyed his sense of humour, even those he fooled with his wrong-un, and tales of his pranks stretched back to his days at Woodville High School on to his years with Port Adelaide and his appearances in the State team.

He made his debut for South Australia in 1919–20 against New South Wales at Adelaide and then took most wickets (35) in the Adelaide district competition the following summer. Most of his initial success in State matches were with the bat, but in December, 1923, against Queensland at Adelaide he had a splendid coup, taking 6 for 40 in the first innings and 6 for 155 in the second, South Australia winning right on time.

At Adelaide in December, 1926, he had another 12-wickets match against Victoria, taking 6 for 88 and 6 for 146, looking apologetically at the Victorian batsmen as they departed. He always acted as if he expected grown men to know all about well disguised and subtlely flighted googlies. In grade cricket he was devastating and took most wickets in an Adelaide season 11 times for Port Adelaide, including a run of nine successive seasons between 1924–25 and 1932–33. He made centuries in grade cricket but his best score in first-class cricket was 56. Williams died at 48 after years of heart trouble.

WILLIAMS, Norman Leslie, 1899–1947

First-Class Averages: Batting, 852 runs at 15.49; Bowling, 122 wickets at 39.09.

A stylish batsman and excellent outfielder for Melbourne University, Victoria and the First AIF team. Willis first came to notice with an innings of 168 for Victorian Colts against New South Wales Colts in 1912–13. For the AIF team in 1919, he was most impressive, scoring 1,652 runs at 41.30 including four centuries, and an innings of 96 v. an England XI at Scarborough. His best scores were 156 n.o. against Leicestershire, when he put on 266 for the fifth wicket with "Nip" Pellew, 129 n.o. v. Worcestershire when, with Pellew his partner again, he helped add 301 unbeaten for the fifth wicket in 2 hours 40 minutes, 130 v. Notts, when he and Oldfield put on 169 for the ninth wicket, and 127 v. Sussex. When the AIF side went to South Africa, he made 94 against Western Province, and 340 runs at 37.77.

WILLIS, Carl Bleackley, 1893–1930

First-Class Averages: Batting, 3,707 runs at 35.64; Bowling, 7 wickets at 50.28.

Willis, who learned cricket at Wesley College where he opened with Roy Park, also was an outstanding schoolboy athlete. He was a flamboyant character, one of the flashiest dressers of his day, noted for fancy haircuts, big gold watches and elegantly tailored clothes. He played Australian Rules football for University and Melbourne.

Back in Australia he made 111 for the AIF against Victoria, and with his friend Allie Lampard proceeded to score heavily for Prahran. He hit 520 runs at 74.50 in his first season and was a leading member of the 1920–21 premiership team. He was made the Prahran captain and the next year scored 598 runs at just under 60.00. In 1921–22, Willis hit 133 for the Rest of Australia v. Australia at Sydney in the Frank Iredale benefit match. For Victoria, he made 100 against NSW at Sydney in 1924–25 and in the same summer scored 104 for Victoria against Canterbury at Christchurch. His nine years with Prahran yielded 2,907 runs at 40.94, with seven centuries. He died at 37 in the NSW country town of Berrigan, a dasher to the last in bush cricket matches.

WILLS, Thomas Wentworth Spencer, 1835–1880

First-Class Averages: Batting, 602 runs at 12.28; Bowling, 121 wickets at 10.09.

A tall, heavily-bearded NSW-born allrounder who, with the assistance of his cousin, Henry Colden Harrison, invented Australian Rules football to prevent cricketers becoming physically soft in winter. Wills, born at Molonglo, near Canberra, was a right-hand batsman, and a right-hand fast or medium-pace bowler of round-armers and under-armers. He captained Rugby School's first XI in England and played for Kent (1855), MCC (1855–56) and Cambridge University (1856), but when he returned home was appalled at the lack of fitness of cricketers in Melbourne. He attributed this to winter inactivity and invented Australian Rules because he considered Rugby football was too rough for cricketers.

Wills was not strictly qualified for Cambridge who found themselves one short for the University match. He had enrolled on the University books and although he had not taken up residence Cambridge played him. He returned home at the end of the year, and immediately represented Victoria, playing so well he was soon made captain. When Queensland became a separate colony in 1859 his father, a former Victorian MLA, was so impressed with opportunities there he sold his home at Geelong and went north with Tom and several employees. The full party of 25 reached Cullinlaringo station at Nogoa, 200 miles from Rockhampton on October 3, 1861. They were immediately pestered by Aboriginals who, they were warned, were dangerous. Wills senr. and his men were armed but had got on so well with Aboriginals in Victoria they were careless.

They were resting from the heat on October 17, when the

1114

Aboriginals took them by suprise and massacred 19 men, women and children, including Tom's father. Tom only escaped because his dray had broken down some distance from the station, and did not reach the scene until the following day. For two years he tried to hold on to his father's tragic investment, but when Parr's England team came to Australia in the summer of 1863–64, he headed for Victoria. He arrived too late for the first match but played almost continuously after that, helping local Victorian teams. He even went to New Zealand to play in three matches for local teams who would have fared far worse without his effective bowling.

Despite the Queensland massacre, he coached Aboriginal teams on his return to Victoria. He captained the Aboriginal team at the Melbourne Cricket Ground on Boxing Day, 1866, and in 1867 took them on tour in NSW. He then ended his association with the team, leaving Charles Lawrence to lead the Aboriginals on their tour of England in 1868.

Wills, who played for the Richmond club, first appeared for Victoria in 1856–57 and played his 16th and last match for the State in 1875–76, aged 40. His drinking, said to have been accentuated by the massacre at Nogoa, was developing into acute alcoholism but he had enough vision in 1878 to join Charles Lawrence, a member of H. H. Stephenson's All England XI of 1861–62, in sponsoring the first Australian team to England as a speculative venture. In 11-a-side matches, Wills scored 356 runs for Victoria at 17.80, best score 58, and took 98 wickets at 8.88, 12 times taking five wickets or more in an innings. Among his best figures were 6 for 26 and 4 for 40 in the 1857 match against NSW, 7 for 44 in 1869 against NSW, and 7 for 48 and 6 for 44 in a 1870–71 match against Tasmania. In matches with or against the odds, he scored 59 runs at 9.83, topscore 20, and took 38 wickets at 8.39.

He had to be placed under restraint because of his drinking bouts, and on May 2, 1880, he eluded his attendant, found a bayonet, and stabbed himself to death, aged 44, a tragic end to one of the most colourful lives in the history of Australian cricket.

T. S. Wills

A useful allrounder who played only twice for his native Victoria but made a big reputation playing for Sussex, Oxford University, the MCC, and for the Gentlemen. He played strokes all round the wicket, fielding splendidly in the slips, and bowled a handy fast-medium pace. He was educated at Scotch College, Melbourne, and at Brighton College, in Sussex, where he played for the County team from 1887 to 1895. He headed the Sussex batting averages in 1886 and 1887 with 59.63 and 54.06 respectively, and captained the County XI in 1887. In all, he scored 1,886 runs at 22.45 for Sussex.

WILSON, George Lindsay, 1868–1920

First-Class Averages: Batting, 2,599 runs at 20.46; Bowling, 34 wickets at 59.64.

Wilson, 5 ft 11 ins, 12 st 7 lb, had an outstanding double for Sussex against Gloucestershire at Bristol in 1893, scoring 117 in the first innings and 92 in the second. His highest score for the County was 174 against Oxford University at Hove in 1895, when he and F. W. Marlow (130) added 303 for the first wicket. He won his Blue for Oxford in 1890 and in 1891 against Cambridge. His two games for Victoria in 1898 produced 102 runs at 34.00, topscore 68. He played for the Melbourne club and was a lawyer by profession.

WILSON, John William, 1922–

First-Class Averages: Batting, 287 runs at 5.74; Bowling, 230 wickets at 30.51.

Tests (1): D.N.B.; 1 wicket at 64.00.

A stocky, deceptive left-arm googly bowler who took wickets consistently in eight seasons of first-class cricket and had one triumphant match for Australia. He threw the ball high, compelling batsmen to produce good strokes to score consistently. Few of the pitches he bowled on suited his methods, but he regularly appeared near the top of the Australian first-class bowling averages. His batting was quite impoverished and he never made 20 runs in a first-class knock.

Wilson was born in Albert Park, Victoria, and began in district cricket with South Melbourne. He played one match for Victoria in 1949–50 without taking a wicket before moving to Adelaide, where he topped the district cricket bowling averages for East Torrens in 1954–55 and 1955–56. He played for South Australia from 1950–51 to 1957–58, six times taking five wickets or more in an innings for the State and at one period forming an intriguing spin-bowling partnership with another left-arm back of the hand bowler, J. S. Manning. In October, 1954, he took 5 for 81 for South Australia against England in Adelaide.

He was a surprise selection for the 1956 Australian tour of England, the selectors gambling that he was the right type for the expected conditions. Captain Ian Johnson gave him every chance, but he ended the tour with just 43 wickets at 23.09. The highspot of his career came in the match at Bristol against Gloucestershire when he took 7 for 11 and 5 for 50, match figures 12 for 61. At one stage in the first innings on a damp, responsive pitch he took six wickets in seven overs without conceding a run. Most of the pitches that summer were dust bowls but he certainly made the most of the one rain-affected strip on which he bowled. Despite his coup at Bristol he was not considered for Tests.

On the way home when Australia played in Pakistan and India he made his Test debut at Bombay. He took 0 for 39 in the first innings and had India's Ramchand caught by Maddocks in the second innings, finishing with 1 for 64 from a match in which he did not bat. He played for another season for South Australia, and has since been active in cricket administration.

Tasmania's best allrounder between 1894 and 1912, a right-handed spinner and batsman of such obvious talents that English authorities like Pelham Warner criticised his omission from Australian teams. He was left out because the selectors of Australian teams for England knew little about him as his duties with the civil service kept him in the Tasmanian hinterland. He played in two Test trials, the first at the age of 30 in February, 1900 and the second in March, 1908, when he had lost the zest of youth.

Windsor was born at Launceston and began his senior career in 1886 with Esk, where C. W. Rock guided him. He took two hat-tricks and was picked to play G. F. Vernon's England team in 1887–88. He surprised himself by scoring 28 and from then on took his batting seriously and developed into a splendid allrounder. He was a completely natural player who seldom practised and when he occasionally wandered into the nets it was mainly to gossip with friends. He had a sad stint on the mainland when he went to the East Melbourne Club in January, 1894, only to find he could not get a game until he was residentially qualified. He did not play in a match and returned to Tasmania after two months.

When the 1899 Australian team for England was being chosen, Joe Darling told the selectors that in the absence of George Giffen and Tom McKibbin, Windsor was the next best spin bowler in Australia and should tour. Windsor missed selection and scored 35 and 6 and took two wickets (Victor Trumper in each innings) for The Rest of Australia v. the Australian XI in a Sydney match staged to raise funds for Australian troops in the Boer War. When he was again overlooked for the Australian team to England in 1905, Windsor's fans in Northern Tasmania, encouraged by a glowing assessment of Windsor's attributes by "Plum" Warner, tried to have him added to the team by offering to pay all expenses, but team manager Frank Laver rejected the idea.

Visiting teams continued to pay tribute to his skills, however, and in March, 1908 he appeared for Australia v. The Rest in another Test trial. Monty Noble paid him the compliment of asking him to bowl first but on a hard true wicket he could not turn the ball. He did score 78, however, in a ninth wicket stand of 225 with Warwick Armstrong. He declined to tour New Zealand with an Australian side some months later. In 1911, he earned high praise again, this time from the South Africans, for his double of 10 wickets and 85 runs in the match against them at Hobart. Tasmanians regarded him as another Trumper, for he was similarly adventurous, ready to experiment with wristy shots. When the Victorian captain T. S. Warne rebuked him in 1912 for changing from off-breaks to leg-breaks, he simply said, "Ah, well, I get more fun out of leg-breaks."

WINDSOR, Edward Arthur Cartwright, 1869–1953

First-Class Averages: Batting, 1,451 runs at 32.24; Bowling, 129 wickets at 29.79.

1117

WOMEN'S CRICKET, IN AUSTRALIA

The first women's cricket match in Australia was played at Bendigo in 1874, according to a report in the Melbourne *Argus*. The players wore calico dresses and red and blue tops. No scores survive, but the players were known to be daughters of the miners. The first match between organised women's clubs was played on Sydney Cricket Ground in 1886 between Fernleas and Siroccos, but again no scores are available. The first inter-State match for women was played in 1890 between Victoria and New South Wales at Sydney, and in 1891 Miss Rosalie Dean made 195 and 104 in each innings of a Sydney Cricket Ground match.

By the 1890s strong Australian teams such as the Snowflakes and Warrnambool Forget-Me-Nots were established in Victoria and the Seafoams in Sydney. Women were warned to tie their hats on securely because catches were often dropped through trying to hold a hat in one hand and make a catch with the other. Stopping the ball with their petticoats was regarded as unsporting. Clubs in both Sydney and Melbourne were members of associations but these were abandoned at the start of World War I.

The Victorian Women's Cricket Association was re-formed in 1922–23 with four clubs and built up to a membership of 39 clubs by the start of World War II. The New South Wales Women's Cricket Association was founded in 1927. Little is known of early women's cricket in Queensland but a State As-

A 1906 women's cricket team from Launceston, Tasmania, wearing the full length skirts in which they played.

sociation was formed in the late 1920s. Western Australia and South Australia formed Associations in the early 1930s. The Australian Women's Cricket Council was formed in 1931, with Victoria, NSW and Queensland as foundation members. South Australia and Western Australia joined in 1935–36.

Inter-State women's matches became a regular feature of the Australian season between the wars and were firmly established when the Australian Women's Cricket Council began negotiations with the Women's Cricket Association in England for an exchange of teams. These two bodies initiated international cricket for women. In 1934–35 an English team captained by Betty Archdale was unbeaten in a programme of 21 matches, winning 15, with six unfinished. The Queensland Women's Cricket Association was largely responsible for the staging in Brisbane of the first women's international between Australia and England. All the 16 members of the English team bought their own equipment and paid their own fares—the boat passages cost £80 each—for a tour that took six months.

The surprise in the England team was the quality of their wicket-keepers, Betty Snowball and Grace Morgan, and the allround skill of Molly Hide and Myrtle Maclagan, who achieved an average of 63.25 in nine tour innings. This included the first-ever century by a woman in international cricket—119 in the Second Test against Australia at Sydney.

The Australian women's cricket team at Lord's in 1976 (L to R): Back, S. Tredrea, J. Lumsden, K. Price, L. Hill, W. Hills, J. Tredrea, R. Thompson, P. May, J. Robinson; Front, M. Lutschini, B. McDonald, A. Gordon (captain), Mrs. L. Thomas (manager), M. Jennings, W. Blunsden, K. Mortimer.

Six-ball overs were adopted throughout the tour and have remained in use in international matches ever since. England's use of the lighter 5 oz ball also was copied. Caps were worn from the start, but it took a few years for divided skirts to replace dresses and knee length socks to replace long white stockings.

Australia returned the visit in 1937 with a 19-match tour of Britain. This team, captained by Margaret Peden, lost only one match, the Second Test. England visited Australia again in 1948–49, under Molly Hide, the team's only defeat being in a Test. In 1951 the second Australian women's team toured Britain under the captaincy of Molly Dive, NSW. The financing of these tours was difficult, with the visitors paying their own fares and the hostess country bearing all the cost of promoting and staging matches, entertaining teams and transporting them to grounds. The hostess country also retained any match profits.

Australia was runner-up in the inaugural women's cricket World Cup in England in 1973, a tournament which attracted teams from five nations. Australia won the second World Cup in India in 1978 against teams from England, New Zealand and India, with the final between Australia and India at Patna watched by a capacity crowd of 35,000. This compared with the crowd of 3,000 which watched the first women's in-

Australia's 1979 women's Test team (L to R): Back, J. Kennane, J. J. Stockton, J. Laing, A. Mitchell (manager), W. Hills, J. Jacobs, W. Weir; Front, S. Fitzsimmons, R. Thompson, M. Lutschini, S. Tredrea (captain), P. Cook, D. Martin.

Copybook bowling action of Betty Wilson, regarded by some experts as the finest allrounder Australian women's cricket has produced.

ternational match, a 60-overs game, on the hallowed field at Lord's in 1976, when England 2 for 162, defeated Australia 161. By now international women's cricket was securely established but was no more immune to political problems than men's cricket. The 1978 World Cup proceeded without Holland and the West Indies, for example, when these countries withdrew at the last minute on political grounds.

Through the years Australia has produced some outstanding women cricketers. Here is a review of the exploits of some of the best known:

PEDEN, Margaret Elizabeth, 1905–1981.

Captain of the Australian women's cricket team in the first ever Test series—between England and Australia. She then led the first Australian women's team to England. The first series was staged in Australia in 1934–35 when Betty Archdale's English team won two Tests, with one unfinished. The second was in 1937 when each country won a Test and the third was drawn. Between them these two series of international matches firmly established the future of international women's cricket.

Peden attended Sydney University, taking a degree in Arts with a diploma in Education. She taught at SCEGGS Redlands and served on the council of Abbotsleigh. She helped found the Australian Women's Cricket Council, the New South Wales Women's Cricket Association, and the Sydney University Women's Cricket Club. She had been responsible for the issuing of the invitation to tour Australia to the English women's cricket team in 1934–35. She was regarded as the most skilful player in the Australian team and opened the batting in four of her six Tests. She had 12 innings in Tests altogether, scoring 87 runs at 8.7, with a topscore of 34. For much of her life she was closely involved with her opposing captain in the first two Test series, Betty Archdale, who was Headmistress of Abbotsleigh.

ANTONIO, Peggy, 1917– A small, dark right-arm leg-spin bowler, useful bat and competent fielder who was one of the first big crowd-pleasers of Australian women's cricket. She played for Victoria at the age of 15 in 1932–33, and in 1934–35 played in all three Tests in the first ever women's Test series against Betty Archdale's English team, taking 12 wickets at 18.25 in the series. In

Australia's other "Thommo," Raelene Thompson in action against England at Edgbaston in 1976.

1937–38, she took 19 wickets at 11.20 in the three Tests against England in England and a total of 50 wickets at 12.00 on the entire tour. Her best figures were 6 for 51 and 3 for 40 against England at Northampton. She retired after she returned from England to marry Edward Howard, having taken 31 wickets in six Tests at 13.90, and scored 128 runs at 11.64, highest score 37. She drew big crowds to matches and always received a favourable press because of her guile and personality. She worked very hard to master spin in the nets but had a carefree approach. She was not aware of her Test figures until someone listed them for her almost 40 years after she retired.

KNEE, Miriam, 1939–

A deceptive right-arm medium-pace bowler who could spin and cut the ball and was a reliable and sound left-hand bat. She was first selected for Victoria in 1961 and played eight

Sharon Tredrea swings a ball to the leg boundary to become the first woman to make 50 at Lord's.

1123

Tests. Against England in 1963 in England, she took 8 for 55 in a Test (5 for 35 and 3 for 22), and in the 1968–69 Test series against England in Australia she took 8 for 68 (5 for 49 and 3 for 19). In 1963 she created a Test record with a six wicket stand of 125 with Mary Allitt. She became vice-captain of the Australian side in 1968–69 and the following season was appointed Victorian captain, a job she held for four summers. She also captained Australia against New Zealand in 1972 and in England in 1973 during the initial Work Cup competition. She was an Australian selector from 1973 to 1979 and helped pick seven Australian teams. In her eight Tests she scored 319 runs at an average of 26.58, highest score 96, and took 35 wickets at 16.29.

PAISLEY, Una Lillian, 1922–1977   A schoolgirl prodigy who played in the highest club grade at the age of 11 and made her debut for Victoria at 15, in 1937. She was a right-hand bat and bowler, coached by her father, and played in 18 inter-State series, 16 of them as Victorian captain. She first won selection for Australia in 1948 for the tour of New Zealand, where she scored a century in her first Test at Wellington. Her 108 helped her achieve a fourth wicket Test partnership record of 163 with Betty Wilson. She scored one other Test century, also against New Zealand, and in 17 Test innings was involved in six partnerships worth 50 or more. She was Australia's vice-captain in 1957 against New Zealand and in 1957–58 against England. She was a Victorian delegate to the Australian Women's Cricket Council for seven years, an Australian selector for three Test series, and a Victorian selector and administrator for more than 15 years. She made 471 runs in 12 Tests at 27.71, and took 19 wickets at 22.47.

TREDREA, Sharon Ann, 1954–   A forceful right-hand bat and right-arm fast bowler whom noted international umpire Dickie Bird said was as fast as most men at her peak. She has recently been forced to reduce her speed and increase her variation because of a persistent back injury. She can cut and swing the ball from the pitch either way. Strong, athletic and attractive, she presents an ideal image for women's sport, remaining modest about her feats and completely unconcerned about statistics. She is an excellent field, Australia's best all-rounder in the 1970s and so far into the 1980s. Sharon was first selected for the Victorian team while still a junior, aged 19, in 1973 and also for Australia in one limited over match against England in the inaugural World Cup. She captained Australia in three Tests against New Zealand in 1979 and also led Australia in the successful defence of the World Cup in 1982 in New Zealand, when Australia won 12 of its 13 matches and drew the other. In seven Tests she had scored 249 runs at 27.66 and taken 29 wickets at 21.89.

1124

Generally accepted as Australia's greatest woman cricketer, an all-rounder who took almost twice as many Test wickets and scored almost twice as many Test runs as her nearest rival. She batted and bowled right-handed and was an outstanding field. She began in Melbourne at the age of 11, when she was watching a women's match and fielded a ball on the boundary, picking up and throwing with such natural skill she was immediately invited to join the local club. She first played for Australia in 1948 in New Zealand and in the only Test created a fourth wicket partnership record of 163 with Una Paisley. In 1948–49 she scored the first century in Tests by an Australian, 111 against England and in the same match took 6 for 23. Her stand of 123 with Molly Dive set a new third wicket partnership record. In England in 1951 she scored 175 runs in three Tests, took 16 wickets, and created a 10th wicket partnership record of 39 with Mavis Jones. She scored two centuries in the three Tests against England in 1957–58, totalling 282 runs and taking 21 wickets. In all, Betty Wilson played 16 Test innings for 862 runs, scoring three centuries and three half-centuries, and was involved in nine partnerships over 50 runs. She took five wickets in an innings four times in securing 66 Test wickets at 11.56. In the 1957–58 Test at Melbourne against England her figures of 7 for 7 included a hat-trick.

WILSON, Betty Rebecca, 1921–

WOOD, Graeme Malcolm, 1956–

First-Class Averages: Batting, 5,488 runs at 36.20; Bowling, 5 wickets at 25.40.

Tests (37): 2,299 runs at 34.31.

An appealing Western Australian left-hand opening batsman whose gifts are sometimes squandered by his impetuous running between wickets. Few batsmen in world cricket hit the ball as sweetly as Wood in full flight, and he has built a commendable record of big opening stands. He fields efficiently close to the wicket and bowls occasional left-arm slows. He has shown pluck to fight his way back into Tests after being dropped from the Australian and Western Australian teams.

Wood, born at East Fremantle, began with the Fremantle club where his father, Malcolm Wood, was president for a time. His brother Dwayne was in the Australian Under-17 side that toured New Zealand in 1977–78. Graeme later joined the Melville club. He has always been a fitness fanatic, practising his footwork at the nets with his father, and working as a physical education teacher. On tour he's the keenest Australian on early morning runs. He has a superb eye and abundant confidence when he is scoring well but has a habit of nervous starts in which he talks to himself, scratches incessantly at his mark, and flexes his knees. A taciturn character off the field, all the tension comes out when he has to decide on tight runs.

He first attracted attention with a breezy 37 against Tony Greig's England team in their warm-up game in Perth against WA before the Centenary Test in Melbourne. When WA lost several players to WSC he got his chance in the State team and in his first season scored 525 runs at 65.63 to finish second in the Shield averages to David Ogilvie. He made his Test debut against India in 1977–78 at Adelaide and in his first six Tests scored 521 runs at 43.42. After his Test baptism (39 and 8) against India he played in all five Tests in the West Indies. In the Third Test at Georgetown, when Australia scored 7 for 362 in the final innings to win by seven wickets, he shared a fourth wicket stand of 251 with Craig Serjeant. Wood was run out for 126, his first Test century, and still his highest.

Among those impressed by Wood's effort was WSC organiser Ian Chappell. "Wood is the sort of player we want in the Australian WSC side," said Chappell. The next season in Australia Wood hesitated about signing an Australian Cricket Board contract before the First Test at Brisbane, but eventually signed and scored 344 runs at 28.66 in the series. It was in this series that doubts first arose about his running between wickets, for his batting was littered with appalling misjudgments, causing team-mates to nickname him the "Kamikaze Kid."

He lost his Test place during the series in India and missed the tour of Pakistan in 1979–80. He also missed selection in the Australian team for the World Cup in England in 1979. Some blamed his omission from the World Cup tour on his delay in signing the ACB contract a year earlier, but his form in India completely vindicated the selectors, for he made

Graeme Wood drives between cover and point against the West Indies at Barbados in 1978.

only 138 runs at 13.80 on the entire tour. When he returned home, he was dropped from the Western Australian team. His career was clearly at crisis point and in an attack on the WA selectors he talked about leaving the State. However, he was striking the ball superbly by the end of the season, and made 213 in the Perth district semi-final followed by 112 in the final.

Fortunately, common sense prevailed and he fought his way back into the Test team. He was only a marginal selection for the Centenary Test at Lord's in 1980 but on the first day of that match battled his way to 112. He followed with 111 in his next Test, against New Zealand at Brisbane, to complete a praise-worthy comeback. By the time he made 125 in the Second Test of the 1980–81 series against India, his Test

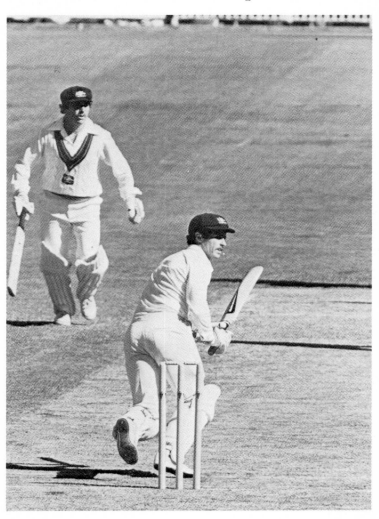

Wood turns Botham down the legside during his century at Melbourne in 1978–79. Alan Border is backing up.

place was assured. He toured England in 1981 under Kim Hughes, played through the series in Australia against Pakistan and the West Indies in 1981–82 and went to New Zealand in 1982 with Greg Chappell's side. Here his familiar problems in running between wickets recurred, but he disciplined himself to finish second on the tour averages with 388 runs from seven innings at 55.43. Only Greg Chappell did better and Wood (100) and Chappell were the only Australian century-makers in the Tests.

WOOD, Reginald, 1860–1915

A left-hand batsman and left-arm medium-pace bowler who was born at Woodchurch, Cheshire, England, but migrated to Australia where he spent the rest of his life teaching aspiring cricketers. He was a useful batsman who hit the ball hard and freely. He played a few times for Lancashire between 1880 and 1884 and was in the Charterhouse XI in 1876. His name began to appear in Melbourne matches around 1886, when he played two matches for Victoria, scoring 34 runs at 11.33, but failing to take a wicket. He was for some time engaged at East Melbourne and later played for the Melbourne club.

In 1886–87, Wood assisted the English team in some of their matches in Australia when W. Barnes sustained a hand injury. He played in one Test for England at Sydney in which he scored 6 and 0. He joined the Albert club in Sydney as a professional in 1889, and died in the Sydney seaside suburb of Manly soon after World War I began.

First-Class Averages: Batting, 235 runs at 15.66. Bowling, 8 wickets at 16.75.

WOODCOCK, Ashley John, 1947–

A sound, stylish right-hand batsman over 10 seasons for South Australia whose sole Test was a disappointing reward for his talents. He was an impressive, clean-cut figure who timed the ball well and enjoyed the short boundaries square of the wicket at Adelaide Oval. but could not produce big scores when a regular Test spot beckoned. He was a physical education master at St Peter's College, Adelaide, and this showed in his athletic fielding and throwing.

Woodcock made his debut for South Australia in 1967–68 against India, scoring 56. He made his initial first-class century, 127, against NSW at Adelaide in February, 1970. The following season he retired hurt on 119 after an impressive opening stand of 250 with Barry Richards against England at Adelaide. A stylish century (141) against Western Australia in Adelaide won him selection in the Third Test in 1973–74 against New Zealand on the same ground. He opened with Keith Stackpole and was the second batsman out with the score at 67, Australia winning a one-sided match by an innings and 57 runs. He was not given another chance, although he toured New Zealand under Ian Chappell in 1973–74.

First-Class Averages: Batting, 4,550 runs at 30.95.

Tests(1): 27 runs at 27.00.

1129

WOODFULL, William Maldon, 1897–1965

First-Class Averages: Batting, 13,392 runs at 65.00; Bowling, 1 wicket at 24.00.

Tests (35): 2,300 runs at 46.00.

A big, stolid, reserved Victorian schoolmaster, a clergyman's son imperturbable in a crisis, who gave Australia memorable service between 1926 and 1934 as an opening batsman and as a captain, most of them years of turmoil in international cricket. He formed with Bill Ponsford one of the most successful opening partnerships in Australia's cricket history. He led Australia to glory in England in 1930 after we had been well beaten under Jack Ryder's captaincy only two years earlier, and he repeated the performance in 1934 in England after England had regained The Ashes in the 1932–33 series.

Woodfull, nicknamed the "Unbowlable" or "The Rock," used barely any backlift with his bat, and on hard, fast pitches was frustrating to dislodge in a period when time had little bearing on match results. He would not have enjoyed limited-over cricket. His runs came from firm clips in front of the wicket and a range of pushes and deflections. At The Oval in 1926 when he made 118 against Surrey his last scoring stroke was his first four. Bowlers who hit his stumps became heroes. When Wally Hammond bowled him in the Fifth Test at Melbourne in 1928–29, it was the first time Woodfull's stumps had been hit in a year.

If Woodfull pulled a rank long hop to the fence, he was cheered as if he had scored a century. In 1928–29, when he made 102 for Australia against England at Melbourne, he hit only three fours, and in 1931–32 his 161 for Australia against South Africa at Melbourne, his highest Test score included only five fours. No wonder English bowlers always liked to see him in his bulky green cap disappear into the pavilion.

Bill Woodfull was born in the small town of Maldon, from which he took his second christian name, and had to overcome muscular troubles that prevented his acceptance in the first AIF. He did not play in a regular team until he was 22, and first played against Englishmen at Ballarat in 1920–21. The following summer he made the Victorian team and began his long pairing with Ponsford. He did not win a place in the Australian side, however, until 1926, but then he played in the next seven international series. One of his pluckiest innings came in 1928–29 at Brisbane when Australia, with two men absent, scored only 66 against England. Woodfull batted through the Australian innings for 30 not out.

Last man chosen in 1926, for the first of his three tours of England, he made more runs on the trip than any of his teammates, 1,809 at 53.35, including 201 against Essex in his first match on English soil. Four years later he returned to England as Australian captain, and against all the odds, won back The Ashes, helped by an unprecedented scoring spree from Bradman, who averaged 98.66 on the tour. In the Lord's Test on the 1930 tour, Australia made her highest Test score until then, 6 for 729, a total that was later exceeded by Ian Johnson's team in the West Indies.

1130

Woodfull's backlift was never pronounced, even in a practice workout.

Woodfull had a habit of being where things were tough, and he brought rare dignity to the Australian captaincy. He was deeply respected by his players, who had an affection for him only equalled by Ian Chappell among our great skippers. When the 1930 team arrived home at Fremantle several players openly expressed their annoyance when Bradman flew ahead of the team and received accolades in capital city appearances that the team felt rightly belonged to Woodfull.

Australia was fortunate that in the midst of intense friction between England and Australia during the Bodyline series that Woodfull was our captain, for he handled temperately a situation that could have ended international cricket. An explosive character like Ian Chappell, for example, would never have allowed his players to be hit as often as Woodfull's players were without a tremendously hostile response.

Woodfull let his feelings be known when the English manager "Plum" Warner came to sympathise with the Australian players who had taken painful blows in the Adelaide Test, but he always regretted that reports of that famous scene leaked out. Having just taken a fierce blow over the heart, Woodfull responded to Warner's commiserations by saying: "There are two teams out there, but only one of them is playing cricket." Warner stormed from the room.

Bill Woodfull lived until he was 68 and to the end refused countless invitations to say anything that would have rekindled the animosity of the Bodyline series. He was a stern schoolmaster right up to his retirement and Keith Miller recalls being punished by him for a playground misdemeanour. In 35 Tests, 25 of them as Australia's captain, Woodfull hit seven centuries and 13 half centuries, highest score 161.

In all first-class matches, Woodfull scored an impressive 49 centuries, highest score 284 for an Australian XI against a New Zealand XI in 1927–28. The figures do not show, however, what an outstanding team batsman he was, forever involved in partnerships that counted. Nor do the figures show the man's courteousness, his sense of decorum and unshakeable commonsense. In many ways he was the most "English" of Australian cricketers, supporting the ethic of fair play in all he did. He once refused to play cricket for Victoria against New South Wales on Christmas Day because he said the day belonged to the family.

WOODS, Samuel Moses James ("Sammy"), 1867–1931 A dual international who excelled in every sport he attempted, a stylish, graceful games player of indomitable spirit. He played for Australia and England at cricket, captained Cambridge University, Somerset and the Gentlemen, and in Rugby is ranked as one of the finest forwards to play for England and Cambridge. He was born at Glenfield, New South Wales, developed his love for sport at Sydney Grammar School and at Royston College, Sydney, where he once took seven wickets with seven balls. He grew to 6 ft 1 in and 13 st 6 lb and went on to Brighton College, England, with his younger brother, H. D. L. Woods.

For Brighton College, Sammy took 14 wickets, all bowled, for 27 runs, v. Lancing College at Lancing in 1886. He also played an innings of 205 for Brighton College v. Next Seventeen at Brighton in 1886. At Cambridge he played in the First XV from 1888 to 1891 and for the First XI which won three and drew one of its four matches against Oxford in that period. He was Cambridge cricket captain in 1890, and in that summer took all 10 wickets in an innings v. C. I. Thornton's XI for 69 runs and 15 in the match for 88. For Cambridge v. Surrey in 1891, he took 14 for 154.

First-Class Averages: Batting, 15,352 runs at 23.43; Bowling, 1,040 wickets at 20.82.

Tests (6): Australia—3, 32 runs at 5.33; 5 wickets at 24.20. England—3, 122 runs at 30.50; 5 wickets at 25.80.

Sammy Woods' immensely powerful physique is evident in this turn of the century shot in London.

By then he had developed into a fast bowler Sir Pelham Warner later was to describe as the most artistic and subtle he ever saw, enormously strong, fast and accurate, with a deadly yorker and a clever slower ball. Woods played for Somerset for 25 years, 1886 to 1910, captained the County from 1894 to 1906 and was secretary of the County for 30 years up until 1923. He lived in Taunton and had the Somerset brogue. All bar one of his 19 centuries in first-class cricket were made for Somerset, his best being 215 out of 282 in 150 minutes v. Sussex at Hove in 1895. Three years later in the corresponding match he scored 143 out of 173 in 135 minutes.

From about 1893 he lost pace as a bowler, but his batting improved rapidly and he ended with an impressive total of 12,637 first-class runs at 25.07 to match his 554 wickets for 23.78 apiece for Somerset. He held 282 catches in first-class matches. He played several times for the 1888 Australian side in England, which had included only 13 players. He played for the Gentlemen from 1888 until 1902, toured America in 1891 and South Africa in 1895–96, each time as a member of a Lord Hawke MCC team, and played in three Tests for England. He visited the West Indies with Sir A. Priestly in 1896 and America with K. S. Ranjitsinhji in 1899.

For Lord Hawke's side v. Gentlemen of Philadelphia in 1891–92 at Philadelphia he took 15 for 86. Woods was popular wherever he went, a genial, burly figure who left Rugby followers discussing with awe his immensely powerful forward play after 13 internationals for England against Scotland, Wales, and Ireland. Among all his remarkable performances, however, Sammy Woods is probably best remembered at Somerset, where his cheery nature, whole-hearted effort whether bowling or batting left a legend that has endured among the cider lovers.

WOOLLEY, Roger Douglas, 1954–

First-Class Averages: Batting, 1,576 runs at 38.43; Dismissals 45 (35 catches, 10 stumpings).

A wicket-keeper batsman who played an important role in Tasmania's five-year build-up to full Sheffield Shield status. He performed consistently well between 1977–78, when Tasmania was admitted to the Shield competition on a restricted basis, and 1981–82, after which Tasmania achieved equal status with the other States. He is a hard-hitting right-hand batsman with a string of long blows for six to his credit and a neat, tidy 'keeper right up to the best mainland standards.

Woolley, a confident, dapper insurance broker from Hobart, has made 11 fifties and two centuries for Tasmania. He began in grade cricket with New Town club in the mid-1970's and spent two seasons playing for Great Harwood in the Ribblesdale League, Lancashire, to further his cricket education. He worked as a plumber's mate to pay expenses for his wife and himself in England. He made a thrilling 141 not out for New

Town soon after his return home, hitting 18 fours and two sixes against South Hobart in a TCA game. He went into the State team soon after, scoring 49 and 55 against Rodney Hogg's pace bowling for South Australia in Hobart.

A week later he made 103 against Queensland at Launceston, the first century in the Shield competition by a Tasmanian-born batsman. In only his third first-class match, Woolley hooked Geoff Dymock for four to bring up his hundred. In 1978–79, he made 99 not out in an unbroken seventh wicket stand of 172 with Jack Simmons against Western Australia to give Tasmania their first Sheffield Shield victory. He took over the wicket-keeper's job when Bruce Doolan broke a thumb and has steadily improved behind the stumps each season. In 1980–81 he tore a medial ligament in the knee playing basketball, which forced him to drop out for most of the season. He bounced back in 1981–82 to head the Tasmanian first-class batting averages with 417 runs at 46.33, including his career highest score, 116, against Queensland at Devonport, sharing a stand of 137 for the fifth wicket with David Boon.

Roger Woolley at the nets, concentrating hard.

WORLD SERIES CRICKET The colourful promotion of international cricket in opposition to that staged by established authority, which began in 1977–78 and lasted for two Australian seasons after media entrepreneur Kerry Packer bought the exclusive services of 66 of the world's best players. The Australian players who joined WSC claimed there had been years of inaction by administrators on claims for better match pay, and a bigger say in the running of the game. The Australian Cricket Board claimed it paid leading players the maximum it could afford and that the State captains Greg Chappell, Doug Walters, Richie Robinson, Ashley Woodcock and Rodney Marsh had unanimously accepted this in December, 1976, just six months before WSC was announced in May, 1977.

Packer lost heavily on WSC in the first season, but built a large and enthusiastic following for his matches in only two years. Packer was assisted by two former Australian captains, Richie Benaud and Ian Chappell, and by the captains of England and Australia, Tony Greig and Greg Chappell, who wrote in his book *The Hundredth Summer*, that Test payments had increased dramatically in the two years before WSC.

Established cricket denied WSC the use of the majority of Australia's cricket grounds, banned some of the players from playing district cricket or practising with the State squads, sacked Greig as England's captain, and enlisted sponsors to put money into cricket for players loyal to the traditional authorities. They could not stop WSC attracting big audiences, both at the grounds and for his television stations. WSC not only drew a new type of cricket spectator, eager to barrack noisily, but it also introduced a long list of innovations, some of them of lasting benefit to the game.

WSC staged cricket's first night games, introduced a white ball, coloured clothing for the players, coloured pads and helmets, battery-operated carts to bring on drinks, and set new standards in public relations by making TV and radio appearances obligatory for WSC players. WSC even commissioned a team of songwriters to compose songs about its teams. "Come on, Aussies, come on" went to the top of the hit parade.

At Sydney WSC spectators were banned from taking alcohol into the SCG. WSC players were over-exposed and many of them spent long periods in country areas in minor matches. WSC's televised matches were notable for superb camera work and for tedious repetition of commercials. The viability of the Sheffield Shield was threatened even further, and WSC created a division among lifelong cricket supporters that was not healed when a settlement was reached with established cricket. In November, 1981, when 27,000 spectators saw Australia beat the West Indies in an incident-packed one-day match at the SCG, the members' stand was almost empty. The cleavage WSC had created between traditional cricket fans and WSC's fence-jumpers remained, with great servants of

1136

the game like Lindsay Hassett, Sam Loxton, Bill O'Reilly and "Stork" Hendry stern critics of the decline in player behaviour that became more obvious with the WSC. Meanwhile the money is rolling in with the rapacious showing of TV commercials. The Australian Cricket Board has become affluent with the peace but is powerless to impose limitations on TV commercials for the relief of cricket followers who decline to expose their families to larrikinism at the grounds.

The ACB waited after the announcement of WSC on May 9, 1977, until September 16, 1977, to issue a statement outlining its case in the whole affair. In the four months the ACB remained silent, claims about how poorly Test players were paid went unchecked. The ACB set the record straight in its statement but much damage had been done by its insistence on remaining silent "while the Australian team was engaged with England in a Test series." The Board pointed out that players in the Centenary Test had received $2,277 each, not $300 as WSC players alleged. Each player on the 35-day tour of New Zealand received $2,430, not "something over $1,200" as the players claimed. The 17 players on the 1977 tour of England received $10,890 and not $6,000, as claimed.

English cricket writers found it particularly difficult to understand the Australian Test players' motives in joining WSC. The English game owed its early progress to an upper class who played cricket and patronised it with social distinctions, a part of the game at all levels. It is not so long ago that English professionals changed in different rooms from amateurs in the same team and only met their team-mates on the field. When the great Australian leg-spinner Bruce Dooland played for Nottinghamshire in the 1950s he was reprimanded by a Notts committeeman for calling the team captain R. T. Simpson "Reg," an action that is totally incomprehensible to Australians.

Australia's international cricket strength has been built on mateship and an underlying common keenness to pick any spare change that was around, if only to compensate for the financial sacrifices in travelling vast distances to play in other countries. Early Australian teams in England played as many matches as possible, sometimes every day, to bring in the money they split up at the end of the tour. They got their rest by refusing to play before noon and after 6 p.m. A writer in the contemporary *Lillywhite* complained that the splendid 1882 Australian side "have seriously and perceptibly aggravated the symptoms of a commercial spirit in cricket." Australians called their players amateurs or used the euphemism "cricketers" but the top players always were alert for financial gain.

This is why World Series Cricket received a sympathetic response in Australia, compared with the outright hostility it aroused in England. For the reasons why so many top players

1137

supported the WSC went back a long time, probably even to 1911–12 when six star players refused to go to England because of the terms offered. Just after World War II Ray Lindwall lost his job by playing for Australia. Members of the great 1948 team found they had lost job opportunities by making that memorable tour of England. More recently Ross Edwards lost his job in a Perth accountancy firm and was forced to quit Test cricket before he wished because of his absences on Australian team trips. The players' discontent over the sacrifices they had to make were well known but the only people who listened to their grievances were the TV comedian Paul Hogan and his manager, John Cornell, who went to Packer with the idea that developed into WSC. The ACB at the time was doing the gentlemanly thing and refusing to negotiate TV rights with Packer's network until an existing contract with the ABC expired, so Packer decided to take on the ACB.

The players were convinced that their complaints were all on view in the Centenary Test at Melbourne in March, 1977, and the success of this masterly promotion strengthened the resolve of those with doubts about signing for WSC. The match attracted 247,873 spectators and $262,086 in gate-money, of which each Australian player received $2,277. More importantly, the Centenary Test showed how progressive the players were in arguing that big cricket demanded professional staging. Even while playing the Centenary Test the WSC players were going over their contracts. In the end Packer was able to pick and choose because so many big names wanted to sign up. Former players Bob Cowper and John Gleeson joined the management committee without fees, and Bill Lawry and Keith Stackpole gave their support as commentators.

Offered the chance to earn up to $30,000 a year playing cricket in Australia, 66 of the world's best cricketers jumped at it. The fact that so many signed at a point when match fees were rising and no organisation existed to stage WSC games, demonstrated how unanimous was the players' discontent and how badly key ACB officials misjudged the players' mood. In retrospect it seems beyond belief that such a group was able to shake traditional cricket to its foundations, but over two years they welded themselves into an organisation that did just that.

Reactions to the formation of WSC were varied. In Melbourne Ray Bright was barred from grade cricket in 1977–78 and had to play for Footscray Technical College to get practice. Richie Robinson played on malthoid as captain-coach of North Alphington to get his practice. In England Tony Greig found his daughter in tears when he went to pick her up at school. She had been excluded from a children's party because of what her father had done. Another of the rebels,

1138

Derek Underwood, said: "It was a terrible time for me and my family. The mental pressures were intense. Not a day passed without my wife, Dawn, and I having long talks about the implications of my decision to sign. I sensed that people considered me disloyal, a traitor, a money-grabber and worse, when the truth is, all I was trying to get was a degree of security for my wife and two daughters."

When the International Cricket Conference announced that they intended to ban all WSC players from official Tests for two years after their last appearance for WSC, Packer took them to court. The High Court hearing in London lasted 31 days and judgment took 5 hours 30 minutes to deliver. The court ruled in Packer's favour, basically on the ground that banning his players was an unreasonable restraint of trade,

Crowds swarm on to the field after an SCG WSC night match.

Kerry Packer going out to bat in a journalists' match at Harrogate in 1977.

leaving the ICC and England's Test and County Cricket Board with more than $A300,000 to pay in court costs. The judge agreed that in the interests of team building selectors should not be instructed whom they should select. The judgment meant that all the English counties with WSC players on their books had to re-engage them.

Kerry Francis Bullmore Packer (1937–), the man who threw Australian cricket into the greatest turmoil in its history, lost millions of dollars on WSC but he also reduced the ACB almost to insolvency. In the two years of WSC Packer showed immense loyalty to his players, defending their decisions to make more money from the game with a toughness his father, the former Sydney newspaper baron, **Sir Douglas Frank Hewson Packer** (1906–1974) would have admired. Sir Frank founded the Australian *Women's Weekly* in 1933 and built Consolidated Press into a conglomerate of TV stations, magazines, book publishing firms, laundries, mail order and dress pattern outfits, and newspapers, but sold off the newspapers to Rupert Murdoch not long before his death. Kerry and his elder brother, **Robert Clyde Packer** (1935–), were to have inherited the empire Sir Frank built, but a few years before his father's death Clyde took a settlement and left Consolidated Press, leaving Kerry as sole heir.

After talks at Lord's with the ICC broke down, Kerry Packer was obliged to stage his first WSC matches on football grounds using prefabricated wickets. Just when it seemed that established cricket would endure the rebellion by restricting WSC to outlying suburbs, Packer pulled off an amazing coup. For reasons it has never clarified, the NSW State Government rushed through parliament changes to the Act that removed the New South Wales Cricket Association's priority over the use of the Sydney Cricket Ground. The SCG Trust then leased the ground to WSC and in a few weeks workmen erected six 250-foot towers that each carried 96 powerful lights and transformed the old ground and the economics of WSC's challenge to established cricket. The lights cost $1.3 million to which it contributed one-third, said the NSW Government.

When the lights went on WSC was accepted. On November 28, 1978, after an acrimonious year of feuding with established cricket, Ian Chappell led the Australian WSC side on to the field for the first match under lights. An astounding evening ensued, before a crowd estimated at 58,000. Packer, who said he would have been happy if 20,000 attended, threw open the gates after 7 p.m. and let people in free so that they would not miss the match. It was apparent he had found a new audience for cricket, people who cheered raucously and joshed the players and brought their freshly painted banners. It has been said that many of them were drunks but this was true only of a very small number in that first big WSC crowd. Signifi-

1140

cantly, a lot of them were family groups, with parents bringing their children. And they all had a good time.

Cricket writers in England tried to down-grade the success of WSC by stressing that the crowds that followed behaved like those at a Beatles' concert. They were certainly different galleries to those at the average England-Australia Test, with many more teenagers present, but they were an audience cricket needed. There were other pluses, too, such as the white ball and the use of 30 metre circles to prevent negative field placings.

Packer lost an estimated $4 million on the first year of WSC but with substantial corporate backing he could absorb that loss. He lost far less the second year and streamlined his organisation as public and media support grew. When the settlement was negotiated with the ACB, Packer got what he had always wanted—exclusive rights to televise big cricket in Australia. WSC players were all paid up and accepted back in the Test teams of their home countries. The ACB, having suffered crippling losses in the two years of WSC, now looked to WSC and its promotional expertise to help.

When the Australian Broadcasting Commission challenged Packer's right to exclusively televise big cricket, he agreed, in an out of court settlement, to allow the ABC to televise all games for two hours each day in the States where they were played. The ABC agreed to pay Packer's network an undisclosed fee for these rights and the Channel 9 network retained TV rights to entire matches. To many people in outlying areas to whom the ABC coverage was almost a way of life, this arrangement was greeted with relief. It left Packer with his cherished TV rights but did not compel cricket fans to listen to his commentators. Indeed the ABC got surprising results when it experimented by showing Channel 9's film of a London Test without sound and urged viewers to combine the film with Alan McGilvray's radio commentary.

Now that the animosity aroused by WSC has faded Packer's PBL Marketing organisation and the ACB appear to be working harmoniously. The cash rewards from the 1981–82 season obviously delighted the Board as they passed back their shares of it to the States. The public seems to have finally realised that the Board distributes profits from home and overseas tours to assist in developing the game at all levels from schools through junior and country associations to grade and district clubs. Not the least of the benefits intense exposure from Channel 9 cameramen has brought is the public acceptance of countries like India, Pakistan and New Zealand, who previously would not have drawn a quorum on Australian tours. With their bank balances looking healthy because of the WSC revenue, the establishment has even accepted coloured clothing and the white ball. Night cricket is treated as a master stroke.

1142

The 66 players who played with the WSC were:

AUSTRALIA (28 players): Ian Chappell (capt), Ray Bright, Greg Chappell, Trevor Chappell, Ian Davis, Ross Edwards, Gary Gilmour, David Hookes, Martin Kent, Bruce Laird, Rob Langer, Dennis Lillee, Ashley Mallett, Mick Malone, Rod Marsh, Rick McCosker, Graham McKenzie, Kerry O'Keefe, Len Pascoe, Wayne Prior, Ian Redpath, Richie Robinson, Jeff Thomson, Max Walker, Doug Walters, Graeme Watson, Dennis Yagmich and Kepler Wessels (a former South African).

WEST INDIES (18): Clive Lloyd (capt), Jim Allen, Richard Austin, Colin Croft, Wayne Daniel, Roy Fredericks, Joel Garner, Gordon Greenidge, Desmond Haynes, David Holford, Michael Holding, Bernard Julien, Collis King, Deryck Murray, Albert Padmore, Vivian Richards, Andy Roberts, Lawrence Rowe.

REST OF THE WORLD (20): Tony Greig (capt), Dennis Amiss, Alan Knott, John Snow, Derek Underwood, Bob Woolmer (England); Eddie Barlow, Garth Le Roux, Mike Proctor, Clive Rice, Barry Richards (South Africa); Asif Iqbal, Imran Khan, Javed Miandad, Mushtaq Mohammad, Sarfraz Nawaz, Haroon Rashid, Zaheer Abbas, Majid Khan (Pakistan), Richard Hadlee (New Zealand).

Thirty players from the Australian and World teams played one three-day and eight one-day games on a tour of New Zealand in November, 1978. The World team to New Zealand contained West Indian cricketers. Australian and West Indies teams, each of 15 players, toured the West Indies from February-April, 1979, where they played five five-day internationals and eight one-day games before record crowds.

The WSC Australians and West Indies' tour of West Indies in 1979 was disrupted by rioting spectators. They forced the second four-day international at Bridgetown, Barbados, to be abandoned as a draw and the fourth four-day international at Georgetown, Guyana, to be reduced to three days after the abandonment of the first day's play.

Many of the on-field innovations introduced by World Series Cricket during their two-year breakaway from official cricket were retained during the first compromise season in 1979–80. They included:

- Games under floodlights.
- Use of white balls and black sightboards for night games.
- Six-ball overs exclusively.
- One white ball bowled from each end of the wicket.
- Field microphones for television coverage.
- Coloured clothing worn by the players and umpires and coloured equipment worn by the players.

Opposite: Tony Greig, one of the masterminds of WSC, during his days with Sussex.

RECORDS OF AUSTRALIAN PLAYERS IN WSC INTERNATIONAL GAMES
(1977–78 and 1978–79 seasons)
BATTING

	Matches	Innings	Not Out	H. Score	Runs	Averages	Centuries	Catches
G. S. Chappell	15	28	1	246*	1578	58.44	5	20
K. C. Wessells	4	8	1	126	291	41.57	1	5
D. W. Hookes	13	24	2	116	789	35.86	1	6
I. M. Chappell	15	29	2	141	873	32.33	1	15
R. S. Langer	2	4	–	45	104	26.00	–	1
B. M. Laird	14	28	1	122	642	23.77	3	10
R. J. Bright	16	29	6	69	541	23.52	–	9
R. B. McCosker	7	14	–	129	306	21.85	1	5
M. F. Kent	10	20	–	78	428	21.40	–	2
R. W. Marsh	16	30	1	102*	603	20.79	1	54
R. Edwards	2	4	–	39	81	20.25	–	4
T. Chappell	4	8	–	41	127	15.87	–	1
M. H. N. Walker	8	15	4	30	168	15.27	–	3
L. S. Pascoe	9	14	6	26*	119	14.87	–	1
I. C. Davis	6	12	–	84	176	14.66	–	2
G. J. Gilmour	8	15	1	36	204	14.57	–	7
R. Robinson	1	2	–	26	28	14.00	–	2
D. K. Lillee	15	26	8	37	226	12.55	–	6
W. Prior	2	3	2	7*	12	12.00	–	1
K. D. Walters	1	2	–	16	21	10.50	–	–
M. F. Malone	1	2	1	7*	7	7.00	–	–
J. R. Thomson	5	8	2	12	39	6.50	–	1
I. R. Redpath	2	3	–	9	16	5.33	–	1

Marsh kept wickets in all 16 of Australia's WSC international games, making 54 dismissals, all caught

BOWLING

	Overs	Maidens	Runs	Wickets	Average
M. H. N. Walker	208.2	42	783	33	23.72
D. K. Lillee	554.1	116	1889	79	23.91
G. S. Chappell	49	8	156	6	26.00
I. M. Chappell	47.4	13	174	6	29.00
R. J. Bright	422.2	97	1257	43	29.23
J. R. Thomson	133	25	476	16	29.75
L. S. Pascoe	242.1	38	960	30	32.00
G. J. Gilmour	263	59	807	24	33.62
M. F. Malone	40	11	109	3	36.33
D. W. Hookes	25	6	94	1	94.00
W. Prior	41	4	232	2	116.00

The above figures incorporate WSC's 16 international games—six in Australia in 1977–78, and one in New Zealand, four in Australia, and five in the West Indies in 1978–79.

WORRALL, John
1863–1937

A highly belligerent all-round sportsman whose fame in Melbourne as a cricketer who could tear an attack apart was matched by his great success as an Australian Rules footballer. Short, wide-shouldered, he was a man of stern but balanced views who later became a highly respected sportswriter for Melbourne newspapers and is sometimes said to have invented the word "Bodyline". He played cricket for Victoria for almost 18 years and for Australia in 11 Tests over 14 year. He twice toured England in Australian teams and

1144

would have gone a third time in 1902 but for a misunder-standing over his availability.

Worrall was born at Maryborough, Victoria, and educated at the local State school. He was a somewhat crude batsman in his early days but he learned quickly and channelled his flair for big hitting into many valuable innings. His scoring in Melbourne grade matches often was spectacular. In 1891–92, he had a knock of 221 not out for Fitzroy Bohemians, and in February 1896, made 417 not out in a total of 922 for Carlton against Melbourne University. He batted on three afternoons for his 417, hitting three fives and 61 fours offering only one chance. In 1911, he made 215 for Carlton v. North Melbourne, adding 357 with T. Warne (130 not out) before a wicket fell.

Jack Worrall made his debut for Victoria in 1883–84 and played 65 times for the State. He made his Test debut in January 1885, in the first of five Test series against England but in a team of brilliant cricketers struggled for his place. English critics thought him misguided in his quest for runs off every ball on his first tour in 1888, but by the time he toured again in 1899 he was a far more disciplined and polished performer. He made 104 v. Yorkshire at Bradford, 100 not out v. Leicestershire at Leicester, and 128 v. Sussex at Hove. In the match against Cambridge University when Australia were set 123 to win, he and Joe Darling got them without loss, at one period scoring 74 in 28 minutes.

At Headingley, Leeds, in June, 1899, he played one of Test cricket's most remarkable innings. Opening up, he made his first 28 runs, 37 of the first 38, 51 out of 62, and finally 76 out of 95 in 75 minutes at the crease. That 76 remained his highest score in a Test career that yielded five innings over 50 runs.

In his long career for Victoria, Worrall batted in every position in the order and scored four centuries. In 1909–10, the VCA appointed him coach to the State's most promising colts, a position in which his experience proved invaluable.

In the press box, he was always helpful to aspiring cricket writers, a seemingly endless sources of anecdotes about W. G. Grace, Billy Murdoch, Spofforth and other great Australians. He had a special place in his memory bank, however, for Victor Trumper and even after Bradman's prodigious scoring feats Worrall always referred to Trumper as the greatest batsman of all.

The legend is that when Worrall went to the First Test at Sydney in 1932 he sought to save money in a cable to his paper in Melbourne by condensing the words "in line with the body" to "bodyline". In Melbourne when his cable was received a sub-editor liked the word "bodyline" and put it up in a headline. It could never have happened after telephones became fashionable, before teleprinters and instant radio, but Worrall's cable possibly gave cricket a word that will endure as long as the game itself.

First-Class Averages: Batting, 4,660 runs at 20.99; Bowling, 105 wickets at 23.10.

Tests (11): 478 runs at 25.15; 1 wicket at 127.00.

WRIGHT, Albert William, 1875–1938

First-Class Averages: Batting, 242 runs at 7.58; Bowling, 110 wickets at 30.81.

A right-arm South Australian leg-spinner who took wickets regularly in Sheffield Shield matches in the decade before World War I. He was the curator at the Adelaide Oval and did a lot of bowling at the nets on the ground and achieved unusual accuracy with his spinners. He was a quiet, modest man who got on with the job of preparing first-class wickets without fuss, and he played all his cricket in the same unpretentious fashion. He was a poor batsman, his six successive ducks in 1905–06 established the world record for unproductive batting, and a fieldsman of such indifference he was not easy to hide in the field.

Wright was serving his apprenticeship under Charlie Checkett at Adelaide Oval and turning out for the Adelaide club in district cricket when he was picked for the South Australian team to play New South Wales in December, 1905 on a strip he had helped prepare. He bowled 40.2 overs in a NSW total of 556, taking 5 for 150. He opened the bowling against Victoria at Melbourne in the following month and took 7 for 66, setting up a South Australian win. His good form continued in 1906–07 when he took 5 for 42 against Victoria and 6 for 91 against NSW. His match bag in the Victorian match was 9 for 96 which enabled SA to win by 319 runs. Wright took 29 first-class wickets that year at 21.24.

He took most wickets in Adelaide district cricket in the 1907–08 and 1909–10 seasons and also topped the bowling averages in 1909–10 (59 wickets at 11.96) but dropped out of the State team when it interfered with his duties as curator. His was a familiar figure at Adelaide Oval walking behind a roller drawn by a mare named "Queenie" who wore specially padded boots. Queenie had been selected for the job by Clem Hill, whose eye for a good horse proved as alert as it was for a loose ball, for Queenie did the job for 20 years until she was replaced by a motorised roller.

Alby Wright was pressed into service again with the State team in 1910–11 when the State was woefully weak in bowling. At Sydney against NSW he opened the bowling with medium-pacer Roy Hill and took 5 for 75 and 6 for 103. At the end of the 1911–12 season he retired for good to concentrate on his wickets and looking after Queenie, a much loved, sunburnt character who devoted himself to establishing Adelaide Oval as one of the best batting wickets in the world.

WRIGHT, Kevin John, 1953–

An alert, tidy red-haired wicket-keeper of trim appearance who did well in 10 Tests for Australia in the absence of Rod Marsh with WSC but has since been unable to regain the job. He is a natural left-hander when he takes the ball, but bats capably right-handed, and has scored two first-class centuries and many runs late in the order. He came originally from

1146

the same club in Perth as Marsh, but moved to South Australia after the 1979–80 season to improve his prospects of regaining the Test place.

Wright, born at North Fremantle, first played for WA in 1974–75 against England, and whenever Marsh was absent. He quickly built a fine record of dismissals with the State team. His chance to appear in Tests came unexpectedly when the selectors omitted John Maclean, Australia's vice-captain in the first four Tests and preferred Wright for the last two Tests against England in 1978–79. He made a splendid impression with his agility and determination behind the stumps. He took six catches in his initial Test and stumped Gooch off Higgs with a delightful piece of work in the Sixth Test, Gooch only momentarily losing his balance to give Wright his chance. His good work continued in the two Tests that followed against Pakistan and he took seven catches in both games.

Wright toured England with Australia's World Cup team in 1979 and played in all six Tests against India later the same year, compiling his highest Test score, 55 not out, in the Fourth Test at New Delhi, and in the Fifth Test at Calcutta his catching was responsible for six of the 14 dismissals in the match. The harsh realities of Test cricket overtook him on his return home from the tour. Wright, Hilditch, Wood and Yardley all lost their Test places as a result of the WSC settlement and so far only Wood and Yardley have regained them. Since he moved to South Australia Wright has improved his batting and in 1981–82 his consistent scoring was a useful aid to his side's Sheffield Shield success. But he missed selection in the Australian team that toured England in 1981 when Steve Rixon was preferred as Marsh's deputy.

First-Class Averages: Batting, 1,932 runs at 27.60; Dismissals 231 (210 caught, 21 stumped).

Tests (10): 219 runs at 16.84; Dismissals 35 (31 caught, 4 stumped).

A tall, fair-haired Toowoomba-born left-arm pace bowler who was regarded as one of the most promising of his type in Australia in the 1930s. He was twice nominated for overseas trips by Australian teams but failed to tour. He played four seasons for Queensland from 1933–34 before a foot injury curtailed his cricket. His 25 matches for Queensland produced a topscore of 29 and best bowling figures of 6 for 33.

Wyeth got his nickname through his ability with his fists as a boy at Toowoomba East Public School. There was no cricket at the school so he organised matches against other schools without help from his teachers. At Toowoomba Grammar School, George ("Boss") Barbour, father of Eric and Robert Barbour, was the headmaster. Wyeth made a careful study of Eric Barbour's book on cricket techniques and this strongly influenced his style. He went into the Queensland Colts team after he entered Queensland University. In 1933–34 he took 6 for 48 for Queensland Colts against NSW Colts.

WYETH, Ezra Robert ("Boxer"), 1910–

First-Class Averages: Batting, 251 runs at 8.09; Bowling, 50 wickets at 43.18.

Before he represented his State, Wyeth received a telegram informing him that he had been chosen in the Australian team to tour New Zealand in 1933–34. Two days later the tour was cancelled. He took 6 for 33 against South Australia at the Gabba in a 1934–35 Shield match. When Vic Richardson took an Australian team to South Africa in 1935–36, only 14 players were named. The selectors wanted another bowler, Wyeth, but the Board of Control insisted that only 14 players should tour.

Wyeth won the Barstow trophy for the best bowler in Brisbane club cricket in his final year at Queensland University, finishing with 7 for 24 against Valley, 7 for 40 and 3 for 23 against Easts, and 7 for 57 against Souths. He became a respected educationist and wrote a definitive history of Education in Queensland, took his doctorate in Educational Psychology at the University of California in 1947, and in 1949 joined the staff of Melbourne University. From there he moved to California State University as a professor of Education. He played frequently in matches with Boris Karloff, C. Aubrey Smith and other film stars, and for three years coached the University of Southern California cricket team.

After the foot injury ended his cricket career, Wyeth became a world authority on lawn bowls. He captained the American team in the world bowls championship at Kyeemagh in Sydney in 1966, and in international tournaments at Brisbane, Sydney and Melbourne in 1981. He won an International Bowling Board Championship in California in 1965. At 72 in 1982 he could reflect on a career in which he had represented Queensland at cricket and lawn bowls and both Victoria and America at lawn bowls.

Y

The popular name for the legendary Australian spectator, **Stephen Harold Gascoigne** (1878–1942), whose boisterous comments and great sense of timing enlivened matches at Sydney Cricket Ground for 30 years. He was a trader in rabbits who trundled a cart around the South Sydney and Balmain areas of Sydney, hawking his rabbits to housewives who appeared at the sound of his bell and argued about how fast he could skin their purchases. His father has been a storekeeper in Oxford before migrating to Australia.

Yabba held court in the centre of The Hill in the days before television and larrikinism, and he was a major reason for The Hill winning a world-wide reputation for knowledgable spectatorship, sadly now but a memory. He was gifted with a voice that carried clearly and precisely to the far corners of the ground. In the Members' Stand, opposite Yabba's stage, he came through like a church bell. Yabba was all for the underdog and had an ex-soldier's vocabulary, dating back to his service in the South African war.

He arrived at the Sydney Cricket Ground carrying a hamper and bottles of beer, a fleshy, open-hearted man close to 6ft tall and around 14 stone, and set up camp looking down the pitch from around mid-on. He wore his hawker's white coat until it became too hot and he removed the coat to show his braces. Admirers surrounded him, shoving drinks into his vast hands but most of the quips with which he entertained them have soured through constant repetition. The generally accepted notion on how he came to be known as Yabba was that this was a corruption of his cry, "Rabbie, wild rabbie", as he wheeled his cart through the back streets.

YALLOP, Graham Neil, 1952–

A stylish, hard-driving Victorian left-handed batsman who in a first-class career that began in 1972–73 has repeatedly had to prove himself. He captained Australia in seven Tests

First-Class Averages: Batting, 7,656 runs at 40.29; Bowling, 7 wickets at 79.28.

Tests (32): 2,101 runs at 36.22; 1 wicket at 116.00.

at a time of intense publicity in the second year of WSC, losing six Tests and winning one, inspiring neither team-mates nor cricket watchers. He has played some notable innings, including six Test centuries, and few batsmen can handle top-class spin bowling better, but since the settlement with WSC he has been unable to command a regular place in the Australian team.

Yallop, born at Balwyn, Victoria, learnt his cricket at Carey, a leading Melbourne Grammar School, where he came under the influence of former English Test star Frank Tyson, then a master at the school. Yallop began as an opening bowler but developed quickly as a batsman who could handle any position in the order from opener to No. 6. In 1972, he toured Sri Lanka with the Australian Schoolboys' side.

After leaving school he went to work in a sports store owned by Tyson's friend Lindsay Hassett, and at Tyson's suggestion went to play for Walsall in the Birmingham League in 1973 after making his debut for Victoria in 1972–73. Yallop made 3,000 runs in a variety of competitions in three seasons and also met his Welsh wife, Helen. He rejected offers from English county clubs—he had appeared for Glamorgan Second XI—to return to Australia and build his reputation with a series of big scores for Victoria.

Yallop narrowly avoids being run out by Derek Randall at Brisbane in 1977–78, providing Jim Fenwick with an outstanding photograph.

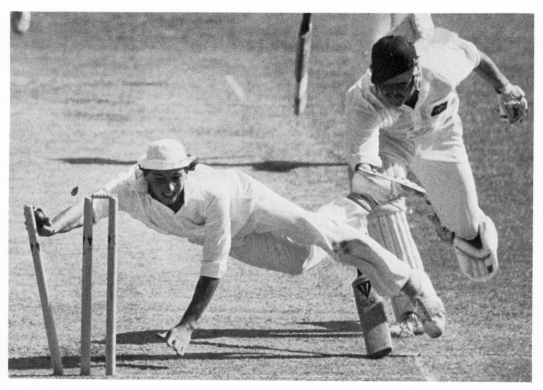

Yallop plays his favourite square cut to the boundary.

A young man in a hurry, he married, opened his own sports goods wholesaling business under the same roof as his father's engineering firm, bought an interest in a sports centre, built a house in the Melbourne suburb of Ringwood. In 1978 he was one of the few players to show any consistency on the West Indies tour with the team led by Bob Simpson, heading the averages with 660 runs at 55.00. He scored 317 of these runs in the Tests at 45.28, best score 118 not out against Guyana at Georgetown in a five hour innings without the helmet he had helped popularise, the innings ending when a bouncer broke his jaw. In 1978–79 he took over the Australian captaincy from Bobby Simpson, whose terms were unacceptable to the Australian Board of Control. Playing in his first Test against England and leading Australia for the first time, he scored 102 in the second innings of the First Test at Brisbane, but from the start he was in trouble with his players and the media.

1151

After an unhappy series during which he clashed openly with the record-breaking fast bowler Rodney Hogg, he was deposed as Australian captain by Kim Hughes for the 1979 tour of India. He had not had a fair go from the media and had not realised the importance of his dealings with them. In 1980–81 he lost the Victorian captaincy to Richie Robinson who returned from WSC. Through all these setbacks even Yallop's sternest critics never doubted his batting skill, particularly against slow bowlers. He has a gift for timing drives and cuts when set, though in England in 1981 Willis and Hendrick made him look suspect facing high, rising deliveries. In the Fifth Test, he hit his most recent Test century, 114 at Manchester, and in the six Tests only Border made more runs for Australia. Yallop had made 17 first-class centuries and is still good enough to reappear for Australia.

YARDLEY, Bruce ("Roo"), 1947–

First-Class Averages: Batting, 2,154 runs at 20.71; Bowling, 258 wickets at 26.49.

Tests (25): 776 runs at 19.90; 95 wickets at 29.66.

A highly-strung Perth allrounder of leathery-skin and combative disposition who has often proved invaluable to Australian teams by taking breathtaking gully catches, dismissing dangerous batsmen, or scoring a brisk 30. He has overcome many setbacks to establish himself as one of Australian cricket's big crowd-pleasers. Spectators sense that he is big cricket's typical Aussie battler and share his joy when he occasionally defies the odds and straight drives great fast bowlers for four or when one of his drifting off-breaks hangs in flight and cleans bowls a Test star.

Cricket is never dull when Yardley is on stage, for he can be mercurial and heroic. His failures bring disappointment akin to personal loss. Yardley was born at Midland, WA, and has played all his club cricket with Midland-Guildford. He made his debut for WA in 1966–67 against Queensland as the new ball partner to Ian Brayshaw, with Colin Guest as first change. When Graham McKenzie, Bob Massie and Sam Gannon returned from other duties he was dropped after just one game. Five years later he was back in the State team as a first change bowler of medium-pace outswingers, with a slower delivery that dipped and cut back. He had begun as a schoolboy bowling leg-spinners, holding the ball between the third and fourth fingers and he used the same fingers when he threw the ball, finding that he could produce an outcurve holding the ball that way.

The Midland-Guildford coach, Keith Slater, suggested that he try bowling off-spinners with his leg-spinner's grip and because it felt comfortable that he stick with the pace bowler's approach.

The combination worked so well that within two years Yardley was back in the State team, drifting the ball away from right-handers and cutting it back. He took wickets con-

Yardley at the nets—showing his unorthodox grip on the ball.

sistently, and in 1976–77 did his Test prospects no harm by scoring 97 not out for WA against NSW. He was tipped as a probable English tourist in 1977 but when the national selectors wanted to watch him the WA selectors made him 12th man.

Yardley finally made his Test debut in 1977–78 against India in the Fifth Test at Adelaide, taking 4 for 134 from 43 overs in the second innings on a good batting wicket, which helped clinch an Australian win. In the West Indies on his first tour in 1978 his spin bowling became an important part of Bob Simpson's attack. A week before the Third Test, with the West Indies 2-0 up and the tour a potential flop, Yardley was flattened by a Colin Croft bouncer in the match against Guyana and taken to hospital. A jagged wound in his head had to be stitched but x-rays cleared him of a skull fracture and two hours after being carried from the field with blood pouring from his head he was back fielding. A headache finally forced him to the dressing-room. In the Third Test he took 3 for 96, including the vital wicket of Kallicharan, and then hit the winning runs as Australia scored 7 for 362 to win by three wickets. The tour was saved.

Yardley took 15 Test wickets on that tour and bowled more overs than any Australian except Jim Higgs. He made his highest Test score in the Bridgetown Test, 74, which he followed with an aggressive 43 in the second innings. He returned home a confirmed allrounder, but was dropped after two Tests in the 1978–79 series against England. The selectors brought him back for the Fifth and Sixth Tests, and although he seldom beat the bat on unresponsive pitches he bowled tidily and hit a fighting 61 not out in the last Test.

Yardley went to India with Kim Hughes' side in 1979, playing in three of the six Tests and taking 10 Test wickets at 38.10. He missed selection for the Centenary Test tour to England in 1980 and the three Tests versus New Zealand in 1980–81, but bounced back to play in two of the three Tests that summer against India. In 1981–82 he was up to his old unpredictable tricks mixing some splendid efforts with bad lapses in technique. He took his career best figures for Tests by taking 6 for 84 in the First Test against Pakistan at Melbourne and improved them as the summer progressed. In the Third Test versus Pakistan he had 7 for 187 off 66 overs. At Sydney in the Second Test against the West Indies he took 7 for 98 and scored 45 when Australia appeared in trouble. In among these outstanding results he kept falling for Joel Garner's fast yorker, a "sucker ball" to anyone trying to make every delivery a half-volley fit for driving. On the last day of the Third Test against the West Indies at Adelaide, Yardley's bowling was the key to the result but Clive Lloyd and Andy Roberts punished him severely to set up a West Indies win and draw the series.

But a slow bowler who cannot take a hammering is unworthy of a national team place, and Yardley went on enthusiastically to three Tests in New Zealand, where he was Australia's leading wicket-taker, with 13 victims at 23.92. Considering his record, however, it would be unwise to suggest that he had finally become an automatic Test selection.

YOUNIS, Ahmed, 1947–

A nuggetty, thickset Pakistani left-handed batsman and left-arm medium pace or slow bowler who played several times for South Australia in 1972–73. He was an unsatisfactory import with the South Australian players, most of whom believed his place should have gone to a young local batsman rather than a player with an unremarkable past overseas. This feeling was partly caused by reports that Younis was to receive $1-a-run while playing for South Australia. He scored 289 runs for South Australia at 26.27, topscore 69 against Victoria, and took 2 wickets at 61.00. He played for Pakistan in two Tests against New Zealand in 1969–70, appeared for Surrey from 1965 to 1978, and for Worcestershire from 1979 to 1982.

Z

ZIEBELL, Keith Percy, 1942–

First-Class Averages: Batting, 506 runs at 36.14; Bowling, 2 wickets at 59.50.

A right-hand batsman and right-arm medium pace for Ipswich, Brisbane Colts and Queensland, who played in nine matches between 1965 and 1967. He scored only one first-class century but what a century it was! At Melbourne in 1966–67 Victoria batted first and scored 573. Queensland made 146 in reply and followed-on. Ziebell went in at No 4 and against all the odds saved the match with an innings of 212 not out, Queensland finishing with 7 for 525.

ZIMBULIS, Anthony George, 1918–1963

First-Class Averages: Batting, 338 runs at 14.01; Bowling, 49 wickets at 39.12.

A prodigious schoolboy spinner of the ball whose right-arm legbreaks failed to achieve consistent accuracy against top-flight batsmen. He made his debut for Western Australia in 1933–34 at 16. He had headed the bowling averages for North Perth the previous summer with 37 wickets at 10.1. He had some remarkable figures in district cricket. He headed the Perth bowling aggregates four times—in 1935–36 when he took 93 wickets at 11.2, in 1937–38 when he took 62 wickets at 13.61, in 1938–39 when he took 73 wickets at 14.8, and again in 1948–49 when he had 67 wickets at 17.9. His best figures in first-class cricket were 5 for 60 against Victoria at Melbourne in 1937–38. He batted right-handed and had a topscore of 43 not out. He was a bowler of rich talent but had the bad luck to appear at a time when Bill O'Reilly, Clarrie Grimmett and Fleetwood-Smith—some of the finest spinners in Australian cricket history—held the slow bowling berths in the national side. He served during World War II as an RAAF pilot and did well in services matches in England.

ADDENDUM

AUSTRALIAN CRICKET BOARD

CHAIRMEN

L. A. Adamson (Vic)	1905–1906	H. Gregory (WA)	1926–1927
E. E. Bean (Vic)	1906–1907	R. A. Oxlade (NSW)	1927–1930
G. P. Barbour (NSW)	1907–1908	Dr A. Robertson (Vic)	1930–1933
Colonel Foxton (Qld)	1908–1910	R. A. Oxlade (NSW)	1933–1936
G. Mostyn-Evans (SA)	1910–1911	Dr A. Robertson (Vic)	1936–1945
C. J. Eady (Tas)	1911	R. A. Oxlade (NSW)	1945–1948
W. P. McElhone (NSW)	1911–1912	Dr A. Robertson (Vic)	1948–1951
E. E. Bean (Vic)	1912–1913	R. A. Oxlade (NSW)	1951–1952
J. Allen (Qld)	1913–1914	R. F. Middleton (SA)	1952–1955
*H. Blinman (SA)	1914	F. M. Cush (NSW)	1955–1957
*J. Allen (Qld)	1914–1918	W. T. Dowling (Vic)	1957–1960
H. Blinman (SA)	1918–1919	Sir Donald Bradman (SA)	1960–1963
H. Bushby (Tas)	1919	E. G. Macmillan (NSW)	1963–1966
H. Gregory (WA)	1919–1920	R. J. Parish (Vic)	1966–1969
H. R. Rush (Vic)	1920–1922	Sir Donald Bradman (SA)	1969–1972
H. Gregory (WA)	1922–1923	T. C. J. Caldwell (NSW)	1972–1973
J. S. Hutcheon (Qld)	1923–1924	T. C. J. Caldwell (NSW)	1973–1975
B. V. Scrymgour (SA)	1924–1925	R. J. Parish (Vic)	1975–1980
H. Bushby (Tas)	1925–1926	P. L. Ridings (SA)	1980–

*H. Blinman was elected chairman in 1914 but J. Allen was caretaker chairman during World War I. From 1892 to 1900 the governing body for cricket in Australia was known as the Australasian Cricket Council. Then in 1905 the Australian Board of Control for International Cricket was formed. In 1973 this body became the Aust. Cricket Board. During World War I A.B.C.I.C. meetings were limited in numbers and frequency (the annual general meeting of 1915 lapsing through lack of quorum) and no meetings of the A.B.C.I.C. were held at all during World War II.

SECRETARIES

W. P. McElhone (NSW)	1905–1910	*W. H. Jeanes (SA)	1927–1954
C. A. Sinclair (NSW)	1910–1911	J. A. Ledward (Vic)	1954–1960
S. Smith Jnr (NSW)	1911–1927	A. R. Barnes (NSW)	1960–1973

AUSTRALIAN CRICKET BOARD

A. R. Barnes (NSW)	1973–1981

*W. H. Jeanes was the first paid secretary of the Board and Messrs. Jeanes, Ledward and Barnes served concurrently as secretary of their state association and Board secretary during their periods of office. In 1976 Alan Barnes retired as NSWCA secretary to concentrate on Board administration.

1157

AUSTRALIAN CRICKET BOARD EXECUTIVE DIRECTOR:
D. L. Richards (Vic)   1980–

AUSTRALASIAN CRICKET COUNCIL
This body, the forerunner to the Australian Board of Control for International Cricket, had its inaugural meeting on September 13, 1892, and disbanded in 1900.

CHAIRMEN
R. Teece (NSW)	1892–93	J. M. Gibson (NSW)	1895–96
R. Best (Vic)	1893–95	F. Grey-Smith (Vic)	1896
G. M. Evan (SA)	1895	W. O. Whitridge	1897–1900

SECRETARIES
J. Portus (NSW)	1892–96	J. Creswell (SA)	1896–1900

BIBLIOGRAPHY

ALTHAM, H. S. *A History of Cricket, volume 1*. George Allen & Unwin, London, 1926.

ARLOTT, John, (ed.). *The Great All-rounders*. Pelham, London, 1968.

ARLOTT, John, (ed.). *The Great Bowlers*. Collins, London, 1969.

BACHELOR, Denzil. *The Book of Cricket*. Collins, London, 1952.

BAILEY, Trevor. *The Greatest of My Time*. Eyre & Spottiswoode, London, 1968.

BARKER, Ralph. *The Great Bowlers*. Chatto & Windus, London, 1967.

BEDSER, Alec and Eric. *Our Cricket Story*. Evans, London, 1949.

BENAUD, Richie. *Way of Cricket*. Hodder & Stoughton, London, 1961.

BIRD, Dickie. *Not Out*. Arthur Barker, London, 1978.

BLANCH, John (ed.). *Ampol's Sporting Records*. Budget Books, Melbourne, 1981.

BOWEN, Rowland. *Cricket, a History*. Eyre & Spottiswoode, 1970.

BRADMAN, Sir Donald. *Farewell to Cricket*. Hodder & Stoughton, London, 1950.

BREARLEY, Mike. *The Ashes Returned*. Hodder & Stoughton, London, 1979.

BRITTENDEN, R. T. *New Zealand Cricketers*. Reed, Wellington, 1961.

CARDUS, Neville. *Australian Summer*. Collins, London, 1973.

CARDUS, Neville. *Cricket All The Year*. Collins, London, 1952.

CHAPPELL, Ian. *My World of Cricket*. Pollard, Sydney, 1974.

COWDREY, Colin. *M.C.C.* Hodder & Stoughton, London, 1974.

DARLING, D. K. *Test Tussles On and Off the Field*. Privately Printed, Hobart, 1970.

DAVIDSON, Alan. *Fifteen Paces*. Souvenir Press, London, 1963.

DE CARVALHO, David and PEARSON, Tony. *Cricket Cocktail*. Old Collegians, Sydney, 1963.

DOCKER, Edward Wybergh. *Bradman and the Bodyline Series*. Angus & Robertson, Brighton, 1978.

DOWNER, Sidney. *100 Not Out*. Rigby, Adelaide, 1972.

DUNSTAN, Keith. *The Paddock That Grew*. Cassell, Melbourne, 1962.

EAGAR, Patrick and ARLOTT, John. *An Eye For Cricket*. Hodder & Stoughton, London, 1979.

FAVELL, Les. *By Hook or By Cut*. Investigator Press, Adelaide, 1970.

FERGUSON, W. H. *Mr Cricket*. Nicholas Kaye, London, 1957.

FINGLETON, Jack. *Ashes Crown the Year*. Collins, London, 1954.

FINGLETON, Jack. *Brightly Fades the Don*. Collins, London, 1949.

FINGLETON, Jack. *Cricket Crisis*. Cassell, Melbourne, 1947.

FINGLETON, Jack. *The Immortal Victor Trumper*. Collins, London, 1978.

FINGLETON, Jack. *Masters of Cricket*. Heinemann, London, 1958.

FRINDALL, Bill. *The Wisden Book of Test Cricket*. MacDonald & Jane, London, 1978.

FRITH, David. *The Archie Jackson Story*. The Cricketer, London, 1974.

FRITH, David. *England Versus Australia*. Richard Smart, Sydney, 1980.

FRITH, David. *The Fast Men*. Van Nostrand Reinhold, London, 1977.

FRITH, David. *The Golden Age of Cricket*. Angus & Robertson, Sydney, 1978.

FRITH, David. *My Dear Victorious Stod*. Privately Printed, London, 1970.

FRY, C. B. *Giants of the Game*. Ward Lock and E. P. Publishing, London, 1910.

GIFFEN, George. *With Bat and Ball*. Ward Lock, London, 1898.

Gordon District Cricket Club's 75th Anniversary Report. Gordon Cricket Club, Sydney, 1980.

GRACE, Radcliffe. *Warwick Armstrong*. Privately printed, Melbourne, 1975.

GRIMMETT, C. V. *Getting Wickets*. Hodder & Stoughton, London, 1930.

GROUT, Wally. *My Country's Keeper*. Pelham, London, 1965.

HALL, Wes. *Pace Like Fire*. Pelham, London, 1965.

HARVEY, Neil. *My World of Cricket*. Hodder & Stoughton, London, 1963.

HAYGARTH, Arthur, ASHLEY COOPER, F. S. and LILLYWHITE, Frederick. *M.C.C. Cricket Scores and Biographies*. Longmans, London, Vols. I to XVI

HAYTER, Reg, (ed.). *The Cricketer International*.

HUTCHEON, E. H. *A History of Queensland Cricket*. Queensland Cricket Association, 1947.

IREDALE, Frank. *33 Years of Cricket*. Beatty Richardson, Sydney, 1920.

JOHNSON, Ian. *Cricket at the Crossroads*. Cassell, London, 1957.

LARWOOD, Harold and PERKINS, Kevin. *The Larwood Story*. W. H. Allen, London, 1965.

LAVER, Frank. *An Australian Cricketer on Tour*. Bell & Sons, London, 1907.

LAWRY, Bill. *Run–Digger*. Souvenir, London, 1966.

LILLEE, Dennis. *Back to the Mark*. Hutchinson, Melbourne, 1974.

McGILVRAY, Alan, (ed.). *The ABC Cricket Year Books*.

MACKAY, Ken. *Slasher Opens Up*. Pelham, London, 1964.

MAILEY, Arthur. *Ten for 66 and All That*. Phoenix Sports Books, London, 1958.

MALLETT, Ashley. *Rowdy*. Lynton, Adelaide, 1973.

MARSH, Rodney. *You'll Keep*. Hutchinson, Melbourne, 1975.

MARTIN-JENKINS, Christopher. *The Complete Who's Who of Test Cricketers*. Rigby, Adelaide, 1980.

MILLER, Keith. *Cricket Crossfire*. Oldbourne, London, 1957.

MILLER, Keith. *Keith Miller on Cricket*. Pelham, London, 1965.

MOODY, Clarence P. *Australian Cricket and Cricketers*. R. A. Thompson, Adelaide, 1894.

MOODY, Clarence P. *Cricket Album of Noted Australian Cricketers*. R. A. Thompson, Adelaide, 1905.

MOODY, Clarence P. *South Australian Cricket Reminiscences of Fifty Years*. R. A. Thompson, Adelaide, 1898.

Mosman Cricket Club's 50th Anniversary Report. Mosman Cricket Club, Sydney, 1958.

MOYES, A. G. *A Century of Cricketers*. Angus & Robertson, Sydney, 1950.

MOYES, A. G. *Australian Cricket: A History*. Angus & Robertson, 1959.

MOYES, A. G. *The Changing Face of Cricket*. Angus & Robertson, Sydney, 1963.

MULLINS, Patrick J. *Cricket in the Tropics*. Brisbane (privately issued).

MULVANEY, D. J. *Cricket Walkabout*. Melbourne University Press, Melbourne, 1967.

O'NEILL, Norman. *Ins and Outs*. Pelham, London, 1964.

PAGE, Roger. *A History of Tasmanian Cricket*. Roger Page, Hobart, 1957.

PEEBLES, Ian. *Straight From the Shoulder*. Hutchinson, London, 1968.

PIESSE, Ken, (ed.). *Cricketer*. Newspress, Melbourne.

PIESSE, Ken. *The Prahran Cricket Club Centenary History*. Prahran Cricket Club, 1979.

POLLARD, Jack. *Bumpers, Boseys and Brickbats*. Murray, Sydney, 1962.

POLLARD, Jack, (ed.). *Cricket—The Australian Way*, Pollard, Sydney, 1980.

POLLARD, Jack. *Six and Out*. Pollard, Sydney, 1980.

RAIJI, Vasant, (ed.). *Victor Trumper*. Vivek Publications, Bombay, 1964.

RICHARDSON, V. Y. *The Victor Richardson Story*. Rigby, Adelaide, 1966.

ROBERTSON-GLASGOW, R. C. *Cricket Prints*. Wernie Laurie, London, 1946.

ROBERTSON-GLASGOW, R. C. *Crusoe on Cricket*. Alan Ross, London, 1966.

1161

ROBERTSON-GLASGOW, R. C. *More Cricket Prints*. Wernie Laurie, London, 1948.

ROBINSON, Ray. *Between Wickets*. Collins, London, 1946.

ROBINSON, Ray. *From the Boundary*. Collins, London, 1951.

ROBINSON, Ray. *On Top Down Under*. Cassell, Sydney, 1975.

ROSENWATER, Irving. *Sir Donald Bradman: A Biography*. Batsford, London, 1978.

ROSS, Alan. *Australia '63*. Eyre & Spottiswoode, London, 1963.

ROWAN, Lou. *The Umpire's Story*. Pollard, Sydney, 1972.

The St. Kilda Cricket Club Centenary Report. St. Kilda Cricket Club, Melbourne, 1956.

SIMPSON, Bobby. *Captain's Story*. Stanley Paul, London, 1966.

SMITH, Sydney. *History of the Tests*. Australasian Publishing Company, Sydney, 1946.

STACKPOLE, Keith and TRENGOVE, Alan. *Not Just For Openers*. Stockwell, Melbourne, 1974.

SWANTON, E. W. and WOODCOCK, John, (ed.). *Barclay's World of Cricket*. Collins, London, 1980.

SWANTON, E. W. *A History of Cricket, volume 11*. George Allen & Unwin, 1938.

SWANTON, E. W. and MELFORD, Michael, (ed.). *The World of Cricket*. Michael Joseph, London, 1966.

TAYLOR, Percy. *The Story of the Carlton Cricket Club*. Carlton Cricket Club, Melbourne, 1956.

TORRENS, Warwick. *Queensland Cricket and Cricketers*. Brisbane, 1981.

TRESIDDER, Phil, (ed.). *Australian Cricket*. Modern Magazines, Sydney,

TRUMBLE, Robert. *The Golden Age of Cricket*. Melbourne, 1968.

TURNER, C. T. B. *The Quest For Bowlers*. Cornstalk Publishing, Sydney, 1926.

WAKELY, B. J. *Bradman The Great*. Nicholas Kaye, London, 1959.

WALKER, Max. *Tangles*. Barry Sparkes, Melbourne, 1976.

WALTERS, Doug. *Looking for Runs*. Pelham, London, 1971.

WARD, Kirwan. *Put Lock On*. Robert Hale, London, 1972.

WARNER, Sir Pelham. *Cricket Between the Wars*. Chatto and Windus, London, 1942.

WARNER, Sir Pelham. *How We Recovered the Ashes*. Chatto and Windus, London, 1905.

WEBBER, Roy. *The Playfair Book of Cricket Records*. Playfair, London, 1951.

WELLINGS, E. M. *Dexter Versus Benaud*. Bailey Bros. & Swinfen, London, 1963.

WINNING, Clifford. *Cricket Balmania*. Balmain Cricket Club, Sydney, 1981.

Wisden's Cricket Almanacks. Sporting Handbooks and MacDonald Jane, London.